Analytical Methods

Interpretation, Identification, Quantification

R Gopalan

Professor and Head (retired), Department of Chemistry, Madras Christian College

K S Viswanathan

Professor and Head, Department of Chemical Sciences, IISER Mohali

Universities Press

ANALYTICAL METHODS: Interpretation, Identification, Quantification

Universities Press (India) Private Limited

Registered Office
3-6-747/1/A & 3-6-754/1. Himayatnagar, Hyderabad 500 029, Telangana, India
e-mail: info@universitiespress.com; www.universitiespress.com

Distributed by
Orient Blackswan Private Limited

Registered Office
3-6-752, Himayatnagar, Hyderabad 500 029, Telangana, India

Other Offices
Bengaluru, Bhopal, Chennai, Guwahati, Hyderabad, Jaipur, Kolkata,
Lucknow, Mumbai, New Delhi, Noida, Patna, Vijayawada

First published 2018

ISBN: 978-93-86235-57-2

Typest in Minion Pro 11/12 by
Bookcraft Publishing Services (I) Pvt Ltd, Chennai

501452

Printed at
Sri Ram Printing Press,Chennai 600 116

Published by
Universities Press (India) Private Limited
3-6-747/1/A & 3-6-754/1, Himayatnagar,
Hyderabad 500 029, Telangana, India

Preface

Analytical Methods: Interpretation, Identification, Quantification, consists of 20 chapters dealing with the concepts, instrumentation, applications and uses of the title subject. A lacuna in teaching and learning of analytical methods in chemistry is the absence of stress on integrating the concepts that students learn in classrooms with the experiments they do in the laboratory. The book has been written with a view to addressing this lacuna. This book will serve as a textbook for students of M.Sc. chemistry. In addition, it can serve as a convenient reference for B.Sc. chemistry students and for candidates taking the UGC–CSIR NET examination.

The spectacular advances in electronic instrumentation and the integration of microprocessors with scientific instrumentation have enabled students in using new-generation scientific gadgets for measuring both physical and chemical data. Such gadgets have rendered analytical analyses both challenging and fascinating, as well as offering the advantage of using small amounts of chemicals—sometimes as low as nanograms. This aspect has been highlighted in every chapter of this book. The exploding modern knowledge in analytical methods cannot be adequately dealt with in a book of this kind. However, the contents of this book are intended to initiate students in concepts, interpretation, identification and quantification in analytical chemistry and enable them to delve deeper into this subject through modern literature. However, the book is undoubtedly intended to address the demands of the syllabi prescribed by universities and autonomous colleges.

The extensive progress in chemical analysis – both in theory and experiments – has been realised by the pioneering works of scientists. Therefore, brief profiles of such pioneers have been included, not only to acknowledge their significant scientific contributions but also to enthuse students to choose careers in analytical chemistry research. Solved problems and exercises given in each chapter are aimed at helping students in extending their comprehension of concepts and preparation for examinations.

The contents of each chapter have been put together in a way to fulfil the basic requirement of college and university students pursuing courses or papers in chemistry, and what they are required to study based on prescribed syllabi. It is hoped that this book will impart a clear comprehension of the fundamentals of the subject and also inculcate a desire to explore the depths of the topics included in this book.

R Gopalan
K S Viswanathan

Acknowledgements

The production of this book involved the assistance and expertise of several persons. The professional guidance extended by Dr Gita S Dattatri, Universities Press, is the principal factor in enabling the publication of this book. We thank her for her expertise in improving the manuscript and patience in dealing with our deficiencies. As a sculptor chisels a stone, she copy-edited and transformed our manuscript into material suitable for printing. We are grateful to Universities Press for their excellent support during the publication of this book.

For some photos from the net, we acknowledge http://commons.wikimedia.org under the terms of the GNU Free Documentation License. Others have been acknowledged at the site of use.

RG acknowledges the assistance received from Usha Sundar, V Srinivasan and S Rakulan in word processing and drawing figures. He acknowledges the encouragement received from his wife, Aruna Gopalan, during the preparation of the manuscript. KSV thanks his wife, Chitra Viswanathan, for her support through the preparation of the manuscript.

The authors welcome suggestions from their readers—both students and teachers.

May 2018

R Gopalan
K S Viswanathan

Contents

1 Introduction to Analytical Chemistry

1.1 WHAT IS ANALYTICAL CHEMISTRY?

Analytical chemistry is a branch of chemistry that deals with the characterisation of matter. Everything around us is made of chemicals, and analytical chemistry involves characterisation of these chemicals. Characterisation of a matter pertains to the following five aspects:

- Identification of the chemicals present in the matter: *qualitative analysis*.
- Separation of the chemicals in the matter; purification of the constituents.
- Determination (estimation) of the chemicals: *quantitative analysis*.
- Determination of the structures of the chemicals: *structural analysis*.
- Promotion of the use of chemicals for improving the quality of life: *applications*.

1.2 STEPS IN ANALYSIS

An analysis is performed systematically adopting standard, well-evolved analytical steps. The following are the major steps in an analysis.

(i) ***Definition of the problem***: The problem has to be defined with answers for the following questions. What is the aim of the analysis—is it qualitative or quantitative? Is it an one-time analysis or a repeated long-term analysis? How accurate and precise should it be?

(ii) ***Selection of a method***: After defining the problem, a method suitable for analysis should be selected. The method is selected to satisfy
- its suitability for the analyte,
- the required degree of accuracy,
- the cost allowable, and
- the speed desirable for the analysis.

(iii) ***Preparation of the sample***: Enough sample containing the analyte should be available for replicate analysis. Then, a suitable quantity should be weighed and treated chemically to render it suitable for identification or estimation. This is the preliminary physico-chemical treatment of the sample. Such a treatment may involve one or more steps comprising drying, calcination, ashing, dissolution, masking the interferants, concentration, pH adjustment, and so on.

Separation: In some cases, the analyte may have to be separated from the sample before analysis. This is essential when the analytical method to be adopted is selective. Physical separation, such as distillation, solvent extraction, chromatography or electrophoresis, or chemical separation such as precipitation or calcination may be required depending upon the nature of the sample.

(iv) ***Analysis***: The analysis required may be qualitative, quantitative or both. Separation and analysis are composite, to be performed in a particular sequence, the sequence being dictated by the nature of the sample. In quantitative analysis, frequently, separation precedes determination of the components of the sample. After separating the components, the different components may have to be estimated by different techniques based on the nature and quantity of the components of the sample. In quantitative methods, calibration of the method, use of control (blank) and replication are important factors that validate the results.

(v) ***Calculation***: The final step in an analytical method is the calculation. The use of proper stoichiometric equations, formulae and computations are important to obtain the correct data. The data thus obtained should be statistically analysed for reliability, and then reported with information on their accuracy.

The usual steps in an analysis are depicted in Fig. 1.1.

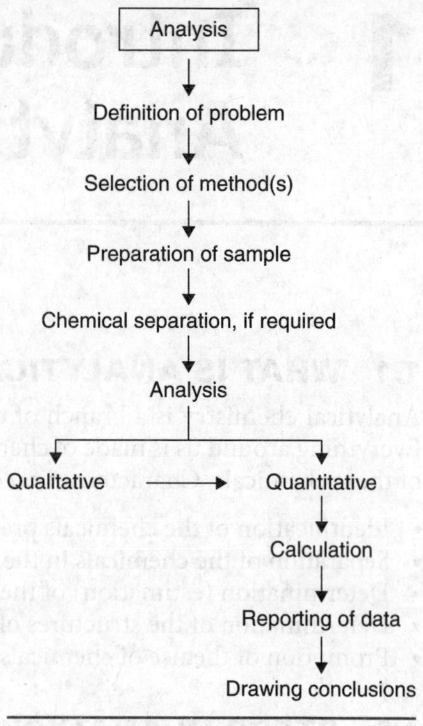

Fig. 1.1 Steps in analysis

1.3 SELECT VOCABULARY IN ANALYTICAL CHEMISTRY

Some important frequently used terms in analytical chemistry are defined for convenience.

- *Analytical chemistry* provides the methods and tools needed for insight into our material world. It also provides answers to basic questions about a material sample—what, where, how much and what structure?
- *Analysts* apply known measurement techniques to well-defined compositional or characterisation questions.
- *Analytical chemistry* is the science of chemical measurement.
- *Chemometrics* is the chemical discipline that uses mathematical and statistical methods to design or select optimal measurement procedures and experiments, and to provide maximum chemical information by analysing chemical data.
- Generally, in analyses, the *concentration* of an analyte is a function of an instrumental response:

  $$C_{\text{analyte}} = f(x)$$

  where C_{analyte} is the concentration of the analyte and $f(x)$ denotes a function of a measured signal x. These two are linearly related:

  $$C_{\text{analyte}} = m\,x + c$$

- The term *analyse* means examination of the sample for a specific purpose, say to identify its constituents, and may also include quantitative procedures.
- The term *determination* is more specific—it means to find out the amount of one of the constituents of the sample; it may also mean the estimation of all of the constituents of the sample.

- Depending upon the *quantity* of the analyte (constituent) in the sample, it can be classified into one of the four *types*:

Major	> 1%
Minor	0.1%–1%
Trace	< 0. 1%
Ultratrace	ppm level

- A sample may be subjected to *complete* or *partial analysis*; In complete or total analysis, all the constituents of the sample are identified and determined. But in partial analysis, only the constituent of interest is determined.
- Some chemicals have to be totally characterised (assayed) before marketing. They are totally analysed and the percentages of all constituents reported on the label (Fig. 1.2). Such labels indicate total assay.

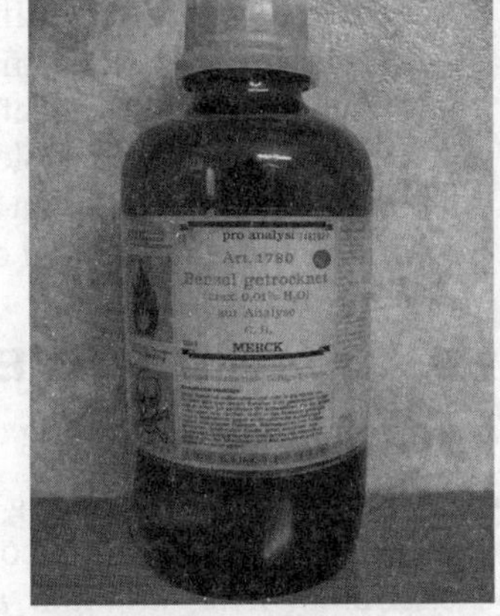

Fig. 1.2 A bottle of benzene

Antoine Lavoisier: the 'Father of Analytical Chemistry'

Born	26 August 1743 Paris, France
Died	8 May 1794 (aged 50) Paris, France
Fields	Biology, chemistry
Influenced by	Guillaume-François Rouelle

Lavoisier was born in Paris in 1743. He became a tax-collector during the reign of King Louis XIV. He practised analytical chemistry as a hobby. He performed several quantitative analyses to prove the law of conservation of mass. He formulated the metric system of measurements and units, helped abolish the false phlogiston theory and improved the nomenclature of chemicals. He performed several experiments on thermodynamics and researched on allotropy.

His contributions to analytical chemistry are considered to be path breaking; therefore, he has been called the 'father of analytical chemistry'. During the French Revolution, on 8 May 1794, he was guillotined for his role as a tax-collector. When Lavoisier was beheaded, his contemporaneous mathematician J L Lagrange commented, 'It took them only an instant to cut off his head, but France may not produce another like him in a century'.

G L Carius, J A R Newlands and M Tsvet are some of the other early chemists who contributed greatly to the development of analytical methods.

- *Speciation*: Speciation is characterisation of chemical species—to ascertain the exact composition of a chemical species. For example, the environmental pollutant, mercury, may be present in the environment, in soil or water in different chemical forms, such as Hg(II)aq, $HgCH_3^+$, $HgOH^+$, a chelate complex, and so on. The degree of the toxic effect of Hg(II) depends upon the nature of the Hg(II) species. Therefore, the analyst is required to identify and estimate the mercury species in a sample. The procedure adopted for this is speciation.

- Speciation is the identification of the exact chemical state of a material. The chemical species are specific forms of an element.
- Speciation of an element is the distribution of an element based on isotopic composition, oxidation state and molecular structure, amongst defined chemical species in a system.
- Speciation analysis is an analytical method of identifying and measuring the quantities of one or more individual chemical species of an element in a sample.

1.4 QUANTITATIVE ANALYTICAL METHODS

The methods of determining analytes are classified into four major types:

- *physical methods* involving measurements of mass, colour, odour, melting point, refractive index, viscosity, thermal conductivity, and so on,
- *electromagnetic radiation methods* involving measurement of absorption, emission and scattering (such as UV, IR, fluorescence, XRD),
- *electric charge methods* involving measurement of voltage, current, conductivity and masses of molecular fragments (mass spectrometry), and
- *magnetic methods* involving measurement of magnetic behaviour (NMR, ESR).

1.4.1 Classical Analytical Methods

The analytical methods used early on – before the invention of instrumentation – are called *classical methods*. In the early years of the study of chemistry, most analyses were carried out by the classical methods. These methods involve

- evaporation,
- calcination,
- precipitation,
- filtration,
- recrystallisation,
- distillation,
- extraction,
- weighing, and so on.

In quantitative analysis, the classical methods include volumetric and gravimetric methods. These classical methods still form the basis in analytical procedures in schools, colleges and research laboratories as well as in industries. Frequently, the modern instrumental methods necessarily have to be preceded by the classical methods.

1.4.2 Modern Methods: Instrumental Analysis

The physical and chemical examination of a material using an instrument is called instrumental analysis. Each instrumental analysis is based on the measurement of a physical property of the sample. Even the simple procedure of the determination of the melting point of a substance using an inexpensive instrument is an example of instrumental analysis. It can be a complicated method using an expensive X-ray spectrometer or an electron microscope (SEM and TEM).

1.4.2.1 Advantages of Instrumental Analyses

Instrumental analyses generally have the following advantages:

- They are more sensitive than the classical methods.
- They offer more selectivity for analysis.
- They can be performed rapidly.
- They can be applied to a mixture without separating the components.
- They are suitable for analysing a large number of batches of analytes routinely, such as materials handled in a quality control laboratory.
- The analyses can be computer-controlled for easy performance, recording of data and also for obtaining precision in data.
- Some of them lend themselves to analysis, preceded by separation, both the processes being performed in one instrumental unit (LC–MS).

1.4.2.2 Disadvantages of Instrumental Analyses

In spite of several advantages, instrumental techniques do have some disadvantages:

- They are expensive.
- The maintenance of the instruments needs special care; in addition, their spare parts are expensive.
- Some techniques are destructive and therefore not ideal for samples which are difficult to acquire.
- The experimenter may find it easy to operate but difficult to master unlike when using a classical method.
- Instrumental readings are influenced – though to a small extent – by certain extraneous factors such as voltage fluctuations, vibrations, deterioration in the performance of some of the instrumental components, noise, and so on. (*Noise* is disturbance that accompanies and affects electrical signals, important in scanning pulse microscopy and in some spectral methods.)

Most instrumental methods are *relative*. Instruments display a signal due to some physical property of the analyte. For example, spectophotometers measure the fraction of electromagnetic radiation from a light source that is absorbed by the sample. This absorption is related to the analyte concentration by comparison against that absorbed by a known concentration of the analyte; this implies that the spectrophotometer must be calibrated. Therefore, the data obtained by this procedure are relative.

1.4.3 Comparison of Analytical Techniques

All the analytical techniques are not identical in all respects—the concentration-sensitivity range for estimation, degree of precision, speed of analysis, and so on, differ significantly (Table 1.1). These variations have to be weighed carefully before applying a technique to an analyte.

1.4.4 Instrumental Signals

In each instrumental analysis, the response or signal produced by the analyte is recorded by the instrument. Generating this signal without any interference and recording it accurately are crucial for collection of reliable and reproducible data. For example, when a coloured species is determined by visible spectroscopy, the absorbance by the species should be unique at a particular wavelength region without any interference, and the spectrophotometer should read the absorbance accurately. The signals used in instrumental analysis are listed in Table 1.2.

Table 1.1 Comparison of analytical techniques

Technique	Range for estimation (mol/L)	Precision (%)	Speed
Volumetry	10^{-4}–10^{-1}	0.1–1	Slow
Gravimetry	10^{-2}–10^{-1}	0.1–0.5	Slow
Visual colourimetry	10^{-6}–10^{-3}	1–2	Slow
Sepctrophotometry	10^{-6}–10^{-3}	1–2	Fast
Potentiometry	10^{-6}–10^{-1}	2–3	Fast
Electrogravimetry	10^{-4}–10^{-1}	0.1–2	Slow
Coulometry	10^{-4}–10^{-1}	0.1–2	Slow
Voltammetry	10^{-8}–10^{-3}	2–5	Moderate
Fluorimetry	10^{-9}–10^{-6}	1–5	Moderate
Atomic spectroscopy	10^{-9}–10^{-3}	2–10	Fast
Chromatography	10^{-9}–10^{-3}	2–5	Fast
Kinetic methods	10^{-6}–10^{-2}	2–5	Slow
Radioactive method	down to 10^{-9}	1–2	Fast

Table 1.2 Signals used in instrumental methods

Signal	Instrumental method(s)
Electromagnetic radiation	
(i) Absorption of radiation	Spectrophotometry and spectroscopy (UV–vis, IR, NMR and ESR)
(ii) Emission of radiation	Emission spectroscopy (X-ray, UV, visible, electron, Auger), fluorescence, phosphorescence and luminescence
(iii) Scattering of radiation	Turbidimetry, nephelometry and Raman spectroscopy
(iv) Refraction of radiation	Refractometry and interferometry
(v) Diffraction of radiation	X-ray, neutron and electron diffraction methods
(vi) Rotation of radiation	Polarimetry, ORD and circular dichroism
Electrical	
(i) Electrical potential	Potentiometry
(ii) Electrical charge	Coulometry
(iii) Electrical current	Polarography and amperometry
(iv) Electrical resistance	Conductometry
Miscellaneous	
(i) Mass/charge ratio	Mass spectrometry
(ii) Reaction rate	Kinetic methods
(iii) Thermal behaviour	Thermal conductivity and enthalpy methods
(iv) Radioactivity	Activation analysis and isotope dilution analysis
(v) Volume	Dilatometry
(vi) Viscosity	Viscometry

Potential instrumental errors: Even an expensive instrument may record spurious data due to

- power fluctuation,
- faulty calibration of read-out device,
- component malfunction,
- variation in temperature, or
- noise (electrical, vibration).

An analyst should design the analysis in such a way that these sources of error are minimised or eliminated.

1.4.4.1 Signal-to-noise Ratio (SNR)

An analytical measurement has two components—*signal* and *noise*. The signal is the information about the analyte being estimated; the noise is the unwanted, extraneous information. Noise reduces the accuracy and precision of an estimation. In addition, it necessitates the use of higher concentration of the analyte for detections.

- *Noise* is a radio (an engineering term); it denotes unwanted instrumental response detected by the ear as noise or static.
- It originates from the random fluctuations of a signal (instrument response).
- Random errors in the response sensitivity of an instrument produces fluctuations in signal.

As the noise increases, the accuracy of the signal (and hence that of the datum) decreases. The effect of noise on the relative error of measurement becomes greater and greater as the quantity being measured decreases in magnitude. This factor is denoted by the signal-to-noise (S/N) ratio. This ratio should be as high as possible to render the measurement reliable. A large noise decreases the reliability of the measured instrumental value. This relationship between the signal and noise is shown in Fig. 1.3. As the S/N ratio increases, the resolution of the signals is better and the data derived from the measurements become accurate. When S/N is 5, the peaks are not distinctly recognisable; when it is 99.5, the peaks are distinctly recognisable.

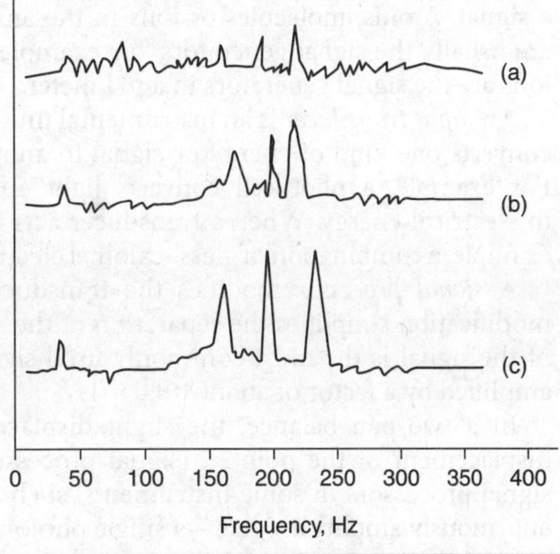

Fig. 1.3 Effect of signal to noise ratio on an NMR spectrum **(a)** $S/N = 5$ **(b)** $S/N = 60$ **(c)** $S/N = 99.5$

1.4.4.2 Sources of Noise in Instrumental Analysis

Noise in instrumental analyses may be *chemical noise or instrumental noise.* Chemical noise arises from variations in chemical compositions in the analyte *during* analysis. Such variations arise from shift in equilibila caused by changes in temperature and pressure. Humidity, light energy, ambient air quality, vibration of the analyte, and so on, may also create chemical noise.

Instrumental noise is caused by the electronic components that constitute the instrument. The origin for this kind of noise is the variation in the functioning of the instrumental components such as transducers, signal processing units, and others.

The noise actually observed in a measurement may be a complex composite of all types of noises. Choosing carefully controlled experimental conditions, pre-treatment of the analyte and the use of a good instrument can minimise noise and maximise the accuracy of the measured readings.

1.4.5 Analytical Instruments

An *analytical instrument* is designed to convert an analytical signal into a directly detectable signal or response. For example, the light transmitted by a solution, after absorbing a part of the incident light is converted to electrical current by a photometer. A current meter is used to measure the current produced and this is quantitatively related to the light transmitted. The production of current from light is done by a photocell. The unit, the photocell, which generates a measurable signal (current), is called the *transducer*. The components that enable an analytical measurement work in the sequence shown in Fig. 1.4.

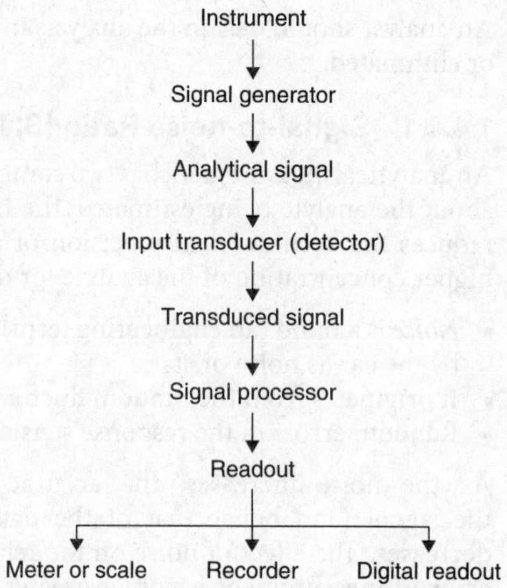

Instrument
↓
Signal generator
↓
Analytical signal
↓
Input transducer (detector)
↓
Transduced signal
↓
Signal processor
↓
Readout
↓
Meter or scale | Recorder | Digital readout

Fig. 1.4 Components of an analytical instrument

A *signal generator* is the species which produces a signal. Atoms, molecules or ions in the analyte are usually the signal generators; for example, H^+ ions are the signal generators in a pH meter.

An *input transducer* is an instrumental unit that converts one kind of energy or signal to another. For example, a photocell converts light energy to electrical energy. When a transducer acts on a chemical signal, it is called a *detector*. For example, a combination of glass–calomel electrodes senses H^+ ions and therefore it is a detector.

A *signal processor* modifies the transduced signal received from the detector. Such a modification simplifies the separation of the signal in the readout instrument. Amplification of the signal is the most commonly used signal processor. For example, electric signals are amplified by a factor of about 10^{10}.

In a two-pan balance, the slight displacement of the beam is made to cause a large displacement of the pointer, (signal processor) in a scale. Photographic films are used as signal processors in some instruments, such as an X-ray machine. A photographic film can enormously amplify a signal—a single photon may produce nearly a trillion silver atoms.

A *readout device* is a transducer; it converts a processed signal to a simple signal that can be observed or recorded by the experimenter. The simple signal formed can be the pointer (needle) moving on a scale. The other common readout devices are cathode-ray tube, pen-chart, digital data display, photographic plate and so on. In expensive instruments, the concentration can be directly read off the instrument.

A *microprocessor* is a computer-based unit that helps programming the instrument for analysis and also gives simplified direct results of the analysis. The experimental parameters, suitable for the analyte, can be set with the help of this unit.

1.4.6 Definitions of Analytical Methods

Generally, analytical techniques are used to identify the analytes and then determine them. Frequently, quantitative analysis is a necessary follow up of qualitative analysis.

In this section, simple definitions of analytical techniques are given. The finer details of each technique and the variations in each technique are considered in subsequent chapters. The term 'metry' derived from the Greek *metria*, means measure.

- An experimental process of determining the weight (amount) of a substance is named with the suffix, metry.

Titrimetry (volumetry): The substance to be analysed is reacted with an appropriate reagent, added as a standard solution (known concentration) and the volume of solution needed for complete reaction is measured.

Volumetry: A gas liberated or absorbed is determined by the measurement of volume and then calculation of its weight is performed.

Gravimetry: The substance being determined is converted into an insoluble precipitate which then is collected and weighed.

Electrogravimetry: The analyte – in the form of a suitable solution – is electrolysed and the material deposited on one of the electrodes is weighed.

Dilatometry: The changes in the volume of a liquid or dimensions of a solid which occur due to change in temperature, fluid absorption, mechanical stress or chemical reaction are measured.

Voltammetry: An electrical technique by which an analyte is estimated by the measurement of current at a microelectrode at a specified voltage.

Coulometry: An electrical technique by which an analyte is determined by the measurement of current (in coulombs) and time needed to complete an electrochemical reaction or to generate sufficient material to react completely with a specified reagent.

Potentiometry: An electrochemical technique by which an analyte is estimated by the measurement of the potential of an electrode in equilibrium with an ion to be determined.

Thermal methods (thermometry): Techniques in which changes in physical and/or chemical properties of a substance are measured as a function of temperature; involves changes in weight or changes in energy.

Spectroscopic methods: Methods which depend on measuring the amount of radiant energy of a particular wavelength absorbed by the sample, or measuring the amount of radiant energy of a particular wavelength emitted by the sample.

Atomic absorption spectroscopy: Involves atomising the specimen, usually by spraying a solution of the sample into a flame, and then studying the absorption of radiation from an electric lamp thus producing the spectrum of the element to be determined.

Turbidimetric and nephelometric methods: A method which involves the measurement of the amount of light stopped or scattered by a suspension of the analyte. They are not absorption methods.

Emission methods: They are techniques in which the sample is heated by direct heat or electricity so that the atoms are raised to their excited states causing them to emit energy. The intensity of the emitted energy is then measured.

Emission spectroscopy, flame photometry and *fluorimetry* belong to emission methods.

Emission spectroscopy: It involves introducing the sample into an inductively coupled plasma nebuliser and then examining the emitted light, which may extend into the UV region.

Flame photometry: This involves the injection of a solution of the analyte into a flame and the characteristic colours produced are used for detecting elements. Quantitative analysis can be carried out by measuring the colour intensities using a spectrometer.

Fluorimetry: This is based on the measurement of radiant energy absorbed or emitted during fluorescence of the analyte molecules. Some molecules fluoresce by the absorption of radiant energy, namely, UV or visible radiation.

Chromatographic methods: A group of methods for separation of mixtures involving differential distribution of the components between two phases; adapted to the identification of the components of mixtures as well as quantitative analysis. In chromatography, one phase is stationary and the other is mobile in a definite direction.

Electrophoresis: This is a separative process, similar to chromatography, but separation of charged species in a mixture is effected by an applied electric field based on the charge to mass ratios; the ions migrate differentially on a special paper leading to their separation. It helps identification also, in addition to separation.

Mass spectrometry: It involves vapourising the analyte using a high vacuum, then, bombarding the vapour by a high-energy electron beam to fragment the molecules into ions of varying size. The positive fragments are then distinguished by accelerating them in an electric field, and deflecting them in a magnetic field where they follow paths defined by their mass/charge ratio and reach the detector and recording instrument. A mass spectrum is a *fingerprint* of a molecule, and therefore this technique can be applied to identify molecules and also determine their structure.

Mössbauer spectroscopy: It involves gamma ray spectroscopy for structural analysis (particular oxidation states) of metallic compounds.

Kinetic methods: They are based on reaction rates, especially the order of a reaction defining the dependence of reaction rates on the concentrations of reacting species.

X-ray methods: Crystalline materials diffract beams of X-rays. This property is the basis for applying the X-ray diffraction technique to determine the crystal pattern and also to identify the components of a solid sample. The wavelengths of the X-ray emission peaks are characteristic of the atomic number and the intensity of the peaks is proportional to the amounts of the element present in the sample.

Radiochemical methods: Radiochemical methods are based upon the radioactivity of active nuclides; these involve the measurement of radioactivity of natural or induced activity. Activation analysis, isotope dilution and radioimmuno-assay are some such methods.

Kinetic methods: Kinetic methods can be adopted, in rare cases, to determine the amount of a substance in solution; this is performed by adding a catalyst to the analyte which will change the analyte to the products, and the change in the absorbance of the solution is used to calculate the amount of the analyte. Such kinetic methods are useful in clinical and physiological chemistry. Conversely, the amount of a catalyst, which is the analyte, can be estimated by measuring the speed of a reaction that is catalysed by the analyte. This is based on the fact that the rate of the catalysed reaction is dependent on the quantity of the catalyst added.

Optical methods: Measurement of the refractive index using a refractometer can help identify an analyte—however, the analyte has to be pure. Even a mixture of two pure liquids can be analysed by this method. Another optical method used in analysis is polarimetry. In this method, the optical rotation of an optically active analyte is measured by a polarimeter for both qualitative and quantitative results.

1.4.7 Calibration

Calibration is a critical examination of the utility of an experimental procedure, checking the reliability of an instrument and the suitability of the chosen method for the analysis. When the instrument response is related to the analyte concentration (mostly linearly), calibration is done by preparing a series of standard solutions of a pure sample of the material (which is being analysed in the sample) and measuring the instrument response to each of these. Then, a calibration curve is drawn by plotting the instrument responses – say, absorbance or conductance – against the various known concentrations of the standard solutions (Fig. 1.5). Then, the concentration of the analyte in the sample is determined using its instrumental response and interpolating this value in the calibration curve.

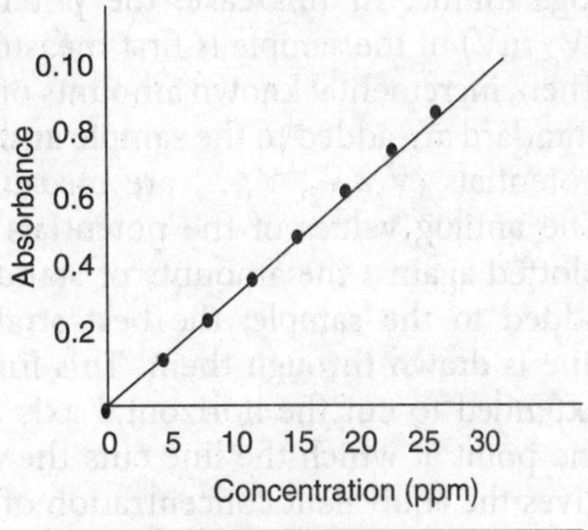

Fig. 1.5 Calibration plot

A calibration curve is a plot of the instrument response as a function of concentration.

The *interpolation* procedure is simple and reliable when the response of the instrument is linearly related to the analyte concentration. This is so for several systems: for example, the relationship between absorbance and concentration of $Ce(IV)_{aq}$. In modern computer-based instruments, the concentration of the analyte is directly displayed digitally.

When the concentrations are very low, the *S*/*N* ratio may render displayed data less accurate. In such cases low-noise amplifiers are used to reduce the internal noise of electronic systems to maximise the *S*/*N* ratio and minimise inaccuracy.

1.4.8 Method of Standard Additions

The instrument response to the analyte may be affected by the *sample matrix* in some cases. In such cases, the environment of the standard should be the same as of the analyte. For example, if an analyte in a sample exists as a component of a mixture, then the standard is prepared in such a way that it has more or less the same type of mixture. However, this procedure is not easy. Then, another method of calibration, called the *method of standard additions* is used. In this method, a portion of the analyte sample is spiked with a known amount of the sample; then the increase in the signal consequent to the addition of the standard is measured. By comparing the instrument responses obtained before and after spiking, the analyte can be determined. In this method, the standard is subjected to the same environment (matrix) as the analyte.

- In adopting the standard additions method, only *small volumes* of concentrated standard should be added to the sample in order to minimise volume corrections. For example, when 100 μL of a 1000 ppm standard is added to 10 mL of the sample, the volume increases only by 1%, and therefore the volume changes can be ignored.
- Another precaution to be taken in the standard additions method is that the concentration increments by spiking should be close to the unknown concentration.

1.4.9 Gran-type Plot

Most instrumental methods offer a linear response to concentrations of the analyte. In some cases, as in potentiometry, the response may by logarithmic. In this case, the potential (V_o mV) of the sample is first measured. Then, incremental known amounts of the standard are added to the sample and the potentials (V_1, V_2, V_3...) are measured. The antilog values of the potentials are plotted against the amounts of standard added to the sample; the best straight line is drawn through them. This line is extended to cut the horizontal axis and the point at which the line cuts the axis gives the equivalent concentration of the unknown. (The horizontal axis is determined from similar measurements on a blank with extrapolation to zero concentration.) The plot obtained in this method is called the *Gran-type plot* (Fig. 1.6). A Gran-type plot transforms a logarithmic response (nonlinear) to a linear plot.

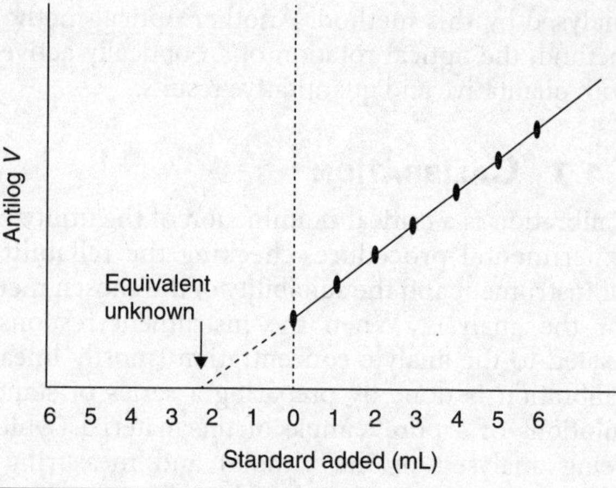

Fig. 1.6 Gran-type plot

1.5 SELECTIVITY

Selectivity of an analytical method is defined as the extent to which it is free from interference by other species present in the sample. Higher the selectivity, the more reliable the results are. Actually, no analytical method is totally free from interference by other species; therefore, when a method is applied to a species, the interference must be minimised by suitable experimental procedures, such as separation, masking, pH adjustment and so on. A highly selective method implies minimum interference.

1.5.1 Interference in Estimations

In an analytical estimation no interference from any species should occur. Ideally, if the analyte sample is totally free from any interfering species, then the estimation would give reliable data. However, this is rarely the case. Then, one of the following procedures should be adopted to solve the problem of interference:

- All the interfering species are separated from the analyte prior to estimation to render ideality in the analyte sample.
- The interfering species are rendered inert towards the reagents used for estimating the analyte. This can be done by sequestrations.
- Reagents that do not react with the interfering species under the selected experimental conditions (pH, temperature and concentration) are chosen.
- Relatively high concentration of the species being estimated is used such that interference imparts only negligible error (well within the range of error expected) in the data.

The selection of these procedures depends upon the nature and amount of the analyte, that of the interfering species and the method used for analysis. When the calibration curve method in an instrumental technique is used in an estimation, accuracy is critically dependent upon how closely the matrix of the standards matches with that of the samples analysed. The *interferents* have to be eliminated from the analyte before the instrumental response.

- *Matrix* is the collection of all the different constituents present in the analyte sample.
- An *interferent* is a species – physical or chemical – in the analyte which interferes with the method of estimation. For example, in spectrophotometric analyses, absorption of incident radiation of wavelengths close to the wavelength of absorption by the analyte species is a physical interference. In the estimation of vanadium at 3082.11 Å by AAS, aluminium which absorbs at 3082.15 Å is an interferent. Chemical interferences originate due to competive reactions between the impurities and the reagent. For example, in the gravimetric determination of nickel in steel with DMG, Fe^{3+} (interferent) is masked with tartaric acid by forming a soluble unreactive iron complex.

Isobaric interference In estimations based on atomic masses, isobaric interferences may occur. For example, in the mass spectrometric analysis of $^{113}In^+$, an isotope of cadmium forming $^{113}Cd^+$ in the mass spectral tube produces an overlapping peak with that of $^{113}In^+$. Only a mass spectrometer with a very high resolution can resolve these two overlapping peaks. Such isobaric overlaps are predictable; from abundance tables, correction for interferences can be applied to arrive at accurate spectral data.

Isobaric interferences may be noticed in Mössbauer spectral methods also.

Swamping In the flame photometric estimation of sodium, potassium interferes. The ionisation of sodium,

$$Na \rightarrow Na^+ + e^-$$

is repressed by the ionisation of K. Sodium analyses of unknown samples containing varying quantities of potassium thus give erroneous results. This problem is overcome by the addition of a large, known quantity of potassium salt to all the solutions—both unknowns and standards; this stamps out variations from one sample to another.

The nature and degree of interference depend upon the nature of the analyte, nature of the interferents and the method of analysis. Minimisation or elimination of interference in an estimation is achieved after careful trials of estimation.

Interference filters In a spectroscopic measurement, the wavelength of the radiation absorbed or measured should be narrow (sharp) to avoid interference and increase accuracy. Filters are used to attain these two requirements, by selecting narrower bandwidths. Such filters are called *wavelength selectors.* These filters can be used for ultraviolet, visible and infrared regions. When a radiation passes through a selected filter, most of the interfering radiation is absorbed by it and only the required radiation passes through it.

1.6 TEMPERATURE: EFFECT ON ANALYTICAL DATA

Several analytical data are temperature dependant—voltage, conductance, volume of fluids, density. Therefore, maintaining a standard temperature is mandatory for reporting reproducible data. In addition, temperature variations may change the nature of the chemicals and reagents used in analysis, imparting uncertainty in the procedure. Many of the modern instruments have temperature-control units for holding samples at a fixed temperature. If a datum is temperature dependent, the temperature at which it was measured should be reported.

1.7 SAMPLING

Sampling is the selection of a representative portion of the sample; the sample should represent all the components of the material and also their amounts in the bulk. For example, if 1 g of a sample is taken from 1000 kg of a bulk material for analysis, the sample, (1 g) should be a true representative of the bulk or gross material.

1.7.1 Solid Samples

A solid, bulk matter is crushed and powdered to obtain a fine powder; this procedure homogenises the material. Then, a portion of the powder is used for analysis. When a bulk matter, such as a hard metal, is analysed, it is cut into tiny pieces – as tiny as possible – and then several such pieces are used for analysis.

Sometimes, a solid sample may have extraneous, adhered matter; these should be detached by washing, degreasing or scrubbing before sampling it.

Solid samples are more likely to be heterogeneous than liquid and gaseous samples.

1.7.2 Liquid Samples

As most of the liquids are homogeneous, sampling them is easy. If a liquid is heterogeneous, say, consisting of two or more immiscible liquids, or containing suspended mater, then, samples have to be obtained with care. The bulk can be stirred well, homogenised, and then sampled.

For flowing liquids, samples have to be collected at different points in the flow system. Samples of water from a lake or pond have to be collected at different locations and also from different depths.

1.7.3 Gaseous Samples

Gaseous samples have to be collected and transported to the testing laboratory in leak-proof containers; special gas containers are commercially available for doing this. In the collection of atmospheric samples, the volumes of gas collected and the rate and duration of sampling are important factors as these affect the nature of samples. Gaseous samples should be analysed soon after bringing them to the laboratories as they can change in composition or leak. On-site analysis of gases gives reliable data.

Gaseous samples are dynamic, and therefore they should be tested soon after collection or on site.

1.7.4 Sample Size

The quantity of the sample containing the analyte, used for the actual analysis, is called the sample size. The sample size depends upon

- the quantity of sample source available,
- the nature of the sample,
- the method adopted for the sample analysis,
- the speed of analysis required, and
- the cost of the procedure.

Depending upon the sample size, the analytical methods are classified as *macro, semimicro, micro* and *ultramicro* (Table 1.3).

Table 1.3 Classification of analytical methods based on sample size

Sample weight (g)	Method
0.1 or more	Macro
10^{-2}–10^{-1}	Meso (semimicro)
10^{-3}–10^{-2}	Micro
10^{-4}	Ultramicro

Nanoscale analysis involves 10^{-10} to 10^{-7} ppm of the analyte. The smaller the sample size, more the skill required of the experimenter for successful analysis. Analysis at the micro-scale is a challenge that can be met only with practice by a skilled experimenter.

1.8 DISSOLUTION OF THE SAMPLE

The dissolution of the sample is an important step in analysis. The medium for dissolution should be so chosen as to dissolve the sample completely, especially when complete analysis in required. The medium for dissolution is chosen in the order: water, a dilute acid, a concentrated acid, a mixture of concentrated acids, a special solvent (such as an organic solvent or a liquid which can chemically react and solubilise the sample). With some solvents, special treatments such as fusion or fusion with an acidic or basic flux prior to dissolution may be required. A basic flux such as Na_2CO_3 or NaOH is suitable for fusing an acidic sample, and an acidic flux such as $NaHSO_4$ is suitable for a basic sample. An oxidising agent such as Na_2O_2 or a reducing agent such as Na_2SO_3 may be required as flux for fusing certain types of samples.

After dissolving the sample, the homogeneity of the solution should be ensured. Keeping the solution aside for an hour or two and checking for any sediments or colloids is a method of checking the nature of the solution prepared.

A heterogeneous solution will give spurious results in replicate analyses.

1.9 DESTRUCTIVE AND NON-DESTRUCTIVE ANALYSES

Some of the analytical methods of analysis are non-destructive while the others are destructive (Table 1.4). When the analyte is expensive or when it is required for further testing, a non-destructive method has to be adopted. For example, the samples in a quality control laboratory may be assayed routinely by a destructive method. On the other hand, an expensive sample, such as a ruby gem, has to be necessarily analysed by a non-destructive method.

Table 1.4 Destructive and non-destructive analytical techniques

Destructive methods	Non-destructive methods
Volumetry	X-ray analysis
Gravimetry	Neutron-activation analysis
Potentiometry	ESR spectroscopy
Coulometry	NMR spectroscopy
Voltammetry	IR, UV–vis spectrocopy
Mass spectrometry	Optical methods
Kinetic methods	Chromatography
Thermal methods	Atomic absorption and emission spectroscopy
Turbidimetry	
Nephelometry	Mössbauer spectroscopy

1.10 REAGENT PURITY

The success of an analytical procedure hinges upon the use of pure chemicals at all stages of analysis. The use of expensive instruments and the adoption of consummate skill will be of no avail if the reagents used are of inadequate purity. Therefore, the experimenter should use chemicals of appropriate analytical grade or *spectroscopic grade*. Aqueous solutions of reagents should be prepared in distilled or deionised water. When extremely high degree of accuracy of results is required, all the chemicals and also the water used must be checked for purity before using them.

Purity grades

Commercial grade
Laboratory grade
Analar grade
Spectroscopic grade

(↓ Increasing purity)

1.11 UNITS OF CONCENTRATION

Expressing concentrations is an important aspect of presenting data in analytical chemistry. The common units used for this purpose are listed in Table 1.5.

Table 1.5 Units of concentration

Unit	Symbol	Definition
Molar	M	$\frac{\text{Moles of solute}}{\text{Litres of solution}}$
Molal	m	$\frac{\text{Moles of solute}}{\text{Kilograms of solvent}}$
Formal	F	$\frac{\text{Gram formula weight of solute}}{\text{Litres of solution}}$
Mole fraction	$\mathcal{N}$	$\frac{\text{Moles of solute}}{\text{Moles of solvent + moles of solute}}$
Normal	N	$\frac{\text{Equivalents of solute}}{\text{Litres of solution}}$
Grams per volume	g/v	$\frac{\text{Grams of solute}}{\text{Litres of solution}}$
Weight percent	wt%	$\frac{100 \times \text{Grams of solute}}{\text{Grams of solvent + grams of solute}}$
Volume percent	vol %	$\frac{100 \times \text{Litres of solute}}{\text{Litres of solution}}$
Parts per million	ppm	$\frac{\text{Milligrams of solute}}{\text{Kilograms of solution}} = \frac{\text{Milligrams}}{\text{Litre}}$
Parts per billion	ppb	$\frac{\text{Micrograms}}{\text{Litre}}$

1.12 APPLICATIONS OF ANALYTICAL CHEMISTRY

Analytical chemistry is applied in several branches of science—chemistry, physics, geology, biology and medicine. It is used in industries, especially chemical industries. Its major uses include

- determining physical properties and chemical compositions,
- determining structures,
- quality control,
- disease diagnosis, and
- research projects.

Chemicals are constituents of every material we use or consume, and therefore the knowledge of the chemical composition of such materials is important. Analytical chemistry is applied in determining the chemical composition and exploitation of materials. The advances in analytical techniques – especially the invention of electronic instruments – have dramatically improved and facilitated analytical procedures. Such advances have promoted the application of analytical chemistry in several areas of science and technology. Thus, it plays an important role in agricultural, clinical, food, environmental, forensic, industrial, metallurgical, geological and pharmaceutical science. The modern methods of processing natural resources and exploiting them for various uses largely depend upon the applications of analytical techniques. In industries, where great stress is laid on quality of materials, analytical techniques play a crucial role in quality control.

Analytical Chemistry and the Nobel Prize

In the twentieth century, the research which led to several Nobel Prizes was based on the classical methods of analytical chemistry. This was so not only in chemistry, but also in biology and medicine. The research works of the Nobel laureates Marie Curie, Pierrie Curie, Joliot Curie, H C Brown, R B Woodward, Emil Fischer, A Von Baeyer, Victor Grignard, Fritz Pregl, Jaroslav Heyrovsky, Willard Libby, George de Hevesy, A J P Martin, R L M Synge, F A Aston are a testimony to this fact. Not only inorganic chemists, but organic chemists also have to adopt analytical techniques in their research. Research in biology and medicine also requires the use of several classical and instrumental analytical techniques. Thus, analytical methods play an important role in scientific research.

I M Kolthoff: Father of Modern Analytical Chemistry

Izaak Maurits Kolthoff

Born	11 February 1894 Almelo, Holland
Died	4 March 1993 (aged 99) St. Paul, Minnesota
Nationality	Dutch-born American
Fields	Analytical Chemistry
Institutions	University of Minnesota
Alma mater	University of Utrecht
Doctoral advisor	Nicholas Schoorl
Notable awards	William H Nichols Medal (1949) Robert Boyle Medal

Izaak Maurits Kolthoff (1894–1993) was born at Almelo, Holland. He developed and perfected several analytical methods of analysis involving acidimetry, alkalimetry, gravimetry, colloids and crystal growth. His pioneering work on acid–base indicators led to the understanding of the functioning of these indicators. Iodometry owes its origin to his extensive experimentation.

Kolthoff published his first research article in 1915 at the age of 21. He migrated to the US and worked as a professor at the University of Minnesota between 1927 and 1962. The popular multi-volume book, entitled *Quantitative Inorganic Analysis*, authored by him and T Ernest Sandell (his colleague at Minnesota USA) is the progenitor of all modern textbooks on analytical chemistry.

His work on potentiometric and conductometric titrations, environmental trace metal analyses, biological sensors, polarographic analyses and ion-selective electrodes is both significant and expansive. His student, James Lingane remarked on the death of Kolthoff, 'Analytical Chemistry has never been served by a more original mind, nor a more prolific pen as Kolthoff's'.

'Theory guides; experiment decides': Schoorl.

2 Analysis and Reporting of Data

2.1 INTRODUCTION

Scientific data are collected and reported in great numbers. Theories and applications of science are based on data. Such data have to be critically analysed with the following questions:

- Are the data accurate?
- Are they reproducible?
- Do they truly represent scientific facts?
- Will they stand the test of scrutiny and permanence?

2.2 ANALYSIS OF DATA

Scientific data should be subjected to certain mathematical and statistical tests before they are accepted and reported. In this chapter, an elementary treatment of some of these tests is given.

The mean A mean value is obtained by dividing the sum of a set of replicate measurements by the number of individual results in the sets. For example, if a titration is repeated four times and the titre values are 10.1, 9.9, 10.0 and 10.2 mL, then

$$\text{Mean} = \bar{x} = \frac{10.1 + 9.9 + 10.0 + 10.2}{4} = \frac{40.2}{4} = 10.05$$

This mean value is also called *arithmetic mean* or *average.*

The median This (M) is a value about which all other values in a set are equally distributed. Half of the values are greater and the other half smaller numerically, compared to the median. For example, in the density values of water determined at a particular temperature, 1.01, 1.02, 1.05, 1.03 and 1.04, the median value is 1.03. When a set of data has an even number of values then the median is the average of the middle pair.

For example, the median for the set, 7.1, 7.4, 7.0, 7.5, 7.2, 6.9 is 7.15.

The median versus the mean

- The median M is an estimate of the central value.
- It is not significantly influenced by extraneous values, as is the mean, $\bar{x}$.
- For only two estimates, the median and the mean are identical.
- For three observations from a normal population, the median is better than the mean of the best two out of three values.
- In statistics, the symbol $\bar{x}$ is used to represent the mean of a small set of replicate data. The symbol μ is used to denote the mean of an infinite collection of data.

Test of significance When a new analytical method has been devised, the results must be compared with the results of an accepted, already well-tested method. Then, statistics is applied to check the differences between the two methods. If the new method has to be accepted as reliable, the difference in the means of the two sets of data – one from the old and the other from the new method – must not be significant. The number of data collected and the spread will decide whether one set of data is significantly different from another.

Not only the difference in the means but also the amount of data collected and the spread decide whether one set of results is significantly different from another set.

2.2.1 Why Resort to Statistics?

Most of the sciences depend on experimentation and observation for their day-to-day applications as well for research and progress. The practice of chemistry involves the collection of data and their analysis leading to inferences at every level. While some of these are essentially qualitative, like the identification of the elements present in an organic compound, most others are quantitative in nature, including the determination of the extent to which the different elements are present in the said compound, leading to its molecular formula. In fact, even where a purely qualitative finding is to be made, it will be of benefit to carry out the exercise as quantitatively as possible.

The success of such endeavours is hindered by the experimental data and the results being rarely reproducible: *replications* under as identical conditions as possible lead to readings that differ by a smaller or greater extent depending on a number of factors, so that exact quantification of the measured attribute is rarely achieved. Instead, one obtains a set of readings, many of which differ at least slightly, with no explicit clue as to which of them is 'correct' or 'true'.

Statistics comes to the rescue here. The Computing Dictionary defines statistics as 'the practice, study or result of the application of mathematical functions to *collections* of data in order to summarise or extrapolate [them]'. Statistics is successful in bringing coherence or consistency to disagreeing data in a set, leading to acceptable estimates and enabling the experimenter to progress in his undertaking.

Errors are the cause for readings/data differing minutely even when the experiment is repeated as carefully as possible with the best of apparatus and measuring instruments. Even the most sophisticated instruments are liable to both systematic and random errors (will be discussed in detail), the technique chosen for the experiment may itself be error-prone, and finally, the skill and application of the worker.

> *The purpose of employing statistics to experimental data is to minimise the impact of the errors and arrive at the best estimates of the quantities under study.*

At this juncture, a distinction between two types of data can be made. One pertains to *invariant readings*, like the weight of an empty crucible. In the same class, but slightly different, is the titre value for, say 10 mL of a given solution A with another B of known concentration using a colour indicator; a repetition necessarily involves the use of a fresh 10 mL aliquot of A, the volume pipetted out will not be exactly the same, the intensity of colour at the endpoint might differ, and the volume of B consumed will differ accordingly. In both the situations, the same value (X) is expected to be measured in every replication, but due to differing errors, different estimates are obtained; which explains why the quantity is assigned the symbol X, usually reserved for variables, though it should be invariant. The values recorded in the trials are then denoted by X_i, where i ranges from 1 to N, N being the total number of trials. Here, only one value is being measured in a number of replications.

There are numerous instances when the measured property of the system undergoes change and is a true variable; the change can be in the time domain, that is, the property changes with time, and at each instant of time when it is measured, different values will be obtained, each, of course, containing errors. Thus, the concentration X of a reactant in a mixture undergoing chemical reaction, changes with time in a manner which can be generally represented, in the simplest case, as:

$$X = f(k, t)$$

where k is a reaction parameter which is to be estimated, t and X being the reaction variables. Usually, X is estimated by an appropriate method only once at each of N instants of the reaction, giving a sequence of N time readings of X, each of which inevitably contains errors. Again, statistical methods are employed to minimise the impact of experimental errors present in the data and arrive at the best estimates of the parameter k. To obtain a more reliable estimate of the parameter, the *entire* experiment, the so-called kinetic run in this case, must be repeated, preferably more than once.

There are also cases where the change does not occur with time. Thus, if the photometric absorbance of a given, stable solution of a substance is measured in the UV–visible region, it is found to vary with the wavelength or frequency of the radiation used and does not change with time. The variations lie in the frequency domain, giving the absorbance spectrum of the substance. A parameter governs the absorbance at *each* wavelength, and best estimates of the same can be obtained by repeating the measurement of the absorbance at the wavelength a number of times and subjecting the data to statistical analysis.

2.2.2 Precision and Accuracy

Precision A datum is said to be precise when it is reproducible. For example, when the weight of a crucible is found to be 20.1081 g, and when every time it is weighed the value is 20.1081 g, the value is precise.

Precision is defined as the agreement between the numerical values of two or more measurements of the same object that have been made in an identical manner. Thus a value is said to be precise when there is agreement between a set of results for the same quantity. However, *a precise value need not be accurate.*

Precision can be expressed in an absolute method or a relative method. In the absolute way, the deviation from the mean $(x_i - \bar{x})$ expresses precision without considering sign. Consider the data in Table 2.1.

Table 2.1 Illustrative data for average deviation

Sample of an organic compound	% of carbon	Deviation from mean $\lvert x_i - \bar{x} \rvert$
1	38.42	0.20
2	38.02	0.20
3	38.22	0.00
$\bar{x} = 38.22$		Average deviation $= \frac{0.40}{3} = 0.133$

The mean value for the data is 38.22%. The average deviation from the mean is 0.133. Smaller the average deviation, greater will be the precision of the value.

Sometimes, a relative method for expressing precision is used. For example, for the first value of 1 in Table 2.1,

$$\text{Relative deviation from mean} = \frac{0.20 \times 100}{38.22} = 0.5233 \approx 0.5\%$$

The relative deviation of a value is its percentage deviation in terms of the mean value of the set.

The difference between the maximum value and the minimum value of the set is called the *range*. This is denoted by the symbol w, and it represents the numerical difference between the highest and lowest result. The value of w is a measure of the precision. For the data in Table 2.1 the value of w is the maximum value minus the minimum value:

> • *Precision is a measure of the agreement among a group of results.*
> • *The precision improves as the square root of the number of measurements.*

$$38.42 - 38.02 = 0.40$$

Accuracy A physical property may be determined or calculated accurately by using a good experimental method. For instance, the Avogadro number N, has been determined more accurately from X-ray diffraction on crystals than from the Brownian movement method.

The dissociation constant for acetic acid is 1.75×10^{-5} at 25°C. In an experiment, if a student arrives at exactly this value, his value is said to be accurate. Accuracy represents the nearness of a measurement to its true value. Any difference between the measured value and the true or correct value is expressed as *error*. Accuracy is nearness to a true value whereas precision is concerned with agreement among the measurements made in the same way. For example, if the actual percentage content of moisture in a chemical sample is 2.12%, and if a student obtains the values 2.01%, 2.02% and 2.01% in a triplicate analysis, the values are precise but not accurate.

The term accuracy is denoted in terms of *absolute error, E*. The E is the difference between observed value x_i and the expected value x_t.

$$E = |x_i - x_t|$$

The best measurement of a datum has the least E value. However, the importance to be attached to E will depend on the reliability of x_t. The value of x_t itself may be subject to uncertainty.

If a student obtains a value of 1.69×10^{-5} for the dissociation constant of acetic acid at 25°C, the absolute error in this determination is

$$E = |1.69 \times 10^{-5} - 1.75 \times 10^{-5}| = 0.06 \times 10^{-5}$$

(The sign is ignored.)

Sometimes, the term *relative error* is used to express the uncertainties in data. Relative error denotes the percentage of error compared to the expected value. For the dissociation constant value reported by the student,

$$\text{Relative error} = \frac{-0.06 \times 10^{-5} \times 100}{1.75 \times 10^{-5}} = -3.4\%$$

The recorded datum has a negative error.

Precision is sometimes expressed by a term called the *standard deviation* σ. This denotes the square root of the mean of the square of the difference between the individual measured values x_i and the mean of the number of measurements, μ.

$$\sigma = \left\{\frac{\Sigma(x_i - \mu)^2}{N}\right\}^{1/2}$$

N is the number of values measured.

This equation is applicable only for a large set of measurements. The value of σ is known as *population standard deviation*. Suppose all measurements are not available and if a random sample is taken, then the standard deviation of the population is estimated using the equation

$$S = \left\{ \frac{\Sigma(x_i - \bar{x})^2}{N-1} \right\}^{1/2}$$

where $\bar{x}$ is the mean of the sample values. The symbol S instead of σ is used here to indicate that the standard deviation obtained is only an approximation of the true value. When $N \to \infty$, $S \to \sigma$.

Another term used to denote precision is the *coefficient of variation* (C.V.). This is given as

$$\text{C.V.} = \frac{(\text{Standard deviation} \times 100)}{\text{Mean}} = \frac{S \times 100}{\bar{x}}$$

Deviation The deviation d_i, of result x_i, is defined as the absolute difference between the result and the mean, that is

$$d_i = |x_i - \bar{x}|$$

The average deviation $\bar{d}$ is defined as

$$\bar{d} = \frac{\sum_{i=1}^{i=N} |x_i - \bar{x}|}{N}$$

Variance The square of standard deviation s^2, is called the variance.

$$s^2 = \frac{\Sigma x_i^2 - N(\bar{x})^2}{N-1} = \frac{\Sigma x_i^2 - (\Sigma x_i)^2/N}{N-1}$$

Problem 2.1 Multiple analysis of an ore of thorium gave the following percentage values for its thorium content: 0.354, 0.361, 0.356, 0.355, 0.358, 0.357, 0.354, 0.357, 0.359, 0.359. From these data, calculate the mean, standard deviation and coefficient of variation.

Solution

Mean $\bar{x} = 0.357$

Standard deviation $s = \frac{\sqrt{\Sigma(x - \bar{x})^2}}{n-1}$

$$= \frac{\sqrt{0.000048}}{\sqrt{9}}$$

$$= \sqrt{0.000053}$$

$$= \pm 0.00728$$

$$\text{C.V.} = \frac{s \times 100}{\bar{x}} = \frac{0.00728 \times 100}{0.357}$$

$$= 2.04\%$$

Thorium percent	$x - \bar{x}$	$(x - \bar{x})^2$
0.354	–0.003	0.000009
0.361	0.004	0.000016
0.356	–0.001	0.000001
0.355	–0.002	0.000004
0.358	0.001	0.000001
0.357	0.000	0.000000
0.354	–0.003	0.000009
0.357	0.000	0.000000
0.359	0.002	0.000004
0.359	0.002	0.000004
$\Sigma x = 3.570$		$\Sigma(x - \bar{x})^2 = 0.000048$

- The mean of several measurements $\bar{x}$ is a more reliable estimate of the true mean than is given by one measurement.
- The greater the number of measurements (n), the closer to the true mean will be the sample average.
- The standard error of the mean s_x is given by

$$s_x = \frac{s}{\sqrt{n}}$$

The precision of a measurement may be improved by increasing the number of measurements.

In Problem 2.1,

$$s_x = \pm\frac{0.0728}{\sqrt{10}} = 0.0023$$

The standard error of the mean decreases as more measurements are made. If twenty measurements were made,

$$s_x = \pm\frac{0.00728}{\sqrt{20}} = 0.0016$$

Various cases of accuracy and precision are denoted in Fig. 2.1.

(a) Excellent precision, excellent accuracy
(b) Low precision, high accuracy
(c) Excellent precision, low accuracy
(d) Low precision, low accuracy

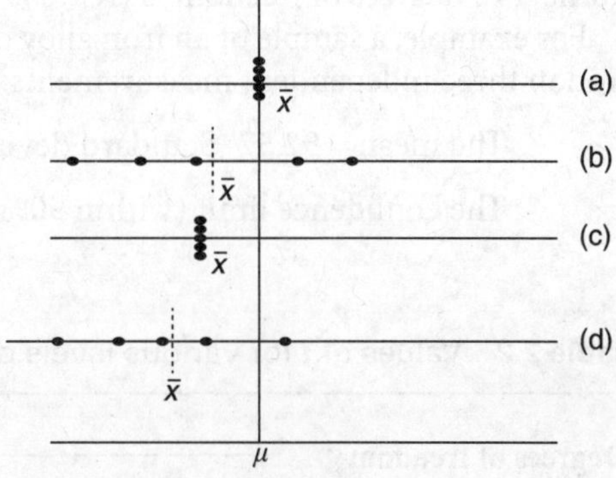

Fig. 2.1 Accuracy and precision (for five measurements)

(i) Case (a) represents excellent precision because the individual measurements are close together. It denotes excellent accuracy also because the measurements agree with the true value, μ.
(ii) Case (b) denotes low precision because the measurements are scattered. It, however, represents high accuracy because the average (mean) value $\bar{x}$ is close to the true value, μ.
(iii) Case (c) indicates excellent precision because the measurements are close together, but poor accuracy because $\bar{x}$ is different from μ.
(iv) Case (d) denotes low precision because the measurements are scattered and also low accuracy because $\bar{x}$ is much different from μ.

Mode The mode x_p, is defined as the value that occurs most frequently.

In the set of data on the replicate measurement of temperature, 70.1, 70.8, 70.1, 69.9, 70.1°C, the mode is 70.1, as it occurs more frequently.

Range The range R, is defined as the difference between the highest and the lowest result in a set of data. It is denoted as

$$R = x_{\text{highest}} - x_{\text{lowest}}$$

The range in the temperature data is 70.8 – 69.9 = 0.9°C.

2.2.3 Confidence Limits

The precision associated with a particular set of data is indicated by the standard deviation. However, a large number of data is required for the standard deviation to provide reliable information about the experimentally determined mean $\bar{x}$. In an ideal case $\bar{x}$ should be equal to the true mean value μ. With statistical theory, we can find out the range within which the true value might fall. Thus limits may be set about the experimentally determined mean $\bar{x}$ within which the true mean is expected to fall with a certain probability. The limits obtained in this manner are called *confidence limits.* For example, applying the statistical theory, if we can conclude from measurements that the true boiling point of ethanol at 760 torr should fall between 77.9°C and 78.4°C then, these two temperatures represent the *confidence limits.* The interval between the confidence limits is known as the *confidence interval.* The confidence interval is derived from the standard deviation and its magnitude depends upon the certainty with which the standard deviation is known.

The confidence limit is expressed as,

$$\text{Confidence limit} = \bar{x} \pm \left(t \frac{S}{\sqrt{N}} \right)$$

The factor t is a statistical factor and it depends on the number of degrees of freedom (N) and the confidence limit (Table 2.2); S is the estimated standard deviation. For the t-factor the number of degrees of freedom is $(N-1)$.

For example, a sample of an iron alloy on analysis gave values of 92.10%, 92.72%, 92.90% of iron in three independent measurements.

The mean = 92.57 Standard deviation, $S = 0.42$

$$\text{The confidence limit (within 90\% range)} = 92.57 \pm (2.92 \times 0.42/\sqrt{3})$$

$$= 92.57 \pm 0.71\ (91.86, 93.28)$$

Table 2.2 Values of *t* for various levels of probability

Degrees of freedom	Factor for confidence interval, %				
	80	90	95	99	99.9
1	3.08	6.31	12.7	63.7	63.7
2	1.89	2.92	4.30	9.93	31.6
3	1.64	2.35	3.18	5.84	12.9
4	1.53	2.13	2.78	4.60	8.60
5	1.48	2.02	2.57	4.03	6.86
6	1.44	1.94	2.45	3.71	5.96
7	1.42	1.90	2.36	3.50	5.41
8	1.40	1.86	2.31	3.36	5.04
9	1.38	1.83	2.26	3.25	4.78
10	1.37	1.81	2.23	3.17	4.59
11	1.36	1.80	2.20	3.11	4.44
12	1.36	1.78	2.18	3.06	4.32
13	1.35	1.77	2.16	3.01	4.22
14	1.35	1.76	2.15	2.98	4.14
∞	1.29	1.65	1.96	2.58	3.29

Estimation of S from w The standard deviation S can be estimated from the range w of the data using the relationship,

$$S = \frac{w}{d}$$

where d is a statistical factor. This factor depends upon the number of measurements or samples (Table 2.3).

Table 2.3 Factors for calculating standard deviation S from spread w employing $S = w/d$

Number of samples, N	d	Number of samples, N	d
2	1.428	9	2.970
3	1.693	10	3.078
4	2.059	11	3.173
5	2.326	12	3.258
6	2.534	13	3.336
7	2.704	14	3.407
8	2.847	15	3.472

Confidence interval denotes the values within which there is a specified probability that the true value will occur.

2.2.4 Errors

A datum error is the difference between the measured and correct value.

Error may be introduced in a measured value of a property by a number of sources. Errors in a measurement will affect the accuracy and precision of the measured quantity and hence the reliability of the data. Errors are of two main types:

(i) Determinate errors
(ii) Indeterminate errors.

The difference between the experimental value and the true value is called the *absolute error*.

2.2.4.1 Determinate Errors or Systematic Errors

These errors are determinable and therefore are avoidable if care is taken. Determinate errors have definite values and are classified into three types:
(i) Instrumental errors, (ii) operative errors and (iii) methodic errors.

(i) ***Instrumental errors***: Instrumental errors are introduced due to the use of defective instruments. For example, an error in a volumetric analysis will be introduced when a 20 mL pipette, which actually measures 20.1 mL, is used. Sometimes, an instrumental error may arise from the environmental factors on the instrument. For example, a pipette calibrated at 20°C, if used at 30°C, will introduce error in volume. Instrumental errors may be largely eliminated by periodically calibrating the instruments and also using appropriate blanks.

(ii) ***Operative errors***: These errors are also called *personal errors* and are introduced because of variation of personal judgments. For example, due to colour blindness, a person may arrive at wrong results in a volumetric or colorimetric analysis. Using incorrect mathematical equations and committing arithmetic mistakes will also cause operative errors. Errors of operators due to carelessness, fatigue or inadequate instruction can also lead to operative errors. Such errors are called *gross mistakes.* Arithmetic mistakes, misplacing numbers and decimals in recording data, reading a scale wrongly, reversing a sign and using a wrong scale are some among the gross mistakes. Frequently, personal errors arise due to bias—human tendency to estimate readings in a direction that improves the precision of the results.

Gross errors: Gross errors are a type of operative error. An error originating due to the carelessness of the experimenter is a gross error. For example, spilling a part of the weighed sample and ignoring it knowingly or unknowingly is a gross error. The following are other examples for gross error:

- When an instrument has two scales on the same panel, the wrong scale is used in recording readings.
- The material being handled gets contaminated during the experiment.
- A positive reading on a meter is recorded as a negative one and vice versa.
- Transposing the numbers in recording a measurement; for example, when the actual reading is 0.0171, it is recorded as 0.0117.

A gross error in a set of replicate measurements can be easily recognised—it appears as an *outlier*. An outlier in a data set is a datum noticeably different from the data in the set. For example, in the data pertaining to a replicate analysis 2.70, 2.65, 2.71, 2.52, 2.72, the datum 2.52 is an outlier.

Some researchers are happy with outliers as they provide them with proof – though false – for advancing preconceived ideas. For example, one or two outliers in say, five sets of data on *x* and *y* may permit the researcher to present them as a smooth curve, though in actuality, *x* and *y* are linearly related.

- *Data of questionable reliability are worthless. A few reliable data, collected carefully, are more dependable than several carelessly collected data.*
- *A proportional error is a determinate error which varies with sample size such that the relative error remains constant.*

Determinate errors may be constant when the absolute value (E) of the error is the same for all examples. For example, when a fixed volume of a reagent containing a constant quantity of an interfering contaminant is used in replicate analysis, the results of the analyses will always be in error by a fixed degree. For example, in the volumetric analysis of vinegar for its acetic acid content, if the vinegar samples are contaminated with a fixed quantity of formic acid, then there would a constant positive error in the results.

Determinate errors may be *proportional errors*, when the relative error (E/μ) is constant, that is, the absolute error E is proportional to the quantity μ of the determined substance. For example, if the concentration of a standard acid solution is in error by +0.5 %, then the apparent amount of the base reacted with it will always be in error by –0.5%, since the volume of the acid required for neutralisation will be 0.5% lower.

Some determinate errors are composite systematic errors; such errors are combinations of constant and proportional errors. Systematic errors of different types are depicted in Fig. 2.2.

(a) Ideal agreement with no determinate errors
(b) Constant positive determinate error
(c) Constant negative determinate error
(d) Proportional positive error
(e) Proportional negative error
(f) Composite: constant error + proportional error

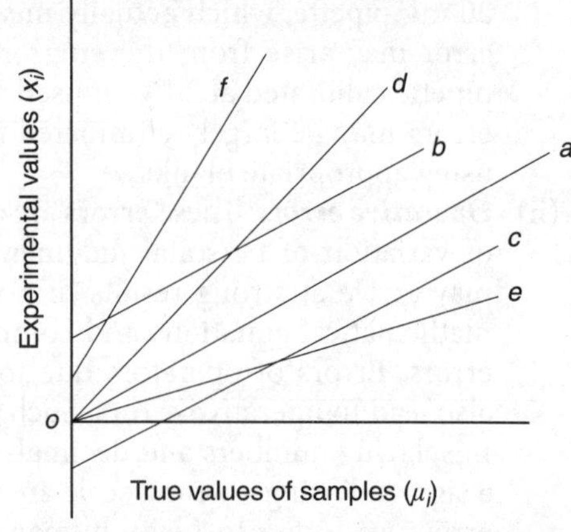

Fig. 2.2 Types of systematic errors

(iii) ***Methodic errors***: These errors are caused by adopting defective experimental methods. For example, in the gravimetric estimation of lead as lead chromate, the method of precipitating lead chromate may involve co-precipitation of impurities. This would lead to spuriously high weight of lead chromate and hence incorrect estimated value of lead.

In volumetric analysis, the use of an improper indicator leading to wrong results is an example for methodic error. Proper understanding of the theoretical background of the experiment is a necessity for avoiding methodic errors. Methodic errors are generally difficult to detect and hence the most serious of the three types of determinate errors.

- To detect systematic errors in an analysis, a known amount of standard is added to a sample and the datum is re-recorded. Invariance of the datum would confirm the absence of any systematic error. Analysis of reference substance, independent of the sample may also help detect systematic errors.
- Determinate or systematic errors are not random; they occur identically in replicate measurements because they originate from identical faulty measurement. For example, when you determine the end point in a titration using an inappropriate indicator, then you obtain a wrong end point. Nevertheless, the end points may be precise—you may obtain identical, but incorrect, end points.
- Determinate errors may be additive or multiplicative, depending on the nature of the error and how the error enters into the calculation.
- A determinate error of constant magnitude is called a *constant error*; its relative value decreases as the size of the sample increases.

Systematic errors: bias ***Bias*** in data is any systematic error rendering the data uncertain. It refers to the tendency of a measurement process to overestimate or underestimate the value. When bias is absent in measurements, then the limiting mean μ_A is the true value x_t.

Number bias is a source of personal systematic error. For example, when recording the readings in a sensitive voltmeter, a person may tend to estimate the position of the needle on the scale with preference for the digits 0 and 5. Similarly, the experimenter may have preference for small digits over large digits and also for even digits over odd digits. When recording burette readings, a person may tend to prefer the reading, say, 21.0 mL when it is actually 21.05 mL.

Systematic errors cause bias in a measurement method. Bias is illustrated by Fig. 2.3. It shows the frequency distribution of replicate results in the analysis of identical samples by two methods that have random errors of identical size. Method A has no bias; in this case, the limiting mean is the true value x_t. Method B has a bias. Such a bias is denoted by

$$\text{Bias} = \mu_B - x_t = \mu_B - \mu_A$$

The bias has a sign; it affects all of the data in a set.

- Systematic errors have a definite value.
- They arise due to definite cause.
- Such errors have the same sign and magnitude for replicate measurements recorded in exactly the same way.

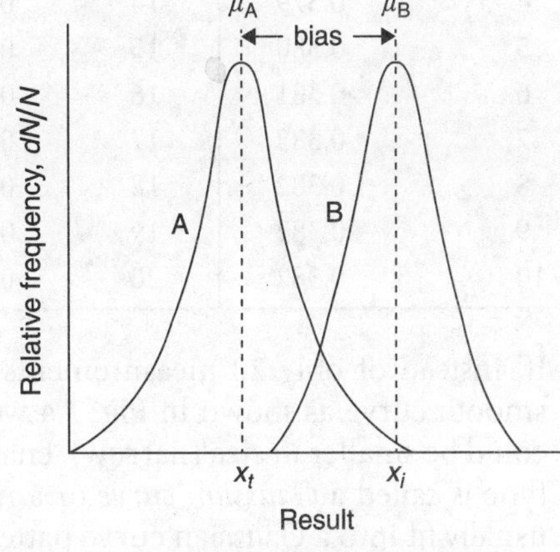

Fig. 2.3 Depiction of bias

2.2.4.2 Indeterminate or Random Errors

The random error E_r for the mean of the small set is given by

$$E_r = \bar{x} - \mu$$

The mean for a finite set of data approaches the true mean where the number of measurements N increases beyond 20 or 30.

Repetitive analytical measurements give a *scatter of data* consequent to random or indeterminate errors. Generally, data scatter on the sample is indicative of random errors. The 20 replicate absorbance measurements of a sample of Ce(IV) aqueous solution are given in Table 2.4. The measured absorbances are directly proportional to [Ce(IV)]. These data have a scatter because of random errors. The distribution of random errors in these data becomes easily discernible on reorganisation of these to equal-size, contiguous data sets (cells) as represented in Table 2.5 (a). Then, the relative frequency of occurrence of data [Table 2.5 (b)] in each cell is plotted to produce a *bar graph* called a *histogram* (Fig. 2.4).

Table 2.4 Absorbance values in the order as recorded

Serial no.	Absorbance	Serial no.	Absorbance
1	0.381	11	0.382
2	0.379	12	0.389
3	0.383	13	0.387
4	0.382	14	0.387
5	0.378	15	0.382
6	0.385	16	0.388
7	0.384	17	0.376
8	0.386	18	0.386
9	0.384	19	0.380
10	0.379	20	0.382

Table 2.5 (a) Absorbance values arranged in increasing order

Serial no.	Absorbance	Serial no.	Absorbance
1	0.376	11	0.383
2	0.378	12	0.384
3	0.379	13	0.384
4	0.379	14	0.385
5	0.380	15	0.386
6	0.381	16	0.386
7	0.382	17	0.387
8	0.382	18	0.387
9	0.382	19	0.388
10	0.382	20	0.389

Table 2.5 (b) Absorbance values grouped in cells

	0.375 – 0.380	0.381 – 0.385	0.386 – 0.390
	0.376	0.381	0.386
	0.378	0.382	0.386
	0.379	0.382	0.387
	0.379	0.382	0.387
	0.380	0.382	0.388
		0.383	0.389
		0.384	
		0.384	
		0.385	
No	5	9	6

If, instead of only 20 measurements, there were a large number of measurements, then, a smooth curve as shown in Fig. 2.4 would be obtained; with a large number of data, the cells could be smaller in size (narrow), enabling us to draw a smooth curve. A smooth curve of this type is called a *Gaussian curve* or a normal error curve. Replicate measurements of a datum usually fit into a Gaussian curve pattern.

The pattern of distribution of data, as revealed by the cells, is called the *frequency distribution*. Taller a bar is in the histogram, more is the frequency distribution for the data in that cell. This distribution is plotted as percentage of measurements. The frequency distribution in a Gaussian curve has the following features.

> *Gaussian, also known as* normal distribution, *is a mathematical function giving the relative frequency of an error as a function of its magnitude. A graph of the function gives a bell-shaped curve.*

- The most frequently observed result is the mean μ of the set of data (denoted in the tallest bar).

- The other results cluster symmetrically around this mean value.
- Small variations from the central mean value occur more frequently than large variations (as revealed by the decreasing heights of the bars on the two sides of the tallest one).
- When systematic errors have been minimised (which is possible), then, the mean of a large set of data approaches the true value.
- Random errors in an analysis can only be minimised but never totally eliminated.
- The ideal μ is obtained from a very large set of data. However, we can perform only two or three replicated measurements; therefore, the μ value from such measurements has significant random error. Smaller the replicate data set, larger is the uncertainty in μ.
- The μ actually means the mean of an infinite set of data; the mean of a small set of data is symbolised by $\bar{x}$. The $\bar{x}$ value approaches μ (*limiting mean*) when the number of replicate measurements N increases.

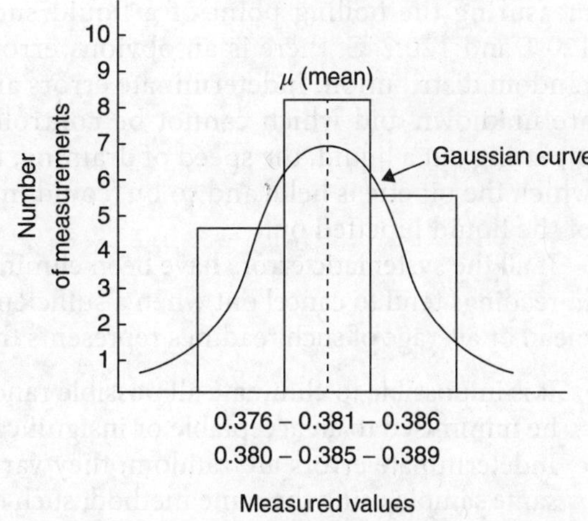

Fig. 2.4 Histogram and frequency program for absorbance measurements of 20 replicate amylase solutions

Problem 2.2 In the determination of titanium in an ore, which actually contains 10.7% of Ti, the following data were obtained:

Weight of ore (g) analysed	% Ti, experimental
0.7720	10.81
2.0000	10.02
0.9182	10.91
1.3271	10.07

Assess the type of error associated with the determination.

Solution

The data are first rearranged in the order of rank in sample weights to understand the trend in the result.

Sample (g)	Ti (g) Expected (10.7%)	Ti (g) Experimental	Absolute error
0.7720	0.0826	0.0835	+0.0009
0.9182	0.0982	0.1002	+0.0020
1.3271	0.1420	0.1336	–0.0084
2.0000	0.2140	0.2004	–0.0136

The error values are not constant; they are random, with different values and also signs. Therefore, the errors are of random type. These errors are therefore indeterminate.

If the method is defective, then there should have been a constant determinate error, of course, eliminating the random errors.

Indeterminate errors Indeterminate errors are the errors which arise in a measurement when all *known* sources of determinate errors have been identified and eliminated. These errors are also called *accidental* or *random errors.* For example, when a student measuring the boiling point of a liquid successively reports the values as 120.0, 119.8, 120.1 and 120.2°C, there is an obvious error in his measurements. These errors follow a random distribution. Indeterminate errors arise from uncertainties in a measurement that are unknown and which cannot be controlled by the experimenter. For example, when pipetting out a liquid, the speed of draining, the angle of holding the pipette, the portion at which the pipette is held, and so on, could introduce an indeterminate error in the volume of the liquid pipetted out.

If all the systematic errors have been eliminated or adjusted for, the random errors present in readings tend to cancel out when a sufficiently large number of readings is taken. Then the mean or average of such readings represents the best estimate of the true value.

- It is impossible to eliminate all possible random errors in an experiment; they can however be minimised to an acceptable or insignificant degree.
- Indeterminate errors are random; they vary from one determination to another with the same sample using the same method; such errors cannot be eliminated.
- Indeterminate errors follow a *normal distribution*—also called *Gaussian curve.* The figure denotes how the error is distributed with reference to the mean. The curve is drawn by plotting the values of standard deviations (σ) for the data on a particular property with reference to the mean value. The symbol σ represents the standard deviation of an infinite population of measurements. The figure shows the spread of the normal population distribution.

Errors in Burette Readings

- The smallest graduation in the common 50 mL burette is 0.1 mL. Students can therefore record burette volumes correctly only up to 0.1 mL. A careful observer may record up to 0.05 mL, though such a graduation has not been marked on the burette. This however, is only an approximation. Recording readings such as 0.01 mL, 0.07 mL using such a burette is not appropriate and reliable. When, such readings of volume are required, a micro-burette has to be used, which may have divisions up to 0.01 mL.
- During a titration, the final burette reading should be recorded at least 30 seconds *after* the final addition of the titrant. This allows for the complete drainage of the liquid from the inner walls of the burette on to the liquid surface inside the burette. Otherwise, one would record a higher volume than the correct one. This precaution is more relevant especially when the titration is preformed rapidly.
- Another common error in titrations involves the presence of a hanging titrant drop at the tip of the burette nozzle. This leads to an erroneously higher burette reading than the correct reading of volume.
- A burette with dirty inner walls produces 'islands' of liquid adhering on the walls, instead of a uniform liquid film—this introduces error in readings.
- The presence of air bubbles in the liquid column in the burette is another common source of error.

2.2.4.3 Rules for Improving Accuracy of Data

- Every instrument used in the analysis must be checked and calibrated.
- Blanks should be used along with the test sample whenever possible.
- A particular measurement should be repeatedly made under stringently identical conditions and its constancy checked.

- All possible personal errors must be predicted and then eliminated in each measurement.
- Errors involving arithmetic mistakes, transposition of numbers in recording the data, reading a scale backward, reversing a sign, using a wrong scale and applying a wrong equation must be avoided. The computing equipment itself must be checked for its soundness.
- The instrument reading must be re-read after the value has been recorded and then the new value must be checked against the one that has already been recorded.
- An experiment for obtaining data should not be performed when the experimenter is tired or has not received complete instructions.

2.2.5 Rejection of Data

Rejection of an observation In analytical chemistry, in replicate measurements, one result in the set may be widely different from the rest. The obviously discordant datum in a set can be rejected without much thought. However, frequently, replicate results do not lend themselves to such clear situations and decisions.

When the number of replicate values is small, rejection of a datum becomes a dilemma. The divergent datum exerts a significant effect upon the mean. In addition, the insufficient data pose a problem in performing reliable statistical analysis of the results.

The 2.5 d rule: A rule applied for rejection of a datum from a set of data is called the 2.5 *d* rule. The following steps are adopted in applying this rule:

- Identify the 'suspect' result.
- Calculate the mean of the 'good' results.
- Then, calculate the average deviation of the 'good' (remaining) results.
- Calculate the deviation of the suspect result from the mean of the 'good' results.
- If the deviation of the suspect result from the mean of the 'good' ones is at least 2.5 times the average deviation of the 'good' results, then, reject the suspect result, else retain it.

The 2.5 *d* rule is associated with a very low limit. Sometimes, another rule, called the *4 d* rule is applied for rejection of data. It is similar to the 2.5 *d* rule, except that the deviation of the suspect result can be 4 times the average deviation of the 'good' results. Therefore, the 4 *d* rule entails less frequent data rejection.

Avoiding Errors in the Use of a Pipette

- When the liquid from a pipette is delivered, the liquid column from the tip to the top graduation should be free from air bubbles.
- The liquid from a pipette should be delivered slowly by opening the top partly and not fully; fast delivery may result in retention of some liquids on the inner walls of the pipette.
- A pipette is graduated to measure the marked volume *excluding* the little liquid retained at the tip after delivery; therefore, this liquid portion should not be forced out by blowing or pricking the pipette tip on the glass surface.
- Hot liquids should never be pipetted out.
- Pipettes should never be heat-dried at high temperatures, > 60°C.
- Pipettes should be washed and rinsed with distilled water immediately after use.
- Solutions should never be allowed to get dry inside a pipette; if this happens, a permanent coating of salt may form on the inner walls and introduce error in the volume.

Problem 2.3 The percentage of tungsten in an alloy was estimated and replicate analyses gave the values 3.12%, 3.17%, 3.13% and 3.10%. The 2 d test may be applied to this set of data to check whether the value 3.17 (suspect) can be discarded.

(i) Calculate the mean and average deviation of the three 'good' results.

	Results		Deviations
	3.12		0.00
	3.13		0.01
	3.10		0.02
Mean	3.12	Average deviation	0.01

(ii) Calculate the deviation of the suspect result from the mean of the three 'good' results:

$3.17 - 3.12 = 0.05$

using the 2.5 d rule,

$2.5 \times 0.01 = 0.025$

As $0.05 > 0.025$ the suspect result (3.17) is rejected.

2.2.5.1 The *Q* Test

Frequently, one or two values in a set of data may appear suspect, and the decision to reject these or not may become difficult. A test called the *Q*-test is applied while making such a decision. The difference between the questionable value and its nearest value is divided by the range of the entire set. The resulting ratio is denoted as *Q*. This *Q* value is then compared with the questionable value. This *Q* value is called the Q_{exp}. If this is greater than Q_{crit} (Table 2.6) it is rejected, and if it is less, it is retained.

For $N = 5$,

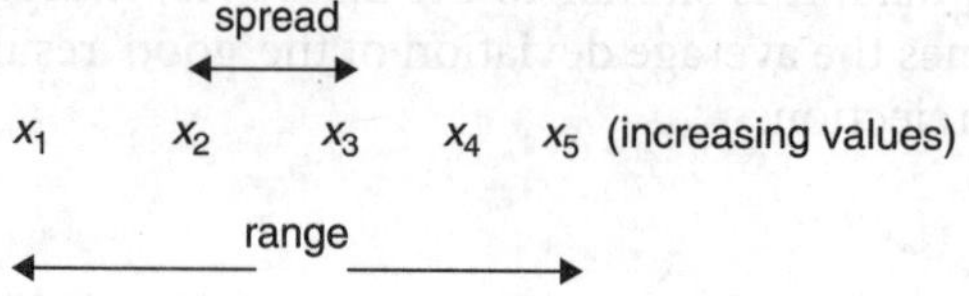

Table 2.6 Critical values* for rejection quotient *Q*

Number of observations	Q_{crit} (Reject if $Q_{exp} > Q_{crit}$)		
	90% confidence	96% confidence	99% confidence
3	0.94	0.98	0.99
4	0.76	0.85	0.93
5	0.64	0.73	0.82
6	0.56	0.64	0.74
7	0.51	0.59	0.68
8	0.47	0.54	0.63
9	0.44	0.51	0.60
10	0.41	0.48	0.57

*Dean R B and Dixon W J, *Anal. Chem.*, 23, 636 (1951).

The *spread* is defined as $x_2 - x_1$; it is the difference between two closest values.
When $N = 3 - 7$, the range is $x_N - x_1$.
x_N is the largest value in the set.
When $N = 8$ or 9, the range is $x_{N-1} - x_1$.
x_{N-1} is the largest value ignoring the largest value of the set.

$$Q = \frac{\text{spread}}{\text{range}}$$

A Q value is always less than 1.

2.2.5.2 Formulae for the *Q* Test

Suspect result	**Formula for the test**
Smallest value, x_1	$Q = \dfrac{x_2 - x_1}{x_N - x_1}$
Largest value, x_N	$Q = \dfrac{x_N - x_{N-1}}{x_N - x_1}$

Problem 2.4 Apply the Q test to each of the following sets of data and determine whether any data should be rejected.

(i) 50.17, 50.23, 49.91, 50.15 (ii) 0.0172, 0.0174, 0.0185, 0.0171

Solution

(i) The value, 49.91 is a suspect value, as it is significantly different from the other three values.

$$Q_{exp} = \frac{49.91 - 50.15}{50.23 - 49.91} = \frac{-0.24}{0.32} = 0.75$$

(The negative sign is ignored, as only the numerical difference matters.)

For $N = 4$, $Q_{0.90} = 0.76$

Q_{exp}, $0.75 < Q_{crit}$ 0.76

Therefore, the value 49.91 should be retained.

(ii) The value 0.0185 appears suspect; it is the largest value.

$$Q_{exp} = \frac{0.0185 - 0.0174}{0.0185 - 0.0171} = \frac{0.0011}{0.0014} = 0.78$$

Q_{exp} $0.78 > Q_{crit}$ 0.76

Therefore, the value 0.0185 should be rejected.

In the case of three replicates, with two coinciding values, $Q_{exp} = 1$. Therefore, the suspect value should always be rejected, regardless of the magnitude of its deviation from the two identical results.

In rare cases, the experimenter may have reasons to retain the suspect value. Then, the median M of the set, instead of the mean is reported; this is because M is insensitive to the divergent value and it is computed considering all the data. The $\bar{x}$ value is very sensitive to a divergent value, especially when N is very small.

Problem 2.5 A beta-active material was analysed for its radioactivity. The first three replicate measurements gave the results, 72.02, 69.12 and 71.90 disintegrations per minute (each is an average per minute, after measuring the activity for a longer period). If a fourth measurement is also made, (i) how large, and (ii) how small can it be so that it is to be rejected under the Q-test at the 0% (two-tailed) confidence level?

Solution

$$Q = \frac{\text{spread}}{\text{range}}$$

$$Q\ 90\% = 0.765$$

$\therefore$ the maximum measurement x_i, satisfies

$$\frac{72.02 - x_1}{69.12 - x_1} = 0.765$$

solving, $x = 81.63$ dpm (upper limit for rejection)

Similarly, the minimum measurement x_i satisfies

$$\frac{69.12 - x_1}{72.02 - x_1} = 0.765$$

Solving, $x_i = 59.97$ dpm (lower limit for rejection)

- The Q-test is a statistical test for examining and discarding an experimental result with a specified probability or confidence.

2.3 REPORTING OF DATA

2.3.1 The Significant Figure

Every measured value has some associated uncertainty. This uncertainty is indicated as the *standard deviation* of the value. *The standard deviation represents the deviation from the mean.* For example, if the E_a value of a reaction is reported as 120 ± 5 kJ mol^{-1}, it means that the correct value can be anything between 115 and 125 kJ mol^{-1}.

Data have to be reported with care, keeping in mind the reliability about the number of figures used. For example, when reporting an E_a value, as many as six decimal numbers can be obtained when one uses a calculator. However, reporting all these decimal numbers is meaningless because, as is generally true, there may be uncertainty about the first decimal itself. Therefore, experimental data should be rounded off so that they contain only the digits known with certainty plus the first uncertain one. If the refractive index of a liquid is known with certainty only up to two decimals, the value should be reported only up to three decimals. This practice is called the *significant figure practice.*

A zero is not a significant figure when used to locate a decimal. However, it is significant when it occurs at the end. For example, 0.0405 has three significant figures, the two zeros (0.0) before the 4 being used to imply only the magnitude; but 0.04050 has four significant figures, the zero beyond the 5 being significant. To make this point clear, the exponential notation is useful. The value 4.05×10^{-2} has only three significant figures, while 4.050×10^{-2} has four significant numbers. The datum, reported as 4.050×10^{-2} indicates that the last 0 is relevant, as it has been evaluated reliably.

The number of significant figures in a given number is found by counting the number of figures from the left to right in the number beginning with the first non-zero digit and continuing until reaching the digit that contains the uncertainty. Each of the following has three significant figures.

646 0.317 9.22 0.00149 20.2

The number of significant figures that should be included in a datum should be decided with care. For addition and subtraction, the number of significant figures can be ascertained by visual inspection. For example, in the summation

$$4.1 + 0.18 + 2.1 = 6.38 = 6.4$$

the second decimal place in the sum value is not significant because of an uncertainty in the first decimal place in the value, 4.1. Therefore, the sum should be reported as 6.4.

When multiplication and division are carried out, it is assumed that the number of significant figures of the result is equal to the number of significant figures of the component quantity that contains the least number of significant figures. For example,

$$\frac{(11 \times 0.122)}{10} = 0.1342 = 0.13$$

This result has to be given only in two significant figures, because two of the component quantities have only two significant figures. However, such rounding off may not be always desirable, especially when such a rounding off leads to magnified uncertainty in the reported value. Rounding off may conceal the original difference between data. To illustrate this, consider the two rate constants, 2.024×10^{-3} and 2.011×10^{-3} s^{-1}. These values differ by 0.013. On rounding off, these will become 2.02×10^{-3} and 2.01×10^{-3} s^{-1}. This difference of one unit may not be a good representation of the values, especially when the two rate constants are expected to be different. Therefore, rounding off of data should be done with care and thought. Logarithms and antilogarithms must be rounded off with care. Otherwise, significant changes in the final value from the real value may occur. For example, log 2.13 is 0.3284. When 2.13 is rounded off to 2.1, the logarithmic value becomes 0.3222, which is appreciably different from 0.3284.

When a number is rounded off to reduce it to a significant number of figures, the rule is that, for a 5 or above in the last figure rejected, the last retained figure is increased by one. Thus 2.736, if rounded to three figures, becomes 2.74; if it is rounded to two figures, it becomes 2.7. In calculations, rounding off should be done at the final stage. This would avoid *rounding errors*. Rounding off at every stage may sometimes significantly alter the final value.

Examples

(i) $13.90 + 0.0080 + 2.0 + 0.082 = 15.99 = 16.0$

(ii) $(15.91 \times 0.0062)/0.081 = 1.20395 = 1.2$

(iii) $(1.0051 - 0.0032)(1.41) = 1.427 = 1.41$

(iv) $(2.87 \times 4.008) + (7.82 \times 1.7) = 1.1503 + 13.294 = 14.4443 = 14.4$

or

$1.15 + 13.3 = 14.45 = 14.5$

Problem 2.6 How many significant numbers are there in each of the following numbers?

(i) 7.045 (ii) 0.0070 (iii) 2.00×104 (iv) π

Solution

(i) Four (ii) two (iii) three (iv) infinity

Examples

Numbers	Number of significant figures
23	2
207	3
1.072	4
0.007	1
0.0010	2
2.00×10^4	3
π	∞

Examples

Calculation		Result in proper number of significant digits
(i) $17.02 + 13.3 + 0.17 =$	30.49	30.5
(ii) $142 - 2.7 =$	139.3	139
(iii) $13.8 \div 10.1 =$	1.366	1.37
(iv) $53.0 + 0.0031 + 0.00002 =$	53.00312	53.0

The concept of significant figures may be summarised as rules. These rules provide only the possible uncertainties in a datum, whereas, it would be prudent to assume that the real uncertainty is greater than that defined by these rules.

Rule 1: A value is reported so that it contains all the digits known with certainty, in addition to a digit that is known only to within ±1.

If the actual uncertainty is calculated, say, as a standard deviation σ, then σ automatically determines the number of significant figures. The value of standard deviation is preferably known to two digits, and this necessitates showing the second uncertain digit also in the original value.

For example, if replicate measurements in an experiment gave an average result of 7.131 and a standard deviation of 0.026, then, the result should be denoted as 7.131 ± 0.026. This shows that only the first two digits, 7 and 1 in the result are certain; the digits 3 and 1 are uncertain. In such a case, the second uncertain digit is shown as a subscript, 7.13_1. If only one digit of the standard deviation has to be retained, the rules of rounding would be applied, and the result would be written as 7.13 ± 0.03.

Rule 2: A zero between non-zero digits (for example, 1.081) is always significant. *Leading zeros* – as in 0.0072 – merely locate the decimal point and are not significant. *Trailing zeros* of integers may or may not be significant. In the following values, 0.317, 0.7001 and 0.004, the zero *before* the decimal point in each case is non-significant.

Values with significant zeros:

30.18203; in this value, as there is uncertainty only in the fifth decimal, the fourth decimal digit 0 becomes significant.

7.860 ± 0.001; in this, uncertainty exists in the third decimal and so the third decimal digit 0 is insignificant.

The scientific power notation can be used to clearly show which trailing zeros are significant.

The datum 70000 can be expressed as 7.000×10^4 to show that it has four significant figures. The datum, 0.00062 can be expressed as 6.2×10^{-4}.

Rule 3: In the addition – and also in subtraction – of a set of values, the number of significant figures in the result is decided by the least certain value; for example, the actual value of

$$12.021 + 3.1 + 211.3 + 0.0041 \text{ is equal to } 226.4251$$

However, it should be shown as 226.4 since the two numbers, 3.1 and 211.3 have no digits beyond the first decimal place.

Similarly,

$$69.0577 - 7.23 + 1.720$$

though amounts to 63.5477, should be expressed as 63.55.

Rule 4: In multiplying and / or dividing a set of values, the number of significant figures in the result should not exceed the number of significant figures in the least precise multiplier or divisor.

For example,

$$\frac{(7.4)(122.7)}{(0.0072)(7298.1)} = \frac{907.98}{52.5463}$$

$$= 17.2796 = 17$$

because the least precise value 7.4 has only two digits.

Rule 5: Logarithms: The number of significant digits in x determines the number of decimal places (the mantissa) in log x.

A logarithm is composed of two parts, a whole number (called the characteristic) and a decimal fraction (called the mantissa). The characteristic is a function of the position of the decimal in the number whose logarithm is being determined; therefore, it is not a significant figure. The mantissa is the same regardless of the position of the decimal; therefore, the digits are significant.

Examples

(i) Express the logarithm of 4.2×10^6.

Characteristic is 5.

Mantissa is 0.6232.

$\log 4.2 \times 10^6 = 5.62$

As there are only two significant figures in 4.2×10^6, the value is reported as 5.62.

(ii) Express the antilog of 2.426

From a log table, 0.4265 is the mantissa of the number 267. The answer should have only three significant figures; therefore, it should be 267 or 2.67×10^2.

(iii) The hydrogen ion concentration of a solution is given as

$$[H^+] = 4.61 \times 10^{-5}$$

Then, $\text{pH} = -\log [H^+]$

$$= -\log [4.61 \times 10^{-5}]$$

$$= -(0.664 - 5) = +4.336$$

Only three decimal places are relevant in the mantissa (0.664) because $[H^+]$ is given up to three significant digits (4.61).

(iv) Consider the reverse calculation of $[H^+]$ from the pH:

$$\text{pH} = 11.2$$

$$\text{Then,} \quad [H^+] = 10^{-\text{pH}} = 10^{-11.2}$$

$$= 10^{-11} \times 10^{-0.2} = 10^{-11} \times \frac{1}{10^{0.2}}$$

$$= 10^{-11} \times \frac{1}{5} = 2 \times 10^{-12}$$

> *It is a good practice to retain an extra figure during the intermediate steps of a calculation and then drop it in the final number.*

The antilog of 0.2 is considered only up to one significant digit, since 0.2 has only one decimal place.

The propagation of errors in arithmetic calculations is summarised in Table 2.7.

Table 2.7 Propagation of errors in arithmetic calculations (*A*, *B* and *C* are experimental variables whose standard deviation are s_A, s_B and s_C respectively)

Type of calculation	Example	Standard deviation of *x*
Addition or subtraction	$X = A + B - C$	$s_x = \sqrt{s_A^2 + s_B^2 + s_C^2}$
Multiplication or division	$X = \frac{(A+B)}{C}$	$\frac{s_x}{X} = \left\{\left(\frac{s_A}{A}\right)^2 + \left(\frac{s_B}{B}\right)^2 + \left(\frac{s_C}{C}\right)^2\right\}^{1/2}$
Exponentiation	$X = A^y$	$\frac{s_x}{X} = y\left(\frac{s_A}{A}\right)$
Logarithm	$X = \log_{10} A$	$s_x = 0.434\left(\frac{s_A}{A}\right)$
Antilogarithm	$X = \text{antilog}_{10} A$	$\frac{s_x}{X} = 2.303\, s_A$

2.3.1.1 Determinate Errors: Maximum Resulting Error

The maximum resulting error is the error in a result computed based on measured quantities. For example, let us assume that a datum *x* has been obtained by computation based on three measured quantities—*A*, *B* and *C*. Then, the absolute determinate errors, α, β and γ in *A*, *B* and *C* are transmitted through addition, subtraction, multiplication and division.

- In addition or subtraction, the *absolute* determinate errors are transmitted directly into the result.
- In multiplication or division, the *relative* determinate errors are transmitted directly into the result.

When $x = A + B + C$, the corrected value of *x* is

$$x + \rho = (A + \alpha) + (B + \beta) + (C + \gamma)$$

When $x = A + B - C$, the corrected value of *x* is

$$x + \rho = (A + \alpha) + (B + \beta) - (C + \gamma)$$

When $x = A\,B/C$, the corrected value of x is

$$x + \rho = \frac{(A+\alpha)(B+\beta)}{(C+\gamma)}$$

Expanding and simplifying the above equation,

$$\frac{\rho}{x} = \frac{\alpha\,BC + \beta AC + \gamma AB}{AB\,(C-\gamma)}$$

Since γ is very small compared to C, the equation can further be simplified to

$$\frac{\rho}{x} = \frac{\alpha}{A} + \frac{\beta}{B} + \frac{\gamma}{C}$$

Illustration for the propagation of determinate errors:

(i) In an analytical experiment,

A = 8.91, B = 4.72 and C = 3.71

The absolute determinate errors

$\alpha = 0.03, \beta = 0.04$ and $\gamma = 0.01$

(ii) Calculate the maximum error in the result computed using the relationship,

$$x = A + B - C$$

$$x = 8.91 + 4.72 - 3.71 = 9.92$$

$$\rho = \alpha + \beta + \gamma = 0.03 + 0.04 + 0.01 = 0.08$$

(iii) Calculate the maximum error in the datum obtained by the relationship,

$$x = \frac{A \times B}{C}$$

$$x = \frac{(8.91 \times 4.72)}{3.71} = 3.67$$

$$\frac{\rho}{x} = \frac{\alpha}{A} + \frac{\beta}{B} + \frac{\gamma}{C}$$

$$= \frac{0.03}{8.91} + \frac{0.04}{4.72} + \frac{0.01}{3.71}$$

$$= 0.00337 + 0.00847 + 0.00270$$

$$= 0.01454 = 0.015$$

$$\frac{\rho}{3.67} = 0.015\ \rho = 0.06$$

Therefore, the maximum error in this calculation, $\rho = 0.06$. The error may be positive or negative.

Problem 2.7 The percentage of a metal in an alloy was estimated volumetrically. Then, the percentage value was computed using the equation,

$$\%\text{ metal} = \frac{20.15\text{ mL} \times 0.1075\text{ meq/mL} \times (51.996/3)\text{ mg/meq} \times 100}{258.5\text{ mg}}$$

$$= \frac{3754.2845}{258.5} = 14.5233$$

What is the correct way of expressing the result?

Solution

(i) The number 3 and 100, being whole numbers, have no uncertainties.

(ii) The burette reading 20.15, assuming 0.1 mL as the least division in the burette, is uncertain to the extent of ± 0.05 mL.

(iii) The datum 0.1075 pertains to a normality, and therefore its uncertainty is likely to be about one part per thousand, ± 0.0001, that is 0.1075 ± 0.0001

(iv) 51.996 is an atomic weight, and therefore, the uncertainty in it is usually ± 1 in the last decimal, 51.996 ± 0.001.

(v) 258.5 is the reading of weight recorded using an analytical balance; the uncertainty is presumably ± 0.2 mg.

(vi) The relative uncertainties in parts per thousand (ppt) are

$$\frac{0.05}{20.15} \times 1000 = 2.48\text{ ppt}$$

$$\frac{0.0001}{0.1075} \times 1000 = 0.93\text{ ppt}$$

$$\frac{0.001}{51.996} \times 1000 = 0.02\text{ ppt}$$

$$\frac{0.2}{258.5} \times 1000 = 0.77\text{ ppt}$$

The sum of the uncertainties = 4.2 ppt

$$\frac{\rho}{14.5233} \times 1000 = 4.2$$

∴ the maximum error, $\rho = 0.06$

Therefore, the result should be rounded to the second decimal, and reported as 14.52. It has uncertainty in the second decimal to the extent, ± 6. Thus, the value can range from 14.46 to 14.58.

Problem 2.8 Express each of the following results to the correct significant digits:

(i) (0.216) (47.27) – (0.111) (11.32) (ii) $4.272 - \log(2.7 \times 10^{-6})$ (iii) (3.728 × 0.011) / 0.271

Solution

(i) The arithmetic value is

$$10.21032 - 1.25652$$

Each product can be given up to three digits:

$$10.21_1 - 1.25_7 = 8.953 = 8.95$$

(ii) The number of decimal places in the log term should be limited to two. Therefore, the answer is

$$4.272 + 5.56_9 = 9.841 = 9.84$$

In log (2.7×10^{-6}), there are only two significant digits; therefore, the mantissa should be considered only up to two decimals.

(iii) $$\frac{(3.728 \times 0.011)}{0.271} = \frac{0.041008}{0.271}$$

$$= \frac{0.0410_1}{0.271} = 0.1513 = 0.151$$

Data Report

Analytical data should be reported with as much information about the accuracy and precision as possible. The following is the recommended method of reporting data:

- *All data concordant*: Report mean and average deviation for two or three values. Report mean and standard deviation for four or more results.
- *Data which are not concordant*: The suspect data should be tested for rejection. If rejection of some data gives concordant data, these concordant data may be reported as stated earlier. If rejection is not possible, report as follows:
    - *Only two results*: report mean and average deviation.
    - *Three results*: report mean and average deviation, if all are divergent, but median if only one is divergent.
    - *Four or more results*: report mean and standard deviation.

2.3.2 Scatter Diagram

An effective way of presenting a trend or relationship is by drawing a *scatter diagram*. This diagram is obtained by plotting two variables *X* and *Y*, one against the other. To illustrate this, the data in Table 2.8 can be considered. A scatter diagram (Fig. 2.5) is drawn using these data. It is customary to plot the independent variable (cause or value from which the prediction is being made) along the X-axis (horizontal). The dependent variable (effect on the thing being predicted) is plotted along the Y-axis (vertical). An examination of the scatter diagram will immediately indicate the trend. Figure 2.5 shows a linear relationship between X and Y. The points corresponding to the data fall close to the line drawn.

2.3.2.1 The Student *t* Test

The student *t* test is a test to ascertain that the results obtained by two different methods indeed measure the same thing. It tests whether there is a statistical difference between the two results. Replicate data are obtained by each method so that two sets of replicate data become available. A statistical *t* value is calculated and compared with a tabulated value for the given number of

Table 2.8 Variation of property X with another property Y

X	Y	X	Y
1	10.0	4	40.2
2	20.5	5	51.0
3	29.8	6	60.5

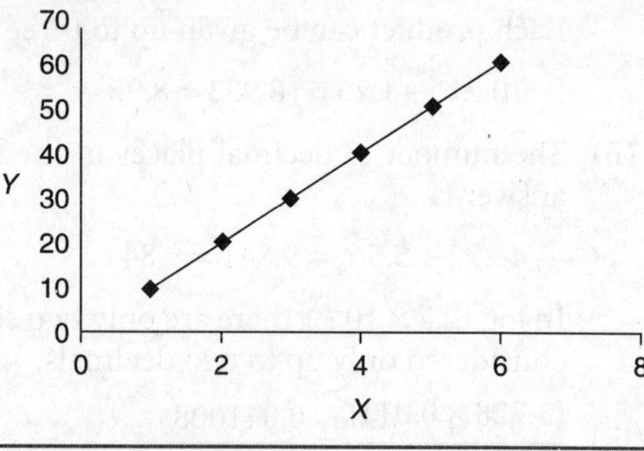

Fig. 2.5 Scatter diagram

tests at the desired confidence level (Table 2.8). If the calculated t value exceeds the tabulated value, then the two results are considered significantly different at that confidence level. Then, the two methods are assumed to give different results. If it does not exceed the tabulated value, then, no significant difference between the two methods is assumed.

- Student's t is a statistical term defined as $\pm t = (\bar{x} - \mu)\sqrt{N}/s$.
- The t-test is a statistical test which shows with a specified probability whether the means of two determinations differ significantly.

Problem 2.9 A sample containing a chloride was subject to replicate analysis. The chloride content results are given as

$$\bar{x} \pm s_x = 7.11 \pm 0.05 \; N_x = 6$$

$$\bar{y} \pm s_y = 7.05 \pm 0.03 \; N_x = 5$$

Do $\bar{x}$ and $\bar{y}$ have a statistically significant difference?

Solution

$$s_p = \sqrt{\frac{(0.05)^2(5) + (0.03)^2(4)}{9}}$$

$$= \sqrt{\frac{(0.0125 + 0.0036)}{9}}$$

$$= \sqrt{0.00179} = 0.0423$$

$$|t| = \frac{|7.11 - 7.05|}{0.0423}\sqrt{\frac{(6)(5)}{11}}$$

$$= 2.341 = 2.34$$

$$2.34 > 2.262 \quad (t_{95.9})$$

Therefore, the difference in the means is statistically significant.

2.3.2.2 The F Test

The F test evaluates differences between the spread of results. It determines if two variances are statistically different. This test has been designed to indicate whether there is a significant difference between two methods based on their standard deviations.

Variance is the square of standard deviation, s^2. F is defined in terms of the variances of the two methods:

> *The variance-ratio test (f-test) is a test to determine if the standard deviations are significantly different; this is performed using the ratio of the variances of two sets of results.*

$$F = \frac{s_1^2}{s_2^2}$$

where $s_1^2 > s_2^2$.

There are two different degrees of freedom, v_1, and v_2. A degree of freedom is $N - 1$.

Statistical tables have been formulated that show how large a difference has to be to confirm that such a difference has not occurred by chance. If the calculated F value exceeds a tabulated F value at the selected confidence level, then a significant variance between the two methods is implied.

Problem 2.10 The antibiotic assay of a fermented broth was done by two methods and the data obtained are given below. Assess the precision of the two methods.

Method 1 (μg/l)	Method 2 (μg / l)
2.3	2.5
2.4	2.6
2.2	2.2
2.1	2.3
2.4	2.7
mean $\bar{x}_1$ 2.28	mean $\bar{x}_2$ 2.46

Solution

$$s_1^2 = \frac{\Sigma(x_{i1} - \bar{x}_1)^2}{N_1 - 1}$$

$$\Sigma(x_{i1} - x_1)^2 = (0.02)^2 + (-0.12)^2 + (-0.08)^2 + (-0.17)^2 + (0.12)^2$$

$$= 0.0004 + 0.0144 + 0.0064 + 0.0289 + 0.0144 = 0.0645$$

$$N_1 - 1 = 5 - 1 = 4$$

$$\therefore \quad s_1^2 = \frac{0.0645}{4} = 0.0161$$

$$s_2^2 = \frac{\Sigma(x_{i2} - \bar{x}_2)^2}{N_2 - 1}$$

$$\Sigma(x_{i2} - \bar{x}_2)^2 = (0.04)^2 + (0.14)^2 + (-0.26)^2 + (-0.16)^2 + (0.24)^2$$

$$= 0.0016 + 0.0196 + 0.0676 + 0.0256 + 0.0576$$

$$= 0.172$$

$$N_2 - 1 = 5 - 1 = 4$$

$$s_2^2 = \frac{0.172}{4} = 0.043$$

$$F = \frac{0.0430}{0.0161} = 2.67$$

(The two variances are so arranged (s_2^2/s_1^2) so that $F > 1$.)

The tabulated F value for $v_1 = 5$ and that for $v_2 = 5$ is 5.05. The calculated F value is less than 5.05; therefore, the two assay methods have the same precision. The standard deviations are from random error alone and do not depend on the sample.

Problem 2.11 Calculate the standard deviation of the result of the following computation:

$$y = \frac{(6.41 \pm 0.03)\,(0.1100 \pm 0.0002)}{(4.98 \pm 0.07)} = 0.1416$$

Solution

The computation involves multiplication and division.

$$\therefore \qquad \frac{s_y}{y} = \sqrt{\left(\frac{0.03}{6.41}\right)^2 + \left(\frac{0.0002}{0.1100}\right)^2 + \left(\frac{0.07}{4.98}\right)^2}$$

$$= \sqrt{0.0000219 + 0.00000331 + 0.000198}$$

$$= \sqrt{0.000224} = 0.01496$$

$$\therefore \qquad s_y = 0.01496 \times 0.1416 = 0.0021$$

$$y = 0.1416 \pm 0.0021$$

2.3.3 Method of Least Squares

A visual examination of Fig. 2.5 indicates that the linearity is good. However, frequently such good linearly related data may not be obtained or may not exist. In such cases the points may deviate from the *best fit*. That is, there would be a scatter of points about a line. To judge the deviation from linearity quantitatively in a scatter diagram, a method called the *Method of least squares* is used. This method offers a more satisfactory way for locating the trend line. This method helps in obtaining a straight line which satisfies two requirements: the algebraic sum of the vertical deviations from the straight line equals zero and the sum of the squares of the vertical deviations is less than the sum of the squares from any other straight line. These conditions limit the line to one position. This 'best' line cannot be drawn by visually judging the positions of points on a graph sheet. The method of least squares is then used to arrive at the best straight line to represent the data. This is achieved by the following steps:

Step 1: ΣX, ΣY, ΣXY, ΣX^2, $\bar{Y}$ and ΣY^2 are calculated. For the data in Table 2.9 these values are 21, 212, 919.2, 91, 35.33 and 9285.58 respectively.

Step 2: These values are then substituted in the following simultaneous equations, where N is the number of pairs of data (six in the example given).

$$\Sigma Y = AN + B\Sigma X$$

$$\Sigma XY = A\Sigma X + B\Sigma X^2$$

These two equations are solved to obtain the values for A and B.

$$A = -0.1067$$

$$B = 10.1257$$

B is known as the regression coefficient or slope. A is the intercept of the regression line on the X-axis. B can be positive (implying that Y increases as X increases), zero (Y remains a constant as X is altered or negative (Y decreases as X increases).

Step 3: Values of Y (Y_{cal}) are then obtained from the given values of X by using the equation,

$$Y_{cal} = A + BX$$

This equation is used to predict the most likely value of Y for a given value of X. For two values of X in Table 4.5 the corresponding Y values are obtained.

$$X = 1, Y_{cal} = 10.019$$

$$X = 5, Y_{cal} = 50.5218$$

Step 4: A line is then drawn using these two pairs of values obtained by calculation. This line is called the *best fit*—the line which truly represents the trend of the data. Another name for this line is *regression line.* The actual points may be found scattered around the line. Sometimes, none of the points may actually fall on the regression line. If the linear relationship between X and Y is good, then the points would be very close to or on the regression line.

Problem 2.12 Two parameters x and y are linearly related. From the following x and y values, determine the linear least squares line.

x =	1	2	3	4	5	6	7	8	9	10
y =	4.7	9.0	13.1	19.4	23.0	26.9	33.0	35.6	40.1	44.6

Solution

First, the values of x_i^2 and $x_i y_i$ are calculated.

The summation values are substituted in the equations,

$$a = \frac{N\sum x_i y_i - \sum x_i \sum y_i}{N\sum x_i^2 - (\sum x_i)^2}$$

$$= \frac{(10 \times 1739) - (55 \times 249.4)}{(10 \times 385) - (55)^2} = 4.45$$

$$b = \frac{\sum x_i^2 \sum y_i - \sum x_i \sum x_i y_i}{N\sum x_i^2 - (\sum x_i)^2}$$

$$= \frac{(385 \times 249.4) - (55 \times 1739)}{(10 \times 385) - (55)^2} = 0.45$$

N	x_i	y_i	x_i^2	$x_i y_i$
1	1	4.7	1	4.7
2	2	9.0	4	18.0
3	3	13.1	9	39.3
4	4	19.4	16	77.6
5	5	23.0	25	115
6	6	26.9	36	161
7	7	33.0	49	231
8	8	35.6	64	285
9	9	40.1	81	361
10	10	44.6	100	446
	$\Sigma x_i = 55$	$\Sigma y_i = 249.4$	$\Sigma x_i^2 = 385$	$\Sigma x_i y_i = 1739$

Therefore, the equation for the regression line is

$$y = 4.45\,x + 0.45$$

The method of least squares is based on the assumptions that:

- the measured values of y correspond to chosen values of x,
- the error in the values of y is independent of the magnitude of x,
- x and y are linearly related to a satisfactory degree, and
- x values are free of error.

Problem 2.13 The data obtained by two students for the percentage chlorine content of an organic compound are given below.

Student 1: 16.44, 16.47, 16.55, 16.48

Student 2: 16.36, 16.37, 16.42, 16.38, 16.37, 16.40

Compare: (i) the standard deviations and (ii) the mean values of the two sets of data.

$\bar{x}_{i(1)}$	$x_{i(1)} - \bar{x}_{(1)}$	$[\bar{x}_{i(1)} - x_{(1)}]^2$
16.44	0.05	0.0025
16.47	0.02	0.0004
16.55	0.06	0.0036
16.48	0.01	0.0001
$\bar{x}_{(1)} = 16.49$	$\Sigma[x_{i(1)} - \bar{x}_{(1)}]^2 = 0.0066$	

$$s_{(1)}^2 = \frac{0.0066}{3} = 0.0022 \qquad s_1 = 0.047$$

16.36	0.02	0.0004
16.37	0.01	0.0001
16.42	0.04	0.0016
16.38	0.00	0.0000
16.37	0.01	0.0001
16.40	0.02	0.0004
$\bar{x}_{(2)} = 16.38$	$\Sigma[x_{i(2)} - \bar{x}]^2 = 0.0026$	

$$s_2^2 = \frac{0.0026}{5} = 0.00052 \qquad s_2 = 0.0228$$

Solution

(i) The standard deviations of the two sets of data are calculated as follows:
$F = 5.41$ for $v_1 = 3$ and $v_2 = 5$ at the 95 % confidence limit.

$$\therefore \quad F_{exp} = \frac{s_1^2}{s_2^2}$$

$$= \frac{0.0022}{0.00052}$$

$$= 4.23 \approx 4$$

The value of F will exceed 5.41 only 5% of the time. Therefore, it is obvious that the value of F is not statistically significant; hence, the t test can be applied to the data.

$$\text{(ii)} \quad s_{1-2} = \frac{\sqrt{(0.0066 + 0.0026)}}{\sqrt{(4+6-2)}}$$

$$= \sqrt{0.00115} = 0.0339 = 0.034$$

$$t = \left[\frac{(16.49 - 16.38)}{0.034}\right] \times \sqrt{\frac{(4 \times 6)}{(4+6)}}$$

$$= 3.235 \times \sqrt{2.4} = 3.235 \times 1.549$$

$$= 5.011 = 5.0$$

The values of t (theoretical) for $v = 4 + 6 - 2 = 8$ are 2.306 and 3.355 at the 95% and 99% confidence levels, respectively.

t experimental > t theoretical at the 99% confidence level; therefore, the difference $\bar{x}_{(1)} - \bar{x}_{(2)}$ 16.49 − 16.38 = 0.11 is statistically significant.

2.3.3.1 Propagation of Errors in Computations

Frequently, in analytical chemistry, the final result is a composite computed value based on more than one datum, a, b, c …, each of which has an associated error. In such a case, the effect of the individual errors associated with a, b, c, …, on the computed quantity y depends on

- how y is related to a, b, c, …,
- the types of errors (determinate or indeterminate).

These facts are summarised in Table 2.9.

Table 2.9 Errors of computed results

Computation	Determinate error	Random error
Addition or subtraction, $y = a + b - c$	$E_y = E_a + E_b - E_c$	$s_y^2 = s_a^2 + s_b^2 + s_c^2$
multiplication or division, $y = ab/c$ general	$\frac{E_y}{y} = \frac{E_a}{a} + \frac{E_b}{b} - \frac{E_c}{c}$	$\left(\frac{s_y}{y}\right)^2 = \left(\frac{s_a}{a}\right)^2 + \left(\frac{s_b}{b}\right)^2 + \left(\frac{s_c}{c}\right)^2$
general, $y = f(a, b, c, \ldots)$	$E_y = \frac{\partial y}{\partial a} E_a + \frac{\partial y}{\partial b} E_b + \cdots$	$s_y^2 = \left(\frac{\partial y}{\partial a}\right)^2 s_a^2 + \left(\frac{\partial y}{\partial b}\right)^2 s_b^2 \ldots$

- In the case of determinate errors, for addition or subtraction, the absolute error of the final result E_y, is determined by the individual absolute determinate errors.
- For multiplication or division, the relative errors of the final result, E_y/y is determined by the relative determinate errors associated with a, b, c …
- For addition or subtraction in the case of random errors, the variance of the final result s_y^2, is determined by the variances of the terms a, b, c …
- For multiplication or division, the square of the relative standard deviation of the final result $(s_y/y)^2$ is determined by the squares of the individual relative deviations.

2.3.3.2 Correlation Coefficient

Correlation coefficient (r) is a quantity that indicates the extent of linearity of a given set of data. It helps to examine the appropriateness of the linear relationship between X and Y. This coefficient is obtained from the equation

$$r = \left(\frac{A\sum Y + B\sum XY - \bar{Y}\sum Y}{\sum Y^2 - \bar{Y}\sum Y}\right)^{1/2}$$

Substituting the various values calculated and simplifying,

$$r = \left(\frac{1794.96}{1795.62}\right)^{1/2} = 0.99$$

The value may be obtained from the following equation also

$$r = \frac{N\sum XY - (\sum X \cdot \sum Y)}{\{[N\sum X^2 - (\sum X)^2][N\sum Y^2 - (\sum Y)^2]\}^{1/2}}$$

The value of 0.99 for r indicates excellent linearity between the two properties represented by X and Y. When the value of r is 1.00 it would mean 'perfect' linearity. Therefore, r value can never be greater than 1.00. Lesser is its value from 1.00, lesser is the linear character of the data. When r is greater than 0.75, the linearity must be considered excellent (Fig. 2.6).

Fig. 2.6 Scale of correlation values

The correlation coefficient is positive when both X and Y increase simultaneously, and it is negative if one increases as the other decreases. Correlation coefficient is usually given only up to two decimal places.

2.3.4 Presentation of Tabulated Data

Representing the data in a tabular form is an important exercise in the practice of science. A table of data should have the following characteristics:

- It should be as brief as possible.
- It should represent the results in a clear and uncomplicated manner.
- The data should be qualified by the correct units.
- The data should be presented according to the significant number convention.
- Repetition of ideas in the form of replicate data should not be a part of the table.
- It should have a title which is brief but comprehensive in qualifying the data.
- The data should be arranged in the table in such a way that a trend is discernible at a glance.
- The table should have a number, so that it can be referred to by this number in the text; for example, Table 2.8.

Presentation of data in a tabular form has several advantages.

- It enables us to present a large body of data in a comprehensible manner with minimum space.
- Visual examination of the table may readily reveal the trend in a property.
- Tabular presentation affords easy comparison of properties.
- Tabulated data are a good source of reference material.

Scientific data, presented in tables, form the basis for writing a report in science. Therefore, tables have to be presented in standard and clear style in reports.

2.3.4.1 Purposes of Tables

Data tables are intended to

- indicate the extent of experiments performed in a study,
- convey the results of experiments clearly,
- render trends – increase, decrease or constancy of a property (measured by experiments) – in a readily discernible manner to the reader.
- help interpret and write discussion of results of experiments and also to draw conclusions.

2.3.4.2 Abbreviations and Symbols in Tables

Use of abbreviations in tables saves space, especially because spaces in table rows and decks are limited. However, only the standard and easily understandable abbreviations should be used. Familiar abbreviations, such as % for per cent, kg for kilogram, ms^{-1} for metre per second, and so on, need no explanation for the readers; but unfamiliar abbreviations need to be defined in notes at the bottom.

Symbols may similarly be used in tables to save space. Familiar symbols such as $<$, $>$, $\neq$, °, ', ", μ, σ, α, ∞, $\rightarrow$, ... need no explanation.

However, the unfamiliar ones, if used, should be defined as head notes or foot notes.

2.3.4.3 Punctuation in Tables

- Minimum punctuation should be used in tables.
- No period is added at the end of the table title.
- A period may be added after the table number. For example,
  Table 2. Isotopes of hydrogen
- No period is necessary at the end of a foot note, unless it is a full sentence.
- Punctuation marks may be avoided in column headings and subheadings.
- Word splits are undesirable in tables. Clear distinctions among 'minus sign', 'hard hyphen' and 'dashes' should be ensured.
- Slashes should be placed correctly without causing ambiguity in data.

2.4 INTERNATIONAL (SI) SYSTEM OF UNITS

Every value of a measurement should be indicated along with its proper units, unless the value is dimensionless. The numerical values of various properties of matter can be expressed in different units. The metric system for indicating the units has now been universally accepted. This system is simple and coherent in which larger and smaller versions of each basic unit can be obtained by multiplying or dividing the unit by ten. This is a decimal system, and can be extended to all branches of science so that everyone can speak the same 'scientific language'.

The General Conference on Weights and Measures made a revision of the metric system in 1960. This system has since been adopted by the scientists all over the world and is called *Le System international d' Units* (International System of Units). This system is based on seven basic units (Table 2.10).

Table 2.10 Basic SI units

Physical quantity	Name of SI unit	Symbol for SI unit
Length	metre	m
Mass	kilogram	kg
Time	second	s
Temperature	kelvin	K
Amount of substance	mole	Mol
Electric current	ampere	A
Luminous intensity	candela	cd

2.4.1 Derived SI Units

Other quantities not represented in Table 2.10 are expressed in derived units. The units are obtained by multiplication or division. For example, area is represented by the derived unit m^2, and volume has the unit m^3. Such derived units are given in Table 2.11. Some units which are not strictly in line with the SI units are also permitted, because of their long-standing common usage (Table 2.12). Certain prefixes are used in the metric system of units and these prefixes modify the magnitude of the unit (Table 2.13).

A clear understanding about the SI units is required for presenting data by the students of science. The SI units are currently used along with the other systems (Table 2.14) and therefore clearly indicating the unit after each datum would avoid uncertainty. The most commonly used units in chemistry are given in Table 2.15.

Table 2.11 Derived SI units

Quantity	Unit	Symbol	Definition
Force	newton	N	kg m s^{-2}
Work, energy, quantity of heat	joule	J	Nm
Pressure	pascal	Pa	N m^{-2}
Electric charge	coulomb	C	As
Power	watt	W	J s^{-1}
Magnetic flux density	tesla	T	kg s^{-2} A^{-1} ($Vm^{-2}s$)
Frequency	hertz	Hz	s^{-1} (cycles per sec)
Electrical potential difference	volt	V	kg m^2 $s^{-3}A^{-1}$ ($JA^{-1}s^{-1} = JC^{-1}$)
Temperature	Deg. celsius	°C	t°C

Table 2.12 Units permitted in conjunction with the SI units

Physical quantity	Unit	Symbol	Definition
Area	barn	b	10^{-28} m^2
Volume	litre	l	10^{-3} $m^3 = dm^3$
Pressure	bar	bar	10^5 Nm^{-2}
Mass	tonne	t	10^3 kg = Mg
Radioactivity	curie	Ci	37×10^9 s^{-1}
Energy	electron volt	eV	1.6021×10^{-19}J
Magnetic flux intensity	gauss	G	10^{-4} Vsm^{-2}

Table 2.13 Prefixes of the units

Name	Symbol	Factor
atto	a	10^{-18}
femto	f	10^{-15}
pico	p	10^{-12}
nano	n	10^{-9}
micro	μ	10^{-6}
milli	m	10^{-3}
centi	c	10^{-2}
deci	d	10^{-1}
kilo	k	10^3
mega	M	10^6
giga	G	10^9
tera	T	10^{12}
peta	p	10^{15}
exa	E	10^{18}

Table 2.14 Equivalence between units

Length		Weight, Mass	
1 inch	2.54 cm	1 oz	28.35 g
1 foot	30.48 cm	1 lb	453.6 g
1 yard	0.9144 m	1 g	2.205×10^{-3} lb
1 mile	1.609 km	1 kg	2.205 lb
1 cm	0.3937 inch	1 amu (u)	1.66041×10^{-27} kg
1 m	39.37 inches		
1 Å	0.1 nm		
Volume		**Heat, Energy**	
		1 cal	4.184 J
		1 erg	1×10^{-7} J
1 qt	0.946 litre	1 erg	2.39×10^{-8} cal
1 gal	3.785 litres	1 eV	1.6021×10^{-19} J
		0°C	273.15 K

2.4.2 Conventions in the Use of SI Units

Internationally accepted styles have to adopted in the use of units in scientific writings.

(i) The symbol for a unit is represented in Roman type.
(ii) No space is given between the letters of a symbol; for example, the letters k and g are written as kg (kilogram) with no space between the two.

(iii) Both the singular and the plural forms of a unit are represented by the same symbol without adding 's' to represent the plural. For example, both 1 gram and 10 grams should have the same symbol g. For example, 10 g and not 10 gs.

(iv) A unit symbol should not be followed by a period (full stop) except when it occurs at the end of a sentence (40 kJ and not 40 kJ.).

(v) Symbols for prefixes for units should also be printed in Roman type without space between the prefix and the unit, as in MeV, not M eV.

(vi) Double prefixes should be avoided, as in giga watt (GW), not kilomega watt (kMW).

(vii) The combination of a prefix and a symbol should be considered as a single symbol, which may be raised to a power without the use of parentheses, as in dm^3.

(viii) More than one slash should not be used in the same unit, as in cal deg^{-1} $mole^{-1}$ and not cal/deg/mole.

(ix) The abbreviated units should be used only when preceded with numeral; in the text without numbers, the units should be written only in the full-expanded form. For example, five kilograms of glucose, not five kg of glucose.

(x) Line-symbols, like square root and cube root, should not be used; instead exponents $( )^{1/2}$ and $( )^{1/3}$ are preferred.

Table 2.15 Units in chemistry

Symbol	Unit	Unit equivalent
Length		
m	metre	–
cm	centimetre	1×10^{-2} m
mm	millimetre	1×10^{-3} m
nm	nanometre	1×10^{-9} m
Å	angstrom	1×10^{-10} m
μ	micron	1×10^{-6} m
mμ	millimicron	1×10^{-9} m
Mass		
kg	kilogram	1×10^{3} g
g	gram	–
mg	milligram	1×10^{-3} g
Volume		
l	litre	–
mL	millititre	1×10^{-3} litre
cm^3	cubic centimetre	1 mL
m^3	cubic metre	–
dm^3	cubic decimetre	–
μl	microlitre	1×10^{-6} litre
Heat		
cal	calorie	–
kcal	kilocalorie	1×10^{3} cal
J	joule	–
kJ	kilojoule	1×10^{3} J
Pressure		
mm Hg	millimetre of mercury	$13.5951 \times 980.665 \times 10^{-2}$ Nm^{-2}
atm	atmosphere	101325 Nm^{-2}
torr	torr	(101325/760) Nm^{-2}

EXERCISES

1. The following results were obtained for a sample of a copper alloy that contains 10.00% Cu. Is the method associated with a determinate error?

Alloy sample taken (g)	Cu estimated (g)
0.5000	0.0492
0.4500	0.0451
0.4000	0.0392
0.3500	0.0346

2. The results obtained in a gravimetric and volumetric determination of Ni (%) in an alloy sample are given below.
   Gravimetric: 37.21 36.92 37.05 37.41 37.01
   Volumetric: 37.11 37.19 36.99 36.91 37.41
   Calculate the 95%, and 99% confidence intervals for the means of the two methods.
3. Apply the *Q* test to test the following results: 2.02, 2.11, 1.98, 1.99, 2.17, 2.14, 2.13.
4. A burette can read volumes down to 0.01 mL. Calculate the smallest volume (in mL) that should be used in a titration so that the volumetric error does not exceed 0.5%.
5. An ethanol sample is known to contain 1.71% of ethanol. The results of replicate analysis gave the values 1.69, 1.72, 1.79, 1.63 and 1.70. Do these data indicate the presence of bias in the method?
6. Calculate the standard deviation of the result of
   $$\frac{[7.12\,(\pm 0.02) - 1.11\,(\pm 0.02)] \times 0.050\,(\pm 0.001)}{617\,(\pm 8) + 209\,(\pm 4) \times 71.2\,(\pm 1.0)}$$
7. Complete and also calculate the absolute deviations of the following computations:
   (a) $x = \log\,[4.00\,(\pm 0.02) \times 10^{-3}] =$
   (b) $x = \text{antilog}\,[2.700\,(\pm 0.002)] =$
8. An amperometric method has a standard deviation of 2.0%. How many replicate measurements are necessary if the standard error of the mean is to be 0.01%?
9. What is the 95% confidence interval for the μ if 21 analyses yield $\overline{x} \pm s_x = 80.0 \pm 3.1$?
10. A sample of commercial glucose was analysed in triplicate. The 95% confidence – level estimate of the true value of the glucose content (in per cent) was calculated to be $\mu \approx 12.1 \pm 2.0$. Assume that the same standard deviation s_x, is found for any set of *N* repeat measurements. How large must *N* be so that the 95% confidence level precision estimate of the mean will be less than 1.0, rather than 2.0 as in the $N = 3$ analysis?
11. A standard method of analysis for the oxides of nitrogen in air samples has a standard deviation of 0.022 ppm.
    (a) Calculate the 95% confidence limit for the mean of four measurements obtained by this method.
    (b) How many measurements should be made if the 95% confidence limit is to be ± 0.012?

References

1. Hastie T, Tibshirani R and Friedman J, *The Elements of Statistical Learning*, Springer, 2011.
2. Blackwell S, *Basic Statistics*, McGraw-Hill, 1969.
3. Hadjiioonnou P, *Problem Solving in Analytical Chemistry*, Pergamon, Oxford, 1962.

3 Separation and Purification Techniques

3.1 SEPARATION TECHNIQUES

Natural materials occur mostly as mixtures. For example, air, water in our environment, ores and minerals, are mixtures. The constituents of a mixture have to be separated for their use and is routinely done in our homes, laboratories and industries.

Separation techniques constitute an important aspect of experimental chemistry. The quest for isolating a chemical in a 100% pure form has resulted in the invention and perfection of innumerable separatory methods. Some are simple and inexpensive such as the age-old technique of filtration, and others such as the computer-aided high performance liquid chromatography, which are modern and expensive.

3.1.1 CALCINATION

Calcination is the process of heating a solid in a crucible or over an open flame without causing fusion (melting), until it is reduced to ashes. It is adopted for bringing about some physical or chemical change.

For example, the conversion of limestone ($CaCO_3$) to calcium oxide by heating is calcination. In metallurgy, it is used for separating the main metallic constituent from the ore for further treatment. It is carried out in furnaces, retorts, fluidised bed reactors or kilns. Calcination or *calcining*, is different from roasting; in roasting, more complex gas–solid reactions occur between the furnace atmosphere and the solids.

Applications of calcination The following are some examples of applications of calcination:

- decomposition of carbonate ores, as in the calcination of limestone to drive off carbon dioxide,
- decomposition of hydrated minerals, as in the calcination of bauxite, to drive off crystalline water,
- decomposition of volatile matter contained in raw petroleum coke, and
- heat treatment to cause phase transformations, as in the conversion of anastase to rutile or devitrification of glass materials.

The product of calcination is called *calcine*, regardless of the actual material thermally treated.

Calcination reactions usually occur at or above the thermal decomposition temperature (for decomposition and volatilisation reactions) or the transition temperature (for phase transitions). This temperature is defined as the temperature at which the standard Gibbs free energy of reaction for a particular calcination reaction is equal to zero. For example, in the calcination of limestone, the decomposition reaction is

$$CaCO_3(s) \longrightarrow CaO(s) + CO_2(g)$$

For this reaction, the standard Gibbs free energy is denoted as

$$\Delta G_r^o = 177\,100 - 158\,T \text{ J mol}^{-1}$$

The standard free energy of reaction is zero in this case when $T = 1121$ K, or 848°C. Therefore, the minimum calcination temperature required for this reaction is 848°C.

3.1.2 Precipitation

Precipitation is an important method of separation in various analytical techniques (extensively dealt with in Chapter 5).

In qualitative analysis, the principle of separation of cations belonging to different groups is essentially based on precipitation of these by adding suitable reagent(s). For example, the addition of dilute hydrochloric acid to a mixture of cations precipitates only mercurous, lead and silver ions. Thus a separation of these from ions Cu^{2+}, Al^{3+}, Zn^{2+} ..., is possible. For the analysis of metals belonging to a particular group in qualitative analysis, separation by precipitation is again very useful. For example, bismuth ions can be separated from copper ions by the addition of NH_4OH. Manganese ions can be separated from zinc ions by the addition of NaOH. This method is so powerful and foolproof that Marie Curie used it to discover and isolate radium from pitchblende in 1902.

In quantitative analysis, estimation of one constituent requires, as a first step, removal of interference from other constituents. Precipitation again comes handy in such cases. For example, from a mixture of copper and nickel ions, copper ions are precipitated as sulphide and removed before nickel is gravimetrically estimated using dimethylglyoxime.

To separate an organic compound from another, we can use precipitation in suitable cases. For example, a carbonyl compound can be precipitated by the addition of Borsche's reagent. This is a convenient method of separating a carbonyl compound from other classes of organic compounds.

Recovery coefficient In an analytical chemical separation, the completeness of the recovery of the analyte A from the sample is important. An efficient separation method results in higher recovery of A from the sample; this factor is denoted by the recovery coefficient, R_A. This is denoted as

$$R_A = \frac{Q_A}{(Q_A)_o}$$

where Q_A is the quantity of A recovered and $(Q_A)_o$ is the initial quantity of A in the sample. In a 100% recovery of A, $R_A = 1$, and such a recovery method is the best for the recovery of A.

Separation coefficient Not only the recovery of A but also its separation from the other constituents of the sample is important in analytical procedures.

R_A may be 1 but it may still be contaminated with the other components of the sample. This fact is defined by another term—*separation coefficient*, The degree of separation of two components A and B is denoted by the separation coefficient $S_{B/A}$. This is defined as

$$S_{B/A} = \frac{Q_B/Q_A}{(Q_B)_o\,(Q_A)_o} = \frac{R_B}{R_A}$$

where Q_A and Q_B are the quantities of A and B that are recovered and $(Q_A)_o$ and $(Q_B)_o$ their corresponding initial quantities in the sample. If $R_A \simeq 1$, then the previous equation simplifies to

$$S_{B/A} \simeq \frac{Q_B}{(Q_B)_o} = R_B$$

3.1.3 Solvent Extraction

Extraction using a solvent is used as a method for separation of dissolved substances from solutions. It can be used for the separation of one constituent from a solid mixture and for the removal of undesired soluble impurities from mixtures.

Extraction with a second solvent is an application of the Nernst distribution law according to which, *at constant temperature a solute distributes itself between two immiscible solvents only in a particular ratio.* When a substance distributes itself between two solvents without the complications of dissociation or association, it is possible to calculate the weight of the substance that can be removed by a series of extractions. If v_1 mL of a solution contains W g of a substance and if the substance is repeatedly extracted with v_2 mL of another solvent, the weight of the substance W_n remaining in the first solvent after n extractions is given by

$$W_n = W\left(\frac{Kv_1}{Kv_1 + v_2}\right)^n$$

where K is the distribution coefficient for the substance between the two solvents. This equation predicts that for a given volume of solvent, the extraction process is more efficient with several extractions with aliquots than a single extraction with all the available solvent. The larger the value of K, the more efficient the extraction.

Consider a solution of two compounds in a solvent. For effective separation of these two compounds by extraction with a second solvent, the distribution coefficient of one should be significantly greater than 1.0 whereas the distribution coefficient of the other should be significantly smaller than 1.0. If this condition is met, one compound will be mainly distributed in one solvent and the other in the second solvent. Physical separation of the two liquids results in a partial separation of the two compounds.

The common solvents used for extraction in the laboratory are diethyl ether, benzene, petroleum ether, chloroform and carbon tetrachloride. A good solvent for extraction should satisfy two important conditions—(i) the substance extracted should be highly soluble in the solvent, (ii) after the extraction, the solvent should be easily separable from the solute.

For the extraction of organic substances, diethyl ether is used because several organic substances are soluble in ether which has a low boiling point that enables its easy removal after extraction. Ether is highly flammable and hence should be handled with care. Diisopropyl ether is better than diethyl ether in this respect (with less flammability) but it is not commonly used because of its very high cost.

The extraction with a second solvent can be carried out in the laboratory with a separating funnel (Fig. 3.1) in which two sharply defined layers are formed. The two layers can be separated by opening the stop-cock and allowing the lower aqueous layer to drain slowly into a breaker.

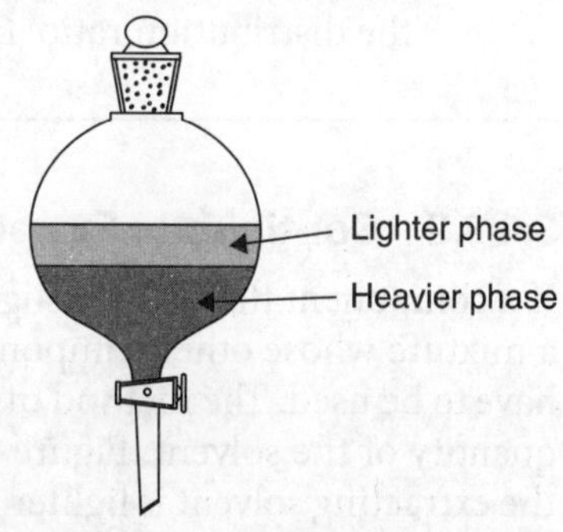

Fig. 3.1 Separating funnel

3.1.3.1 Extraction by Chemically Active Solvents

When an organic compound is extracted from an aqueous solution by ether, the efficiency of extraction is markedly increased by the addition of a salt like sodium chloride since the salt decreases the solubility of an organic substance in water.

Sometimes a reagent which reacts chemically with a compound may be used to extract the latter. This method is generally employed either to remove small amounts of impurities in an organic compound or to separate the components of a mixture. Some examples are:

- An aqueous solution of sodium bicarbonate may be used to extract an organic acid from an ether solution. The sodium salt of an acid is soluble in water but is insoluble in the organic solvent. The aqueous layer is separated and then treated with a mineral acid to regenerate the organic acid.
- A dilute solution of HCl may be used to extract an organic base from an organic solvent. The hydrochlorides of organic bases are water-soluble and hence get transferred to the aqueous layer.
- Cold concentrated sulphuric acid may be used to remove unsaturated hydrocarbons present in saturated hydrocarbons; similarly alcohols and ethers present in alkyl halides can be separated with sulphuric acid. In the former case, soluble sulphonated products are formed whereas in the latter case, alkyl hydrogen sulphates or addition complexes that are soluble in the concentrated acid are produced.

Problem 3.1 A 100.0 mL portion of a 0.100 M aqueous solution of the weak acid HA is extracted with 100.0 mL of CCl_4. After the extraction, a 25.0 mL aliquot of the aqueous phase was titrated with 0.1000 M NaOH to an end point of 15.6 mL. Calculate the distribution ratio of HA.

Solution

Let x be the molarity of HA in the aqueous phase after extraction.

Then,

$$25.0 \text{ mL} \times x \text{ mmol/mL} = 15.6 \text{ mL} \times 0.1000 \text{ mmol/mL}$$

$$\therefore \quad x = \frac{15.6 \times 0.1000}{25.0} = 0.0624$$

$$100 \text{ mL} (0.100 - 0.0624) \text{ mmol/mL}$$

$$= 3.76 \text{ mmol of HA was extracted in to 100 mL of } CCl_4$$

$$\therefore \quad \text{the distribution ratio } D = \frac{3.76/100}{0.0624/100} = 6$$

3.1.3.2 Continuous Extraction

If a component that is only slightly soluble in the extracting solvent has to be separated from a mixture whose other components are essentially insoluble, large quantities of solvent would have to be used. The method of continuous extraction can be used in such cases with a smaller quantity of the solvent. Figure 3.2 shows the apparatus used for continuous extraction when the extracting solvent is lighter than the original solution containing the solute. The extracting solvent is kept in a flask which is heated. The vapours condense and the liquid solvent drains into the vessel containing the solute to be extracted. After extracting a little of the solute, the extracting solvent being lighter rises to the top. When the level exceeds a certain limit, it drains once again into the original flask from where it is vapourised and then utilised for extraction once again.

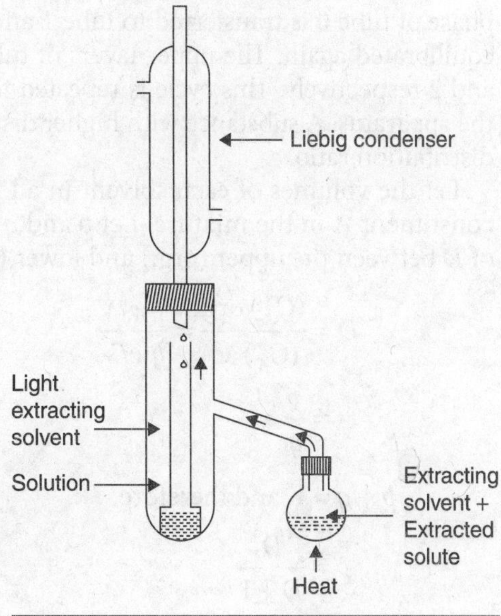

Fig. 3.2 Continuous extraction apparatus

3.1.3.3 Soxhlet Extraction

For separation of the component(s) of a solid mixture by continuous extraction, a Soxhlet apparatus (Fig. 3.3) is used. The solid is kept in the porous thimble and the extracting solvent is taken in the boiling flask. When the solvent is heated to reflux, the distillate drains into the porous thimble and extraction occurs. As more and more solvent collects in this chamber, the solution empties into the boiling flask by a siphoning action. Pure solvent continuously gets vapourised from the boiling flask and the cycle of condensation of the vapour, extraction of the components and draining of the solution into the boiling flask goes on.

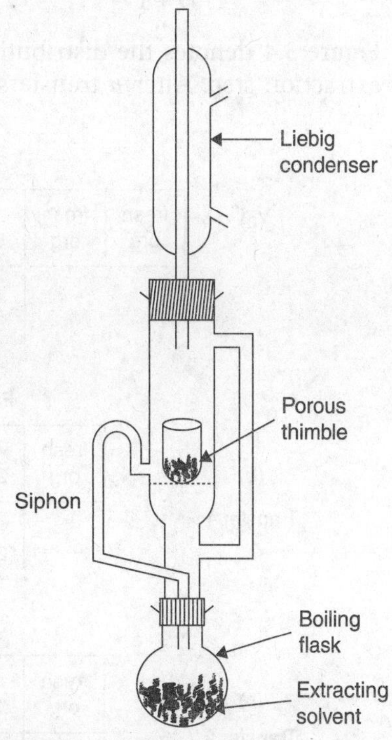

Fig. 3.3 Soxhlet extractor

3.1.3.4 Craig Extraction

Craig extraction is the separation of solutes on the basis of differences in their partitioning between two solvents. Unlike in a countercurrent separation - during which two phases move - only one phases moves in the Craig separation; therefore, it is called also *pseudocountercurrent extraction*. This process was devised by Lyman C Craig.

Theory The Craig method is a liquid–liquid extraction for the separation of substances with different distribution coefficients (ratios). An apparatus devised by Craig, now called the Craig apparatus, is used for the separation. It consists of a series of glass tubes (labelled 0, 1, 2...) that are made and arranged such that the light liquid phase is transferred from one tube to the next easily. The liquid–liquid extractions occur simultaneously in all tubes of the apparatus. The assembly of several Craig tubes is operated electromechanically. (The design and operator of the Craig tube can be seen at. https://cao.chen.ufl.edu)

The lower (heavier) phase of the two-phase solvent system, say, water–hexane, is the stationary phase (water), whereas the upper phase is the mobile phase (hexane). Initially, tube number 0 contains a mixture of substances to be separated in the heavier solvent; all the other tubes contain equal volumes of the same heavier solvent. Now, the lighter solvent is added to tube 0, extraction takes place and the phases are allowed to separate. The upper phase of tube 0 is transferred to tube 1 and fresh solvent is added to tube 0, and the phases are equilibrated again. The upper layers of tubes 0 and 1 are simultaneously transferred to tube 1 and 2 respectively. This cycle is repeated to continue the extraction through the other tubes of the apparatus. A substance with higher distribution ratio moves faster than the one with a lower distribution ratio.

Let the volumes of each solvent in all the tubes be equal (V), and let w be the weight of a constituent A in the mixture. Let p and q represent the fraction of A with a distribution ratio of D between the upper (org.) and lower (aq.) phase. Then,

$$D = \frac{(C_A)\,\text{org}}{(C_A)\,\text{aq}} = \frac{pw/V}{qw/V}$$

$$= \frac{p}{q}$$

$p + q = 1$, and therefore

$$p = \frac{D}{D+1}$$

$$q = \frac{1}{D+1}$$

Figure 3.4 denotes the distribution of fractions of solute (A) in successive tubes after each extraction step. After n transfers or equilibrium cycles, the total fraction of A in each tube

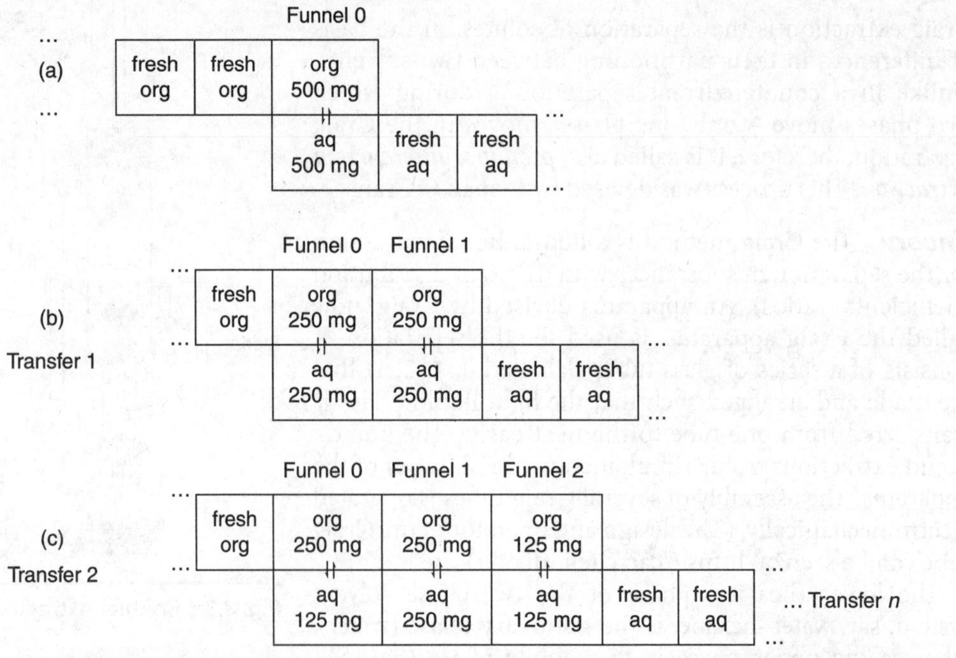

Fig. 3.4 Representation of distribution of fractions of a solute in successive Craig tubes (a) 1000 mg of solute distributed between organic and aqueous layers equally as $D = 1$, (b) Distribution after 1 transfer, (c) Distribution after 2 transfers

corresponds to the terms of the binomial expression $(p + q)^n$, as the ratio $D = p/q$ must be maintained for each tube after the equilibration step.

Therefore, the total fraction of solute in tube x after n transfers is given by

$$f_{n,x} = \frac{n!}{x!\,(n-x)!}\, p^x q^{n-x}$$

Substituting the values of p and q from the previous equations,

$$f_{n,x} = \frac{n!}{x!\,(n-x)!} = \frac{D^x}{(D+1)^n}$$

This equation shows that the greater the difference of the distribution ratio of the constituents, the better will be the separation. The number of Craig tubes required in an assembly will have to be more as the distribution ratios of the constituents of the mixture are closer. For most of the separations, 20 tubes may be sufficient.

Applications of Craig extraction Though the Craig method has been superceded by more convenient chromatographic methods, it may be used in several separations:

- separation of metals after forming chelate complexes which are soluble in organic phase, and
- organic natural products.

3.1.3.5 Rotary Evaporation

Rotary evaporation is a separation method used to remove solvents from samples by gentle evaporation. This method was invented by Lyman C Craig. In a rotary evaporator, the mixture is taken in a flask, a part of the distillation assembly (Fig. 3.5). The volatile solvent is distilled off under low pressure or vacuum. The flask is rotated gently by a motor without exposing the inner system to the atmosphere. This method is actually distillation under reduced pressure, the additional feature being the rotation of the flask containing the mixture. The evaporator is known also as a *rotavap.*

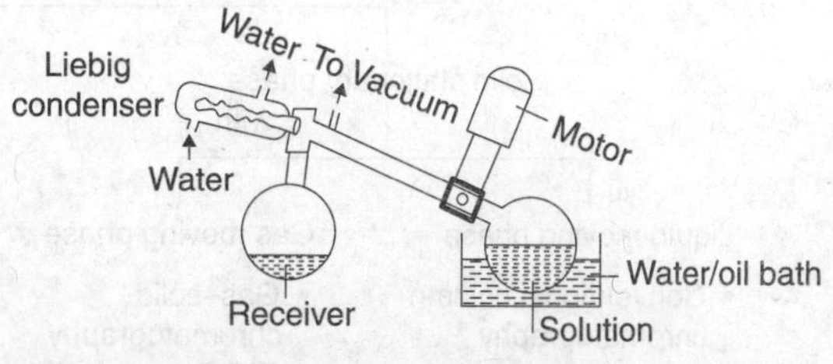

Fig. 3.5 Craig's rotavap apparatus

Advantages: The centrifugal force and the frictional force between the wall of the rotating flask and the liquid sample create a thin film of warm solvent being spread over a large surface. The gentle rotation of the flask and the resulting swirling of the liquid avoid bumping and promote smooth, steady and speedy distillation.

Solvents such as ethers, alcohols, DMF and DMSO can be conveniently separated from samples by this method.

Glassware with flaws, when used in a rotavap may lead to explosion. Unstable compounds such as nitro compounds may explode inside the system.

3.2 CHROMATOGRAPHY

Chromatography is based on the general principles of phase distribution. The method involves selective removal of the components from one phase when it flows past a second stationary phase. The stationary (fixed) phase is generally a column or strip through which the moving phase flows. The removal of a component by the fixed phase from the flowing phase is essentially an equilibrium process. Separation of two or more components is possible when the equilibrium constants for the distribution of these components between the two phases vary. Expressed simply, the molecules of a substance which interact strongly with the fixed phase will move slowly through the column whereas substances which do not interact strongly are carried through more rapidly. This results in the migration of components into separate regions, referred to as the *bands* of the fixed phase.

Chromatography was invented by the Russian botanist Mikhail Tswett who employed this technique to separate plant pigments like chlorophylls and xanthophylls using a column of calcium carbonate. Since the separated components appeared as coloured bands on the column, the name chromatography was given by the inventor of this technique (*chroma* means colour). As of now, chromatography encompasses a diverse group of separation methods that makes possible separation, purification and identification of closely related components of a mixture. The only common factor of all these separation methods is that these employ a stationary phase and a mobile phase.

- Chromatography is a physical method of separation of mixtures.
- In chromatography, the components of a mixture are distributed between two phases, one being a stationary bed of large surface area, the other being a fluid that percolates through the stationary bed.
- Chromatography is of different types depending on the nature of the two phases used:

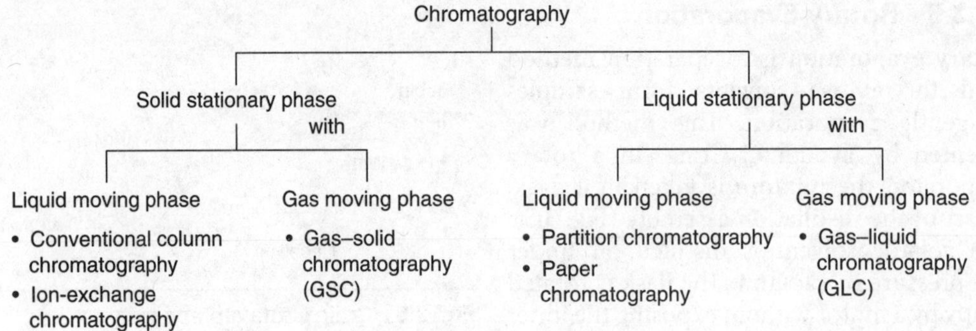

There are three types of chromatographic methods depending on the nature of the fixed phase.

(i) ***Adsorption chromatography*** A solid which is insoluble in the solvents chosen may be used as the fixed phase. The mode of interaction between the components of the mixture and the fixed phase is adsorption. Hence the method is called adsorption chromatography. The adsorption could be caused by electrostatic attraction, complexation, hydrogen bonding, van der Waals' forces, and so on.

(ii) ***Partition chromatography*** The fixed phase may be a solid on which a liquid is very firmly adsorbed to form the stationary phase. Distribution of components of a mixture could occur between the adsorbed liquid and the flowing liquid (mobile phase) because of differences in solubility. The adsorbed liquid should be immiscible with the flowing liquid. This technique is referred to as partition chromatography.

In paper chromatography, a paper strip is used as the 'column' through which the mixture in an organic solvent flows. Since a layer of adsorbed water carried by the paper acts as the fixed phase, this method is regarded as a kind of partition chromatography. A filter paper or a chromatographic paper automatically incorporates in it water adsorbed from the atmosphere.

(iii) ***Ion-exchange chromatography*** This involves an exchange of ions of like sign between a solution and an essentially insoluble solid in contact with the solution. The mobile phase could be a liquid (which can percolate through the fixed phase by forces of gravity or capillary forces) or a gas which can be forced through the fixed phase by pressure.

3.2.1 Column Chromatography

This technique is a type of solid–liquid adsorption chromatography. The fixed phase is a solid and the mobile phase a liquid. The basis of separation is selective adsorption of the components present in the liquid phase on the solid.

A column such as the one shown in Fig. 3.6 is used. According to the scale of the experiment, columns from a few mm to several cm in diameter are used. A long, thin column ensures best separation in many difficult cases but large quantities of readily separable substances can be separated more rapidly using a wide column. The column is packed with an active solid such as alumina or silica gel. Apart from these two substances, charcoal, magnesia, calcium carbonate, starch, sucrose, talc and fluorisil (fluorinated silicon polymer) are also used as solid adsorbents. For a good separation, the solid adsorbent should be of uniform particle size and of high specific area, a property which can contribute to rapid equilibrium of the solute between the two phases.

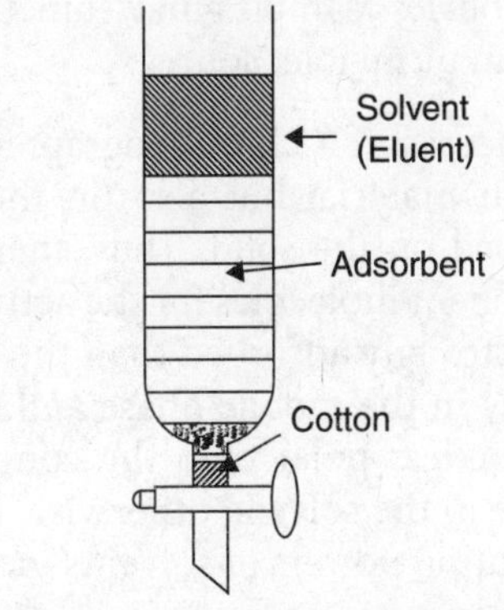

Fig. 3.6 Chromatography column

The column should be filled with the adsorbent very carefully because air gaps may lead to: (i) mixing of separated zones and (ii) channels through which the solution can flow unchanged. The adsorbent is usually made into a slurry with a liquid such as petroleum ether, poured into the column and allowed to settle. During the packing, continual tapping of the column with a pencil or a glass rod may help form an evenly packed column. After packing the column with the adsorbent, a small portion of the sample solution (mixture) is poured on the top. The sample gets adsorbed at the top of the column. An eluting solvent is then allowed to flow through the column. This solvent carries with it the components of the mixture. Because of the selective adsorption capacity of the solid phase, the components move down the column at different rates. The progressive separation of the components into bands is shown in Fig. 3.7.

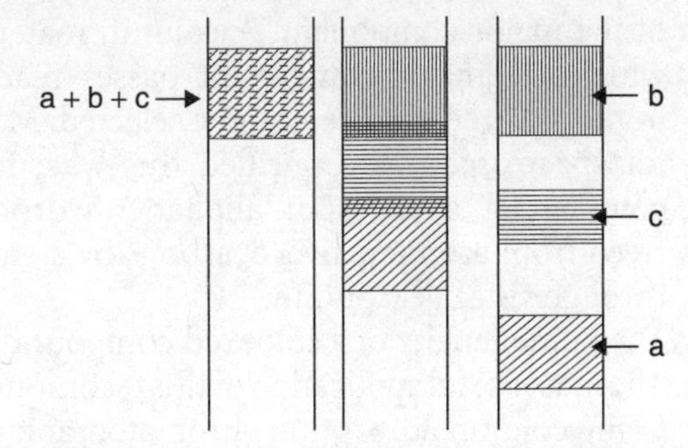

Fig. 3.7 Separation of components into bands

The separated components may be recovered from the column in two ways.

(i) The solvent can be sent through the column until the bands are eluted from the bottom of the column and collected in different containers. Removal of the solvent by a suitable method gives the pure components of the mixture.

(ii) If the solid can be extruded from the column in one piece, the portion of the solid containing different bands may be cut out separately and extracted with appropriate solvents. This method is more difficult than the first.

- The bands may be directly observed only with coloured materials. In dealing with colourless materials, the chromatographic experiment is followed by collecting a series of fractions of eluent of constant volume, say 10 mL. The solvent is then evaporated to check whether any solute is present. The different components are obtained in different containers, though each component may be distributed among several containers. Even though the method is tedious, this is generally adopted.
- With a few colourless materials, the separation can be attempted with coloured derivatives; for example, mixed aldehydes and ketones can be converted into dinitrophenylhydrazones and then separated.
- Colourless samples may sometimes be made visible on the column by fluorescence excited by an ultraviolet source.

The success of a chromatographic separation depends not only on the proper choice of the column material but also on the proper selection of solvent(s). The solvent also may be adsorbed on the solid. Thus, there is a competition between the solvent molecules and the component molecules for the active centres on the solid. If the solvent is more polar and hence more strongly adsorbed than the components of the mixture, the latter would remain almost entirely in the mobile phase and little separation would occur. Therefore, the eluting solvent must be less polar than the components of the mixture. Besides, the components must be soluble in the solvent; otherwise, the components remain permanently adsorbed on the solid. The eluting powers of solvents increase in the order,

$$n\text{-}C_6H_{14} < CCl_4 < C_6H_6 < CHCl_3 < C_2H_5O\,C_2H_5 < CH_3COCH_3 < C_2H_5OH < H_2O$$

The best solvent for a particular mixture is chosen only by trial and error. A mixture of two solvents is sometimes found to be more useful than individual solvents.

Applications of column adsorption chromatography

- This technique is used to remove small amounts of impurities whose structures differ widely from that of the major component. A column material through which the major component passes readily but the impurities get adsorbed can be selected. Many solvents for spectroscopy are purified this way; for example, commercial samples of aliphatic hydrocarbons are freed from aromatic hydrocarbons by a single passage through silica gel column.

For a demonstration in a class, separation of syn- and anti-azobenzene may be attempted. A 50 mL burette may be used to prepare a column of alumina (about 15 g). Petroleum ether may be used as the solvent.

- The homogeneity of a coloured compound can be tested easily.
- The most useful application of this technique is separation of structurally similar compounds.
- Using column adsorption chromatography, even gases can be separated. In this technique, referred to as *Gas Adsorption Chromatography*, a 'carrier' gas such as nitrogen replaces the solvent. The method is normally applied to the separation of mixtures of gases or low boiling hydrocarbons.

3.2.2 High Performance Liquid Chromatography (HPLC)

HPLC involves the use of tightly packed columns containing small particles (a few micrometer diameter) of the stationary phase. The use of small particles provides greater surface area for the sample components; this increases the separation efficiency of the column. In other respects, it is similar to gas chromatography.

As the column is packed with fine particles, the flow of solvent through the column is very slow. To overcome this problem in HPLC, high pressure (6000 psi) is applied on the inlet of the column with a pump; the outlet is at atmospheric pressure. Hence, this method is also known as *high pressure liquid chromatography*. Using the pump, the flow-rate is adjusted to be about 0.01 to 10 cm^3 per minute. Figure 3.8 (a) describes a HPLC instrument.

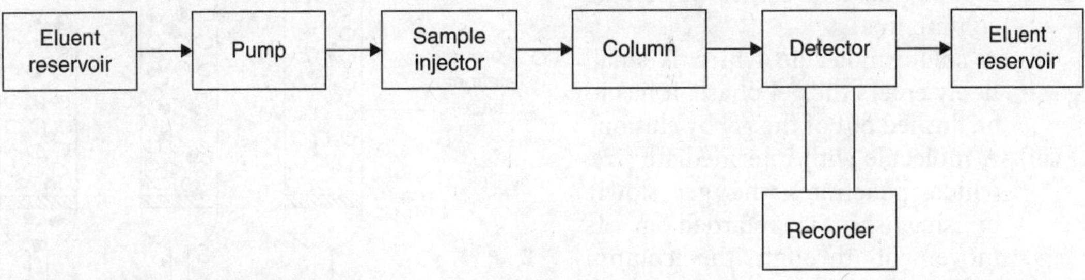

Fig. 3.8 (a) HPLC Block diagram

Several separation mechanisms can be employed in HPLC—partition, adsorption, ion exchange and size exclusion. However, partition mechanism is the most widely used in this method.

Adsorption-HPLC separation of isomeric nitroanilines on a silica column is depicted in Fig. 3.8 (b). Ion exchange-HPLC can be used for separating metal ions. For example, a mixture of Cu^{2+}, Zn^{2+} and Cd^{2+} can be separated by this method.

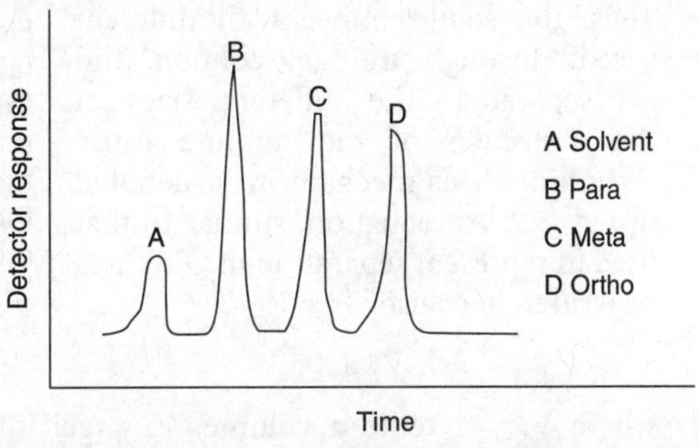

Fig. 3.8 (b) HPL chromatogram for isomeric nitroanilines

Advantages of HPLC

- It is extremely efficient in separation.
- A wide variety of materials can be analysed by this method.
- It requires only a few microlitres or micrograms of the analyte.

However, the HPLC instrument is expensive.

3.2.3 Size Exclusion Chromatography (SEC)

SEC is used for separating molecules according to their size. When SEC is performed in aqueous solvents on water-soluble species, it is called *gel filtration chromatography.* When performed in non-aqueous solvents, it is called *gel permeation chromatography* (GPC). The mechanism of separation in these two methods is the same. They are based on the relative pore sizes of the stationary phase compared to the size (volume) of the solute molecules with no chemical interation between the solute and stationary phase.

3.2.3.1 Mechanism of Size Exclusion Chromatography

SEC involves the following processes:

- The solutes – the components of the mixture – get distributed between the aqueous phase *within* the gel and the external mobile aqueous phase.

- The distribution between the two liquid phases is not identical for the solutes.
  (i) A solute molecule which is big cannot penetrate the gel and tends to remain in the mobile aqueous phase. It moves rapidly through the mobile phase. It comes out of the column first.
  (ii) A solute molecule which is small freely enters the gel phase; it has to be flushed out of the gel by elution.
  (iii) A molecule with intermediate size, which penetrates the gel slowly or sluggishly is retarded in its movement through the column unlike the big molecule, which readily moves through the column.
- Thus, the solutes move with different speeds through the gel column and get separated. The different sizes of the molecules of the mixture cause separation. This mechanism in denoted in Fig. 3.9. An equation, similar to that used to represent separation in GLC, can be written here also:

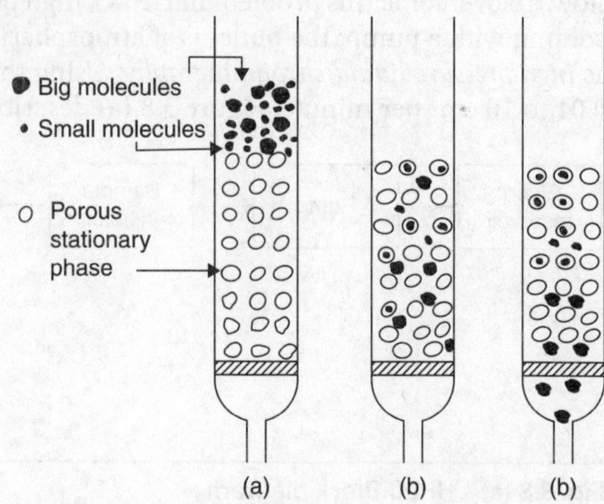

Fig. 3.9 Stages in gel filtration chromatography. **(a)** The mixture just poured over the gel, **(b)** A stage at which big molecules of the mixture move down the column and the small molecules are retarded due to penetrating into the gel, **(c)** Well-separated components; the big molecules moving out of the column.

$$V_R = V_o + K\,V_L$$

where V_R = retention volume, V_o = gel interstitial or void volume, K = distribution coefficient and V_L = volume of water within the gel available for accepting solutes. For a solute which is completely excluded from the gel, $K = 0$ and $V_R = V_o$.

For a solute which readily enters the gel, $K = 1$ and $V_R = V_o + V_L$. For molecules of intermediate sizes which can penetrate the gel to some extent but not freely, K is between 0 and 1.

SEC is suitable for separating an enzyme from other proteins. A Sephadex-G-100 gel filtration column is commonly used for such separations.

3.2.4 Affinity Chromatography

Affinity chromatography is the separation of molecules based on their biological functions. It particularly uses subtle conformational differences among similar biological macromolecules for their effective separation. This technique involves the following steps:

- A column is packed with a matrix specially prepared to attract and attach a specific biomolecule of interest in the mixture. The matrix (adsorbent) is not an inert martial such as silica or alumina (used in conventional chromatography); it is specially prepared with a covalently bonded biospecific ligand.
- The mixture containing the desired molecule is dissolved in a suitable solvent. This solution is made to percolate through the column. Adsorption occurs, which actually is not a simple physical adsorption. The biomolecule attaches itself to the matrix via the biospecific ligand forming a complex. The ligand on the matrix is stereospecific and therefore it traps only one kind of conformer from the mixture. The other molecules, which have no interaction with the ligand, quickly pass through the matrix.

- A solvent, used to prepare the solution of the mixture is then trickled through the column to free it completely from the unbound constituents of the mixture. Now the column matrix contains only one constituent of the mixture.
- Then, the adsorbed constituent is eluted with a suitable eluent. The biomolecules detach themselves from the matrix (ligand) and are collected as a solution. The regenerated column is now ready for the next cycle of separation.
- Affinity chromatography is a *biospecific process*; it is a separation process that uses a very highly selective or specific interaction among biological macromolecules.
- These interactions are based on conformational aspects of structure and not on size, charge or solubility which are used in conventional methods separation.
- The vital step in this method is the immobilisation of a particular component of the mixture on a gel matrix.

Agarose, a polysaccharide, and a component of agar obtained from seaweed, can serve as an inert matrix in affinity chromatography. Its suitability to serve as a matrix is enhanced by synthetically cross-linking the molecules and activating it by introducing some functional groups on it; this improves the interaction between the matrix and the biomolecule to be separated.

- Pure biological materials required for immunological studies can be obtained by affinity chromatography. An example for this is the isolation of bovine prothrombin from cattle blood.
- Enzymes, such as trypsin and rennin can be purified by this chromatography.
- Proteins, which are important in the study of molecular biology, can be isolated and purified by affinity chromatography.

3.2.5 Column Partition Chromatography

This method depends on the distribution of solutes between a mobile solvent and a second liquid, firmly attached to the solid adsorbent. Martin and Synge have separated amino acids using a column of silica with a mixture of chloroform and butanol as the mobile medium. The method can be used only when the solutes are water soluble because generally water is used as the second solvent. However, in such cases, paper chromatography is more convenient. Therefore, column partition chromatography is not widely used.

3.2.6 Thin Layer Chromatography

Thin layer chromatography (TLC), involves the same principles as those of column chromatography. It is a form of solid-liquid adsorption chromatography. In TLC, separation takes place on a layer of finely divided solid that is fixed on a flat surface.

3.2.6.1 Preparation of TLC Plates

The same solid adsorbents used for column chromatography are employed for TLC. Silica and alumina are widely used. A thin layer plate is prepared by spreading an aqueous slurry of the finely ground solid on the clean surface of a glass or rigid plastic. A small amount of a

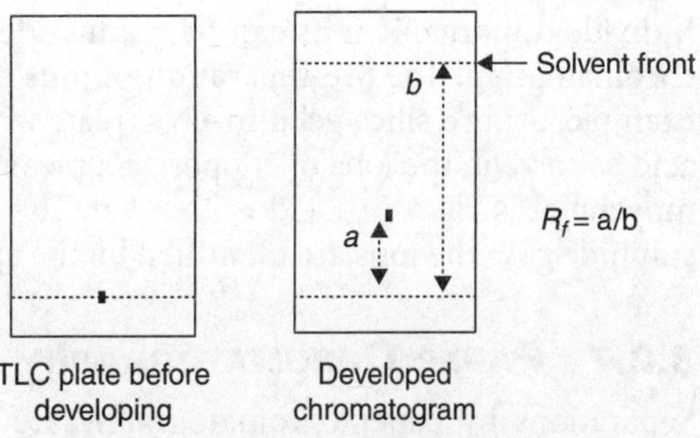

Fig. 3.10 Thin-layer chromatogram

binder (for example, plaster of Paris, calcium sulphate or starch) is incorporated into the slurry to increase adhesion of the solid particles to the glass and also to one another. The plate is then heated in an oven for about 30 minutes and cooled inside the oven itself. Care is taken to avoid exposing the surface to the atmosphere to prevent water adsorption.

3.2.6.2 Plate Development

A drop of the solution containing the mixture to be separated is placed near one edge of the plate and its position is marked with a pencil. The plate is then placed in a container (developing chamber) with enough solvent to come to a level just below the original sample spot. The chamber is kept closed with a flat glass plate. The solvent migrates up the plate carrying with it the components of the mixture at different rates. After the solvent has reached almost the top edge of the plate, the latter is removed and dried. Coloured materials appear as dots in the chromatogram (Fig. 3.10).

A number of methods are available for locating the spots of colourless materials. Irradiation of the plate with ultraviolet light will permit location of spots of compounds that exhibit fluorescence. There are some detecting agents, which when sprayed on the chromatograms, make the spots readily visible; for example, sulphuric acid and potassium permanganate solution. Iodine is another good detecting agent. In this case the plate is kept in a vessel saturated with iodine vapour. Iodine is adsorbed by many organic compounds and consequently brown spots appear on the chromatogram. Ninhydrin (2,2-dihydroxyindane-1,3-dione) is a commonly used colouring agent. It produces a deep blue or purple colour (Ruhemann's purple) with ammonia, primary amines and secondary amines.

Under a given set of conditions (adsorbent, solvent, layer thickness) the rate of movement of a compound with respect to the rate of movement of the solvent front is a property characteristic of the compound. This property, represented by the symbol R_f (*Retention front*) is obtained by dividing the distance travelled by the substance by the distance travelled by the solvent front from the original spot.

Applications of TLC

- Since the technique is easy and can be done rapidly, it is ideal for routine analysis of the composition of a mixture. A great advantage of this method is that only a very small quantity of the sample (approximately 10^{-9} g) is required.
- TLC may be used to find out the best eluting agent for column chromatography.
- A semi-quantitative estimate of the amount of a component present in a mixture can be obtained by a comparison of the area of a spot with that of a standard.

3.2.6.3 TLC of Inorganic Ions

Individual inorganic ions can be readily identified by the common detection reactions on a chromatogram. The pre-separation of ions into groups by classical methods is desirable. For example, using a silica gel thin-layer plate with a mixture of *n*-butanol and 1.5 N hydrochloric acid as solvent, the ions of copper group can be separated and identified. The sequence of ion movement is Hg > Bi > Cd > Pb > Cu. The plate is inserted into a tank filled with hydrogen sulphide gas. The ions are identified by the appropriate coloured spots.

3.2.7 Paper Chromatography

Separations by paper chromatography are performed in the same way as with thin-layer plates, but paper chromatography is based on a slightly different principle. Specially-prepared papers which are reproducible with respect to porosity and thickness are employed. Such papers contain sufficient adsorbed water that paper chromatography can be classified as *liquid–liquid partition chromatography.*

The experimental set-up for paper chromatography is shown in Fig. 3.11. About a milligram of the mixture in solution is spotted onto the paper, which is then dipped into the developing solvent. The paper is hung in a vertical configuration within a wide-mouthed bottle which contains a 1-cm layer of solvent.

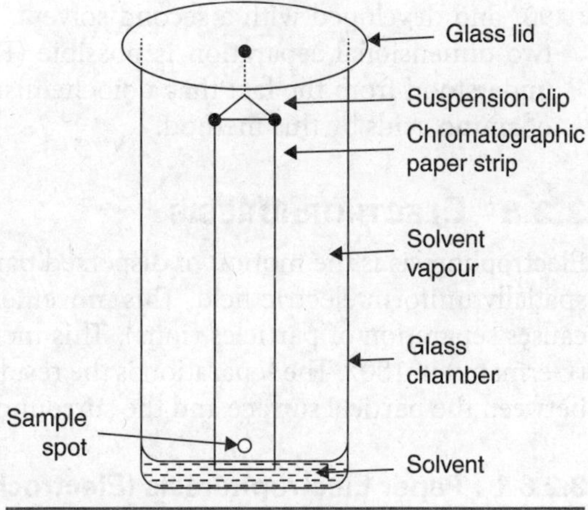

Fig. 3.11 Paper chromatography

The solvent rises by capillary attraction and the components are carried with it at different rates. When the solvent almost reaches the top edge of the paper, the paper is removed and dried in an oven. The separated spots, if colourless, may be rendered visible by treatment with an appropriate reagent.

Applications of paper chromatography

- Compounds may be identified by comparison of their R_f values. The R_f values are far more reproducible with paper chromatography than with TLC. This is because papers are made to correct specifications. If a mixture is separated along with spots of the likely components, presence or absence of the latter in the mixture can be inferred by a direct comparison of the R_f values.
- Since the method is very simple, it is ideally suited for rapid analysis of reaction mixtures and hence is a valuable tool in the hands of the organic chemist.

> - *There are two factors that govern the choice of paper. If the solutes are strongly adsorbed and hence slow-moving, a thin paper is used. To handle large quantities, a thick paper is generally preferred.*
> - *A basic limitation of the method is that capillary attraction can lift the solvent front only up to a height of 30 cm. In attempting complicated separations, where there is not much of a difference in rates, a descending method, in which the solvent is siphoned downward from a trough through the paper, is used.*

- It is not necessary to have only water as the stationary phase in paper chromatography. Other liquids can be made to displace the water adsorbed on the paper. A paper treated with paraffin oil can be used for reverse phase chromatography in which the mobile phase is water.
- Specially made papers are available which contain an adsorbent or an ion-exchange resin. Adsorption paper chromatography and ion-exchange paper chromatography are performed with such papers.
- When separation is incomplete with any one developing solvent, a two-dimensional paper chromatographic method is used.
- The initial spot is placed near one corner of a square sheet and the chromatogram is developed in the usual way with one solvent. The paper is dried, turned through

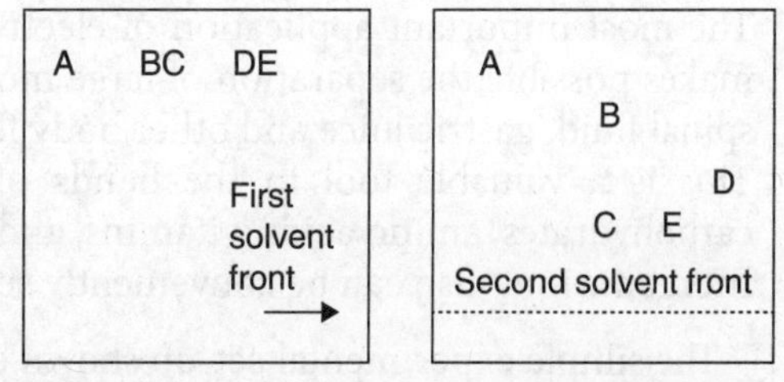

Fig. 3.12 Two-dimensional chromatography

90° and developed with a second solvent. By a proper choice of two solvents, a complete two-dimensional separation is possible (Fig. 3.12). The efficiency of the method can be understood from the fact that a biochemist could separate a mixture containing a number of amino acids by this method.

3.2.8 Electrophoresis

Electrophoresis is the motion of dispersed particles relative to a fluid under the influence of a spatially uniform electric field. This movement is called an *electrokinetic phenomenon* and it causes separation of particles (ions). This method of separtation was invented by F F Reuess (Germany) in 1807. The separation is the result of the presence of a differential charge interface between the particle surface and the surrounding field.

3.2.8.1 Paper Electrophoresis (Electrochromatography)

This is not strictly a branch of chromatography but its applicability is very similar to that of paper chromatography. Paper chromatography cannot be applied for substances of high molecular weight such as proteins or peptides since their separations are very slow. In such cases, eletrophoresis is the alternative. The experimental set-up is shown in Fig. 3.13.

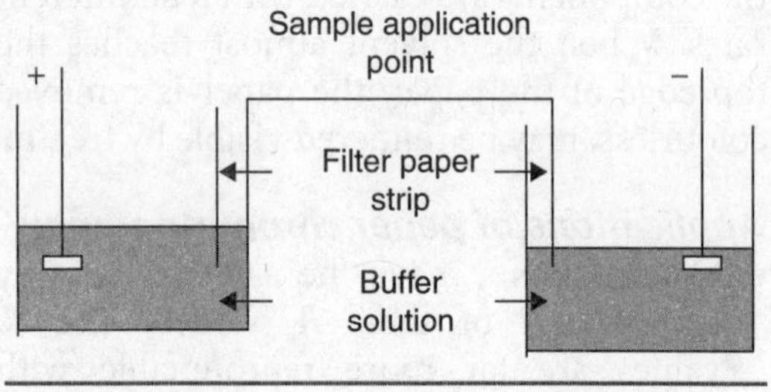

Sample application point
+
−
Filter paper strip
Buffer solution

Fig. 3.13 Electrochromatography apparatus

A strip of paper is held horizontally between two containers filled with a buffer mixture. The paper is soaked with buffer. The sample to be separated is placed at the centre of the strip. A high dc potential, depending upon the nature of the component species, is applied across the electrodes dipping in the buffer solution. The components of the mixture separate by virtue of moving at different speeds in the applied electric field. The paper acts merely as a porous supporting material which prevents remixing by diffusion of the separated components. After passing the current for a suitable period, the paper is removed and dried. The separated zones are rendered visible by spraying a suitable reagent.

This method applies only to substances such as acids, bases, amino acids and proteins which carry charge in a buffer of suitable pH. Careful choice of the buffer is an essential requirement of electrochromatography. In general the pH of the buffer should be roughly in the middle of the pK_a range of the components to be separated. To apply the technique to water-insoluble substances, the aqueous buffers can be replaced by organic buffers such as pyridine–acetic acid or trimethylamine–formic acid.

Applications of electrophoresis

- The most important application of electrophoresis is in clinical diagnosis. The technique makes possible the separation of large molecules such as proteins present in serum, urine, spinal fluid, gastric juice and other body fluids.
- This is a valuable tool in the hands of a biochemist interested in the separation of carbohydrates, amino acids, vitamins, and so on.
- Inorganic ions also can be conveniently separated using electrochromatography.

(i) The simple experimental set-up shown earlier can be slightly modified to suit large-scale separations (Fig. 3.14).

A sheet of paper is clamped vertically between two strips which form the electrodes. The solution containing the components flows continuously on to the paper at the point D. Separation occurs in the vertical direction under the influence of gravity. When the potential is applied, simultaneous separation occurs in the horizontal direction as well. The components are, therefore, fanned out and can be collected separately.

(ii) In addition to paper as the supporting medium, other materials such as cellulose acetate membranes, cellulose powders, starch gels, glass powders, and ion-exchange resins are used as solid supports in electrochromatography.

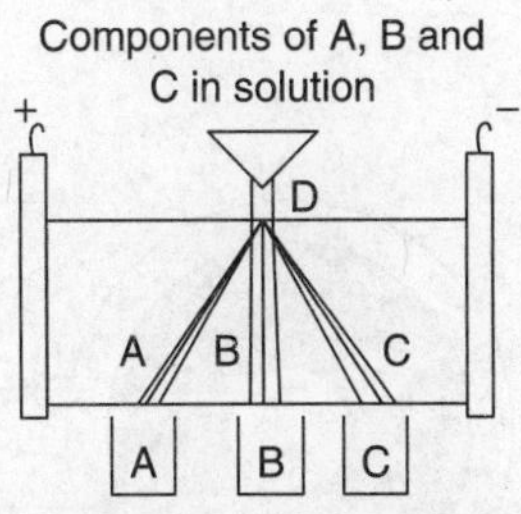

Fig. 3.14 Large-scale electrochromatography

3.2.9 Capillary Electrophoresis

Capillary electrophoresis (CE) is a separation method in which smaller, more positively charged ions are made to migrate rapidly, whilst the more negatively charged ions migrate slowly through a capillary tube in an applied electric field.

3.2.9.1 CE apparatus

The apparatus used for CE is shown in Fig. 3.15. The mixture of electrolytes is injected at one end of a capillary tube, packed with fused silica. The silica is wetted with an appropriate electrolyte solution. The two ends of the capillary tube are kept dipped in electrolyte buffer solutions, the same solution as in the capillary. A small volume of the mixture is introduced at one end of the capillary tube. Platinum electrodes immersed in the two buffer solutions are connected to a direct current high voltage source; this source delivers currents up to 250 μA at voltages in the range 1000–30000 V.

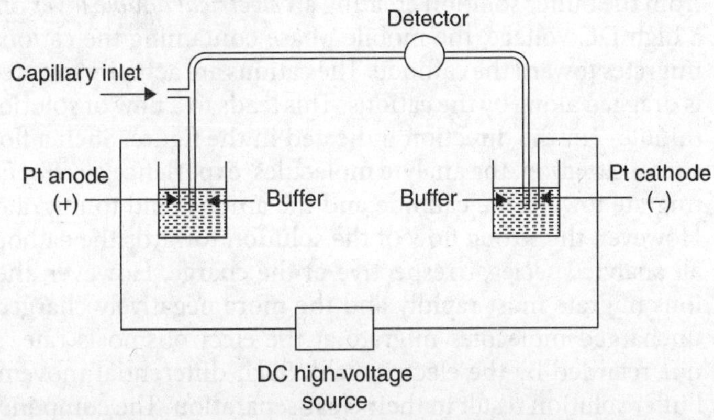

Fig. 3.15 Capillary electrophoresis apparatus

A detector is placed near one end of the capillary tube—it may be a UV absorbance detector. A focussed beam is passed through the capillary tube and the emerging beam is collected by an optical fibre coupled to a photomultiplier tube. As each component passes through the region of detection in the tube, a peak is recorded. Instead of a UV detector, a fluorescence detector – with laser sources – may be used. This detector is capable of detecting very low quantities of the components, down to 10^{-21} mole (zeptomoles).

3.2.9.2 Mechanism of CE

The capillary tube is made of fused silica Fig. 3.16 (a). Its outer walls are coated with a polyamide for imparting strength to the tube. Its inner walls have a layer of silanol groups (SiOH). The tube is filled with a buffer. Above pH 2, the silanol group ionises to produce a negative charge

- *CE can analyse at nanolitre (10^{-9}) range of samples.*
- *It is associated with one million theoretical plates.*
- *It can detect materials even at zeptomole level.*

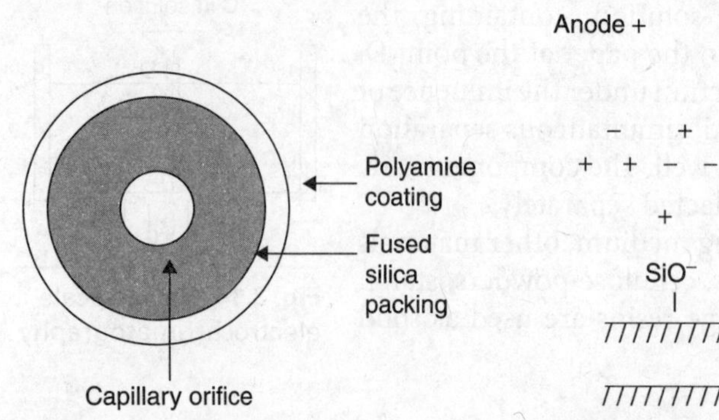

Fig. 3.16 (a) Capillary tube for CE (enlarged depiction)

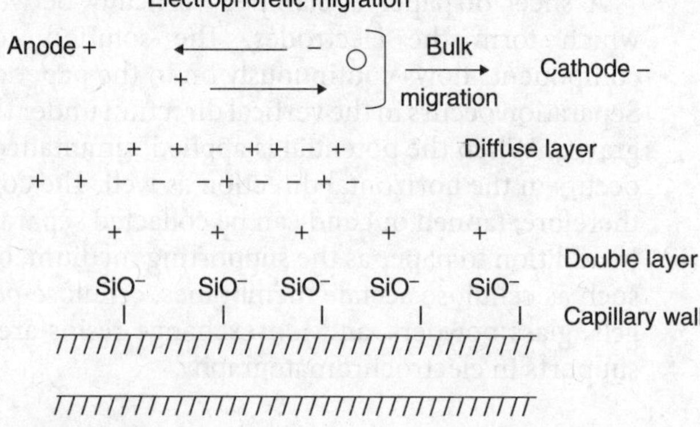

Fig. 3.16 (b) Mechanism of CE separation

on the capillary surface. Such a charge is called *zeta potential.* This potential attracts cations from the buffer solution creating an *electrical double layer* on the walls of the tube. On applying a high DC voltage, the mobile phase containing the cations in the diffuse outer double layer migrates toward the cathode. The cations are actually solvated, and therefore the buffer solution is dragged along by the cations. This leads to a flow of solution – several hundred nanolitres per minute – in the direction indicated in the figure. Such a flow is called *electro-osmotic flow.* In such a situation, the analyte molecules experience *electrophoretic mobility*, namely, the cations migrate toward the cathode and the anions tend to migrate toward the anode [Fig. 3.16 (b)]. However, the strong flow of the solution towards the cathode results in unidirectional flow of all analyte species, irrespective of the charge. However, the smaller, more positively charged ions migrate most rapidly and the more negatively charged anions migrate most slowly. The uncharged molecules migrate at the electroosmosis rate, since they are neither accelerated nor retarded by the electric field. Such differential movements of the various species in the buffer solution result in their clear separation. The components of the mixture can be collected separately guided by the detector response.

The electophoretic mobility u_i for an ion in CE is given by

$$u_i = \frac{z}{6\pi\eta r}$$

where z = number of ionic charges on solute, η = solution viscosity and r = ionic radius. The value of u_i is positive for a cation and negative for an anion. The number of plates n, is given by

$$n = \frac{u_{i_{\text{net}}} V}{2D}$$

- *CE is not a chromatographic technique.*
- *The separation mechanism of CE is called* molecular diffusion broadening.
- *The separation efficiency of CE is 10–100 times better than that of HPLC.*

where V is the applied voltage and D is the solute diffusion coefficient ($cm^2\ s^{-1}$). The value n increases with applied voltage. For large molecules such as proteins, the diffusion coefficient D is small and therefore n increases; this implies that the separation efficiency increases. In CE, unlike in column chromatography, the number of plates is independent of the column length.

Advantages of CE

- CE is suitable for separating multi-ion mixtures.

- It can be used for separating cations and anions and also neutral species.
- The speed of separation is high.
- The resolution and sensitivity are high.
- It is an inexpensive method.

3.2.10 Ion-Exchange Chromatography

Ion-exchange is a process involving exchange of ions of like sign between a solution and a solid in contact with the solution. The ion-exchange properties of clays and zeolites have long been known. But several synthetic materials which act as ion-exchangers have been made since 1935. Today ion-exchange resins are the most widely used packing in column chromatography. Ion-exchange chromatography is a special name given to column chromatography when the stationary phase is an ion-exchange resin.

Synthetic ion-exchange resins are high molecular weight polymeric materials containing a large number of ionic functional groups per molecule. Cation-exchangers contain sulphonic acid groups ($RSO_3^-H^+$) or carboxylic acid groups ($RCOO^-H^+$). Anion-exchange resins contain amines attached to the polymer molecule $RN(CH_3)_3^+ OH^-$.

Ion-exchange chromatography found its first major application in the separation of rare earths. A column was packed with an acid resin and treated first with hydrochloric acid to make sure that all exchange points were occupied by hydrogen ions. A mixture of rare earths as their chlorides was sent down the column. This resulted in the displacement of hydrogen ions by rare earth cations. The rare earth ions could then be eluted one after another. Since elution with water was very slow, a solution of citric acid was used as eluting solvent. The cations moved at different rates depending on the stability of the corresponding complex with citric acid.

There are two distinct advantages in ion-exchange chromatography:

(i) Since the capacity of the resins for exchange is quite high, it is easy to handle as much as 0.1 g of the sample at a time.
(ii) The recovery of ions from the column can be virtually complete (quantitative) which is an important factor in dealing with expensive materials and in quantitative work.

A mixture of amino acids can be separated using sulphonated polystyrene as the stationary phase. After application of the sample to the column, dilute sodium hydroxide solution can be used to elute the various amino acids. The reactions on the column are:

$$RSO_3H + B \rightarrow RSO_3^- \bullet BH^+ \text{ (salt)}$$

$$RSO_3^- \bullet BH^+ + OH^- \rightarrow RSO_3^- + H_2O + B$$

(B = amino acid)

3.2.11 Gas Liquid Chromatography (GLC or GLPC)

In accordance with the recommendation of the Hydrocarbon Research Group of the Institute of Petroleum, USA, gas–liquid partition chromatography (GLPC) is referred to as gas–liquid chromatography. Since the discovery of the technique in 1952, its applications have increased so rapidly that GLC has become today an essential part of any well-equipped organic chemistry laboratory.

In GLC, the mixture to be separated is vapourised and sent through a column by a flowing inert gas such as hydrogen or helium. The inert gas is called the *carrier gas*. The gaseous mixture is the mobile phase. The column is packed with a solid on the surface of which is adsorbed a liquid of very low volatility. This liquid serves as the fixed phase. The components of the mixture move through the column at different rates due to selective phase distribution between the two phases and thus get separated.

In general, low boiling and highly volatile components move through the column faster than low volatile components because, to a rough approximation, the higher the vapour pressure of a gas, the lower its solubility in a liquid. Apart from volatility, polar interactions significantly affect the solubility of a solute in a solvent.

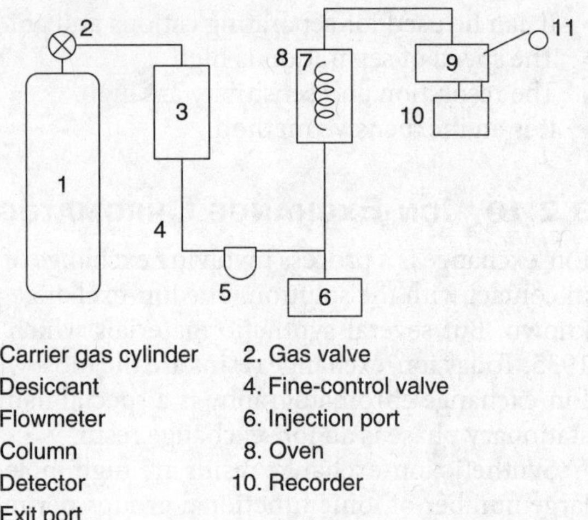

Fig. 3.17 Schematic diagram of a gas chromatograph

Numerous instruments for GLC are available commercially. The basic components of a gas–liquid chromatograph are shown in Fig. 3.17.

The column is kept in an oven whose temperature is controlled by a thermostat and heating elements. The sample is introduced into the flow system at the injection port. This unit is individually heated to facilitate vaporisation of the sample. As the vapourised sample is swept into the column by the carrier gas, its components separate into individual bands in the carrier gas and pass into the detector.

A relatively simple detection system consists of an instrument called *katherometer* which measures changes in the thermal conductivity of the gas stream [Fig. 3.18 (a)]. The instrument consists of an electrically heated wire which forms one arm of a Wheatstone bridge. The wire assumes a steady temperature and resistance when the pure carrier gas flows over it. As the separated components reach the wire, its temperature increases as a result of a decrease in thermal conductivity of its surroundings. The consequent change in

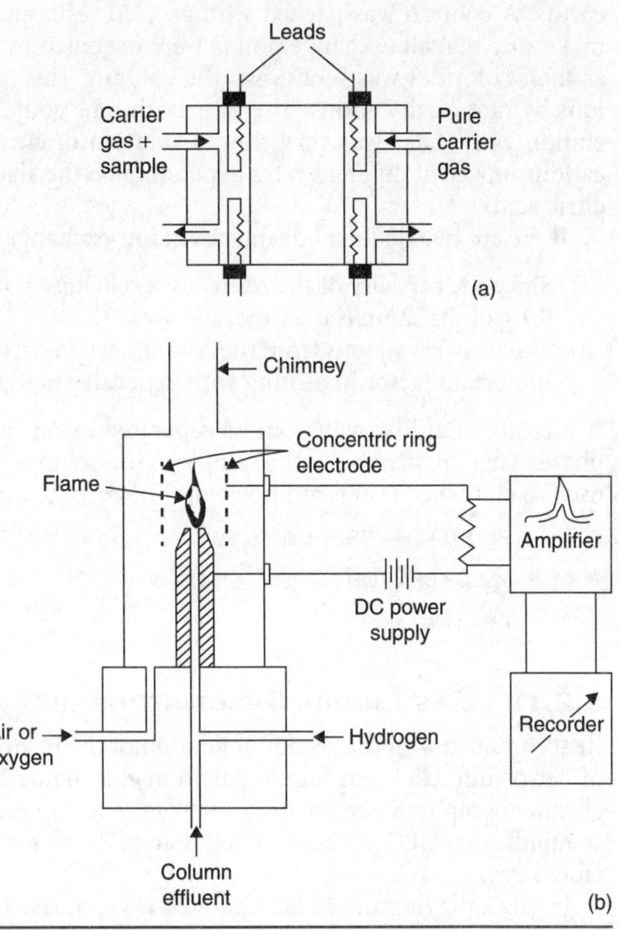

Fig. 3.18 GLC detector systems **(a)** Thermal conductivity detector **(b)** Flame ionisation detector and circuitry

resistance is measured by the bridge. The change in resistance is proportional to the concentration of the component. The bridge is coupled to a pen recorder and the chromatogram consists of a plot of concentration of the component in the carrier gas *versus* time. A typical chromatogram is shown in Fig. 3.19.

- The thermal conductivities of hydrogen and helium are roughly six to ten times greater than those of most organic compounds. The presence of even traces of other materials causes a relatively large decrease in thermal conductivity. That is why these two carrier gases are preferred to nitrogen and carbon dioxide, whose thermal conductivity values are in the same range as those of most organic substances.

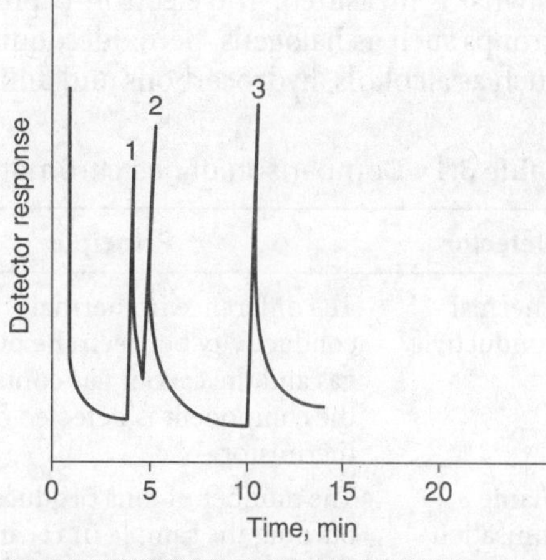

Fig. 3.19 A typical gas chromatogram, three peaks denoting three components of the mixture

The choice of the stationary liquid phase depends on the types of compounds to be separated. The best choice would be a liquid that gives rise to significant differences in the partition coefficients of the components to be separated. Squalene, polyethylene glycol, diethylene glycol adipate, diethylene glycol succinate and butanediol succinate are some of the substances commonly used as stationary phases. The liquid is coated on the solid support by dissolving the liquid in a low-boiling solvent and mixing the solid with this solution. Evaporation of the solvent leaves the solid granules evenly coated.

3.2.11.1 Detection Systems

The solute concentration in a carrier gas at any instant is only a few parts per thousand. The detector system that is used, therefore, should be sensitive enough to respond to such low concentrations. Also, the interval during which a component passes through the detector is usually one second or less. The detector, therefore, should be capable of exhibiting its full response within this period. More than a dozen different types of detectors are used. The most widely used of these are the *thermal conductivity detector*, the *flame ionisation detector* and the *electron-capture detector*. The first of these has already been described.

Flame ionisation detector Many organic compounds, when pyrolysed at the temperature of a hydrogen – or an air – flame, produce ionic species. These ions can be collected and the resulting ion current measured. An electrometer must be employed for measurement of current since the latter would be very small because of the high resistance of the flame.

The hydrogen-flame detector is a very popular and sensitive detector. A schematic diagram of flame ionisation detector is shown in Fig. 3.18 (b). The hydrogen-flame detector is more expensive than the thermal conductivity detector but is much more sensitive than the latter.

Electron-capture detector This functions in the same way as a proportional counter for the measurement of X-radiation. The effluent from the column is allowed to pass over a β-emitter such as nickel-63. An electron from the emitter causes ionisation of the carrier gas and production of an innumerable number of electrons. A constant standing current results from this ionisation process in the absence of organic molecules. However, in the presence of organic molecules that tend to capture electrons, a decrease in the current is expected and this is what is measured. The electron-capture detector is very sensitive towards a few functional groups such as halogens, peroxides, quinones and nitro groups but insensitive to compounds such as alcohols, hydrocarbons and amines.

Table 3.1 Comparison of gas chromatograph detectors

Detector	Principle	Application	Limitations
Thermal conductivity	The difference in thermal conductivity between the pure carrier gas and the carrier gas containing the component is detected by a thermistor	Suitable for both organic and inorganic mixtures	Sensitive to both changes in temperature and gas flow; least sensitive
Flame ionisation	The number of ions produced on burning the sample in H_2 and air is detected as current on an electrode	Suitable for organic compounds; unsuitable for many inorganic species	Very sensitive
Electron capture	Reducible species of the mixture in the carrier gas capture electrons produced from Ar gas by particles. The detector senses reduction in the flow of electrons to the anode.	Suitable for O, P, S, X, N compounds, insecticides and pesticides; low response to ethers and hydrocarbons	Extraordinarily sensitive

3.2.11.2 Chromatographic Column Materials

A variety of solid phases are used for packing chromatographic columns. The solid used in the column should have certain characteristics.

- It should be inert; it should not react either with the stationary phase coated on it or with the mobile phase or with the constituents of the analyte.
- It should be porous and have uniform pore diameter.
- Its surface area should be large.
- Its particles should be of regular shape with good mechanical strength to permit an efficient, well-packed column.
- It should be inexpensive.
- Several chromatographic solid supports are available commercially (Table 3.2).

Table 3.2 Chromatographic column solid supports

Solid support	Characteristics	Commercial names
Diatomite	Silica material composed of skeletons of microscopic algae	Chromosorb P, Gas chrom R, Anakrom ABS, Gas chrom Q
Porous organic polymers	Have different chemical structures; serve as stationary phase directly, as well as support phase	Chromosorb century series, Poropak, Tenax
Glass beads	Have roughened (texurised) surfaces	–
Sieved Teflon	Inert toward corrosive components in the analyte	–

3.2.11.3 Column Packings

Column packings used to consist of a stationary phase physically adsorbed onto a porous silica support. In such a system, the pressure and shearing effects of the mobile liquid flowing through the column led to 'bleeding' of the stationary phase off the solid support. Therefore, in modern methods, the stationary phase is 'chemically bonded' to a porous silica support thus preventing bleeding. Chemical bonding between the two is achieved by reacting the hydroxyl groups on the surface of the silica support with an organochlorosilane.

$$-\underset{|}{\overset{|}{Si}}-OH + Cl\,Si\,(CH_3)_2\,R \longrightarrow -\underset{|}{\overset{|}{Si}}-O-\underset{CH_3}{\overset{CH_3}{Si}}-R + HCl$$

The R groups render the silica surface hydrophobic. The polarity of the R groups varies depending upon their nature (Table 3.3).

The packing materials are prepared as small porous spheres with large surface area and uniform diameter.

Table 3.3 Some silica column packings with chemically bonded organosilanes

R Group	Formula
Octadecyl	$C_{18}H_{37}-$
Octyl	$C_8H_{17}-$
Ethyl	C_2H_5-
Benzyl	$C_6H_5CH_2-$
Alkycyano	$N\equiv C(CH_2)_n-$
Alkylamino	$H_2N(CH_2)_n-$

3.2.11.4 Stationary Phases

The stationary phase is a material coated on the surface of a solid support such as silica. The stationary phase may be bonded on to the silica surface. Such a combination of solid support with a bonded stationary phase is known as *bonded-phase columns.* Such columns are more efficient separators than the ones containing coated columns. Some of the commonly used materials for bonding on silica columns are listed in Table 3.4.

Table 3.4 Some commonly used bonded-phase stationary materials

Phase	Temperature range used for separation (°C)
Methyl silicone	60–300
Phenylmethyl silicone	60–300
Trifluoropropyl silicone	50–220
Polyethylene glycol (Carbowax)	20–230

Capillary columns A capillary column is a column of very small inner diameter. The inner walls of this column are coated with a stationary phase; such a column is known as wall-coated open tubular capillary (WCOT) column or simply capillary column. They are long and provide excellent separation. They are suitable for separating even a mixture of several constituents. They can be made of glass or stainless steel.

Wide-bore capillary columns This type of column is an open-tubular column with an inside diameter of about 0.5 mm and a length of 15 m. Its separatory efficiency is less than that of capillary columns but more than that of packed columns. It is easy to prepare, and liquid samples can be easily injected into it.

3.2.11.5 Plate Theory

The *plate theory* is the assumption that the movement of substance A through a chromatographic column involves movement through successive equilibration chambers. Such equilibration chambers are called *theoretical plates.* A theoretical plate is the volume of the column required for an equilibrium between the stationary and the mobile phases. The equilibrium is described by the distribution ratio or distribution coefficient, *K.* This ratio is denoted by the equation,

$$K = \frac{C_s}{C_M}$$

where C_s and C_M are the concentrations of substance A in the stationary and the mobile phases, respectively. The mobile phase is a liquid in column chromatography and a gas in gas chromatography.

The same equilibrium may also be described by the ratio (k') of the moles of a substance in the stationary phase to its moles in the mobile phase:

$$k' = \frac{C_s V_s}{C_M V_M}$$

$$k' = K \frac{V_s}{V_M}$$

where V_s = volume of the stationary liquid phase, V_M = dead (void) volume of the column and k^1 = *capacity factor* or *mass distribution ratio*.

A theoretical plate is an imaginary concept; it is not related to real column parameters. However, it helps understand the column parameters. Each theoretical plate has a definite length, called the *height equivalent* (*h*) *to a theoretical plate* (HETP). It is given as

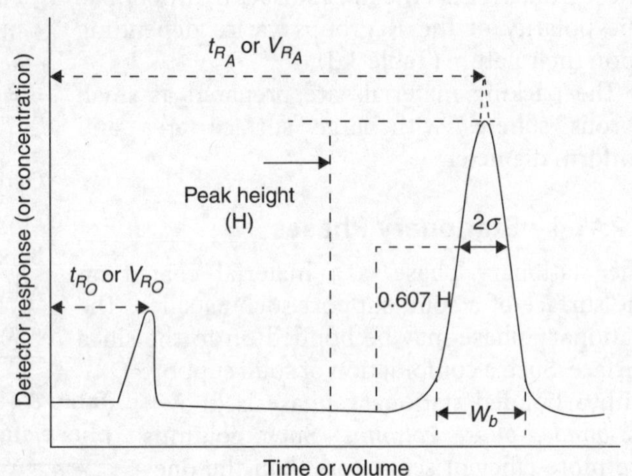

Fig. 3.20 Chromatogram of a mixture of two components

$$h = \frac{L}{n}$$

where L is the length of the column and n is its theoretical *plate number*. In a separation, the equlibria experience an inertia, and therefore an inability to instantaneously re-establish the distribution equilibrium at each point of the column. The efficiency of separation increases as n of theoretical plates increases. The value of n should be the highest possible for separating two components of a mixture, when the two differ only slightly in their distribution coefficients.

The detector at the outlet of the chromatographic column gives a signal proportional to the quantity of the substance eluted per unit time. When the detector response or the proportional concentration of the substance in the gaseous phase is plotted against time or volume of the gaseous phase, a chromatographic peak is obtained. Each peak denotes one constituent in the mixture being analysed. A typical chromatographic plot for a mixture of two substances (A and B) is represented in Fig. 3.20. Substance A is eluted immediately after the passage of the eluent through the column, indicating that it is not distributed between the stationary and the mobile gaseous phases; it remains in the gaseous phase ($K = 0$). But substance B is distributed between the two phases, and therefore eluted from the column after substance A.

Dead time, t_M: This is the time that elapses between the injection of an inert substance which is not distributed between the two phases, such as air, and the appearance of the maximum peak. $t_M = t_{R_o}$ in Fig. 3.20.

Retention time, T_R: This is the time that elapses between the injection of the sample at the inlet of the column and the appearance of the maximum of the peak. It is relevant to each peak. It is related to k':

$$t_R = t_M (1 + k')$$

When a gas has no affinity for the column material, that is, when it does not remain adsorbed on the column material, $k' = 0$. This is so with an inert gas.

Then, $t_R = t_M$

Retention volume V_R: This is the volume of a carrier gas required for the elution of a substance; it is represented by the equation,

$$V_R = t_R F_C$$

where F_C is the flow rate of the carrier gas, measured at the column temperature and outlet pressure (atmospheric pressure).

Adjusted retention time, t'_R: This is given by the equation

$$t'_R = t_R - t_M$$

Adjusted retention volume, V'_R: This is denoted by the relation

$$V'_R = V_R - V_M$$

where V_M is the dead volume of the column.

$$V_M = t_M F_C$$

Corrected retention volume, V^o_R: This is given by the relation

$$V^o_R = j\, V_R$$

where j is the pressure drop correction factor, given by the relation.

$$j = 1.5\left(\frac{p^2 - 1}{P^3 - 1}\right)$$

$$p = \frac{p_i}{p_o}$$

where p_i and p_o are the pressures of the carrier gas at the inlet and the outlet of the column, respectively.

The adjusted retention time and the adjusted retention volume are generally used for identification of substances.

Retardation factor, R_f: This factor denotes the ratio of velocities of the movement of the sample and the carrier gas; it is given by the relation.

$$R_f = \frac{L/t_R}{L/t_M}$$

$$= \frac{t_M}{t_R} = \frac{V^o_M}{V^o_R}$$

Peak height, H: This is the distance between the peak maximum and the baseline corresponding to zero concentration or quantity of the eluted substance A.

Peak width, w_b: This is the distance between the points of intersection of the tangents, drawn at the inflection points of the peak and the baseline. Assuming that the peak has the shape of a Gaussian curve,

$$w_b = 4\sigma$$

where σ is the standard deviation of the distribution, denoted by the Gaussian curve; σ is equal to the half-width of the peak at a height equal to $H/\sqrt{e} = 0.607\,H$.

Relative retention, α: This is the ratio of the adjusted retention times or volumes of the substance A being analysed and a reference substance B.

$$\alpha = r_{B/A} = \frac{t'_{R_B}}{t'_{R_A}} = \frac{t_{R_B} - t_M}{t_{R_A} - t_M}$$

$$\alpha = r_{B/A} = \frac{V'_{R_B}}{V'_{R_A}} = \frac{V_{R_B} - V_M}{V_{R_A} - V_M}$$

> *A major limitation of the GLC is that the sample must have an appreciable vapour pressure at the temperature of the column. This condition precludes many kinds of non-volatile samples from this chromatographic method.*

The value of α gives a measure of the possibility of separating A and B. α is independent of the length of the column, the flow rate of the carrier gas and the quantity of the liquid stationary phase.

> - *If the column length is too long, the pressure required to create sufficient gas flow rate will have to be high.*
> - *Longer the column, longer is the time taken for elution.*
> - *The optimum column length is selected based on preliminary experiment.*

Length of column With identical experimental conditions, the number of theoretical plates is proportional to the length of the column. Therefore, a way of improving resolution is using a longer column. The separation of two peaks, $t_{R2}-t_{R1}$ is directly proportional to the distance that the two solutes migrate. The width of an elution band increases directly with the square root of the distance. When the column length is increased, two bands will separate faster than they broaden, and the resolution will improve.

Applications of GLC

- GLC is used for the separation of mixtures and identification of the components from a quantity called *retention time*. The time taken by a given component to pass from the injection port to the detector is known as its retention time. For any given column and a set of conditions (flow rate and temperature), the retention time is a characteristic property of the compound and therefore may be used to identify the latter (similar to R_f value).
- GLC provides a convenient method of quantitative analysis of small amounts of mixtures, provided the identities of all the components are known. The area under the peak in a chromatogram is proportional to the concentration of the component responsible for that peak.
- GLC can be used for the purification of a compound as an alternative to distillation. As the vapour of the compound comes from the exit port, it may be collected and condensed.

3.2.11.6 Qualitative Analysis by GLC

The components of a mixture can be identified by GLC based on the adjusted retention time t'_R or the adjusted retention volume V'_R. These two parameters depend not only on the nature of a component but also on the experimental conditions such as temperature, carrier gas velocity and the quantity of the liquid phase. Reproducible parameters can be obtained only when these experimental conditions are kept precisely constant. Therefore, the identification of a substance is better achieved by applying the concept of *Kováts retention index* I, which is independent of experimental factors. This index denotes the relative retention of a substance with respect to linear alkanes, which are taken as reference materials. The Kováts index is expressed as

$$I = 100 \frac{\log t'_{R,X} - \log t'_{R,Z}}{\log t'_{R,Z+1} - \log t'_{R,Z}} + 100\, Z$$

$t'_{R,X}$, $t'_{R,Z}$ and $t'_{R,Z+1}$ are the adjusted retention times for substance x and the alkanes with z and $z+1$ carbon atoms respectively. z is so chosen such that $t'_{R,Z} < t'_{R,X} < t'_{R,Z+1}$. For example, for benzene, $I = 650$; therefore, benzene behaves like a linear alkane with 6.50 carbon atoms. It is eluted between n-hexane and n-heptane. The value of t'_R and V'_R change when the experimental conditions are changed; however, as I is a ratio, it does not change with experimental conditions. Thus, Kováts index is a reliable index for identifying substances.

Among the members of a homologous series, say a series of straight chain alkanols, the logarithm of the retention volume is a linear function of the number of carbon atoms under identical experimental conditions (Fig. 3.21).

Such a relationship can be used to identify a compound.

Most of the inorganic compounds, being non-volatile, are not suitable for GLC analysis.

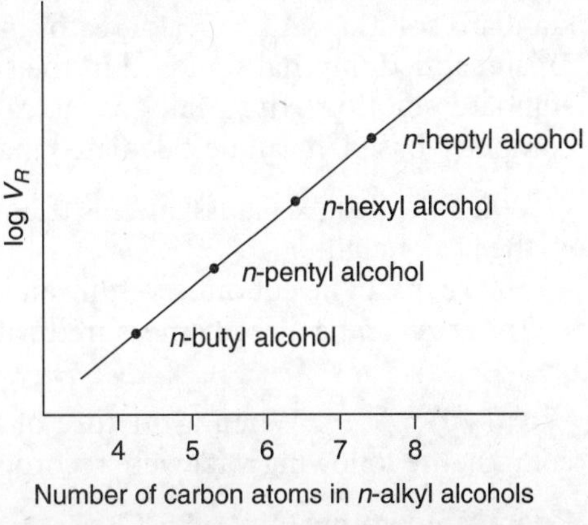

Fig. 3.21 Retention volume versus carbon atoms

3.2.11.7 Quantitative Analysis

GLC can be applied to quantitative analysis as well. The area of a chromatographic peak is proportional to the quantity of a component, under constant experimental conditions. When the identity of a component in a mixture has been established, a calibration GLC is performed using known quantities of that component; then, the calibration data (curve) can be used to determine the unknown concentration by comparison. When the t'_R values are small, sharp and narrow peaks are obtained whose heights are directly related to the amount of the components; however, the peak area is a more precise measure of quantity of a compound than the peak height.

Assuming that the detector responses are identically sensitive to all components in a mixture, the relative areas of the peaks are equal to the relative quantities of the components. However, this is rarely so; the sensitivity of the thermal conductivity detector is different for different substances; it varies with the nature of the substances. With a flame ionisation detector, it varies with the number of carbon atoms in the molecule of the component. Granting such variations in responses, an empirical factor, called *response factor* (F) is evaluated for each component adopting constant experimental conditions. This factor is given by the equation

$$F = \frac{C/C'}{A/A'}$$

where C and C' are the concentrations of the component and the standard respectively and A and A' are the corresponding peak areas.

The method of internal standard is applied when changes in experimental conditions are inevitable. Then, the relative areas of the peaks for two components X and Y in the analyte are constant and independent of the flow velocity of the carrier gas. In this method, the concentration (C_X) of the component X in the sample is given by the relation,

$$C_x = \left(\frac{A_X}{A_S}\right) C_{XS} \left(\frac{A_{IS}}{A_{ISS}}\right)$$

where, A_X = peak area of substance X in the sample, A_S = peak area of substance X in the standard solution, A_{IS} = peak area of internal standard in the standard solution, A_{IIS} = peak area of added internal standard in the sample and C_{XS} = concentration of substance X in the standard solution. The peak area is calculated automatically when the GLC instrument is computer-based. It can be calculated manually also.

- When the peak is Gaussian, it is triangulated, the width $w_{1/2}$ is measured and multiplied by the peak height h.
- The peak can be cut out carefully and the paper weighed.
- The area can be directly measured with a planimeter or calculated with an integrator.

Problem 3.2 When a mixture of two substances A and B was separated with a GLC column, the following data were recorded:

Room temperature (air)	25°C	Outlet pressure	760 torr
Column temperate	80°C	Volume of stationary liquid phase	4.0 mL
Inlet pressure	1300 torr	Flow rate of carrier gas at 25°C	20.0 mL/min

Retention times:

air	0.32 min
A	5.0 min
B	6.0 min

Calculate (i) the corrected retention volumes for the air and A and B, (ii) the retardation factors for A and B, (iii) the distribution coefficients for A and B at 80°C and (iv) the separation factor for A and B.

Solution

(i) The pressure drop correction factor,

$$j = 1.5\left(\frac{p^2 - 1}{p^3 - 1}\right)$$

$$= 1.5\left[\frac{(1300/760)^2 - 1}{(1300/760)^3 - 1}\right] = 0.721$$

Retention volume, $V_R = t_R F_C$

$$V_R^o = jV_R$$

For air, $V_{air}^o = V_M^o = j\, t_R F_C \left(\frac{T_{column}}{T_{air}}\right)$

$$= 0.721 \times 0.32 \times 20.0 \left(\frac{353}{298}\right) = 5.5$$

$$V_{RA}^o = 0.721 \times 5.0 \times 20.0 \left(\frac{353}{298}\right) = 85.4 \text{ mL}$$

$$V_{RB}^o = 0.721 \times 6.0 \times 20.0 \left(\frac{353}{298}\right) = 102.5 \text{ mL}$$

(ii) Retardation factor

$$R_F = \frac{V_M^o}{V_R^o}$$

$$R_{F_A} = \frac{5.5}{85.4} = 0.064$$

$$R_{F_B} = \frac{5.5}{102.5} = 0.054$$

(iii) The distribution coefficient

$$K = \frac{V_R^o - V_M^o}{V_s}$$

$$K_A = \frac{V_{R_A}^o - V_M^o}{V_s} = \frac{85.4 - 5.5}{4.0} = 20.0$$

$$K_B = \frac{V_{R_B}^o - V_M^o}{V_s} = \frac{102.5 - 5.5}{4.0} = 24.3$$

(iv) The separation factor

$$\alpha = \frac{t_{R_B} - t_M}{t_{R_A} - t_M} = \frac{6.0 - 0.32}{5.0 - 0.32} = 1.21$$

Problem 3.3 A mixture of two components X and Y is separated isothermally by GC, using a 2.00 m column having 6000 theoretical plates. The flow rate used is 20.0 mL /min. Air, which is not adsorbed on the column emerges in 40.0 s. Peak X emerges in 4.0 min and peak

Y emerges in 10.0 min. Calculate (i) the base widths of peaks X and Y (ii) the fraction of time that Y spends in the mobile phase while passing through the column and (iii) the value of H for the column used.

Solution

(i) The number of theoretical plates associated with a given peak is given by the relation

$$n = 16\,(t_R/w)^2$$

where t_R is the retention time and w is the width of the peak at its base.

$$\therefore \quad w = \frac{4t_R}{\sqrt{n}}$$

$$w_X = \frac{4 \times 240}{\sqrt{6000}} = 12 \text{ s}$$

$$w_Y = \frac{4 \times 600}{\sqrt{6000}} = 31 \text{ s}$$

(ii) The mobile phase for any substance in this experiment lasts 40 s, the time required for the air peak to emerge. As Y remains for 10 min in the column, the desired fraction is

$$\frac{40}{60 \times 10} = 0.07$$

(iii) $H = \dfrac{L}{n}$

$$\frac{200 \text{ cm}}{6000 \text{ plates}} = 0.033 \text{ cm/plate}$$

Versatility of GC

Gas chromatography is a versatile technique as it can be applied to separate and determine many compounds of the types:

- gases,
- covalent, organic solids and liquids, containing up to 25 carbon atoms,
- volatile organometallic compounds,
- simple volatile inorganic compounds, and
- suitably derivatised products of nonvolatile or unstable compounds.

GC cannot be applied to

- nonvolatile, ionic compounds,
- salts,
- macromolecules, and
- thermally labile molecules.

3.2.12 Programmed-Temperature GLC

In GLC, the temperature of the column is raised *during* the chromatographic run. Initially, the column is kept at a lower temperature, suitable for the separation of the lower members of a series of components, which have lower boiling points (more volatile). Then, the temperature is increased to suit the separation of the higher members, which have higher boiling points. Satisfactory elution of these two classes of the components requires the application of such differential temperature. When the column temperature is much higher than the boiling points of the components, the components tend to rush out of the column together instead of one after another. In programmed-temperature GLC, the temperature is increased linearly with time, at a certain rate. In a computerised chromatographic machine, the initial temperature, the rate of temperature increase and the final temperature can all be selected at the beginning of the experiment and these are automatically attained sequentially by the column.

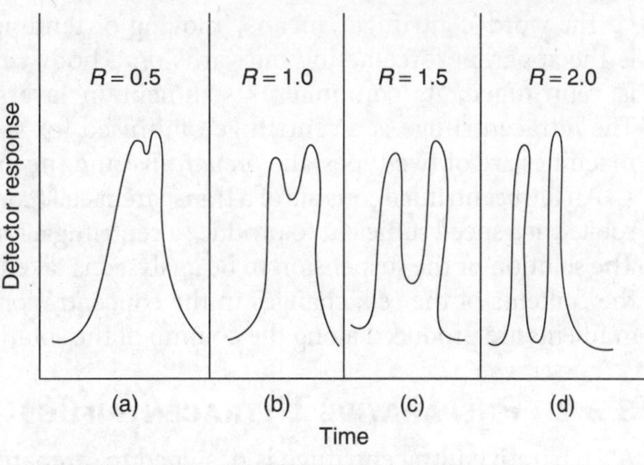

Fig. 3.22 Isothermal chromatogram

A mixture of normal hydrocarbons does not get separated properly by the isothermal method, whereas it gets separated well by the programmed-temperature method. Figure 3.22 shows how temperature programming of separation increases resolution in the GLC separation of a mixture of three components and Fig. 3.23 shows gas chromatograms of a mixture of three components with widely different boiling points.

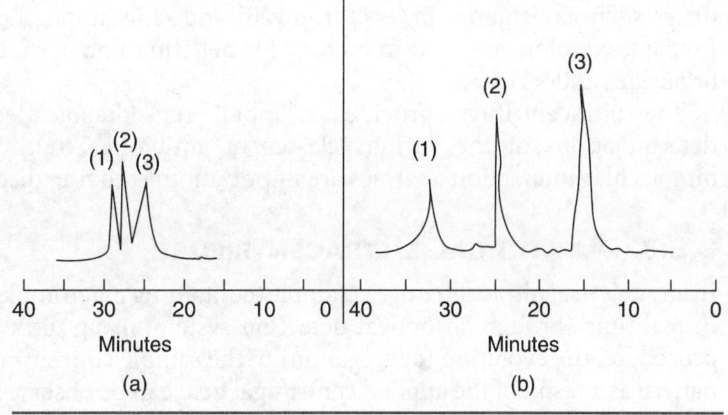

Fig. 3.23 Programmed-temperature chromatogram
(a) Isothermal **(b)** Temperature-programmed

3.2.13 Gas Chromatography–Mass Spectrometry (GC–MS)

The interfacing of a GC aparatus and and a mass spectrometer is called the GC–MS method. In this sysem, the mixtue is first separated by the GC apparatus and the separated components are automatically made to flow into the MS apparatus for mass analysis. Such a system is called a *hyphenated system*. In a GC–MS system, the entire eluent from the capillary GC column is led directly into the ion source of the mass spectrometer, creating direct coupling of the two systems. It is a powerful analytical tool for separating and characterising complex mixtures.

3.3 CENTRIFUGAL METHODS

3.3.1 Ultracentrifugation

Ultracentrifugation involves subjecting a material to an exceedingly high centrifugal force, which will separate and sediment the molecules of the substance or *subcellular* components. An ultracentrifuge is a machine capable of spinning a material at more than 50,000 revolutions per minute.

The word 'centrifugal' means, 'moving or tending to move from centre'. Centrifugal force is the apparent force acting outwards on a body revolving round a centre. When a mixture is centrifuged, its components sediment in layers according to their molecular weights. The ultracentrifuge is a centrifuge optimised for spinning a rotor at very high speeds. Such machines are of two types, the *preparative* and the *analytical ultracentrifuge.*

An ultracentrifuge consists of a transparent cell (container) mounted on a rotor. The cell can be rotated at a speed sufficient to produce a centrifugal force from 500 to 40,000 times that of gravity. The solution or the suspension to be analysed is taken in the cell. As the centrifugal force acts on the contents of the cell, changes in the concentration take place in the solution; concentration gradients are produced along the column of the solution according to molecular weights.

3.3.2 Preparative Ultracentrifuge

A preparative ultracentrifuge is designed to 'prepare' – actually separate – a component from a natural biomaterial. For example, human serum lipoproteins can be separated from a serum sample. The instrument can be used for the determination of quantitative binding of certain drugs such as gentamycin, erythromycin and chloramphenicol to human serum proteins. Preparative rotors are used in biology for pelleting fine particulate fractions, such as cellular organelles and viruses.

The ultracentrifuge provides a rapid, reproducible technique for protein-binding determinations of the various classes of antibiotics to serum protein molecules. Such bimolecular interaction analyses are important in studying diseases.

3.3.3 Analytical Ultracentrifuge

In an analytical ultracentrifuge, a sample (containing macromolecules) being spun is monitored in real time through an optical detection system, using ultraviolet light absorption. By this procedure, the evolution (aggregation) of the sample concentration versus the axis of rotation pattern as a result of the applied centrifugal field can be observed. This pattern can be recorded by computerisation of the machine. The observations are used to study sedimentation velocity and sedimentation equilibrium. The velocity data can be interpreted to give shape and molar mass of macromolecules, as well as their size distribution. In addition, these data can be used to understand chemical equlibria between macromolecules.

Sedimentation equilibrium distributions in the centrifugal field are characterised by the Boltzmann distributions. Therefore, the data in these experiments can give the molar masses of the macromolecules and, for reacting mixtures, chemical equilibrium constants.

- Analytical ultracentrifugation can furnish several kinds of information on macromolecules, polymers (both natural and synthetic), viruses, and so on. Such information includes:
  - gross shape,
  - size distributions,

- conformational changes,
- stoichiometry of association of species, and
- equilibrium constants.

- Analytical ultracentrifugation is a classical method in biochemistry and molecular biology.
- Sedimentation, effected by ultracentrifugation, can provide basic hydrodynamic and thermodynamic information for nearly any molecule, in a wide range of solvents and over a wide range of solute concentrations.
- This method is useful in analysing industrial polymers.

Theodor Svedberg (1884–1971)

The analytical ultracentrifuge was invented by Svedberg in 1923. His centrifuge enabled biologists to separate and unravel several characteristics of biomolecules.

Svedberg was born in Sweden in 1884. He worked as a professor at Uppsala and then became the director of the Gustaf Werner Institute of Nuclear Chemistry. His work was mainly on colloids and macromolecules. He invented the ultracentrifuge to study the sedimentation of proteins and other polymers. He authored several papers and books which guide researchers even now. He received the John Ericsson Medal (1942), the Berzelius Medal (1944) and the Franklin Institute Medal (1949). For his work on the disperse systems, especially proteins, he received the Nobel Prize in 1926. Painting and study of plants were his hobbies.

Edward Greydon Pickels modified Svedberg's centrifuge for operations under vacua. In this centrifuge, the friction generated at high speeds is reduced, thereby improving separation of the components. In addition, this machine was designed for maintaining constant temperature. In 1946, Pickels co-founded Spinco, a company for making and marketing ultracentrifuges based on his invention.

Source: By Unknown - http://www.nobelprize.org/nobel_prizes/chemistry/laureates/1926/svedberg.html, Public Domain, https://commons.wikimedia.org/w/index.php?curid=550336

3.4 PURIFICATION TECHNIQUES

The chemical and physical aspects of purification of matter are interesting. The purification techniques have undergone vast improvements with the development of modern technology. Though expensive instruments are sometimes used for purifying a compound, the underlying principles are simple and well-known. For example, the well-known principle of adsorption–desorption is used in chromatography. In spite of the availability of modern gadgets for separation and purification of chemicals, simple and inexpensive techniques like distillation, filtration and sublimation continue to remain indispensable in all laboratories and industries.

3.4.1 Desiccants and Drying

A desiccant or a drying agent is a substance which has the ability to combine with moisture from the surrounding atmosphere. The drying power of desiccants varies and no desiccant can keep the air within a closed desiccator perfectly dry. Desiccants are frequently used to dry solids and to remove water from organic liquids.

3.4.1.1 Types of Desiccants

Drying agents may be divided broadly into those that

- combine with water reversibly,
- react chemically with water by a non-reversible process giving rise to a new water-free compound.

Anhydrous calcium chloride is an example for the first type and metallic sodium is an example for the second type of desiccant.

3.4.1.2 The Relative Efficiencies of Desiccants

Some desiccants are more effective than others. The relative efficiency of a desiccant is assessed from the amount of moisture it can absorb from one litre of moist gas, air or nitrogen. The relative efficiencies of the common drying agents are shown in Table 3.5. These were determined by passing humidified nitrogen over the desiccant and trapping the water which escaped (unabsorbed by desiccant) in a cold trap immersed in liquid nitrogen. By using a large volume of nitrogen, the weight of water was obtained by direct weighing. The smaller the amount of moisture remaining per litre of nitrogen, the more effective the desiccant is. From the table, it is evident that magnesium perchlorate is a much more effective desiccant than the commonly used anhydrous calcium chloride.

The efficiency of a desiccant can be expressed in another way as well. It is the weight of water that can be removed by one gram of the desiccant. This is called its *drying capacity*. In general, substances that form hydrates ($CuSO_4$, $CaCl_2$, and so on) have good drying capacities.

Table 3.5 Comparative efficiencies of some drying agents

Drying agent	Residual water per litre of nitrogen (μg)
$Mg(ClO_4)_2$, anhydrous (*anhydrone*)	0.2
$Mg(ClO_4)_2$ 1–1.5 H_2O	1.5
BaO, porous	2.8
Al_2O_3	2.9
P_2O_5	3.6
$CaCl_2$ anhydrous (dried at 127°C)	67
$CaSO_4$, anhydrous (*drierite*)	67
Silica gel	70
Ascarite (NaOH on an asbestos base)	93
$CaCl_2$, anhydrous (dried at 245°C)	137
NaOH	513
CaO	656
KOH	939

3.4.1.3 Drying Power and Temperature

The vapour pressures of the various hydrate systems increase with temperature. The pressures of calcium chloride at various temperatures are given in Table 3.6. *As the vapour pressure*

Table 3.6 Vapour pressure of calcium chloride systems

Temp. (°C)	Pressure (mm)	Solid phases
-55.0	0.0	Ice–$CaCl_2$•$6H_2O$
29.2	5.7	$CaCl_2$•$6H_2O$–β-$CaCl_2$•$4H_2O$
29.8	6.8	$CaCl_2$•$6H_2O$–α-$CaCl_2$•$4H_2O$
38.4	7.9	β-$CaCl_2$•$4H_2O$–$CaCl_2$•$2H_2O$
175.5	842.0	$CaCl_2$•$2H_2O$–$CaCl_2$•H_2O

increases, the ability of a desiccant to hold moisture decreases. Therefore, the efficiency of desiccants decreases with a rise in temperature. At high temperatures certain desiccants actually undergo dehydration. If the vapour pressure of a desiccant is greater than that of the substance being dried at a particular temperature, no drying will occur.

High boiling organic liquids should not be distilled from drying agent systems which have appreciable vapour pressures. At the boiling points, the drying agents would release moisture and the distillate will be contaminated with water.

3.4.1.4 Regeneration of Desiccants

Desiccants may be regenerated, made anhydrous after use if they are expensive. However, the regeneration of some desiccants is difficult and time-consuming. Therefore, regeneration is done only when it is absolutely necessary, and used desiccants are best discarded. A simple method of regenerating a desiccant involves heating it to above the temperature at which it becomes anhydrous. For example, calcium sulphate can be regenerated by maintaining it at about 273°C for several hours. Regeneration of calcium chloride, phosphorus pentoxide and potassium hydroxide is difficult and normally not done. Silica gel can be regenerated by heating it to 120°C, and then bringing it to room temperature in a moisture-free chamber.

3.4.1.5 Choice of Desiccant

The choice of a desiccant for drying a particular substance depends upon the following:

- the degree of drying required,
- the nature of the drying agent,
- the nature of the substance being dried,
- cost of the desiccant, and
- the speed of drying desired.

In using a desiccant, the absence of any reaction between it and the substance being dried should be ensured. For example, an acidic desiccant should not be used for drying amines. Similarly, a basic desiccant cannot be used to dry acids (Table 3.7).

Table 3.7 Drying agents for organic liquids

Class of organic liquid	Recommended drying agent
Hydrocarbons	Calcium chloride, sulphuric acid (saturated hydrocarbon only) phosphorus pentoxide (aromatic hydrocarbon only)
Alkyl halide	Calcium chloride, phosphorus pentoxide
Alcohols	Sodium carbonate
Aldehydes, ketones	Sodium carbonate
Esters	Sodium carbonate, calcium chloride
Amides	Sodium carbonate, sodium hydroxide
Nitriles	Sodium carbonate
Amines	Sodium carbonate
Ethers	Phosphorus pentoxide, sodium metal
Aryl halides	Phosphorus pentoxide
Acids	Sodium sulphate, calcium sulphate
General	Magnesium sulphate (except amines), Sodium sulphate, drierite, molecular sieves

Sometimes, a coloured substance is added to the desiccant to indicate the state of the desiccant. When the desiccant has absorbed a considerable amount of water, the colour of the added substance changes, which can indicate at a glance that the desiccant has to be replaced.

Sulphuric acid: This is a good desiccant but the danger of its splashing and spilling presents a practical drawback. Therefore, it is rarely used.

Porous barium oxide: This is a satisfactory desiccant, but this swells as it absorbs moisture so that a large space inside the desiccator must be provided for its expansion.

Anhydrone: It is anhydrous magnesium perchlorate; it is an efficient drying agent.

Calcium chloride: This is an inexpensive and widely used desiccant. Its low equilibrium vapour pressure indicates that it has a high capacity for drying.

$$CaCl_2 + H_2O \rightleftharpoons CaCl_2{\bullet}H_2O \quad 0.3\text{ mm}$$

Its drying action is fast. It cannot be used with certain classes of organic compounds, for example, alcohols, because it forms complexes with these. This can be safely used with hydrocarbons, and alkyl and aryl halides.

Sodium sulphate: Anhydrous sodium sulphate also has a high capacity for drying. However, its action is slow. Therefore, the substance to be dried should be kept in contact with the desiccant at least overnight. This is a general drying agent for a wide variety of organic compounds, because it is inert. It is usually used as a powder, not as granules, for preliminary drying.

Phosphorus pentoxide: When extreme drying conditions are required, phosphorus pentoxide is used. This substance is placed in a small dish inside the desiccator to prevent the possibility of the desiccator cracking when the partially exhausted phoshphorus pentoxide is washed out. It is effective but handling it is inconvenient. In addition, an insulating film of phosphoric acid, formed by initial absorption of moisture, makes it less effective for subsequent absorption.

Magnesium sulphate: This is a very useful drying agent. It is commonly used for drying organic liquids. It gets hydrated in six steps:

$$MgSO_4 + H_2O \rightleftharpoons MgSO_4{\bullet}H_2O \quad 1\text{ mm, at }25°\text{C}$$

$$MgSO_4{\bullet}H_2O + H_2O \rightleftharpoons MgSO_4{\bullet}2H_2O \quad 2\text{ mm}$$

$$MgSO_4{\bullet}2H_2O + 2H_2O \rightleftharpoons MgSO_4{\bullet}4H_2O \quad 5\text{ mm}$$

$$MgSO_4{\bullet}4H_2O + H_2O \rightleftharpoons MgSO_4{\bullet}5H_2O \quad 9\text{ mm}$$

$$MgSO_4{\bullet}5H_2O + H_2O \rightleftharpoons MgSO_4{\bullet}6H_2O \quad 10\text{ mm}$$

$$MgSO_4{\bullet}6H_2O + H_2O \rightleftharpoons MgSO_4{\bullet}7H_2O \quad 11.5\text{ mm}$$

Drierite: This is the commercial name for anhydrous calcium sulphate. Its drying action is rapid but it has only a limited drying capacity because it forms only a hemihydrate, $2CaSO_4{\bullet}H_2O$, combining with only 6.6% of its weight of water. A large quantity of it must therefore be used. The vapour pressure of the system is only 0.004 mm at 25°C.

$$2CaSO_4 + H_2O \rightleftharpoons 2CaSO_4{\bullet}H_2O$$

The residual water content of the substance dried would therefore be very low. It is employed for drying alcohols, esters, ketones and acids. If the water content of an organic liquid is high, a preliminary drying with another desiccant such as anhydrous magnesium sulphate, or anhydrous sodium sulphate, which can absorb a higher proportion of water is required.

Copper sulphate: This is a drying agent of moderate efficiency. White anhydrous copper sulphate becomes blue on absorption of water and gets hydrated. This is used sometimes to detect moisture in organic solvents. When copper sulphate is shaken with a wet organic solvent, such as benzene at 25°C, the water will first combine to form the monohydrate. When sufficient anhydrous copper sulphate is used, the effective concentration of water in the solvent is reduced to about 1 mm of ordinary water vapour. However, this desiccant cannot remove water completely. The monohydrate is far less effective than the anhydrous compound for the removal of water.

$CuSO_4 + H_2O \rightleftharpoons CuSO_4{\cdot}H_2O$ 0.8 mm, at 25°C

$CuSO_4{\cdot}H_2O + 2H_2O \rightleftharpoons CuSO_4{\cdot}3H_2O$ 5.6 mm

$CuSO_4{\cdot}3H_2O + 2H_2O \rightleftharpoons CuSO_4{\cdot}5H_2O$ 7.8 mm

> *A low value of equilibrium vapour pressure indicates a good drying capacity of the substance on the left hand side of the equation.*

Molecular sieves: These are modern drying agents and are useful for drying almost all classes of organic compounds. Molecular sieves are synthetic or naturally occurring substances, characterised by the presence of 'cavities' or 'holes' within their molecular structures, which may be penetrated only by gaseous molecules small enough to enter these cavities. Small water molecules can also be trapped in these cavities. Molecular sieves have high capacities for rapidly removing water from a system. Water is absorbed as water of hydration. The hydrated sieves can be regenerated by heating these at 300–320°C. Molecular sieves are aluminosilicates and their pore sizes range from 0.3 to 0.4 nm.

3.4.1.6 Technique of Drying

Liquids should always be dried in a container that can be stoppered (Erlenmeyer flask). The liquid is kept shallow over the drying agent. The amount of drying agent to be used should be decided carefully after considering the amount of liquid being dried, the proportion of water in the liquid and the drying capacity of the desiccant. Too little desiccant would mean incomplete drying and too much would result in loss of the liquid itself due to absorption by the desiccant. When the drying action is slow, keeping aside the liquid being dried in contact with the desiccant overnight is advisable. The desiccant should be filtered off before distilling the liquid. Otherwise, during distillation the desiccant might release the 'absorbed' water which might distil off with the liquid being dried.

> - *Silica gel, alumina and calcium sulphate desiccant are impregnated with a cobalt salt so that they function as self-indicators; where these desiccants become exhausted, their colour changes from blue to pink.*
> - *The ordinary desiccator [Fig. 3.24 (a)] used by students was designed by Scheibler. It is provided with a porcelain plate having holes to support crucibles. The plate rests on a constriction situated roughly halfway up the wall of the desiccator. Instead of the porcelain plate, a rounded wire gauze may also used.*
> - *A vacum desiccator [Fig. 3.24 (b)] has a pump attached to it for evacuating the inside of the desiccator. Evacuation accelerates and enhances drying.*

3.4.1.7 Drying of Solids

The solid product in the Buchner funnel, during filtration, should be pressed down with a flat spatula-blade to remove as much solvent as possible. The solid may be washed with alcohol to remove water from it provided the solid is insoluble in alcohol. Steam or hot air should not be used for drying solids because at high temperatures the solids may melt or decompose. Drying in a desiccator over calcium chloride is simple but slow. Vacuum drying is an efficient and safe drying method for solids.

3.4.1.8 Precautions in Using a Desiccator

- The desiccator should always remain closed, except briefly when something is placed in it or removed from it.

- The lid should be placed on the table with its inner side facing upward to avoid the grease ring collecting dust from the table surface.
- When a hot object, such as a crucible, is placed in it, about 10 seconds should elapse for the air inside the desiccator to expand before putting the lid in place; otherwise, re-opening the desiccator would be difficult.
- The lid should always be slid open or shut gently. If the lid is removed quickly, air may rush into the partially evacuated desiccator and blow away the material dried.
- A vacuum desiccator is kept inside a protective wire cage during its use to avoid accident to the user due to implosion.

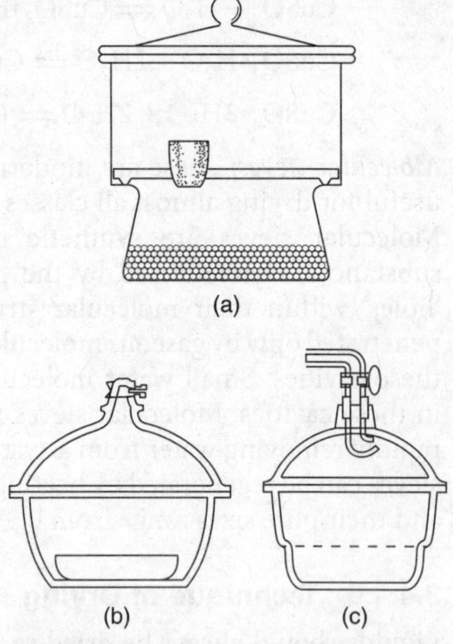

Fig. 3.24 **(a)** Desicator; **(b), (c)** Two types of vaccum desiccator

3.4.1.9 Dry Boxes

A dry box or a *glove box* is a plastic or metal box with clear glass or plastic windows on the upper side and also on the sides. Rubber or plastic gloves are fitted using airtight seals through the front side of the box. Manipulations inside the box may be carried out by introducing the hands into the gloves. A tray of desiccant placed inside the box maintains a dry atmosphere.

- Dry boxes are used for handling materials that are very sensitive to atmospheric oxygen or moisture.
- Reactions in an inert atmosphere may be performed inside such boxes by passing a slow stream of nitrogen.
- Highly toxic materials may also be safely manipulated inside glove boxes.

3.4.2 Distillation

Distillation is the most common method of purifying liquids. This technique comprises two steps—vaporisation and recondensation.

Theory of distillation *Vapour pressure*: A liquid contained in a closed space will evaporate, giving off its vapour until the vapour attains a definite pressure. This pressure depends only upon the temperature. The vapour at this condition is said to be *saturated.* The vapour pressure of a liquid in contact with its own liquid is a constant at a given temperature. It is independent of the absolute amount of liquid and of vapour present in the system. The vapour pressure is expressed in terms of the height of mercury column which will produce an equivalent pressure.

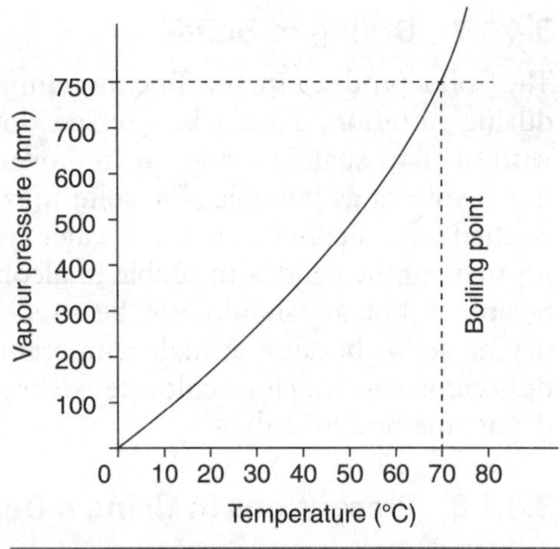

Fig. 3.25 A typical vapour pressure *versus* temperature plot for a liquid

As the temperature rises, the vapour pressure of a liquid increases. A typical vapour pressure *versus* temperature graph is shown in Fig. 3.25. When the vapour pressure is equal to the total pressure exerted on the surface of a liquid, the liquid boils. Under this condition, the temperature does not rise further even when the liquid is kept boiling. On increasing the supply of heat to the boiling liquid, the rate of bubble-formation is increased and the heat of vaporisation is absorbed. The temperature at which the liquid boils is called the boiling point of the liquid.

The boiling point of a liquid is defined as the temperature at which the vapour pressure of the liquid is equal to the external pressure exerted at any point upon the liquid surface. This external pressure may be exerted by atmospheric air or by any other gas or vapour. The boiling point at a pressure of 760 mm of mercury (standard atmospheric pressure) is called the *normal boiling point.* When this pressure on the surface is reduced, the boiling point is lowered. The pressure on the liquid surface can be reduced by connecting the vessel containing the liquid to a pump. The boiling point is dependent upon the external pressure and, therefore, the pressure at which the boiling-point is recorded should be specified. *Usually the normal boiling point is given without specifying the value of pressure, 760 mm.*

Boiling points at selected pressures: The boiling point of a liquid at any selected pressure can be calculated from the vapour pressure–temperature curve. These two are related by the equation,

$$\log p = A + B/T$$

where p is the vapour pressure, T is the temperature on the absolute scale and A and B are constants. When $\log p$ is plotted against $1/T$, a straight line is obtained (Fig. 3.26). The straight line can be drawn with just two values of $\log p$ and the corresponding values of T. The value of p corresponding to any absolute temperature or *vice versa* can be obtained from the graph.

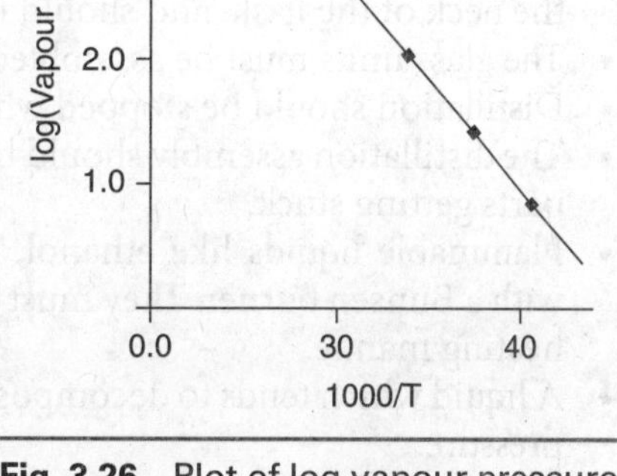

Fig. 3.26 Plot of log vapour pressure with reciprocal temperature

Very rarely, the atmospheric pressure is exactly 760 mm. Therefore, the observed boiling point should be converted to normal boiling point (at 760 mm). The following equation is used for this purpose.

$$\Delta t = 0.00012\,(760 - p)\,(t + 273)$$

where Δt is the correction in degree centigrade to be made in the observed boiling point t, and p is the barometric pressure.

For associated liquids, such as water, alcohols and acids, the following expression is used

$$\Delta t = 0.00010\,(760 - p)\,(t + 273)$$

Technique of distillation The set-up used for distillation is shown in Fig. 3.27. The capacity of the distillation set should be decided by the amount of liquid to be distilled. When the boiling point is very high, a short air condenser can be used instead of a Liebig's condenser.

The liquid during distillation must be boiled steadily. Boiling chips (unglazed porcelain bits) are added to prevent bumping by emitting small quantitites of air and promote regular boiling. The boiling chip should be added to the cold liquid before the beginning of the distillation. If it is added to a heated liquid, a lot of vapour will be formed suddenly and this would eject the hot liquid through the mouth of the flask. If the distillation has been interrupted, a fresh boiling chip should be added before heating is resumed.

The following aspects should be borne in mind while distilling a liquid:

- A round-bottom flask and not a flat-bottom flask should always be used for smooth boiling.
- Heating must be slow and uniform either with a small flame or by an electrical heater.
- The main fraction which distils at the boiling point should be collected separately, rejecting the first (head) and the last (tail) portions, which are likely to be impure.

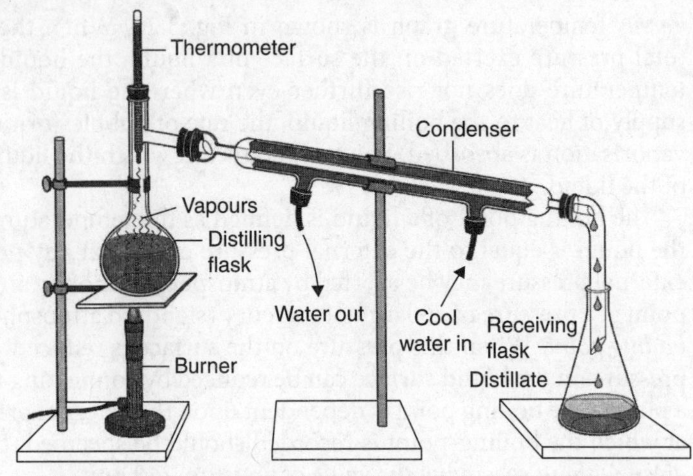

Fig. 3.27 Apparatus for distillation

- In clamping a flask in which a liquid is distilled, the clamp should hold the flask at the coolest part of the neck to prevent cracking.
- The bulb of the thermometer should be below the position where the side tube is fused into the neck of the flask, and should not be immersed in the liquid.
- The glass units must be assembled tightly to avoid leakage of vapour or liquid.
- Distillation should be stopped when some liquid is left in the flask.
- The distillation assembly should be dismantled when it is slightly warm to avoid the various parts getting stuck.
- Flammable liquids like ethanol, benzene and carbon disulphide should never be heated with a Bunsen burner. They must be distilled with a steam-bath or with a controlled electric heating mantle.
- A liquid which tends to decompose at its boiling point should not be distilled at atmospheric pressure.

3.4.2.1 Fractional Distillation

When a mixture of two liquids is boiled, the vapour phase is richer in the more volatile component than the boiling liquid with which it is in equilibrium at any given temperature. For example, if component A is more volatile than component B,

$$\frac{\text{Partial pressure of A}}{\text{Partial pressure of B}} > 1$$

Therefore,

$$\frac{\text{Mole fraction of A in the vapour phase}}{\text{Mole fraction of B in the vapour phase}} > \frac{\text{Mole fraction of A in liquid phase}}{\text{Mole fraction of B in liquid phase}}$$

This is the basis of fractional distillation and is used to separate liquids which are miscible with one another. The boiling points of the two liquids should be far removed from each other. For example, a mixture of benzene and toluene boiling at 80°C and 110°C respectively can be separated by fractional distillation. This method is similar to an ordinary distillation except that the distillation unit has a *fractionating column*. A fractionating column is designed to provide a continuous series of partial condensation of the vapours and the partial vaporisation of the condensate and its effect is similar to a number of separate distillations. The column can simply be a long tube attached to the top of the distillation flask. In this arrangement, as a mixture of the vapours of the two liquids rises in the column, the vapour of the higher boiling liquid will condense and fall back into the flask, whereas the vapour of the lower boiling liquid alone will go to the top of the column and escape into the condenser. For efficient separation, the vapour mixture should be exposed to a large surface area inside the column.

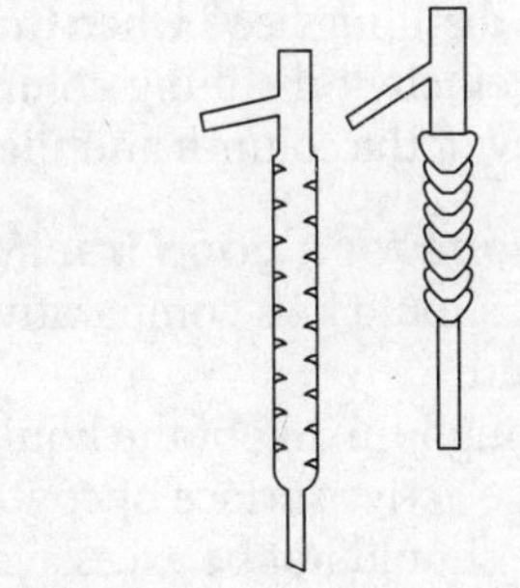

Fig. 3.28 Sidney Young columns

This is achieved by a special type of column devised by Sidney Young (Fig. 3.28). It comprises either rod and disc, or a pear-shaped still head. These have the advantage that a fairly good separation can be accomplished by one distillation. Sometimes, a long column packed with glass beads can be used. This is called the *Hempel column*.

In fractionating, it is essential that the distillation should proceed slowly and evenly. It should always be possible to count the individual drops as they pass into the receiver. The ratio of the number of drops of liquid flowing back down the column to the number collected in the receiver is called the *reflux ratio*. For efficient distillation, where compounds boiling within a few degrees of one another are to be separated, this ratio should be 100:1.

Example: Fractionation of benzol Benzol is a mixture of several compounds, benzene and toluene being the major components. These two can be obtained from benzol by fractional distillation. The mixture is distilled by heating the flask electrically, care being taken that the ebullition is quite regular and that the condensed liquid does not drop into the receiver at a more rapid rate than one drop per second. Separate fractions are collected every 3° or 5°. Any distillate passing over between 80.2° and 81.2°C will be rich in benzene. Pure toluene will distil over at 110.6°C. Each component must be collected at as close a temperature range as possible. Complete separation is not possible in one distillation. The fractionated liquids should be repeatedly fractionated to improve the purity of a component.

If two liquids form an *azeotrope*, complete separation is impossible by fractional distillation. All that can be accomplished in this case is the separation of the excess of one constituent from the mixture of constant boiling point. For example, water and alcohol form an azeotropic mixture and hence complete separation of this mixture is not possible by fractional distillation.

Figure 3.29 indicates distillation curves for a two-component system. Figure 3.29a represents an ideal situation. Portion CD represents the distillation of one liquid alone and EF that of the other liquid alone. As soon as one component is completely distilled, the boiling temperature rises sharply, which is indicated by the section DE. Figure 3.29b is the curve obtained with

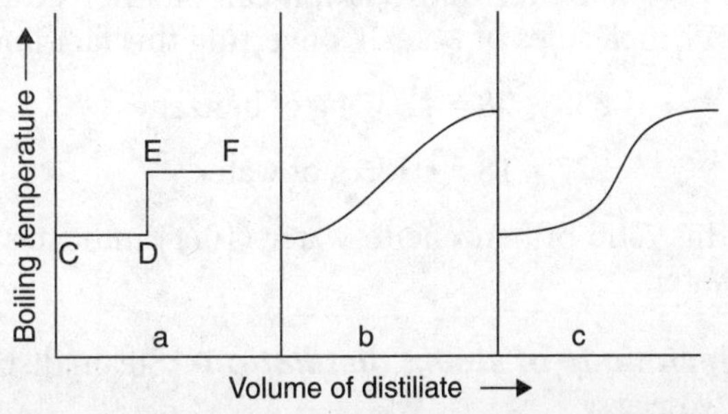

Fig. 3.29 Distillation curves for a two-component system. **(a)** Ideal fractional distillation, **(b)** Simple distillation, **(c)** Efficient fractional distillation

a simple distilling head when the fractionation is not sharp. Figure 3.29c indicates the situation with an efficient distilling column. The actual curve obtained will vary depending upon the efficiency of the column and the difference between the boiling points of the two components.

Conditions for a good fractionation

- There should be a comparatively large amount of liquid continuously *returning* through the column.
- Thorough mixing of the liquid and vapour should occur.
- A large active surface of contact between liquid and vapour should be available.
- There should not be excessive cooling in the column.

3.4.2.2 Steam Distillation

The separation and purification of volatile organic compounds, which are immiscible with water, is accomplished with the help of steam distillation. This method is applicable only to substances which have an appreciable vapour pressure at 100°C or just below it. In this technique, a current of steam is blown through the substance to be distilled. The steam escapes from the substance carrying with it only the volatile component, which is being separated from the impurities.

When two miscible liquids distil together, the boiling temperature is between the boiling points of the two components. This is not so with two immiscible liquids since each exerts its own vapour pressure. This mixture of miscible liquids will boil when the combined vapour pressure is equal to the external pressure and always below the boiling point of the lower boiling component. Furthermore, the distillate will have a constant composition as long as there is some of each of the components present in the distillation flask. The ratio of immiscible components, A and B, in the distillate is given by the formula,

$$\frac{\text{Mole A}}{\text{Mole B}} = \frac{\text{VP of A (at boiling)}}{\text{VP of B (at boiling)}}$$

Consider a mixture of benzene and water, two immiscible liquids. As the temperature is raised, the sum of the two pressures reaches the atmospheric pressure, and at this temperature, the mixture boils. But this temperature is less than 80°C, the boiling point of benzene. Actually, the temperature is 69.3°C, and the partial pressure of benzene is 533 mm and that of water is 227 mm (when the atmospheric pressure is 760 mm). Therefore, a mixture of benzene and water will distil at 69.3°C until one or the other material is exhausted in the distillation flask. Thus, passing steam through benzene will remove benzene as a distillate and this operation is called steam distillation.

From the Avogadro law, it can be inferred that 533 molecules of benzene distil for every 277 molecules of water. Converting this fact into moles and into grams we get,

$$533 \times 78 = 41{,}574 \text{ g of benzene}$$

$$227 \times 18 = 4{,}186 \text{ g of water}$$

This ratio of benzene to water (10/1) indicates that 100 g of benzene will distil with 10 g of water.

Technique of steam distillation Steam distillation is accomplished in one of the following two ways:

(i) The organic compound to be distilled is placed in a round-bottom flask fitted with a Claisen head which is equipped with a still-head connected to a water-cooled condenser

(Fig. 3.30). The Claisen head prevents splattering of the mixture into the condenser during distillation. Steam, produced externally in a steam generator is passed via a long tube reaching almost the bottom surface of the distillation flask. Water may condense in the distillation flask, filling it to inconvenient levels. This problem is avoided by gently heating the distillation flask with a Bunsen burner, or connecting a bent adapter between the steam generator and the distillation flask.

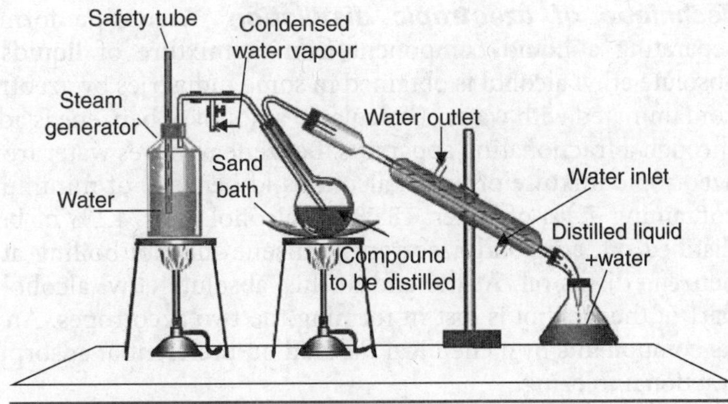

Fig. 3.30 Steam distillation apparatus

(ii) Instead of passing steam through the liquid, water can be added to the organic compounds to be distilled in the distillation flask. This mixture is then heated directly to generate steam in situ. This method is suitable for steam distilling small amounts of liquids.

Precautions: Steam should be turned off only after opening the pinch clamp on the bent adapter exit tube. Otherwise, due to development of vacuum in the distillation flask, the distilled liquid from the receiver will shoot back into the track.

Steam distillation provides a method of separation of volatile liquids and also volatile solids which are insoluble in water from non-volatile substances under comparatively mild conditions. Steam distillation is used in some chemical industries. For example, steam-volatile turpentine is separated from crude pine resin by this technique. When the volatile turpentine and other components are carried away by steam, a mixture called rosin is left as a non-volatile residue. Similarly, peppermint oil is obtained by steam distillation of the crushed peppermint plant. The volatile components of several plants (essential oils) have been recovered by steam distillation—these materials have been commercially important for hundreds of years. Turpentine, orange oil, peppermint oil and oil of cloves are some among these.

Steam distillation is not suitable for substances which decompose upon prolonged contact with steam or hot water, react with water or have a vapour pressure of 5 mm or less at 100°C. Steam distillation requires large amounts of heat compared to other methods of distillations. This point has to be borne in mind in using this method in industries.

3.4.2.3 Azeotropic Distillation

An *azeotrope* is a mixture of two or more miscible liquids having a constant boiling point and a constant composition. For an azeotrope, the composition of the liquid phase is identical with that of the vapour phase. For example, a mixture containing 80% by weight of chloroform and 20% by weight of acetone boils at 64.7°C. This is an azeotropic mixture. Several other liquids form azeotropes: water–ethyl alcohol, water–pyridine, benzene–cyclohexane and phenol–aniline. The boiling point of an azeotrope may be lower than that of its components and such an azeotrope is called an *azeotrope of minimum boiling point*. Water (100°C) and ethanol (78.3°C) form a minimum boiling (78.15°C) azeotrope. The boiling point of an azeotrope may be higher than that of its components. Such an azeotrope is called a *maximum boiling azeotrope*. For example, water (100°C) and formic acid (100.8°C) form an azeotrope of maximum boiling point (107.1°C).

Technique of azeotropic distillation Azeotrope formation is sometimes used for separating a liquid component from a mixture of liquids by distillation. For example, absolute ethyl alcohol is obtained in some industries by azeotropic distillation. To the alcohol contaminated with water, a calculated amount of benzene is added and the mixture is distilled through a fractionating apparatus. Benzene removes water from alcohol by forming a ternary azeotropic mixture of water, alcohol and benzene of minimum boiling point (64.85°C) and containing 7.4% of water, 18.5% of alcohol and 74.1% of benzene. Once this azeotrope is distilled off, a second azeotrope, benzene–alcohol boiling at 68.25°C, containing 32.4% of benzene distils off. At the end of this, absolute ethyl alcohol distils over. In this method, a part of the alcohol is lost in forming the two azeotropes. An azeotrope may be broken into its components by a chemical method or, preferential adsorption, or fractional extraction or fractional freezing.

Benzene can be freed from moisture by azeotropic distillation. Adding a calculated amount of ethanol and distilling the mixture will remove all the water in the form of a ternary azeotrope.

Solids can sometimes be dried by azeotropic distillation. The wet solid is dissolved in a non-aqueous solvent which can form an azeotrope with water. Then water is removed by azeotropic distillation. The solid would remain in the non-aqueous solvent free from moisture. It can be recovered in a dry form by evaporating the solvent.

3.4.2.4 Distillation in Vacuum

The boiling point of a liquid is that temperature at which the total vapour pressure is equal to the external pressure. From this, it follows that when the external pressure, the pressure above the liquid is reduced, the boiling point will be decreased. When vacuum is applied (pressure ~0), the boiling point should be the minimum. At intermediate pressures the boiling points would be intermediate.

Need to adopt distillation under diminished pressure

- Certain liquids have very high boiling points and therefore distillation of these under vacuum is easy; distillation of these under atmospheric pressure would be slow and laborious.
- In many cases, boiling points at atmospheric pressure are too high to be desirable, because the compound being distilled may get oxidised, undergo molecular rearrangement or decompose.
- Sometimes, the impurities present in the liquid may catalyse some reactions or may themselves react with the liquid at high temperatures.

Technique of vacuum distillation For distillation under reduced pressure, the distillation assembly consists of a distillation unit with a provision for connecting an aspirator (water pump) or a mechanical oil pump. An aspirator reduces the pressure to about 25 mm and oil pump to below 1 mm. The flask should be made up of

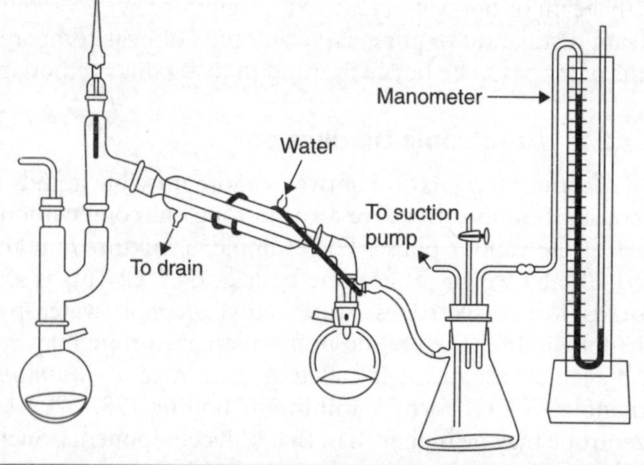

Fig. 3.31 Apparatus for distillation under reduced pressure

stout glass; otherwise due to low pressure inside, it may collapse. The distillation assembly (Fig. 3.31) should be tightly assembled with no loose joints.

Bumping is much more pronounced in distillations under diminished pressures than in ordinary distillations. Another way of avoiding bumping (other than boiling chips) is to have a glass tube fitted to the neck of the flask. This tube drawn out at its lower end to a capillary which dips into the liquid, can be closed by means of a piece of rubber tubing and small screw clamp at its upper end. With this arrangement the passage of air into the distilling flask is easily regulated. The pressure inside can be read with a manometer connected to the system between the pump and the distillation unit.

Two useful approximations of the effect of reduced pressure on boiling points are the following:

(i) When the pressure is reduced from 760 mm to 25 mm, the boiling point of a high boiling liquid (250–300°) is reduced by about 100–125°.

(ii) Below 25 mm, each time the pressure is halved, the boiling point is reduced by about 10°. More accurate estimates of boiling points at different pressures may be made from the actual pressure *versus* boiling point curve. The exact boiling points at different pressures can also be calculated using the integrated form of the Clausius–Clapeyron equation.

3.4.3 Recrystallisation

Recrystallisation is an important and common method of purifying solids. In this method, the impure solid is dissolved in a hot solvent to the point of supersaturation and on cooling, pure crystals of the substance are formed, the impurities remaining in solution. The crystals thus formed are then filtered and dried.

3.4.3.1 Steps in Recrystallisation

The purification of a solid by recrystallisation is based upon differences in the solubilities of the substance being isolated and the impurities present in the crude sample. The method involves the following steps:

- Dissolving the impure substance in a suitable solvent at or near the boiling point.
- Filtering the hot solution from insoluble particles and dust.
- Allowing the hot solution to cool when the dissolved substance crystallises out.
- Separating the crystals from the mother liquor.
- Drying the solid.
- Checking the purity of the recrystallised sample.

These steps are repeated with a sample until the melting point remains unchanged.

3.4.3.2 Solvent for Recrystallisation

The success of recrystallisation depends upon the selection of a proper solvent. An ideal solvent for recrystallisation should have the following characteristics:

- A high solvent-power for the substance to be purified at elevated temperatures and a low solvent-power at room temperature.
- It should either dissolve the impurities readily or to only a small extent; when the impurities are highly soluble, they will not recrystallise on cooling the solution and if they are insoluble, they can be filtered off.
- It should yield well-formed crystals of the purified compound.

- It must be capable of easy removal from the crystals of the purified compound. This is possible when it has a low boiling point.
- It should not interact chemically with the substance.
- It should be inexpensive.

Table 3.8 Common solvents for recrystallisation

Solvent	Boiling point (°C)	Solvent	Boiling point (°C)
Water	100	Benzene	80
Methanol	64	Petroleum ether	60–90
Ethanol	78	Toluene	111
Acetic acid	118	Xylene	139
Methylene chloride	40	Acetone	56
Carbon tetrachloride	77	Chloroform	61

Water, ethyl alcohol, acetone, chloroform, benzene, light petroleum and acetic acid are some of the common solvents used for recrystallisation (Table 3.8). Methylene chloride, cyclohexane, pyridine and nitrobenzene are some among the less commonly used solvents.

In some cases, recrystallisation does not take place rapidly, which may be due to the absence of suitable nuclei for crystal growth. Scratching the vessel below the surface of the solution with a glass rod will promote recrystallisation in such cases. Sometimes, cooling the solution in an ice–salt mixture may lead to recrystallisation. The solution may be seeded with a crystal of the same substance to initiate recrystallisation. Sometimes, mixed solvents or solvent pairs are used especially when the substance is far too soluble in one solvent and much too insoluble in another solvent, to permit satisfactory recrystallisation. The two solvents used must be miscible with each other. Alcohol–water, alcohol–benzene, benzene–light petroleum and acetic acid–water are some such mixed solvents used.

Sometimes, crystallisation may be carried out by adding a few pieces of solid carbon dioxide. This produces cold spots in the solution, aiding the formation of crystals. Leaving the solution in a refrigerator may be adopted when other techniques fail to promote crystallisation.

3.4.3.3 Hot Filtration

When a hot solution is filtered to remove the insoluble impurities, the solution may cool and crystallisation begin before completion of filtration. This is avoided by adopting the method

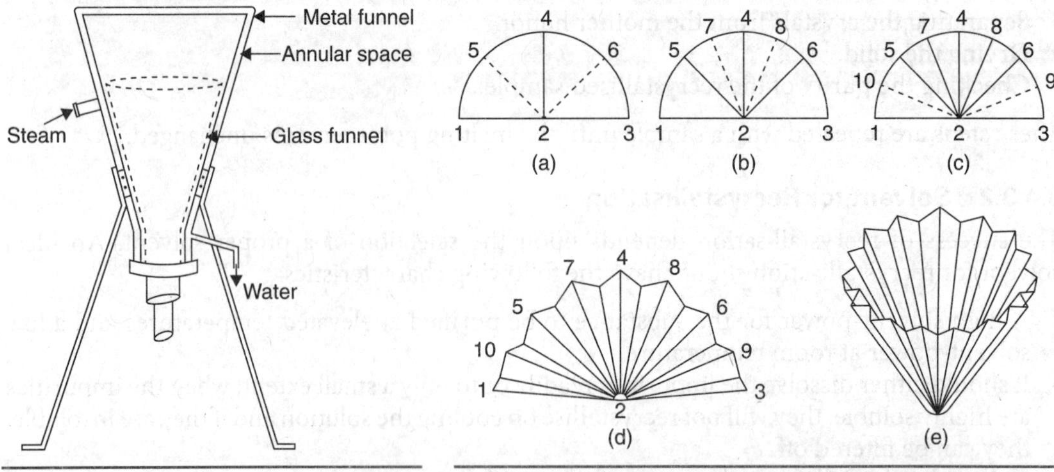

Fig. 3.32 (a) Apparatus for hot filtration

Fig. 3.32 (b) Steps in making fluted filter paper

of hot filtration. The glass funnel is kept inside a double-walled metal funnel which is placed on the neck of a conical flask (Fig. 3.32a). Steam is circulated through the annular space in the metal funnel so that the solution remains hot during filtration. Using a *fluted filter paper,* which allows rapid filtration, crystallisation inside the funnel is avoided (Fig. 3.32b).
When the crystals are filtered, it is customary to rinse them with some of the cold solvent used in the recrystallisation. In general, crystallisation should be done from an Erlenmeyer flask and not from a beaker. The design of the conical flask is such that it prevents *evaporative creep* of the materials up the flask walls and to permit the flask to be corked and stored without loss of solvent by evaporation. It is easy to swirl a conical flask containing a solution without spilling, which is impossible with a beaker.

After filtering the crystals, a second crop of crystals can usually be obtained by cooling the mother liquid in ice water or by concentrating the solution by boiling away some of the solvent and cooling. The crystals thus obtained may not be as pure as the first.

3.4.3.4 Drying the Crystals

Most of the solvent admixed with the crystals may be evaporated by allowing the aspirator to pull air through the funnel for a few minutes. Complete drying is accomplished by air drying for a few hours or by placing the sample inside a dessicator. When there is no risk of decomposition, the solid may be dried in an oven, keeping the oven temperature at least 20° below the melting point of the substance.

3.4.3.5 Removal of Colouring Matter During Recrystallisation

Frequently, crude organic products contain coloured impurities which are not eliminated by recrystallisation. Sometimes, the hot solution of the substance is turbid owing to the presence of resinous impurity or very fine suspension of an insoluble impurity, which cannot always be removed by simple filtration. These impurities can be removed by boiling the substance in solution with a little decolourising charcoal for 5–10 minutes, and then filtering the solution while hot. Resinous and finely divided impurities are *adsorbed* by charcoal so that colourless or white precipitate can be obtained from the filtrate. The decolourisation can be done in either aqueous or organic medium. An excess quantity of charcoal must be avoided, since it may adsorb a part of the compound that is being purified. Animal charcoal is an inexpensive and commonly used decolourising material. It is also called *bone black* or *bone charcoal.* Activated decolourising charcoal prepared from birch wood has excellent decolourising power and is marketed under the trade name *Norit.*

The Art of Recrystallisation

The technique of recrystallisation, though appearing simple, is tricky. This has to be mastered only by practice with patience. The following precautions are helpful in successfully recrystallising a sample:

- The minimum amount of solvent must be used.
- The boiling or hot solution must be rapidly filtered if there are insoluble impurities.
- During recrystallisation, the solution should not be disturbed.
- Flammable solvents should be heated using a water bath.
- A single recrystallisation may not always give a pure substance. Repeated recrystallisations may then be done.

3.4.4 Sublimation

Sublimation is a process of a solid getting directly converted into its vapour on heating without becoming a liquid. This happens below the melting point of the solid. The vapour on condensation gives back the solid. Sublimation is an alternative to crystallisation for the purification of some solids. The differing vapour pressures of the substance which sublimes and the impurities help in purifying a substance using sublimation.

3.4.4.1 Principle

The process of sublimation can be understood by studying the pressure–temperature phase diagram for a substance that sublimes (Fig. 3.33). The figure relates the solid, liquid and vapour states of the substance with pressure and temperature.

At the triple point, solid, liquid and vapour coexist. For a solid to pass directly into vapour without the intermediate formation of a liquid phase, the pressure of the vapour must not be allowed to exceed that of the triple point. This can be done if the vapour pressure at the triple point is fairly high and consequently the rate of vaporisation will be considerable. Under these conditions, purification of the solid by sublimation at atmospheric pressure is possible.

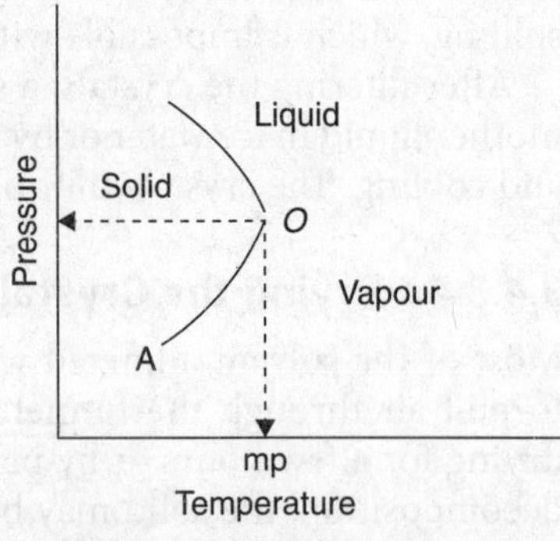

Fig. 3.33 Phase diagram for a sublimation

Example: Camphor has a triple point at 179°C and an equilibrium pressure of 370 mm. When it is slowly heated below 179°, it will vaporise without melting and if the vapour is deposited on a cold surface, the pressure will be kept below 370 mm and hence vaporisation will continue until all the solid has disappeared. Condensation occurs on the cold surface directly because the pressure is below that at the triple point.

3.4.4.2 Technique of Sublimation

A simple form of apparatus for sublimation is shown in Fig. 3.34. The substance to be sublimed is placed in an evaporating dish. A narrow ring of pyrex glass is fitted near the rim, which supports a filter paper with a number of small holes made in an upward direction. A funnel with a plug of glass wool in the stem is kept inverted over the paper. The dish is gently heated. Vapours escape through the holes in the paper and condense on the upper surface of the filter paper and also on the walls of the funnel. Heating is stopped when most of the material in the dish has vapourised. The supply of heat should be such that the funnel does not become hot. The rate of sublimation may be increased by applying very gentle suction at the stem of the funnel. This will draw the vapour into the condensing chamber.

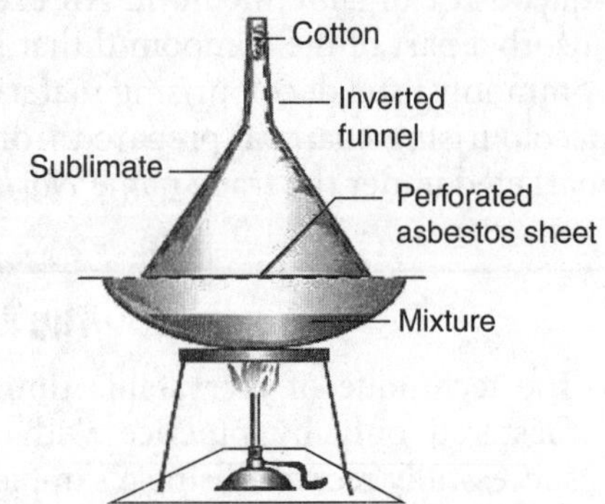

Fig. 3.34 Apparatus for sublimation

3.4.4.3 Types of Sublimation

(i) *Simple sublimation*: A simple sublimation is conducted at atmospheric pressure. For example, hexachloroethane attains a vapour pressure of 760 mm below its melting point. Attempt to heat solid hexachloroethane above 180°C (760 mm) in an unstoppered vessel will cause an outgoing of the vapour and the whole material will sublime and escape into the atmosphere.

(ii) *Sublimation under reduced pressure*: This can be carried out by using the apparatus shown in Fig. 3.35. The cold finger is fitted into the larger tube by means of rubber stopper and carries a disc slightly smaller in diameter than the outer tube. The pressure can be reduced by a water or an oil pump. The impure material is taken in the wider tube. On heating gently, either with a small flame or over an oil bath, the substance sublimes and collects on the cold surface of the disc.

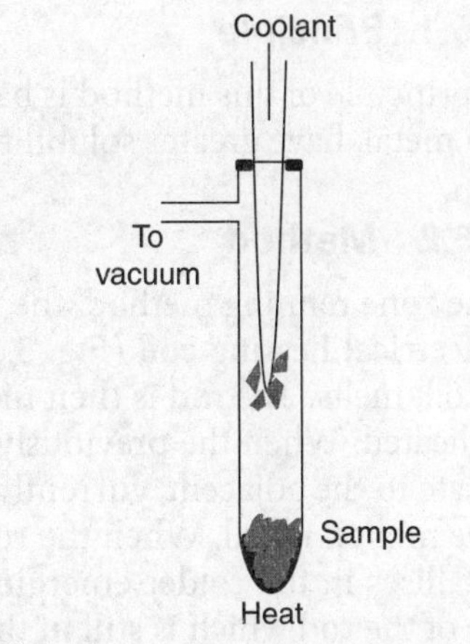

Fig. 3.35 Cold finger sublimation

(iii) *Vacuum sublimation*: Very few organic compounds exhibit a vapour pressure adequate for sublimation at atmospheric pressure. Reduced pressure (vacuum) is needed to increase the rate of evaporation of the solid. This method is similar to the use of vacuum distillation for high boiling liquids. Most solids melt at temperatures below those at which their vapour pressures reach 760 mm. Naphthalene and phthalic anhydride belong to this type. These sublime readily under reduced pressure and this technique is called vacuum sublimation. Sublimation under high vacuum is effective for separating a substance from a mixture.

(iv) *Entrainer sublimation*: This is a technique of subliming a substance (which must otherwise be sublimed under vacuum) at atmospheric pressure below the melting point by introducing an inert gas as an entrainer. The vapour of the substance is swept by the inert gas into a condenser where it crystallises.

3.4.4.4 Advantages of Sublimation

- Sublimation is a convenient and rapid method for purification of solids when impurities are either non-volatile or considerably more volatile than the desired compound.
- In distillation, volatile impurities tend to dissolve in the newly formed distillate as the distillate is formed in the condenser; in sublimation this is impossible as crystals are formed directly from the vapour, the impurity molecules still remaining as vapour.
- The apparatus required for sublimation is simple and inexpensive.

Sublimation is restricted to relatively non-polar substances having symmetrical structures. In these cases, crystal forces are weaker and vapour pressures are higher. These properties increase the ease with which a molecule can escape from the solid to the vapour phase. In a symmetrical structure, the electron density is symmetrically distributed making dipole moments smaller and intermolecular attractions weaker. A smaller dipole moment implies a higher vapour pressure. van der Waals forces also influence the ease of sublimation, but to a lesser extent compared to electrostatic forces. When the van der Waals forces are of high magnitude as with large molecules, the substance is less likely to sublime.

3.4.5 Zone Refining

This is a process for the purification of certain materials, especially elements. This method is actually *fractional crystallisation*; the impurities tend to remain dissolved in the molten metal rather than in the solid metal. *Zone melting* is another name for this process.

3.4.5.1 Principle

The principle of this method is based on the fact that the impurities in a sample of an element, say a metal, have greater solubility in the molten element than in the solid element.

3.4.5.2 Method

In the zone refining method, the impure metal, in the form of a rod, is made to move through an electrical heating coil (Fig. 3.36). The portion of the rod exposed to the heating effect of the coil, melts. The rod is then moved in one direction so that the adjacent portion of the rod gets heated. When the previously heated molten portion cools, the impurities in that portion migrate to the adjacent, currently heated (molten) portion of the rod. The impurities dissolve in the molten metal. When the rod emerges from the heating coil, it cools and the pure metal crystallises in the colder emerging rod end, with the impurities migrating to the hot molten zone of the rod which is still in the heating coil. The metallic crystal lattice formed on cooling does not accommodate the impurities. When the molten zone containing more impurities than the cold zone reaches the end of the rod, it is allowed to cool. The process of heating and cooling of the rod is repeated to allow the migration of all the impurities to one end of the rod. Then the impure end is cut off and discarded. The remaining metal is 99% pure.

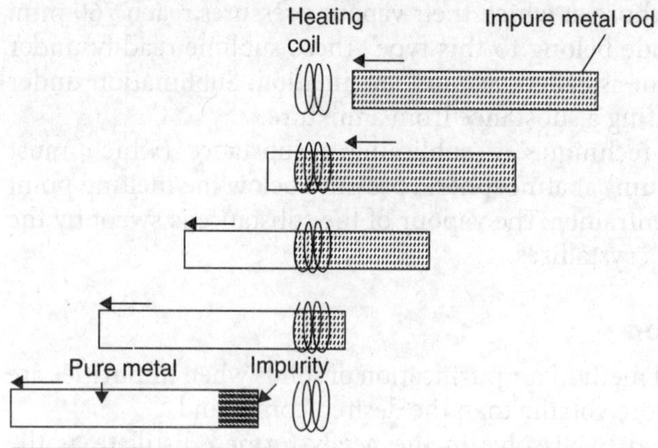

Fig. 3.36 (a) Zone-refining technique for purifying metals

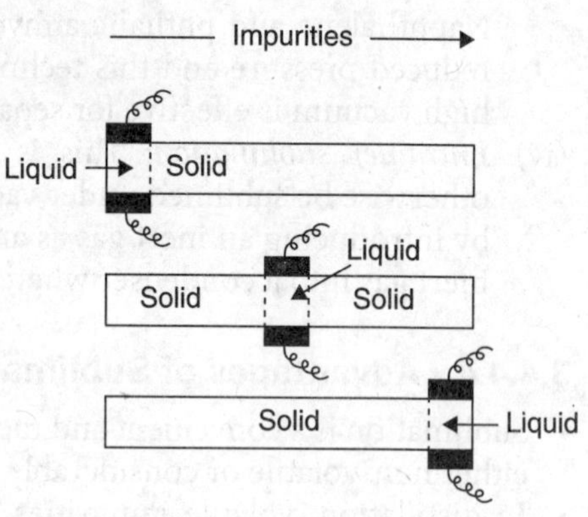

Fig. 3.36 (b) Zone-refining: Three stages in one pass of the heating zone

3.4.5.3 Heating methods

The heating in zone refining can be carried out with one of the following devices—electrical resistance coil, induction heater, electric arc, electron beam, radiation source, plasma, solar heater, laser and peltier heater (heat produced by electric current flowing across a junction between two different conductors).

> *In zone refining or zone purification, a narrow molten zone is moved slowly along the complete length of the specimen to bring about impurity segregation.*
>
> *It is based on the differences in compositions of the liquid and solid in equilibrium.*

3.4.5.4 Applications of Zone Refining

Pure silicon – with impurities only at ppm level – required for the electronic industries, is obtained by zone refining. Ge and Ga are also purified by this method. Ta,W, Mo and Be are the other elements which are produced in high purity by zone refining. This method of purification can be applied to elements, alloys, semiconductors and some inorganic and organic compounds.

This purification method is used for producing extremely pure semi-conductor silicon required for rectifiers and transistors in electronic industries. Silicon can be purified to contain less than one part of impurities in 10,000 million parts of silicon. In zone refining, all discontinuities in the lattice of the material disappear with the formation of a large single crystal of silicon.

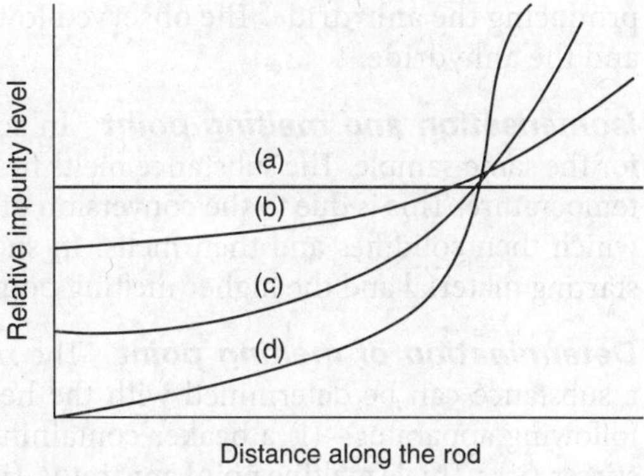

Fig. 3.37 Impurity levels plotted against the distance for repeated zone passing in zone refining. **(a)** Impure material at the beginning, **(b)** After 5 passes, **(c)** After 20 passes, **(d)** After 50 passes.

3.4.6 CRITERIA AND TESTS FOR PURITY

A substance purified by any of the techniques described in the previous sections of this chapter has to be checked for its purity. The following physical properties are used for checking the purity of substances—(i) melting point (mp), (ii) boiling point (bp), (iii) refractive index (*n*) and (iv) density (d).

These properties have long been utilised in identification and characterisation of organic compounds. Only very rarely may more than one compound exhibit the same value for any of these properties. Spectroscopic and chromatographic data are also sometimes used to check the purity of substances.

3.4.6.1 Melting Point

The melting point of a substance is the temperature at which the liquid and solid phases exist in equilibrium with each other. The melting point of a pure substance is a constant and not affected by experimental conditions. It is an *intensive property*—not dependent on the quantity of the substance used. The presence of impurities almost invariably lowers the melting point. Therefore, if the observed melting point of a substance is the same as that expected, the substance is taken as pure.

In dealing with an unknown compound, it is usual to crystallise it repeatedly until its melting point is no longer affected by subsequent recrystallisations. As a rule, the compound will then have a sharp, definite melting point and is considered pure. A few substances have indefinite melting points. They begin to soften at a certain temperature and get completely molten only at a much higher temperature. However, as a rule, a melting point which is not sharp is due to the presence of an impurity.

Decomposition and melting point The rate of heating may affect the melting point of a substance. For example, the melting point of phthalic acid has been given in the books at various temperatures ranging from 180° to 200°C. This variation is especially possible when a substance decomposes on heating. In such a case, it is advisable to raise the temperature of the bath to nearly the actual melting point and then introduce the substance and quickly raise the temperature until melting occurs. If the substance and thermometer are placed in a cold bath and the temperature slowly raised, a lower melting point is obtained for phthalic acid. The reason is that as the acid is heated it loses water, producing the anhydride. The observed lower melting point is that of a mixture of the acid and the anhydride.

Isomerisation and melting point In some rare cases, two melting points are observed for the same sample. The substance melts first, solidifies and then melts once again at another temperature. This is due to the conversion of the substance at its melting point into an isomer which then solidifies and then melts. In such a case, the lower melting point is that of the starting material and the higher melting point that of the isomer.

Determination of melting point The melting point, of a substance can be determined with the help of one of the following apparatus—(i) a beaker containing a liquid and a stirrer, (ii) a Thiele melting point apparatus, (iii) an electrically heated metal block.

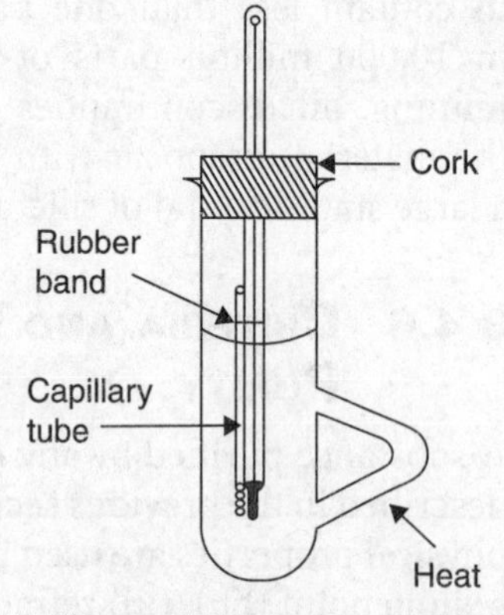

Fig. 3.38 Thiele melting point apparatus

Procedure One end of a capillary tube of about three inches is sealed by introducing it into the edge of a Bunsen burner. The dry substance whose mp has to be determined is taken on a watch glass. The open end of the capillary tube is pressed gently on the solid, when some substance will enter the capillary tube. The tube is then filed gently with the spine of a test tube brush. This will shift the solid to the sealed end of the tube. These processes are repeated until solid accumulates in the capillary tube to a length of about 2–3 mm. The capillary tube is then attached to a calibrated thermometer with a rubber band so that the substance is alongside the bulb. The thermometer–capillary tube assembly is kept in a beaker containing an oil (paraffin oil can be used; use of sulphuric acid is better avoided due to the risk of splashing on the body). This assembly is kept on a wire gauze and the oil is gently heated with a microburner. The oil is kept stirred with a thin glass stirrer. The temperature at which the solid becomes a liquid is carefully noted.

Fig. 3.39 Melting point apparatus

Thiele melting point apparatus In this apparatus (Fig. 3.38), heating of the liquid is carried out with a microburner at the triangular side tube. This ensures a steady rise in temperature. The heating fluid actually gently circulates due to convection. The danger of overheating is avoided in this method. The heating rate is usually about 2° per minute.

Electrically heated metal block The substance in the capillary tube is heated by placing it in the cavity of a metal block (Fig. 3.39). A hole is provided to insert the thermometer which helps to note the temperature accurately. The metal block is heated electrically with a coil beneath it. The heated substance is observed through a built-in magnifying glass. The rate of heating can be controlled by a rheostat.

Precautions in melting point determination The following precautions should be followed in melting point determination:

- Only a small amount of the substance should be used. The common mistake is to use too much material; then the temperature of the bath may rise through several degrees whilst the whole of the substance is melting unless the temperature is carefully regulated.
- Commercial thermometers may be inaccurate to an extent of 2°–3°. They must be calibrated before use. The thermometers can be checked for correct calibration by determining the melting points of pure samples of compounds of known melting points. Naphthalene (81°C), benzoic acid (122°C), urea (133°C) and *p*-nitrobenzoic acid (239°C) are some of the readily available compounds that may be used for calibrating thermometers.
- The temperature of the bath must be raised slowly by means of a microburner; rapid heating may lead to inaccurate melting points.
- If the whole of the mercury thread of the thermometer is not immersed in the hot liquid, the temperature read on the thermometer would not be the correct melting point. It should be corrected with the formula,

$$t_{cor} = t + 0.000156\, a\, (t - t_0)$$

where 0.000156 is the apparent coefficient of expansion of mercury in glass, a is the length of thread measured in degrees not immersed in the hot liquid, t is the melting point as read and t_0 is the mean temperature of the thread above the liquid. When a short thermometer is used with a range of 50°, this correction is not a necessity.

Factors which affect melting point The observed melting point is dependent on a number of factors such as sample size, state of subdivision of the sample and heating rate, in addition to its purity.

Mixture melting point The method of mixture melting point (mmp) is used to ascertain the purity of a solid. To the sample of the solid a small proportion of an authentic sample of the same compound is added and then the melting point of the 'mixture' determined. If this mp is the same as that of the sample prepared, then the sample is taken to be pure.

3.4.6.2 Boiling Point

The boiling point of a pure substance under a particular pressure is a constant, and therefore this property can be used to check the purity of a liquid. Dissolved impurities in a liquid increase its boiling point.

Determination of boiling point The bp of a liquid can be determined using the apparatus shown in Fig. 3.27. Frequently, wrong techniques lead to inaccurate recording of boiling points. Only when there is a constant passage of the boiling liquid from the distilling flask to the outlet, the thermometer will record the correct boiling point. This is achieved by a steady heating so that the thermometer bulb comes into contact with sufficient boiling vapour.

Precautions in determining boiling point The following precautions should be followed in determining the boiling points of various liquids:

- The whole of the thermometer bulb should be exposed to the hot vapour during distillation. The thermometer is so arranged such that the bulb is just below the side tube. It should not be immersed in the liquid.
- Superheating of the vapour must be avoided. When a low boiling liquid is boiled on a water bath, the steam issuing may surround the flask and superheat the vapour. As a rule, a small direct flame from a microburner is the best. The flame should be directed in such a way that it comes into contact with only the portion of the flask filled with liquid.

- The bulb of the thermometer should always be covered with a film of pure liquid produced by the condensation of vapour over the thermometer. This thin film of liquid will be in equilibrium with the pure vapour and hence the correct boiling point is registered.
- Bumping should be avoided by adding boiling chips.

Micro boiling point This method uses only a micro quantity of a liquid for determining the bp. Seal one end of a capillary tube and join the sealed end to the sealed end of another capillary tube. Cut the capillary tube 1 cm below the joint. Take a few drops of the liquid, whose bp has to be determined in a 4-mm tube and place the capillary prepared inside it, so that the joint is near the bottom of the 4-mm tube. The liquid level in the tube must be just above the joint in the capillary tube. Attach this tube-capillary tube unit to a thermometer with a rubber band. Immerse this in a paraffin oil bath (Fig. 3.40).

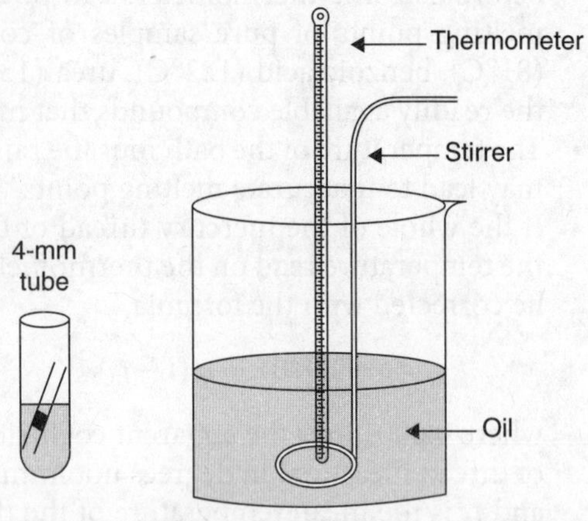

Fig. 3.40 Apparatus for micro method of determining boiling point

The temperature is raised rapidly till a continuous stream of bubbles comes out of the capillary tube. The heating is stopped and bath temperature allowed to come down. The rate of bubbling will decrease and then stop. The temperature is noted at this stage and this is the bp of the liquid. At the exact temperature when bubbles stop forming and escaping from the bottom portion of the capillary tube, the pressure inside the tube is equal to the atmospheric pressure. This temperature is the boiling point.

3.4.6.3 Refractive Index

The velocity with which light travels in different media is not a constant. This leads to the bending of a beam of light as it passes through the interface of two different media. The change in the 'speed' of light causes this bend. This is called *refraction*. The angle of refraction is dependent on the density, type of molecule and the temperature of the media as well as the wavelength of light. Air is chosen as the standard medium. With reference to this medium, different media bend light to different angles. When all angles of refraction are measured at the same temperature with the same wavelength of light with reference to air, the measured angle is a property of the second medium. This property is used as an identifying characteristic of the substance constituting that medium.

Instead of the angle of refraction, another quantity called refractive index (n) is actually reported. The refractive index is given by the equation,

$$n = \frac{\sin i}{\sin r}$$

where i is the angle of incidence and r is the angle of refraction (Fig. 3.41). Monochromatic light gives more precise values of n than white light, and therefore indices of refraction are reported for the D-line of sodium (λ = 589.3 nm). This fact is

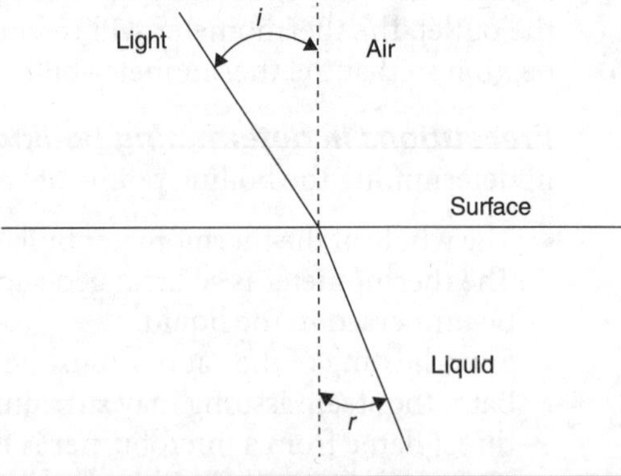

Fig. 3.41 Refraction of light

indicated by a subscript and the temperature by a superscript. A typical notation of refractive index is η_D^{20} which means that the index is measured at 20°C for the sodium D-line. Refractive indices are measured with an instrument called a refractometer.

A pure liquid has a constant refractive index at a particular temperature. Even traces of impurities alter this value, and therefore measuring the refractive index of a sample will indicate whether the sample is pure or not. The measured index may be compared with that obtained with a pure sample of the same compound or with the reported literature value.

3.4.6.4 Density

The density of a substance is occasionally used to check the purity of the substance. Density is a measure of concentration of matter. This is reported in units of grams per millilitre at 20°C. The density of a liquid is measured using a small container called a pycnometer (Fig. 3.42) whose volume is accurately known.

The pycnometer is weighed accurately and then filled with the liquid whose density is to be determined. The temperature of this is brought to 20°C, the volume is readjusted, if necessary, and then weighed. The density may be calculated by dividing the weight in grams by the volume in millilitres.

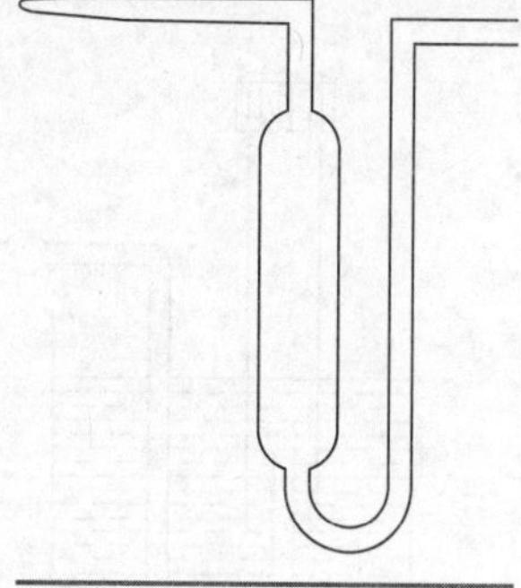

Fig. 3.42 Pycnometer

3.4.6.5 Spectral Absorption

The spectrum, for example, the infrared spectrum, of a compound can serve as its identity, especially the fingerprint region (6–15 μm). A molecule can be identified by a comparison of its unique absorption in this region with a catalogued known spectrum. The presence of impurities introduces a non-match between the recorded and expected spectra. Similarly, the mass spectrum or the NMR spectrum may also prove the purity of a material. The chromatogram may also be checked to authenticate the purity of material.

3.5 MICRO-SCALE APPARATUS

Small is Beautiful, in Chemistry Also (Abstracted from: Gopalan R, Small is beautiful in chemistry also, *Resonance*, 1997, p. 82).

Chemistry is very much an experimental science. Students can appreciate the various concepts of chemistry only by conducting laboratory experiments. These experiments necessarily involve the use of a large number of chemicals that are used and washed down the sink. This implies more expenditure for laboratory work in chemistry than for any other subject.

The prices of chemicals have increased phenomenally during the last few decades. However, the laboratory budget in our educational institutions has not been enhanced in proportion to the price-hike for chemicals. This imbalance between the prices and budget has led to a considerable qualitative and quantitative decrease in chemistry practical experiments in most of the educational institutions in our country. In several colleges, post-graduate students do only a few experiments in a year, implying a serious erosion in the quality of chemistry education.

There is, therefore, an urgent need to circumvent this deficiency in the chemistry laboratory work. An excellent way to solve this crisis involves miniaturising the chemistry experiments. Each experiment has to be planned using micro quantities of the chemicals involved. This would require replacement of the currently used glassware by micro-glassware. The adoption of micro-scale methods would save a lot of money, which in the long run would be manifold compared to the initial expenditure incurred on new micro-glassware.

Several advantages would accrue on switching over from the present macro-scale to the micro-scale of experimentation:

- Handling smaller apparatus and lesser chemicals requires greater skill in students; therefore, the practical work would be more challenging than it is now. It would also impart a better training for them.
- Larger number of experiments for each class can be prescribed with the same budget.
- Cleaning, drying and maintenance of the micro-glassware would be easy and convenient.

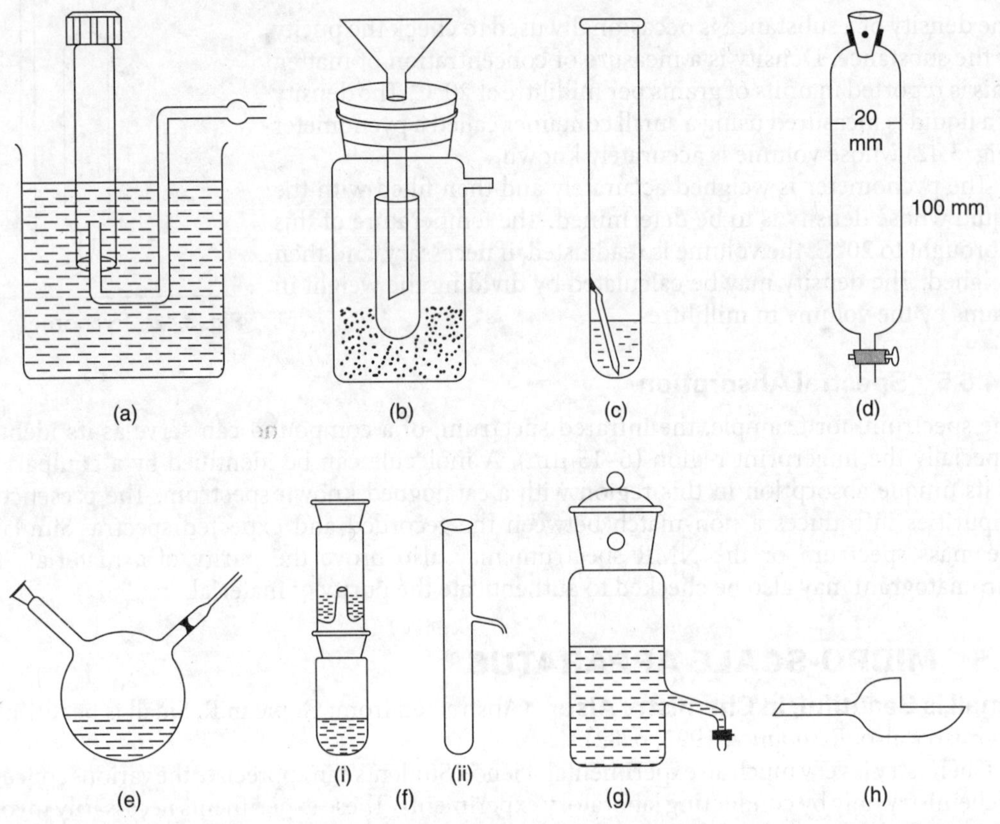

Fig. 3.43 Micro-scale apparatus. **(a)** Gas collector. This can be used for collecting and testing small quanitites of gases such as CO_2, H_2S, SO_2, hydrocarbons, and so on, **(b)** Micro filter assembly. This is suitable for filtration of 1–3 ml of material **(c)** Micro boiling point apparatus. A sample of 0.5 ml of the substance is sufficient for determining the boiling point. (The method is described in B N Campbell and M Mecarthy Ali, Organic chemistry expriments, Brooks/Cole. Pub. Co. California, p. 83, 1994), **(d)** Mini-separating funnel, **(e)** Two-necked flask for small-scale crystallisation and hot filtration. It has a sinter fused into one arm. This is suitable for a variety of organic laboratory operations, to be used with an air condenser, a Liebig condenser or as such, **(f)** (i) Micro distillation unit for liquids of a few ml quantity (ii) Micro distillation tube for liquids less than 1 ml, **(g)** Liquid weighing bottle. It has a side-arm with a stop-cock for draining a liquid. There is a hole in the neck and another hole in the hollow stopper. These two holes are made concentric by turning the stopper for drawing the liquid through the stop-cock. The bottle is weighed before and after drawing the liquid into a receiver to know the weight of the liquid drawn, **(h)** Weighing funnel.

- The cost of replacing smaller, broken glassware would be less than that of large glassware.
- The micro-apparatus set requires smaller storage space and therefore the laboratories can be better organised and used by more students.
- Students, using only small quanitites of chemicals, would be less exposed to health hazards.
- The pollution of the laboratory during the practical class and also the pollution of the environment from the laboratory wastes would be substantially reduced.
- The quantity of fuel needed for heating the reactants can be reduced.

Chemistry teachers, who traditionally prescribe large scale use of chemicals, may find it difficult to accept this concept of miniaturisation of experiments. But micro-scale experiments prepare the students for modern research, which generally involves handling chemicals in milligram quantities. Of course, teachers need to be innovative to utilise the advantages of miniaturised equipment.

Small is not only beautiful but also rewarding both for chemistry teachers and students. Failure to adopt miniaturisation would mean continued fall in the standard of chemistry laboratory work as the prices of chemicals are only expected to rise further without any proportionate rise in the laboratory budget.

Any conventional laboratory glassware can be miniatured. For example, enormous quantities of chemicals can be saved using semi-micro test tubes of 5 mm inner diameter and 80 mm height. An elongated tube (without a bulb) with 25 mm diameter and 150 mm length could serve as a separating funnel. Melting points can be determined using semi-micro Thiele tubes of 25 mL capacity. Glass spatulas can be made from glass rods by forming a cavity at one of its ends. Some micro-scale apparatus are represented in Fig. 3.43.

EXERCISES

1. Rationalise the following:
   (a) An ion-association complex such as $H_3O^+FeCl_4^-$ is effectively extracted by methyl isobutyl ketone but is not extracted to any extent by toluene.
   (b) Chromatographic peaks resemble a normal distribution curve.
   (c) Sometimes, chromatographic solid supports are silanised (treated with an organic silicon compound).

2. A sample of drinking water is contaminated with $CHCl_3$. A 100 mL sample of this water is shaken with 1.0 mL of *n*-hexane; 63% of $CHCl_3$ is extracted into hexane. Calculate the percentage of chloroform extracted when 10.0 mL of the water sample is shaken with 1.0 mL of hexane.

3. Outline the experimental steps needed for separating a mixture of
   (a) alanine, valine and threonine
   (b) benzene, toluene and benzoic acid
   (c) water, ethanol and butanol.

4. If the distribution ratio for substance A is 8.0, what is the minimum number of 10.0 mL portions of ether that must be used to extract 99.9% of substance A from 10.0 mL of an aqueous solution that contains 0.0800 g of substance A? What weight of A is removed with each extract?

5. The theoretical plate numbers for a gas chromatographic system are 61.4, 98.7 and 91.3 for linear gas velocities of 0.41, 1.52 and 3.12 cm s^{-1}, respectively. Calculate the maximum possible theoretical plate number for this system. What is the carrier gas velocity needed to achieve it?v

6. A mixture containing 1.50 m mol of *o*-xylene and 1.25 m mol of *p*-xylene is dissolved in the appropriate solvent and the solution is analysed by GC. The area of the *o*-xylene peak is 2.22 cm^2, whereas

the area of the *p*-xylene peak is 2.42 cm². A sample containing 1.25 mmol of *o*-xylene and *x* mmol of *p*-xylene is analysed similarly to produce peaks of areas 1.90 cm² and 1.21 cm², respectively. Calculate (a) the response factor for *o*-xylene relative to *p*-xylene (reference compound, internal standard), and (b) the value of *x*.

7. For a mixture of A and B, $V_s = 1.4$ mL, $V_M = 2.3$ mL, $K_A = 10.0$ and $K_B = 42.0$. The column used contains 30 theoretical plates. Calculate the retention volumes for A and B. Comment on the effectiveness of the separation.

8. Calculate the length that a column must have for the quantitative separation of substances A and B ($R = 1.62$), when V_M 9.2 mL, $V_{R_B} = 100$ mL, $\alpha = 1.10$ and $h = 0.120$ cm.

9. For two columns of equal length, the constants A, B and C of the van Deemter equation have the following values:

	A (cm)	B (cm²/s)	C (s)
Column 1	0.20	0.48	0.06
Column 2	0.260	0.40	0.13

(a) If the flow velocity of the carrier gas is 1.2 cm /s, which of the two columns would have the larger theoretical plate number?
(b) Calculate the optimum velocity for each of the two columns.

10. In the gas chromatogram of a 10.0 mg sample of A containing an impurity B, the peak corresponding to B has an area of 0.60 cm². When 4.0 mg of pure B was injected, the peak area is 5.21 cm². Calculate the percentage purity of the sample.

11. 50.0 mL of a 0.100 M solution of a compound X, in $CHCl_3$ is extracted successively with three fresh portions of water, each 20.0 mL.

$$K_p = \frac{X_{CHC_B}}{X_{water}} = 6.20$$

Calculate the distribution of X between $CHCl_3$ and the third portion of water.

4 Principles of Volumetric Analysis

4.1 INTRODUCTION

Volumetric analysis is the measurement of the volume of a solution of known concentration required to react completely with the *analyte*. An analyte is the component (element, compound or ion) in a sample whose amount is determined by a chosen method. For example, if the amount of Fe(II) present in a sample of its aqueous solution is determined, then Fe(II) is the analyte. Volumetric analysis is known also as *volumetric titrimetry*. The term *metry* means amount or weight; in titrimetry the amount (weight) is calculated from volumes of the reacting substances.

The advantages of volumetric analysis are:

- it is the least expensive among the analytical determinations,
- it is carried out using simple apparatus,
- it is a rapid method,
- it is accurate; when it is done carefully, an accuracy of ~0.5% can be achieved,
- it has an extensive range, that is, several types of analytes – acids, bases, oxidants, reductants and complexable species – can be estimated, and
- it lends itself to a variety of techniques such as visual titrimetry, conductometry, voltametry and spectrophotometric titrimetry.

It is thus a common technique practised in the laboratories of schools, colleges, research laboratories and industries.

4.1.1 VOCABULARY OF VOLUMETRY

Standard solution A standard solution is a reagent of known concentration that is used in volumetric analysis. Such a solution is known also as a *standard titrant*.

Titrant A titrant is a solution taken in the burette and added to the analyte.

Analyte The substance being titrated is called the *titrand* or *analyte*. An analyte is the substance to be estimated.

Titration A titration involves the addition of a standard solution from a burette or other liquid-dispensing apparatus to a solution of the analyte until the reaction between the two is complete. The volume of the titrant added to complete the reaction is the difference between the initial and final burette readings.

Equivalence point The equivalence point in a titration is the stage at which the amount of added titrant is chemically (stoichiometrically) equivalent to the amount of analyte in the sample. For example, in the titration of aqueous sodium hydroxide (base) with hydrochloric acid, the equivalence point is reached when one mole of the acid has been added to one mole of the base. One mole of HCl is required for complete reaction with one mole of NaOH. At the equivalence point, the reaction between the analyte and titrant is complete.

In the titration of sodium hydroxide with sulphuric acid, the equivalence point is reached on adding half a mole of the acid to one mole of the base since H_2SO_4 is a dibasic acid.

End point The equivalence point in a titration is the theoretical point at which the reaction is expected to be complete. However, it cannot be determined experimentally. Usually, in titrations, the equivalence point is inferred by observing some physical change that occurs in the reaction solution at this point—this is called the end point of the titration. In most titrations, the end point and the equivalence point do not coincide; the end point is slightly further from the equivalence point due to two reasons: (i) the inadequacy or insensitivity of the physical change that signals the end point and (ii) the limitation in our ability to observe the end point.

- The end point is what is actually observed and the equivalence point is what should ideally be observed.
- The convergence of the end point and the equivalence point confers accuracy to a titration.

Titration error The difference in volume or mass between the equivalence point and the end point is the titration error. It is called an error because the volume of the titrant added to note the end point is slightly higher than the volume required to reach the equivalence point. In volumetric methods, the titration error E_t is given by $E_t = V_{end} - V_{equ}$ where, V_{end} is the actual titrant volume added to notice the end point and V_{equ} is the theoretical (stoichiometric) volume required to reach the equivalence point. When titrations are done carefully, the titration error is minimum, well within the experimental error. In such titrations, the extra amount of titrant added should not be greater than 0.1 mL. In such cases, the percentage error in the titration is very small.

Problem 4.1 In a titration of 20.0 mL of aqueous sodium hydroxide with 0.10 N hydrochloric acid, the observed end point is 22.7 mL, whereas the equivalence point is 22.5 mL. Calculate the percentage error in the mass of hydrochloric acid per litre of the analyte for this titration.

$$\text{The normality of NaOH } (aq) \text{ as per the end point} = \frac{22.7 \times 0.10\text{ N}}{20.0} = 0.1135\text{ N}$$

$$\text{The mass of HCl/L} = 0.1135 \times 36.45\text{ g} = 4.1371\text{ g}$$

$$\text{The mass of HCl/L as per the equivalence point} = \frac{22.5 \times 0.10\text{ N}}{20.0}\ 36.45 = 4.1006\text{ g}$$

$$\%\text{ error in mass per litre} = \frac{(4.1371 - 4.1006) \times 100}{4.1006} = 0.9$$

As the reacting volumes are proportional to the equivalent, the percentage error can be calculated directly from the volumes:

$$\frac{(22.7 - 22.5) \times 100}{22.5} = 0.9\%$$

Indicators An indicator is a chemical added to the analyte solution to cause an observable physical change at or near the equivalence point. Usually, large changes in the relative concentration of analyte or titrant occur in the equivalence point region. Such changes in concentration cause a change in the appearance (say colour) of the indicators. The appearance or disappearance of turbidity in the analyte solution may also signal the end point in some titrations.

Indicators are of different types: acid–base, redox, adsorption, turbidity, self and instrumental (Table 4.1). The indicator for a titration is selected based on the chemical nature of the analyte and the titrant.

An instrument that records or indicates a certain property of the solution that changes in a characteristic way during the titration, can be used to detect the end point. Voltmeter, ammeter, ohmmeter, colourimeter, pH meter, refractometer and temperature recorder are some such instruments. When an instrument is used, a dramatic change in the reading is observed at the equivalence point; such a change signals the end point. No chemical indicator is necessary in this case.

Table 4.1 Types of indicators

Type of titration	Mode of action	Indicator	Example titration
Acid–base	Colour change from acidic to basic medium	Phenolphthalein	HCl–NaOH
Redox	Colour change from oxidised to reduced form	Ferroin	Fe(II)–Ce(IV)
Adsorption	Colour of indicator changes due to adsorption	A soluble chromate	Cl^-–$AgNO_3$
Self	Titrant or analyte is coloured	$KMnO_4$	Fe(II)–$KMnO_4$
Instrumentally detectible property	A sudden change—an increase or decrease in a property	Conductance	AcOH–NaOH

Primary standard A primary standard in volumetry is a highly pure compound that serves as a reference material. Based on the concentration of a solution of a primary standard, the concentrations of analytes can be calculated. The accuracy of titrimetry is critically dependent on the properties of the primary standard. The requirements for a primary standard are:

- should be highly pure (with a purity close to 100%),
- should lend itself to a simple method of checking its purity,
- should be stable in air and at room temperatures, and also in solution during its titration,
- composition should be constant; it should not get hydrated in humid atmosphere or lose its water of hydration in dry atmosphere,
- should be inexpensive,
- should be soluble in the titration medium (aqueous medium is commonly used),
- molar mass should preferably be large so that the relative error associated with weighing the standard is minimised, and
- routine use in laboratories should not cause hazards such as toxicity and flammability.

Not many compounds satisfy all these requirements, and therefore only a few compounds serve as primary standards. For example, anhydrous sodium carbonate, oxalic acid dihydrate, ferric alum, copper sulphate pentahydrate, boric acid and sodium hydrogencarbonate are primary standards.

Secondary standard Some compounds of lesser purity must sometimes be used as standards instead of a primary standard; such compounds are called *secondary standards*. The purity of the secondary standard is determined before it is used. For example, potassium permanganate or iodine can serve as a secondary standard. A secondary standard cannot be weighed and used directly without checking the normality of its solution.

Standard solutions A standard solution is a solution of known concentration. It is prepared by weighing the required amount of a primary standard, dissolving it in a solvent (usually pure water) and making up the solution to a desired volume. For example, 5.300 g of analar $NaHCO_3$ dissolved in water and made up to 1000 mL is a standard (0.1 N) solution. The preparation of standard solutions is an important part of all volumetric methods. The accuracy of its concentration influences the success of the analysis.

Preparation of a standard solution This procedure can be explained using standard sodium carbonate solution as an example. Let us assume that 100 mL of 0.1000 N sodium carbonate solution is required for an experiment. The equivalent weight of anhydrous sodium carbonate (Na_2CO_3) = 53 g.

The weight of 0.1000 N Na_2CO_3 required for 100 mL of its solution

$$= \frac{53}{10 \times 10} \text{ g} = 0.53 \text{ g}$$

Therefore, if we weigh exactly 0.5300 g of Na_2CO_3 and dissolve it in water and then make up the volume of the solution to exactly 100 mL, then the solution would be exactly 0.100 N. However, it is inconvenient to weigh *exactly* 0.5300 g of Na_2CO_3; therefore, about 0.53 g is taken in a dry, clean weighing bottle and weighed accurately (w_1 g). Then, the salt in the bottle is transferred to a beaker and the empty bottle is weighed (w_2 g). The exact weight of sodium carbonate transferred to the beaker is ($w_1 - w_2$) g. The carbonate in the beaker is dissolved in water and then the solution is made up exactly to 100 mL in a standard flask. The normality of the solution thus made is

$$\frac{w_1 - w_2}{53} \times \frac{1}{10 \times 10}$$

In volumetric analysis, the strength of a standard solution need not be a round figure (such as 0.1000 N or 0.0500 N). It is necessary to know the exact strength; for example, it could be 0.1108 N or 0.0984 N.

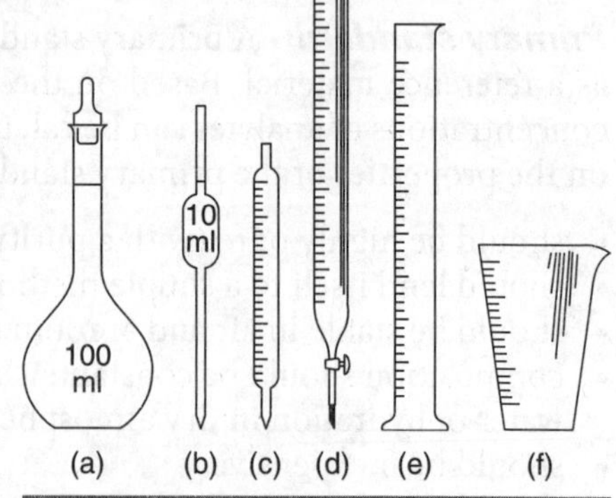

Fig. 4.1 Graduated glassware: **(a)** Standard flask **(b)** Pipette **(c)** Graduated pipette **(d)** Burette **(e)** Measuring cylinder **(f)** Graduated beaker

The ideal standard solution The ideal standard solution for a titrimetric method should have the following properties. It should

- be stable so that its concentration remains constant during use,
- react rapidly with the analyte so that the time required between additions of the aliquot of the reagent is minimum,
- react completely with the analyte to produce reliable end points, and
- undergo a selective reaction with the analyte that can be denoted by a simple balanced equation.

Erlenmeyer, Richard August Carl Emil (1825–1909)

Born	1825 Germany
Died	1909

Erlenmeyer was a German pharmacist. He was born in Wiesbaden, Germany in 1825. He first started studying medicine compelled by his father. He happened to listen to the lectures of Liebig, a renowned chemist of his time. Astonished by the captivating and scholarly lectures of Liebig, Erlenmeyer switched to the study of chemistry! He came under the intellectual spell of great chemists, Kolbe, Bunsen and Kekule. He and Kekule moved to Heidelberg and pursued research in chemistry. Not satisfied with the types of glass containers available at that time for conducting reactions, Erlenmeyer designed in 1861 a conical flask, now called the Erlenmeyer flask. This eponymous flask, widely used now in every chemistry laboratory in the world offers several advantages.

- It has a wide bottom and therefore is stable when placed on the laboratory table.
- As its bottom is broad, it holds more amount of the liquid and also offers a large area for heating.
- Its neck is narrow, suitable for holding the flask firmly and conveniently and also helps in easy swirling.
- Its narrow neck and the sloping sides prevent splashing of the liquid on swirling.
- A coloured liquid contained at the broad bottom transmits uniform colour intensity which helps identify the end point properly in a titration.
- When it has a ground-joint neck with a stopper, it can safely contain the contents including volatile ones.
- It is convenient for recrystallisation.

The features of the Erlenmeyer flask have thus rendered it a celebrated logo of chemistry.

- The asbestos embedded wire gauze, used for uniform heating by the Bunsen flame was also invented by Erlenmeyer.
- He contributed richly to the development of organic chemistry. He was the first to synthesise isobutyric acid, tyrosine and several other aliphatic compounds. He enunciated the Erlenmeyer rule, according to which 'all alcohols in which the hydroxyl group is attached directly to a double-bonded carbon atom easily transform to aldehydes or ketones'.
- He established the structure of naphthalene, thus proving, for the first time, the existence of compounds with fused benzene rings.
- The terms, 'monovalent', 'divalent' and 'unsaturated' were coined by him.

His contributions to chemistry are monumental.

Few reagents satisfy all these requirements. For example, aqueous potassium dichromate is an ideal standard solution and is thus often used in titrimetry.

Standardised solution A solution prepared from a substance which is not a primary standard and whose normality has been determined by titration with a standard solution prior to its use is a *standardised solution.*

Graduated glassware The glass apparatus – pipette, burette, standard flask, and so on used in titrimetry – are collectively called graduated glassware (Fig. 4.1).

4.1.2 Standardisation of Solutions

Standardisation is the determination of the concentration of a solution by titrating a measured volume of the solution. When a solution is prepared with a primary volumetric standard, the concentration of the solution can be calculated from the weight of the solute and the volume of the solution made. But, a solution of a secondary volumetric standard or any other solution to be used has to be standardised—this is done by titrating it with another solution of known concentration.

The accuracy of a titrimetirc method depends on the accuracy of the concentration of the standard solution used in the titration. Two methods are used for the standardisation of volumetric solutions:

Direct method In this method, a carefully weighed quantity of a primary standard is dissolved in a suitable solvent and diluted to an exactly known volume in a volumetric flask. The resulting solution is then a standard solution.

Standardisation method In this method, the titrant is standardised by titrating it against a measured volume of another standard solution. For example, NaOH(*aq*) can be standardised by titrating a definite volume (say 10.0 mL) against HCl(*aq*) of known concentration. Standardisation may also be effected by titrating the solution against a weighed quantity of a primary standard in the solid form. For example, HCl(*aq*) can be standardised by titrating it with $Na_2CO_3(s)$.

A titrant that is standardised against a primary standard solution or against a secondary standard (of known strength) is called a *secondary standard solution.* The concentration of a secondary standard is subject to more uncertainty than that of a primary standard. Therefore, preparing a standard solution by the direct method is reliable; however, in the absence of a primary standard, titrants have to be necessarily standardised.

The mineral acids, such as hydrochloric, sulphuric and perchloric are not primary standards. The commercial samples are usually diluted appropriately and then standardised against a primary standard or a standardised titrant.

Problem 4.2 What volume of a commercial sample of H_2SO_4 (M = 16.21) is required for preparing 250 mL of 0.5 N of this acid?

Solution

Normality of $H_2SO_4 = 16.21 \times 2 = 32.42$

The dilution ratio for preparing 0.5 N acid = 32.42 : 0.5

= 64.84 : 1

Therefore, for 250 mL of 0.5 N acid, the volume of commercial sample required

$$\frac{250}{64.84} = 3.86 \text{ mL}$$

Problem 4.3 What volume of HCl solution, that has a density of 1.20 g/mL and contains 37% HCl by weight, is required to prepare one litre of an approximately 0.200 N HCl solution?

Solution

The normality of the original HCl solution

$$N_{HCl} = \frac{\frac{1000\text{ mL}}{1} \times 1.20\text{ g/mL} \times \left(\frac{37}{100}\right)\text{g HCl/g}}{36.46\text{ g HCl/eq}} = 12.18\text{ eq/L}$$

Let x be the volume of the original HCl solution required

Then, 12.18 meq/mL × x = 0.200 meq/mL × 1000 mL

$$\therefore \quad x = \frac{0.200 \times 1000}{12.18}\text{ mL} = 6.4\text{ mL}$$

Back titration Sometimes, the volumetric reaction is too slow for a titration to be carried out directly by adding the titrant A to combine exactly with the amount of analyte B in solution. In such a case, a measured volume of A is added that is in excess of that theoretically needed to react with B. The excess A is back-titrated with a standardised reagent C that will react rapidly with A. Let this correspond to the end point V_1.

$$\text{A} + \text{B} \xrightarrow{\text{slow}} \text{Products} + \text{Excess A}$$

$$\text{Excess A} + \text{C} \longrightarrow \text{Products}$$

A *blank* titration with the same volume of A (added for the reaction) is performed; let this end point correspond to V_2 mL. Then $(V_2 - V_1)$ mL is the volume of reagent C corresponding to the amount of B. Then,

$$(V_2 - V_1)_C \times N_C = V_B \times N_B$$

From this relationship, the normality and hence the amount of B can be determined.

4.2 CONCENTRATION UNITS

The concentrations of volumetric standard solutions are expressed in the unit of either *normality* (C_N) or *molarity* (C).

4.2.1 NORMALITY

The normality of a solution is the number of equivalents of a solute contained in 1 litre of solution. It is also the number of milliequivalents in 1 mL. For example,

(i) The normality of aqueous sodium carbonate containing 5.2995 g of Na_2CO_3 solute in 1 litre of the solution = 5.2995/52.995 = 0.10 N. (The equivalent weight of Na_2CO_3 is 52.995.)

(ii) The normality of NaOH (*aq*) containing 0.3800 g of NaOH solute in 100 mL of the solution

$$= \frac{0.3800}{100} \times 1000 \times \frac{1}{39.9968} = 0.0950$$

(The equivalent weight of NaOH is 39.9968.)

(iii) The normality of an aqueous solution of $KMnO_4$ is 0.050 N. Then, the amount of the solute present in 100 mL of its solution

$$= 31.607 \times \frac{0.050}{1} \times \frac{100}{1000} = 0.1580 \text{ g}$$

(The equivalent weight of $KMnO_4$ is 31.607.)

For a solution of species A, the normality C_N is given by the equations,

$$C_N = \frac{\text{no. of meq A}}{\text{no. of mL solution}}$$

$$C_N = \frac{\text{no. of eq A}}{\text{no. of L solution}}$$

When the concentration of a solution is very low, the milliequivalent (meq) unit is useful; it is one-thousandth of an equivalent.

Problem 4.4 Calculate the weight of pure oxalic acid dihydrate, $(COOH)_2 \cdot 2H_2O$ required to prepare 500 mL of a 0.02 N standard solution.

The molar mass of $(COOH)_2 \cdot 2H_2O = 126.064$

As oxalic acid is a dibasic acid, its equivalent weight = (molar mass/2), that is, 126.064/2.

For preparing 1 L of 1 N acid, 63.032 g of the acid is required.

Therefore, for preparing 500 mL of 0.02 N solution, the weight of the acid required

$$= 63.032 \times \frac{0.02 \text{ N}}{1 \text{ N}} \times \frac{500 \text{ mL}}{1000 \text{ mL}} = 0.6303 \text{ g}$$

Therefore, 0.6303 g of the acid should be dissolved in water and then the solution made up to 500 mL.

4.2.1.1 Treatment of Titration Data

The following examples show the treatment of titration data based on the normality unit.

(i) ***Calculation of the normality of a solution:*** Exactly 25.0 mL of an HCl solution required 24.8 mL of 0.1126 N NaOH to give an end point with phenolphthalein indicator. Calculate the normality of the HCl solution.

$$V_{HCl} \times N_{HCl} = V_{NaOH} \times N_{NaOH}$$

$$25.0 \times N_{HCl} = 24.8 \times 0.1126\ N$$

$$N_{HCl} = \frac{24.8 \times 0.1126\ N}{25.0}$$

$$= 0.1117\ N$$

- 1 litre of a 1 N solution of A reacts completely with 1 litre of a 1 N solution of B.
- In titrations, complete reactions occur in equivalents.

(ii) ***Calculation of milliequivalents of an analyte:*** How many milliequivalents of H_2SO_4 are required to react completely with 100 mL of 0.200N aqueous $Ba(OH)_2$?

Equivalent weight of sulphuric acid = 49.036

Equivalent weight of barium hydroxide = 85.657

1000 mL of 1 N $Ba(OH)_2$ = 1 eq of H_2SO_4 = 1000 meq of H_2SO_4

$$100\text{ mL of } 0.200\text{ N } Ba(OH)_2 = 1000\text{ meq} \times \frac{100\text{ mL}}{1000\text{ mL}} \times \frac{0.200\text{ N}}{1\text{ N}}$$

$$= 20\text{ meq}$$

(iii) ***Calculation of percentage purity:*** An impure sample of $NaHCO_3$ was used in a titrimetry. Exactly 5.000 g of this sample required 483.2 mL of 0.100 N aqueous hydrochloric acid for neutralisation. What is the percentage purity of $NaHCO_3$?

1 equivalent weight of HCl (36.461 g) = 1 equivalent weight of $NaHCO_3$ (84.0056 g)

$$483.2\text{ mL of } 0.100\text{ N HCl} = \frac{483.2\text{ mL}}{1000} \times 0.100\text{ N equivalent of HCl 1000 mL}$$

$$= 0.04832\text{ equivalents}$$

The same number of equivalents of $NaHCO_3$ must be present in 5.000 g of the sample.

$$0.04832\text{ equivalent of } NaHCO_3 = 0.04832 \times 84.0058\text{ g}$$

$$= 4.0591\text{ g}$$

Thus, 5.000 g of the impure sample contains 4.0591 g of $NaHCO_3$.

Therefore, the percentage purity of the sample

$$= \frac{4.0591}{5.000} \times 100 = 81.2$$

4.2.2 Molarity

The molar concentration (C_X) of the solution of the chemical species X is the number of moles of that species that is contained in one litre of the *solution* (not one litre of the solvent). The unit of molar concentration is molarity, M; it has the dimensions of mol L^{-1}. Molarity also denotes the number of the millimoles of a solute per millilitre of solution.

$$C_X = \frac{\text{no. mol solute}}{\text{no. litre of solution}} = \frac{\text{no. m mol of solute}}{\text{no. mL of solution}}$$

$$\text{Amount of substance in moles} = \frac{\text{mass of the substance in grams}}{\text{molar mass}}$$

$$\text{Molar mass} = \text{gram/mole}$$

When amounts are small, the unit *millimole* is used:

$$1 \text{ millimole} = 1 \text{ mole}/1000$$

Problem 4.5 5.0000 g of pure NaCl was dissolved in water and then made up to exactly 500 mL. Calculate the molarity of this solution.

Solution

$$\text{The number of moles of NaCl dissolved} = \frac{5.0000}{58.4428} = 0.0856$$

$$\text{Therefore, the molarity} = \frac{0.0856}{(0.5)} = 0.1712$$

Problem 4.6 The titration of 0.4242 g of pure $Na_2C_2O_4$ (134.00 g/mol) consumed 86.62 mL of $KMnO_4(aq)$. Calculate the molarity of the $KMnO_4$ solution.

The chemical reaction involved is

$$2MnO_4^- + 5C_2O_4^{2-} + 16H^+ \longrightarrow 2Mn^{2+} + 10CO_2 + 8H_2O$$

Solution

This equation indicates that the stoichiometric ratio is

$$2 \text{ moles of } KMnO_4 = 5 \text{ moles of } Na_2C_2O_4$$

$$\text{No. of moles of } Na_2C_2O_4 \text{ reacted} = \frac{0.4242}{134.00} = 0.003166$$

Then, $$\text{the no. of moles } KMnO_4 \text{ consumed} = \frac{0.003166 \times 2}{5} = 0.0012664$$

$$= 0.0012664 \times 168.034 \text{ g of } KMnO_4$$

$$= 0.2128 \text{ g}$$

$$86.62 \text{ mL of } KMnO_4 \text{ contains } 0.2128 \text{ g of } KMnO_4$$

$$1000 \text{ mL of } KMnO_4 \text{ will contain} = \frac{0.2128 \times 1000}{86.62} = 2.4567 \text{ g}$$

Then, $$\text{the molarity of } KMnO_4 \text{ solution} = \frac{2.4567}{\text{molar mass}} = \frac{2.4567}{168.034} = 0.0146$$

4.2.3 Molality

Molality is another unit used to express concentration. The molality of a solution is the number of moles of a solute contained in 1000 *grams* of the solvent. A one molal solution contains one mole of solute in 1000 g of solvent. For example, when 1 mole of NaCl is dissolved in 1000 grams of water, then the concentration of the resulting solution is 1 molal (1 m). As the quantity of the solvent pertains to weight, this concentration unit is temperature-independent (on the other hand, the volume of a liquid changes with temperature; therefore, M and N are temperature-dependent) *Molality does not change with temperature.*

Problem 4.7 The molality of a glucose solution required for an experiment should be 0.1. How much of glucose (in grams) has to be dissolved in 1 g of water to prepare this solution?

Solution

The molar mass of glucose, $C_6H_{12}O_6$ is 180.1548 g. Therefore, for a 0.1 molal solution with 1000 g of water, the amount of glucose required.

$$= 180.1548 \times 0.1 \text{ g}$$

Then, for 1 g of water the amount of glucose required $= \dfrac{180.1548 \times 0.1}{1000} = 0.0180$ g

---

Mole: A mole is the formula weight of a substance expressed in grams:

$$\text{moles} = \frac{\text{g}}{\text{formula wt}}$$

Molar concentration: The molar concentration (or molarity) M of a solution is the number of moles of solute present in 1 litre of solution:

$$M = \frac{\text{moles}}{\text{litres}}$$

$$\text{litres} \times M = \text{moles}$$

$$\text{moles} \times \text{formula weight} = \text{g}$$

$$\text{litres} \times M \times \text{formula weight} = \text{g}$$

Millimole: A millimole is the formula weight of a substance expressed in milligrams:

$$\text{mmoles} = \frac{\text{mg}}{\text{formula wt}}$$

Molar concentration: The molar concentration (or molarity) M of a solution is the number of millimoles of solute present in one millilitre of solution:

$$M = \frac{\text{mmoles}}{\text{mL}}$$

$$\text{mL} \times M = \text{mmoles}$$

$$\text{mmoles} \times \text{formula weight} = \text{mg}$$

$$\text{mL} \times M \times \text{formula weight} = \text{mg}$$

Note that g mol^{-1} is the same as mg $mmol^{-1}$; g L^{-1} the same as mg mL^{-1}, and mol L^{-1} the same as mmol mL^{-1}. The expressions in the right column (mmoles, millilitres, milligrams) are preferred to those in the left column (moles, litres, grams) because most analytical titrations are concerned with small quantities of solutions and chemicals. For example, it is easier to say 'twenty-two millilitres' and write '22 mL' than it is to say 'twenty-two thousandths of a litre' and write '0.22 L'. The chance of error in writing 4.7 mmoles is less than that in writing 0.0047 mole.

4.2.4 Titer

The titer is the weight (in mg) of analyte that is the chemical equivalent of 1 mL of the titrant.

For example, if a potassium dichromate solution has a titer of 1.9005 mg Fe, each millititre of potassium dichromate will react with 1.9005 mg iron. Then, the weight of the iron titrated is obtained by simply multiplying the volume of titrant used by the titer. The titer can be expressed in terms of any form of the analyte; for example, milligrams of Fe, FeO or Fe_2O_3.

Problem 4.8 A standard solution of $K_2Cr_2O_7$ contains 3.2652 g of $K_2Cr_2O_7$ per litre. Calculate its titer in terms of Fe(II).

Solution

Fe^{2+} reacts with $Cr_2O_7^{2-}$ as per the equation

$$6Fe^{2+} + Cr_2O_7^{2-} + 14H^+ \longrightarrow 6Fe^{3+} + 2Cr^{3+} + 7H_2O$$

$$6 \text{ moles of Fe(II)} \equiv 1 \text{ mole of } K_2Cr_2O_7 \equiv 6 \text{ equivalents of } K_2Cr_2O_7$$

$$\text{The strength of } K_2Cr_2O_7 \text{ solution} = \frac{3.2652}{48.9315} = 0.06673 \text{ N}$$

$$1000 \text{ mL of 1 N dichromate solution} \equiv 1 \text{ mole of Fe(II)}$$

$$1 \text{ mL of 0.6673N dichromate solution} \equiv \frac{1}{1000} \times 0.06673 \text{ mole of Fe(II)}$$

$$\equiv 0.00006673 \text{ mole of Fe(II)}$$

$$\equiv 0.00006673 \times 55.847 \text{ g} \equiv 3.7 \times 10^{-3} \text{ g}$$

$$\equiv 3.7 \text{ mg of Fe(II)} = \text{titre}$$

Problem 4.9 Calculate the NH_3 titer of a 0.100 N solution of HCl.

Solution

The reaction between NH_3 and H^+ is

$$NH_3 + H^+ \longrightarrow NH_4^+$$

$$1000 \text{ mL of 1 N HCl} \equiv 17 \text{ g of } NH_3$$

$$1 \text{ mL of 0.100 N HCl} \equiv \frac{17 \text{ g}}{1000 \text{ mL}} \times 1 \text{ mL} \times \frac{0.1000 \text{ N}}{1 \text{ N}} \equiv 0.0017 \text{ g}$$

$$\equiv 1.7 \text{ mg of } NH_3$$

Hence, the NH_3 titer of HCl solution is 1.7 mg. This means that 1 mL of this HCl solution will neutralise 1.7 mg of NH_3.

$$\text{Titer } T = 0.1000 \text{ meq/mL} \times 17.0 \text{ mg/meq } NH_3 = 1.7 \text{ mg}$$

(For H^+, equivalent = 1; for 0.100 N HCl, milliequivalent = 0.1000)

The titer denotes the extent to which a titrant can react with an analyte. For a particular analyte, the titer of a titrant depends on the strength of the titrant. For example, the titer for 0.1 N HCl is different from the titer for 0.2 N HCl for an analyte, say NaOH.

If the normality of a solution is expressed as N and its volume of the solution in litres as V, then NV is equal to the number of equivalents of solute in the given volume of solution.

$$V\text{ (litres)} \times N\text{ (equiv/litre)} = \text{no. of equivalents}$$

or $$V\text{(mL)} \times \frac{N\text{ equiv/litre}}{1000\text{ mL/litre}} = \text{no. of equivalents}$$

4.2.5 Formality

The term *formality* is used for expressing the concentrations of ionic salts that do not exist as molecules in the solid or in the solution phase. The concentrations of their solutions are given as *formal* (F). Formality is numerically the same as molarity. For example, consider a solution of NaF(*aq*). In solution, NaF is almost completely ionised into Na^+(*aq*) and F^-(*aq*). Therefore, expressing the concentration of NaF(*aq*) in M – which implies that the solution contains molecules of NaF – is not accurate. In such a case, formality can be used. When a solution of NaF(*aq*) is said to be 0.1 F, it means that it has been prepared by dissolving 0.1 mole of NaF(*s*) in sufficient water to give a solution of 1 L. Thus, formality is used for describing concentrations of made-up solutions (that is, total analytical concentration). The formality of a solution is the number of gram formula weights of solute used in preparing one litre of the solution. For example, a solution prepared with 41.9882 g of NaF in one litre of the solution is a 1 F solution.

$$\text{F} = \frac{\text{Number of formula weights of solute}}{\text{Litres of solution}}$$

The formal concentration term gives definite information about how a solution has originally been prepared, but it does not necessarily indicate what happens to the particular solute after it dissolves. For example, a 1 F acetic acid solution in water does not contain 1 mol of undissociated acetic acid molecules because some of the molecules would have undergone dissociation. Therefore, such a solution cannot be precisely called a 1 M acetic acid solution. In such cases, the term formality is used. Because of the complex nature of aqueous solutions, the term formal rather than molar may be preferred. However, these two are used interchangeably.

Problem 4.10 A solution of oxalic acid dihydrate has NaOH titer of 10.00 mg mL^{-1}. Calculate the formality of the oxalic acid solution.

Solution

Oxalic acid and NaOH react according to the equation

$$H_2C_2O_4 + 2OH^- \longrightarrow C_2O_4^{2-} + 2H_2O$$

The equivalent weight of oxalic acid (a dibasic acid) is one-half of its molecular weight (1/2 × 126.0 = 63.0)

$$1\text{ mL of oxalic acid dihydrate} = 10.00\text{ mg NaOH}$$

$$1000\text{ mL of oxalic acid} = 10.00 \times 1000 = 10000\text{ mg (10 g) NaOH}$$

$$\therefore \quad \text{Normality of oxalic acid} = N_{NaOH} = \frac{10}{40} = 0.25\text{ N}$$

The amount of oxalic acid per litre = 0.25 N × 63 = 15.75 g

$$\therefore \qquad \text{Formality} = \frac{15.75}{126} = 0.125$$

4.2.6 Parts Per Million (ppm)

This unit of concentration is the number of parts of a component in 1 million parts of a mixture:

$$\text{ppm} = \frac{w}{w + w_0} \times 10^6$$

where w is the number of grams of solute and w_0 the number of grams of solvent. This unit is used for expressing very low concentrations. Therefore, the value of w is negligible compared to that of w_0; then,

$$\text{ppm} = \frac{w}{w_0} \times 10^6$$

For example, when 1 litre of an aqueous solution contains 1 mg of a solute, then the solute concentration

$$= \frac{1\ \text{mg}}{1000 \times 1000\ \text{mg}} = 1\ \text{ppm}$$

because 1 litre of water weighs 10^6 mg.

Problem 4.11 A medicinal solution contains 0.01207 g of potassium sulphate (K_2SO_4) in 1 litre. Express the concentration of potassium metal present in ppm.

Solution

The formula weight of $K_2SO_4 \equiv 174.25$

$$1 \text{ formula weight of } K_2\,SO_4 \equiv 2 \times 39.0983 \text{ g of K} \equiv 78.1966 \text{ g of K}$$

$$0.01207 \text{ g } K_2\,SO_4 \equiv \frac{78.1966}{174.25} \times 0.01207 \text{ g K}$$

$$\equiv 0.00542 \text{ g K} \equiv 5.42 \text{ mg K}$$

Therefore, the concentration of K in ppm in the solution = 5.42.

4.3 CALCULATION OF EQUIVALENT WEIGHTS

Equivalent weights have to be known for the preparation of primary standard solutions and for calculating amounts of substances in the analyte.

- The equivalent weight of a substance depends upon the type of reaction it undergoes in the titrations.

- A substance may have two or three equivalent weight values depending on the reactions in the titrations.
- It is not necessarily the same as the molar mass.

Equivalent weight of an acid It is the weight in grams of the acid required to furnish 1 mol (1.0088 g) of H^+.

$$1 \text{ eq of HCl} = 1 \text{ mole} = 36.5 \text{ g of HCl}$$

$$1 \text{ eq of } H_2SO_4 = \frac{1}{2} \text{ mole} = 49 \text{ g of } H_2SO_4$$

One mole of H_2SO_4 gives two moles of H^+ and therefore its equivalent weight is half of its molecular weight.

$$1 \text{ eq of } H_3PO_4 = \frac{1}{3} \text{ mole} = 97.9855 \text{ g}$$

We can titrate the first two protons of H_3PO_4 separately. The third is too weak to titrate. Then the equivalent weight of the acid is 1/2 mole = 146.978 (ignoring the third proton). Therefore, the equivalent weight of an acid is its formula weight divided by the number of reactive hydrogen atoms present in it. Such values for some acids, commonly used in titrimetry, are given in Table 4.2.

Table 4. 2 Equivalent weights of some acids

Acid	Formula	No. of replaceable hydrogens	Molar mass	Equivalent weight
Hydrochloric	HCl	1	36.46	36.46
Nitric	HNO_3	1	63.02	63.02
Sulphuric	H_2SO_4	2	98.08	49.04
Oxalic	$H_2C_2O_4 \bullet 2H_2O$	2	126.07	63.03
Phosphoric	H_3PO_4	3	98.00	32.66
Orthoboric	$B(OH)_3$	1	61.83	61.83
Formic	HCOOH	1	46.026	46.03
Acetic	CH_3COOH	1	60.05	60.05

Problem 4.12 Calculate the milliequivalent of oxalic acid dihydrate.

Solution

The molar mass of $(COOH)_2 \cdot H_2O$ = 126.064 g. It is a dibasic acid; therefore, its equivalent weight = 1/2 (molar mass) = 1/2 (126.064) g = 63.032 g.

$$1 \text{ milliequivalent} = \left(\frac{\text{equivalent}}{1000}\right) \text{g} = \left(\frac{63.032}{1000}\right) \text{g} = 0.063032 \text{ g}$$

Orthoboric acid $B(OH)_3$ is a weak monobasic acid though its molecule has three hydrogens.

$$B(OH)_3 + 2H_2O \rightleftharpoons H_3O^+ + B(OH)_4^-$$

Therefore, its equivalent weight is its molar mass, 61.8307 g. This shows that the equivalent weight of a substance cannot be guessed merely from its formula but can be known only from the actual reaction it undergoes in a titration.

Equivalent weight of a base It is the weight of the base (in grams) which reacts completely with 1 mole of H^+ (1 equivalent weight of an acid). It can also be defined as the weight of the base that will give one mole of OH^- ions. For example, 39.9967 g of NaOH gives one mole of OH^- (17.0069). Therefore, its equivalent weight is 39.9967 (its molar mass).

$$NaOH + HCl \longrightarrow NaCl + H_2O$$

This equation shows that the reaction between the acid and the base is balanced, and that one mole of the acid reacts with 1 mole of the base. With HCl or NaOH, the molar mass is also its equivalent weight. Thus, the equivalent weight of a substance can be calculated by writing the balanced (stoichiometric) equation between the analyte and titrant. The equivalent weights of some bases are listed in Table 4.3.

Table 4.3 Equivalent weights of some bases

Base	Molar mass	Equivalent weight
NaOH	39.9971	39.9971
KOH	56.1057	56.1053
$Ca(OH)_2$	79.0946	37.0473
$Ba(OH)_2$	179.3446	85.6723
NH_3	17.0304	17.0304
$C_6H_5NH_2$	92.1283	92.1283
$NaHCO_3$	84.0069	84.0069
Na_2CO_3	105.9888	52.9944
$CaCO_3$	100.0892	50.0446

Now, consider the reaction between the base baryta, $Ba(OH)_2$ and HCl:

$$Ba(OH)_2 + 2HCl \longrightarrow BaCl_2 + H_2O$$

This balanced equation shows that one mole of $Ba(OH)_2$ reacts completely with 2 moles (2 equivalents) of HCl. Therefore, the equivalent weight of $Ba(OH)_2$ is one-half of its molar mass, as it has two hydroxyl groups.

$$\frac{1}{2}(\text{molar mass}) = \frac{1}{2} \times 171.3438$$

$$= 85.6719 \text{ g}$$

$$\text{Equivalent weight} = \frac{\text{Molar mass}}{\text{equiv/mole}}$$

One equivalent of any acid will neutralise one equivalent of any base. The equivalents of acids and bases are represented in Table 4.4 by means of neutralisation reactions.

Table 4.4 Equivalents of acids and bases

Acid		Base		Products
HCl 1 eq mol^{-1}	+	KOH 1 eq mol^{-1}	$\longrightarrow$	$KCl + H_2O$
2 HCl 1 eq mol^{-1}	+	$Ca(OH)_2$ 2 eq mol^{-1}	$\longrightarrow$	$CaCl_2 + 2H_2O$
HCl 1 eq mol^{-1}	+	NH_3 1 eq mol^{-1}	$\longrightarrow$	NH_4Cl
H_2SO_4 2 eq mol^{-1}	+	2NaOH 1 eq mol^{-1}	$\longrightarrow$	$Na_2SO_4 + 2H_2O$
H_3PO_4 3 eq mol^{-1}	+	3NaOH 1 eq mol^{-1}	$\longrightarrow$	$Na_3PO_4 + 3H_2O$
H_3PO_4 2 eq mol^{-1}	+	2NaOH 1 eq mol^{-1}	$\longrightarrow$	$Na_2HPO_4 + 2H_2O$

Equal volumes of solutions of acids and bases of equal normalities will exactly neutralise each other. If the normality of one solution is not known, it can be determined from the volume of the other solution used in the reaction, using the relationship,

$$V_1N_1 = V_2N_2$$

where 1 and 2 denote the two solutions.

Problem 4.13 Calculate the mass of H_2SO_4 contained in 1 mL of commercial concentrated sulphuric acid that is 35.4 N. What is its molarity?

Solution

The number of equivalents in 1 mL of 35.4 N acid

$$= NV = (35.4\ \text{eq}^{-1})\left(\frac{1}{1000\ \text{litre}}\right) = 0.0354\ \text{eq}$$

The equivalent weight of H_2SO_4 is one-half the molecular weight; it is $\frac{98.0}{2} = 49.0\ \text{g eq}^{-1}$

Then, 0.0354 equiv

$$= (0.0354 \times 49.0)\ \text{g} = 1.7346\ \text{g}$$

$$\text{Molarity} = \frac{\text{Weight per litre}}{\text{Molar mass}}$$

$$= \frac{(1.7346 \times 1000)}{98.0} = 17.7\ \text{M}$$

Equivalent weight of an oxidant The equivalent weight of an oxidant is the weight of the oxidant that reacts with (accepts) 1 mole of electrons.

For example, consider the redox reaction between Fe^{2+} and MnO_4^- in acidic medium:

$$5Fe^{2+} + MnO_4^- + 8H^+ \longrightarrow 5Fe^{2+} + Mn^{2+} + 4H_2O$$

$$\underset{+7}{MnO_4^-} \longrightarrow \underset{+2}{Mn^{2+}}$$

One formula weight of MnO_4^- reacts with 5 moles of electrons; therefore the equivalent weight is 1/5 (formula weight). Then its equivalent weight

$$= \frac{\text{Molecular mass of } KMnO_4}{5}$$

$$= \frac{158.0323}{5} = 31.6065\ \text{g}$$

The oxidant $K_2Cr_2O_7$ is frequently used in titrimety. For example, it reacts with Sn(II) according to the equation,

$$Cr_2O_7^{2-} + 3Sn^{2+} + 14H^+ \longrightarrow 3Sn^{4+} + 2Cr^{3+} + 7H_2O$$

$$Cr_2O_7^{2-} \longrightarrow 2Cr^{3+}$$

One $Cr_2O_7^{2-}$ species accepts six electrons to form two Cr^{3+} ions:

$$2\ \text{Cr(VI)} \xrightarrow{6e^-} 2\ \text{Cr(III)}$$

Therefore, the equivalent weight of $Cr_2O_7^{2-}$

$$= \frac{\text{Formula weight}}{6}$$

For $K_2Cr_2O_7$ it is $\frac{(293.5888)}{6} = 48.9315$ g

Equivalent weight of a reductant It is the weight of the reductant which gives one mole of electrons. For example, in the reaction between Ce^{4+} and Fe^{2+},

$$Ce^{4+} + Fe^{2+} \longrightarrow Ce^{3+} + Fe^{3+}$$

one electron is transferred from Fe^{2+} to Ce^{4+}. Hence the equivalent weight of Fe^{2+} is the same as the formula weight. Similarly, the equivalent weight of Ce(IV) is its formula weight. In the redox reaction,

$$Cr_2O_7^{2-} + 6Fe^{2+} + 14H^+ \longrightarrow 2Cr^{3+} + 6Fe^{3+} + 7H_2O$$

the equivalent weight of the $Cr_2O_7^{2-}$ species is one-sixth of the formula weight, as each $Cr_2O_7^{2-}$ accepts a total of six electrons ($2Cr^{6+} \rightarrow 2Cr^{3+}$). When $SnCl_2$ is used in this titration instead of Fe^{2+}, then the equivalent weight of $SnCl_2$

$$= \frac{189.596}{2} = 94.798 \text{ g}$$

Problem 4.14 Each of the following equations represents a redox titrimetric method. Balance each equation and calculate the equivalent weight of the underlined species.

(i) $\underline{H_3AsO_3} + I_2 + H_2O \longrightarrow HAsO_4^{2-} + I^- + H^+$

(ii) $K_2Cr_2O_7 + \underline{[Fe(CN)_6]^{4-}} + H^+ \longrightarrow Cr^{3+} + [Fe(CN)_6]^{3-} + H_2O^+ + K^+$

Solution

(i) $H_3AsO_3 + I_2 + H_2O \longrightarrow HAsO_4^{2-} + 2I^- + 4H^+$

As (+III) → As(+V) I(0) → I^- (−1)
2-electron change 1-electron change

Therefore, the equivalent weight of H_3AsO_3 is one-half of its molar mass;

$1/2 \times 125.943 = 62.9712$

(ii) $K_2Cr_2O_7 + [Fe(CN)_6]^{4-} + 14H^+ \longrightarrow 2Cr^{3+} + 2[Fe(CN)_6]^{3-} + 7H_2O + 2K^+$

As it is a one-electron change, Fe(II) to Fe(III), the equivalent weight of $[Fe(CN)_6]^{4-}$ is its molecular weight.

Problem 4.15 A titration involves the following redox reaction,

$$Mn^{2+} + S_2O_8^{2-} + 4H_2O \longrightarrow MnO_4^- + 2\,SO_4^{2-} + 8H^+$$

Calculate the equivalent weight of Mn^{2+} used in the form, $MnSO_4$. How many mmoles of $S_2O_8^{2-}$ are needed to react with 1 meq of Mn^{2+}?

Solution

From the equation, the equivalent weight of $MnSO_4$ should be

$$= \frac{\text{molar mass}}{5} \text{ (five electrons are transferred in the reaction)}$$

$$= \frac{150.99}{5} = 30.198 \text{ g}$$

According to the stoichiometric equation, 1 mole of $S_2O_6^{2-}$ is required for reacting with 5 equivalents of Mn^{2+}. Therefore, the no. of mmoles of $S_2O_8^{2-}$ required for reacting with 1 mequiv of Mn^{2+},

$$= \frac{1 \text{ mmol } S_2O_8^{2-}}{5 \text{ mequiv } Mn^{2+}} = 0.2 \text{ mmole}$$

Problem 4.16 A 1.0000 g sample of an alloy of tin was dissolved in an oxidising acid, and the tin(IV) in the resulting solution was reduced to tin(II). Titration of the tin(II) solution required 40.20 mL of 0.1000 N $K_2Cr_2O_7$. Calculate the percentage of tin in the alloy.

Solution

In this titration, Sn(II) is oxidised to Sn(IV); this is a two-electron reaction. Therefore, the equivalent weight of Sn is 1/2 (atomic weight) = 1/2 × 118.69

$$= 59.35$$

Therefore, 1000 mL of 1N $K_2Cr_2O_7$ $\equiv$ 59.35 g Sn

40.20 mL of 0.1000 N $K_2Cr_2O_7$ $\equiv 59.35 \times \left(\frac{40.20}{1000}\right) \times 0.1000$ N g Sn

$$\equiv 0.2386 \text{ g}$$

Thus, 1 g of the alloy contains 0.2386 g Sn. Then, the percentage of tin present in the alloy

$$= \frac{0.2386}{1.0000} \times 100 = 23.9$$

The balanced chemical reaction (equation) should always be considered in calculating the results of a titration. To understand this, let us consider the titration of phosphoric acid with sodium hydroxide.

The formula of the acid H_3PO_4 might indicate that it is tribasic and its equivalent weight is one-third of its formula weight. However, the third hydrogen is too weakly acidic and hence it does not react when titrated with NaOH. By using phenolphthalein indicator, two hydrogens are titrated. Therefore, in this titration,

$$\text{Equivalent weight of } H_3PO_4 = \frac{\text{Formula weight}}{2}$$

$$H_3PO_4 \longrightarrow Na_2HPO_4$$

$$= \frac{98.00}{2} = 49.00$$

With methyl orange indicator, the end point corresponds to the reaction of only one hydrogen of H_3PO_4.

$$H_3PO_4 \longrightarrow NaH_2PO_4$$

Then, the equivalent weight of the acid will be the formula weight itself (98.00).

4.3.1 Classification of Reactions in Titrimetry

There are four types of reactions involved in titrimetry.

(i) *Neutralisation reactions, or acidimetry and alkalimetry*: The titration of a free base or a salt of a weak acid with a standard acid is *acidimetry*. The titration of a free acid or an acid formed by the hydrolysis of the salt of a weak base with a standard base is *alkalimetry*.
(ii) *Oxidation-reduction*: These are redox reactions involving transfer of electrons among the reacting substances. The standard solutions are either oxidising or reducing agents.
(iii) *Complex formation reactions*: These titrations involve the reaction between a metal ion and a complexing agent to form a coordination compound. In such titirations, a metal ion indicator is used to detect the equivalence point.
(iv) *Precipitation reactions*: The reaction of the analyte with the titrant produces a precipitate in a precipitation titration. It does not involve change in oxidation state.

4.4 THEORIES OF TITRATIONS

The most important aspect of carrying out titrations is the correct detection of end points because this influences the accuracy of results. The theories of detecting end points are discussed in this section.

4.4.1 Acid–Base Titration

Acid–base titrations are of different types.

4.4.1.1 Strong Acid Versus Strong Base

An acid–base titration involves a neutralisation reaction in which an acid is reacted with an equivalent amount of a base. At the end point, the neutralisation is theoretically 100%. The end point signals the completion of the reaction.

Titration curve By constructing a titration curve, we can explain how end points can be detected. A titration curve is drawn by plotting the pH of the solution being titrated as a function of the volume of the titrant added.

The titrant is always a strong acid or a strong base; it is taken in the burette. The analyte is a strong base or an acid, or a weak base or an acid. In the case of a titration involving a strong acid versus a strong base, both the titrant and the analyte are completely ionised. An example for this is the titration of hydrochloric acid with sodium hydroxide;

$$H^+Cl^- + Na^+OH^- \longrightarrow H_2O + Na^+ + Cl^-$$

The H^+ and OH^- combine to form H_2O, the other ions Na^+ and Cl^- remain unchanged; the net result of neutralisation is the conversion of HCl to a neutral solution of NaCl. The titration curve of this reaction is drawn by plotting pH values against volumes of NaOH solution added to HCl during the titration. The curve for 100 mL of 0.1 N HCl titrated with 0.1 N NaOH is shown in Fig.4.2.

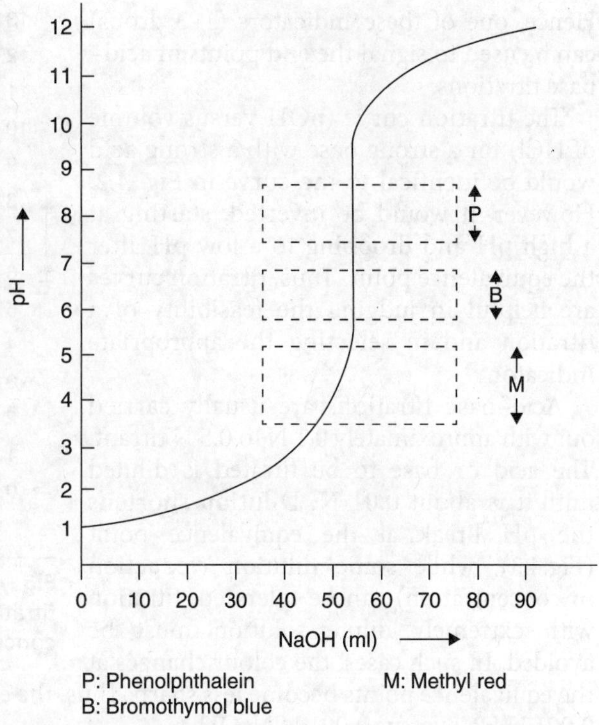

Fig. 4.2 Titration curve for 100 mL of 0.1 N HCl versus 0.1 N NaOH

At the beginning of the titration, only 0.1 N HCl is present making the pH 1.0. As the titration proceeds, a part of the H^+ ions are removed from solution as H_2O; the concentration of H^+ gradually decreases. At 90% neutralisation – after the addition of 90 mL NaOH – only 10% of H^+ remains. The H^+ concentration at this point is 10^{-2} M, and the pH has risen by only one pH unit (pH 1 to pH 2). The volume changes are neglected for simplicity of understanding. As the equivalence point approaches – the point at which a stoichiometric amount of NaOH has been added – the H^+ concentration gets rapidly reduced. At the equivalence point, the neutralisation is complete and no H^+ remains; only neutral NaCl is present in the medium; therefore, the pH rises to 7.0. On further addition of NaOH, the OH^- concentration increases and therefore the pH rapidly increases immediately after the equivalence point; it then levels off between 10^{-2} and 10^{-1} N of OH^-. Thus, the pH remains fairly constant on either side of the equivalence point, but it changes markedly very near the equivalence point. Therefore, the measurement of the pH or some property related to the pH can indicate the equivalence point of the titration. The equations governing the different portions of the titration curve for a strong acid with a strong base are given in Table 4.5.

Table 4.5 Equations pertaining to a strong acid (HX) or strong base (BOH) titration

Fraction F titrated	Strong acid		Strong base	
	Present	**Equation**	**Present**	**Equation**
F = 0	HX	$[H^+] = [HX]$	BOH	$[OH^-] = [BOH]$
0 < F < 1	HX/X^-	$[H^+]$ = [remaining HX]	BOH/B^+	$[OH^-]$ = [remaining BOH]
F = 1	X^-	$[H^+] = \sqrt{K_w}$	B^+	$[H^+] = \sqrt{K_w}$
F >1	OH^-/X^-	$[OH^-]$ = [excess titrant]	H^+/B^+	$[H^+]$ = [excess titrant]

The 'boxed' areas in Fig. 4.2 are the 'ranges' over which the three visual indicators change colour. The large increase in pH at the equivalence point causes colour changes in these indicators.

Hence, one of these indicators (1–3 drops) can be used to signal the end points in acid–base titrations.

The titration curve (pOH versus volume of HCl) for a strong base with a strong acid would be identical to the curve in Fig. 4.2. However, it would be inverted, starting at a high pH and dropping to a low pH after the equivalence point. Thus, titration curves are helpful in judging the feasibility of a titration and in selecting the appropriate indicator.

Acid–base titrations are usually carried out with approximately 0.1 N to 0.5 N titrant. The acid or base to be titrated is diluted until it is about 0.01 N. Dilution shortens the pH break at the equivalence point (Fig.4.3); while some dilution (reduction in concentration) can be tolerated, titration with extremely dilute solution must be avoided. In such cases, the colour changes at the equivalence points become less sharp. Thus, the equivalence point pH break is the least for 0.001 N HCl versus 0.001 N NaOH.

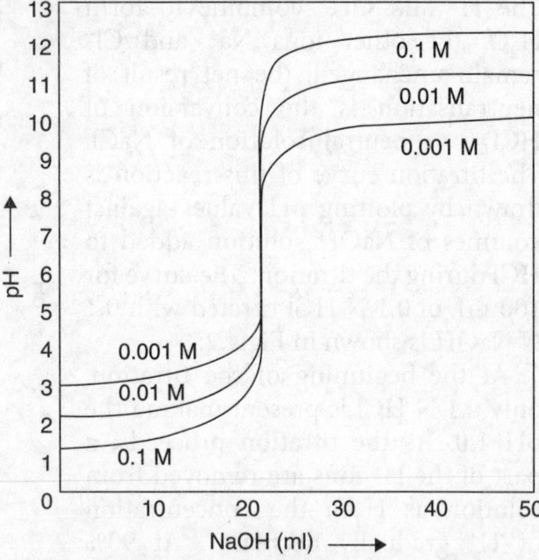

Fig. 4.3 Titration curve for hydrochloric acid titrated with sodium hydroxide at different concentrations

4.4.1.2 Weak Acid Versus with Strong Base; Weak Base Versus Strong Acid

Consider a weak acid of the neutral type (HA) or of the charged type (BH^+); it reacts with a strong basic titrant such as sodium hydroxide to form the conjugate base, A^- or B.

$$HA + OH^- \longrightarrow A^- + H_2O$$

$$BH^+ + OH^- \longrightarrow B + H_2O$$

The shape of such a titration curve will depend on the value of the ionisation constant and to a lesser extent on the concentration of the acid titrated.

A plot of the titration curve for 0.10 N benzoic acid (a weak acid) with sodium hydroxide (a strong base) from 0% to 100% is shown in Fig. 4.4. At 0% titration, the solution has only benzoic acid; it is weakly acidic with a pH of about 3. On adding NaOH, the pH increases; near the equivalence point and immediately after the equivalence point, the pH increases sharply. The pH levels off as more NaOH is added after the equivalence point.

Titration of a weak base with a strong acid An example for this type of reaction is the titration of sodium benzoate with hydrochloric acid.

$$A^- + H^+ \longrightarrow HA$$

$$C_6H_5COO^- + H^+ \xrightarrow[\text{(HCl)}]{} C_6H_5COOH$$

The titration curve in this case is traced by starting at the pH of A^- (Fig. 4.4) and retracing the curve from right to left (A^- to HA). On adding hydrochloric acid beyond the equivalence point, the pH will decrease further and then level off as shown on the left-portion of the figure. The end point in this titration is not very sharp because A^- is a weak base. The curve will be in the reverse position but without a sharp change.

Notes about titration curves

- At the midpoint in any titration (halfway between HA and A^- or between BH^+ and B), the pH is always equal to the pK_a of the acid.
- In the titration of any acid, the sharpness of the pH break at the end point decreases as the K_b of the acid becomes smaller. For weak acids with K_a = 10–9, the end point break is so slight that titration in aqueous solution is not reliable.
- The magnitude (the height) of the break depends on both the concentration of the acid and the concentration of the base.
- In the titration of bases, the titration becomes more accurate as the K_a of the conjugate acid becomes smaller; this is because the K_b becomes larger.

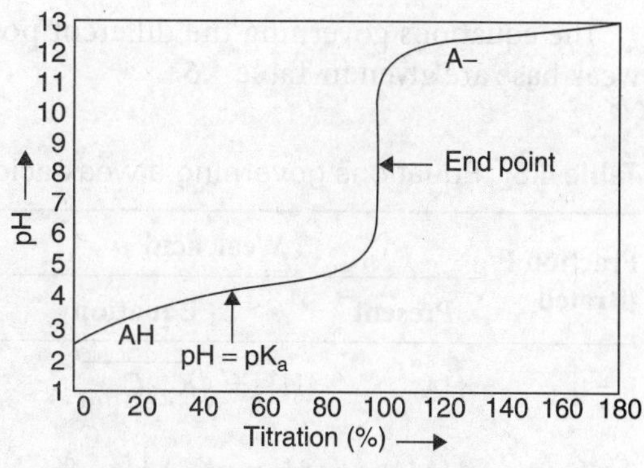

Fig. 4.4 Titration of 0.1 M benzoic acid with 0.1 N sodium hydroxide

Titration of two acids or two bases of different strengths A mixture of two acids can be titrated and estimated only if the strong acid reacts first and gives a pH break at its equivalence point. Then, the weak acid reacts and gives a second pH break at its equivalence point. For example, a mixture of HCl and CH_3COOH, with appreciable difference in acid strengths can be estimated by titrating the mixture against NaOH (Fig. 4.5). The first break (lower portion) in the curve corresponds to HCl neutralisation and the second one corresponds to CH_3COOH neutralisation. A titration in which a separate end point is obtained for each of two or more constituents in a mixture is called a *differentiating titration.*

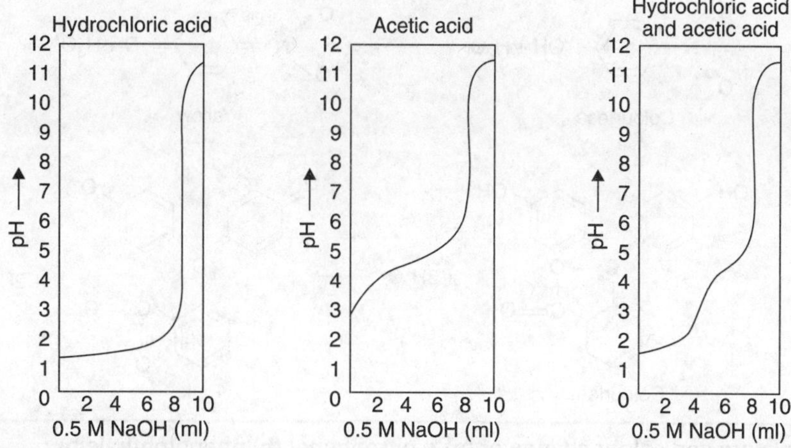

Fig. 4.5 Titration curves for the differentiating titration of hydrochloric and acetic acids with sodium hydroxide

A mixture of acetic acid and lactic acid cannot be estimated by titration with an alkali as their K_a values do not differ appreciably. Their individual titration curves are very similar, and the curve for the mixture shows only one pH break when the sum of the two acids has been neutralised.

A diprotic acid can be titrated against a strong base to give two breaks in its titration curve provided its two acid constants K_1 and K_2 differ appreciably (K_1/K_2 should be greater than 10^3). The sharpness of the first break increases as this ratio becomes larger.

The equations governing the different portions of the titration curve for a weak acid or a weak base are given in Table 4.6.

Table 4.6 Equations governing a weak acid (HA) or weak base (B) titration

Fraction F titrated	Weak acid		Weak base	
	Present	**Equation**	**Present**	**Equation**
$F = 0$	HA	$[H^+] = \sqrt{K_a \cdot C_{HA}}$	B	$[OH^-] = \sqrt{K_b \cdot C_B}$
$0 < F < 1$	HA/A⁻	$pH = pK_a + \log \dfrac{C_{A^-}}{C_{HA}}$	B/BH⁺	$pH = [pK_w - pK_b] + \log\left(\dfrac{C_B}{C_{BH^+}}\right)$
$F = 1$	A^-	$[OH^-] = \sqrt{\dfrac{K_w}{K_a} \cdot C_{A^-}}$	BH^+	$[H^+] = \sqrt{\dfrac{K_w}{K_b} C_{BH^+}}$
$F > 1$	OH^-/A^-	$[OH^-]$ = [excess titrant]	H^+/BH^+	$[H^+]$ = [excess titrant]

4.4.2 Acid–Base Indicators

As already described, a large change in pH occurs when equivalence points are reached in acid–base titrations; this change is used for detecting the equivalence point. Some organic acids and bases have different colours in their undissociated and ionic forms. For example, *p-nitrophenol* is colourless in its undissociated form but yellow in its ionic form.

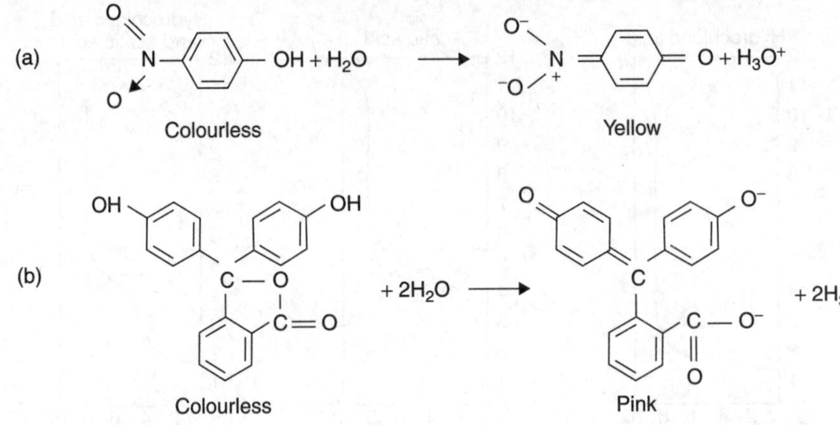

Fig. 4.6 Structure and colour change of **(a)** *p*-nitrophenol **(b)** phenolphthalein

Phenolphthalein is a diprotic acid; it is colourless. It dissociates to its colourless monoanion first and then to its coloured dianion. The dianion is a conjugated system and it is red (Fig. 4.6).

Methyl orange is a base and is yellow in its molecular form. On forming its conjugate acid with a proton, it becomes pink (Fig. 4.7).

Such molecules that change colour at the neutralisation point are called *visual indicators.*

Molecules or ions having conjugated systems absorb light of longer wavelengths compared to molecules in which no conjugated system exists. The light absorbed is often in the visible region of the spectrum. Let an acidic indicator be denoted as HIn and a basic inditator as InOH. Their dissociations are represented as

$$HIn + H_2O \longrightarrow H_3O^+ + In^-$$

$$InOH \longrightarrow In^+ + OH^-$$

The dissociation constant for the acid

$$K_a = \frac{[H_3O^+][In^-]}{[HIn]}$$

$$\log K_a = \log [H_3O^+] + \log[In^-] - \log[HIn]$$

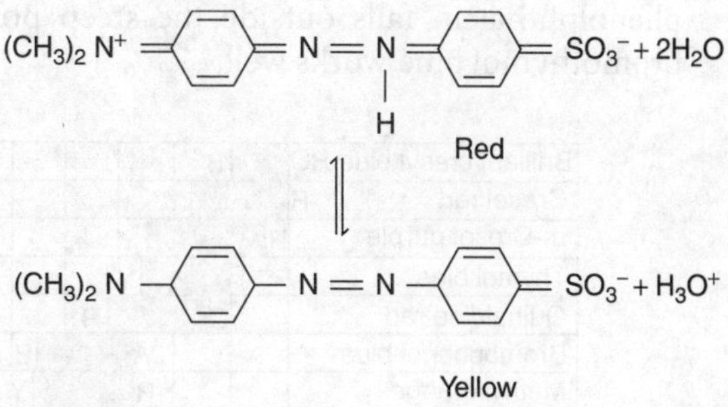

$(CH_3)_2N^+$ = ⟨ ⟩ = N — N(H) — ⟨ ⟩ — $SO_3^- + 2H_2O$ Red ⇌ $(CH_3)_2N$ — ⟨ ⟩ — N = N — ⟨ ⟩ — $SO_3^- + H_3O^+$ Yellow

Fig. 4.7 Methyl orange

The last equation can be written as a *Henderson–Hasselbalch* equation:

$$pH = pK_a + \log \frac{[In^-]}{[HIn]}$$

The indicator changes colour over a pH range. This transition range depends on the ability of the observer to detect small colour changes. With indictors in which both forms are coloured, generally only one colour is observed if the ratio of the concentration of the two forms is 10:1; only the colour of the more concentrated form is observed. Form this fact, the pH transition range required to go from one colour to the other can be calculated.

When only the colour of the unionised form is seen, $[In^-]/[HIn] = 1/10$

$$pH = pK_a + \log\frac{1}{10} = pK_a - 1$$

When only the colour of the ionised form is observed,

$$\frac{[In^-]}{[HIn]} = \frac{10}{1}$$

$$pH = pK_a + \log\frac{10}{1} = pK_a + 1$$

Therefore, the pH in going from one colour to the other has changed from $(pK_a - 1)$ to $(pK_a + 1)$. This is a pH change of 2. Thus, most indicators require a transition range of about two pH units. During this transition, the colour observed is a blend of the two colours. Midway in the transition, the concentrations of the two forms are equal, and hence $pH = pK_a$. This shows that the pK_a of the indicator should be close to the pH of the equivalence point.

Weak base indicators show a similar transition range; the pOH midway in the transition is equal to pK_b; the pH equals $14 - pK_b$. The colours and transition ranges of some commonly used indicators are shown in Fig. 4.8. The following are the highlights.

- The pH range is less than two units in some cases.
- Some colours are prominent; hence they can be easily and clearly seen during titrations.
- Some indicators change from colourless to coloured species or vice versa; such a transition is easier to see and hence the end points are sharp (phenolphthalein, colourless–pink). Thus, this indicator is preferred for strong acid–base titrations. However, in dilute solutions,

phenolphthalein falls outside the steep portion of the titration curve; in such a case, bromothymol blue works well.

Indicator	Colour change
Brilliant cresyl blue	RO – B; B – Y
Cresol red	R – Y; Y – R
m-Cresol purple	R – Y
Thymol blue	R – Y; Y – B
Quinaldine red	C – R
Bromophenol blue	Y – B
Methyl orange	R – Y
Congo red	B – R
Bromocresol green	Y – B
Methyl red	R – Y
Chlorophenol red	Y – R
4-Nitrophenol	C – Y
Bromocresol purple	Y – P
Bromothymol blue	Y – B
Neutral red	R – O
Phenol red	Y – R
1-Naphtholphthalein	Y – B
Phenolphthalein	C – R
Thymolphthalein	C – B
Alizarin yellow R	Y – RO
Tropaeolin O	Y – O

Fig. 4.8 Titrimetric indicators: colour change intervals

4.4.2.1 Amount of Indicator

Since an indicator is an acid or a base (though weak), the amount of indicator added should be minimum so that it does not contribute appreciably to the pH and so that only a small amount of (excess) titrant will be required to cause a change in colour. The colour change will be sharper when the concentration of the indicator is lower because less acid or base is required to convert it from one form to the other. However, sufficient indicator must be added to impart

W Ostwald

The first useful theory of indicator was suggested by W Ostwald in 1895 based on the concept that indicators are very weak acids or bases. During his time, the concept of pH was not established. Ostwald simply proposed acid–base inter-conversion of indicator molecules. This theory was improved after the development of the pH scale by S P L Sorensen (1909) and the establishment of structures of indicators. Thus Ostwald's theory was the basis for later theories of indicators.

Source: By Nicola Perscheid - http://www.gettyimages.co.uk/detail/news-photo/ostwald-wilhelm-chemist-philosopher-germany-obtained-the-news-photo/537147985, Public Domain, https://commons.wikimedia.org/w/index.php?curid=44052385

a colour to the solution that is easily visible. Generally, a very dilute (say 0.1% wt/vol) solution of the indicator is prepared; a few drops of it are used. For example, two drops (0.1 mL) of 0.01 M indicator (0.1 % solution with F wt = 100) is equal to 0.01 mL of 0.1 M titrant. This is unlikely to cause any error in the titration.

4.4.2.2 Indicator Colour Change Interval

Neutralisation indicators (acid–base indicators) change colour according to the hydrogen ion concentration of the solution. The chief nature of these indicators is that they change from a predominantly acid colour to predominantly alkaline colour. This change is not sudden and abrupt, but occurs within a small pH *range* (usually about two pH units). This is called the *colour change interval* of the indicator. The position of the colour change interval in the pH scale depends on the indicator. For most acid–base titrations, the indicator should be carefully selected so that it shows a distinct colour change at a pH close to the equivalence pH. The colour changes and pH ranges of certain indicators are given in Table 4.7.

Table 4.7 Colour change and pH ranges of certain indicators

Indicator	pH range	Colour	
		In acid	In base
Phenolphthalein	8.3–10.0	Colourless	Red
Methy orange	2.9–4.6	Red	Orange
Methyl red	4.2–6.3	Red	Yellow
Thymol blue	1.2–2.8	Red	Yellow
Congo red	3.0–5.0	Blue	Red
p-Nitrophenol	5.0–7.0	Colourless	Yellow
Phenol red	6.8–8.4	Yellow	Red
Cresol red	7.2–8.8	Yellow	Red
Alizarin yellow R	10.1–12.1	Yellow	Orange-red

4.4.2.3 Choice of Acid–base Indicators

In a neutralisation titration, the equivalence point can be detected properly only when the pH changes by approximately two units near the stoichiometric end point produced by the addition of a small volume of the titrant. The pH change on both sides of the equivalence point can be seen from the titration curve. This pH change should bring about a change of colour of the indicator. The indicator is so chosen that it changes its colour at or near the equivalent point. The choices of suitable indicators may now be listed.

(i) *Strong acid and strong base:* Any indicator, which has the range between pH 4.5 and 9.5 may be used for 0.1 M or more concentrated solutions. When the concentration is 0.01 M, the pH range is smaller, 5.5–8.5. If the solution has dissolved CO_2, it should be boiled to expel CO_2, cooled and then titrated; otherwise, an indicator with a range below pH 5 should be used when carbonic acid would not interfere.

(ii) *Weak acid and strong base*: Thymol blue, thymolphthalein or phenolphthalein can be used.

(iii) *Weak base and strong acid*: Methyl red, methyl orange, bromocresol green or bromophenol blue is a suitable indicator for this titration.

(iv) *Weak acid and weak base*: The neutralisation curve for this titration does not have a sharp rise indicative of the equivalence point. Therefore, this type of titration should be avoided. A mixed indicator, for example, neutral red–methylene blue is suitable. This indicator exhibits a colour change over a very narrow pH range. For example, diluted ammonia solution can be titrated against ethanoic acid using this mixed indicator.

- When an indicator does not give a sharp end point, then an equal volume of a blank solution, containing the same quantity of the indicator and final product is prepared.

The end point is assumed to be attained when the colour of the solution exactly matches with the colour of the blank.

- No indicator may work satisfactorily with some sets of acids and bases, for example, dark coloured acids and bases. In such cases, potentiometry or coulometry may be adopted.
- Certain titrations, which are not feasible in aqueous medium, may be performed well in a non-aqueous medium. Changes in degrees of acidic and basic properties render a non-aqueous medium better suited for neutralisation. Solubility may be another factor for choosing a non-aqueous medium for titrations; some organic substances which are insoluble in water, require non-aqueous media for titrations.
- The selection of the indicator becomes more critical as the solution becomes more dilute.
- The best indicator for a titration is the one whose pK_a is nearest the equivalence point pH.

4.4.2.4 Mixed Indicators

The colour change extends over two units of pH with an ordinary acid–base indicator, and therefore it is not very sharp. For a sharp colour change over a narrow and selected pH range, a mixture of two indicators is used for some titrations. The two indicators selected for a mixture should have their pK'_{In} values very close and their overlapping colours complementary at an intermediate pH value. Some examples are discussed below.

(i) *Neutral red and methylene blue*: This mixed indicator gives sharp colour change from violet blue to green in passing from acid to alkaline solution at pH 7. The indicator solution is prepared by mixing equal volumes of 0.1% solutions of the two in ethanol. This indictor may be used to titrate ethanoic acid with ammonia solution or vice versa. In this case, both acid and base have approximately the same strength and hence the equivalent point lies at pH $\approx$ 7. This titration has to be performed with an indicator of very narrow pH range because the salt formed undergoes hydrolysis and the titration curve is almost flat.

(ii) *Thymol blue and cresol red*: A mixture of thymol blue (three volumes of a 0.1% aqueous solution of the sodium salt) and cresol red (1 volume of a 0.1% aqueous solution of the sodium salt) is used for the titration. It changes from yellow (in acid) to violet (in base) at pH 8.3. It may be used for the titration of carbonate to the hydrogencarbonate stage.

(iii) *Phenolphthalein and 1-naphtholphthalein*: This mixed indicator is prepared by mixing 3 volumes of a 0.1% ethanolic solution of phenolphthalein with 1 volume of a 0.1% ethanolic solution of 1-naphtholphathein. It changes from pale rose (in acid) to violet (in base) at pH 8.9. It may be used for the titration of phosphoric acid to the diprotic stage. The equivalence point lies at pH 8.7.

4.4.3 Redox Titrations

A redox titration is the titration of a reducing agent with an oxidising agent. The following are some common redox titrations:

Fe(II)	versus	$KMnO_4$
Oxalic acid	versus	$KMnO_4$
H_2O_2	versus	$KMnO_4$
NO_2^-	versus	$KMnO_4$
As(III)	versus	Ce(IV)
Fe(II)	versus	Ce(IV)
Fe(II)	versus	$K_2Cr_2O_7$

A number of inorganic and organic substances can be determined by titration with a standard solution of an oxidising or a reducing titrant. Certain conditions have to be fulfilled for quantitative determination by oxidation–reduction titrimetry.

- The analyte should be in a particular oxidation state. For example, iron has to be in its divalent state for its determination using $KMnO_4$ or $K_2Cr_2O_7$. Therefore, this condition sometimes necessitates a preliminary chemical treatment of the analyte. For example, if the analyte is in the Fe(III) state, then it has to reduced to the Fe(II) state. Zinc metal, coated with zinc amalgam is usually used for this reduction.

$$2\,Fe^{3+} + Zn \rightleftharpoons 2\,Fe^{2+} + Zn^{2+}$$

- The redox reaction that occurs during the titration should be quantitative and irreversible; only then stoichiometric calculation is possible.
- The redox reaction must be fast for direct titration. For example, the redox reaction between Fe(II) and $KMnO_4$ is fast enough for direct titration. When the reaction is slow, an indirect titration may be adopted. In this procedure, a measured excess of the standard oxidising solution is added to the sample and sufficient time is allowed for completion of the reaction. Then, the excess (unreacted) oxidant is *back-titrated* with a standard reducing solution that reacts rapidly with the oxidant. For example, in the determination of phenol with bromine, bromination is not very fast. Hence, in this determination, standard bromate–bromide solution is added in excess, and the excess is determined by the indirect iodine method.
- The end point must be easily and clearly detectible. A visible indicator is necessary for this. Alternatively, a potentiometric end point detection method can be adopted.

4.4.3.1 Redox Indicators

Redox indicators are of several types.

(i) A *self indicator* that is a coloured reagent – analyte or titrant – may act as its own indicator. For example, potassium permanganate solution is so deeply coloured that a slight excess of this reagent in a titration can be easily detected.

(ii) A *specific indicator* is a substance which reacts in a specific way with one of the reagents to produce a colour in a titration. For example, starch indicator forms a deep blue colour with iodine; thiocyanate ion indicator forms a red colour with Fe(III).

(iii) An *external indicator* is used when no internal indicator is available. The end point is detected by spot test; a negligible portion of the reacting solution is added to the indicator on a spot plate, and the colour developed indicates the end point. The ferricyanide ion is an external indicator used in the titration of Fe(II) with potassium dichromate. Fe(II) and ferricyanide ion react to form iron(II) ferricyanide (Turnbull's blue).

(iv) The *change of potential* values during a redox titration can be measured and then a titration curve – potential versus volume of titrant – is drawn. The equivalence point is indicated by a dramatic change in this curve.

(v) A *true redox indicator* is an indicator which itself undergoes oxidation–reduction. The oxidised and reduced forms of such an indicator have different colours. At the equivalence point, either due to its oxidation or reduction, a colour change occurs signalling the completion of the titration.

Let us designate an indicator molecule as In. Then, the redox couple is

$$In^{+} + e^{-} \longrightarrow In$$

Oxidised form Reduced form

Colour 1 Colour 2

The equation to calculate the potential of this system is

$$E = E_i^0 - 0.059 \log \frac{[In]}{[In^+]}$$

Where E_i^o is the standard potential of the indicator couple.

When $[In]/[In^+]$ is 10 or greater, only colour 2 can be seen; when this ratio is one or less, only colour 1 can be seen. Therefore,

$$\text{Colour 2:} \quad E = E_i^0 - 0.059 \log \frac{10}{1}$$

$$= E_i^0 - 0.059$$

$$\text{Colour 1:} \quad E = E_i^0 - 0.059 \log \frac{1}{10}$$

$$= E_i^0 + 0.059$$

subtracting, $\Delta E = \pm 2 \times 0.059 = \pm 0.12$ V

This calculation shows that a change in potential of about 0.12 V is needed to bring about a change in colour of the indicator. This potential is called the *transition potential.* Theoretically, the transition potential represents exactly 50% conversion of one form of the indicator to the other. However, this is not always the case; it is because the two coloured forms of the indicator are not equally intense to the eye. With ferroin for example, the formal potential is +1.06 V; however, the visual end point can be seen clearly (deep red to pale blue) only when the potential reaches about +1.11 V. The transition potentials of some redox indicators are given in Table 4.8.

Table 4.8 Transition potentials of some redox indicators

Indicator	Colour of reductant	Colour of oxidant	Transition potential (V)	Condition
Diphenylamine	Colourless	Violet	0.76	1 M H_2SO_4
Diphenylbenzidine	Colourless	Violet	0.76	1 M H_2SO_4
Diphenylamine-sulphonic acid	Colourless	Red-violet	0.85	Dil. acid
Ferroin	Red	Faint blue	1.11	1 M H_2SO_4
Methylene blue	Colourless	Blue	0.53	1 M acid

4.4.3.2 Structural Chemistry of Redox Indicators

The colour changes observed with redox indicators at the equivalence point are due to structural changes in the indicator molecules. The redox indicators used are organic molecules; they undergo structural changes upon getting oxidised or reduced. This can be illustrated with ferroin indicator which is the iron(II) complex of the organic compound 1,10-phananthroline (Fig. 4.9).

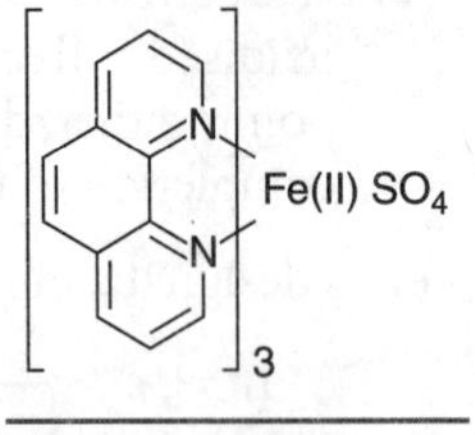

Fig. 4.9 Structure of ferroin indicator

Each of the two nitrogen atoms in 1,10-phenanthroline has an unshared pair of electrons that can be shared with the Fe(II) ion. Three such ligand molecules get attached to one Fe(II) ion to form a blood-red complex ion. This complex can be oxidised to the corresponding light blue Fe(III) complex with the same structure. Therefore, a sharp colour change from red to blue occurs on oxidation of the complex.

$$\underset{\text{(blue)}}{[Ph_3Fe]^{3+}} + e^- \longrightarrow \underset{\text{(red)}}{[Ph_3Fe]^{2+}} \quad E^0 = 1.06\ \text{V}$$

The indicator is prepared by mixing equivalent quantities of iron(II) sulphate and 1,10-phenanthroline. The resulting Fe(II) complex sulphate is called ferroin. The Fe(III) complex sulphate is called *ferriin.* The colour change actually occurs at about 1.11 V (not at 1.06 V), since the colour of ferroin is so much more intense than that of ferriin.

4.4.3.3 Calculations

For calculations in redox titrations, the normality unit is used. The equivalent weight of a substance involved in a redox reaction is the formula weight of the substance divided by the number of electrons transferred in the redox reaction.

$$\text{Equivalent weight} = \frac{\text{Formula weight } (w_f)}{\text{No. of } e^- \text{ transferred}}$$

The redox reactions commonly involved in titrations that are given below illustrate this concept.

Reaction	No. of e^- transferred	Equivalent weight of reactant
$Fe^{2+} \longrightarrow Fe^{3+} + e^-$	1	$w_f/1$
$KMnO_4 + 5e^- \longrightarrow Mn^{2+}$	5	$w_f/5$
$Na_2S_2O_3{\bullet}5H_2O \longrightarrow 1/2\ S_4O_6^{2-} + e^-$	1	$w_f/1$
$H_2S \longrightarrow SO_4^{2-} + 8e^-$	8	$w_f/8$ [S(–II) to S(+VI)]
$Cr_2O_7^{2-} + 6e^- \longrightarrow 2Cr^{3+}$	6	$w_f/6$
$Ce^{4+} + e^- \longrightarrow Ce^{3+}$	1	$w_f/1$

Problem 4.17 A sample of iron ore contains 60% Fe. Calculate the weight of the ore sample used when 25.6 mL of 0.1000N $K_2Cr_2O_7$ is required for titration of the solution of the ore sample.

Solution

$$1000\ \text{mL}\ 1\ \text{N}\ K_2Cr_2O_7 \equiv 55.847\ \text{g Fe}$$

$$25.6\ \text{mL}\ 0.1000\ \text{N}\ K_2Cr_2O_7 \equiv 55.847 \times \frac{25.6}{1000} \times 0.1000 = 0.1430\ \text{g}$$

$$60\%\ \text{Fe} = 0.1430\ \text{g}$$

$$\text{Weight of ore sample taken} = \frac{0.1430 \times 100}{60} = 0.2383\ \text{g}$$

Problem 4.18 25.0 mL of a solution of Fe(III) containing 40.000 g of $(NH_4)_2SO_4 \cdot Fe_2(SO_4)_3 \cdot x\,H_2O$ per litre is reduced to Fe(II) and then titrated with 25.4 mL of $K_2Cr_2O_7$ solution, containing 4.0012 g of $K_2Cr_2O_7$. Find out the value of *x*.

Solution

The normality of the dichromate solution

$$N_{K_2Cr_2O_7} = \frac{4.0012}{(294.19/6)} = 0.0816$$

The amount of $(NH_4)_2SO_4 \cdot Fe_2(SO_4)_3$ in the alum sample taken

$$= (25.4 \times 0.0816)\left(\frac{0.5320}{2}\right) = 0.5513 \text{ g}$$

Therefore, per cent of $(NH_4)_2\,SO_4 \cdot Fe_2(SO_4)_3$

$$= \frac{0.5513 \times (1000/25) \times 100}{40} = 55.13$$

Hence, the per cent of H_2O in the alum

$$= 100.00 - 55.13 = 44.87$$

$$= \frac{18.015x}{(18.015x + 532.02)} \times 100 = 44.87$$

$$x = 24$$

With a titrant such as $KMnO_4$, the equivalent weight has to be calculated carefully based on the number of electrons transferred in the titration. This number can vary depending on the experimental conditions and the nature of products.

Acidic	$KMnO_4 \rightarrow Mn^{2+}$	: 5-electron reaction
Neutral	$KMnO_4 \rightarrow Mn^{4+}$	: 3-electron reaction
Basic	$KMnO_4 \rightarrow MnO_4^{2-}$	: 1-electron reaction
In the presence of F^-	$KMnO_4 \rightarrow Mn^{3+}$	: 4-electron reaction

Thus, the same oxidant $KMnO_4$ will have four different equivalent weights in four types of reactions.

4.4.4 Iodometric and Iodimetric Titrations

Iodine is a solid that is insoluble in water. However, it is extremely soluble in aqueous potassium iodide. The iodine reacts with iodide ion and forms a soluble anionic complex.

$$I_2 + I^- \longrightarrow I_3^-$$

This reaction increases the solubility of iodine. I_3^- is deep red-brown and soluble in water. Pure samples of iodine are available in the market. However, iodine cannot serve as a primary standard as its solutions are not very stable; slight changes in concentration occur over a few hours due to the volatility of iodine. Solutions of iodine should therefore be standardised just prior to their use as titrants. A solution of iodine can be prepared by dissolving a carefully weighed portion of elemental iodine in an aqueous iodide solution. Though I_3^- is the actual species of iodine that exists in such solutions, for convenience in calculations it is referred to as I_2. The standard reduction potential of iodine indicates that it is a weak oxidising agent:

$$I_2 + 2e^- \longrightarrow 2I^- \; E^0 = +0.535V$$

However, several substances can be determined by titration with a standardised iodine solution. The mild oxidising nature of iodine is actually an advantage, namely, for titrations where a more powerful titrant might lead to non-stoichiometric oxidations and errors in titrations. Two types of titrations are carried out with iodine:

- direct titrations and
- indirect titrations.

4.4.4.1 Direct Titrations

The titration of iodine (oxidant) solution with an analyte (reductant) is called a direct titration. *Iodimetry* is another name for this type of titrimetry. Some of the direct titration reactions with iodine are listed in Table 4.9.

Table 4.9 Some direct titrations with iodine as titrant

Analyte	**Proudcts**
$2S_2O_3^{2-}$	$S_4O_6^{2-} + 2I^-$
$SO_3^{2-} + H_2O$	$SO_4^{2-} + 2H^+ + 2I^-$
H_2S	$S + 2I^-$
As(III)	As (V) + $2I^-$
Sn(II)	Sn (IV) + $2I^-$
Sb(III)	Sb (V) + $2I^-$
$2[Fe(CN)_6]^{4-}$	$2[Fe(CN)_6]^{3-} + 2I^-$
$C_6H_8O_6$ (Ascorbic acid)	$C_6H_6O_6 + 2H^+ + 2I^-$ (Dehydroascorbic acid)

Direct iodine titrations are carried out in neutral or acidic solutions. At pH values higher than 11, the stoichiometry of iodine titrations is uncertain because at this pH iodine is oxidised to hypoiodite (IO^-). Hypoiodite is unstable and forms the iodate (IO_3^-). In some titrations with iodine, the pH is critical. For example, in the titration of As(III), the reaction is smooth in slightly alkaline medium. However, in strongly acidic solution, the reaction occurs in the reverse direction:

$$H_3AsO_4 + 2I^- + 2H^+ \longrightarrow H_3AsO_3 + I_2 + H_2O$$

Problem 4.19 A standard solution of 0.2000 g of As_2O_3 (primary standard) required 42.1 mL of an iodine solution. Calculate the normality of the iodine solution.

Solution

The reaction involved in the titration is

$$\overset{III}{H_3AsO_3} + H_2O + [I_3]^- = \overset{V}{HAsO_4^{2-}} + 4\,H^+ + 3I^-$$

This involves a change in the oxidation number by 2 per As and a total of 4 per As_2O_3 molecule.

$$\therefore \quad \text{meq } I_2 = \text{meq } As_2O_3$$

Then, $42.1\text{ mL} \times \dfrac{\text{N meq } I_2}{\text{mL}}$

$$= \frac{200 \text{ mg } As_2O_3}{(197.84/4) \text{ mg } As_2O_3/\text{meq}}$$

(Molecular weight of $As_2O_3 = 197.84$)

$$\therefore \quad N_{I_2} = \frac{200}{(197.84/4) \times 42.1} = 0.096 \text{ meq/mL}$$

4.4.4.2 Indirect Titrations

In an indirect titration (called *iodometry*), an excess of potassium iodide solution is added to the sample. The I^- in KI reduces the oxidising chemical in the analyte resulting in the formation of an equivalent amount of free iodine. The 'liberated' iodine is then titrated with standardised sodium thiosulphate solution. The general equation for indirect titrations is represented as

(i) Analyte (oxidant) + I^- (excess) $\longrightarrow$ Analyte (reduced) + I_2

(ii) $I_2 + S_2O_3^{2-} \longrightarrow S_4O_6^{2-} + 2I^-$

The iodine formed in reaction (i) is equivalent to the amount of oxidising agent in the sample. In this reaction, the iodide (KI) added is in large excess; it is not a standard solution. The iodine liberated is then titrated with sodium thiosulphate; iodide and tetrathionate ions are the products.

Some of the indirect titrations with iodine are listed in Table 4.10.

Table 4.10 Some indirect iodine titirations

$Cr_2O_7^{2-} + 6I^- + 14H^+$	$\rightarrow$	$2Cr^{3+} + 3I_2 + 7H_2O$
$Cl_2 + 2I^-$	$\rightarrow$	$2Cl^- + I_2$
$Br_2 + 2I^-$	$\rightarrow$	$2Br^- + I_2$
$ClO^- + 2I^- + 2H^+$	$\rightarrow$	$Cl^- + I_2 + H_2O$
$IO_3^- + 5I^- + 6H^+$	$\rightarrow$	$3I_2 + 3H_2O$
$IO_4^- + 7I^- + 8H^+$	$\rightarrow$	$4I_2 + 4H_2O$
$2Cu^{2+} + 4I^-$	$\rightarrow$	$2CuI(s) + I_2$

4.4.4.3 Starch Indicator

Starch is used as an indicator in both direct and indirect titrations involving iodine. Starch forms a blue complex with iodine. The disappearance of the blue colour shows the end point. As iodine is consumed in the titration, the complex is decomposed. When all the iodine has been lost from the complex, the blue colour is lost.

$$\text{Colourless starch} + I_2 \rightarrow \text{Blue starch–iodine complex} \xrightarrow[\text{end point}]{S_2O_3^{2-}} \text{Colouless starch}$$

The deep blue colour that develops is due to the absorption (trapping) of iodine into the helical chain of β-amylose, a macromolecular component of starch. The so-called *soluble starch*, available commercially, consists primarily of β-amylose; the α-amylose, present along with β-amylose in natural starch is removed in preparing the soluble starch. The interaction between the α-amylose and iodine is not readily reversible and therefore its presence in starch is undesirable to get a clear end point.

Aqueous starch suspensions decompose within a few days, primarily because of bacterial action. The products of this decomposition obscure the end point, and may also consume iodine. The addition of a little HgI_2 or chloroform – a bacteriostat – inhibits the decomposition of starch.

Certain precautions have to be followed in using starch as indicator. They are given below.

(i) The starch solution should be freshly prepared. Old starch solutions do not mark end points sharply.

(ii) Unlike other indicators, a relatively larger quantity of starch is needed; 1–2 mL should be used.

(iii) Starch indicator should not be added until most of the iodine has been titrated. As the titration of I_2 with $S_2O_3^{2-}$ proceeds, a pale yellow colour develops, indicating that most of the iodine has been consumed by $S_2O_3^{2-}$. Starch is added at this stage; this is just prior to the end point. If it is added too soon – at the beginning of the titration – iodine is *adsorbed* onto the starch, making the end point slow and difficult to detect. In addition, I_2 can decompose starch.

(iv) The starch solution should be free from lumps of starch. It is prepared as a consistent (homogeneous) solution by adding soluble starch powder slowly to boiling water with vigorous stirring. The hot solution is cooled and then used.

4.4.4.4 Oxygen Error

In the indirect iodine methods, oxygen from the air oxidises iodide to iodine.

$$4I^- + O_2 + 4H^+ \longrightarrow 2I_2 + 2H_2O$$

Therefore, the reactant solution may have a little more iodine than that produced by the analyte; this aerial oxidation gives high results. The magnitude of this error increases with increasing acidity of the analyte solution. This problem is solved by adding a little sodium bicarbonate to the analyte solution; this produces a blanket of CO_2 above the solution, excludes atmospheric oxygen and avoids oxidation by O_2. Instead of $NaHCO_3$, solid CO_2 may be used.

4.4.4.5 Sodium Thiosulphate

- $Na_2S_2O_3$ is not a primary standard; therefore, it has to be standardised before use. This standardisation can be carried out with standard $K_2Cr_2O_7$ (primary standard) or potassium iodate.
- It is one of the few reducing agents that is not oxidised by air. Therefore, it has a long shelf-life.
- In the titration against iodine, each thoisulphate ion offers one electron.

$$2S_2O_3^{2-} \longrightarrow S_4O_6^{2-} + 2e^-$$

- The quantitative conversion of thiosulphate ion to tetrathionate ion requires a pH of 7.
- It is available both in the anhydrous form (f. wt = 158.11) and in the pentahydrate form (f. wt = 248.19).
- About 0.1 g of Na_2CO_3 is added to the solution of sodium thiosulphate before adjusting the volume in the standard flask. This prevents its decomposition to sulphur. It should be standardised every time it is used.
- It is inexpensive.

4.4.5 Complexometric Titrations

The formation of a complex by the analyte species may form the basis of a titrimetric determination. Such a method is called *complex formation* or *complexometric titration*. For example, the complex formation between Ag^+ and CN^- can be used for estimating silver using cyanide.

$$Ag^+ + 2CN^- \longrightarrow Ag(CN)_2^-$$

An aqueous solution of Ag^+ (analyte) can be titrated with a standard CN^- solution and then the Ag^+ determined. The reagents used for complex formation are mostly organic compounds that contain several electron-donor groups. Most of these reagents are chelate-forming. For example, glycine forms a chelate with Cu(II). Therefore, a Cu(II) solution can be titrated with glycine solution.

- The complexes formed in titrations should be soluble in the medium used. Insoluble complexes obscure end points.
- Multidentate ligands, especially those having four or six donor groups, have two advantages over unidentate ligands: (i) They generally react more completely with cations and hence produce sharper end points. (ii) They react with cations (analytes) forming 1:1 complexes in a single-step process. On the contrary, complex formation with unidentate ligands usually involves two or more steps. Consider, for example, the titration of a metal ion M with a coordination number four with a quadridentate ligand L:

$$M + L \longrightarrow ML \text{ (For simplicity, charges are not denoted)}$$

As the ligand solution is added, the concentration of the free metal ion will decrease (–log M = pM; this will increase). The titration curve shows that the change in pH in the equivalence point region is large and therefore, the end point is sharp and clean, (Fig. 4.10a). When another ligand L′ which reacts with the same metal as per the equation,

$$M + 4L' \longrightarrow ML'_4$$

is used (1:4 ratio combination), the change in pM near the equivalence point is not significant (Fig. 4.10b), and hence the end point is not sharp. Therefore, multidentate ligands are preferred as titrants in complexometric titrations.

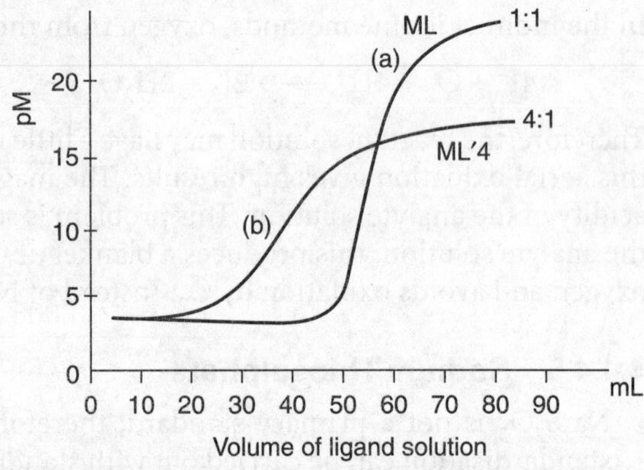

Fig. 4.10 Reaction of a metal with a ligand: **(a)** quadridentate ligand L **(b)** unidentate ligand L

Most metal cations other than alkali metals are suitable for complexometric titrations. Such titrations are convenient and accurate. In many cases, these titrations have replaced the time-consuming gravimetric methods.

Choice of titrant (i) For titration of a metal ion with a ligand, the formation constant of the complex must be large so that the titration reaction will be stoichiometric and quantitative. (ii) For detecting the end point clearly, there must be a sharp change in the metal ion concentration at some stoichiometric point in the titration; multidentate ligands produce such sharp changes. (iii) The ligand must be soluble in water. (iv) The ligand must be inexpensive. (v) A suitable indicator must be available.

4.4.5.1 Ethylenediaminetetraacetic Acid (EDTA)

Ethylenediaminetetraacetic acid (EDTA) or (ethylenedinitrilo)tetraacetic acid is the most widely used complexometric titrant.

It possesses six sites for bonding with a metal ion—four COOH groups and two N atoms. It is a *hexadentate ligand.*

Acidic properties of EDTA EDTA can be denoted as H_4Y, as it has four acidic hydrogens. The various species arising from its dissociation are denoted by H_3Y^-, H_2Y^{2-}, HY^{3-} and Y^{4-}. The relative amounts of these five species in a solution vary as a function of pH. In moderately acidic medium (pH 3–6), H_2Y^{2-} predominates; when the pH is greater than 10, the ion Y^{4-} is formed as the major species.

Standard EDTA solution The solubility of the acid form of EDTA is not appreciable in water; therefore, it cannot be used as such for preparing titrimetric solutions. However, its disodium salt Na_2H_2Y is soluble in water; thus it is suitable for preparing the titrant solutions. It is commercially available in its dihydrate form. Standard EDTA solutions are prepared by dissolving weighed quantities of $Na_2H_2Y{\cdot}2H_2O$ and diluting up to the mark in a volumetric flask. The acid itself can be used for preparing standard solution by dissolving an exact weighed amount in the minimum amount of aqueous NaOH required for complete dissolution and then the solution is made up to a definite volume.

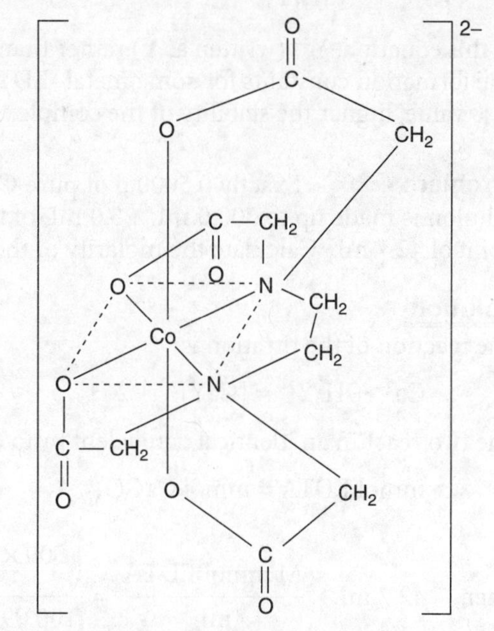

Fig. 4.11 Cobalt(II)–EDTA Complex

Metal ion–EDTA complexes EDTA combines with metal ions in a 1:1 ratio regardless of the charge on the cation. It forms stable chelates with metals ions. A cage-like structure results on complexation as several complexing sites of EDTA bind the metal; the cation is surrounded and isolated from solvent molecules due to bonding with the ligand. The structure of a metal–EDTA complex is denoted in Fig. 4.11. Six donor atoms, (four oxygen and two nitrogen atoms) of the ligand are bonded to the metal ion. When the disodium salt of EDTA reacts with a metal ion, say Mg^{2+}, hydrogen ions are liberated.

(i) $Na_2H_2Y \longrightarrow 2Na^+ + H_2Y^{2-}$
(ii) $H_2Y^{2-} + Mg^{2+} \longrightarrow MgY^{2-} + 2H^+$

Because of the liberation of H^+, the solution is buffered to prevent a large change in pH during titration. Increasing acidity weakens the complex by protonating the Y species. As $[H^+]$ increases, the amount of uncomplexed EDTA increases [reaction (ii) is reversed].

The strength or stability of complexes with EDTA differs for different metal ions. The formation constant (stability constant) is a measure of the strength of the complex. The complexation reaction is

$$M^{2+} + Y^{4-} \longrightarrow MY^{2-}$$

For simplicity, it is written without charges as,

$$M + Y \longrightarrow MY$$

Table 4.11 Formation constants of some metal–EDTA complexes

Metal ion	log K_{MY}	Metal ion	log K_{MY}
Fe^{3+}	25.1	Co^{2+}	16.3
Th^{4+}	23.2	Al^{3+}	16.1
Cr^{3+}	23.0	Ce^{3+}	16.0
Bi^{3+}	22.8	La^{3+}	15.4
Cu^{2+}	18.8	Mn^{2+}	14.0
Ni^{2+}	18.6	Ca^{2+}	10.7
Pb^{2+}	18.0	Mg^{2+}	8.7
Cd^{2+}	16.5	Sr^{2+}	8.6
Zn^{2+}	16.5	Ba^{2+}	7.8

Then the formation constant

$$K_{MY} = \frac{[MY]}{[M][Y]}$$

In this equation, Y^{4-} (written as Y) rather than H_2Y^{2-} is considered the reactive EDTA species. The formation constants for some metal–EDTA complexes are given in Table 4.11. Larger the K_{MY} value, higher the stability of the complex.

Problem 4.20 Exactly 0.5000 g of pure $CaCO_3$ is dissolved in 1 : 1 HCl solution and the solution is made up to 500.0 mL. 25.0 mL of this is titrated with an EDTA solution to an end point of 42.7 mL. Calculate the molarity of the titrant.

Solution

The reaction of the titration is

$$Ca^{2+} + H_2Y^{2-} = [CaY]^{2-} + 2\,H^+$$

The two react in an identical equivalent ratio (1 : 1).

$$\therefore \quad \text{mmol EDTA} = \text{mmol } CaCO_3$$

$$\text{Then,} \quad 42.7 \text{ mL} \times \frac{\text{M mmol EDTA}}{\text{mL}} = \frac{\left(500 \times \dfrac{25.00}{500} \text{ mg } CaCO_3\right)}{(100.09 \text{ mg } CaCO_3/\text{mmol})}$$

$$\therefore \quad M_{EDTA} = 0.00584$$

4.4.5.2 Effect of pH on EDTA Titrations

The complexation equilibrium of the EDTA titrations,

$$M^{2+} + Y^{4-} \rightleftharpoons MY^{2-}$$

is pH-dependent, as the pH of the solution influences the stability of MY^{2-}. Only some metal chelates are stable enough to allow titrations in an acid solution; others require an alkaline solution. The more stable the complex, the lesser is the pH at which the titration can be performed. The calcium chelate is too weak to be titrated in acid solution, while the mercury chelate is strong enough to be titrated in acid. The minimum pH values at which different metals can be titrated with EDTA are shown in Fig. 4.12. The smaller the formation constant K_f, the more alkaline the solution must be for an accurate end point. For Ca^{2+}, a pH of about 8 or above is necessary; but for Fe^{3+}, it is about 2 as the K_f for Fe^{3+} is higher than the K_f for Ca^{2+}.

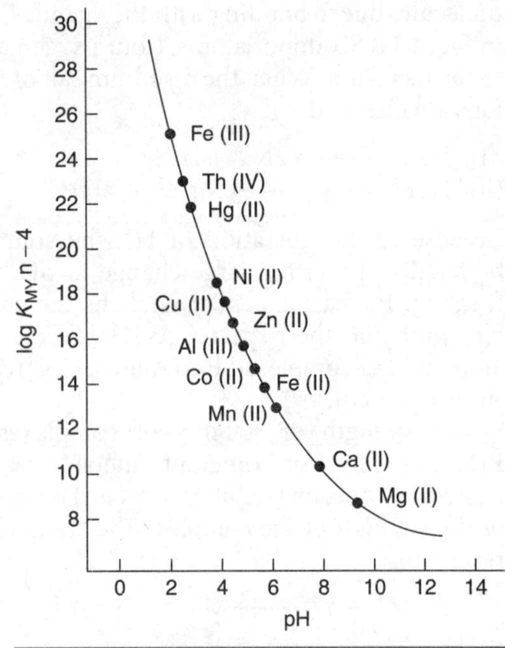

Fig. 4.12 Minimum pH required for titration of some metal ions with EDTA

All the metals will react at high pH range, but some of them, such as Fe^{3+} and Th^{4+}, will form their insoluble hydroxides.

4.4.5.3 Back Titration with EDTA

Back titration is a method where the concentration of an analyte is determined by adding a known amount of an excess reagent to a definite volume of an analyte. The unreacted excess reagent is then titrated with another standard titrant. This titration indicates how much of the added reagent was actually used by the analyte. Some metals cannot be directly titrated with the standard EDTA solution: (a) they may precipitate with the EDTA solution, (b) they may form inert complexes, or (c) a suitable metal indicator may not be available. In such cases, back titration is useful. An excess of EDTA solution is added to the analyte buffered to a suitable pH, and the unreacted excess of EDTA is back titrated with a standard metal ion solution, such as Mg^{2+} or Zn^{2+}.

Metal ions such as Al^{3+}, Fe^{3+}, Ni^{2+} and Ti^{4+} react slowly with EDTA, and so direct titration is slow; in addition, the direct titration shows several false, fading end points. Therefore, these ions are determined rapidly and accurately by back titration.

4.4.5.4 Metal Ion Indicators

A metal ion indicator is used for visual detection of the end point in an EDTA titration. Such an indicator should fulfill the following criteria.

(i) The colour reaction should be specific or at least selective (applicable only to a few selected metals).
(ii) The indicator should be very sensitive to metal ions – that is to pM – so that the colour change occurs as near the equivalence point as possible.
(iii) The colour of the free indicator and that of the metal–indicator complex should be distinctly different.
(iv) The colour reaction must be such that the solution is strongly coloured before the end point, when nearly all the metal ion is complexed with EDTA.
(v) The metal–indicator complex should be stable enough to avoid dissociation and consequent lack of sharp colour change.
(vi) The metal–indicator complex should be less stable than the metal–EDTA complex to ensure that all the metal ions from the former are abstracted by EDTA at the end point.
(vii) All of the criteria (i–vi) should be fulfilled within the pH range at which the titration is conducted.

Some of the metal ion indicators are listed in Table 4.12.

- The pH of the solution is critical to many EDTA titrations; limits of ±0.5 pH is necessary for several metals.
- These titrations are preferably performed with 0.25 mmol of the metal ion in a volume of 50–150 mL of solution. Higher metal ion concentrations obscure the end point.
- The use of 30–50 mg of a 1% solid mixture of indicator – potassium nitrate – is satisfactory for most of the titrations. A higher amount of the indicator darkens the colour of the solution before the end point and decreases the sharpness of the end point.
- In many EDTA titrations, the colour change in the neighbourhood of the end point is slow. This problem is eliminated by efficient stirring of the reaction mixture with a magnetic stirrer and also warming it to 40°C.

Table 4.12 Metal ion indicators

Chemical name	Commercial name (colour index)	Titratable metal ions	pH range	Colour change at end pint in titration
Eriochrome Black T or Solochrome black (C1 14645)	1-(1-Hydroxy-2-naphthylazo)-6-nitro-2-naphthol-4-sulphonate	Mg, Mn, Zn, Cd, Hg, Pb, Ca	10	red → blue
Ammonium salt of pupuric acid	Murexide (CI 56085)	Cu, Ni, Co, Ca, lanthanons	10–11	yellow → blue (Ni, Co) orange → blue (Cu) red → blue violet (Ca)
3'3-[(N,N-) di(carboxymethyl)-aminomethyl]-*o*-cresol sulphonthalein	Xylenol orange	Bi, Th, Zn, Co Cd, Pb, Sn, Ni, Mn	1–2 4–6	red → lemon yellow
Dibromopyrogallol-sulphonphthalein	Bromopyrogallol red	Several cations	2–3	blue → claret red
4-Methoxy-4'-aminodiphenyl amine	Variamine blue (C1 37255)	Fe(III)	3	blue → yellow
2-Hydroxy-1-(2-hydroxyl-4-solpho- 1-naptithylazo)-3-naphthoic acid	Patton and Reeder's indicator (HHSNNA)	Ca	12–14	wine red → blue
1-(2-hydroxy-5-sulphophenyl)- 3-phenyl-5-(2- carboxyphenyl)- formazon	Zincon	Ca in presence of Mg, EGTA as titrant	10	blue → orange red
Cyclotris-(1-azo-8-hydroxynaphthalene-3-6-disulphonic acid)	Calcichrome	Ca, CDTA as titrant	11–12	pink → blue
Thymolsulphonphthalein di (methylimine diacetic acid)	Methylthymol blue	Zn Th, Zr, Hf	6 0–2	blue → yellow blue → yellow
Thymolphltalein di (methylimine diacetic acid)	Thymolphthalexone	Mn, Ca, Sn	10	blue → pink

- Detection of the end point visually needs careful observation. The photometric method gives a more accurate end point.

4.4.5.5 Complexometric Titrations with Other Complexing Agents

A few complexing agents, other than EDTA can also be used in complexometric titations. Ethyleneglycolbis(2-aminoethyl ether)-N,N,N′,N′-tetraacetic acid (EGTA), and 1, 2-diamino-cyclohexane-N, N, N_1' N_1' -tetraacetic acid (CDTA) are two such important titrants.

Examples

(i) Calcium, in the presence of magnesium, can be determined with EGTA. The stability constant for the calcium–EGTA complex is about 1×10^{11} whereas that for magnesium–EDTA complex is only about 1×10^{5}; therefore, magnesium does not interfere in the titration of calcium. Zincon indicator is used in this titration. This indicator gives an indirect end point based on the reaction,

$$Zn\,EGTA^{2-} + Ca^{2+} \longrightarrow Zn^{2+} + Ca\,EGTA^{2-}$$

The liberated zinc ions form a blue complex with the indicator. At the end point, the blue zinc–indicator complex is decomposed and the solution becomes orange-red:

$$ZnIn^{-} + H_2EGTA^{2-} \rightleftharpoons Zn\,EGTA^{2-} + HIn^{-}$$

(ii) Calcium in the presence of barium can be determined using CDTA. The stability constants of the complexes of these two metals with CDTA differ appreciably (log K for Ca = 12.5, for Ba = 7.88). Therefore, calcium can be titrated with CDTA in the presence of barium without any interference (with EDTA, the stability constants are too close for this determination). The indicator calichrome, specific for calcium, is used in this titration.

- Complexing agents such as EDTA, EGTA, CDTA, and so on, used in complexometric titrations are known as *complexones*.
- The complexones have proved to be versatile analytical reagents in several industrial laboratories.

4.4.5.6 Determination of Hardness of Water

An important industrial application of complexometric titrations is the determination of hardness of water using EDTA. Calcium and magnesium salts cause hardness of water. Titration of a sample of water against EDTA using solochrome black indicator gives the total hardness (due to both calcium and magnesium, but expressed in parts of $CaCO_3$ per million of water). The calcium content alone can be determined by titration of the water sample with EDTA using Patton and Reader's indicator or by titration with EGTA. The magnesium content can then be calculated from the total hardness.

$$\text{Hardness} = \frac{(\text{mL of EDTA})\,(\text{M of EDTA})\,(100.09)\,(1000\ \text{mL}/\ell)}{\text{mL of sample}}$$

4.4.5.7 Types of EDTA Titrations

(i) ***Direct titration:*** In direct titration, the metal ion to be estimated is buffered to the required pH and then titrated directly with the standard EDTA solution. Any interfering metal ion present with the analyte is sequestered with an auxiliary complexing agent, such as tartrate, citrate or triethanolamine. For example, Ba can be determined by direct titration at pH 11.5–12.7 using thymol blue–potassium nitrate indicator. Similarly, Bi can be determined directly using xylenol orange–potassium nitrate mixture.

(ii) ***Substitution titration:*** Substitution titration is used for a metal ion which does not react with a metal ion indicator or which forms a complex more stable than those of calcium and magnesium. Such a metal ion M^{n+} to be estimated is treated with a known excess of magnesium–EDTA complex solution. Then, the following reaction occurs.

$$M^{n+} + Mg\,Y^{2-} \rightleftharpoons (MY)^{(n-4)+} + Mg^{2+}$$

The amount of magnesium ion liberated is equivalent to the M^{n+} present; the liberated Mg^{2+} is titrated with a standard EDTA solution using a suitable indicator.

This method is used for the estimation of calcium. When this metal is estimated by direct titration using, say solochrome black, a poor end point is obtained; but, the substitution method offers a clear end point and accurate result.

(iii) ***Other methods***

- Fluoride can be determined by precipitating it as lead chlorofluoride, isolating and dissolving the precipitate in dilute nitric acid, and then titrating the solution (lead in it) at pH 5–6 with EDTA using xylenol orange indicator.

- Sulphate is estimated by first converting it to $BaSO_4$ or $PbSO_4$, then adding excess EDTA to the isolated precipitate and titrating the excess EDTA with a standard zinc solution using solochrome black as indicator.
- Phosphate is estimated by converting it to $Mg(NH_4)PO_4{\bullet}6H_2O$, dissolving the product in dilute hydrochloric acid and then adding excess EDTA. The unreacted EDTA is titrated with standard magnesium ion solution at pH 10 using solochrome black indicator.

4.4.5.8 Spectrophotometric EDTA Titrations

The detection of the equivalence point by following the change in absorbance by the solution is called spectrophotometric or *photometric titration.*

Principle A spectrophotometric titration is possible only when one of the species – the analyte, titrant or product – has a characteric absorption which can be measured accurately at a chosen wavelength. During the titration, the absorbances are recorded corresponding to the volumes (concentrations) of the titrant added. Then the absorbance values are potted against the volumes of titrant added. A sharp change in this graph indicates the equivalence point.

Conditions for photometric titrations

- The analyte, the titrant or the titration product should absorb radiation.
- The absorbance monitored during the titration should be distinctively different when the other species also absorb.
- The absorbing species should obey Beer's law; only then, the titration curve will offer linearity required for extrapolation to the end point.
- The analyte and the titrant should not undergo photolytic changes.

Volume correction As the volume of the solution changes during a photometric titration, it is necessary to correct the absorbance for volume changes. Therefore, each absorbance value is multiplied by $(V + v)/V$, where V is the original volume of the solution and v is the volume of the titrant added.

Examples

(i) *Copper(II) versus EDTA:* Aqueous Cu(II) can be titrated with aqueous EDTA, monitoring the titration at 745 nm. At this wavelength, the copper–EDTA complex has greater molar absorption coefficient than aqueous copper(II). The titration is performed at pH 2.4 using acetate buffer. As the titration proceeds with incremental additions of standard EDTA, the absorbance increases consequent to the formation of the strongly absorbing complex. Then, beyond the equivalence point, when all the Cu(II) species have been complexed, the absorbance becomes a constant. On plotting absorbance against the volume of titrant added, two straight lines are obtained; the intersection of these represents the end point (Fig. 4.13).

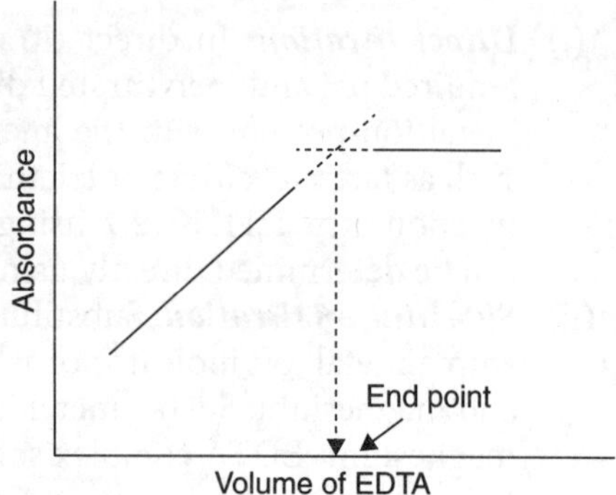

Fig. 4.13 Spectrophotometric titration of copper(II) with EDTA

(ii) *Iron(III) versus EDTA:* In this estimation, first Fe(III) is complexed with salicylic acid. This soluble complex is deep coloured, but less stable than the colourless Fe(III)–EDTA complex. Therefore, when EDTA titrant is added to a known volume of the Fe(III)–salicylic acid solution, the absorbance steeply decreases. The Fe–EDTA complex is progressively converted to the Fe–salicylic acid complex. After the equivalence point, the absorbance becomes a constant. The intersection of the two straight lines – the first sloping and the second horizontal – gives the end point (Fig. 4.14). The titration is performed at pH 2.4 using sodium ethanoate–ethanoic acid buffer. The absorbance values are noted at 525 nm. At the chosen pH, Zn, Cd, Sn, Mn, Cr and Al do not interfere with this estimation. However, Pb, Bi, Co, Ni and Cu interfere.

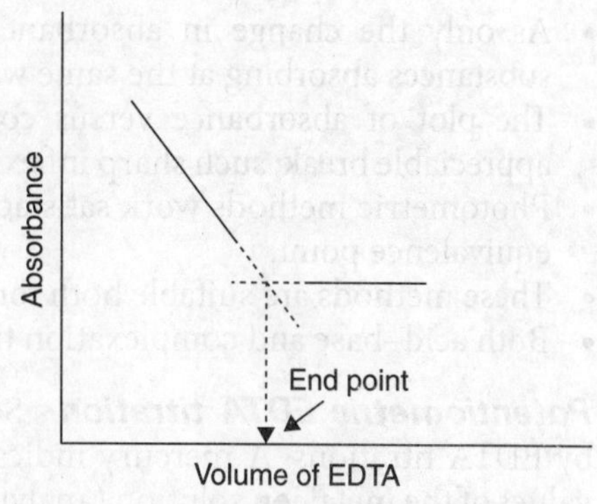

Fig. 4.14 Spectrophotometric titration of iron(II)–salicylic acid with EDTA

Apparatus Spectrometric titrations can be performed with the apparatus shown in Fig. 4.15. A special titration cell made from perspex sheet, which completely fits into the cell compartment is used. A stirrer and a microburette are fitted on the cell through two openings on the lid of the cell. Monochromatic light is made to pass through two quartz windows. All the surfaces of the cell, except the quartz windows are covered with black paper to exclude extraneous light from falling on the absorbing solution. The effect of dilution is minimised using a concentrated titrant.

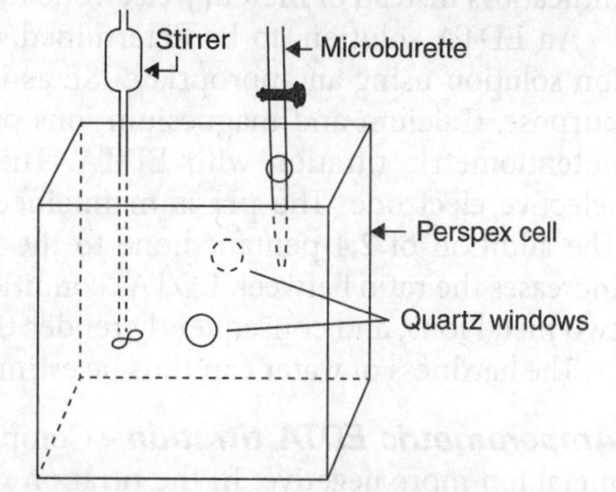

Fig. 4.15 Apparatus for spectrophotometric titrations

EDTA titration *Mixture of metal ions:* An aqueous mixture of two metal ions can also be titrated with EDTA titrant. In such a case, the metal ion–EDTA complex of higher stability reacts first. For example, when a mixture of $Fe^{3+}(aq)$ and $Cu^{2+}(aq)$, is titrated with EDTA, the Fe^{3+} ion with higher stability constant ($10^{25.1}$) reacts first, and then Cu^{2+} with a lesser stability constant ($10^{18.8}$) reacts. The two end points can be detected spectrophotometrically. This titration is performed at pH 1.8 and a wavelength of 748 nm. The titration curve is shown in Fig. 4.16. The initial horizontal portion of the graph denotes the titration of Fe^{3+}. The ascending portion denotes the titration of Cu^{2+}. The end points can be read from the graph by dropping vertical lines drawn from (*a*) and (*b*). V_1 is the volume of EDTA corresponding to Fe^{3+} equivalent and $(V_2 - V_1)$ that corresponding to Cu^{2+}.

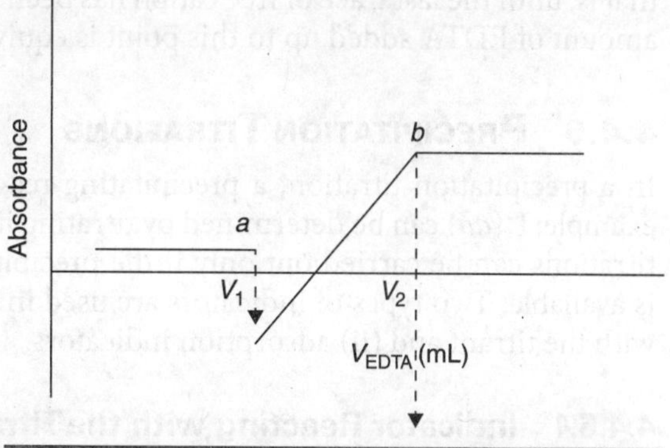

Fig. 4.16 Spectrophotometric titration of Fe^{3+} and Cu^{2+} with EDTA

Advantages of spectrometric titrations Spectrometric titrations have several advantages.

- They are precise.

- As only the change in absorbance is necessary for estimation, the presence of other substances absorbing at the same wavelength does not interfere.
- The plot of absorbance versus concentration plot in a photometric titration gives an appreciable break; such sharp inflexion points are not observed in potentiometric titrations.
- Photometric methods work satisfactorily even when the reactions are incomplete near the equivalence point.
- These methods are suitable both for aqueous and non-aqueous media.
- Both acid–base and complexation titrations can be performed by the photometric method.

Potentiometric EDTA titration Some metal ions can be determined potentiometrically by EDTA titrations. A mercury indicator electrode is used in such determinations. The emf values of the metal ion solution (analyte) is measured by adding incremental volumes of EDTA solution to it. The end point is obtained by drawing the first derivative curve ($\Delta E/\Delta V$).

Halide ions interfere in theses titrations. Ion selective electrodes (ISEs) can be used as indicators instead of mercury electrode for determining copper, cadmium and calcium.

An EDTA solution, to be determined, can be directly titrated with a standardised metal ion solution using an appropriate ISE as indicator. A copper ISE is commonly used for this purpose. Calcium and magnesium ions present in a sample of water can be determined by potentiometric titration with EDTA. The two end points are detected using calcium ion selective electrode. The pH is maintained with tris-(hydroxymethyl)aminomethane buffer. The addition of 2,4-pentanedione to the reacting mixture of calcium and magnesium ions increases the ratio between EDTA's conditional (apparent or altered) stability constants for the two metal ions, and consequently render the two end points clearly independent.

The hardness of water can thus be estimated by potentiometric EDTA titration.

Amperometric EDTA titration Complex formation renders the half-wave potential of a metal ion more negative. In the titration of a metal ion with a complexing agent, say EDTA, the electrode potential is adjusted to a value between that of the half-wave potential of the uncomplexed ion and that of the complex; then the EDTA solution is slowly added to the solution of the metal ion. The diffusion current steadily falls until it equals the residual current, that is, until the last trace of free cation has been complexed. This point is the end point and the amount of EDTA added up to this point is equivalent to the amount of metal present.

4.4.6 Precipitation Titrations

In a precipitation titration, a precipitating reagent is used for determining the analyte. For example, $I^-(aq)$ can be determined by titrating it with $Ag^+(aq)$; AgI precipitate is formed. Such titrations can be carried out only if the precipitating reaction is fast and a suitable indicator is available. Two types of indicators are used in precipitation titrations: (i) indicators reacting with the titrant and (ii) adsorption indicators.

4.4.6.1 Indicator Reacting with the Titrant

The Mohr method The Mohr method for determining chloride serves as an example for an indicator reacting with the titrant. Immediately after the equivalence point, the indicator reacts with the titrant to form a coloured precipitate; this signals the end point. An example of the Mohr method is the titration of chloride with silver nitrate using potassium chromate as indicator. As $Ag^+(aq)$ is added to the chloride containing a small amount of $CrO_4^{2-}(aq)$ indicator, only Cl^- reacts and forms AgCl(s). When the precipitation of the chloride is complete, the first excess of silver ions react with chromate to form a red precipitate of silver chromate.

$$Ag^+ + Cl^- \longrightarrow AgCl(s) \qquad \text{Titration reaction}$$

$$2Ag^+ + CrO_4^{2-} \longrightarrow \underset{\text{(red)}}{Ag_2CrO_4(s)} \qquad \text{End point reaction}$$

The end point is the first permanent darkening of the yellow chromate colour of the medium and also over the precipitate. The end point is not as sharp as might be desired. Some excess silver nitrate must be added to form enough silver chromate to be seen over the heavy white precipitate and yellow chromate solution. This makes it necessary to determine an *indicator blank* and subtract this from the volume of silver nitrate used in titrating the sample.

The indicator is prepared by dissolving 5 g of potassium chromate in 100 mL of water. 1 mL of the indicator is used, so that its concentration in the actual titration is only 0.0025–0.005 M. The concentration of the chromate indicator is important. If too much indicator is added, the end point occurs before the equivalence point; if the amount of indicator is not enough, the end point comes late.

A pH of about 8 is necessary for this titration; in acidic solutions, a part of the indicator is converted to $HCrO_4^-$ which is undesirable to obtain the correct end point. Solid calcium carbonate provides pH 8 that is required for this titration. When the solution is more alkaline, silver carbonate or silver hydroxide will be precipitated marring the titration. The Mohr titration is useful for determining chloride in drinking water.

The Mohr method cannot be applied to the titration of iodide or thiocyanate because of the difficulty of clearly observing the colour change of potassium chromate and also adsorption process. Eosin can be successfully used for these titrations.

Problem 4.21 A 0.5000 g sample of a mixture of NaCl and KCl is titrated with 0.0500 M $AgNO_3$. The titer value is 40.4 mL. Calculate the percentages of the two chlorides in the mixture.

Solution

Let the amount of NaCl in the mixture be x g.

Then, the amount of KCl in the mixture = $(0.5000 - x)$ g

$$\frac{x \text{ g NaCl}}{0.05844 \text{ g/m mol}} + \frac{(0.5000 - x)\text{ g KCl}}{0.07456 \text{ g/m mol}}$$

$$= 40.4 \text{ mL} \times \frac{0.050 \text{ m mol}}{\text{mL}}$$

$$\therefore \qquad x = \frac{(0.5000 - x)}{0.07456} \times 0.05844 \text{ g} = 0.3919 \text{ g}$$

Then, the amount of KCl in the mixture = 0.5000 – 0.3919 = 0.1081 g

$$\%\text{NaCl} = \frac{0.3919}{0.5000} \times 100 = 78.4$$

$$\%\text{KCl} = \frac{0.1081}{0.5000} \times 100 = 21.6$$

Mohr, Karl Friedrich (1806–1879)

The salt $FeSO_4 \bullet (NH_4)_2SO_4 \bullet 6H_2O$ is known as Mohr's salt in honour of Karl Fredrich Mohr, a Prussian Chemist-cum-pharmacist. He was a chemist par excellence who performed pioneering experiments in analytical chemistry. He introduced the use of the Mohr salt and oxalic acid as primary standards in volumetry. He designed the pinchcock, cork borer, an improved version of the chemical balance and graduated pipette among several apparatus. He was the first to design ingeniously a burette; he attached one end of a rubber tube to a graduated pipette and attached a small glass nozzle to the other end of the tube; he then fixed his pinchcock (Mohr's clip) to the rubber tube. This assembly was the precursor for the present–day burette, which has a glass tap replacing the rubber tube and the pinchcock of the Mohr burette. The technique of titration was born in 1855 thanks to the burette designed by him.

Mohr was the first scientist to enunciate clearly the law of conservation of energy in 1837.

Mohr's contribution to analytical chemistry is epochal.

Source: By Ralph Oesper - Journal of Chemical Education, pages 1357 – 1363, 1927, Public Domain, https://commons.wikimedia.org/w/index.php?curid=3749533

Problem 4.22 6.25 g of a sample of common salt is dissolved in distilled water and made up to a litre. 25.0 mL of this solution requires 26.4 mL of decinormal silver nitrate at the end point. What is the percentage of sodium chloride in the sample of common salt?

Solution

$$Ag^+ + Cl^- \longrightarrow AgCl$$

$$NaCl \equiv AgNO_3$$

58.5 g ≡ 1000 mL of 1 N solution

∴ weight of sodium chloride in 1 litre of the solution.

$$= 58.5 \times \frac{(26.4 \times 40 \times 0.1)}{1000} \text{ g} = 6.18 \text{ g}$$

Then, percentage of sodium chloride in the sample

$$= \frac{6.18}{6.25} \times 100 = 98.9$$

The Volhard method This is another example for precipitation titrations. This is an indirect titration procedure for determining anions (Cl^-, Br^-, SCN^-) that precipitate with silver. In this procedure, a measured excess of $AgNO_3$ is added to the anion in nitric acid medium. Then the excess of Ag^+ is determined by back titration with standard potassium thiocyanate solution.

$$X^- + Ag^+ \longrightarrow AgX + \text{Excess } Ag^+$$

$$\text{Excess } Ag^+ + SCN^- \longrightarrow AgSCN$$

The end point is detected by adding iron(III) as ferric ammonium sulphate, which forms a soluble red complex with the first excess of the titrant.

$$Fe^{3+} + SCN^- \longrightarrow Fe\,(SCN)^{2+}$$

If the precipitate AgX is less soluble than AgSCN, it need not be filtered off before titrating the unreacted Ag^+; such is the case with I^-, Br^- and SCN^-. However, in the case of I^-, the indicator is added only after all the I^- ions have been precipitated, since it would otherwise be oxidised by the iron(III). If the precipitate is more soluble than AgSCN, it will react with the titrant and produce a very obscure and high end point. It happens in the case of AgCl.

$$AgCl + SCN^- \longrightarrow AgSCN + Cl^-$$

Therefore, the precipitate has to be filtered off, and then the filtrate titrated with SCN^-. Alternatively, instead of filtering out the silver chloride precipitate, nitrobenzene can be added and the contents shaken vigorously. Nitrobenzene is immiscible with water and heavier than water. It coagulates and coats the silver chloride precipitate so that AgCl cannot react with the aqueous layer of solution during the titration. The excess silver nitrate remains in the aqueous layer and is titrated – without loss – with standard thiocyanate. The Volhard method is satisfactory only when

- the indicator does not form a compound with the titrant, and
- no colour-reaction occurs when the first drop of the titrant is added.

4.4.6.2 Adsorption Indicators

In the adsorption indicator method for halide ions [$Ag^+(aq)$ versus Na^+X^-], the end point reaction occurs on the surface of the silver halide precipitate. The precipitation of the silver halide is the stoichiometric titration reaction. The end point reaction occurs between silver(I) and a coloured indicator anion, for example, dichlorofluorescein.

$$Ag^+ + X^- \longrightarrow AgX(s) \quad \text{Titration reaction}$$

$$Ag^+ + AgX(s) + In^- \longrightarrow \underset{\text{(Red)}}{AgX{:}\,Ag^+\,In^-(s)}$$

(In$^-$ is the anionic indicator species)

During the titration – before the end point – the halide ion is in excess and is adsorbed on the surface of the precipitate as the primary adsorbed ion. In this situation, the In^- is repelled from the negatively charged precipitate.

$$\underset{\text{(Titrant)}}{Ag^+} + \underset{\text{(Analyte)}}{2X^-} \longrightarrow [\underset{\substack{\text{Primary}\\\text{layer}}}{AgX{:}\,X^-}\;\underset{\substack{\text{Secondary}\\\text{layer}}}{{:}Na^+}](s)$$

Beyond the equivalence point, the excess of titrant added causes an abrupt change on the surface of the precipitate. Now, Ag^+ is the primary adsorbed ion (as all the Cl^- ions have already reacted); therefore, the surface of the precipitate has a positive charge. This results in the adsorption of In^- as a counter ion on the surface of the precipitate.

$$\underset{\text{(Yellow)}}{AgX{:}\,Ag^+(s)} + In^- \longrightarrow \underset{\text{(Red)}}{[AgX : Ag^+ : In^-](s)}$$

Immediately after the end point, a colour change occurs on the surface of the precipitate (white to red) due to adsorption. It should be noted that In^- is yellow but all of it remains in solution before the equivalence point. The indicator forms a coloured complex with silver(I) on the surface of AgX. Such a complex is too unstable to be formed in solution whereas it has appreciable stability on the surface of the solid precipitate.

$$\underset{\substack{\text{(In solution)}\\ \text{Unstable}}}{Ag^+ + In^- \longrightarrow AgIn} \quad \underset{\text{Stable}}{AgX(s) \rightleftharpoons [AgX: Ag\,In](s)}$$

- The indicator anion In^- must not displace the primary adsorbed ion (X^-) during the titration. Too strong an adsorption results in such displacement. But, it must be adsorbed as the counter ion at the end point.
- Fluorescein can be used as an indicator for titrating any of the halides because it will not displace the halide from $[AgX:X^-](s)$.
- When the pH is low, the [In] is reduced and a clear end point will not be observed.
- The adsorption indicator method produces a sharp end point and is accurate; therefore it is excellent for determining halides.
- Most of the end points in adsorption titrations do not coincide with the equivalence point, and therefore the titrant should be standardised by the same titration as used for the sample. In this way, the errors will nearly cancel if about the same amount of titrant is used for both the standardisation and analysis.
- Photodecomposition of AgX, which is catalysed by the adsorption indicator, causes error in the titration. However, by proper standardisation, accuracies of one part per thousand can be achieved.
- Maximum surface area of the precipitate for adsorption is required for adsorption indicators.
- The titration of chloride with fluorescein is called the *Fajans method*.

Some adsorption indicators are listed in Table 4.13.

Table 4.13 Adsorption indicators

Indicator	Titration	Condition	Colour change at end point: Solution	→ Precipitate
Fluorescein	Cl^- with Ag^+	pH 7–8	yellow green	pink
Dichlorofluorescein	Cl^- with Ag^+	pH 4	yellow green	red
Eosin	SCN^- with Ag^+	pH 2	pink	red violet
Bromophenol blue	Cl^-, Br^-, I^-, with Hg^{2+}	0.1 M solution	blue	violet
Thorin	SO_4^{2-} with Ba^{2+}	pH 1.5–3.5	colourless	green

4.5 COMMON ERRORS IN VOLUMETRY

The common errors in volumetry are:

- adopting wrong stoichiometry,
- committing arithmetic errors,

- not caring for weighing errors,
- using an inappropriate indicator,
- titrating beyond the end point,
- using an impure primary standard,
- not noting the formula of the primary standard correctly,
- committing errors in pipetting solutions,
- using uncalibrated pipette, burette and volumetric flaks, and
- incorrectly reading volumes, absorbances, electrical quantity, and so on.

4.5.1 Titration in Non-aqueous Solvents

A non-aqueous solvent is used for a titration because of one or more of the following reasons:

- the reactants are insoluble in water,
- the reaction is not stoichiometric in aqueous medium, but it is so in a non-aqueous medium, and
- the acidic or basic nature or the reactivity of the reagents is enhanced in non-aqueous medium, aiding the reaction.
- Different types of non-aqueous solvents are used in titrimetry.

Aprotic solvents are chemically neutral and unreactive; they have low dielectric constants and do not cause ionisation of solutes; and they do not react with acids and bases. They are used in titrations merely based on solubility considerations, that is, to dissolve the reactants and products. Carbon tetrachloride is such a solvent.

Protophilic solvents are proton-abstracting. For example liquid ammonia, a protophilic solvent, is used in the titration of a weak acid. This solvent enhances the strength of the weak acid; it has a *levelling effect* on acids, that is, it increases the strength of weak acids to the level of the strength of strong acids.

A *protogenic* solvent, such as anhydrous hydrogen fluoride, is used as a solvent in the titration of weak bases. Such solvents enhance the basic strength by their ability to produce H^+ required by the base.

An *amphiprotic* solvent, that is acidic and readily donates a proton, such as ethanoic acid, is used for the titration of a weak base with a very strong acid, such as perchloric acid. Though this solvent is an acid, it accepts a proton from the strong perchloric acid:

$$CH_3COOH + HClO_4 \rightleftharpoons CH_3COOH_2^+ + ClO_4^-$$

Then, $CH_3COOH_2^+$ can easily give up its proton to react with a base; this ability enhances the strength of the weak base. Therefore, titration between weak bases and perchloric acid can be performed in ethanoic acid solvent.

Titrations in non-aqueous solvents are useful for substances which give poor end points in aqueous solutions or which are insoluble in water. *Differential titrations*, that are titrations for determining the proportions of components in mixtures of acids or bases, can be performed in non-aqueous solvents which do not exert a levelling effect. The indicators used in titrations in aqueous medium can be used in titrations in non-aqueous media also. For highly coloured solutions, potentiometric titrations can be adopted. Titrations in non-aqueous media are useful for determining mixtures of primary, secondary and tertiary amines, and other organic acids. Glacial ethanoic acid, acetonitrile, alcohols, dioxin and dimethyl formamide are the commonly used non-aqueous solvents in titrations.

EXERCISES

1. 25.0 mL of a solution of oxalic acid was titrated with 0.1007 N NaOH solution. The end point for this titration was 30.1 mL. Another 25.0 mL of the same oxalic acid reacted with 32.2 mL of a $KMnO_4$ solution in acidic medium ($MnO_4^- \rightarrow Mn^{2+}$). Calculate the normality of the $KMnO_4$ solution.
2. What volume of H_2SO_4 solution, that has a density of 1.835 g/mL and contains 93.0% H_2SO_4 by weight, must be diluted with water to prepare 1 litre of an approximately 2 N H_2SO_4 solution?
3. A 0.1251 g sample of iron ore is dissolved in acid. To this solution, 50.0 mL of 0.0511 M EDTA solution is added and the excess of unreacted EDTA is back-titrated with 18.2 mL of 0.0502 M Zn^{2+} solution. What is the percentage of Fe_2O_3 in the ore?
4. A solution is prepared by mixing 20.0 mL of 0.0500 M NaOH solution with 30.0 mL of 0.0100 M Na_2CO_3. Calculate the normality of the mixture with respect to (a) phenolphthalein indicator (b) methyl orange indicator.
5. A 0.1614 g sample of a 10% pure dibasic organic acid is neutralised with 21.4 mL of 0.1008 M NaOH. Calculate the molecular weight of the acid.
6. 0.575 g of magnesium is reacted with 50 mL 1 N H_2SO_4. How many mL of 0.0912 N KOH would be required to neutralise the excess acid?
7. 25.0 mL of a solution containing oxalic acid and sodium oxalate required 14.8 mL of 0.1 N NaOH solution for neutralisation, and 30.2 mL of 0.1025 N $KMnO_4$ for oxidation in acidic conditions at about 60°C. Calculate the number of grams of each (anhydrous) constituent per litre of the solution.
8. 25.0 mL of a solution containing ferrous sulphate and ferric sulphate require 18.5 mL 0.1 N $KMnO_4$ solution for oxidation in acidic condition. After complete reduction by zinc amalgam, 25.0 mL of the solution requires 32.6 mL of the same $KMnO_4$ solution. Calculate the number of grams of each anhydrous sulphate per litre of the solution.
9. 6.150 g of $BaCl_2 \cdot xH_2O$ are dissolved in water and the solution made up to 500 mL. 25.0 mL of this solution is treated with a moderate excess of sodium sulphate solution, after which 25.2 mL of 0.100 N $AgNO_3$ solution is needed to neutralise the chloride in solution. Calculate the value of x.
10. How many grams of $CuSO_4 \cdot 5H_2O$ must be dissolved in water and made up to 1 litre of solution so that 25 mL of the solution will liberate from acidified KI solution enough iodine to react with 37.7 mL of N/10 $Na_2S_2O_3$?
11. 50.0 mL of 0.1002 M EDTA solution is added to a solution containing 0.0780 g of lead, and the excess unreacted EDTA is backtitrated with 0.012 M $MgSO_4$ solution. Calculate the volume of $MgSO_4$ solution required for neutralisation.
12. Calculate the hardness of a water sample, 100 mL of which required 20 mL of EDTA. 20.0 mL of calcium chloride solution, whose strength is equivalent to 1.05 g of $CaCO_3$ per litre, required 30.0 mL of EDTA solution.
13. 10.000 g of a mixture of potassium iodide and iodate are made up to one litre of aqueous solution. 25.0 mL of the solution is added to sufficient potassium iodide solution to ensure excess of iodide and then acidified. The liberated iodine requires 27.6 mL of 0.100 N sodium thiosulphate solution for reduction. Calculate the percentage of potassium iodate in the mixture.
14. 25.0 mL of $Hg^{2+}{}_2$ (aq) is titrated with 0.0500 M NaI(aq). Calculate pI after the addition of 10.0 mL of the titrant. The K_{sp} for $Hg_2I_2(s)$ is 4.5×10^{-29}.
15. A 0.621 g sample of NaH_2PO_4 is titrated with 0.120 M NaOH and the end point required 28.1 mL. Calculate the percentage purity of the sample.

5 Principles of Gravimetric Analysis

5.1 INTRODUCTION

Gravimetric analysis is the estimation of an analyte based on measurement of weights. It involves the following steps:

- taking a known weight of the material containing the analyte,
- separating the analyte from the interfering constituents of the original material,
- converting the analyte into a precipitate in pure form using a suitable precipitant,
- isolating and drying the precipitate formed,
- weighing the pure dry precipitate, and
- calculating the weight of the analyte based on the weight of the precipitate formed.

The success of gravimetric analyses hinges upon:

- selecting an appropriate precipitant,
- avoiding interference in precipitation, and
- isolating the precipitate in its pure form, suitable for weighing.

For example, consider the gravimetric estimation of nickel. It involves the following steps:

- the analyte containing nickel is brought into solution by a suitable chemical treatment,
- any interfering constituent in the solution is either eliminated or sequestered,
- the treated solution containing Ni(II) is reacted with slightly more than the required quantity of the chosen precipitant, say dimethylglyoxime; nickel-dimethylglyxime complex, $Ni(C_4H_7O_2N_2)_2$, is formed,
- the precipitated complex is isolated, dried and weighed,
- from the knowledge of the formula of the complex and the relative atomic masses of the constituent elements in the formula, the quantity of nickel in it can then be calculated.

Advantages of gravimetric analysis The gravimetric method has the following advantages.

- It is an accurate and a precise method.
- It is an *absolute method* as it involves a direct measurement without requiring any calibration.
- It can be applied to several analytes, both inorganic and organic, cationic and anionic.
- A particular analyte can be gravimetrically determined with more than one precipitant.
- It requires only inexpensive apparatus.

Disadvantages of gravimetric analysis This method, however, has the following disadvantages.

- It is a macroscopic method requiring relatively large quantities of the analyte, at least in grams.

- It is a laborious method, involving several steps—weighing, dissolution, filtration, precipitation, washing and drying.
- The choice of the precipitant for a particular analyte is restricted as it should fulfill all the conditions for analysis.

Gravimetric factor A factor called the *gravimetric factor* is used for directly calculating the percentage of an analyte. This factor is the number of grams of an analyte per one gram of the precipitate formed.

$$\text{Gravimetric factor} = \frac{\text{a formula weight of analyte}}{\text{a formula weight of precipitate}}$$

$$\text{Weight of analyte} = \text{weight of precipitate} \times \text{gravimetric factor}$$

$$\text{Percentage of analyte in the sample} = \left(\frac{\text{weight of precipitate} \times \text{gravimetric factor}}{\text{weight of sample}}\right) 100$$

The gravimetric factors for some analytes are listed in Table 5.1.

Table 5.1 Some gravimetric factors

Analyte	Precipitate	Gravimetric factor	Weight ratio (g/g)
Pb	$PbCrO_4$	$Pb/PbCrO_4$	207.2/323.19
CaO	$CaCO_3$	$CaO/CaCO_3$	56.08/100.09
FeS	$BaSO_4$	$FeS/BaSO_4$	87.91/233.40
Cr_2O_3	Ag_2CrO_4	$Cr_2O_3/2Ag_2CrO_4$	99.99/631.46
$UO_2(NO_3)_2 \cdot 6H_2O$	U_3O_8	$3\ UO_2(NO_3)_2/U_3O_8$	1182.12/842.09
Ni	$Ni(DMG)_2$	$Ni/Ni(DMG)_2$	58.71 /288.94
Fe	Fe_3O_4	Fe/Fe_3O_4	(3 × 55.847)/231.539
Ag	AgCl	Ag/AgCl	107.868/143.32
MgO	$Mg_2P_2O_7$	$2MgO/Mg_2P_2O_7$	0.3623
P_2O_5	$Mg_2P_2O_7$	$P_2O_5/Mg_2P_2O_7$	0.6377
Zn	$Zn(C_{10}H_8ON)_2$	$Zn/Zn(C_{10}H_8ON)_2$	65.39/381.75

Problem 5.1 A 2.000 g sample of a rock containing metallic lead, iron and copper was chemically treated to dissolve the three metals. The solution containing these three was then used for gravimetric estimation of the metals. The estimations yielded 0.3188 g $PbSO_4$, 0.7282 g Fe_2O_3 and 0.4787 g CuCNS. Calculate the percentages of the three metals in the rock.

Solution

$$\text{The amount of lead in the rock} = \frac{0.3188}{303.26} \times 207.2 = 02178\ \text{g}$$

$$\therefore \quad \text{Per cent of lead} = \frac{0.2178}{2.000} = 100 = 10.9$$

$$\text{The amount of Fe in the rock} = \frac{0.7272 \times 111.69}{159.69} = 0.5086\ \text{g}$$

$$\therefore \quad \text{Per cent of Fe} = \frac{0.5086}{2.000} \times 100 = 25.4$$

$$\text{The amount of Cu in the rock} = \frac{0.4787}{121.63} \times 63.546 = 0.2501\ \text{g}$$

$$\therefore \quad \text{Per cent of Cu} = \frac{0.2501 \times 100}{2.000} = 12.5$$

Problem 5.2 A 1.0020 g sample of Pb_3O_4, contaminated by an inert matter, gave 1.3215 g of $PbSO_4$ in a gravimetric method. Calculate the percent of Pb_3O_4 and also the per cent of Pb in the sample.

Solution

The per cent of Pb_3O_4 in the sample

$$= 1.3215\ \text{g PbSO}_4 \times \frac{685.57\ \text{g Pb}_3\text{O}_4/(3 \times 303.25)\text{g PbSO}_4}{1.0020\ \text{g sample}} \times 100 = 99.4$$

$$\text{The per cent of Pb in the sample} = 99.4\%\text{Pb}_3\text{O}_4 \times \frac{(3 \times 207.19)\ \text{g Pb}}{685.57\ \text{g Pb}_3\text{O}_4} = 90.1$$

5.1.1 Calculation on Dry Basis and As-received Basis

When chemical industries receive raw materials, it is necessary to know the per cent of a constituent in the sample as it is received. Such samples may contain moisture (*hygroscopic water*). Then, the results of gravimetric analysis are expressed on an *as-received basis.* Such results are useful in assessing the economic value of the raw material. However, the sample is usually dried prior to the analysis because the moisture content of the samples may not be uniform or it may be difficult to handle moist samples. In addition, the moisture content may change during the estimation of the sample. Drying of the sample is carried out by heating it at 105–110°C for 1–2 h in an oven with a thermostat. Alternatively, some samples can be air-dried at room temperature. In such cases, the results are reported on *dry basis.*

The per cent moisture alone (% A_{moist}), the weight per cent of the constituent A on the as-received basis ($A_{a.r}$) and the per cent of A on a dry basis (A_d) are interrelated by the equation

$$\%\ A_d = \frac{(\%\ A_{a.r} \times 100)}{(100 - \%\ A_{moist})}$$

5.1.2 Direct and Indirect Gravimetry

Gravimetric methods of chemical analysis are either direct or indirect. In the direct method, the constituent A being determined is separated from the other components of the sample in the form of a pure substance, which can either be A itself or a compound B (formed from A) of known and definite composition, from the weight of which the amount of A can be calculated. Only rarely do gravimetric methods involve the separation of the constituent A directly and weighing it; frequently, A is converted to another chemical form B and separated.

For example, the nickel (A) content of a nickel alloy can be determined gravimetrically by converting the nickel to its DMG complex (B).

In an indirect gravimetry, two pure chemical substances are isolated from the sample and weighed together. Then, by further chemical treatment of the two substances or by analysis of a new sample, additional data are obtained, from which the amount of one of the constituents is calculated; that of the other one is calculated by difference.

Model Gravimetry

The estimation of Ag^+ or Cl^- as AgCl(*s*) essentially involves the reaction,

$$Ag^+ + Cl^- \longrightarrow AgCl\downarrow$$

This method is ideal for gravimetry because of the following facts.

- AgCl is insoluble in water; its solubility is only 1.4 mg/l at 30°C.
- A small mass of analyte, Cl^- yields a large mass of precipitate.
- AgCl is formed in curds or lumps that can easily be collected, dried and weighed.
- The precipitate is not hygroscopic.
- The reaction is sensitive and goes to completion.
- Silver chloride has no water of crystallisation.
- It is dried readily and totally just above 100°C.

Problem 5.3 A 1.3356 g sample of limestone on chemical treatment and gravimetry gave 0.0639 g of a mixture of Fe_2O_3 and Al_2O_3 (limestone is mainly constituted by $CaCO_3$). The Fe_2O_3 content of limestone was found to be 1.81%. Find out the per cent of Al_2O_3 in limestone.

1.3356 g of limestone contained 0.0639 g of $Fe_2O_3 + Al_2O_3$,

That is, $\frac{0.0639}{1.3356} \times 100 = 4.78\%$

Hence, % $Al_2O_3 = 4.78 - 1.81 = 2.97\%$

Problem 5.4 A 0.4300 g sample consisting of $BaCl_2$, KCl and $CaCO_3$ was chemically treated and 0.4050 g of a mixture containing only $BaCl_2$ and KCl was obtained. This mixture consumed 40.5 mL of 0.1200 M $AgNO_3$ solution for the quantitative precipitation of chloride. Calculate the per cent of Ba and K in the sample.

Let the amount of $BaCl_2$ in the sample be *x* mmol and the amount of KCl be *y* mmol.

The molecular weight of $BaCl_2 = 208.25$

The molecular weight of KCl = 74.56

$\therefore$ $208.25\,x + 74.56\,y = 405.0$

x mmol of $BaCl_2$ = 2*x* mmol of chloride

y mmol of KCl = *y* mmol of chloride

$\therefore$ $2x + y = (40.5 \text{ mL})\ (0.1200 \text{ mmol } AgNO_3/L) = 4.86$

Solving the two equations,

$x = 0.7212, y = 3.4176$

Then $\% \text{ Ba} = \frac{(0.7212 \text{ mmol BaCl}_2)(137.34 \text{ mg Ba/mmol BaCl}_2) \times 100}{430 \text{ mg sample}} = 23.03$

$$\% \text{ K} = \frac{(3.4176 \text{ mmol KCl})(39.10 \text{ mg K/mmol KCl}) \times 100}{430 \text{ mg sample}} = 31.08$$

5.2 PRECIPITATE FORMATION

5.2.1 Methods of Obtaining the Precipitate

The precipitate or solid for weighing can be obtained by one of the following methods:

- Volatilisation
- Electrodeposition and
- Reacting two solutions and filtering the precipitate.

Of these three, the last one is the most commonly adopted method. It is important to understand the nature of the precipitation reaction and also the subsequent interactions between the precipitate and solution.

5.2.2 Conditions for Precipitation

Four requirements must be fulfilled for quantitative estimation by precipitation.

(i) The desired constituent must be precipitated quantitatively. This means that the concentration of the constituent left in solution must be a negligible fraction of the original total amount, that is, the precipitation should yield a precipitate which is so slightly soluble that the constituent is left in solution at a concentration level that would not be detectable within the weighing limits of the analytical balance (0.0001 g or less).

(ii) The precipitate must be pure; at the time of final measurement of weight, it must be of known purity. At the time of its formation, the precipitate must not include significant quantities of any other substance. If some extraneous substances are associated with the precipitate, they must be readily removable by washing and drying.

(iii) The precipitate must be in a physical form suitable for subsequent handling; it should consist of particles which are large enough to be filtered.

(iv) The weighing form of the precipitate, after drying and ignition, should be of a known and constant composition.

5.2.3 Choice of Precipitants

A *precipitant* is a reagent added to a solution to form a precipitate with the constituent being determined. For example, when nickel is estimated as the nickel dimethylglyoxime complex, DMG is the precipitant. The selection of a precipitant is vital for success in gravimetric analysis. However, the choice of precipitants is limited for a metal ion since only one or two precipitants satisfy all the requirements indicated above.

The common precipitants may be classified into two types: (a) inorganic precipitants and (b) organic precipitants. For example, aluminium may be precipitated with the inorganic precipitant ammonium hydroxide or with the organic precipitant oxine (8-hydroxyquinoline). Some important inorganic precipitants are listed in Table 5.2.

Table 5.2 Common inorganic precipitants

Precipitant	Substance estimated	Weighed form	Precipitant	Substance estimated	Weighed form
HCl	Ag	AgCl	KI	Bi	BiOI
$AgNO_3$	Cl^-	AgCl	H_2S	Zn	ZnO or $ZnSO_4$
$BaCl_2$	SO_4^{2-}	$BaSO_4$		Sb	Sb_2O_3
H_2SO_4	Ba	$BaSO_4$		As	As_2S_3
	Pb	$PbSO_4$	KIO_3	Ce	CeO_2
H_2SO_4	Ba	$BaSO_4$	$NH_3(aq)$	PO_4^{3-}	$(NH_4)_3[PMo_{12}O_{40}]$ or $P_2O_5{\bullet}24MoO_3$
NH_4SCN	Cu	CuSCN	NH_4OH	Be	BeO
$(NH_4)_2HPO_4$	Mg	$Mg_2P_2O_7$	$Pb(NO_3)_2$	Cr	$PbCrO_4$
$(NH_4)_2HPO_4$	Mn	$Mn_2P_2O_7$	SO_2	Se	SeO_2
$NH_3(aq)$	Al	Al_2O_3	$AgNO_3$	CN^-	Ag CN
	Fe	Fe_2O_3			

5.2.3.1 Advantages of Using Organic Precipitants

- The precipitates formed with organic precipitants are often very insoluble in water making the degree of separation highly quantitative.
- The precipitate has a high formula weight relative to the metal ion being separated, so that a small weight of the metal being estimated gives a large precipitate weight. This allows high sensitivity in the detection of the metal involved, with less errors in weighing.
- Organic precipitates have a large particle size and therefore can be easily filtered and washed.
- Organic precipitates frequently are more easily dried than inorganic precipitates because of their reduced tendency to hold water.

5.2.3.2 Disadvantages of Using Organic Precipitants

- Drying of organic precipitates sometimes results in a dried product of uncertain composition. This may be due to partial decomposition or volatilisation during drying.
- Organic precipitants are generally less soluble in water compared to inorganic precipitants. This creates a problem of preparing the organic precipitant solution, requiring the use of an organic solvent. For example, DMG is insoluble in water and has to be prepared in alcohol.
- Organic precipitants are more expensive than inorganic precipitants.

Therefore, the selection of a precipitant for estimating a particular analyte should be done after carefully considering all of these aspects.

5.2.3.3 Types of Organic Precipitants

These are of two types—(i) chelating precipitants and (ii) ion-associating precipitants.

Chelating precipitants These form ring-complexes called chelates of high molecular weight, with a metal ion. The chelating agent will contain both acidic groups (replaceable hydrogens) and coordinating groups (atoms with unshared electron pairs). The nature of the chelate precipitate formed will be dependent upon the size, oxidation number and coordination number of the metal ion. Table 5.3 indicates the various chelating precipitants commonly used in gravimettic analyses and also the metal ions which are estimated by these precipitants. The chelating precipitants are usually very specific, reacting with only one or two metal ions under specific experimental conditions. For example, DMG reacts in acid solution with only palladium and in slightly acid to slightly basic solution with only nickel.

Table 5.3 Chelating precipitants

Precipitant	Metal ion precipitated	Remarks
Dimethylglyoxime	Ni(II)	Excess reagent should be avoided since it itself would precipitate
Anthranilic acid	Cu(II) Cd(II), Ni(II), Cu(II)	Sodium salt of the acid is used
8-Hydroxyquinoline	Mg(II)	–
Quinaldic acid	Cu(II), Cd(II)	–
Salicylaldoxime	Cu(II)	–
Cupferron	Fe(III), Cu(II)	Precipitated from acid medium in cold aqueous solution.
α-Benzion oxime	Cu(II)	In diluted ammonia solution
α-Nitroso-β-naphthol	Co(II)	No interference from Ni(II)

Ion-associating precipitants

Certain organic precipitants ionise in aqueous solution to form anions and cations. These ions then react with some oppositely charged species in solution producing insoluble compounds. The product is mainly ionic in character and not ring-structured. The precipitate can be dried and weighed easily. A typical example of ion-associating precipitant is tetraphenylarsonium chloride $(C_6H_5)_4As^+Cl^-$. This precipitates Hg^{2+} quantitatively and hence is used in its estimation.

$$2(C_6H_5)_4As^+Cl^- + HgCl_4^{2-} \longrightarrow [(C_6H_5)_4As]_2\,HgCl_4(s) + 2Cl^-$$

This precipitant is cationic and it combines with anionic species. It is called an *anion-precipitant*, because it precipitates an anion. Oxalic acid is a *cation-precipitant*. It can be used for estimating Ca^{2+} and Mg^{2+}.

Specific and selective precipitants Certain precipitants are highly specific in their reactions and can therefore be used to separate a particular metal ion from a mixture. Such a precipitant is called a specific precipitant. *A specific precipitant is capable of precipitating a particular species quantitatively no matter what other substances may be present in solution.* This is an ideal case and is rarely possible. In practice, some precipitants are selective. *A selective precipitant is one which can precipitate a small group of ions in the presence of certain specified ions.* For example, OH^- is a selective precipitant, capable of precipitating a few metal ions as their hydroxides, other metal ions forming soluble hydroxides. In some cases, selectivity of a precipitant is achieved by carrying out the precipitation under specific, carefully controlled conditions such as pH and temperature. For example, oxine can precipitate almost all metals, but it can be made selective by pH control, and be made to precipitate either aluminium or magnesium from a mixture of metal ions.

A specific precipitant is an ideal substance and in practice does not exist. Certain precipitants may, however, be considered close to ideal specificity. DMG, for example, may be considered as a specific precipitant in precipitating palladium or nickel. Gravimetric reagents, with a few notable exceptions, are not very specific but are only selective. They tend to form precipitates with groups of ions. Each ion, within any group, will then interfere with the analysis of any other ion in the group, unless a preliminary separation is performed. Therefore, gravimetric procedures are less specific than volumetric procedures.

5.2.4 Sequestering Agents (Masking Agents)

The introduction of a reagent to eliminate interference by a substance in an estimation is called masking or sequesteration. *Masking is defined as the process in which a substance, without physical separation, of the substancce or its reaction products, is so transformed that it does not interfere with a particular reaction involved in estimation.* The reagent thus added is called a masking or sequestering agent. Masking agents may be used in volumetry, gravimetry, solvent extraction, or any other analytical method.

Generally, the masking agent forms highly stable, soluble complexes with the interfering species. For example, in EDTA titrations, the cyanide ion is employed as a masking agent for estimating magnesium and calcium in the presence of Cd, Co, Cu, Ni and Pd. All of the latter ions form stable, soluble cyanide complexes and these complexes do not react with EDTA. In the iodometric estimation of copper, iron which will interfere is rendered inactive by the addition of the masking agent F^-, which forms a stable complex with Fe(III). This complex of iron(III), unlike free Fe(III), will not oxidise I^-.

Masking agents are used in certain gravimetric estimations as well. For example, both Mg^{2+} and Cu^{2+} combine with oxine. However, Cu(II) can be masked by the addition of CN^-. Cu(II) is converted to a stable, non-reactive, soluble cyanide complex.

$$Cu^{2+} + 4CN^- \longrightarrow [Cu(CN)_4]^{2-}$$

Thus Mg(II) can be gravimetrically estimated with oxine in the presence of Cu(II) by sequesteration. Ca(II), Mg(II), Pb(II) and Mn(II) can be estimated gravimetrically with suitable reagents in the presence of Cd(II), Zn(II), Hg(II), Cu(II), Co(II), Ni(II) and Ag(I) by masking the latter group of ions with cyanide. There are other masking agents which are less frequently used—triethanolamine masks Ti(IV) and Fe(III), I^- masks Hg(II), F^- masks Sn(II).

Demasking is a process in which the masked substance regains its ability to enter into a particular reaction. For example, the cyanide complex of zinc is demasked by treating it with formaldehyde–acetic acid solution.

$$[Zn(CN)_4]^{2-} + 4H^+ + 4HCHO \longrightarrow Zn^{2+} + 4\, HOCH_2CN$$

The use of masking and selective demasking agents permits the successive gravimetric estimations of metals from a solution.

5.3 SEPARATIONS IN GRAVIMETRIC ANALYSIS

Frequently, the interfering species have to be separated from the sample, using a suitable reagent, before the analyte is reacted with the precipitant.

- In the estimation of Mg(II) as phosphate in a sample containing Ca(II), the interfering calcium ions are first separated as calcium oxalate using ammonium oxalate.
- Al(III) and Ir(III) are separated as hydroxides using aqueous ammonia in the estimation of Cu(II) with thiocyanate.
- Cu(II) is separated as its sulphide by passing H_2S in acidic medium before estimating Ni(II).

5.4 SOLUBILITY PRODUCT AND PRECIPITATION

When a substance is said to be insoluble in water, it actually means that its solubility is negligible. Even a highly insoluble precipitate like lead chromate is soluble in water to a minute extent. In other words, some lead and chromate ions will remain solvated. In a gravimetric estimation, such minute amounts of a precipitate getting dissolved can be neglected because it is an extremely small fraction of the total precipitate weight. Such minute quantities in solution can be related to a term called solubility product, K_{sp}. For example, for AgCl, this is given as

$$K_{sp} = [Ag^+][Cl^-]$$

This value for AgCl at 25°C is 1.78×10^{-10}. Only when the value of the ionic product exceeds 1.78×10^{-10}, AgCl will start appearing as a precipitate in water.

The solubility product is the ultimate value attained by the ionic concentration product when equilibrium has been established between the solid phase of a sparsely-soluble salt and the solution. When the product of the concentrations of the ions in solution is made to exceed the solubility product by the addition of a reagent, the precipitation of the salt will result. Thus the solubility product concept has an important bearing upon precipitation from solution.

When the solubility product constant is very low for a substance, gravimetric estimation involving the weight of that precipitate can be adopted because the error due to the solubility of the precipitate will be low. For example, for Cu(I) thiocynate at 25°C, K_{sp} equals 4.8 $\times 10^{-15}$. This implies that, in one litre of water at 25°C, the amount of Cu(I) thiocyanate remaining dissolved is 6.9×10^{-8} g. This is such a small quantity compared to the usual amounts of precipitate involved in the estimation that it will *not* introduce any detectable error in the estimation.

More insoluble the precipitate, the better it is suited for its formation and weighing in a gravimetric analysis. Precipitates with very low solubility product constants are highly insoluble. Some such solids, used in gravimetry are listed in Table 5.4.

Table 5.4 Solubility product constants of highly insoluble salts

Salt	K_{sp} (25°C)	Solubility S (mol/l)
$PbSO_4$	1.6×10^{-8}	1.3×10^{-4}
CaC_2O_4	2.6×10^{-9}	5.1×10^{-5}
AgCl	1.8×10^{-10}	1.0×10^{-5}
AgBr	4×10^{-13}	6×10^{-7}
$PbCrO_4$	1.8×10^{-14}	1.3×10^{-7}
AgI	1×10^{-16}	1×10^{-8}
$Al(OH)_3$	2×10^{-32}	5×10^{-9}
$Fe(OH)_3$	4×10^{-38}	2×10^{-10}
Ag_2S	2×10^{-49}	4×10^{-17}
HgS	4×10^{-53}	6×10^{-27}
Ag_2CrO_4	1.9×10^{-12}	1.1×10^{-12}
$ZnCO_3$	2×10^{-11}	1.2×10^{-5}
$PbCl_2$	1.6×10^{-5}	3.9×10^{-2}
CaF_2	1.7×10^{-10}	1.9×10^{-4}
$BaSO_4$	1.5×10^{-9}	1.1×10^{-5}
CuSCN	4×10^{-14}	6.9×10^{-9}

Problem 5.5 Calculate the concentration of added Ag^+ needed to just begin precipitation of AgCl in a 1.0×10^{-2} M solution of NaCl at 25°C.

Solution

The K_{sp} of AgCl at 25°C is 1.8×10^{-10}

$$\therefore \quad [Ag^+]\,(1.8 \times 10^{-2}) = 1.8 \times 10^{-10}$$

$$[Ag^+] = \frac{1.8 \times 10^{-10}}{1.0 \times 10^{-2}} = 1.8 \times 10^{-8}$$

Therefore, the concentration of added Ag^+ must just exceed 1.8×10^{-8} M to start precipitation.

Consider a 0.10 M $FeCl_3$ solution. The pH required to precipitate $Fe(OH)_3$ from this solution can be calculated.

$$Fe(OH)_3 \rightleftharpoons Fe^{3+} + 3\,OH^-$$

$$[Fe^{3+}]\,[OH^-]^3 = 4 \times 10^{-38}$$

$$[0.10]\,[OH^-]^3 = 4 \times 10^{-38}$$

$$\therefore \quad [OH^-] = \sqrt[3]{\frac{4 \times 10^{-38}}{0.10}}$$

$$= \sqrt[3]{400 \times 10^{-39}} = 7 \times 10^{-13}\ M$$

$$pOH = -\log(7 \times 10^{-13}) = 12.2$$

$$\therefore \quad pH = 14.0 - 12.2 = 1.8$$

This calculation indicates that $Fe(OH)_3$ can precipitate in acid solution itself. Similarly, the pH at which other hydroxides precipitate can be calculated.

5.5 FACTORS WHICH AFFECT SOLUBILITY OF PRECIPITATES

Temperature Heat is absorbed as most solids dissolve. Therefore, the solubility of precipitates increases with increasing temperature. Solubility products for most sparingly soluble compounds increase at higher temperatures. The solubility product for AgCl is about a hundred fold (21.5×10^{-10}) greater at 100°C than at 5°C (0.21×10^{-10}).

Solvent composition The nature of solvent influences the solubility of most inorganic substances. It is markedly less in mixtures of water and organic solvents than in pure water.

Rate of precipitate formation Precipitation reactions are often slow, several minutes or even several hours being required to attain equilibrium. This is used to accomplish separations that would not be possible if equilibrium were approached rapidly. For example, calcium can be separated from magnesium by precipitation as the oxalate, though magnesium also forms an oxalate of comparable solubility. However, the equilibrium for magnesium oxalate formation is attained at a much slower rate than that for calcium oxalate formation. Calcium oxalate, free of contamination by magnesium oxalate, can be obtained if it is filtered shortly after precipitation. If the precipitate remains in contact with the solution for a long time, it will be contaminated with magnesium oxalate.

Common ion effect The solubility of a slightly soluble salt is decreased by the presence of an ion which is in common with one of the ions of the slightly soluble salt. For example, in the precipitation of AgCl from a solution of $AgNO_3$ using KCl as the precipitant, the addition of an excess of KCl will serve to reduce the molar solubility of AgCl due to common ion effect. However, the solubility of AgCl becomes significantly large in solutions containing a high chloride concentration, such as 1.0 M or above, owing to the formation of $AgCl_2^-$ and $AgCl_3^{2-}$ species. The benefit of the common ion effect in suppressing the solubility of a precipitate is lost in the need to wash the precipitate thoroughly to remove the common ion.

Consider the equilibrium in water involving the slightly soluble electrolyte, $BaSO_4$:

$$BaSO_4(s) \rightleftharpoons Ba^{2+}(aq) + SO_4^{2-}(aq)$$

When another electrolyte, say Na_2SO_4, containing a common ion is added to the saturated solution of $BaSO_4$ in equilibrium, the equilibrium is shifted in favour of $BaSO_4(s)$. Such a shift is in accord with the Le Chatelier principle. This shift is called the common ion effect. This effect is applied in precipitation reactions in gravimetry; a small excess of reagent is added to decrease the solubility of the sparingly soluble substance (weighed in gravimetry). This practice assures quantitative precipitation and offers accurate gravimetric data.

Diverse ion effect Many sparingly soluble salts show an increased solubility in the presence of increased concentrations of certain salts having no ion in common with those of the sparingly soluble salt. Thus AgCl is more soluble in KNO_3 solution than in water. *This effect is called the diverse ion or neutral salt effect.* In the precipitation of AgCl, high excess of KCl will tend to increase the molar solubility of AgCl due to diverse ion effect, K^+ ion being the diverse ion. This effect is in addition to the common ion effect due to it. Therefore, very large excesses of the precipitating ion is avoided in gravimetric analysis.

The salt effect is known also as the *uncommon ion effect*. As the total ionic concentration of a solution increases, interionic interactions become significant. The salt effect on the equilibrium of slightly soluble salt tends to increase the solubility. The comparison between the salt effect and the common ion effect is depicted in Fig. 5.1.

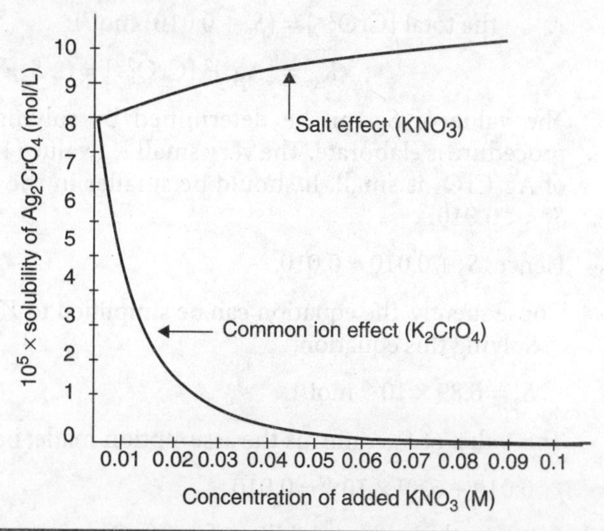

Fig. 5.1 Comparison of salt effect with common ion effect

For a given concentration of a diverse ion, the increase in solubility increases with the charge of the diverse ions. For example, with the same concentration, an SO_4^{2-} ion with two charges, increases the solubility of a slightly soluble salt more than the NO_3^- ion, with a single charge.

The value of the solubility product K_{sp} is a function of the ionic strength μ of the solution. For example, the K_{sp} for $BaSO_4$ at $\mu = 0$ is 1.5×10^{-9} mol/L, but its K_{sp} in 0.010 M KNO_3 ($\mu = 0.010$) increases to 3.9×10^{-9} mol/L.

Problem 5.6 Calculate the molar solubility of Ag_2CrO_4 in (i) water (ii) 0.010 M Na_2CrO_4 solution and (iii) 0.010 M $AgNO_3$ solution. K_{sp} for Ag_2CrO_4 is 1.90×10^{-12} (assume that chromate does not hydrolyse).

Solution

(i) The molar solubility of Ag_2CrO_4

$$S_1 = (m + x)\sqrt{\frac{K_{sp}}{m_m x_x}}$$

where K_{sp} is the solubility constant, m and x are the numbers of cations and anions in the salt.

$$\therefore\ S_1 = \sqrt[3]{\frac{1.9\times10^{-12}}{2^2\times1^1}}$$

$$= \sqrt[3]{\frac{1.9\times10^{-12}}{4}} = 7.8\times10^{-5}\ \text{mol/L}$$

(ii) Let S_2 be the molar solubility of Ag_2CrO_4 in the presence of Na_2CrO_4.

$[Ag^+] = 2S_2$ as there are two Ag^+ ions in solution.

CrO_4^{2-} ions in solution are contributed by two sources, Ag_2CrO_4 and Na_2CrO_4.

$[CrO_4^{2-}]$ from $Ag_2CrO_4 = S_2$ mol/L

$[CrO_4^{2-}]$ from $Na_2CrO_4 = 0.010$ mol/L

$\therefore$ the total $[CrO_4^{2-}] = (S_2 + 0.010)$ mol/L

$$K_{sp} = [Ag^+]^2\,[CrO_4^{2-}] = (2\,S_2)^2\,(S_2 + 0.010)$$

The value of S_2 can be determined by solving this cubic equation; however, the procedure is elaborate. The very small K_{sp} value (1.9×10^{-12}) indicates that the solubility of Ag_2CrO_4 is small. It should be smaller in the presence of excess CrO_4^{2-}. Therefore, $S_2 << 0.010$.

Hence, $S_2 + 0.010 \approx 0.010$.

Consequently, the equation can be simplified to $K_{sp} = (2S_2)^2\,(0.010) = 1.9\times10^{-12}$
Solving this equation,

$S_2 = 6.89\times10^{-6}$ mol/L

This value of S_2 confirms the assumption made, because

$0.010 + 6.89\times10^{-6} \approx 0.010$

(iii) Let S_3 be the molar solubility of Ag_2CrO_4 in presence of $AgNO_3$

Then, $[Ag^+] = 0.010 + 2S_3$

$[CrO_4^{2-}] = S_3$

Therefore, $(0.010 + 2S_3)^2\,S_3 = 1.9\times10^{-12}$

As $S_3 << 0.010$, it can be ignored inside parentheses.

$\therefore\ (0.010)^2\,S_3 = 1.9\times10^{-12}$

$S_3 = 1.9\times10^{-8}$ mol/L

The results reveal that

- The solubility of Ag_2CrO_4 decreases in the presence of common ions, Ag^+ and CrO_4^{2-}.
- However, the decrease is more in the presence of Ag^+ than the decrease in the presence of same amount of CrO_4^{2-}. This enhanced influence of Ag^+ is due to the presence of two Ag^+ ions compared to only one CrO_4^- ion in Ag_2CrO_4.

The Na^+ and NO_3^- ions are *diverse ions*; they do not directly influence the solubility. However, they increase the ionic strength of the solution and are expected to slightly increase the solubility of Ag_2CrO_4.

5.5.1 LIMITATION OF K_{sp} CONCEPT

The concept of K_{sp} discussed so far is strictly applicable only to sparingly soluble salts. In these cases, the use of ionic concentrations in the equilibrium equation is valid, as these concentrations are very low. With moderately or highly soluble salts, their saturated solutions have high concentrations of ions and therefore, instead of ionic concentrations, only *ionic activities* should be used in the equation. For them, the molar concentrations and ionic activities (effective concentrations) are not the same. For more soluble salts, the dynamic equilibrium constant obtained from using activities is denoted as K.

- A solubility product constant is the product of the concentrations of the ions appearing in the chemical equation for the solubility equilibrium, with each term raised to the power given by the coefficient in the equation. For example, for the equilibrium

  $$Bi_2S_3(s) \rightleftharpoons 2\ Bi^{3+}(aq) + 3\ S^{2-}(aq)$$

  $$K_{sp} = [Bi^{3+}]^2\ [S^{2-}]^3$$

- A common ion reduces the solubility of a sparingly soluble solute. When a small volume of a clear, concentrated solution of KI is added to a clear saturated solution of PbI_2, a small quantity of $PbI_2(s)$ precipitates—this is due to common ion effect.
- A diverse ion causes *salt effect*, slightly increases the solubility of a sparingly soluble salt.
- The concept of solubility product is applicable only to sparingly soluble salts.

Problem 5.7 An aqueous solution is a mixture of Cd^{2+}, Cu^{2+} and Mn^{2+}, each of 0.020 M concentration. Which sulphide(s) will precipitate if the solution is saturated with $H_2S(aq)$?

Solution

$$H_2S(aq) \rightleftharpoons 2H^+(aq) + S^{2-}(aq)$$

In a saturated solution of H_2S,

$$[S^{2-}] = 1.0 \times 10^{-14}\ M$$

Since each ion concentration is 0.020 M, each ion product,

$$[M^{2+}]\ [S^{2-}] = (0.020)\ (1.0 \times 10^{-14}) = 2.0 \times 10^{-16}$$

Let Q be the reaction quotient.

$$Q_{CdS} = [Cd^{2+}]\ [S^{2-}] = 2.0 \times 10^{-16}$$

For CdS, $K_{sp} = 8 \times 10^{-27}$

As $Q_{CdS} > K_{sp}$, CdS precipitates.

$$Q_{CuS} = [Cu^{2+}]\ [S^{2-}] = 2.0 \times 10^{-16}$$

For CuS, $K_{sp} = 6 \times 10^{-36}$

As $Q_{CuS} > K_{sp}$, CuS precipitates.

$Q_{MnS} = [Mn^{2+}]\,[S^{2-}] = 2.0 \times 10^{-16}$

For $MnS,\ K_{sp} = 2 \times 10^{-13}$

As $Q_{MnS} < K_{sp}$, MnS does not precipitate.

5.5.2 Effect of pH

The pH of the solution affects the solubility of a salt of a weak acid. The H^+ ion combines with the anion of the salt to form the weak acid, and increases the solubility of the salt. For example, the molar solubility of CaC_2O_4 is 1.3×10^{-9} whereas in a solution with 1.2×10^{-4} [H^+ M], it increases to 6.7×10^{-5} mol/L.

The pH is an important factor in the formation of precipitates in gravimetric analysis. It is chosen to ensure complete precipitation and stability of the precipitate. For example, the various metal oxinates have to be precipitated at different pH conditions, depending upon the effect of pH on their stabilities (Table 5.5).

Table 5.5 The pH ranges for precipitation of metal oxinates

Metal	Initial precipitation pH	Complete precipitation pH
Al	2.9	4.7–9.8
Ca	6.8	9.2–12.7
Cu	3.0	> 3.3
Ir(III)	2.5	4.1–11.2
Mg	7.0	> 8.7
Ni	3.5	4.6–10.0
Ti	3.6	4.6–8.6
Zn	3.3	> 4.4

5.5.3 Effect of Complexation

Complexation increases the solubility of a sparingly soluble salt in water. The increase in solubility depends upon the nature of the complexing agent, its concentration and formation constant of the complex. For example, the sparingly soluble AgCl(*s*) dissolves on adding aqueous ammonia to it.

5.5.4 Effect of Other Factors

The nature of the solvent and the particle size of the sparingly soluble salt also affect the solubility. Freshly precipitated colloidal particles are more soluble than larger particles. Ageing a precipitate decreases its solubility. That is why, in gravimetry, precipitates are allowed to stand for some time, to allow for formation of larger particles and render the precipitate more filterable.

5.6 THEORIES OF PRECIPITATION

5.6.1 Types of Precipitates

In gravimetric analyses, different types of precipitates are formed. They are formed through different mechanisms and have to be treated differently.

5.6.2 Nucleation and Crystal Growth

The formation of a precipitate is a physical process as well as a chemical process. The physical process consists of two steps—nucleation and crystal growth. Nucleation is the formation of the smallest particles of a precipitate capable of spontaneous growth. Crystal growth is the deposition of ions from the solution on the surfaces of solid particles formed in nucleation. Nucleation precedes crystal growth. The number of particles and the particle size of a given mass of precipitate are determined by the number of nuclei formed in the nucleation step.

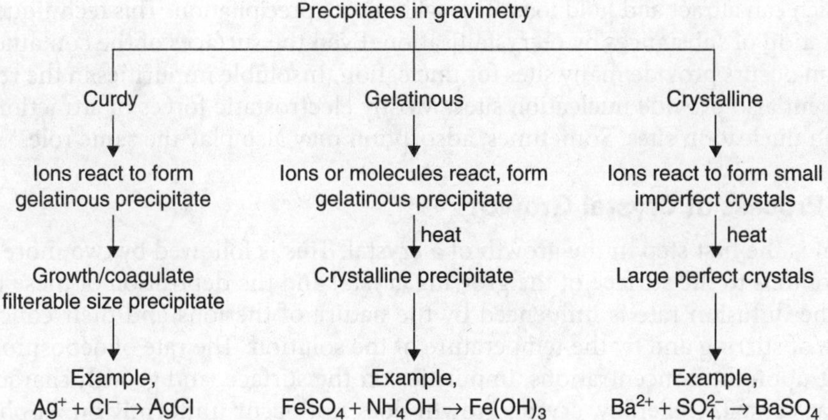

The von Weimarn ratio Von Weimarn found out that the particle size of precipitates is inversely proportional to the relative supersaturation of the solution during precipitation process. This fact is denoted as

$$\text{Relative supersaturation} = \frac{Q - S}{S}$$

where Q is the concentration of the mixed reagents before precipitation occurs and S is the solubility of the precipitate at equilibrium.

Supersaturation It is a condition in which the solution phase contains more of the dissolved precipitate than can be in equilibrium with the solid phase. It is a temporary condition. This state is lost when precipitation starts. The ratio, $(Q - S)/S$ gives the rate of precipitation also.

$$\text{Rate of precipitation} = \frac{(Q - S)}{S}$$

The number of nuclei formed is directly proportional to the extent of supersaturation, $(Q - S)/S$, existing at the time of nucleation. In general, the larger the extent of supersaturation, the smaller will be the size of the individual particles of the precipitate. *Therefore, it is important to have the solutions diluted before precipitation to promote the formation of large crystals.* Larger the crystal size, the easier will be its handling in gravimetry.

To mimise supersaturation and obtain large crystals,

- precipitation is carried out from dilute solutions,
- the precipitating reagent is diluted and added slowly, with effective stirring; these procedures reduce Q, and
- precipitation is done from hot solutions: this increases S; then the mixture is cooled for quantitative precipitation.

5.6.2.1 Spontaneous and Induced Nucleation

The large clusters of ions can join in a supersaturated solution to form a nucleus and this process is called *spontaneous nucleation*. However, spontaneous nucleation is not common. In solution, some sites can attract and hold ions. These sites act as centres at which nucleation and crystal growth are promoted. This nucleation is called *induced nucleation*. Nucleation does not occur readily with some solutions, and in such cases a few particles of a precipitate are deliberately added, which can attract and hold ions. This will initiate precipitation. This technique is used in the purification of substances by recrystallisation. Even the surfaces of the container in which the reaction occurs provide many sites for nucleation. Insoluble impurities in the reagents and in the solvent also provide nucleation sites. Mostly electrostatic forces of attraction hold ions together on nucleation sites. Sometimes, adsorption may also play the same role.

5.6.2.2 Process of Crystal Growth

Nucleation is the first step in the growth of a crystal. This is followed by two more steps—the diffusion of ions to the surface of the growing crystal and the deposition of these ions on the surface. The diffusion rate is influenced by the nature of the ions and their concentrations, by the rate of stirring and by the temperature of the solution. The rate of deposition of ions is dependent upon the concentrations, impurities on the surface, and growth characteristics of a particular crystal. Generally, crystal growth does not occur uniformly on all phases of the crystal and therefore perfect geometrical shapes are rarely formed in precipitation processes. On certain phases, preferential growth may occur. Preferential growth on corners may result in irregularly branched crystals called *dendrites*. The shape of precipitated particles is markedly influenced by the presence of impurity ions, probably because they inhibit or aid growth on certain phases. The physical phenomena of nucleation and crystal growth are related to satisfactory requirements of precipitation and quantitative separation of chemical species. Physical form, purity and solubility of a precipitated phase are influenced by nucleation and crystal growth.

5.6.3 Purity of Precipitates

The purity of a precipitate is a vital aspect for successful gravimetric determination. The precipitate may be contaminated with one or more other substances because those other substances are themselves insufficiently soluble in the mother liquid. A precipitated phase can become contaminated with substances from its mother liquid even when the equilibrium solubilities of those other substances are not exceeded. There are different ways by which this contamination can occur.

The surface of a precipitate has positive and negative centres and these may attract negative and positive ions from the medium. Such ions, attracted by the precipitate would get adsorbed on the surface of the precipitate. This causes contamination of the precipitate, and is called *adsorption-contamination.*

Paneth–Fajans–Hahn law This law gives an idea of the nature of adsorption. According to this law, a precipitate preferentially adsorbs that ion which forms the least soluble compound with a lattice ion. For example, calcium oxalate preferentially adsorbs magnesium ions rather than sodium ions because magnesium oxalate is less soluble than sodium oxalate. Ion adsorption is selective; it depends on the nature of electrical attraction, concentration of ions in solution, size of ion, in addition to the solubility as indicated by the Paneth–Fajans–Hahn law.

5.6.3.1 Co-precipitation

The process of precipitates of impurities getting associated with the precipitate (being separated for estimation) is called co-precipitation. Co-precipitation by direct adsorption is likely to be negligible because the specific area of crystalline precipitates is relatively small. There are two other forms of co-precipitation—*inclusion* and *occlusion.* Inclusion is the process of impurities being randomly distributed in the form of individual ions or molecules throughout the crystal. As a crystal is formed during precipitation, some impurities can get attracted and trapped within

T W Richards, USA, 1868–1928

Born	1868 USA
Died	1928

The accurate determination of atomic weights was a challenging and laborious task for early chemists. They used simple and inexpensive apparatus for the gravimetric determinations of atomic weights. The atomic weights of 55 of the 92 elements known at that time were determined gravimetrically. Richards T W (Harvard University) received the 1914 Noble Prize for the atomic weight determination of silver, chlorine and nitrogen.

He determined the atomic weight of over 30 elements with a high degree of accuracy. Though such determinations appear simple now, and may be performed even by undergraduate students, these were considered pioneering research in the 1900s.

He invented the nepholometer.

According to Richards, 'Every substance must be assumed to be impure, every reaction must be incomplete, every method of measurement must be associated to contain some constant error until proof to the contrary can be obtained. As little as possible must be taken for granted'.

This is a well acknowledged truth in chemistry.

the growing crystal lattice. This type of contamination is *occlusion contamination*. Occlusion is a non-homogeneous distribution of impurities present within the imperfect crystal lattice of the precipitate. Occlusion occurs when whole droplets of solutions containing impurities are trapped by a rapidly growing crystal. Contaminants are located within the crystal and therefore washing will not remove these impurities from the precipitate. Occlusion can be significantly lessened by a lower precipitation rate. When precipitation is slow, the impurities will have sufficient time to escape from the precipitate before they become entrapped. Digestion of the precipitate for several hours is effective in eliminating contamination by occlusion.

In co-precipitation, the precipitation of an otherwise soluble substance along with an insoluble precipitate takes place. The insoluble precipitate and the impurity may precipitate simultaneously or one after the other. However, it is possible to precipitate one component under such conditions that all other components would be expected to remain completely in solution, on the basis of the solubility principle. In practice, co-precipitation always occurs to some extent. Even in a highly accurate work, as in the carefully prepared precipitate of silver chloride, some co-precipitation would occur, though insignificant. It may be significant in some cases, as in the precipitation of hydrous ferric oxide.

Mechanisms of co-precipitation Co-precipitation may occur in one or more of the following ways of which the first three have already been discussed—(i) surface adsorption, (ii) occlusion, (iii) inclusion and (iv) isomorphous replacement.

Isomorphous replacement An ion in a crystal of the precipitate may be replaced by an impurity ion of similar size and shape—this phenomenon is isomorphous replacement. Here, the impurity is permanently incorporated into the crystal lattice and cannot be removed by washing. Removal of the offending ion likely to take part in isomorphous replacement before precipitation of the desired compound is one way of avoiding this kind of contamination. Another way is to dissolve the precipitate and re-form it under more favourable conditions. For example, $BaSO_4$ gets contaminated with alkali metal ions. The ions K^+ and Ba^{2+} have comparable radii (1.33 nm and 1.35 nm respectively) and therefore isomorphous replacement is possible.

5.6.3.2 Post-precipitation

This is another type of precipitate contamination. Post-precipitation is the precipitation of an impurity from its supersaturated solution some time after the appearance of a primary precipitate which is being determined. For example, when calcium is determined as its oxalate, and if the solution contains magnesium ions, magnesium oxalate will be precipitated slowly on calcium oxalate. Post-precipitation is greater when the precipitate is kept in contact with the mother liquid longer. It occurs with sparingly soluble substances which form supersaturated solutions. These substances usually have an ion in common with the primary precipitate (oxalate in the example cited).

The surface of a precipitate has positive and negative centres and these may attract negative and positive ions from the mother liquid. Such attracted ions would get adsorbed on the surface and thus contaminate the precipitate.

Differences between post-precipitation and co-precipitation

- In post-precipitation, the contamination increases as the precipitate is kept in contact with the solution longer, but with co-precipitation it decreases with time.
- With post-precipitation, contamination increases the faster the solution is agitated. The reverse is true with co-precipitation.
- The magnitude of contamination by post-precipitation is generally much greater than that by co-precipitation.

Procedures to minimise occlusion

- The precipitate is ignited at high temperature when, due to internal pressure, the pockets holding the occluded impurity may rupture and release the impurity.
- The solution is kept dilute with respect to all components so that the mother liquid which is trapped will not contain much solute.
- The precipitation is carried out under conditions that promote slow growth of crystals, thus minimising the formation of flaws and voids within the crystal.
- The precipitation may be performed under conditions in which the precipitate has appreciable solubility and then it is allowed to recrystallise slowly.

Methods to minimise surface adsorption

- The solution from which the precipitate is formed should be made dilute.
- The precipitate should be formed as large crystals. This is promoted by slow precipitation, stirring during mixing and using dilute solutions.
- The precipitate should be formed from a hot solution, so that the solubility of the impurities is high. This would decrease the tendency for the formation of colloidal particles and decrease the attraction between the impurity ions and the ions on the surface of the precipitate. The adsorption of foreign ions, which results in the formation of relatively insoluble compounds with the ions of the precipitate, can be prevented at high temperatures.

- Highly charged ions tend to co-precipitate. These may be removed prior to precipitation.
- Precipitation may be done with a reagent such that no other ions in the solution are of the same size as any lattice ion in the precipitate; otherwise, surface adsorption would occur.
- The precipitate is digested so that crystals undergo recrystallisation to form larger, fewer crystals with correspondingly less surface area.

5.6.3.3 Effect of Digestion

Digestion is carried out by allowing the precipitate to stand for several hours (sometimes up to 24 hours) at room temperature or at slightly higher temperatures, in contact with the solution from which it was formed. This promotes complete precipitation in the form which can be readily filtered. During digestion, small particles tend to pass into solution and then redeposit on the larger particles. Digestion thus promotes the formation of regular crystal shapes with lesser surface area. Hence co-precipitation by adsorption would be less. During digestion, the impurities trapped in some pockets may also escape from these places, making the precipitate less impure.

5.6.3.4 The Ostwald Ripening

The process of digesting the precipitate to obtain larger crystals is called the Ostwald ripening. This is depicted in Fig. 5.2. Digestion promotes dissolution of small crystals and recrystallisation on the surfaces of large crystals, leading to larger crystals. It also promotes *agglomeration*, that is, cementing of smaller crystals to bigger ones.

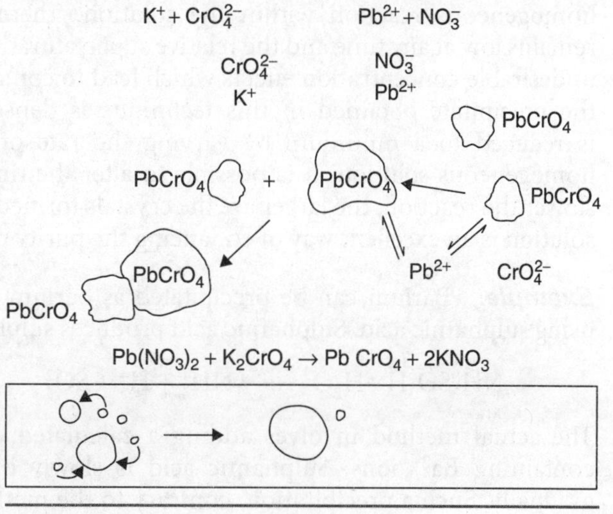

Fig. 5.2 Ostwald ripening of precipitate

Many small crystals form in a system initially but slowly disappear except for a few that grow large, at the expense of the small crystals. The smaller crystals serve as 'nutrients' for the larger crystals. As some crystals grow, the area around them is depleted of smaller crystals. Ostwald ripening is a spontaneous process and is energetically favourable. Though smaller crystals are kinetically favoured, larger ones are thermodynamically favoured. Large crystals with greater volume-to-surface area ratio represent low energy states.

The recrystallisation of water within ice cream which gives ice cream a gritty crunchy texture is an Ostwald ripening process.

5.6.3.5 Perfect Precipitation Practice

- Precipitation should be carried out in dilute solution to minimise the error due to co-precipitation.
- The reagents should be mixed slowly and with constant stirring. This will keep the degree of supersaturation low, promoting the growth of large crystals.
- A slight excess of the reagent is generally required to ensure complete precipitation.

- Precipitation is carried out in hot solutions, provided the product is thermally stable. At higher temperatures, the solubility is increased with a consequent reduction in the degree of supersaturation. In addition, coagulation is assisted and sol formation is decreased.
- The completion of precipitation should be ascertained by adding a few drops of the precipitant through the side of the beaker and observing for absence of fresh precipitate formation in the clear supernatant liquid.
- Crystalline precipitates should be digested preferably overnight, except in those cases where post-precipitation may occur. Digestion on the steam bath is desirable. However, digestion has no effect upon amorphous or gelatinous precipitates.
- The precipitate should be washed with an appropriate dilute solution of an electrolyte. Pure water may cause peptisation.
- If appreciable co-precipitation is a possibility, the precipitate should be dissolved in a suitable solvent and then reprecipitated.

5.7 PRECIPITATION FROM HOMOGENEOUS MEDIUM

In this technique, the precipitant is not added as such, but it is slowly generated by a homogeneous reaction within the solution. Therefore, the concentration of the reagent remains low at any time and the relative supersaturation is always low. This situation avoids the undesirable concentration effects which lead to contamination of the precipitate. In addition, the precipitate obtained in this technique is dense and easily filterable. Co-precipitation is reduced to a minimum by varying the rate of reaction producing the precipitant in homogeneous solution. It is possible to alter the time of appearance of the precipitate. The slower the reaction, the larger are the crystals formed. Thus, precipitation from homogeneous solution is an excellent way of enhancing the purity of a precipitate.

Example: Barium can be precipitated as barium sulphate from a homogeneous medium using sulphamic acid. Sulphamic acid produces sulphate ion on hydrolysis.

$$NH_2SO_3H + H_2O \longrightarrow NH_4^+ + H^+ + SO_4^{2-}$$

The actual method involves adding a calculated excess of sulphamic acid to a solution containing Ba^{2+} ions. Sulphamic acid is slowly hydrolysed, and this precipitates $BaSO_4$ gradually. Such a precipitation, contrary to the method involving the addition of a sulphate directly, produces pure, coarsely crystalline barium sulphate. In Table 5.6 are given the representative methods of precipitation from homogeneous medium; the precipitants are highlighted with underlines.

Table 5.6 Precipitation from homogeneous media

Precipitant	Reagent	Precipitant generation reaction	Metal precipitated
OH^-	Urea	$(NH_2)_2CO + 3H_2O \rightarrow CO_2 + 2NH_3 + \underline{2NH_4OH}$	Al, Fe, Sn
SO_4^{2-}	Dimethyl sulphate	$(CH_3O)_2SO_2 + 2H_2O \rightarrow 2CH_3OH + \underline{SO_4^{2-}} + 2H_3O^+$	Ba, Pb
PO_4^{3-}	Trimethyl phosphate	$(CH_3O)_3PO + 3H_2O \rightarrow 3CH_3OH + \underline{H_3PO_4}$	Zr, Hf
$C_2O_4^{2-}$	Ethyl oxalate	$(C_2H_5)_2C_2O_4 + 2H_2O \rightarrow 2C_2H_5OH + \underline{H_2C_2O_4}$	Ba, Ra
S^{2-}	Thioacetamide	$CH_3CSNH_2 + H_2O \rightarrow CH_3CONH_2 + \underline{H_2S}$	Sb, Mo, Cu, Cd

5.7.1 Cation-Release Method

In each of the examples given in Table 5.6, an anionic precipitant is slowly generated, which then reacts with a cation to form a precipitate. Sometimes, precipitation from a homogeneous medium may involve the reverse; a cation may be slowly generated, which then combines with an anion to form a precipitate. An example of this is the precipitation of SO_4^{2-} by the soluble Ba–EDTA 1:1 complex in the presence of H_2O_2. At 80°C, the peroxide releases barium ions by oxidising the organic ligand. The barium ions then form barium sulphate precipitate.

5.8 WASHING OF PRECIPITATE

Before drying, washing of the precipitate is necessary to remove the soluble compounds that are adhered to the precipitate. In this process, only surface impurities will be removed. Pure water is not generally used because it may peptise a precipitate, leading to loss of a part of the precipitate. A solution of some electrolyte is preferably used for washing. This should have a common ion with the precipitate to reduce solubility errors and should be easily volatilised in the preparation of the precipitate for weighing. To fulfill these conditions, ammonium salts, ammonia solution, and dilute acids are commonly employed. If the precipitate is insoluble under hot conditions, hot wash solutions are preferred because of the greater solubility of the foreign ions and the increased speed of filtration.

5.8.1 Types of Wash-Solutions

Wash solutions are of three types:

(i) *Solutions which prevent the precipitate from becoming colloidal and passing through the filter.* This tendency is observed with gelatinous or flocculated precipitates. A solution of an electrolyte like an ammonium salt is used for washing such precipitates.

(ii) *Solutions which reduce the solubility of the precipitates.* If the wash solution has an ion common with an ion in the precipitate, the solubility of the precipitate will be less in the wash solution. For example, dilute ammonium oxalate solution is used for washing calcium oxalate. Sometimes, organic solvents like ethanol and ether may be used for washing. These are safe solvents because most of the precipitates are insoluble in these.

(iii) *Solutions which prevent the hydrolysis of salts of weak acids and bases.* A tendency to hydrolyse is shown by a precipitate which is a salt of a weak acid. The product of such hydrolysis will be a base. The wash liquid must therefore be basic. For example, $MgNH_4PO_4$ hydrolyses to give acid phosphate ion HPO_4^{2-} and hydroxide ion, and therefore it should be washed with dilute aqueous ammonia.

The loss of precipitate due to solubility is minimised by using the least quantity of wash solution. *Washing should be carried out efficiently by using many small portions of liquid rather than a few large portions.* Qualitative tests must be made upon portions of the filtrate for some foreign ion which is present in the original solution and washing stopped at the appropriate stage. For example, in the estimation of silver chloride, the washing of the precipitate is continued with dilute nitric acid until the filtrate is free from chloride ion.

5.8.2 Ideal Characteristics of Wash Liquids

- It should have no solvent action upon the precipitate, but dissolve foreign (impurity) substances easily.

- It should have no dispersive action on the precipitate.
- It should form no volatile or insoluble product with the precipitate.
- It should be easily volatilised at the temperature of drying of the precipitate.
- It should not contain any substance which is likely to interfere with subsequent determination of constituents in the filtrate.
- It should be non-toxic, considering the fact that it is washed down the drain and volatilised during drying of the precipitate.

5.9 WATER IN GRAVIMETRIC ANALYSIS

Understanding the association of water with the precipitate is an important aspect of gravimetric analysis. The precipitate may be associated with water in five ways.

(i) The water from the solution can be *physically retained* by the precipitate.
(ii) Water may be *adsorbed* on the precipitate.
(iii) Water may be *occluded*—present in solid solution or in cavities within crystals.
(iv) *Sorbed* water may be associated with the precipitate, especially with precipitates having a large internal surface.
(v) Water can be a part of the *hydrated* precipitate—water of crystallisation.

The removal of all of these forms of water is necessary for the reliable estimation of an analyte. In rare cases, the precipitate may be weighed in its hydrated form, provided it is stable at the temperature of drying. For example, in the estimation of manganese using diammonium hydrogen phosphate, the crystalline precipitate with the formula, $MnNH_4PO_4 \cdot H_2O$ is weighed at 105°C. Elimination of all forms of water to obtain stoichiometrically pure dry precipitate is crucial in gravimetry. The temperature for drying the precipitate is so chosen as to ensure completeness of drying without any decomposition of the product.

5.9.1 Drying of Precipitate

The temperature at which a precipitate has to be dried can be ascertained from the knowledge of the thermogravimetric curve for that substance. The temperature range used for drying should be high enough to volatilise water and other volatile impurities but must be well below the decomposition temperature. The precipitate is brought to a specified temperature and maintained at that temperature for a definite time to ensure a constant weight for the precipitate.

- Thermal decomposition consequent to drying the precipitate at a higher temperature than the required temperature is a common source of error in gravimetry.

5.9.2 Temperature for Drying Precipitate

The temperature at which the precipitate has to be dried is chosen based on the following criteria.

- The compound obtained by precipitation should not decompose.
- The weighable, chemical form of the precipitate should be totally free of water.
- Repeated drying of the precipitate should give a constant weight.

The temperature suitable for drying – satisfying these criteria – can be determined, as already stated, from a study of the thermometric curves for the substance precipitated. Usually, the precipitate is thermally stable at a range of temperature and therefore it can be dried by maintaining a narrow temperature range, ± 5°C, well below its decomposition temperature, but above 100°C.

5.9.3 Fractional Precipitation

Fractional precipitation is the selective precipitation of a single ion or a group of ions from a mixture of ions. It is called also *controlled precipitation*; such precipitations are done by choosing the experimental conditions so that the solubility product is exceeded for only one ion of the mixture, though the other ions in the mixture can also form precipitates with the reagent.

An example for fractional precipitation is the separation of the cations of the second group from the cations of the third group by S^{2-} ion in acid medium, $[H^+]$ being 0.1 to 0.3 M. Similarly, Fe^{3+} can be separated from Mg^{2+} quantitatively using aqueous ammonia. Carbonates can also be separated by fractional precipitation, and so also chlorides. These principles are used in gravimetry in the determination of certain ions.

The primary condition for fractional precipitation is that, the two or more constituents to be separated, should differ significantly in their solubility. This implies that their K_{sp} values should be significantly different.

Example: Consider the separation of $CrO_4^{2-}(aq)$ and $Br^-(aq)$ by the use of $Ag^+(aq)$. The equilibria involved are

$$Ag_2\,CrO_4(s) \rightleftharpoons 2\,Ag^+(aq) + CrO_4^{2-}(aq) \qquad K_{sp} = 2.4 \times 10^{-12}$$

$$Ag\,Br(s) \rightleftharpoons Ag^+(aq) + Br^-(aq) \qquad K_{sp} = 5.0 \times 10^{-13}$$

As the K_{sp} values differ significantly, fractional separation of CrO_4^{2-} and Br^- is possible. On adding $Ag^+(aq)$ to the solution mixture, Br^- will react first and $AgBr(s)$ will precipitate, as this salt has a lower K_{sp} value.

5.10 ANALYTES IN GRAVIMETRY

Different types of analyte species – cations, anions, inorganic and organic – can be determined by gravimetry.

5.10.1 Gravimetry of Metals

The precipitants and the chemical formulae for products obtained by precipitation processes in gravimetric determinations for some metallic cations are listed in Table 5.7.

Table 5.7 Gravimetry of some metals

Metal ion	Precipitant	Product formula	Drying temperature (°C)
Aluminium	8-hydroxyquinoline (oxine)	$Al(C_9H_6ON)_3$	130
Ammonium	sodium tetraphenylborate	$NH_4[B(C_6H_5)_4]$	100
Antimony	pyrograllol	$Sb(C_6H_5O_3)$	105
Arsenic	hydrogen sulphide	As_2S_3	105
Barium	sulphuric acid	$BaSO_4$	600–800
Beryllium	ammonium hydroxide	BeO	1000 (ignite)
Bismuth	potassium iodide	BiOI	110

(Continued)

Table 5.7 Continued

Metal ion	Precipitant	Product formula	Drying temperature (°C)
Cadmium	quinaldic acid	$Cd(C_{10}H_6O_2N)_2$	125
Calcium	ammonium oxalate	$CaC_2O_4{\bullet}H_2O$ or $CaCO_3$	110 475
Cerium	potassium iodate	CeO_2	500 (ignite)
Chromium	lead nitrate	$PbCrO_4$	120
Cobalt	mercury(II) chloride and ammonium thiocyanate	$Co[Hg(SCN)_4]$	100
Copper	ammonium thiocyanate	CuSCN	110–120
Gold	sulphur dioxide	Au metal	800 (ignite)
Iron	methanoic acid and urea	Fe_2O_3	ignite at 850
Lead	chromium nitrate and potassium bromate	$PbCrO_4$	120
Lithium	sodium aluminate	$2Li_2O{\bullet}5Al_2O_3$	500–550
Magnesium	8-hydroxyquinoline	$Mg(C_9H_6ON)_2$	155–160
Manganese	diammonium hydrogen phosphate	$MnNH_4PO_4{\bullet}H_2O$ or $Mn_2P_2O_7$	100–150
Mercury	thionalide	$Hg(C_{12}H_{10}ONS)_2$	105
Molybdenum	8-hydroxyquinoline	$MoO_2(C_9H_6ON)_2$	130–140
Nickel	dimethylglyoxime	$Ni(C_4H_7O_2N_2)_2$	120
Palladium	dimethylglyoxime	$Pd(C_4H_7O_2N_2)_2$	110
Platinum	methanoic acid	Pt metal	ignite
Potassium	sodium tetraphenylborate	$K[B(C_6H_5)_4]$	120
Selenium	sulphur dioxide	Se metal	100–110
Silver	hydrochloric acid	AgCl	130–150
Sodium	zinc uranyl ethanoate	$NaZn(UO_2)_3-(C_2H_3O_2)_9 \cdot 6H_2O$	55–60
Strontium	potassium dihydrogenphosphate	$SrHPO_4$	120
Tellurium	sulphur dioxide	Te metal	105
Thallium	potassium chromate	Tl_2CrO_4	120
Thorium	sebacic acid	ThO_2	700–800
Tin	N-benzoyl-N-phenylhydroxylamine	$(C_{13}H_{11}O_2N)_2SnCl_2$	110
Titanium	tannic acid and phenazone	TiO_2	100 (dry), 1000 (ignite)
Tungsten	tannic acid and phenazone	WO_3	800–900 (ignite)
Uranium	cupferron	U_3O_8	1000
Vanadium	silver nitrate and sodium ethanoate	Ag_3VO_4	110
Zinc	8-hydroxyquinaldinate	$Zn(C_{10}H_8ON)_2$	130–140
Zirconium	mandelic acid	ZrO_2	900–100 (ignite)

5.10.2 Salt-like Precipitates

Some organic precipitants form salt-like precipitates with some inorganic ions. For example, oxalic acid forms an insoluble salt with Ca^{2+} and this reaction is suitable for the gravimetric estimation of calcium. Some examples of such gravimetry are given in Table 5.8.

Table 5.8 Gravimetry with salt-like precipitates

Reagent	Analyte
Oxalate	Ca^{2+}
Sodium tetraphenylboron	K^+
Benzidine	SO_4^{2-}
Tetraphenylarsonium chloride	Tl^+
Arsonic acid	Sn^{4+}, Th^{4+}, Zr^{4+}

5.10.3 Gravimetric Estimation of Anions

Some anions in analytes can also be estimated gravimetrically. In each of these estimations, the precipitant consists of a cation which forms a stable precipitate of definite composition with the anion. Some examples for such estimations are listed in Table 5.9.

Table 5.9 Gravimetric estimation of anions

Anion	Precipitant	Formula of of precipitate	Conditions
Chloride	silver nitrate	AgCl	–
Bromide	silver nitrate in nitric acid	AgBr	–
Iodide	silver nitrate	Ag I	dry below 150°C
Nitrate	nitron	$C_{20}H_{16}N_4$•HNO_3	dry at 105°C
Nitrite	potassium permanganate, nitron	$C_{20}H_{16}N_4$•HNO_3	nitrite is first oxidised
Sulphate	barium chloride	$BaSO_4$	–
Phosphate	ammonim molybdate	$(NH_4)_3[PMo_{12}O_{40}]$ or P_2O_5•24 MoO_3	dry at 200–400°C or heat to 800–825°C
Oxalate	calcium chloride	$CaCO_3$ or CaO	–
Cyanide	silver nitrate	AgCN	dry at 100°C; No heating > 100°C
Thiocyanate	copper sulphate	CuSCN	dry at 110–120°C

5.11 ERRORS IN GRAVIMETRIC ANALYSIS

Gravimetic analysis requires skill and practice for avoiding errors and obtaining accuracy. The common errors that occur are:

- the use of a defective balance and careless weighing,
- incomplete separation of the analyte from the sample,
- incomplete precipitation of the product to be weighed,
- contamination of the precipitate with the precipitant and other materials,
- incomplete drying of the precipitate,
- decompostion of the precipitate due to high temperatures, or its partial or total chemical transformation during the experiment,
- employing wrong stoichiometric equation in calculation, and
- partial loss of precipitate due to the use of defective apparatus (say, a crucible through which the precipitate passes) or spurting of the reaction mixture during digestion or faulty filtration process.

Problem 5.8 In the gravimetric estimation of a chloride, the precipitate AgCl was partly photo-reduced to Ag during filtration and drying. The precipitate contained 0.007% of elemental silver by weight. Calculate the relative error in the percentage of chloride in the sample.

Solution

Let the weight of the precipitate be x g. Then, it is a mixture of 0.993 x g of AgCl and 0.007 x g of Ag.

$$0.007x \text{ g Ag} = (0.007x)\left(\frac{143.32}{107.87}\right) \text{g AgCl}$$

$$= (0.007x)\ (1.3286) \text{ g AgCl}$$

$$= 0.0093x \text{ g AgCl}$$

Therefore, 0.0093 x g of AgCl has been lost due to photo-reduction. Hence, the weight of AgCl before decomposition

$$= (0.993\ x + 0.0093\ x) \text{ g} = 1.0023\ x \text{ g}$$

∴ The relative error

$$= \frac{x - 1.0023\ x}{1.0023\ x}$$

$$= \frac{x}{1.0023\ x} - \frac{1.20023\ x}{1.0023\ x}$$

$$= 0.998 - 1.197 = -0.2\%$$

This is a negative error; the weight of the precipitate is less than what it should have been.

5.12 GUIDELINES FOR GRAVIMETRY

- Use analar grade reagents.
- Ensure that the precipitation is quantitative; achieve this by choosing appropriate experimental conditions and adding sufficient precipitant.
- Carry out precipitation in dilute solution to avoid co-precipitation of impurities.
- Mix the reagents slowly with continuous stirring; this avoids supersaturation and promotes the growth of large crystals.
- Carry out precipitation in hot solutions to reduce degree of supersaturation.
- Digest the precipitate on a steam bath to avoid co-precipitation of impurities and also to help in the formationof an easily filterable precipitate.
- Wash the precipitate with the appropriate dilute solution of an electrolyte to remove impurities.
- If necessary, dissolve the precipitate in a suitable solvent and reprecipitate it; this enhances the purity of the precipitate.
- Adopt if possible, precipitation from a homogenous solution.
- Dry the precipitate carefully at an appropriate temperature to drive off all the adhering solvent, without decomposing the precipitate.

5.13 APPLICATIONS OF GRAVIMETRIC ANALYSIS

- Every element in the periodic table can be determined gravimetrically.
- Gravimetry is an important experimental procedure in chemical laboratories and industries.
- Some organic compounds can also be gravimetrically determined. For example, cholesterol forms a precipitate (complex) with digitonics (an organic saponin).
- Several pharmaceutical compounds can be estimated gravimetrically either by isolating their pure forms without a chemical reactant or by conversion of their sodium salts to acid forms.
- C and H in organic compounds are determined gravimetrically.

5.14 CRUCIBLES: TYPES, CARE AND USE

Crucibles are an important apparatus in gravimetry. They should be carefully selected to suit the type of precipitate and the method of processing the precipitate. Different types of crucibles are used for collecting and weighing the precipitates (Fig. 5.3). These are mainly of two types.

(i) Crucibles made of silica or porcelain are used when the precipitates are ignited to constant weights with a Bunsen burner.

(ii) Sintered crucibles are used for precipitates which are weighed after drying in an air oven.

Crucibles are expensive. They should be handled properly for obtaining reliable gravimetric data. They should never be touched but must always be handled with a pair of tongs. They should not be placed on the table but only on a clean tile.

Porcelain crucibles They are usually 3–4 cm in diameter. They should be carefully heated with a small flame in order to avoid fracture before being heated to a high temperature. They are suited for heating the precipitates to very high temperatures. Porcelain crucibles are suitable for use up to temperatures 1000–1200°C. Hydrofluoric acid, sodium hydroxide, sodium peroxide and alkali carbonates attack porcelain and therefore substances containing these materials should not be contained in such crucibles. These crucibles can be cleaned with warm concentrated acids.

Silica crucibles They are more expensive than porcelain crucibles. However, they may be safely exposed to sudden changes of temperature without any risk of fracture. Silica crucibles must not be used for alkalis or hydrofluoric acid because these chemicals attack silica. Certain precipitates tend to adhere strongly and permanently to these crucibles and hence these crucibles should be carefully cleaned immediately after use.

Platinum crucibles Platinum crucibles are marketed in various shapes and sizes. The choice of the crucible for an experiment is decided by the quantity of the precipitate handled. These are very expensive and hence their use is very much restricted to cases where they are indispensable. These crucibles can be more readily and more uniformly heated to redness than porcelain crucibles. The following rules and precautions must be observed with regard to these crucibles:

- They must not be exposed to a luminous flame since this will cause the platinum metal to lose its lustre and become brittle owing to the formation of platinum carbide.
- Compounds of lead, silver, zinc, tin, bismuth, arsenic and antimony must not be heated in these when there is any possibility of reduction to the metallic state. These metals, having low melting points, may alloy with platinum. Phosphates should not be ignited in a platinum crucible. If phosphorus is formed during ignition it will combine with platinum rendering it brittle.

- Hydroxides, nitrates, nitrites and alkali cyanides should not be fused in platinum crucibles because these react with platinum.
- Evaporation or fusion involving the formation of chlorine, bromine or iodine must not be performed in platinum crucibles because these elements attack platinum.
- The crucible should not be squeezed or scratched. A bright surface should be maintained by burnishing it with sand.
- Adhering substances or stains can be removed by boiling a little concentrated hydrochloric acid in the crucible. Then the crucible should be rinsed with distilled water and dried.

Gooch crucible A Gooch crucible is made of porcelain with the bottom perforated with a number of small holes. It is usually fitted into a glass adaptor (Gooch funnel) by means of a narrow rubber ring, the adaptor passing through the rubber stopper of a filter flask. The bottom of the crucible is covered with asbestos. This covering is done by shaking asbestos fibre bits with water and pouring the mixture into the crucible. The water drains leaving the asbestos as a thin cover at the bottom. A Gooch crucible is used usually for drying precipitates only up to about 250°C, because above this temperature the asbestos loses its weight. This crucible is preferable to filter paper for filtering solutions, such as potassium permanganate, which attack paper.

Sintered crucible In this crucible, instead of the asbestos fibre, a fixed layer of sintered glass particles is used as the filtering medium. The body of the crucible is made of crack-resistant glass and a porous disc of sintered glass is fused into the body. The filter disc is made in varying porosities indicated by numbers from zero to five.

Porosity:	0	1	2	3	4	5
Pore diameter (μm):	200–250	100–120	40–50	20–30	5–10	1–2

Smaller the porosity number, the less suitable is the sinter for filtering fine particles of precipitate. For filtering precipitates of moderate particle size, porosity 3 is suitable. For fine particles such as $BaSO_4$, porosity 4 must be used.

A sintered crucible is also fitted into an adaptor and then into a flask in the same manner as a Gooch crucible. Sintered crucibles are convenient to handle because they are sturdy and remain nearly constant in weight. However, they should not be heated above 200°C. Gelatinous precipitates cannot be filtered through sintered crucibles because the filter pores tend to get clogged with such precipitates.

Precipitates from a sintered crucible may be gently removed by means of the bristles of a test tube brush and water. The sintered portion should never be scratched with glass rod or spatula because scratching will permanently damage the filtering medium. Particles in the pores of the filter can be dislodged by drawing water through it in the reverse direction or by dissolving the solid in a suitable solvent. Caustic alkali should not be used for cleaning because it attacks the sinter. Concentrated acids may be used for cleaning. Acetone is convenient for cleaning and rapid drying. EDTA solution is particularly useful for removing precipitates such as barium sulphate and lead chromate. A new crucible should always be conditioned before being used in a determination. This is done by treating it repeatedly with warm hydrochloric acid, washing and drying until weight constancy is attained.

Rose crucible A rose crucible is used when a precipitate has to be ignited in an atmosphere of a gas, say, hydrogen, carbon dioxide or oxygen. It has provision for passing a gas through it during fusion.

Seven Steps in Gravimetric Analysis

- Dry and weigh the sample.
- Dissolve a suitable weight of the sample in a suitable liquid.
- Add the precipitant in slight excess.
- Coagulate the precipitate by digestion.
- Filter off the precipitate.
- Wash the precipitate
- Dry and weigh the precipitate to a constant weight.

Potpourri

- Ammonium ion can be gravimetrically determined by precipitating it as $(NH_4)_2PtCl_6$. The precipitate is ignited to platinum metal, which is then weighed.

$$(NH_4)_2PtCl_6 \xrightarrow{\Delta} Pt + 2\,NH_4Cl + 2\,Cl_2$$

- A common error in the gravimetric analysis of $Ni(DMG)_2$ – as also in other gravimetric analyses – is the addition of excess of the precipitant. This increases adsorption.
- Peptisation, which is the reverse of coagulation, is avoided by washing the precipitate with an electrolyte in gravimetric analyses. The electrolyte is then volatilised by heating.
- The atomic weights of several elements were determined accurately in the eighteenth and nineteenth centuries by gravimetric analysis bringing fame to some chemists.
- More selective the precipitation reaction in a gravimetric analysis, less is the interference by impurities and other materials present in solution.
- Selection of proper pH for precipitation ensures quantitative precipitation.
- $Fe(OH)_3$ actually precipitates in acid solution due to its small K_{sp}!
- Performing gravimetric estimations requires refined experimental skill and therefore these experiments are a means for training a chemist.
- *Volatilisation gravimetry* involves decomposition of the sample and measurement of the mass of the residue (analyte).
- *Sinter* is to cause to become a coherent mass by heating without melting.

EXERCISES

1. 2.1020 g of an alloy of nickel was brought to solution, and the solution made up to 500 mL. A 50 mL aliquot of this solution was used for gravimetric estimation of Ni after eliminating the other constituents. It yielded a Ni–DMG precipitate of 0.2512 g in a dry condition. Calculate the percentage of Ni in the alloy.

2. A sample contains only CaC_2O_4 and CaO. A 1.2278 g sample of this mixture is heated at 900°C; a residue of CaO weighing 0.8595 g was obtained. What are the percentages of CaC_2O_4 and CaO in the sample?

3. What weight of a steel sample must be used for analysis so that each milligram of $BaSO_4$ precipitate obtained represents 0.100% sulphur in the sample?

4. Calculate the weight of a metal bromide sample – which contains 22.0 % Br^- – that must be taken for gravimetric analysis in order to obtain 0.4080 g of AgBr precipitate.

5. In a gravimetric analysis of a chloride, the precipitate AgCl was weighed erroneously with incomplete drying. The chloride content was then calculated to be 21.4%, whereas the correct value was 20.9%. What was the percent moisture in the precipitate?

6. A sample of limestone contains $MgCa(CO_3)_2$ and also silicates, iron and aluminium compounds. Write a flowchart for the sequential gravimetric estimation of the constituents of this sample.

7. Calculate the gravimetric factor for
(a) S weighed as $BaSO_4$ (b) P weighed as $Mg_2P_2O_7$ (c) C_6H_5Cl weighed as AgCl

8. 0.915 of an impure sample of barium chloride crystals, $BaCl_2 \cdot x\,H_2O$, were dissolved in hot water and then a slight excess of silver nitrate solution was added. The precipitated silver chloride, after filtration, washing and drying at about 120°C, weighed 1.077 g. Find the value of *x*.

9. 2.456 g of a mixture of potash alum and anhydrous potassium sulphate was dissolved in a small quantity of water and heated. Ammonium chloride and ammonia were added to complete the precipitation of aluminium hydroxide. The precipitate was filtered off, washed and heated to obtain alumina. The residue weighed 0.170 g. Calculate the percentage of anhydrous potassium sulphate in the mixture.

10. Calculate the gravimetric factor for the following:
(a) P analyte in the precipitate Ag_3PO_4
(b) Bi_2S_3 analyte when it is estimated as $BaSO_4$
(c) P estimated as $P_2O_5{\bullet}24MoO_3$

11. Calculate the stoichiometric amount of K_2CrO_4 in grams required to precipitate completely Ag^+ as $Ag_2CrO_4(s)$ from a 50 mL 0.120 M $AgNO_3(aq)$.

12. Write a flow chart for separation and gravimetric estimations of the components of each of the flowing alloys:
(a) brass (b) bronze (c) sterling silver (d) manganin (e) alnico

13. Outline a gravimetric method for determining
(a) platinum (IV) (b) uranium (VI) (c) cerium (IV)

14. All the oxygen in a 0.655 g sample of a pure oxide of iron is eliminated by reduction with hydrogen. The residue then weighs 0.4725 g. What is the empirical formula of the oxide?

15. In a gravimetric estimation of magnesium as oxinate, a student actually weighed the dihydrate. But, he calculated the result assuming the precipitate to be anhydrous. What is the percentage error in his calculation?

16. A.0.203 g sample of $MgCl_m \cdot nH_2O$ was dissolved in water and then titrated with 0.100 mol dm^{-3} silver nitrate to an end point of 20.0 mL. Another portion of the sample lost 53.2% of its mass when heated in a stream of hydrogen chloride, leaving a residue of anhydrous magnesium chloride. Find the values of *m* and *n*.

17. A 1.0000g sample of a mixture of NaCl and KCl was dissolved in water and the aqueous solution treated with $AgNO_3(aq)$. The dry AgCl weighed 2.107 g. Calculate the %Na and %K in the sample.

18. Write an essay on the contributions by the 19th century chemists on evolving gravimetric techniques.

19. A 1.0000 g sample containing 75% potassium sulphate (F.W. 174.25) and 25% MSO_4 is dissolved and the sulphate precipitated as $BaSO_4$ (F.W. 233.39). The weight of $BaSO_4$ obtained is 1.4900 g. Calculate the atomic weight of M.

20. From the modern literature, outline the gravimetric determination procedures for the lanthanide elements.

6 Thermoanalytical Methods

6.1 THERMOANALYTICAL METHODS

Many properties of matter are temperature dependent. Density, refractive index, surface tension and magnetic behaviour have significant temperature coefficients. In general, the measurement of these properties at different temperatures does not provide analytical information. However, there are some properties, which when measured as a function of temperature, provide useful information. *Thermal analysis* includes a group of techniques in which a physical property of a substance and/or its reaction products is measured as a function of temperature whilst the substance is subjected to a controlled temperature programme. The techniques used to obtain such information on some property as a function of temperature are called *thermoanalytical* or *thermometric* methods. In each of these techniques, the results are recorded as a curve called a *thermogram*, which is characteristic of the analyte. Some important thermoanalytical methods and the properties measured are listed in Table 6.1.

Table 6.I Thermoanalytical methods

Method	Property measured	Thermogram	Apparatus used
Thermogravimetric analysis (TGA)	Change in weight	Weight (w) versus temperature (T)	Thermobalance
Derivative thermo-gravimetry (DTG)	Rate of change of weight	dw/dt versus temperature (T) (t = time)	Thermobalance
Differential thermal analysis (DTA)	Heat evolved or absorbed	ΔT versus temperature (T)	DTA apparatus
Thermometric Titration (TT)	Change of temperature	Temperature (T) versus volume (V)	Titration calorimeter
Differential scanning calorimetry (DSC)	Difference in heat energy	Differences in heat flow (calories or joules) versus sample temperature (T)	Calorimeter

6.2 THERMOGRAVIMETRIC ANALYSIS (TGA)

6.2.1 Principle

This is a technique in which the change in weight of a substance with temperature over a period of time is followed. The temperature is increased at a constant rate for a known initial weight of the substance and changes in weight are accurately recorded at different times. When the weights are plotted against temperature, a curve characteristic of the substance studied is obtained. Such a curve is called a *thermogravimetric curve* or a *thermogram.* It is called also *pyrolysis curve.* The sample should be ignited up to a temperature range where the curve is flat, that is, where the weight is constant over a wide temperature range. This confirms that all the thermal changes have been completed for the sample.

6.2.2 Thermal Analysis of Silver Nitrate

Figure 6.1 represents the TGA curve for silver nitrate. The horizontal (plateau) portion in the curve indicates no weight change and the plunging portion (inflexion) indicates weight change corresponding to decomposition. The weight of the substance remains constant up to 473°C, indicating that silver nitrate is thermally stable up to this temperature. At 473°C, it starts losing its weight indicating that decomposition starts at this temperature. It decomposes to NO_2 and O_2.

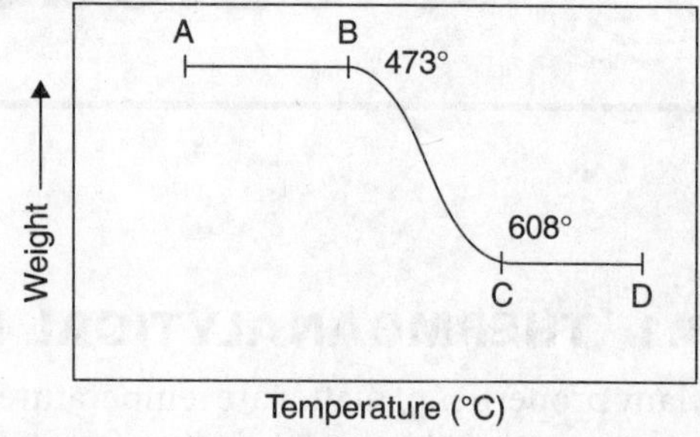

Fig. 6.1 The thermogram for silver nitrate

$$2AgNO_3 \longrightarrow 2Ag + 2NO_2 + O_2$$

The loss in weight continues up to 608°C, and the weight of the sample remains constant beyond this temperature. This is shown by the portion of the curve CD. The portion between 473 and 608°C (BC) represents the decomposition of silver nitrate. Therefore, the decomposition is complete at 608°C, leaving metallic silver as the stable residue. Thus, the thermogram of silver nitrate clearly indicates the decomposition temperature range for silver nitrate. The temperature interval between B and C is called the *reaction interval*; this represents the temperature region in which a particular decomposition takes place. This example shows how the thermal behaviour of a material can be studied by TGA.

6.2.3 Methods of Obtaining Thermograms

Thermograms may be constructed in different ways. Sometimes, in a thermal analysis, the weight change is recorded against the time instead of temperature, keeping the rate of heating constant. The weight change may be recorded in one of the following ways: (i) actual weight loss, (ii) percentage weight loss, (iii) weight loss in terms of molecular mass unit, or (iv) rate of change of weight (with time) (dw/dt) each plotted against temperature (T).

Temperature measurement The crucial aspect of thermogravimetry is the accurate recording of temperature during thermal analysis of the sample. A thermocouple can be immersed in the sample for accurate temperature response; however, this introduces the risk of catalytic decomposition of the sample (the thermocouple, made of metals, can decompose the sample). In addition, the sample may get contaminated and weighing errors may occur. To avoid these problems, a small thermocouple is located inside the sample holder as close as possible to the sample, without contacting the sample. This arrangement is not free from problems; the recorded temperatures usually lag or lead the actual sample temperatures.

In modern thermobalances, a computerised temperature control unit is used. It automatically compares the voltage output of the thermocouple with a set of voltage versus temperature data stored in a read-only memory. The voltage applied to the heater is then automatically adjusted by the microprocessor based on the difference between the temperature of the thermocouple and the temperature specified in the read-only memory. This procedure gives excellent agreement between the specified temperature progress and the actual temperature of the sample. The modern TGA instruments give a reproducibility of ±1°C in duplicate analyses.

6.2.4 Derivative Thermogravimetry (DTG)

DTG is a method in thermal analysis. The curve obtained by plotting the rate of change of weight *dw/dt* with temperature (*T*) is called the derivative thermogravimetric curve (*t* is time). This method is useful for a complicated decomposition where weight changes occur at close temperatures. *DTG curves have better resolution than TGA curves.*

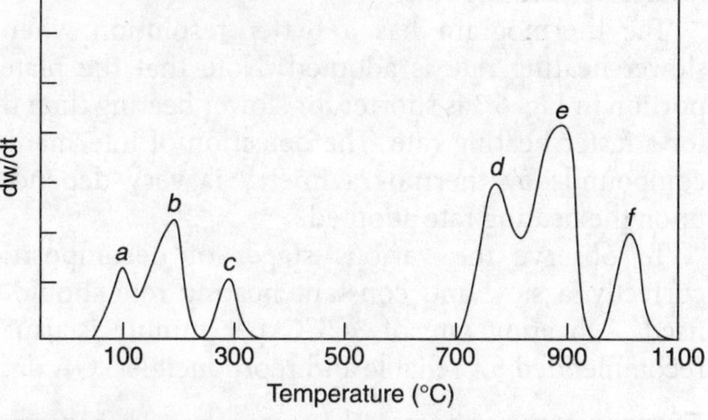

Fig. 6.2 Derivative thermogravimetric curve $CuSO_4{\bullet}5H_2O$

Figure 6.2 represents the derivative thermogravimetric curve for copper sulphate pentahydrate. It is a seemingly simple salt, but undergoes complicated multi-step thermal decomposition. Each peak represents a thermal decomposition step. The thermogram has six peaks indicating that there are six decomposition steps when $CuSO_4 \cdot 5H_2O$ is heated. These can be clearly understood by thermal analysis.

These steps are given below:

$$CuSO_4{\bullet}5H_2O \longrightarrow CuSO_4{\bullet}3H_2O + 2H_2O$$

$$CuSO_4{\bullet}3H_2O \longrightarrow CuSO_4{\bullet}H_2O + 2H_2O$$

$$CuSO_4{\bullet}H_2O \longrightarrow CuSO_4 + H_2O$$

$$2CuSO_4 \longrightarrow 2CuO{\bullet}SO_3 + SO_2 + \tfrac{1}{2}O_2$$

$$2CuO{\bullet}SO_3 \longrightarrow 2CuO + SO_2 + \tfrac{1}{2}O_2$$

$$2CuO \longrightarrow Cu_2O + \tfrac{1}{2}O_2$$

6.2.5 Factors which Influence the Thermogram

The thermal decomposition of a compound and the precise temperature region for each reaction mainly depend on the chemical nature of the compound. However, some experimental conditions also influence the thermogram. The heating rate, furnace atmosphere, crucible geometry and sample characteristics are the experimental factors which influence the decomposition.

Heating rate The temperatures of decomposition for some substances depend on the heating rate. Usually, when the heating rate is high, the decomposition temperature is also high. This effect is shown in Fig. 6.3 which denotes the TGA for a single-step reaction of a substance. The curve *ab* represents the decomposition curve at a slow heating rate; the curve *cd* denotes that at a faster heating rate. Let T_a and T_b be the starting and final temperatures of the reaction for slow heating rate and T_c and T_d those for fast heating rates. Then,

$$T_a < T_c$$

$$T_b < T_d$$

Generally, $(T_b - T_a) < (T_d - T_c)$

indicating that the decompostion temperature is higher for a faster heating rate.

The thermogram has a better resolution when a slower heating rate is adopted. Note that the plateau portion in Fig. 6.3 is shorter for slower heating than that for a faster heating rate. The detection of intermediate compounds by thermogravimetry is very dependent upon the heating rate adopted.

To observe the various stages of decomposition correctly, a slow and constant heating rate should be used. A heating rate of 3–5°C per minute is usually recommended for reliable and reproducible TGA data.

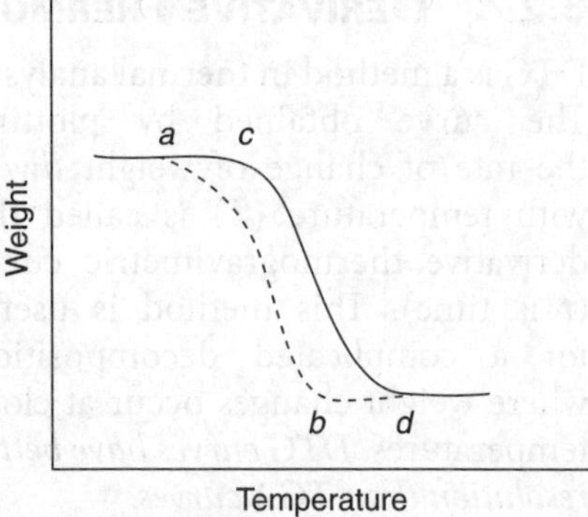

Fig. 6.3 Effect of heating rate on reaction temperature *a–b* slow heating rate, *c–d* fast heating rate

Furnace atmosphere The atmosphere in the furnace surrounding the sample has a profound effect on the decomposition temperature of the sample. One of the following atmospheres can be used inside the furnace: (i) static air—maintaining ordinary air inside the furnace as outside, (ii) dynamic air—compressed air from a cylinder passed through the furnace at a steady rate and (iii) nitrogen atmosphere—pure nitrogen gas passed from a cylinder providing an inert atmosphere.

Crucible geometry The crucible geometry influences the slope of the thermogravimetric curve. Therefore, the use of a flat-shaped crucible is recommended to obtain reproducible thermograms. The diffusion of gases formed during analysis and better thermal uniformity within the sample are facilitated by a flat-shaped crucible with lesser 'height' of the sample.

Sample characteristics The thermogram of a substance is influenced by the weight, the particle size and the mode of preparation of the substance. For example, $Mg(OH)_2$ prepared by precipitation has a thermogram different from the one for a naturally occurring sample. *Small sample weight and small uniform particle size* are generally recommended to facilitate diffusion of gaseous products through the solid sample. Using a small sample weight eliminates the existence of temperature gradient throughout the sample. The use of large crystals may result in apparent, very rapid weight loss during heating. This is found to be due to mechanical loss of a part of the sample by its forcible ejection from the sample container during the evolution of a gas (decrepitation). A compressed, compact sample usually decomposes at a higher temperature than a loose sample. The surface area of the sample in TGA is maximised to improve weight loss resolution and temperature reproducibility.

Heat of reaction This will alter the difference between the sample temperature and furnace temperature and thus affect the thermogram. An exothermic change will cause the sample temperature to lead the furnace temperature. An endothermic change will make the sample temperature lag the furnace temperature. A few preliminary simple experiments for measuring the furnace and the sample temperatures will provide the necessary information on the effect of heat of reaction on the thermogram. Then, necessary corrections in the thermogram can be introduced. Condensation of volatile products on the cooler sides of the container will introduce serious errors in the TGA data, and therefore this should be checked and eliminated.

6.2.6 TGA Instrument

An important development in the history of thermogravimetry was the designing of a thermobalance (Fig. 6.4) by the Japanese scientist Kotaro Honda. This historic apparatus is called *Honda's apparatus*, and this was subsequently modified to more refined instruments.

A typical thermobalance is described here. AB and CD are the two arms of the balance beam. The crucible E, made of platinum, is suspended with platinum wires from *A*. The spiral S, attached to D and also to the bottom of a Dewar flask (F) prevents oscillation of the beam during heating. This arrangement acts as a damper. The sample temperature is measured by means of a platinum/platinum–rhodium thermocouple. Changes in weights are found out by finding the beam deflection on adding a known weight to the pan.

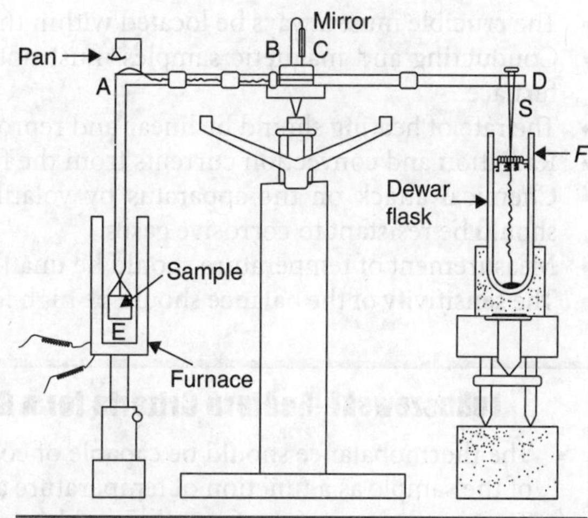

Fig. 6.4 Honda's balance

The thermogravimetric instrument essentially consists of

- a furnace that can be heated so that the temperature rises linearly with time,
- a precision thermobalance, and
- a recorder.

The sample is kept in the crucible E which is inside a furnace. The crucible is actually suspended in a platinum–rhodium stirrup attached to the beam of a balance. The entire furnace compartment can be water-cooled. The compartment is flushed with an inert gas. A known weight of the sample is taken in the crucible. The furnace temperature is then raised at a slow and steady rate. The temperature of the sample and the corresponding weight are accurately and precisely noted continually. In a modern instrument, the thermogram is automatically recorded by a pen recorder. Highly advanced electronics-based, expensive TG units are now available. Figure 6.5 represents an outline of such a TGA unit.

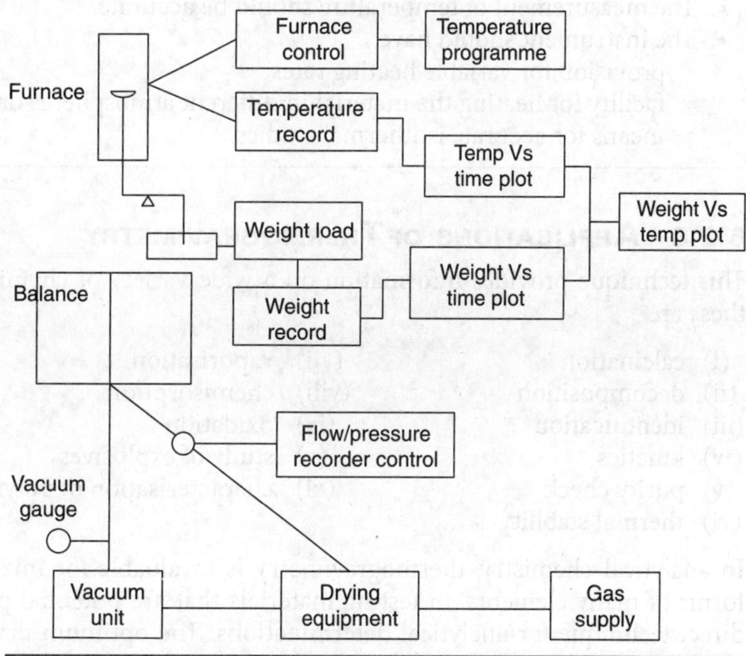

Fig. 6.5 Schematic representation of a modern TGA unit

6.2.7 Precautions Required in the Use of a Thermobalance

- The hot zone of the furnace should be of uniform temperature to within 5°C and for a reasonable volume.

- The crucible must always be located within the hot zone.
- Conducting and magnetic samples must not interfere with the electrical winding of the furnace.
- The rate of heating should be linear and reproducible.
- Radiation and convection currents from the furnace must not affect the weighing unit.
- Chemical attack on the apparatus by volatile products must be prevented; the balance should be resistant to corrosive gases.
- Measurement of temperature should be unaffected by the hot furnace.
- The sensitivity of the balance should be high for recording small changes in sample weights.

Lukaszewski–Redfern Criteria for a Good Design for a Thermal Balance

- The thermobalance should be capable of continuously registering the change in weight of the sample as a function of temperature and time.
- The temperature of the furnace should reach the maximum desired value for complete reaction.
- The rate of heating should be linear and reproducible.
- The sample holder should be maintained in a uniform hot zone.
- The measurement of temperature should be accurate.
- The instrument should have
  - provision for variable heating rates,
  - facility for heating the material in different atmospheres or in vacuo, and
  - means for accurate isothermal studies.

6.2.8 Applications of Thermogravimetry

This technique provides information on a wide variety of chemical investigations. Some of these are

(i) calcination
(ii) decomposition
(iii) identification
(iv) kinetics
(v) purity check
(vi) thermal stability
(vii) vaporisation
(viii) chemisorption
(ix) oxidation
(x) study of explosives
(xi) characterisation of polymers

In analytical chemistry, thermogravimetry is invaluable for investigating suitable weighing forms of many elements, in testing materials that are potential primary standards, and as a direct technique for analytical determinations. The optimum drying range for an analytical precipitate can be ascertained from its thermogram.

The thermoanalytical methods find applications in several industrial researches and analyses. Among these are cement, glass, polymer, drug, structural composites and ceramic industries. Chemical materials used in these industries are routinely characterised by thermoanalytical methods.

Problem 6.1 Microcosmic salt has the composition $Na(NH_4)HPO_4 \cdot 4H_2O$. Its TGA shows a three-stage decomposition giving $NaPO_3$ as the final thermally stable product. The following are the data obtained from its TGA. Interpret these results.

Stage	*Weight of residue (mg)*
Initial	8.3626
I	5.4802
II	4.7990
III	4.0784

Solution

m.wt of $Na(NH_4)HPO_4 \cdot 4H_2O = 209.065$

In stage I, the loss of weight = (8.3626 – 5.4802) = 2.8824 mg

This loss in weight is likely to be due to the salt losing its water of hydration partly or fully.

The wt/mole ratio can indicate what exactly has been eliminated at this stage:

Assuming the loss H_2O molecule(s),

$$\frac{8.3626}{209.065} = \frac{2.8824}{x\ 18.015}$$

where x is the number of water molecules lost and 18.015 is the m.wt of H_2O.

$$x = \frac{2.8824}{18.015} \times \frac{209.065}{8.3626} = 4$$

This value confirms that all the four H_2O molecules are lost at stage I:

$$Na(NH_4)HPO_4 \cdot 4H_2O \longrightarrow Na(NH_4)HPO_4 + 4H_2O$$

m.wt: (209.065) (137.005) (4 × 18.015)

The weight/mole ratio for stage II is

$$\frac{5.4802}{137.005} = \frac{0.6812}{y}$$

$\therefore \quad y = 17.03$

This y value exactly corresponds to the m.wt of NH_3; therefore, $Na(NH_4)HPO_4$ must have eliminated a molecule of NH_3 at this stage:

$$Na(NH_4)HPO_4 \longrightarrow NH_3 + NaH_2PO_4$$

m.wt: 137.065 17.031 119.974

The weight/mole ratio for stage III is

$$\frac{4.799}{119.974} = \frac{0.7206}{z}$$

$z = 18.0148$

The value of z indicates the loss of a water molecule; hence, the decomposition step is

$$NaH_2PO_4 \longrightarrow NaPO_3 + H_2O$$

m.wt: 119.974 101.959 18.0148

Therefore, the complete thermal process for the salt is

$$Na(NH_4)HPO_4{\bullet}4H_2O \longrightarrow Na(NH_4)HPO_4 + 4H_2O$$

$$\downarrow$$

$$H_2O + NaPO_3 \longleftarrow NaH_2PO_4 + NH_3$$

Problem 6.2 The thermogravimetry of a 100 mg pure sample of cobalt metal in air is given in Fig. 6.6. Find the molecular formula of its oxide formed in this analysis.

Solution

The TGA curve indicates that the metal gains weight starting at about 250°C.

The weight gain continues up to about 700°C and then remains constant. This shows that the oxide formation is completed at about 700°C. Cobalt is known to form oxides on heating in air.

The constant weight attained by the sample is 135 mg, the gain in weight being 35 mg. Let the oxide formed be designated as Co_xO_y.

$$\underset{100\text{ mg}}{Co} + O_2 \longrightarrow \underset{135\text{ mg}}{Co_xO_y}$$

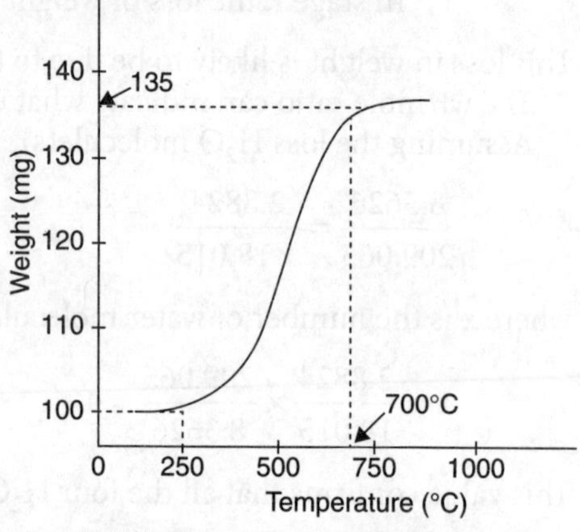

Fig. 6.6 The TGA curve for 100 mg of cobalt metal in air atmosphere

The following are the possible oxides formed by cobalt, and the corresponding cobalt metal/ oxide molar mass ratios:

Oxide	*Molar mass ratio* (Co/oxide)
CoO	$\dfrac{58.993}{74.932} = \dfrac{100}{176.96}$
Co_2O_3	$\dfrac{117.866}{165.883} = \dfrac{100}{147.73}$
$Co_3O_4 (CoO{\bullet}Co_2O_3)$	$\dfrac{176.799}{240.795} = \dfrac{100}{136.20}$

The calculated ratio for Co_3O_4 (100/136.20) agrees with the experimental value (100/135); therefore, the oxide formed in the TGA is Co_3O_4.

6.2.8.1 Thermogravimetric Analysis of Calcium Oxalate Monohydrate

The thermogram for this compound is shown in Fig. 6.7. Successive plateaux in the figure correspond to the formation of anhydrous salt, calcium carbonate and calcium oxide.

$$CaC_2O_4{\bullet}H_2O(s) \longrightarrow CaC_2O_4(s) + H_2O$$

$$CaC_2O_4(s) \longrightarrow CaCO_3(s) + CO(g)$$

$$CaCO_3(s) \longrightarrow CaO(s) + CO_2(g)$$

The thermogram indicates that loss of water begins at 100°C, loss of CO at 400°C and loss of CO_2 at 660°C.

In the gravimetric estimation of calcium, Ca(II) ions are precipitated as calcium oxalate. As the oxalate is thermally unstable, it cannot be dried and weighed. Therefore, it is converted to either calcium carbonate or calcium oxide and then the product is weighed. The temperatures suitable for these processes are found out by a thermogravimetric analysis of the oxalate. A suitable heating temperature is indicated by a plateau on the curve. The precipitate can be heated to obtain the carbonate at about 600 K or the oxide at about 1000 K.

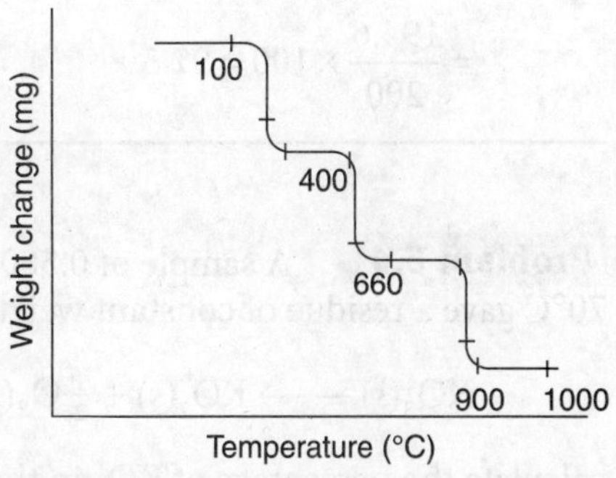

Fig. 6.7 Thermogravimetric analysis of calcium oxalate monohydrate (heating rate: 4° per min)

Magnesium oxalate behaves differently compared to calcium oxalate on heating. It simultaneously loses CO_2 and CO, not step-wise as does the calcium salt (Fig. 6.8a).

The route of formation of certain precipitates influences their thermal behaviour as revealed by their TGA curves. For example, the TGA curve for aluminium hydroxide obtained by precipitation with aqueous ammonia is different from that obtained with urea (Fig. 6.8b, c).

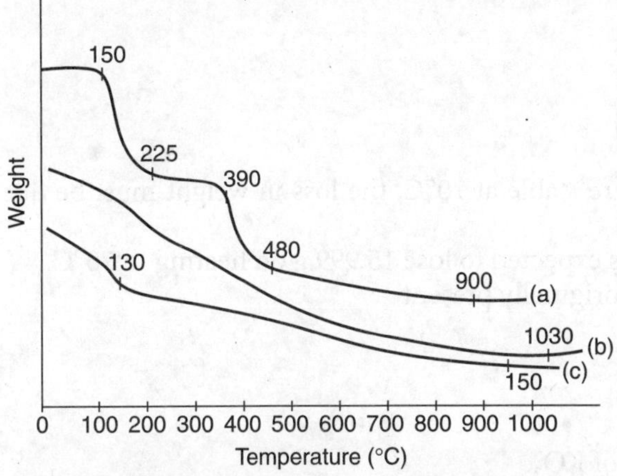

Fig. 6.8 Thermograms of **(a)** magnesium oxalate monohydrate, **(b)** aluminium hydroxide precipitated with aqueous ammonia and **(c)** aluminium hydroxide precipitated with urea.

Problem 6.3 The TGA curve of 200 mg of an impure sample of $CaC_2O_4 \cdot H_2O$, containing a thermally inert impurity, shows a mass loss of 24 mg at 140°C corresponding to loss of water. Calculate the percentage (*w*/*w*) of $CaC_2O_4 \cdot H_2O$ in the sample.

Solution

The reaction that occurs at 140°C is

$$CaC_2O_4 \cdot H_2O(s) \longrightarrow CaC_2O_4(s) + H_2O(g)$$

One millimole of $CaC_2O_4 \cdot H_2O$ will produce one millimole of water.

$$\frac{24 \text{ mg}}{18.015 \text{ mg}} = 1.332 \text{ millimole of water}$$

∴ The sample must have contained 1.332 millimole of $CaC_2O_4 \cdot H_2O$, that is

$$1.332 \times 146.12 \text{ mg} = 194.6 \text{ mg}$$

∴ Percentage of $CaC_2O_4 \cdot H_2O$ in the sample

$$= \frac{194.6}{200} \times 100 = 97.3$$

Problem 6.4 A sample of 0.500 g of potassium ozonide (KO_3) on thermal analysis up to 70°C gave a residue of constant weight 0.426 g. Assuming the reaction

$$KO_3(s) \longrightarrow KO_2(s) + \tfrac{1}{2}O_2(g)$$

calculate the percentage of KO_3 in the sample.

Solution

$$\begin{array}{llll} & KO_3(s) & \xrightarrow{70°C} KO_2(s) + & \tfrac{1}{2}O_2 \\ \text{m.w:} & 87.095 & 71.096 & 15.999 \end{array}$$

Assuming that $KO_2(s)$ and the impurities are stable at 70°C, the loss in weight must be due only to decomposition of $KO_3(s)$.

As per the equation, 87.095 g of $KO_3(s)$ is expected to lose 15.999 g on heating to 70°C. For a loss of 0.074 g, the amount of KO_3 originally present

$$= \frac{87.095}{15.999} \times 0.074 = 0.403 \text{ g}$$

0.500 g of the sample contains only 0.403 g of KO_3.

$$\therefore \quad \text{The percentage purity} = \frac{0.403}{0.500} \times 100 = 80.6$$

6.2.8.2 Decomposition of Complexes

The decomposition sequence of a complex salt can be found out by its thermogravimetric behaviour. For example, the TGA of $[Co(NH_3)_6]Cl_3$ indicates the following decomposition sequence for this complex.

$$6\,[Co(NH_3)_6]Cl_3 \xrightarrow{190°C} 3\,CoCl_2 + 3\,(NH_4)_2[CoCl_4] + N_2(g) + 28\,NH_3(g)$$

$$3\,(NH_4)_2[CoCl_4] \xrightarrow{280°C} 6\,NH_4Cl + 3\,CoCl_2$$

A coordination complex may undergo a multi-step thermal decomposition. All these steps can be precisely understood from its thermogram.

The thermal analysis of the complex $[Ln(PMVP)_3{\bullet}H_2O{\bullet}C_2H_5OH]{\bullet}H_2O$, (where Ln = trivalent lanthanides such as La, Ce, Nd, Sm, Gd, Er and PMVP = 1-phenyl-3-methyl-4-valonyl-2-pyrazoline-5-one) indicates that one of the H_2O molecules is coordinated and the other is non-coordinated (water of hydration). The thermogram indicates that the non-coordinated water is lost first, and then the complex decomposes. (Ref. Costamagna J et al., *Coordination Chemistry Reviews*, 119, 67, 1992.)

6.2.8.3 Study of Polymers

An important industrial application of TGA is the study of polymers. TGA provides information about the thermal stability and decomposition mechanism of polymers. Each polymer decomposes in a characteristic pattern. The TGA curves of polyvinyl chloride (PVC) and low density polyethylene (LDPE) are given in Fig. 6.9. PVC is stable up to about 220°C (curve *a*). It undergoes a two-stage decomposition, one in the 220–250°C range and the other in the 380–450°C range. LDPE, on the other hand is thermally more stable (curve *b*); it remains unaffected up to about 350°C and then undergoes a single step decomposition in the 350–450°C range. Curve *c* denotes the TG of polyethylene that has been formulated (blended) with fine carbon black. This blended polymer has more stability than the unblended polyethylene; it is stable up to 400°C. Thermal analyses are thus useful in characterising and formulating synthetic polymer raw materials required for various industrial applications.

The TG curve for nylon 66 shows that there is no change in the weight of the polymer up to 377°C in air atmosphere; then there is substantial loss in weight which indicates decomposition with attendant formation of volatiles. The decomposition temperature is slightly higher (385°C) in nitrogen atmosphere. These TG data are useful for selection of polymers for applications.

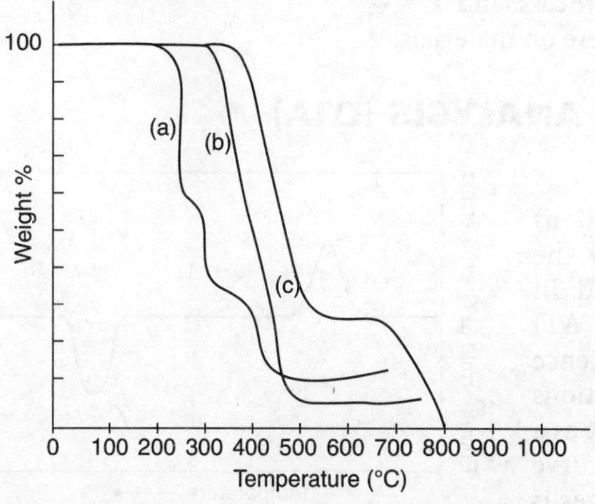

Fig. 6.9 Thermograms of polymers **(a)** PVC **(b)** LDPE **(c)** carbon-black blended polythene

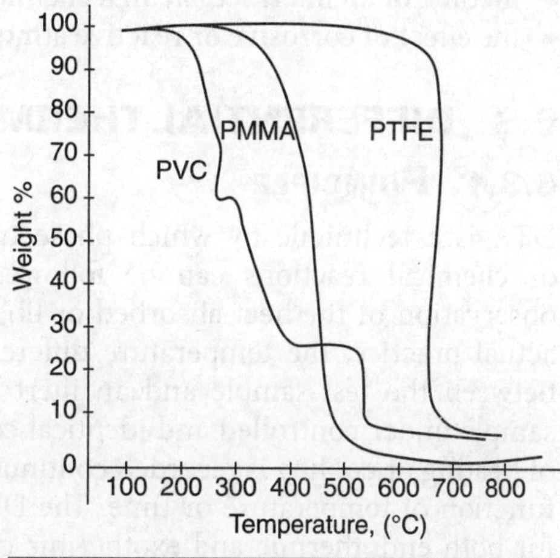

Fig. 6.10 TGA curves for some high temperature polymers

6.2.8.4 Evaluation of High Temperature Polymers by TGA

Certain polymers or polymer composites are made especially for high temperature applications. Such materials are called high temperature polymers. For example, certain grades of PVC and polymethylene methacrylate (PMMA) serve as industrial high temperature polymers. Such materials can be evaluated for their thermal stability before moulding them into industrial products. Figure 6.10 shows the TGAs of high temperature PVC, PMMA and PTFE (polytetrafluoroethylene). The curves indicate that PVC is thermally stable up to about 250°C, PMMA is stable up to about 350°C and PTFE is stable up to about 600°C. Thus, the order of thermal stability is PTFE > PMMA > PVC.

- DTA curves can offer information about composition, melting behaviour, degree of crystallinity, effect of additives, glass-transition process, thermal stability, polymer reactions, and so on, pertaining to polymers.

- DTA is applied in the industrial control processes for formulating polymers with tailored qualities.

6.2.9 Versatility of TGA

TGA can be applied to the following studies:

- establishment of composition of materials,
- decomposition studies,
- rate of thermal degradation,
- oxidative stability,
- assessment of polymer flammability,
- thermal stabilities,
- fingerprinting polymers,
- evaluation of moisture content,
- determination of volatiles,
- gas evolution from materials,
- estimation of ash content,
- lifetime of an intermediate in a chemical process, and
- the effect of corrosive or reactive atmosphere on materials.

6.3 DIFFERENTIAL THERMAL ANALYSIS (DTA)

6.3.1 Principle

DTA is a technique by which phase transitions or chemical reactions can be followed by the observation of the heat absorbed or liberated. In actual practice, the temperature difference (ΔT) between the test sample and an inert reference sample under controlled and identical conditions of heating or cooling is recorded continuously as a function of temperature or time. The DTA curve for both endothermic and exothermic changes is shown in Fig. 6.11.

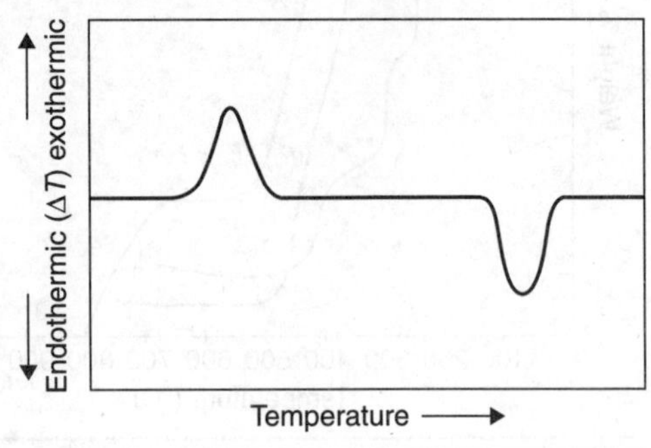

Fig. 6.11 A typical DTA curve

- In an endothermic change, the temperature of the sample lags behind the temperature of the reference since heat is required for a transition. When the transition is complete, thermal diffusion brings the sample to zero ΔT, creating a depression in the DTA curve.
- For an exothermic process, an elevation in the DTA curve is observed.
- Fusion, change in the crystalline state and other physical changes of the sample during heating give sharp endothermic peaks.
- Dehydration is indicated by a broad endothermic peak.
- Certain chemical changes such as oxidative degradations, aided by oxygen, show exothermic peaks.
- *Peak areas*: Peak areas in a differential thermogram depend upon the mass of the sample m, the enthalpy ΔH, of the physical or chemical change and certain geometric and heat conductivity factors. These variables are related by the equation.

$$A = -k\, G\, m\, \Delta H$$

$$= -k'\, m\, \Delta H$$

In this equation, A is the peak area, k is a constant related to the thermal conductivity of the sample and G is a calibration factor that depends upon the sample geometry. The negative sign in the equation implies an exothermic enthalpy change. For a given sample, k' is a constant under constant experimental conditions; then, the mass of the analyte can be calculated from known ΔH; the enthalpy can be calculated from known k' and m.

6.3.1.1 Calorimetric DTA

The modern methods of quantitative DTA are a type of 'calorimetric method'. They provide direct calorimetric information. In calorimetric DTA as opposed to conventional DTA, the temperature sensors are placed outside the sample and reference; in addition, the sample and reference weights are smaller (0.1 to 10 mg).

Calorimetric DTA is of three types:

(i) In the first type, the temperature difference between the sample and the reference is recorded, as in normal DTA, but the conditions of experiment are close to equilibrium.
(ii) In the second type, the difference between the energies required to maintain the same temperature in the sample and reference is recorded.
(iii) In the third type, the difference between the *heat fluxes* into the sample and into the reference before the attainment of a steady state is measured. This measurement is done using a microcalorimeter.

6.3.2 DTA Instrument

In a typical DTA apparatus, one set of thermocouple junctions is inserted into an inert material (aluminium oxide) which does not change in any manner through the temperature range to be studied. On constant heating, any transition or thermally induced reaction in the sample will be recorded as a peak or dip in an otherwise straight line. An endothermic process will cause the thermocouple junction in the sample to lag behind the junction in the inert material, which would develop a voltage. An exothermic change will develop a voltage of opposite sign.

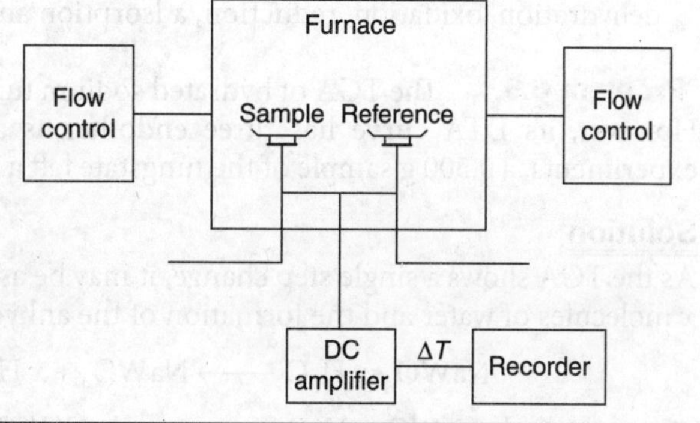

Fig. 6.12 Schematic representation of DTA instrument

The commercially available DTA unit has five basic components:

(i) sample and reference holder with thermocouple assembly,
(ii) a furnace assembly,
(iii) a furnace power programmer and controller,
(iv) gas-flow-controller system, and
(v) DC amplifier and recorder.

A schematic representation of such a unit is shown in Fig. 6.12. Dual thermocouples are used to measure the difference in temperature between the sample and the reference material, both of which are heated in a furnace operated by a temperature programmer and controller. The outputs from the differential thermocouple are amplified and fed into the recorder.

6.3.3 Applications of DTA

6.3.3.1 DTA of Calcium Oxalate Monohydrate

Figure 6.13 is a DTA curve showing the decomposition of calcium oxalate monohydrate. Thermogram. (*a*) represents the decomposition in carbon dioxide atmosphere. This has three peaks corresponding to the successive elimination of H_2O, CO and CO_2. These three steps of weight loss correspond to the three endothermic processes. Each process requires energy to break the bonds and thus is endothermic. Curve (*b*) represents the DTA diagram for the same compound in air. The second peak in this curve is sharply exothermic, but corresponds to the same weight loss as in the carbon dioxide atmosphere. This peak represents the exothermic burning of carbon monoxide in air at the temperature of the furnace.

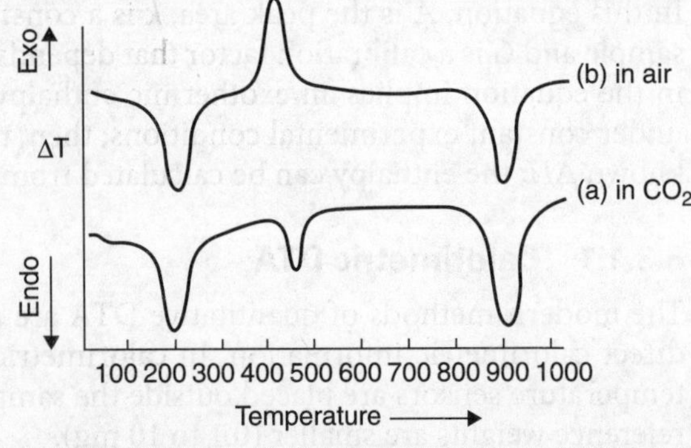

Fig. 6.13 DTA diagram for the decomposition of calcium oxalate monohydrate

- Derivative thermograms (DTG) can give information only about weight changes, whereas DTA will indicate changes in energy, irrespective of constancy or change in weight.
- DTA can provide information on a slew of processes such as fusion, de-solvation, dehydration, oxidation, reduction, adsorption and solid state reactions.

Problem 6.5 The TGA of hydrated sodium tungstate shows a single step change at 81°C. However, its DTA curve has three endotherms at 81°C, 585°C and 697°C. In both the experiments, a 0.500 g sample of the tungstate left a residue of 0.4412 g. Interpret these results.

Solution

As the TGA shows a single step change, it may be assumed that this change denotes the loss of x molecules of water and the formation of the anhydrous salt, $NaWO_4$.

$$NaWO_4 \cdot x\,H_2O \longrightarrow NaWO_4 + x\,H_2O$$

$$\text{1 mole } NaWO \cdot x\,H_2O \longrightarrow \underset{(270.825\text{ g})}{\text{1 mole } NaWO_4} + \underset{(x\ 18.015\text{ g})}{x \text{ moles } H_2O}$$

$$0.500\text{ g } NaWO_4 \cdot xH_2O \longrightarrow 0.4412\text{ g } NaWO_4 + 0.0588\text{ g } H_2O$$

$$\therefore \quad \frac{0.4412}{270.825} = \frac{0.0588}{x\ 18.015}$$

$$0.00163 = \frac{0.00326}{x}$$

$$x = \frac{0.00326}{0.00163} = 2$$

Therefore, the formula of the hydrated salt is $NaWO_4 \cdot 2H_2O$.

The two endotherms – second and third – shown by the DTA correspond to changes without any weight loss. One should represent a crystalline phase change (at 585°C) and the other the melting (at 697°C) of $NaWO_4$.

6.3.3.2 Thermal Analysis of Calcium Acetate Monohydrate

Figure 6.14 represents the TGA and DTA thermograms of $(CH_3COO)_2Ca \cdot H_2O$. The TGA curve (*a*) indicates three stages of decomposition corresponding to

$$Ca(CH_3COO)_2 \cdot H_2O \longrightarrow Ca(CH_3COO)_2 + H_2O$$

$$Ca(CH_3COO)_2 \longrightarrow CaCO_3 + CH_3COCH_3$$

$$CaCO_3 \longrightarrow CaO + CO_2$$

The dehydration occurs between 200 and 250°C. The decomposition of the anhydrous salt takes place beyond 400°C. The final reaction producing CaO and CO_2 starts at about 500°C.

The DTA curve (*b*) shows that the dehydration is an endothermic change. The anhydrous salt is stable up to temperatures of approximately 350–400°C, beyond which endothermic decomposition reaction occurs. (The thermograms indicate the reactions in oxygen atmosphere.)

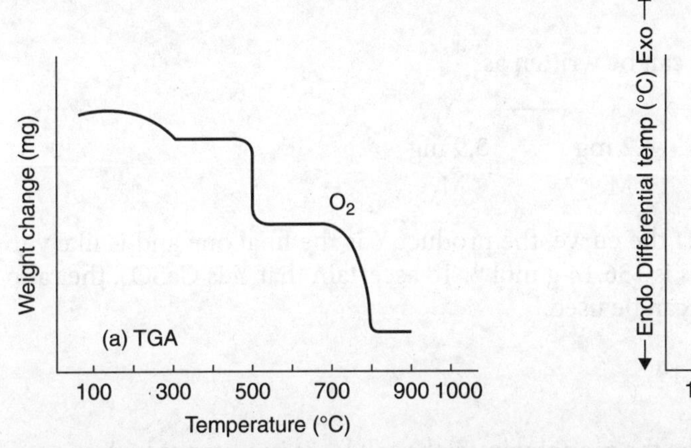

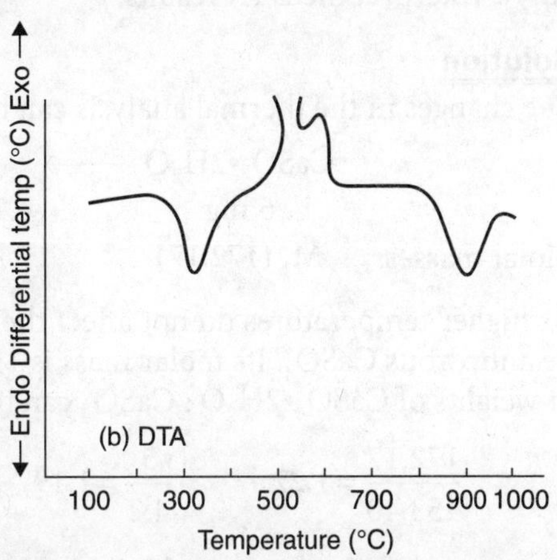

Fig. 6.14 Thermal analysis of calcium acetate monohydrate

Problem 6.6 The DTA of a pure sample of $Al(OH)(HCOO)_2 \cdot 0.5\ H_2O$ is shown in Fig. 6.15. The initial mass of 50 mg was reduced to a constant mass of 35.52 mg at the end of the analysis. Interpret the curve.

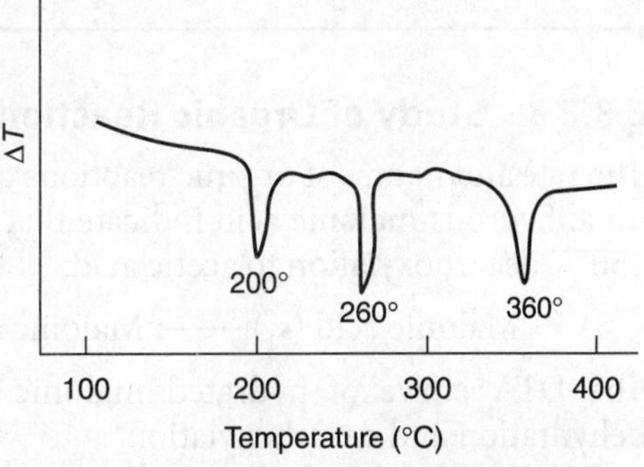

Fig. 6.15 DTA curve for $Al(OH)(HCOO)_2 \cdot 0.5\ H_2O$

Solution

Let us assume that the compound is finally decomposed to stable Al_2O_3.

$$\underset{143.26}{Al(OH)(HCOO)_2 \cdot 0.5\ H_2O} \longrightarrow \underset{101.961}{Al_2O_3}$$

143.026 g of the initial substance is expected to give a residue of 101.961 g. If the assumption that the final product is Al_2O_3, then,

$$\frac{101.961}{143.26} \text{ must be equal to} = \frac{35.52}{50}$$

This is so; 0.713 ≈ 0.710

Therefore, the final residue must be Al_2O_3.

The formation of Al_2O_3 is complete at 360°C.

The curve shows two more steps of decomposition before the formation of Al_2O_3. The one at 200°C is likely to be the loss of 0.5 H_2O.

$$Al(OH)(HCOO)_2{\bullet}0.5\,H_2O(s) \xrightarrow{200^\circ C} Al(OH)(HCOO)_2(s) + 0.5\,H_2O(g)$$

The other decomposition at 260°C is likely to be that of $Al(OH)(HCOO)_2$ to $Al(OH)_3$:

$$Al(OH)(HCOO)_2(s) \xrightarrow{260^\circ C} Al(OH)_3(s) + 2\,CO(g)$$

Problem 6.7 The DTA of 5 mg of calcium sulphate dihydrate shows two endotherms, one at 150°C and the other at 200°C. The first endotherm corresponds to a weight loss of 0.8 mg and the second a total of 1.1 mg. Higher temperatures do not have any effect on the curve. Interpret the DTA results.

Solution

The changes in the thermal analysis can be written as

	$CaSO_4{\bullet}2H_2O$	⟶	X	⟶	Y
	5 mg		4.2 mg		3.9 mg
Molar masses:	M_1 (172.17)		M_2		M_3

As higher temperatures do not affect the curve, the product Y is the final one and is likely to be anhydrous $CaSO_4$. Its molar mass is 136.14 g mol^{-1}. To ascertain that Y is $CaSO_4$, the ratio of weights of $CaSO_4{\bullet}2H_2O : CaSO_4$ can be used.

$$\frac{172.17}{153.40} = 1.22 \qquad \frac{5}{4.2} = 1.19$$

As these two ratios agree, X should be the monohydrate; the salt loses its water of hydration in two steps. Y should be anhydrous calcium sulphate.

$$CaSO_4{\bullet}2H_2O \longrightarrow CaSO_4{\bullet}H_2O \longrightarrow CaSO_4$$

6.3.3.3 Study of Organic Reactions

The rate and nature of organic reactions can be studied by DTA. For example, the DTA results on anhydrous malonic acid indicate that at about 70°C, it undergoes phase transition and at 150°C decarboxylation to acetic acid.

$$\text{Malonic acid } (s_1) \longrightarrow \text{Malonic acid } (s_2) \longrightarrow \text{Acetic acid } (l)$$

The DTA curve of hydrated malonic acid has three peaks corresponding to its m.p, dehydration and decarboxylation.

DTA is helpful in finding melting points, boiling points, decomposition temperatures and decomposition patterns of several organic compounds. For example, the DTA curve of benzoic acid at atmospheric pressure (Fig. 6.16) shows two peaks, the first representing its m.p and the second its b.p; the acid is thermally stable.

Another example for DTA-based study of organic reactions is the study of the thermal behaviour of L-glutamic acid in the presence of air; the DTA data reveal the following sequence of changes:

$H_2N — CH — COOH$

$CH_2 CH_2 COOH$

$O = $ N $— COOH$

H

N

H

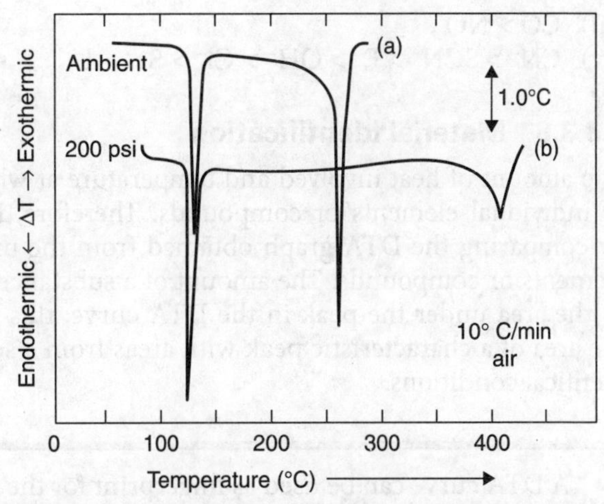

Fig. 6.16 Differential thermogram for benzoic acid. Curve **(a)**: atmosperic pressure; Curve **(b)**: at 200 lbs/in²

6.3.3.4 Study of Catalysts

The change in the chemical states of a catalyst may be studied by thermogravimetric techniques. A mixture of Zn and $ZnCrO_4$ is used as catalyst in the synthesis of methanol. The weight–temperature curve of the catalyst obtained during the reaction indicates that its composition is changed to $ZnO•ZnCrO_4•H_2O$ in the initial stage and then to $3.3\ ZnO•ZnCrO_4$.

DTA has been used in the study of not only catalysts but also catalytic reactions. As all catalysed reactions are accompanied by enthalpy changes, DTA is a versatile method for studying such changes. This is illustrated in Fig. 6.17, where a closed system containing reactants in the presence of a catalyst gives a sharper DTA peak (curve *a*) at a lower temperature than does the same system in the absence of catalyst (curve *b*). The peak areas are the same since the same amount of heat is involved in the catalysed and uncatalysed reactions. Curve *a* shows that in the presence of the catalyst, the reaction is completed in a smaller temperature and time interval because of the lower energy barrier to be crossed. The formation of organic adducts catalysed by Al_2O_3 has been studied by DTA; the data show that the catalyst facilitates easier reactions.

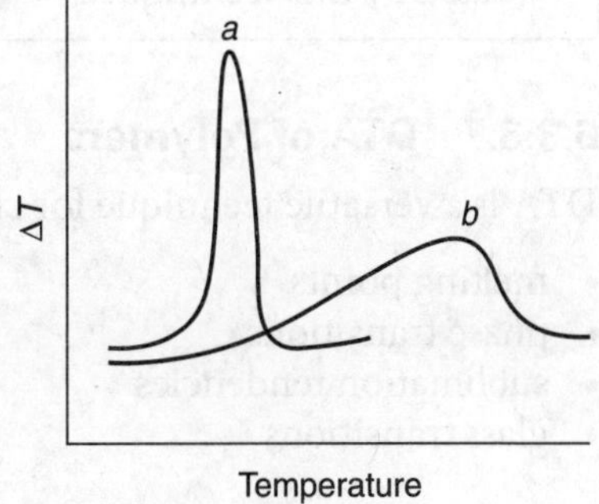

Fig. 6.17 DTA curves for **(a)** a catalysed reaction; **(b)** the same reaction, uncatalysed

6.3.3.5 Trends in Ligand Stabilities

TGA and DTA can give information on the thermal stabilities of groups inside the coordination sphere. In a complex, having more than one type of ligand, which one is eliminated earlier on heating can be found out from the weight loss of the complex with increasing temperature. Moeller, using such thermal data, arrived at trends in stabilities of certain groups of ligands inside the coordination sphere.

Decreasing stability:

(i) $NH_3 > RNH_2 > R_2NH > R_3N$

(ii) $H_2O > ROH > R_2O > RCOR > RCHO$

(iii) CO > NO
(iv) $CN^- > SCN^- > F^- > OH^- > Cl^- > Br^- > I^-$

6.3.3.6 Material Identification

The amount of heat involved and temperature at which changes take place are characteristic of individual elements or compounds. Therefore, identification of a substance is achieved by comparing the DTA graph obtained from the unknown sample with those from known elements or compounds. The amount of a substance present in a composite sample is related to the area under the peak in the DTA curve; this amount can be calculated by comparing the area of a characteristic peak with areas from a series of standard samples analysed under identical conditions.

- A DTA curve can be used as fingerprint for the identification of materials.
- It can be used for quantitative analysis.
- It is used for the study of phase diagrams, heat changes and decomposition of materials in various furnace atmospheres.
- It is widely used in pharmaceutical and food industries. As drugs and food items are affected by changes in temperature, these studies are of great applicability in their storage.
- Characterisation of cement minerals and environmental toxins can be carried out by DTA.
- Ancient bone remains can be dated by DTA; other archaeological artefacts can also be dated by this technique.

6.3.3.7 DTA of Polymers

DTA is a versatile technique for characterising polymers. It can provide valuable data on their

- melting points
- phase transitions
- sublimation tendencies
- glass transitions
- crystal transitions
- crystallisation conditions
- thermal stabilities
- nature of decomposition products

6.3.3.8 DTA of Dacron

The DTA curve of Dacron, (polyethylene terephthalate) fibre is shown in Fig. 6.18. This reveals the following characteristics of Dacron, useful for fibre processing.

- For the undrawn polymer, the T_g appears at 77°C and this is followed by the crystallisation peak at 136°C and the melting peak at 261°C; for the drawn fibre, T_g is barely evident and little or no crystallisation precedes melting.
- Drawing Dacron into fibre suppresses the glass transition effect.

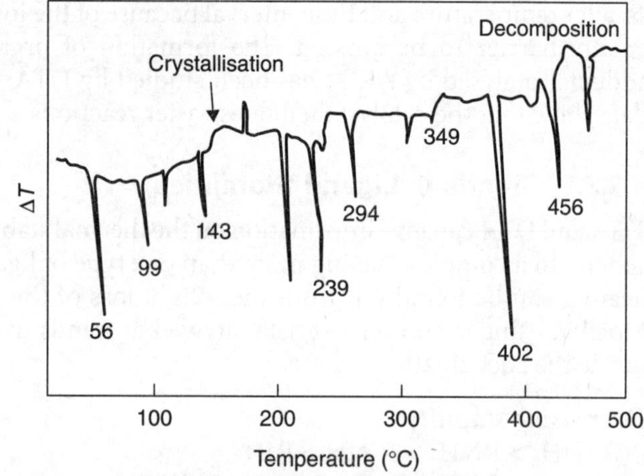

Fig. 6.18 DTA curve for Dacron (polyethylene terephthalate) fibre

- The ambient atmosphere influences the course of decomposition. For the drawn fibre, the decomposition in air starts at 470°C whereas in nitrogen atmosphere, it starts only beyond 500°C.

6.3.3.9 Decomposition Temperatures of Fibres

The thermal stability of fibres is a crucial property for their use in industrial products. DTA is useful in ascertaining this property, particularly the decomposition temperatures. Such DTA data on some polymeric fibres are given in Table 6.2. Among these fibers, polypropylene has the highest thermal resistivity.

Table 6.2 Decomposition temperatures of fibres

Fibre	Endothermic decomposition	
	Commencement (°C)	Peak (°C)
Acetate	300	342
Viscose rayon	290	330
Nylon 66	345	403
Dacron	390	420
Polypropylene	400	447
Spandex	305	337

The DTA of a mixture of LDPE, polypropylene (PP) and polytetraflouroethylene (PTFE) is shown in the Fig. 6.19. The three peaks denote the melting points of the three polymers. PTFE shows an additional peak (*d*) which corresponds to a transition in its crystal structure. This shows that PTFE is isomorphic. Therefore, DTA is useful for identifying polymers from the melting point peaks and also for studying their crystalline phase transformations.

6.3.3.10 Measurement of Heat Capacity

C_P, the heat capacity of a substance under constant pressure can be measured using the DTA curve. It is given by the equation,

$$C_P = K^1\left(\frac{T_2 - T_1}{m\,H}\right)$$

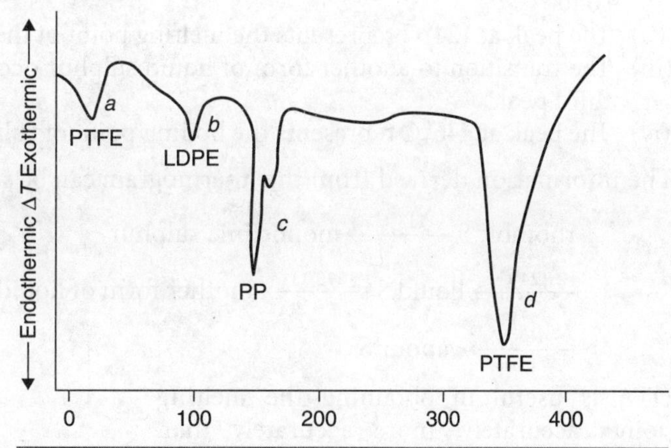

Fig. 6.19 DTA curve for mixture of LDPE, PP and PTFE

where T_1 and T_2 are the differential temperatures generated when the apparatus is first used without any sample and then with the test sample respectively, H is the heating rate, K^1 is a constant determined by calibration against standard substances and m is the mass of the sample analysed.

6.3.3.11 Study of Reaction Kinetics by DTA

DTA can be applied for studying some reaction kinetics. The rate of such a reaction can be monitored by loss in weight of the reactant isothermally with time.

Example

(i) The mineral *brucite,* $Mg(OH)_2$ undergoes thermal dehydroxylation to *periclase,* MgO:

$$Mg(OH)_2 \xrightarrow{\text{heat}} MgO + H_2O$$

The DTA is recorded by maintaining the brucite sample at a fixed high temperature in vacuum. The decreasing weight of the residue is recorded with time. From the recorded data, certain kinetic parameters have been calculated. The order of the reaction has been calculated to be 0.5 and E_a (kcal/mol) about 25.

(ii) The kinetics of decomposition of benezenediazonium chloride has also been studied by DTA. The reaction is represented as

$$C_6H_5N{:}\,NCl \xrightarrow{H_2O} N_2 + C_6H_5Cl$$

This is a heterogeneous reaction. The results show that the reaction follows first order kinetics. The rate data fit a linear Arrhenius plot.

6.3.3.12 Study of Thermal Behaviour of Nuclear Fuel

DTA has been employed in the study of nuclear fuel elements (uranium and thorium oxides). Such studies are useful in understanding the behaviour of fuels at high temperatures usually attained inside nuclear reactors. Certain ceramic oxides, useful for nuclear radiation protection, have also been studied by DTA for better use of such ceramics.

6.3.3.13 Study of Phase Diagrams

DTA can be applied to construct phase diagrams and study phase transitions. The DTA analysis of sulphur, for example, reveals the following about its phase transitions.

(i) The peak at 113°C corresponds to the transition from rhombic solid to monoclinic solid.
(ii) The peak at 124°C represents the melting point of the monoclinic form.
(iii) The transition to another form of liquid sulphur occurs at 179°C as represented by the third peak.
(iv) The peak at 446°C represents the boiling point of sulphur.

The information derived from this thermogram can be summarised as

$$\text{rhombic S} \xrightarrow{113°C} \text{monoclinic sulphur}$$

$$\xrightarrow{124°C} \text{liquid S} \xrightarrow{179°C} \text{another form of liquid S}$$

$$\xrightarrow{446°C} \text{vapour S}$$

DTA is useful in obtaining the melting points accurately, more accurately than by the capillary tube method; the melting points of the allotropes of sulphur have been determined by DTA.

6.3.3.14 Phase Transition Studies in Metals by DTA

Several metals undergo phase transitions. An insight into such transitions can be obtained by DTA. Figure 6.20 shows the DTA curve for uranium metal obtained in argon atmosphere. The curve shows that the phase at lower temperatures called the α phase, passes on to the β phase and on further heating the γ phase is formed.

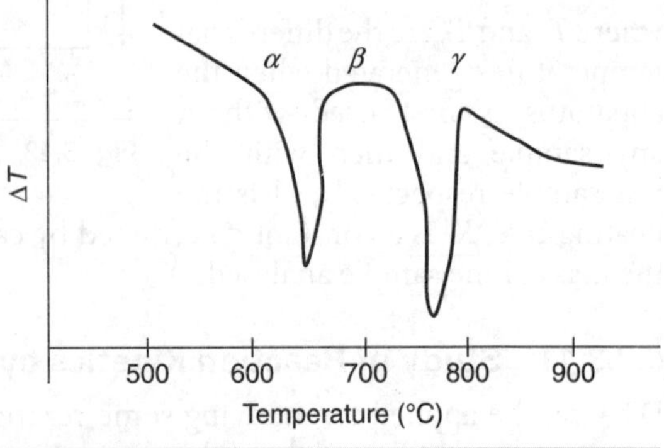

Fig. 6.20 DTA curve for uranium metal in argon atmosphere

$$\alpha\text{-U} \xrightleftharpoons{668 \pm 1°C} \beta\text{-U} \xrightleftharpoons{775 \pm 2°C} \gamma\text{-U}$$

6.3.4 Evolved Gas Analysis (EGA)

EGA is a modified or hyphenated method of TGA. In this method, the gas evolved in a controlled thermal decomposition is led into a mass spectrometer and qualitatively and quantitatively analysed. The mass spectral data are then collated with the TGA data for better understanding of the thermal behaviour of the analyte. For example, dolomite $CaMg(CO_3)_2$, on TG–MS analysis, indicated that it decomposed to yield CO_2 at 780–900°C. This method gives more accurate data than TGA. Simultaneous measurement of two or more properties for the same sample can provide more useful information than sequential analysis. TG–DTA and TG–MS are two such methods. They are applied in characterising pharmaceuticals, polymers and natural industrial raw materials.

6.4 THERMOMETRIC TITRATIONS

6.4.1 Principle

Practically all chemical reactions are accompanied with heat effect and therefore it is possible to follow the course of a reaction by observing the heat liberated. Thermometric titration (TT) is such a technique. This involves the measurement of the change of temperature of a solution during titration as a function of the volume of the titrant added. The change in temperature is due to heat changes during the reaction. The end point in a thermometric titration is indicated by a sharp break in the temperature versus volume curve.

Thermometric titrations are carried out under adiabatic conditions to minimise the heat-exchange between the system and the surroundings. This can be done in a small Dewar flask. The titrant is added from a thermostated automatic burette at a constant rate into the thermally insulated vessel containing the solution to be estimated. The temperature is noted after each addition of the titrant. The temperature of the system is read accurately with a thermistor-thermometer.

Conditions for thermometric titration Thermometric titrations can be adopted only when certain conditions are fulfilled.

- The reaction should be accompanied by heat change that can be measured.
- The heat of dilution of the product should be negligible.
- The reaction should be a simple, one-step change.
- The transfer of heat between the titration vessel and its surroundings should be prevented.

6.4.2 Thermometric Titration Instrument

Figure 6.21 is a schematic representation of a thermometric titration unit. It consists of (i) a motor-driven thermostated burette, (ii) a thermally insulated adiabatic titration vessel (Dewar flask), (iii) a thermistor bridge set and (iv) a recorder. A known volume of the solution to be estimated is taken in the Dewar flask. The tip of the burette is dipped into the solution in the vessel. The vessel is covered by a thick, insulating material containing holes for inserting the thermistor, the burette and the stirrer. The titrant is added at a constant rate while the solution in the Dewar flask is constantly stirred. The thermistor assembly is connected to one arm of a Wheatstone bridge and its resistance is recorded directly on a recorder. The temperature-measuring thermistor unit should be capable of measuring a temperature change of 0.01°C.

The titrant should be 10–100 times more concentrated than the solution in the Dewar flask, so that the titration can be done by the addition of only a small quantity of the titrant.

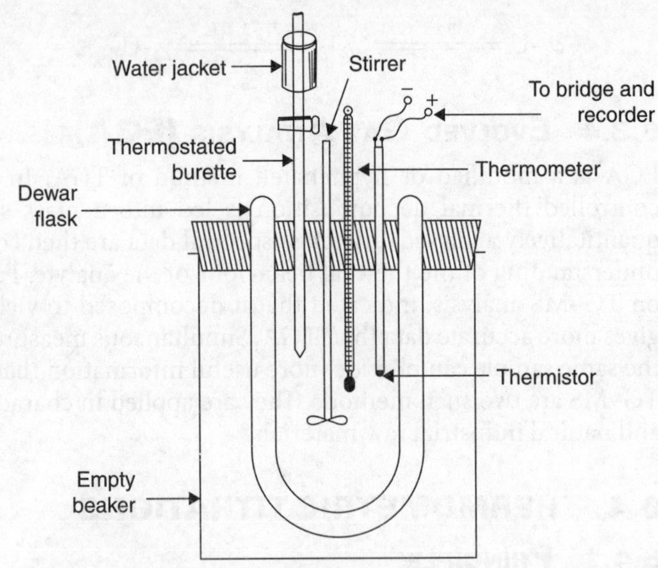

Fig. 6.21 Thermometric titration apparatus

6.4.3 Applications of Thermometric Titrations

Several types of titrations have been followed successfully by the thermometric method. These include neutralisations of both strong and weak acids, precipitations, redox reactions and complex formations. These titrations can be carried out in aqueous or non-aqueous media. Besides in water, thermometric titrations have been reported in acetic acid, carbon tetrachloride, benzene and nitrobenzene. The sensitivity of the technique is enhanced by the use of organic solvents because of their low specific heats. The precision of a thermometric titration is usually ±1%. It can be applied to estimating mixtures of analytes by the change in temperature ΔT during the titration using the relationship

$$\Delta T = \frac{-n\,\Delta H}{K} = \frac{Q}{K}$$

where n is the number of moles of the reactant, K is the effective heat capacity of the system, and Q is the total amount of heat evolved or absorbed.

In a modification of thermometric titration, an excess of the titrant of known concentration is directly and rapidly added to a known volume of the analyte. The resulting rise in temperature is then measured, which is directly proportional to the concentration of the analyte. A calibration can be performed by measuring the rise in temperatures with different standard solutions of the substance being estimated. This method is called the *direct injection method.*

6.4.3.1 Titration of Hydrochloric Acid with Sodium Hydroxide

A known volume of hydrochloric acid to be estimated is taken in the Dewar flask. The titrant NaOH solution is added from the burette. Temperature readings are recorded for different volumes of the titrant added. The thermogram is obtained by plotting temperature *versus* titrant volume (Fig. 6.22). The neutralisation point is indicated by a sharp inflexion point D. *Thermometric titrimetry* is one of the few methods of titration not based solely on consideration of the free energy change ΔG, and hence on the equilibrium

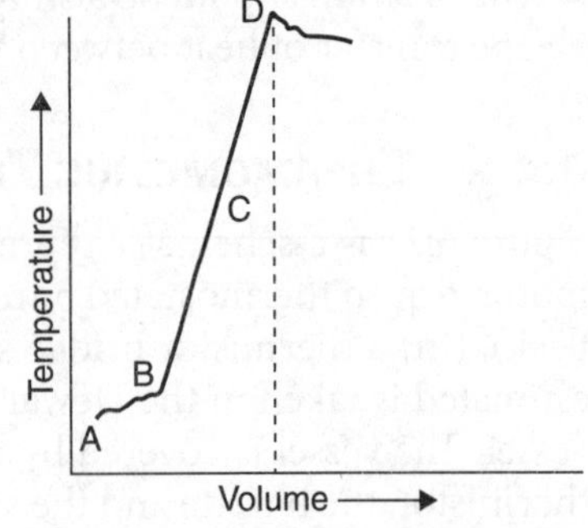

Fig. 6.22 The thermogram for the titration of hydrochloric acid with sodium hydroxide

constant of the reaction. ΔH and not ΔG, is measured in this method. Hence this titration may give useful results even when ΔG is less negative, zero or positive. For example, for the neutralisation of boric acid,

$$H_3BO_3 + OH^- \longrightarrow H_2BO_3^- + H_2O$$

$\Delta G = -6.5$ cal mol^{-1}, too small a value.

For the titration of boric acid against sodium hydroxide, which cannot be successfully done by any method that depends on the pH, the thermometric method can be adopted successfully.

6.4.3.2 Thermometric Titration of Butyllithium

Butyllithium (BuLi) can be titrated thermometrically with butanol, the product being lithium butoxide:

$$n\text{-BuLi} + n\text{-BuOH} \longrightarrow n\text{-BuOLi} + n\text{-BuH}$$

Toluene is used as the solvent in this titration. The chart drive is energised at $t = 0$, and initially a straight line is obtained. At time $t = 1$ min, a motor-driven syringe is made to start delivering the standard titrant, n-butyl alcohol. An increase in temperature occurs until an inflection point is reached; then, the temperature decreases slowly. The rate of delivery by the syringe is constant; therefore, from the time taken for inflection, the volume of titrant required for neutralisation can be found out.

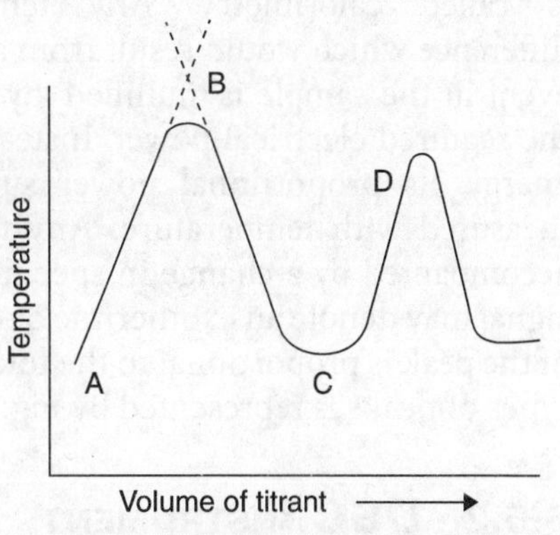

Fig. 6.23 Thermometric titration curve for the titration of a mixture of Ca^{2+} and Mg^{2+} with EDTA

6.4.3.3 Complexometric Titrations

Consider, for example, the titration of calcium and magnesium with EDTA. The stability constants of the chelates differ only by less than two orders of magnitude. Thus, a titration based on an indicator can give only the sum of the concentrations of the two ions. However, for the reaction of Mg^{2+} with EDTA, the enthalpy is +5.5 kcal/mol whereas that for the Ca^{2+} reaction is −5.7 kcal/ mol. This distinct difference in ΔH values makes it possible for the adoption of thermometric titration for estimating these two ions. The titration curve for this mixture is shown in Fig. 6.23. The titration is started at A and shows a calcium end point extrapolated to B and a magnesium end point at C. Typical examples of thermometric titrations are listed in Table 6.3.

Table 6.3 Typical examples of thermometric titrations

Type	Analyte	Titrant
Acid-base	NaOH	HCl
	H_3PO_4	NaOH
	C_5H_5N	HCl
Redox	Fe^{2+}	$Cr_2O_7^{2-}$ or MnO_4^-
	$H_2C_2O_4$	MnO_4^-
	H_2O_2	Ce^{4+}
Precipitation	Ag^+	Cl^-
	Pb^{2+}	$H_2C_2O_4$
	Hg^{2+}	I^-
	Cu^{2+}	EDTA
	Ca^{2+}	EDTA

6.5 DIFFERENTIAL SCANNING CALORIMETRY

6.5.1 Principle

Differential scanning calorimetry (DSC) was invented by E S Watson and M J O'Neill in 1962. A differential scanning calorimeter measures energy directly and provides for precise measurement of heat capacity. DSC is an excellent tool to study biomolecules in their natural environments since it directly measures heat changes that occur in them during controlled increase or decrease in temperature.

In DSC, differences in energy between a reference and a sample are measured as a function of sample temperature while the two are subjected to a controlled temperature programme. (In DTA, differences in temperature are measured.) As the heat energy is measured, this method is called calorimetry. Any temperature difference which would result from a thermal event in the sample is 'nullified' by applying the required electrical power. Instead of heat energy, its proportional power supplied is measured with temperature. Any transition accompanied by a change in specific heat produces a discontinuity in the power signal. The signal may denote an exothermic or endothermic change in the form of a dip or peak. The area of the peak is proportional to the total enthalpy change. A typical DSC curve showing the two types of peaks is represented by Fig. 6.24.

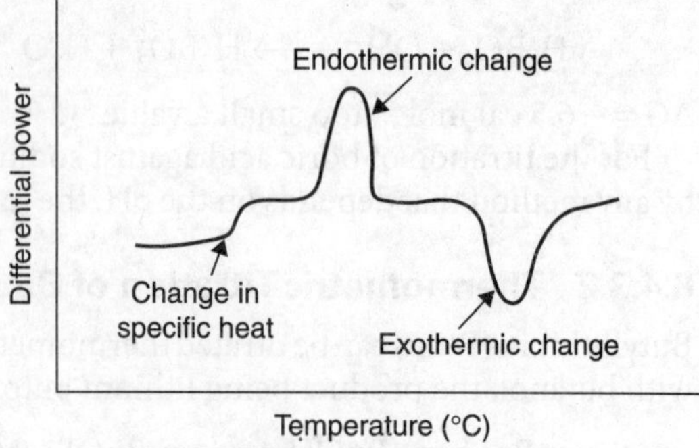

Fig. 6.24 Typical DSC curve

6.5.2 DSC Instrument

When a sample undergoes a transition (decomposition, phase change or isomerisation), it loses or gains thermal energy. This causes a thermal gradient (difference) between the sample and reference; this gradient is nullified by adding thermal energy to the reference or sample or removing thermal energy from the reference or sample. Such a procedure maintains exactly the same temperature in both. The energy input or withdrawal, which is precisely equivalent in magnitude to the energy absorbed or released in a particular transition is measured using a sensitive electronic instrument. Thus, it is a direct calorimetric measurement.

Two types of experiments are usually adopted in DSC: (i) In *power-compensated DSC*, the sample and reference are heated by separate heaters to change their temperatures linearly by ensuring that the two temperatures are identical at any moment. (ii) *Heat flux DSC* is the other type in which the difference in the heat flow into the sample and reference is measured as the sample temperature is increased or decreased linearly. These two methods provide the same information; however, the instrumentations required for these are different.

Power-compensated DSC A schematic of a power-compensated DSC is shown in Fig. 6.25. *S* and *R* are two independent but identical heaters for heating the sample and reference respectively. These two heaters are small, designed for rapid rates of heating, cooling and equilibration. The furnaces are housed inside large temperature-controlled heat sinks S_1 and S_2. The sample and reference holders are kept above the furnaces.

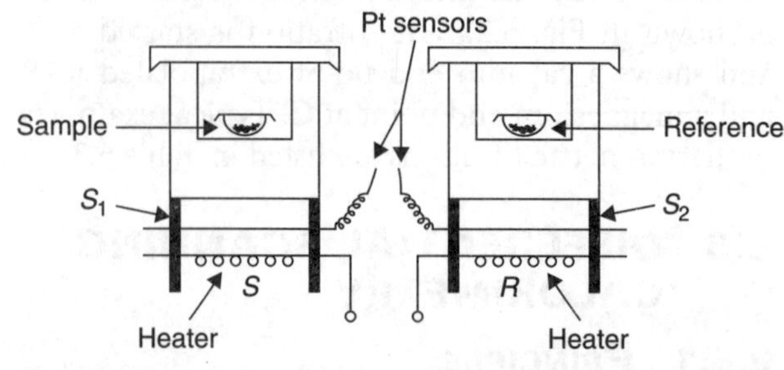

Fig. 6.25 Schematic of a power-compensated DSC instrument

Platinum resistance thermometers are embedded in the sample and reference materials to measure the temperatures of the two materials continuously.

The platinum resistance sensors produce signals which are fed into a differential amplifier via a computer circuit. This circuit is designed to determine which of the two signals is greater. The temperature difference between the sample and reference causes a difference in the signal strengths. Then, the amplifier output adjusts the power input to the two furnaces in such a way that their temperatures are kept identical. This ensures that the sample and reference are isothermal throughout the analysis. The difference in power input to the two furnaces is transmitted to the microprocessor. Such differences are automatically plotted as milliwatts against the sample temperatures.

Heat flux DSC A schematic of a heat flux DSC cell is represented in Fig. 6.26. An electrically heated constantan thermoelectric disk (*D*) is used to heat the sample (*S*) and reference (*R*) materials, kept in a single furnace. These two materials are contained in small aluminium pans placed over the heating disk. The pans conduct heat into the sample and reference. The differential heat flow to the sample and reference is monitored by thermocouples formed by the junction between the constantan platform and alloy disks attached to the underside of the platform. The differential heat flow into the pans is directly proportional to the difference in output of the two thermocouple functions. The temperature of the sample is estimated by means of the bimetallic thermistor unit under the sample disk.

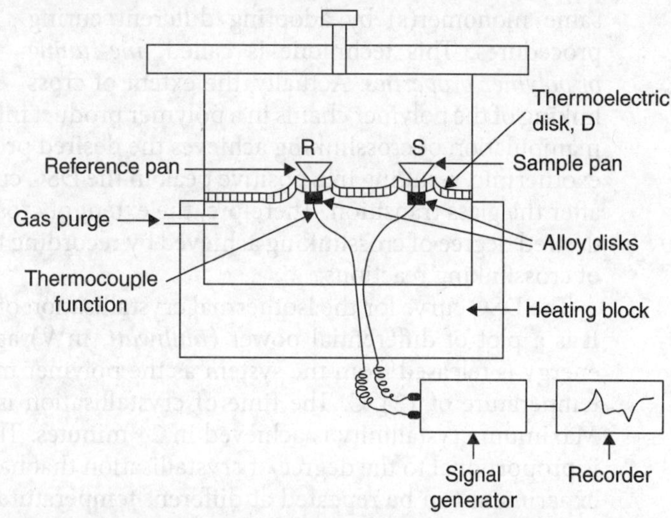

Fig. 6.26 Schematic of a heat flux DSC instrument

6.5.3 Applications of DSC

6.5.3.1 Study of Polymers

(i) ***Kinetics of glass transition:*** DSC can be used to study crystallisation of glasses. The data are analysed using the Johnson–Mehl–Arvami equation:

$$x = 1 - \exp\{-k\,t^{n}\}$$

where x is the volume ratio of transformation at time t, k is the crystal formation rate as a function of temperature change and n is a constant for a particular mechanism of transition. The term k is temperature-dependent since it is a function of nucleation and growth rate of the transformation product.

A typical DSC graph for a glass transition is represented in Fig. 6.27. The transition from the crystalline to the amorphous state is accompanied by a heat of fusion. At T_g, the crystalline compound becomes amorphous. The transition occurs over a range of temperature; the midpoint on the inflection $(t_1 - t_2)$ is taken as T_g.

In DSC (and also in DTA), the peak area A depends on the sample mass m, the heat change ΔH and an empirical constant K:

$$A = \pm \Delta H m K$$

For DSC, the constant K is determined from a standard of high purity with an accurately known enthalpy of fusion (ΔH_f). Pure indium metal is used as the standard. Then, K is calculated from the peak area obtained from the melting endotherm of indium.

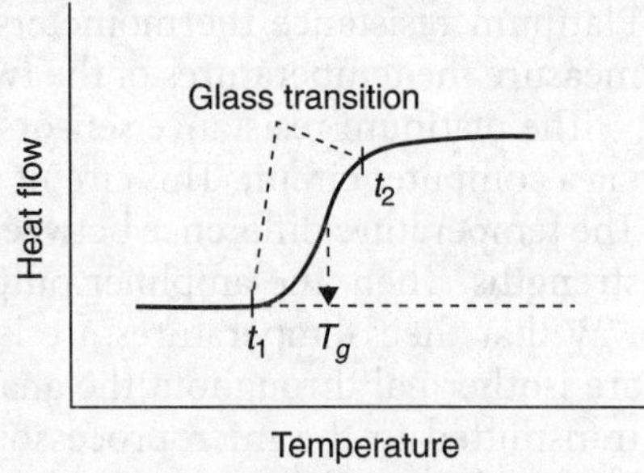

Fig. 6.27 Typical DSC curve for glass transition of a polymer

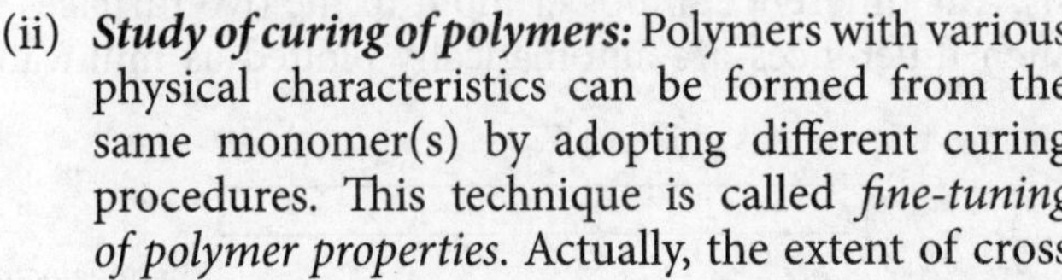

(ii) ***Study of curing of polymers:*** Polymers with various physical characteristics can be formed from the same monomer(s) by adopting different curing procedures. This technique is called *fine-tuning of polymer properties*. Actually, the extent of cross linking of the polymer chains in a polymer product influences its properties and therefore manipulation of crosslinking achieves the desired properties. Crosslinking reactions are exothermic, resulting in a positive peak in the DSC curve; such peaks usually occur soon after the glass transition. Therefore, the extent of crosslinking can be monitored and the desired degree of crosslinking achieved by recording the DSC curves during the progress of crosslinking reactions.

The DSC curve for the isothermal crystallisation of polyethylene is shown in Fig. 6.28. It is a plot of differential power (*milliwatt*, mW) against time of crystallisation. Heat energy is released from the system as the polymer melt forms crystals at an isothermal temperature of 124°C. The time of crystallisation is 24 minutes for a mass of 10 mg. Maximum crystallinity is achieved in 24 minutes. The area under the exothermic peak is proportional to the degree of crystallisation that has occurred at this temperature. The experiment can be repeated at different temperatures to understand the crystallisation behaviour of the polymer and then a suitable temperature is chosen for the industrial production of the polymer.

DSC experiments are usually conducted in the temperature scan mode, that is, measuring the heat energy as the temperature is varied. In a few cases, it is conducted isothermally by scanning the differential power against time.

(iii) ***Purity check of polymers:*** DSC curves can indicate the purity of a polymer as the temperature range over which a mixture of compounds (polymer + impurities) melts is

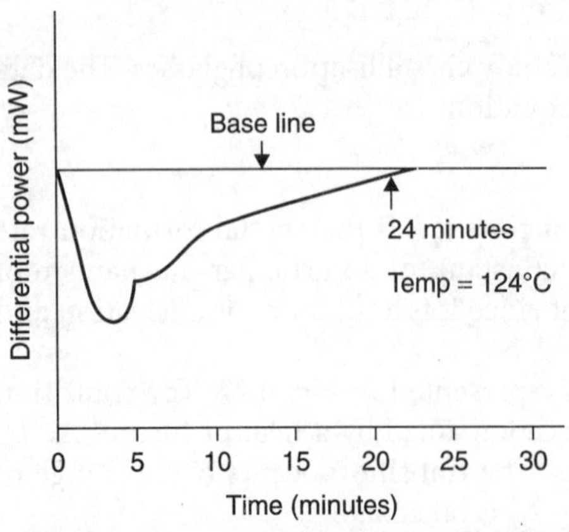

Fig. 6.28 DSC curve for the isothermal crystallisation of polyethylene

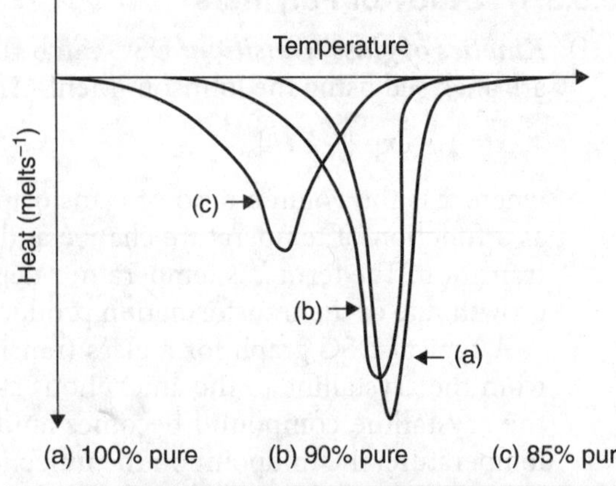

Fig. 6.29 DSC curves of samples of a polymer with different purities (temperature scan mode)

dependent on their relative amounts. The DSC curve (Fig. 6.29) shows a freezing point depression for an impure polymer. Impure polymers produce broad DSC peaks. The DSC curve of the sample is compared with that of a pure sample. The presence of impurities in the sample is reflected in a shift of the position and altered shape (broadening) of the curve.

The total DSC curve for a polymer is shown in Fig. 6.30. It shows three changes:

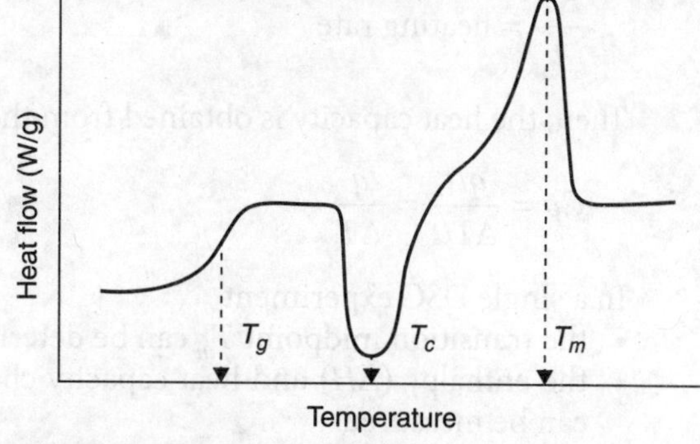

Fig. 6.30 DSC curve for a polymer. T_g: glass transitation temperature; T_c: crystallisation temperature; T_m: melting temperature

- The curve shows an upward shift. This denotes the glass transition. Polymers have a higher heat capacity above their glass transition temperatures than the values below these temperatures. This change in heat capacity shown by the steep portions of the curve can be used to record the T_g value. This change does not occur suddenly, but occurs over a temperature range; therefore, the middle of the inclined line is taken to be the T_g.
- Above the glass transition, the polymer molecules have a lot of mobility. When they reach the right temperature beyond T_g, they move into a very ordered arrangement called the crystalline state. Normally, with small molecules, higher temperatures disrupt crystallinity, but with polymers, the molecules tend to be ordered after acquiring some energy at moderately higher temperatures. When polymers change to the crystalline state, they give off heat. This fact is revealed by the big dip (exothermic) in the DSC curve. The temperature at the lowest point of the dip is considered to be the polymer's crystallisation temperature, T_c. The area of the dip is a measure of the latent heat of crystallisation. The DSC curve of an amorphous polymer will thus indicate whether or not it can form crystals. Not all polymers can form crystals and in such cases no dip in the DSC curve would be obtained. For example, amorphous atactic polystyrene does not crystallise on heating.
- When the polymer is heated beyond its T_c, it eventually undergoes another thermal transition, called melting. It melts at a temperature T_m, when the polymer lattice breaks apart. The chains get loose of their orderly arrangements and begin to move freely at T_m. When the polymer crystal melts, they absorb heat required for melting, and therefore the temperature would not rise. Thus, the extra heat flow during melting is shown as a big peak in the DSC plot. The heat energy absorbed at this transition denotes the latent heat of melting (fusion). The area under the peak is proportional to this heat. This is an endothermic transition. The temperature at the top of the peak is taken as the melting point of the polymer. Only those polymers which have both amorphous and crystalline domains show all the three transitions. Therefore, DSC can indicate whether a polymer is amorphous or crystalline or part amorphous and part crystalline. Several polymers are part amorphous and part crystalline. The ΔH_m (proportional to peak area) can be used to calculate the proportion between these two states in the polymer.

(iv) ***Heat capacity of a polymer:*** The heat capacity C_p, of a polymer is a property useful to determine the use of the polymer. This can be evaluated for it from its DSC analysis. The heat supplied q per unit time (q/t) is the heat flow.

$$\frac{\text{heat}}{\text{time}} = \frac{q}{t} = \text{heat flow}$$

The temperature increase (ΔT) of the polymer per unit time is the heating rate.

$$\frac{\Delta T}{t} = \text{heating rate}$$

Then, the heat capacity is obtained from the relation,

$$Cp = \frac{q/t}{\Delta T/t} = \frac{q}{\Delta T}$$

In a single DSC experiment

- the transition midpoint T_m can be determined; and
- the enthalpy (ΔH) and heat capacity change (ΔC_p) associated with a transformation can be measured.

DSC is extensively used in the study of polymers. It enables us to

- know what happens when a polymer is heated,
- understand the nature of the thermal transitions,
- estimate the relative extent of crystallinity and amorphousness,
- determine its glass transition temperature (T_g) and crystallisation temperature (T_c),
- measure the heat of crystallisation and the related quantity, the heat of melting, ΔH_m,
- determine the melting point T_m of the polymer,
- evaluate the heat capacity C_p, and
- ascertain its purity.

6.5.3.2 Study of Metals and Alloys

DSC is increasingly used in the characterisation of alloys with reference to the following characteristics:

- solidus and liquidus temperatures,
- phase transitions,
- crystal dislocations,
- grain growth,
- crystallisation and
- crystal defects.

6.5.3.3 Study of Liquid Crystals

Some materials on undergoing transition from solid to liquid go through a third state, which displays properties of both the phases. Such an intermediate state is called the *liquid crystalline state*.

$$\text{solid} \longrightarrow \text{liquid crystal} \longrightarrow \text{liquid}$$

The intermediate state is called also the *anisotropic liquid* or *mesomophous state*. Using DSC, it is possible to observe small energy changes that occur as a material transitions from a solid to a liquid crystal, and from a liquid crystal to an isotropic liquid.

6.5.3.4 Study of Oxidation States

DSC can be applied to study the relative stability of the oxidation states of a species. In such a study, first, the sample in a particular oxidation state is kept in a closed chamber isothermally (at constant temperature) in nitrogen atmosphere and its DSC plot is recorded. The nitrogen atmosphere ensures that the species retains its oxidation state during the DSC study. Then, the nitrogen atmosphere is changed to oxygen atmosphere and the sample again brought to the previously maintained temperature. Now, the new DSC curve is recorded; any oxidation that occurs is observed as a deviation in the baseline of the DSC curve. Such DSC analyses are useful for determining the stability and optimum storage conditions for oxidatively mobile compounds. Metal complexes, where the metals can exhibit variable valences have been subjected to such studies.

6.5.3.5 Evaluation of Enthalpies of Transitions

The DSC curve can be used to calculate enthalpies of transitions. This is done by integrating the peak corresponding to a given transition (Fig. 6.31). The enthalpy of transition (ΔH_t) can be expressed by the equation

$$\Delta H_t = K A$$

where K is the calorimetric constant and A is the area under the curve. The calorimetric constant will vary from instrument to instrument, and can be evaluated by analysing a well-characterised sample with a known enthalpy of transition.

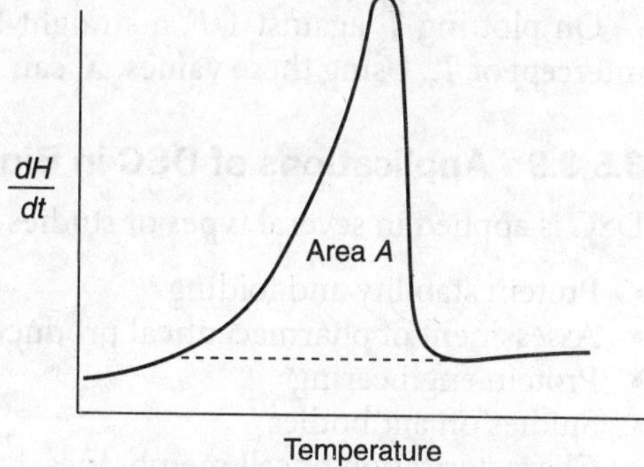

Fig. 6.31 DSC curve for the evaluation of the enthalpy of transitation of a solid

6.5.3.6 Study of Proteins

Protiens get denatured on heating. Denaturation is a consequence of rupture of inter- and intramolecular bonds in proteins. DSC on proteins can provide information on temperature of denaturation (T_d) and enthalpy of denaturation (ΔH_d). ΔH_d is calculated from the area under the transition (natural to denatured) peak. The denaturation temperatures are measures of the thermal stabilities of proteins. The data from DSC on proteins are used in the characterisation and applications of these polymers.

6.5.3.7 Purity Check by DSC

DSC can be applied for purity check on chemicals, as the DSC curve is a fingerprint of a chemical. The presence of impurities in a chemical alters the curve. From the curve, the percentage purity can also be calculated. However, the following factors have to be reckoned with in purity check:

- Manual calculations of purity from the DSC scans are lengthy and laborious; therefore, appropriate computer software should used.
- Not all samples are suitable for purity determination; decomposition of the sample can produce an altered endotherm, even when the sample is pure; if the compound under study and the impurities form a solid solution, then also, the endotherm will be altered.
- The sample (the major component) should exist in the solid state as a single phase.

6.5.3.8 Determination of Purity of Drugs

The purity of a drug can be accurately determined by DSC. The m.p of the drug is altered by impurities present in the drug; the m.p becomes lower and melting occurs in a range. The DSC curve of the impure sample is interpreted applying the modified form of the van't Hoff equation:

$$T_s = T_o - \frac{RT_o^2 X_i}{\Delta H_f}\left(\frac{1}{F}\right)$$

where, ΔH_f = heat of fusion of pure drug (J mol^{-1}), R = gas constant (8.314 J mol^{-1} K^{-1}), T_s = sample melting temperature (K), T_o = theoretical m.p. (K) of pure compound, X_i = mole fraction of impurity, F = fraction of sample melted at T_s.

On plotting T_s against $1/F$, a straight line is obtained with a slope of $RT_o^2\ X_i/\Delta H_f$ and an intercept of T_o. Using these values, X_i can be calculated.

6.5.3.9 Applications of DSC in Biological Studies

DSC is applied in several types of studies on biological species:

- Protein stability and folding
- Assessment of pharmaceutical products
- Protein engineering
- Studies on antibodies
- Characterisation of cell membranes, lipids, nucleic acids and micellar systems
- Relationship between structure and stability of bimolecules
- Study of interaction among bimolecules.

EXERCISES

1. A 1 g sample of a mixture of calcium and barium salts was dissolved in a suitable medium, and the Ca^{2+} and Ba^{2+} ions in the solution were precipitated as $CaC_2O_4 \cdot H_2O$ and $BaC_2O_4 \cdot H_2O$. The mixture of oxalates was then analysed thermogravimetrically. At the 320–400°C range, the residue weighed 0.6100 g and at the 580–620°C range, it weighed 0.5122 g. Calculate the percentages of Ca and Ba in the sample.

2. 0.500 g of pure $[Co(NH_3)_6]Cl_3$ was subjected to TGA. Draw the expected thermal analysis graph. Calculate the weight of the residue at each stage of the decomposition.

3. The DTA of ammonium nitrate in nitrogen atmosphere shows three endotherms at 55°, 130°, 172°C. Explain the data.

4. A 1.000 g sample of calcium hydroxide on thermal analysis lost 0.0788 g without change in its molecular composition. The product then lost in two stages 0.1803 g and 0.1801 g to form a stable residue. Interpret these data.

5. Predict and sketch the TGA curve for (a) dolomite (b) cinnabar (c) white lead.

6. Exactly 1.000 g $FeCl_3 \cdot 6H_2O$ on thermal analysis produced 0.767 g of a residue at T_1°C and then 0.600 g of a residue at T_2°C, with no loss in weight on further heating. Predict its decomposition pattern.

7. $Ca_2P_2O_7$ on heating loses a molecules of P_2O_5 and forms the very heat stable compound $Ca_3(PO_4)_2$. Assuming the decomposition temperature to be T, sketch and explain the DTA curve for 0.25 mg sample of the pyrophosphate.

8. The DTA curve for manganese phosphinate monohydrate $Mn(PH_2O_2)_2 \cdot H_2O(s)$ in vacuum consists of five peaks, the first and fifth being endothermic and the other three being exothermic. Predict the thermal behaviour steps undergone by this salt.

9. Illustrate the application of thermometric titration method in the titrations of ion-combination reactions.

Suggested Reading

1. Brown M E, *Thermal Analysis: Techniques and Applications*, Chapman and Hall, New York, 1988.
2. Wunderlich B, *Thermal Analysis*, Academic Press, San Diego, 1990.
3. Mendham J, Denney R C, Bannes J D and Thomas M, *Vogel's Textbook of Quantitative Chemical Analysis*, Pearson Education Asia, Delhi, 2000.
4. Mackenizie R C, *Differential Thermal Analysis*, Vol. 1, 2, Academic Press, London, 1972.

7 Electroanalytical Methods

7.1 CONDUCTOMETRY

Electrochemistry deals with the relationship between electrical energy and chemical reactions. Electroanalytical chemistry involves applications of electrochemistry in separation, identification and estimation of chemicals. In addition, it is used for quality control and manufacture of industrial products.

Electrical conduction The flow of electricity through a conductor involves the transfer of charges from a point of higher negative potential to one of lower potential. This transfer occurs by one of the two mechanisms—*electronic conduction* or *electrolytic conduction.*

Electronic conduction Electronic conduction involves conduction by direct transfer of electrons through the conductor under the influence of an applied potential. For example, electronic conduction takes place in solid copper and solid cadmium sulphide. The resistance of an electric conductor to current passage can be determined by applying Ohm's law to the conductor. According to Ohm's law, the strength of an electric current flowing through a conductor (that is, the quantity of electricity flowing per second) is determined by the difference in potential applied across the conductor and by the resistance offered by the conductor to the current. This is denoted mathematically as

$$I = \frac{E}{R}$$

where I is the strength of the current (in amperes) flowing through a resistance R (in ohms) under an applied potential difference E (in volts). This equation indicates that the current strength is directly proportional to the difference in potential and inversely proportional to the resistance. The proportionality constant in this equation is made unity by an appropriate choice of units.

Electrolytic conduction Electrolytic conduction involves the transfer of electrons through the migration of positive and negative ions towards the electrodes. For example, in molten NaCl, electrolytic conduction takes place. Unlike during electronic conduction, chemical changes occur during electrolytic conduction.

In dealing with solutions in electrochemistry, the term *conductance* (L) is used. It is the reciprocal of electrical resistance.

$$L = \frac{1}{R}$$

L is expressed in ohm^{-1}, denoted by Ω^{-1} (omega inverse), as resistance is measured in ohms, Ω.

In an ionic solution, the cations and the anions are free to move and both can transport charge. When a current is passed through such a solution, the ions carry the current. The ability of the ions in solution to carry current is called *conductivity*. The conductivity of a solution depends on the numbers of cations and anions present and also the mobility of these ions.

The resistance R (ohms) of a conductor is directly proportional to its length l (cm) and inversely proportional to its cross-sectional area, A (cm^2).

$$R\alpha = \frac{l}{A} \qquad \therefore R = \rho \frac{l}{A}$$

where ρ is called the *resistivity* (or *specific resistance*) of the substance; ρ is characteristic of the material which conducts current. Resistivity is the resistance offered by a specimen 1 cm in length having a cross-sectional area of 1 cm^2.

When dealing with electrolytic solutions in chemistry, conductance is more relevant and useful than resistance. Therefore, conductance (reciprocal of resistance), or *specific conductance* (*conductivity*), κ is used in chemistry.

$$\kappa = \frac{l}{AR}\ \text{ohm}^{-1}\ \text{cm}^{-1}$$

It is the conductance between opposite faces of a 1-cm tube of material. If an emf of 1 V is applied to the opposite faces of a 1-cm cube of a material, the current flowing (in amperes) is numerically equal to κ.

The *specific conductance* is the conductance of a solution taken in a cell in which the electrodes are unit distance apart and have unit area each. The *specific conductance* (kappa) is the reciprocal of the resistivity:

$$\kappa = \frac{l}{\rho} = \frac{l}{AR}$$

The dimensions of specific conductance

$$= \frac{\text{length}}{\text{resistance} \times \text{area}}$$

$$= \frac{\text{cm}}{\Omega \times \text{cm}^2} = \Omega^{-1}\ \text{cm}^{-1}$$

(if the unit metre is used, it is Ω^{-1} m^{-1}).

The SI unit for reciprocal ohms (ohm^{-1} or Ω^{-1}) is Siemens (S) and that for l/A is m^{-1}; therefore the conductance is usually expressed in Sm^{-1}.

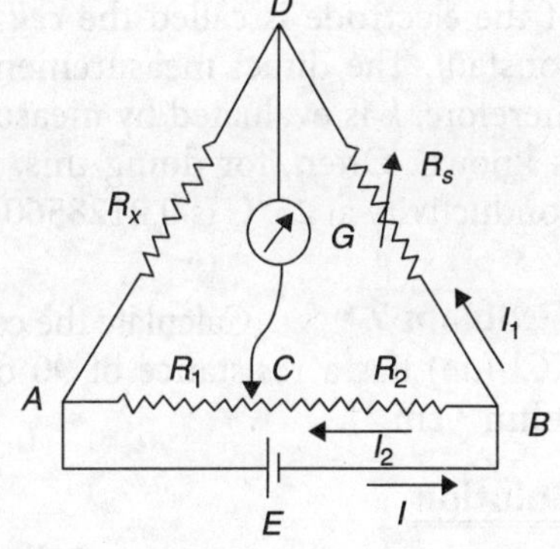

Fig. 7.1 Apparatus for measurement of specific conductance (Wheatstone bridge circuit)

7.1.2 Measurement of Specific Conductance (κ)

The specific conductance of an electrolyte solution is calculated after measuring its resistance. The resistance is measured using a Wheatstone bridge circuit (Fig. 7.1). R_x is the resistance to be measured which is connected to one arm of the bridge. R_s is a variable resistance in the other arm. AB is a uniform slide wire across which a contact point C can be moved. This contact is moved along the resistance wire until no current from the alternating current source E flows through the galvanometer G. At this stage, R_s (known resistance), R_1 (resistance from A to C) and R_2 (*resistance* from C to B) are noted.

R_x can be calculated based on the following facts. When the current I from the source reaches point B, it divides itself into two parallel paths and two currents, I_1 and I_2. As these currents traverse along the resistance, potential drop occurs. When the bridge is balanced by moving C, the potential drop from B to C equals that from B to D. At this balanced condition, D and C are at the same potential and therefore no current flows through the branch containing the galvanometer. This situation is expressed mathematically as

$$R_s I_1 = R_2 I_2$$

Similarly, $R_x I_1 = R_1 I_2$

Dividing the second pair by the first,

$$\frac{R_x I_1}{R_s I_1} = \frac{R_1 I_2}{R_2 I_2} \quad \therefore \frac{R_x}{R_s} = \frac{R_1}{R_2}$$

$$R_x = \left(\frac{R_1}{R_2}\right) R_s$$

Then, using this R_x value, the conductivity (specific conductance) is calculated from the equation.

$$\kappa = \left(\frac{l}{A}\right)\frac{1}{R_x} \qquad (7.1)$$

The term l/A, the ratio of the length between the two electrodes and the cross-sectional area of the electrode is called the *cell constant k*. For a particular conductivity cell, it remains a constant. The direct measurement of l and A to obtain the cell constant is not convenient; therefore, k is evaluated by measuring the resistance of a standard solution whose κ (kappa) is known. Often, for doing this, a standard solution (0.10 mol dm^{-3}) KCl (*aq*) is used. Its conductivity at 25°C is 0.0128560 $ohm^{-1}\ cm^{-1}$.

Problem 7.1 Calculate the cell constant of a conductance cell with which a 0.100 mol dm^{-3} KCl (*aq*) has a resistance of 90 ohms. The κ (kappa) for this solution is 0.0128560 S cm^{-1} ($ohm^{-1}\ cm^{-1}$).

Solution

$$\kappa \text{ S cm}^{-1} = \frac{\text{Cell constatnt}}{R}$$

$$0.0128560 \text{ S cm}^{-1} = \frac{\text{Cell constatnt}}{90 \text{ ohm}}$$

$$\therefore \quad \text{Cell constant} = 90 \times 0.0128560 = 1.157 \text{ cm}^{-1}$$

Problem 7.2 When a solution with κ = 1.300 S m^{-1} was placed in a cell, its resistance measured 160 Ω. The area of the electrodes is 1.60×10^{-4} m^2 each. Calculate the distance between the electrodes and also the cell constant.

Solution

$A = 1.60 \times 10^{-4}\ m^2$

$R = 160\ \Omega$

$\kappa = 1.300\ S\ m^{-1}$

$$\text{Specific conductance } \kappa = \text{cell constant} \left(\frac{l}{A}\right)\left(\frac{1}{R}\right)$$

$$\begin{aligned}\text{Cell constant} &= \kappa R \\ &= (1.300\ Sm^{-1})\ (160\ S^{-1}) \\ &= 208\ m^{-1}\end{aligned}$$

$$\text{Cell constant} = \frac{l}{A}$$

$$\therefore \quad 208\ m^{-1} = \frac{l}{1.60 \times 10^{-4}\ m^2}$$

$$\begin{aligned}\therefore \quad l &= 208\ m^{-1} \times 1.60 \times 10^{-4}\ m^2 \\ &= 3.328 \times 10^{-2}\ m\end{aligned}$$

Problem 7.3 The specific conductance of 0.1 N KCl (*aq*) at 298 K is 1.28 Sm^{-1}. The measured resistance for a cell containing this solution is 108 Ω. Calculate the cell constant for the cell used.

Solution

$$\begin{aligned}\text{Cell constant} &= \text{Specific conductance} \times R \\ &= 1.289\ Sm^{-1} \times 108\ \text{ohm} = 139\ m^{-1}\end{aligned}$$

7.1.3 Conductance Cells

Various types of cells are used for measuring conductance; such cells differ in shape and structure. Two main types of cells are commonly used—the *cup-type* (Fig. 7.2) and the *dip-type* (Fig. 7.3). They are made of pyrex glass with two platinum electrodes fused into the glass. The relative positions of the two electrodes are fixed. They are coated with a fine layer of platinum black, which eliminates polarisation effects due to the passage of current. For a solution of high conductance, these electrodes are placed widely apart, while

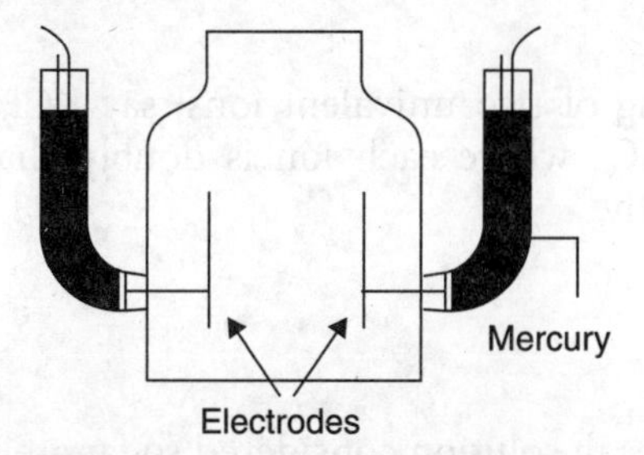

Fig. 7.2 Cup type conductance cell

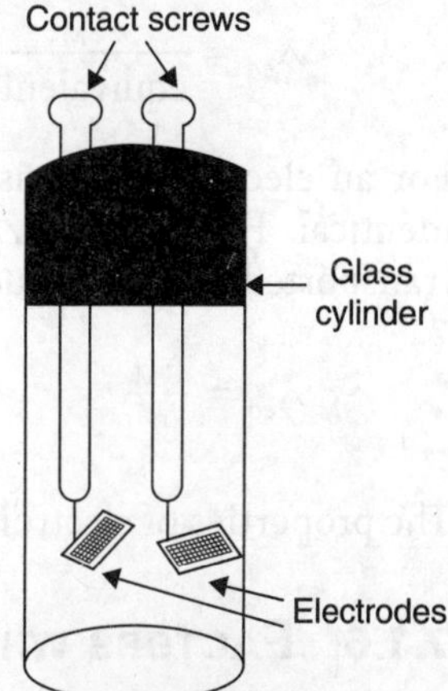

Fig. 7.3 Dip-type conductance cell

for a poorly conducting solution, they are placed close to each other. The solution whose conductance has to be measured is poured into the cup-type cell whereas the dip-type cell is kept dipped into the solution taken in a beaker. In the cup-type cell, electrical contacts are made through mercury, whereas in the dip-type the wires can be directly connected to screws at the top of the cell.

7.1.4 Equivalent Conductance

The equivalent conductance of an electrolyte is defined as the conductivity of a volume of solution containing one gram equivalent of the dissolved electrolyte—the solution being placed between two parallel electrodes 1 cm apart and large enough to contain between them, the whole of the solution. The equivalent conductance is denoted by $\wedge_{eq}$.

$$\wedge_{eq} = \frac{1000}{C}\kappa \tag{7.2}$$

The unit for $\wedge_{eq}$ is S cm^2 eq^{-1} (CGS); S m^2 eq^{-1} (SI); therefore, S m^2 eq^{-1} = 10^4 S cm^2 eq^{-1}.

7.1.5 Molar Conductance

The conductance of a sample solution depends on the concentration of the ions it contains. Generally the conductance is expressed as *molar conductance.* It is denoted by the symbol $\wedge_M$ (capital lambda, with subscript M).

The molar conductance is the conductance expected of the solution of 1 molar concentration.

$$\text{Molar conductance, } \wedge_M = \frac{1000}{C}\kappa = \frac{\text{electrical conductance (S cm}^{-1})}{\text{molarity (mol cm}^{-3})}$$

$\wedge_M$ has the units S cm^2 mol^{-1} and is used for comparing the conductances of different solutions.

Relationship between equivalent conductance and molar conductance:

$$\text{Equivalent conductance} = \frac{\text{Molar conductance}}{\text{Number of equivalents present in 1 mol of electrolyte}}$$

$$\therefore \quad \wedge_{eq} = \frac{\wedge_M}{\text{equivalents}}$$

For an electrolyte consisting of two univalent ions, say KCl, the values of $\wedge_{eq}$ and $\wedge_M$ are identical. However, in $ZnSO_4$ where each ion is doubly charged, two units of charge are transported and consequently,

$$\wedge_{eq} = \frac{\wedge_M}{2}$$

The properties of electrolytes in solution considered so far are summarised in Table 7.1.

7.1.6 Factors which Influence Conductance

The conductance of an electrolyte solution is influenced by several factors:

(i) the nature of the electrolyte—weak or strong,

Table 7.1 Some electrolyte properties

Property	Symbol	Unit	Defining relationship
Resistance	R	Ohm	$R=\frac{E}{I}$
Specific resistance	ρ	Ohm-cm	$\rho = R(A/l)$
Conductance	L	Ohm^{-1} or (mho) or S	$L=\frac{1}{R}$
Specific conductance or conductivity	κ	$Ohm^{-1}cm^{-1}$or $S\ cm^{-1}$	$\kappa=\frac{1}{\rho}=\frac{1}{R}\left(\frac{l}{A}\right)$
Cell constant	k	cm^{-1}	$k=\frac{l}{A}$
Equivalent conducance	$\wedge_{eq}$	$S\ cm^2\ eq^{-1}$	$\wedge_{eq}=\frac{1000}{C}\kappa$
Molar conductance	$\wedge_M$	$S\ cm^2\ mol^{-1}$	$\wedge_M = \kappa V_M$
Limiting ionic conductance	$\wedge_\infty$	$S\ cm^2\ mol^{-1}$	$\wedge_\infty = \lambda_\infty^+ + \lambda_\infty^-$

(ii) the concentration of the solution,
(iii) the temperature; as the temperature increases, ion mobility increases and hence the conductance,
(iv) the ion size; increasing ion size increases interionic interactions and therefore the conductance decreases,
(v) the nature of interionic interactions; as this becomes strong, the mobility of the ions is inhibited thereby decreasing the conductance, and
(vi) the nature of the solvent; higher the viscosity, lesser is the conductance; higher the ion–solvent interaction, lesser is the conductance.

7.1.6.1 Variation of Conductance with Dilution

According to the Arrhenius theory, when a solution is diluted, the dissociation of the electrolyte increases, producing more number of ions. Therefore its equivalent and molar conductances increase. (The molar or equivalent conductance denotes the contribution towards conductivity by all the ions present in solution.) However, *dilution decreases the number of ions per unit volume* though the total number of ions in the bulk of the solution increases. Therefore, the specific conductance decreases on dilution (κ denotes the conductance per 1 cm^3 of the solution). At a particular high dilution, when the electrolyte is 100% dissociated, the equivalent conductance will be the maximum and is called the *equivalent conductance at*

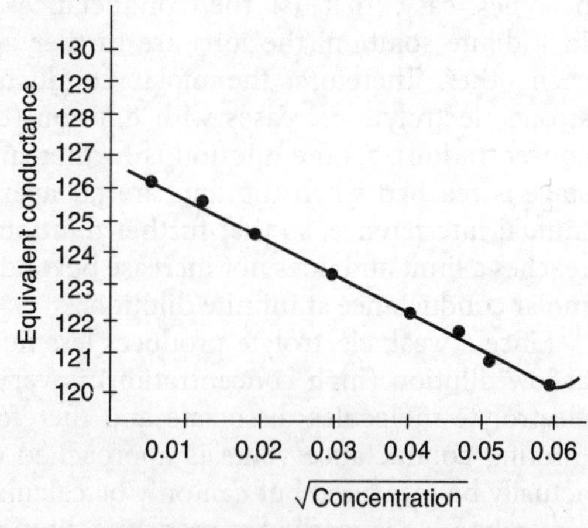

Fig. 7.4 Plot of $\wedge$ versus $\sqrt{C}$

infinite dilution $\wedge_\infty$. When the equivalent conductance of a strong electrolyte (say NaCl) is plotted against the square root of its concentration, a linear plot is obtained (Fig. 7.4); then its $\wedge_\infty$ can be obtained by extrapolating this line to cut the y-axis. With strong electrolytes there is thus a linear relationship between the extent of dissociation and $\sqrt{C}$. However, with a weak electrolyte, the plot of $\wedge$ versus $\sqrt{C}$ is curved; therefore, it cannot be extrapolated to obtain $\wedge_\infty$.

The $\wedge$ versus $\sqrt{C}$ relationship is based on the Debye–Huckel–Onsager equation:

$$\wedge = \wedge_\infty - (A + B\wedge_\infty)\sqrt{C}$$

In this equation A and B are constants, $\wedge$ is the equivalent conductance measured at concentration C and $\wedge_\infty$ is the equivalent conductance at infinite dilution. The above equation can be rewritten as

$$\wedge = \wedge_\infty - \text{constant}\sqrt{C} \tag{7.3}$$

Therefore, on extrapolating the $\wedge$ versus $\sqrt{C}$ plot to cut the *y*-axis, $\wedge_\infty$ can be obtained.

7.1.6.2 Strong and Weak Electrolytes

A strong electrolyte, on dissolution in water, gets highly dissociated producing a large number of ions. A weak electrolyte dissolves in water to produce only a small number of ions. In a concentrated solution of a strong electrolyte, the ions are very close to each other. A positive ion in such a solution is closely surrounded by a sphere of negative ions due to the attraction between the oppositely charged ions; similarly, a negative ion is closely surrounded by a sphere of positive ions. When an electric field is applied to such a solution, the movement of a positive ion towards the cathode is inhibited by the neighbouring negative ions and vice versa. When this concentrated solution is diluted, the influence of the ions of opposite charge on a cation or an anion decreases and consequently its movement becomes easy, that is, the conductance increases. In a dilute solution, the ions are further apart from each other. Therefore, the molar conductance of a strong electrolyte increases with dilution (decreasing concentration). As the dilution is further increased, a stage is reached when the ions are far apart with no mutual interference, so that further dilution has no effect; the molar conductance therefore reaches a limit and does not increase beyond this stage. This *limiting conductance* is called the molar conductance at infinite dilution $\wedge_\infty$.

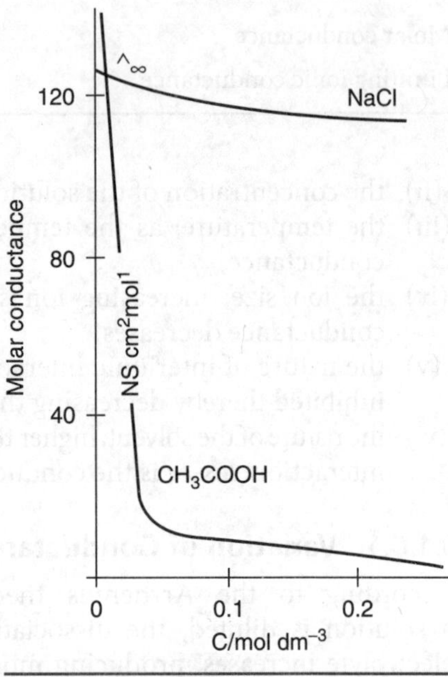

Fig. 7.5 The plot of $\wedge_M$ versus *C* for NaCl and CH_3COOH

Since a weak electrolyte produces less number of ions in solution, its molar conductance at low dilution (high concentration) is very low. As the dilution is increased, more of the electrolyte molecules dissociate and therefore the conductance increases. In this case, the limiting conductance value is approached only gradually with dilution; this value cannot actually be measured but can only be calculated as an approximation. In the case of a strong electrolyte, $\wedge_\infty$ is reached at moderate dilution because, even at this dilution, the dissociation is almost 100%. But with a weak electrolyte, $\wedge_\infty$ can be approached only at extremely high dilution as the electrolyte does not readily dissociate. The effects of dilution on the molar conductances of a strong electrolyte (NaCl) and a weak electrolyte (CH_3COOH) are depicted in Fig. 7.5.

7.1.6.3 The Degree of Dissociation of a Weak Electrolyte

The conductance of a weak electrolyte gives a measure of its degree of dissociation. The degree of dissociation $\alpha = \wedge/\wedge_\infty$. The equivalent conductance of a weak electrolyte shows a marked dependence on the concentration unlike that of a strong electrolyte (Fig. 7.5). This can be understood by considering a weak electrolyte, ethanoic acid. Its conductivity is very low at high concentration, increases gradually with decreasing concentration initially and increases steeply at very low concentrations.

This trend implies that a weak electrolyte is poorly dissociated at high concentration; however, high dilution (low concentration) promotes high dissociation, which is expressed by the term *degree of dissociation*. The value of α is a function of the electrolyte concentration. For an electrolyte AB, with concentration of C, the concentration of $A^+ = \alpha C$ and the concentration of $B^- = \alpha C$; then, the concentration of the undissociated AB = $(1 - \alpha)C$. At high concentrations of the weak electrolyte (very low ionisation), α is very low; at low concentrations (high ionisation), α is close to unity. A value of 1 for α means 100% dissociation.

7.1.6.4 Ostwald's Dilution Law

For the dissociation of ethanoic acid, a weak electrolyte,

$$CH_3COOH\,(aq) \rightleftharpoons CH_3COO^-\,(aq) + H^+\,(aq)$$

the equilibrium constant

$$K_a = \frac{[CH_3COO^-\,(aq)]\,[H^+\,(aq)]}{[CH_3COOH(aq)]}$$

When 1 mol of CH_3COOH is present in a solution of volume V, at equilibrium

$$= \frac{[CH_3COOH(aq)]}{\text{mol dm}^{-3}} = \frac{1-\alpha}{V}$$

$$\frac{[CH_3COO^-\,(aq)]}{\text{mol dm}^{-3}} = \frac{\alpha}{V}$$

$$\frac{[H^+\,(aq)]}{\text{mol dm}^{-3}} = \frac{\alpha}{V}$$

$$\therefore \quad K_a = \frac{(\alpha/V)(\alpha/V)}{(1-\alpha)/V} = \frac{\alpha^2}{(1-\alpha)/V}$$

$$= \frac{\alpha^2 C}{(1-\alpha)} \quad (\text{as } 1\,\text{mol}/V = C)$$

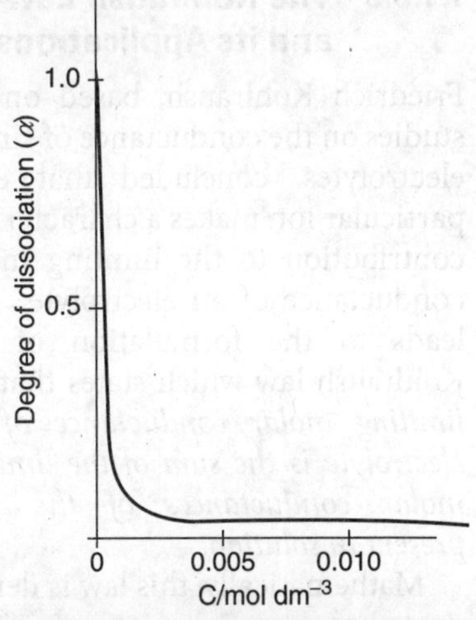

Fig. 7.6 Dependence of degree of dissociation on concentration for a weak electrolyte

However, $\alpha = \dfrac{\Lambda}{\Lambda_\infty}$

Substituting this value for α in the previous equation,

$$K_a = \frac{(\wedge/\wedge_\infty)^2 C}{(1-\wedge/\wedge_\infty)} \tag{7.4}$$

Using this equation, the equilibrium constant of a weak electrolyte can be calculated after measuring its conductance. This equation, first developed by Wilhelm Ostwald is called *Ostwald's dilution law.*

The dependence of the degree of dissociation of a weak electrolyte (CH_3COOH) on its concentration is depicted in Fig. 7.6.

Problem 7.4 For 0.100 M ethanoic acid at 25°C, Λ has been measured to be 5.22 S cm², Λ_∞ = 390.71 S cm². From these data, calculate the degree of dissociation of the acid and K_a.

Solution

$$\alpha = \frac{\wedge}{\wedge_\infty} = \frac{5.22}{390.71} = 0.01336$$

$$K_a = \frac{\alpha^2 C}{(1-\alpha)} = \frac{(0.01336)^2 \times 0.100}{1-0.01336}$$

$$= \frac{1.7849 \times 10^{-5}}{0.9866} = 1.81 \times 10^{-5}$$

7.1.6.5 The Kohlraush Law and its Applications

Friedrich Kohlraush, based on his studies on the conductance of strong electrolytes, concluded that each particular ion makes a characteristic contribution to the limiting molar conductance of an electrolyte. This leads to the formulation of the Kohlraush law which states that *the limiting molar conductance of an electrolyte is the sum of the limiting molar conductances of the ions present in solution.*

Table 7.2 Values of some limiting ionic conductivities at 25°C

Ion	λ_∞ (S cm² mol⁻¹)	Ion	λ_∞ (S cm² mol⁻¹)
H^+	350	F^-	55
OH^-	198	K^+	73
CO_3^{2-}	139	Na^+	50
Ca^{2+}	119	Li^+	39
Mg^{2+}	106	CH_3COO^-	41
Br^-	78	SO_4^{2-}	160
I^-	77	NO_3^-	72
Cl^-	76		

Mathematically, this law is denoted as

$$[\wedge_\infty(AB) = \lambda_\infty(A^+) + \lambda_\infty(B^-)]$$

where $\wedge_\infty(AB)$ is the limiting molar conductance of the electrolyte AB, $\lambda_\infty(A^+)$ is the limiting molar conductance of A^+ and $\lambda_\infty(B^-)$ is the limiting molar conductance of B^-.

The law, also called the *Kohlraush law of independent ionic migration* can be stated in a simpler manner as 'the conductance of a solution is the sum of the individual contributions from the positive and negative ions'.

The values of the individual ionic contributions to the conductance (λ_∞ values) are obtained by a method of trial and error, after measuring the $\wedge_\infty$ for various electrolytes, and applying the additivity principle. A more satisfactory method for evaluation of λ_∞ values involves measuring the transference number of ions present in the electrolyte; these numbers denote the speeds with which the ions move under the influence of an applied potential gradient and are related to the ionic conductance. The values of the ionic conductivities (λ_∞) obtained by these procedures are given in Table 7.2.

The values of λ_∞ are helpful in theoretically calculating the $\wedge_\infty$ values for dilute solutions of strong electrolytes. For example,

(i) $\wedge_\infty (KBr) = \lambda_\infty (K^+) + \lambda_\infty (Br^-)$

$$= 73 + 78 = 151 \text{ S cm}^2 \text{ mol}^{-1}$$

(ii) $\wedge_\infty (K_2SO_4) = 2\,\lambda_\infty\, K^+ + \lambda_\infty (SO_4^{2-})$

$$= (2 \times 73) + 160$$

$$= 306 \text{ S cm}^2 \text{ mol}^{-1}$$

The degree of dissociation of a weak electrolyte (AB) can be evaluated from the known $\wedge_\infty$ values and the measured $\wedge$ value as follows:

$$\alpha = \frac{\wedge}{\wedge_\infty} = \frac{\wedge}{\lambda_\infty (A^+) + \lambda_\infty (B^-)}$$

Problem 7.5 The limiting molar conductivities of the three strong electrolytes NaCl, NaOH and NH_4Cl are 126.4, 248.4, 149.8 S cm^2 mol^{-1} respectively. Calculate $\wedge_\infty$ for the weak electrolyte NH_4OH.

Solution

$$-[\lambda_\infty(Na^+) + \lambda_\infty(Cl^-)] = -126.4$$

$$[(\lambda_\infty Na^+) + \lambda_\infty(OH^-)] = 248.4$$

$$[\lambda_\infty(NH_4^+) + \lambda_\infty(Cl^-)] = 149.8$$

$$[\lambda_\infty(NH_4^+) + \lambda_\infty(OH^-)] = 271.8 = \wedge_\infty$$

Therefore, $\wedge_\infty\, NH_4OH = 271.8 \text{ ohm}^{-1} \text{ cm}^2$

7.1.7 Applications of Conductance Measurements

Some applications of conductance measurements are:

- to distinguish between weak and strong electrolytes,
- to determine the degree of dissociation of acids,

- to determine the solubilities of sparingly soluble salts, and
- titrimetric determinations.

The first two applications have already been discussed; the other applications are considered in the following sections.

7.1.7.1 Determination of the Solubilities of Sparingly Soluble Salts

The solubility of a sparingly soluble salt such as $BaSO_4$ or AgCl can be evaluated from conductance measurements. First the specific conductance of a pure sample of water is measured (κ_{H_2O}). Then this water is used to prepare a saturated solution of the sparingly soluble salt at a fixed temperature. An aliquot of the solution that is above the undissolved excess salt is taken out and its specific conductance measured ($\kappa_{\text{salt soln}}$). Then, the specific conductance of the salt alone is

$$\kappa_{\text{salt}} = \kappa_{\text{salt soln}} - \kappa_{H_2O}$$

The equivalent conductance of the salt

$$\wedge_{eq} = \frac{1000}{C}\kappa_{\text{salt}}$$

where C is the concentration of the salt in equivalents per dm^3. As the solubility of the salt is very low, the solution must be very dilute and consequently the salt is assumed to be completely dissociated; therefore, the equivalent conductance can be equated to the equivalent conductance at infinite dilution ($\wedge_\infty$).

$$\therefore \quad \wedge_{eq} = \frac{1000}{C}\kappa_{\text{salt}}$$

$$\wedge_\infty = \lambda_\infty^+ + \lambda_\infty^-$$

The value of $\wedge_\infty$ can be calculated from the values of λ_∞^+ and λ_∞^- obtained from standard tables. Then, the solubility C can be calculated by measuring the κ_{salt} of the solution:

$$C = \frac{1000\,\kappa_{\text{salt}}}{\Lambda_\infty}$$

7.2 CONDUCTOMETRIC TITRATIONS

The detection of the end point in the titration of an analyte with a titrant by monitoring the change in the conductance of the solution is called a *conductometric titration*. This can be illustrated with a few examples.

Titration of a strong acid HCl (aq) with a strong base NaOH (aq) The conductance of a known volume of hydrochloric acid is measured. Then a solution of sodium hydroxide is added from a burette. After adding each definite volume (say 0.1 or 0.2 mL) of the base, the conductance of the reaction solution is measured. Initially, the conductance of the solution (containing highly mobile H^+ ions) is high. As NaOH is added, the number of H^+ ions decreases because of the reaction $H^+ + OH^- \rightarrow H_2O$; H^+ ions are replaced by slower moving Na^+ ions and consequently the conductance decreases progressively. The decrease in conductance continues until the end point of the titration. At the end point, the concentration of H^+ ions is negligible.

Beyond this point, on adding NaOH, the excess OH^- ions being added increase the conductance sharply. Plotting the conductance against the volume of NaOH generates a graph as shown in Fig. 7.7. The minimum point in this graph denotes the endpoint. This point is the intersection of the two lines.

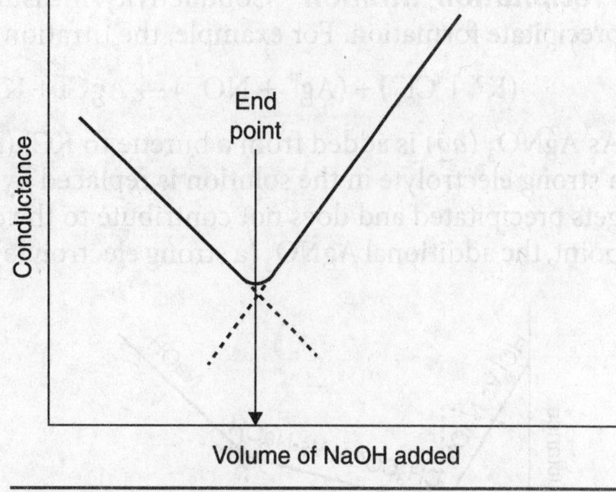

Fig. 7.7 Conductometric titration curve: Strong acid versus strong base

Titration of a weak acid (CH_3COOH) with a strong base (NaOH) Figure 7.8 represents the titration of a weak acid (CH_3COOH) with a strong base (NaOH).

$$CH_3COOH + (Na^+ + OH^-) \rightarrow$$
$$CH_3COO^- + Na^+ + H_2O$$

In this titration, the conductance is initially low as CH_3COOH is a weak electrolyte. As NaOH is added, the strong electrolyte formed ($CH_3COO^-Na^+$) increases the conductance steadily. Beyond the end point, the conductance rises very sharply, as the excess base added is a strong electrolyte. The end point is the intersection of the two straight lines.

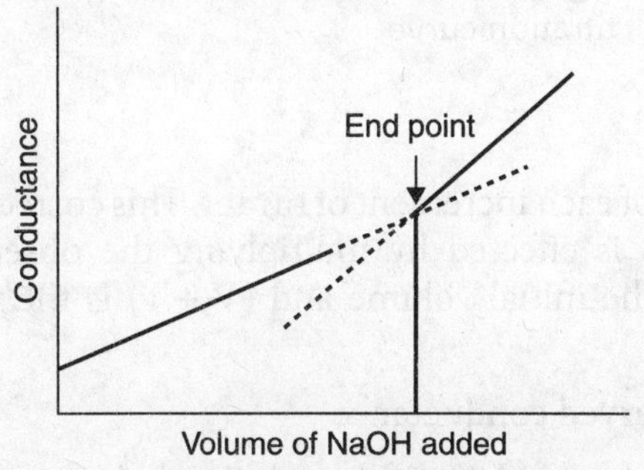

Fig. 7.8 Conductometric titration curve: Weak acid versus strong base

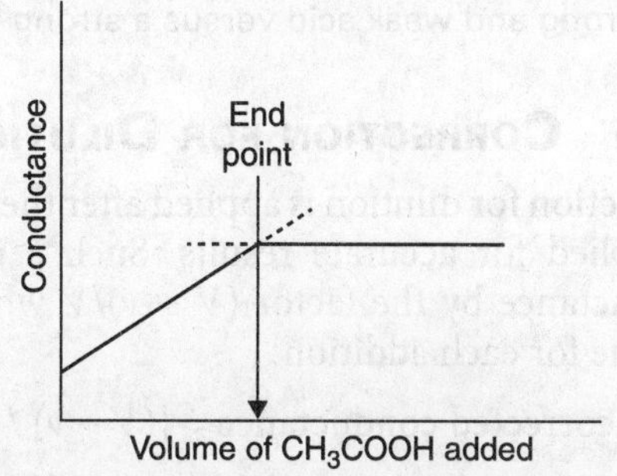

Fig. 7.9 Conductometric titration curve: Weak base versus weak acid

Titration of a weak base (NH_4OH) with a weak acid (CH_3COOH) Figure 7.9 denotes the titration curve of a weak base (NH_4OH) with a weak acid (CH_3COOH). As CH_3COOH is added to NH_4OH, the conductance increases as the salt CH_3COONH_4 is more dissociated than NH_4OH. After the end point, the conductance remains almost constant as the excess weak acid added is weakly ionised. Thus the end point is represented by a pronounced change in the slope of the graph.

Titration of a mixture of a strong acid and a weak acid Figure 7.10 denotes the titration of a mixture of HCl and CH_3COOH against NaOH. As NaOH is added to the mixture of the acids, the stronger acid HCl gets neutralised first. This leads to a decrease in the conductance. Once all the HCl has been neutralised, CH_3COOH starts getting neutralised. During this, there is a small increase in the conductance. Beyond this endpoint, the addition of excess NaOH, a strong electrolyte, increases the conductance steeply. Thus, the two inflexion points on the graph corresponding to the two sudden changes in slopes represent the two endpoints.

Precipitation titration Conductivity measurements can be used for titrations involving precipitate formation. For example, the titration of KCl (*aq*) with $AgNO_3$ (*aq*):

$$(K^+ + Cl^-) + (Ag^+ + NO_3^-) \rightarrow AgCl + K^+ + NO_3^-$$

As $AgNO_3$ (*aq*) is added from a burette to KCl (*aq*), no change in conductance occurs as KCl, a strong electrolyte in the solution is replaced by another strong electrolyte KNO_3 (since AgCl gets precipitated and does not contribute to the conductance of the solution). Beyond the end point, the additional $AgNO_3$ (a strong electrolyte) steeply increases the conductance (Fig. 7.11).

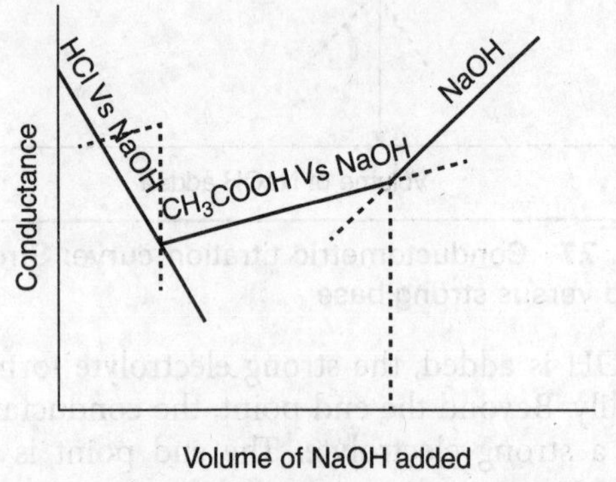

Fig. 7.10 Conductometric titration curve: Mixture of a strong and weak acid versus a strong base

Fig. 7.11 Conductometric precipitation titration curve

7.2.1 Correction for Dilution

Correction for dilution is applied after the addition of each increment of titrant. This correction is applied for accurate results. Such a correction is effected by multiplying the observed conductance by the factor $(V + v)/V$ where V is the initial volume and $(V + v)$ is the final volume for each addition.

Thus, corrected conductance = $[(V + v) / V] \times$ Observed conductance

When the total volume of the titrant added does not exceed 2% of the solution being titrated, no such correction is necessary.

7.2.2 Advantages of Conductometric Titration

- It can be used even when the reactants are coloured, in which case no commonly used indicator would work satisfactorily.
- It is suitable for very low concentrations of the reactants, unlike in conventional titrimetry.
- The titration of a weak base with a weak acid, which cannot be carried out successfully with an indicator, can be done by the conductance method.
- It can also be used for precipitation titrations with precision.
- A mixture of analytes (say, Cl^- and I^-) can be easily determined by this method.
- The end point is determined graphically and is accurate; it does not require the special precautions usually vital for visual identification of end points.

7.3 POTENTIOMETRY

Electrical energy and chemical energy are interconvertible; likewise chemical reactions and the flow of electricity are related. The study of these relationships constitutes electrochemistry.

Chemical reactions involving electricity are called *electrochemical reactions*. These reactions are of two types:

(i) *Induced electrolytic reactions*: When non-spontaneous reactions are forced to occur by the passage of electricity through the reactants, they are called induced electrolytic reactions. For example, on passing electricity through acidified water, a chemical reaction – the decomposition of water – occurs.

$$2H_2O \rightarrow 2H_2 + O_2$$

(ii) *Spontaneous oxidation–reduction reactions*: In these redox reactions, as the two reactants interact, product formation and electricity generation also occur.

$$Cu^{2+}\,(aq) + Zn\,(s) \rightarrow Cu\,(s) + Zn^{2+}\,(aq)$$

Electrochemical reactions and electrical energy have great practical applications in modern life; some such applications are:

- electrolytic production of metals and their compounds,
- electrochemical methods of studying industrial materials,
- manufacture of batteries, and
- physiological studies on nerve actions in living systems.

7.3.1 Metallic and Electrolytic Conductors

The passage of electricity through a substance is electrical conductance; it involves movement of electrons. When a substance allows such movement of electrons or ions, it is called an *electrical conductor*. Electrical conductors are of two types—*metallic conductors* and *electrolytic conductors*.

7.3.1.1 Metallic Conductors

An electron can move from one end of a metallic wire to the other. This kind of transport of electrons is called electrical conduction. In a solid, such as a copper wire, electrical conduction involves the free movement of electrons in the metallic lattice without any movement of the lattice atoms; this type of conduction is called *metallic conduction*. In metallic conduction, electricity is carried exclusively by electrons, the atomic nuclei remaining stationary. Metallic conduction is also known as *electronic conduction*. Metals, alloys, certain metallic salts and graphite are some of the solids which are electronic conductors and certain gases are also electronic conductors.

7.3.1.2 Electrolytic Conductors

On passing electricity through molten (liquid) sodium chloride, the Na^+ ions migrate towards the negative electrode (cathode) and the Cl^- ions migrate towards the positive electrode (anode). In this case, the passage of electricity through matter results in the actual transfer of matter (unlike in metallic conduction). This type of conduction is called *electrolytic conduction*. Liquid NaCl is an electrolytic conductor. The migration of matter (actually ions) in an electrolytic conductor results in changes in concentration and also sometimes in the visible formation of materials at the points where electricity enters and leaves the liquid. Electrolytic conductors are of two main types:

(i) pure polar substances, such as acetic acid, fused NaCl and so on, and

(ii) solutions of certain polar substances such as aqueous sodium chloride, aqueous copper sulphate and so on.

Electrochemistry is primarily concerned with the electrolytic conductors.

7.3.1.3 Mechanism of Electrolytic Conduction

Neither molten NaCl nor NaCl (*aq*) contains free electrons (contrary to a metal); then how do they conduct electricity? This question can be answered by considering the changes that occur on passing electricity through say, NaCl (*l*) (Fig. 7.12). In NaCl (*l*), the salt ionises producing Na^+ and Cl^- ions. On passing a direct current through the two metal electrodes, the electrodes acquire electrical charges. Each electrode attracts to itself ions of the opposite polarity available in the solution, and thus the positive ions migrate to the cathode and the negative ions to the anode. Each electrode is consequently surrounded by a layer of ions of opposite charge. Each Cl^- ion close to the anode, transfers an electron to the anode and gets oxidised to Cl. This electron gained from the anion flows through the external circuit and is delivered at the cathode. At the cathode, this electron is gained by an Na^+ ion to get reduced to Na. Each time a negative ion gets oxidised, another Cl^- ion from the solution moves on to take its place on the anode. Similarly, on the reduction of each Na^+ at the cathode, another Na^+ from the solution moves on to the cathode. The overall effect of these changes is the occurrence of a redox reaction:

Anode (oxidation): $2Cl^- (l) \rightarrow Cl_2 (g) + 2e^-$

Cathode (reduction): $Na^+ (l) + e^- \rightarrow Na (l)$

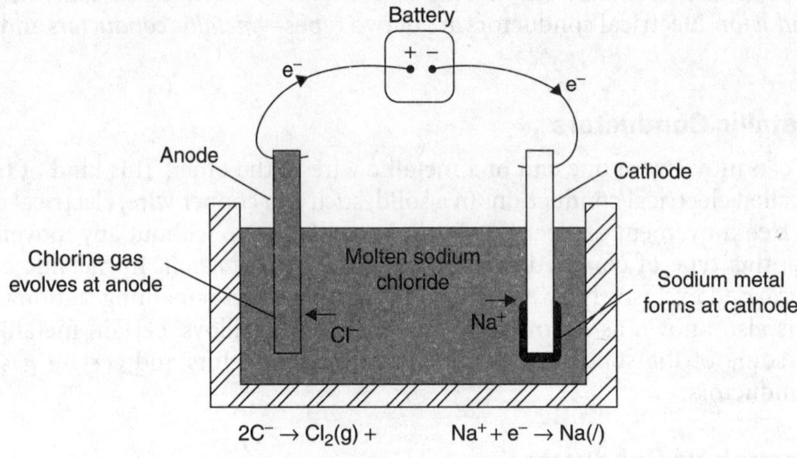

Fig. 7.12 Electrolysis of molten sodium chloride

This redox reaction results in the migration of ions toward the electrodes and the flow of electrons through the wires of the external circuit. The migration of ions through the liquid is called electrolytic conduction. The molten NaCl is decomposed to liberate Na (*l*) and Cl_2 (*g*), and this process is called *electrolysis*. In electrolysis, a non-spontaneous chemical change is forced to occur by the application of an electrical voltage across a pair of electrodes that dip into the liquid system.

The apparatus consisting of a container for the electrolyte into which the electrodes are dipped is called an *electrolytic cell.*

7.3.1.4 Galvanic Cell

In an electrolytic cell, electricity forces a non-spontaneous chemical change to occur. As a complementary process, in a system, a spontaneous chemical change producing electricity can occur. As a consequence of the chemical change, electrons flow through the electrical circuit. Such chemical systems are called either *galvanic cells* or *voltaic cells*. For example, when metallic zinc is dipped in aqueous copper sulphate, a redox reaction occurs.

$$Cu^{2+} (aq) + Zn (s) \rightarrow Cu (s) + Zn^{2+} (aq)$$

In this redox reaction, chemical energy is converted into electrical energy. This reaction can be denoted as a pair of redox *half reactions*.

$$Cu^{2+} (aq) + 2e^- \rightarrow Cu (s)$$

$$Zn (s) \rightarrow Zn^{2+} (aq) + 2e^-$$

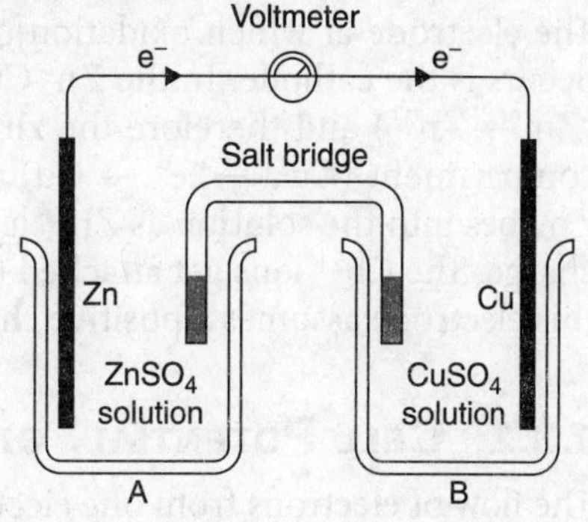

Fig. 7.13 Galvanic cell: copper–zinc

In this galvanic cell, Cu^{2+} is reduced and Zn is oxidised (Fig. 7.13). The container A has a zinc electrode dipped in aqueous zinc sulphate. The container B has a copper electrode dipped in aqueous copper sulphate. The two electrodes are connected by a wire through a voltmeter. An inverted U-tube containing KCl solution in gelatin connects the two containers—this is called the *salt bridge* and it provides an electrically conducting medium between the two solutions. The openings of the U-tube are loosely plugged with cotton to prevent the KCl solution from dripping into the container; it however allows the cations and the anions to move across. As the redox reaction progresses, electrons flow externally from the Zn electrode (anode) to the Cu electrode (cathode).

When the zinc metal is directly dipped into a solution of Cu^{2+}, the reaction occurs at the surface of zinc, no useful flow of electrons generating electricity would occur. On the contrary, electricity generation is achieved by using *half-cells*; in this arrangement, the electrons have to travel through the wire and produce electricity. Such a galvanic cell can then function as a source of electricity.

- *Faradaic current* is the current directly due to electrode reactions. This current is carried across the electrode–solution interfaces by electron transfer reactions involving redox couples.

7.3.1.5 The Role of Salt Bridge

The two solutions, Zn^{2+} (*aq*) and Cu^{2+} (*aq*) have to be separated in two compartments in the galvanic cell. If they are kept together, Cu^{2+} would directly react at the Zn electrode and the electrons would not be forced to flow through the external circuit. This problem is solved by using a salt bridge. Although the two solutions have to be separated to generate electricity, the complete isolation of the two species would produce electrical imbalance at the electrodes and then the electron flow would stop. Such an imbalance is prevented by the KCl in the salt bridge. The K^+ ions diffuse into one half-cell to balance the excess negative charge, while the Cl^- ions diffuse into the other compartment to balance the positive charge. The salt bridge solution is made of an electrolyte whose ions do not react with the ions of the solutions or with the electrodes.

- A salt bridge is a U-shaped glass tube containing an 'inert' electrolyte such as KCl or KNO_3 mixed with a gel such as gelatin or agar agar.
- It connects the solutions of two half-cells and completes the cell circuit.
- It prevents transference or diffusion of the solutions from one half-cell to the other.
- It keeps the solutions of the two half-cells electrically neutral.

7.3.1.6 Electrode Signs in Galvanic Cells

The electrode at which oxidation occurs is the anode and the electrode at which reduction occurs is the cathode. In the Zn–Cu galvanic cell, oxidation occurs in the zinc compartment ($Zn \rightarrow Zn^{2+}$) and therefore the zinc electrode is the anode, reduction occurs at the copper compartment ($Cu^{2+} + 2e^- \rightarrow Cu$) and therefore the copper electrode is the cathode. When Zn goes into the solution as Zn^{2+} leaving two electrons, the zinc electrode acquires a negative charge. The Cu^{2+} ions get attached to the copper electrode before becoming Cu and therefore this electrode assumes a positive charge.

7.3.2 Cell Potential, emf

The flow of electrons from one electrode to the other in a galvanic cell indicates that there is a voltage difference between the two electrodes. This voltage difference between the electrodes is called the *electromotive force* (emf). It is denoted by the symbol *E*. It can be measured by connecting a voltmeter between the two electrodes. The emf of a galvanic cell is measured in volts (V); it is called the *cell voltage* or *cell potential* (E_{cell}).

The emf is the force with which electrons move through the wire. The volt denotes the energy representing the flow of electric charges when the emf is 1 volt; then the passage of 1 coulomb would be able to effect 1 joule of work.

$$1 \text{ volt} = \frac{1 \text{ joule}}{\text{coulomb}}; \quad 1\text{ V} = \frac{1\text{ J}}{\text{C}}$$

The cell emf depends on the concentrations of the ions in the cell, the temperature and the partial pressures of gases that might be involved in the cell reactions.

Therefore, for comparing the cell emf values, these are expressed with reference to standard cell conditions—ion concentrations at 1 M, temperature at 25°C and partial pressures of gases at 1 atm. The emf at these standard conditions is called the *standard cell potential*, denoted as E^0_{cell}.

The emf is an *intensive property* and is therefore independent of the volume of the solution and the weight (size) of the electrodes.

7.3.2.1 Measurement of emf

The emf of a cell can be measured using a potentiometer, operating on the Poggendorff principle. In this apparatus, the potential generated by the galvanic cell is balanced by an opposing potential (voltage from a storage battery) from within the potentiometer. The opposing potential is varied and when the two potentials are equal, no current flows. At this point the cell potential is equal to the opposing emf, which is read from the voltmeter attached in the circuit. The measured voltage is the maximum emf of the galvanic cell.

A potentiometer (Fig. 7.14) consists of a working cell C. This is a storage battery of constant emf which must be larger than the emf of the cell to be measured. The battery is connected across the ends of a uniform conductor AB of high resistance. The cell X, which is under study is connected to A, with the poles in the same direction as the cell C, and then through a galvanometer G to a sliding contact SC. This contact can be moved along AB which is a straight platinum wire of uniform thickness. The position of SC is adjusted until D when no current flows through the galvanometer. Then, the fall of potential between A and D due to the cell C is exactly compensated by the emf of X, which is E_x. Using a switch, the cell X is now replaced by a standard cell S of known emf equal to E_s. The sliding contact is readjusted until a point of balance is reached at D′. The decrease of potential between A and D′ is equal to E_s as the conductor AB is uniform.

$$\frac{E_x}{E_s} = \frac{\text{AD}}{\text{AD}'}$$

$$E_x = \frac{\text{AD}}{\text{AD}'} \times E_s$$

E_s is known, AD and AD′ can be measured. Therefore, the emf of the unknown cell, E_x can be calculated.

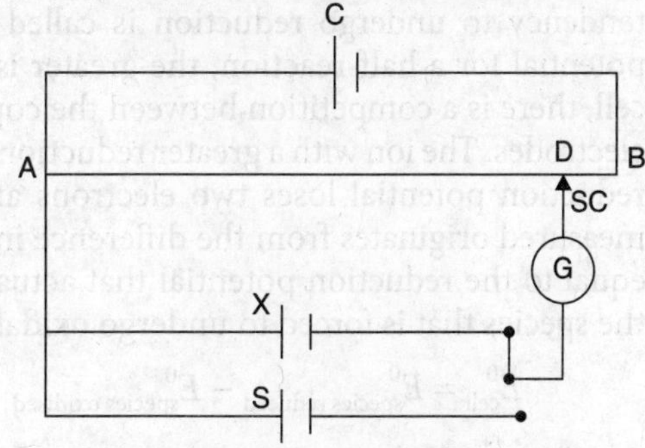

Fig. 7.14 Potentiometer: Measurement of emf

The commercial potentiometer consists of a number of resistance coils with a movable contact, and has a slide wire for fine adjustment. The calibration is effected with a standard cell of known emf. The emf of the unknown cell is read directly with an accuracy of 0.1 millivolt from the built-in sensitive voltmeter.

7.3.2.2 Cell Diagrams

A cell diagram is a simple notation used to provide important information about a galvanic cell. For example, the zinc–copper cell is denoted as:

$$\underbrace{\overset{1}{\text{Zn }(s)}\ |\ \overset{2}{\text{Zn}^{2+}}\ \overset{3}{(1.00\text{ M})}}_{\text{half-cell}}\ \overset{4}{||}\ \underbrace{\overset{5}{\text{Cu}^{2+}}\ \overset{6}{(1.00\text{ M})}\ |\ \overset{7}{\text{Cu }(s)}}_{\text{half-cell}}$$

1. anode
2. electrolyte in the half-cell
3. concentration of Zn^{2+} electrolyte in the half-cell
4. salt bridge
5. electrolyte in the other half-cell
6. concentration of Cu^{2+} electrolyte in the half-cell
7. cathode

The cell diagram consists of two half-cell diagrams connected by a salt bridge. The single bar between the electrode and electrolyte symbols (Zn | Zn^{2+}) in the cell diagram denotes the phase boundary, between the solid electrode and the solution.

The emf of a combination of two half-cells is the difference between the emf of the half-cell on the right-hand side minus the emf of the half-cell on the left-hand side. The half-cell with the more negative electrode potential should be shown as the left-hand half-cell.

For the Cu–Zn electrode cell (Daniell cell), the zinc half-cell has a standard electrode potential of –0.76 V and the copper half-cell +0.34 V. Therefore, the zinc half-cell becomes the left-hand side cell in cell depiction.

7.3.3 Reduction Potentials

In the zinc–copper cell, both Zn^{2+} and Cu^{2+} have a tendency to get reduced.

$$Zn^{2+}(aq) + 2e^- \rightarrow Zn(s)$$

$$Cu^{2+}(aq) + 2e^- \rightarrow Cu(s)$$

Each of these half-cell reactions has a natural tendency to proceed from left to right; this tendency to undergo reduction is called the *reduction potential.* The larger the reduction potential for a half-reaction, the greater is the tendency to undergo reduction. In the actual cell, there is a competition between the copper and zinc ions for acquiring electrons from the electrodes. The ion with a greater reduction potential, in this case Cu^{2+}, wins. Zinc, with a lower reduction potential loses two electrons and gets oxidised. Therefore, the potential actually measured originates from the difference in the tendencies of the two ions to get reduced. It is equal to the reduction potential that actually gets reduced minus the reduction potential for the species that is forced to undergo oxidation. This is denoted as

$$E^0_{\text{cell}} = E^0_{\text{species reduced}} - E^0_{\text{species oxidised}}$$

For the zinc–copper cell,

$$E^0_{\text{cell}} = E^0_{Cu^{2+}/Cu} - E^0_{Zn^{2+}/Zn}$$

Where, E^0_{cell} = measured emf, $E^0_{Cu^{2+}/Cu}$ = standard reduction potential for copper, and $E^0_{Zn^{2+}/Zn}$ = standard reduction potential for zinc.

$E^0_{Cu^{2+}/Cu}$ is larger than $E^0_{Zn^{2+}/Zn}$ and therefore E^0_{cell} is positive.

When the concentrations of both Cu^{2+} and Zn^{2+} ions are 1.00 M each at 25°C, the emf of the cell (Fig. 7.13) is 1.10 V. This voltage is the cumulative value of the two single electrode potentials. It is impossible to measure the *absolute single electrode potential.* When the sign of the reduction potential is changed, it would denote the *standard oxidation potential,* that is, the potential for the reverse single-cell reaction. Each half-cell potential is called a *single electrode potential.*

7.3.4 Determination of Single Electrode Potentials

An electrochemical reaction is the sum of two electrode reactions, an oxidation and a reduction. Similarly, the emf of every cell is composed of two individual single electrode potentials; the algebraic sum of these potentials is equal to the total emf of the cell.

Experimentally, only the difference in potentials between two electrodes can be measured. The hydrogen electrode, whose potential at all temperatures is taken as zero, can be used as the reference electrode

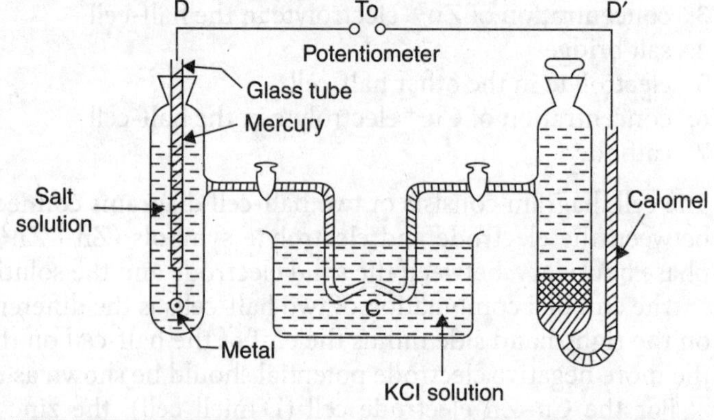

Fig. 7.15 Apparatus for the determination of single electrode potential

for determining the emf. The preparation and use of the standard hydrogen electrode is experimentally difficult and therefore, secondary auxiliary *reference electrodes* are widely used in electrochemistry. The *calomel electrode* is one such electrode.

For determining the single electrode potential of an electrode, it is combined with the standard calomel electrode (Fig. 7.15). The two electrodes are combined with a salt bridge C consisting of a beaker filled with 1 N or saturated potassium chloride solution; the side arms of the two electrodes are dipped into the salt bridge solution. Electrical contact is made by wires D and D′. With the help of a potentiometer, the emf of the cell is measured.

7.3.4.1 Calculation of Single Electrode Potentials

This calculation can be described with an example, say, the Cd/Cd^{2+} electrode.

$$Cd/Cd^{2+}\ (a = 1)\ //\ KCl\ (1\ N),\ Hg_2Cl_2\ (s)/Hg$$

In this combination of the two electrodes, cadmium is oxidised and the calomel is reduced.

$$\text{Negative electrode: } Cd\ (s) \rightleftharpoons Cd^{2+}\ (a = 1) + 2e^-$$

$$Hg_2Cl_2\ (s) + 2e^- \rightleftharpoons 2\ Hg\ (l) + 2\ Cl^-\ (1\ N)$$

At 25°C, the emf for this cell is measured to be 0.6830 V. For the reduction of calomel the emf at 25°C is $E_C = +0.2800$ V.

Therefore,

$$E = E_{Cd} + E_C$$

$$0.6830 = E_{Cd} + 0.2800$$

$$E_{Cd} = 0.6830 - 0.2800$$

$$= 0.4030\ V$$

The reaction and the corresponding standard (single) electrode potential for the Cd/Cd^{2+} $(a = 1)$, electrode are

$$Cd(s) = Cd^{2+}\ (a = 1) + 2e^-$$

$$E_{25°C} = 0.4030\ V$$

7.3.5 Standard Hydrogen Electrode

If one of the single electrode potentials for the Cu^{2+}/Zn^{2+} system is known, then using the measured emf, the other single electrode potential can be calculated. To do this, the hydrogen electrode has been arbitrarily assigned a potential value of 0.00 V; this is called the *standard hydrogen electrode* (SHE). The SHE (Fig. 7.16) is used to determine the single electrode potentials of other systems. It consists of a platinum wire encased in a glass sleeve. Hydrogen gas is passed through this sleeve at 1 atm. pressure. A platinum foil is attached to one end of the wire, at the open end of the sleeve. This foil is coated with a black, smooth layer of finely-divided platinum, which serves as the catalyst for the electrode reaction.

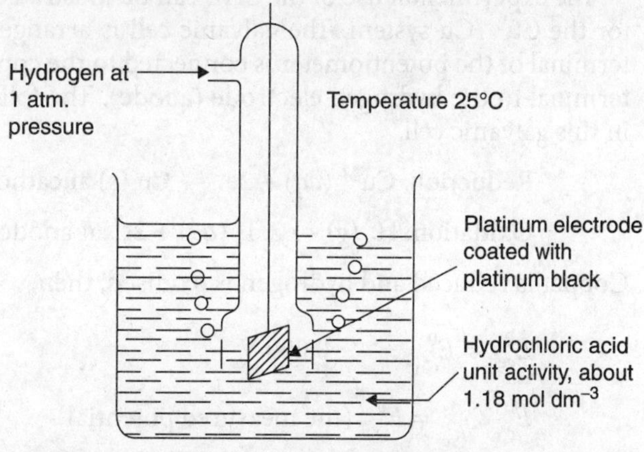

Fig. 7.16 Standard hydrogen electrode

$$2H^+ (aq) + 2e^- = H_2 (g)$$

This electrode is immersed in an acidic solution with $[H^+] = 1.00$ M at 25°C. By convention, the SHE is assigned a reduction potential $E^0_{H^+/H_2}$ of 0.000 V at all temperatures. A species which is more easily reduced than H^+ has a positive E^0 value and a species which is less easily reduced than H^+ has a negative E^0 value. For example, the reduction $Cu^{2+} + 2e^- \rightarrow Cu$ is easier than the reduction of H^+ and therefore its standard electrode potential is positive (+0.34 V).

The cell is written as

$$\text{Pt}, H_2 / H^+ (a = 1) \;\vdots\;\vdots\; Cu^{2+} (a = 1)\ Cu$$

7.3.5.1 Use of SHE

The SHE is paired with another half-cell in a galvanic cell to determine the single electrode potential of the coupled half-cell. If the coupled half-cell has a reduction potential greater than that for the hydrogen electrode (E^0 is positive), the hydrogen species are forced to undergo oxidation.

$$H_2 (g) \rightarrow 2H^+ (aq) + 2e^-$$

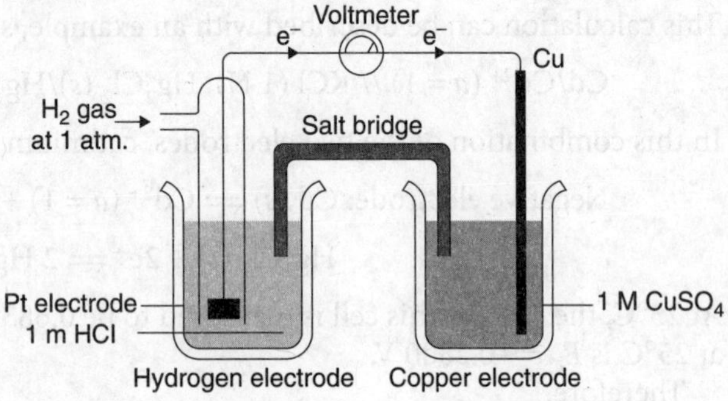

Fig. 7.17 Cu/SHE galvanic cell

On the contrary, if the reduction potential of the coupled half-cell is less than 0.000 V (E^0 is negative), then the hydrogen species undergoes reduction.

$$2H^+ (aq) + 2e^- \rightarrow H_2 (g)$$

This would lead to the oxidation of the coupled species.

The experimental use of the SHE can be illustrated by considering the determination of E^0 for the Cu^{2+}/Cu system. The galvanic cell is arranged as indicated in Fig. 7.17. The positive terminal of the potentiometer is connected to the copper electrode (cathode) and the negative terminal to the hydrogen electrode (anode). The following spontaneous half-reactions occur in this galvanic cell.

Reduction: $Cu^{2+} (aq) + 2e^- \rightarrow Cu (s)$ at cathode

Oxidation: $H_2 (g) \rightarrow 2H^+ (aq) + 2e^-$ at anode

Copper is reduced and hydrogen is oxidised; then,

$$E^0_{cell} = E^0_{Cu^{2+}/Cu} - 0.000 \text{ V}$$

$$E^0_{Cu^{2+}/Cu} = E^0_{cell} \text{ (the measured potential)}$$

The experimental value for this E^0_{cell} is +0.34 V; the positive E^0_{cell} indicates that Cu^{2+} is more easily reduced than H^+.

There are some metal species which are less easily reduced than H^+ (*aq*), for example, Ni^{2+}. When a half-cell with such a metal is coupled with the SHE, in the galvanic cell arrangement, the SHE has to be connected to the positive terminal and the metal half-cell to the negative terminal of the potentiometer. In the nickel–hydrogen cell, the spontaneous half-cell reactions are:

Reduction: $2H^+ (aq) + 2e^- \rightarrow H_2 (g)$ cathode

Oxidation: $Ni (s) \rightarrow Ni^{2+} (aq) + 2e^-$ anode

The measured E^0_{cell} for this system is 0.25 V. Then,

$$0.25 = E^0_{H^+/H_2} - E^0_{Ni^{2+}/Ni}$$

$$E^0_{Ni^{2+}/Ni} = (0.000 - 0.25) \text{ V}$$

$$= -0.25 \text{ V}$$

7.3.5.2 Uses of Reduction Potentials

- The direction of spontaneous cell reactions can be predicted using the reduction potentials. For example, the cell potential and the spontaneous cell reaction for the Ni/Cu cell can be predicted using the reduction potentials for the nickel and copper electrodes.

$$Cu^{2+} (aq) + 2e^- \rightarrow Cu (s) \quad E^0_{Cu^{2+}/Cu} = +0.34 \text{ V}$$

$$Ni^{2+} (aq) + 2e^- \rightarrow Ni (s) \quad E^0_{Ni^{2+}/Ni} = -0.25 \text{ V}$$

The higher value of the copper electrode potential indicates that Cu^{2+} is more readily reduced than Ni^{2+}. Then the reaction occurring in the cell must be:

$$Ni (s) + Cu^{2+} (aq) \rightarrow Ni^{2+} (aq) + Cu (s)$$

Then, $E^0_{cell} = E^0_{Cu^{2+}/Cu} - E^0_{Ni^{2+}/Ni}$

$$= +0.34 \text{ V} - (-0.25 \text{ V})$$

$$= +0.59 \text{ V}$$

This value of + 0.59 V is actually the value measured experimentally for the Ni/Cu cell, thus proving the validity of the method of predicting E^0 values. The cell reaction between the nickel and copper species indicated above is spontaneous.

Consider now the Ag/Cu cell. Let us find out whether Ag would be able to reduce Cu^{2+}.

$$Cu^{2+} (aq) + 2Ag \rightarrow Cu (s) + 2Ag^+ (aq)$$

$$E^0_{cell} = E^0_{Cu^{2+}/Cu} - E^0_{Ag^+/Ag}$$

$$= +0.34 \text{ V} - (+0.80 \text{ V})$$

$$= -0.46 \text{ V}$$

The E^0 of the cell is negative and, therefore, the reaction indicated above would not occur; actually the reverse reaction

$$2Ag^+ (aq) + Cu (s) \rightarrow 2Ag (s) + Cu^{2+} (aq)$$

would be spontaneous with $E^0_{cell} = -(-0.46 \text{ V}) = +0.46 \text{ V}$

- The reduction potential is an *intensive property*, therefore $E^0_{Ag^+/Ag}$ is not multiplied by 2 here, though in the balanced equation for cell reaction, two Ag atoms are involved.

- The sign of the emf of the cell indicates whether a redox reaction is spontaneous or not. If the emf of the cell is positive, then under standard state conditions, the redox reaction is spontaneous in the forward direction. If it is negative, then the redox reaction is spontaneous in the *opposite direction*.

Problem 7.6 Considering the following half-reactions,

$Fe^{3+} + e^- = Fe^{2+} \quad E^0 = 0.771\ V$

$I_3^- + 2e^- = 3I^- \quad E^0 = 0.536\ V$

calculate the cell voltage for a possible reaction between the two.

Solution

The Fe^{3+}/Fe^{2+} potential is more positive than the I_3^-/I^-. The overall cell reaction will be:

$$2\ Fe^{3+} + 3I^- = 2\ Fe^{2+} + I_3^-$$

$$E^0_{cell} = E_{cathode} - E_{anode}$$

$$= E^0_{Fe^{3+},Fe^{2+}} - E^0_{I_3^-,I^-}$$

$$= 0.77V - 0.536\ V = +0.235\ V$$

Cell conventions

- A cell consists of two half-cells.
- The cell emf $E^0_{cell} = E^0_{right} - E^0_{left}$
- Arbitrarily, the SHE is assigned an emf of 0.000 V.
- The standard electrode potential of a half-cell is measured by combining it either with a standard hydrogen electrode or an *auxiliary electrode (reference electrode).*
- The standard hydrogen electrode or the more negative electrode is shown on the left-hand side of the cell.
- The more negative half-cell releases electrons to the circuit.

7.3.6 Standard Reduction Potentials

Employing the SHE, the standard reduction potentials of several half-cells have been evaluated (Table 7.3).

Table 7.3 Standard reduction potentials at 25°C

Half-reaction			E^0(V)
$Li^+ (aq) + e^-$	→	$Li\ (s)$	−3.05
$K^+ (aq) + e^-$	→	$K\ (s)$	−2.93
$Ba^{2+} (aq) + 2e^-$	→	$Ba\ (s)$	−2.90
$Sr^{2+} (aq) + 2e^-$	→	$Sr\ (s)$	−2.89
$Ca^{2+} (aq) + 2e^-$	→	$Ca\ (s)$	−2.87

(Continued)

Table 7.3 Continued

Half-reaction			E^0(V)
$Na^+ (aq) + e^-$	→	$Na (s)$	−2.71
$Mg^{2+} (aq) + 2e^-$	→	$Mg (s)$	−2.37
$Be^{2+} (aq) + 2e^-$	→	$Be (s)$	−1.85
$Al^{3+} (aq) + 3e^-$	→	$Al (s)$	−1.66
$Mn^{2+} (aq) + 2e^-$	→	$Mn (s)$	−1.18
$2H_2O + 2e^-$	→	$H_2 (g) + 2OH^- (aq)$	−0.83
$Zn^{2+} (aq) + 2e^-$	→	$Zn (s)$	−0.76
$Cr^{3+} (aq) + 3e^-$	→	$Cr (s)$	−0.74
$Fe^{2+} (aq) + 2e^-$	→	$Fe (s)$	−0.44
$Cd^{2+} (aq) + 2e^-$	→	$Cd (s)$	−0.40
$PbSO_4 (s) + 2e^-$	→	$Pb (s) + SO_4^{2-} (aq)$	−0.31
$Co^{2+} (aq) + 2e^-$	→	$Co (s)$	−0.28
$Ni^{2+} (aq) + 2e^-$	→	$Ni (s)$	−0.25
$Sn^{2+} (aq) + 2e^-$	→	$Sn (s)$	−0.14
$Pb^{2+} (aq) + 2e^-$	→	$Pb (s)$	−0.13
$2H^+ (aq) + 2e^-$	→	$H_2 (g)$	0.00`
$Sn^{4+} (aq) + 2e^-$	→	$Sn^{2+} (aq)$	+0.13
$Cu^{2+} (aq) + e^-$	→	$Cu^+ (aq)$	+0.15
$SO_4^{2-} (aq) + 4H^+ (aq) + 2e^-$	→	$SO_2 (g) + 2H_2O$	+0.20
$AgCl (s) + e^-$	→	$Ag (s) + Cl^- (aq)$	+0.22
$Cu^{2+} (aq) + 2e^-$	→	$Cu (s)$	+0.34
$O_2 (g) + 2H_2O + 4e^-$	→	$4OH^- (aq)$	+0.40
$I_2 (s) + 2e^-$	→	$2I^- (aq)$	+0.53
$MnO_4^- (aq) + 2H_2O + 3e^-$	→	$MnO_2 (s) + 4OH^- (aq)$	+0.59
$O_2 (g) + 2H^+ (aq) + 2e^-$	→	$H_2O_2 (aq)$	+0.68
$Fe^{3+} (aq) + e^-$	→	$Fe^{2+} (aq)$	+0.77
$Ag^+ (aq) + e^-$	→	$Ag (s)$	+0.80
$Hg_2^{2+} (aq) + 2e^-$	→	$2Hg (l)$	+0.85
$2Hg^{2+} (aq) + 2e^-$	→	$Hg_2^{2+} (aq)$	+0.92
$NO_3^- (aq) + 4H^+ (aq) + 3e^-$	→	$NO (g) + 2H_2O$	+0.96
$Br_2 (l) + 2e^-$	→	$2Br^- (aq)$	+1.07
$O_2 (g) + 4H^+ (aq) + 4e^-$	→	$2H_2O$	+1.23
$MnO_2 (s) + 4H^+ (aq) + 2e^-$	→	$Mn^{2+} (aq) + 2H_2O$	+1.23
$Cr_2O_7^{2-} (aq) + 14H^+ (aq) + 6e^-$	→	$2Cr^{3+} (aq) + 7H_2O$	+1.33
$Cl_2 (g) + 2e^-$	→	$2Cl^- (aq)$	+1.36
$Au^{3+} (aq) + 3e^-$	→	$Au (s)$	+1.50
$MnO_4^- (aq) + 8H^+ (aq) + 5e^-$	→	$Mn^{2+} (aq) + 4H_2O$	+1.51
$Ce^{4+} (aq) + e^-$	→	$Ce^{3+} (aq)$	+1.61

(Continued)

Table 7.3 Continued

Half-reaction			E^0(V)
$PbO_2\ (s) + 4H^+\ (aq) + SO_4^{2-}\ (aq) + 2e^-$	→	$PbSO_4\ (s) + 2H_2O$	+1.70
$H_2O_2\ (aq) + 2H^+\ (aq) + 2e^-$	→	$2H_2O$	+1.77
$Co^{3+}\ (aq) + e^-$	→	$Co^{2+}\ (aq)$	+1.82
$O_3\ (g) + 2H^+\ (aq) + 2e^-$	→	$O_2\ (g) + H_2O\ (l)$	+2.07
$F_2\ (g) + 2e^-$	→	$2F^-\ (aq)$	+2.87

The following are the important features of this set of data:

(i) The hydrogen electrode is placed at the middle of the series of half-cells with an arbitrary value (standard) of 0.000 V.

(ii) Species which are more difficult to get reduced are placed above hydrogen; the redox potentials for these species are negative.

(iii) Species which are more easily reduced than hydrogen are placed below hydrogen; the redox potentials for these species are positive.

(iv) The half-cell reaction

$$F_2\ (g, 1\ atm.) + 2e^- \rightarrow 2F^-\ (aq) \qquad E^0 = +2.87\ V$$

has the highest E^0 value and, therefore, F_2 has the greatest tendency to get reduced; it is consequently the strongest oxidising agent.

(v) The half-cell reaction

$$Li^+\ (aq) + e^- \rightarrow Li\ (aq) \qquad E^0 = -3.05\ V$$

has the least (most negative) E^0 value and therefore, Li^+ is reduced with most difficulty; Li metal therefore, is the strongest reducing agent.

(vi) The species listed at the top (right sides of arrows) of the series are good reducing agents and those listed at the bottom (left sides of arrows) of the series are good oxidising agents.

(vii) Each of the cell reactions listed in the Table 7.3 is reversible. The direction of each half-cell reaction depends upon the other half-cell reaction with which it is coupled. For example,

$$2H^+ + 2e^- \rightleftharpoons H_2$$

proceeds in the forward direction when it is coupled with the Zn^{2+}/Zn half-cell but the backward reaction occurs when it is coupled with Cu^{2+}/Cu.

(viii) The data in this table are useful for predicting whether a given galvanic cell reaction would be spontaneous. Any species listed on the left of a given half-reaction will react spontaneously with a species listed on the right of a reaction located above it in the table. This is called the *redox potential diagonal rule*. Thus Ag^+ would spontaneously react with Zn. The nature of several inorganic reactions can be predicted with these E^0 data.

> - *A voltaic cell generates electrical energy.*
> - *An electrolytic cell uses electrical energy.*

(ix) Metallurgical methods can be chosen based on these data. For example, copper can be produced by the electrolysis of aqueous copper sulphate, but aluminium cannot be obtained similarly. Copper is more readily reduced ($E^0 = +0.34$ V) than H_2O ($E^0 = -0.83$ V) but, H_2O gets more readily reduced than aluminium ($E^0 = -1.66$V). This implies that when $Al^{3+}\ (aq)$ is electrolysed, the H_2O gets electrolysed but not $Al^{3+}\ (aq)$.

(x) The E^0 values can be used for calculating equilibrium constants for metallic systems in solution.

(xi) The emf of a cell is the algebraic sum of the single electrode potentials, provided each emf value carries a sign corresponding to the reaction as it actually occurs at the electrode.

Problem 7.7 Calculate the standard emf of the cell:

$Zn\ (s) \mid Zn^{2+}\ (aq) \mid\mid Cl^-\ (aq) \mid Cl_2\ (g) \mid Pt$

Solution

$$E^0_{Zn^{2+}/Zn} = -0.76\ V$$

$$E^0_{Cl^-/Cl^{2+}/Pt} = +1.36\ V$$

$$E^0_{cell} = +1.36\ V - (-0.76\ V) = 2.12\ V$$

Problem 7.8 Considering the following electrode potentials,

$Zn^{2+}\ (aq) + 2e^- \rightarrow Zn\ (s) \qquad E^0 = -0.76\ V$

$2Fe^{3+}\ (aq) + 2e^- \rightarrow 2Fe^{2+}\ (aq) \qquad E^0 = +0.77\ V$

find out whether or not the following reaction is spontaneous.

$Zn^{2+}\ (aq) + 2Fe^{2+}\ (aq) \rightarrow Zn\ (s) + 2Fe^{3+}\ (aq)$

Solution

$$E^0_{cell} = -0.76 - 0.77 = -1.53\ V$$

This value being negative, the reaction as written is non-spontaneous.

7.3.6.1 Electrodes

Anode	*Cathode*
Oxidation occurs	Reduction occurs
Attracts anions	Attracts cations
Electrons leave cell	Electrons enter cell
Negative in voltaic cell	Negative in electrolytic cell

7.3.6.2 Effect of Concentration on Cell emf

The cell emf is dependent on the concentrations of the reactants and products; that is the reason for quoting E_{cell} values with reference to standard concentrations (1 M). The cell emf and also the direction of the cell reaction can be changed by the concentrations of the reactants.

7.3.7 Relationship Between the Cell emf and Concentrations

The Nernst equation Consider the redox reaction of the type

$$aA + bB \rightarrow cC + dD$$

The free energy change ΔG of this reaction under non-standard conditions is given by the equation

$$\Delta G = \Delta G^0 + RT \ln Q$$

ΔG^0 is the free energy change for the reaction at standard conditions and Q is the reaction quotient (Q is the value of the mass action expression obtained by substituting the initial concentrations in the equilibrium constant expression).

Using the common logarithm,

$$\Delta G = \Delta G^0 + 2.303\ RT \log Q$$

But $\Delta G = -nFE^0$

Substituting this in the equation for ΔG,

$$-nFE = -nFE^0 + 2.303\ RT \log Q$$

This reduces to $\left[E = E^0 - \frac{2.303}{nF} R\,T \log Q\right]$

$$Q = \left[\frac{[\text{red}]}{[\text{ox}]}\right]$$

This equation is called the *Nernst equation.*

It is better to use activities instead of concentrations in the Nernst equation. This equation is commonly used in electroanalytical applications.

W H Nernst

Walther Hermann Nernst (1864–1941) was a German chemist. His research included work on electrolytes and thermodynamics. He enunciated the third law of thermodynamics, for which he was awarded the Nobel Prize in chemistry in 1920. His contributions in solid state chemistry and photochemistry are also significant. He invented the Nernst glower used in the IR spectrometer. He invented the electric piano.

Source: By Unknown (Mondadori Publishers) - http://www.gettyimages.co.uk/detail/news-photo/portrait-of-the-german-chemist-and-physicist-walter-hermann-news-photo/141553142, Public Domain, https://commons.wikimedia.org/w/index.php?curid=41260080

From the Nernst equation, it is clear that as the concentrations of the species involved in a voltaic cell change, Q changes and consequently E changes. If all the ionic concentrations in the cell are 1 M and the partial pressure of any gas involved in calculating Q is 1 atm., then Q becomes 1 and therefore $E = E^0$; under this situation, the cell reaction is said to take place under standard conditions.

Problem 7.9 A solution is 10^{-2} M in $Cr_2O_7^{2-}$ and 10^{-2} M in Cr^{3+}. The pH of the solution is 2. Calculate the potential of the half-reaction.

Solution

$$Cr_2O_7^{2-} + 14\,H^+ + 6e^- \rightleftharpoons 2\,Cr^{3+} + 7H_2O$$

$$E = E^0_{Cr_2O_7^{2-},Cr^{3+}} - \frac{0.059}{6}\log\frac{[Cr^{3+}]^2}{[Cr_2O_7^{2-}]+[H^+]^{14}}$$

$$= 1.33 - \frac{0.059}{6}\log\frac{(10^{-2})^2}{(10^{-2})(10^{-2})^{14}}$$

$$= 1.33 - \frac{0.059}{6}\log 10^{26}$$

$$= 1.33 - 26\left[\frac{0.059}{6}\right]$$

$$= 1.33 - 0.26 = 1.07\text{ V}$$

7.3.8 Nernst Equation and Overvoltage (Overpotential)

If the potential of an electrode is different from its reversible potential E_{rev} as calculated from the Nernst equation, the electrode is said to be *polarised.* The amount of polarisation is the overpotential η, of the electrode:

$$\eta = E - E_{rev}$$

The term *overvoltage* pertains to a complete cell, while the term *overpotential* is applicable to a single electrode. [This is similar to the *potential* of a single electrode and the emf (cell voltage) of a complete cell].

Overpotential is of two types: (i) *concentration polarisation* or *concentration overpotential* and (ii) *activation overpotential.* Concentration polarisation arises when the rate of reduction (or oxidation) at an electrode is so rapid that the concentration of reducible (or oxidisable) substance is different at the electrode's surface in comparison to that in the bulk of the solution. Concentration overpotential can be minimised or eliminated by efficient stirring of the electrolyte and by *applying* only a small current density. (The current density is amperes per square centimetre of electrode surface.)

The potential at an electrode has to be raised over the reversible potential by a certain amount to cause the passage of a measurable current at the electrode. This current shift is called

Table 7.4 Overpotential of hydrogen and oxygen

Current density amperes / cm²	Hydrogen		Oxygen	
	Smooth Pt	Platinised Pt	Smooth Pt	Platinised Pt
0.001	0.024	0.015	0.72	0.40
0.01	0.068	0.030	0.85	0.52
0.10	0.29	0.041	1.28	0.64
1.00	0.68	0.048	1.49	0.77

activation overpotential. The activation overpotential depends on the material discharged and the nature of the electrode. It is very low for plating metals on a platinum electrode. It has a value of several tenths of a volt for discharging certain gases at an electrode. For any given electrode, it is influenced by the condition of the electrode surface, the amount of current flowing and other factors. The overpotential values of hydrogen and oxygen are given in Table 7.4.

Overpotential may be observed at both electrodes. It is more positive for oxidation at the anode and more negative for reduction at the cathode:

η_a is + in sign

η_c is – in sign

For electrolysis, the voltage necessary is given by the equation,

$$E = (E_a + \eta_a) - (E_c + \eta_c) + iR$$

where E_a and E_c are the reverse potentials at the anode and cathode calculated from standard reduction potentials based on the Nernst equation. The term *iR* represents the voltage drop caused by the cell resistance; it is small. It is called the *iR* drop.

- Over potential is the difference between the experimentally measured potential and the reversible (equilibrium) potential calculated based on the Nernst equation.
- *E* is always smaller then E_{rev} because polarisation always reduces the electrode potential of a system.

7.3.9 Applications of the Nernst Equation

7.3.9.1 Calculation of the Potential of a Cell Under Non-standard Conditions

This can be illustrated by the following problem:

Calculate the emf of the zinc–copper cell at 25°C under the following conditions:

$$Zn\ (s)\ |\ Zn^{2+}\ (aq)\ (0.50\ M)\ ||\ Cu^{2+}\ (0.010\ M)\ |\ Cu\ (s)$$

The cell reaction is

$$Zn\ (s) + Cu^{2+}\ (0.010\ M) \rightarrow Cu\ (s) + Zn^{2+}\ (0.50\ M)$$

The Nernst equation for this reaction is

$$E = 1.10\ V - \frac{0.0592\ V}{2}\log\frac{[Zn^{2+}]}{[Cu^{2+}]}$$

$$= 1.10\ V - 0.0296\ V \log (0.50/0.010)$$

$$= 1.10\ V - 0.0296\ V \log 50$$

$$= 1.05\ V$$

7.3.9.2 Determination of an Unknown Concentration in a Galvanic Cell

By measuring the *E*° for a cell containing a known concentration of one of the ionic species involved, the concentration of the other ionic species can be determined. Consider the cell,

$$\text{Mg}(s) \mid \text{Mg}^{2+}(aq, 1\text{ M}) \mid\mid \text{Ag}^{+}(aq, x\text{ M}) \mid \text{Ag}(s)$$

$$x = [\text{Ag}^+]$$

To determine the concentration of Ag^+ (*aq*), the potential of the cell is determined; let it be 2.0 V.

$$E_{\text{cell}} = E^0_{\text{cell}} \frac{0.0592\text{ V}}{2} \log \frac{[\text{Mg}^{2+}]}{\text{Ag}^+}$$

Substituting the values of E_{cell} and E^0_{cell},

$$2.0\text{ V} = 3.17 - \frac{0.0592\text{ V}}{2} \log \frac{(1\text{ M})}{[\text{Ag}^+]^2}$$

$$2.0\text{ V} = 3.17 - 0.0296\text{ V} \log \frac{(1\text{ M})}{[\text{Ag}^+]^2}$$

$$\log \frac{(1\text{ M})}{[\text{Ag}^+]^2} = \frac{2.0\text{ V} - 3.17\text{ V}}{0.0296\text{ V}} = \frac{1.17}{0.0296} = 39.5$$

$$\therefore \quad \log(1\text{ M}) - 2\log[\text{Ag}^+] = 39.5$$

$$-\log[\text{Ag}^+] = \frac{39.5}{2}$$

$$[\text{Ag}^+] = 3.2 \times 10^{-40}$$

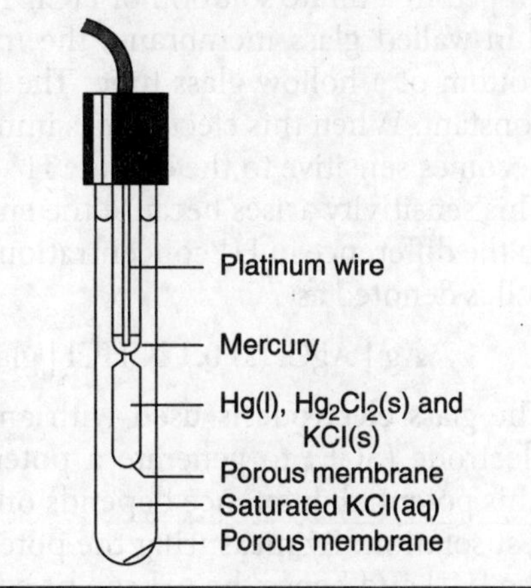

Fig. 7.18 Saturated calomel electrode

7.3.9.3 Calculation of the pH of a Solution

The pH of a solution can be calculated from the measurement of emf. The emf of a cell in which a hydrogen electrode constitutes one half-cell is proportional to the logarithm of the hydrogen ion concentration, and hence is proportional to the pH. Therefore, to measure the pH, a cell is set up with a hydrogen electrode dipping into the test solution, the other half-cell being a saturated calomel electrode (SCE) (Fig. 7.18) in contact with the solution:

calomel/test solution/hydrogen electrode

For this cell,

$$E = E^0 - \left(\frac{2.303\,RT}{F}\right)\log[\text{H}^+]$$

$$= E^0 - (0.0592)\log[\text{H}^+]$$

$$= E^0 + (0.0592) \times (-\log[\text{H}^+])$$

$$= E^0 + (0.0592) \times \text{pH (since } -\log[\text{H}^+] = \text{pH)}$$

$$\text{pH} = \frac{(E - E^0)}{0.0592}$$

The standard emf of this cell (saturated calomel electrode) E^0 is –0.246 V. The last equation can be used to calculate the pH of the solution from the value of E.

7.3.9.4 Glass Electrode

A glass electrode (Fig. 7.19) is an *ion-selective electrode*; it is sensitive to H^+ ions. It is therefore used to measure $[H^+]$. It consists of a silver wire covered with a layer of silver chloride which is kept dipped in a dilute solution of HCl. The acid is entrapped in a very thin-walled glass membrane, the membrane being sealed at the bottom of a hollow glass tube. The $[H^+]$ inside this electrode is a constant. When this electrode is immersed in a solution of $[H^+]$, it becomes sensitive to the outside H^+ concentration in the solution. This sensitivity arises because the emf of this electrode is sensitive to the difference in H^+ concentrations inside and outside of it. This cell is denoted as

$$\text{Ag} \mid \text{AgCl}\ (s)\ 0.1\ \text{N HCl} \mid \text{glass electrode} \mid \text{test H}^+ \text{ solution}$$

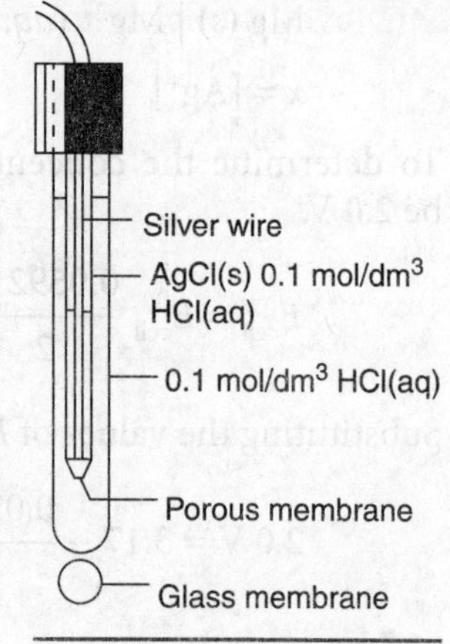

Fig. 7.19 Glass electrode

The glass electrode is used with another reference electrode (SCE) to generate a potential difference. This potential difference depends on the $[H^+]$ of the test solution. By measuring the potential difference, the $[H^+]$ and hence the pH can be evaluated.

The hydrogen electrode is difficult to set up because of the need to bubble hydrogen gas. Therefore, a *glass electrode* is used for pH measurements. The glass electrode is sensitive to hydrogen ion concentration and its potential is proportional to the pH. Thus, the cell adopted for the pH measurements is

$$\text{Calomel / test solution / glass electrode}$$

In a commercial pH meter, the scale of the voltmeter that measures the emf of the cell is calibrated to indicate the pH directly. The emf of this cell varies linearly with the pH of the solution. The experimental arrangement for the pH measurement is shown in Fig. 7.20.

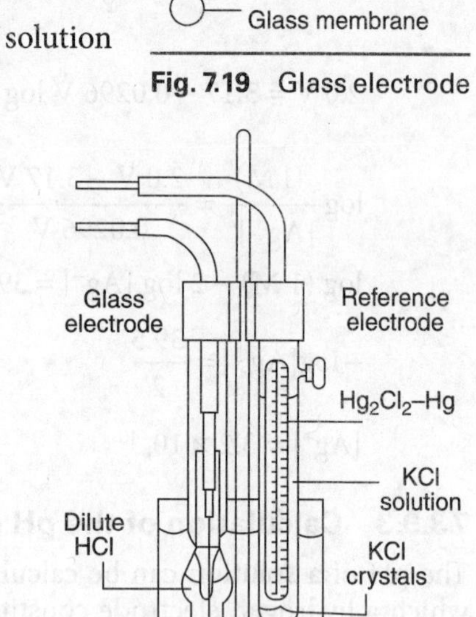

Fig. 7.20 Experimental set-up for pH measurement

7.3.9.5 Saturated Calomel Electrode (SCE)

The calomel electrode is a *subsidiary reference electrode*. It is easier to construct and more convenient to use when compared to the SHE. It consists of mercury in contact with a solution of potassium chloride saturated with mercurous chloride (Hg_2Cl_2: calomel). It is a *metal-insoluble metal salt electrode*. Different concentrations of KCl can be used, so that the cell can give rise to different potentials. When it is saturated with KCl, the electrode is called *saturated calomel electrode (SCE)*. The word 'saturated' refers to KCl; calomel is saturated in all calomel electrodes. The potential of the calomel electrode with saturated KCl is –0.246 V at 25°C. This potential is determined by making use of the standard potential of the Ag, AgCl (s), Cl^- electrode. The commercial SCE is compact, in the shape of a pen and is convenient to use. This can be directly dipped into the solution of the other electrolyte system. The electrical contact between the two solutions occurs at the loose ground point of the calomel electrode tip. The porous tip (frit) is a salt bridge.

The cell notation for the SCE is

$$Cl^- \text{ (4 M)} \mid Hg_2Cl_2(s) \mid Hg(l) \mid Pt$$

It is based on the redox reactions

$$Hg_2^{2+} + 2e^- \rightleftharpoons 2Hg(l)$$

$$E^0_{Hg_2^{2+}/Hg} = +0.80 \text{ V}$$

$$Hg_2Cl_2 + 2e^- \rightleftharpoons 2Hg(l) + 2Cl^-$$

$$E^0_{Hg_2Cl_2/Hg,\, Cl^-} = +0.27 \text{ V}$$

The SCE is used in pH measurement, cyclic voltammetry and several aqueous electrochemical systems. As it involves the use of mercury, which introduces health hazards, the Ag/AgCl electrode has replaced SCE in several applications.

Problem 7.10 The emf of the voltaic cell (at standard conditions)

$$Hg_2^{2+}(aq) + H_2 = 2\text{ Hg }(1) + 2H^+(aq) \text{ is } 0.850 \text{ V}$$

Evaluate the maximum electrical work of this cell when 1.00 g of H_2 is consumed.

Solution

The half-cell reactions of this system are

$$Hg_2^{2+}(aq) + 2e^- \rightleftharpoons 2\text{ Hg }(l)$$

$$H_2(g) \rightleftharpoons 2H^+(aq) + 2e^-$$

Therefore, $n = 2$

The maximum work of the cell

$$\omega_{max} = nF\,E_{cell} = 2 \times 96500 \text{ C} \times 0.850 \text{ V} = 164050 \text{ V C} = 164050 \text{ J}$$

The positive sign for work indicates that work is done by the cell, with loss of energy from the cell. This energy corresponds to the consumption of 1 mol (2.02 g) of H_2.

∴ The energy that corresponds to the consumption of 1.00 g of H_2

$$= \frac{1.00}{2.02} \times (164\,050 \text{ J}) = 81212 \text{ J} = 81.2 \text{ kJ}$$

Problem 7.11 The standard potential of the calomel electrode is 0.268 V. The E^0 for Hg/Hg_2^{2+} electrode is 0.789 V. calculate K_{sp} for Hg_2Cl_2.

Solution

For $Hg_2^{2+} + 2e^- \rightleftharpoons Hg$

$$E = 0.789 - \frac{0.059}{2}\log\frac{1}{a_{Hg_2^{2+}}} \qquad \text{(a)}$$

For $Hg_2Cl_2 + 2e^- \rightleftharpoons 2Hg + 2Cl^-$

$$E = 0.268 - \frac{0.059}{2} \log (a_{Cl^-})^2 \qquad \text{(b)}$$

$$K_{sp} = (a_{Hg_2^{2+}})(a_{Cl^-})^2$$

$$E = 0.268 - \frac{0.059}{2} \log \frac{K_{sp}}{a_{Hg_2^{2+}}} \qquad \text{(c)}$$

$$= 0.268 - \frac{0.059}{2} \log K_{sp}$$

$$- \frac{0.059}{2} \log \frac{1}{a_{Hg_2^{2+}}} \qquad \text{(d)}$$

From Eqs (a) and (d),

$$0.789 = 0.268 - \frac{0.059}{2} \log K_{sp}$$

$$\therefore \quad K_{sp} = 2.4 \times 10^{-18}$$

7.3.9.6 Silver–Silver Chloride Electrode

This electrode consists of a silver wire or a silver-plated platinum wire, coated electrolytically with a thick layer of silver chloride. The wire is kept dipped into a potassium chloride solution of known concentration which is saturated with silver chloride. Saturated potassium chloride solution is most commonly used; however, the KCl solution could be of 0.1 M or 0.01 M concentration. The potential of the electrode depends on the activity of the chloride ions in the KCl solution; the values at 25°C are

Saturated KCl : 0.999 V

1.0 M KCl : 0.227 V

0.1 M KCl : 0.290 V

This electrode is also a useful reference electrode.

Problem 7.12 Calculate the potential of the cell consisting of a silver electrode dipping in a silver nitrate solution with $a_{Ag^+} = 0.0200$ M and a SCE reference electrode.

Solution

$$E_{cell} = E_{indicator} - E_{ref}$$

$$= E^0_{Ag^+, Ag} - 0.059 \log \frac{1}{a_{Ag^+}} - E_{SCE}$$

$$= 0.799 - 0.059 \log \frac{1}{0.0200} - 0.242$$

$$= 0.799 - 0.100 - 0.242 = 0.457 \text{ V}$$

7.3.9.7 Quinhydrone Electrode (QHE)

A mixture of quinone $C_6H_4O_2$ (Q), and hydroquinone $C_6H_4(OH)_2$ (QH_2), in the presence of hydrogen ions constitutes a reversible oxidation–reduction system.

$$QH_2 \rightarrow Q + 2H^+ + 2e^-$$

The reduction potential of this system is given by the equation

$$E = E^0_{QH_2} + \frac{RT}{2F} \ln \left[\frac{a_Q a_{H^+}}{a_{QH_2}} \right] \qquad (7.5)$$

This equation indicates that the potential of the system depends on the hydrogen ion activity of the system. Therefore, this electrode can be used for the determination of pH. In solutions, the activities of Q and QH_2 are constant. E^0 for this cell has a value of 0.6996 V at 25°C. For determining the pH of a solution, the cell used is

$$\text{Reference electrode // } H^+ [a_{H^+}]Q, \frac{QH_2}{Pt}$$

The saturated calomel electrode can be used as the reference electrode. The solution whose pH has to be measured is saturated with quinhydrone. A strip of Pt immersed in the solution serves as an electrode.

Advantages of quinhydrone electrode

- pH values up to 8 can be measured accurately using this electrode. (In solutions of higher pH, oxidation of QH_2 by air and ionisation of QH_2 as an acid introduce errors.)
- The electrode can be used even in the presence of ions of many metals without interference (unlike the hydrogen gas electrode).
- It can be adapted for pH measurements in non-aqueous media also.

7.3.10 Concentration Cells

The electrode potential of the cell depends on the concentrations of the ions used. The Nernst equation indicates that a cell can produce an emf even if its half-cells differ only in concentrations of the electrolyte. A cell may be constructed using two half-cells consisting of the same substance but differing in ion concentrations. Such a cell is called a *concentration cell*. For example, two half-cells containing different concentrations (say 0.10 M and 1.0 M) of zinc sulphate can be combined in a galvanic cell (Fig. 7.21).

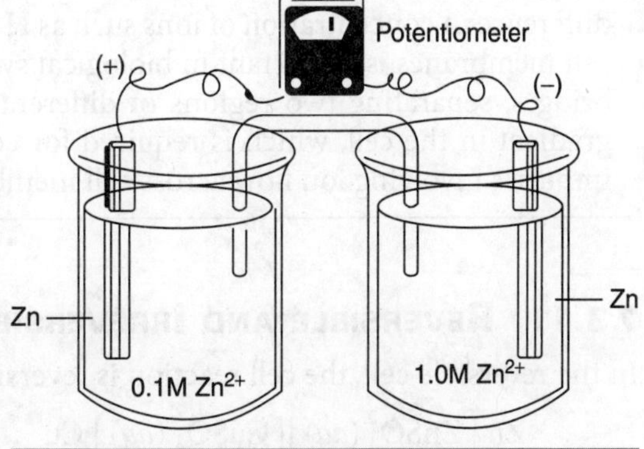

Fig. 7.21 Concentration cell: zinc

The two solutions are connected by a salt bridge. The two zinc electrodes are joined by a piece of wire. The cell reactions in this cell can be understood by applying the Le Chatelier principle to the equilibrium

$$Zn^{2+}(aq) + 2e^- \rightleftharpoons Zn(s)$$

As the concentration of Zn^{2+} increases, the reduction to Zn should be favoured. This implies that in the cell, reduction would occur in the half-cell containing the higher concentration of Zn^{2+} ions. Oxidation would occur in the other half-cell containing the lesser concentration of Zn^{2+} ions. The cell diagram for this system is

$$Zn(s) / Zn^{2+}(aq, 0.10\ M) / KCl / Zn^{2+}(aq, 1\ M) / Zn(s)$$

The half-cell reactions are

Oxidation: $Zn(s) \rightarrow Zn^{2+}(aq, 0.1\ M) + 2e^-$

Reduction: $Zn^{2+}(aq, 1.0\ M) + 2e^- \rightarrow Zn(s)$

Overall reaction: $Zn^{2+}(aq, 1.0\ M) \rightarrow Zn^{2+}(aq, 0.1\ M)$

The emf of the cell

$$E = E^0 - \left(0.0591\frac{V}{n}\right)\log\frac{[Zn^{2+}]_{dil}}{[Zn^{2+}]_{conc}}$$

The E^0 for a cell consisting of the same electrode and ions of the same type is zero.

$$E = \left(-0.0591\frac{V}{2}\right)\log\left(\frac{0.10}{1.0}\right)$$

$$= -0.0296\ V\ (\log 10^{-1}) = +0.0296\ V$$

The emf value of a concentration cell is small. It decreases continually as the cell is operated. The two cell concentrations approach each other because of the natural tendency for the two concentrations to equalise. When the concentrations of the ions in the two half-cells are the same, the emf is zero.

Membrane Cell

Concentration cell in nerve cell: The existence of an electrochemical gradient due to the difference in concentration of ions such as H^+, K^+, Na^+ and so on, within and outside nerve cell membranes is important in biological systems. The biological membranes act like salt bridges, separating two regions of different ion concentration. This produces a voltage gradient in the cell, which is required for certain physiological processes, such as nerve impulses involving ion flow across cell membranes.

7.3.11 Reversible and Irreversible Cells

In the reversible cell, the cell reaction is reversible. Consider, for example, the cell

$$Zn \mid ZnSO_4(aq) \parallel CuSO_4(aq) \mid Cu$$

This is the Daniell cell. The two metals in this cell are separated by a porous partition. Under this condition, neither metal is attacked. When the two metals are connected by a wire, a current flows in the circuit due to a galvanic reaction.

$$Zn\ (s) + Cu^{2+}\ (aq) \rightarrow Zn^{2+}\ (aq) + Cu\ (s)$$

If this cell is connected to an external source of emf which is adjusted exactly to balance the emf of the cell, there would be no flow of current in the cell and there would be no chemical reaction. If the external emf is decreased by an infinitesimally small amount, a current will flow from the cell and a chemical change takes place.

$$Zn\ (s) + Cu^{2+}\ (aq) \rightarrow Zn^{2+}\ (aq) + Cu\ (s)$$

On the other hand, if the external emf is increased over the emf of the cell by a small amount, the current in the cell now passes in the reverse direction and also the cell reaction occurs in the opposite direction.

$$Zn^{2+}\ (aq) + Cu\ (s) \rightarrow Zn\ (s) + Cu^{2+}\ (aq)$$

This cell therefore is called a reversible cell. A cell is reversible if it satisfies the conditions of thermodynamic reversibility, namely,

- the driving and opposing forces of the change be only infinitesimally (very little) different from each other, and,
- the process should be reversible by applying a force infinitesimally greater than the one causing a reaction in the system.

The Daniell cell satisfies these two conditions and is therefore a reversible cell.

Consider the cell consisting of zinc and copper electrodes immersed in dilute sulphuric acid:

$$Zn\ |\ \text{dilute}\ H_2SO_4\ |\ Cu$$

When the two electrodes are short-circuited, zinc dissolves in dilute sulphuric acid with the evolution of hydrogen.

$$Zn\ (s) + H_2SO_4 \rightarrow ZnSO_4 + H_2\ (g)$$

The H_2 (*g*) escapes from the cell and therefore the cell reaction cannot be reversed. This cell is an irreversible cell. The thermodynamic reversibility requires a state of equilibrium at every stage of the process; in this case the spontaneous reaction at the electrodes indicates that the system is not in equilibrium.

- The electrode reactions in a cell occur either in the forward or reverse direction when the external emf is increased or decreased by an infinitesimally small value.
- A galvanic cell is said to be reversible when its reactions are thermodynamically reversible. It will behave as a reversible cell when the current passed or drawn is extremely small.

7.3.12 Potentiometric Titrations

In a potentiometric titration, the end point is detected by determining the volume at which a relatively large potential (*E*) change occurs as the titrant is added to the analyte. Figure 7.22 shows the apparatus used for such a titration. An indicator electrode (glass electrode) and a reference electrode (calomel electrode) are used in this method. The titration can be performed manually or automated with a recorder. In a manual titration, the potential is measured after the addition of each successive increment of the titrant. The resulting potential values are plotted

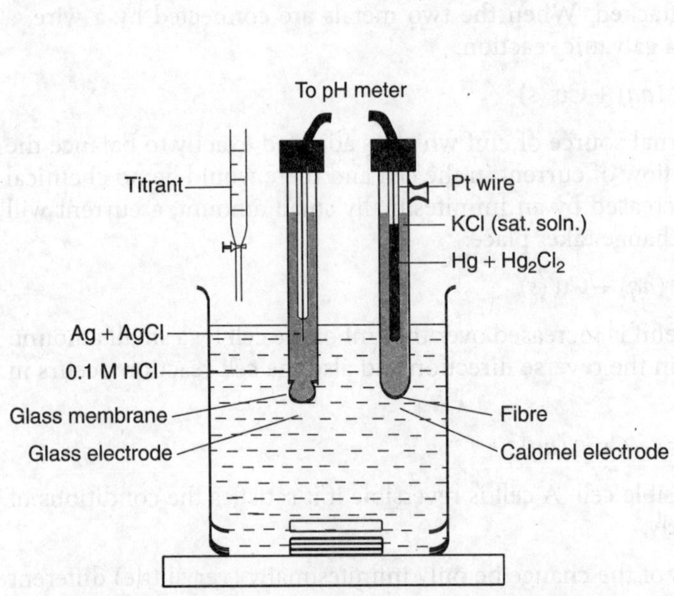

Fig. 7.22 Apparatus for potentiometric acid–base titration with glass–calomel electrode pair

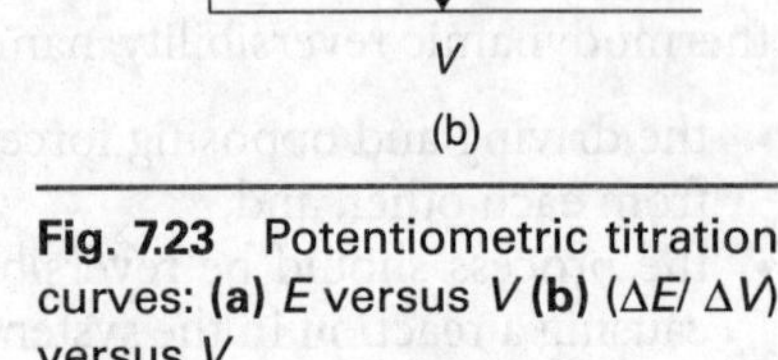

Fig. 7.23 Potentiometric titration curves: **(a)** E versus V **(b)** ($\Delta E/\Delta V$) versus V

against volumes of titrant added to give a titration curve (Fig. 7.23 a). A vertical line passing through the midpoint of the steep portion of the curve is drawn. The intersection point of this line with the volume axis gives the volume of the titrant required for completion of the reaction.

Finding the midpoint of the steep section of the curve is not always easy. Therefore, a better method of determining the end point is to plot $\Delta E/\Delta V$ (change in potential with change in volume) versus V (Fig. 7.23 b). The volume at the equivalence point is determined by dropping a vertical line from the peak to the volume axis.

- Potentiometric titrations can be performed for acid–base reactions, redox reactions and precipitation reactions.
- This method is suitable even for small volumes of analytes.
- It is a reliable method offering accurate results.
- It does not require any chemical indicator.
- It can be performed rapidly and with a large set of analytes.
- Potentials during titrations can be accurately measured using a pH meter also.

7.3.12.1 Redox Titration

Titration of Fe(II) with dichromate This is a redox titration in which the platinum electrode (indicator) and the calomel electrode (reference) are used. Prepare a standard solution of potassium dichromate by weighing accurately about 1.25 g of the pure, dry salt. Dissolve it in water and make up the solution to 250 mL in a volumetric flask. Fill the burette with this solution. Weigh accurately a sample of about 1.5 g of pure iron(II) ammonium sulphate. Dissolve it in about 100 mL of distilled water and add about 10 mL of concentrated sulphuric acid. Insert a platinum wire and an SCE into the iron solution. The platinum wire serves as the positive electrode. Add about 5 mL of the dichromate solution from the burette and then measure the potential. Continue the titration, recording the volume and potential, until about 10 mL of excess titrant is added. Plot the potential values against volume of the titrant. Draw one more graph, $\Delta E/\Delta V$ versus V. From the graphs, find the volume of dichromate required for the equivalence point. Then, from the weight of iron (II) ammonium sulphate and the volume of dichromate, calculate the normality of the dichromate solution. Compare this value with the normality calculated from the weight of dichromate dissolved in 250 mL of solution. Repeat the titration to check the validity of the first titration.

7.3.12.2 Precipitation Titration

Titration of Cl^- with Ag^+ A polished silver wire is used as the indicator electrode and a calomel electrode is used as the reference electrode for this titration. However, the calomel electrode is placed separately in a saturated potassium nitrate solution taken in a vessel. If it is directly placed in the chloride solution to be titrated, silver chloride would precipitate. The two solutions are connected by a salt bridge containing potassium nitrate. Pipette out exactly 20 mL of the chloride solution to be estimated into a 100 mL beaker. Add about 5 mL of the standardised silver nitrate solution from the burette to the chloride solution and then measure the potential. Continue the titration, recording the potential and the volume of silver nitrate until about 10 mL of excess titrant is added.

Titration of a mixture of chloride, bromide and iodide with silver(I) The potential of a silver electrode is measured as various volumes of silver nitrate are added to a known volume of a mixture of Cl^-, Br^- and I^-. The p_{Ag} for each volume of titrant is calculated from a_{Ag^+} using the equation,

$$p_{Ag} = \log a_{Ag^+}$$

where, approximately, $a_{Ag^+} = [Ag^+]$. (In dilute solutions, the activity and concentration of a species may be equated.) $\log a_{Ag^+}$ is a function of the potential (E), as denoted by the equation,

$$E = 0.800 + 0.059 \log a_{Ag^+}$$

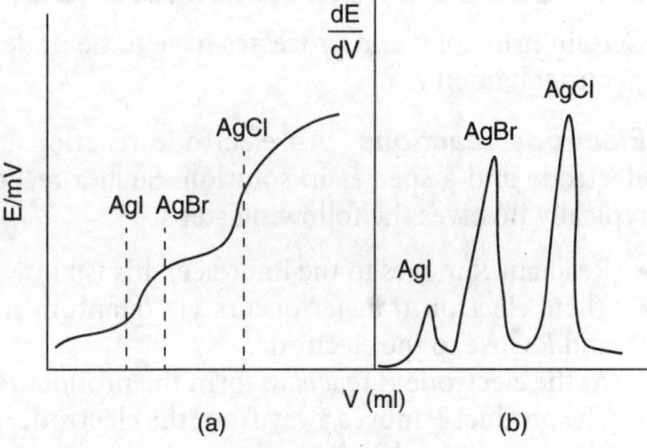

Fig. 7.24 Potentiometric titration curve of $I^- + Br^- + Cl^-$ with Ag^+ **(a)** E versus V **(b)** dE/dV

The data thus obtained are plotted as shown in Fig. 7.24. A separate potentiometric break is obtained for each halide. Therefore, the three equivalence points and hence the concentrations of halides can be calculated.

During the titration, the iodide reacts first because its silver salt is the least soluble. Then, the bromide reacts; finally, the chloride reacts. This method is not very accurate as co-precipitation of the more soluble halide occurs during the precipitation of the less soluble one. For example, AgBr may be coprecipitated with AgI.

- Potentiometric titrations are similar to using a pH meter to obtain the titration curve for an acid–base reaction.
- In a potentiometric titration, the potential difference between an indicator electrode and a reference electrode is plotted against the volume of titrant added.

- Potentiometric titrations can be performed using the SHE as the reference electrode. However, SCE is less bulky and more convenient to use. Each voltage measured during a titration represents the difference in potential between the indicator and reference electrodes:

  $$E_{\text{measured}} = E_{\text{ind}} - E_{\text{ref}}$$

  With a SCE,

  $$E_{\text{ind}} = E_{\text{measured}} + 0.246$$

- In a redox titration, at 50% of the reaction,

  $$E_{\text{measured}} = E_{\text{ind}} - 0.059 \log \log\left(\frac{50}{50}\right)$$

  $$\therefore \quad E_{\text{measured}} = E_{\text{ind}}$$

  In any oxidation–reduction titration at 50% titration, $E = E^0$ (the standard redox potential for the substance being titrated.
- Potentiometric end point is widely applicable.
- This method is more accurate than methods using indicators.
- It is useful for titration of coloured or turbid solutions.
- It can be used for detecting and estimating several species in a solution.
- However, this is a more time-consuming method.

7.4 ELECTROGRAVIMETRY (EG)

Certain principles and processes have to be understood before dealing with the technique of electrogravimetry.

Electrode reactions An electrode reaction involves the transfer of charge between an electrode and a species in solution. Such a reaction is usually referred to as electrolysis; it typically involves the following steps:

- Reactant R moves to the interface; this is known as *mass transfer*.
- Then, electron transfer occurs via quantum mechanical tunneling between the electrode and R close to the electrode.
- At the electrode R reacts to form the product P.
- The product P moves away from the electrode, allowing migration of fresh R to the surface.
- The reaction at the electrode usually involves one or two electrons.

An example for an electrode reaction is

$$Ag^+ \text{ (solution)} + e^- \text{ (electrode)} \rightarrow Ag \text{ (electrode surface)}$$

This is a one-electron electrode process. An example for a two-electron electrode process is

$$Cu^{2+} + 2e^- \rightarrow Cu^0$$

For every Cu^{2+} reduced, two electrons flow. Flow of electrons generates current. The current generated is proportional to the number of electrons flowing. By measuring the flow of current, the number of Cu^{2+}, that is $[Cu^{2+}]$ can be calculated.

In this electrode process, as the product is a metal (M^0), it is deposited on the electrode surface (Fig. 7.25 a). If the product were an ion or a soluble one, it would migrate to the solution from the surface of the electrode after reaction. For example, when Cr(VI) gets reduced to Cr(III) at the electrode, Cr(III) will remain dissolved in solution (Fig. 7.25 b). Electrode processes are carried out by the application of a voltage suitable for the process.

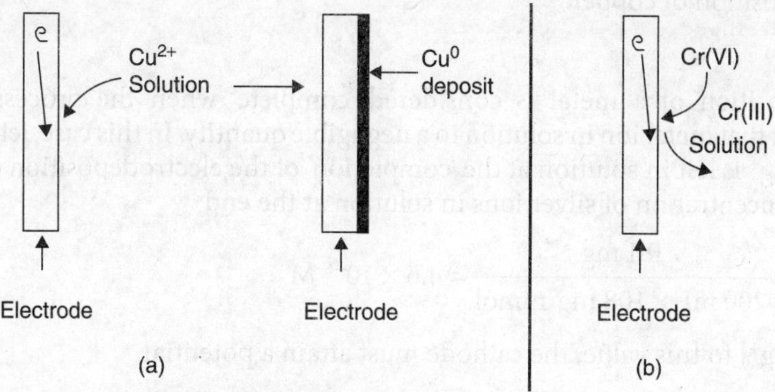

Fig. 7.25 Depiction of electrode processes

Principle When electricity is passed through a solution of an electrolyte containing the analyte, usually a metal ion, say M^+, the M^+ ions migrate to the cathode and get deposited on this electrode. The difference in weights of the cathode before and after complete deposition gives the weight of M deposited. Electrogravimetry requires the use of carefully controlled experimental conditions to deposit an element electrolytically upon a suitable electrode.

- The applied potential in EG is controlled at a particular range to effect deposition of a particular metal, avoiding the electrolysis of other materials that may be present in the sample. Therefore, EG is also called *controlled potential electrolysis.*
- Electrogravimetry (EG) is the determination of an element by depositing it upon a suitable electrode electrolytically. For example, the silver present in a solution of silver nitrate can be estimated by EG.

Electrolysis requires that the electroactive species reach the electrode surface for reaction. This may occur by three mechanisms:

- migration under the influence of an electric field,
- convection effected by stirring, and
- diffusion due to concentration differences between the liquid on the electrode surface and the bulk of the solution.

Decomposition potential The minimum external potential that must be applied to effect continuous electrolysis of the electrolyte is called the *decomposition potential* of the electrolyte (Fig. 7.26). As the applied potential is increased, initially a small increase in current occurs. When the potential reaches the decomposition potential, the current suddenly increases. This increase indicates the onset of electrolysis, say, the deposition of the metal on the cathode.

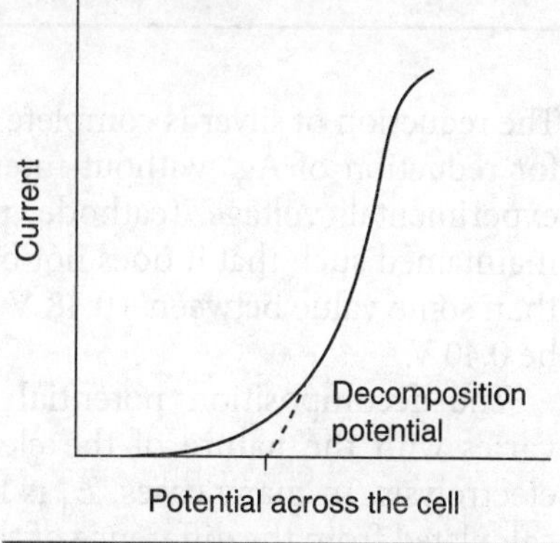

Fig. 7.26 Decomposition potential curve

The minimum external emf which must be applied between the two electrodes of an electrolytic cell to bring about continuous electrolytic decomposition of an electrolyte is the *decomposition potential* or *decomposition voltage.*

Problem 7.13 200 mL of a solution contains about 0.05 M of Ag^+ and 0.05 M of Cu^{2+}. Find out under what experimental conditions silver can be deposited on a platinum electrode without the deposition of copper.

Solution

The electrodeposition of a metal is considered 'complete' when the process reduces the concentration of that metal ion in solution to a negligible quantity. In this case, let it be assumed that 0.1 mg of Ag^+ is left in solution at the 'completion' of the electrodeposition of silver.

The molar concentration of silver ions in solution at the end

$$[Ag^+] = \frac{0.1\ \text{mg}}{200\ \text{mL} \times 108\ \text{mg/mmol}} = 4.6 \times 10^{-6}\ \text{M}$$

For lowering $[Ag^+]$ to this value, the cathode must attain a potential

$$E_{cathode} = +0.80 - 0.06 \log\left[\frac{1}{4.6 \times 10^{-6}}\right]$$

$$= +0.80 - 0.06 \log 217391$$

$$= +0.80 - (503372 \times 0.06)$$

$$= +0.80 - 0.032 = +0.48\ \text{V}$$

The concentration of Cu^{2+} is 0.05 M. Therefore, the potential of an electrode which can be in equilibrium with this ion

$$E_{cathode} = +0.34 - \frac{0.06}{2} \log \frac{1}{0.05}$$

$$= +0.34 - 0.03 \times 1.3010$$

$$= +0.34 - 0.03903 = +0.30\ \text{V}$$

Hence, for reduction of Cu^{2+} to Cu^0, the cathode must be more negative than +0.30 V.

The reduction of silver is complete at +0.48 V. Therefore, for reduction of Ag^+ without interference by Cu^{2+}, the experimental voltage (cathode potential) should be maintained such that it does not become more negative than some value between +0.48 V and +0.30 V. It could be 0.40 V.

Table 7.5 Overvoltages of metals

Metal	Overvoltage (V)
Cu, Ag, Au	0.35
Zn, Cd, Hg	0.70
Al	0.50
Sn, Pb	0.45
Sb, Bi	0.42
Cr, Mo, W	0.32
Mn	0.25
Fe, Ni, Rh, Pt, Ir	0.18

The decomposition potential E_d of an electrolyte varies with the nature of the electrodes used for the electrolysis. In many cases, E_d is higher than the value calculated from the difference of the *reversible* electrode potentials. Theoretically, only a voltage of 1.23 V is required for electrolysing water using Pt electrodes; in reality, it requires 1.7 V. The difference, 0.47 V, is the overpotential (overvoltage). The higher observed potential implies that the decomposition is accompanied by a relatively large *polarisation*. The polarisation depends on the nature of the electrodes. For the electrolysis of H_2SO_4 with lead electrodes, the E_d is 2.2 V but, it is only

1.7 V with platinum. The potentials can be experimentally determined by coupling each electrode with a calomel electrode and measuring the emf of this combination.

The hydrogen overvoltage being dependent on the electrodes varies with the metals (Table 7.5). If H^+ ions are also present, both H^+ and M^+ ions would compete for getting discharged at the electrode. The ion with more positive potential than H^+ will be discharged first. This is the case with Ag^+ and Cu^{2+}. This enables electrogravimetry of these metals even in the presence of H^+.

- The excess voltage over the calculated back emf is called the *overpotential.*
- Overpotential may occur at the anode as well as at the cathode. The decomposition voltage E_d is therefore given as

  $$E_d = E_{\text{cathode}} + E_{\text{oc}} - (E_{\text{anode}} - E_{\text{oa}})$$

  where E_{oc} and E_{oa} are overpotentials at the cathode and anode respectively.
- The higher overpotential of hydrogen is an advantage in EG of metals, such as cadmium and zinc. Cd^{2+} and Zn^{2+} get deposited from aqueous solutions without H^+ getting simultaneously reduced.

If the deposition potential of a metal is above that of hydrogen in the electrochemical series, that is, if it is less positive or more negative than that of hydrogen, hydrogen would be evolved at the cathode. However, in calculating the discharge potential, the hydrogen overvoltage at the cathode must also be considered. In addition, the overvoltage of the metal should be considered. The discharge potential of a metal at 298 K is given by

$$E = E^0 + \frac{0.059}{n}\log a - \omega_m$$

where ω_m is the overvoltage of the metal.

For example, consider the electrodeposition of zinc from a solution containing Zn^{2+} ions at $a = 1$ and a pH = 4.

Theoretical (reversible) discharge potential of zinc = – 0.76 V

E for hydrogen = –0.236 V

Overpotential for hydrogen = 0.70 V

$$E_{H_2} = -0.059\,\text{pH} - \omega_{H_2}$$
$$= -0.936\ \text{V}$$

Since this value is more negative than that for Zn (–0.76), Zn will be deposited first without evolution of H_2. Increasing current density increases ω_{H_2}; on increasing the pH, E_{H_2} becomes more negative. Therefore, by adjusting these two factors, the current efficiency for the deposition of zinc can be promoted. With nickel, ω_{H_2} on the nickel electrode is 0.18 V and E_{H_2} will then be less negative than E_{Zn}.

$$E_{Ni} = -0.250$$

$$E_{H_2} = -0.059 \times 4 - 0.18\ \text{V} = -0.416\ \text{V}$$

Since this value is more negative than E_{Ni}, nickel gets deposited first.

Overvoltage is influenced by

- *Current density*: ω increases with *i*.
- *pH:* Very low pH or very high pH leading to high $[H^+]$ or high $[OH^-]$ alters the nature of the electrolyte and therefore influences the overpotential.
- *Temperature*: Increasing temperature decreases ω.
- *Pressure*: At high pressures, hydrogen overvoltage is only slightly affected, but at low pressures, it increases on copper, nickel and mercury cathodes.
- *Surface:* Increasing surface area decreases ω. On a smooth polished surface, the overvoltage is greater than that with a rough, pitted surface.
- *Impurities*: The presence of impurities on the cathode may increase or decrease the overvoltage.
- Electrodes.
- Nature of electrolyte.
- Surface tension of the solution.

7.4.1 Laws Which Govern Electrodeposition

Electrodeposition is governed by three laws.

(i) *Ohm's law:* This law relates current (I), electromotive force (E) and resistance (R):

$$I = \frac{E}{R}$$

(ii) *Faraday's first law:* According the this law, the amount (w) of a substance liberated or dissolved at the electrodes of a cell is directly proportional to the quantity of electricity which passes through the solution.

$$w = e\,i\,t$$

where e is a constant called *electrochemical equivalent, i* is current and t is time.

(iii) *Faraday's second law:* According to this law, the amounts of different substances liberated or dissolved by the same quantity of electricity are proportional to their relative atomic or molar masses divided by the number of electrons transferred in their respective electrode processes.

Problem 7.14 Calculate the amount of metallic copper produced in the electrolysis of a copper(II) sulphate solution during 5.5 hours at a steady current of 80 amperes.

Solution

The amount of electricity used for the electrolysis

$$= \text{current (amperes)} \times \text{time (seconds)}$$

$$= \frac{1 \text{ coulomb}}{1 \text{ amperes}} \times \frac{1 \text{ faraday}}{96500 \text{ coulombs}}$$

$$= (80 \times 5.5 \times 60 \times 60) \times \frac{1 \text{ coulomb}}{1 \text{ amperes}} \times \frac{1 \text{ faraday}}{96500 \text{ coulombs}}$$

$$= 16.4 \text{ faradays}$$

The electrolytic reaction,

$$Cu^{2+} + 2e^- \rightarrow Cu(s)$$

Equivalents in EG

- The coulomb is a *quantity* of electricity.
- Electric current is the *rate of flow* of electricity; it is measured in amperes.
- $\text{amperes} = \dfrac{\text{coulombs}}{\text{seconds}}$; $i = \dfrac{C}{t}$
- $\text{equivalents deposited} = \dfrac{\text{coulombs}}{96487} = \dfrac{i\,t}{96487}$
- $\text{equivalents} = \dfrac{\text{grams}}{\text{equivalent}} = \dfrac{\text{grams} \times n}{\text{formula wt}}$

n = number of electrons involved in the reduction.

$$\therefore \quad \frac{\text{grams} \times n}{\text{formula wt}} = \frac{i\,t}{96487}$$

$$\therefore \quad t = \frac{96487 \text{ grams} \times n}{i \text{ (formula wt)}}$$

The time necessary to deposit a given weight of a metal can be calculated using this equation.

shows that 2 faradays of electricity will produce 1 mole (63.55 g) of Cu.

$\therefore$ weight of copper formed

$$= 16.4 \text{ faradays} \times \frac{63.55}{2 \text{ faradays}} = 521 \text{ g}$$

Problem 7.15 Calculate the mass of copper deposited by the passage of 2.6 A of current for 520 s, through a 2.1 M solution of $CuSO_4$.

Solution

Appling Faraday's laws, the mass of Cu deposited

$$= (520 \text{ s})(2.6 \text{ C/s})\left(\frac{1 \text{ mol } e^{-1}}{96500 \text{ C}}\right)\left(\frac{1 \text{ mol Cu}}{2 \text{ mol } e^{-1}}\right)(63.5 \text{ g/mol Cu})$$

$$= \frac{85852}{193000} = 0.44 \text{ g}$$

Problem 7.16 How much current is required to deposit 1.00 g of gold per hour on the cathode from a solution containing a salt of gold (III)?

Solution

The quantity of current required

$$= (1.00 \text{ g Au/h})\left(\frac{1 \text{ mol Au}}{197 \text{ g Au}}\right)\left(\frac{3 \text{ mol } e^{-1}}{\text{mol Au}}\right)\left(\frac{96500 \text{ C}}{\text{mol } e^{-1}}\right)\left(\frac{1 \text{ h}}{3600 \text{ s}}\right)$$

$$= \frac{289500}{709200} = 0.41 \text{ A}$$

7.4.2 Requirements for Electrogravimetry

(i) The deposition of the substance (analyte) must be quantitative.
(ii) The deposit must be inert; it must not change in its weight during analysis due to some spontaneous reaction.
(iii) The deposit must be of known composition.
(iv) The deposit must adhere firmly to the electrode so that the electrode can be rinsed, dried and weighed without loss of deposit.

7.4.2.1 Apparatus

The experimental system used for EG is given in Fig. 7.27. A known volume of the electrolyte (analyte) is taken in a cell. The two electrodes are held in the electrolyte. The cathode is the electrode on which the metallic analyte is deposited by reduction. It is connected to the negative terminal of the energy source. The anode is the terminal at which oxidation occurs. It is attached to the positive terminal of the energy source.

The electrodes are made of platinum gauze; the openness of the gauze permits the circulation and therefore uniformity of the solution. The solution is stirred using a magnetic stirrer. A DC source rated at 3–15 V, a variable resistance, an ammeter and a voltmeter are connected as shown in Fig. 7.27. The electrolyte cell may be heated over a hotplate when the deposition has to be carried out from a hot electrolyte. A paddle-shaped electrode may be used for providing a large surface for deposition of metal.

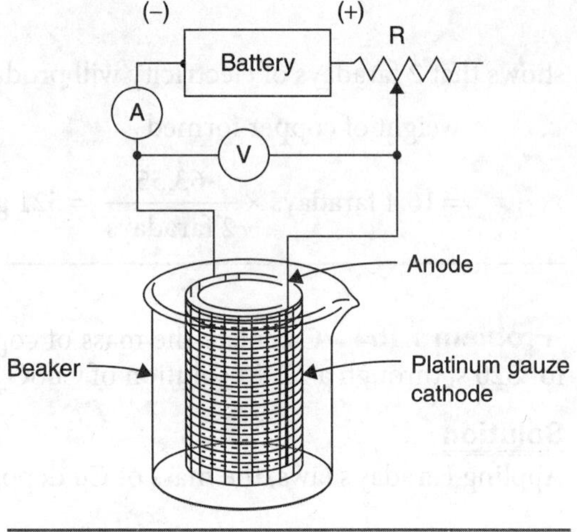

Fig. 7.27 Experimental arrangement for electrogravimetry

7.4.2.2 Cell Reactions in EG

The reduction of the metal ion is the main cell reaction during electrolysis. In addition, other reactions may occur—co-deposition of other metals present in the electrolyte, water itself may decompose to hydrogen and oxygen which may interfere with the deposition of the metal on the cathode. Thus, complications may arise in EG, and to avoid these, the conditions for electrolysis have to be carefully controlled.

7.4.3 Electrolytic Separation of Metals

Metal ions with positive reduction potentials may be separated from metal ions with negative reduction potentials. For example, the potentials for copper and cadmium are

$$Cu^{2+} + 2e^- \rightleftharpoons Cu \quad +0.337\ V$$

$$Cd^{2+} + 2e^- \rightleftharpoons Cd \quad -0.403\ V$$

Therefore, a mixture of Cu^{2+} and Cd^{2+} can be separated by electrogravimetry.

If a current is passed through a solution containing Cu(II), H^+ and Cd(II), copper will be deposited first at the cathode. As the copper deposits, the electrode potential decreases; when it equals the potential of the hydrogen ions (0.00 V) hydrogen gas will get evolved at the cathode. As long as hydrogen is evolved, the potential at the cathode will remain constant; it will not become sufficiently negative for the deposition of cadmium. As long as there is water in the electrolytic cell, cadmium will not be deposited; therefore in an aqueous medium, copper gets separated as deposit from cadmium (remaining in solution). This separation occurs without the need for external control of the cathode potential.

7.4.3.1 Separation of Silver and Copper

These two metals have positive reduction potentials; however, the potentials differ considerably (Ag +0.779 V, Cu +0.337 V) and therefore can be readily separated.

The separation and estimation of metals by EG is carried out under carefully selected and controlled experimental conditions (Table 7.6).

Table 7.6 Some electrolytic separations

Mixture	Electrolyte	Ampere (A)	Voltage (V)
Cu^{2+}– Ni^{2+}	H_2SO_4, Cu is deposited first; neutralise with NH_3; then Ni is deposited	2–4 4	3–4 3–4
Cu^{2+}– Pb^{2+}	HNO_3,Cu is deposited on cathode, PbO_2 on anode	1.5–2.0	2
Cd^{2+}–Zn^{2+}	HCl, pH 1.5, Cd is deposited first, then add 4 N NaOH, 1 g KCN, 10 mL ammonia, Zn is deposited	3	1–2

7.4.4 Constant Current Method

The details about electrogravimetry at constant current are given in Table 7.7. Usually, a platinum cathode is used on which the metal gets deposited. However, some of the metals deposited cannot be readily distinguished on a platinum surface and it is difficult to note when the deposition is complete. In such cases, a platinum cathode, which has been plated with copper before the initial weighing, is used. Then, the deposit on the cathode electrode surface becomes clearly visible.

For Cd^{2+}, Co^{2+}, Pb^{2+}, Ni^{2+} and Zn^{2+} a platinum cathode plated with copper is used. When lead is deposited from nitric acid solutions, PbO_2 is deposited on the *anode*, which can be weighed for estimation.

7.4.4.1 Separation of Cu^{2+}, Ni^{2+} and Zn^{2+}

To a suitable aliquot of the mixture, add 5 mL HNO_3 and 10 mL water. Evaporate the mixture to expel HNO_3 and then dilute the reduced volume of the solution to 100 mL. Add 5 mL concentrated HCl and 1 g hydrazine hydrochloride to the solution. Electrolyse it at –0.4 V for 30 minutes. Weigh the cathode for the copper. Neutralise the remaining solution with ammonia and then add 20 mL excess ammonia and also 2 g Na_2SO_4. Electrolyse the solution at –0.25 V at 75°C; weigh the cathode for Ni. Then, electrolyse the remaining solution at room temperature for 30 minutes at 2 amp to deposit Zn.

Table 7.7 Conditions for determining metals by electrogravimetry

Ion	Electrolyte	Ampere (A)	Voltage (V)
Cu^{2+}	Sulphuric acid–nitric acid	2–4	3–4
Cd^{2+}	Potassium cyanide	1.5–2	2.5–3
Co^{2+}	Ammonical sulphate	4	3–4
Pb^{2+}	Tartrate buffer	2	2–3
Ni^{2+}	Ammoniacal sulphate	4	3–4
Ag^{+}	Potassium cyanide	0.5–1.0	2.5–3
Zn^{2+}	Potassium hydroxide solution	4	3.5–4.5

7.4.4.2 Separation of Metals with Slightly Differing Standard Potentials

The electro-separation of metals with similar standard potentials is more difficult. This difficulty is solved by decreasing the concentration of one of the ions by complexation; this converts the free ion into a stable complex which is not reduced at the electrode. The other uncomplexed metal ion then gets deposited without any interference. For example, copper (II) and cadmium (II) can be separated by adding CN^- to the mixture. Copper forms a stable complex and cadmium alone is deposited.

7.4.5 Controlled Potential Method

This method is used for separating and determining the components of alloys (Table 7.8). For example, an alloy of Cu–Bi–Pb–Sn can be solubilised in an acid medium and then the metals are separated in the sequence Cu, at –0.3 V, Bi at –0.4 V, Pb at –0.6 V and Sn at –0.65 V (versus the standard calomel electrode). Examples for separation of metals by this method are given in Table 7.8.

Table 7.8 Electrogravimatric separations with controlled cathode potential

Metal	Electrolyte	$E_{cathode}$ vs SCE (V)	Separated from
Copper	Tartrate–hydrazine–Cl^-	–0.3	Bi, Cd, Pb, Ni, Sn, Zn
Cadmium	Ethanoate buffer	–0.8	Zn
Nickel	Tartrate–NH_4OH	–1.1	Al, Fe, Zn
Lead	Tartrate–hydrazine–Cl^-	–0.6	Cd, Fe, Mn, Ni, Sn, Zn
Silver	Ethanoate buffer	+0.1	Cu
Antimony	Hydrazine–HCl	–0.3	Pb, Sn

Advantages of EG

- Small quantities of metals can be estimated by EG.

- A mixture of metallic ions in solution can be separated easily, without involving several steps of chemical separation methods.
- The method leads to accurate determinations, ±0.1%.
- The apparatus required for EG are simple.
- The separation is quick.
- It is a low-energy process.
- EG is used in industries for:
  - selective deposition (separation) of metals,
  - analysis of minerals,
  - making nanostructural materials; for example, wires consisting of alternating magnetic and non-magnetic layers, each only a few millimetres thick,
  - making metal-coated organic polymers used in biotechnological research, and
  - estimating toxic metallic pollutants in environmental engineering.

Comparison between coulometry and EG

- Both are good methods for determining electroactive species.
- EG is more procedural than coulometry.
- Coulometry is a better method as it includes both electrochemical reactions in which a gas is formed and reactions in which both reactant and product are soluble species.
- Coulometry offers a method for accurately measuring quantities of species too small to be weighed or titrated by ordinary methods.

7.5 AMPEROMETRY

Principle Amperometry involves measurement of current (amperes) under constant applied voltage. When the *migration current* is eliminated, the *limiting current* depends only on the rate of diffusion of electroactive material from the bulk of the solution to the electrode surface.

Therefore, diffusion current = limiting current – residual current

The migration current is eliminated by the addition of a supporting electrolyte. The diffusion current is proportional to the concentration of the electroactive material in the solution.

7.5.1 AMPEROMETRIC TITRATIONS

If some of the electroactive material is reacted by the addition of a reagent, the diffusion current will decrease—this is the principle made use of in amperometric titrations.

- In an *amperometric titration,* the diffusion current is measured as a function of the volume of the titrant at a constant voltage. Then, the diffusion current values are plotted against volumes of titrant. The end point is the point of intersection of two straight lines denoting the change of current before and after the equivalence point.
- Polarography is the basis of amperometric titrations. The current is measured in the diffusion current region of a current–voltage curve. In this region, the current is independent of the potential of the indicator electrode because of an extreme state of concentration polarisation at the electrode. At the electrode surface, the concentration of the material undergoing electrode reaction is maintained at practically equal to zero; the current is limited by the supply of fresh material to the electrode surface by diffusion. The rate of diffusion and hence the current, is proportional to the concentration of diffusing substance in the bulk of the solution.

- *Condition for amperometric titration:* At least one of the participating reagents, or analyte, or products of the reaction should be oxidisable or reducible at a microelectrode.

Let us study an example of such a titration.

7.5.1.1 Electrode for Amperometric Titrations

The indicator electrode used for amperometric titrations may be a dropping mercury electrode or a rotating metal microelectrode.

The rotating metal electrode consists of a short length of wire, usually platinum, protruding 5–10 mm from the wall of a piece of glass tubing. The glass tubing is bent at right angles, a short distance from the end of the stem in order to sweep an area of the solution with the wire. The electrode is mounted on the shaft of a motor and rotated at a constant speed of about 600 rpm. The rotating electrode *decreases* the diffusion layer thickness and thereby increases the sensitivity and the attainment of a steady diffusion state. The limiting current may be up to about 20 times larger than that with a dropping electrode; it is proportional to the *one-third* power of the number of revolutions per minute above 200 rpm.

- A stationary electrode with a magnetic stirrer to drive the solution to the electrode, exhibits the same response as a rotated electrode.
- The larger currents attained with a rotating electrode allow correspondingly smaller concentrations to be measured without a loss in accuracy.
- Where the discharge of hydrogen interferes, a dropping mercury electrode, with its larger value of hydrogen overpotential, must be used.

7.5.1.2 Titration of Pb^{2+} with SO_4^{2-}

The lead ion is reducible whereas the sulphate ion is non-reducible. A known volume of Pb^{2+}(*aq*) is taken and SO_4^{2-}(*aq*) is added in equal aliquots; after each such addition, the diffusion current is measured.

If the voltage is maintained at any value on the diffusion–current plateau, the current will be i_o. On continuous addition of the sulphate ion solution, the lead ions are removed *from the solution* as insoluble lead sulphate and are therefore not available for reduction at the electrode. Therefore, the cathodic current decreases (i_1, i_2, i_3, … i_r). The current i_r denotes the residual current, that is, only the current flowing due to the supporting electrolyte.

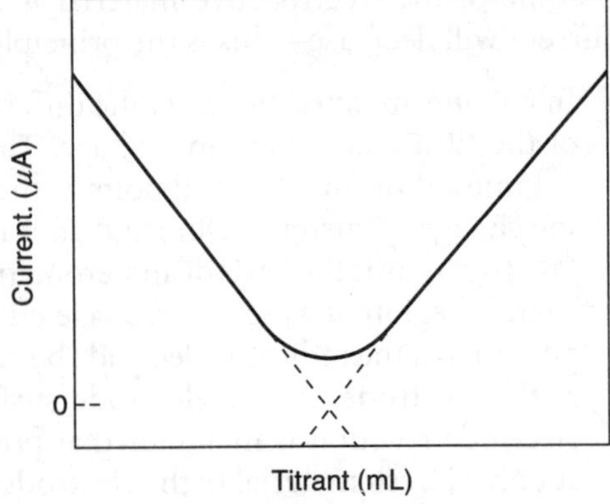

Fig. 7.28 Amperometric titrations curve for Pb^{2+} with SO_4^{2-}

Procedure Take a known volume of the analyte (Pb^{2+}) solution in a titration cell and assemble the apparatus (Fig. 7.28). Add a sufficient quantity of the supporting electrolyte to the analyte solution. The cathode is a dropping mercury electrode and the anode a saturated calomel electrode. The dissolved oxygen is removed from the solution by passing a slow stream of pure nitrogen for about 15 minutes. The applied voltage is adjusted to the desired value, and the initial diffusion current (i_o) is noted. A known volume (V_1) of the standardised sulphate solution is added to the cell from a microburette and nitrogen gas is bubbled through the mixture for about two minutes to

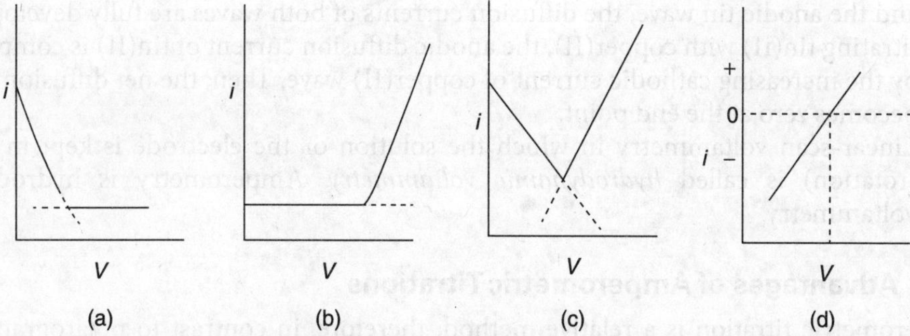

Fig. 7.29 Typical amperometric titration curves **(a)** analyte is reduced, reagent is not, **(b)** reagent is reduced, analyte is not, **(c)** both reagent and analytle are reduced, and **(d)** analyte gives an anodic diffusion current.

expel oxygen from the mixture and also to effect complete mixing. Now, the current (i_1) and the burette readings are noted.

Then, incremental volumes of the sulphate solution are added and current values noted on each addition (i_2 to i_5). The current values (i_0 to i_5) are plotted against the volumes of sulphate added. The plot will consist of two linear portions; their intersections denote the end point (Fig. 7.29a).

Note: To minimise errors due to volume change during the titration, the titrant is made 10–20 times more concentrated than the analyte. In addition, this reduces the introduction of more dissolved oxygen.

7.5.1.3 Amperometric Titration Curves

Amperometric titration curves typically conform to one of the forms shown in Fig. 7.29.

(a) In this case, only the material titrated gives a diffusion current. The titrating reagent is not electroactive. It removes the electroactive analyte from the solution. Therefore, as the titration proceeds, the diffusion current decreases. After the equivalence point, there is no change in current. For example, the titration of lead ions with sulphate ions.

(b) In this case, only the titrating reagent and not the analyte, is electroactive. Therefore, until it is added in excess, beyond the equivalence point, no change in the reading is observed. After the equivalence point, the excess titrant produces current (Fig. 7.29b). For example, the titration of sulphate ions with lead or barium ions.

(c) In this case, both the reagents give rise to diffusion current, as both are electroactive. Up to the equivalence point, the two regents react and lead to a decrease in current. After the equivalence point, the titrant produces diffusion current. A V-shaped curve is obtained (Fig. 7.29c). For example, the titration of lead ions with chromate ions.

(d) In this case, the analyte gives an *anodic* diffusion current. At the equivalence point, the current changes to cathodic due to the presence of excess titrant. The point of zero current is the end point. For example, the titration of chloride ions with silver ions.
   - An amperometric titration without any chemical reaction is also possible. For example, copper(II) and tin(II) in a tartrate medium at pH 4 do not react. However, Cu(II) is cathodically reduced to Cu(0) and Sn(II) species is anodically oxidised to Sn(IV). These two, therefore produce independent current–voltage curves (Fig. 7.29d). At an applied potential, midway between the half-wave potential of the cathodic copper wave

and the anodic tin wave, the diffusion currents of both waves are fully developed. On titrating tin(II) with copper(II), the anodic diffusion current of tin(II) is compensated by the increasing cathodic current of copper(II) wave. Then, the net diffusion current becomes zero at the end point.

- Linear-scan voltammetry in which the solution or the electrode is kept in motion (rotation) is called *hydrodynamic voltammetry.* Amperometry is hydrodynamic voltammetry.

7.5.1.4 Advantages of Amperometric Titrations

- Amperometric titration is a relative method; therefore, in contrast to polarography, it is associated with fewer interfering variables.
- The electrode characteristics are not important in this method; the capillary characteristics of a dropping electrode need not be predetermined.
- A rotating electrode can be used for reproducible results. The absence of current oscillations on using rotating electrodes permits the use of rugged micrometers for the measurement of current.
- In this method, each branch of the titration curve is the average of the recorded points, which offers a higher accuracy than polarography.
- The accuracy of the titrant delivery mainly determines the error in the end point.
- It is a more sensitive method than either the conductometric or potentiometric methods. Traces of analytes down to 10^{-6} M can be determined with good precision.

7.5.2 Amperometric Titration with Complexants

Amperometic titrations can be adopted for titrating a metal ion with a complexing agent. For example, Bi(III) can be titrated with standard EDTA at a pH of 1–2. The potential of the indicator electrode (−0.16 to −0.20 V versus SCE) is such that Bi(III) is reduced, but the Bi–EDTA complex and the titrant are not. The current decreases linearly (Fig. 7.29a) as EDTA is added; during this stage [Bi(III)] decreases. At the equivalence point, when all the free Bi(III) has been complexed, the current does not change; this is indicated by the linear portion of the curve. In the titration of Mg(II) with oxine ($E = 1.6$ V versus SCE), only the complexation agent gets reduced. Therefore, the current remains constant in the beginning, as the added oxine is used for complexation without undergoing reduction. After the equivalence point, oxine gets reduced, contributing to the current. The titration current resembles that in Fig. 7.29b.

7.6 VOLTAMMETRY

- Voltammetry is electrolysis on a microscale, using a micro working electrode (for example, a platinum wire).
- It is a current–voltage method.
- In this method, the potential of the micro working electrode is varied and the resulting current is recorded as a function of applied voltage. The resulting record is a *voltammogram.*
- On applying a potential, the electroactive species (reducible or oxidisable) in the solution will be electrolysed. The reaction occurs when the applied potential becomes sufficiently negative or positive for reaction.
- If the solution is dilute, the current will reach a limiting value.
- The limiting current is proportional to the concentration of the species.

- A voltammetric cell is actually an electrolytic cell in which the electrochemical reaction occurs due to the applied potential.
- A limiting current is reached because the analyte is being electrolysed as fast as it can diffuse to the electrode.
- In a voltammetric measurement, the solution can be recovered unchanged due to the passage of only small currents.
- The potential at which the analyte is electrolysed is a qualitative identification of the analyte.
- The height of the voltammetric wave is proportional to the number of electrons involved in the electrolytic reaction.
- In all electrochemical methods, with the exception of potentiometry, a supporting electrolyte is added to the electrolytic solution. The concentration of the supporting electrolyte is at least 100-fold greater than the concentration of the analyte; such a concentration prevents or minimises the migration current.

7.6.1 Stripping Voltammetry

Principle Stripping voltammetry (SV) is a two-step determination of the concentration of a species by electrodeposition. The first step is the deposition of the analyte species. The deposited material is then electrolytically stripped (removed) from the electrode surface and determined by the current peak produced during the stripping process.

The limit of detection in DC polarography is about 10^{-5} M; this sensitivity can be improved by a factor of 2–10 using differential pulse polarography (down to 100 μg/ kg). In stripping voltammetry, the detection limit is lower than these limits. In the stripping analysis, more ions from a given solution reach the small layer of liquid close to the working electrodes and react, unlike in polarographic methods. This enhances the detection limit to 1 μg/ kg^{-1}.

The deposition step can either be (i) a cathode process where metal ions are reduced at a mercury electrode to give an amalgam or (ii) an anodic process where Hg is oxidised to Hg^+, and this then reacts with the analyte ions to form an insoluble product as a film on the electrode surface. This product is then stripped back into solution by a negative potential (cathode).

Deposition: A negative potential is applied to the solution.

$$M^{n+} + ne^- \longrightarrow M^0 \xrightarrow{Hg} \text{Amalgam}$$

Stripping: The potential is scanned from negative to positive value.

$$\text{Amalgam} \longrightarrow M^{n+} + ne^-$$

This is called *anode stripping voltammetry* (ASV), because, in the stipping step, the potential is altered from a negative to a positive value.

Deposition:

$$Hg \longrightarrow Hg^+ + e^-$$

$$2Hg^+ + 2X^- \longrightarrow \underset{\text{(deposit)}}{Hg_2X_2}$$

Stripping:

$$Hg_2X_2 + 2e^- \longrightarrow 2Hg + 2X^-$$

In the stripping process, the potential–current graph forms a peak at the reduction or oxidation potential of the species deposited on the electrode. This peak height is proportional to the amount of material deposited on the electrode and hence to the amount of the analyte.

Accurate results are obtained in SV only when

- the surface area of the electrode is conditioned for efficient deposit formation,
- corrected potential is applied during the two steps,
- correct duration of the deposition step is ensured, and
- proper rate of stirring of the solution (neither two low nor too fast) is adopted.

Apparatus: A polarographic apparatus with DME and provision for stirring the solution can be used for SV. In the concentration step, a small mercury volume is used compared to the volume of the analyte solution and efficient stirring is necessary to quicken the deposition. In the stripping step, a fast voltage scan is performed but without producing peak tailing. The cell used should have provision for eliminating dissolved oxygen and remain closed during the SV process. A magnetic stirrer is used for efficient stirring.

7.6.1.1 Applications

SV can be applied for determining several metals—Cd, Sn, Zn, Cu, Pb, Au and Ag. For example, the stripping voltammogram for Cd is shown in Fig. 7.30.

- Voltammetry is a type of electroanalytical method that involves the measurement of *electrical current* as a function of *applied electrical potential.*
- The magnitude of the measured current is proportional to the concentration of the analyte (oxidisable or reducible).
- Voltammetry at a dropping mercury electrode is polarography.

There are three forms of voltammetry:

(i) Potential step voltammetry (PSV),
(ii) Linear sweep voltammetry (LSV), and
(iii) Cyclic voltammetry (CV).

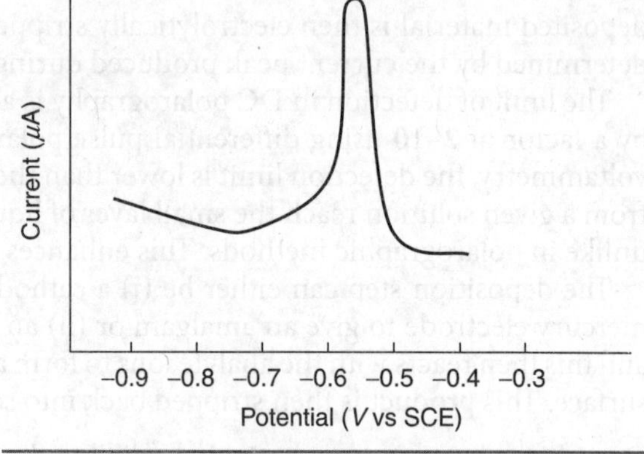

Fig. 7.30 Stripping voltammogram for cadmium

In each of these methods, voltages are applied to the electrodes and the corresponding current flows are recorded. The voltages are applied in different modes in these techniques.

7.6.2 Potential Step Voltammetry

In potential step voltammetry (PSV), the applied voltage is increased from V_1 to V_2 in a single step (not increased gradually, Fig. 7.31a). The resulting current (i) is then measured as a function of time. Consider the reaction

$$Cd^{2+}(\text{solution}) + 2e^- \longrightarrow Cd(s)$$

Initially, the voltage is set at V_1 such that the reduction is thermodynamically unfavourable. Then the voltage is increased to V_2 at which reduction of Cd^{2+} ions close to the electrode structure is favourable. At this stage, the current response is shown in Fig. 7.31b. The current rises instantaneously (a to b) and then starts decreasing as a function of time.

Just before stepping up the voltage, the surface of the electrode is completely covered in the reactant and the solution below has a constant composition. On stepping up the voltage, Cd^{2+} is converted to Cd^0, and therefore a large current flows. Fresh reactant then approaches the

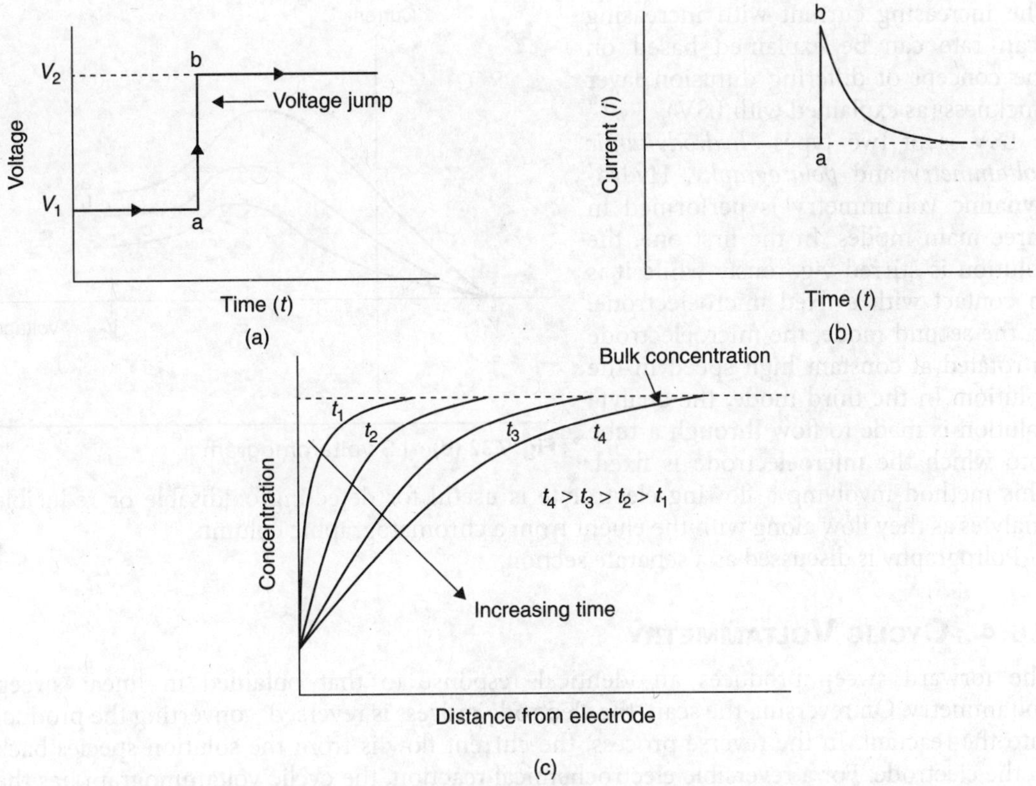

Fig. 7.31 Potential step voltammetric curves **(a)** Voltage vs time plot **(b)** Current vs time plot **(c)** Concentration vs electrode distance plot for various time periods.

electrode surface from the solution by diffusion and the reaction continues. With the progress of reaction, the amount of Cd^{2+} decreases in solution and the concentration gradient also decreases (Fig. 7.31c). With decreased supply of Cd^{2+} to the electrode, the current decreases. Therefore, the current is related to the bulk concentration of the reactant and therefore the analyte can be estimated.

7.6.3 Linear Sweep Voltammetry

In linear sweep voltammetry (LSV) a fixed potential range is applied. Unlike with PSV, in LSV the voltage is scanned from a lower limit to the upper limit, V_1 to V_2 (Fig. 7.32a). A typical linear sweep voltammogram is shown in Fig. 7.32b. In addition, in this method, the current response is plotted as a function of voltage whereas in PSV, current is plotted against time.

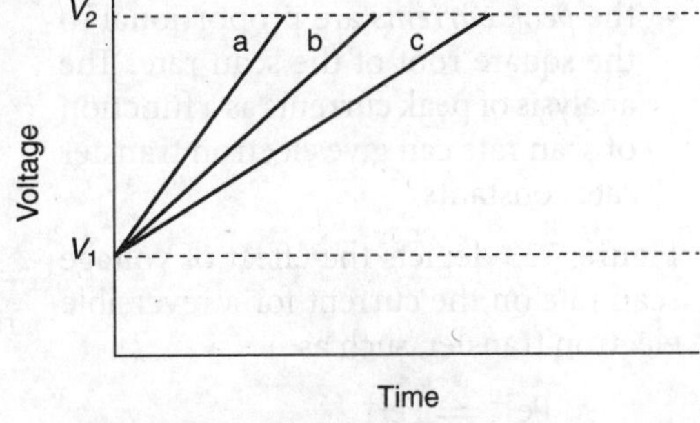

Fig. 7.32 (a) Linear increase of potential with time in LSV for three scan rates (a > b > c)

The properties of an LS voltammogram depend on

- the rate of the electron transfer reaction,
- the chemical reactivity of the electroactive species, and
- the voltage scan rate.

The increasing current with increasing scan rate can be explained based on the concept of differing diffusion layer thickness (as explained with LSV).

LSV is of two types—*hydrodynamic voltammetry* and *polarography*. Hydrodynamic voltammetry is performed in three main modes. In the first one, the solution is stirred vigorously while it is in contact with a fixed microelectrode. In the second mode, the microelectrode is rotated at constant high speed in the solution. In the third mode, the analyte solution is made to flow through a tube into which the microelectrode is fixed.

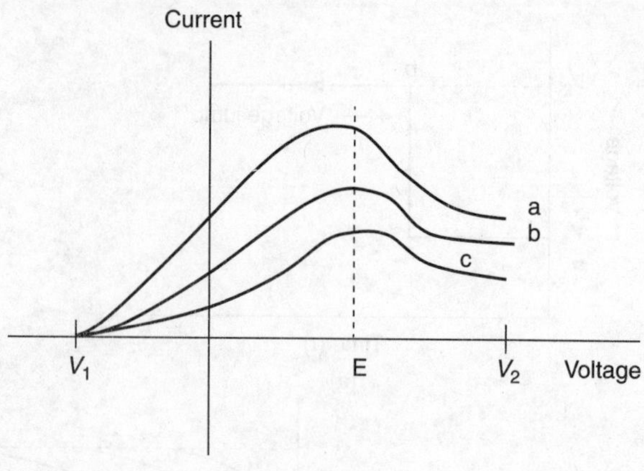

Fig. 7.32 (b) LS voltammogram

This method involving a flowing electrolyte is useful for detecting oxidisable or reducible analytes as they flow along with the eluent from a chromatographic column.

Polrography is discussed as a separate section.

7.6.4 Cyclic Voltammetry

The forward sweep produces an identical response to that obtained in linear sweep voltammetry. On reversing the scan, the electrode process is reversed, converting the product into the reactant. In the reverse process, the current flow is from the solution species back to the electrode. For a reversible electrochemical reaction, the cyclic voltammogram has the following features:

- the voltage separation between the two current peaks (forward and backward reactions) is distinct,
- the voltage scan rate does not shift the positions of *peak voltage*,
- the ratio of the peak current is one, and
- the *peak currents* are proportional to the square root of the scan rate. The analysis of peak currents as a function of scan rate can give electron transfer rate constants.

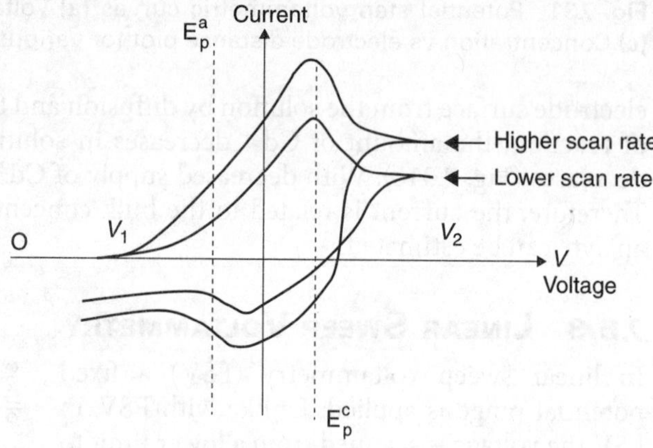

Fig. 7.33 Effect of scan rate on the current for a reversible electrode reaction

Figure 7.33 depicts the effect of voltage scan rate on the current for a reversible electron transfer, such as

$$Fe^{3+} \rightleftharpoons Fe^{2+}$$

The increasing current with increasing scan rate can be explained based on the concept of differing diffusion layer thickness (as explained with LSV).

Cyclic voltammetry is a modified version of normal polarography; in CV, a fast scan is effected in two directions, namely from O to *V* and back to O. The applied potential is rapidly varied in the O–*V*–O volt region. In this scan, as the potential is applied in two directions, two curves are obtained (Fig. 7.34). One curve is the cathodic reduction wave and the second is the anodic oxidation wave. The two curves are equal in magnitude. They are approximately vertically aligned. The two curves constitute a cyclic polarographic curve; this indicates that the electrode reaction is a reversible reaction. The peak-to-peak separation with reference to the potential axis is designated as ΔE_p (mV). It is directly related to the number of electrons transferred in the reversible reaction. It is given by

$$\Delta E_p = \frac{2.22\,RT}{nF} = \frac{57.0}{n}$$

$$\text{The number of electrons, } n = \frac{57.0}{\Delta E_p}$$

CV is performed with electrodes of small surface area in unstirred solution; the process produces a very small redox current. When the current is small, the ohmic drop IR is small even for poorly conducting solutions. As the capacitance involved is low, fast scan rates are possible (a few kVs^{-1}). The quick scan eliminates any contribution to current by diffusion.

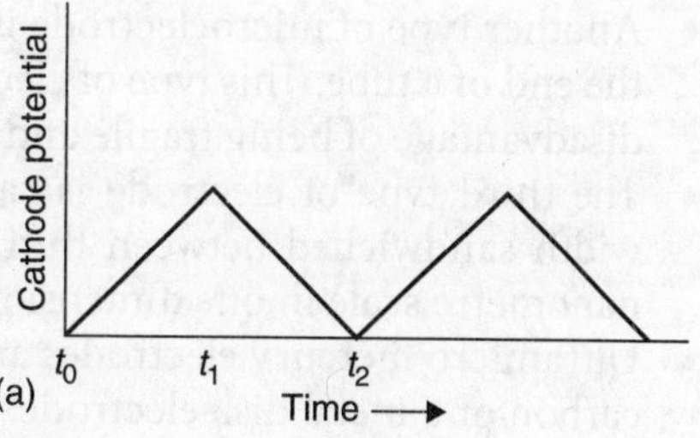

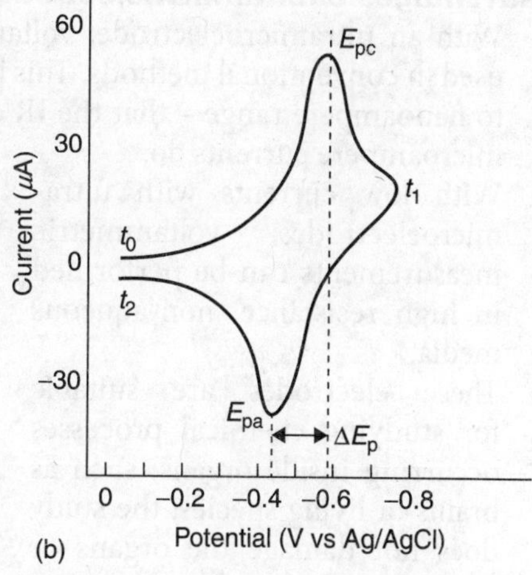

Fig. 7.34 Cyclic voltammetric curve

7.6.4.1 Advantages of CV

- It is suitable for studying reversible electrode processes.
- It can be applied to the study of kinetics of fast reactions.
- The number of species participating in the reaction sequence can be found out by CV.
- It can provide information of reaction mechanisms.

7.6.4.2 Disadvantages of CV

- The instrument is more expensive than that used for conventional polarography.
- The scan rate, in addition to the concentration of redox species, may influence the magnitude of the waves produced, leading to errors. However, CV offers a rapid location of redox potentials of the electroactive species.
- It gives only qualitative information about electrochemical reactions.

7.6.5 Voltammetry using Ultramicroelectrodes

Ultramicroelectrodes are smaller than 20 μm. Such electrodes are also called *microscopic electrodes.*

- An example for ultramicroelectrode is the carbon fibre electrode; it consists of a conducting carbon fibre (radius 5 μm) sealed in an insulating fine capillary tube. The fibre is cut flush with the ends of the tubes. Instead of carbon fibre, gold or platinum wire may also be used.

- Another type of microelectrode is the cylindrical type. It consists of a wire extending from the end of a tube. This type of electrode offers the advantage of larger currents but it has the disadvantage of being fragile and difficult to clean and polish.
- The third type of electrode is called band electrode; it is made of a metal film of 2 nm width sandwiched between thin glass insulators. Such electrodes can be fabricated on a nanometre scale in one dimension; the magnitude of their currents increases with length.
- Ultramicro mercury electrodes are formed by eletrodeposition (coating) of the metal on to carbon or a metal disk electrode.

Advantages of ultramicroelectrodes

- With an ultramicroelectrode, voltammetry need not employ the three-electrode system used in conventional methods. This is because the currents are so small – in the picoampere to nanoampere range – that the IR drop does not distort the voltammetric waves the way microampere currents do.
- With low currents with ultra-microelectrodes, voltammetric measurements can be performed in high resistance, non-aqueous media.
- These electrodes are suitable for studying chemical processes occurring inside organs, such as brains of living species; the study does not damage the organs or interfere with their function.
- High speed measurements enabled by these electrodes help study intermediates in rapid electrochemical processes.

7.7 POLAROGRAPHY

Polarography is an electroanalytical method used to study the composition of dilute electrolytic solutions by plotting current–voltage curves. In this technique, the voltage applied to a small polarisable electrode is increased in the range of 0–2 V and the resulting changes in current through the solution are noted. The general name for this method is *voltammetry*. The term polarography is used when a dropping mercury cathode is used. The dropping mercury electrode is referred to as the *working electrode* in polarography. It is also referred to as the *indicator electrode or microelectrode.*

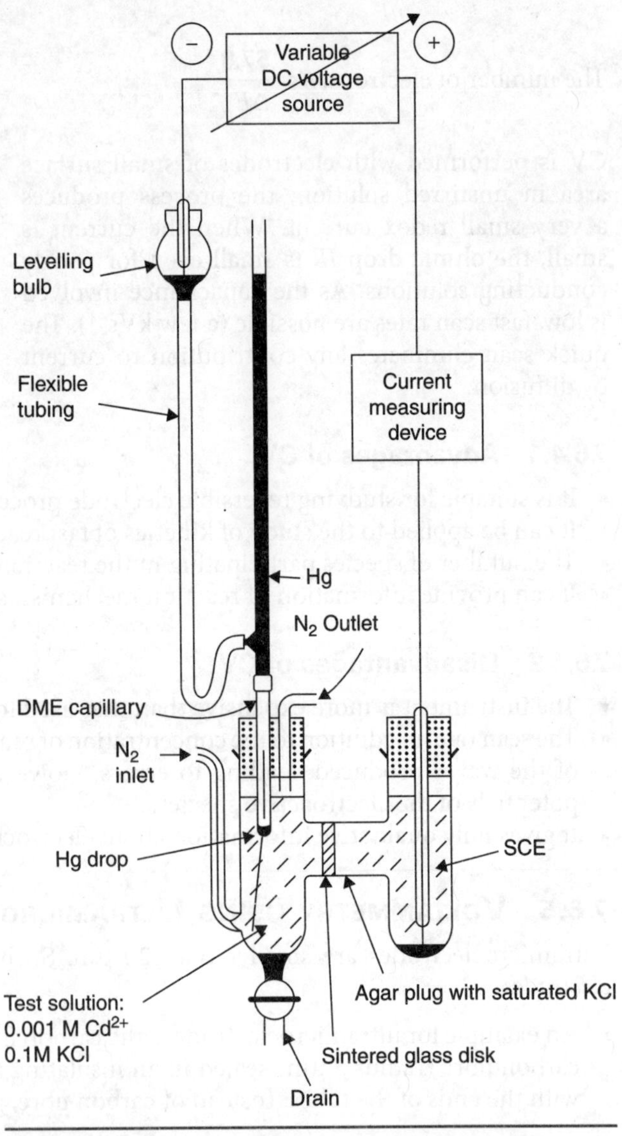

Fig. 7.35 Polarographic experimental assembly

The polarographic experimental assembly (Fig. 7.35) is similar to the one used in potentiometry. This method was invented by Heyrovsky in the year 1922. The electrodes are connected to a variable voltage source. A very sensitive ammeter or galvanometer, provided with a shunt, is included in the circuit. The potential at the working electrode is measured by a voltmeter relative to the reference electrode.

The working electrode is the dropping mercury electrode which uses mercury in the form of a succession of tiny droplets emerging from a glass capillary. The construction and handling of the dropping mercury electrode (dme) is done very carefully. However, there are a few advantages to offset this inconvenience. One apparent advantage is that the surface of the electrode remains pure and clean as it is continually being renewed. The second advantage is the very high hydrogen ovetvoltage on the mercury cathode. Cations of metals such as iron, zinc and so on, can be reduced to free metals. The reference electrode must be constructed in such a way that it has as low a resistance as possible. This is essential because currents of very low magnitude are measured in polarography. In addition, the metal–solution interface at the anode must have a large area so that the polarisation effects are minimum.

Heyrovsky

Polarography was invented in 1922 by Heyrovsky, a Czechoslovakian chemist. This method was widely used immediately after its invention by both organic and inorganic chemists. It has found excellent applications in many fields of research.

He demonstrated, for the first time, that electrochemical experiments could offer data of a high degree of precision and reproducibility. The classical polarography of Heyrovsky paved the way for the invention of several modern electroanalytical methods. Heyrovsky received a Nobel prize in 1959 for this invention.

Source: By Heyrovsky_Jaroslav.jpg: archiv ÚFCH J.Heyrovského AV ČR, v.v.i.derivative work: Materialscientist (talk) - This file was derived from Heyrovsky Jaroslav.jpg:, CC BY-SA 3.0, https://commons.wikimedia.org/w/index.php?curid=18262036

7.7.1 Principle of Polarography

When a current–voltage curve is plotted for a solution, it is seen that a small current flows even before the decomposition of the solution begins. The origin of this current is shown to be the continual charging of mercury drops to the applied potential, and the reduction of impurities present in the system. This current is known as the *residual current* and this increases linearly with the applied voltage. When the potential is increased sufficiently to cause reduction of the electroactive material, the ions undergoing reduction may reach the surface of the electrode either by migration in the electrical field caused by applied voltage or by diffusion. In a polagraphic experiment, the former is completely eliminated by the addition of a strong solution of another electrolyte known as the *supporting electrolyte*. It is the ions of the supporting electrolyte that carry all the current, even though it is the electroactive material that undergoes reduction at the dropping mercury electrode. The ions of the supporting electrolyte should have a higher discharge potential than the ion(s) under investigation. When the migration current MN, is practically reduced to zero by using a supporting electrolyte, the current–voltage curve (also known as *polarogram*) takes the shape shown in Fig. 7.36.

The rising portion of the curve MN, is known as a *polagraphic wave*. The number of waves present in a polarogram will be exactly equal to the number of different species in the solution which can be reduced at the dropping mercury electrode.

- The potential corresponding to the point of inflexion of the curve, that is, half way up the polarographic wave is called the *half-wave potential*, $E_{½}$. The half-wave potential is characteristic of the ion that gets reduced at the dropping mercury electrode.
- The wave height represents the *diffusion current* and is a function of the concentration of the ion that is reduced. Therefore, not only a particular ion can be qualitatively identified from its $E_{½}$ value but also its concentration in the solution can be determined from the wave height.

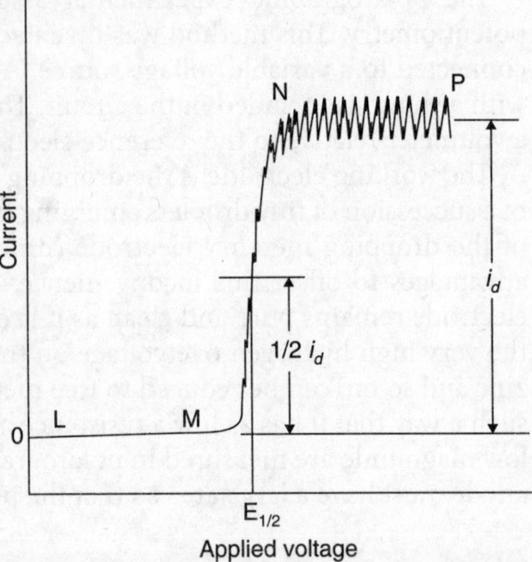

Fig. 7.36 A typical polarogram

It can be shown that the current *i*, at any point on the polarographic wave is related to the potential $E_{½}$ by the following expression,

$$E = E_{1/2} + \frac{0.059}{n}\log\left[\frac{(i_d - i)}{i}\right] \qquad (7.6)$$

where i_d is the diffusion current and *n* is the number of electrons required to reduce the electroactive material. This equation is very useful in organic polarography. To postulate a suitable mechanism for the electroreduction, the value of *n* is required. This is readily obtained by plotting *E* versus log $[(i_d - i)/i]$

7.7.2 Diffusion Current: The Ilkovic Equation

The diffusion current lies in the plateau region of a polarogram; hence it is independent of potential. The magnitude of the diffusion current i_d, depends on several factors; this fact is denoted by the *Ilkovic equation*:

$$i_d = 706\, n\, C\, D^{1/2}\, m^{2/3}\, t^{1/6} \qquad (7.7)$$

where, i_d = maximum value of the diffusion current during the life of the mercury drop, 706 is the resultant of several constants, *n* = number of electrons involved in the reaction, *C* = concentration of the electroactive substance in millimoles per litre, *D* = diffusion coefficient of the ion in square centimetres per second, *m* = mass of dropping mercury in milligrams per second, *t* = time between two consequtive drops in seconds.

This equation indicates that i_d is proportional to the concentration of an electroactive material in the bulk of the solution, when *t* and the temperature of the solution are kept constant (*D* is dependent on temperature). Some polarographic half-wave potentials are given in Table 7.9.

The currents of many polarographic waves tend to go through a maximum – a disturbing tendency – before returning to the plateau region. This disturbance is avoided by the addition of a surface-active agent, such as gelatine. Such a reagent is called a *maximum suppressor*. The data in Table 7.9 have been obtained in the presence of gelatine.

Table 7.9 Some polarographic half-wave potentials (supporting electrolyte: 0.1 M KCl)

Reaction	$E_{1/2}$ vs SCE
Cu (II) → Cu	+0.04
Pb (II) → Pb	−0.40
Cd (II) → Cd	−0.60
Zn (II) → Zn	−1.00
Ni (II) → Ni	−1.10
Mn (II) → Mn	−1.51

- Voltammetric methods using a dme are called polarography.
- Polarography was the first type of voltammetry to be invented and used.
- It differs from hydrodynamic voltammetry in two aspects:
    - *Convection* is avoided; therefore, the polarographic limiting currents are controlled by diffusion alone rather than by both diffusion and convection. In the absence of convection, polarographic limiting currents are one or more orders of magnitude smaller than hydrodynamic limiting currents.
    - A dme, instead of a fixed electrode, is used. This offers a fresh electrode surface continually, during electrode reaction.

7.7.3 Quantitative Polarographic Analysis

- Several species – both inorganic and organic – can be estimated polarographically.
- Two methods are available for the determination of concentration of an electroactive substance in a solution using polarography.

(i) *Wave height–concentration plots:* The principle of this method is that the wave height, which is a measure of diffusion current, is directly proportional to the concentration of the species undergoing reduction at the dropping mercury electrode. Standard solutions of different concentrations of the substance under investigation are subjected to polarographic analysis, keeping the composition of the supporting electrolyte and other experimental conditions the same. The wave height is measured in each case and plotted against the corresponding concentration. The wave height is determined for the solution in which the concentration is to be determined. From the graph, the concentration can be read by interpolation. For example, estimation of cadmium ion.

A series of standard solutions of cadmium sulphate with concentration of Cd^{2+} equal to 0.001, 0.002, 0.004, 0.005 and 0.008 M are prepared. Ten mL of each one of these solutions is mixed with 25 mL of a 0.1 M solution of KCl and the polarogram recorded. The wave height (or i_d) is measured for each concentration and is plotted against concentration. The test solution is also subjected to a similar polarographic analysis. Knowing the wave height (or i_d) of the test solution, the concentration can be read from the graph by interpolation.

Note To get accurate results, it is necessary to exclude dissolved oxygen from the system by passing an inert gas such as nitrogen through the solution, because dissolved oxygen can be reduced at the dme.

Interference by oxygen: Oxygen is electroactive; it undergoes two types of reduction at the dme.

$$O_2 + 4H^+ + 4e^- \rightarrow 2H_2O \qquad E^0 = 1.23V$$

$$O_2 + 2H^+ + 2e^- \rightarrow H_2O_2 \qquad E^0 = 0.70V$$

Therefore, for reproducible $E_{1/2}$ values for analytes, the test solution should be freed from dissolved oxygen. This is effected by passing an electro-inactive gas (sparging) N_2 of high purity, through the solution and eliminating the dissolved oxygen.

(ii) *Method of standard addition:* The solution under investigation is first subjected to polarographic analysis after which a known volume of the standard solution of the same substance is added and a second polarogram taken. Let i_1 be the diffusion current of the test solution of volume V_1 mL and of concentration C_1. Similarly let i_2 be the diffusion current for the second polarogram, that is, after the addition of V_2 mL of a standard solution of concentration C_2. Since the diffusion current is proportional to the concentration,

$$i_1 = kC_1$$

$$i_2 = k\frac{V_1C_1 + V_2C_2}{V_1 + V_2}$$

Thus $$k = i_2\frac{(V_1 + V_2)}{V_1C_1 + V_2C_2}$$

From these two equations, it is possible to calculate C_1.

$$C_1 = \frac{i_1V_2C_2}{[(i_2 - i_1)(V_1 + V_2) + i_1V_2]}$$

Both the methods can be applied to solutions in which the concentrations of the electroactive materials are as low as 10^{-3} to 10^{-4} M.

Advantages of DME

- Zinc and cadmium can be estimated from acidic solutions even though their thermodynamic potentials indicate that deposition of these metals at other electrodes would occur with simultaneous evolution of hydrogen.
- Solid, stationary electrodes change their character during a deposition, giving unreliable results. This is a consequence of adsorbed or deposited impurities. This problem does not occur with the dme, as the system provides new metal surface continually.
- With the dme, reproducible average currents are quickly realised at any given potential regardless of whether this potential is approached from lower or higher settings.

Disadvantages of DME

- The polarographic determinations with the dme can be used only for small amounts of substances, and are associated with a relative error of 1% or more. (Amperometry is suitable for larger amounts of analytes.)
- Mercury is easily oxidised; this limits the use of the electrode as an anode. When the potential is greater than +0.4 V, Hg(0) gets oxidised to Hg(I) and this gives a wave that masks the curves of other oxidisable species.
- A non-faradaic residual or charging current limits the sensitivity of the classical polarographic method to concentrations of about 10^{-5} M. At lower concentrations, the diffusion current is lower than the residual current, leading to inaccurate diffusion current data.
- The dme is messy to use. Sometimes, clogging in the capillary may break the current measurement. Because mercury is toxic, it has to be handled with care, avoiding spills.

7.7.4 Applications of Polarography

7.7.4.1 Inorganic Polarographic Analysis

- Most metallic cations, including alkali cations (which are difficult to reduce), can be polarographically estimated. With alkali cations, as they are reducible only at high potentials, a supporting electrolyte which is electro-inactive at the high potential should be used. Tetraalkylammonium halides are suitable as supporting electrolytes in these analyses.
- The choice of the supporting electrolyte influences the success of a polarographic estimation. A proper choice of the supporting electrolyte enhances the selectivity of the method. For example, the waves for iron(III) and copper(II) interface when KCl is used as the supporting electrolyte. However, clear, well-separated waves are obtained if KF is used instead of KCl. The fluoride ion shifts the half-wave potential of iron(III) by –0.5 V, without altering that of copper(II).
- Inorganic ions such as bromate, iodate, dichromate, vanadate, selenite and nitrite are also electroactive and can be estimated polarographically. In these reductions, H^+ also takes part and therefore pH is a critical factor in the estimation; buffering to a fixed pH is necessary to obtain reproducible data in each case.
- Polarography is applied in the study of metal complexes; their compositions and characteristics can be determined.

7.7.4.2 Effect of Complex Formation on Polarographic Waves

- Polarographic half-wave potentials are affected by complexing species. For example, $E_{1/2}$ for uncomplexed Cd^{2+} is –0.59 V whereas it is –1.18 V on complexing the cadmium ions with CN^- species.
- The half-wave potential for the reduction of a metal complex is more negative than that for the reduction of the corresponding simple metal ion (Table 7.10).
- The negative shift in potential on complexing metal ions enables the elucidation of the composition of the complex ion and the determination of its formation constant, provided that the electrode reaction is reversible.

Table 7.10 Effect of complexing agents on polarographic half-wave potentials at the dme

Ion	$E_{1/2}$ (Non-complexing Medium) (V)	$E_{1/2}$ (Complexing medium) (V)		
		1 M CN^-	1 M Cl^-	1 M NH_3 + 1 M NH_4Cl
Cu^{2+}	+0.02	*	+0.04	–0.24
Cd^{2+}	–0.60	–1.18	–0.64	–0.81
Zn^{2+}	–1.00	*	–1.00	–1.35
Co^{2+}	–	–1.45	–1.20	–1.29
Ni^{2+}	–1.10	–1.36	–1.20	– 1.10

*No reduction occurs before involvement of the supporting electrolyte.

7.7.4.3 Determination of Stability Constants for Complexes

Principle The $E_{1/2}$ value of a simple metal ion shifts when it gets complexed. The magnitude of this shift depends on the concentration of the ligand used. By measuring the $E_{1/2}$ values as a function of the concentration of the ligand, the equilibrium constant for the formation of complexes (stability constant) can be computed. Consider the redox equation,

$$\text{Ox} + ne^- \rightarrow \text{Red}$$

where 'Ox' and 'Red' are the oxidised and the reduced forms of a metal ion. The corresponding Nernst's equation is:

$$E = E^0 + \left(\frac{0.059}{n}\right)\log\left\{\frac{[\text{Ox}]}{[\text{Red}]}\right\} \tag{7.8}$$

The complexation of the metal ion with a p number of ligand L, could be represented as,

$$\text{Ox} + p\text{L} \rightleftharpoons \text{OxL}_p$$

so that the equilibrium constant, $K = \dfrac{[\text{OxL}_p]}{[\text{Ox}][\text{L}]^p}$

or $\quad [\text{Ox}] = \dfrac{[\text{OxL}_p]}{K[\text{L}]^p}$

Substituting for [Ox], we get,

$$E = E^0 + \left(\frac{0.059}{n}\right)\log\frac{[\text{OxL}_p]}{K[\text{L}]^p[\text{Red}]} \tag{7.9}$$

The half-wave potential ($E_{1/2}$) is the potential at which one-half of all the oxidised form that reaches electrode surface is reduced. Therefore, when the potential E is equal to $E_{1/2}$, [Ox] = [Red] for the simple metal ion and $[\text{OxL}_p]$ = [Red] for the complex. Incorporating these results in Eqs 7.8 and 7.9, we get for the reduction of simple ion,

$$E_{1/2} = E^0 \tag{7.10}$$

and for complex ion, $E_{1/2} = E^0 + \left(\dfrac{0.059}{n}\right)\log\left(\dfrac{1}{\text{K}[\text{L}]^p}\right)$ (7.11)

Subtracting Eq. 7.11 from Eq. 7.10,

$$E_{1/2}(\text{simple ion}) - E_{1/2}(\text{complex ion}) = \left(\frac{0.059}{n}\right)\log \text{K}[\text{L}]^p$$

or $$\Delta E_{1/2} = \left(\frac{0.059}{n}\right)\{\log \text{K} + p\log[\text{L}]\} \tag{7.12}$$

Thus, the $E_{1/2}$ values for the simple metal ion and for a series of solutions containing a fixed metal ion concentration with different ligand concentrations are measured. When the $\Delta E_{1/2}$ values are plotted against the log[L] values, a straight line is obtained. The slope of the line is $0.059p/n$ from which p can be calculated. Substituting this value for p in Eq. 7.11, a series of values for K can be obtained according to the concentration of the ligand used. Finally, the average of all the K values is taken as the *equilibrium constant* or the *stability constant* of the complex. This procedure was evolved by J J Lingane (*Chem. Rev.* 29, 1, 1941).

7.7.4.4 Organic Polarographic Analysis

(i) Several organic functional groups are reducible polarographically, and therefore can be estimated by this method (Table 7.11).

(ii) Even oxidisable organic functional groups can be analysed using platinum, gold or carbon microelectrodes.

(iii) The half-wave potential of an organic compound is pH dependent. In addition, the product of reaction may change with change in pH. For example, benzaldehyde is reduced to benzyl alcohol at pH 8, with $E_{1/2} = -1.4$ V.

$$C_6H_5CHO + 2H^+ + 2e^- \rightarrow C_6H_5CH_2OH$$

When the pH is less than 2, hydrobenzoin is formed with $E_{1/2} = -1.0$ V.

$$2C_6H_5CHO + 2H^+ + e^- \rightarrow C_6H_5\ CHOH\ CHOH\ C_6H_5$$

At intermediate pH values, both the products are obtained, as indicated by two waves.

(iv) Several organic compounds are insoluble in water; therefore, they cannot be estimated in the aqueous medium. Then, an organic solvent such as ethanol, acetic acid or dioxane can be used. Lithum salts or tetraalkylammonium salts are used as supporting electrolytes with such organic solvents.

(v) An organic compound may produce more than one wave as it can undergo step-wise reduction or simultaneously two types of reduction.

(vi) The carbonyl group (aldehydes, ketones and quinones) produce polarographic waves. Aldehydes are reduced at lower potentials than ketones. Conjugation in the carbonyl compound reduces the $E_{1/2}$ value.

(vii) Simple aliphatic and aromatic monocarboxylic acids are not reduced. However, keto, aldehydic and dicarboxylic acids are reduced, each giving a characteristic polarogram.

(viii) Organic halides are reduced to hydrocarbons.

(ix) Nitro, nitroso, amine oxide and azo groups are reducible at the dme.

(x) Organic peroxides and epoxides are polarographically active.

(xi) The carbon–carbon double bond, when conjugated with another double bond, an aromatic ring or an unsaturated group, gets reduced.

(xii) Hydroquinones and mercaptans give anodic waves.

Table 7.11 Half-wave potentials of some organic functional groups

Functional group	$E_{1/2}$ (V)
$-C\equiv C-$	−2.3
$-C=C-$	−2.3
C = O	−2.2
S – S	−0.3

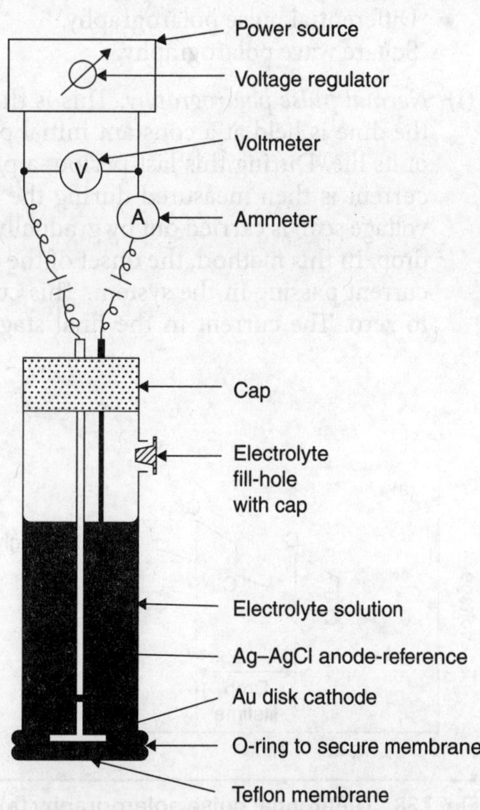

Fig. 7.37 The Clark voltammetric sensor

(xiii) Certain biological organic molecules are also reducible polargraphically. For example, ascorbic acid in fruit juices can be polarographically determined.

The Clark voltammetric sensor L C Clark Jr devised a sensor for estimating dissolved oxygen in aqueous solutions. It is actually a voltammetric cell (Fig. 7.37) which consists of a platinum disk cathode working electrode, fixed inside a cylindrical insulator. The anode is a ring-shaped silver metal electrode. The tubular insulator and electrodes are mounted in a second cylinder that contains a buffered electrolyte solution of potassium chloride. A thin (20 nm) oxygen-permeable membrane of Teflon or polyethylene is fixed at the bottom of the tube by an O-ring. When the sensor is immersed in a stirred solution containing dissolved oxygen, the oxygen diffuses through the membrane into the electrolyte; then from the electrolyte it diffuses to the cathode and gets reduced to water. The current produced in this electrode reaction is measured and equated to dissolved oxygen content of the analyte.

7.7.5 Pulse Polarography

The apparatus used for conventional linear polarography is inconvenient. It has poor detection limits and is slow. These limitations are overcome in pulse polarography.

- In pulse polarography, the current is measured at a time when the difference between the desired faradaic current and the interfering charging current is large.
- Pulse polarography is of different types:
  - Normal pulse polarography,
  - Differential pulse polarography,
  - Square wave polarography.

(i) *Normal pulse polarography*: This is the simplest polarographic method. The potential of the dme is held at a constant initial potential except during the last 50–60 milliseconds of its life. During this last period, a pulse of higher potential is applied to the drop. The current is then measured during the last 20 milliseconds of the drop life. The required voltage scan is carried out by gradually increasing the potential applied to each successive drop. In this method, the onset of the pulse is marked at first by a sudden rise in the total current passing in the system. This current is the condenser current which soon decays to zero. The current in the final stages of the drop life is due to the faradaic process;

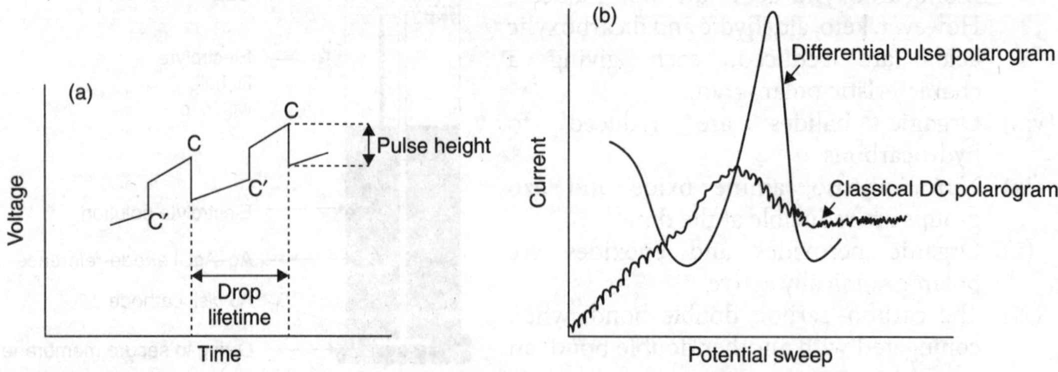

Fig. 7.38 Differential pulse polarography **(a)** Voltage–time graph for pulse wave form **(b)** A typical differential pulse polarogram compared with a classical DC polarogram

this current is proportional to the analyte concentration. The polarogram obtained in this method consists of a *stepped curve* instead of the saw-tooth pattern obtained in the conventional polarogram.

(ii) *Differential pulse polarogoraphy*: In this method, a pulse (say, of 50 mV) is applied during the last 50 milliseconds of the life time of the mercury drop. The pulse and drop are synchronised. Two current measurements are recorded for each mercury drop, one x milliseconds prior to the DC pulse and the other exactly x milliseconds after the DC pulse. To synchronise the pulse with the drop, the drop is detached at an appropriate time by a mechanical means. The difference in current (Δi) per pulse is recorded as a function of the linearly increasing voltage. When the values of Δi are plotted against voltage values, a curve results (Fig. 7.38). It consists of a peak, the height of which is directly proportional to concentration.

7.7.5.1 Advantages of Differential-pulse Polarography

- In this procedure, individual peak maxima can be observed for substances with $E_{1/2}$ values differing by as little as 0.05 V. On the contrary, in conventional polarography, a potential difference of at least 0.2 V is required for resolution of the polarographic waves.
- It is a sensitive method; the detection limits with this method are two to three orders of magnitude lower than those for classical polarography.
- This method offers highly accurate values in the determination of trace concentrations of heavy metal ions.

(iii) *Square wave polarography*: Square wave polarography is a type of pulse polarography. It offers great speed and high sensitivity. The complete polarogram can be recorded in about 10 milliseconds. In this method the scan is done during the last few milliseconds of the life of a single drop of mercury of the dme; during the scan, the charging current is constant. Detection limits for square wave polarography are in the range 10^{-7} to 10^{-8} M. This method is useful for detecting the components separated by liquid chromatography. It is incorporated in detectors for HPLC.

7.8 COULOMETRY

Principle A coulometric analysis is the estimation of a substance by the measurement of the quantity of electricity (the number of coulombs), needed for the quantitative electrochemical reaction of the substance. In this method, the number of coulombs required is measured, and therefore, it is called *coulometry.* The quantity of the reactant is calculated from Faraday's laws of electrolysis. This calculation requires a known current efficiency; that is, the relationship between the number of coulombs of electricity and the number of equivalents of substances oxidised or reduced.

Direct method In direct coulometry, the substance to be determined is oxidised or reduced directly at one of the electrodes. For example, copper can be determined coulometrically at a constant applied voltage. The electrode reactions are the same as when copper is determined by electrogravimetry. The current decreases as the electrolysis proceeds. This decrease is because of decrease in the concentration of copper in solution. When the reduction of copper is complete, the current becomes negligibly small.

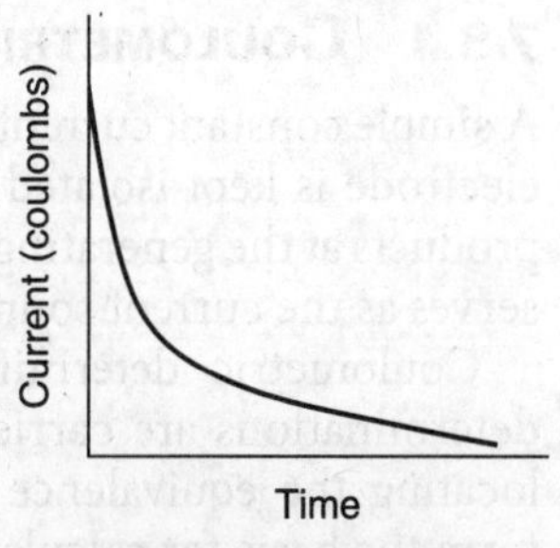

Fig. 7.39 A coulometric current–time curve

The current values are plotted against time (Fig. 7.39). Then, the number of coulombs of electricity can be calculated from the area under the curve, which is proportional to the number of coulombs used.

Indirect methods These methods are actually *coulometric titrations*. In a coulometric titration, a redox 'titrant' is generated at a constant rate by the anodic or cathodic electrolysis of a reagent added to the reaction mixture in high concentration. The generated titrant reacts with the analyte stoichiometrically. The high concentration of the added reagent from which the titrant is generated stabilises the potential of the working electrode and hence prevents side reactions and loss of current efficiency.

Example Iron(II) can be determined by constant current coulometry. Initially, a large excess of cerium(III) solution is added to an acidic solution of the sample. At the working electrode, cerium(III) is oxidised to cerium(IV), which immediately reacts with iron (II):

$$\text{Ce(IV)} + \text{Fe(II)} \rightarrow \text{Ce(III)} + \text{Fe(III)}$$

Because of the availability of a large amount of Ce(III) for oxidation at the anode, the potential is stabilised below that at which cerium(IV) oxidises water to oxygen, and also below that at which O_2 is produced electrolytically. Thus, side reactions are avoided. The equivalence point is determined using a visual indicator. The number of coulombs required to reach the equivalence point is noted, which is proportional to the concentration of Fe(II) in the analyte. The equivalence point can be detected using a potentiometer also.

Other reducing agents, such as arsenic(III), antimony(III), uranium(IV) and hydrazine can be coulometrically estimated. These species can be oxidised by bromine; bromine oxidant is produced electrolytically in the reaction mixture by oxidising bromide ion at a platinum electrode:

$$2\,Br^- \rightarrow Br_2 + 2e^-$$

$$\text{Reducing analyte} + Br_2 \rightarrow \text{products}$$

Phenol can be coulometrically determined by reacting it with the bromine generated; the reaction is actually bromination. Chlorine and iodine can also be generated electrochemically and then made to react with various species in coulometric determinations.

- Indirect coulometric methods are referred to as *coulometric titrations* though no burette and standard solution are used.
- The number of coulombs of electricity required for the reaction is measured, and this is equated to the concentration, applying Faraday's law of electrolysis.

7.8.1 Coulometric Apparatus

A simple constant current coulometric apparatus is depicted in Fig. 7.40. The second (counter) electrode is kept isolated from the sample solution to avoid reoxidation or reduction of the products at the generating electrode or in the sample solution. A constant–voltage transformer serves as the current source.

Coulometric determinations at controlled potential are time consuming. Therefore, determinations are carried out at *constant current.* A known constant current, a means of locating the equivalence point and an electric stopwatch for measuring the time elapsed form the basis for calculating the number of coulombs used for complete reaction (up to the equivalence point), and hence the amount of the analyte. The occurrence of side reactions during analysis in some cases limits the application of the direct method. In such cases, a

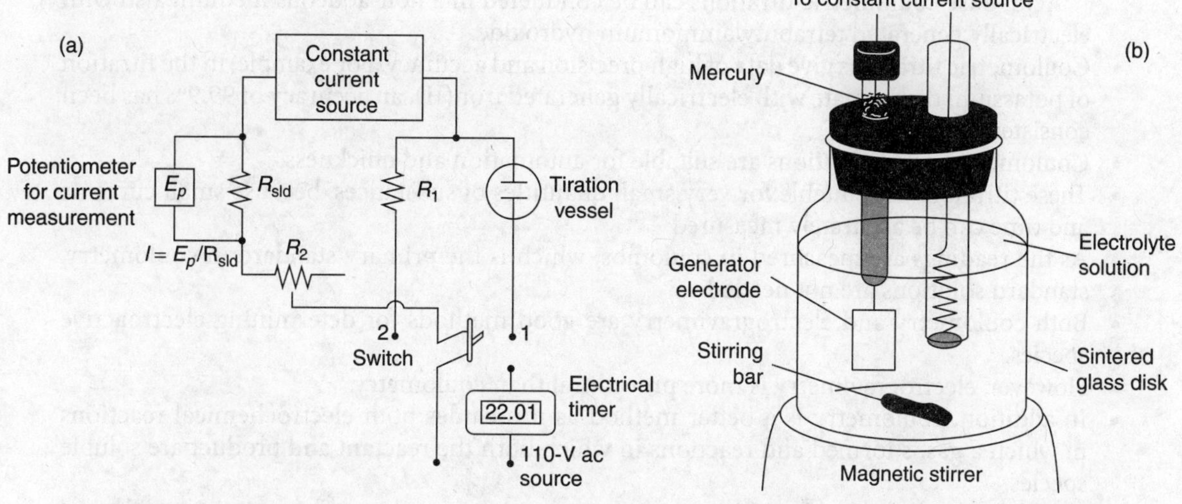

Fig. 7.40 Coulometric apparatus **(a)** Schematic of a coulometric titration **(b)** A typical coulometric titration cell

constant current efficiency cannot be maintained. For example, in the direct coulometric oxidation of iron(II), a side reaction, the oxidation of water to oxygen, occurs; this increases the potential, which does not occur in a constant current method.

Direct coulometric analysis of thin films or plated deposits can be carried out by electrolytic stripping, the reverse of electroplating. The equivalence point in such an analysis is indicated by an inflection in the voltage-time curve.

7.8.2 Advantages of Coulometric Methods

- In the indirect coulometric method, the titrating species is used as soon as it is formed; therefore, the method is suitable for unstable reactants. For example, silver(II), an unstable titrant can be generated by the anodic oxidation of silver(I) and then used to estimate cerium(III) and vanadium(IV).
- Even, complexometric titration by coulometry is possible. For example, the cathodic reduction of Hg(II)–EDTA complex releases EDTA reagent.

  $$\text{Hg–EDTA} + 2e^- \rightarrow \text{Hg}^0 + \text{EDTA}$$

  The electrolytically released EDTA can then be titrated with ions of a metal present in the same electrolytic solution.
- Acid–base titrations with very small amounts of reactants can be accurately conducted using coulometry. An acid can be estimated with electrically generated hydroxide ions. In this method, unlike with the conventional volumetry, the titrant is free from interfering carbonate impurities. An excess of sodium bromide is added to the sample solution. Hydroxide ions are produced at the cathode:

  $$2\,H_2O + 2e^- \rightarrow H_2 + 2\,OH^-$$

  At the anode, Br^- is oxidised. The anode is kept isolated in a tube with a sintered glass disk (Fig. 7.40b) to avoid the interference due to the neutralisation reaction by the anodic oxidation products.

Acid–base coulometric titrations can be conducted in a non-aqueous medium also with electrically generated tetrabutylammonium hydroxide.

- Coulometric titrations give data of high precision and accuracy. For example, in the titration of potassium dichromate with electrically generated iron(II), an accuracy of 99.9% has been consistently achieved.
- Coulometric determinations are suitable for automation and quickness.
- These titrations are suitable for very small quantities of substances, because small currents and time can be accurately measured.
- As the readings are measured in coulombs, which is the primary standard in coulometry, standard solutions are not needed.
- Both coulometry and electrogravimetry are good methods for determining electroactive species.
- However, electrogravimetry is more procedural than coulometry.
- In addition, coulometry is a better method as it includes both electrochemical reactions in which a gas is formed and reactions in which both the reactant and product are soluble species.
- Coulometry offers a method for accurately measuring quantities of species too small to be weighed or titrated by ordinary methods.

7.9 GLOSSARY

Amperometry is measurement of current; the current measured is proportional to the analyte concentration.

Anode (positive electrode) The electrode at which oxidation occurs in an electrochemical cell.

Cathode (negative electrode) The electrode at which reduction occurs in an electrochemical cell.

Cell constant The ratio of the length between the two electrodes and the cross-sectional area of the electrode = l / A.

Cell diagram The notation of representing a galvanic cell indicating

- the nature of the electrodes,
- the nature of the solutions in contact with the electrodes,
- which of the half-cells is the anode and which is the cathode, and
- the reactants and products in each of the half-cells.

Cell potential (E_{cell}) The emf produced by a galvanic cell.

Honour List of Electrochemists

Scientist	*Honour*
Alessandro Volta	Volt unit Voltaic cell Voltmeter
Luigi Galvani	Galvanic cell Galvanic potential Galvanometer Galvanisation
Michael Faraday	Farad unit Faraday paradox Faraday rotation
Georg Ohm	Ohm unit Ohm's law
Charles Coulomb	Coulomb's law Coulomb (Unit for electrical energy)
Andre Marie Ampere	Ampere (Unit for current)

Chemical cell The cell in which the emf is due to a chemical reaction.

Concentration cell The cell in which the emf is due to the free energy decrease consequent to the transfer of matter from one part of the cell to the other.

Conductance (L) The reciprocal of the electrical resistance ($L = I / R$).

Conductometric titrations Titrations carried out by finding endpoints of titrations by monitoring changes in the conductance of reaction mixtures during titrations.

Coulomb (C) The SI unit for electrical charge.

Coulometric titration is a method of determining an analyte by measuring the time required for an electrolytic process at constant current. This method is called also as *titration with electrons.*

Coulometry is the measurement of coulombs (quantity of electricity) to determine an analyte, undergoing an electrochemical reaction.

Electrochemistry The study of relationship between chemical reactions and electricity.

Electrogravimetry is the deposition of a metal onto a weighed platinum cathode and then reweighing to determine the quantity of the metal.

Electrolytic cell A specially-designed apparatus for conducting chemical reactions at electrodes during electrolysis.

Electrolytic conduction The passage of current through a liquid due to the movement of ions.

Electrolytic conductor One in which transfer of charge (current conduction) occurs by migration of ions towards the electrodes.

Electromotive force (emf) The difference of potential which causes a current to flow from the electrode of higher potential to that of lower potential. It is expressed in volts (V). The emf denotes the energy available per coulomb.

Electronic conductor One in which electrical conduction occurs by direct migration of electrons through the conductor under the influence of an applied potential.

Equivalent conductance (Λ_{eq}) of an electrolyte The conductance of a volume of solution containing one equivalent weight of dissolved substance when placed between two parallel plates 1 cm apart, and large enough to contain between them all of the solution. It is never determined directly, but calculated from the specific conductance.

Faraday (F) One unit of electrical charge, which is equal to 96500 coulombs. It denotes the charge on 1 mole of electrons.

1 mole e^- = 96500 C

Galvanic cell or voltaic cell A chemical system involving a spontaneous chemical change which occurs with electron flow though an electrical circuit, generating electricity.

Gibbs–Stockholm convention In this, the half-reaction is always written as a reduction.

Glass electrode An ion selective electrode, sensitive to H^+. It consists of a silver wire covered with a layer of silver chloride that dips into a dilute solution of HCl.

Half-reaction Denotes one half of the reaction in a redox reaction, either oxidation or reduction; no half-reaction can occur in isolation.

Indicator electrode is the one that measures the analyte.

Ion selective electrode is an electrode of the membrane or solid state type whose potential responds selectively to the activity of a particular ion.

Ionic conductance (λ^+, λ^-) The conductance contribution by an ion.

Irreversible cell A cell in which the chemical changes occurring cannot be reversed.

Kohlrausch's law of independent migration of ions At infinite dilution, when dissociation for all the electrolyte molecules is complete and where all interionic effects disappear, each ion migrates independently of its co-ion, and contributes to the total equivalent conductance.

Limiting conductance ($\wedge_\infty$) of an electrolyte Maximum conductance observable at infinite dilution of an electrolyte. It is also called *equivalent conductance* at *infinite dilution*. It is the sum of the ionic conductances at infinite dilution.

Metallic conduction or electronic conduction The passage of electricity through a metal involving only the movement of electrons.

Molar conductance (Λ_M) The conductance of that volume of solution which contains 1 mol of the solute and is placed between two parallel electrodes 1 cm apart, and having sufficient area to hold the whole of the solution.

Nernst equation $E = E^0 - \dfrac{RT}{nf} \ln Q$

Ohm's law $I = E/R$, where I is the strength of a current flowing through a resistance R under an applied potential E.

Overpotential is the additional voltage beyond the decomposition potential; it is the iR drop that must be applied to overcome slow kinetic steps in electrolysis reactions.

Oxidation The loss of electrons; for example, Zn (s) $\rightarrow Zn^{2+} + 2e^-$

pH of a solution The negative logarithm of hydrogen ion concentration

$$pH = -\log [H^+]$$

Polarogram is a plot of current vs dme potential.

Polarography is a special type of voltammetry where the working electrode is a dme.

Potentiometer An instrument used to measure the emf of a cell.

Redox reaction Involves gain of electrons for one species (reduction) and loss of electrons for another species (oxidation). In such a reaction, the total electron loss is equal to the total electron gain.

Reduction potential The measure (in volts) of the intrinsic tendency of a half-reaction to proceed in the direction of reduction. For example, Zn^{2+} (*aq*) + $2e^- \rightarrow$ Zn (*s*). The larger the reduction potential of a half-reaction, the greater is the tendency to undergo reduction.

Reduction The gain of electrons; for example, $Cu^{2+} + 2e^- \rightarrow$ Cu (*s*)

Reference electrodes are metal–metal salt types, the Hg–Hg_2Cl_2 (calomel) and the Ag/AgCl electrodes are the common ones; the potential of a reference electrode is constant.

Reversible cell A cell in which the driving and opposing forces differ only infinitesimally and the chemical change occurring in it is reversible.

Salt bridge A U-shaped tube filled with an electrolyte such as KNO_3 or KCl in gelatin, which allows intermigration of ions between the two half-cells and consequently maintains ionic charge (electrical) balance in the two half-cells.

Saturated calomel electrode A subsidiary reference electrode which consists of mercury in contact with a saturated solution of KCl saturated with Hg_2Cl_2 (calomel).

Single electrode potential The potential of oxidation or reduction occurring in a cell; the algebraic sum of the two individual single electrode potentials of a cell is the total emf of the cell.

Specific conductance (κ) of a conductor The reciprocal of its specific resistivity. It denotes the conductance of 1 cm cube of material; it is expressed in reciprocal ohms or mhos per centimeter.

Specific resistivity (ρ) It depends on and is characteristic of the nature of the conductor.

Standard electrochemical cell A cell which has a reproducible potential constant with time, and well known.

Standard hydrogen electrode (SHE) The electrode of the hydrogen half-cell with the hydrogen gas in its standard state (1 bar pressure) and the hydrogen ion concentration 1 mol dm^{-3} (the pH = 0).

Supporting electrolyte is an 'inert' electrolyte in high concentration that 'swamps out' the attraction or repulsion of the analyte ion at the charged electrode.

The standard cell potential (E°) The cell potential when all ion concentrations in the cell are 1 M, all partial pressures of gases are 1 atm and the temperature of the cell is 25°C.

Volt (V) A measure of the energy that is capable of being extracted from the flowing electric charge.

Voltammetry is electrolysis in which the current is recorded as a function of the potential of the working electrode.

Working electrode is the electrode where the reaction of interest occurs. This will be the cathode if a reduction is being studied or the anode if an oxidation is being studied.

EXERCISES

1. For the galvanic cell Zn (*s*) | Zn^{2+} (0.100 M) ||Pb^{2+} (*x* M) |Pb (*s*), the measured potential is 0.45 V at 25°C. The standard cell potential for this cell is 0.64 V. Calculate the concentration of Pb^{2+}.
2. Calculate the pH of a solution whose potential at 25°C measured with a hydrogen electrode at 768 torr (after correcting for the vapour pressure of water) is –0.35 V (relative to the normal hydrogen electrode).
3. The standard potential of the silver/silver bromide electrode is 0.073 V. What is the solubility product of silver bromide?
4. What is the quantity of electricity required to deposit the copper completely from 100 mL of 0.1 M copper sulphate solution? If a current of 3.0 amp is used for this deposition, what is the time needed for complete deposition?
5. In a coulometric titration of lactic acid [$CH_3CH(OH)COOH$] with coulometrically generated OH^- at a constant current of 20.0 mA, the analyte required 200 seconds for titration. Calculate the amount of lactic acid present in the sample.
6. An organic compound on polarographic analysis produced a cathodic wave at $E_{1/2} = -0.42$ V versus the SCE. Explain how the number of electrons *n* involved in the cathodic wave can be determined. What parameters of the polarographic system should be known for finding the value of *n*.
7. Outline a coulometric proceduce for determining (a) Fe(III) (b) Ce(IV) and (c) oxine.
8. 50 mL of 0.100 M Fe^{2+} solution in 1.00 M $HClO_4$ is titrated with 0.010 M $Cr_2O_7^{2-}$ solution. Calculate the potential in the solution (vs SHE) at 10, 20, 40 and 50 mL titrant added.
9. A test solution of lead(II) has a limiting current of 6.02 μA. To 10.0 mL of this test solution, 1.0 mL of a 1.00×10^{-3} M lead(II) solution is added; the limiting current of the mixture is 11.5 μA. Calculate the concentration of lead(II) in the test solution.

8 Polarimetry

8.1 INTRODUCTION

Polarimetry is a method of chemical analysis based on the optical activity of the substance being determined. This method can be used for both organic and inorganic materials.

There are many molecules whose structures are not superimposable on their mirror images since these molecules lack symmetry in their structure. The molecule and its non-superimposable mirror image counterpart are known as enantiomers. Their properties are identical except in one physical property—they rotate the plane of plane polarised light to the same degree but in opposite directions. Such compounds are known as *optical isomers.* For example, (+) lactic acid and (–) lactic acid are optical isomers (*enantiomers*). The optical rotation value (the extent of rotation of the plane polarised light) depends upon the number of molecules that the plane polarised light comes across as it passes through the solution. This value also depends on the wavelength of the light used and the temperature.

Invention of Polarimetry

- Polarimetry was invented by E L Malus (1775–1812), a French engineer.
- Another Frenchman J B Biot (1774–1862), found that molecules such as sugar could rotate polarised light.
- In 1874, the Dutch chemist J H van't Hoff proposed that the tetrahedral structure of carbon compounds was responsible for the optical activity.

8.2 PLANE POLARISED LIGHT

Ordinary light is one in which the electric and magnetic vectors vibrate in all possible orientations perpendicular to the line of propagation; this is said to be non-polarised (Fig. 8.1a). Ordinary non-polarised light can be converted into plane-polarised light (in which the vectors vibrate in only one plane) by passing it through a polarised or calcite material (Fig. 8.1b). Plane polarised light is composed of two components—left and right-circularly polarised light (Fig. 8.2). The vectors representing left- and right-circularly polarised light are shown in a different way in Fig. 8.3. The resultant sum is also shown in the same figure.

The two components of the plane polarised light travel with the same velocity in an optically inactive material. The optically inactive material has the same refractive index for both the components of light. But in the case of optically active compounds, the two components of the plane polarised light travel with different velocities in the medium. This phenomenon is known as *circular*

(a) (b)

Fig. 8.1 (a) Non-polarised light (b) Polarised light

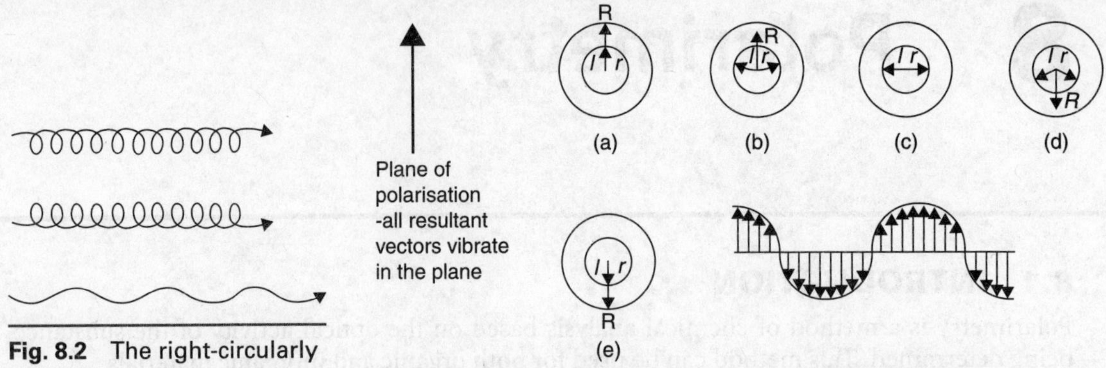

Fig. 8.2 The right-circularly and left-circularly polarised lights and their resultant

Fig. 8.3 The resultant of the left- and the right-circularly polarised lights

birefringence. The optically active compound is said to be *circularly birefringent*, that is, it has different refractive indices for left- and right-circularly polarised light. Since the two components travel with different velocities in the medium, when they come out of it, they begin to vibrate in a plane which is different from the original plane. If the left-circularly polarised light travels faster than the right-circularly polarised light, the resultant will still vibrate in a plane but it will be tilted to the left of the original plane by an angle α (Fig. 8.4). The angle of rotation is given by the equation,

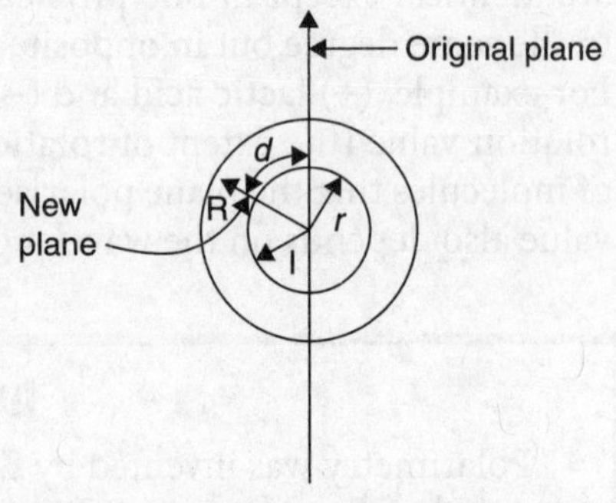

Fig. 8.4 Optical rotation due to circular birefringence

$$\alpha = \frac{(n_r - n_l)\pi}{\lambda}$$

where n_r and n_l are the refractive indices of the medium for the right and left-circularly polarised light and λ is the wavelength of the light employed. The compounds which allow the right-circularly polarised light to travel faster through them than the left-circularly polarised light are known as *dextrorotatory* and have positive α-values; compounds which allow the left-circularly polarised component to travel faster through them are known as *laevorotatory* and have negative α-values.

If the optically active medium absorbs one of the components of the light more than the other, then due to unequal absorption, the resultant vector sum will trace an elongated ellipse and the light is said to be *elliptically polarised* (Fig. 8.5). This phenomenon is known as *circular dichroism.*

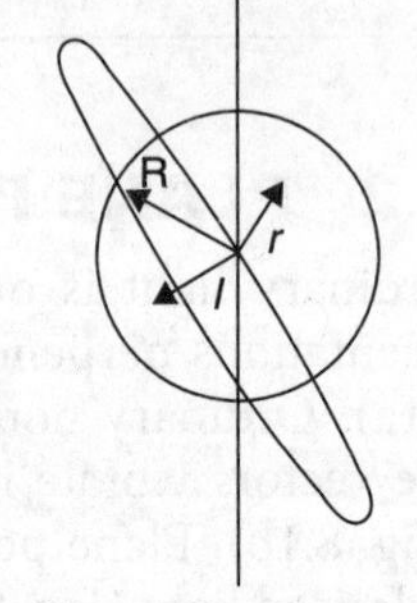

Fig. 8.5 Elliptically polarised light

8.2.1 Factors that Determine the Angle of Rotation

For a given substance, the angle of rotation depends upon the following factors:

- nature of the optically active substance,
- nature of the solvent,

- the length of the column through which light passes,
- the concentration (or density) of the solution,
- the temperature,
- the presence of traces of optically active impurities, and
- the wavelength of light used.

8.3 INSTRUMENTATION

A polarimeter is used to measure the angle of rotation of an optically active compound. There are four principal components in a polarimeter (Fig. 8.6).

(i) *The light source*: This consists of incandescent gaseous sodium metal, which produces monochromatic light of wavelength 589 nm (the sodium D line).
(ii) *Nicol prism*: This consists of two optically pure calcite crystal prisms joined together. This is known as the polariser.
(iii) *Glass tube*: In this tube, the sample is taken either as a neat liquid or as a solution.
(iv) *A second Nicol prism*: This is rotatable and is attached with a vernier scale which measures the angle of rotation in degrees. This prism is known as the analyser.

The light from the sodium lamp vibrates in the *x*, *y* and *z* planes. This non-polarised light enters the polariser and becomes plane polarised light. This plane polarised light passes through the optically active solution and is rotated by an angle α. The light will not be seen by the viewer unless the analyser prism is rotated through an angle α. The scale attached to the analyser records the angle of rotation in degrees.

The light emerging from the analyser can be detected either visually or by a photocell. A comparison of the angular orientation of the analyser as measured with the empty cell and then with the cell filled with solution will give a measure of the rotation of the polarised light by the sample.

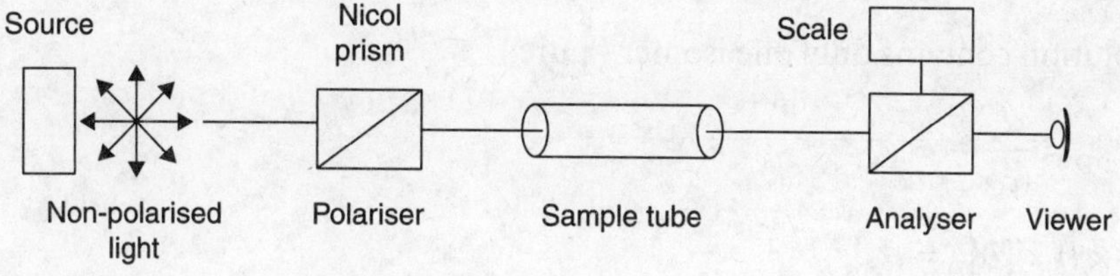

Fig. 8.6 Polarimeter: a schematic diagram

8.3.1 LIGHT SOURCES IN A POLARIMETER

Traditionally, a mercury or deuterium lamp was used as the light source. Now, other light sources such as xenon, tungsten and halogen, with appropriate filters are used in polarimeters. These sources are less expensive than deuterium and in addition have a long life and also broad wavelength emission range.

The degree of optical rotation depends upon the cell length l and the concentration of the solution c in grams per millilitre of solution. The specific rotation at 20°C, using sodium light, is then given by

$$[\alpha]_D^{20} = \frac{\alpha}{lc}$$

where l = length in decimeter, c = concentration in g/ml, α = experimentally observed rotation in degrees.

- Polarimetry may be applied to either qualitative or quantitative investigations.
- The calculation of the specific rotation helps to identify the unknown substance.
- The concentration of a given optically active material can be calculated from its specific rotation.

Problem 8.1 The observed rotation is +9.3° for a solution which has a concentration of 15 g in 100 ml of solution, in a 20.0 cm long tube. Calculate the specific rotation.

$$l = 20\text{ cm} = 2.0\text{ dm} \quad c = \frac{15}{100} = 0.15\text{ g/ml}$$

Therefore, $$[\alpha]_D = \frac{9.3}{(2.0 \times 0.15)} = +31°$$

The molecular rotation $[\phi]$ is given by

$$[\phi] = \frac{[\alpha]_D M}{100}$$

where $[\alpha]$ is specific rotation and M is the molecular weight of the optically active compound.

Enantiomeric excess (EE) The difference between the percentages of two mirror-image isomers present in a solution is called enantiomeric excess.

% EE = % of major isomer – % of minor isomer

When a solution contains only one isomer ('pure'),

$$[\alpha]_D = \frac{\alpha_{obs}}{(c \times l)}$$

$$\therefore \quad (c \times l) \times [\alpha]_D = \alpha_{obs}$$

Assume that for a pure solution the observed specific rotation is +40°, then, for a mixture containing 60% of the (+) form and 40% of the (–) form, the specific rotation will be

$$0.2 \times 40 = 8°$$

(as EE = 60 – 40 = 20 = 0.2 fraction). From the measurement of the optical rotation, the isomeric composition can be calculated.

8.4 OPTICAL ROTATORY DISPERSION

The variation of optical rotation with the wavelength of the light is termed Optical Rotatory Dispersion (ORD). The plot of rotation values *versus* wavelength (λ) results in ORD curves. There are two different types of ORD curves—*plain curves* and *Cotton effect curves* (anomalous curves).

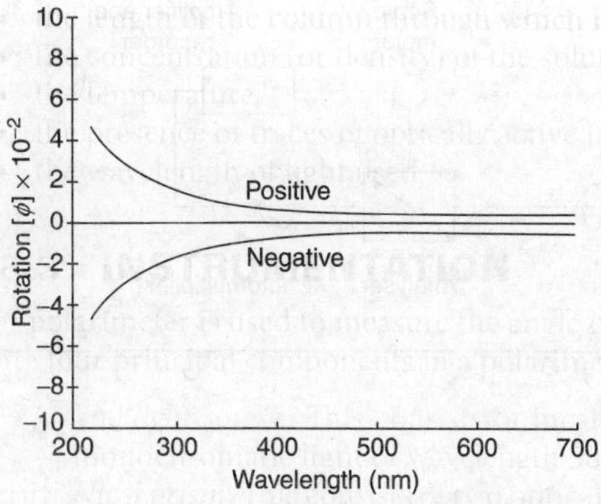

Fig. 8.7 ORD—Plain curves

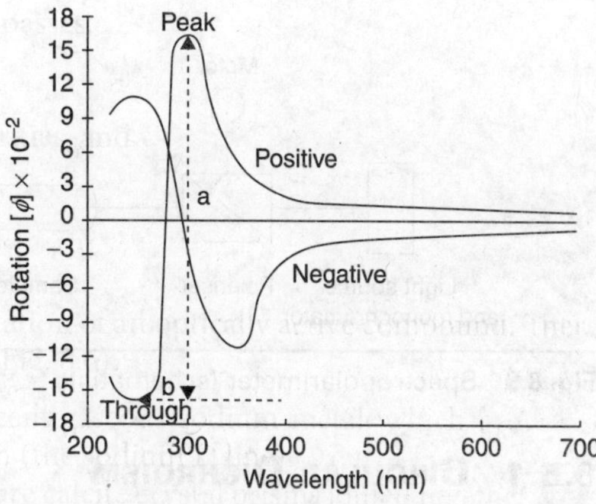

Fig. 8.8 ORD—Cotton effect curves

8.4.1 Plain Curves

Plain curves are obtained when the compound under study has no absorption band within the wavelength region used. Plain curves are further classified into positive and negative curves. If the rotation of the compound becomes positive as the wavelength of the light is decreased, then it is known as a positive plain curve and if it becomes negative with decreasing wavelength, it is known as a negative plain curve (Fig. 8.7).

8.4.2 Cotton Effect Curves (Anomalous Curves)

If the optically active compound absorbs some portion of light in the wavelength region used, then Cotton effect curves result. These curves exhibit two extrema known *as maxima* and *minima* (Fig. 8.8).

On approaching from the longer wavelength regions to the shorter wavelength regions, if a peak is obtained first it is known as *positive cotton effect curve* and if a trough is obtained first it is known as *negative cotton effect curve;* the vertical distance from the peak to the trough is known as amplitude *a*, and the horizontal distance is known as breadth *b* of the curve.

8.5 SPECTROPOLARIMETRY

A spectropolarimeter is designed to give data both on light absorption and optical rotation by a molecule. Certain molecules having *symmetrical functional groups* attached to *asymmetric centres* absorb light in the visible and ultraviolet regions. Such molecules give rise to Cotton effect curves. For example, molecules with azide, xanthate, nitrate, dithiocarbonate, sulphoxide, conjugated double bonds, carbonyl group and heterocyclic aromatic groups behave like this. The change in position of attachment of these groups in a molecule has dramatic effect on the ORD curve. For example, different ORD curves are obtained for cholestan-1-one and cholestan-2-one. Such curves, in conjunction with spectral data are useful for characterising certain molecules.

ORD measurements are taken in a spectropolarimeter (Fig. 8.9). ORD studies are generally used in the determination of absolute configuration if the conformation is known and for the determination of the conformation if the absolute configuration is known for a compound.

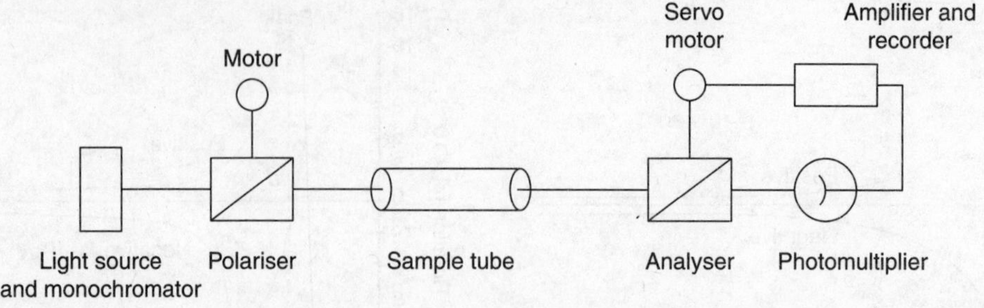

Fig. 8.9 Spectropolarimeter (schematic)

8.5.1 Circular Dichroism

As indicated earlier, circular dichroism is the result of differential absorption of right and left circularly polarised light by the sample and it can be measured in terms of either the difference in absorption or by the extent of ellipticity of the polarised beam. It gives almost the same kind of stereochemical information as ORD and since its effect is only seen in the region of the absorption band, its use is more specific than ORD. Circular dichroism has been applied mainly to distinguish *cis* and *trans* isomers in steroids. For example, 3-keto-5α-steroids (A/B *trans* ring fusion) and 3-keto-5β-steroids (A/B cis ring fusion) can be distinguished by means of their respective circular dichroism curves, molar ellipticity versus wavelength (Fig. 8.10).

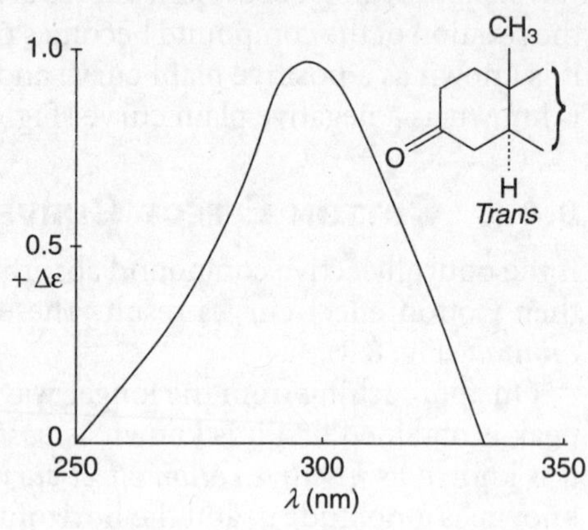

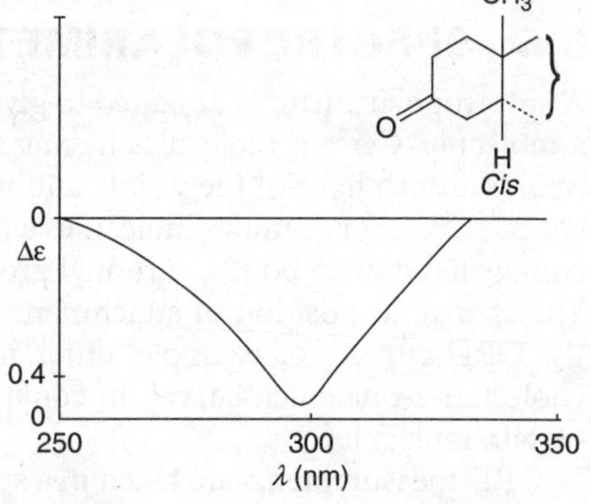

Fig. 8.10 Distinguishable curves showing circular dichroism of *trans* and *cis* monoketo steroids

- For wavelengths that are absorbed by the optically active sample, the two circularly polarised components will be absorbed to different extents. Such an unequal absorption is known as CD. CD causes incident linearly polarised light to become elliptically polarised.
- ORD and CD are related, just like ordinary absorption and dispersion are. If the entire optical rotatory dispersion spectrum is known, the circular dichroism spectrum can be calculated, and vice versa.
- ORD and CD are known as *chiroptical properties.*
- ORD curves are useful in the determination of conformations. For example, the chair and boat conformations of cyclohexanes, the two interconvertible chair forms of substituted cyclohexanes, and the axial and equatorial conformations of substituents in steroid molecules have all been studied by ORD curves.
- Rotary dispersion curves are useful in establishing the presence of carbonyl groups in compounds in which their presence is difficult to prove by chemical means; for example in 11-oxosteroids. Similarly, acetoxyl and carbonyl

groups are difficult to distinguish by spectrophotometry, but can be clearly recognised by different ORD curves.

8.6 APPLICATION OF OPTICAL ROTATION METHOD IN THE DETERMINATION OF RATE CONSTANTS

8.6.1 KINETIC POLARIMETRY

The kinetics of reactions involving changes in optical rotation with time during reactions can be studied by polarimetry. Such methods are called kinetic polarimetry. The measurement of optical rotation against time is called *rotography*. The change in rotation is related to the concentration of one of the species in the reacting solution and therefore rate data may be evaluated by kinetic polarimetry. Enzyme-catalysed reactions of natural products can be conveniently studied by this technique.

Acid-catalysed mutarotation of glucose The conversion of α-glucose to β-glucose is an example of mutarotation:

$$\alpha\text{-glucose} \rightleftharpoons \beta\text{-glucose}$$

The acid-catalysed mutarotation of glucose is a first order reaction. The specific rotations of α- and β-glucose are +110° and +19° respectively. On standing, either of the pure isomers gives an equilibrium mixture of the α and β-forms with a specific rotation of 52.5°. The change in value of specific rotation is known as mutarotation. This means that during conversion of either α or β-glucose into a mixture of the two, the optical rotation changes with time. This provides a method for following the reaction.

A 20% solution of glucose in 0.2 N hydrochloric acid is taken in the polarimeter tube. The angle of rotation is noted after every two minutes for a period of half an hour. The final reading is taken after two hours. If α_0 is the initial angle of rotation, α_t is the angle of rotation at time t, and α_∞ is the final angle of rotation, then $(\alpha_0 - \alpha_\infty)$ is proportional to a and $(\alpha_t - \alpha_\infty)$ is proportional to $(a - x)$. The rate constant for this reaction is given by,

$$k_1 = \frac{2.303}{t} \log \frac{a}{a-x}$$

$$k_1 = \frac{2.303}{t} \log \frac{(\alpha_0 - \alpha_\infty)}{(\alpha_t - \alpha_\infty)}$$

Hence a plot of log $(\alpha_t - \alpha_\infty)$ versus t is linear; from the slope k_1 can be calculated.

Inversion of cane sugar The hydrolysis of cane sugar with dilute acids gives an equimolecular mixture of D(+) glucose and D(–) fructose. This is also a pseudo first order reaction. When water is taken in large excess, its concentration will remain almost constant during the reaction. Cane sugar is dextrorotatory and the mixture of glucose and fructose is laevorotatory. Hence the reaction can be followed by measuring the optical rotation of the solution at various time intervals.

$$\underset{\text{Cane sugar}}{C_{12}H_{22}O_{11}} + H_2O \xrightarrow{H^+} \underset{\text{Glucose}}{C_6H_{12}O_6} + \underset{\text{Fructose}}{C_6H_{12}O_6}$$

A 20% cane sugar solution and 1.0 N hydrochloric acid solution are kept in a constant temperature bath. When both the solutions have attained the temperature of the bath,

20 ml of cane sugar solution is mixed with an equal volume of hydrochloric acid in a separate vessel, shaken well and the mixture immediately transferred into a polarimeter tube with a thermostatic arrangement. The optical rotation value is noted immediately and also at the end of every twenty minutes for about three hours. The final reading can be taken after 24 hours. If the initial angle of rotation is α_0, at a time t, α_t and the final value α_∞, then $(\alpha_0 - \alpha_\infty)$ is proportional to the initial concentration of cane sugar and $(\alpha_t - \alpha_\infty)$ is proportional to the concentration of unreacted cane sugar after the time interval t. Then, the rate constant k_1 is given by the expression,

$$k_1 = \frac{2.303}{t} \log \left[\frac{\alpha_0 - \alpha_\infty}{(\alpha_t - \alpha_\infty)} \right]$$

From this expression, k_1 can be calculated.

8.6.2 Relative Strengths of Two Acids

The strengths of two acids can be compared by following the kinetics of hydrolysis of cane sugar. Since the reaction is catalysed by acids, the rate of the reaction is directly proportional to the concentration of the acids used. Two reactions are carried out under identical conditions; one with acid HCl(1) and the other with the acid HCl(2). The rate constants for these two reactions are determined.

Rate constant for the first reaction k_1, is proportional to $C_{HCl(l)}$

Rate constant for the second reaction k_2 is proportional to $C_{HCl(2)}$

$$\frac{k_1}{k_2} = \frac{C_{HCl(1)}}{C_{HCl(2)}}$$

From this, the relative strengths of two acids, HCl(1) and HCl(2), can be calculated.

8.7 POLARIMETRY IN CARBOHYDRATE CHEMISTRY

Polarimetry is widely used in studying the chemistry of carbohydrates. Sugar solutions can be analysed by polarimetry and accurate chemical data on them obtained. The molecular configurations of carbohydrates and also those of other organic molecules greatly influence the biological activities of these compounds; therefore, polarimetry is a useful tool in biochemical research on carbohydrates.

The information obtained by ORD has shown that minor changes in configuration of a molecule markedly alter its dispersion properties. Based on the properties of compounds of known configuration, the absolute configurations of some other molecules can be determined; thus, the various isomers of a molecule can be identified by ORD data.

ORD data are applied for understanding the nature and role of sugar, steroids, amino acids, polypeptides and proteins.

8.7.1 Saccharimetry

Saccharimetry is the determination of sugar solutions of high concentrations. A saccharimeter uses white light and can be used only with sugar solutions (a polarimeter is operated with sharply monochromatic light). In visible light, quartz has almost the same rotatory dispersion as sucrose. This fact is applied in fabricating a saccharimeter. By positioning a quartz wedge in the light path, a variable light path through quartz is obtained. When measuring the concentration of a sugar solution, the wedge is pushed into a point where it exactly compensates the rotation by sugar solution. The linear displacement of the wedge is measured, which is calibrated and directly related to sugar concentration. In a saccharimeter, the analyser and the polariser are kept fixed in orientation; only the light path length is varied.

A potassium dichromate filter is used to compensate for the minor difference between the rotatory dispersion of quartz and of sugar. Saccharimeters are used to measure *sugar degrees* (°S), an internationality accepted scale for expressing sugar concentrations.

A pure sucrose solution containing 26 grams of sucrose in 100 ml of pure water at 20°C measured in a saccharimeter with a light path length of 200 mm with white light and potassium dichromate filter is assigned a sugar degree of 100. It is denoted as 100°S.

- Polarimetry is a sensitive non-destructive technique for measuring the optical activity exhibited by inorganic or organic compounds.
- A compound is considered to be optically active if linearly polarised light is rotated when passing through it.
- Visual saccharimeters are known as *polaroscopes.*

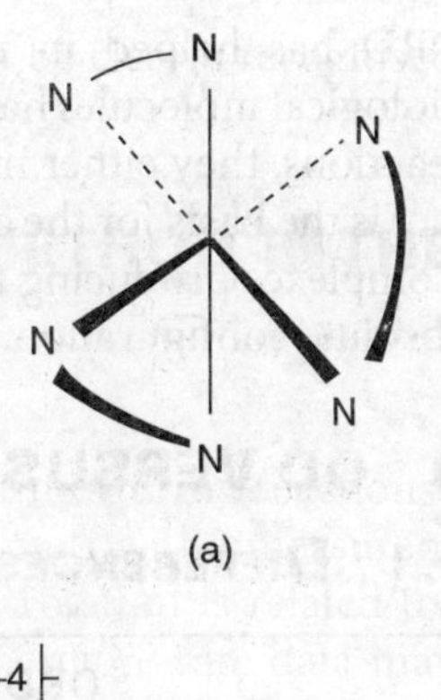

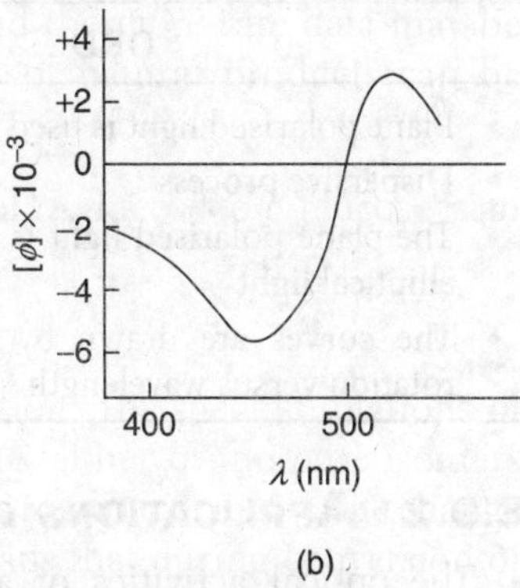

Fig. 8.11 (a) The absolute configuration **(b)** ORD spectrum of ∧-$[Co(en)_3]^{3+}$

8.8 ORD AND METAL COMPLEXES

ORD has been used to find out the absolute configuration of metal complexes.

- If in analogous metal complexes, corresponding electronic transitions show Cotton effects of the same sign, the complexes have the same optical configuration.
- If the complex is initially laevorotatory, the ORD curve falls to a minimum, rises rapidly to a maximum, and then slowly falls. If the complex is initially dextrorotatory, the effect is reversed with the ORD curve rising first to a maximum, then falling, and so on. These denote positive and negative cotton effects respectively.

The ${}^1A_{1g} \rightarrow {}^1T_{1g}$ transition holds only for perfect O_h symmetry and so the ${}^1T_{1g}$ level is split into ${}^1A_2$ and ${}^1E$. Therefore, there are two transitions, ${}^1A_1 \rightarrow {}^1E$ and ${}^1A_1$ to ${}^1A_2$. For example, tris(ethylenediamine) cobalt(III) has D_3 symmetry and so the ${}^1T_{1g}$ level is split into ${}^1A_2$ and ${}^1E$. Since the trigonal compound is small, a separate band for each transition cannot be distinguished in the ordinary absorption spectrum. However, the two transitions do follow different selection rules and can be distinguished in CD spectra.

Complex	ν (cm⁻¹)	$\varepsilon_l - \varepsilon_r$	Absolute configuration
(+)-$[Co(en)_3]^{3+}$	20280	+2.18	∧
	23310	−0.20	
(−)-$[Co(en)_3]^{3+}$	20280	−2.18	Δ
	23310	+0.20	

- ORD has helped in understanding several aspects of enzyme stereochemistry. Most biological molecules have one or more chiral centres. When they undergo enzyme-catalysed reactions, they either maintain or reverse the chirality at one or more of these centres. This fact is the basis for the application of ORD and CD in the study of such biological reactions.
- Complexes producing the same sign of CD for a particular absorption band have the same absolute configuration.

8.9 OD VERSUS CD

8.9.1 Differences between ORD and CD

ORD	CD
• Plane polarised light is used	• Circularly polarised light is used
• Dispersive process	• Absorptive process
• The plane polarised light is not converted to elliptical light	• The circularly polarised light used is converted to ellipticity
• The curves are drawn by plotting specific rotation versus wavelength	• The curves are drawn by platting rolar ellipticity versus wavelength

8.9.2 Applications of ORD and CD

- The optical activities of amino acids, polypeptides, proteins, steroids, antibiotics and terpenes have been determined.
- The stereochemistry of aliphatic amino acids has been established based on their unique Cotton effect.
- The stereochemistry of steroids has been established unequivocally based on specific rotation measurements; in one form of a steroid, the specific rotation increases with decreasing wavelength (positive curve) while in the other form, it decreases with increasing wavelength (negative curve).

8.9.3 Specific Applications of ORD

- As specific rotation is a reliable measure of concentration, ORD is applied in quantitative analysis.
- It is applied in the assignment of absolute configurations.
- Conformational studies can be made with this technique.
- Cotton effect data can be used to derive information on equilibrium systems; the extent of reaction and the speed of attainment of equilibrium can be ascertained.

8.10 FARADAY EFFECT

In the absence of magnetic fields, only chiral substances exhibit ORD and CD. In a magnetic field, even substances that have no chiral centres rotate the plane of polarised light. This behaviour, first proved by M Faraday is called the *Faraday effect* or *magnetic optical rotation.* The wavelength dependence of the Faraday effect is known as *magnetic optical rotatory dispersion.* Also, in regions of absorption, magnetic circular dichroism is possible.

Optical rotation is an indispensable quality and identity assay for a wide range of chemicals in several industries. Organic chemists test the effectiveness of catalysts in asymmetric synthetic processes. Food, drug and flavour industries apply polarimetry as a quality control method for raw materials and finished products. Polymer industries also use this method for charactersing biopolymers and synthetic polymers.

- Cotton curves were first described by the French Physician Aimé Cotton (1869–1951).
- Carl Djerassi (USA) and William Klyne (USA) classified the ORD curves into plain curves and Cotton effect (anomalous) curves.
- W Moffett (USA) first formulated the *octant rules* connecting the sign of the Cotton effect with absolute configurations studying cyclohexanone derivatives.

EXERCISES

1. The (+) enantiomer of a compound X has an optical rotation of 100°. A sample of X has an optical rotation of 65°, what is the composition of the sample?
2. The pure (+) enantiomer of a compound shows an optical rotation of 22°. If a sample of this compound contains 40% of the (+) enantiomer and 50% of the (–) enantiomer what is its optical rotation?
3. A compound synthesised in a laboratory was analysed to be 100% pure. A solution of 0.05 g of this compound in 2.0 ml of methanol was contained in a 1.0 dm cell. Three polarimetric readings, 1.12°, 0.920° and 0.890° were then recorded.
   (a) Calculate its $[\alpha]$.
   (b) What is its EE?

9 Spectroanalytical Techniques: Atomic Absorption Spectroscopy, Flame Emission Spectrometry

9.1 INTRODUCTION

The use of optical emission or absorption in analytical estimations is a very popular method, as would have been and will be observed in the many discussions in this book. The optical process can be broadly classified into molecular and atomic absorption (or emission). The major difference between the two processes is that molecular absorption (or emission) bands are generally broad, with bandwidths being typically in nanometres. The rather large widths of the molecular transitions are generally due to the overlap of the many rotational–vibrational (rovibronic) transitions in the electronic transitions. The atomic transitions in the gas phase, on the other hand have relatively small widths, with typical atomic linewidths being fractions of nanometres, as atomic species do not have any rovibronic transitions to contend with. The operative word here is *gas phase*, as the linewidths in solution and solid phases are broad and the advantage of narrow linewidths is obtainable only in gas phase experiments. The narrow linewidths of the atomic transitions can be used to advantage to differentiate two atomic species that have closely lying electronic transitions. For example, the atomic transitions of atomic Fe and B occur around 249.2 and 249.7 nm. The wavelength at which the atomic transitions occur can be determined by quantum chemical techniques, which will not be discussed here, as it is beyond the scope of this book.

9.2 ABSORPTION AND EMISSION SPECTROMETRY

In a spectrochemical analysis, two modes are used to probe the elemental concentration—absorption and emission. In absorption, light of an appropriate frequency that is resonant with an atomic transition of the species in question, is incident on the sample and attenuation of light intensity due to absorption is measured. This attenuation in intensity is related to the concentration of the analyte through the Beer–Lambert law. Alternatively, in emission spectroscopy, the atomic sample is excited and the emission that results when the excited atomic species returns to the ground state is measured. The intensity of the atomic emission is related to the analyte concentration.

History of AA Methods

Alan Walsh

- Kirchoff (German) and Bunsen (German) in 1860 first conducted experiments on spectrochemical analysis.
- Alan Walsh (Melbourne, 1916–1998) first described the AAS method using a prototype double beam absorption spectrometer.
- The first commercial AA spectrometer was developed and sold by Perkin–Elmer.
- Flame emission spectroscopy became very popular in 1955.
- Dramatic modernisation of AA method was effected in 1976 by applying computer technology to instrumental analyses.

Source: By CSIRO, CC BY 3.0, https://commons.wikimedia.org/w/index.php?curid=35442780

9.2.1 Term States and Spectral Transitions in Atoms

It would be instructive at this point to consider, as an example, the energy levels of the alkali atoms, to understand the excitation/emission schemes encountered in these experiments. The alkali atoms have an outer electronic configuration of ns^1, which corresponds to a ground state, with a term symbol, $^2S_{1/2}$. A term symbol is designated as $^{2S+1}L_J$, where L is the total orbital angular momentum, which for the S state is 0. The S in the 2*S*+1 (in the superscript), refers to the spin angular momentum, and *J* to the total angular momentum. Elementary textbooks on spectroscopy may be consulted for methods to derive term symbols, given an electron configuration. On excitation, the outer electron can be excited to the first higher energy orbital n*p*^{1}, which corresponds to a term state ^{2}P. Due to the coupling of the spin and orbital motion, the ^{2}P state splits into two spin-orbit doublets, $^2P_{1/2}$ and $^2P_{3/2}$. The subscript, as explained earlier, refers to the value of the total orbital angular momentum quantum number *J*. In the case of alkali metals, where the occupied *p* level in the excited state is less than half full (that is, a *p*^{1} configuration), the term state with the lower *J* turns out to be lower in energy. These energy levels for Li and Na are shown as an energy level diagram in Fig. 9.1. The difference in energy between the two spin-orbit components is a function of the atomic number *Z*, of the element; the higher *Z* elements show a larger spin-orbit splitting. The absorption in the alkali atom therefore would correspond to the atomic transition $^2S_{1/2} \rightarrow {}^2P_{1/2}$ and $^2S_{1/2} \rightarrow {}^2P_{3/2}$.

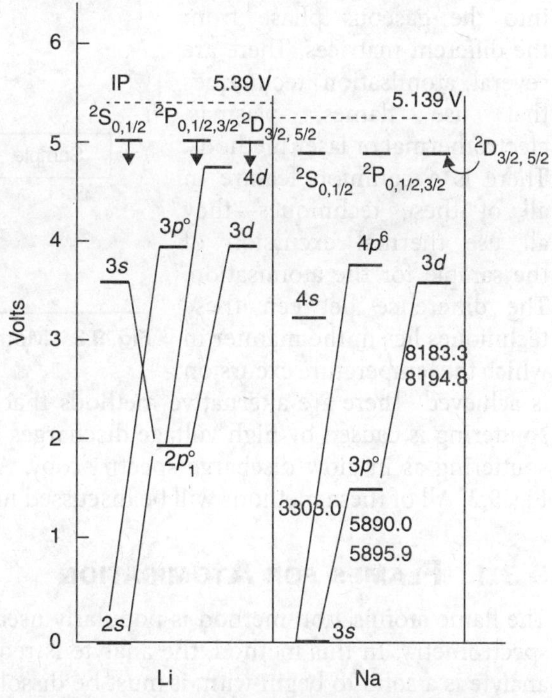

Fig. 9.1 Energy level diagram for Li and Na

Likewise, emission from the excited level of the alkali atoms would be the reverse of the above transitions; $^2S_{1/2}\leftarrow^2P_{1/2}$ and $^2S_{1/2}\leftarrow^2P_{3/2}$. The doublet in the atomic emission of sodium, at 589.0 and 589.6 nm, are the transitions from the two closely spaced spin orbit doublets. There are many compilations that list the important atomic transitions, their wavelengths, term state assignment and their intensities [1]. These compilations can be consulted when deciding on the atomic transition to be used for a spectrochemical exercise.

9.3 ATOMISATION METHODS

In atomic spectroanalytical experiments, the strategy is to bring the analyte atoms into the gas phase. As mentioned earlier, it is in the gas phase that the advantage of small linewidths can be obtained. There are a number of methods that are used for the atomisation process which we shall discuss. The analyte may be in the form of a solution or a solid to begin with, and the atomisation process must be so designed to bring the analyte into the gaseous phase from the different matrices. There are several atomisation techniques that use flames, plasmas, electrothermal or laser methods. There is a common feature in all of these techniques—they all use thermal excursion of the sample for the atomisation. The difference between these techniques lies in the manner in which the temperature excursion is achieved. There are alternative methods that use atom sputtering for atomisation. Atom sputtering is caused by high voltage discharges such as in spark source spectroscopy or ion sputtering as in glow discharge spectroscopy. A summary of these techniques is shown in Fig. 9.2. All of these methods will be discussed in this chapter.

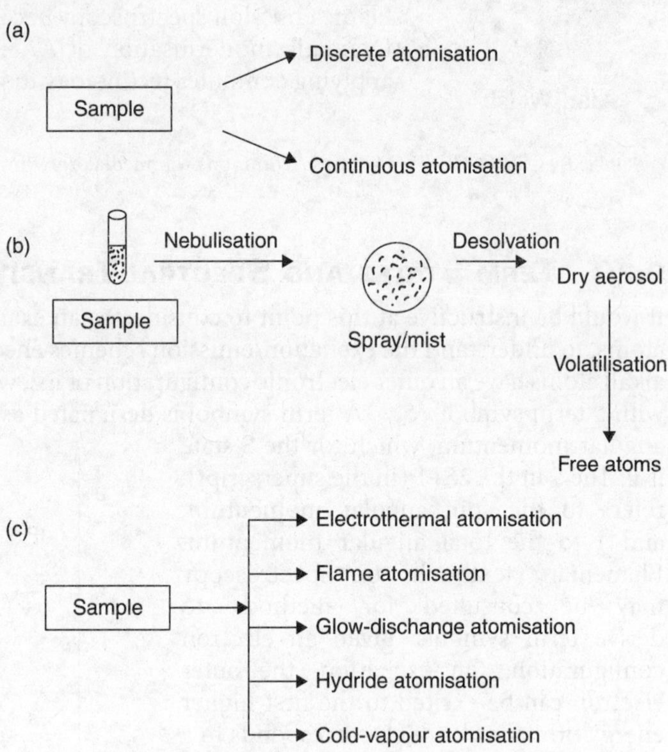

Fig. 9.2 Methods of atomisation of samples in AAS

9.3.1 Flames for Atomisation

The flame atomisation method is popularly used in atomic absorption and atomic emission spectrometry. In this method, the analyte is required to be in the form of a solution. If the analyte is a solid to begin with, it must be dissolved or digested to bring it into solution. For this solution to be fed into the flame where it can be atomised, a nebuliser is used. A nebuliser is a device that converts the solution into a mist – very much like the one used in deodorant or insecticide sprays – it is this mist that is introduced into the flame for atomisation. The nebuliser that is commonly employed for this purpose is the concentric tube nebuliser

(Fig. 9.3). In this nebuliser, a high pressure gas flows through the outer tube while the analyte solution flows through the central capillary tube. As a result of the high flow of the gas through the outer tube, the solution is sucked up due to the Bernoulli effect and exits through the tip of the capillary. The solution that exits from the capillary is broken up into small droplets and is then introduced into the flame. For the operation of the flame, a fuel and an oxidant are required. The oxidant is usually sent at high flow through the outer concentric tube and serves the dual purpose of nebulising the sample and also as an oxidant. The sample aerosol mixed with the oxidant enters the flame burner where it is mixed with the fuel and the flame is ignited. The flame burner that is usually employed is the laminar flow burner. A number of baffles are placed in this burner through which the oxidant/sample aerosol and the fuel pass through. The baffles allow only the finest droplets to pass through while the larger drops are drained out and collected in a container. The fine droplets are then led through the burner which is shaped in the form of a slot where it is ignited to form the flame. Figure 9.4 shows the construction of a laminar flow burner. It is this flame that serves as the atom reservoir for atomic absorption or emission spectrometry.

To understand the role of the flame in the atomisation process, it is important to understand the flame structure and the different zones constituting the flame (Fig. 9.5). The sample aerosol mixture enters at the bottom of the flame where the solvent evaporates. The desolvated particles then enter the central and hottest part of the flame where they are converted to gaseous atoms and, to a lesser extent, to ions. The temperature in this region is hot enough to cause some excitation of the atoms too and this forms the basis of emission spectrometry. It is in this region of the flame where the actual spectrometric

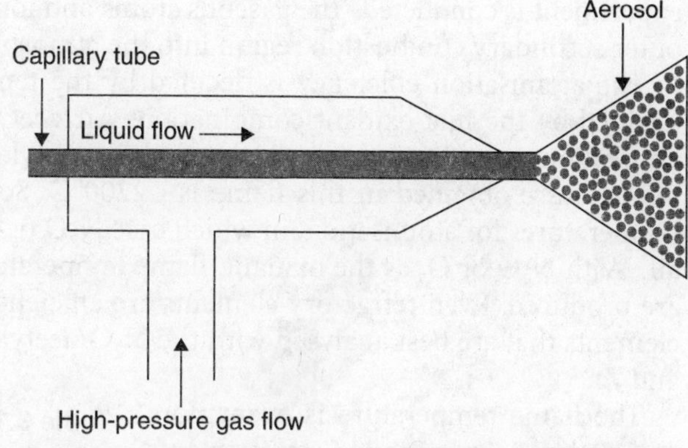

Fig. 9.3 A concentric tube nebuliser

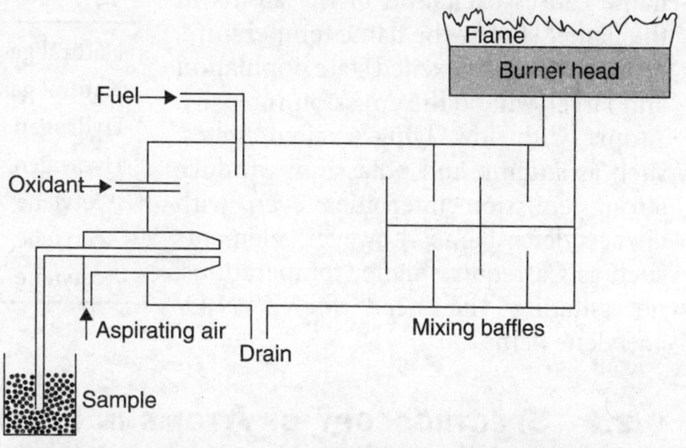

Fig. 9.4 Laminar flow, burner for atomic absorption

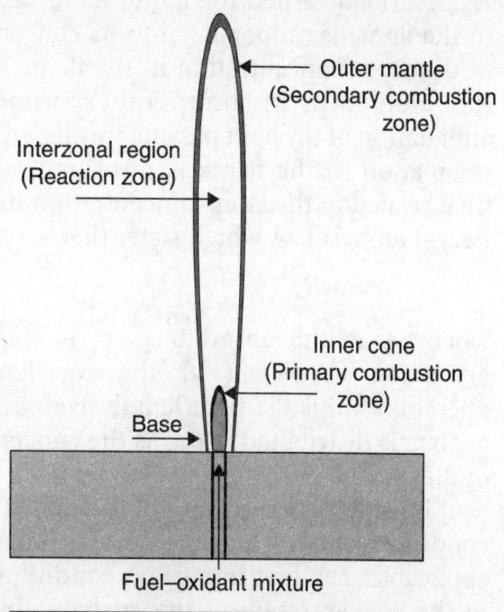

Fig. 9.5 Structure of a flame

experiment is conducted. The gaseous atoms and ions that entered the flame, exit through the outer secondary combustion region into the atmosphere, from where it is removed.

The atomisation efficiency is decided by the temperature of the flame, which in turn is decided by the fuel/oxidant combination. Air/acetylene flame is commonly used in atomic absorption experiments where the fuel is acetylene and air serves as the oxidant. The temperature obtained in this flame is ~2200°C. Some elements, such as Sr, require higher temperatures for atomisation, in which case N_2O or O_2 is substituted as the oxidant instead of air. With N_2O or O_2 as the oxidant, flame temperatures of ~2800°C and 3000°C respectively, are produced. Even refractory elements are efficiently atomised at these temperatures. A few elements that are best analysed with the N_2O/acetylene flame are Al, Ba, Be, Mo, Si, V, Ti, W and Zr.

The flame temperature is even more of an issue in emission experiments (Table 9.1). The high temperature of the flame causes excitation of the atoms in the flame. Higher the flame temperature, higher will be the excited state population and larger will be the emission intensity. Atoms with low lying excited states, such as sodium and potassium produce strong emission intensities even with air/acetylene flame; however, elements such as Ca require higher temperatures, necessitating the need for a N_2O/acetylene flame.

Table 9.1 Fuels used in flame spectroscopy

Fuel	**Oxidant**	**Flame temperature range (°C)**
Natural gas	Air	1700–1900
Natural gas	Oxygen	2700–2800
Hydrogen	Air	2000–2100
Hydrogen	Oxygen	2500–2700
Acetylene	Air	2100–2400
Acetylene	Oxygen	3050–3150
Acetylene	Nitrous oxide	2600–2800

9.3.2 Spectroscopy of Atoms in Flames

9.3.2.1 Beer–Lambert Law and its Applicability

As described earlier, the flame serves as an atom reservoir. The concentration of the atoms in the flame is proportional to its concentration in the analyte solution. Hence, the estimate of the atom concentration in the flame would be a measure of the analyte concentration in the solution. In an absorption experiment, the attenuation of the light passing through the atom population in the flame is measured, which is then related to the atom concentration using the Beer–Lambert law, which states that

$$A = \varepsilon_\lambda l C$$

where A is the absorbance, ε_λ is the molar extinction coefficient at the wavelength of operation λ, l is the path length over which the analyte is distributed and C is the concentration of the analyte.

It is important at this point to understand the conditions under which the Beer–Lambert law is applicable. The first important condition relates to the concentration of the analyte. The law is

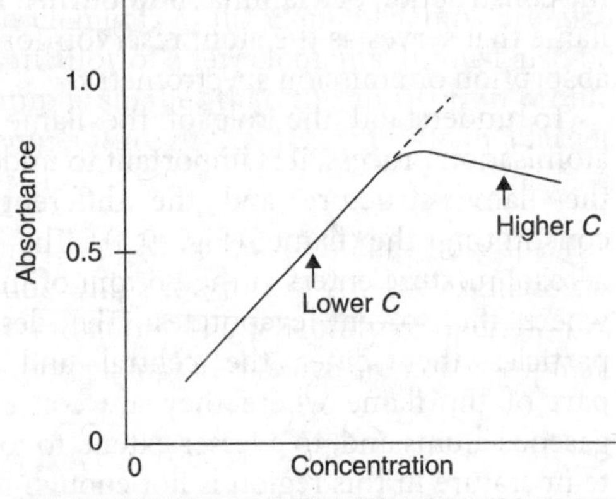

Fig. 9.6 The Beer–Lambert law: non-linearity at higher concentrations

applicable only at low concentrations of the analyte, where a linear dependence of absorbance with concentration is observed. At higher concentrations of the analyte, a non-linearity is observed (Fig. 9.6), and hence these concentration ranges must be avoided in analytical spectrometry.

Another important factor that is implicitly necessary for the observance of the Beer–Lambert law is that the radiation used for the absorption experiment must be 'truly monochromatic'. However, there is no such thing as a truly monochromatic radiation and all radiation sources, however narrow, have a finite spectral width. If we now assume that the spectral width is composed of wavelengths ranging from λ_1 to λ_2, then the different wavelengths constituting the radiation source will each have absorptivities applicable at the particular wavelength. If it turns out that the absorptivities are vastly different at different wavelengths, the measured absorbance for this polychromatic radiation will no longer have a linear dependence on concentration. On the contrary, if the absorptivities at the different wavelengths are nearly the same, a linear dependence of measured absorbance on concentration will be observed. To achieve this condition, it is necessary that the radiation source be as narrow in its spectral width as possible and preferably be centred at the peak of the absorption profile, where the absorptivities change very little over a small wavelength interval (Fig. 9.7).

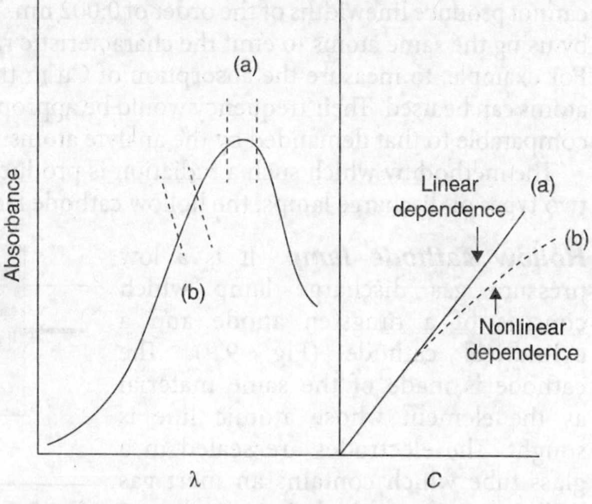

Fig. 9.7 Deviation of the Beer–Lambert law with polychromatic radiation **(a)** ε varies very little with wavelength **(b)** ε varies significantly with wavelength.

In addition to the problem of non-linear dependence of absorbance on concentration, if radiation sources of large spectral widths are used, there is also the problem of poor sensitivities. Let us look at this issue in a little more detail. The spectral linewidth of the absorbing gaseous atoms in the flame, as mentioned earlier, is very small, of the order of 0.002 nm. If the probe radiation is ten times larger in spectral bandwidth (say ~0.02 nm), then most of the radiation constituting the probe radiation will not even be absorbed by the sample atoms. The change in intensity of the probe radiation due to absorption will be small, as only a small part of the probe radiation will even be capable of being absorbed by the sample atoms (Fig. 9.8). The small change in intensity will consequently result in poorer sensitivity. It is therefore clear that the spectral width of the

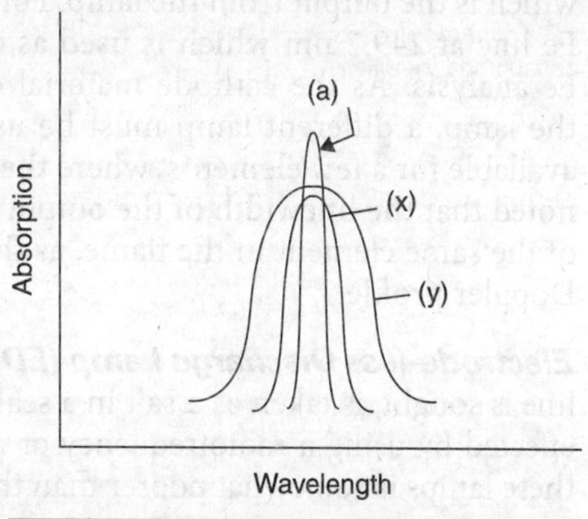

Fig. 9.8 Effect of linewidth of source radiation on sensitivity of absorption. **(a)** Sample absorption spectrum. **(x)** Emission spectrum of source *x*. **(y)** Emission spectrum of source Y.

probe radiation must be small and comparable with the width of the absorption profile of the sample atoms in the flame.

9.4 SOURCES FOR ATOMIC ABSORPTION

The small linewidth demanded by the above arguments, rules out the possibility of using a broadband source such as Xe together with a monochromator, because such an arrangement cannot produce linewidths of the order of 0.002 nm. This problem was solved quite ingeniously by using the same atoms to emit the characteristic radiation as those which are being probed. For example, to measure the absorption of Cu in the flame, radiation emitted by excited Cu atoms can be used. Their frequency would be appropriate and the spectral width would also be comparable to that demanded by the analyte atoms in the flame.

The method by which such a radiation is produced is by using discharge lamps. There are two types of discharge lamps, the hollow cathode lamp and the electrode-less lamps.

Hollow cathode lamp It is a low pressure gas discharge lamp which consists of a tungsten anode and a cylindrical cathode (Fig. 9.9). The cathode is made of the same material as the element whose atomic line is sought. The electrodes are sealed in a glass tube which contains an inert gas at low pressure, which is typically ~1 torr. A potential of a few hundred volts is applied between the electrodes. Under these conditions of voltage and gas pressure, the typical current drawn is 5 mA. The Ar contained in the discharge lamp is ionised and is drawn towards the cathode where it collides with the cathode with sufficient energy to sputter the material constituting the cathode. (Sputtering is a process in which atoms or ions are ejected from the surface of a material by a beam of charged particles.) The sputtered atoms from the cathode, some of which are excited, emit their characteristic atomic line which is the output from the lamp. For example, a Fe cathode would emit the characteristic Fe line at 249.7 nm which is used as the radiation source for absorption experiments for Fe analysis. As the cathode material defines the spectral line that can be obtained from the lamp, a different lamp must be used for each element. Multi-element lamps are also available for a few elements, where the cathode is an alloy of a few elements. It must also be noted that the linewidth of the output from the lamp is smaller than the absorption profile of the same element in the flame, as the higher temperature in the flame results in a larger Doppler profile.

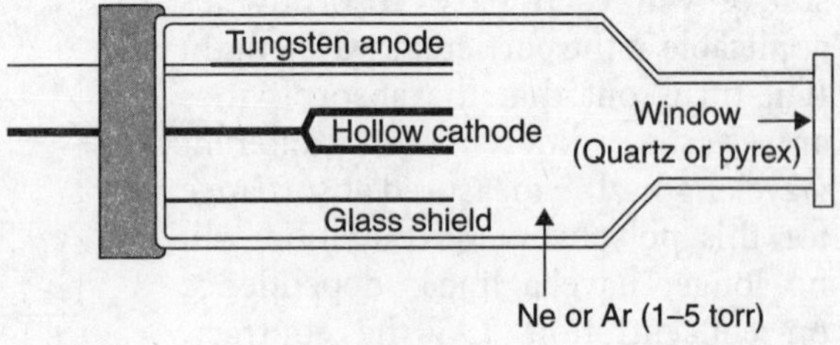

Fig. 9.9 Hollow cathode lamp

Electrode-less Discharge Lamp (EDL) These are lamps where the element whose spectral line is sought, is taken as a salt in a sealed quartz tube with a few torr of Ar. The excitation is effected by using a radiofrequency or a microwave radiation. The reliability of operation of these lamps is somewhat poorer than the hollow cathode lamps and hence are not as popular.

9.5 INSTRUMENTATION OF THE AAS

Having learnt about the hollow cathode lamp which is the light source, and the flame which serves as a sample reservoir, it is now appropriate to discuss the instrumentation of the atomic absorption spectrometer and the actual experimentation on this spectrometer (Fig. 9.10). The sample solution is aspirated with the nebuliser into the flame, as discussed earlier. The emission line from the hollow cathode lamp is directed through the flame containing the analyte atoms, which absorb the light. However, to measure the absorbance, which is log (I_t/I_o), it is required to measure both I_o, which is the intensity of the radiation before it traverses the flame, and I_t which is the intensity after its journey. While the most obvious way to measure I_o would be to measure the intensity of the radiation from the hollow cathode lamp without the flame, say by turning the flame off, it would be inconvenient to do so. Instead, the light from the lamp is deflected away from the flame and directed to take a path to the detector without traversing the flame (Fig. 9.10). The beam therefore traverses two different paths; path 1 is through the flame when measuring I_t, and another, a circuitous path 2, away from the flame, when measuring I_o. The position of a flip mirror (A) decides if the light from the hollow cathode lamp traverses path 1 or 2. Such an arrangement is called the double beam spectrometer and is a popular configuration in commercial AAS instruments.

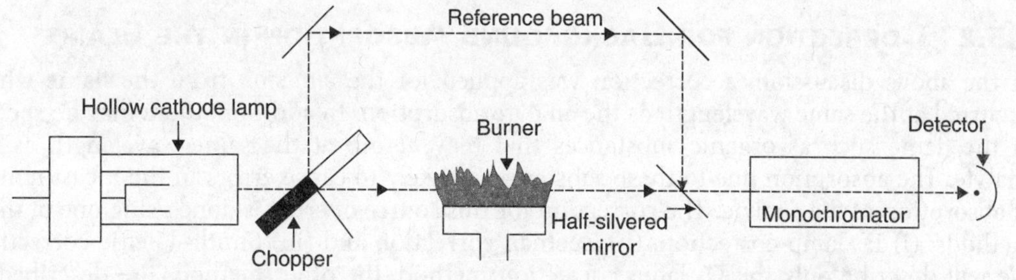

Fig. 9.10 A double-beam atomic absorbtion spectrophotometer: Block diagram

9.5.1 Correction for Background Emission from the Flame

The light, after it traverses through or around the flame, is directed onto a photomultiplier to measure the intensities I_t and I_o, at the selected wavelength λ_a, appropriate for the element in question. However, the intensity measurements pose some further problems. In addition to the light from the hollow cathode lamp, the flame also emits radiation over a wide range of wavelengths, which constitutes a baseline intensity at the photomultiplier and which must be corrected in the measurement of the absorbance. The first step in the correction process is to use a monochromator (or a filter) to discriminate against all the wavelengths other than that corresponding to the wavelength of the hollow cathode lamp. With the monochromator in place, the only radiation reaching the photomultiplier would be that from the hollow cathode lamp, which constitutes the signal and the small slice of radiation from the flame at the same wavelength. Part of the background from the flame is due to a small fraction of the analyte atoms which are excited in the flame and which emit at the wavelength at which the monochromator is set. While the monochromator significantly reduces the background emission from the flame by rejecting all those wavelengths where $\lambda \neq \delta\lambda_a$, where $\delta\lambda_a$ is the small bandwidth around the wavelength λ_a, the emission within this bandwidth is not rejected by the monochromator. The amount of light from the flame naturally would be dependent on the bandwidth of the monochromator.

The background emission from the flame within this bandwidth must be corrected for an accurate determination of the absorbance and is done using a modulation technique. In this technique, the source radiation from the hollow cathode lamp is modulated using a chopper, which causes the intensity from the hollow cathode lamp to fluctuate at the frequency of the chopper and results in a time varying signal at the detector. The intensity of the radiation from the flame is, on the contrary, unmodulated and constitutes only a DC signal at the detector. An electronic detection scheme that rejects the DC signal and only amplifies and records the time-varying signal is employed. Using a combination of a monochromator and a phase sensitive detection scheme, the background emission from the flame is completely rejected.

It must be noted that in a monochromator, the spectral line of a given element is selected by the appropriate positioning of the grating and the selected line is made incident onto a photomultiplier tube. If another element is to be monitored, the grating position is changed (as also the hollow cathode lamp source) and the corresponding line of the newly chosen element is made incident on the PMT. Consequently, each element is monitored sequentially. When several elements have to be monitored, this sequential monitoring method can prove to be a disadvantage, as the time taken for a complete analysis can be long. Furthermore, the amount of solution required for the complete analysis is also large, which can be a problem, where only a limited amount of the analyte solution is available.

9.5.2 Correction for Background Absorption in the Flame

In the above discussion, a correction was applied for the *emission* from the flame which occurred at the same wavelength as the analyte absorption. In addition, there may be species in the flame such as organic substances that may *absorb* at the same wavelength as the analyte. The absorption due to these substances is likely to cause errors in the measurement of absorption of the analyte. The correction for this source of error is done using one of three methods: (i) D_2 lamp correction, (ii) Zeeman correction and (iii) Smith–Hieftje correction. We will describe only the D_2 lamp correction method; the other methods are described in detail in the references [2].

9.5.2.1 D_2 Lamp Correction Method

In this method, a D_2 lamp which is a source of continuum radiation over the ultraviolet region, is used. The lamp is used in a configuration shown in Fig. 9.11. The rotating chopper allows the light from the hollow cathode lamp and the D_2 lamp to pass alternately through the flame. This procedure enables measurement to be made on the absorption in the flame of the radiation from the hollow cathode lamp and the D_2 lamp. The absorption of the D_2 radiation is then subtracted from that measured for the hollow cathode lamp. It must be remembered that the analyte species will also absorb the radiation from the D_2 lamp and hence if this absorption is to reflect the absorption of *only* the interfering species in the lamp, the bandwidth of the D_2 radiation must be made larger than that of the atomic absorption of the analyte line, so that the broad band absorption of the interfering species is monitored. Towards this end, the slit width of the radiation from the D_2 lamp is kept sufficiently wide so that the broadband radiation effectively monitors the interfering species in the flame, which is then subtracted from the absorption from the hollow cathode lamp so that the absorption of the analyte is accurately measured.

The standard addition method, described earlier, should be used whenever interferences are suspected, which will help identify and compensate these interferences.

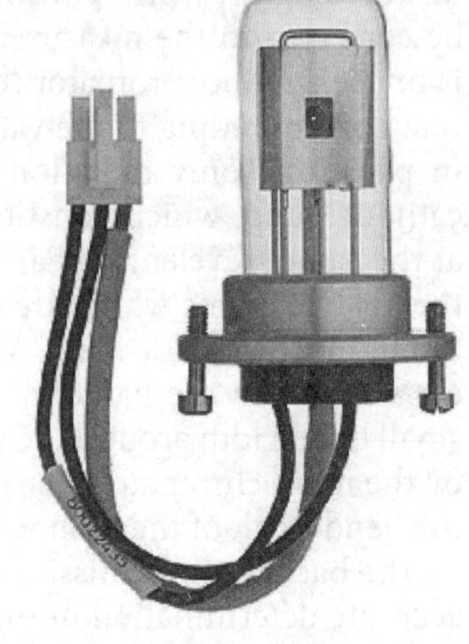

Fig. 9.11 Deuterium lamp

Let us now summarise all the problems that we encountered in the instrumentation of the atomic absorption spectrometer and how each of them was addressed.

- The analyte had to be atomised and brought into the gas phase for analysis. This was achieved using a combination of a nebuliser and a flame.
- A narrow linewidth source had to be used for a successful estimation of the atomic absorbance—a hollow cathode source was used.
- I (intensity of light after passing through the sample) and I_0 (intensity of light when no analyte was present) had to be measured to estimate absorbance—a double beam spectrometer was used.
- Emission from the flame falling on the photomultiplier had to be corrected for—a monochromator and phase-sensitive detection were used.
- Absorption of non-analyte species in the flame occurring at the same wavelength as the analyte had to be corrected for—D_2 lamp correction was used.

The above points summarise the working of the atomic absorption spectrometer.

9.5.3 Interferences in AAS

In the conduct of the AAS analysis, one has to contend with interferences of many types. One of the chief sources of interference is that due to another element having an absorption close to that of the analyte—spectral interference. For example, the absorption line of Cu at 224.7 nm is very close to that of Sn at 224.6 nm and consequently the absorption measurement can be affected by the interfering species. In such cases, an alternative line may be chosen for the analyte. In the above example, the Cu line at 324.7 nm and that of Sn at 235.0 nm can be chosen.

Another source of interference is due to specific chemistry occurring in the analyte solution. For example, in the analysis of alkaline earth metals, the presence of sulphates can cause the concentrations of some elements to be underestimated as the insoluble sulphates of these elements can cause poor sample introduction into the flame. These problems are addressed by varying the conditions in preparing the aqueous solution of the analyte.

9.6 Graphite Furnace AAS

As an alternative to flame AAS, graphite furnace AAS (GFAAS) is used. In this method, the flame is replaced by a graphite furnace. A small volume (~2 μL) of the sample is placed on a graphite plate that is located inside the graphite furnace (Fig. 9.12). The temperature of the furnace is then raised in stages, using programmed electrical heating, to an eventual temperature of ~3000°C. This technique is therefore also referred to as *electrothermal evaporation*. In the initial phase of the temperature excursion, the solvent is evaporated, following which the sample is ashed at a somewhat higher temperature. Finally, the sample is atomised and this atom source is then probed as in flame AAS using a hollow cathode lamp source.

GFAAS has several advantages over the flame technique. In GFAAS, a solid or a slurry can also be used as the analyte, unlike in a flame where only solution samples can be used. The solid or the slurry is placed on the graphite plate and subjected to a temperature excursion for analysis. The GFAAS also displays superior detection limits over the flame method. The reason for the superior detection limit stems from the fact that the entire sample placed on the graphite plate is evaporated as a pulse, thus providing a high atom concentration in a short period of time, which can be effectively analysed. Unlike the flame technique, this method does not suffer from the large flame emission background, which also contributes to the superior detection limit for this method. The detection limits in GFASS is typically about 100-fold superior to flame AAS. Furthermore, only a few μL of the sample is necessary for an analysis in GFAAS, unlike several mL required in the flame method.

The GFAAS method however suffers from a few disadvantages. The precision in this method is inferior to that observed in a flame method. The dynamic range is also smaller in the GFAAS technique and this technique is therefore employed when smaller detection limits are necessitated.

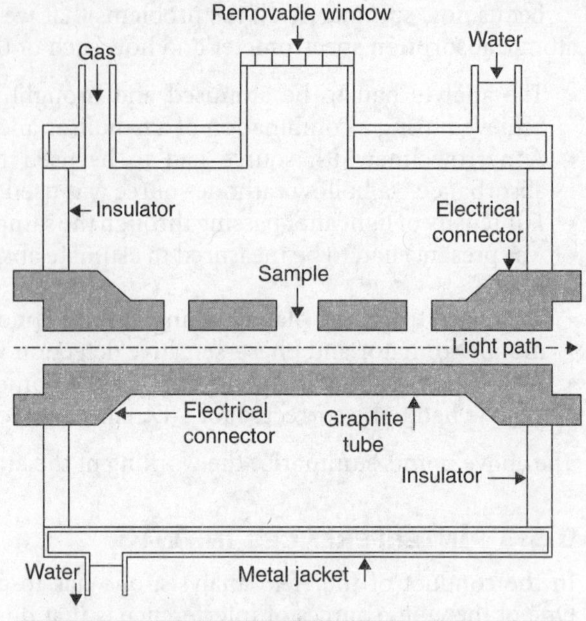

Fig. 9.12 Graphite tube furnace

9.7 HYDRIDE GENERATION AAS

Where the analytes form volatile hydrides, the technique of hydride generation comes in very handy. In this method, the analyte solution, say of As or Ge, is treated with a reducing agent such as sodium tetrahydroborate to form a volatile hydride, such as AsH or GeH. The volatile hydride is then introduced into the flame (Fig. 9.13). The volatility of the hydride allows for an efficient introduction of the analyte into the flame without the need for nebulisers. The detection limit of this technique is also superior to that observed in flame AAS.

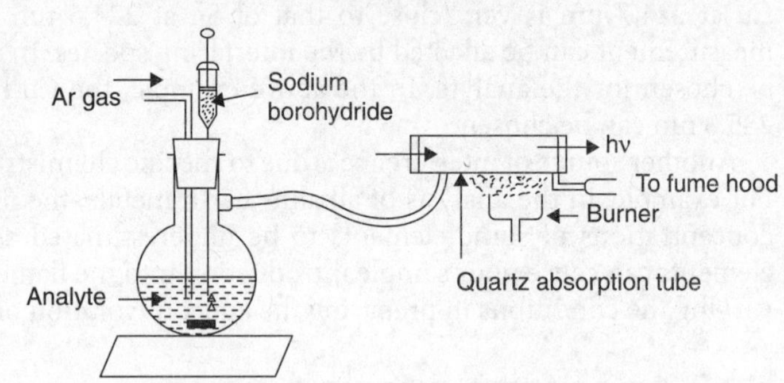

Fig. 9.13 Apparatus set-up for hydride generation for AAS

9.8 FLAME EMISSION SPECTROMETRY

Until now, we have been dealing with absorption spectrometry. One can also monitor the emission from excited atoms for analysis, as the emission intensity is proportional to the analyte concentration. With almost an identical experimental set up used for flame AAS, one can also perform atomic emission experiments. As in AAS, the analyte is nebulised into the flame where atomisation takes place. Due to the flame temperature of a few thousand degrees, a fraction of the analyte atoms are excited and eventually emit their characteristic line. The fraction of the analyte atoms that are excited is given by the Boltzmann distribution law,

$$N_1 = N_0\left(\frac{g_0}{g_T}\right)\exp\left(\frac{-\Delta E}{kT}\right)$$

where N_1 and N_0 are the populations, g_0 and g_T are the degeneracies for the states 1 and 0 respectively, ΔE is the energy difference between the two states, T is the temperature (in kelvin) and k is the Boltzmann constant. It can be seen that the population of the excited state is dependent on the temperature. Higher the flame temperature, the larger is the excited state population and greater will be the emission intensity. Likewise, smaller the energy difference ΔE, the larger is the population of the excited state. Consequently, atoms with low lying excited states (small ΔE), such as alkali atoms, are good candidates for emission experiments. Emission experiments for some elements are conducted in flames, used for absorption spectrometry, where the temperatures are ~2500°C. In this method, the flame is oriented at right angles to the optical axis.

The detection limits are superior in emission experiments for a number of elements, compared with those in absorption experiments (the width of atomic emission peaks is about 10^{-3} nm).

9.9 INDUCTIVELY COUPLED ATOMIC EMISSION SPECTROMETRY

While the flame is used for emission experiments, plasmas which provide much higher temperatures such as 10,000 K have a unique place in emission experiments. The high temperatures in the plasma result in a large excited state population and therefore a large emission intensity and consequently excellent detection limits. One of the most popular plasma sources is the inductively coupled plasma, referred to as ICP (Fig. 9.14). The technique of monitoring optical emission in an ICP is often referred to as ICP-OES (ICP-optical emission spectrometry) or ICP-AES (ICP-atomic emission spectrometry).

While a flame is sustained by the combustion of a fuel which is a chemical process, ICP is sustained by coupling electrical energy into the medium using a radiofrequency (RF) source. The RF source is usually of about 1 kW power and a frequency of 27 MHz. It consists of three quartz tubes around which a Cu tube is wound. The Cu tube serves as the induction coil which couples the energy from the radiofrequency source into the medium, which is usually Ar. The Ar is passed through these tubes at flow rates that range from 10 to 20 L/min. To initiate the plasma, electrons are seeded into Ar using a Tesla coil. The seeded electrons are accelerated under the influence of the radiofrequency field, and cause ionisation and excitation in Ar to produce a plasma, whose temperature is typically 10,000 K. The plasma is contained well within the walls of the quartz torch, by a tangential flow of Ar through the outermost tube; insufficient flow of this gas in the outer tube can cause the torch to contact the plama leading to a melting of the torch. (A plasma is a gas containing high concentrations of cations and electrons.)

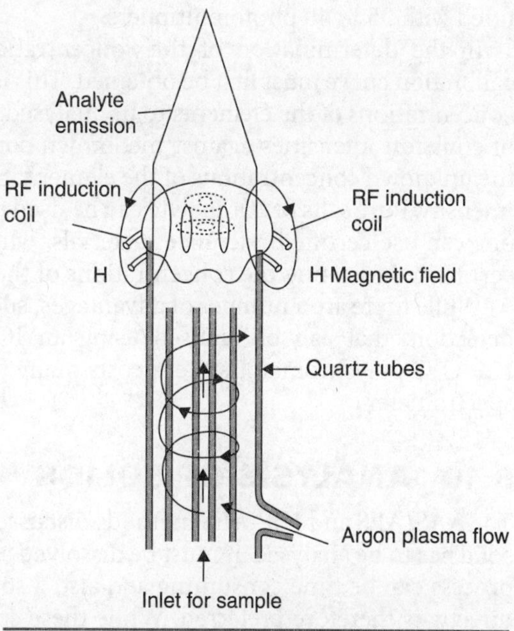

Fig. 9.14 Inductively coupled argon plasma source

The analyte sample is aspirated into the plasma through the central tube where it is atomised and excited, and emits its characteristic emission line which can be monitored. Since the temperature of the plasma is significantly high compared with that of the flame, the fraction of atoms that are excited in the plasma is quite large which leads to a large emission intensity in an ICP. Consequently, much smaller concentrations can be measured in an ICP than in a flame emission technique. Typical detection limits in the ICP-OES technique are ~50 to 100 ng/L. The higher temperature of the plasma also leads to complete atomisation and interferences due to molecular species that are observed in flames, are less of a problem in ICP.

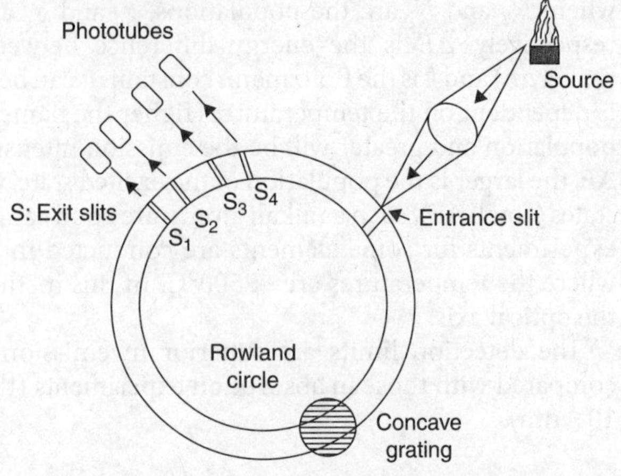

Fig. 9.15 Polychromator spectrometer

The emission from the plasma is collected and focused onto the entrance slit of a spectrometer. The technique is made versatile by using a polychromator instead of a monochromator. We have seen earlier that in a monochromator, analysis is perfomed sequentially, that is, one element after another. In a polychromator, a number of elements are monitored simultaneously. This is achieved by mounting a number of photomultiplier tubes at the positions where the atomic lines of the various elements are focused (Fig. 9.15). The locus of points where the emission lines of the various elements are focused is known as the *Rowland circle*. This arrangement allows for a simultaneous monitoring of a number of elements, thereby reducing the time of analysis and also the requirement of the amount of analyte. It is not unusual to have polychromators fitted with 35 to 40 photomultipliers.

In the determination of the concentration of the elements in the analyte solution, a calibration curve must first be obtained. This is done by aspirating solutions containing known concentrations of the elements to be analysed and measuring their emission intensities. A plot of emission intensities against the known concentrations is made, which is used to estimate the unknown concentrations of the element in an analyte solution from its measured emission intensity. Pure salts of the analyte can be used to prepare the calibration standards; alternatively one can use certified reference materials, which are solutions of analyte that are sold with a certificate indicating the concentrations of the element in question.

While there are a number of advantages, such as superior detection limits and multielement detection, that can be realised using an ICP, the cost is not certainly one of them. An ICP-OES polychromator system costs many times more than an atomic absorption/emission spectrometer.

9.10 ANALYSIS OF SOLIDS

The AAS/AES and ICP-AES methods discussed thus far, can handle only solution samples. If a solid has to be analysed, it must be dissolved and converted to a solution prior to analysis. This process can be time consuming and also a source of errors. A method that can handle solids directly is therefore preferred. While these spectrometric methods use the same principle of atomic emission and subsequent detection using a monochromator or a polychromator, they are different in the way they handle sample atomisation and excitation. Spark source atomic emission spectrometry and glow discharge spectrometry are two popular methods that handle solid samples directly without dissolution.

9.10.1 Spark-source Emission Spectrometry

In this technique, the solid sample is made the anode in a discharge set up. A counter electrode, usually tungsten, is placed opposite the sample. A high voltage is now applied across these electrodes when it produces a discharge. As a result of this discharge, atoms are sputtered from the surface of the sample and enter the electric discharge. Discharge sputtering is therefore the atomisation process in this method. After atomisation the atoms enter the discharge, where they are excited and emit their characteristic atomic line. The details of the experimental set up are shown in Fig. 9.16.

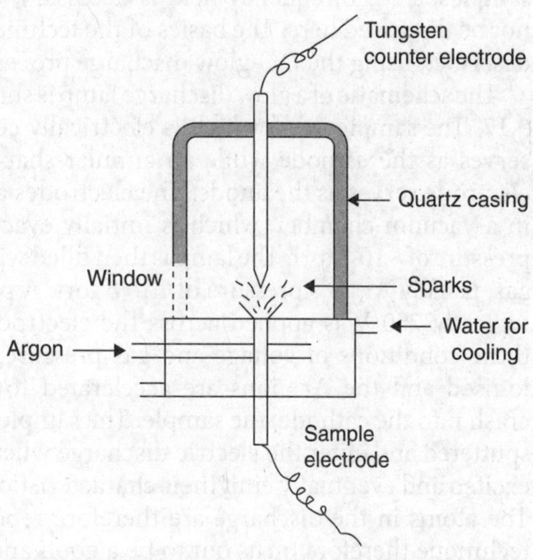

Fig. 9.16 Spark source for spark-emission atomic spectrometry

The sample is first polished to obtain a flat surface and then placed on the spark stand, with the tungsten electrode located opposite the sample. The discharge is produced in the form of a number of unidirectional AC sparks; the unidirectionality is ensured through the use of a diode in the circuit. Argon is flushed through the discharge region and a potential is then applied across the electrodes. The flow of Ar is required to provide an inert atmosphere in the dischcarge zone and also to flush the sputtered material out of the discharge region. The emission from the sample is focused onto the entrance slit of a polychromator for analysis. The emission is collected for a desired number of sparks and the signal is then averaged. The emission is collected over a large number of sparks to obtain the desired precision in the intensity values which would translate to a precision in the eventual concentration values.

The advantage of this technique is that it does not necessitate the dissolution of the solid sample. The composition of a number of elements in the sample can be simultaneously determined through the use of a polychromator. This technique is particularly useful for the compositional characterisation of steels and other metal alloys. However, for the determination of the concentrations of the elements in sample, it is required to first obtain a calibration curve (as in the solution method). Samples containing precisely known amounts of the elements in question are used to obtain the calibration; these can be purchased as certified standards. While this technique has a number of advantages, the requirement of certified standards can sometimes pose a difficulty. The matrix constituting the analyte sample and that of the certified standard must be similar for the analysis to be accurate. For example, for the analysis of steel samples, certified steel standards must be used. Hence, it is necessary for the analytical laboratory to procure standards that have a similar matrix as the samples that are to be analysed. The ease of analysis of solid samples has made this technique particularly useful in the steel industry.

9.10.2 Glow Discharge Spectrometry

This is yet another method that is used for the analysis of solids, without the need for dissolution. Unlike the spark source technique, which is an atmospheric pressure discharge, glow discharge is a low pressure discharge, where the discharge is usually sustained at a gas pressure of typically a few torr. If the sample is electrically conducting, a DC voltage would suffice for sustaining the discharge; for electrically non-conducting samples, a radiofrequency field is necessary, which will not be discussed here. The basics of the technique will be described using the DC-glow discharge process.

The schematic of a glow discharge lamp is shown in Fig. 9.17. The sample itself, which is electrically conducting, serves as the cathode while an annular-shaped copper electrode serves as the anode. The electrodes are housed in a vacuum chamber, which is initially evacuated to a pressure of ~10^{-3} torr. The lamp is then filled with an inert gas, usually Ar, to a pressure of 1 to 5 torr. A potential of typically 750 V is applied across the electrodes. Under these conditions of voltage and gas pressure, the Ar is ionised and the Ar^+ ions are accelerated towards and crash into the cathode, the sample. The sample atoms are sputtered and enter the electric discharge where they are excited and eventually emit their characteristic radiation. The atoms in the discharge are therefore representative of the sample composition and this technique therefore turns out to be a good analytical technique for the analysis of solids. It is noteworthy to recognise that the emission in the discharge is produced in the region which is called the negative glow region, which is a field-free region. Consequently, the linewidths in the glow discharge processes are narrow as they do not suffer from Stark broadening, which is otherwise an important broadening mechanism in discharge processes.

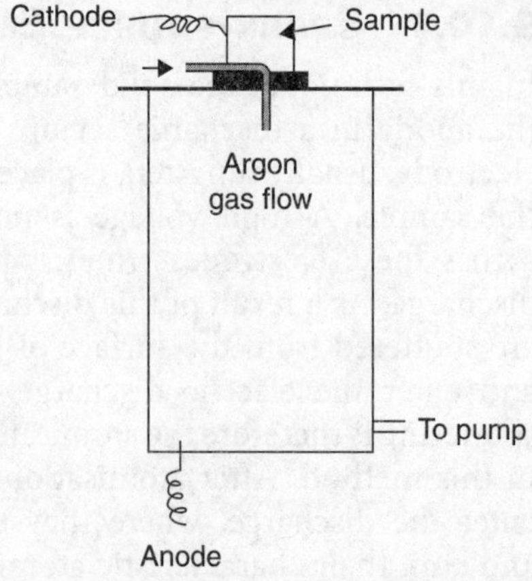

Fig. 9.17 Glow discharge atomiser (schematic)

While the glow discharge process is useful for the bulk compositional analysis of solids, it also has the added advantage that provides compositional information as a function of depth from the surface. This is possible, as the sputtering process occurs layer by layer and the material from the sample enters the discharge progressively from the surface as the sputtering proceeds. The emission from the sample is therefore recorded as a function of time, with the emission from the initial times occurring from nearer the surface while those at later times are from deeper into the sample. If the sputtering rate is known, the emission as a function of time can be converted to emission as a function of depth. This aspect is particularly important when studying corrosion of samples as the composition in these samples vary with the depth from the surface, and depth profiling can throw light on the corrosion processes. This aspect is also useful to study thin films and their compositions.

EXERCISES

1. Rationalise the following:
   (a) The first step in all atomic spectroscopic methods is atomisation.
   (b) Both emission and absorption atomic spectra are affected by variations in flame temperature.
   (c) The spectrum of an atom is different from that of its ions.
   (d) Both Doppler broadening and pressure broadening are temperature dependent.

2. Define the following with reference to AAS:
   (a) Sputtering
   (b) Modulation
   (c) Radiation buffer

3. Explain the following with reference to AAS:
   (a) Ionisation suppression (b) Protective agents (c) Releasing agents
4. Discuss the theory of interferences in AAS and the procedures adopted to suppress or eliminate such interferences. Cite examples.
5. List and explain 'flame variables' with reference to AAS and AES.
6. Outline the principle of
   (a) Cold-vapour absorption determination (b) Inductively-coupled AES
   (c) Spark-source AES
7. How do the following units of the atomic spectrometer function?
   (a) Laminar flow burner (b) Concentric tube nebuliser
   (c) Hollow cathode lamp (d) Electrothermal atomiser
8. Describe how the mercury pollutant present in a bird's egg can be determined by atomic absorption spectroscopy.
9. Explain the principle and advantages of plasma emission spectroscopy.
10. What is the role of an internal standard in flame emission methods?
11. An electrothermal atomiser is more sensitive than a flame ioniser—explain.
12. A metal ion present as an aqueous solution was determined by AAS as per the following experimental procedure.

Analyte solution taken (mL)	Standard solution (20 ppm) added (mL)	Made up to (mL)	Measured absorbance
20	0.0	50	0.150
20	5.0	50	0.237
20	10.0	50	0.361
20	15.0	50	0.483
20	20.0	50	0.582

Calculate the amount of the metal ion (in ppm) present in the analyte solution.

13. Explain the principle of functioning of a hollow-cathode lamp.
14. With examples, explain interferences in determining metallic ion by atomic spectroscopic methods.
15. In flame emission spectrometry of a plant cell fluid for potassium , two (*a* and *b*) 1-mL aliquots of the fluid are added to 10 mL portions of water separately. 10 mL of 0.100 M KCl solution is then added to the diluted solution (*a*). This produced an arbitrary emission signal of 70.2. The blank solution (*b*) produced a signal of 24.2. Calculate the amount of potassium in the cell fluid.
16. Explain how the Maxwell–Boltzmann expression is applied in understanding the wavelength parameters in atomic spectral methods.
17. Explain the following:
   (a) A sharp-line source is preferred for atomic absorption spectroscopy.
   (b) Absorption spectra of atomic species consist of discrete lines of specific wavelength rather than broad bands as for molecular species.
   (c) In AAS, electrothermal atomisers have high sensitivity compared to other types of atomisers.
18. Explain why the radiation source in AA instruments is modulated.

References

1. Payling R and Larkins P, *Optical Emission Lines of the Elements*, John Wiley & Sons, Chichester, England, 2000.
2. (a) Merdham J, Derrey R C, Barnes J D and Thomas M J K, *Vogel's Textbook of Quantitative Chemical Analysis*, Pearson Education, 2000.
   (b) Skoog D A, Holler F J and Nieman T A, *Principles of Instrumental Analysis*, Thomson, Singapore, 1988.

10 Fluorescence Spectroscopy

10.1 INTRODUCTION

An atom or a molecule that has been excited from its ground state to a state of higher energy, returns to the ground state after a finite period of time. During the process of returning to the ground state, the excited species disposes off the energy initially provided to it, through a variety of ways. If the excess energy is disposed off as light, it is referred to as luminescence, or more generally as a radiative process. Alternatively, the energy could be disposed off to the surrounding medium as heat, a process known as non-radiative decay. Yet another pathway is one where the excess energy is used to break a chemical bond initiating a chemical process; such a process would give rise to photochemical reactions. These processes are summarised pictorially in Fig. 10.1. The initial excitation itself can be effected by a variety of methods—using electric discharge, light, heat, chemical reactions and so on. The specific case, where excitation is initiated by light and the return of the excited species to the lower levels is monitored, also through light emission, is referred to as fluorescence spectroscopy. Other modes of excitation and emission processes will be discussed elsewhere in the book.

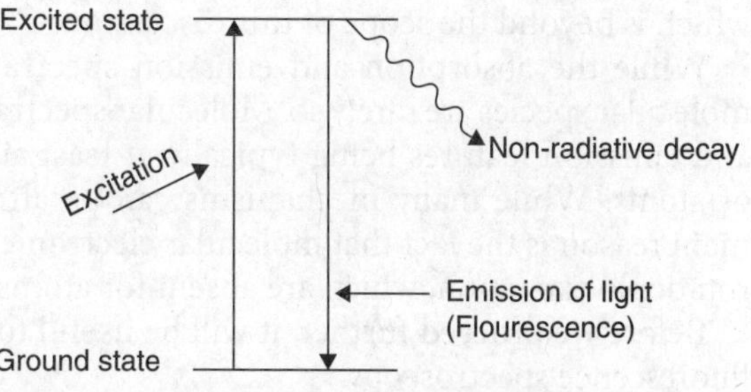

Fig. 10.1 Scheme showing excitation, fluorescence and non-radiative decay channels

When the atom or molecule absorbs the excitation radiation, the energy can be absorbed into any of the degrees of freedom in the molecule – vibrations, rotations or electronic – depending on the wavelength used. Where ultraviolet or visible light is used, as is usually done in the case of fluorescence spectroscopy, electronic excitation is the *primary* event. Of course, along with electronic excitation, there could be accompanying vibrational and rotational excitation. What one implies by electronic excitation is that one of the electrons in the atom or molecule is promoted from its ground state configuration to a configuration of higher energy. For example, the electronic configuration of Na is $1s^2 2s^2 2p^6 3s^1$. If the Na atom absorbs energy, the outermost electron, that is the 3*s* electron which is the easiest to excite, can be excited to a higher lying orbital, say the 3*p*, with the excited Na atom now having a configuration, $1s^2 2s^2 2p^6 3p^1$. This configuration, however, being of a higher energy than the ground state, cannot survive for ever and before long, the electron that was excited returns to the stable 3*s* level. In the process, Na emits light of yellow colour, characteristic of the sodium lamps seen in the streets. (The above discussion is more accurately conducted using the concepts of term symbols, but for now, it is sufficient to discuss as above.)

10.2 EXCITATION AND EMISSION SPECTRUM

The wavelength at which a given species absorbs or emits is characteristic of that species. The excitation and emission processes have therefore been used to qualitatively and quantitatively characterise the species. For example, Ti has a characteristic emission at 337 nm while Si has one at 224 nm. Emission at these wavelengths can therefore be ascribed to the presence of these elements. The various colours observed in the flame test is also based on the characteristic emission of the elements in question; for example, the emission at 584 nm is responsible for the yellow colour in the flame test for Na, while the emission near 670 nm causes the crimson red colour in the flame test for Li. The characteristic absorption and emission wavelengths stem from the discrete and unique energy level structure for each element in the periodic table. Theoretical methods can be used to calculate the energy level diagram of the elements, which is beyond the scope of this discussion.

While the absorption and emission spectra of atomic species are sharp, the spectra of molecular species are rarely so. Molecular spectra are broad with the envelope of the absorption and emission features being typically at least an order of magnitude larger than the profiles of atoms. While many mechanisms can be attributed to this broadening in molecules, the main reason is the fact that molecular electronic excitation is accompanied by vibrational and rotational excitation, which are absent for atoms.

Before we proceed further, it will be useful to learn some of the terms used in the study of fluorescence spectroscopy.

Excitation wavelength It is the wavelength that is used to cause excitation of the species, which then eventually emits light. The excitation wavelength is quite naturally a wavelength at which the species in question absorbs strongly.

Emission wavelength It is the wavelength at which the excited species emits and returns to a lower state. By the energy conservation rule, the emission wavelength can never be shorter than the absorption wavelength; at best the two can be equal, in which case it is called resonance fluorescence. Usually, the emission occurs at longer wavelengths than absorption, referred to as a Stokes shift (Fig. 10.2). The reason for this Stokes shift is explained later in this chapter when discussing the Jablonski diagram.

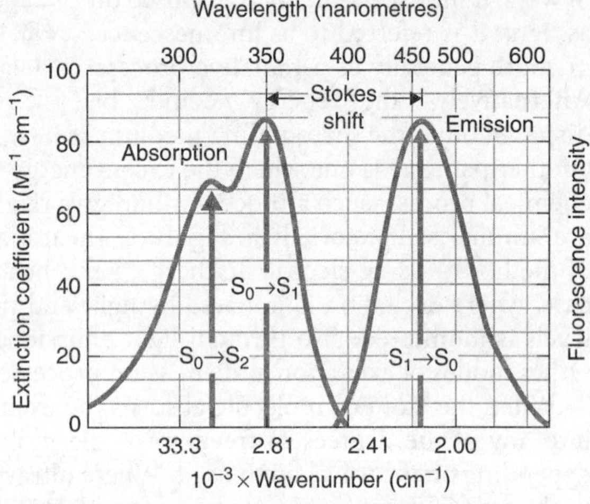

Fig. 10.2 Absorption and emission spectra of quinine; it can be seen that the emission occurs at longer wavelengths compared with the absorption–the Stokes shift

10.2.1 LIFETIME OF EXCITED STATES

As we saw earlier, the process of fluorescence emission rests on the fact that excited states have a finite lifetime. The lifetimes of the excited states can vary from picoseconds (10^{-12} s) to many seconds. The lifetime of a state depends on many factors, such as the species in question, excited state energies, and the effect of solvent or surrounding medium in which the excited species is located. One or more of these factors essentially decide the probability of a transition from the excited to the lower state and, in turn, the lifetime of the excited state; smaller the probability, greater would be the lifetime.

It is worthwhile understanding the concept of 'lifetime' in some detail. An excited state of Tb^{3+} in aqueous solution is known to have a lifetime of about 150 μs. This certainly does not mean that if 100 ions of Tb^{3+} are excited, they would *all* 'live' for a period of exactly 150 μs in the excited before decaying to the lower state! The concept of lifetime here has the same connotation as it does in demography. If a statement was made that the lifespan of an Indian was 65 years, it certainly does not mean that every Indian lives up to the age of 65 and dies on his 65th birthday! That certainly would not be a happy birthday! It simply means that the average age is 65, with some living close to and may be over 100 years, while there may be many unfortunate ones who die early in their lives. The lifetime of 150 μs simply means likewise. There are many Tb^{3+} ions that would decay immediately after excitation (the ones that die young) while there may be a few Tb^{3+} ions that would stay excited for a period well over 150 μs before returning to the lower state. The average of all these individual lifespans of the Tb^{3+} ions that were excited, would work out to 150 μs. It is therefore important to realise that the concept of lifetime is an average concept.

In many processes (though not all), the population of the excited state decays following an exponential function (recall radioactive decay). The population at any instant t , $N(t)$, in such cases, is given by the equation:

$$\frac{N_t}{N_0} = \exp\left(\frac{-t}{\tau}\right) \tag{10.1}$$

where $N(0)$ is the population at time, $t = 0$, and τ is a constant that determines how quickly the given excited system decays and has the unit of time. This equation is exactly what we derive as the rate equation for first order kinetics. If we plot $N(t)$ as a function of time t, we would get a decaying exponential (Fig. 10.3). The constant τ is the time constant of the process and can also be considered as the excited state lifetime. The reciprocal of the lifetime would be a measure of the rate of the process—the smaller the lifetime, the faster the rate of the process under consideration. From Eq. 10.1, we can derive an alternative definition for lifetime. If we set $t = \tau$, $N(t) = N(0).(1/e)$; in other words, τ is the time during which the population drops to $1/e$ of the original value.

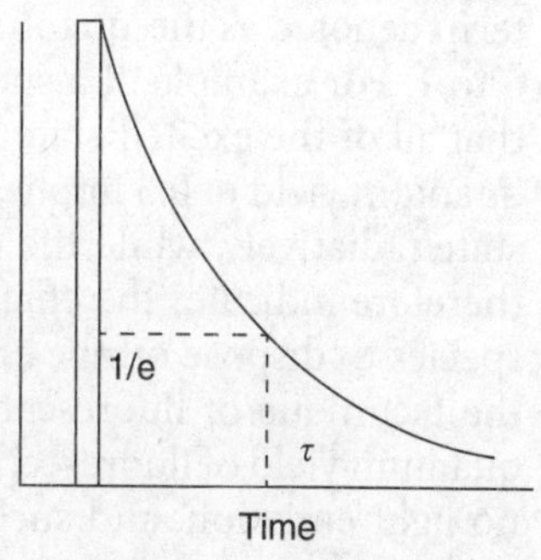

Fig. 10.3 A plot showing the fluorescence decay with time.

Now that we know how to express the time dependence of the excited state population, we will see how this dependence can be used to show that lifetime is really the average time spent by the species in the excited state. Assume N_j atoms or species reside in the excited state, for t_j seconds before they return to the lower state; that is, $N_j(t)$ is the number of atoms that live for a period of t_j seconds. The average time spent by all the atoms is then given by Eq. 10.2, which is simply the way averages are computed.

$$<t> = \frac{\Sigma t_j N_j(t)}{\Sigma N_j(t)} \tag{10.2}$$

For large N and small time intervals, when the variable t can be considered continuous, the summation can be replaced by an integral. Furthermore, $N(t)$ can be substituted using Eq. 10.1 to yield the following.

$$<t> = \frac{\int N_0 \exp\left(\frac{-t}{\tau}\right) t\, dt}{\int N_0 \exp\left(\frac{-t}{\tau}\right) dt} \tag{10.3}$$

$$= \frac{\int t \exp\left(\frac{-t}{\tau}\right) dt}{\int \exp\left(\frac{-t}{\tau}\right) dt} \tag{10.4}$$

This integration can be seen to yield $<t> = \tau$, indicating that τ is simply the *average* lifetime.

Conceptually, the methods to measure excited state lifetimes parallels the method that we learn in chemical kinetics; however, given the short lifetimes (or extremely fast decay rates) encountered in spectroscopy, the instrumentation employed for fluorescence lifetime measurements turns out to be sophisticated.

10.2.2 Quantum Yield of Fluorescence

We had seen earlier that an excited atom or molecule can choose to decay to the ground state either by emitting a photon (a radiative decay channel) or by disposing off the excess energy as heat to the surrounding (a non-radiative decay channel). Some of the excited molecules or atoms can decay to the ground state radiatively, while others may choose to do so non-radiatively. Of the excited species, the fraction that decays radiatively, is given by a term denoted as the 'quantum yield of fluorescence', a number that obviously must range from 0 to 1. For example, if a species is determined to have a quantum yield of 1, it simply means that all of the excited state species return to the lower state by emitting photons. However, a quantum yield of 0.5 implies that only half of the excited state population decays to the ground state radiatively, while the other half decays non-radiatively. Quantum yield of fluorescence therefore indicates the efficiency with which the radiative process is employed by the excited species to dispose off the energy which it received through the excitation process. Obviously, the technique of fluorescence spectroscopy would work well with systems that have a high quantum yield of fluorescence. A system with a quantum yield of fluorescence of 0 would imply no light emission, and such systems would be poor candidates for study using fluorescence spectroscopy.

10.2.3 Jablonski Diagram

All of the concepts that we have discussed thus far can be illustrated in a diagram that is popularly referred to as the Jablonski diagram (Fig. 10.4). Since the diagram depicts vibrational energy levels in the energy disposal scheme, it naturally refers to molecules, since atoms do not have vibrational degrees of freedom. The various steps involved in this process are the following. Energy is first absorbed by the molecule, which prior to excitation, thermally populates the various vibrational energy levels of the ground electronic state, dictated by the Boltzmann equation. The absorption of energy causes excitation, which results in molecules from the various vibrational levels of the ground electronic state (S_0) to be promoted to the various vibrational levels of the excited electronic state (S_1), dictated by the Franck–Condon principle. (For a treatment of the Franck–Condon principle see Ref. 1.) The excitation therefore results in both electronic excitation and rotational–vibrational excitation. In the excited electronic state, the molecules first relax through vibrational relaxation, as a result of which they quickly get to the lowest vibrational level of the *excited electronic state*. In other words, very quickly, the molecules pool into the lowest vibrational state of the excited electronic state. That is, the electron still resides in the higher energy orbital, while the molecules have disposed off the excess vibrational energy to the surrounding medium through a non-radiative process. The lowest vibrational level of the excited electronic level, may be somewhat long-lived and from here the molecule may take one of many decay channels. The excited molecule may return to the ground electronic state *radiatively* and this $S_1 \rightarrow S_o$ process is called *fluorescence*. The rate and quantum yield of fluorescence are determined by the radiative lifetime of the excited state. Following fluorescence, which vibrational levels of the ground electronic state the molecules will reach, will be dictated again by the Franck–Condon principle. The molecules that reach high vibrational levels of the ground electronic state, will eventually relax through a non-radiative process to the lower vibrational levels of the ground electronic state, for the process to start all over again. From Fig. 10.4, it is clear that, as a result of the vibrational relaxation processes occurring in the excited state and the fact that the molecules end up in high vibrational levels of the ground electronic state during the radiative process, the emission wavelength must be longer than the absorption wavelength. This is the Stokes shift that we referred to earlier. From the lowest vibrational level of S_1, the molecule also has other decay channels that it can choose from, in addition to what was mentioned above. It could transfer to the lowest triplet state (T_1), a process referred to as *inter-system crossing.* The $S_1 \rightarrow T_1$ transition is a non-radiative process and involves a flip of the spin of the electron. From the T_1 state, the molecule may return to S_0 by the emission of a photon, which is called *phosphorescence*. However, this is a slow process, as single-triplet transition is forbidden due to the spin selection rule. Yet another pathway available for the molecule in the lowest vibrational level of S_1 is *internal conversion*, which is a non-radiative process, in which the electron returns to the ground state without the emission of light. In short, the molecule in the S_1 state may decay radiatively, or through inter-system crossing (ISC) or internal conversion (IC), each with its own time constants or lifetime, given by τ_R, τ_{ISC}, τ_{NR} respectively. Which of these processes is dominant, depends on the particular system. The quantum yield of fluorescence basically gives us the relative importance of the radiative process over the other non-radiative processes. Obviously, the process with the smallest lifetime (or the fastest rate) would dominate the scenario.

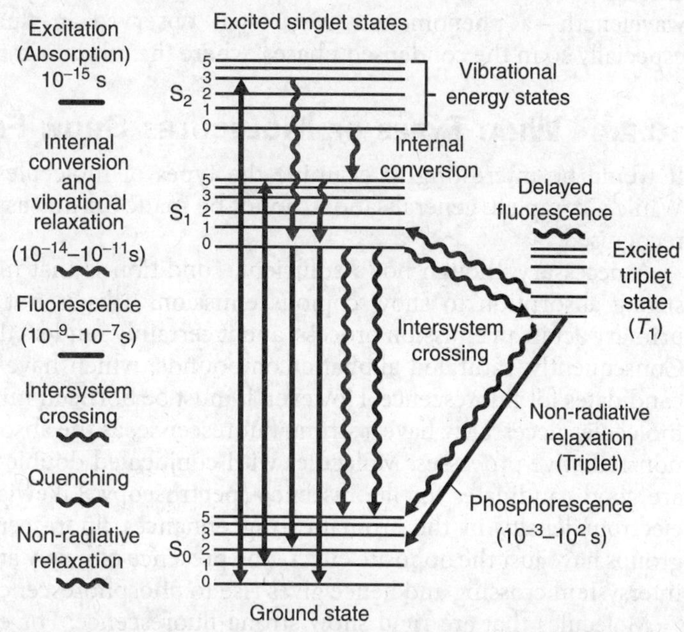

Fig. 10.4 The Jablonski diagram showing the various channels operative in a photo excitation and de-excitation process of molecules

Fluorescence emission is fast (10^{-5} s or less) in contrast to phosphorescence emission which is slow and may last for several minutes or even hours.

The above discussion also highlights another important fact about fluorescence spectra. Irrespective of which level the molecule was initially excited to, a quick relaxation process brings it to the lowest vibrational level of the excited electronic state from where fluorescence emission is observed. In other words, it does not matter what excitation wavelength is used; eventually the molecules will always fluoresce from the lowest vibrational level of the excited electronic state. Emission spectra would therefore be independent of the excitation wavelength—a phenomenon very often observed in fluorescence spectroscopy. This is especially so in the condensed phases, where the relaxation referred to above is fast.

10.2.4 What Types of Molecules Show Fluorescence

It would be interesting to examine the types of molecules that show strong fluorescence. While a complete generalisation cannot be made on this aspect, certain general rules can be recognised.

A necessary, though not a sufficient, condition is that molecules must have a reasonably strong absorption to show copious emission. This is not surprising as absorption is the primary act in an emission process, and it certainly renders this process as efficient as possible. Consequently, saturated aliphatic compounds, which have weak absorptions, are not good candidates for fluorescence. However, it must be borne in mind that not all strongly absorbing molecules necessarily have a strong fluorescence, as the absorbed energy may be dissipated in non-radiative processes. Molecules with conjugated double bonds and aromatic compounds are good candidates for fluorescence spectroscopy. Likewise, any substituent that increases electron density in the aromatic ring enhances fluorescence, while electron withdrawing groups have just the opposite effect. The presence of heavy atoms in the molecules encourages intersystem crossing and hence gives rise to phosphorescence at the expense of fluorescence.

Molecules that are rigid show strong fluorescence. For example phenolpthalein does not show any fluorescence, while a similar molecule fluorescein, shows a strong fluorescence, so much so, that it has come to be named as such. The difference in the two molecules (Fig. 10.5) is that, fluorescein is a rigid molecule due to the C–O bond, while the absence of such a bond in phenolphthalein makes it floppy. Floppy molecules tend to have vibrations that drain away the excited state energy through non-radiative processes, and hence show poor fluorescence. Aromatic molecules such as furan and pyridine do not fluoresce but quinoline and indole (rigid molecules) do.

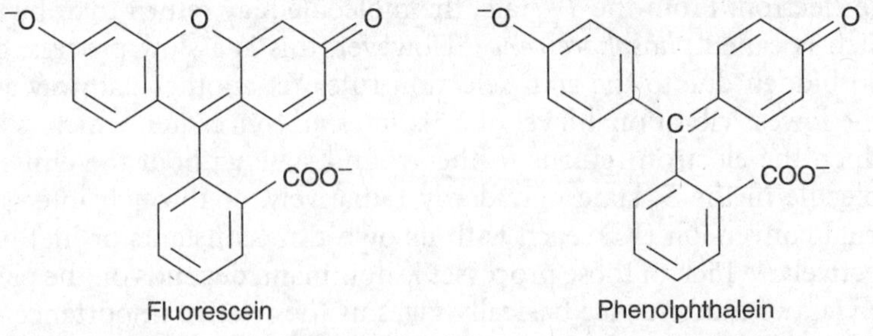

Fig. 10.5 Structure of fluorescein and phenolphthalein; the former is a rigid molecule and shows intense fluorescence

10.3 EXPERIMENTAL ASPECTS

Experiments on fluorescence may be conducted in one of two modes—steady state fluorescence or time resolved fluorescence. In the first mode, the sample is excited by a continuous emission source and the fluorescence emitted by the molecules is also monitored continuously. In this mode, no information on dynamics, such as the lifetime of excited states, is sought nor can be obtained. In the time resolved mode, the excitation source is either pulsed or modulated and the emission is collected, synchronised to the time dependent behaviour of the excitation source. In this mode, information on lifetimes or energy transfer dynamics can be obtained.

10.3.1 Steady State Fluorescence

We will first discuss the instrumentation used in steady state fluorescence spectroscopy (Fig. 10.6). The fluorescence spectrometer or fluorimeter, consists of two monochromators—an

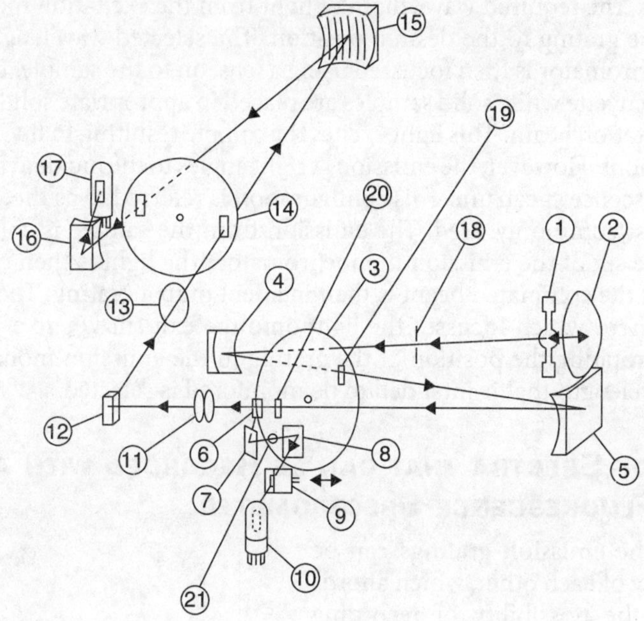

1. Xenon lamp, 150 W
2. Condenser ellipsoidal mirror, (SiO_2 coated)
3. Excitation slit assembly
4. Concave mirror
5. Concave diffraction grating (for excitation)
6. Beam splitter quartz plate
7. Teflon reflector No. 1
8. Teflon reflector No. 2
9. Optical attenuator
10. Monitor photomultiplier, R 212-09
11. A couple of light-collecting lenses
12. Cell
13. Light-collecting lens
14. Emission slit assembly
15. Concave diffraction grating (for emission)
16. Concave mirror
17. Photometric photomultiplier, R 452-01
18. Focus
19. Entrance slit
20. Exit slit
21. Light beam balancing aperture

Fig. 10.6 Schematic of the instrumentation used in steady state fluorescence spectroscopy

excitation monochromator and an emission monochromator. The excitation monochromator provides a beam of light of the desired wavelength to excite the sample molecules; the emission monochromator integrates the fluorescence emitted by the sample as a function of wavelength.

The excitation monochromator, which is used to select the wavelength to be employed for exciting the molecule, consists of an excitation source such as a Xe lamp, which has an output over wide wavelength range, typically 200–700 nm. The polychromatic light from the excitation source is efficiently collected and collimated using a system of mirrors. The collimated light is then incident on a grating which causes the dispersion of light. The light from the grating is then allowed to pass through a slit and is then directed onto the sample. The slit controls the amount of light falling on the sample and is usually chosen in a trade off between the amount of light incident on the sample and the wavelength resolution or the bandwidth of the incident beam. Small slit widths yield small bandwidths or better wavelength resolution, while at the same time limit the amount of light incident on the sample, which in turn results in lower fluorescence intensity. The required wavelength of light from the excitation monochromatic is chosen by rotating the grating to the desired position. The selected wavelength of light from the excitation monochromator is then focussed using a lens, on to the sample. If the sample is a liquid, it is taken in a cuvette while solid samples are placed in appropriate solid sample holders in the path of the excitation beam. This light excites the sample resulting in fluorescence, which is emitted in all directions. However, the emission at right angles to the incident beam is sampled for recording a fluorescence spectrum. This configuration is referred to as the T-geometry and is the one that is most commonly used. The emission from the sample is collected by a lens and focussed onto the slit of the emission monochromator. The light is then collimated using a concave mirror and the collimated beam is then incident onto a grating. The dispersed light falls on a concave mirror which focusses the light onto the exit slit where a photomultiplier tube is mounted. By rotating the position of the grating in the emission monochromatic, the specific emission wavelength that is intended to be monitored is selected.

10.3.2 Types of Spectra that can be Recorded with a Steady State Fluorescence Spectrometer

The excitation and the emission gratings can be rotated independently of each other, which affords the experimentalist the possibility of recording different types of spectra, each providing a unique set of information.

First, the excitation wavelength (λ_{exc}) is selected by rotating the grating in the excitation monochromator to a predetermined position. Keeping this position of the grating in the excitation monochromatic constant, it is possible to continuously vary the position of the grating in the emission monochromator, over a range of wavelengths. This experiment would achieve the excitation of a sample at a predetermined wavelength and allow monitoring of the intensity of the emission over a desired wavelength range. Such a spectrum would constitute an *emission*

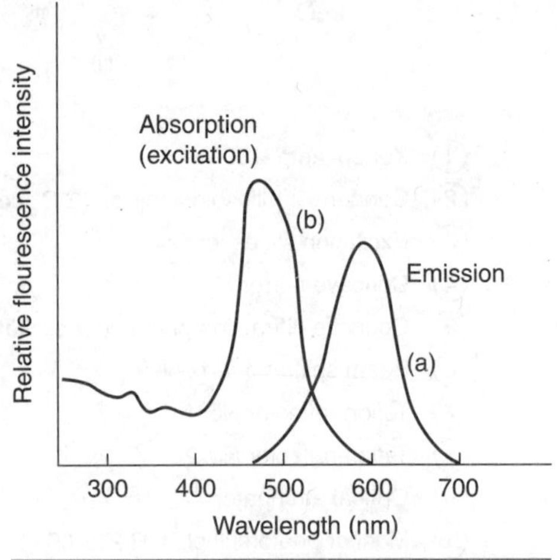

Fig. 10.7 The emission **(a)** and excitation **(b)** spectrum of a compound *X*

spectrum (Fig. 10.7). This provides information on the range of the lower states studied in a fluorescence process.

Alternatively, one can keep the position of the grating of the emission monochromator fixed, (thereby monitoring emission from the sample at a fixed wavelength, λ_{em}), and then scan the excitation monochromatic over a range of wavelengths. The spectrum thus obtained, where we record the fluorescence intensity from the sample as the excitation wavelength is scanned, is referred to as an *excitation spectrum*. This process records the different excited states involved in the fluorescence process. Obviously, if the absorption of the sample is large at a given wavelength, the fluorescence emission would also be large at this excitation wavelength relative to a wavelength where the absorption is small. Barring complications, the excitation spectrum can be expected to mimic an absorption spectrum of the sample. An example of an excitation spectrum and the corresponding absorption spectrum of a compound is shown in Fig. 10.7.

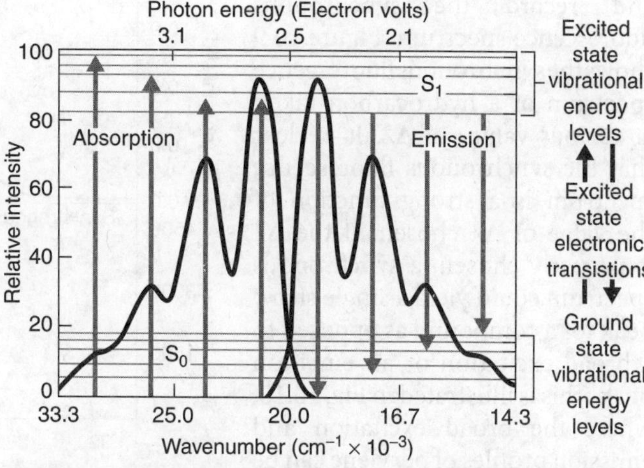

Fig. 10.8 Absorption and emission spectrum of perylene, illustrating that the emission spectrum appears to be the mirror image of the absorption spectrum

A common observation in fluorescence spectroscopy is that excitation spectra are often the mirror images of the emission spectra. This can be seen in Fig. 10.8, shown for the case of perylene. The reason why this mirror image rule works is that, in most cases the vibrational spacing in the upper and lower levels are about the same and the upper state potential curve lies almost vertically above the ground state. Exceptions to this rule, though, are not uncommon.

There is a third mode of recording a fluorescence spectrum, in which both the excitation and emission monochromators are scanned *simultaneously*. A spectrum thus recorded is a *synchronous fluorescence spectrum*. As an example, one can start the scan of the emission monochromator at say, 500 nm, while starting the scan of the excitation monochromator at 300 nm. The $\Delta\lambda$ is thus set equal to 200 nm and this difference is maintained constant right through the scan. One could maintain any desired difference

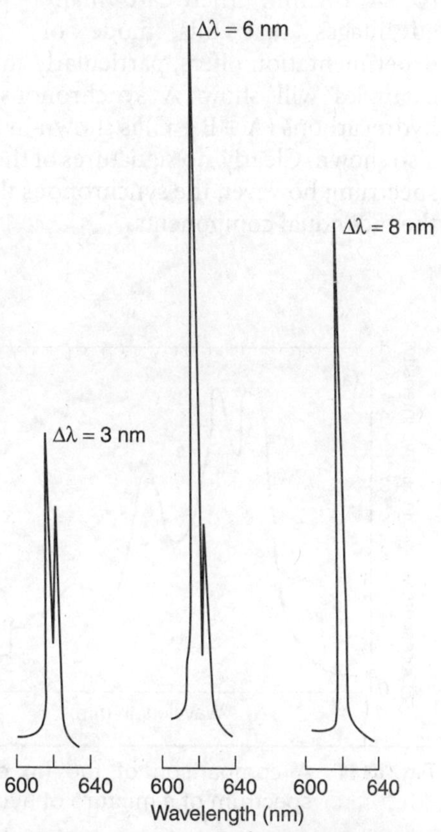

Fig. 10.9 A synchronous fluorescence spectrum of diindeno-[1,2, 3-c, d-1′, 2′, 3′-1, m] perylene at three different values $\Delta\lambda$

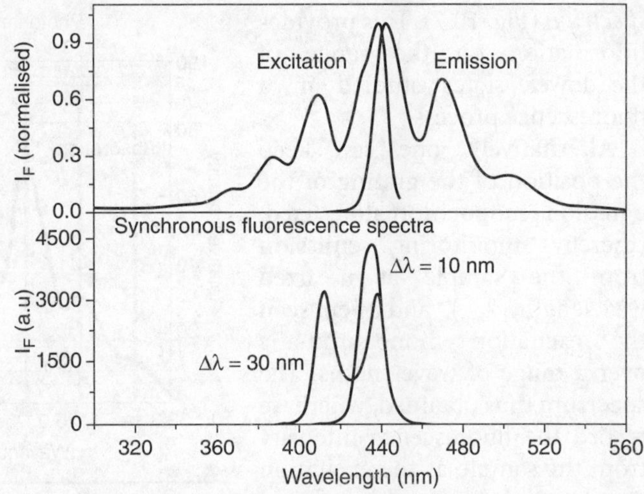

Fig. 10.10 Spectra of the emission, excitation and synchronous fluorescence of perylene in ethanol, where the $\Delta\lambda$ has been chosen to be 3 nm

and record the synchronous fluorescence spectrum. Figure 10.9 shows the synchronous fluorescence spectrum of a hydrocarbon taken at various values of $\Delta\lambda$. It is clear that the synchronous fluorescence spectrum is a strong function of the value of $\Delta\lambda$ chosen. If the $\Delta\lambda$ is properly chosen, a synchronous spectrum could yield a single sharp peak for a compound as opposed to a broad excitation or an emission peak. This is illustrated in Fig. 10.10, where the broad excitation and emission profiles of perylene can be compared with a single sharp peak in the synchronous fluorescence spectrum recorded choosing $\Delta\lambda$ = 10 nm. There are many advantages that this mode of experimentation offers, particularly in the realm of analytical spectroscopy, as the following examples will show. A synchronous fluorescence spectrum (b) of a mixture of three hydrocarbons (A + B + C) is shown in Fig. 10.11. The emission spectrum (a) of the mixture is also shown. Clearly, no signatures of the individual components are observable in the emission spectrum; however, the synchronous fluorescence spectrum shows clear signatures of each of the individual components.

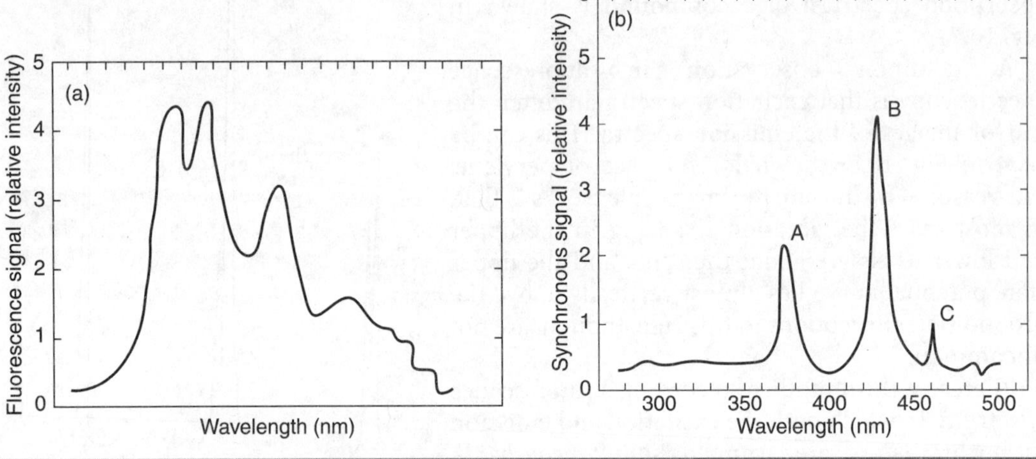

Fig. 10.11 A comparison of the **(a)** emission spectrum and **(b)** synchronous fluorescence spectrum of a mixture of hydrocarbons

10.4 TIME RESOLVED FLUORESCENCE

In the previously described steady state experiments no dynamical information was sought. However, in time resolved fluorescence, information on the lifetime of the excited states and energy transfer process can be obtained. Time resolved fluorescence can be studied by one of two methods—pulsed technique and phase modulation; both of which will be discussed briefly.

10.4.1 Pulsed Technique

In this method, the sample is excited by a *short* pulse of light, with typical pulse widths of micro- or nanoseconds. (The pulse width has now been extended to pico and femtoseconds, where ultra-fast processes are studied.) This short excitation pulse populates the excited state on the time scale of the duration of the exciting pulse. The excited state population will now de-excite and produce fluorescence emission which has a time profile. All the emission from the sample can be allowed to fall on a photomultiplier or the emission can be dispersed using a monochromator and specific wavelengths can be monitored. The time profile of the emission from the sample is converted to a current pulse by a fast photomultiplier which is now monitored as a function of time.

Of course, the time constant of the detection process must be short compared with the dynamics of the emission process that is being monitored. For example, if the emission process has a lifetime of 50 ns, the detection process must be capable of keeping pace on this time scale. It would be futile trying to study nanosecond dynamics, with detection equipment that has a time constant of the order of μs. The slow detection system would simply average out the time information and would serve no useful purpose. The response of the detection system depends on the response time of the detector used, such as a photomultiplier tube (PMT) and the signal acquisition device such as digital storage oscilloscope. PMTs with small response times and digital storage oscilloscopes with large bandwidths must be used to obtain a detection system with good time resolution. The speed of data handling of a digital storage oscilloscope is given by the bandwidth of the scope. When handling fast pulses, it is also imperative to understand concepts in electronics that deal with transmission of short pulses, as a proper choice of cables and connectors with the right impendence is essential. An improper choice could give rise to artifacts such as pulse ringing—a phenomenon in which a single pulse travels back and forth in the cable to produce multiple pulses arising out of mismatched impendence in transmission lines. A detailed discussion of such concepts is beyond the scope of this book; the discussion given above is only to highlight the need to understand such concepts when setting up time resolved experiments.

The above discussion also implies that the temporal pulse width of the exciting light pulse must be short compared with the rate of the process being monitored. One can easily imagine the problem that arises when one uses a pulse of microseconds to study a nanosecond process! A good part of the fluorescence response would be underway even before the excitation is complete. In such cases, the fluorescence temporal profile would be convoluted with the excitation pulse and is a needless complication.

A variation of the above experiment is single photon counting. In the experiment discussed above, a single pulse of light causes the excitation of a large number of species resulting in the emission of a large number of photons. This has a time profile that is monitored. Alternatively, one can excite a small number of atoms or molecules, such that on an *average*, no more than one photon is emitted in every pulse. Note the use of the term 'average'; this implies that there may be excitations that cause no photon emission, while some may lead to just one photon and extremely rare instances where more than one photon is emitted following an excitation. The photon emission is recorded using a sensitive PMT and detection system. The trick in such experiments is to distinguish between noise in the PMT which always exists and the small increase in signal levels following the incidence of a photon on the PMT. This discrimination between noise and signal is achieved using electronic devices such as constant fraction discriminators, which are triggered only by signals above a certain threshold. The threshold is judiciously set to discriminate between noise and signal and hence only events corresponding to photon emission are recorded. A number of excitation pulses are made incident on the sample; some excitations cause photon emission immediately after excitation (recall the discussion on lifetimes) while in some cases the emission may occur somewhat later. A complete record of a large number of photon emissions would yield the emission profile of the sample as a function of time; very much like that obtained in the earlier experiment where a single strong pulse causes instantaneous excitation of a number of molecules leading to photon emission. The concept to be understood here is that the process of simultaneous excitation of N molecules and monitoring the decay (in time) of this sample, is equivalent to N individual excitations of the same species and monitoring 'single photon' emission.

In single photon emission experiments, it is necessary to keep the excitation intensity low and obtain no more than one photon in every excitation process. If more than one photon were to be emitted by the same excitation pulse, it is likely that when processing the signal from the first photon, the later photons may be ignored—a problem referred to as *pulse pile up*.

10.4.2 Phase Modulation

This is an alternative experimental method to measure lifetimes of excited states. In this method, the excitation of the sample is carried out using a modulated excitation source. The modulation profile could be sinusoidal in nature, with the modulation frequency being ω. Modulation means, the intensity of the excitation beam follows a time variation. The emission from the sample would also be modulated likewise. If the lifetime of the excited state were to be *zero*, the emission and the excitation beams would be in phase. However, as the excited state has a definite lifetime, the emission from the sample would be somewhat retarded in time compared to the excitation beam; in other words, there would be a phase difference between the two beams. Furthermore, the emitted light would also be demodulated. The phase shifts and demodulation are then used to determine excited state lifetimes. The experiment therefore consists of monitoring the emission from the sample and measuring the phase difference of this emission relative to that of the excitation beam and the demodulation factor. The lifetime of the excited state is given by the relation:

$$\omega\tau = \tan\theta$$

where τ is the excited state lifetime, ω is the modulation frequency and θ is the phase difference of the emission relative to that of the excitation beam. The demodulation factor m is given by;

$$m = (1 + \omega^2\tau^2)^{-1/2}$$

Using the measured values of θ and m, the excited state lifetime can be derived.

Where complex multiple de-excitation processes occur, measurements of θ and m yield only an effective lifetime. In order to resolve the individual process, the measurements of θ and m would have to be made at various modulation frequencies.

10.5 CONCENTRATION DEPENDENCE OF THE FLUORESCENCE INTENSITIES

Fluorescence intensities are strongly dependent on the concentration of the emitting species and this dependence makes it a useful tool in chemical analysis. The spectrum in Fig. 10.12, shows a plot of the fluorescence intensity of uranium at various concentrations. It is clear that the fluorescence intensity increases with the concentration of the flurophores. It should be borne in mind that this linearity is only assured at low concentrations and deviations from linearity can be quite pronounced at high concentrations. The linear dependence of fluorescence intensity on concentrations can be understood from the following analysis.

The primary act in any fluorescence experiment is absorption, and the efficiency of absorption will therefore be an important factor in deciding the fluorescence intensity. The light absorbed by the sample is given by Beer–Lambert's equation:

$$T = \frac{I}{I_0} = \exp(-\varepsilon Cl) \tag{10.3}$$

where ε = absorptivity, C = concentration of the absorbing species, l = path length of the cell, I = intensity of light transmitted through the sample, I_0 = intensity of light incident on the sample and T = fraction of light transmitted.

From Eq. 10.3, one can write the *fraction* of light absorbed as

$$\frac{1-I}{I_0} = 1 - \exp(-\varepsilon Cl) \tag{10.4}$$

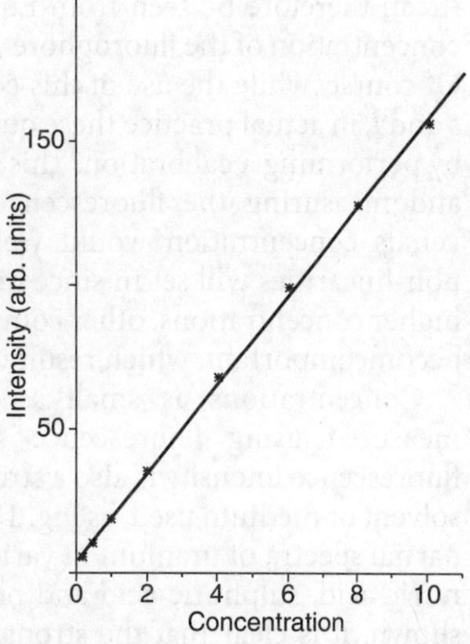

Fig. 10.12 A plot of the fluorescence intensity of the fluorophore as a function of the fluorophore concentration, showing the linear dependence.

The amount of light absorbed by the sample is given by $(I_0 - I)$, which can be expressed as

$$I_0 - I = I_0[1 - \exp(-\varepsilon\, Cl)] \tag{10.5}$$

The fluorescence intensity observed I_f, will naturally be dependent on the amount of absorbed light. In addition, I_f will also be dependent on the quantum efficiency, ϕ_f which you will recall, determines what fraction of the molecules that were excited will return to the ground state by emission of fluorescence. The observed fluorescence intensity will also depend on the instrumental factors such as the monochromator efficiency, detector efficiency, sampling geometry, and so on. All these factors – amount of light absorbed $(I_0 - I)$, quantum efficiency (ϕ_f) and instrumental parameters (ξ) – can be grouped together to express an equation for I_f, as follows;

$$I_f = \xi \cdot \phi_f \cdot (I_0 - I) \tag{10.6}$$

Substituting Eq. 10.5 in Eq. 10.6, we obtain,

$$I_f = \xi \cdot \phi_f \cdot I_0[1 - \exp(-\varepsilon\, Cl)] \tag{10.7}$$

The term $[1 - \exp(-\varepsilon\, Cl)]$ can be expanded as a series as follows;

$$1 - \exp(-\varepsilon\, Cl) = \varepsilon\, Cl - (\varepsilon\, Cl)^2/2! \tag{10.8}$$

For small values of $\varepsilon\, Cl$ (which arises for small concentrations or path lengths or absorptivities), square terms and higher in $\varepsilon\, Cl$, can be neglected. Equation 10.6 then reduces to

$$I_f = \xi \cdot \phi_f \cdot I_0(\varepsilon\, Cl) \tag{10.9}$$

It can therefore be seen from Eq. 10.9, that the fluorescence intensity is proportional to the concentration of the fluorophore. It is this dependence that is exploited in analytical chemistry. Of course, while the use of this equation demands a knowledge of quantities such as ξ, ϕ_f, I_0, ε and l, in actual practice these quantities are combined into one constant which is determined by performing a calibration. This is achieved by taking known concentrations of the substance and measuring the fluorescence at each concentration; a plot of fluorescence intensity versus concentration would yield the working analytical curve. At high concentrations, non-linearities will set in since higher order terms in Eq. 10.8 can no longer be neglected. At higher concentrations, other complications, such as inner filter effects and quenching may also become important, which result in deviations from Eq. 10.9.

Concentrations as small as a ng/mL can be measured using fluorescence spectroscopy. The fluorescence intensity is also a strong function of the solvent or medium used, as Fig. 10.13 will show. The partial spectra of uranium in various media—water, nitric acid, sulphuric acid and phosphoric acid are shown. It is clear that the strongest fluorescence is observed in phosphoric acid, which therefore is the medium of choice for the flourimetric estimation of uranium. These differences arise due to the interaction of the solvent with the fluorophore. It is therefore necessary that a judicious choice of the solvent be made in fluorimetric estimations.

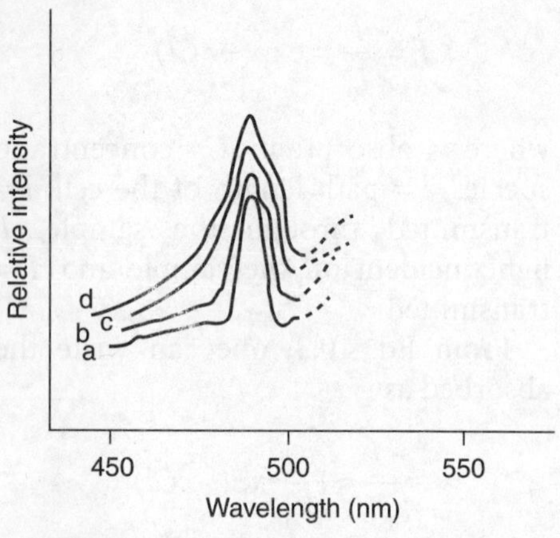

Fig. 10.13 Effect of solvent medium in the fluorescence intensity of uranium nitrate (only one of the spectral absorptions in each solvent is shown) **(a)** water **(b)** nitric acid **(c)** sulphuric acid and **(d)** phosphoric acid.

Changes in fluorescence intensities and wavelength of emission also result from changes in solvent polarities. The most striking example is that of PRODAN [6-propionyl-2-(N-N-dimethyl) naphthalene]. The spectrum of this compound changes dramatically as the solvent is varied. The emission in fact changes from 390 nm in cyclohexane to 530 nm in water. These changes arise because of the differences in the dipoles of the ground and excited states, which in turn arise due to the reorganisation of the electrons on optical excitation. The energy corresponding to say, λ_1 would cause excitation of the molecule from the ground state to the excited state, which we will assume has a greater dipole than the ground state. Soon after excitation, the polar solvent molecules sense the creation of a dipole and recorganise themselves to effectively interact with the newly created dipole. This causes the energy of the excited molecule to become lower after solvent reorganisation than it was soon after excitation. This process itself would lead to a solvent-induced Stokes shift in addition to the Stokes shift we saw earlier that arises due to the vibrational relaxation process. The extent of the solvent-induced Stokes shift would be a strong function of the differences in the dipole moment between the ground state and the excited state and the polarity of the solvent. Strongly polar solvents lead to a large solvent-induced Stokes shift. This concept has been used in biological applications to determine the polarity of the environment of the biological fluorophore.

10.5.1 Fluorescence Quenching

The fluorescence emission of a fluorophore is influenced also by the presence of other species in the solution. Figure 10.14a shows the fluorescence spectrum of uranium in phosphoric acid, where the concentration of uranium was maintained at 50 μg/mL. Figure 10.14b shows the fluorescence of the same concentration of uranium in the phosphoric acid medium, *but in the presence of 160 μg/ml of* Eu^{3+}. It is clear that in the presence of Eu^{3+}, the fluorescence intensity of uranium is significantly diminished. This decrease in intensity occurs due to a process known as fluorescence quenching. Collisions between the uranium and Eu^{3+} causes the excited uranium to be deactivated, not by emission of a photon, but by losing its energy to the colliding partner through a non-radiative process, thereby decreasing the fluorescence intensity. This process is also referred to as *dynamic quenching.* It is clear that the fluorescence intensity of uranium is reduced in the presence of the quencher compared to the intensity observed without the quencher. If the process of quenching is not recognised, the decreased fluorescence intensity might be interpreted as a smaller uranium concentration. It is therefore imperative to recognise quenching when it does occur.

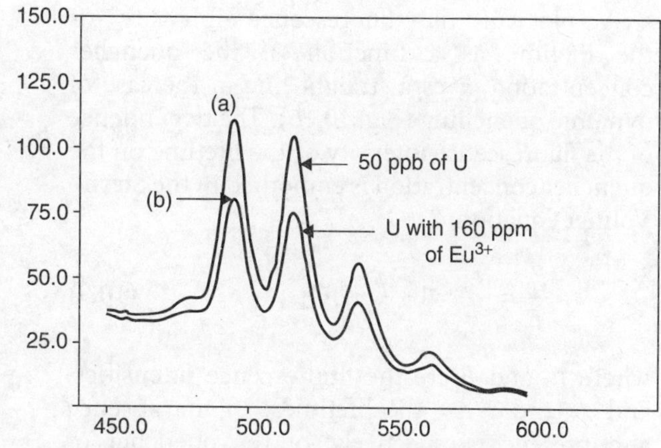

Fig. 10.14 (a) Fluorescence of uranium nitrate in phosphoric acid; **(b)** fluorescence of the same concentration of uranium in phosphoric acid, but in the presence of Eu^{3+}, to indicate the effect of quenching.

One of the methods to recognise and quantify dynamic quenching is through the measurement of lifetime of the fluorophore in the presence and absence of the quencher. Since the excited state population is reduced through collisions, in addition to a decrease in fluorescence intensity, the excited state lifetime is also decreased in dynamic quenching. Figure 10.15 shows the time resolved fluorescence decay of Eu^{3+} with and without the quencher; it is clear that in the presence of the quencher, the lifetime of the fluorophore is reduced. The decrease in the lifetime of the fluorophore with and without the quencher is a measure of the decrease in the fluorescence due to the quencher and this information can be used to correct for the decrease in fluorescence intensity due to quenching, so that the fluorophore concentration is not underestimated. This method is used in analytical chemistry wherein, in addition to the intensity of the flurophore emission, the lifetime of the fluorescence is also measured. The decrease in the fluorescence lifetime of the flurophore, relative to that of the unquenched fluorophore, is then used as a measure of the quenching process.

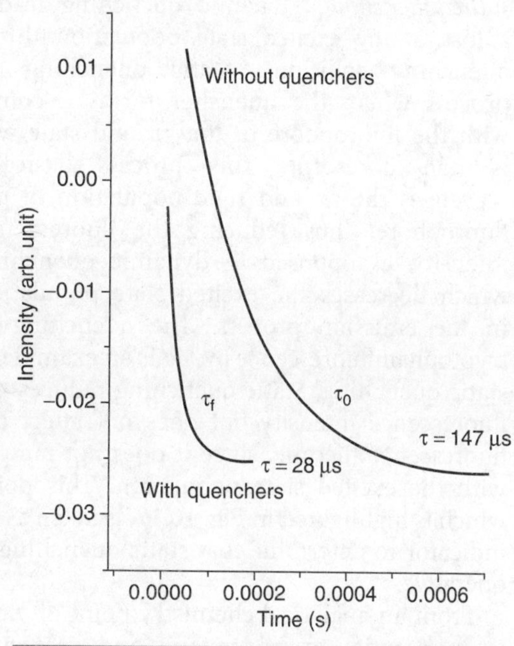

Fig. 10.15 A plot of the fluorescence lifetime of the fluorophore with and without quencher, to demonstrate dynamic quenching.

A plot of the fluorescence intensity or the lifetime as a function of the quencher concentration gives a straight line in the case of dynamic quenching (Fig. 10.16). The dependence of the fluorescence intensity or the lifetime on the quencher concentration is embodied in the Stern–Volmer equation:

$$\frac{F_0}{F} = \frac{\tau_0}{\tau} = 1 + k_q \tau_0 [Q] \tag{10.9}$$

where F_o and F are the fluorescence intensities, and τ_o and τ are the lifetimes, in the absence and presence, respectively, of the quencher of concentration $[Q]$, and k_q is the bimolecular quenching constant.

In addition to dynamic quenching, there is yet another mechanism for fluorescene quenching—*static quenching*. Dynamic quenching leads to a loss of the excited state population through quenching collisions. Static quenching is a process where the quencher forms a complex with the fluorophore in the ground state which is non-fluorescent. This process basically scavenges the ground state population of the fluorophore, thus reducing the fluorescence intensity, as opposed to dynamic quenching which decreases the excited state population in the emission process. The quenching of tryptophan fluorescence by Hg is an example of static quenching. Static quenching reduces the fluorescence intensity but does not affect the fluorescence lifetime, since it does not tamper with the excited state population. This point which is highlighted in Fig. 10.17, is taken as an indicator to determine that static quenching is operative.

From an analytical chemistry point of view, it is essential to understand and recognise quenching when it occurs, as otherwise the reduced fluorescence intensity may be interpreted as simply occurring from a reduced fluorophore concentration. In other words, if fluorescence quenching is not recognised, the concentration of the flurophore may be underestimated.

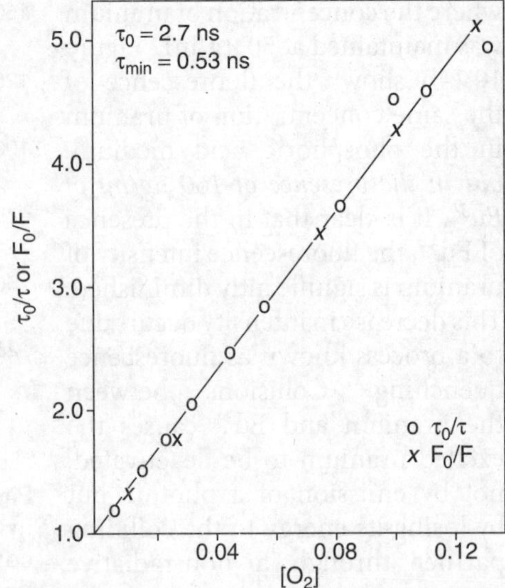

Fig. 10.16 Dynamic quenching: A plot of the fluorescence intensity and lifetime relative to the values in the absence of the quencher (F_0 and τ_0) as a function of the quencher concentration.

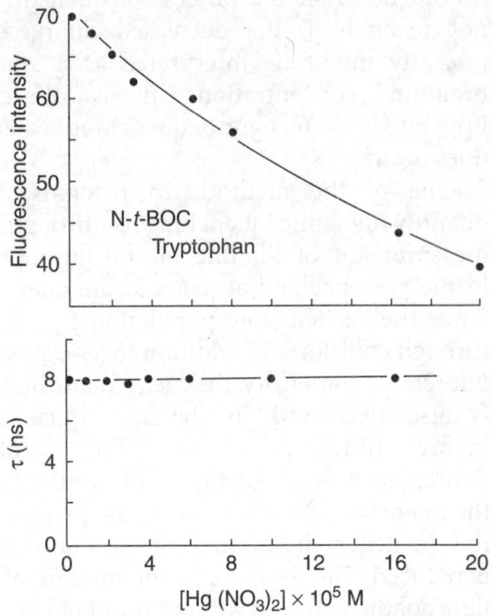

Fig. 10.17 Static quenching: A plot of the fluorescence intensity and the lifetime as a function of quencher concentration for static quenching.

10.5.2 Fluorescence Enhancement

The above discussion was directed towards factors that contribute to a decrease in fluorescence intensity of the fluorophore. Likewise, conditions can be created where the fluorescence intensity of the fluorophore can be enhanced. Such studies where fluorescence enhancement is observed are useful as they can be employed to obtain superior detection limits in fluorescence estimations.

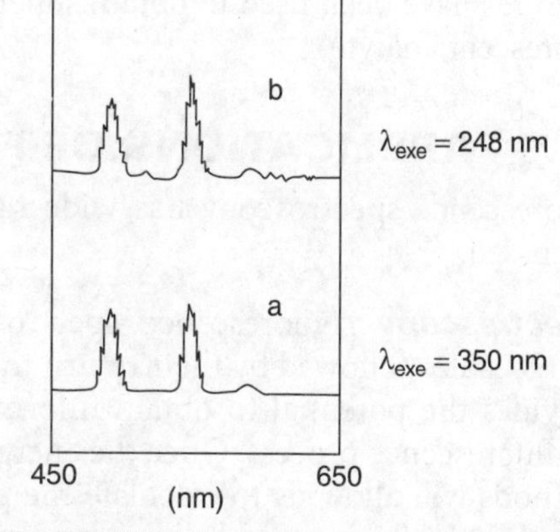

Fig. 10.18 Fluorescence spectra of Tb^{3+} **(b)** with and **(a)** without the addition of a sensitising ligand, benzoic acid, to demonstrate the phenomenon of ligand sensitized fluorescence enhancement. Intensity scales are the same in both figures. In both cases, the intensities are about the same, but the Tb^{3+} concentration used to record the spectrum (b) is about three orders of magnitude smaller than that used for spectrum (a). The fluorescence enhancement is therefore obvious.

One of the most popular methods used to obtain fluorescence enhancement is ligand sensitisation. In this experiment, the species that is probed, say Tb^{3+} ion, is complexed with a ligand such as benzoic acid. It has been observed that the fluorescence of the Tb^{3+} ion is enhanced by about 1000 times in the presence of benzoic acid (Fig. 10.18). In this figure are shown the fluorescence emission spectra for both uncomplexed Tb^{3+}, and Tb^{3+} complexed with benzoic acid. The fluorescence intensities shown in the two traces are about the same, but it must be noted that the concentration of Tb^{3+} is about three orders of magnitude smaller in the experiments where it was complexed with benzoic acid. Hence the fluorescence enhancement of about 1000 times is evident.

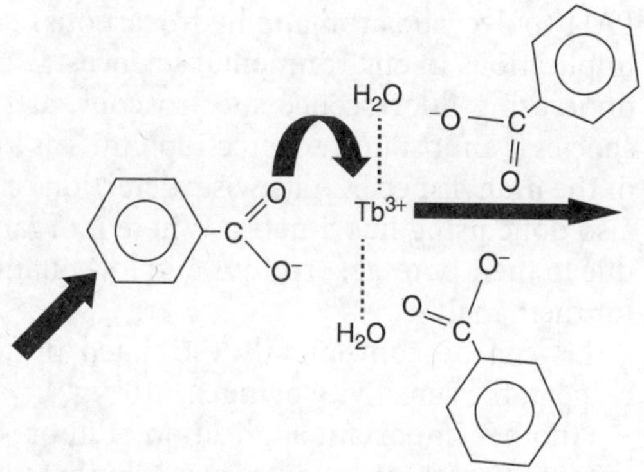

Fig. 10.19 A schematic showing the energy transfer processes in ligand sensitised fluorescence. The ligand absorbs the excitation light and transfers the energy eventually to the coordinated metal, which then emits it characteristic fluorescence.

The fluorescence enhancement arises due to the following process. The light is first absorbed by the ligand, benzoic acid, which has an absorption cross-section far higher than that of the lanthanide ion. The energy absorbed by the ligand raises it to the S_1 electronic state, from where the ligand might eventually find itself in the triplet state, T_1. If the triplet state has an energy close to the energy of the excited state of the lanthanide, an efficient energy transfer takes place between the triplet state of the ligand and the lanthanide, leading to an excitation of the lanthanide ion. From this excited state, the lanthanide then fluoresces giving rise to its fluorescence. The absorption cross-section of the ligand being strong and the eventual energy transfer to the lanthanide ion also being efficient, the lanthanide ion is more efficiently pumped to its excited state through this process rather than a direct absorption of light by the lanthanide ion. The ligand basically serves as an antenna in coupling light to the lanthanide (Fig. 10.19). This process is referred to as ligand sensitisation and it offers over a 1000-fold enhancement of fluorescence intensity. Such methods have been used to obtain superior detection limits in fluorescence estimation of the fluorescent analyte.

10.6 APPLICATIONS OF FLUORESCENCE SPECTROSCOPY

Fluorescence spectroscopy has wide ranging applications, some of which will be now be discussed.

Spectroscopy Fluorescence spectroscopy involves excitation of molecules to higher energy states followed by their return to the ground state. The study of fluorescence therefore provides the potential to obtain information on the energy levels of the states involved in the fluorescence process. Once the energy level information is obtained, quantum mechanical methods will allow us to calculate the potential energy curves of the states involved. Hence the study of fluorescence allows for the basic study of the potential surfaces. For example, fluorescence spectroscopy of the simple I_2 molecule has enabled the characterisation of the various electronic states of this molecule. Time resolved fluorescence, furthermore, allows one to obtain the dynamics of the relaxation process of the states.

Analytical chemistry The estimation of analytes in trace quantities is one of the most significant applications of fluorescence spectroscopy. Using fluorescence spectroscopy, limits of detection down to picograms/mL have been reported. This amounts to detecting material as low as parts per trillion. Of course, as explained above, underestimation of concentrations of analytes due to quenching must be taken into account, but the discussions above will show that there are prescribed methods available for this quenching.

Fluorescence measurements have greater sensitivity than absorbance measurements.

Using fluorimetry, both organic and inorganic compounds may be analysed. For example, PAH (polycyclic aromatic hydrocarbons) can be sensitively estimated, which has important implications in environmental sciences. Estimation of uranium as the uranyl ion, is routinely done using fluorescence spectroscopy, as the quantum yield of fluorescence for the uranyl species is almost unity. Detection limits as low as ng/mL have been reported for the estimation of the uranyl species. Likewise, detection of lanthanides, such as Tb^{3+}, Eu^{3+}, Dy^{3+} and Sm^{3+}, is also done using fluorimetry. Where inorganic ions are not amenable to fluorimetric analysis, due to their poor absorptions and low quantum yields, we use methods of ligand sensitisation for their analysis.

Li^+ can be conveniently estimated by fluometry at 370 nm with a 8-hydroxyquinoline reagent, the sensitivity being 2×10^{-7} g.

Another important application of fluorescence is in remote monitoring of analytes such as those in hazardous environments. In these cases, the excitation light is delivered to the analyte through optical fibre cables and the emitted fluorescence is then collected and transported thorugh optical fibres to a spectrometer kept some distance away from the hazardous sample. This method greatly facilitates the analysis of hazardous samples in the industry as it eliminates the need to collect such samples and bring it to the laboratory for analysis. The analysis of uranium in reprocessing streams in the nuclear industry is one such application.

Biology Proteins are often studied using fluorescence spectroscopy. This study becomes possible as three of the amino acids – tryptophan, tyrosine and phenylalanine – are fluorescing molecules. The study of the fluorescence from these amino acids can lead to important information about the structure of the proteins themselves. For example, depending on the three-dimensional structure of the proteins, these amino acids may be exposed to aqueous or lipid phases. Whether they are exposed to aqueous or lipid phases can be determined by studying the emission characteristics from these amino acids.

Pharmaceuticals Many pharmaceutically active compounds such as the tranquiliser reserpine exhibit strong fluorescence. Therefore fluorimetry provides for a sensitive detection and quantification of such compounds.

10.6.1 Advantages of Fluorescence Spectroscopy

Before closing the discussion on fluorescence spectroscopy, it would be worthwhile to summarise the advantages of this technique.

Absorption spectroscopy measures differences in light intensities as light traverses the sample. In fluorescence spectroscopy, emission from the sample at a wavelength different from that used for excitation, is monitored. The emission intensity (and not the *difference* in the light intensity, as in absorption), is proportional to concentration of the probe species. This aspect makes the fluorescence method more sensitive than absorption.

While absorption spectroscopy is characterised by the use of the one wavelength parameter—the absorption frequency, in fluorescence, uses two wavelengths to characterise the sample—the excitation and the emission wavelength. Furthermore, the emission lifetimes add another dimension to the detection parameters. This immediately increases the selectivity of the technique. It is likely that two substances may have the same absorption wavelength, but less likely that they would have the same absorption and emission wavelengths. In the unlikely case where the excitation and emission wavelengths happen to be nearly the same for a set of species, there is always the possibility of resolving their emission in the time domain. It is highly unlikely that the two species would have the same excitation and emission wavelengths as well as the same emission lifetimes. The multiparameter nature of the fluorescence technique leads to high degree of selectivity.

The dynamics of the emission process being dependent on the environment of the fluorophore, this technique becomes extremely useful in probing the environment of the species under study.

The sensitivity of fluorescence detection has given rise to the technique of *single molecule detection*. This involves detecting a single molecule present in the probe volume! This technique has become possible with the advent of lasers, which with its high intensity has pushed limits of detection to amazingly low levels. The problem one would envisage with detecting single molecules in the probe volume is that, in the same volume there would exist solvent molecules far in excess of the probe molecule and the light emission or scatter from the solvent molecules must be distinguished from that emitted by the probe molecule. There now exist experimental techniques to do exactly that. The experimental technique of single molecule detection will be described in detail in the chapter that deals with laser techniques.

Who's who in fluorescence

- *Alexander Edmond Becquerel* (1820–1891, France) He invented the phosphorscope, using which he discovered phosphorescence in several substances.
- *Aleksander Jabłoński* (1898–1980, Poland) (Father of phosphorescence) He proposed energy diagrams, now known as Jablonski energy diagrams to explain the kinetics and spectra of fluorescence.
- *Johan Sebastian Ploem* (1927–, Dutch) He is a physicist who invented the epi-illumination cube used in modern fluorescence spectrometers.
- *George Gabriel Stokes* (1819–1903, UK) He first proposed the term 'fluorescence' after studying the fluorescence of several molecules. The wavelength shifts in fluorescence are now known as Stokes shift, in his honour.

- *Gregorio Weber* (1916–1997, England) He is considered the promoter of modern fluorescence spectroscopy. He devised the model of phase-modulation fluorescence. He reported the classical technique of calculating the absolute quantum yield of fluorescence.

EXERCISES

1. Rationalise the following:
   (a) Fluorescence is favoured by regidity in organic molecules.
   (b) In most molecules, the quantum efficiency of fluorescence decreases with increasing temperature.
   (c) The relative fluorescence intensity for benzonitrile is 20 where as that for benzoic acid is only 3.
   (d) The excitation spectrum and the fluorescence spectrum for a compound are often mirror images.
2. Illustrate the effect of substituents on the fluorescence of benzene compounds.
3. Dissolved oxygen in the analyte solution reduces the intensity of fluorescence: rationalise this observation.
4. Explain the following:
   (a) Self-quenching fluorescence
   (b) Internal conversion in fluorescence
   (c) Vibrational relaxation
5. Discuss the experimental conditions that influence the quantum efficiency of fluorescence.
6. Arrange the following in the increasing order of fluorescence quantum yield under identical experimental conditions: aniline, fluorescein, oxine and iodobenzone. Explain.
7. Explain critically how fluorometry complements spectrophotometry for the determination of cations.
8. Write an account of the quantitative methods in molecular fluorescence spectrometry.
9. A solution of a heterocyclic compound was dissolved in sufficient 0.10 M HCl and the solution made upto 500 mL. 20.0 mL of this solution was diluted to 100.0 mL with the acid solution. Its fluorescent intensity measured at 347.5 nm indicated an intensity of 300 on an arbitrary scale. Under identical experimental conditions, a standard solution of the heterocycle (60 ppm) showed an intensity reading of 120. Calculate the quantity of the heterocycle in the analyte solution.
10. Distinguish between (a) resonance fluorescence and sensitised fluorescence (b) fluorescence quenching and fluorescence enhancement.
11. Explain the factors which determine the fluorescence quantum yields.
12. Outline the principle of
    (a) Phase-resolved fluorescence spectroscopy
    (b) Fluorescence correlation spectroscopy
    (c) Pulsed fluorescence spectroscopy
13. Explain how the Jablonski diagram is applied in understanding the theory of fluorescence spectroscopy.
14. A fluorescence spectrum can be recorded by different modes: explain.
15. Citing a journal article, illustrate the application of fluorescence spectroscopy in characterising drug molecules.

11 Infrared Spectroscopy

11.1 INTRODUCTION

The vibration of bonded atoms and molecules is often a good indicator of the properties of the system. For example, two balls attached by a spring will vibrate with a characteristic frequency which is descriptive of the properties of the spring, such as the spring constant and the masses of the balls attached to them. Molecular systems behave likewise. Two atoms coupled to each other through a bond, the equivalent of the spring, vibrate (even at temperatures of absolute zero!), and this vibrational act of the system can be used to understand the properties of the system. The frequency with which the molecule vibrates is characteristic of the structure and nature of bonding in the molecule; this fact is used to great advantage in the study of the molecular properties. For a diatomic molecule, the vibrational frequency ω, is given by

$$\omega = \left(\frac{1}{2\pi}\right)\left(\frac{k}{\mu}\right)^{1/2} \tag{11.1}$$

where k is the force constant of the bond and μ is the reduced mass. Clearly, the nature of the bond and hence the magnitude of k and the mass of the system, influence the vibrational frequency. Stronger force constants and lighter atomic masses give rise to larger vibrational frequencies. It is this dependence of the force constant on the vibrational frequency that lays the foundation for the study of molecular structure and bonding using vibrational spectroscopy. As we will see later, this technique is not only used to study fundamental aspects of molecular structure and bonding but has also been extensively and routinely used in analytical chemistry for qualitative and quantitative characterisation of materials and molecules.

While experimentation in vibrational spectroscopy is now well established, it might just be instructive to examine the daunting task that we have taken upon ourselves when we decided to probe molecular vibrations. A simple molecule such as H_2 has a vibrational frequency of ~4100 cm^{-1}. This bond vibrates about 10^{14} times a second, which is a vibration once every ~10^{-14} s. The atom is displaced about a few picometres during every vibration. It is also possible for molecules to execute vibrations in which the bond angles are altered; the angular displacements in such vibrations is only of the order of a few degrees. (Of course, angular displacements become relevant only for molecules that have at least three atoms.) These displacements seem to be so insignificant, that one would seem to have no hope of physically observing them. However, we do not necessarily have to see the miniscule displacements of atoms to study molecular vibrations. The interaction of radiation with molecules provides us with a powerful tool to 'see' the molecular vibrations. When the frequency with which the atoms in the molecules vibrate, matches with the frequency of the electromagnetic radiation to which it is exposed, a resonance condition is established. Other things being favourable, which we shall see later, the electromagnetic radiation is absorbed by the molecule; very much the way a tuning fork of a certain frequency will start to vibrate, in resonance, with another already-vibrating tuning fork of the same frequency. The absorption of radiation can be monitored to identify molecular vibrations.

11.1.1 Region of the Electromagnetic Spectrum

The region of the electromagnetic radiation that resonates with molecular vibrations is the infrared region—between 2.5 and 500 μm in wavelength. For the sake of convenience and experimental significance, this region is further subdivided. The first is the region between 2.5 and 25 μm which is the mid-infra region, while the second is the region between 15 and 1000 μm, which is the far-infrared region. These numbers are also often expressed in units of reciprocal lengths, or wavenumbers. The mid-infrared region, in such units, ranges from 4000 to 400 cm^{-1}, while the far-infrared region is between 700 and 10 cm^{-1}. In terms of frequency, the mid-infrared region corresponds to 1.2×10^{14} s^{-1} to 1.2×10^{13} s^{-1}, while the far-infrared region is the region spanning roughly 2×10^{13} s^{-1} to 3×10^{12} s^{-1}. It is essential to be conversant with the different units used to describe molecular vibrations.

Organic chemists are often interested in the mid-infrared region as most of the functional groups of organic molecules vibrate with frequencies that are in resonance with the frequency of the electromagnetic radiation in this region. The far-infrared region is of great interest to inorganic chemists.

11.2 NATURE OF MOLECULAR VIBRATIONS

The vibration in a diatomic molecule is rather simple; there is only one way in which the atoms can vibrate. If one of the two atoms were to be kept fixed, the second atom can only vibrate in a to-and-fro motion relative to the first, along the line of the bond. However, for triatomic and larger molecules, the vibrational pattern that the molecule executes gets complex. Take the simplest triatomic case—water. This molecule, as we all know, is V-shaped. This molecule can fundamentally vibrate in three ways (Fig. 11.1). First, is the *symmetric stretch*, in which the two H–O bonds pull simultaneously outwards (or inwards), as indicated by the arrows. The second is the *asymmetric stretch*, in which one H–O bond pulls outwards, while the other pulls inwards, or vice-versa. In both the vibrational patterns, the H–O bond length constantly changes during the vibrational motion, while H–O–H bond angle is barely affected. The third is the *bend*, in which the two H atoms move towards or away from each other, thereby constantly altering the H–O–H bond angle during the vibration, while barely affecting the H–O bond length. These three ways in which this molecule vibrates are called the *normal modes*. These three modes are not unique to water; *any* triatomic bent molecule would vibrate in these modes, be it HOCl or H_2S.

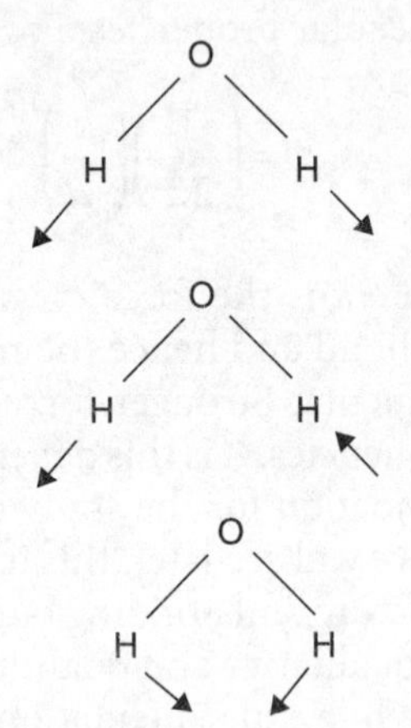

Fig. 11.1 Normal vibrational modes of the H_2O molecule

11.2.1 Normal Modes

What is so special about the three vibrational modes of water that we discussed? In other words, what do normal modes really mean? Assume for a moment, that we could 'hang' a molecule of water in front of us and 'observe' it vibrate. Would we see it doing a symmetric stretch or an asymmetric stretch or a bend? Or would it alternate between these three modes—once doing a symmetric stretch for a while and then shifting to a bend and then onto an asymmetric stretch, only to return to one of the other modes, a little later? In fact we would see none of this; the molecule of water would in fact perform a very complex motion that would be completely confusing! However, it can be shown that whatever the water molecule does, its motion can be resolved into a linear combination of the three modes that we mentioned earlier. Very much like the complicated dance motion of a performing artist can be resolved into basic dance steps! In the realm of the molecular dance, the fundamental dance steps are the normal modes. The normal modes serve as a basis for representing any complex vibrational motion that the molecule may perform. The number of normal modes that a non-linear molecule has is given by $3N–6$, where N is the number of atoms. For a linear molecule, the number of normal modes are $3N–5$. That is the reason we have three normal modes for non-linear triatomic water while we have four for the linear triatomic CO_2 molecule. How these normal modes are arrived at, is beyond the scope of this discussion and textbooks on normal coordinate analysis may be consulted for this purpose.

We noted earlier that interaction of infrared radiation with molecules serves as a tool to observe molecular vibration. A diatomic molecule has only one mode of vibration and let us assume, for a moment, that this vibration occurs at a frequency of 6×10^{13} s^{-1}, which corresponds to 2000 cm^{-1} or to a wavelength of 5 μm. This molecule has a vibration that will be resonant only with just that region of the electromagnetic radiation at 5 μm and assuming that other things are favourable, this region of the radiation will be absorbed. Imagine that we shine on a diatomic molecule, polychromatic infrared radiation with wavelengths ranging from 2.5 μm to 25 μm. If we now have a detector, that monitors the intensity of the radiation with and without the sample molecules and detect those regions of the electromagnetic radiation that have a reduced intensity as a result of the transit through the sample molecules, the vibrations in the molecules can be detected.

However, a mere resonance condition between the frequency of the electromagnetic radiation and the vibrational frequency does not ensure that the radiation will be absorbed; there are certain *favourable* conditions required for the absorption as alluded to earlier. While the resonance condition is a necessary condition, it certainly is not a sufficient condition. This 'favourable condition' has to do with the dipole moment of the molecule, which we will now discuss.

A dipole is formed when a positive and a negative charge of magnitude Q are separated by a distance r; the dipole moment of this separated charge pair is given by Qr. In ionic bonds and polar covalent bonds, there is a charge separation and such bonds give rise to a dipole that arises from the different electronegativities of the constituent atoms. For example, in water there is a dipole moment associated with each of the O–H bonds, with the negative end of the dipole pointing to the oxygen. Bonds in homonuclear molecules such as H–H or Cl–Cl have no associated dipole moment, as these bonds do not involve any charge separation, as both atoms have identical electronegativities. Considering water which has two O–H bonds, each of which has an associated dipole moment, the net dipole moment can be calculated from simple vector mathematics. The resultant dipole moment would be that of the H_2O molecule. It is obvious that the two dipoles which make an angle of ~105° would vectorially add up to a net dipole moment that is non-zero. In the case of CO_2, while each C–O bond would have non-zero dipole moment, due to the different electronegativities of carbon and oxygen, the molecule would have a zero dipole moment, as the individual dipoles are oriented 180° to each other and hence would vectorially cancel each other out.

While we have learnt to derive the dipole moment of molecules in their equilibrium configuration, we need to examine what happens to the dipole moment of the same molecule while it executes each of its normal vibrations. As the distances between the constituent atoms continuously change during a vibration, the individual bond dipole moments may also change—how this change affects the overall molecular dipole during a vibration needs to be considered.

First take the case of H_2, the simplest of all cases. In this case, since there is no charge separation ($Q = 0$), the dipole moment of the molecule is zero. Altering r during the vibration has no influence, since Q continues to be zero, and the dipole moment of the molecule turns out to be zero at every point in the vibration. Consider HCl, a heteronuclear diatomic molecule in which there is obviously a charge separation. As the vibration progresses, r is continuously altered—larger than the equilibrium value during the stretching phase, and smaller during the contraction phase. The dipole moment of the molecule consequently *changes* during the course of the vibration in HCl. The CO_2 molecule has four normal modes of vibrations (Fig. 11.2), one of which is a symmetric stretch. In this mode, the two oxygen atoms move away or towards the central carbon atom, in phase. Consequently, even though the individual bond dipoles may change during a vibration, the two dipoles are *always* equal and oriented exactly opposite to each other, leading to no net change in the molecular dipole moment during the course of the vibration, which is always zero. On the other hand, the asymmetric stretch and the bending vibrations would result in a change in the dipole moment of the CO_2 molecule, as the vibration occurs. It can therefore be seen that for the same molecule, certain vibrations cause a *change* in the dipole moment of the molecule during a vibration, while there may be others that do not. It can be shown that any vibration that changes the dipole moment of the molecule, leads to absorption of the infrared electromagnetic radiation at the resonant frequency and such vibrations are said to be *infrared active*. These are vibrations that will cause an attenuation of the radiation at the particular frequency of the vibration, as the radiation passes through the sample molecules. Vibrations that do not cause *changes* in the molecular dipole moment during the vibration, do not lead to any absorption of the infrared electromagnetic radiation, even though the resonance condition is met. Such vibrations are referred to as *infrared inactive*. Of course, all hope of studying such infrared inactive vibrations is not lost, as there are other experimental techniques such as Raman spectroscopy, which may help in probing such vibrational modes (Chapter 12). Which vibrational modes are infrared active can be derived by using concepts in group theory, which is beyond the scope of the discussion here. Suffice it to say, that the symmetry of the molecule plays an important role in deciding which vibrations will be infrared active.

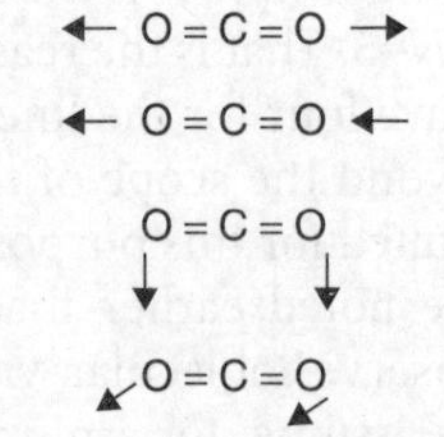

Fig. 11.2 Normal modes of vibration in the CO_2 molecule

It should be noted that CO_2 has two bending modes, one in which the oxygen atoms move in the plane of the paper, while in the second they move perpendicular to the plane of the paper. These are two distinct vibrational motions but have the same vibrational frequency and are referred to as *degenerate modes*. It is seen with symmetric molecules, such as CO_2.

It may be added that variations of bending vibrations such as those referred to as the *rocking*, *wagging*, *scissoring* and *twisting* are also encountered in a number of molecules (Fig. 11.3). These are merely bending vibrations, in which the motions of atoms mimic a rocking motion of a cradle or the wag of a tail.

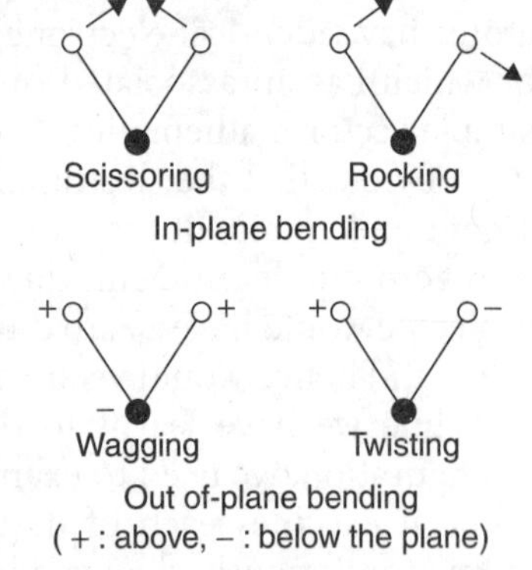

Fig. 11.3 Variation of bending vibrations of CO_2 molecule

The infrared spectra are usually plotted as transmittance as a function of the infrared frequencies—frequencies where the sample absorbs the least have the largest transmittance, while at frequencies where the absorption is the strongest show small transmittance. Alternatively, the spectra can also be plotted in terms of absorbance, (which is a measure of the light absorbed), as a function of the infrared frequencies. The relation between absorbance and transmittance is:

$A = -\log T$, where A is the absorbance and T is the transmittance of the sample.

Problem 11.1 Carbon–carbon absorption peak occurs in the infrared region for molecules of the type A but not for molecules of the type B. Explain.

A: $R(R)C{=}C(R)R^*$

B: $R(R)C{=}C(R)R$

Solution

In B, the structure is symmetrical; the carbons carrying the double bond are symmetrically substituted with two R groups each. In this molecule, no dipole moment change is expected with the vibration. Therefore, no C–C absorption peak is expected for this molecule. In A, the substitution around the C=C is unsymmetrical; change in the dipole moment is expected with the vibration and therefore, C–C absorption peak occurs.

Problem 11.2 Which of the following compounds are IR active?

(i) 1-butene (ii) 2,3-dimethyl-2-butene (iii) 2,3-dimethyl-2-hexene

Solution

For absorption by a molecule in the infrared region, the dipole moment of the molecule must change when vibration occurs. When a vibration is not accompanied by a change in dipole moment, no absorption band would be observed.

(i) $H(H)C{=}C(H)CH_2CH_3$

(ii) $CH_3(CH_3)C{=}C(CH_3)CH_3$

(iii) $CH_3(CH_3)C{=}C(CH_3)CH_2CH_2CH_3$

(i) This has a dipole moment along the carbon–carbon double bond. As this bond is stretched, the dipole moment changes (increases) and this produces an absorption band in the infrared region.

(ii) This molecule has a symmetrical structure. Therefore, it does not have a dipole moment along the carbon–carbon double bond. When the bond is stretched, no dipole moment results. Therefore, it is infrared inactive.

(iii) When this molecule stretches, only a negligible change in dipole moment results. Therefore, only an extremely weak absorption band is formed for the stretching vibration of the carbon–carbon double bond.

11.3 STRUCTURAL ELUCIDATION: CHARACTERISTIC FREQUENCIES OF GROUPS

In the previous sections, we discussed vibrational modes in simple molecules. Larger molecules have correspondingly a larger number and more complex vibrational patterns or normal modes. However, even in such complex cases, vibrations very often show patterns that are characteristic of groups of atoms present in a molecule. Figure 11.4 shows the infrared spectra of hexane and dodecane. While these molecules are clearly different from

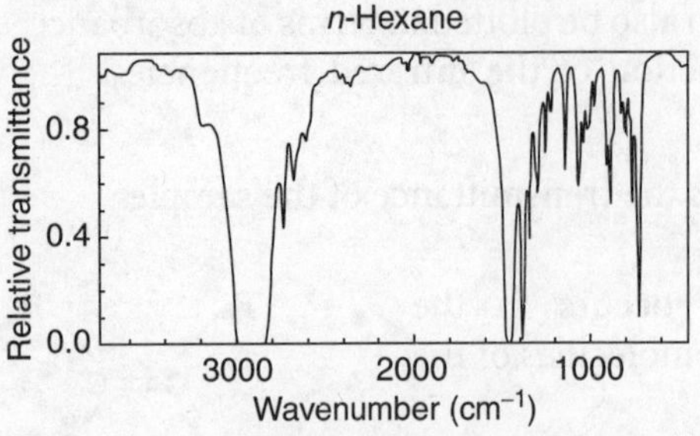

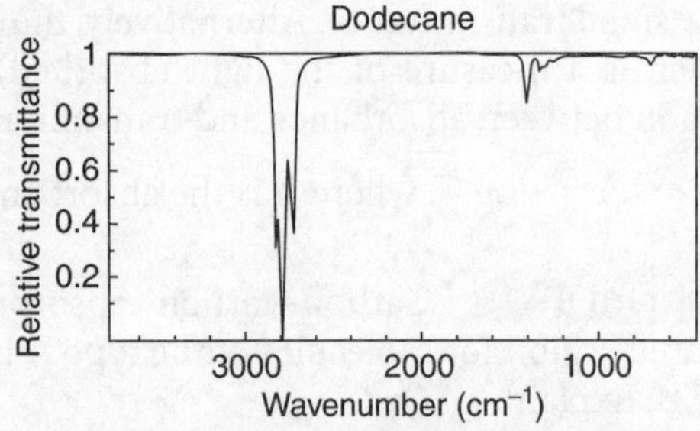

Fig. 11.4 IR spectra of hexane and dodecane

each other, their spectra show remarkable similarities such as the features near 2900 and 1400 cm^{-1}. The similarities arise from the fact that both these molecules have C–H and C–C groups, and the features at 2900 and 1400 are due to these clusters of atoms. Similarly, Fig. 11.5 shows the spectra of ethanol and propanol with similar features at 3300, 2900, 1400 and 1050 cm^{-1}, due to the vibrations of the O–H, C–H, C–C and C–O groups respectively. The feature at 1400 cm^{-1} is due to the C–C group; this is shown by recording the spectra of methanol (in which this group is absent) and this is true for the feature at 1400 cm^{-1} (Fig. 11.5 a, b, c). Figures 11.5a and d show the spectra of ethanol and dimethyl ether, which are functional group isomers. Clearly the two spectra are remarkably different. The spectrum of ethanol shows features due to the O–H, C–H and C–O groups at 3100, 2900 and 1100 cm^{-1} respectively. The ether, on the other hand, shows features only at 2900 and 1100 cm^{-1}, due to the C–H and C–O groups, while the feature at 3100 cm^{-1} is clearly absent. Infrared spectroscopy is such as a powerful tool as it enables the identificaon of groups present in the molecule.

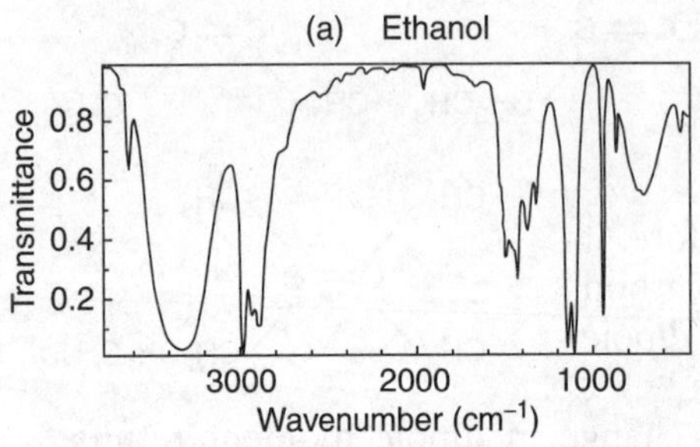

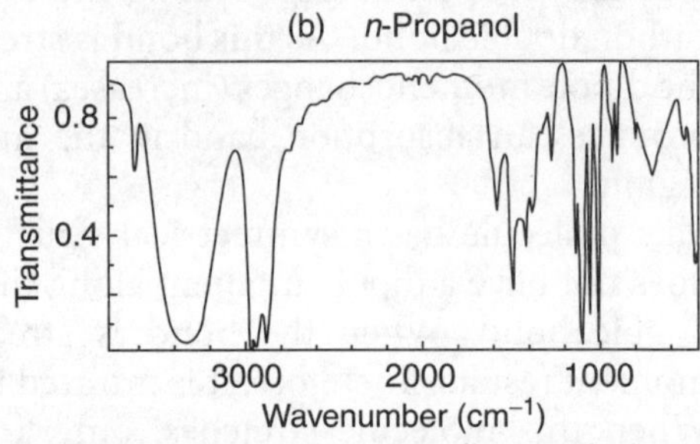

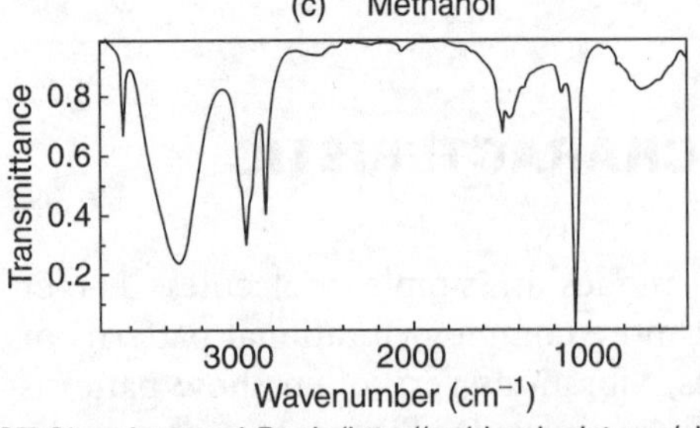

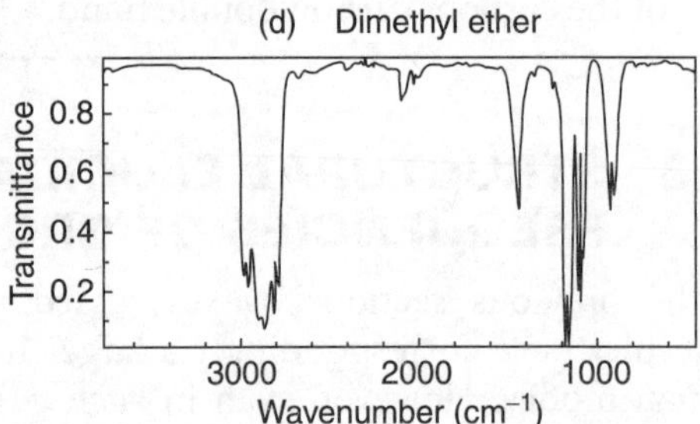

Fig. 11.5 IR spectra of ethanol, propanol, methanol and dimethyl ether

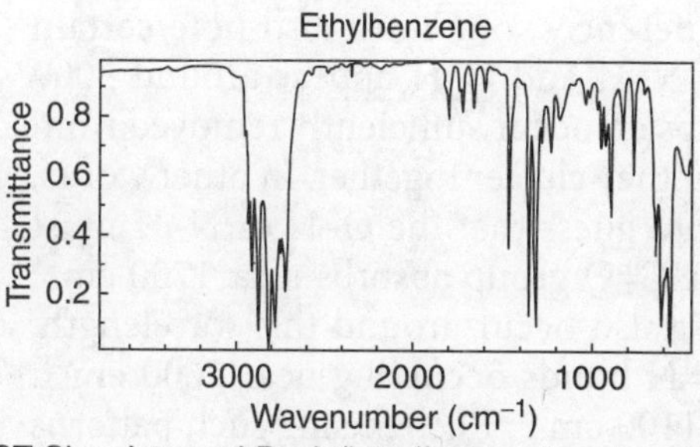

NIST Chemistry webBook (http://webbook.nist.gov/chemistry)

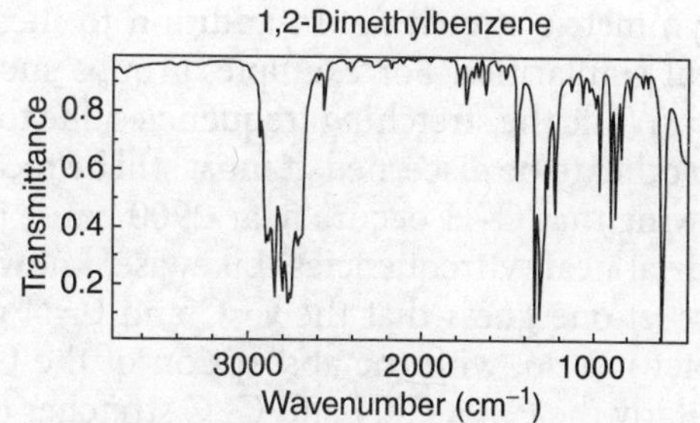

NIST Chemistry webBook (http://webbook.nist.gov/chemistry)

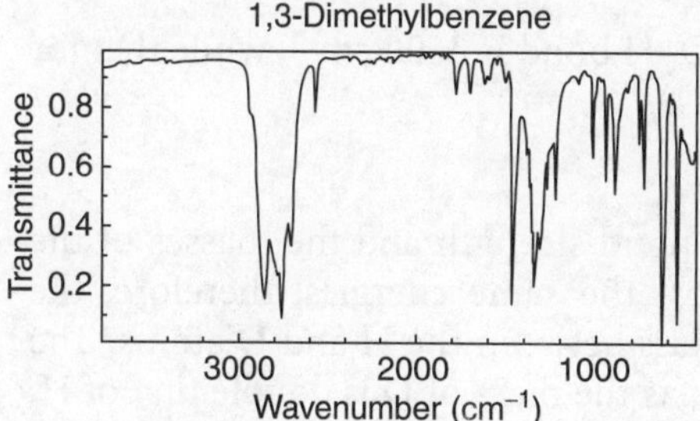

NIST Chemistry webBook (http://webbook.nist.gov/chemistry)

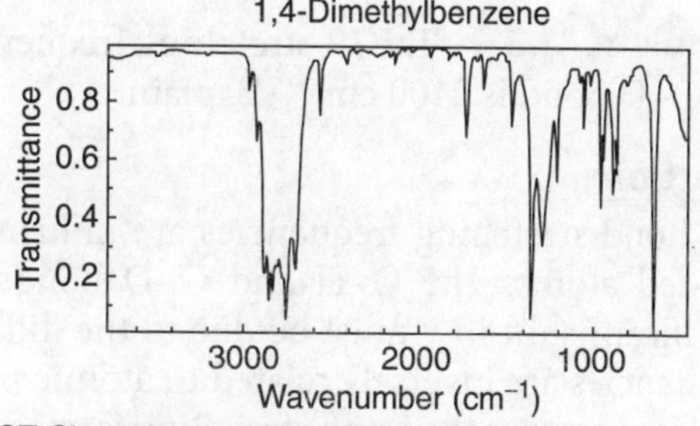

NIST Chemistry webBook (http://webbook.nist.gov/chemistry)

Fig. 11.6 IR spectra of ethylbenzene and its isomers, *o*-, *m*- and *p*-dimethylbenzene

The remarkable similarities observed in the IR absorption between different compounds may at the same time be both surprising and disturbing. It is surprising that the same functional groups in different molecules vibrate more or less at the same frequencies, which allows one to determine grossly the nature of the groups present in the molecule. It is also disturbing that if such similarities exist, would the technique be useful enough to determine closely related compounds? While we cannot ensure that closely related compounds may be differentiated using infrared spectroscopy in every single instance, there are subtle differences in the spectra of such compounds that makes this technique quite useful. Figure 11.6 shows the spectra of ethyl benzene and its isomers, *o*-, *m*- and *p*-dimethylbenzene. While there may be gross similarities in these spectra, there are sufficient differences for one to be able to differentiate them from one another.

Figure 11.7 lists the frequencies of the various functional groups that are normally encountered. While the data appear enormous, certain trends can be observed with regard to vibrational frequencies and which must be recognised. The stretching frequencies occur at shorter wavelengths (or higher energies) than bending frequencies. For example, the C–H stretching occurs near 2900 cm^{-1} while the C–H bending occurs near 1000 cm^{-1}.

Among the stretches, the asymmetric stretch occurs at higher energies relative

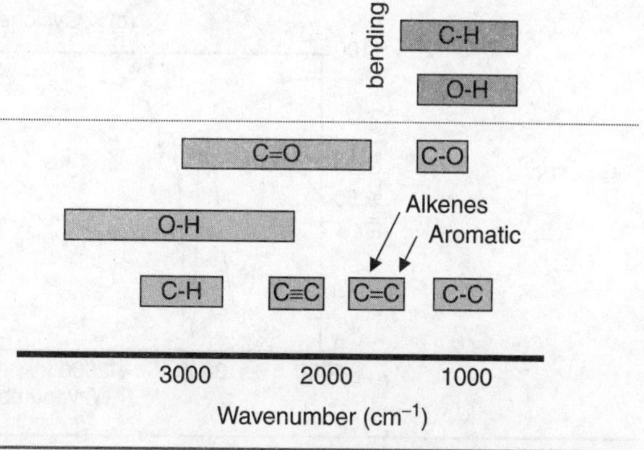

Fig. 11.7 Infrared frequencies of the various groups

to symmetric stretching. In addition to these broad differences, one must also note certain useful similarities. For example, groups such as O–H, N–H and C–H appear around 3000 cm^{-1}. While the stretching frequencies due to these groups do occur sufficiently removed from each other to be discerned, it must still be recognised that they cluster together. In other words, knowing that C–H occurs near 2900 cm^{-1}, is sufficient to guess that the O–H or N–H must occur at nearby frequencies. Likewise, knowing that the C=O group absorbs near 1700 cm^{-1} must let one guess that the C=C and C=N groups must also occur around this wavelength. In fact it is so, with the absorption of the C=C and C=N bonds occurring near 1600 cm^{-1}. Similarly the C–O, C–N and C–C stretches occur near 1100 cm^{-1}. Recognising such patterns is both interesting and essential in the exercise of assigning infrared features.

Problem 11.3 The IR stretching frequency for the O–H bond is 3600 cm^{-1}, while that for the O–D bond is 2100 cm^{-1}. Explain.

Solution:

The bond stretching frequencies are influenced by the bond strength and the masses of the bonded atoms. The O–H and O–D bonds have almost the same energies; therefore, the significant shift in v must be due to the difference in mass between the H and D atoms. The frequencies are inversely related to atomic masses; thus, as the mass of D is double that of H, the frequency of the bond stretching is decreased from 3600 to 2100 cm^{-1}.

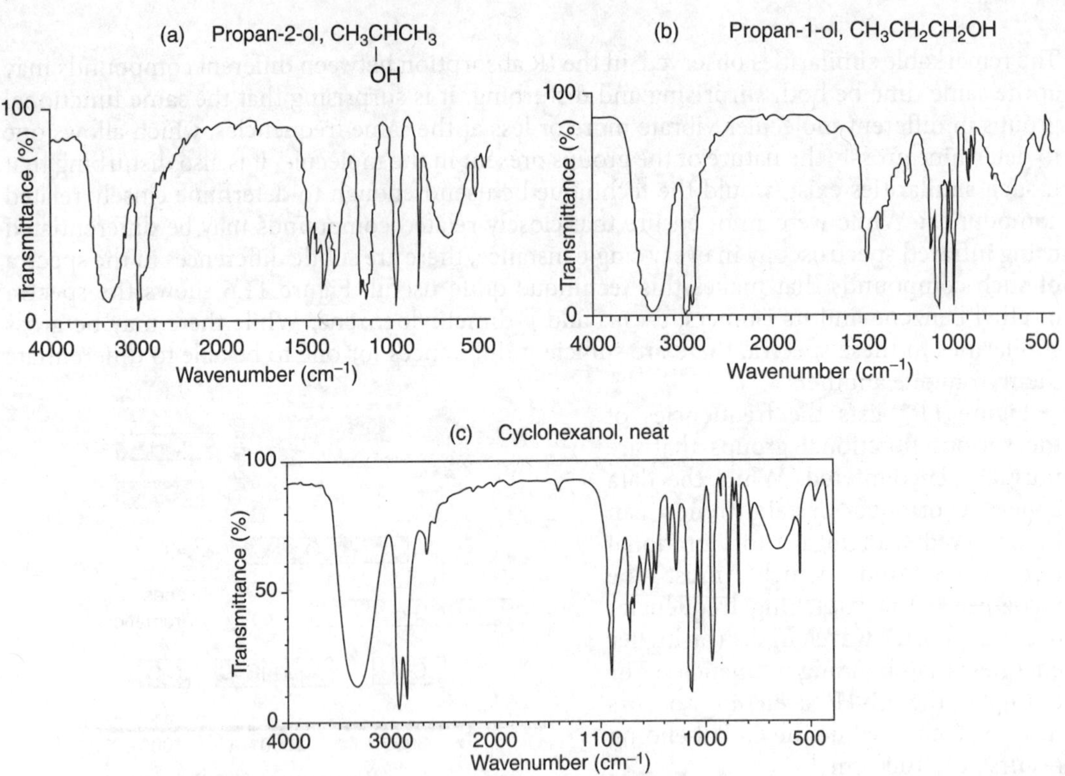

Fig. 11.8 IR spectra of compounds to show utility of the finger print region

While the region of the spectrum from 4000 to 1200 cm^{-1} provides information on the functional groups in the molecule and is therefore referred to as the *functional group region*, the region between 1200 and 900 cm^{-1} is usually complex and cannot be assigned to specific groups in the molecule. This region however manifests subtle differences among the spectra of different molecules and can therefore be used to identify uniquely specific molecules. This region has therefore been referred to as the *fingerprint region*. An examination of Fig. 11.8 will show why this nomenclature of 'fingerprint region' is justified. Although these three spectra are of hydroxyl compounds, they have distinctly different spectral features in the fingerprint region. This aspect of IR spectroscopy is applied for identifying the actual molecules in spite of their identical functional groups.

The region longer than 900 cm^{-1} (900 to 400 cm^{-1}) is referred to as the aromatic region. Bands due to C–H bending occur in this region. This region also provides information on the number of substitutions and their positions in the aromatic ring. It must however be remembered that several other groups also have vibrational frequencies in this region, such as the C–Cl bond, and assignments must therefore be made with caution. It would be more accurate to say that absence of peaks in this region would rule out aromatic compounds, but presence would have to be dealt with in a cautious manner as the spectra in Fig. 11.9 will show. Figure 11.9a shows the spectrum of an aromatic compound, with strong features being observed in the aromatic region. Figure 11.9b shows strong features in the same region but the compound is not aromatic. Figure 11.9c shows the absence of features in the same region and quite convincingly indicates a non-aromatic compound.

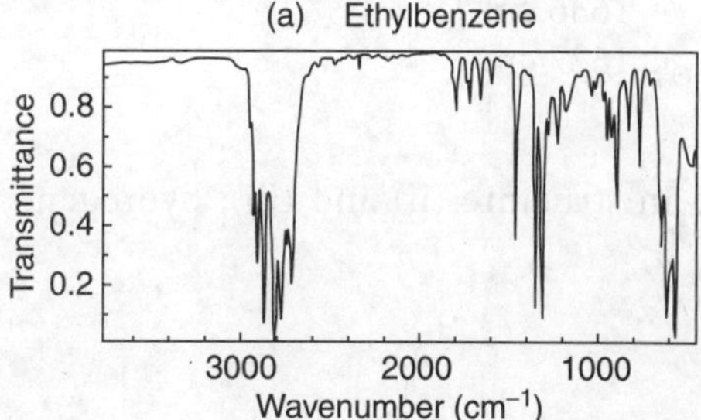

NIST Chemistry webBook (http://webbook.nist.gov/chemistry)

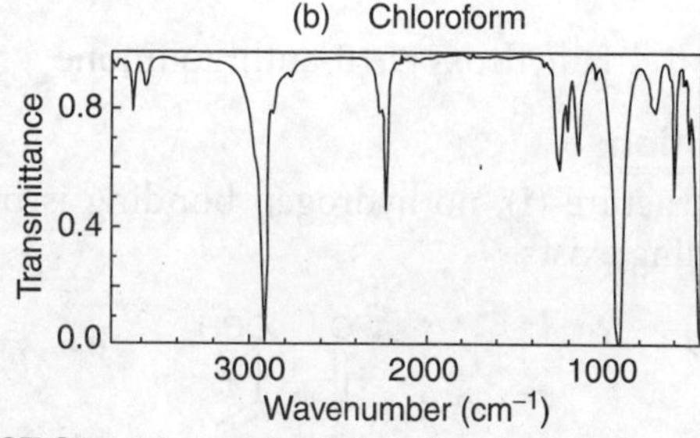

NIST Chemistry webBook (http://webbook.nist.gov/chemistry)

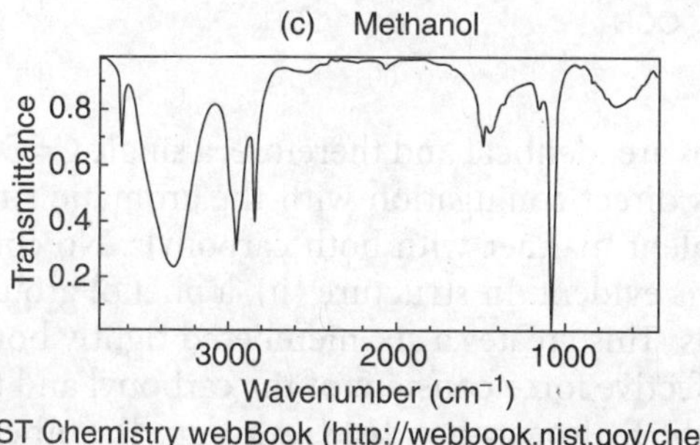

NIST Chemistry webBook (http://webbook.nist.gov/chemistry)

Fig. 11.9 IR spectra in the aromatic region **(a)** aromatic compound **(b)** non-aromatic compound with peaks in this region **(c)** non-aromatic compound with no peaks in this region

11.3.1 IR Spectra and Hydrogen Bonding

IR spectroscopy is a diagnostic tool for hydrogen, its presence, strength and location in the molecule.

The hydroxyl groups of alcohols and phenols are easy to recognise in infrared spectra by their O–H stretching absorptions. Such bands are very sharp in the 3590–3650 cm^{-1} region, if the molecule is not hydrogen bonded. Formation of hydrogen bonding in these molecules broadens the O–H stretching absorptions and broad bands are obtained at 2500–3000 cm^{-1} region. For example, a sharp absorption occurs at ~3550 cm^{-1} for phenol in dilute solutions attributed to 'free', unassociated OH group. When the concentration of phenol is increased or when a neat sample is used, this peak is replaced by a broad bond at 3200–3550 cm^{-1}, region consequent to intermolecular hydrogen bonding.

Similar broadening of N–H stretching absorptions are observed with amines from their original sharp peaks at 3300–3500 cm^{-1} region consequent to intermolecular hydrogen bonding.

Intramolecular hydrogen bonding can also be confirmed by IR spectroscopy. This type of bonding produces sharp and well defined O–H stretching bonds, unlike the broad one observed with intermolecular hydrogen bonding. Intramolecular hydrogen bonds are independent of concentration, unlike intermolecular bonds.

Problem 11.4 Rationalise the following IR spectral data:

(i) 1,4-Dimethoxy-9,10-anthraquinone $\nu_{C=O}$: 1675 cm^{-1}
(ii) 1-Hydroxy-4-methoxy-9,10-anthraquinone $\nu_{C=O}$: 1675 cm^{-1}, 1636 cm^{-1}
(iii) 1,4-Dihydroxy-9,10-anthraquinone $\nu_{C=O}$: 1627 cm^{-1}

Solution:

In structure (i), no hydrogen bonding is possible. But, in structure (ii) and (iii), hydrogen bonding exists.

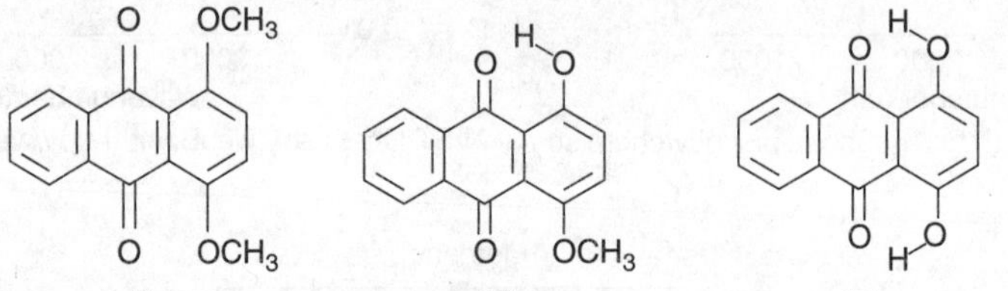

O OCH3 O OCH3 (i)

H O O O OCH3 (ii)

H O O O O H (iii)

Thus in (i), both C=O groups are identical and therefore, a single C=O frequency at 1675 cm^{-1} occurs. This value indicates direct conjugation with the aromatic ring; the methoxy groups are conjugated in an equivalent manner with both carbonyls. No coupling between the two carbonyls through the ring is evident. In structure (ii), a phenol group is present in the place of one of the $-OCH_3$ groups. This creates a six-membered tightly bonded H-bond ring. This is expected to reduce the effective force constant of the carbonyl and therefore, the frequency is reduced to 1636 cm^{-1} for the hydrogen-bonded CO group. The other non-hydrogen bonded CO absorbs at 1675 cm^{-1}. In structure (iii), with two OH groups, both the CO groups are hydrogen bonded. Therefore, there is a single reduced CO stretching frequency, namely 1627 cm^{-1}. In (ii) and (iii), the decrease in stretching frequency (40–50 cm^{-1}) is attributed to strong internal hydrogen bonds.

11.3.2 Infrared Spectroscopy in Inorganic Chemistry

IR spectroscopy is extensively applied in the structural studies of inorganic molecules, both simple and complex. Extensive structural studies on metal complexes, especially metal carbonyls, by IR spectroscopy have provided incisive details on structures of those species. The frequency of the IR absorption associated with a C–O stretching vibration is a measure of the strength of the bond. The frequency values on carbonyls are used to ascertain the nature of bonding between the ligands and the metal. The extent of M–C π bonding may also be determined by the IR frequency values.

Problem 11.5 Explain the following IR spectroscopic data:

Carbonyl species	ν_{CO}/cm^{-1}
$[Mn(CO)_6]^+$	~ 2090
$[V(CO)_6]$	~ 2000
$[V (CO)_6]^-$	~ 1860

Solution:

These carbonyls are iso-electronic. The decrease in frequency values indicates a decrease in C–O bond strength and reduction in bond order. The bond order and, hence, the bond strength for C–O in a carbonyl depends on the extent of metal → carbon π bond.

$M-C\equiv O^-: \leftrightarrow {}^+M=C=\ddot{O}:$ when the extent of metal → carbon π bonding increases, the C–O bond order/strength decreases ($C\equiv O$ to $C=O$). Therefore, the frequency will decrease.

In $[Mn(CO)_6]^+$, the shift of electrons from metal to carbon for forming a π bond is inhibited and therefore, the C–O bond is close to $C\equiv O$. This produces a higher ν of CO absorption. In $V(CO)_6$, a partial M–C π bonding is possible which decreases the bond order in CO and therefore, the CO absorption frequency decreases to ~2000 cm. In $[V(CO)_6]^-$, because of the negative charge, shift of electrons from metal to carbon for π-bond formation is easy and therefore, the CO absorption is further decreased.

(As the metal–carbon π bond character increases, the carbon–oxygen π bond character decreases.)

Problem 11.6 A complex of the metal M having the formula $M[(CH_3)_3P]_2(CO)_4$ exists in two isomeric forms. One shows four IR bands at 2016, 1915, 1900 and 1890 cm^{-1}, whereas, the other shows only one strong band at 1890 cm^{-1}. Explain these data.

Solution:

The data indicate that the two isomers have different symmetries; there is a direct relationship between the symmetry of a carbonyl molecule and the number of IR active CO stretching modes. The isomer which shows four CO stretching bonds should be the *cis*-isomer. The one with only one bond should be the *trans*-isomer. In the *cis*-isomer, four distinct forms of CO stretching vibrations are possible, all of which can absorb IR radiation. In the *trans*-isomer, of the four stretching modes only two can absorb IR radiation. These form a degenerate vibration and being equivalent, have the same frequency. Therefore, for this isomer only a single strong band at 1890 cm^{-1} is observed.

11.4 QUANTIFICATION USING INFRARED SPECTROSCOPY

In addition to providing information on the structural aspects of molecules, infrared spectroscopy can also be used for quantification. There exists a linear relation between *absorbance* (*A*) and concentration, as given by the Beer–Lambert relation,

$$A = \varepsilon \times c \times l$$

where ε is the absorption cross-section for the absorption at a particular wavelength, c is the concentration of the sample and l is the path length or the length through which the infrared radiation traverses the sample. The above relation holds good only for small absorbance values; where the absorbance is very strong, non-linear effects set in and the linear dependence between A and c no longer holds good. The absorbance of the C–Cl vibration in CCl_4 at 700 cm^{-1} was monitored to draw the concentration versus absorbance plot. It can be seen that as the concentration increases, the absorbance increases linearly but only up to a point, beyond which non-linearity sets in. The above discussion clearly highlights the utility of the infrared spectroscopic technique for the qualitative and quantitative examination of materials.

Quantitation is also possible if the sample contains more than one species with overlapping spectra. Principles of chemometrics, such as chemical analysis, are now widely used in such cases to arrive at the concentrations of the various components present in the mixture.

In general, it must be noted that the Beer–Lambert law holds good for absorption in any region of the wavelength, be it infrared, microwave or UV-visible. It must be seen as a relation that describes absorption in general.

11.5 EXPERIMENTAL ASPECTS

Fourier Transform Infrared Spectrometers

In the present day context, Fourier transform instruments have become ubiquitous and indispensable. While dispersive instruments (where the light is spatially dispersed with prisms or gratings) were used in earlier times, Fourier transform instruments, which use the concept of interferometry, have now monopolised infrared spectroscopy.

Fourier Transform Infrared (FTIR) spectroscopy is based on the use of a Michelson interferometer (or variations of this method). This was the famous experimental technique that was devised by Michelson and Morley to study the existence (or not) of the ether concept in the propagation of light.

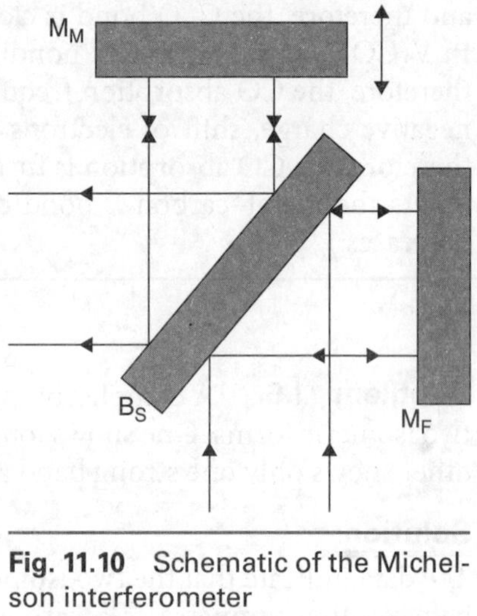

Fig. 11.10 Schematic of the Michelson interferometer

In this method (Fig. 11.10), light from an infrared source is directed onto a beam-splitter (B_S), where the light beam splits into two. The beam-splitter is a partially metal-coated mirror, which transmits half the light falling on it and reflects the other half. The transmitted and the reflected beams travel a certain distance before they are reflected back by mirrors M_F and M_M, and recombine at the beam-splitter. The recombined beam then falls on an infrared detector, where the intensity of the infrared beam is monitored. In this set up, the mirror M_F is fixed while the mirror M_M traverses to and fro, a predetermined distance d.

To understand the working of the FTIR, let us begin by assuming that both mirrors, M_F and M_M, are equidistant from the beam splitter and that a monochromatic beam of wavelength λ is incident on the beam splitter. The light beam is split at the beam-splitter and the two light beams travelling to mirrors M_F and M_M and back, travel the same distance. These beams therefore arrive at the beam splitter in phase, resulting in constructive interference; the detector consequently records a significant intensity. If, however, the movable mirror M_M is moved a distance $\lambda/4$ away from the beam-splitter, the beam traversing the distance to the movable mirror M_M and back to the beam-splitter travels a distance $\lambda/2$ greater than the beam travelling to the fixed mirror M_F and back. The two beams therefore arrive at the beam-splitter shifted in phase by $\lambda/2$ and consequently suffer destructive interference, signaled by the detector as a reduced intensity. As the movable mirror is further moved, the signal at the detector varies sinusoidally as conditions of constructive and destructive interference are alternately met during mirror traverse. It can be quickly realised that the frequency of the sinusoidal variation of the intensity as a function of mirror movement must depend on the *wavelength* of the light, since different wavelengths would require the moving mirror M_M to be positioned at different points for constructive or destructive interference. A Fourier transformation of the signal at the detector yields the wavelength information of the light used in this exercise. What the detector sees is *intensity* as a function of *distance* (of the mirror position from the beam splitter). A Fourier transformation yields information on intensity as a function of wavelength, or more correctly intensity as a function of cm^{-1} or $(distance)^{-1}$.

The above feature is characteristic of Fourier transformation which maps onto an inverse domain. In this case, a function in the distance domain is mapped onto a $(distance)^{-1}$ domain. Such an inverse mapping must be recognised whenever Fourier transformation is encountered, such as when studying FT-NMR. From the above discussion we realise that the accuracy of the wavelength information obtained following a Fourier transformation, depends on the accuracy of the mirror position information which serves as the raw data for the FT. It is therefore necessary that the mirror position be tracked accurately in real time, as the intensity of the modulated infrared beam is acquired by the detector. This tracking of the mirror position is done using a He–Ne laser. (For details on how the mirror position is tracked during its traverse, books on FTIR may be consulted.)

If we now extend this experiment using two wavelengths of light, λ_1 and λ_2, each wavelength would result in a sinusoidal variation characteristic of each of the wavelengths; the intensity variation at the detector would be the resultant of the two sinusoidal variations. Once again, the Fourier transformation, which is basically a *frequency picking* technique from a complex waveform, would yield the wavelength information of the two wavelengths employed. In a real life situation, a polychromatic radiation is used to record the infrared spectrum. As we said earlier, if the experiment is done in the mid-infrared region, the region spanned is from 2.5–25 μm or 4000–400 cm^{-1}. When this range of wavelength is incident onto the interferometer, a complex waveform is seen at the detector. A Fourier transformation of this complex waveform then yields the required wavelength information. When a sample is placed in the path of the infrared beam, specific wavelengths which are resonant with the allowed molecular vibrational transitions, are absorbed. A Fourier transformation therefore yields the absorption spectrum.

The basic difference between a conventional dispersive instrument and the FT method must be understood. In a conventional dispersive instrument, one wavelength after another is made incident on the sample and the spectrum is recorded in a sequential manner. In the FT method, all wavelengths are allowed to fall on the sample simultaneously and spectra corresponding to all the wavelengths are recorded at once. This process considerably reduces the time taken to record a spectrum using the FT method and is referred to as the *Fellget* or the *multiplex advantage*. Furthermore, in conventional instruments, slits limit the amount of light falling on the detector, particularly at high resolutions, when narrow slit widths are used. The FT method uses no such slits and therefore does not limit the amount of infrared radiation falling on the detector. This advantage is referred to as the *Jacquinot* or *throughput advantage*.

A detailed treatment on the advantages of FT over conventional dispersive instruments can be found in texts on FT spectroscopy.

Of course, what has been explained here is just the basic instrumentation. Details of data acquisition and data processing which involve concepts of *apodisation*, *zero filling*, and so on, are beyond the scope this text.

11.6 SAMPLING METHODS IN INFRARED SPECTROSCOPY

Liquids, gases and solids can be examined using infrared spectroscopy. Each phase has its unique challenges which must be considered by the infrared spectroscopist.

11.6.1 Liquids

Liquids are by far the easiest to handle. When a liquid sample, say benzene, is used without any dilution with a solvent, the spectrum thus recorded is referred to as the *neat* liquid spectrum. Alternatively, the sample may be diluted in a solvent, and the solution may then be used to record an infrared spectrum. Liquids are taken in liquid sampling cells, which are of two types—*fixed pathlength cells* and continuously *variable pathlength cells*. The fixed pathlength cells consist of two infrared transmitting windows, such as KBr, which are placed in a liquid cell holder at a fixed distance from each other. The distance between the windows is usually determined by the use of appropriate Teflon spacers or gaskets. The space between the windows is filled with the liquid to be examined. A gasket or an O-ring ensures that no liquid leaks out from the cell. Windows of various path lengths can be employed by simply varying the thickness of the spacer. Different pathlengths are usually employed depending on the absorbance or concentration of the sample. For dilute solutions or samples with poor infrared absorptions, a larger pathlength cell may be required to obtain good spectra, relative to a situation where the sample is either concentrated or neat or has a strong infrared absorption. Alternatively, liquid cells where the distance between the windows can be continuously varied are also employed. When the distance between the windows is very small, the spectrum that is recorded may usually show annoying interference fringes.

11.6.2 Solids

One of the popular methods of recording infrared spectra of solids is the KBr pellet technique. In this method, the sample is finely ground in a mortar along with KBr, the sample concentration in KBr being ~1%. The finely ground mixture of the sample in KBr is then pressed into a pellet using a hydraulic press. The pellet is then loaded onto a pellet sample holder and the spectrum of the sample is recorded.

While this method is very popular and convenient for most organic compounds, it has its pitfalls. Sometimes, the sample may be refractory and hard to grind as a fine powder. In such cases, the relatively coarse particle texture can lead to scattering of the infrared radiation, resulting in spectra with a sloping baseline. In fact, a sloping baseline is an indication of scattering losses from the sample. In some cases, where the cation in the inorganic compound can be exchanged with the K^+ of KBr, the identity of the sample is altered, which may lead to erroneous results. In such cases, alternative sampling technique, such as *diffuse reflectance spectroscopy*, may be employed.

The special characteristics of KBr and ZnSe that allow their use for pelletisation:

- KBr does not absorb IR radiation and therefore does not interfere with absorption by the sample. Being ionic, it transmits throughout most of the IR region with only a lower cut-off of about 400 cm^{-1}.

- It is inert towards most samples.
- Bands due to the mulling agent (nujol) are eliminated.
- It has the property of cold flow (glass-like transparent or translucent property) on applying pressure to the finely powdered material.
- It has good resistance to mechanical shock which renders the pellet non-fragile.
- It is inexpensive and available in the pure form commercially.
- Most of these characteristics are true of ZnSe as well, however, it is not inexpensive.
- ZnSe has a wide transmission wavelength range (0.45 μm to 21.5 μ).
- Both are affected by moisture (disadvantage).

An alternative sampling method for solids, is to grind the sample and mix it with a mineral oil nujol (a mixture of various straight chain hydrocarbons) to form a suspension and record the spectrum of this suspension. This is referred to as the *nujol mull technique*. It has the disadvantage that the mull itself presents strong features of the C–H vibrations and hence is not the preferred method for studying hydrocarbons. However, where functional group analysis is required covering regions that do not interfere with the C–H groups, this method is quite useful.

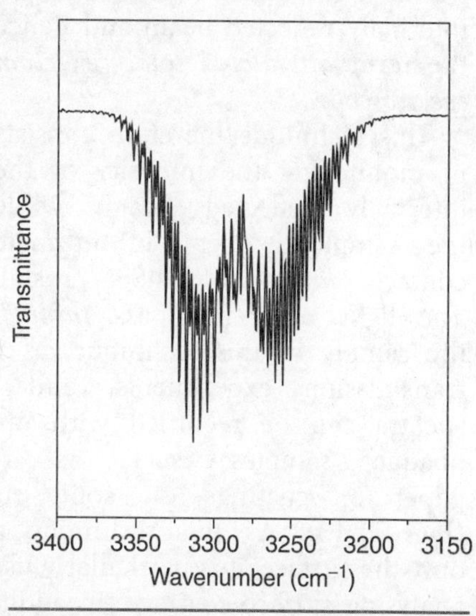

Fig. 11.11 Gas phase IR spectrum of acetylene

11.6.3 Gases

Spectra of gases or vapours of volatile materials can be recorded using infrared gas cells. Cells of various pathlengths, such as 15–30 cm can be used. These cells are fitted with infrared windows such as KBr or ZnSe. The cell is first evacuated and is then filled with the sample under study, to the desired pressure. Gas-phase spectra, particularly for small molecules, show fine structure due to the molecular rotations, as can be seen in the spectrum of acetylene (Fig. 11.11).

11.7 ATTENUATED TOTAL REFLECTION SPECTROSCOPY (ATR)

While the above sampling methods are routinely used, one may often encounter samples that cannot be studied using any of the methods described above. For example, thick samples such as rubber or paper cannot be examined using the transmission method described above. In such cases, the technique of *attenuated total reflection spectroscopy* is extremely useful. This technique uses the principle of total internal reflection. Assume light is incident on the face of a ZnSe crystal (Fig. 11.12). The light traverses into the ZnSe and hits the surface at point 1. At this point, light is incident on a boundary between ZnSe and air. The ZnSe is denser relative to air, and if the angle of incidence in the denser medium were to be greater than the critical angle, total internal reflection would occur and the light would be

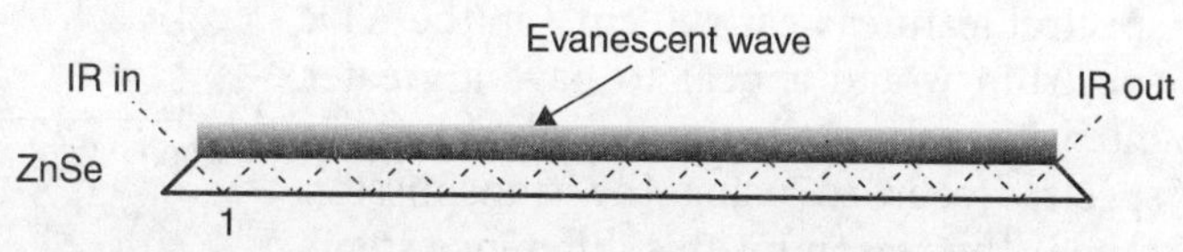

Fig. 11.12 Diagram illustrating the working of attenuated total reflection

reflected back into the ZnSe medium. However, the electric field of light would penetrate into the rarer medium, decaying exponentially with distance from the interface. This field that penetrates the rarer medium when total internal reflection occurs, is called an *evanescent field*. If a sample were to be kept in close contact with the ZnSe crystal, the evanescent field would interact with the sample. Furthermore, if the sample has an absorption at a given wavelength, the evanescent field corresponding to that particular wavelength would be absorbed by the sample. Correspondingly, the intensity at that wavelength would be reduced in the internally reflected beam and hence the term *attenuated total reflection spectroscopy*.

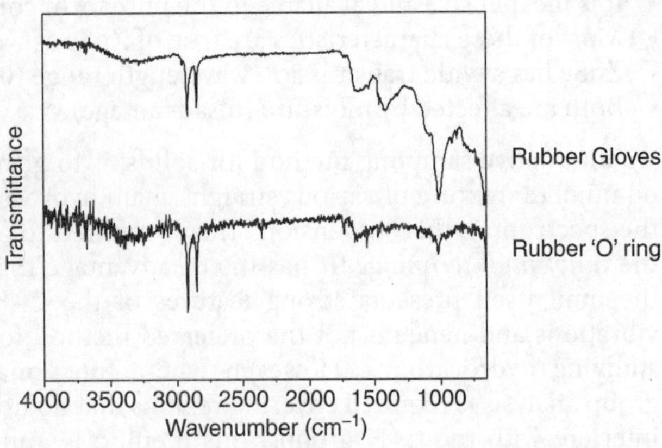

Fig. 11.13 ATR-IR spectra of rubber glove and O-ring

This technique therefore consists in monitoring the intensity of the internally reflected beam, while the sample is kept in intimate contact with the ZnSe crystal. The light need not pass *through* the sample in this technique, as in the transmission experiments, and hence spectra can be recorded with optically opaque samples, such as rubber, paper or coatings on solid surfaces (Fig. 11.13). As this technique probes only the surface, it is particularly useful in analysing surface coatings. In addition to ZnSe, Ge and KRS5 (thallium bromoiodide) crystals are also used to perform the ATR experiment; the condition being that the material must be infrared transmitting and have a large refractive index to cause total internal reflection.

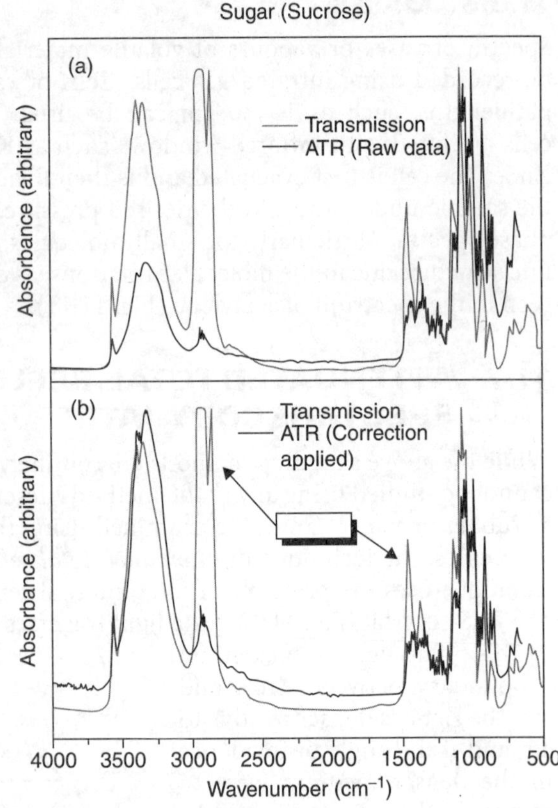

Fig. 11.14 Comparison of ATR with transmission spectra to show ATR correction

The spectrum of a sample recorded using the transmission mode and the ATR mode, would look somewhat different, with respect to the relative intensites of the infrared peaks, even though one would expect to observe identical spectra with the two techniques. Specifically, the spectral features near 400 cm^{-1} in the ATR spectrum would appear to have a greater intensity relative to those observed in spectra recorded using the transmission mode. The reason for this difference stems from the fact that the infrared radiation penetrates a greater depth into the sample at longer wavelengths in the ATR experiment, resulting in somewhat larger pathlengths at the longer wavelengths and hence greater intensities. In the transmission mode, no such artifacts exist and a constant pathlength is sampled over the entire wavelength range. These artifacts in ATR spectra are easily corrected using the functional dependence on the sample depth probed on the wavelength of light (Eq. 11.2).

$$d_p = \frac{\lambda_1}{(2\pi\sqrt{\sin^2\theta - n_{21}^2})} \tag{11.2}$$

where d_p is the depth of penetration of the evanescent wave into the sample, λ_1 is the wavelength of the infrared radition, θ is the angle of incidence and n_{21} is the refractive index of the ATR crystal. This is referred to as ATR correction (Fig. 11.14).

In addition to the dependence on wavelength, the sample depth probed also depends on the angle of incidence of the beam incident on the ZnSe-sample interface. This dependence is used to great advantage in arriving at the concentrations of samples as a function of depth, by simply recording their spectra as a function of incidence angle.

11.8 WINDOW MATERIALS, SOURCES AND DETECTORS

From the point of view of experimental infrared spectroscopy, it is necessary to be familiar with the various materials used as windows for infrared spectroscopy. Likewise, it is also necessary to learn about the sources and detectors used in infrared spectroscopy.

11.8.1 Window Materials

Any material used as windows in spectroscopic measurements must be transparent over the wavelength range of interest. The most popular window materials used in infrared spectroscopy are KBr, NaCl, CsI, ZnSe, KRS5 and Ge. These materials offer the best transmission over the infrared range, with each material possessing its own advantages and disadvantages. For example, KBr is transparent over the range 5000–400 cm^{-1} while ZnSe cuts off around 650 cm^{-1}, thus providing for a smaller working range. However, ZnSe is resistant to moisture, while KBr being hygroscopic is affected in humid environments and needs to be repolished. The choice of the window material must therefore be made keeping in mind the application and constraints in handling. The working range of each of the window materials is given in Fig. 11.15.

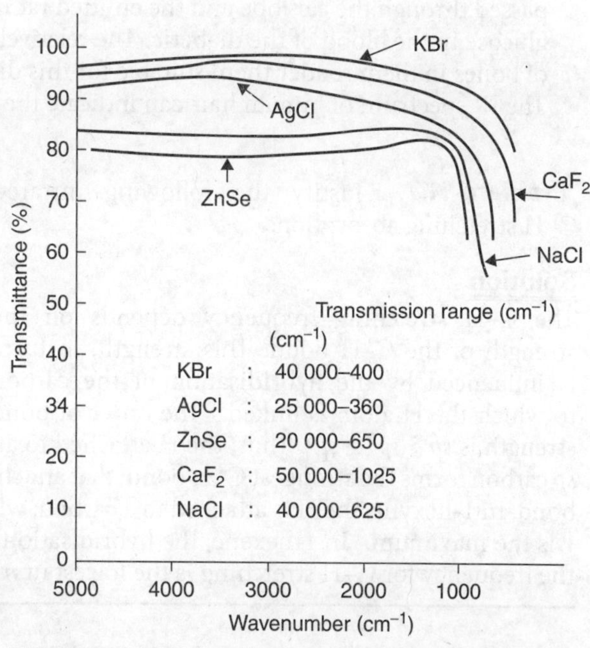

Fig. 11.15 Working range of IR window materials

11.8.2 Sources

The most popular infrared source is a simple SiC bar heated to about 2000°C. The bar, also referred to as the Globar source, serves as a blackbody emitter and provides the infrared radiation required for vibrational spectroscopic measurements. Other sources are the Nernst glower (essentially a mixture of Zr, Y and Th oxides) and incandescent wires.

11.8.3 Detectors

Thermocouples, bolometers and pyroelectric detectors are most commonly employed in infrared spectroscopy. It may be noted that all of these are heat-measuring devices and not surprisingly so as infrared radiation essentially produces heat in the material on which it is incident. While thermocouples were the preferred detectors in conventional dispersive instruments, pyroelectric detectors [deuterated triglycine sulphate, $(H_2NCH_2COOH)_3 \bullet H_2SO_4$] are used in modern FT infrared instruments. The choice is determined based on factors such as sensitivity and response times.

11.9 FAR-IR SPECTROSCOPY

While the discussion so far has concentrated mostly on aspects of mid-infrared spectroscopy, a good number of the inorganic and organometallic compounds show features in the far infrared region, between 700 and 15 μm. Transitions from valence to conduction bands also often fall in this region. The instrumentation and choice of window materials are specific to this region. For example, polyethylene, mylar N and diamond provide a choice of window materials. Likewise, the instrumentation of the FT spectrometers also has its unique aspects such as the use of the step-scan technique, which will not be discussed here.

- IR can be applied in the blood glucose test. When a harmless dose of near infrared light is passed through the ear lobe and the emitted radiation is recorded, it can give the amount of glucose in the blood of the diabetic. The relatively small thickness of the lobes and absence of bones in them render them suitable for this diagnosis.
- The IR spectrum of human hair can indicate the prevalence of certain diseases in a person.

Problem 11.7 Justify the following infrared C–H stretching absorptions:

Molecule	Stretching frequency C–H (cm^{-1})
1-hexyne	3320 (≡ C–H)
1-hexene	3080 (=C–H)
n-octane	2985 (>C–H)

Solution

The C–H stretching frequency depends on the strength of the C–H bond. This strength, in turn, is influenced by the hybridisation of the carbon to which the H atom is linked. The order of bond strength is $sp > sp^2 > sp^3$. Thus, the H attached to an sp carbon forms the strongest C–H bond; that attached to an sp^3 carbon forms the weakest C–H bond. In 1-hexyne, the H is attached to a carbon, which has sp hybridisation and therefore, the v is the maximum. In 1-hexene, the hybridisation is sp^2 and in *n*-octane, it is sp^3. Therefore, the frequency for C–H stretching is the lowest in *n*-octane.

Problem 11.8 Account for the following IR spectral data:

Solution

The decreasing stretching frequency from HCHO to CH_3CHO and to CH_3COCH_3 is because of the +I effect of the methyl group. The CH_3 group increases the degree of polarisation of the C=O bond to C–O and thus weakens the bond. This weakening reduces the ν. In acetone, the two methyl groups effect greater weakening of the C=O bond and consequently the ν for it is the lowest.

Molecule	C=O stretching frequency (cm^{-1})
HCHO	1735
CH_3CHO	1730
$CH_3CO\ CH_3$	1715

EXERCISES

1. State whether each of the following is true or false and explain why.
   (a) Methanol can be used as solvent for sample preparation in UV spectroscopy, but not in IR spectroscopy.
   (b) The C–H stretching band of octane is very strong.
   (c) The C = O absorption frequency for butyraldehyde is lower than that for salicylaldehyde.
2. Explain the following stretching frequencies.
   C – H 2853–2962 cm^{-1}
   C = C 1620–1680 cm^{-1}
   C ≡ C 2100–2260 cm^{-1}
3. Which one in each of the following pairs is expected to show a higher C = O stretching frequency?
   (a) *cis*-cinnamic acid: *trans*-cinnamic acid
   (b) acetic acid: acetone
   (c) acetic acid (neat): acetic acid (extremely dilute solution in CCl_4)
4. A compound X (molecular formula, $C_6H_{12}O_2$) on heating with P_2O_5 gives Y ($C_{12}H_{22}O_3$). The infrared spectrum of Y shows prominent peaks at 2950–2850, 1830, 1761 and 1415 cm^{-1}. Explain the spectrum of Y and identify X.
5. Explain why the IR spectra of benzene and its derivatives show characteristic absorption bands in three regions.
6. Draw the possible vibrational excitations in Cl – CH = CH – COOH.
7. Explain the observation that *trans*-4-octene does not show any IR absorption for its carbon–carbon double bond.
8. Why are the IR frequencies for the ester carbonyls 20–40 cm^{-1} higher than those for simple aliphatic carbonyls?
9. A complex of metal M having the formula $M[(CH_3)_3P]_2(CO)_4$ exists in two isomeric forms. One shows four IR bands at 2016, 1915, 1900 and 1890 cm^{-1}, whereas the other shows only one strong band at 1890 cm^{-1}. Explain.
10. Illustrate how hydrogen bonding affects IR spectra.
11. Predict the important IR spectral features of
    (a) camphor (b) vitamin C (c) aspirin
12. Compare the N–H IR absorption frequencies of aliphatic amines and aromatic amines.
13. Why do IR vibrational absorptions appear as bands rather than as lines?

14. With two examples, substantiate that IR and Raman spectral methods an complementary.
15. Write a critical account of the uses of various windows in IR spectroscopy.
16. Discuss quantitative IR spectroscopy.
17. Explain 'dedicated application of IR (quantitative) spectrometry', citing the working of breath analysers used by the traffic police.
18. Explain the baseline method of determining absorbance.
19. Discuss the principle of determining the composition of a mixture of these isomeric *o*–, *m*– and *p*-xylenes by IR spectrometry.

12 Raman Spectroscopy

12.1 INTRODUCTION

In earlier discussions on infrared and fluorescence spectroscopy, the primary process of photon–molecule interaction was absorption. The molecule absorbed a photon and was consequently raised to an excited state. The experiments involved observing the absorption or emission process when the molecule returns to its ground state.

There is yet another process of photon–molecule interaction, which turns out to be an important tool to study molecular processes. In this process, the photon is not absorbed or emitted, but is scattered by the molecule. New insights into molecular properties may be obtained by a study of this process. The experimental demonstration came from the work of C V Raman and his associate, K S Krishnan, working then at the Indian Association for the Cultivation of Sciences at Kolkata, in 1928. This work earned for Raman, the coveted Nobel Prize in Physics in the year 1930.

We come across scattering when we study Compton scattering through an experiment that was performed by A H Compton in 1923, that demonstrated the particle aspect of a photon. In this experiment, Compton studied the scattering of X-ray photons from the electrons of graphite and observed that the wavelength of the scattered photons was different from that of the incident photons. The change in the photon wavelength could be calculated, assuming that the scattering process occurs as if it were between particles. The optical analogue of this effect is the Raman effect, in which Raman observed that in some of his experiments, the wavelengths of the incident radiation were modified by their passage through the sample. The changes in the wavelength that he had observed, he concluded, must be due to a scattering phenomenon in his experiments and thus was discovered the *Raman effect*. He announced these findings to the scientific community on February 28, which today is celebrated as the National Science Day, in honour of this remarkable finding of Raman.

Scattering of light is all pervasive. The blue colour of the oceans, and the bright red sunrise and sunset are all consequences of scattering and the dependence of scattering efficiency on the wavelength of light.

12.2 BASIC ASPECTS OF THE RAMAN PROCESS

Assume that a light of wavelength λ_i is incident on the sample. This photon can suffer the same fate as described in earlier discussions - absorption - which we will not consider here. In addition, the incident photon and the molecule can interact, following which a photon can be produced due to scattering. Following the scattering process, the molecule can be left in exactly the same energy state as it was before the scattering process; in this case, as a result of the energy conservation principle, the energy of the scattered photon would be exactly the same as the incident photon. The wavelength of the photon after scattering λ_f, therefore, turns out to be equal to λ_i, the wavelength of the incident photon—a process called *Rayleigh scattering*, which is an elastic scattering process.

It is also possible for the scattering process to be inelastic, in which case the energy of molecule is altered as a result of the scattering process. If as a result of the scattering, the molecule gains energy from the photon, the molecule will be left in a higher energy state. Energy conservation then demands that the scattered photon has an equivalent loss of energy or in other words, the scattered photon would have a wavelength longer than the incident photon. This process is called the *Stokes process*, in analogy with the Stokes shift in fluorescence, in which the emitted light is of a longer wavelength. Alternatively, the scattering process can leave the molecule in a lower energy state, in which case the scattered photon would now have a correspondingly higher energy and would have a shorter wavelength compared with the incident photon; this process is called an *anti-Stokes process*. For the anti-Stokes lines to occur, the molecule must lose energy to the photon in the scattering process, which therefore necessitates the molecules to be in a higher energy state before the scattering process; since a molecule in the ground state can lose no further energy in any process. This necessity of the molecule to be in a higher energy state is important when we later discuss the relative intensities of the Stokes and the anti-Stokes lines. In summary, the scattering process can produce a photon of the same wavelength (Rayleigh scattering), a longer wavelength (Stokes radiation) or a shorter wavelength (anti-Stokes radiation), compared to the incident radiation.

It is essential to keep in mind that the process under discussion is a scattering process which is quite different from an absorption or an emission process discussed earlier. The consequences of this fundamental difference will become obvious in the next section, as the discussion on the Raman technique proceeds.

12.3 INTERACTION OF RADIATION WITH MOLECULES IN THE RAMAN PROCESS

For a molecule to interact with a photon, we have seen earlier that there must be a time-varying electric or magnetic component of the molecule when it interacts with light. For an absorption or emission process, it was the dipole moment of the molecule that was responsible for the photoprocess. We have seen while studying infrared spectroscopy, that the molecule must show a change in the dipole moment during its vibration for it to absorb the infrared photon. In the scattering process, it is the polarisability of the molecule that comes into play. Polarisability is the ability of the electron cloud in the molecule to distort in the presence of an electric field. As a result of the polarisation, a dipole moment may be induced in the molecule, referred to as the *induced dipole moment*. Since it is the polarisability of the molecule that initiates the photon–molecule interaction in a scattering process, molecules that have no dipole moment can still produce photon scattering, even though they may not be able to absorb a photon. In this way, the scattering process allows one to probe molecules that cannot be observed in a simple absorption or emission process and is therefore complementary in our studies on molecular phenomena.

If the applied electric field is E, the induced polarisation P is given by,

$$P = \alpha E \tag{12.1}$$

where α is the polarisability. We can express the electric field of the electromagnetic radiation as

$$E = E_0 \cos (2\pi \nu t) \tag{12.2}$$

where ν is the frequency of the electromagnetic radiation used.

The question that arises now is, how to represent the term α in Eq. 12.1. For this purpose, we must recognise the dependence of α on molecular processes, such as vibration. We will discuss this aspect using vibrations, but the discussion will apply equally well for other degrees of freedom, such as rotations. Let us consider the H_2 molecule for this discussion. Let us assume that the molecule is initially at its equilibrium internuclear position, r_e. At this position, the electron cloud of the molecule can be polarised to a certain extent. Let us say the polarisability is α_0 at the equilibrium internuclear distance. As the molecule vibrates and reaches its outer turning point (its extreme distended position), the electron cloud is more easily polarisable, as it is somewhat further away from the attractive forces of the nuclei. On the other hand, at the inner turning point, the polarisability will be smaller than that at the equilibrium position. It is therefore clear that as the molecule vibrates, the polarisability changes during vibration, even though the permanent dipole moment of the molecule is zero at all times during vibration. This variation in polarisability during vibration can be expressed as follows

$$\alpha = \alpha_0 + \beta \cos(2\pi \nu_\nu t) \tag{12.3}$$

where ν_ν is the vibrational frequency of the molecular vibration. If we now introduce Eqs 12.2 and 12.3 in Eq. 12.1, we get

$$P = [\alpha_0 + \beta \cos(2\pi \nu_\nu t)]\,[E_0 \cos(2\pi \nu t)] \tag{12.4}$$

$$= \alpha_0 E_0 \cos(2\pi \nu t) + \beta E_0 [\cos(2\pi \nu_\nu t) \cos(2\pi \nu t)] \tag{12.5}$$

The second term in Eq. 12.5 is a product of two cosines and can be simplified to give

$$P = \alpha_0 E_0 \cos(2\pi \nu t) + \beta E_0 [\cos\{2\pi(\nu - \nu_\nu)t\} + \cos\{2\pi(\nu + \nu_\nu)t\}] \tag{12.6}$$

The first term in Eq. 12.6 is a term where the polarisation is unmodulated by the molecular vibration as it does not contain ν_ν; and corresponds to the Rayleigh process where the frequency of the scattered radiation is the same as that of the incident radiation, ν. The next two terms show a modulation of the polarisation at frequencies $(\nu - \nu_\nu)$ and $(\nu + \nu_\nu)$. The term containing the $(\nu - \nu_\nu)$ term corresponds to the inelastic scattering process where the frequency of the scattered radiation is shifted to lower frequencies and can be correlated to the Stokes process. Likewise, the term containing the $(\nu + \nu_\nu)$ term corresponds to the anti-Stokes process. The frequency of the scattered radiation, $(\nu - \nu_\nu)$ and $(\nu + \nu_\nu)$, is shifted from the frequency of incident radiation by ν_ν, which is exactly the vibrational frequency of the molecule. Hence, recording the frequencies of the scattered radiation provides information on the vibrational modes of the molecules, very much on the lines of what is obtained in infrared spectroscopy. Figure 12.1 shows the infrared and Raman spectra of CCl_4, and the similarity in the two spectra is obvious.

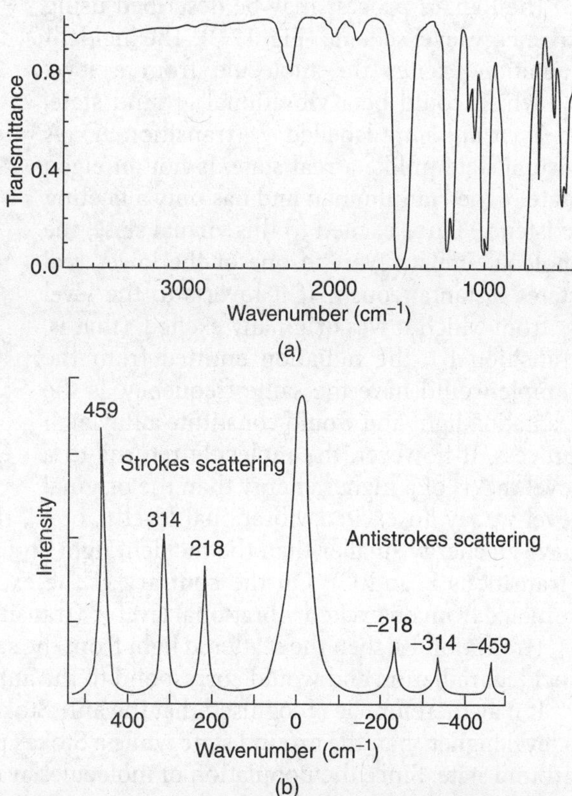

Fig. 12.1 Comparison of **(a)** infrared and **(b)** Raman spectra of CCl_4

While these are similar, the differences inherent in the two processes must be clearly understood. The first is the fundamental difference discussed earlier with regard to the mechanism of the two processes. While modulation of the polarisability during a vibration is responsible for Raman scattering, changes in the dipole moment during vibration produce infrared absorption. The second difference lies in the experimental aspects. In infrared spectroscopy the radiation used and detected is in the infrared region, while in Raman spectroscopy, the radiation used and detected is in the visible region, for which sensitive detectors are available, such as the photomultipliers and charge coupled device (CCD).

Raman spectroscopy also has another important advantage over infrared absorption spectroscopy. Aqueous solutions do not pose problems due to solvent interference when recording Raman spectra since water is a poor scatterer. On the contrary, water which has strong infrared absorption is not an attractive choice when recording infrared spectra. This advantage is particularly important in biological sciences where aqueous solutions are often encountered and where Raman spectroscopy is the technique of choice.

It must also be noted that Eq. 12.1 is somewhat more profound than it appears. It is not always that the direction of the induced dipole moment is in the same direction as the electric field. It would apply for simple cases such as H_2, due to the symmetry of the molecule. However, in less symmetric cases, the direction of the induced moment can be in a direction different from that of the applied field and Eq. 12.1 reduces to a matrix form, where α would now be the polarisability tensor.

The Raman process may be described using an energy level scheme (Fig. 12.2). The incident radiation excites the molecule from a level v_0, which could be a vibrational ground state, to a *virtual state* labelled v_i (transition A). A virtual state unlike a real state, is not an eigen state of the Hamiltonian and has only a fleeting existence. Once excited to this virtual state, the molecule must revert to one of the lower real states instantaneously. If it reverts to the level v_0 from which it was originally excited, (that is, transition B), the radiation emitted from the sample would have the same frequency as the excitation light and would constitute a Rayleigh process. If however, the molecule returns to a level that is of a higher energy than the original level v_0, say an excited vibrational level v_1 or v_2, the scattered light from the sample would have an energy smaller than the incident light and hence would constitute the Stokes process (transitions B and C). On the contrary, if the excitation of the Raman process were to be initiated from an excited vibrational level v_1 (transition E) and terminated on a lower level, say v_0, (transition F), then the scattered light from the sample would be of a higher energy than the incident radiation and would correspond to the anti-Stokes radiation.

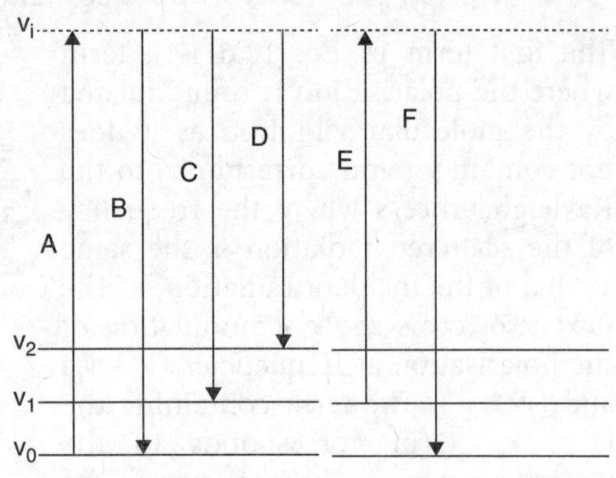

Fig. 12.2 Raman processes showing the generation of the Rayleigh, Stokes and anti-Stokes lines

It may therefore be recognised that the anti-Stokes process must necessarily originate from a level higher than the ground state while a Stokes process would generally originate from the ground state. Since the population of molecules available in the higher energy level is smaller than that available in the higher energy states, the intensities of Stokes process would always be higher than those for the corresponding anti-Stokes process in the same molecule.

It should also be seen from Fig. 12.2, that the transition from $v_0 \leftrightarrow v_1$ can be observed both as a Strokes line (transition A + C in Fig. 12.2) or as an anti-Stokes line (E + F in Fig. 12.2).

Problem 12.1 In the Raman spectrom of the HCl molecule, the successive rorational Stokes lines are separated by 41.4 cm^{-1}. Calculate the moment of inertia and internuclear distance in H–Cl (μ for HCl = 1.627×10^{-27} kg).

Solution

The rotational constant

$$4\,B = 41.4 \qquad \therefore\ B = 10.35$$

$$B = \frac{h}{8\pi^2 Ic} = 10.35$$

$$\therefore \qquad I = \frac{h}{8\pi^2 \times 10.35 \times c} = 2.7036 \times 10^{-47}\ \text{kg m}^2$$

$$I = \mu r^2$$

Therefore, the internuclear distance $r = \left[\dfrac{I}{\mu}\right]^{1/2}$

$$= \left[\frac{2.7036 \times 10^{-47}}{1.627 \times 10^{-27}}\right]^{1/2} = 1.289 \times 10^{-10}\ \text{m} = 0.1289\ \text{nm}$$

12.4 MOLECULAR SYMMETRY AND THE RAMAN PROCESS

In the above discussion, the molecule chosen for the discussion of the Raman process was homonuclear diatomic H_2. The discussion concluded that the vibration of H_2 can be observed through changes in polarisability or in other words, the vibrational spectrum of H_2 can be recorded in a Raman process. The same vibration, it can be recalled while studying infrared spectroscopy, was silent, as the vibration does not induce changes in dipole moment and hence is not observed in infrared spectroscopy. Raman and infrared spectroscopy can often therefore be complementary, especially with molecules such as H_2. More specifically, molecules which have a centre of symmetry, such as H_2, CO_2 and C_6H_6 exhibit this phenomenon, where vibrations that can be observed in the infrared cannot be seen in the Raman and vice versa. Figure 12.3 shows the infrared and Raman spectra of C_6H_6, which clearly shows the features appearing in the infrared are missing in the Raman and vice versa. An application of group theoretical principles (which is beyond the scope of this book) elegantly rationalises this phenomenon, which is referred to as the *rule of mutual exclusion.*

This phenomenon often helps establish the structure of a molecule. For example, stilbene exists in two geometric isomeric forms—*cis* and *trans*. The isomeric form *trans*-stilbene has a centre of symmetry while the *cis* form does not. Hence the principle of mutual exclusion will be exhibited by the *trans* structure but not by the *cis* structure. Figure 12.4 shows the infrared and Raman spectra of both *cis*- and *trans*-stilbene. The IR and Raman spectra of stilbenes are shown in Fig. 12.4. The IR (a) and Raman (c) spectra have absorption peaks indicating some asymmetric vibrational features associated with the structure. Therefore, these are the spectra of *cis*-stilbene. With no symmetry, the spectra of the *cis*-isomer are expected to show such vibrational absorptions. The IR (b) and Raman (d) spectra of *trans*-stilbene do not show the vibrational features like those of *cis*-stilbene. Spectra (b) and (d) substantiate the operation of the mutual exclusion principle implying the existence of a centre of symmetry in the *trans*- structure.

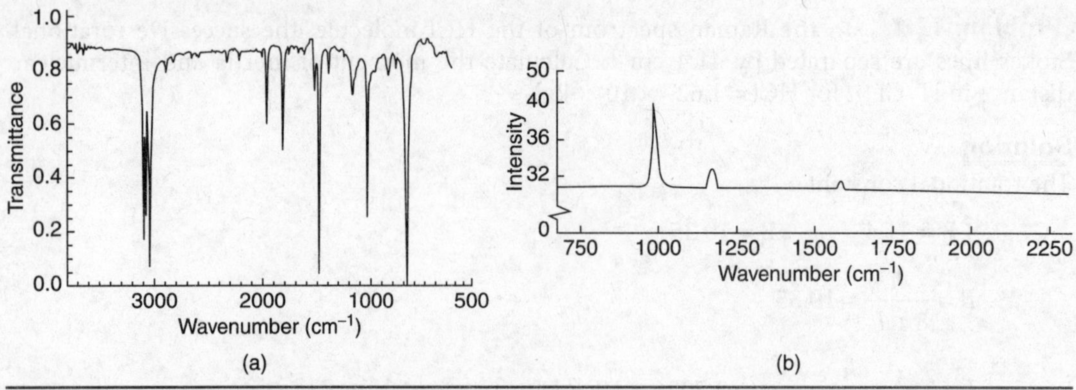

Fig. 12.3 **(a)** IR and **(b)** Raman spectra of benzene

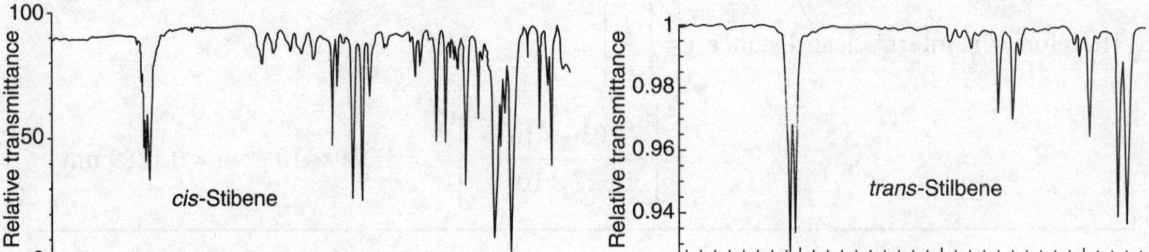

Fig. 12.4 IR spectra of **(a)** *cis*-stilbene **(b)** *trans*-stilbene, Raman spectra of **(c)** *cis*-stilbenel and **(d)** *trans*-stilbene.

Exclusion rule: If a molecule has a centre of symmetry, IR and Raman active vibrational modes are mutually exclusive. If a vibration is IR active, it cannot be Raman active and vice versa.

12.4.1 Experimental Details

The recording of a Raman spectrum involves the use of an excitation source, which in earlier times were discharge lamp sources. The photons from the light source were incident on the sample. The light scattered at right angles were collected, passed through a monochromator and detected. All three processes, Rayleigh, Stokes and anti-Stokes, can be examined and recorded. The Rayleigh process would be the strongest, followed by the Stokes and the anti-Stokes. The intensity of the anti-Stokes process is invariably weak and to discriminate this signal from background scattered light, the use of double-monochromators, (which used two gratings) was common.

The Raman experiments today are carried out using lasers. It may even be said that Raman spectroscopy has had a new lease of life due to the advent of the lasers. A laser is used to excite the sample and the scattered radiation is then collected at right angles. The high intensities attainable using a laser is the advantage when recording weak Raman signals. The weak signals must still be discriminated from the strong Rayleigh scattered light. For this, spectrometers with high quality holographic gratings and multiple monochromators are used to reject the unwanted radiation. A filter, such as a notch filter, is also used to discriminate against the strong Rayleigh scatter. The monochromator is usually fitted with an electric radiation transducer such as a photomultiplier tube or a charge-coupled device (CCD). The use of array detectors such as a CCD has become popular as it allows for a range of wavelengths to be recorded at once, thereby reducing the time of data acquisition compared with a photomultiplier, where the signal is acquired at each wavelength sequentially. Figure 12.5 shows a typical Raman instrumentation, where each component discussed can be identified.

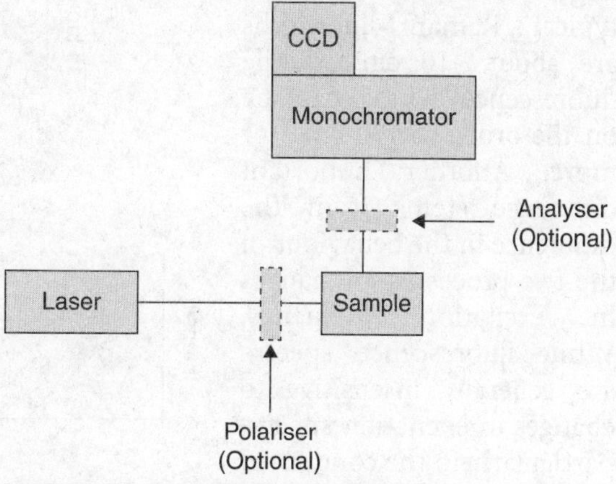

Fig. 12.5 Schematic of the instrumentation of a Raman spectrometer. Polariser and analyser are optional and are used when performing depolarisation ratio experiments (Section 3.2).

Typical lasers used for Raman excitation are Ar^+ laser (λ = 488.0 or 514.5 nm), Kr^+ (λ = 530.9 or 647.1 nm), helium–neon laser (632.8 nm) and the fundamental of the Nd:YAG laser (λ = 1064 nm). The choice of the excitation laser wavelength is dependent on a few factors such as sample decomposition and suppression of unwanted fluorescence.

Shorter wavelength lasers produce strong Raman scattering as the scattering process is proportional to the fourth power of the frequency of the excitation beam. However, shorter wavelengths may produce photodecomposition of the sample. To overcome this problem, experiments are usually carried out by ejecting the solution through a capillary so that a fresh aliquot of the solution is exposed to the laser beam. Alternatively, long-wavelength lasers are used to avoid the problem of sample decomposition.

The use of short-wavelength lasers also introduce the problem of molecular fluorescence, which can often be an annoying interference in a Raman experiment, since the radiation used in the Raman scattering process may also cause fluorescence. The fluorescence can often be so strong that the detection of the Raman process becomes rather difficult. To alleviate this problem, long-wavelength lasers are used for excitation—such as the He–Ne laser (632.8 nm). At these wavelengths, normally no electronic states get excited to give rise to fluorescence. Figure 12.6 shows the fluorescence and Raman spectra of a dye, Sudan I. The Raman spectra were recorded using two different excitation wavelengths, 481 and 632 nm. The lack of fluorescence at the longer excitation is obvious. The disadvantage of poorer Raman scattering cross sections with these long-wavelength lasers is compensated by the fact that the lasers can be used at higher laser intensities.

It will be relevant at this point to compare fluorescence and the Raman process. The linewidths in fluorescence are generally larger than in Raman; typical Raman linewidths are about ~10 cm^{-1}, while fluorescence bands can be on the order of 100 cm^{-1} or more. Another important difference stems from the difference in the behaviour of the two processes to changes in excitation frequency. While fluorescence spectra are generally insensitive to changes in excitation spectra particularly in the condensed phase, the scattered radiation from a Raman process shifts with changes in the excitation frequency such that, the shift in frequency between the scattered radiation and the excitation radiation is constant and which is a signature of the molecule under study.

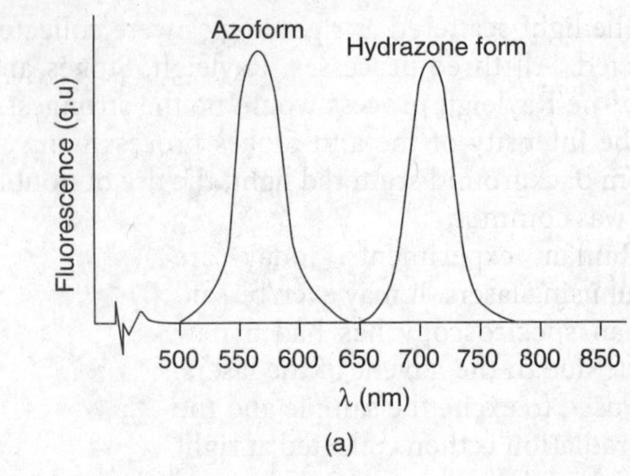

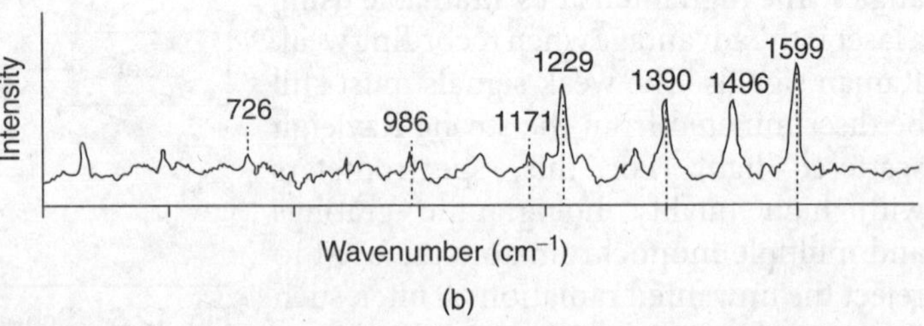

Fig. 12.6 A comparison of the **(a)** fluorescence (in ether) and **(b)** Raman spectra of Sudan I

The Nd:YAG laser operated at the 1064 nm infrared line is also a popular excitation source, particularly in Fourier Transform Raman spectrometers. Low probability of sample decomposition, lack of molecular fluorescence and amenability for the use in a Michelson interferometer in the Fourier Transform instrument have made this wavelength quite popular. However, the long wavelength Nd:YAG laser has one particular disadvantage—water absorbs in this region of the spectrum, which makes handling of aqueous solutions rather difficult at these wavelengths. One of the major advantages of Raman spectroscopy is that it can be applied to aqueous solutions as water is a rather poor scatterer, while aqueous solutions cannot be handled in IR spectroscopy. The use of lasers such as the Nd:YAG laser therefore somewhat offsets this advantage.

12.4.2 Polarisation Aspects of Raman Spectroscopy

In all the discussions thus far, no attention was paid to the polarisation of the incident and the scattered beam. The excitation source was assumed to be unpolarised. If polarised light sources are used for the Raman excitation, new insights into molecular phenomena can be obtained. The polarisation dependence of the scattered radiation in Raman spectroscopy can often provide information on the symmetry properties of the scattering species and that of the vibrations. To take advantage of this aspect, the experiments are conducted using polarised light for excitation. A discussion on how these experiments are carried out will be relevant at this point.

Light, as we know, is a form of electromagnetic radiation; this implies that as the light propogates, say in the *z* direction, the electric field vector would be oscillating in a direction perpendicular to the propagating direction, while the magnetic field would be oscillating in a direction perpendicular to both the direction of propagation and the direction of oscillation of the electric field. The solid lines in Fig. 12.7 show *one* possibility for the direction of the three vectors, that is, electric and magnetic field vectors and the propagation vector. However, this configuration of vectors is not the only possibility; for a given direction of propagation, there are an infinite number of ways in which the electric and magnetic field vectors can line up, fulfilling the condition of the mutual orthogonality of the three vectors mentioned above. Another such possibility is shown in the same figure, where the electric and magnetic vectors are shown in broken lines. A beam of light that propagates assuming all the different possibilities for the electric and magnetic field direction is called unpolarised light. If however, the propagating light beam is restricted to assume only one orientation for the electric field vector which then automatically constrains the magnetic field vector to also assume a fixed direction, the beam of light is referred to as polarised light. Experimentally, this can be achieved by passing unpolarised light through a polariser.

Fig. 12.7 Relative orientations of the electric and magnetic vectors with respect to the direction of propagation of light

If the electric field is restricted to oscillate in the direction parallel to the *z* axis (that is, in the *yz* or *xz* planes), shown as a solid arrow in Fig. 12.8, it is referred to as vertically polarised light. However, if it is restricted to oscillate in a direction perpendicular to the *z* axis (that is, the *xy* plane), shown by a broken arrow, it is referred to as horizontally polarised. We will use this coordinate specification in further discussions on the use of polarised light in Raman spectroscopy.

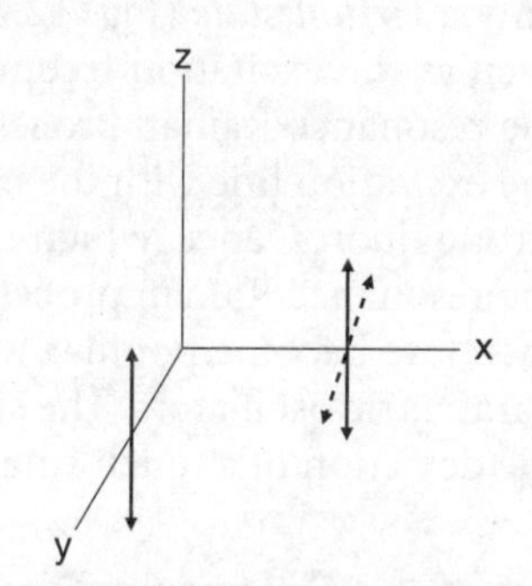

Fig. 12.8 Coordinate system showing the direction of vertically and horizontally polarised beams

If the excitation beam for Raman excitation is polarised, say vertically, then one can gain useful information by measuring the intensity of the Raman scattered beam that is polarised vertically (which would be parallel to the polarisation of the excitation beam) and horizontally (which would be perpendicular to the polarisation of the excitation beam). The intensity of the scattered beam is determined in both the parallel and perpendicular directions. The intensities in the parallel and perpendicular directions are denoted as $I_{\parallel}$ and $I_{\perp}$ respectively. The ratio of the intensities ($I_{\perp}/I_{\parallel}$) is referred to as the depolarisation ratio ρ. A small value for ρ implies that the direction of polarisation of the excitation beam is more or less maintained in the scattering process, while a large value for this ratio means that there is a scrambling of rotation of the polarisation in the scattering process. A classical treatment of the Raman process (beyond the scope of this text), shows that if the vibration is non-symmetric, maximum values for this ratio ρ would be 6/7, while vibrational transitions which are totally symmetric would yield much smaller ratios. The ν_1 vibration of CCl_4 at 459 cm^{-1} is a totally symmetric mode corresponding to the symmetric motion of all the four chlorine atoms away (or towards) the central carbon, a mode called the breathing mode and corresponding to the A_1 representation of the T_d point group. The symmetric nature of this vibration is confirmed by the observation that this mode shows a depolarisation ratio of 0.005. At the same time, the vibrational mode corresponding to the ν_3 mode at 775 cm^{-1} has a depolarisation ratio of 0.71 and is therefore concluded to belong to the non-totally symmetric mode. This mode actually corresponds to the B_2 representation. This example clearly shows the utility of the polarisation aspects in Raman spectrum for vibrational assignments.

12.5 MODIFIED RAMAN PROCESSES

12.5.1 Resonance Raman Spectroscopy

It was mentioned earlier that as the excitation frequency is changed, the frequency of the scattered photon also changes to keep the shift a constant, the shift being equal to, say a vibrational frequency in the molecule. The dependence of the Raman spectrum on the excitation frequency is not always as simple as discussed above. As the excitation frequency is changed, it can sometimes overlap with an absorption of the molecule. If the excitation frequency overlaps with a molecular absorption, the Raman process becomes significantly enhanced and this process is then termed as a *resonance Raman process*. The difference between this process and the normal Raman process is that, in the resonance process the molecule is raised to an excited electronic state while in the normal process, the upper state accessed is only a *virtual state* (Fig. 12.2). A significant enhancement in the Raman process can be seen even as the excitation frequency begins to overlap with the fringes of molecular absorption; the resonance Raman process is often conducted under these conditions. A strong overlap of the excitation line with the molecular absorption is often judiciously avoided, as it may lead to strong fluorescence, which can often mask the observation of the Raman process. The use of the resonance Raman process calls for the availability of a tunable excitation source and it has therefore become popular with the advent of tunable lasers such as the dye laser and optical parametric oscillators. The stronger cross sections for the resonance Raman process allows for the detection of a much smaller concentration of the analyte through this process.

12.5.2 Surface Enhanced Raman Spectroscopy (SERS)

It has been observed that a significant enhancement in the Raman cross section is also produced when the sample is adsorbed on colloidal particles of metals such as gold or silver. An enhancement of the Raman signal by 4 to 5 orders of magnitude is often observed when the molecule of interest is adsorbed on a metal surface compared to the Raman signal of the same sample in a bulk solution. The actual physics of this process is only now being slowly understood, and the enhancement is attributed to an increased polarisability of the molecule adsorbed on the surface or an increased electric field experienced by the adsorbed molecule. The increased polarisability can occur due to the interaction of the adsorbed molecule with the metal surface, which can alter the electronic distribution in the molecule. Alternatively, the laser can interact with the metal surface leading to surface plasmon resonances that can eventually cause an increase in the electric field experienced by the molecule. From Eq. 12.1, it is clear that an enhancement in either the polarisability or the electric field can increase the strength of the Raman signal. Analytical advantages of this technique have been exploited for quite some time now. Combined with the advantages of laser excitation and other processes such as resonance Raman effects, the detection limits obtained using SERS have made this an useful analytical tool. However, the interpretation of the SERS spectra can pose challenges as the spectra can often be very different from those obtained from normal solution phase.

12.5.3 Higher Order Raman Processes

The intensity of the laser sources has made it possible to observe higher order Raman processes. Let us look back at Eq. 12.1 which essentially is not complete. For stronger electric fields, such as that obtained in a laser, the equation must involve higher powers of the electric field and is therefore written as

$$P = \chi_1 E + \chi_2 E^2 + \cdots \quad (12.7)$$

The α in Eq. 12.1 is equivalent to χ_1 in Eq. 12.7. The values of χ_2 and coefficients of higher powers of the electric field are much smaller than χ_1 and the higher order terms therefore assume importance only for large values of E. With weak conventional light sources, the first order term alone is important and thus, it was used during the discussion on conventional Raman spectroscopy. However, with the advent of high power laser sources, the effects of the higher powers of the electric field in the scattering process can be observed. As a result, higher order Raman processes such as Stimulated Raman Scattering (SRS), Coherent Anti-Stokes Raman Spectroscopy (CARS) and Coherent Stokes Raman Spectroscopy (CSRS) have become important areas of study. As an example of the higher order Raman process, we will discuss the generation of the CARS signal.

12.5.3.1 Coherent Anti-Stokes Raman Spectroscopy (CARS)

In this experiment, the sample is irradiated with two laser beams of frequency ω_1 and ω_2. The experiment is an example of wave mixing, where the scattered Raman scattering occurs at a frequency $(2\omega_1 - \omega_2)$, as shown in the energy level scheme. Quite clearly, the frequency of the scattered radiation is higher than the frequencies of the two incident beams and therefore is not masked by any fluorescence that the sample may emit. Fluorescence always occurs at smaller frequencies compared to those of the excitation beam. Furthermore, the scattered radiation is coherent, and is emitted as a collimated beam; thus justifying the nomenclature of the process. The intensity of the CARS signal is significantly greater than a normal Raman process and hence provides the advantage of improved detection limits.

The CARS signal is observed when the difference $(\omega_1 - \omega_2)$ matches a vibrational transition in the molecule. Consequently, one of the frequencies ω_1 is fixed while the second frequency is varied using a dye laser. As this frequency is tuned, strong CARS signals are observed when the difference $(\omega_1 - \omega_2)$ matches a vibrational (or rotational) frequency of the molecule. The two laser beams are focussed into the sample, using an appropriate lens L, making an angle 2β. Due to reasons of momentum conservation, which is also referred to as phase matching, the emerging scattered radiation at the frequency, $(2\omega_1 - \omega_2)$, emerges at a specific angle. Consequently, as shown in Fig. 12.9, this beam can be easily spatially resolved from the incident beams and detected. Discrimination of the scattered beam therefore does not require wavelength dispersing devices, which is an added advantage of this technique. Since the frequency of the scattered beam is greater than that of the incident beam, it is referred to as an anti-Stokes process. As mentioned earlier, it must be remembered that these higher order Raman processes can be observed only with strong laser excitation sources.

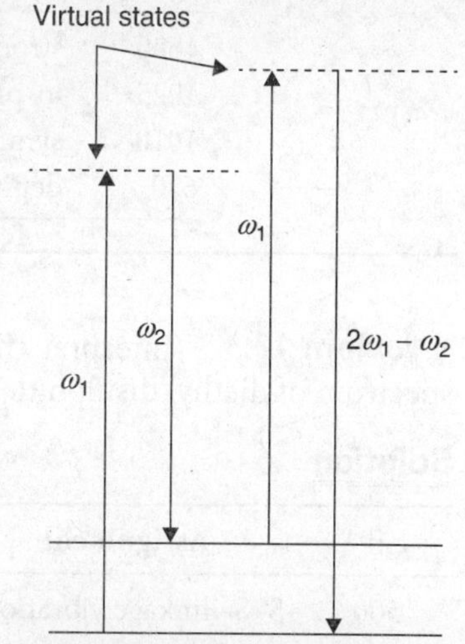

Fig. 12.9 Energy level scheme for the CARS process

CARS has found interesting applications in studies on combustion and atmospheric chemistry, as this technique has the sensitivity to probe transient species. For example, the dynamics of the dissociation of O_3, via absorption through the Hartley bands which occur between 210 nm and 310 nm, and its subsequent production of excited O_2 (a $^1\Delta_g$) and O ($^1D_2$) was established through the use of CARS.

12.6 APPLICATIONS OF RAMAN SPECTROSCOPY

Raman spectroscopy finds vast applications in various branches of physics, chemistry and biology. Since different substances can often show unique Raman signatures, this technique is an excellent analytical tool for the characterisation of materials. For example, paints made up of pigments have unique Raman features. Hence, forensic science has often used this tool to identify or confirm the source of paints in investigations. Analysis of paints has also been used in the study of art materials to fix the age of a painting or identify the authenticity of an art piece. Raman spectroscopy finds a place of importance in these analyses due to the non-destructive nature of analysis—a necessary criterion in the analysis of art samples.

The ability of Raman spectroscopy to fingerprint materials is being exploited in the industry to confirm the purity of starting materials, process monitoring and purity of finished products. For example, in the polymer industry, unsaturated carbon compounds are used. These ethylenic compounds are better observed in the Raman as the C=C bonds are stronger in the Raman than in the IR. The polymerisation process which involves in the conversion of a C=C bond to a C–C bond can be easily followed, by keeping track of the concentration of the ethylenic compound.

In biology, Raman spectroscopy is fast becoming an important tool due to the fact that the spectra can be recorded in aqueous solutions. The use of lasers further makes it possible to focus the excitation beams to small spot sizes, making it possible to use Raman spectroscopy in the microscopy mode. This tool is now used quite commonly for the studies of single bacterial cells.

Problem 12.2 Account for the following data recorded in the Raman spectrum of styrene (monomer):

Wave number: 1620 1025 1010 620 cm^{-1}

Solution

$\bar{\nu}$	Assignment
1620	strong deformation mode: symmetric ring stretching
1025	in-plane hydrogen bending vibration
1010	symmetric ring-stretching vibration
620	depolarised in-plane bending vibration

Problem 12.3 Interpret the Raman spectrum of diethyl disulphide.

Solution

ν cm^{-1}	Assignment
500	–S–S– linkage vibration
660	–C–S– stretching
2610	–S–H stretching
2950	–C–H stretching

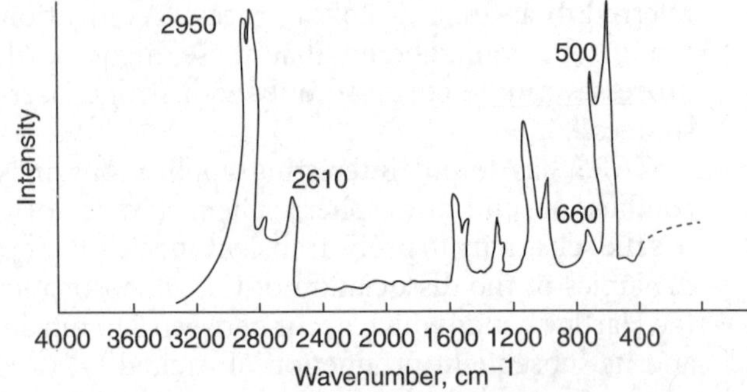

12.6.1 Raman Spectra of Inorganic Compounds

Raman spectroscopy is used for the characterisation of several inorganic species. This method is superior to IR as inorganic species can be studied in aqueous solutions as opposed to the IR method. The existence of metal–metal bonds and confirmation of the stereochemistry of inorganic molecules are two important applications of Raman spectroscopy. The Raman-active metal–metal vibrational peaks occur at 100–700 cm^{-1}, a region difficult to experimentally study by the IR method.

12.6.1.1 Metal–Metal Bonds

The presence of metal–metal bonds in some inorganic species has been established by Raman spectroscopy. For example, a vibrational Raman line at 169 cm^{-1} occurs for aqueous mercurous ion. Independent Hg^{+} cannot be Raman active; therefore, the Raman line at 169 cm^{-1} must be due to the presence of Hg–Hg bond in the mercurous species. Actually, the mercurous species occurs as $(Hg - Hg)^{2+}$.

The proof that some other metal ions, such as those of argentous and thallous, also exist as dimeric species, has been provided by Raman spectroscopy.

Raman spectroscopy, coupled with IR spectroscopy, confirms the formation of mercury species such as Hg_3^{2+} and Hg_4^{2+} on dissolving Hg in ASF_5 in liquid SO_2.

12.6.1.2 Raman Spectroscopy and Nature of Bonds

Raman spectroscopy is used as a diagnostic tool to study the nature of bonds in simple inorganic molecules such as halides. For example, NaCl, AgCl, and $BaCl_2$ do not show Raman lines; these halides, being electrovalent, are strongly ionic and have no vibrational modes. Halides, such as $ZnCl_2$, $SiCl_4$ and PCl_3 show prominent Raman lines indicating the existence of metal–chlorine bonds in them; these are covalent. CdI_2 shows a faint Raman line because it has partial ionic character.

12.6.1.3 Coordination Compounds

An important application of Raman spectroscopy is the determination of the composition, structure and stability of coordination compounds. For example, the work by Fujiwara and Tasumi (*J. Phys. Chem.*, Vol. 90:2,1986) on resonance Raman spectrum of chlorophyll *a* in *n*-hexane shows three bands at 1612–1606, 1554–1551, and 1529–1527 cm^{-1}. These data are used to infer that the Mg atom of chlorophyll *a* is five-coordinated (with one axial ligand). On the other hand, when the spectrum is recorded in methanol, the Mg atom is six-coordinated, with two axial ligands. The Raman spectrum of chlorophyll *b* shows that it behaves in the same manner as chlorophyll *a* with respect to axial coordination by solvent molecules.

Raman spectroscopy has also wide-ranging applications in inorganic chemistry. Many of the metal–oxygen and metal–carbon vibrations occur in the far-infrared region of the spectrum, which are not observed in the more commonly studied region of the infrared, namely the mid-infrared. However, these regions are easily studied by Raman spectroscopy. For example, Raman spectra of VO_4^{3-}, $Al(OH)_4^{-}$, $Si(OH)_6^{2-}$ and $Sn(OH)_6^{2-}$ confirmed the structures of these species containing M–O bonds. Furthermore, the ability of the Raman technique to study aqueous solutions also makes this technique popular with inorganic chemists.

Problem 12.4 The Raman spectrum of aqueous nitric acid consists of a band at 1050 cm^{-1}. This band is less intense when the acid is concentrated compared to that in aqueous alkali nitrates of the same concentration: rationalise this.

Solution

The absorption at 1050 cm^{-1} is due to the symmetric stretching mode of the nitrate ion. The lower intensity of this band at high concentration compared to that in aqueous alkali nitrates is an evidence for the existence of undissociated HNO_3 molecules. The band intensity is observed to be proportional to the degree of dissociation of the molecule.

12.6.1.4 Quantitative Analysis

The intensity of a Raman line is measured in terms of an arbitrarily chosen reference (standard) line, that of CCl_4 at 459 cm^{-1}. This line is studied before and after the spectral recording of the sample. The recorded height of the sample peak is divided by the average of the heights of the dual traces of the CCl_4 peak. This gives *scattering coefficients*, which are proportional to the quantity of analyses. Both the standard and the sample are used in cells of identical dimensions. The intensity of Raman lines is directly proportional to the scattering coefficient and hence to the number of scatterer molecules. The sensitivity of Raman analysis is10^4 Pa (100 torr).

12.6.2 Advantages of Raman Spectroscopy

- Raman spectra appear simpler than IR spectra because in the former, the overtone and combination bands are weak unlike in the latter.
- The Raman intensity is directly proportional to the concentration of the active species rendering determination easy.
- Aqueous solutions can be used in this method, unlike in the IR method.
- It is well-suited for the analysis of organic polar compounds which differ in skeletal structure.
- Glass cells are conveniently used in this method whereas salt cells are required in the IR method.

Commercial sources of Raman spectrometers are now quite abundant and this has largely added to the routine utility of this important tool. Raman spectroscopy has had a new lease of life since the lasers were discovered.

EXERCISES

1. Define the following:
   (a) Raman scattering
   (b) Rule of mutual exclusion
   (c) Resonance Raman spectroscopy

2. Explain the following spectral data recorded for $TiCl_4$.

Absorption (wave number cm^{-1})	**IR**	**Raman**
119	—	strong
139	medium	medium
388	—	very strong (polarized)
490	very strong	medium
506	very weak (shoulder)	weak

3. Predict and explain the Raman spectrum of ClO_3^-.

4. With two examples, explain the application of Raman spectroscopy in the study of conformational analysis.

5. Write a critical account of the relative uses of IR and Raman spectral methods in measuring the vibrational frequencies of carbon–heteroatom bonds.

6. The use of lasers in Raman spectroscopy has enhanced the applications of this spectroscopy vastly: justify this with examples.

7. Citing literature sources, explain the application of Raman spectroscopy in *combustion and flame diagnostics*.

8. Account for the following:
   (a) A molecule must be anisotropically polarisable to show a rotational Raman spectrum.
   (b) Resonance Raman spectroscopy is preferable to vibrational spectroscopy for studying certain bond stretching modes.
   (c) Raman spectra have isotope effects.
   (d) The ratio of anti-Stokes and Stokes intensities increases with temperature.

9. Both IR and Raman spectroscopy have selection rules based on the symmetry of the molecule: substantiate this with two examples.

10. How are the weak Raman signals improved?

11. Write the principle of surface-enhanced Raman spectroscopy (SERS)?

12. None of the normal modes of vibration of benzene can be both infrared and Raman active: explain.

13. Which one of the following cannot show a pure rotational spectrum: CH_3CH_3, N_2O, SF_6. Explain.

14. Why is resonance Raman spectroscopy preferable to vibrational spectroscopy for studying the O–O stretching mode?

15. State whether each of the following is true or false explaining your choice.
   (a) For a vibration to be Raman active, there must be a change in the polarisability tensor.
   (b) If a molecule has a centre of symmetry, IR and Raman active vibrational modes are mutually exclusive.
   (c) In IR spectroscopy the excitations are detected by *absorption* of characteristic frequencies; but in Raman spectroscopy the excitations are detected by characteristic *shifts* in frequencies of the scattered light.

16. It is impossible for a molecule with a centre of symmetry to have a vibration that is both IR and Raman active. Explain.

17. Illustrate how isotopic substitution in a molecule can be used to assign some Raman frequencies.

18. Explain the application of Raman spectroscopy in the assignment of structures, choosing XeF_4 and isomeric xylenes as examples.

19. Discuss the application of character tables in the analysis of Raman spectra.

20. Citing literature, summarise the refinement of Raman spectroscopy by modern instrumentation.

13 Absorption Spectroscopy (UV–Vis Spectroscopy)

13.1 INTRODUCTION

Absorption spectroscopy has already been discussed in other contexts, such as infrared and atomic absorption spectroscopy. In infrared absorption, excitation of light resulted in excitation of vibrational levels. Since different functional groups in molecules have characteristic absorption frequencies, this technique was used to characterise the functional groups in molecules. In atomic absorption spectroscopy, absorption of light caused an electronic excitation in atoms, which was used to identify and quantify the analyte, which was in its atomic state. Electronic excitation in molecules is also extensively used to characterise and quantify molecular species. This technique employs radiation in the ultraviolet (~200 nm to ~350 nm) and visible regions (~350 nm to ~900 nm) of the electromagnetic spectrum and the technique is often referred to as *UV-visible spectroscopy*.

13.1.1 Wavelengths Used

In addition to the commonly employed regions of the electromagnetic radiation mentioned above, electronic excitation is also carried out, though not commonly, using radiation in the vacuum ultraviolet (<190 nm) involving highly excited electronic levels. Likewise, near-infrared (~1000 nm to 2500 nm) radiation which involves low lying electronic levels is also employed. The lowest energy transition (that is, the transition occurring at the longest wavelength) in a molecule is due to a transition between the *highest occupied molecular orbital* (HOMO) and the *lowest unoccupied molecular orbital* (LUMO). Electronic excitation in molecules is always accompanied by changes in vibrational and rotational levels (Fig. 13.1) and hence molecular absorption bands are usually broad. Excitation of electrons in molecules can be from any one of the molecular orbitals—bonding, antibonding or non-bonding.

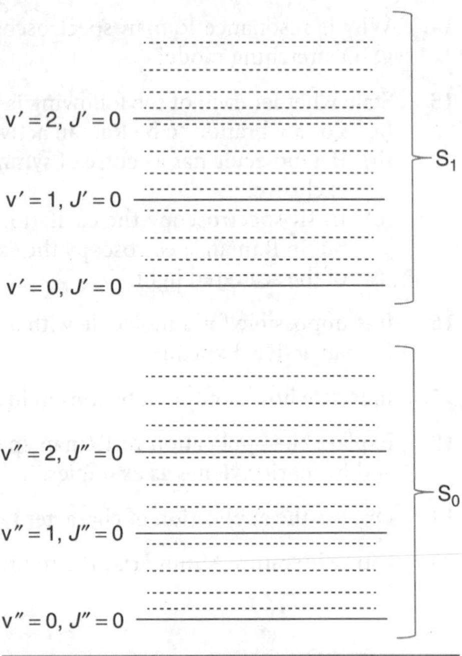

Fig. 13.1 Rotational and vibrational levels in two electronic states

13.1.2 TYPES OF TRANSITIONS

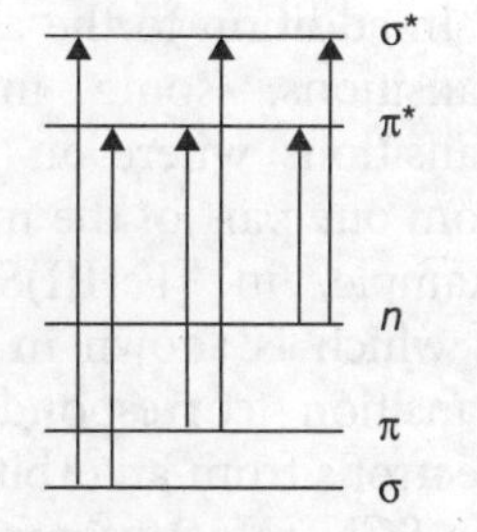

Fig. 13.2 Molecular orbitals and the corresponding transitions involved in molecular absorption

Figure 13.2 shows the molecular orbital diagram, where σ and π levels correspond to the bonding orbitals, while the σ^* and π^* levels refer to the antibonding levels. The same figure also depicts the possible electronic transitions, such as the $\pi \rightarrow \pi^*$ and $\sigma \rightarrow \sigma^*$. In alkanes, which have only σ bonds, the only possible transition would be the $\sigma \rightarrow \sigma^*$ transition. In alkenes, on the other hand, which have both σ and π bonded electrons, the possible transitions are $\sigma \rightarrow \sigma^*$ and $\pi \rightarrow \pi^*$ transitions. It can be seen from the energy level diagram, that the $\sigma \rightarrow \sigma^*$ transition would occur at high energies or shorter wavelengths compared to the $\pi \rightarrow \pi^*$ transition. Typically, the $\sigma \rightarrow \sigma^*$ transitions occur in the vacuum ultraviolet region of the electromagnetic spectrum, that is, <190 nm, while the $\pi \rightarrow \pi^*$ transitions normally occur near 250 nm. The wavelength of the $\pi \rightarrow \pi^*$ transition shifts to longer wavelengths as the length of the conjugated π system increases. For example, while the $\pi \rightarrow \pi^*$ transition in ethylene occurs near 175 nm, that for buta-1,3-diene is observed at 215 nm. Aromatic systems such as benzene show a $\pi \rightarrow \pi^*$ transition at even longer wavelengths near 260 nm, while for naphthalene the transition occurs near 300 nm.

The shift to longer wavelengths with increase in conjugation is explained in a straightforward manner using the *particle in a box* approach, one of the first problems solved in quantum chemistry. The longer the box, the smaller are the differences between energy levels and hence longer are the observed transition frequencies.

In molecules containing heteroatoms, such as ketones, the presence of non-bonding electrons on the heteroatoms, such as oxygen, allows for the excitation of these non-bonded electrons to π^* and σ^* orbitals, giving rise to $n \rightarrow \pi^*$ and $n \rightarrow \sigma^*$ transitions. The $n \rightarrow \pi^*$ transition, if it does occur, will be observed at the wavelengths longer than the $\pi \rightarrow \pi^*$ and $\sigma \rightarrow \sigma^*$ transitions in the molecule. For example, in acetone the $\pi \rightarrow \pi^*$ transition is observed at 195 nm, while the $n \rightarrow \pi^*$ transition occurs at 274 nm (Fig. 13.3). Furthermore, the $\pi \rightarrow \pi^*$ transition is seen to be considerably stronger than the $n \rightarrow \pi^*$ transition, which is typical.

The occurrence of these transitions lends important clues to the structure of the molecule in question and hence in qualitative analytical chemistry, these transitions often serve to identify the analyte in question.

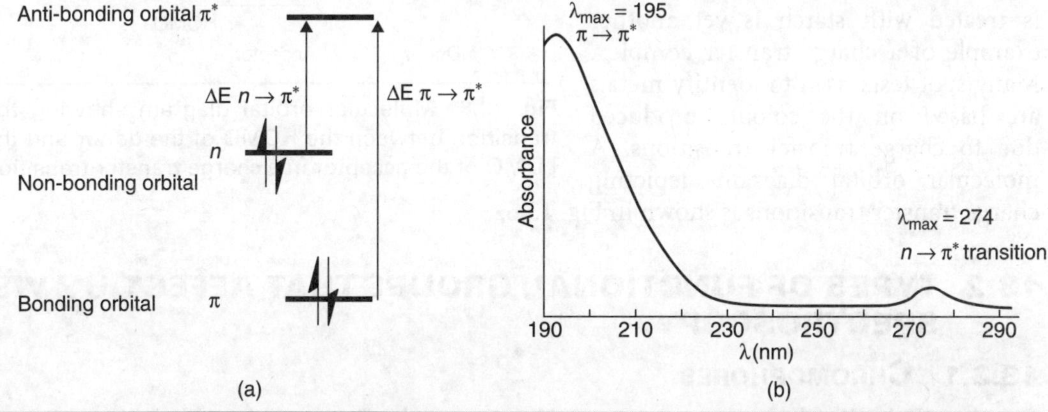

Fig. 13.3 **(a)** Electronic transitions in acetone **(b)** UV absorption spectrum of acetone

In addition to the above type of electronic transitions, some molecules also exhibit transitions where an electron is transferred from one part of the molecule to another. For example, in $[Fe(III)SCN]^{2+}$ (the spectrum of which is shown in Fig. 13.4), the intense transition corresponds to the transfer of electrons from an orbital primarily located on the SCN moiety to an orbital on Fe^{3+}. More specifically, the transition occurs between the HOMO of the donor and the LUMO of the acceptor, in the complex. Such transitions, which are usually intense, are called *charge transfer transitions.* They have typical molar absorptivities in the range 50,000 L mol^{-1}cm^{-1} which is orders of magnitude greater than, say a $\pi \rightarrow \pi^*$ transition. Due to their very large intensities, the charge transfer transitions are often used for trace level detection in analytical chemistry. For example, Fe^{3+} can be detected at sub ng/mL concentrations using the $Fe(SCN)_3$ complex. Another example of a charge transfer transition is that occurring in $KMnO_4$, the absorption spectrum of which is shown in Fig. 13.5. The purple colour of this compound results from the charge transfer transition involving the transfer of an electron from an oxygen-centred orbital to a Mn-centred orbital in the MnO_4 ion. Organic ligands such as 2,2'-bipyridine and 1,10-phenanthroline are also excellent candidates for charge transfer with metals such as Pd and Fe, respectively. The blue colour produced when iodine is treated with starch is yet another example of a charge transfer complex. Many spot tests used to identify metals are based on the colours produced due to charge transfer transitions. A molecular orbital diagram depicting charge transfer transitions is shown in Fig. 13.6.

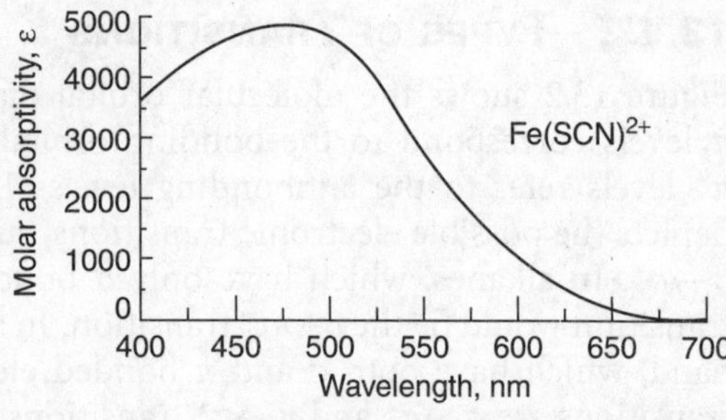

Fig. 13.4 Absorption spectrum of $Fe(SCN)^{2+}$

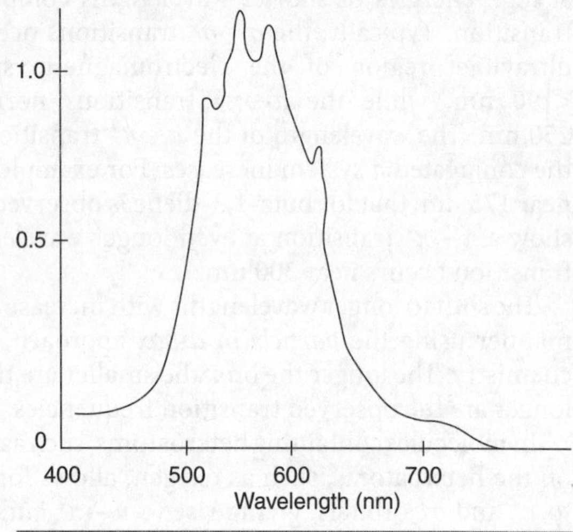

Fig. 13.5 Absorption spectrum of aqueous $KMnO_4$

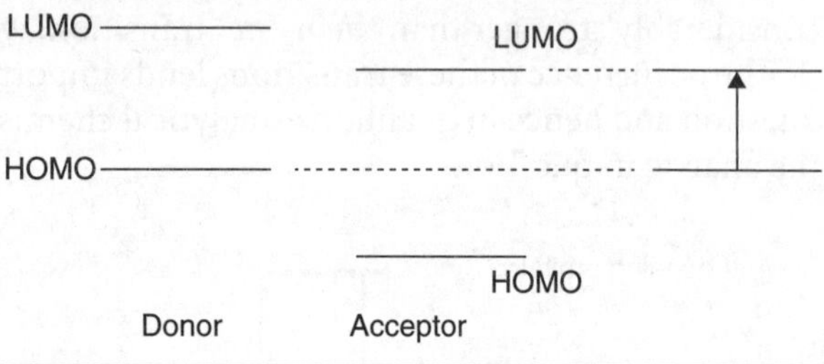

Fig. 13.6 Molecular orbital diagram showing the transition between the HOMO of the donor and the LUMO of the acceptor in a charge transfer transition

13.2 TYPES OF FUNCTIONAL GROUPS THAT AFFECT UV-VIS SPECTROSCOPY

13.2.1 Chromophores

Based on the earlier discussions, we can see that groups that have π and non-bonding electrons can give rise to electronic transitions in the ultraviolet and visible regions. Such groups are called *chromophores*. Some of the common chromophoric groups together with their transition wavelengths are given in Table 13.1. It is also possible that more than one of these chromophores may be present in a molecule in way that there exists a conjugation between them. In such instances, the absorption may become stronger than when either of the chromophores are present alone, and may also occur at longer wavelengths. Such shifts to long wavelengths are called *bathochromic shifts*; when the shift occurs to shorter wavelengths it is referred to as a *hypsochromic shift*. These shifts are as shown.

Table 13.1 Transitions in common functional groups in organic molecules and the corresponding transition frequencies

Group	Transition wavelength	Type of transition
C=C	175 nm	$\pi \rightarrow \pi^*$
C=O	280 nm	$n \rightarrow \pi^*$
–COOH	210 nm	$n \rightarrow \pi^*$
$-NO_2$	280 nm	$n \rightarrow \pi^*$
–NO	650 nm	$n \rightarrow \pi^*$

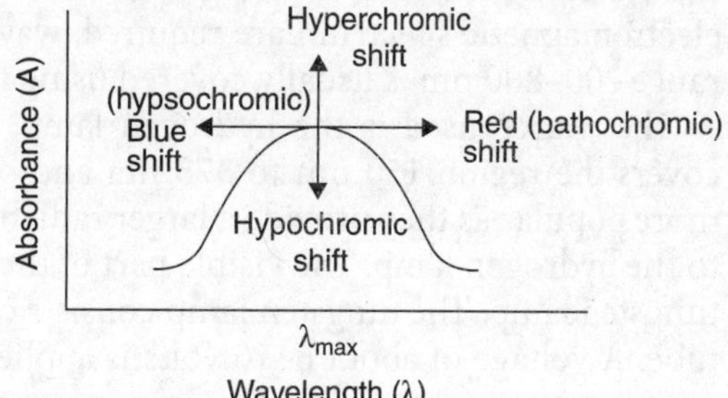

13.2.2 Auxochromes

There are some groups, such as OH, CH_3 and NH_2, which do not themselves absorb strongly in the ultraviolet or visible regions, but when present along with a chromophore can intensify or alter the transition due to the chromophore. Such groups are called *auxochromes*. The effect that the *auxochromophore* can have on the transition depends largely on the polarity of the auxochrome. For example, the presence of a CH_3 group will cause a bathochromic shift of hardly about 5 nm, while NH_2 attached to the benzene ring can influence the spectrum drastically. This can be observed by comparing the spectral data of benzene (C_6H_6) and aniline ($C_6H_5NH_2$). Benzene in hexane absorbs at 184, 204 and 254 nm. The $—NH_2$ substituent in benzene increases the wavelength (204 → 230; 254 → 280 nm) and the intensity of the absorption peaks since $—NH_2$ is an auxochrome.

While it is outside of the scope of the present text, the maximum in the absorption spectrum of an organic compound can be predicted reasonably well using rules that have been deduced, based on the chromophoric groups present in the molecule. A discussion on these apsects can be found in the references cited (1, 2).

13.2.3 Solvents

Solvents can also alter the absorption spectra of compounds, and it is therefore essential that when reporting spectra, the solvents used must be mentioned. Solvents of low polarity and molecules that are non-polar show little effect, while polar solvents can interact with polar molecules causing changes in the spectral characteristics. For example, the spectrum of phenol in methanol and hexane are remarkably different (Fig. 13.7). Hydrogen bonding

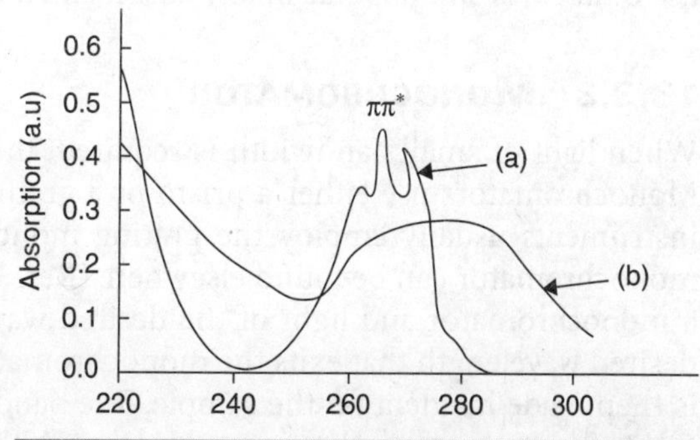

Fig. 13.7 UV absorption spectra of phenol in **(a)** *n*-hexane and **(b)** methanol.

interactions between the solvent and solute causes band broadening and consequent loss of the vibronic sructure. Hydrogen bonding leads to loss of spectral structure.

13.3 INSTRUMENTATION OF UV–VIS SPECTROPHOTOMETER

The instrumentation of a spectrophotometer is very similar to the atomic absorption spectrometers (Chapter 9). The various parts of the spectrophotometer are: (i) light source, (ii) wavelength selection device, (iii) sample holder, (iv) detector and readout system.

13.3.1 Radiation Source

The radiation source must be capable of delivering light of reasonable intensity over the wavelength range covering 200 nm to about 800 nm. If near-infrared regions of the electromagnetic spectrum are required, wavelengths longer than 1000 nm are necessary. The range 200–800 nm is usually covered using two light sources.

The source used is the hydrogen lamp, or more commonly the deuterium lamp which covers the region 150 nm to 375 nm and serves as the source of UV. Deuterium lamps are more popular as they provide a larger radiant power over the wavelength of interest compared to the hydrogen lamp. The visible part of the spectrum (~375 nm to 800 nm), is provided by a tungsten lamp. The tungsten lamp consists of a thin coiled tungsten wire in a low pressure gas tube. A voltage of about 6–10 volts is applied across the tungsten wire when the heated wire serves as a source visible radiation.

13.3.2 Wavelength Selection Device

The simplest of wavelength selection devices is the absorption filter, which consists of a coloured glass—the colour of the glass determining the wavelength of light that is absorbed by the filter. Consequently, the filter allows a certain region of wavelength that is transmitted and therefore available for an absorption experiment. For example, a potassium permanganate solution is purple, which implies that it absorbs the complementary green colour. Hence, to perform an absorption experiment on potassium permanganate, a filter that transmits green light would be required. Filters that transmit light longer than a certain wavelength (λ_c) and none shorter, are called *long-pass filters*. Likewise, filters that transmit light shorter than the cut-off wavelength (λ_c) and none longer than it are called *short-pass filters*. Filters which transmit light over a certain region of wavelength are also available and are called *band-pass filters*. While filters are inexpensive, they do not provide monochromatic light. However, the use of filters is still popular in low cost instruments.

13.3.3 Monochromator

When light of small bandwidth is required, the use of a monochromator becomes essential. Monochromators use either a prism or a grating for wavelength dispersion, but present day instruments usually employ the grating monochromator. A discussion on the design of a monochromator can be found elsewhere (Ref. 3). The light from the source is passed through a monochromator and light of the desired wavelength is chosen by tuning the grating. The desired wavelength that exits the monochromator through the exit slit of the monochromator is then made incident on the sample. The bandwidth of the radition ($\Delta\lambda$) that emerges from the monochromator is determined by the width of the slit.

13.3.4 Sample Holder

Samples for absorption spectrophotometry are usually in the form of a gas or neat liquids or solutions. Cells are designed with varying pathlengths, but a 1-cm pathlength cell is the most commonly used. However, where only limited sample is available or where the absorbance is very high, cells with smaller pathlength such as 0.1 cm, are also employed. The cells are called *cuvettes* and are made of quartz, glass or plastic. Glass and plastic cuvettes can be used for experiments in the visible region. However, glass and plastic absorb in the ultraviolet and cannot therefore be used in this region; quartz cuvettes are a necessity. The spectrophotometric cells are usually clear and of optical quality along two opposite sides; while the other two sides need not be of optical quality. In contrast, it must be noted that cells used for fluorescence spectroscopy are of optical quality on all four sides, since in fluorescence, the light is detected at an angle of 90° to the incident beam.

13.3.5 Detectors and Readout Device

Spectrophotometers use either a photomultiplier tubes (PMT) or array detectors, such as photodiode arrays (PDA) or charge-coupled devices (CCD). The PDA have a poorer sensitivity compared to the PMT. However, array detectors offer the advantage of providing simultaneous detection at a number of wavelengths and hence reduce detection time compared to PMT detection, or provide comparable detection times. There is also an improvement in the signal to noise ratio. However, the use of an array detector can increase the cost of the machine, and hence a PMT detector is the popularly used detector. The output of the detector is then amplified and processed for storage on a personal computer. The personal computers are provided with software for data processing and display.

13.4 TYPES OF UV-VISIBLE SPECTROPHOTOMETERS

The basic experiment of absorption spectrophotometry consists in first recording the intensity of the *reference* beam, which is the intensity of the beam passing through just the cuvette containing the solvent. The intensity of the beam after passing through the sample or the analyte is then measured, which is the intensity of the *sample* beam. From the two measurements, the absorbance of the sample is obtained. Instruments employ two different techniques to record the intensities of the reference beam and the sample beam—the single beam spectrophotometer and the double beam spectrophotometer.

13.4.1 Single Beam Spectrophotometer

In this configuration (Fig 13.8), a single beam is used for recording the spectrum of both the sample and the reference. First, the cuvette filled with the solvent is placed in the path of the beam and the detector output is recorded and stored. The sample is then placed in the cuvette and the spectrum again recorded. The spectrum of the sample is then arrived at by subtracting the two outputs. The development of computer based instrumentation has now made it easy to store the reference spectrum making the single beam instruments more reliable and popular, in view of their simplicity.

13.4.2 Double Beam Spectrophotometer

In one form of the double beam spectrophotometer, the radiation from the source is split into two beams—one passing through a reference arm which contains a cuvette containing the solvent, and the other beam passing through the sample arm containing a cuvette filled with

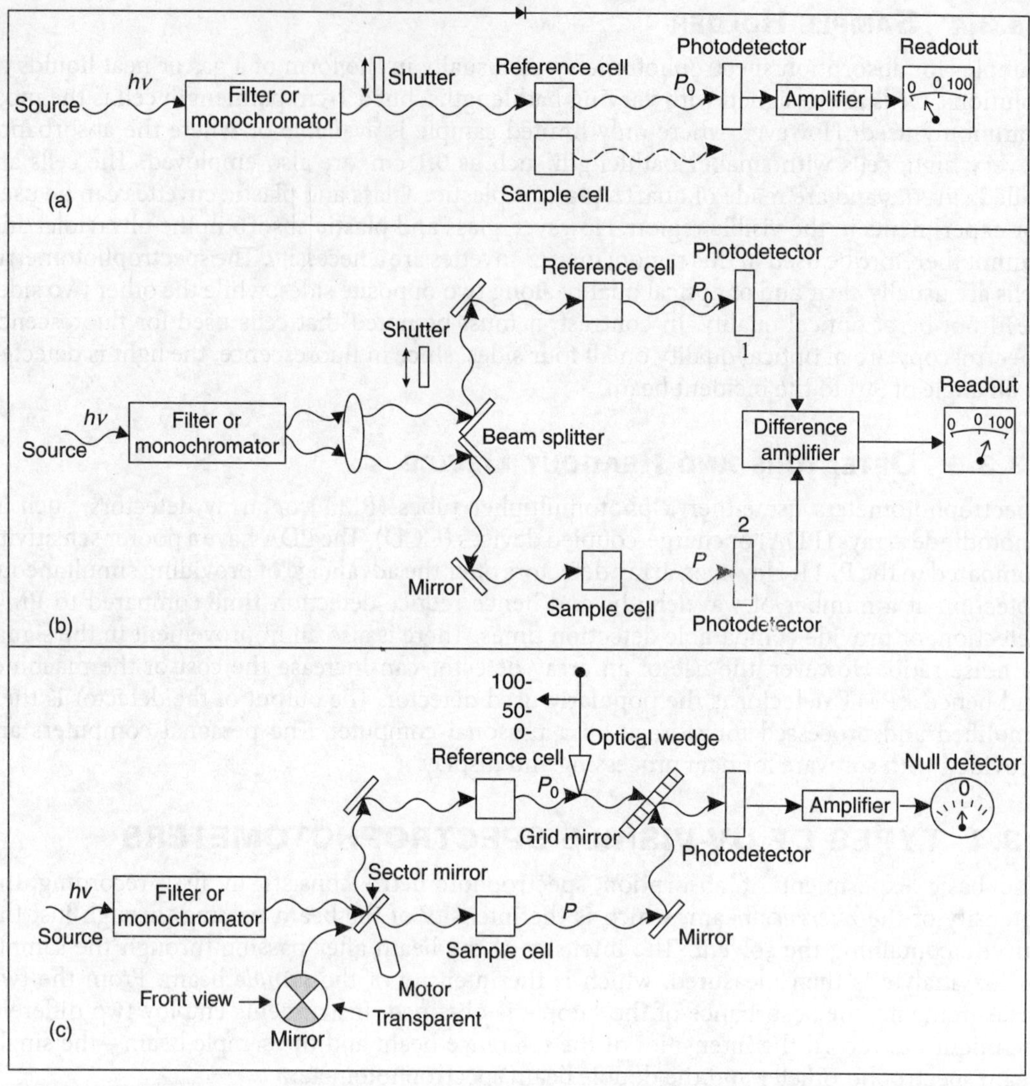

Fig. 13.8 Optical configuration of **(a)** Single beam spectrometer **(b)** Double beam (in space) spectrometer and **(c)** Double beam (in time) spectrometer

the sample in an appropriate solvent. This type of configuration is referred to as a *double beam in-space spectrometer*. Two matched photomultipliers measure the intensity of both the arms; the signals put out by the two photomultipliers is then processed to obtain the absorbance.

Another configuration of the double beam spectrometer employs the double beam in time method. In this configuration, the optical beam is not split, but is diverted alternately towards the sample cell and the reference cell by a rotating mirror. A single detector records the intensity of the beam as it traverses through the sample and the reference, which is then ratioed to obtain the absorption spectrum. This configuration has the advantage that matched photomultiplier detectors, which are difficult to achieve, are avoided.

In a variation of the above described spectrometers, the photomultiplier is replaced by a diode array, which measures the intensity of a range of wavelengths simultaneously. In a PMT based system, each wavelength is measured sequentially and consequently the acquisition period is longer than in an array based system. Alternatively, for similar acquisition times, diode array spectrometers provide a superior signal to noise compared with a PMT based spectrometer.

13.5 ANALYTICAL APPLICATIONS OF UV-VIS SPECTROPHOTOMETER

13.5.1 Qualitative Analysis

We know that since the UV–vis absorption varies with the functional groups in molecules, it can provide useful information on the structure of a molecule. While infrared, NMR and mass spectra provide more detailed and unambiguous information on structural aspects of molecules, UV–vis spectroscopy can often provide valuable information on molecules containing conjugated π systems and systems containing hetero atoms. For example, an absorption in the region 200–350 nm is often a clear indication of the presence of unsaturation in the molecule. Studies on a large number of organic molecules led Woodward, Hoffmann, Fieser and Scott to establish empirical rules for predicting the λ_{max} for an unsaturated molecule. λ_{max} is the wavelength that gives the highest absorbance reading for a given substance. The sensitivity of absorption by the substance is maximum at this wavelength. The absorption spectrum is also sensitive to the polarity of the solvent, as this can alter the energy levels in a molecule (Fig. 13.7). This technique is often used in biology to probe the microenvironment of biologically important species.

13.5.2 Quantitative Analysis

UV–vis spectroscopy finds extensive applications in analytical chemistry, as the absorption due to a molecule is proportional to its concentration within the regime of applicability of Beer–Lambert's law. The advantage of this technique is its relative simplicity, selectivity, precision and excellent detection limits. It is possible to estimate analytes down to concentrations of a few tenths of parts per million. For example, $KMnO_4$ has a strong absorption around 525 nm, which can be used to estimate permanganate down to about 0.2 ppm, with a relative standard deviation of about ~2%. This method uses the time-honoured method of first preparing standard solutions of various known concentrations and recording the absorbance for each of these solutions at the λ_{max}. A calibration curve is then drawn, which must exhibit linearity if the concentrations are chosen within the Beer–Lambert's applicability, which must always be ensured. The concentration of the unknown is then calculated from the calibration graph. Statistical analysis can then be performed to arrive at the standard deviations in the estimated concentrations.

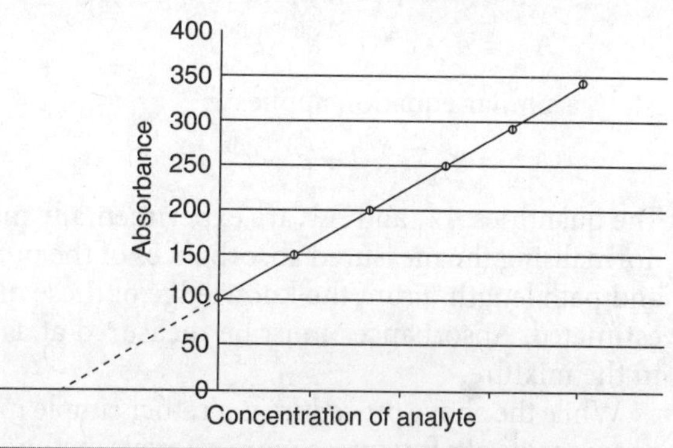

Fig. 13.9 A calibration curve to demonstrate the technique of standard addition

Not uncommonly, the analyte solution may consist of some interfering species which may alter the absorption of the analyte species. Since the standards that are prepared are not likely to contain this interferent, the calibration graph would be inappropriate for use in calculating the concentration of the unknown analyte. In such situations, the method of standard addition is employed. In this method, a known amount of the standard is added to the aliquot of the unknown sample and the absorbance is measured. To a second aliquot of the unknown, a higher amount of the standard is added, say, twice of what was added in the first experiment, and the absorbance is again measured. The experiment is repeated for variable additions of the standard to different aliquots of the solution of the analyte. A plot is then made of the absorbance against added analyte. The first sample is one where no standard is added. If Beer's law is obeyed, a straight line is obtained and extrapolation of the line to intersect the X-axis (on the negative side) is then done. The point of intersection with the X-axis then gives the concentration of the analyte in the original unknown solution (Fig. 13.9).

13.5.3 Analysis of Multi-component Systems

Multi-component analysis can also be carried out using spectrophotometry. Towards this end, we need the absorbance of the two species at least at two wavelengths. For example, if a solution contains a mixture of $K_2Cr_2O_7$ and $KMnO_4$ with absorption maxima at 440 nm and 540 nm respectively, it is possible to estimate the concentration of the two species. The simplest case would be one where at the λ_{max} of the first compound, the second compound has negligible absorption and vice versa. The problem then reduces to two individual estimations of the constituents. However, it is often likely that the second component has a non-negligible absorption at the λ_{max} of the first compound and hence this must be accounted for. Assume that the molar absorptivity for component A at the wavelength of its maximum absorption (λ_1^A) is ε_1^A. Also assume the molar absorptivity for component B at the wavelength of its maximum absorption (λ_2^A) is ε_2^A. Now, let us assume that the molar absorptivity of A at λ_2 is ε_2^A and that for B at λ_1 is ε_1^B. Hence the absorption at λ_1 is caused by both species A and B, with molar absorptivities ε_1^A and ε_1^B. Likewise the absorption at λ_2 is caused by A and B, with molar absorptivities ε_2^A and ε_2^B. If the molar absorptivities are known for the two species at the two wavelengths, the individual concentrations of A and B in the mixture can be computed as follows.

The measured absorbance of the mixture at λ_1 (due to both constituents) is denoted as $A\lambda_1$, which can be written as

$$A_{\lambda_1} = A_{\lambda_1}^A + A_{\lambda_1}^B \tag{13.3}$$

where $A_{\lambda_1}^A$ and $A_{\lambda_1}^B$ are the absorbances of constituent A and B respectively at λ_1. Similarly, the absorbance at wavelength λ_2 for the mixture is given by

$$A_{\lambda_2} = A_{\lambda_2}^A + A_{\lambda_2}^B \tag{13.4}$$

Since A is given by εcl by Beer–Lambert's law, the above expression can be rewritten as

$$A_{\lambda_1} = \varepsilon_{\lambda_1}^A \cdot c^A \cdot l + \varepsilon_{\lambda_1}^B \cdot c^B \cdot l \tag{13.5}$$

At λ_2, a similar equation applies

$$A_{\lambda_2} = \varepsilon_{\lambda_2}^A \cdot c^A \cdot l + \varepsilon_{\lambda_2}^B \cdot c^B \cdot l \tag{13.6}$$

The quantities $A\lambda_1$ and $A\lambda_2$ are experimentally measured, while $\varepsilon_{\lambda_1}^A$ and $\varepsilon_{\lambda_1}^A$ can be obtained by normalising the measured absorbances of the pure components A and B to unit concentration and path length. From the knowledge of these quantities, the concentrations c^A and c^B can be estimated. Absorbances must be measured at as many wavelengths as there are components in the mixture.

While the above procedure is a rather simple method for estimating the concentrations of the components of a mixture, a more rigorous method involves fitting the complete spectrum of each pure component to the measured spectrum of the mixture. This is akin to doing a least squares fit with an over-determined data set rather than solving a set of equations to determine unknowns.

13.5.4 Derivative Spectrum

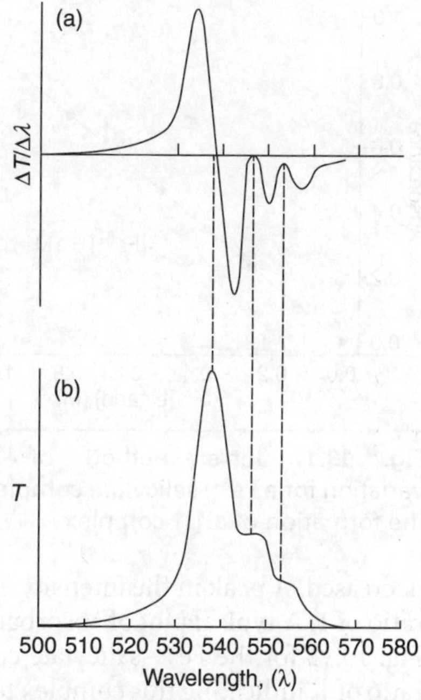

Fig. 13.10 **(a) Absorption spectrum (b) Derivative spectrum of $KMnO_4$**

It has also been recognised that very often, instead of using the raw absorption spectra, it may be more advantageous to use derivative spectra. As shown in Fig. 13.10, spectral features that are not well resolved in the absorption spectrum appear better resolved in the derivative spectrum. It can be seen that features that appear as shoulders in the zeroth order spectrum can now be clearly identified. The peak maximum in the absorption spectrum has a slope of zero, which corresponds to points where the curve cuts the X-axis in the first derivative spectrum; consequently, identification of peak maximum in the absorption spectrum is unambiguous when the derivative spectrum is used. Multi-component samples are therefore better analysed using derivative spectra. However, the process of taking derivatives increases the noise in the spectra and this can be a disadvantage. It is therefore imperative that spectra with excellent signal to noise ratio must be acquired when derivative spectroscopy is to be used. Derivative spectroscopy is also very useful when dealing with scattering samples, which cause a sloping baseline, which in turn can mask small features. This aspect is particularly handy when dealing with absorption of peptide samples which can have a lot of scatter. The presence and the number of individual amino acids such as tryptophan, tyrosine and phenylalanine can be estimated using derivative absorption spectroscopy. High order derivatives, such as second and third order derivatives, have also been used in some cases.

13.5.5 Stoichiometry of Complexes

Very often it is required to determine the stoichiometry of metal–ligand complexes. For example, Fe^{3+} forms a complex with ligands such as salicylic acid, 1,10-phenanthroline and thiocyanate. It is necessary to know if the complex formed is ML or ML_2 or higher, where M is the metal and L is the ligand.

13.5.5.1 Method of Continuous Variation

UV–vis spectrometry offers a convenient method for the determination of metal–ligand complexes known as *Job's method of continuous variation*. In this method, solutions with varying molar proportions of the metal and the ligand are prepared while keeping the total concentration of the metal and the ligand a constant in all the solutions. Let us assume that solutions are prepared at the following metal to ligand molar ratios: 1:9, 4:6, 7:3 and 9:1. If the metal–ligand complex is of 1:1 stoichiometry, the concentration of the complex in the first solution (1:9) will be determined by the metal concentration, which is the limiting reagent. The absorbance of this solution is measured. In the second solution, the concentration of the complex will increase as the concentration of the limiting reagent is increased, which can be observed by an increase in the complex absorption. However, in the third solution, the ligand is now the limiting reagent and the complex concentration now starts to show a decrease in intensity and which further decreases in the last solution, as the proportion of the ligand is

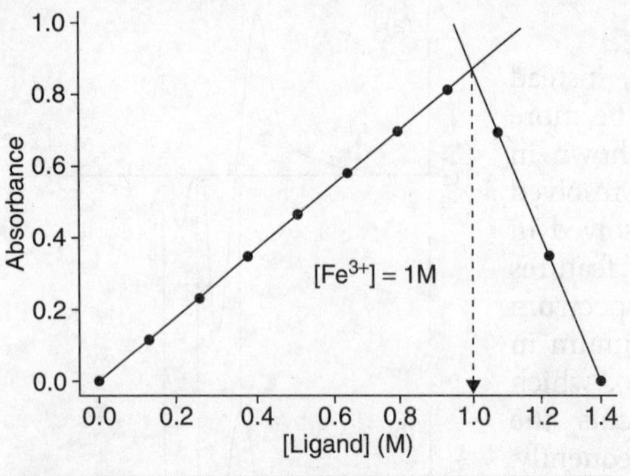

Fig. 13.11 Job's method of continuous variation for a Fe^{3+}–salicylate complex, showing the formation of a 1:1 complex

Fig. 13.12 Salicyate ligand concentration (M) per mole of cation

decreased. A peak in the intensity of the absorption of the complex is obtained at metal–ligand ratio of 1. A typical plot of absorbance of the complex against metal to ligand ratio is shown in Fig. 13.11 for the Fe^{3+}–salicylate complex, where the peak is observed at an Fe^{3+} to salicylate ratio of 1, indicating this complex to have a 1:1 stoichiometry. For an ML_2 complex, the peak in the absorbance in the Job's plot, will be observed at a metal to ligand ratio of 1:2. This method is therefore a convenient technique for determining stoichiometry of complexes.

13.5.5.2 Mole Ratio Method

In another variation of the method, the concentration of one of the reagents, usually the metal ion, is held constant while the ligand concentration is varied. With an increase in the ligand concentration, the concentration of the complex increases, as indicated by an increase in the absorption of the metal–ligand solution. Beyond the equivalence point, a further increase in the concentration of the ligand does not lead to any significant increase in the absorption, as no more complex is produced. A plot of absorption against ligand concentration therefore produces two straight lines with different slopes, a fast rising straight line before the equivalence point and a slowly rising line afterwards. The two straight lines intersect at the concentration indicating the stoichiometry of the complex (Fig. 13.12), for Fe^{3+}–salicylate.

Problem 13.1

(i) Calculate the frequency of a radiation whose wavelength is 420 nm.
(ii) Calculate the wavelength of a radiation whose energy is 9.8×10^{-19} J.
(iii) What is the wave number of the radiation whose wavelength is 275 nm?

Solution

(i) Frequency, $\nu = \dfrac{c}{\lambda}$

$$= \frac{3.0 \times 10^{8}\ \text{ms}^{-1}}{(420\ \text{nm})/(10^{-9}\text{m}/1\ \text{nm})} = 7.14 \times 10^{-14}\ \text{s}^{-1}$$

(ii) $E = \dfrac{hc}{\lambda}; \lambda = \dfrac{hc}{E}$

$$= \frac{(6.63 \times 10^{-34} \text{ Js/particle})(3.0 \times 10^{8} \text{ ms}^{-1})}{(9.8 \times 10^{-19}) \text{ J}}$$

$$= 2.0296 \times 10^{-7} \text{ m} = 203 \text{ nm}$$

(iii) $\bar{\nu} = \frac{1}{\lambda} = \frac{1}{275 \times 10^{-9} \text{ m}} = 3.64 \times 10^{6} \text{ m}^{-1}$

$$= 3.64 \times 10^{4} \text{ cm}^{-1} = 36400 \text{ cm}^{-1}$$

Problem 13.2 Predict the longest wavelength electronic transition in each of the following:

(i) N_2 (ii) C_6H_8 (iii) CH_4

Solution

Electronic excitation in a molecule can be of one of the following types:

$\sigma \rightarrow \sigma^*$

$\pi \rightarrow \pi^*$

$n \rightarrow \pi^*$

$n \rightarrow \sigma^*$

...

$\sigma \rightarrow \pi^*$

$\pi \rightarrow \sigma^*$

The wavelength of the absorbed light depends on the difference in energy between two electronic states; smaller the energy difference longer the wavelength. In each molecule, promotion of an electron from the highest occupied MO (HOMO) to the lowest unoccupied MO (LUMO) occurs.

	transition is expected to have the longest wavelength
(i) $N \equiv N$	$n \rightarrow \pi^*$
(ii) C_6H_8	$n \rightarrow \pi^*$
(iii) CH_4	$\sigma \rightarrow \sigma^*$

Problem 13.3 Identify the chromophore(s) and oxochrome(s) present in each of the following:

(i) $HS–CH_2–CH=CH–CH_2F$ (ii) $Cl–CH_2–CO–CH_2–Cl$

(iii) Br, OH

(iv)

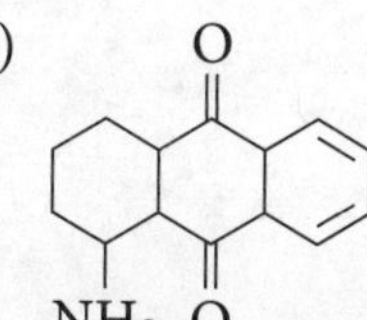

(v) HO, OH

Solution

(i) Chromophores –S– C=C
Oxochrome F

(ii)	Chromophores	>C = O
	Oxochromes	Cl, Cl
(iii)	Chromophores	configuration (double bond)
	Oxochromes	OH, Br
(iv)	Chromophores	>C = O, >C = O, configuration
	Oxochrome	$-NH_2$
(v)	Chromophore	C_6H_4 -(ring)
	Oxochromes	OH, OH

Problem 13.4 Applying the Woodward–Fieser rules, calculate the λ_{max} for

(i) Br (ii)

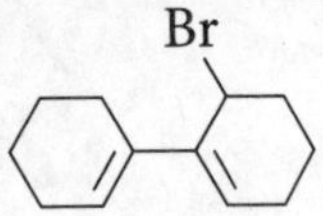

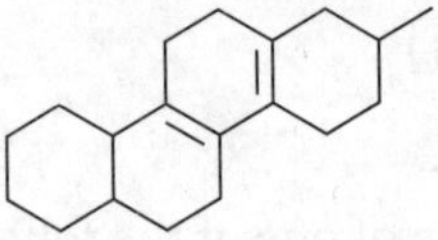

Solution

(i)

Parent ring	217 nm
ring residue (4 × 5)	20 nm
bromine	17 nm
λ_{max} =	254 nm

(ii)

homoannular diene	253 nm
double bond extending conjugation	30 nm
ring residue (8 × 5)	40 nm
Methyl group	5 nm
λ_{max} =	328 nm

Problem 13.5 A solution containing two absorbing species (p and q) was spectrophotometrically analysed at two wavelengths using a cell of 1.00 cm path length. The absorbances of the solution at λ_1 and λ_2 are 0.930 and 0.185 respectively. The molar absorptivity of the compound p was 12500 L g^{-1} cm^{-1} at λ_1 and 248 L g^{-1} cm^{-1} at λ_2 and that of component q was 330 L g^{-1}cm^{-1} at λ_1 and 10,000 L g^{-1}cm^{-1} at λ_2. Calculate the concentration of the individual components.

Solution

Applying the Beer–Lambert law for this mixture,

At $\lambda_{1,}\ A_1 = \in_{p1} C_p + \in_{q1} C_q$ (path length l = 1)

$\therefore$ $0.930 = 12500\ C_p + 330\ C_p$ (1)

At $\lambda_{2,}\ A_2 = \in_{p2} C_p + \in_{q2} C_q$ (path length 1 = 1)

$\therefore$ $0.185 = 248\ C_p + 10000\ C_q$ (2)

$$\therefore \quad C_q = \frac{0.185 - 248\ C_p}{10000}$$

Substituting this in (1)

$$0.930 = 12500\ C_p + 330\left(\frac{0.185 - 248\ C_p}{10000}\right)$$

or $$0.930 = \frac{330 \times 0.185}{10000} + C_p\left(12500 - \frac{330 \times 248}{10000}\right)$$

or $$0.930 = 0.006105 + 12491.8\ C_p$$

$$C_p = \frac{0.930 - 0.006105}{12491.8} = 7.39 \times 10^{-5}\ \text{M}$$

$$\therefore \quad C_q = \frac{0.185 - (248 \times 7.39 \times 10^{-5})}{10000}$$

$$= \frac{0.185 - 0.01833}{10000} = 1.66 \times 10^{-5}$$

Problem 13.6 Explain the following UV absorption spectral data:

Compound	λ_{max} nm
biphenyl	249
2-methylbiphenyl	237
2, 2[1]-dimethylbiphenyl	220

Solution

The ability to attain coplanar configuration decreases with ortho substitution in the conjugated biphenly system. This would lead to destablisation of the excited state. This can account for the decrease in λ_{max} with methyl substitution.

Problem 13.7 The λ_{max} for $CH_2{=}CH{-}CH{=}CH_2$ occurs at 217 nm whereas that for RCH=CH–CH=CHR occurs at 233 nm. Explain. (R = alkyl group)

Solution

The alkyl substitution in $CH_2{=}CH{-}CH{=}CH_2$ has caused a red shift as indicated by increase in λ_{max}. This may be attributed to the electron releasing nature of alkyl-groups which increases the polarisability of the conjugated system. The increased polarisability reduces the energy of the π–π^* tansition.

Problem 13.8 Explain why the β-carotene present in carrots absorbs in the visible region.

Solution

β-carotene has a large number of double bonds. These double bonds shift the λ_{max} to a high value, 455 nm. This absorption is in the visible region and therefore, β-carotene is coloured orange. The red skin of tomatoes is due to the presence of a highly conjugated 13-double bond compound, lycopene. This molecule has its λ_{max} at 505 nm, in the visible region.

EXERCISES

1. Rationalise the following:
   (a) The UV absorption spectrum of *o*-cresol dissolved in *n*-hexane consists of a fine structure; however, its spectrum in ethanols consists of a broad absorption without fine structure.

(b) The λ_{max} ($n \rightarrow \pi^*$) absorptions for the CH_3X molecules are in the order $CH_3Cl < CH_3Br < CH_3I$.
(c) The extent of conjugation in organic molecules can be inferred from their electronic spectra.

2. Explain the following data:

	λ_{max} (nm)	ε (cm^2 $mole^{-1}$)
cis–stilbene	280	10 500
trans–stilbene	295	27 000

3. Rationalise the following:
(a) $[Co(H_2O)_6]^{2+}$ is pink-red in acid solution, while $[CoX_4]^{2-}$ is blue.
(b) The electrons in quinine are more easily promoted to higher energy levels than the electrons in benzene.
(c) The energy required for $\sigma \rightarrow \sigma^*$ transition occurs in the far ultraviolet region.

4. Describes the method of spectrophotometric determination of Hg(II) by the thiocyanate method.

5. (a) Calculate the frequency of radiation whose wavelength is 420 nm.
(b) What is the wavelength of the radiation whose energy is 10.1×10^{-19} J?

6. At 525 nm in a 1.000-cm cell, the absorbance of a 5.25×10^{-5} M $KMnO_4$ solution is 0.124. Calculate the molar absorptivity ε. Also calculate the per cent transmittance of the same solution at 525 nm in a 2.000-cm cell. (The density of the solution is 1.000 g/mL.)

7. Ferroin, $[Fe(C_{12}H_8N_2)_3]^{2+}$, a red complex of Fe(II), obeys Beer's law in the concentration range 0.1 to 5 ppm Fe(II). For a 3.50 ppm standard Fe(II)–complex solution the absorbance is 0.682. The absorbance of a test solution of the complex has an absorption of 0.412. Calculate the concentration of iron in the test solution.

8. Calculate the expected λ_{max} for each of the following:

(a) $CH_2=C(CH_3)-CH=C(CH_3)-CH_3$

(b) [1-vinylcyclohexene structure]

(c) C_6H_5–CO–CH_3

(d) $CH_2=CH$–CO–CH_3

9. Discuss with examples, the deviations of Beer's law.

10. Illustrate the spectral effects of introducing chromophones to a molecule.

11. Predict and explain the electronic transitions in $C_6H_5-N=N-C_6H_5$.

12. Define and illustrate each of the following spectral shifts:
(a) bathochromic (b) hypsochromic (c) hyperchromic (d) hypochromic

13. With an example, explain charge transfer absorption bands.

14. List the characteristies required of a solvent to be used in UV spectroscopy.

15. Explain how UV spectroscopy is diagnostic of hydrogen bonding.

16. Explain why a polar solvent shifts the $\pi \rightarrow \pi^*$ transitions to longer wavelengths, whereas it shifts the $n \rightarrow \pi^*$ transitions to shorter wavelengths.

17. Sketch and explain the expected photometric titration curve for Fe^{3+} with SCN^-, using a green filter. List the sources of error in this determination.

18. Outline the principle of Job's method of ascertaining the composition of a metal complex formed between M^{n+} and L^-.

19. With examples, explain the Woodward–Fieser rules.

20. Calculate the λ_{max} value for

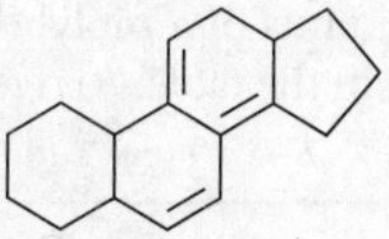

21. Express the following absorbance data in per cent transmission.
(a) 0.444 (b) 1.321 (c) 0.0222

22. The molar absorptivity of a compound is 2.04×10^3 L cm^{-1} mol^{-1}. Calculate the concentration of the compound in solution required to produce a transmittance of 10.22% in a 2.00 cm cell.

23. What is a B-band shift? Illustrate.

24. The ionisation energy for the process

$$Na^+(g) \rightarrow Na^{2+}(g)$$

is 47.3 eV. Calculate the wavelength of radiant energy involved in this process.

25. Calculate the expected λ_{max} for each of the following :

(a) 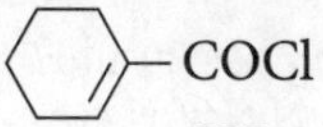 COCl (b) 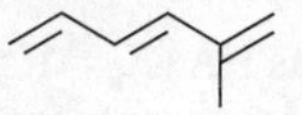 (c)

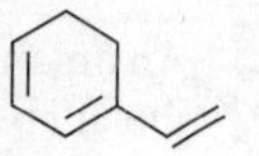

(d) $CH_2=C(CH_3)-CH=C(CH_3)-CH_3$ (e) 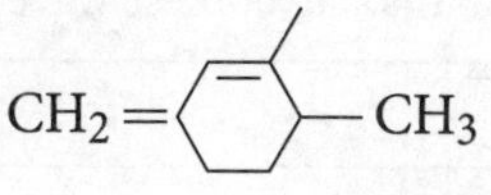 $CH_2=$ ... $-CH_3$

26. Applying the Woodward–Fieser rules, predict the λ_{max} value for each of the following:

(a) $CH_3-CH=CH-CH=CH-CH_3$ (b) $H_2C=C(CH_3)COCH_3$ (c) Vitamin C

27. Among each of the following group of molecules, which would exhibit the electronic absorption of longest wavelength?

(a) (i) 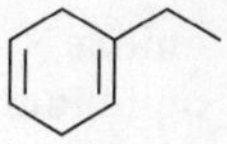 (ii) 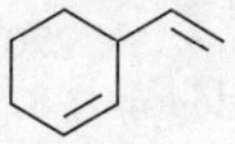 (iii)

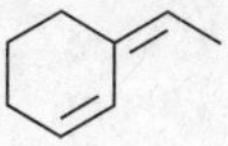

(b) (i) $CH_2=CH-CH_2-CH=CH_2$
(ii) $CH_2=CH-CH=CH-CH_3$
(iii) $CH_2=CH-CH=CH-CH=CH_2$

(c) (i) $CH_2=CH-CO-CH_2-CH_3$
(ii) $CH_2=CH-CO-CH=CH_2$
(iii) $CH_2=CH-CH_2-CH=CH_2$

28. For a chromophoric compound with molar absorptivity, 3120 L mol^{-1} cm^{-1} (at $\lambda = 510$ nm), the intensity of the incident and the transmitted light were observed to be the readings 68 and 16 respectively on a linear scale, when measured using a 2.00 cm cuvette. Calculate the concentration of the test compound.

29. Construct the calibration line for the various concentrations of aqueous Cu(II) salt with the corresponding absorbances at a particular wavelength given below.

[Cu (II)] mM:	1.00	2.00	4.00	6.00	8.00	10.00
Absorbance:	0.120	0.238	0.47	0.68	0.838	0.95

From this calibration line, find out the concentration of the test solution of the same Cu(II) salt whose absorbance is 0.55 at the same wavelength, by interpolation.

30. For solutions containing various amounts of a molybdenum salt, the observed reading which is proportional to absorption are given in the table. Arrive at the equation for a straight line through the data points.

Conc. of Mo salt (mg/L):	1.00	3.00	5.00	7.00	9.00
Instrumental reading, R:	14.6	35.7	44.8	61.5	80.0

The volume of EDTA required to complex all Cu^{2+} present can be found by plotting a graph of Absorption Vs V_{EDTA}

31. A 50 ml solution of Fe^{3+}–salicylic acid complex is titrated with 0.10 M EDTA. During the course of titration the salicylic acid ligand in the above complex is replaced by EDTA. The titration is followed at 525 nm where the Fe^{3+}–salicyclic acid complex absorbs and Fe^{3+}–EDTA complex does not. Calculate the concentration of Fe^{3+} in the solution from the titration data given below:

Volume of EDTA added (mL)	0.00	0.10	0.30	0.50	0.70	0.90	1.10	1.30
Absorption	0.000	0.090	0.180	0.275	0.350	0.373	0.00	0.00

32. An organic acid represented as HA ($K_a = 1.42 \times 10^{-5}$) absorbs at wavelengths 420 and 510 nm. The molar absorptivity of this acid at these wavelengths is 0.1 N HCl and 0.1 N NaOH are given below.

	$\in_{420}$	$\in_{510}$
H A (0.1 N HCl)	620	7120
A^- (0.1 N NaOH)	20,600	960

Predict the absorbance of a 200×10^{-5} M solution of this acid at these wavelengths when measured using a 1-cm cell.

33. The λ_{max} for acetone in *n*-hexane occurs at 280 nm whereas that in water at 265 nm. What is the reason for this change in λ_{max}?

34. Account for the following UV λ_{max} values:

(a) benzene	255 nm	(b) phenol	270 nm	(c) aniline	280 nm
phenol	270 nm	phenoxide ion	287 nm	anilinium ion	254 nm

35. Explain the following:
(a) The UV absorption peaks are usually broader than the IR absorption peaks.
(b) Ultraviolet spectroscopy and visible spectroscopy are called electronic spectroscopy.
(c) The electronic spectrum can indicate how extensively conjugated an organic molecule is.
(d) The major absorption wavelength of *p*-nitrophenol is red-shifted from 320 nm to 400 nm on basifying it. Explain.

REFERENCES

1. Skoog D A, Holler F J and Nieman T A, *Principles of Instrumental* Analysis, Thomson, Banglore, 1998.

2. Silverstein R M, Bassler C G and Morrill T C, *Spectrometric Identification of Organic Compounds*, Wiley International, New York, 1996.

3. Willard H H, Merit L L Jr, Dean J A and Settle F A Jr, *Instrumental Methods of Analysis*, VI Ed., Ch.2, CBS Publishers, New Delhi, 1996.

14 Nuclear Magnetic Resonance Spectroscopy

14.1 INTRODUCTION

Many of the spectroscopic techniques that have been discussed earlier, dealt with transitions between vibrational and electronic energy levels. While nuclear spins do influence the spectroscopy referred to above, through nuclear spin statistics, the nuclear spins are not explicitly probed in these experiments. Explicit study of the nuclear spins is performed in *nuclear magnetic resonance* (NMR) *spectroscopy*. NMR spectroscopy has been used extensively as a characterisation tool in many problems in chemistry and biology. It has in fact become a powerful tool in medical diagnosis too, where it is referred to as magnetic resonance imaging or MRI.

14.2 THEORY OF NMR

To begin the discussion on NMR, let us consider a hydrogen nucleus. Assume that the *hydrogen nucleus is isolated* and does not have any electron in its proximity. This assumption is critical to the development of the application of the NMR technique, as we will see later. The proton has a spin of ½, and hence the nuclear spin of hydrogen, which has just one proton, is ½. This spinning nucleus has a charge +1 and hence generates a magnetic moment. This magnetic moment has two orientations; these two orientations are degenerate in the absence of a magnetic field. However, when a magnetic field is applied, the degeneracy is lifted. The orientation in which the magnetic moment is aligned with the applied field is lower in energy compared to the orientation aligned against the field. It may be noted that for an electron which also has a spin of ½, the reverse is the case, that is, the orientation of the magnetic moment of the spinning electron against the field is lower in energy, as the electron has a charge opposite to that of a proton. The two orientations are defined by the quantum number m_i, which takes on values of +½ and −½, with the former being aligned to the orientation with the

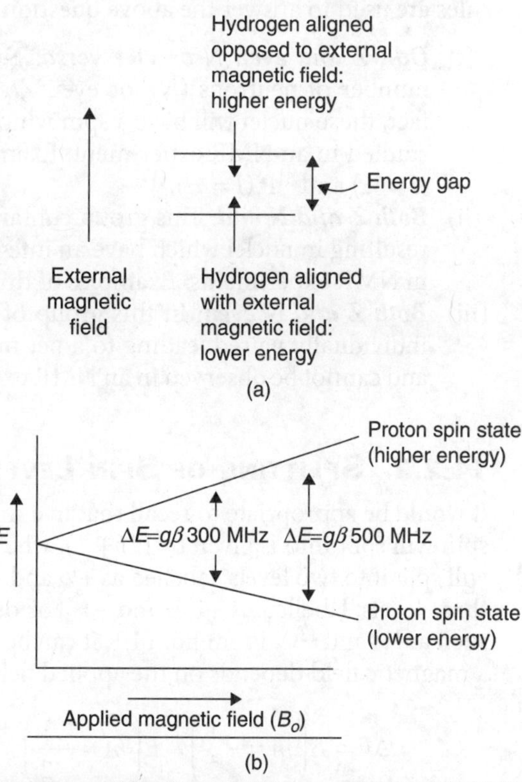

Fig. 14.1 **(a)** The two orientations of the magnetic moment of a proton in an applied magnetic field **(b)** the dependence of the energy of the two orientations of a proton on the applied magnetic field strength.

field and the latter aligned against the field (Fig. 14.1a). The energy difference between the two orientations depends on the strength of the magnetic field (Fig. 14.1b). In addition to the dependence on the applied magnetic field, the splitting of the energy levels for the two orientations of the magnetic moment also depends on the particular nucleus in question, and varies from one nucleus to the other, manifested through the constant γ, referred to as the gyromagnetic or magnetogyric ratio. The energy of the level m_i is given by Eq. 14.1.

$$E_i = -m_i \gamma \hbar B_o \qquad (14.1)$$

where m_i refers to the level defining the orientation of the magnetic moment, γ is the magnetogyric ratio in units of radians per second per tesla (rad.s^{-1}. T^{-1}) and B_o is the applied magnetic field in tesla.

14.2.1 Nuclei that can be Studied

While the above discussion used the spinning *hydrogen* nucleus as an example, it is not the only nucleus that can be studied using this technique. There are other nuclei that can be probed using this technique. However, for a nucleus to be studied by this technique, it must have a non-zero nuclear spin, as only such nuclei have levels that get split in the presence of a magnetic field. Nuclei which have zero nuclear spin are said to be NMR inactive. The question that arises is, what determines if a nucleus will have a non-zero nuclear spin? Some simple rules are used to answer the above question.

(i) ***Odd Z and even N or vice versa***: Nuclei with odd number of protons (Z) and even number of neutrons (N); or even Z and odd N, will have a non-zero nuclear spin. In fact, these nuclei will have a spin which is an integer multiple of (½). Such nuclei can be studied in an NMR experiment. Examples of this group are ^{1}H (I = ½), ^{13}C (I = ½), ^{19}F (I = ½) and ^{31}P (I = ½).

(ii) ***Both Z and N odd***: This group contains an odd number of both protons and neutrons, resulting in nuclei which have an integral nuclear spin. Such nuclei can also be observed in NMR experiments. Examples of this group are ^{2}H (I = 1), ^{14}N (I = 1) and ^{10}B (I = 3).

(iii) ***Both Z and N even***: In this group of nuclei, all the spins of protons and neutrons are individually paired leading to a net nuclear spin of zero. Such nuclei are NMR inactive and cannot be observed in an NMR experiment. Examples of such nuclei are ^{12}C and ^{16}O.

14.2.2 Splitting of Spin Levels

It would be appropriate to recall that in a magnetic field, the number of levels that the nuclear spin will split into is given by ($2I$ + 1), where I is the nuclear spin. Hence a hydrogen nucleus will split into two levels, labelled as +½ and −½. However, a ^{2}H nucleus with I = 1 will split into three levels, labelled as +1, 0 and −1. For our discussion, we will consider only spin ½ nuclei such as ^{1}H and ^{13}C. From Eq. 14.1, it can be seen that the splitting between the energy levels in a magnetic field depends on the applied field strength.

$$\Delta E = E\left(m = -\frac{1}{2}\right) - E\left(m = +\frac{1}{2}\right) \qquad (14.2)$$

Combining Eq. 14.2 with Eq. 14.1 we get,

$$\Delta E = \gamma \hbar B_o \qquad (14.3)$$

For example, for the ^{1}H nucleus for which $\gamma = 267.512 \times 10^6$ rad.s^{-1}. T^{-1}, the difference in energy between the +½ and −½ states in a magnetic field of 9.25 T, can be calculated from Eq. 14.1 to be 2.62×10^{-25} J. It must be noted that even when a strong magnetic field is applied, the energy difference between the two states is orders of magnitude smaller compared with energy differences between states encountered in rotational, vibrational or electronic spectroscopy.

The energy difference in Eq. 14.3 can be expressed in units of s^{-1} by dividing Eq. 14.3 by h, Planck's constant, yielding

$$\nu = \frac{\gamma B_o}{2\pi} \tag{14.4}$$

It can be seen that the energy difference of 2.62×10^{-25} J in 9.25 T field corresponds to 400 MHz, which is the radiofrequency region. In terms of angular frequency, Eq. 14.4 can be rewritten as

$$\omega = \gamma B_o \tag{14.5}$$

Now that we know the energy difference between the two spin states, the population in these states can be calculated using the Boltzmann equation. In the above example, for a field of 9.25 T and a temperature of 298 K, the population in the higher energy −½ state turns out to be 0.99994 of the population in the ground +½ state. The difference in the population is just about 30 parts per million, which is exceedingly small.

The nearly equal population in the two spin states leads to a problem, which we will now address. When a radiation of the appropriate frequency is made incident on the sample, transitions occur between the ground and the excited spin states. However, the population difference being small (of the order of 30 ppm), the population in the two states will become equal very quickly. At this point, absorption of radiation will cease leading to cessation of the experiment. This condition is referred to as *saturation*. In other words, the absorption experiment cannot be sustained for long. However, the process of relaxation (which we will discuss later) causes the nuclei in the higher energy state to return to the lower energy state and therefore restores the population difference to enable the absorption experiment to be sustained.

To summarise the above discussion, a magnetic field is applied to a nucleus with a spin $I \neq 0$; say for example the H nucleus with a spin $I = ½$. As a result of the magnetic field, the degeneracy between the different spin orientations of the spinning H nucleus is lifted, with the magnetic moment oriented along the field being lower in energy than that oriented against. Transition, in the radiofrequency region, can now occur between these two spin states, which is the basis for the NMR experiment.

14.3 MECHANISM OF ABSORPTION OF RF

It is now important to discuss the mechanism that leads to the absorption of the radiofrequency radiation. In the presence of a magnetic field applied, say in the z direction, it can be shown from quantum mechanics that, the spinning nucleus cannot have its magnetic moment vector oriented in the direction of the field, but must be oriented at an angle to the field direction. This is a consequence of the Heisenberg uncertainty principle. Very similar to a spinning top oriented at an angle to the vertical, this vector however does not stay static but precesses or revolves around the applied direction. The frequency at which this vector precesses around the field direction is given by Eq. 14.2, and is called the *Larmor precession frequency*.

$$\omega = \gamma B_o \tag{14.6}$$

It can be seen that the Larmor precession frequency given by Eq. 14.6 is exactly the same as the angular frequency corresponding to the transition frequency between the two spin states given by Eq. 14.5. It is the resonance between the precessional motion of the magnetic moment vector around the magnetic field and the radiation, with a frequency equal to the energy difference between the two spin states, that causes absorption of the radiation, causing the spin +½ nuclei to make a transition to the upper −½ level.

As we saw earlier, the precessional frequency or the frequency of the radiation causing the excitation is typically of the order of a few hundred MHz, at magnetic fields of a few tesla. NMR spectrometers are referred to by this frequency. For example, a 400 MHz NMR spectrometer implies a transition frequency of 400 MHz for a *hydrogen* nucleus in the magnetic field used in the spectrometer, which approximately would be ~9.25 T. Of course in the same spectrometer, the ^{13}C nuclei would absorb at a frequency of approximately 100 MHz as the gyromagnetic ratio γ, for the ^{13}C nucleus (67.264×10^3 rad $s^{-1}T^{-1}$) is about ¼ the value of that for the ^1H nucleus (267.512 rad.s^{-1}.T^{-1}).

14.3.1 Utility of the Technique

The utility of the NMR technique stems from the fact that the hydrogen nucleus, which was assumed to be a bare nucleus with no electrons in its proximity, is really a hypothetical situation. In reality, the hydrogen nucleus in molecules has electrons around it. The presence of these electrons alters the situation; this is what makes the NMR technique so powerful. The electrons surrounding the hydrogen nucleus, in response to the applied field, circulate, which in turn produces an induced magnetic field ($B_{induced}$) which opposes the implied magnetic field. As a consequence, the hydrogen nucleus does not experience the field that is actually applied ($B_{applied}$) but an effective field that is somewhat smaller, given by the equation

$$B_{effective} = B_{applied} - B_{induced}$$

As a result, the reduced effective field causes the nucleus to precess at frequencies lower than that corresponding to a bare nucleus. To what extent the precessional frequency of a *real* nucleus differs from that of an hypothetical bare nucleus depends on the electron density around the *real* nucleus. Clearly, in chemical compounds the electron density around the hydrogen nucleus is different depending on the atoms or groups of atoms to which it is attached. For example, a hydrogen atom attached to a carbon as in the methyl ($-CH_3$) group, will have an electron density around it which will be different from that of a hydrogen atom in a methylene ($-CH_2$) group or that in a hydroxyl (–OH) group. Consequently, each of these hydrogen atoms in different environments will experience a different *effective* fields for a fixed applied magnetic field. Each of these hydrogen nuclei, therefore, will have unique transition frequencies, which is what NMR identifies.

To examine the above issue in a little more detail, it can be seen that the higher electronegativity of the oxygen atom in the hydroxyl group will draw electrons away from the hydrogen atom attached to it. The induced field due to the electron circulation will therefore be less compared to that for a hydrogen atom attached to a carbon atom (since the electronegativity of carbon is less than that of oxygen). For a fixed applied magnetic field, the hydrogen in the hydroxyl group will have a higher transition frequency in the NMR than that of the hydrogens in the methyl group. It is this dependence of the NMR transition frequency on the environment of the proton that makes this technique so powerful in characterising chemical compounds and deriving molecular structure information.

14.4 PERFORMING THE ACTUAL EXPERIMENT

The NMR experiment can be performed in a number of different ways. The magnetic field can be kept constant and an RF field of progressively varying frequencies can be applied to the sample, which is called the *frequency sweep* mode. For a given magnetic field, protons in different environments, such as –OH, $-CH_3$ and $-NH_2$, have different transition frequencies, and hence absorption can be monitored as a function of the frequency of the applied RF radiation.

Alternatively, the RF can be fixed, and the magnetic field can be continuously varied, so that protons in different environments can progressively come into resonance with the RF radiation, which is referred to as the *field sweep mode*. The varying magnetic field option for a fixed RF was the routinely used option in conventional NMR spectrometers. Of course, modern NMR machines use an entirely different method for acquiring spectra which relies on the technique of Fourier Transformation, which is beyond the scope of this text. Modern FT-NMR machines also use large magnetic fields, such as ~9 T, which requires the use superconducting magnets and therefore the use of cryogenic liquids such as liquid He and liquid N_2.

Let us now discuss how exactly the experiment is carried out to measure the precessional frequencies of the various ^1H nuclei present in a molecule. Of course, for a given RF, the various nuclei will come into resonance at different magnetic fields, and the problem is one of measuring the applied magnetic fields as each nucleus undergoes resonance. However, instead of measuring the absolute magnetic field, one can measure the difference in magnetic fields where the nuclei in question and a reference nucleus absorb. What the reference nucleus is, will be discussed shortly. For now let us simply understand that we can measure ΔB for a nucleus with respect to a reference nucleus, instead of B for the nucleus in question. It turns out that the measurement of the difference is far more precise and convenient than the measurement of the absolute fields. Due to various instrumental factors, there will always be a small drift in the absolute fields which makes it difficult therefore to measure them precisely but differences will remain constant, and hence this strategy is adopted. For example, if the reference nucleus R absorbs at a field B_R and the nucleus in question absorbs at B_N, we would measure $B_R - B_N$ rather than B_N for the nucleus of interest. Likewise, the signal for every nucleus is measured as the difference from B_R.

14.4.1 REFERENCE SIGNAL

The above strategy is implemented by incorporating into the sample of interest, a compound which would give a single absorption (that is, has only one type of ^1H nucleus) and all other signals are then measured relative to this signal. Any drift in instrumental parameters will shift all of the frequencies, but the difference from this reference compound will be the same. The signal can then be displayed in terms of this difference, $B_R - B_N$ or $\nu_R - \nu_N$, which we shall define as $\Delta\nu$. This shift is also referred to as the *chemical shift*. By definition, the signal of the reference compound will occur at a value of zero difference. All other signals will be measured against this reference and will occur at frequencies lower or higher than that of the reference compound. The difference is denoted as as $\delta\nu_N$ and defined as $\nu_N - \nu_R$ measured in units of Hz, where ν_R and ν_N are the Larmor precessional frequencies of the reference and sample nuclei.

14.4.2 TMS

What can serve as a good reference compound is the next question we address. Obviously, the reference must be inert and not interact with the compound of interest. It must be soluble in solvents commonly used in NMR, such as $CDCl_3$ or C_6D_6. It would also be advantageous if this compound can be removed easily from the sample solution in case the sample is required after the analysis. Importantly, the reference must give a simple spectrum with a single peak. A compound that satisfies all the above conditions is tetramethylsilane [$(CH_3)_4Si$], commonly referred to as TMS. This compound has 12 equivalent hydrogen nuclei and hence provides a single strong peak in the ^{1}H-NMR spectrum that can be used as a reference signal (Fig. 14.2). Since the Si atom is more electropositive than carbon, the electron density around the hydrogens will be somewhat larger relative to those found in exclusively carbon compounds. Consequently, the hydrogen atoms in TMS experience a lower field and the resonances for TMS almost always occur at higher applied fields compared to carbon compounds. Only hydrogens attached to strongly electropositive elements such as Li, would show signals more upfield to that shown by TMS.

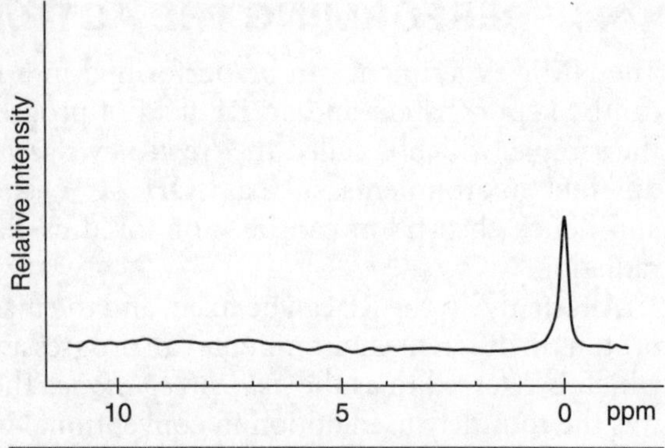

Fig. 14.2 ^{1}H-NMR spectrum of TMS

TMS also has four equivalent carbon atoms and hence serves as a good reference marker for ^{13}C-NMR spectra as well. The only drawback of this reference compound is that it is insoluble in water and hence alternative reference compounds must be used when aqueous solutions are used.

14.4.3 Chemical Shift

From the above discussion, we know that hydrogens attached to a given carbon absorb at a definite field which is measured as the difference from the field at which TMS absorbs ($\Delta\nu$). However, this difference is a function of the magnetic field at which the spectrometer operates. For example, at an applied field of 2 T, if $\Delta\nu$ is 400 Hz for the hydrogens in a given compound, the same compound would show a $\Delta\nu$ of 800 Hz at a field of 4 T. In other words, the shift is a function of the applied field in the spectrometer. This can be annoying as different spectrometers would yield different shifts and unless one knows the operating field of the machine, data cannot be compared between machines.

To overcome this difficulty, the chemical shift has been defined as $\Delta\nu/\nu$, where ν is the frequency of the bare hydrogen resonance and which depends on the applied field. If a hydrogen absorbs 400 Hz from the resonance of TMS, and the operating frequency of the machine is 400 MHz, the ratio is 1×10^{-6} and is expressed as 1 ppm. In a low field machine, say 100 MHz, the resonance of the hydrogen in question will appear 100 Hz from the TMS resonance and the ratio will still turn out to be 1 ppm. In other words, the definition of the chemical shift as a ratio makes this value independent of the field at which the machine operates and hence chemical shift values can be compared between machines, without knowing their operating field. All resonances in NMR are therefore expressed in values of ppm, and are *referred to as δ values*. Earlier literature used the τ scale where, $\tau = 10 - \delta$.

As mentioned earlier, the power of the NMR technique stems from the fact that the electron density around a hydrogen atom differs markedly depending on its environment. A methylene hydrogen has an electron density different from that of a methyl hydrogen and hence the two groups have different resonances. Likewise, a hydroxyl hydrogen has a very different resonance compared to a phenyl hydrogen and can therefore be clearly differentiated.

14.4.4 Substituent Effect on Shielding and Deshielding of Protons

Two factors cause different chemical shifts: (i) deshielding due to reduced electron density effected by electronegative groups and (ii) anisotropy effected by π-bonds. An electron-withdrawing group such as –F deshields a proton leading to increase in δ value for that proton (downfield shift away from TMS peak). The deshielding effect by substituents follows their electron-withdrawing capacities or electronegativities:

Substituent	Electronegativity	
F	4.0	↑
O	3.5	
N	3.0	
Cl	3.0	• Increasing deshielding • Increasing δ • Shift to downfield
Br	2.8	
I	2.5	
P	2.2	
H	2.1	

The higher the electronegativity difference between H and its surrounding atoms, the higher the chemical shift. This is because the higher the electronegativity difference, the lower the electron density is around the H; the proton experiences more deshielding leading to higher chemical shift.

- Electronegative substituents decrease the shielding of methyl protons.

CH_3–X	δ(ppm)
CH_3–H	0.23
CH_3–F	4.3 (Least shielded H)
CH_3–Cl	3.05
CH_3–Br	2.68
CH_3–OCH_3	3.2
CH_3–$N(CH_3)_2$	2.2
CH_3–CH_3	0.9
CH_3–$Si(CH_3)_3$	0.0 (Most shielded H)

14.4.5 Computing the Number of Similar Atoms

The area under the absorption peak is dependent on the number of hydrogens that are in the same environment. Hence, one can obtain not only the nature of the hydrogen but also its number. The 12 hydrogens of the TMS serve as a good calibration standard for the quantitative determination for the number of each type of hydrogen. In analysing the NMR spectrum, we therefore look for the δ value at which a given hydrogen absorbs to identify the group to which it belongs, (methyl, methylene, phenyl, and so on) and the area under its absorption peak to determine its number. We do not have to measure the area as modern spectrometers integrate the peak area and directly indicate the number of hydrogens present in that given group.

Table 14.1 gives the δ value (in ppm) at which each type of hydrogen absorbs. This serves as a good reference to identify the nature of the hydrogen or the group to which it belongs. For example, methane gives just one peak in the NMR spectrum as all the hydrogens are equivalent and all absorb at the same frequency, a frequency that would occur downfield of that shown by

TMS. Integration will also indicate that there are four hydrogens of a given type in methane, which suffices to identify the molecule beyond doubt. Likewise, ethane will also give a single peak as all the six hydrogens are equivalent. However, propane, has two types of hydrogens, six equivalent methyl hydrogens and two equivalent methylene hydrogens. Hence, the NMR spectrum of propane would show two signals, the methyl appearing closer to the TMS signal compared to the methylene. Integration also shows that the methyl hydrogens are six in number while the methylene hydrogens are two in number. The NMR spectrum completely identifies the structure of the molecule. Let us consider butane, which has two isomers, *n*-butane and 2-methylpropane. In the first isomer, there are two types of hydrogens—6 methyl hydrogens and 4 methylene hydrogens. The NMR spectrum of this compound would yield two peaks with the integration showing the respective number of hydrogens. For the second isomer, the NMR spectrum will again yield two peaks, one corresponding to the methyl hydrogens of which there will now be 9, while a second NMR signal will correspond to the single hydrogen attached to the tertiary carbon. While the number of NMR peaks for the two isomers will be the same, namely two, the integration will yield different results. Based on the NMR spectrum alone, it will be possible to unambiguously differentiate between the two isomers.

Table 14.1 ^{1}H-NMR chemical shift values for typical proton groups

Proton type	Chemical shift range (ppm)
1° Alkyl, RCH_3	0.8–1.0
2° Alkyl, RCH_2R	1.2–1.4
3° Alkyl, R_3CH	1.4–1.7
Allylic, $R_2C{=}C(CH_3)R$	1.6–1.9
Benzylic, $ArCH_3$	2.2–2.5
Alkyl chloride, RCH_2Cl	3.6–3.8
Alkyl bromide, RCH_2Br	3.4–3.6
Alkyl iodide, RCH_2I	3.1–3.3
Ether, $ROCH_2R$	3.3–3.9
Alcohol, $HOCH_2R$	3.3–4.0
Ketone, $RC(=O)CH_3$	2.1–2.6
Aldehyde, $R{-}C(=O)H$	9.5–9.6
Vinylic, $R_2C{=}CH_2$	4.6–5.0
Vinylic, $R_2C{=}C(H)R$	5.2–5.7
Aromatic, ArH	6.0–9.5
Acetylenic, $RC{\equiv}CH$	2.5–3.1
Alcohol hydroxyl, ROH	0.5–6.0
Carboxylic, $R{-}C(=O)OH$	10–13
Phenolic, ArOH	4.5–7.7
Amino $R{-}NH_2$	1.0–5.0

14.5 VERSATILE TECHNIQUE

Figures 14.3 (a)–(e) show the NMR spectra of a few compounds and their assignments to demonstrate the power of this technique. An NMR spectrum reveals:

(i) The number of types of protons in the molecule from the number of signals.
(ii) The magnetic field strength at which each type of proton absorbs energy, undergoing resonance.
(iii) The values of chemical shifts for protons caused by shielding and deshielding effects (the environment the hydrogen atoms are in).
(iv) The number of protons of each type present in the molecule, arrived at by integration (ratio of the peak areas) of the spectrum.
(v) The presence of enantiotropic and diastereotopic hydrogens in the structure.
(vi) The structure of the molecule, based on (i) to (iv).

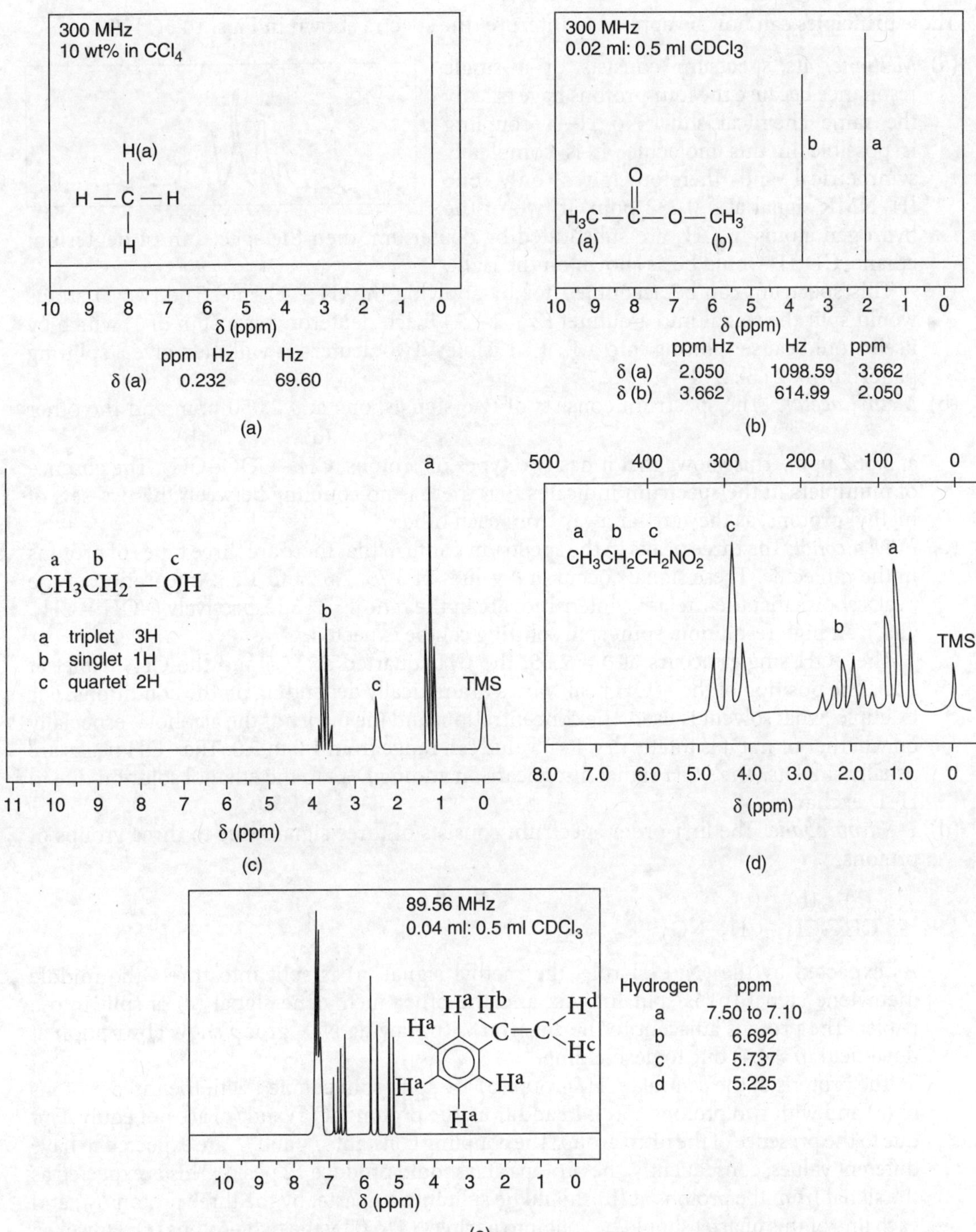

Fig. 14.3 Typical NMR spectra (^1H) **(a)** methane **(b)** methyl acetate **(c)** ethyl alcohol **(d)** 1-nitropropane **(e)** styrene.

These principles can now be applied to interpret the spectra shown in Figs. 14.3(a)–(e)

(a) *Methane:* Its spectrum consists of a single resonance because the four protons have exactly the same chemical shift. No H–H coupling is possible in this molecule. It is completely symmetrical and therefore gives only one ^{1}H–NMR signal at δ 0.232 ppm. If two of the hydrogen atoms in CH_4 are substituted by deuterium, then the spectrum of deuterium ethane, CD_2H_2 would be as shown on the right.

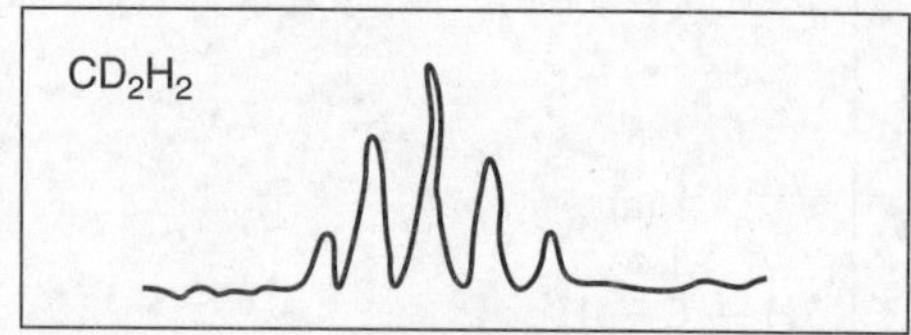

This spectrum can be accounted for by applying the (N + 1) rule. The two D atoms would split the signal into a quintet ($2 \times 2 + 1$). Each deuteron has a spin of 1, which by itself would cause splitting into a 1 : 1 : 1 triplet. Two deuterons will then give a splitting pattern of 1 : 2 : 3 : 2 : 1.

(b) *Methyl acetate:* The spectrum consists of two signals, one at δ 2.050 ppm and the other at 3.662 ppm. This shows that it has two types of protons, $\overset{(a)}{CH_3}$–COO–$\overset{(b)}{CH_3}$. The absence of multiplets in the spectrum indicates that there is no coupling between the two sets of methyl protons, as they are far away from each other.

(c) *Ethyl alcohol:* The three peaks in the spectrum confirm that there are three types of protons in the molecule. These signals occur at δ values of 3.75, 2.62 and 1.25. Integration of the peaks shows that their relative intensities are in the ratio 1 : 2 : 3 respectively (–O$\underline{H}$, –C$\underline{H}_2$, C$\underline{H}_3$). At high resolution, spin–spin splitting can be expected.

The –O$\underline{H}$ singlet occurs at δ = 2.65, the C$\underline{H}_2$ quarted at 3.75 and the C$\underline{H}_3$ triplet at 1.25. The position of the —O$\underline{H}$ peak varies dramatically depending on the conditions; For example, what solvent is used, the concentration, and the purity of the alcohol—especially on whether or not it is totally dry. Its δ value can range from 1.0 to 5.0. The –O$\underline{H}$ peaks are usually singlets. The –O$\underline{H}$ signal disappears on adding D_2O to the ethanol solution due to H–D exchange.

(d) *1-Nitropropane:* The first-order spectrum consists of three signals due to three groups of protons.

(a) (b) (c)
CH_3–CH_2–CH_2–NO_2

As expected by the (N + 1) rule, the methyl signal (a) is split into three, the middle methylene signal (b) is split into six and the other methylene signal (c) is split into a triplet. The protons adjacent to the electron withdrawing NO_2 group show absorption at downfield ($\delta \approx 4.4$) due to deshielding.

The protons of the central –CH_2 group (b) are spin–spin coupled with the three protons of (a) and with two protons at (c). In addition, the protons at (a) and (c) are not equivalent due to the presence of the nitro group. The coupling constants J_{ab} and J_{bc} are expected to have different values; consequently, the protons at *b* should produce 12 peaks. This is expected as the signal from the protons at (b) should be split into a quartet by the three protons (a) and each line of this quartet should be split into a triplet (4×3) by the two protons (c). However, in the actual spectrum, 12 peaks are not observed for the b-protons. Presumably, this is because the coupling constants are such that the peaks are so close and fall on each other.

(e) *Styrene:* The spectrum consists of four signals indicating the presence of four types of hydrogen. The ring protons (a) do not couple to the hydrogen atoms on the side chain (b, c, d protons). The protons on the side chain (vinyl protons) are nonequivalent, and therefore they give three independent signals.

14.5.1 Fine Structure of Signals

Let us consider for simplicity, the spectrum of propane (Fig. 14.4) to discuss the issue of the peak splitting. We saw earlier that this compound yields two signals, one for the terminal methyl hydrogens and one for the methylene hydrogens. While the methyl hydrogens absorb, they in fact can *see* a different environment on the adjacent methylene carbon. The two hydrogens on the methylene carbon can both have the same spin (say +½), alternatively they can both have −½, or it is possible that one of the hydrogens has a spin of +½ while the other has a spin of −½. There is yet another possibility where the first hydrogen has a spin of −½ while the second has a spin of +½, or, the orientation of the first hydrogen can be +½ and that of the second can be −½. The last two orientations are really similar and lead to the same consequence. In other words, the absorbing methyl hydrogens can be seen to have three distinct orientations of the spin of the adjacent methylene hydrogens (Fig. 14.4). When the adjacent hydrogens have their moments aligned in the direction of the applied field, the field experienced by the absorbing hydrogen is now somewhat enhanced. Alternatively, when the two hydrogens have their fields oriented against the field, the field experienced by the absorbing hydrogens is now lower. Where the two hydrogens have opposite orientations, they cancel each other out, and the absorbing hydrogens experience the field due to the electron distribution alone. Hence the single peak of the methyl hydrogen is now split into three peaks for the above reasons. However, the central peak is taller than the flanked peaks, as the central peak is due to the (+)(−) orientation of which there are two possibilities (that is, [+][−] or [−][+]) while there is only one possible orientation for the [+][+] and [−][−] situation. Hence the two peaks at the flanks are about the half the intensity of the central peak in the split pattern. It is therefore obvious that the splitting pattern indicates the *number of hydrogens on the adjacent carbon*. Hence, while the δ value indicates the nature of the absorbing hydrogens, and integration its number, the splitting pattern tells us of the number of hydrogens on the adjacent carbon (Fig. 14.5). It can be seen that a methyl group actually splits the signal into a quartet. In general it can be concluded that n equivalent adjacent hydrogens split the signal into $n + 1$ peaks. The splitting pattern arising from adjacent hydrogens is shown in Fig. 14.6.

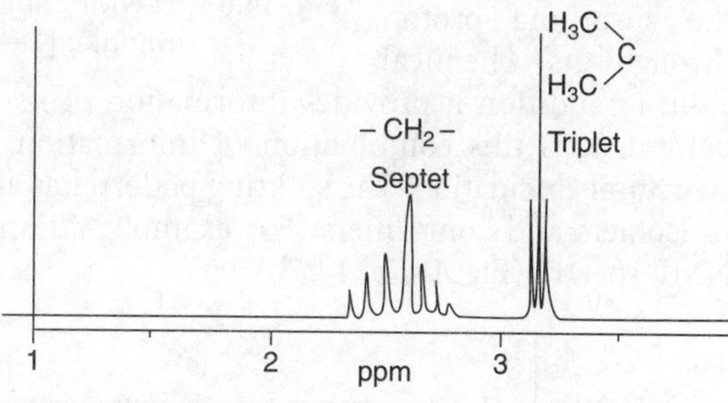

Fig. 14.4 The ^{1}H - NMR spectrum of propane

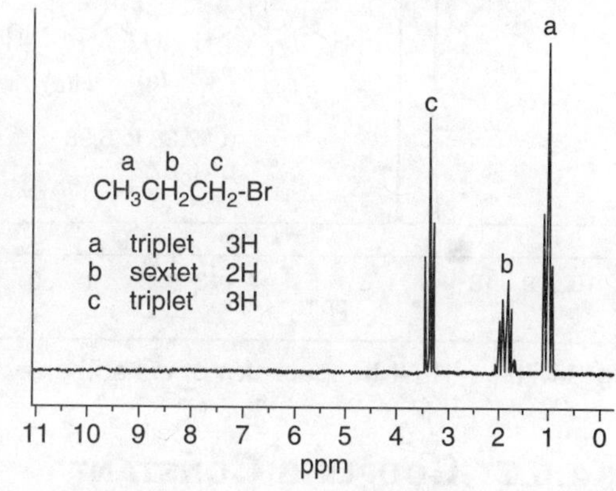

Fig. 14.5 The NMR spectrum of propyl bromide

Let us now consider a situation where the fate of a proton signal is examined due to the presence of n equivalent hydrogens on one adjacent carbon and m equivalent protons on another adjacent carbon. For example, $CH_3CH_2CH_2Br$. The central methylene protons are flanked by three equivalent protons on the terminal methyl group and 2 equivalent protons on the bromomethyl group. Let us now examine the splitting pattern of the central methylene protons for such a system. One can consider that the three equivalent methyl protons would split the signal of the two methylene protons into a quartet (according to the $n + 1$ rule). Each of the features of this quartet would be split into a triplet by the two protons on the bromomethyl group, leading to a final pattern which would be a triplet of a quartet (Fig. 14.6).

Number of equivalent protons causing splitting	Number of peaks: multiplicity	Ratios of area
0	1 (singlet)	1
1	2 (doublet)	1 1
2	3 (triplet)	1 2 1
3	4 (quartet)	1 3 3 1
4	5 (quintet)	1 4 6 4 1
5	6 (sextet)	1 5 10 10 5 1
6	7 (septet)	1 6 15 20 15 6 1

Fig. 14.6 ^{1}H-NMR splitting pattern by adjacent protons (Pascal's triangle: N + 1 rule)

It is therefore clear that the NMR spectrum provides information of the absorbing proton through its chemical shift. In addition it provides information of its neighbouring protons through the splitting pattern. It is this combination of information that makes NMR such a powerful tool in structural elucidation. The splitting pattern has also been applied in the structural elucidation of isomers and conformers. For example, *cis* and *trans*-stilbene can be recognised by their NMR spectra (Fig. 14.7a, 14.7b).

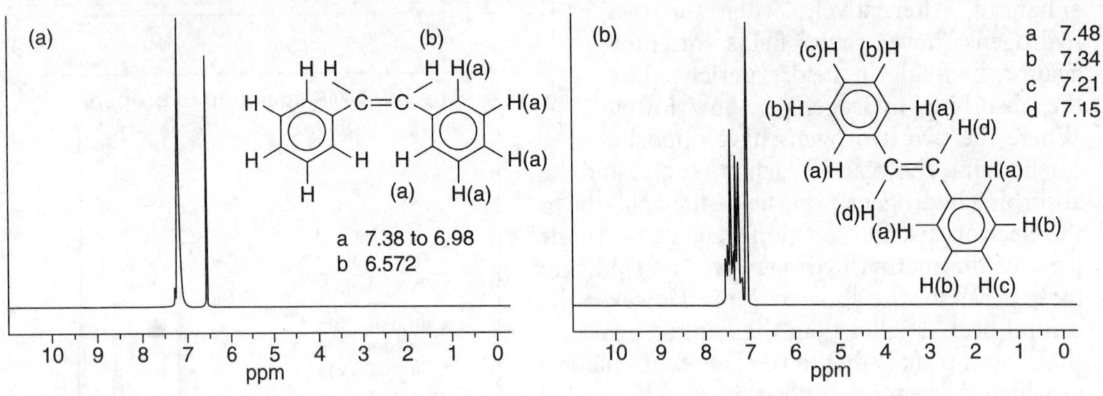

Fig. 14.7(a) ^{1}H-NMR spectrum of *cis*-stilbene **Fig. 14.7(b)** ^{1}H-NMR spectrum of *trans*-stilbene

14.5.2 Coupling Constant

The splitting that is observed in most compounds is roughly of the order of a few Hz and is dependent on the coupling between the adjacent protons and not on the operating field of the spectrometer. The coupling constant is denoted by *J*. The coupling constant is also strongly dependent on the spatial orientation of the adjacent protons. Hence *trans* and *cis*-isomer can be differentiated by their splitting patterns and the coupling constants, as the spatial orientation of the two methyl groups is different in the *cis* and *trans* isomers.

14.5.3 NMR Spectral Parameters

- *Splitting of proton spin levels* occurs on applying a magnetic field, leading to different energy levels for the proton.
- *Nuclear magnetic resonance* is a condition when the frequency of the rotating magnetic field equals the frequency of the precessing nucleus.

- *Units of NMR:* Chemical shift δ is the difference in parts per million (ppm) between the resonance frequency of the observed proton and TMS hydrogens.
- *Signal strength* is the magnitude or intensity of NMR resonance signals, represented along the vertical axis of the spectrum; it is proportional to the molar concentration of the sample.
- *Integration* is an instrumental process of recording the areas of the peaks of the NMR signals, the ratios of the areas being proportional to the ratio of the types of nuclei in molecule.
- *Anisotropy* is the existence of a non-uniform magnetic field around the nucleus due to the effect of electronegative groups, π-systems and hydrogen bonding.
- *Spin–spin interaction* or splitting is the interaction between the spins of neighbouring nuclei in a molecule causing splitting of the signal. It is called spin–spin coupling.
- *The (N + 1) rule* is a guideline for predicting the multiplicity (splitting) of an NMR signal.
- *Coupling constant* is the distance between the peaks in a given multiplet; it is a measure of the splitting effect.
- *NMR spectrum* is a plot of intensity of NMR signals versus magnetic field (frequency) with reference to TMS.
- *Shielding* of the nucleus under study from the external magnetic field occurs due to high electron density around that nucleus; then the signals occur upfield (close to TMS signal) in the spectrum. The opposite effect is deshielding, when the nucleus is exposed more to the applied magnetic field due to low electron density around it; then its signals appear downfield (away from the TMS signal).

14.6 NMR STUDIES ON INORGANIC COMPOUNDS

NMR studies of a large number of inorganic compounds – both simple molecules and metal complexes – have provided valuable structural information. Unlike with organic compounds, the spectrum of each compound is unique. Also, several magnetic nuclei are involved in the magnetic resonance studies on inorganic compounds—H and other magnetic nuclei such as ^{11}B, ^{17}O, ^{19}F, ^{31}P, ^{119}Sn and ^{195}Pt.

A few examples are considered in the following section. Some resonance parameters pertaining to the NMR spectroscopy of some atoms, other than hydrogen and carbon are given in Table 14.2.

Table 14.2 Resonance parameters for inorganic nuclei

Isotope	Spin	Reference	Chemical shift Range (ppm)
^{11}B	3/2	$BF_3{\bullet}H_2O$	100 to –150
^{15}N	1/2	$MeNO_2$	1100 to –400
^{19}F	1/2	$CFCl_3$	550 to –250
^{31}P	1/2	H_3PO_4	250 to –250
^{17}O	5/2	D_2O	1120 to –40
^{127}I	5/2	KI	4000 to –1000
^{115}Sn	1/2	Me_4Sn	700 to –1900
^{195}Pt	1/2	Na_2PtCl_6	200 to –6500

14.6.1 Metal Hydrides

^1H-NMR is useful in understanding the interaction between hydrogen electrons and metal orbital electrons in metal hydrides. The proton NMR signals of hydride ligand bound to transition metals are considerably upfield from TMS (0 to –60 ppm). For example, ^1H chemical shift for $H_2Fe(CO)_4$ is –11, while typical values for organic compounds are downfield from TMS (0 to +15 ppm). The large difference with hydrides compared to organic compounds is the result of paramagnetic contributions from the proximate transition metal. The extent of such paramagnetic contributions can be correlated with ^1H chemical shift values in a set of hydrides.

14.6.2 Fluxional Molecules

A molecule that switches from one structure to another on varying the temperature is a fluxional molecule. This behaviour can be studied by NMR spectroscopy. For example, the proton magnetic resonance spectrum of $(\eta'-C_5H_5)_2(\eta^5-C_5H_5)_2Ti$ shows a single line in its ^1H-NMR spectrum at 62°C. This indicates equality of all the ring protons. This is possible only if the metal migrates from one site to another within each ring. In this dynamic process, the four ligands are rendered equivalent. However, as the temperature is lowered, the signal broadens and gradually splits into two lines which sharpen into equal-intensity singlets at −27°C. At this temperature, the interconversions between mono-and pentahapto ligands occur slowly so that both configurations are observable in the spectrum (Fig. 14.8).

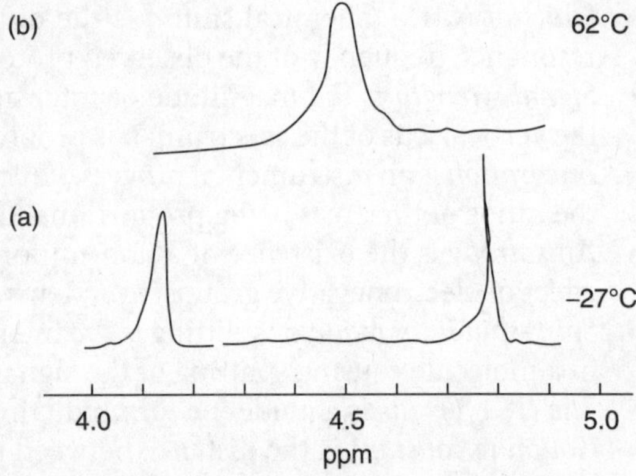

Fig 14.8 ^1H-NMR spectrum of $(\eta'-C_5H_5)_2(\eta^5-C_5H_5)_2Ti$ **(a)** at −27°C **(b)** at 62°C (adapted from Huheey J E, et al., *Inorganic Chemistry: Principle of Structure and Reactivity*, Addison-Wesley Pub. Co., Massachusetts, 1993)

Similarly, the fluxional behaviour of tetramethyl-allene tetracarbonyliron(0) has been proved by its ^1H-NMR spectrum. Its spectrum consists of a single peak at room temperature, but at −60°C, it consists of three independent peaks in the ratio 1:1:2. this proves that all its twelve protons are structurally identical at room temperature due to the molecule experiencing a time-averaged equal chemical environment. The low-temperature spectrum is accounted for by assuming that of its twelve hydrogens, three are *cis*, three *trans* and the remaining six are in a plane perpendicular to the C–Fe bond (Fig. 14.9).

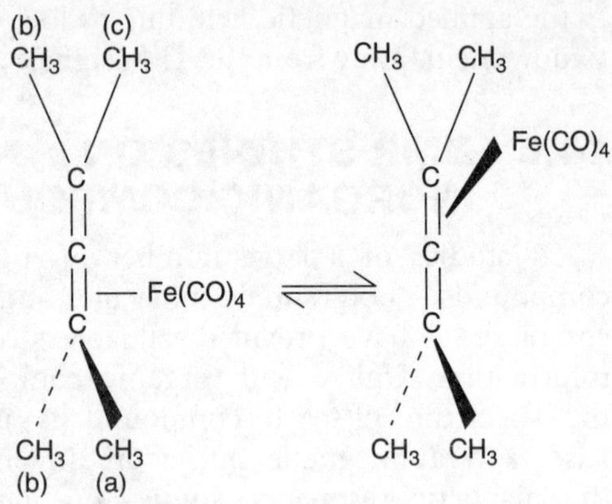

Fig. 14.9 Tetramethylallene tetracarbonyl iron(0)

14.6.3 ^{17}O-NMR in the Study of Exchange Reactions

In some metal complexes, water ligands may get exchanged with water molecules in the medium. The rate of such exchanges can be determined using $H_2{}^{17}O$ and applying ^{17}O-NMR:

$$[M(H_2O)_x]^{z\pm} + H_2{}^{17}O \rightarrow [M(H_2O)_{x-1}\,H_2{}^{17}O]^{z\pm} + H_2O$$

chemical shifts of bulk and coordinated water and consequently, the line width data from the ^{17}O NMR can be used to calculate the rate of H_2O exchange.

14.6.4 ^{19}F-NMR

The chemical shift values for ^{19}F NMR spectra are difficult to predict. Shifts are sensitive to electronegativity, oxidation state and stereochemistry of the neighbouring atoms. Solvents significantly affect these values. For recording the ^{16}F-spectra, $CFCl_3$ is used as reference. The chemical shift values span a wide range, from 0 to 900 ppm. ^1H-^{19}F coupling is strong.

Example:

$C^{19}FCl_3$: singlet
$CH_3{}^{19}F$: quartet
$CH_2{}^{19}F_2$: triplet
$CH_3COCH_2{}^{19}F$: singlet (H-decoupled)
: quartet of triplet (H-coupled)

14.6.4.1 BrF_5

The ^{19}F spectrum of this compound consists of two peaks, one doublet and one quintet with an intensity ratio of 1:4. This substantiates that four F atoms are equivalent and one is different. This is consistent with a square pyramidal structure.

14.6.5 ^{31}P-NMR

^{31}P is the only naturally occurring isotope for phosphorus. Its *I* value is ½, and it is magnetically similar to ^1H. H_3PO_4 is used as the standard for recording the ^{31}P spectra. The chemical shift values are high with reference to the standard, +250 to –250 ppm.

14.6.5.1 ^{31}P-NMR Spectrum of PCl_5

As a solution in CS_2, the ^{31}P spectrum of this compound consists of a single resonance at about 80 ppm, as expected for the single phosphorus atom.. However, in solid state the spectrum shows two intense peaks, indicating the presence of two types of P atoms. This is due to disproportionation of PCl_5 to $[PCl_4^+][PCl_6^-]$, leading to two different chemical environments for the two P atoms. The δ values are 95 (PCl_4^+) and 280 (PCl_6^-) ppm.

14.7 APPLICATIONS OF NMR SPECTROSCOPY

14.7.1 Identification

As discussed above, NMR is a tool that can be used to identify organic compounds unambiguously. Geometrical isomers can also be distinguished from each other using the fine structure. There are many textbooks on organic spectrometry that will provide a detailed treatment on the use of NMR for determining the structure of the compounds.

14.7.2 Polymers

In recent times, the use of high field and multidimensional NMR has become an extremely powerful tool for the structural elucidation of long chain polymers, such as proteins and nucleic acids. A quick survey of the Nobel prizes for chemistry that have been awarded in recent times for such studies will highlight the importance of such applications.

14.7.3 Dynamics of Chemical Processes

NMR can also be utilised to study the dynamics of chemical processes. A wide range of time scales can be probed using NMR, ranging from simple hydrogen exchange and conformer interconversions (which can be in the millisecond timescales), to rotational motions and folding–unfolding processes in complex proteins, where the dynamics can be in the picosecond timescales. Of course, the actual NMR experiments that need to be performed vary widely depending upon the timescales that are encountered.

Consider for example, the spectrum of ethanol. This compound is expected to show three peaks, one for the methyl protons, one for the methylene protons and one for the hydroxyl protons. Furthermore, each of these peaks will also be split due to the coupling with the adjacent protons. The methyl protons are expected to show a triplet due to the coupling with the two methylene protons on the adjacent carbon. Likewise, the methylene protons are expected to show a multiplet, which actually would be a doublet of a quartet. This occurs because the three adjacent methyl protons will split the CH_2 protons into a quartet and each feature in this quartet will be split further into a doublet due to the single adjacent hydroxyl proton. The hydroxyl proton will be split into a triplet due to the two adjacent CH_2 protons.

In reality, this spectrum will only be seen if anhydrous ethanol is taken. If the ethanol contains traces of moisture, the resulting spectrum is different and simplified. The methylene protons show only a quartet (and not a multiplet) and the hydroxyl proton shows only a singlet. This simplification occurs because the protons in the hydroxyl group of ethanol undergo a rapid exchange with the protons of H_2O. This exchange scrambles the spin of the OH proton—the spin of the hydroxyl proton is not fixed but can change during the exchange. An upspin can be exchanged for a downspin during an exchange and back again during a subsequent exchange. In other words, the adjacent CH_2 protons do not see a constant spin on the OH proton but a constantly varying spin. When the water concentration is low and the exchange dynamics is slow, this will give rise to a broadening as the time spent in each spin state is limited. However, when the water concentration is increased and the exchange dynamics speeds up, the CH_2 group observes only an average spin on the OH group and hence the multiplet which should have resulted from the coupling with the OH proton collapses and one observes only the coupling of the CH_2 protons with the CH_3 group. Likewise, the OH group which at low water concentrations shows a broadening, becomes a sharp singlet as the dynamics increases. This behaviour of the coupling process has been used to study the dynamics processes that fall with the time regime of the NMR process.

Another example of the study of dynamics is conformational interconversion. N,N-dimethylformamide (DMF) is a classic example of such a process. In this molecule, one of the methyl groups lies in proximity to the carbonyl group while the other methyl group is *trans* to the carbonyl. Consequently, the chemical shift of the two methyl groups would be different and one does observe two peaks that can be assigned to the methyl proton, provided the two conformers do not interconvert. However, if the rate of conformer interconversion is enhanced by raising the temperature, one would again observe a broadening of the lines, as long as the kinetics of the interconversion $k_{conversion}$, is comparable to the difference to the chemical shifts between the two methyl features, Δv. At even higher temperatures, when the rate is enhanced further so that $k_{conversion}$ is larger than Δv, a single peak is observed for the two methyl peaks, and this occurs midway between the two features seen in the slow conversion limit.

Faster dynamics in the nanosecond and picosecond region can also be studied using multidimensional NMR techniques. This has been used to great advantage in the study of many biological processes.

14.7.4 Medicine

NMR spectroscopy has found widespread applications in diagnostic medicine and is referred to as *Magnetic Resonance Imaging* or MRI. The technique can differentiate diseased tissues from normal tissues. Therefore, it has been used extensively in the detection of conditions such as cancer, ligament damage and vascular problems. Furthermore, the technique is safe as it does not use ionising radiation such as that used in CT scans.

Problem 14.1 A ^{1}H-NMR signal occurs at 180 Hz using a 60-MHz instrument. Calculate the value of this signal. Calculate the frequency at which the same signal would occur in a 100 MHz instrument.

Solution

$$\text{The chemical shift} = \frac{\text{Observed shift from TMS (Hz)}}{\text{Frequency of spectrometer}} \times 10^6 \text{ ppm}$$

$$= \frac{180 \text{ Hz}}{60 \times 10 \text{ Hz}} \times 10^6 \text{ ppm } = 3 \text{ ppm}$$

The δ value for a given proton is constant, irrespective of the instrument used.

$$\therefore \quad 3 \text{ ppm} = \frac{\text{observed shift (Hz)}}{100 \times 10 \text{ Hz}} \times 10^6$$

$$\therefore \quad \text{Observed shift} = 3 \text{ ppm} \times 100 \text{ Hz} = 300 \text{ Hz}$$

∴ the same signal would occur at 300 Hz, when it is recorded with a 100-MHz instrument.

Problem 14.2 The ^{1}H-NMR spectrum of a compound has two peaks, which are separated from the TMS peak by 270 Hz and 306 Hz in a 90-MHz instrument. Calculate their chemical shift values. How many Hertz would separate them from the TMS peak, when the spectrum is re-recorded in a 100-MHz spectrometer?

Solution

$$\text{Chemical shift} = \frac{\text{Distance of peak from TMS (Hz)}}{\text{Spectrometer frequency (MHz)}} \text{ ppm}$$

$$\therefore \quad \delta_1 = \frac{270}{90} = 3.0$$

$$\delta_2 = \frac{306}{90} = 3.4$$

The δ value for a particular type of protons is a constant. It is a field-independent number. On changing the spectrometer frequency, only the position of a particular signal with reference to the TMS signal would vary in the spectrum. For the first signal,

$$3.0 = \frac{\text{Distance of peak from TMS (Hz)}}{100}$$

$$\therefore \quad \text{Distance} = 300 \text{ Hz}$$

For the second signal,

$$3.4 = \frac{\text{Distance of peak from TMS (Hz)}}{100}$$

$$\therefore \quad \text{Distance} = 340 \text{ Hz}$$

Problem 14.3 Which of the following do not contain all-equivalent protons?

(i) $ClCH_2CH_2Cl$ (ii) $(CH_3)_3CC(CH_3)_3$ (iii) $Br–CH_2CH_2Br$

(iv) 1,2,4,5-tetrachlorobenzene (Cl, Cl, Cl, Cl on benzene ring) (v) C_6H_5D (benzene ring with D) (vi) cyclohexanol (cyclohexane ring with OH)

(vii) $C_6H_5CH{=}CHC_6H_5$ (viii) $CH_3–CO–CH_2–CH_2–CH_3$

Solution

(v), (vi), (vii) and (viii) do not contain all-equivalent protons.

Problem 14.4 Explain the following proton NMR chemical shift values:

Compound	δ ppm (for hydroxylic proton)
RO–H	2–3.5
ArO–H	5–10
RCOO–H	10–15

Solution

The increasing value from RO–H to RCOO–H indicates increasing de-shielding of the hydroxylic proton. This is in accord with increasing acidity. In RCOO–H, the proton is expected to exist with appreciable positive charge and therefore, it is de-shielded. RO–H is least acidic and therefore, its proton with least positive charge has its chemical shift at higher fields.

The exact chemical shift of the hydroxylic proton depends on the strength of the hydrogen bonding, the nature of R or Ar, and the acidity of the O–H group.

Problem 14.5 How many signals are expected in the NMR spectrum of each of the following?

(i) $CH_3CH_2CHBr_2$ (ii) $(CH_3)_3C–OCH_3$ (iii) Nitrobenzene

(iv) Chlorocyclobutane (v) $CH_2{=}CHCl$ (vi) $CH_3CHBrCHBr_2$

Solution

(i) Three — (a) (b) (c) $CH_3–CH_2–CHBr_2$

(ii) Two — (a) H_3C, (a) H_3C, (a) H_3C $>C–O–CH_3$ (b)

(iii) Three — NO_2 on benzene ring; ortho H (a), (a); meta H (b), (b); para H (c)

(iv) Five — chlorocyclobutane: H(c), (a)H, H(a), H(d), H(e), (b)H, H(b), Cl

(v) Three — (a)H, H(c) / C=C / (b)H, Cl

(vi) Three — (a) (b) (c) $CH_3CHBrCHBr_2$

Problem 14.6 How many ^{1}H-NMR signals are expected in the spectrum of

(i) 2,2,3,3-tetramethylbutane (ii) chloroethane

Solution

(i) All the protons in this structure are equivalent; therefore, only one ^{1}H-NMR signal is expected for this.

H_3C CH_3
CH_3–C–C–CH_3
H_3C CH_3

(ii) CH_3–CH_2–Cl

The most stable conformation for this molecule is the staggered arrangement :

The three hydrogens of the CH_3 group are denoted with symbols b1, b2 and b3. In the staggered conformer, one of the methyl hydrogens (H_{b3}) is anti to the chlorine atom. This hydrogen may be expected to have a chemical shift different from the two gauche hydrogens (H_{b1} and H_{b2}).

Cl, H_{b1}, H_{b2}, H_{a1}, H_{a2}, H_{b3}

Actually, it is not so; all the three methyl hydrogens produce only one signal. This is because the methyl group rotates fast around the C–C axis and averages the signal for H_b hydrogens. This rotation is fast on the NMR time scale. The NMR spectrometer is incapable of resolving the difference between H_{b3} and the other two hydrogens of the methyl group. Only an average of the two signals (one for H_{b3} and the other for equivalent H_{b1} and H_{b2}) is recorded by the spectrometer.

The equilibrium of the environments of the three methyl protons can be depicted using the Newman projection:

Cl, H_{b1}, H_{b2}, H_{a1}, H_{a2}, H_{b3} ⇌ Cl, H_{b2}, H_{b3}, H_{a1}, H_{a2}, H_{b1} ⇌ Cl, H_{b3}, H_{b1}, H_{a1}, H_{a2}, H_{b2}

Problem 14.7 How many signals are expected in the proton-decoupled CMR spectrum of each of the following?

(i) Propylbenzene (ii) Toluene (iii) Mesitylene

Solution

(i) C_6H_5–CH_2–CH_2–CH_3 (labels: (a) CH_3, (b) CH_2, (c) CH_2, (d) ipso, (e) ortho, (f) meta, (g) para)

Seven signals

(ii) C_6H_5–CH_3 (labels: (a) CH_3, (b) ipso, (c) ortho, (d) meta, (e) para)

Five signals

(iii) Mesitylene (labels: (a) CH_3, (b), (c))

Three signals

Problem 14.8 Predict and explain the proton NMR signals expected for alcohol methine proton for the stereoisomers *cis*-4-*t*-butylcyclohexanol and *trans*-4-butylcyclohexanol.

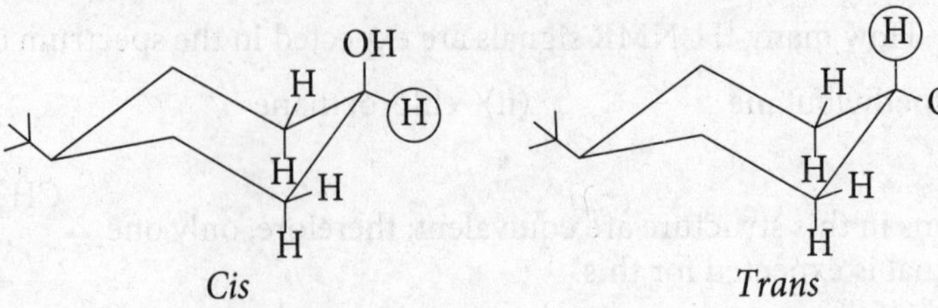

Cis *Trans*

Solution

The alcohol methine proton in the *cis*-isomer is equatorial and, thus, should have a dihedral angle of 60° to all the four adjacent protons. Hence, this should produce a quintet (assuming no coupling between the methine proton and hydroxyl proton). The alcohol methine proton in the *trans*-isomer is axial and, thus, should have a dihedral angle of 180° to each of the two adjacent axial protons and a dihedral angle of 60° to each of the two adjacent equatorial protons. This diastereoisomer should produce a triplet of triplets. The actual spectrum confirms these predictions.

Problem 14.9 At 200 K, the ^{19}F NMR spectrum of IF_5 consists of a doublet (4F) and a quintet (1F). As the temperature is raised, the spectrum is changed to a 5F singlet—explain.

Solution

The iodine of IF_5 has a lone pair of electrons. This lone pair is likely to occupy one of the vertices in the structure to minimise electron–electron repulsion:

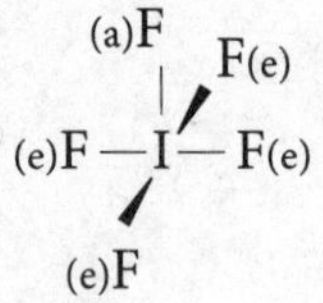

Thus, there are two types of fluorine in this geometry; F(e) equatorial and F(a) axial. The quintet results by the coupling of F(a) to 4 F(e). The four equivalent equatorial fluorine atoms produce a doublet.

The collapse of the spectrum into a single signal at higher temperature indicates that all the F atoms become indistinguishable structurally. This must be due to the fluorine atoms exchanging positions, among themselves rapidly. This is a fluxional molecule.

EXERCISES

1. Explain how tetramethylsilane serves as a good reference compound in PMR spectroscopy.
2. What would be the NMR signal for $LiCH_3$ relative to the TMS peak?
3. Explain the following proton NMR data:

Complex	^1H (ppm)
$H_2Fe(CO)_4$	−11
$[HFe(CO)_4]^-$	−9

4. The addition of HBr to CH_3–CH_2–CH=CH_2 may or may not follow the Markovnikov rule, depending on the experimental conditions. Explain how this can be verified using ^1H NMR spectroscopy.

5. The proton NMR spectrum of *t*-butylfluoride in liquid sulphur dioxide shows a doublet at δ 1.3. On adding antimony pentafluoride to this solution, this doublet is replaced by a singlet at δ 9.35. Explain.

6. Predict and explain the number of signals in the ^{13}C NMR spectrum of
   (a) 1,2-dimethylcyclohexane (b) 1,1,2,2-tetrabromocyclopropane
   (c) cyclooctane (d) methylbenzene (e) tetramethylsilane

7. Comment on the following:
   (a) The distinction between aldehydes and ketones is best achieved in practice from their PMR spectra.
   (b) The PMR value for $CH_2{=}CH_2$ is 5.8, whereas that for $CH{\equiv}CH$ is 2.9.

8. The proton NMR spectrum of menthol shows three methyl doublets. Explain.

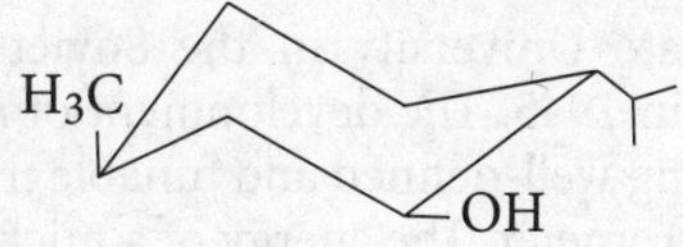

9. The value of the NMR vicinal coupling constant (*J*) is an excellent criterion for identifying stereo-structures of alkenes. Explain.

10. For which one of the following does the proton NMR spectrum show long-range coupling?
   (a) $H_3C{-}CH_3$ (b) $H_3C{-}CHCl{-}CH_3$ (c) $H_2C{=}CH{-}CH_3$ (d) $CH_3{-}CH_2{-}CH_2{-}CH_2F$

11. Predict the total number of peaks that would appear in the ^{13}C NMR spectra of the following molecules:
   (a) Pentanol (b) Diethylether (c) 1-amino-2-methylpropane

12. The infrared spectrum of ClF_3 indicates six strong absorptions. Its ^{19}F NMR spectrum contains two fluorine signals. Explain.

13. The magic angle spinning ^{13}C-NMR spectrum of $Fe(CO)_5$ in the solid state consists of a single absorption at −26°C but two signals, with relative intensity of 2.3, at −118°C. Explain.

14. Predict and interpret the ^1H-NMR spectrum of diborane.

15. Citing journal references, write an essay on the application of ^1H-NMR spectroscopy in the structural studies of coordination compounds.

16. Outline the development of modern instrumentation in NMR spectroscopy. How has this development refined the NMR spectral data?

17. The ^1H-NMR spectrum of the borohydride ion (BH_4^-) is given below. Interpret this spectrum. (The element boron has two isotopes, both of which are NMR-active:

   ^{10}B (I = 3, 20%) and ^{11}B (I = 3/2, 80%).

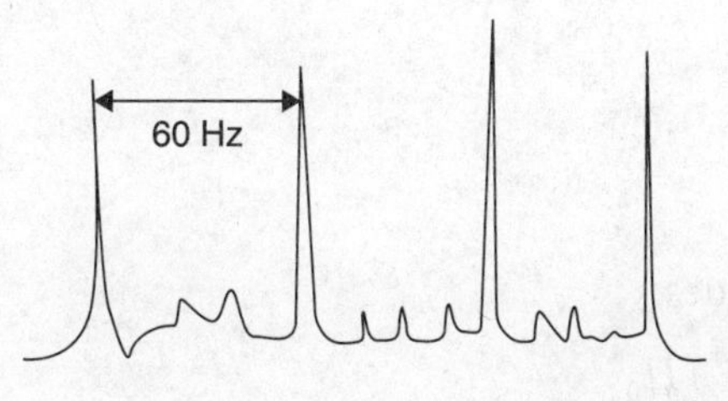

15 Electron Spin Resonance Spectroscopy

15.1 INVENTION OF EPR

Yevgeny Zavoisky at Kazan State University in the Soviet Union first detected electron paramagnetic resonance (EPR) in 1945. The development of *radar* soon after 1945 led to the invention of devices for producing well-defined and tunable microwave sources. Such sources were then used in the EPR spectrometer. The energy of a microwave radiation corresponds to a detectable splitting of the electronic spin states. Since the 1980s, with the advancement of electronic instrumentation, sophisticated modern EPR spectrometers have been commercially made. Now EPR spectroscopy can be studied at a wide range of radiation frequencies and magnetic fields.

The degenerate spin energy states of spin-free electrons cause resonance on absorption of energy and therefore, this method is also known as *electron spin resonance* (ESR) spectroscopy.

15.2 PRINCIPLE OF ESR SPECTROSCOPY

The spin quantum number of an unpaired electron is ½. This electron may exist in either of the two degenerate energy states, +½ or −½. On applying a magnetic field, the degeneracy is lifted. The electron can undego a transition from its lower energy state ($m_s = -½$) to its higher energy state ($m_s = +½$) by absorbing radiation. Such an absorption occurs in the microwave region (400 mμ). ESR spectroscopy is thus an absorption spectroscopy. Radiation of microwave frequency induces transitions between magnetic energy levels of electrons with unpaired spins. The magnetic energy splitting occurs due to a static magnetic field.

When an external, static magnetic field H_0 is applied, two energy levels are established for a spin-free electron. These two levels have an energy separation of ΔE. This is given by

$$\Delta E = \frac{\mu_e H_0}{M_S} = h\nu \tag{15.1}$$

where μ_e = electron magnetic moment and M_S = angular momentum quantum number (+½ or −½)

Rearranging Eq. 15.1,

$$\nu = \frac{\mu_e H_0}{h M_S} \tag{15.2}$$

Substituting the constant values,

$$\nu = \frac{(9.285 \times 10^{-4}\,\text{JT}^{-1})\,H_0}{(6.626 \times 10^{-34}\,\text{Js})\,(1/2)}$$

$$= (2.803 \times 10^{10}\,\text{s}^{-1}\,\text{T}^{-1})\,H_0$$

The SI unit of magnetic field strength is weber per metre-square—*tesla* (T).

$$1 \text{ tesla} = 1 \text{ weber/(metre)}^2 = \text{Wb/m}^2$$

$$10000 \text{ gauss (G)} = 1 \text{ T}$$

On expressing the magnetic field in kilogauss, the resonance frequency for transition from one spin state to the other for a free electron (in MHz) becomes

$$\nu = 2803\, H_0$$

Normally, ESR measurements in solution are made with an exciting frequency of 95000 MHz and a magnetic field strength of 34000 G. The typical energy involved is 1 cal mol^{-1}. Figure 15.1 indicates the establishment of two energy levels for the unpaired electron in an applied magnetic field. The lower energy state has the spin magnetic moment aligned in the direction of the magnetic field and corresponds to the quantum number, $M_S = -½$.

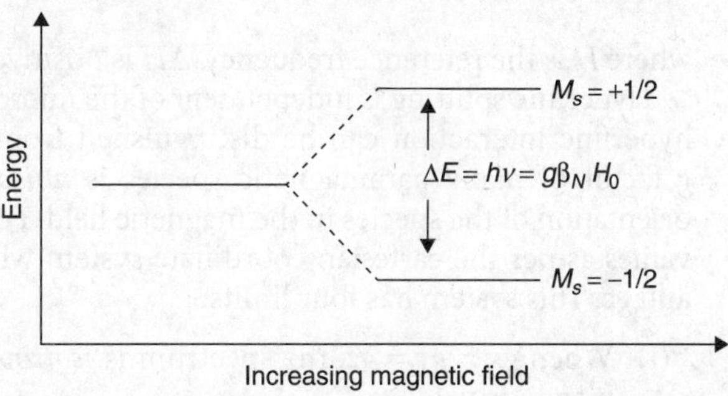

Fig. 15.1 Splitting of an electron energy state by applied magnetic field

$$\Delta E = h\nu = g\,\beta_N\, H_0 \tag{15.3}$$

where h = Planck's constant, ν = frequency of radiation, β_N = Bohr magneton (9.274×10^{-24} J T^{-1}) and H_o = strength of the magnetic field.

The term g is known as the *g-factor*. It is a unitless measure of the intrinsic magnetic moment of the electron. When the electron is free, not influenced by its environment, its g value g_e is 2.0023.

15.2.1 The *g* Factor

The g, called the *spectroscopic splitting factor*, is a function of the electron's environment. For a free electron its value is 2.0023. It varies for an unpaired electron present on different species. The position of the signal is indicated by the g value. Changes in g value from that of a free electron is the result of interactions of the electron with the orbital angular momentum by neighbouring nuclei. The modified g can then be calculated by rearrangement of Eq. 15.3:

$$g = \frac{h\nu}{\beta_N H_0}$$

Since, h, ν and β_N remain constant during an EPR experiment, g values decrease as H_0 increases. The concept of g is comparable with that of the chemical shift in NMR.

- Therefore, the g value is dependent upon the chemical environment of the spin-free electron.
- If an electron in a species is able to move freely due to complete delocalisation, the g value is close to that of a free electron.
- When movement for the spin-free electron is restricted by total localisation, then the g value is quite different from 2.0023.
- In liquids, the paramagnetic species collide among themselves and therefore have a single g value (isotropic); this is a proof for randomisation of the interactions among the molecules.
- In paramagnetic solids, randomisation is not possible and therefore, the g values are different along the coordinate axes, x, y and z.

To obtain the g value of a paramagnetic molecule, the sample and the reference (example: α, α'-diphenyl-β-picrylhydrazyl, DPPH) are taken in two separate sample tubes and placed in a dual sample cavity of the spectrometer. Then, the PMR spectrum is recorded; it will show two signals with a field separation of ΔH. The g value for the molecule is then given by

$$g = g_{\text{ref}}\left(1 - \frac{\Delta H}{H}\right)$$

where H is the reference frequency. ΔH is positive if the analyte has its centre at a higher field.

Hyperfine splitting is independent of the microwave frequency applied; therefore, a nuclear hyperfine interaction can be distinguished from the effects of differences in g factors. The g factor of many paramagnetic species is *anisotropic*; this implies that it depends on the orientation of the species in the magnetic field. For anisotropic species, the g factor takes three values as per the cartesian coordinate system which is symmetric along the diagonal, gx, gy and gz. This system has four limits:

(i) When $gx = gy = gz$, the spectrum is *isotropic*; it is not dependent on orientation in the magnetic field.

(ii) When $gx = gy > gz$, the spectrum is *axial;* the two equivalent g values are known as g_{I} while the singular value is known as g_{II}. The spectrum has a small peak at low field and a large peak at high field.

(iii) When $gx = gy < gz$, the spectrum is axial as with (ii), but is shortened in the xy plane. It consists of a large peak at low field and a small peak at high field.

(iv) When $gx \neq gy \neq gz$, the spectrum is *rhombic*; it consists of three large peaks corresponding to the different components of g. For example, X-irradiated Fe:O_2 complex with an electron addition exhibits such a spectrum, with g values of 2.27, 2.17 ad 1.95 (Table 15.1).

Table 15.1 Proportionality factors (g) of some species

Species	g value
Free e^-	2.0023 (g_e)
$\bullet CH_3$	2.0026
Anthracene cation	2.0028
Anthracene anion	2.0029
Cu(acac)$_2$	2.13
VO(acac)$_2$	1.968
$[MoO(SCN)_5]^{2-}$	1.935
Cr(III)	2.000

- The g factor is a dimensionless constant.
- Free radicals have g values that are fairly close to 2.0023, characteristic of a *free* electron.
- Some transition metal ions such as Co^{2+} and Cu^{2+} have g values significantly different from 2.
- A trend – though slight – is observed in the g values for organic radicals: g of radicals with halogens or peroxy group is greater than the g of radicals with N or O.

Problem 15.1 Calculate the EPR frequency of a spin-free electron in a magnetic field of 0.367 T; free electron $g = 2.0023$ $\beta_N = 9.273 \times 10^{-24}$ JT^{-1}.

Solution

The EPR frequency of a spin-free electron is obtained from the equation,

$$hv = g\,\beta_N\,H_0$$

$$\nu = \frac{g\beta_N H_0}{h} = \frac{2.0023 \times 9.273 \times 10^{-24} \times 0.367}{6.626 \times 10^{-34}}$$

$$= 10000 \times 10^6 \text{ Hz} = 10000 \text{ MHz}$$

Origin of EPR Spectrum

A compound containing an unpaired electron

↓ Exposed to an external magnetic field

The energy levels of the unpaired electron are split by the field

↓ Exposed to constant-frequency microwave radiation

Electron undergoes transition by absorbing radiation

↓ Absorption of energy is recorded

An EPR spectrum

- Unlike in most spectroscopic methods, the frequency of the radiation is held constant while the magnetic field is varied to promote a transition and then the spectrum is obtained in EPR spectroscopy.
- Electron paramagnetic resonance pertains to molecules with unpaired (spin-free) electrons. For example, the molecule NO (*g*) with a spin-free electron undergoes electron paramagnetic resonance.
- Such a resonance can be observed as a spectrum, known as the *EPR spectrum*. The study of such spectra is *EPR spectroscopy*.
- The resonance pertaining to the spin-free electron is a consequence of absorption of energy by the molecule. Therefore, it is an absorption spectroscopic method.
- This spectroscopy is known also as *electron spin resonance* (ESR) spectroscopy because the resonance arises from degenerate spin energy states of the spin-free electron.
- This spectroscopy is similar to nuclear magnetic resonance spectroscopy; in the former, absorption energy lifts the degeneracy for the spin-free electron while in the latter, it occurs for the nuclei.
- The quantum transition in this procedure involves changes in the spin of electrons in an applied magnetic field.
- EPR originates from spin-free electrons in inorganic and organic species. A spin-free electron behaves like a small magnetic bar when placed in a magnetic field. It orients itself parallel to the applied strong magnetic field. On acquiring energy from microwave radiation, the electron orients itself against the applied magnetic field. This effect causes Zeemann splitting, when the energy difference between the lower and the higher energy level matches the microwave energy. At this condition, energy is absorbed and an EPR resonance occurs. Such a resonance can be observed and recorded by the spectrometer. This spectroscopy is occasionally referred to as *Electron Magnetic Resonance* (EMR).
- A deuterium nucleus behaves similar to a hydrogen nucleus in the EPR spectrum, as both nuclei have the same *I*.

15.2.2 EPR Spectrum

Transition from the lower spin energy state to the higher spin energy state can be recorded as an ESR spectrum. The ESR spectrum of a free electron has a single absorption peak (Fig. 15.2a). However, the resonance lines are recorded as first derivative spectrum for sharpness and clarity (Fig. 15.2b).

- Absorptions in EPR spectroscopy are usually broad; therefore, the spectrum is better recorded as a derivative spectrum (a plot of rate of change of absorption versus field strength). Such a first derivative spectrum can give accurate measure of the spacing between the peaks.

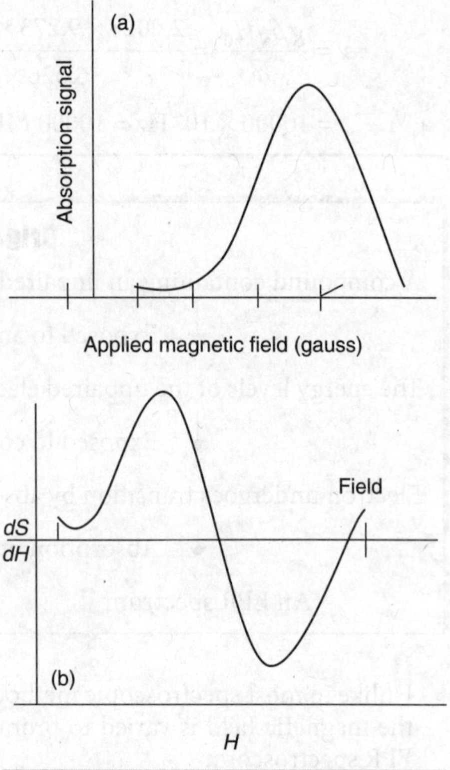

Fig. 15.2 EPR spectrum **(a)** Resonance absorption **(b)** Derivative spectrum

15.2.3 EPR Hyperfine Splitting (Electron–Nucleus Coupling)

The nuclei of the atoms in a molecule or species have their intrinsic fine magnetic moments. Such magnetic moments produce an internal magnetic field. Such fields are sufficiently intense to influence the electronic magnetic field. The interaction between nuclei and electrons results in local magnetic fields. These interactions are called *hyperfine interactions*. With such interactions, the energy level of the electron is expressed as

$$E = g\, m_B\, B_o\, M_S + a\, M_S\, m_I$$

where m_I is the nuclear spin quantum number and a is the hyperfine coupling constant.

Consequent to magnetic interactions between the electron and the nuclei, more than one spectral line can be observed in the EPR spectrum. For example, in the hydrogen atom, the electron is associated with a nucleus of $I = ½$. In the presence of an external magnetic field, the lower electron spin energy state ($m_S = -½$) is associated either with the nuclear spin, $m_I = +½$ or $m_I = -½$. Therefore, the lower energy state of the electron is split into two sub-energy states.

The sub-energy state with $m_S = -½$, $m_I = +½$ has a lower energy than the sub-energy state with $m_S = -½$, $m_I = -½$. Similarly, the higher energy state ($m_S = +½$) is also split into two energy states, the lower energy state ($m_S = +½$, $m_I = -½$) and the higher energy state ($m_S = +½$, $m_I = +½$).

- When the nuclear spin is I, then $(2I + 1)$ energy levels are possible for each value of m_S.
- The multiplicity of absorption pattern, that is the hyperfine structure is given as $(2NI + 1)$, where I is the spin number of the coupled nucleus and N the number of chemically equivalent coupled nuclei.
- The *selection rules* for the allowed EPR transition is

$$\Delta m_I = 0 \text{ and}$$

$$\Delta m_S = \pm 1$$

Applying the selection rules, the following transitions are allowed for the hydrogen electron:

$$m_S = -\frac{1}{2}, m_I = +\frac{1}{2} \longrightarrow m_S = +\frac{1}{2}, m_I = +\frac{1}{2}$$

$$m_S = -\frac{1}{2}, m_I = -\frac{1}{2} \longrightarrow m_S = +\frac{1}{2}, m_I = -\frac{1}{2}$$

Thus, each EPR signal of the hydrogen electron is split into a doublet. In total, 4 hyperfine spectral lines are obtained (Fig. 15.3).

- The energy separation (distance) between two adjacent split signals is known as *hyperfine splitting constant a*. It is measured in Hz.
- When one unpaired electron interacts with one nucleus, the number of EPR lines is $2I + 1$.
- When one unpaired electron interacts with N *equivalent* nuclei, the number of EPR lines is $2NI + 1$.
- When one unpaired electron interacts with non-equivalent nuclei (N_1, N_2 ...), the EPR spectrum becomes a complex multiplet.

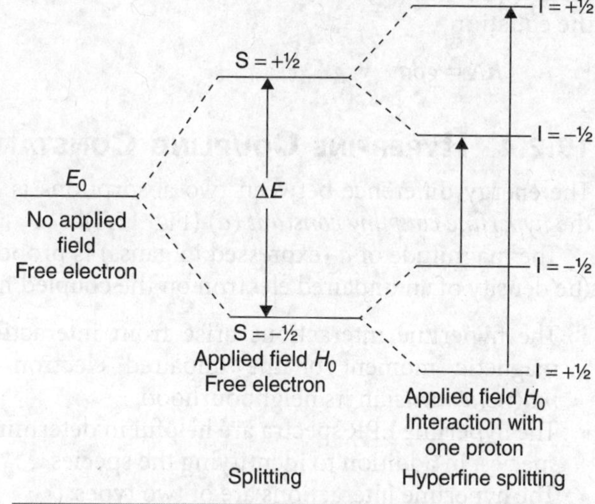

Fig. 15.3 EPR hyperfine splitting for a hydrogen electron

Consider the species, *α,α'*-diphenyl-*β*-picrylhydrazyl (DPPH) radical:

It has a single unpaired electron, providing a very simple energy level structure. *I* for *N* = 1; the two nitrogen nuclei (N–N nitrogens) are equivalent; therefore, the number of lines expected in the spectrum is $2NI + 1 = 5$. Actually, its spectrum has five lines with the intensity ratio 1:2:3:2:1. Free radicals of this type have *g* factors close to that of a free electron (2.0023). The *g* value for the hydrazyl has been calculated to be 2.0036.

- When an unpaired electron couples to a single nucleus, the lines have the same intensity (example: H). When it couples to more than one nucleus, the relative intensity of each line is determined by the interacting nuclei (example: $\bullet CH_3$).
- When coupled to nuclei of $I = ½$, the intensity of each line follows Pascal's triangle;

1
1 1
1 2 1
1 3 3 1
1 4 6 4 1
1 5 10 10 5 1

Hyperfine couplings are of two types:

(i) coupling of the electron magnetic moment to the magnetic moment of the atomic nucleus carrying it (between • and X in $\dot{X}$–Y),
(ii) coupling of the electron to a nucleus of a different atom (between • and Y in $\dot{X}$–Y).

The second type of coupling is known as *super hyperfine splitting.*

The hyperfine splitting constant, known as *a*, can be determined by measuring the distance between each of the hyperfine lines. This value can be converted into Hz (A) using the equation,

$$hA = g\beta a$$

15.2.4 Hyperfine Coupling Constant

The energy difference between two absorptions is known as the *hyperfine coupling constant* (*a*) (Fig. 15.4).

The magnitude of *a* (expressed in gauss) is proportional to the density of an unpaired electron on the coupled nucleus.

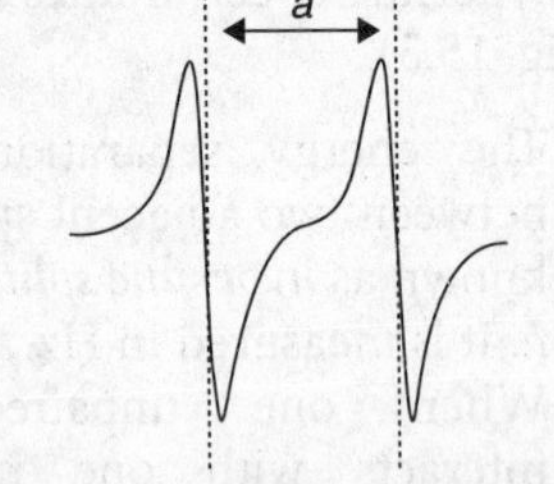

Fig. 15.4 Hyperfine coupling constant

- The hyperfine interactions arise from interaction of the magnetic moment of the unpaired electron with the *magnetic nuclei* in its neighbourhood.
- The hyperfine EPR spectra are helpful in determining the spatial structure of paramagnetic species, in addition to identifying the species.
- The hyperfine interactions are of two types:
  - the *anisotropic* (dipolar) interactions and
  - the *Fermi contact* interactions.

The dipolar interaction is that between two dipoles, the electron spin magnetic moment and the nuclear magnetic moment. This depends upon the shape of electronic orbital and the mean distance between the interacting electron and nucleus. This type of interaction helps in determining the position of a paramagnetic species in a solid lattice.

The Fermi interaction arises from the electrons in *s* orbitals. Such interactions are called *isotropic*; they depend on the presence of a finite unpaired electron density at the position of the nucleus; they do not depend on the orientation of paramagnetic species in the magnetic field. No Fermi contact interaction is possible when the *s* electron density is zero.

The isotropic hyperfine coupling constant A(Hz) is given by

$$A = -83\pi <\mu_n \mu_e> .| \psi(0)|2$$

where μ_n = nuclear magnetic moment, μ_e = electron magnetic moment and $\psi(0)$= electron wave function at the nucleus.

The right-hand side of the equation denotes the unpaired spin density.

- The nuclear hyperfine spectra arise from both the interaction of nucleus and their positions in the molecule and also the extent to which a part or the entire molecule is free to reorient itself according to the direction of the external magnetic field.

The relative intensities of the lines in hyperfine spectra according to the unpaired electrons interacting with multiple *equivalent* nuclei are given below:

Number of equivalent nuclei	Relative intensities
0	1
1	1 : 1 : 1
2	1 : 2 : 3 : 2 : 1
3	1 : 3 : 6 : 7 : 6 : 3 : 1
4	1 : 4 : 10 : 16 : 19 : 16 : 10 : 4 : 1
5	1 : 5 : 15 : 20 : 45 : 51 : 45 : 20 : 15 : 5 : 1
6	1 : 6 : 21 : 40 : 80 : 116 : 141 : 116 : 80 : 40 : 21 : 6 : 1
	Relative intensities of each line when $I = 1$

The complexity of the EPR spectra increases with increasing number of nuclei.

15.2.5 Hyperfine Interaction Rules

The rules for splitting of EPR spectral lines by nuclei are the same as for NMR.

Z	*A*	*I*	EPR splitting	Example
Even	Even	0	Not active	^{12}C
Odd	Even	Integer	Active	^{14}N
Odd	Odd	Fraction	Active	^{23}Na

15.2.6 Line Width

- The unpaired electron not only interacts with the externally applied magnetic field but also interacts with the magnetic fields of the atomic nuclei in its neighbourhood. These interactions cause finite line width ΔB.
- From the line width and the line intensity data, information about the spin environment can be obtained.
- Thus, the line width and the line intensity are dependent upon the electron spin exchange between identical and non-identical molecules; the interaction of molecules nearby carrying unpaired electrons; and the chemical exchange between the paramagnetic molecule and its environment.
- The resonant absorption is not always narrow as the absorption does not always occur at a precise value. The actual line width ranges from a few milligauss for free radicals in solution to over 1000 gauss for some transition metal compounds in the solid state.

15.3 EPR Spectrometer

15.3.1 Microwave Radiation Source

The detectable splitting of the electronic spin states corresponds to a microwave radiation. Therefore, in an EPR spectrometer, a microwave radiation source is used. This radiation is formed and amplified by a *klystron* which also tunes waves to a precise frequency, amplitude and phase. *Waveguides* (*coaxial cables*) direct the waves into the resonant cavity. Waveguides are open air, rectangular brass channels with precise dimensions that correspond to the wavelength of the radiation that is to be propagated. Coaxial cables are suitable for most of the

EPR studies requiring low power, low frequency microwave radiation. The dimensions of the waveguides and the resonator are specific to the microwave frequency.

For observing resonance, the frequency of the microwaves must correspond to the splitting of the spin states of the electron, the splitting being determined by the strength of the magnetic field. Consequently, the strength of the magnetic field is dependent on the frequency of radiation used, and vice versa. Thus the experimental unit has to adopt a corresponding combination of microwave energy, magnetic field strength, and resonator and waveguide dimensions. This occurs in the waveguide unit.

Microwaves of different frequencies ranging from 1 GHz to 170 GHz may be used in EPR spectrometers. The majority of EPR spectrometers operate in the 8–12 GHz (called the X band) range. This range is suitable to observe many EPR transitions, and it does not require high magnetic field strength. As the magnetic field strength is increased, the spin states are split further, spreading apart transitions that are close in energy.

15.3.2 Resonator

The resonator is a component for holding the sample in an EPR spectrometer. It is actually a cavity. Its dimensions correspond to the specific wavelength of microwave radiation that is to be used in the spectral study. With X-band frequencies, for example, the wavelength of the electromagnetic wave is about 3 cm. Therefore, the resonator cavity has dimensions of about 3 cm, for allowing microwaves to resonate in the cavity. The sample is placed in a central location in the cavity, where it can absorb the maximum energy from the magnetic field of the microwaves.

15.3.3 Detector

The detector in an EPR spectrometer is usually a *reflection spectrometer*. It measures the amount of radiation that is reflected back, out of the resonator. When a transition occurs, the level of reflected microwave energy changes. Such energy changes are automatically recorded in the instrument in the form of a spectrum. The magnetic field strength is changed gradually to allow various transitions and the transitions are recorded concurrently. A diode is used to measure the reflected energy.

15.3.4 Electromagnet

A variable field strength electromagnet is used in an EPR spectrometer. The strength of the applied field can be varied precisely, quickly and consistently. Usually, the field strength is swept in the range 0–4000 gauss (0–0.4 tesla). This range covers all transitions. When the strength matches the energy of a transition, that transition gets recorded.

Heat is generated when a significant amount of current is passed through the electromagnet for a field sweep; therefore, the magnet is cooled by a flowing stream of water around the magnet. The sample is kept in the cavity at the centre of the electromagnet.

- In a D-band spectrometer, the frequencies are about 130 GHz. It has a superconducting electromagnet. The magnet is cooled to about 4 K with liquid helium. Such a magnet is required when transitions can be effected in spin states only with high frequency microwaves (0–8 T sweep).
- Greater population difference in the split spin state is obseryable only on cooling the sample to ultra-cold temperatures. Many transitions can be recorded with high signal level at such low temperatures.

- In some modern EPR spectrometers, pulsed microwave energy is used to selectively effect transitions of a paramagnetic substance. Two such instruments are known as Electron Spin Echo Envelope Modulation (ESEEM) spectrometer and Hyperfine Sublevel Correlation Spectrometer.
- An advanced model of EPR spectrometer is Electron Nuclear Double Resonance (ENDOR) spectrometer; the spectra obtained with this instrument provide precise information about nuclei surrounding an unpaired electron.

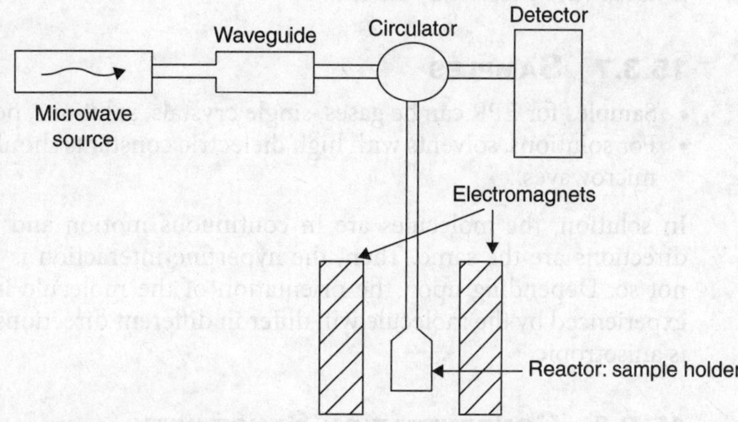

Fig. 15.5 Block-diagram of an EPR spectrometer

A block-diagram of an EPR spectrometer is depicted in Fig. 15.5

15.3.5 Continuous Wave EPR Spectroscopy

This is the conventional EPR spectroscopic technique. In this (CW EPR), the sample is continuously illuminated with microwave radiation of fixed frequency. As the applied magnetic field strength is swept through a selected range, various transitions occur.

15.3.6 Sensitivity of EPR Spectroscopy

At equilibrium, the population (n) of the various energy levels can be predicted by applying the Boltzmann distribution:

$$\frac{n_{\text{upper}}}{n_{\text{lower}}} = e^{-\mu H_0/IkT}$$

where k = Boltzmann constant, μ = Bohr magneton, H_0 = external magnetic field strength in gauss, T = absolute temperature and I = spin number.

The Bohr magneton is about 1000 times larger than the nuclear magneton. Therefore, the spin magnetic moment of the electron is about 1000 times larger than the nuclear magnetic moment. This is reflected in the energy difference between the upper state and the lower state; the difference is greater in the case of electrons than in the case of protons when a magnetic field of same strength is applied.

The excess population of the lower energy level over that in the upper energy level is very small for a single spin system. This ratio is governed by the *Boltzmann distribution*; this is similar to that in NMR. For a free electron at room temperature, the relative ratio of the population of upper-to-lower energy levels is about 0.998 (for a magnetic nuclear spin ½ in a field of 14.09 kG, the distribution calculation gives a population ratio of 0.9999904 at room temperature). The much greater *population difference* in ESR imparts superior sensitivity when compared with NMR. The sensitivity can be further enhanced by recording the spectrum at low temperatures; solids down to liquid helium temperatures have been studied by ESR. (This is not always possible by NMR.)

15.3.7 Samples

- Samples for EPR can be gases, single crystals, solutions, powders and frozen solutions.
- For solutions, solvents with high dielectric constants should not be used as they will absorb microwaves.

In solution, the molecules are in continuous motion and therefore the interactions in all directions are the same. Then, the hyperfine interaction is isotropic. In the solid state, it is not so. Depending upon the orientation of the molecule in the crystal, the magnetic field experienced by the molecule will differ in different directions. Then, the hyperfine interaction is anisotropic.

15.3.8 Concentration Sensitivity

The sensitivity at room temperature of X-band ESR spectrometers is expressed as

$$N_{\min} = 1 \times 10^{11} \frac{\Delta H}{\sqrt{\tau}}$$

where $N_{\min}$ is the minimum number of detectable spins per gauss, ΔH is the width between deflection points on the derivative absorption curve, τ is the time constant of the deflecting system which is inversely proportional to the bandwidth of the detection circuit.

Concentrations of samples of the order of 10^{-9} M are satisfactory for recording the spectrum. For aqueous solutions, 10^{-7} M is the lower limit. For determining structure and quantitative analysis, a concentration of 10^{-6} M is satisfactory. The noise level in the spectrometer due to crystal noise and klystron noise are the limiting factors for instrument sensitivity. The sensitivity is higher for the use of higher magnetic field strengths. For example, a K-band spectrometer is much more sensitive than an X-band spectrometer.

15.3.9 Calibration of EPR Spectra

EPR spectra can be calibrated with a reference material—it has to be a free radical, EPR-active. DPPH is an excellent reference standard for this spectroscopy because it gives a sharp, well-defined EPR spectrum. In addition to DPPH, Fremy's salt [potassium nitrodisulphonate, $K_2NO(SO_3)_2$] and $CuSO_4 \bullet 5H_2O$ (*s*) can serve as standards.

15.4 APPLICATIONS OF EPR SPECTROSCOPY

15.4.1 Detection of Odd-electron Molecules

An odd-electron molecule provides a unique EPR spectrum. For example, the spectrum of nitric oxide, an odd-electron molecule is unique. Similarly, NO_2 and ClO_2, both odd-electron molecules can be identified in the gas phase by ESR spectroscopy.

15.4.2 Detection of Free-radical Reaction Intermediates

The formation and reaction of free radical intermediates of reactions can be ascertained by recording the ESR spectra of reaction mixtures, during the course of the reaction. Short-lived free radical intermediates, which cannot be isolated, can be detected with clarity by the ESR method.

15.4.3 Estimation of Paramagnetic Species

The quantity of a paramagnetic species in a mixture can be estimated by recording the ESR spectrum of the mixture. The other species in the mixture should be ESR-inactive. The intensity of the ESR spectrum is a measure of the amount of the active species in the mixture.

- This procedure is a convenient method for the estimation as the species does not have to be isolated from the mixture,
- It is suitable for estimating even traces (micrograms) of paramagnetic species.

Paramagnetic metal ions M^{n+} with concentrations to the lower limit of 10^{-6} M can be determined by this method. The concentration of a paramagnetic substance is proportional to the spectral intensity:

$$\text{Concentration} \propto \text{intensity} \propto \int_{-\infty}^{+\infty} f(x)\,dx$$

where $f(x)$ denotes the absorption curve. Calibration curves can be recorded with standard solutions of the analyte. The peak heights can then be compared to determine amounts of analytes.

15.4.4 Detection of Conduction Electrons

Solutions of alkali metals in liquid ammonia contain solvated electrons. Such electrons, called conduction electrons, render the solutions highly conducting. These conduction electrons can be studied by the EPR spectrum of the solutions. The quantity of conduction electrons formed and the changes they undergo in the presence of other species can be ascertained by EPR spectroscopy.

The formation of conduction electrons in some metal lattices on alloying them with other metals has also been studied by the EPR method.

15.4.5 Study of Naturally Occurring Substances

ESR spectroscopy is used in some industries which process natural raw materials. The method pertains to identification and estimation of materials routinely by this method. For example, ruby, an expensive gemstone can be characterised by its ESR spectrum. A saleable ruby gem (Al_2O_3:Cr) should have only traces of chromium and its brilliance depends upon this. PMR is used to determine its chromium content non-destructively and hence the value of the gem too. Other natural materials such as dolomite, quartz, haemoglobin, petroleum, coal and rubber are also characterised by the ESR technique.

15.4.6 Study of Coordination Compounds

EPR spectroscopy is extensively applied in studying metal complexes. It can establish (i) the electron configuration of the metal ion in coordination with ligands (ii) the presence of spin-free electrons in the complex (iii) the nature of metal–ligand bonding and (iv) the interaction of the unpaired metal electrons with the magnetic nuclei on the ligands.

For example, the EPR spectrum of $K_2Ir_2Cl_6$ shows hyperfine splitting substantiating the unpaired electron on the Ir ion interacting with the Cl nuclei. This interaction leads to partial delocalisation of the metal electron over the ligands.

The EPR spectrum of Cu(II) proves that it has an odd electron (d^9); the absence of any EPR signal for Cu^+ (d^{10}) shows that electron pairing is complete in this ion. Ligands with nuclei having non-zero spins – such as nitrogen – cause hyperfine EPR splittings. Such splittings are proportional to the number of such atoms bonded to Cu(II). EPR spectra can in addition, give some information on the geometry of copper complexes.

The ESR spectrum of $[Fe(CN)_5NO]^{3-}$ consists of three lines of equal intensity. This can be explained assuming that the spin-free electron present in it interacts with the nitrogen nucleus ($I = 1$) in NO. The *g* values for transition metal components vary largely due to spin-orbit coupling and zero-field splitting; the values range from −1.4 to 3.0. The *g* value is not a constant. It is a tensor quantity that changes with the environment of the electron.

The hyperfine splitting pattern can be used to calculate the spin of a nucleus. For example, the EPR spectrum of a complex containing one manganese ion has six lines.

$$\therefore \quad 2NI + 1 = 6$$

$$N = 1 \text{ atom (Mn)}$$

$$\therefore \quad 2I + 1 = 6; \quad 2I = 5; \quad I = \frac{5}{2}$$

Therefore, the nuclear spin of Mn is 5/2.

In metal complexes, *g* values depend upon the following factors:

- operating frequency,
- concentration of spin-free electron,
- ground state term of the ion,
- symmetry of the field,
- intrinsic magnetic field,
- crystal field splitting,
- Jahn-Teller distortion and
- zero-field splitting.

For Cu(II), the nuclear spin $I = 3/2$; therefore, hyperfine splitting results in four lines of intensity 1 : 1 : 1 : 1. For Cu(II) ligated to four symmetric $I = 1$ nuclei such as ^{14}N, the spectrum would consist of nine lines with intensities 1 : 8 : 28 : 56 : 70 : 56 : 28 : 8 : 1 due to super hyperfine splitting.

The ESR spectra of anhydrous ferric chloride ($FeCl_3$) and that of hydrated ferric chloride ($FeCl_3.6H_2O$) are different. This indicates that the bonds to the Fe atoms are different in these two salts. Anhydrous ferric chloride is a simple compound whereas its hydrated salt is a coordination compound.

15.4.6.1 Identification of Oxidation States

A metal such as Cu, can be present in different oxidation states when bonded to natural molecules in living cells. This can be ascertained by the ESR spectra of complex molecules.

- The metal, bonded to protein molecules is found to be divalent while in certain active enzyme–copper complexes it is monovalent as revealed by ESR spectra.

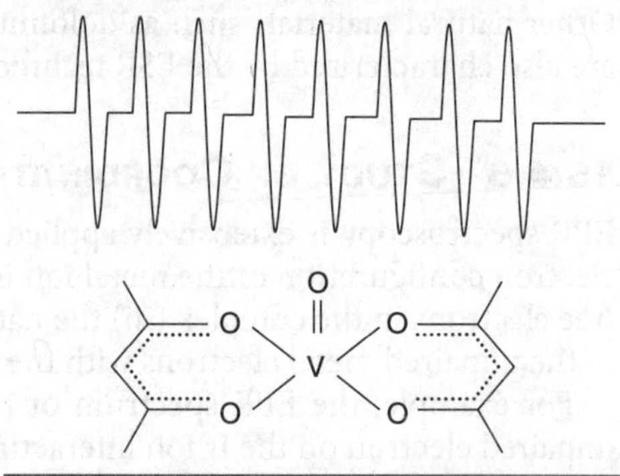

Fig. 15.6 The EPR spectrum of $VO(acac)_2$

15.4.6.2 $VO(acac)_2$

The spectrum of vanadyl acetylacetonate consists of eight lines of equal intensity (Fig. 15.6).

For V, $I = \frac{7}{2}$; therefore, $(2I+1) = \left(2 \times \frac{7}{2} + 1\right) = 8$

EPR spectroscopy has been extensively applied in the study of biologically important transition metal complexes. The nuclear spins and EPR hyperfine patterns of some bio-transition metals are given in Table 15.2.

Table 15.2 EPR hyperfine patterns for some bio-transition metals

Metal ion	Isotope *A*	Spin	Splitting (lines)
Fe (III)	54	0	1
Co (II)	59	7/2	8
Ni (II)	58	0	1
Cu (II)	63	3/2	4
V (IV)	51	7/2	8
Mn (II)	55	5/2	6

15.4.7 Study of Rapid Electron Exchange Reactions

Certain reactions involving electron exchange are very rapid. Their kinetics and mechanisms cannot be studied by the conventional methods. In some such cases, EPR spectroscopy can be used. Electron exchange reactions occur between metal complexes. In such cases, EPR spectra can give information about (i) the rate of electron exchange (ii) changes in electron configurations in the complexes and also (iii) the mechanism of exchange. It can be used to study transient paramagnetic species generated in situ. For example, $VOCl_2\ (PEt_3)_2$ and $[Ti\ (C_6H_6)]^-$ are formed during certain electron exchange reactions. These species cannot be isolated as their existence is only transient. However, their formation, nature and life time can be known by recording their EPR spectra in the reaction mixture.

15.4.7.1 EPR Spectrum of Pyrazine Anion

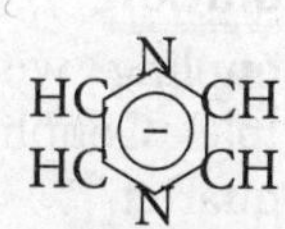

Pyrazine anion

This is an unstable anion, formed in situ at low temperatures.

The electron is delocalised over the entire ring. It couples with two equivalent nitrogens ($I = 1$).

$$\therefore \quad 2NI + 1 = [2(2)(1)] + 1 = 5$$

This should form a spectrum consisting of a quintet. But further coupling occurs with four equivalent hydrogens ($I = 1/2$).

$$\therefore \quad 2N + 1 = \left(2 \times 4 \times \frac{1}{2}\right) + 1 = 5$$

Therefore, the actual spectrum is a quintet of quintets with intensity ratio 1 : 4 : 6 : 4 : 1.

15.4.8 Study of Organic Free Radicals

Organic free radicals can be characterised by their EPR spectra. A free radical has a characteristic spectrum revealing its identity. Such radicals are formed and studied in situ at low temperatures. Commonly they are formed in electrolytic and radiochemical reactions.

15.4.8.1 The EPR Spectrum of the Methyl Radical $\bullet CH_3$

The methyl radical is a one-electron system. This spin-free electron interacts with three equivalent protons. The energy levels in the presence of the applied magnetic field is shown

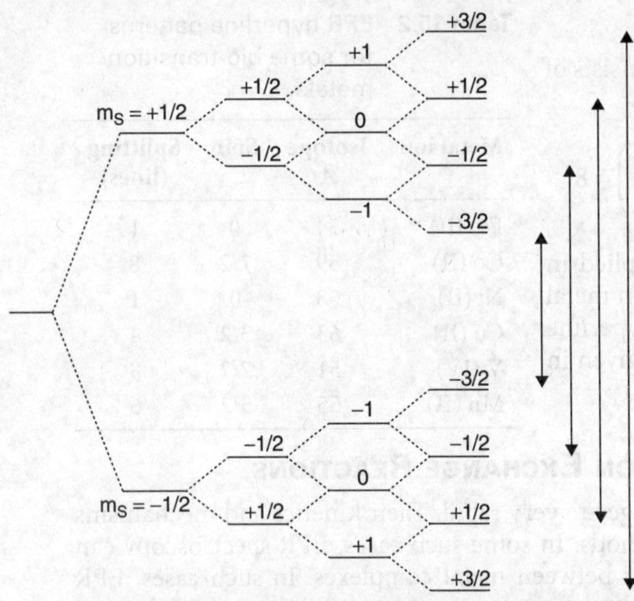

Fig. 15.7(a) EPR hyperfine splitting for the methyl radical

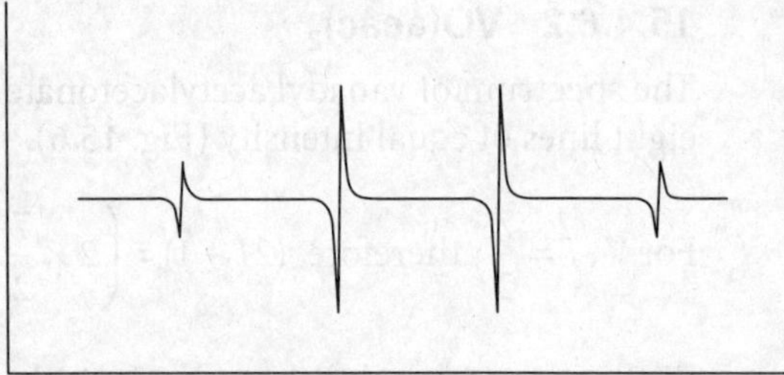

Fig. 15.7(b) The EPR spectrum of the methyl radical

in Fig. 15.7a. Applying the selection rule, four transitions are possible. These transitions produce a quartet spectrum for the radical (Fig. 15.7b).

The methyl radical is a one-electron species. Its signal is split into $(2NI + 1) = (2 \times 3 \times ½) + 1 = 4$ signals (quartet) (Fig. 15.7b). The intensity ratio is 1:3:3:1.

Problem 15.2 Predict the EPR spectrum of the $CH_3–CH_2^{\bullet}$ radical.

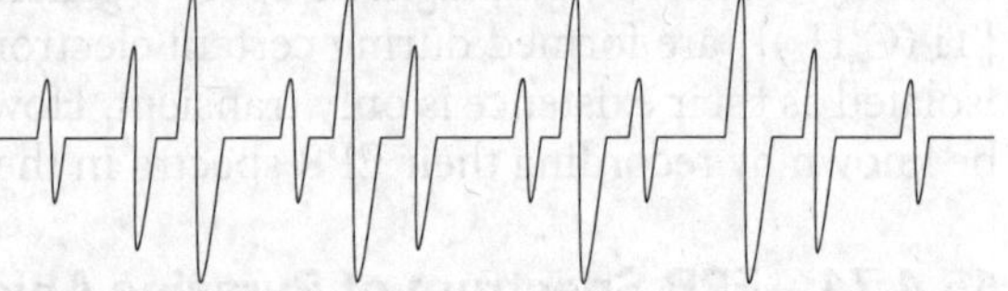

Fig. 15.8 The ESR spectrum of the ethyl radical

Solution

Coupling with CH_2 should produce a triplet. Coupling with CH_3 should produce a quartet.

If $^aCH_2 > {}^aCH_3$, the spectrum would be a triplet of quartets (12 lines).

If $^aCH_2 < {}^aCH_3$, the spectrum would be a quartet of triplets (12 lines)

Actually $^aCH_3 = 2.69$ mT and $^aCH_2 = 2.24$ mT; thus a $^aCH_2 < {}^aCH_3$

Therefore, the actual spectrum is a quartet of triplets.

15.4.8.2 The EPR Spectrum of the Benzene Radical Anion

In $[C_6H_6\bullet]^-$, the spin-free electron is delocalised over all six carbon atoms. Therefore, it is coupled with six equivalent H nuclei. This would result in seven spectral lines. The relative line intensities would be 1 : 6 : 15 : 20 : 15 : 6 : 1 (Fig. 15.9).

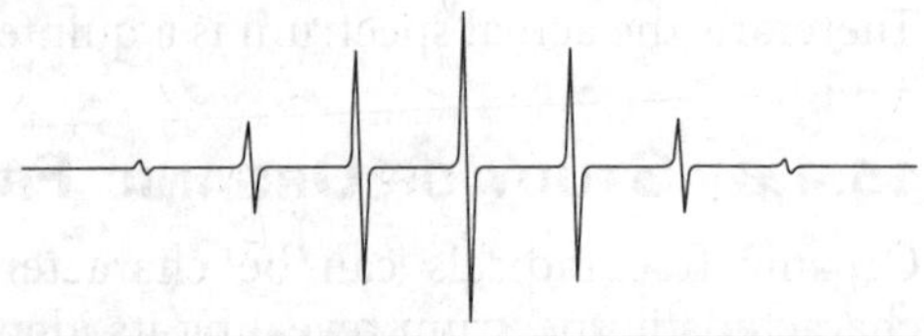

Fig. 15.9 The EPR spectrum of $C_6H_6^{-\bullet}$

The interaction between a hydrogen atom and an unpaired electron is maximum when the carbon–hydrogen bond and orbital are coplanar. The hyperfine splitting by hydrogen is important only at the 1- or 2-position in an alkyl radical:

$$\underset{4}{—CH_2}—\underset{3}{CH_2}—\underset{2}{CH_2}—\underset{1}{\dot{C}H}—R$$

However, the hyperfine splitting by the β-hydrogens in acyclic systems is very weak. Hyperfine splitting by the β-hydrogens is significant in rigid cyclic molecules. When the spin-free electron is proximate to a system of double bonds as in methylbenzene, the double bond character is partially transferred to the single bond and the hyperfine coupling constants become high. Some values of hyperfine splitting constants are given in Table. 15.3.

Table 15.3 Some hyperfine coupling (splitting) constants

Species	Hyperfine splitting constants (gauss)
$H_2\dot{C}{-}H$	23
$H\dot{C}{-}H$	15
$CH_3{-}\dot{C}{-}H$	27, 22
$(CH_3)_3\dot{C}$	23
$H_2C{=}\dot{C}{-}H$	13
$O{=}\dot{C}H$	137
$\bullet CH_2OH$	19
$CH_3\dot{C}HOH$	22
Naphthalene radical anion (positions 1, 2)	(1)5.0 (2)1.9

Table 15.3 Continued

Species	Hyperfine splitting constants (gauss)
Benzene radical anion $[C_6H_6]^-$	3.8
Toluene radical anion (CH_3)	$CH_3 : 0.8$ $o{-}H : 5.1$ $m{-}H : 4.3$ $p{-}H : 0.6$
$[NO_2(a)\text{–}C_6H_4\text{(b, c)}\text{–}N(d)H\,H(e)]^-$	(a) 12 (b) 3 (c) 1 (d) 1 (e) 1

15.4.9 Study of Reaction Mechanisms

Reactions which occur through free radicals may be studied by EPR spectroscopy. For example, the mechanism of the polymerisation of peroxide-initiated acrylic acid has been established by the EPR method. Employing a *flow-system* for the polymerisation, the formation, identification and destruction of free radical intermediates in the reaction have been done by recording the EPR spectra of the reaction mixture. Each free radical in the mixture has a unique spectrum and therefore it can be fingerprinted. Such a study establishes the following mechanism for this polymerisation:

$$\underset{\text{Peroxide}}{-O{-}OH} \longrightarrow \bullet OH$$

$$\bullet OH + CH_2{=}C(H)(COOH) \longrightarrow$$

$$\underset{\text{Initial radical}}{HOCH_2{-}\dot{C}(H)(COOH)} \xrightarrow{CH_2{=}C(H)(COOH)}$$

$$HOCH_2-CH(COOH)-CH_2-\dot{C}(H)(COOH) \xrightarrow[\text{acid molecules}]{\text{More acrylic}}$$

Propagating radical

$$HO\,[CH_2\,CH\,COOH]_n\,CH_2-\dot{C}(H)(COOH) \xrightarrow{\text{A radical}} \text{Polymer}$$

(i) The •OH from the peroxide initiates the formation of the initial organic radical.
(ii) The initial organic radical reacts with a monomer molecule to form a propagating radical.
(iii) The propagating radical reacts with more number of monomer molecules promoting polymerisation.
(iv) When a long polymeric radical is formed, it traps a free radical to form the final polymer molecule; the polymer formation stops at this stage.
(v) Two propagating radicals may react, terminating the polymerisation.

The reaction mixture has the following EPR spectral features:

(i) A spectrum identifying the •OH radical.
(ii) A hyperfine spectrum identifying the initial radical. This spectrum consists of a pair of overlapping triplets (originating from $>\dot{C}H$ unit interacting with the two equivalent methylene protons).
(iii) Another spectrum characteristic of the propagating radical has also been observed.
(iv) Though both the spectra (ii) and (iii) pertain to the site, $>\dot{C}H$, their splitting constants differ; this is obviously due to different lengths of the initial radical and the propagating radical.
(v) The intensities of these two spectra decrease with the progress of polymerisation because the quantities of the two types of radicals decrease due to their reactions forming the polymeric molecule.

15.4.10 Proteins

Heme and non-heme iron proteins have high-spin ferrous ions in their structures. The EPR spectra of these molecules have proved the integer spin state of the metal ions. The mononuclear ferrous sites of myoglobin and transferrin, and the polynuclear ferrous sites of ferredoxin II and aconitase have all been well-characterised by their EPR spectra.

EPR is performed on proteins carrying paramagnetic ions (cofactors), such as Mn^{2+}, Fe^{3+} and Cu^{2+} attached to the protein/enzyme structure. The site of attachment, the role of the ion in the biological process, the changes the ion undergoes during cell reactions can all be understood by EPR spectroscopy. Enzymatic reactions involving *nitrogenase, tyrosinase* and so on, have been studied with EPR data.

Site-directed spin labelling (SDSL) is a method for studying the structure and local dynamics of proteins using ESR. It is based on the specific reaction of spin labelled amino acids.

A spin label can provide the details about the biological changes undergone by a protein. This method is useful for studying macromolecules, such as proteins, enzymes and synthetic polymers.

15.4.11 EPR Spectroscopy and Spin Labelling

Biological cell processes involve complex multiple steps. Obtaining precise information on such processes is difficult. Spin labelling is a method of attaching a free radical to a particular site of a biological reactant to monitor the status of the labelled reactant by its ESR spectrum during the cell's bioprocesses. The ESR data are used to derive insight into the physical and chemical characteristics of the biomolecules in the neighborhood of the labelled site.

An example of a spin label is the NO group containing a spin-free electron. Stable molecules containing NO can be synthesised and studied by the EPR spectroscopy. One such molecule is 2,2,6,6-tetramethyl-4-piperadone-l-oxyl; its EPR spectrum has a 3-line hyperfine spectrum. This can be explained based on the interaction of the NO electron with the nuclear spin of the nitrogen atom ($I = 1$).

O
H_3C CH_3
H_3C N CH_3
O·

15.4.12 Structural Investigation

EPR spectroscopy is not suited for determining molecular structures, because it provides information only about the electron distribution and electron–electron interaction in a molecule. However, in a few cases, the method can provide details on molecular symmetry by comparative interpretation of the EPR data. This spectroscopy is useful for obtaining information about the structure, geometry and molecular symmetry of some transition metal complexes.

15.5 ADVANTAGES OF EPR SPECTROSCOPY

- It is a non-destructive method.
- It is a direct and useful method of investigating the properties of species with unpaired electrons.
- The sample needed for recording the spectrum can be prepared by a simple procedure.
- EPR is highly sensitive to the local electronic structure, oxidation state and the proximity of magnetic nucleus to the site carrying the unpaired electron.
- A wide variety of samples, from simple organic and inorganic compounds to complex biomolecules such as proteins can be analysed by this spectroscopy.
- It has high sample-specificity.
- Hyperfine interactions can provide information about the sample, such as the number of atoms, and as well as the identity of atoms in a molecule. They can provide the distances of atoms from the unpaired electron in the molecule.

15.6 COMPARISON BETWEEN EPR AND NMR

- EPR spectra are recorded using microwaves (3–400 GHz), whereas NMR spectra involve radiofrequency (300–1000 MHz).
- In EPR, the frequency is kept constant, while the magnetic field is varied. The reverse procedure is used in NMR; the magnetic field is kept constant while the radiofrequency is varied.
- The relaxation times of electron spins are very low, unlike those of nuclear spins. Therefore, EPR spectroscopy, unlike NMR spectroscopy, is performed at low temperatures (less than 10 K).
- EPR spectroscopy is about 1000 times more sensitive than NMR spectroscopy because of the higher frequency of electromagnetic radiation used in EPR in comparison to NMR.
- EPR spectroscopy originates from the interactions between the unpaired electrons and the applied external magnetic field. NMR spectroscopy originates from interactions among the magnetic fields of individual atoms.

- NMR spectroscopy does not usually provide useful information on paramagnetic substances, but the EPR spectra of such substances provide additional information. The EPR coupling patterns provide information about the number and type of nuclei coupled to the electrons. The values of *a* can be used to understand the extent of delocalisation of the electrons; the *g* factors can confirm whether the unpaired electrons in a complex species originate from the metal atoms or the bonded ligands.
- EPR is a versatile method applicable to transition metal ions and complexes, organic free radicals, cations and anions, triplet states, conduction electrons in metals and crystals.
- It complements information obtained by NMR spectroscopy.
- It provides information of hyperfine interactions; of number and type of nuclei coupled to the electrons.
- It indicates the extent to which the unpaired electrons are delocalised in the molecular structure.
- EPR is extensively used in the study of structure of transition metal complexes and also geometries (locations) of defects in crystals.
- The application of EPR spectroscopy is restricted to species with spin-free electrons. Not many such species are stable. Short-lived species with spin-free electrons may be generated in reactions and they have to be stabilised at very low temperatures, before recording their spectra.
- EPR spectra are highly dependent on the local electronic structure, oxidation state of atoms and the proximity of magnetic nuclei to the other magnetic atoms.

EXERCISES

1. Predict the main features of the EPR spectrum of di-μ-oxo Mn(III /IV)-phenanthroline.
2. When an EPR spectrometer uses an 8-mm microwave radiation (Q band), what magnetic field is required to satisfy the resonance condition?
3. A radical anion has $g = 2.0011$. At what field will resonance be noticed in a spectrometer operating at 10.0 GHz?
4. Predict the number of absorption lines in the ESR spectrum of
   (a) $[\dot{O}C_6H_4O]^-$
   (b) Vanadium
   (c) Pyrazine radical $C_4N_2H_4^-$
5. Interpret the following EPR spectrum obtained for aqueous Mn^{2+} solution:

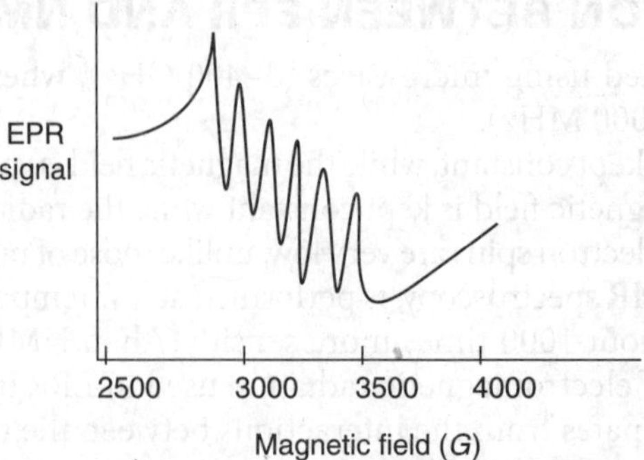

6. $Cu^{2+}(I = 3/2)$ has one unpaired electron. When it is coordinated by one nitrogen atom ($I = 1$) and one OH ($I = 1/2$) group, how many lines are expected in its EPR spectrum?

7. Predict the EPR spectrum of 2, 2, 6, 6-tetramethyl-1-1-piperidinyloxyl (TEMPO).

8. Predict the number of lines in the ESR spectrum of
(a) $[CCl_2H]^\bullet$ (b) $[CCl_2D]^\bullet$

16 Mass Spectrometry

16.1 INTRODUCTION

Mass spectrometry is used to identify a molecule by the analysis of positive ions produced by electron bombardment of the molecule. The masses of the positive ions are recorded in the mass spectrometer. By considering the combination of these ions, as in a jig-saw puzzle, the original molecule is reconstructed.

In the case of a mixture of elements, or a mixture of isotopes of an element, cations of the atoms are formed. These are separated and their masses determined.

- *Atomic mass spectrometry* is the mass spectral analysis of elements.
- *Molecular mass spectrometry* is the mass spectral analysis of molecules—organic, biological and inorganic.

On bombarding a molecule with electrons, mostly, singly-charged positive ions are produced. These ions are separated on the basis of their mass-to-charge ratio and then identified. This technique is predominantly applied to organic molecules. The molecular weight can be obtained by mass spectrometry with very high accuracy. From this value, the exact molecular formula can be deduced. In addition, definite fragments/groups within the molecule can be identified.

16.2 MASS SPECTROMETER

16.2.1 PRINCIPLE

A mass spectrometer is a device in which a substance is bombarded with an electron-beam of energy of about 70 eV. The positive ion fragments that are produced get separated on passing through an electric and magnetic field in vacuum, and their masses are recorded as a spectrum. The energy used for the bombardment is sufficient to break all the bonds in the molecule. This record of ion-masses versus their relative abundance is called the *mass spectrum*.

When a charged particle moves in a suitably oriented magnetic field, the radius of curvature of the path of the ion is decided by its mass. Therefore, ions of different masses will move in different paths in the magnetic field and thus get separated (Fig. 16.1).

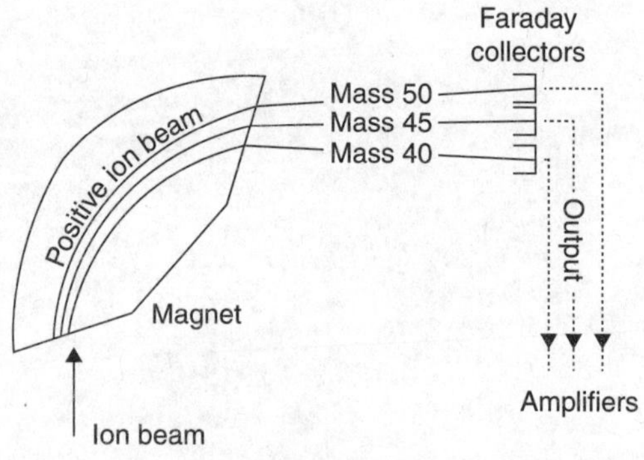

Fig. 16.1 Effect of magnetic field on ions of different masses

16.2.2 Aston's Mass Spectrograph

One of the early models of the mass spectrograph was devised by Aston in 1919. This device was an improvement of Thomson's positive ray apparatus. In Thomson's apparatus, positive ions were deflected in planes at right angles by the applied electric and magnetic fields; but in Aston's apparatus, the deflections were in the same plane but in opposite directions (Fig. 16.2). The positive ions pass through two narrow slits S_1 and S_2. This produces a thin beam. This beam of mixture of ions is spread by the electric field applied across the plates P_1 and P_2. A portion of the beam escapes through a small aperture in S_3 and passes between the poles of a large electromagnet.

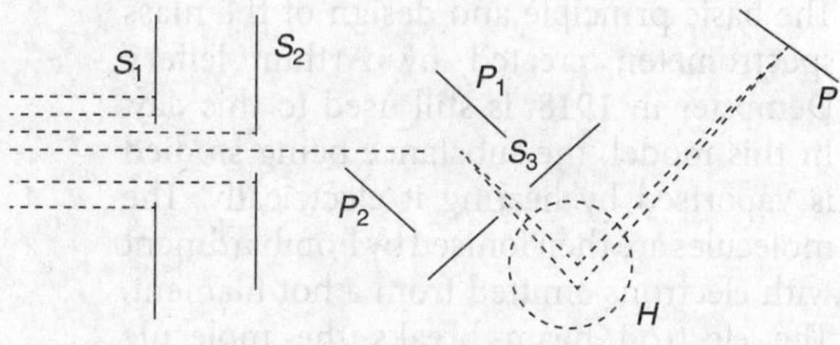

Fig. 16.2 Aston's mass spectrograph

The magnetic field (*H*) is so arranged that it bends the rays in the opposite direction to that of the electric field, but in the same plane. The beam is then brought to a focus on a photographic plate *P*. A sharp line is produced on this plate for each type of ion. Development of the plate would show a series of lines called the mass spectrum. Each line in the spectrum corresponds to ions of a particular *m*/*e* value. By altering the strengths of the deflecting fields, the range of the spectrum can be varied and particular masses can be studied. Figure 16.3 represents the mass spectrum of boron recorded by Aston's mass spectrograph; (a) represents the spectrum when a photographic plate is used and (b) that when ion-current is measured. Natural boron has 19.6% of B^{10} and 80.4% of B^{11}, and therefore the intensities of the spectral lines for these two isotopes are in the ratio 1:4.

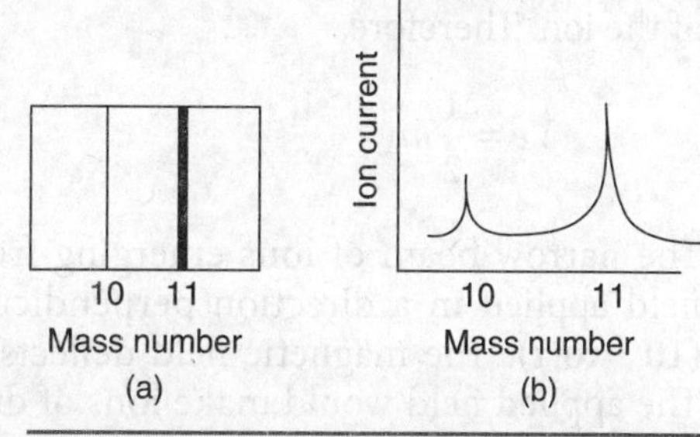

Fig. 16.3 The mass spectrum of boron

F W Aston

Francis William Aston (1877–1945), a British chemist and physicist, was given the 1922 Nobel Prize in chemistry for his work in mass spectrometry. He devised the first mass spectrograph and demonstrated how isotopes could be efficiently separated. He enunciated the *whole-number rule*. According to this rule, 'the mass of the oxygen isotope being defined as 16, all the other isotopes have masses that are very nearly whole numbers'. This rule helped development of theories of nuclear energy. Aston, in 1936 itself, predicted the tapping of enormous energy from the atomic nucleus. He was an avid mountaineer, a cyclist and motor racer. He played the piano, violin and cello with professional finesse.

16.2.3 Dempster's Mass Spectrometer

The basic principle and design of the mass spectrometer, created by Arthur Jeffery Dempster in 1918, is still used to this day. In this model, the substance being studied is vaporised by heating it electrically. The molecules are then ionised by bombardment with electrons emitted from a hot filament. The electron beam breaks the molecule producing positive ions. These ions are then accelerated by applying a variable electric field between P_1 and P_2 (Fig. 16.4). The accelerated ions are made to emerge through a slit S_1 and these emerging ions have the same energy. If V is the potential difference of the applied electric field, a positive ion carrying a charge e will acquire energy Ve in passing between P_1 and P_2. This energy is kinetic in nature and equivalent to ½ mv^2 where m is the mass and v is the velocity of the ion. Therefore,

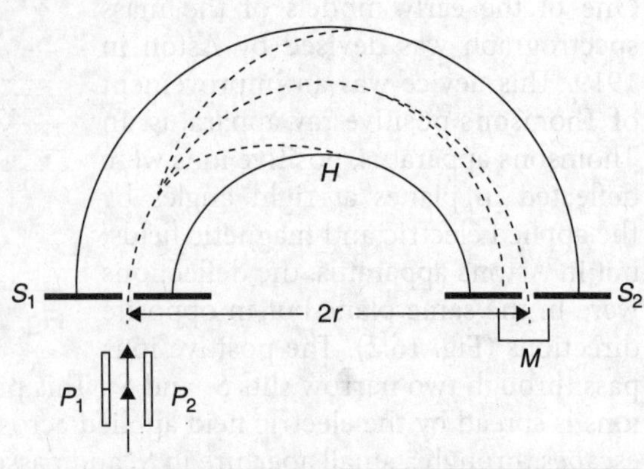

Fig. 16.4 Dempster's mass spectrometer

$$Ve = \frac{1}{2}mv^2 \tag{16.1}$$

The narrow beam of ions emerging from the slit is then exposed to a constant magnetic field applied in a direction perpendicular to the plane of the diagram in a vacuum tube (10^{-7} torr). The magnetic field deflects the ion and makes it traverse a semicircular path. The applied field would make ions of different masses traverse different semicircular paths. Thus the ions are spread out into beams of different curvatures and separated. The slit S_2 being very narrow will allow only ions of suitable mass (describing a particular path) to pass through it. Such ions fall on the plate M, which is connected to a meter for measuring ion-current. The ion-current produced can be recorded as a line on a graph sheet using an electronic instrument.

When a charged particle moves in a suitably oriented magnetic field (H), the radius of curvature (r) of the path of the ion is related to the charge (e), mass (m), velocity (v) of the ion and is given by the equation.

$$\frac{e}{m} = \frac{v}{Hr} \tag{16.2}$$

Combining Eqs 16.1 and 16.2 and eliminating v,

$$\frac{m}{e} = \frac{H^2 r^2}{2V} \tag{16.3}$$

Only those ions moving in a path of definite radius r can pass through the slit S_2 and get recorded. Equation 16.3 indicates that V and H would decide which particle of suitable m/e would pass through S_2. If V and H are kept constant, only ions of a particular m/e having a path radius of r can enter S_2. When H or V is changed, another beam of ions of different m/e would be able to pass through S_2. By this technique, ions can be separated and identified.

16.2.4 The Components of a Mass Spectrometer

Sample handling system, ionisation chamber, acceleration chamber, analysis tubes and magnet, ion collector, amplifier and recorder are the major components of a mass spectrometer. In the *sample handling system,* a small amount of the compound is vaporised and then pumped into the ionisation chamber where the gas molecules are bombarded at right angles by electrons. The ions produced get accelerated in the same chamber. The *analyser tube* is an evacuated, curved (180°) metal tube through which the ion beam passes to the collector. The magnetic pole pieces are mounted perpendicular to the plane of the diagram to give a stable uniform magnetic field as ions are accelerated.

The *ion collector* has collimating slits to collect the ions. These ions are then made to impinge on the collector to produce a signal which is amplified by a vacuum tube.

The recorder is a galvanometer assembly. This can be connected to an electronic unit, which can record the signals as a series of peaks or lines on a pen chart. In a typical instrument, the angle of deflection (60°, 90°, 180°) and hence the radius are fixed for a given analyser tube so that H or V must be varied to focus the ions of varying m/e on the detector. Increasing the accelerating voltage focusses successively lighter ions on the detector. Increasing the magnetic field focusses successively heavier ions on the detector.

16.2.5 Inductively Coupled Plasma (ICP) Source

ICP sources are used for cation analysis in modern mass spectrometers. In this ion source technology, a 'flame' of plasma is used to atomise the sample molecules and also to ionise the atoms in these molecules. The plasma is produced from argon gas, since the first ionisation energy for argon is higher than the first ionisation energy of any other element (except He, O, F, Ne), but lower than the second ionisation energy of all except the most electropositive metals. The heating is carried out by a radiofrequency current passed through a coil surrounding the plasma.

Ion Source Technologies

The positive ions of the analyte molecules may be produced by different methods:

- Electron ionisation
- Chemical ionisation
- Electrospray ionisation
- Matrix-assisted laser ionisation
- Plasma-assisted ionisation
- Glow discharge ionisation
- Spark ionisation
- Thermal ionisation

What happens to a molecule when it is bombarded with electrons? Initially a positively charged ion is formed by the loss of an electron from the molecule.

$$M + e^- \rightarrow M^{\bullet+} + 2e^-$$

$M^{\bullet+}$ is called the *molecular ion* or *parent ion.* The molecular ion is produced by the removal of an electron from an electron pair. Therefore it is not a mere cation but a free radical–cation and is represented with a positive sign and a dot. The parent ion can further break into smaller ions *called fragment ions.* The resulting array of deflected ions is called the fragmentation pattern.

$$\text{(Parent ion) } M^{\bullet+} \rightarrow m_1^+, m_2^+, m_3^+, \ldots$$

The function of a mass spectrometer is to separate these ions and estimate the relative abundance and mass of each constituent ion. Several smaller or bigger ions may be produced depending on the size and nature of the original molecule. These ions are separated by deflection in a variable magnetic field according to their masses and charges. They generate a current called the ion-current at the collector. The ion-current is proportional to the relative abundance. A *plot of relative abundance against m/e* is called *the mass spectrum.* Since most ions have unit positive charge, *m/e* is often equivalent to *m*. Neutral molecules and free radicals, which may also be formed on electron bombardment, cannot be detected in the spectrometer. Corresponding to *all* the ions of a particular *m/e*, a line or a peak is obtained. The intensity of the peak is proportional to the concentration of the ion responsible for that particular peak.

In the mass spectrum, the masses of the positively charged fragments (including the parent ion) *versus* their relative concentrations are recorded. The most intense peak in the spectrum, called the *base peak,* is assigned an intensity value of 100%, and the intensities of the other peaks including the parent peak are reported as percentages of the base peak. The parent peak, of course, could be the base peak as it happens many a time.

16.2.6 Double-Focussing Mass Spectrometer

In the working of the magnetic analyser, it is assumed that all the ions of the same *m/e* have the same energy. In reality, this is not true, creating problems for accurate focussing. In the modern *double-focussing instrument,* magnetic analysis is preceded by an electrostatic analysis to ensure that all the ions of same *m/e* have the same energy or speed. This aids in accurate focussing at the collector plates. Ions, whose masses differ by as little as a few ppm, can be separated in a high resolution double-focussing spectrometer. A O Nier, in 1940, designed a mass spectrometer based on this principle of double-focussing.

A O Nier (1911–94)

Alred Otto Carl Nier was an American Physicist who pioneered the development of mass spectrometry. U-235 was separated from its natural ore using a mass spectrometer by Nier for the first time. Even the current MS instruments use the instrumental configuration developed by Nier, now called the Nier–Johnson geometry. His poor and unlettered parents were German immigrants. He joined the University of Minnesota mainly due to the determination of his parents to give him a good education. He became a top-ranking physicist.

The three molecules, C_6H_{12}, C_5H_8O and $C_4H_8N_2$ all have the same nominal mass (84.0 u); however, these can be distinguished using a double-focussing high-resolution mass spectrometer that easily identifies mass values accurately to four decimal places.

Formula:	C_6H_{12}	C_5H_8O	$C_4H_8N_2$
Mass:	84.0939	84.0575	84.0688

16.2.7 Time-of-flight Mass Spectrometer

Positive ion analysers, without depending on a magnetic field, have been used in modern mass spectrometers. This type of instrument is based on the fact that after acceleration, ions of different masses have the same energy and therefore different velocities. A pulse of electrons is passed in cycles (0.25 microseconds) instead of continuously, to ionise the molecules. The ions formed are accelerated and then passed through a tube to the detector without applying a magnetic field. Ions having different speeds reach the detector at different times. The detector signals the arrival of each group of ions separately and these signals can be recorded on a chart or seen on a screen. This type of a mass spectrometer is called a time-of-flight mass spectrometer. The advantages of this technique are:

- very low concentration, as low as 10^{-12} g of a substance is sufficient, and
- a substance in the gas, liquid or solid form can be used.

The disadvantages of all types of mass spectrometry are:

- The destruction of the sample during analysis.
- The high cost of the instrument.
- A mass spectrometer cannot distinguish between geometric isomers of a compound. For example both *cis-* and *trans*-1,2–dichloroethene give identical mass spectra. Similarly it cannot distinguish between optical isomers. Likewise, the *ortho-*, *meta-* and *para*-isomers of an aromatic compound cannot be distinguished by their mass spectra.
- The analysis requires highly pure compounds. Non-volatile compounds are not suitable for analysis. Mass spectrometry does not directly give structural information.

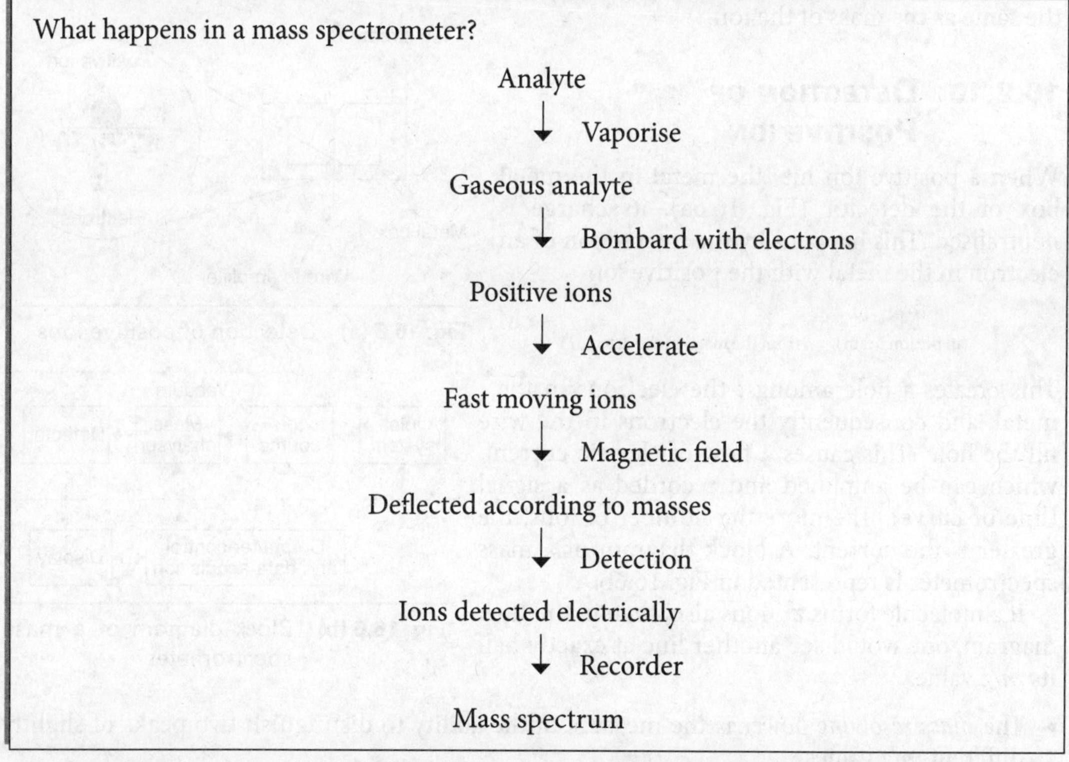

The need for vacuum The ions produced in the ionisation chamber have a free run (remain unchanged) through the machine without hitting air molecules only in vacuum.

The air-free environment in the path of the fragmented ions causes the noise due to other volatile compounds in air to be reduced. Vacuum increases the sensitivity of the instrument.

16.2.8 Acceleration

The ionisation chamber is highly positive; therefore, the positive ions formed are repelled from it. The ions are made to pass through three slits (Fig. 16.5). The slit 3 is at 0 volt; the slit 2 is kept at some intermediate voltage. The positive ions come out of slit 3 as a finely focussed beam.

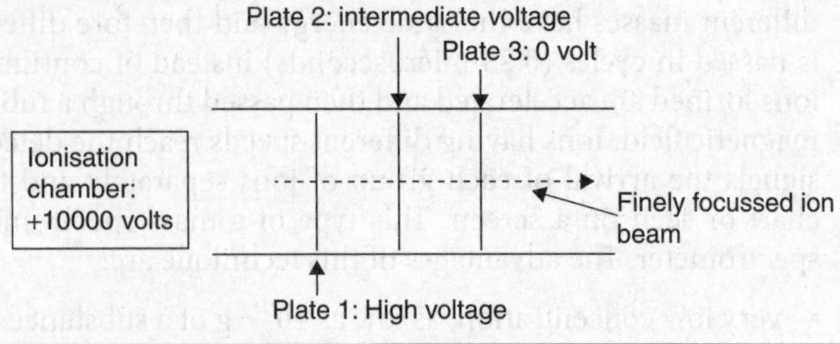

Fig. 16.5 Acceleration of positive ions

16.2.9 Deflection

Mass Lower the mass of the ion (lighter), more is the deflection.

Charge Higher the charge, more is the deflection.

These two factors of deflection are combined into the mass/charge ratio (m/z or m/e). For example, if an ion has a mass of 40 and a charge of +1, its $m/z = 40$. Another ion of mass 60 and charge +1 has an m/z value of 60. Then, the first ion will be deflected more than the second ion. As most of the ions formed in a mass spectrometer have a charge of +1 each, m/z ratio will be the same as the mass of the ion.

16.2.10 Detection of Positive Ion

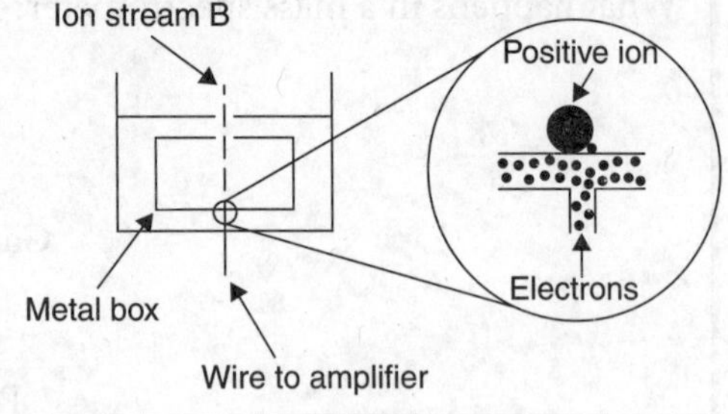

Fig. 16.6 (a) Detection of positive ions

When a positive ion hits the metal in the metal box of the detector (Fig. 16.6a), its charge is neutralised. This happens by the interaction of an electron in the metal with the positive ion.

$$\underset{\text{(in the ion beam)}}{M^+} + \underset{\text{(from the metal in the detector)}}{e^-} \rightarrow M$$

This creates a hole amongst the electrons in the metal, and consequently the electrons in the wire fill the hole. This causes a flow of electric current, which can be amplified and recorded as a signal (line or curve). The more the number of ions, the greater is the current. A block diagram of a mass spectrometer is represented in Fig. 16.6b.

If a molecule forms z^{2+} ions also, then in the stick diagram, one would see another line at exactly half its m/z value.

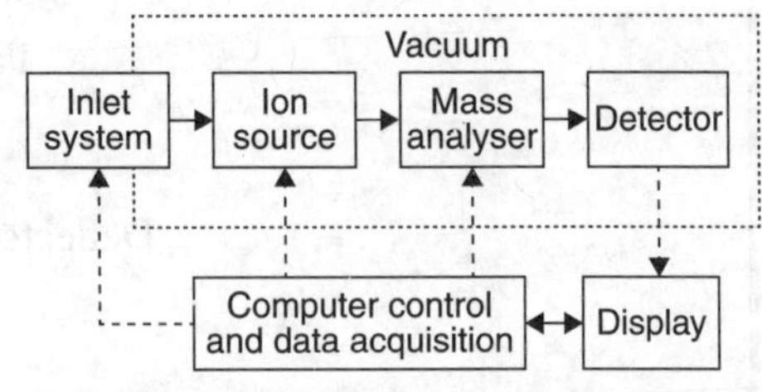

Fig. 16.6 (b) Block diagram of a mass spectrometer

- The *mass resolving power* is the measure of the ability to distinguish two peaks of slightly different m/z values.
- The *mass accuracy* is the ratio of the m/z measurement error to the true m/z. It is expressed in ppm.
- The *mass range* is the range of m/z that can be measured by a mass spectrometer.

- The *linear dynamic range* is the range over which an ion signal is linear with analyte concentration.
- The *speed* is the time frame of the experiment for one mass spectral analysis.

16.3 THE MASS SPECTRUM

The parent ion disintegrates in 10^{-10}–10^{-8} seconds to give smaller ions. A number of fragment ions are thus formed, and each of these can break into smaller fragments. In some of the techniques such as electron inonisation, smaller fragments may rearrange or collide in different combinations. A few of the parent ions may remain intact to reach the detector and get recorded as a peak. From this, the molecular weight of the compound can be obtained. A mass spectrum is a presentation of the positive ions produced versus their relative concentrations. The molecular peak is identified by reducing the ionising voltage (energy of electron beam) to 10–15 eV, at which energy further fragmentation of the molecular ion is avoided. This reduces the intensities of other peaks and the molecular peak stands out.

16.3.1 Line Diagram

The line diagram is a style of depicting the mass spectrum. It shows ion-intensities as a series of vertical lines (Fig. 16.7). The important peaks have *m*/*e* values written at the top.

16.3.1.1 Types of Ions

When a molecule *A* is bombarded with an electron beam of moderate energy, the following primary processes are possible.

$$A + e^- \rightarrow A^+ + 2e^-$$

$$A + e^- \rightarrow A^{n+} + (n+1)e^-$$

$$A + e^- \rightarrow A^-$$

These will be followed by the formation of different types of ions.

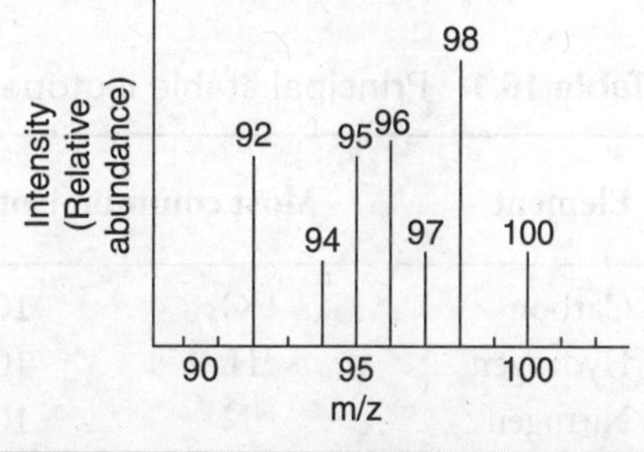

Fig. 16.7 Mass spectrum of natural molybdenum (line diagram)

Parent ion This is an ion produced by the removal of an electron from the original molecule. For example,

$$CH_3CH_2OH \rightarrow [CH_3CH_2OH]^{+\bullet} + e^-$$

The parent ion is also called the *molecular ion.* This is an important ion since its *m*/*e* value gives the molecular weight of the analyte from which its molecular formula can be inferred. Highly reactive compounds do not form a stable parent peak. Even if it is present, its intensity is weak. This is because the bonds are readily broken in the parent ion giving fragment ions. Compounds which are thermodynamically stable, for example, benzene, are more likely to form an intense parent peak than those that are unstable, such as, $(CH_3)_3COH$. The ion of highest mass may not be the parent ion. Isotopic ions will have *m*/*e* greater than the parent ion.

- The *parent peak* is the peak of highest mass number except for the *isotope peaks.*
- The *base peak* is the peak of highest intensity.

Fragment ions These are the ions produced by bond breakages in the parent ion or molecule. The number of fragment ions produced from a molecule depends on the size and nature of the molecule. As many as even a hundred fragment ions may be produced from a large molecule.

Rearrangement ions These ions may be produced from some molecules by bond breakage accompanied by transfer of hydrogen atoms or groups like alkyl, aryl, and so on. For example,

$$[(CH_3)_2CHCH_2]^{+\bullet} \rightarrow CH_3CH_2^+ + \bullet C_2H_5$$

Thus, in the mass spectrum of *iso*-butane, a strong peak appears at *m/e* 29 due to $CH_3CH_2^+$, which is not expected without rearrangement.

Isotope ions Carbon has one part of ^{13}C out of 100 parts. Therefore the ion CH_3^+, for example, will show a peak at *m/e* 16 in addition to the normal peak at *m/e* 15. Similarly for ^{15}N, ^{17}O, ^{18}O, ^{2}H, and so on, weak additional or *satellite peaks* are obtained for ions containing these atoms. Usually the peak with the highest intensity at the high mass region of the spectrum corresponds to the molecular peak. This peak is always accompanied by satellite peaks at M + 1 and M + 2 because of the presence of isotopes of chemical elements. Each of C, N and H, has a principal heavier isotope of one mass unit greater than the most common isotope. Therefore, the presence of these elements (Table 16.1) in a compound will give rise to a small isotopic peak $(M + 1)^+$, one unit greater than the molecular ion. For oxygen, sulphur, chlorine and bromine, the principal heavier isotope is two mass units greater than the most common isotope. Hence, the presence of any of these elements in a compound gives a peak at $(M + 2)^+$.

$(M + 1)^+$ elements: C, H, N

$(M + 2)^+$ elements: O, S, Cl, Br

Table 16.1 Principal stable isotopes of common elements

Element	Most common isotope		Natural abundance of other isotopes (based on 100 atoms of most common isotope)	
Carbon	^{12}C	100	^{13}C	1.08
Hydrogen	^{1}H	100	^{2}H	0.016
Nitrogen	^{14}N	100	^{15}N	0.38
Oxygen	^{16}O	100	^{17}O	0.04
			^{18}O	0.20
Fluorine	^{19}F	100	–	–
Sulphur	^{32}S	100	^{33}S	0.78
			^{34}S	4.40
Chlorine	^{35}Cl	100	^{37}Cl	32.5
Bromine	^{79}Br	100	^{81}Br	98.0
Iodine	^{127}I	100	–	–

Figure 16.8 shows the mass spectrum of water. The *m/e* values of 18, 17 and 16 represent H_2O^+, OH^+, and O^+ respectively. The peak at *m/e* 19 is due to $H_2{}^{17}O^+$ and the peak at 20 is due to $H_2{}^{18}O^+$. The relative intensities of M^+ and $(M + 1)^+$ or $(M + 2)^+$ peaks depend on the abundance ratios of the isotopes in the molecule. The isotope peaks are useful for determining the molecular formula of a compound knowing the relative natural abundances of isotopes. The relative intensity of an isotope peak expected for a particular formula can be calculated. If this agrees with that observed, the molecular formula assumed is considered to be correct. For example, a peak at *m/e* 44 may represent either CO_2^+ or $C_3H_8^+$. The relative intensity of the $(M + 1)^+$ peak for CO_2^+ should be 1.12 while that for

$C_3H_8^+$ should be 3.36. By checking the intensity of the $(M+1)^+$ peak in the actual spectrum of the compound under study, the choice between CO_2^+ and $C_3H_8^+$ can be decided.

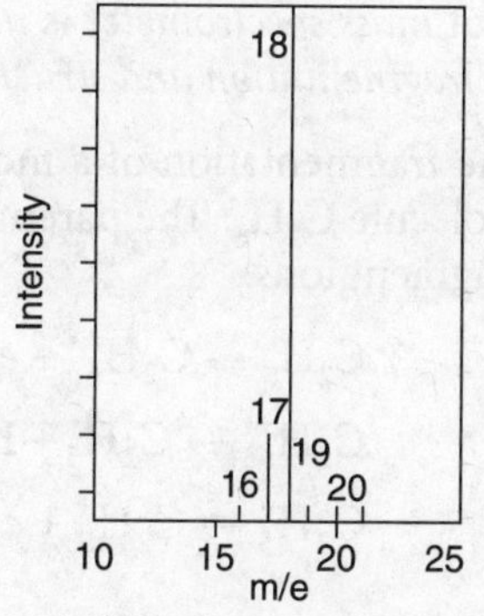

Fig. 16.8 The mass spectrum of water

Doubly-charged ions Generally, electron bombardment of a molecule produces singly-charged ions; occasionally, doubly-charged ions may be produced. Such a doubly-charged ion will show a peak at half its true mass; for example, the $^{16}O^{++}$ peak will appear at *m/e* 8. Such ions produce an abrupt change in the peak spacing in the spectrum and thus can be recognised. Multiple-charged ions are commonly formed from compounds with hetero atoms.

Metastable ions Some ions decompose during their flight in the instrument after nearly complete acceleration but before complete mass analysis. These unstable ions are called metastable ions and they usually produce broad peaks at non-integer *m/e* values. Because of the large width of their peaks, they cause no trouble in the *m/e* assignment of other ions.

Ion–molecule complex ion A fragment ion may collide with a molecule in the ionisation chamber producing an unexpected ion. This ion will have a higher *m/e* compared to the parent ion. For example,

$$CH_3OH + H^+ \rightarrow CH_3OH_2^+$$

Peaks for such complex ions are very weak. On increasing the pressure of the system, the intensity of such a peak is increased due to increased concentration of the complex ion and thus the formation of such an ion can be recognised.

Negative ions In addition to positive ions, negative ions may be produced during electron bombardment. The following are such possibilities with a molecule AB:

$AB + e^- \rightarrow AB^-$ (resonance capture)

$AB + e^- \rightarrow A\bullet + B^-$ (dissociative resonance capture)

$AB + e^- \rightarrow A^+ + B^- + e^-$ (ion-pair production)

Negative ions are not recorded by the instrument.

16.3.2 Calibration

The mass spectrum is characteristic of the compound; therefore a pure compound can be characterised by its fragmentation process. Since mass spectra are dependent on experimental conditions for reproducibility, identical conditions have to be used, preferably the same instrument. The masses of ions recorded in the mass spectrum are calculated by calibrating the spectrum. Normally, air is a component undergoing ionisation along with the substance chosen for fragmentation in a mass spectrometer. Air produces peaks at *m/e* 28 (N_2^+) and *m/e* 32 (O_2^+) with the intensity ratio 4:1. From the relative positions of other peaks with reference to these two peaks in the spectrum, the masses of the other ions can be obtained. Therefore, the presence of pairs of peaks in this low mass region separated by 4 *m/e* units and with intensity ratios of 4 (low mass):1 (high mass) is due to air in the machine. These peaks serve as starting points for identifying the masses of other peaks.

- *A mass spectrometer is useful in determining the molecular weight of a substance, its mode of fragmentation and structure.*

The fragmentation of a molecule in the mass spectrometer may be illustrated with a simple molecule C_2H_6. The parent molecular ion is formed first, which then decomposes to various fragment ions.

$$C_2H_6 \rightarrow C_2H_6^{+\bullet} + e^-$$
$$C_2H_6^{+\bullet} \rightarrow C_2H_5^{\bullet} + H^+$$
$$C_2H_5^{\bullet} \rightarrow C_2H_5^{+} + e^-$$

$$C_2H_5^{+\bullet} \rightarrow C_2H_4^{+} + H^{\bullet}$$
$$C_2H_5^{+\bullet} \rightarrow C_2H_3^{+} + 2H^{\bullet}$$
$$C_2H_5^{+\bullet} \rightarrow C_2H_2^{+} + 3H^{\bullet}$$

The mass spectrum of a compound is a *fingerprint* of that compound. For example, 2-methylpropane may break in a limited number of ways producing a characteristic fragmentation pattern. Consider, for example, *iso*-butane. Breakage of this molecule at *a*, *b* or *c* will produce the major ion fragment at *m/e* 43. Breakage at *a* and *b*, or *c* and *a*, or *c* and *b* would give a fragment at *m/e* 28.

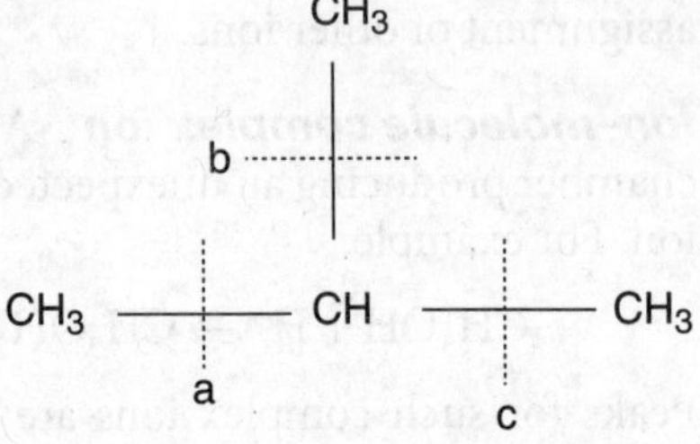

The mass spectrum of NH_3 is simple (Fig. 16.9). The possible fragmentation pattern for NH_3 is

$$\underset{m/e}{NH_3} \xrightarrow{-e^-} \underset{17}{[NH_3]^{+\bullet}} \xrightarrow{-H^\bullet} \underset{16}{[NH_2]^{+}} \xrightarrow{-H^\bullet} \underset{15}{[NH]^{+\bullet}} \xrightarrow{-H^\bullet} \underset{14}{[N^+]}$$

There are peaks at *m/e* 17, 16, 15 and 14 corresponding to the four ions represented here. In addition, there is a small peak at *m/e* 18, $(M + 1)^+$. This is due to the presence of a small amount of $^{15}NH_3$ in the sample.

Figure 16.10 is the mass spectrum of CH_4. The peaks at *m/e* 16, 15, 14, 13 and 12, correspond to CH_4^+ CH_3^+, CH^+, and C^+ respectively. The peak at *m/e* 17 is the isotopic peak due to $^{13}CH_4$. The isotopic peaks help in the determination of the molecular formula. For every 100 CH_4,

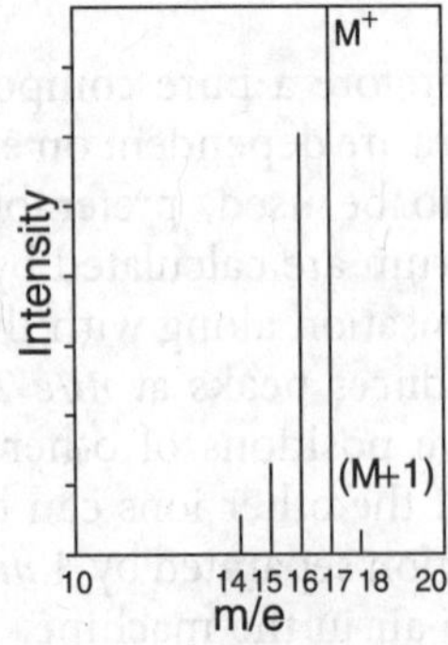

Fig. 16.9 The mass spectrum of ammonia

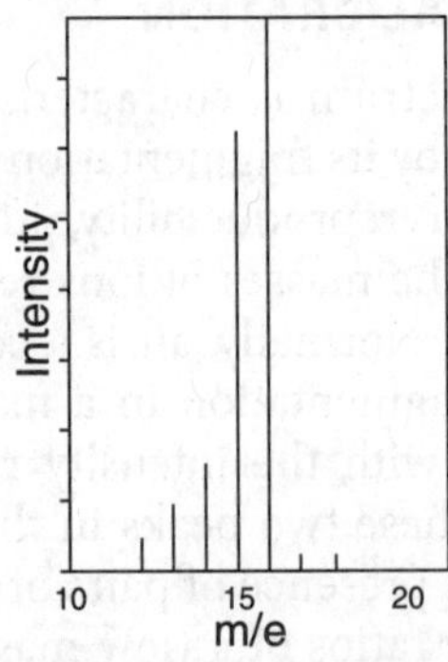

Fig. 16.10 The mass spectrum of methane

there will be 1.08 molecules of $^{13}CH_4$ and 4 × 0.016 molecules of C^2H_4. Therefore, these heavier isotopes will contribute an (M + 1) peak with an intensity of 1.14% of the intensity of the molecular ion (1.08 + 4 × 0.016 = 1.14%). This agrees well with what is observed in the spectrum of CH_4 which contains a peak at *m/e* 17 with an intensity of 1.15%.

16.4 APPLICATIONS OF MASS SPECTROMETRY

Different compounds, even if they are chemically similar, give quite different breakdown patterns. This technique is now extensively used in the analysis of organic compounds. Its uses include

- identification and analysis of mixtures,
- detection of impurities,
- determination of molecular weights,
- determination of molecular structure by reconstructing it from the fragment ions,
- investigating reaction mechanisms with labelled compounds, and
- evaluation of bond energies and ionisation potentials.

16.4.1 Determination of Molecular Formula

The accurate molecular weight of a compound can be obtained from its mass spectrum using a high resolution instrument. Consider an organic compound *X* whose molecular mass is 100. Based on this and other evidence, let us assume that the choice could be narrowed to either $C_6H_{12}O$ or $C_4H_4O_3$. The high resolution mass spectrum of this compound gives a value of *m/e* = 100.08871 for M^+ indicating that the compound is $C_6H_{12}O$. If it were $C_4H_4O_3$, the value would be100.01602. This gives a method of determination of molecular weights accurately up to four decimals with double-focussing spectrometers. For example, the ions $C_2H_4^+$, N_2^+ and CO^+ have the same mass number 28 and these would give the same peak at 28 mass units in a low resolution spectrum. Their accurate masses are 28.0313, 28.0061and 27.9949 respectively, which differ only in decimals. However, these can be separated in a high resolution instrument and their masses recorded precisely from their three independent peaks.

Deuterium ion $^2H^+$ has a mass of 2.014741. Hydrogen molecule ion, H_2^+ has a mass of 2.016290, very close to the value of $^2H^+$. But these two ions are recorded as two independent spectral lines in a high resolution mass spectrometer. In the spectrum, they are closely placed due to low mass difference. Such mass spectral lines are called *mass line doublets.*

A doubly charged positive ion will behave in the same way as a singly charged ion of half the mass. For example, in a low resolution instrument it is difficult to separate the ions CH_3OH^+ and SO_2^{2+} because the *m/e* value for the two ions is the same (32) and this instrument can resolve only ions which differ by at least one unit of *m/e*. The exact *m/e* values of these ions are 32.0262 (CH_3OH^+) and 31.9809 (SO_2^{2+}) which differ slightly. This difference is sufficient enough for their separation in a high resolution spectrometer.

The presence of isotopes also creates problem of identity with low resolution. For example, $^{12}C_2H_2^+$ and $^{12}C^{13}CH^+$ both have

Table 16.2 The mass spectrum of an organic compound

m/e	Intensity (as % of the base peak)	*m/e*	Intensity (as % of the base peak)
27	34	65	8
39	11	78	24 (M^+)
41	22	79	0.8
43	100 (base)	80	8
63	26		

an *m/e* of 26. Their actual masses differ in the third decimal place and these can be resolved and identified only with a high resolution instrument.

The molecular formula of a compound with a modest number of atoms can be determined in the following way. If the M^+ peak is not the base peak in the spectrum of an unknown compound, the intensities of the $[M+1]^+$ and $[M+2]^+$ peaks are recalculated to express them as percentages of the intensity of the M^+ peak. Consider, for example, the spectral data of an organic compound represented in Table 16.2.

The M^+ peak (*m/e* 78) is not the base peak. Therefore, the intensities of the peaks at *m/e* 78, 79 and 80 are calculated as a percentage of the peak at *m/e* 78. This is done by dividing the intensity of each peak by the intensity of the M^+ peak (24) and multiplying by 100.

m/e	intensity (% of M^+)
78	$24/24 \times 100 = 100$
79	$0.8/24 \times 100 = 3.3$
80	$8/24 \times 100 = 33.3$

Then the following points are applied to find out the molecular formula:

The relative abundance of the $(M + 1)^+$ peak indicates the number of carbon atoms.

$$\text{Number of carbon atoms} = \text{Relative abundance of } \frac{(M+1)^+}{1.1}$$

$$\text{For the compound under consideration, the number of carbon atoms} = \frac{3.3}{1.1} = 3.$$

[^{13}C is responsible for the $(M + 1)^+$ peak with its natural abundance of 1.1%]. The $(M + 2)^+$ peak has a high intensity of 33%. This value rules out the presence of the M + 2 atoms, ^{18}O and ^{34}S which would have given a much less $(M + 2)^+$ peak intensity. The satellite peak intensity 33.3% is likely to be due to ^{37}Cl whose natural abundance is 32.5%. Therefore, the compound has 3 carbon atoms and one chlorine atom. This accounts for a mass of 71. After establishing the numbers of C and halogen atoms, appropriate number of oxygen atoms may be added, if necessary. Since only 7 *m/e* units remain to be accounted, the presence of oxygen and nitrogen are ruled out. There must be seven hydrogen atoms. Hence the molecular formula is C_3H_7Cl.

In the next stage, having established the molecular formula, the structure of the compound is determined. The fragmentation pattern and the *m/e* values are carefully correlated to arrive at the structure. The base peak has an *m/e* value of 43 which is 35 units less than that of M^+. This indicates that the Cl readily breaks away from the molecule giving $C_3H_7^+$ which is likely to be a propyl group. It is difficult to decide between, *n*-propyl and *iso*-propyl at this stage. Both these groups can give the *m/e* values listed here. The proton *nmr* spectrum of the compound can be used to decide the correct structure.

Very rarely is mass spectrometry alone helpful in establishing the structure. This should be supplemented with spectroscopic data to confirm the structure.

16.4.1.1 The Nitrogen Rule

According to this rule, a *compound containing an even number of nitrogen atoms or zero nitrogen atoms gives a molecular ion with an even mass number; if the molecule contains an odd number of nitrogen atoms, its molecular ion has odd mass number.*

H_2NNH_2	even	N	$M^+ = 32$
$H_2N(CH_2)_2NH_2$	even	N	$M^+ = 60$
$H_2N{\bullet}C_6H_4{\bullet}NH_2$	even	N	$M^+ = 108$
C_6H_6	zero	N	$M^+ = 78$
CH_3NH_2	odd	N	$M^+ = 31$
$C_6H_5NH_2$	odd	N	$M^+ = 93$

16.4.2 Detection of Isotopes and Their Relative Abundance

In the spectrum of a compound containing an element which has more than one stable isotope, more than one peak for each fragment having this element will be obtained. For example, in the mass spectrum of CH_3Br, two peaks of equal intensity at *m/e* 94 and 96 are obtained. These correspond to $(CH_3{}^{79}Br)^+$ and $(CH_3{}^{81}Br)^+$. From the relative peak intensities the relative abundance of ^{79}Br and ^{81}Br can be calculated:

$$\%\ ^{79}Br : \%\ ^{81}Br = 50.5 : 49.5$$

16.4.3 Separation of Isotopes

The basic principle of the mass spectrometer involves electromagnetic separation of isotopes. This instrument is suited for separating isotopes ranging from micrograms to kilograms. Therefore, certain stable isotopes in pure form are obtained by this technique. These can be used as *tracers* or *isotopic tags;* for example, H-2, C-13, N-15, O-17 and O-l8. Table 16.3 gives the exact masses of certain isotopic nuclei. Figure 16.11 is the mass spectrum of titanium. Its natural sample has five stable isotopes, which can be separated by a mass spectrometer.

Table 16.3 Exact masses of nuclei

Isotope	Mass	Isotope	Mass	Isotope	Mass
^{1}H	1.00783	^{16}O	15.9949	^{34}S	33.9679
^{2}H	2.01410	^{17}O	16.9991	^{35}Cl	34.9689
^{12}C	12.00000	^{18}O	17.9992	^{37}Cl	36.9659
^{13}C	13.00336	^{19}F	18.9984	^{79}Br	78.9183
^{14}N	14.0031	^{32}S	31.9721	^{81}Br	80.9163
^{15}N	15.0001	^{33}S	32.9715	^{127}I	126.9045

16.4.4 Identification of Compounds: Fingerprint Analysis

Under fixed experimental conditions, the mass spectrum of a particular compound is invariable like its IR, UV and NMR spectra. Figure 16.12 is the mass spectrum of *n*-hexane. Thus, a given compound can be identified by comparing its spectrum with the spectra of known compounds. This method is called *fingerprint analysis.* Therefore, by comparing the mass spectrum of a test compound with those compiled already in the literature, the test compound can be identified. One such compilation is that published by the National Institute of Standards and Technology (NIST, USA).

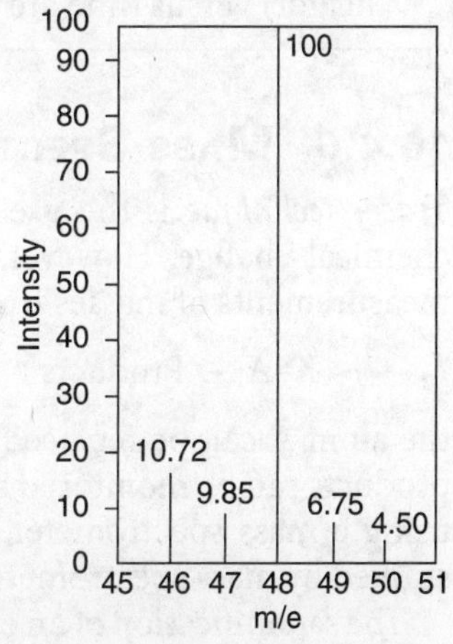

Fig. 16.11 Mass spectrum of natural titanium

16.4.5 Quantitative Analysis of Mixtures

To find the composition of a mixture, the spectrum of each pure component is recorded. The intensities of spectral lines of the pure components are compared with the intensities obtained with the mixture to calculate concentrations. In this method, the concentrations of the components can be obtained without separating them. A mixture of even 25–30 components can be analysed by this method. Very low concentrations – as low as a few μg – can also be accurately determined.

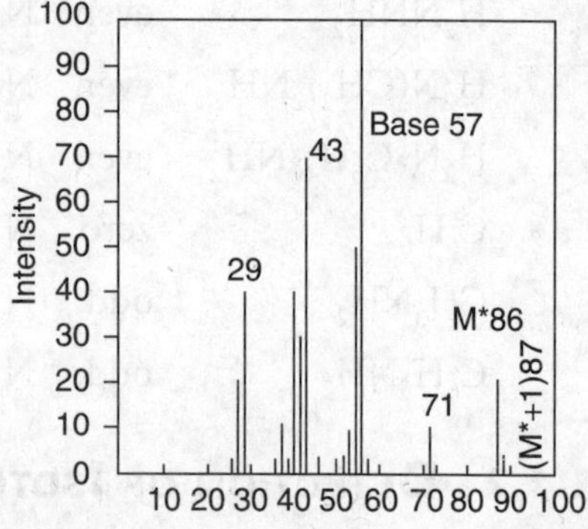

Fig. 16.12 Mass spectrum of *n*-hexane

Application of Mass Spectrometry in Gold Finger Printing

Thieves who steal gold jewellery melt it to destroy its identity. However, mass spectrometry can be applied in identifying the origin of gold and apprehend the thieves.

Extremely minute amounts of cadmium, lead, tellurium and zinc remain in gold samples isolated from the minerals. The proportion of these impurities is characteristic of the place of the gold mine.

The gold sample, confiscated from the alleged thief is analysed mass spectrometrically. A tiny spot – 0.01cm in diameter and depth – of the sample is heated with a high power laser. The vapour formed is swept into a mass spectrometer using argon gas, and its mass spectrum recorded. Then, the spectrum is compared with the spectra of gold samples of various regions (pre-recorded and available in literature). Then, the place of origin of the stolen gold can be known.

- MS measures weight electronically and displays results in the form of a mass spectrum.
- MS serves as an important tool in the hands of chemists. It is widely used for structure determination in conjunction with NMR and IR spectroscopy. Impurity detection and kinetic studies are its other two important applications. The concentration of intermediates (ions) can be monitored by a mass spectrograph and plots of log (peak height) versus time are used for obtaining rate data.

16.4.6 Mass Spectrometry and Tracer Technique

Tracer technique is the use of an isotope – radioactive or otherwise – as a tag to follow a chemical change. However, the mass spectrometric technique is concerned with only the measurements of masses irrespective of their radioactive nature. In the reaction,

$$\text{X–A} \rightarrow \text{Products}$$

the atom A can be replaced by its heavy non-radioactive isotope A*. The change of X–A* to products can be monitored by following the concentration of A* in the reactant or the product using a mass spectrometer. In addition to following a reaction, its mechanism can also be studied by mass spectrometry.

The saponification of an ester by alkali can be considered to illustrate this. Two mechanisms, alkyl-oxygen cleavage and acyl-oxygen cleavage are possible for this reaction. The choice between the two can be made by hydrolysing the ester with $^{18}OH^-$.

$$CH_3–CO–O–R + {}^{18}OH^- \rightarrow CH_3–CO–O^- + R–{}^{18}O–H \text{ alkyl oxygen fission} \quad (16.4)$$

$$CH_3–CO–O–R + {}^{18}OH^- \rightarrow CH_3CO^{18}O^- + R–OH \text{ acyl oxygen fission} \quad (16.5)$$

For example, when amyl acetate was hydrolysed using $H_2{}^{18}O$, ^{18}O was present only in acetic acid confirming that the second mechanism (Eq. 16.5) operates. The location of the ^{18}O is determined by the mass spectrometer.

Mass spectrometry in conjunction with other spectral methods has become an excellent tool for determining structures of organic molecules. The breaking patterns for organic molecules are largely dependent on the relative strengths of bonds in them, the relative stabilities of possible fragment ions for each molecule and the complexities of each molecule.

16.4.6.1 General Principles of Fragmentation

(i) When a molecule can undergo alternative fragmentations, splitting usually occurs in all ways. Among the possibilities, the one leading to the most stable carbonium ion or free radical is predominant. A molecular peak is observed for most of the molecules.

(ii) The stability order of molecular ions is,

Aromatics > conjugated acyclic compounds > alicyclics > *n*-hydrocarbons > ketones > ethers > branched chain hydrocarbons > alcohols.

(iii) The ease of removal of an electron from the molecule to form a molecular ion is influenced by the nature of the electron; the order is lone-pair electron > π-electron > σ-electron.

(iv) An ion may rearrange when a hydrogen atom is involved in a six-membered cyclic transition state when 1,2-shifts are involved.

(v) The major peaks near the molecular ion are examined and their *m/e* values are listed. The study of successive M-*m/e* values, where M is the molecular mass would indicate successive breakages in the molecule. The *m/e* and M – *m/e* values are compared with a list of common fragments. Then predicting the fragmentation pattern, the structure of the compound can be arrived at.

(vi) The fragmentation pattern revealed by the mass spectrum can by used to understand the relative stabilities of ions, mechanisms of elimination of H_2, H_2O, CO_2, NH_3 and so on, as well as rearrangement reactions.

16.4.6.2 Fragmentation Patterns for Organic Compounds

The type of fragmentation of a molecule and the nature of the ion produced depend on the functional group of the molecule. Hence certain general cleavage patterns can be predicted for each class of compounds. In this section, only the cleavages characteristic of the functional groups and not complete cleavage patterns are considered.

The presence of a functional group, particularly one having a heteroatom Y with non-bonding valence electrons (Y = N, O, S or halogen), can change the fragmentation pattern of a compound. The heteroatom 'localises' the radical cation component of the molecular ion on itself. This precludes the formation of the other types of molecular ions. The driving force for this localisation is the fact that a non-bonding electron from the heteroatom can more easily be removed than an electron which is a part of the covalent bond.

The localisation of the reactive moiety favours certain fragmentation patterns. This can be understood by considering the general example of a molecular ion $M^{+\bullet}$, bearing a hetero-atom:

$M^{+\bullet}$ $\qquad$ $R–\overset{\bullet+}{\underset{\bullet\bullet}{Cl}}\colon$ or $R–\overset{\bullet+}{\underset{\bullet\bullet}{O}}–R'$

Molecular ion

$$\text{or} \quad R\text{–}\ddot{N}R_2^{\bullet+} \quad \text{or} \quad R_2C{=}O^{\bullet+}$$

These are all 'localised' molecular ions. Depending upon the nature and structure of these ions, three kinds of cleavages are possible. For example, consider R–CH_2–Y, where Y is a hetero atom:

(i) C–Y cleavage

$$R\text{—}CH_2\text{—}\dot{Y}^{+} \longrightarrow R\text{—}CH_2^{\oplus} + \ddot{Y}^{\bullet} \quad \text{Even-electron ion}$$

(ii) α-cleavage

$$R\text{—}C\text{—}\dot{Y}^{+} \longrightarrow R^{\bullet} + {>}C{=}\overset{+}{Y} \quad \text{Even-electron ion}$$

(iii) H–Y elimination

$$\begin{matrix} C\text{—}H \\ | \\ C\text{—}\dot{Y}^{+} \end{matrix} \longrightarrow \begin{matrix} C \\ \vdots^{+} \\ C \end{matrix} \quad \begin{matrix} H \\ | \\ Y \end{matrix} \quad \text{Odd-electron ion}$$

The charge distributions shown here are common; however, for each cleavage process, the charge may sometimes be carried by the other, neutral species and consequently, both fragment ions are observed. The alpha-cleavage is favoured for nitrogen, oxygen and sulphur compounds. Thus, functional groups influence the fragmentation pattern of organic molecules.

The general patterns of fragmentation characteristic of functional groups may now be considered.

Alkanes Fragmentation of an alkane molecule occurs preferentially at the branched carbon atoms. This is due to the order of stability of carbonium ions, 3° > 2° > 1°. Among side chains, the heaviest one is fissioned first. *n*-Alkanes produce a series of peaks differing by 14 mass units, that is, loss of [CH_2]. For example, the spectrum of *n*-butane has peaks at *m/e* 57, 43, 29, 15 corresponding to $C_4H_9^+$, $C_3H_7^+$, $C_2H_5^+$, CH_3^+ respectively. The parent peak is always present for *n*-alkanes whose intensity decreases with increasing chain length. Greater the branching, less is the probability of appearance of the molecular ion because ready breakage occurs at the branched carbon chain. For example,

$$[CH_3\text{–}\underset{\underset{C_2H_5}{|}}{CH}\text{–}CH_2\text{–}CH_3]^{+\bullet} \rightarrow CH_3\text{–}CH^{+}\text{–}CH_2\text{–}CH_3 + \bullet C_2H_5$$

No peak corresponding to the molecular ion occurs in this case.

Alkenes The mass spectra of alkenes are characterised by peaks for C_nH_{2n-1} (27, 41, 55…) and C_nH_{2n} (28, 42, 56…). The molecular ion tends to undergo allylic cleavage, that is, the C–C bond is broken at the β-position to the double bond.

$$[CH_2{=}CH{-}CH_2{-}R]^{+\bullet} \rightarrow R^{\bullet} + CH_2{=}CH{-}CH_2^{+}$$
$$\alpha \quad \beta$$

The positive charge remains with the fragment containing the double bond, since the allyl ion is stabilised by resonance. When the alkene is sufficiently long to form a six-membered cyclic transition state involving a γ-hydrogen, two smaller alkenes are produced by rearrangement. This is called *McLafferty rearrangement.* The positive charge may remain with one of the alkenes formed.

Alkyl halides The molecular ion is readily formed by the loss of an electron from a lone-pair on the halogen group. For a chloride or a bromide, an (M + 2) peak appears due to the presence of the heavier isotope of Cl or Br. The intensity of M^+ is in the order RI > RBr > RCl > RF. As the size of R in R–X increases, bond breakage is favoured and hence the intensity of the parent peak decreases. Aliphatic fluorides show a typical peak at M–HF (M – 20). Aliphatic chlorides also readily lose HCl, showing a peak at (M – 36).

$$[RCH_2CH_2X]^+ \xrightarrow{\text{F or Cl}} [R{-}CH{=}CH_2]^+ + HX$$
$$[RCH_2CH_2X]^+ \longrightarrow RCH_2\overset{+}{C}H_2 + X$$
$$[RCH_2CH_2X]^+ \xrightarrow{\text{Br or I}} RCH_2 + CH_2{=}X^+$$

Alcohols Primary and secondary alcohols give weak molecular peaks and for a tertiary alcohol this peak is usually absent, due to ready cleavage of a *t*-alcohol. A long chain alcohol shows a peak at M – 18 due to the loss of a molecule of water and formation of a cyclic ion. Generally, intense peaks are present corresponding to the product of β-cleavage.

$$\left[H_3C{-}\underset{CH_3}{\overset{CH_3}{\underset{|}{\overset{|}{C}}}}{-}OH\right]^{+\bullet} \longrightarrow \dot{C}H_3 + \begin{matrix}H_3C\\CH_3\end{matrix}\!\!>\!C{=}\overset{+}{O}H$$

Acids, esters and amides These molecules tend to undergo similar fragmentations. The initial step is α-cleavage involving breaking away of OH, OR or NH_2.

$$[CH_3{-}CH_2{-}COOH]^+ \rightarrow CH_5CH_2CO^+ + {}^{\bullet}OH$$
$$m/e\ 74 \qquad 57\ (M-17) \qquad 17$$

$$[CH_3COOCH_3]^+ \rightarrow CH_3{-}CO^+ + CH_3O^{\bullet}$$
$$m/e\ 74 \qquad 43\ (M-31) \qquad 31$$

$$[CH_3{-}CH_2{-}CONH_2]^+ \rightarrow CH_3CH_2CO^+ + NH_2^{\bullet}$$
$$m/e\ 73 \qquad 57\ (M-16) \qquad 16$$

Therefore, strong peaks at (M – 17), (M – 31) and (M – 16) are indicative of the –OH, $-OCH_3$ and $-NH_2$ groups respectively. Removal of OH and COOH from the parent ion gives characteristic strong peaks in the spectra of fatty acids. Aromatic acids form strong peaks corresponding to the stable fragments, $ArCO^+$ and Ar^+.

Aldehydes and ketones The hydrogen of the aldehyde group is readily cleaved because the aldehydic C–H bond is weak. Therefore, the molecular peak usually has a low intensity.

$$\underset{M}{[CH_3CHO]^{+\bullet}} \rightarrow \underset{M-1}{[CH_3\text{–}CO)^+} + H^\bullet$$

The cleavage giving acylium ion is also easy.

$$[CH_3CHO)^{+\bullet} \rightarrow CH_3^\bullet + \underset{(m/e\ 29)}{H\text{–}C{\equiv}O^+}$$

Therefore, the presence of M – 1 and *m/e* 29 are characteristic of aldehydes. For ketones, the molecular ion peaks are intense. Loss of heavier groups occurs predominantly. For methyl ketones, the acylium ion $CH_3C{\equiv}O^+$ (*m/e* 43) is the base peak. Both aldehydes and ketones produce alkyl groups on further fragmentation.

$$[CH_3\text{–}CO\text{–}CH_3]^+ \rightarrow CH_3C{\equiv}O^+ + CH_3^\bullet$$

$$CH_3C{\equiv}O^+ \rightarrow CO^+ + CH_3^\bullet$$

A carbonyl compound can undergo the McLafferty rearrangement.

Figure 16.13 is the mass spectrum of pentan-2-one. Explain this spectrum.

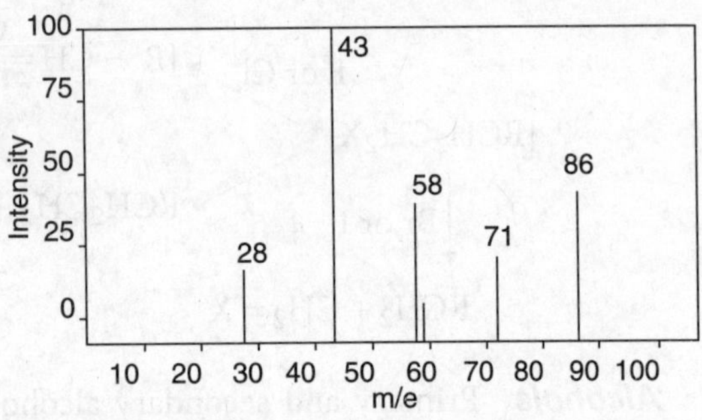

Fig. 16.13 Mass spectrum of pentan-2-one

Solution

The fragmentation scheme expected for pentan-2-one is shown below:

$$\underset{M^+ = 86}{[CH_3COCH_2CH_2CH_3]^{+\bullet}} \longrightarrow [CH_3COCH_2CH_2]^+ + {}^\bullet CH_3$$

$$\downarrow$$

$$\underset{43}{[CH_3C\equiv O:]^+} + \underset{43}{\bullet CH_2CH_2CH_3}$$

As the molecule contains γ-hydrogens, a McLafferty rearrangement is likely:

$$H_2C(H)\text{–}H_2C\text{–}CH_2\text{–}C(=O)\text{–}CH_3 \longrightarrow \underset{28}{CH_2{=}CH_2} + \underset{58}{\left[H\text{–}O\text{–}C(=CH_2)\text{–}CH_3\right]^{+\bullet}}$$

The actual spectrum substantiates this fragmentation pattern.

For a compound containing an odd number of nitrogen atoms, the molecular weight is odd. An amine undergoes ready β-cleavage producing $CH_2{=}^+NH_2$ (*m/e* 30).

$$[\text{R–CH}_2\text{–NH}_2]^{+\bullet} \rightarrow \text{R}^\bullet + \text{CH}_2\text{=}\overset{+}{\text{N}}\text{H}_2$$
(base peak)

Aromatic hydrocarbons The mass spectra of simple aromatic compounds are mainly characteristic of that of benzene. Benzene shows peaks at 78 $(C_6H_6)^{+\bullet}$, 77 $(C_6H_5)^+$, 53 $(C_4H_5)^+$, 51 $(C_4H_3)^+$, 50 $(C_4H_2)^+$ and 39 $(C_3H_3)^+$.

The following mass spectral data are the best clues to the presence of an aromatic compound:

- The high percentage abundance of the ion with *m/e* 77 $(C_6H_5)^+$.
- The presence of peaks at m/e 65 $(C_5H_5)^+$, 53 $(C_4H_5)^+$, 51 $(C_4H_3)^+$, 50 $(C_4H_2)^+$ and 39 $(C_3H_3)^+$.
- The presence of doubly charged molecular ion peaks at *m*/2*e* (the possibility of removal of two electrons from two sites from the parent aromatic molecule is high).

Ethers and phenols Figure 16.14 typifies the splitting pattern of ethers and Fig. 16.15 that of phenols.

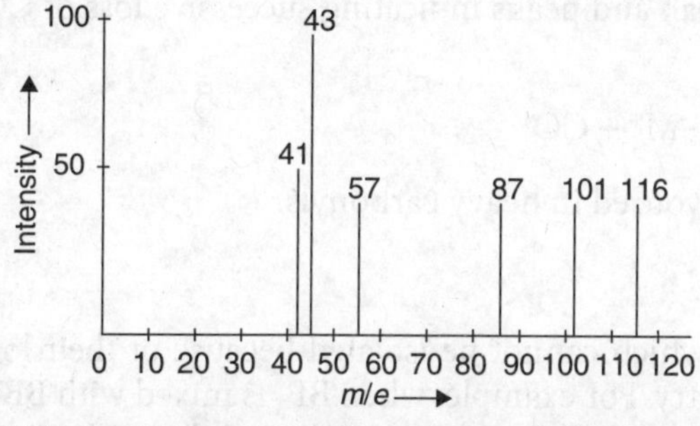

Fig. 16.14 The mass spectrum of *sec*-butyl isopropyl ether

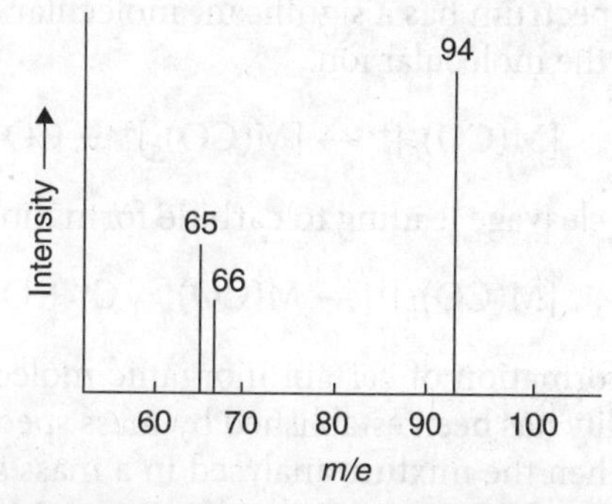

Fig. 16.15 Mass spectrum of phenol

Proteins The two primary methods for ionisation of whole proteins are Electrospray Ionisation (ESI) and Matrix Assisted Laser Desorption Ionisation (MALDI).

In the ESI–MS, tiny droplets of the sample are ionised and then analysed individually by a mass spectrometer. The tiny droplets containing the protein macromolecules are formed by forcing the solution of the analyte through a highly charged capillary needle.

In the MALDI mode, the sample is contained is an inert organic matrix (for example, 2,5-dihydroxybenzoic acid) and irradiated under vacuum with light from a pulsed laser. The matrix efficiently transfers energy from the laser to the sample promoting ionisation. When a MALDI–TOF instrument is used, every ion produced is efficiently recorded by the instrument.

Two approaches are used for characterising proteins. In the first, intact proteins are ionised by either of the two techniques, and then introduced into a mass analyser. This approach is called 'top-down' strategy of protein analysis. In the second, proteins are enzymatically digested into smaller peptides using proteases such as trypsin or pepsin, either in solution or in gel after electrophoretic separation. Then, the peptide products are introduced into the mass analyser. If the characteristic fragmentation pattern of peptides is used for the identification of the proteins, the method is called *peptide mass fingerprinting* (PMF); if the identification is performed using the sequence data determined in tandem MS analysis, it is called *de nova sequencing*. These procedures of protein analysis through peptides are also referred to as the 'bottom-up' approach.

16.4.7 Application of MS in Pharmacokinetics

Pharmacokinetics is a branch of pharmacology, and it involves the determination of the fate of substances administered externally to a living organism. It gives information on mechanisms of absorption and distribution of drugs in the body. In addition, it provides information about the rate of absorption of a drug, duration of effectiveness, the chemical changes of the drug in the body and also the effects and routes of excretion of the metabolites of the drugs.

Mass spectrometry is helpful in the study of pharmacokinetics because of the complex nature of the matrix (such as blood and urine) and the need for high sensitivity to study low doses and also for specificity. LC–MS and triple quadrupole mass spectrometers are suitable for such studies (Section 16.5).

16.4.8 Inorganic Mass Spectrometry

This technique is applied to find the structures of some inorganic compounds also, especially complex compounds. The mass spectrometric data help understand the structure, reactivity and preparative uses of complexes. Consider, for example, $M(CO)_6$ where M is V, Mn or Co. The spectrum has a significant molecular ion peak and peaks indicating successive loss of CO from the molecular ion.

$$[M(CO)_6]^{+\bullet} \rightarrow [M(CO)_5]^{+\bullet} + CO \rightarrow ...., M^{+} + CO^{\bullet}$$

C–O cleavage leading to carbide formation is favoured in heavy carbonyls.

$$[M(CO)_n]^{+\bullet} \rightarrow M(CO)_{n-1}\ C^{+} + O^{\bullet}$$

The formation of certain inorganic molecules, which cannot be isolated because of their low stability has been established by mass spectrometry. For example, when BF_3 is mixed with BBr_3 and then the mixture analysed in a mass spectrometer, the spectrum indicates the presence of BBr_2F and BF_2Br in the mixture. Peaks at *m/e* 190 and 129 were obtained. The formation of these was explained, assuming an exchange reaction involving a four-centre intermediate, $B_2Br_3F_3$.

$$BF_3 + BBr_3 \rightarrow [B_2Br_3F_3] \rightarrow BF_2Br + BBr_2F$$

16.5 TYPES OF MASS SPECTROMETRY

16.5.1 Spark Source Mass Spectrometry

In spark source mass spectrometry, the atomic constituents of the sample are converted to gaseous ions by a high potential (≈ 30 kV), radio-frequency spark. The gaseous positive ions formed are then accelerated into the analyser by a DC potential. This method is useful for quantitative analysis of ions from ^{7}Li upto ^{238}U. It is reliable down to ppb level; thus, it is a highly sensitive version of MS.

16.5.2 Secondary Ion Mass Spectrometry (SIMS)

In SIMS, accelerated non-analyte ions are made to bombard atoms in the analyte. Ions from the analyte are produced by this bombardment. It is useful for surface analysis, namely, studying the composition of solid surfaces (from a few angstroms to a few tens of angstrom thickness). The surface to be analysed is bombarded with a beam of 5 to 20 keV ions such as Ar^+, Cs^+, N_2^+ or O_2^+. This bombardment produces positive ions of surface constituents. These positive ions are then drawn into a spectrometer for mass analysis. As the ions formed from the surface by the impact of ion beam (say Ar^+) are secondary ions, this method is called secondary ion mass spectrometry. SIMS is useful in detailed studies of solid surfaces.

16.5.3 Tandem Mass Spectrometry

Tandem mass spectrometry involves two mass spectrometers in series connected by a chamber. This chamber is known as a *collision cell.* The sample is *sorted* and *weighed* in the first mass spectrometer. Then the molecules are broken into pieces in the collision cell, and the pieces sorted and weighed in the second mass spectrometer.

In one method of tandem mass spectrometry, the precursor masses are scanned in the first analyser. An ion or a group of ions can be selected and analysed in the second mass spectrometer. This method offers a means of analysing complex molecules such as, proteins, polysaccharides, oligonucleotides and arriving at the identities of their sequencing units.

16.5.4 Hyphenated MS (Combined Chromatography–Mass Spectrometry)

In this method, the mass resolving and mass determining capabilities of mass spectrometry are enhanced by combining MS with chromatography.

GC–MS This is a common *hyphenated* mass spectrometry. In this method, a gas chromatograph is used to separate different components of the analyte. The stream of separated components is fed online into the ion source of the mass spectrometer. The ion source consists of a filament which emits electrons; these electrons ionise the compounds. The ions formed undergo fragmentation. The ions and fragments pass into the mass spectrometer's analyser and get detected.

LC–MS This is liquid chromatography–mass spectrometry hyphenated technique. In this method, the compounds are separated chromatographically before they are introduced to the ion source and mass spectrometer. The mobile phase in this method is a liquid, a mixture of water and an organic solvent (instead of gas used in GC). An *electrospray* ionisation is used in LC–MS.

IMMS This is ion mobility spectrometry–mass spectrometry. In this hyphenated method, a mixture of ions is separated by *drift time* through a neutral gas under an applied electrical potential gradient; then the separated ions are introduced into a mass spectrometer. The drift time is a measure of the radius of the ion-path relative to the charge of the ion.

HPLC–MS High performance liquid chromatography–mass spectrometry involves the direct inflow system. The eluent from a microprobe HPLC column with relatively low flow rates is fed directly into the MS ion source. Alternatively, the liquid effluent from the column is converted to a fine mist or spray and then led into the ion source unit. The HPLC–MS helps in analysing complex mixtures that give complicated spectral patterns in simple mass spectrometry.

16.5.5 Laser Microprobe Mass Spectrometry (LMMS)

LMMS is used for surface analysis. In this method, ionisation and volatilisation are carried out by a pulsed, neodymium YAG laser. Another laser, He–Ne laser ($\lambda = 633$ nm) serves as illumination for visually choosing the area on the surface of the material to be analysed. This method has a very high sensitivity (down to 10^{-20} g). It can be applied to analysing surfaces of organic, inorganic and biological matrixes. One micrometre of the surface is sufficient for analysis. LMMS is typically used in the determination of

- Na/K concentration ratios in nerve fibres,
- calcium distribution in retinas,
- composition of silicates,
- constituents in coal mine dust,
- amino acids, and
- composition of polymer surfaces.

Types of Mass Spectrometry

MALDI–TOF	: Matrix-assisted laser desorption/ionisation source with a time-of-flight mass analyser
TIMS	: Thermal ionisation mass spectrometry
SSMS	: Spark source mass spectrometry
LMMS	: Laser microprobe mass spectrometry
ICP–MS	: Inductively coupled plasma–mass spectrometry
AMS	: Accelerator mass spectrometry

16.5.6 Atom Probe

An atom probe is an instrument that combines time-of-flight mass spectrometry and field ion microscopy (FIM). This method is helpful for mapping the location of individual atoms in a matrix.

Problem 16.1 What should be the resolving power of the mass spectrometer which can produce two distinct signals corresponding to the two ions CH_3OH^+ and $N_2H_4^+$ with *m/e* values accurate to four decimals?

Solution

The accurate masses are calculated first:

CH_3OH	^{12}C	12.0000
	^{16}O	15.9949
	^{1}H	4.0318
		32.0267
N_2H_4	^{14}N	28.0061
	^{1}H	4.0318
		32.0379

The difference between these two masses is

$$32.0379 - 32.0267 = 0.0112$$

To obtain the exact masses up to the fourth decimal, the spectrometer should have a resolving power of one part in 10,000 (1/10,000 = 0.0001). However, the two signals for these two ions can be obtained even with a resolving power of one part in 1000.

Problem 16.2 What resolving power is needed for a mass spectrometer to separate a CH_2N^+, $C_2H_4^+$ doublet?

Solution

For CH_2N^+, the *m/e* is calculated as

one carbon	$1 \times 12.0000 =$	12.0000
two hydrogens	$2 \times 1.0079 =$	2.0158
one nitrogen	$1 \times 14.0031 =$	14.0031
		28.0189

For $C_2H_4^+$, *m/e* is calculated as

two carbons	$2 \times 12.00000 =$	24.0000
four hydrogens	$4 \times 1.00794 =$	4.0318
		28.0318

The resolving power (R_p) of a mass spectrometer is defined as the ratio $M/\Delta M$, where M is the mass number of two closely placed peaks and ΔM is the difference between the actual masses of the two fragments representing the doublet.

$$R_p = \frac{28}{28.0318 - 28.0189} = \frac{28}{0.0129} = 2171$$

The required resolving power is 2171.

Problem 16.3 What is the probable composition of a molecule of mass 142, whose M+1 peak intensity is 1.1% of that of the parent peak?

Solution

The ^{12}C: ^{13}C abundance ratio is 100:1.1. The observed intensity of 1.1% for the (M + 1) peak indicates that the molecule has only one carbon. The large molecular mass 142, even though there is only one carbon atom, must be due to the presence of a heavy atom. If the only carbon is assumed to be present as CH_3, the unaccounted mass is $142 - (12 + 3) = 142 - 15 = 127$. This may be due to an iodine atom. The molecule is probably CH_3I.

Problem 16.4 The mass spectrum of a transition metal carbonyl has peaks at *m/e* = 504 (M^+), 476, 448 and decreasing every 28 units down to 168 and then at 112 and 56. Identify the carbonyl.

Solution

The successive differences in masses of unit 28 between 504 and 112 indicate the successive loss of CO ligands.

$$504 - 168 = 336$$

The number of CO ligands in the complex = 336/28 = 12. The *m/e* = 168 should represent the moiety containing the metal atoms. Since the final *m/e* is 56, the metal should be Fe. The values at *m/e* 112 and 168 should correspond to Fe_2 and Fe_3 species respectively. Therefore, the metal carbonyl is $Fe_3(CO)_{12}$.

Problem 16.5 Predict the *m/e* value for the base peak in the mass spectrum of each of the following:

(i) ethylcyclopentane (ii) methylcyclohexane
(iii) 3-methylpentane (iv) *t*-butyl alcohol
(v) 2-chlorobutane

Solution

(i) This is likely to produce the cyclopentyl ion in abundance by the easy cleavage of the ethyl group from the ring:

$$\text{C}_5\text{H}_9\text{–CH}_2\text{–CH}_3 \longrightarrow \text{C}_5\text{H}_9^{+\bullet},\ m/e = 69$$

Therefore, the base peak is expected at *m/e* = 69.

(ii) The base peak is likely to be the cyclohexyl fragment:

$$[\text{C}_6\text{H}_{11}\text{–CH}_3] \longrightarrow \text{C}_6\text{H}_{11}^{\bullet+} + {}^{\bullet}\text{CH}_3$$

C_6H_{11}
m/e = 83

(iii) The formation of the secondary carbocation in abundance (base peak) is expected with this molecule.

$$\left[\text{CH}_3\text{–CH}_2\text{–}\underset{\text{CH}_3}{\text{CH}}\text{–CH}_2\text{–}\overset{+}{\text{CH}_3}\right]^{\bullet} \longrightarrow \text{CH}_3\text{–}\overset{+}{\text{CH}_2}\text{–}\underset{\text{CH}_3}{\text{CH}} + \bullet\,\text{CH}_2\text{–CH}_3$$

m/e = 57

(iv)

$$(\text{H}_3\text{C})_3\overset{+\bullet}{\text{C}}\text{–OH} \longrightarrow (\text{CH}_3)_3\text{C}^+ + \dot{\text{O}}\text{H}$$

(base peak *m/e* = 57)

(v)

$$\left[\text{CH}_3\text{–}\underset{\text{Cl}}{\text{CH}}\text{–CH}_2\text{–CH}_3\right]^{+\bullet} \longrightarrow [\text{CH}_3\text{–CH–CH}_2\text{CH}_3]^+ + \text{Cl}\bullet$$

m/e = 57

The stable secondary carbocation is likely to constitute the base peak.

Problem 16.6 Predict and explain the mass spectral fragmentation data for H_2O.

Solution

The molecular weight for H_2O is 18. Hence, a peak at $m/e = 18$ is expected. The molecule is stable and therefore the intensity of M^+ peak should be high. H_2O is expected to undergo the following fragmentation pattern:

$$H_2O \rightarrow [H_2O]^{+\bullet} \xrightarrow{-H^\bullet} [OH]^+ \xrightarrow{-H^\bullet} [O]^+$$

Satellite (isotope) peaks are expected at $m/e = 19$ and 20.

m/e 19: H^2HO

m/e 20: $H_2{}^{18}O$

Problem 16.7 Calculate the approximate intensities for the $M^+ : (M+2)^+$ peaks for

(i) C_2H_5Cl (ii) CH_3Br (iii) $Cl{-}CH_2{-}CH_2{-}SH$

Solution

(i) C_2H_5Cl
In this molecule, only Cl contributes to the $(M+2)^+$ peak.

$^{35}Cl : {}^{37}Cl$ abundance is 100 : 32.5

Therefore, this should also be the ratio of the intensities of the M^+: $(M+2)^+$ peaks.

(ii) CH_3Br
The isotopic abundance ratio for $^{79}Br : {}^{81}Br = 100 : 98$
Therefore, the $(M+2)^+$ peak would have 98% of the intensity of the M^+ peak.

(iii) $Cl{-}CH_2{-}CH_2{-}SH$
In this molecule, two elements, Cl and S have isotopes.

$^{35}Cl : {}^{37}Cl = 100 : 32.5$

$^{32}S : {}^{34}S = 100 : 4.4$

Therefore the intensity of the $(M+2)^+$ peak would be 36.9% of that of the molecular peak.

Problem 16.8 Explain the following:

(i) The mass spectrum of toluene and that of cycloheptatriene are identical.
(ii) CH_3CO^+ fragment is an important species formed in the mass spectral analysis of acetophenones. The relative abundances of this species with acetophenone, *p*-nitroacetophenone and *p*-aminoacetophenone are 1 : 4.5 : 0.26. Explain.

Solution

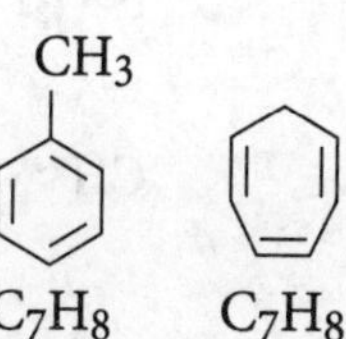

(i) Cycloheptatriene readily forms the more stable aromatic tropylium ion $C_7H_7^+$ (6π-electron species) during its mass spectral analysis. Toluene is expected to initially form the $C_6H_5{-}CH_2^+$ ion. This may then transform itself to the tropylium ion and then undergo fragmentation. Such a process would then produce a mass spectrum identical with that of cycloheptatriene. Whenever an aromatic molecule forms the benzyl cation

$C_6H_5CH_2^+$, it converts itself to the tropylium cation. This fact has been proved by deuterium labelling of $C_6H_5–CH_2–CH_2–R$ at the α position and then studying its mass spectrum.
(α) (β)

(ii) The formation of CH_3CO^+, an electron deficient fragment, would be favoured by an electron withdrawing NO_2 group but hindered by an electron releasing *amino* group. Therefore, its intensity is maximum for the nitro-compound and minimum for the amino- compound.

Problem 16.9 The mass spectrum of a compound has a molecular ion peak with a relative intensity of 61.5% and an (M + 1) peak with a relative intensity of 6.6%. How many carbon atoms are present in this compound?

Solution

The natural abundance ratio for carbon is $^{12}C : {}^{13}C = 98.89\% : 1.11\%$

The relative abundance of (M + 1) = number of carbon atoms × 0.011 × relative abundance of M

Therefore, number of carbon atoms

$$= \frac{\text{Relative abundance of } (M+1)}{0.011 \times \text{relative abundance of M}}$$

$$= \frac{6.6}{0.011 \times 61.5} = 9.8 \approx 10$$

Therefore, the number of carbon atoms in the compound is 10.

Problem 16.10 The following data have been obtained in the mass spectral analysis of methane. Explain.

m/e	Intensity
1	0.4
2	0.2
12	2.8
13	8.0
14	16.0
15	86.0
16	100.0
17	1.1

Solution

The base peak ($m/e = 16$) corresponds to the molecular ion

$$CH_4 \longrightarrow [CH_4]^{+\bullet} + e^- \quad m/e = 16$$

This ion would then undergo fragmentation:

$$[CH_4]^{+\bullet} \longrightarrow CH_3^+ + H^\bullet \quad m/e = 15$$

$$CH_3^+ \longrightarrow [CH_2]^{+\bullet} + H^+ \quad m/e = 14$$

$$[CH_2]^{+\bullet} \longrightarrow CH^+ + H^\bullet \quad m/e = 13$$

$$CH^{+\bullet} \longrightarrow [C]^+ + H^\bullet \quad m/e = 12$$

Occasionally, an organic ion may eject an ionised hydrogen molecule, giving rise to a weak peak at $m/e = 2$.

$$[\dot{C}H_4]^+ \longrightarrow \dot{C}H_2 + [H_2]^+$$
$$m/z = 2$$

The $m/e = 17$ represents the (M + 1) isotopic peak.

Problem 16.11 How can the following be distinguished from their mass spectra?

(i) 3-methyl-2-hexanone form 4-methyl-2-hexanone
(ii) 3-pentanone and 2-pentanone

Solution

(i) $CH_3\text{-}CH_2\text{-}CH_2\text{-}CH(CH_3)\text{-}CO\text{-}CH_3$ (3-methyl-2-hexanone) $CH_3\text{-}CH_2\text{-}CH(CH_3)\text{-}CH_2\text{-}CO\text{-}CH_3$ (4-methyl-2-hexanone)

Both can undergo the McLafferty rearrangement but produce different fragments as shown.

$$\left[H_3C-C(=O)-CH(CH_3)-CH_2-CH_2-CH_3\right]^{\bullet+} \longrightarrow \left[CH_3-C(OH)=CH-CH_3\right]^{\bullet+} + CH_3-CH=CH_2$$

m/e 114 → 72 + 43

$$\left[CH_3-C(=O)-CH_2-CH(CH_3)-CH_2-CH_3\right]^{\bullet+} \longrightarrow \left[CH_3-C(OH)=CH_2\right]^{\bullet+} + CH_3-CH=CH-CH_3$$

$m/e = 58$ 56

(ii) 3-pentanone has no γ-hydrogen and therefore it cannot undergo the McLafferty rearrangement. But 2-pentanone having a γ-hydrogen can undergo this rearrangement.

$CH_3\text{-}CH_2\text{-}CO\text{-}CH_2\text{-}CH_3$: McLafferty rearrangement is not possible.

$$\left[H_3C-C(=O)-CH_2-CH_2-CH_2\right]^{\bullet+} \longrightarrow \left[CH_3-C(OH)=CH_2\right]^{\bullet+} + CH_2=CH_2$$

$m/z = 58$ 28

A peak $m/ = 42$ is indicative of 2-pentanone; no such peak would be obtained with 3-pentanone.

Problem 16.12 Rhenium exists in two isotopic forms; ^{185}Re and ^{187}Re with abundances 37% and, 63% respectively. Bromine exists as ^{79}Br (51%) and ^{81}Br (49%).

(i) In how many isotopic forms can the ion $(ReBr)^+$ exist?
(ii) Calculate the relative abundances of the various $(ReBr)^+$ species?

Solution

(i) $(ReBr)^+$ can exist in four isotopic forms:

$$(^{185}Re^{79}Br)^+, (^{185}Re^{81}Br)^+, (^{187}Re^{79}Br)^+, (^{187}Re^{81}Br)^+$$

(ii) The abundance of $(^{185}Re\ ^{79}Br)^+$

$$= [\%\text{ abundance of } ^{185}Re)\ (\text{fractional abundance of } ^{79}Br)$$
$$= 37\% \times 0.51 = 19\%$$

Similarly, the other abundances can be calculated:

$$(^{185}Re^{81}Br)^+ = 37\% \times 0.49 = 18\%$$
$$(^{187}Re^{79}Br)^+ = 63\% \times 0.51 = 32\%$$
$$(^{187}Re^{81}Br)^+ = 63\% \times 0.49 = 31\%$$

Two species, $[^{187}Re^{79}Br]^+$ and $^{185}Re^{81}Br$ have the same mass, 266 and therefore only three signals are expected in the spectrum.

Problem 16.13 Two metastable peaks at $m_1^* = 94.8$ and $m_2^* = 59.2$ are present in the mass spectrum of *p*-anisidine. Explain.

Solution

A metastable peak is due to an ion which undergoes fragmentation in its path from the ion source to the recorder. Such an ion has a lifetime of 10^{-6} to 10^{-5} s. It is denoted by the symbol m^*. It produces a diffuse (broad) peak of low intensity and thus can be easily recognised in the mass spectrum. As a metastable ion has a short lifetime, the ion (of mass m_1^*) is actually accelerated, but a different ion m_2^* (called a *daughter ion*) passes through the magnetic analyser and gets recorded. The resulting peak is located neither at m_1 nor at m_2 in the spectrum, but at mass m^*. This is given by

$$m^* = \frac{m_2^{*2}}{m_1^*}$$

The metastable ions have great theoretical importance and furnish valuable information about *mass spectral reactions*. These principles can now be applied to the metastable peaks of *p*-anisidine.

The parent ion itself is expected to be metastable; if it is assumed to fragment during its flight in the magnetic analyser into B, then a metastable peak

$$m_2^* = \frac{108^2}{123} = 94.8. \text{ is justifiable}$$

If the ion, B is assumed to be metastable, then it can produce a daughter ion C.

Then, $m_1^* = \frac{80^2}{108} = 59.2$

which can account for the second metastable peak.

The metastable ions provide the link between the parent and the fragment ions.

Problem 16.14 What conclusion can be drawn from each of the following mass spectral features?

(i) The mass spectrum of a compound has a large $(M{-}H_2O)^+$ peak.
(ii) The mass spectrum of a compound does not contain an $(M + 1)^+$ peak.
(iii) For many organic compounds (not containing Cl, S, Br and other isotopically mixed atoms), the $(M{+}l)^+$ peak has a height (relative to M^+) '*n*' times 1.1%, in which '*n*' is the number of carbon atoms present in the molecule.

Solution

(i) The compound is likely to be an alcohol which easily eliminates water (M. wt. 18).
(ii) This indicates that the compound does not contain any carbon atom; the presence of carbon atom(s) in a molecule would produce an (M + 1) peak because of contribution by ^{13}C atom.
(iii) The relative abundance of $^{12}C : {}^{13}C = 100 : 1.11$. Therefore, for each carbon present in the molecule, the contribution to the $(M{+}1)^+$ peak intensity is 1.1%. For example, the (M + 1) peak intensity for C_6H_6 is expected to be $6 \times 1.1\% = 6.6\%$ of that of the parent peak.

Table 16.4 Common fragment ions*

m/*e* value	Ion commonly associated with the mass	Possible inference
15	CH_3^+	–
18	$H_2O^{\bullet +}$	–
26	$C_2H_2^{\bullet +}$	–
27	$C_2H_3^+$	–
28	$CO^{\bullet +}$, $C_2H_4^{\bullet +}$, $N_2^{\bullet +}$	–
29	CHO^+, $C_2H_5^+$	–
30	$CH_2NH_2^+$	Amine
	NO^+	Nitro compound
31	CH_2OH^+	Primary alcohol
36/38 (3 : 1)	$HCl^{\bullet +}$	Chloro compound
39	$C_3H_3^+$	–
40	$Ar^{\bullet +}$, $C_3H_4^{\bullet +}$	–
41	$C_3H_5^{\bullet +}$	–

(Continued)

*Ref. Mendham J, Denney R C, Barnes, J D and Thomas M J K, *Vogel's Textbook of Quantitative Chemical Analysis*, 5th Edition, Pearson Education, Singapore, 2000.

Table 16.4 Continued

m/e value	Ion commonly associated with the mass	Possible inference
	$C_2H_3N^{\bullet+}$	Aliphatic nitrile
43	$C_3H_7^+$	Propyl compound
	CH_3CO^+	Acetyl compound (example, methyl ketone)
	$C_2H_6N^+$	Aliphatic amine
	$^+NH_2{=}C{=}O$	Primary amide
45	$CH_3OCH_2^+$	Methyl ether
	CH_3CHOH^+	Alcohol
47	$CH_2{=}SH^+$, CH_3S^+	Thio compound
50	$C_4H_2^{\bullet+}$	Aromatic compound
51	$C_4H_3^+$	Aromatic compound
55	$C_4H_7^+$	
56	$C_4H_8^+$	
57	$C_4H_9^+$	Butyl compound
	$C_2H_5CO^+$	Ethyl ketone, propionate ester
58	$CH_2{=}C(OH)CH_3^{\bullet+}$	Ketone[a]
	$C_3H_8N^+$	Amine
59	$COOCH_3^+$	Methyl ester
	$CH_2{=}C(OH)NH_2^{\bullet+}$	Primary amide[a]
	$C_2H_5CH{=}OH^+$	$C_2H_5CH(OH){-}R$
	$CH_2{=}O{-}C_2H_5^+$ + isomers	Ether
60	$CH_2{=}C(OH)_2^{\bullet+}$	Carboxylic acid,[a] sugar
61	$CH_3CO(OH_2)^+$	Alkyl acetate
	$C_2H_5S^+$	Thio compound
65	$C_5H_5^+$	Aromatic compound
66	$H_2S_2^{\bullet+}$	
69	CF_3^+	Fluorocarbon
70	$C_5H_{10}^+$	
71	$C_5H_{11}^+$	$C_5H_{11}{-}R$
	$C_3H_7CO^+$	Propyl ketone, butyl ester
72	$CH_2{=}C(OH)C_2H_5^{\bullet+}$	Ketone[a]
	$C_4H_{10}N^+$	Amine
73	$C_4H_9O^+$	Alcohol, ether
	$(CH_3)_3Si^+$	Trimethylsilyl derivative
	$COOC_2H_5^+$	Ethyl ester
74	$C_3H_6O_2^{\bullet+}$	Methyl ester[a]
		Carboxylic acid

(*Continued*)

Table 16.4 Continued

m/e value	Ion commonly associated with the mass	Possible inference
75	$C_6H_3^+$	Disubstituted benzene
	$(CH_3)_2Si{=}OH^+$	Trimethylsilyl ether
76	$C_6H_4^+$	Benzene derivative
77	$C_6H_5^+$	Monosubstituted benzene
78	$C_6H_6^{\bullet+}$	Monosubstituted benzene
79/81 (1 : 1)	Br^+	Bromo compound
80/82 (1 : 1)	$HBr^{\bullet+}$	Bromo compound
83/85/87 (9 : 6 : 1)	$HCCl_2^+$	Chloroform
85	$C_4H_9CO^+$	$C_4H_9CO{-}R$
91	$C_7H_7^+$	Aromatic (possibly benzylic) compound
92	$C_6H_6N^+$	Substituted pyridine
91/93 (3 : 1)	$C_4H_8Cl^+$	Alkyl chloride
93/95 (1 : 1)	CH_2Br^+	Bromo compound
94	$C_6H_6O^{\bullet+}$	$C_6H_5O{-}R$
99	$C_5H_7O_2^{\bullet+}$	Ethylene ketal
105	$C_6H_5CO^+$	Benzoyl compound
122	$C_6H_5COOH^{\bullet+}$	Alkyl benzoate
123	$C_6H_5COOH_2^+$	Alkyl benzoate
127	I^+	Iodo compound
128	$HI^{\bullet+}$	Iodo compound
135/137 (1 : 1)	$C_4H_8Br^+$	Bromo compound
141	CH_2I^+	Iodo compound
147	$(CH_3)_2Si{=}O{-}Si(CH_3)_3$	Trimethysilyl ether
149	$C_8H_5O_3^+$	Dialkyl phthalate

[a]McLafferty fragment.

Table 16.5 Common losses from the molecular ion*

Ion	Species often associated with mass lost	Possible inference
M – 1	$H^\bullet$	Aldehydes, acetals, alkynes
M – 15	$CH_3^\bullet$	Acetals, methyl derivatives
M – 16	$O^\bullet$	Aromatic nitro compounds, *N*-oxides, sulphoxides
	$NH_2^\bullet$	Aromatic amides
M – 17	$OH^\bullet$	Carboxylic acids

(*Continued*)

*Ref: Mendham J, Denney R C, Barnes, J D and Thomas M J K, *Vogel's Textbook of Quantitative Chemical Analysis*, 5th Edition, Pearson Education, Singapore, 2000.

Table 16.5 Continued

Ion	Species often associated with mass lost	Possible inference
	NH_3	Amines (rare)
M – 18	H_2O	Alcohols, acids, aliphatic aldehydes, steroid alcohols and ketones
M – 19	F•	Fluoro compounds
M – 20	HF	Fluoro compounds
M – 26	C_2H_2	Aromatic compounds
M – 27	HCN	Aromatic nitriles, nitrogen heterocycles
M – 28	C_2H_4	Ethyl ester or ether, *n*-propyl ketone
	CO	Quinone, phenol, oxygen heterocycle
M – 29	$C_2H_5^•$	Ethyl group
	CHO•	Aromatic aldehydes, phenols
M – 30	CH_2O	Aromatic methyl esters
	NO	Aromatic nitro compounds
M – 31	$CH_3O^•$	Methyl ester, dimethyl acetal or ketal
M – 32	CH_3OH	Methyl ester
M – 33	$H_2O + CH_3$	Short-chain unbranched primary alcohols, steroid alcohols
	HS•	Thiols
M – 34	H_2S	Thiols
M – 35/37	Cl•	Chloro compounds
M – 36/38	HCl	Chloro compounds
M – 40	$^•CH_2CN$	Aliphatic nitriles and dinitriles
M – 41	$C_3H_5^•$	Propyl ester
M – 42	C_3H_6	Butyl ketone, propyl ether
	CH_2CO	Methyl ketone, acetates, *N*-acetyl compounds
M – 43	$C_3H_7^•$	Propyl ketone
	$CH_3CO^•$	Methyl ketone
	HNCO	Purines, dioxopiperazine
M – 44	CO_2	Anhydrides, cyclic imide, unsaturated esters, carbonates
M – 45	•COOH	Carboxylic acids
	$C_2H_5O^•$	Ethyl ester, acetal or ketal
M – 46	C_2H_5OH	Ethyl ester
	NO_2	Aromatic nitro compounds
	$CO + H_2O$	Carboxylic acids
M – 47	CH_2SH, CH_3S	Aliphatic thiols
M – 48	CH_3SH	Methyl thioester
	SO	Aromatic sulphoxides
M – 55	$C_4H_7^•$	Butyl ester
M – 56	C_4H_8	Butyl compounds, pentyl ketones
	CO + CO	Quinone

EXERCISES

1. Predict the increasing order of peak intensities of molecular ions for the following, under identical mass spectral analysis conditions: 2-Methybutane, *n*-hexane, neopentane and ethane.

2. Rationalise the following:
   (a) Long-chain fatty acids undergo McLafferty rearrangement.
   (b) For ethers, molecular ion peaks are weak.
   (c) The mass spectra of nitro–compounds have peaks at $m/z = 30$ and $m/z = 46$.
   (d) The mass spectrum of methylphenyl ketone has two intense peaks at $m/z = 105$ and $m/z = 77$.

3. An alkene A, on treatment with BH_3 and then with NaOH and H_2O_2 produces a primary alcohol B. The mass spectrum of B has a feeble parent ion peak at m/z 56. Predict the structures of A and B. Write the complete fragmentation pattern for A.

17 Laser Techniques

17.1 INTRODUCTION

Ever since Ted Maiman built the first ruby laser in 1961, spectroscopy has undergone a sea-change. We have seen that Raman spectroscopy in particular has obtained a new lease of life with the advent of lasers. In this chapter we will discuss new analytical techniques that have become possible purely because of the lasers.

17.2 WHY LASERS

We have seen that light sources such as inert gas discharge and incandescent lamps are used in absorption and fluorescence spectroscopy and hollow cathode lamps in atomic absorption spectroscopy. Lasers have properties that are uniquely different from these conventional light sources and therein lies the basis for the applications of lasers in analytical chemistry. Lasers are distinctively different from conventional light sources in that they are highly collimated, intense and monochromatic. Conventional light sources can be collimated using optical devices such as lenses and apertures and can be made monochromatic using dispersion devices such as gratings. However, the process of collimation using apertures and monochromatisation using gratings reduces the intensity of the light beam from conventional sources. However, the laser beam is collimated, intense and monochromatic, which sets it apart from discharge and incandescent sources.

This difference in properties arises fundamentally from the high degree of coherence which the laser beam possesses, unlike conventional sources. Laser beams possess both spatial and temporal coherence. *Spatial coherence* is the correlation in phases at two points on the wave front. Beams with a large spatial coherence display a high degree of collimation. Likewise, *temporal coherence* is the correlation in phase that exists between two points in time. Temporal coherence imparts monochromaticity to the beam—beams with large temporal coherence are highly monochromatic. Lasers display coherence properties because of the mechanism by which they are produced. While conventional light sources are produced by spontaneous emission, lasers are produced by stimulated emission which imparts to them the coherence that they display. It is this coherence that is the underlying cause for a number of applications of lasers to analytical chemistry and spectroscopy.

We will discuss the applications of lasers in analytical chemistry where each of the properties, intensity, monochromaticity and collimation, is taken advantage of. But before we discuss the applications of lasers to analytical techniques, we will first study the working of a laser.

17.2.1 WORKING OF A LASER

Conventional light sources, such as the incandescent lamp, discharge lamps, candles, and so on, produce light when atoms constituting the light source are excited to a higher energy state, which then return to the ground state *spontaneously* by emitting light (Fig. 17.1a). The process of spontaneous emission in these light sources is incoherent; which means that the emission of a given photon does not bear any definite phase relation with that of any other photon; the emission process is essentially random. Incoherent sources exhibit divergence, which is why the light bulb in our homes, lights up the entire room, and thankfully so! The process of spontaneous emission also produces light over a wide spectral range, the spectral width being decided by a number of broadening mechanisms.

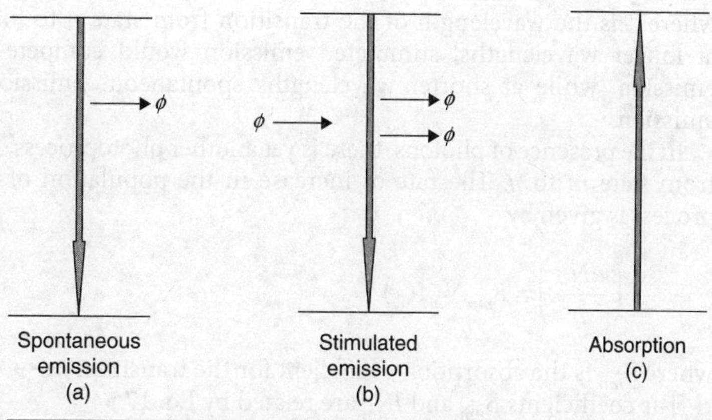

Fig. 17.1 Energy level scheme showing **(a)** spontaneous emission, **(b)** stimulated emission and **(c)** absorption

In addition to spontaneous emission, there is yet another process by which an excited state can decay to the ground state—radiatively. This is the process of *stimulated emission* (Fig. 17.1b). In the process, the excited state is driven to the lower state by a *driver photon*. The driver photon stimulates the emission in the excited molecule, causing it to emit a photon. The condition for the occurrence of this process is that the driver photon should possess the same frequency as the emitted photon. Furthermore, the emitted photon is in the same direction as the driving photon with both the photons being coherent. The coherence leads to the stimulated emission process with a high degree of collimation. Stimulated emission beams can travel long distances with only a small increase in their beam diameters. In addition, stimulated emission produces beams with narrow frequency widths.

It must be kept in mind that while stimulated emission is produced in the presence of a driver photon, there is still a probability of spontaneous emission occurring under these conditions. The relative probabilities of spontaneous and stimulated emission when both processes are possible can be evaluated (which will now be discussed). The rate of spontaneous emission from the state m to state n, is given by the Einstein coefficient A_{nm} (Eq. 17.1), which gives the rate of depletion of the excited state n.

$$-\left(\frac{dN_n}{dt}\right) = A_{nm}N_n \tag{17.1}$$

In Eq. 17.1, N_n is the population of the excited state. Similarly, the rate of stimulated emission is given by the Einstein coefficient B_{nm} in Eq. 17.2.

$$-\left(\frac{dN_n}{dt}\right) = B_{nm}N_nI(\nu) \tag{17.2}$$

where $I(\nu)$ is the intensity of light that drives the stimulated emission process. Since the atoms or molecules in an excited state can decay through both spontaneous and stimulated processes, one can evaluate the ratio of A_{nm} and B_{nm} (Eq. 17.3).

$$\frac{A_{nm}}{B_{nm}} = \left(\frac{8\pi h}{\lambda^3}\right) \tag{17.3}$$

where λ is the wavelength of the transition from state n to m. It is clear from Eq. 17.3 that at longer wavelengths, stimulated emission would compete effectively with spontaneous emission, while at shorter wavelengths spontaneous emission dominates over stimulated emission.

In the presence of photons, there is yet another photoprocess, namely absorption (Fig. 17.1c), from state m to n. The rate of increase in the population of state n due to the absorption process is given by

$$\left(\frac{dN_n}{dt}\right) = B_{mn} N_m I(\nu) \tag{17.4}$$

where B_{mn} is the absorption coefficient for the transition $m \rightarrow n$.

The coefficients B_{mn} and B_{nm} are related by Eq. 17.5

$$B_{mn} = \left(\frac{g_m}{g_n}\right) B_{nm} \tag{17.5}$$

where g_m and g_n are the degeneracies of states m and n.

17.2.2 Principle of Laser Action

In order to understand laser action in a material, let us first consider the photophysics that occurs in a molecule with just two levels. At any temperature, the population in the two levels is dictated by the Boltzmann distribution law,

$$\frac{N_i}{N_j} = \left(\frac{g_i}{g_j}\right) \exp\left(\frac{-\Delta E}{kT}\right) \tag{17.6}$$

where N_i and N_j are populations in the levels i and j at temperature T, ΔE is the energy difference between the two states, k is the Boltzmann constant and g_i and g_j are the statistical weights of the two states. Usually at a given temperature, the population of the molecules in the lower energy state will be higher than that in the higher energy state. If a photon, whose energy matches the energy difference between the two states is incident on the molecule, it can cause either absorption or stimulated emission. However, since the population in the lower energy state is usually larger, there is a larger probability for absorption to occur and hence a molecule is likely to be excited to the higher energy state. As the absorption continues, eventually a point is reached where the population in the two states becomes equal. At this point, the probabilities of absorption and stimulated emission are equal. This condition is referred to as saturation. No further increase in the population of the excited state can occur after this point. For stimulated emission to dominate over absorption, it is essential that the population of the higher energy state be larger than that in the ground state, which we have just seen, cannot occur in a two-level system.

Let us now consider a three-level system (Fig. 17.2). If as before, a photon is incident on the system whose energy matches the energy difference between levels 1 and 2, a molecule will be excited to level 2. If now this excited molecule can relax quickly to level 3, whose lifetime is reasonably long, then there will be a propensity for the population to build up in level 3. Eventually, this state may have a population that exceeds that in the ground state, a condition that is referred to as population inversion. Under these conditions, a photon whose energy equals that of the energy difference between the states 3 and 1, is more likely to cause stimulated emission between these levels rather than absorption. In other words, a population inversion that can be achieved in this 3-level system, can lead to a stimulated emission between levels 3 and 1. In stimulated emission, a photon is incident on the sample with a population inversion, but two photons are emitted—one the incident photon and the other caused by stimulated emission. The stimulated emission process therefore leads to an amplification of light, which forms the basis of laser action.

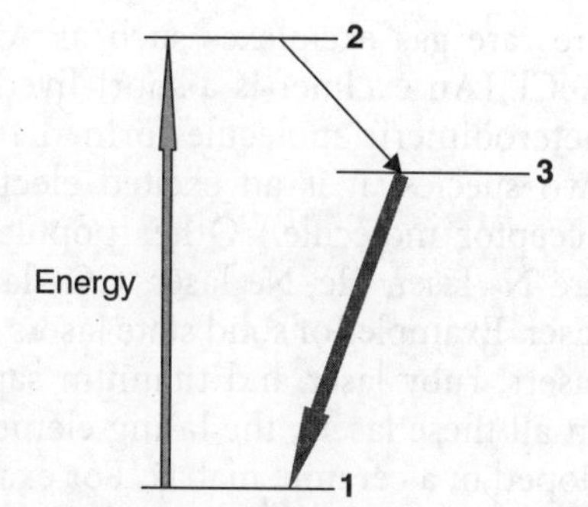

Fig. 17.2 A three level energy system to demonstrate laser action

Stimulated emission process produces photons that have a high degree of coherence, which therefore causes laser light to manifest properties of coherent light. Spontaneous emission on the other hand, is a process where each photon is emitted independent of the other, leading to this form of light having little coherence. The difference in properties of the laser light compared with sources such as the light bulb (discussed earlier), is due to this fundamental difference in the way each source produces light—stimulated emission in the case of lasers and spontaneous emission in the case of the light bulb.

17.2.3 Types of Lasers

The first broad classification of lasers may be considered on the basis of the *pulsed* or *continuous nature* of the laser beam. Continuous wave lasers or CW lasers, such as He–Ne lasers, Ar^+ lasers and CO_2 lasers, have a nearly constant beam intensity. The beam intensity is measured in watts. In pulsed lasers, the laser beam is produced in short bursts of light. The laser pulse is characterised by pulse energy, temporal pulse width and repetition rate. Pulse energy is usually expressed in joules/pulse. Lasers with pulse widths ranging from milliseconds to femtoseconds are available. Shorter pulse widths are generally employed where fast dynamical processes need to be studied. For pulsed lasers, the power of the laser is quoted either as the *peak power* or *average power*. The two definitions are necessary because of the pulsed nature of the laser output.

The *peak power* is the power delivered by the laser during the time the laser pulse is on and is defined as the energy per pulse divided by the temporal pulse width. For example, a laser pulse that has 10 mJ/pulse and a pulse width of 10 ns, delivers a peak power which is equal to 10 mJ/10 ns or 1 MW. This power, it must be remembered, is delivered only during the period the laser pulse is on. The *average power* is defined as the pulse energy multiplied by the repetition rate. The same laser system if running at a repetition rate of 10 Hz would deliver an average power of 100 mW (10 mJ × 10 Hz).

The huge difference in the peak and average power is because of the short pulse width and the low repetition rate. While the laser delivers a large power during every pulse, it really is off most of the time, which is referred to as having a small duty cycle, and hence has a small average power. Repetition rates can vary from a few Hz (as in the Nd:YAG laser) to a few hundred Hz (as in excimer lasers). Methods to produce pulsed lasers are discussed in textbooks on lasers and the reader is referred to such treatments.

Lasers can also be classified as gas lasers, solid state lasers and liquid lasers, based on the state of the lasing medium. Examples of gas lasers are *excimer* lasers, where the lasing media are rare gas exciplexes such as ArF, KrF and XeCl. (An excimer is a short-lived dimeric or heterodimeric molecule formed from at least two species. It is an excited electron donor–acceptor molecule.) Other popular gas lasers are N_2 laser, He–Ne laser, CO_2 laser and Ar^+ laser. Examples of solid state lasers are Nd:YAG lasers, ruby laser and titanium sapphire laser. In all these lasers, the lasing element is an ion doped in a ceramic matrix. For example, in the Nd:YAG laser, Nd^{3+} is doped at concentrations of ~1 atom per cent in yttrium aluminum garnet. Similarly, Cr^{3+} is doped in Al_2O_3 in the ruby laser. An example of a laser where the lasing medium is a liquid, is the dye laser. Table 17.1 lists the various popular lasers and their corresponding lasing wavelengths.

Table 17.1 Some popular lasers with their corresponding wavelengths

Laser	Wavelength
CO_2	10.6 μm
N_2	337.1 nm
He–Ne	632.8 nm
XeCl	308 nm
KrF	248 nm
ArF	193 nm
Ar^+	488 nm and 514.5 nm
Nd:YAG	1064 nm

Lasers have been used in analytical chemistry and each application uses one or more of the unique properties of lasers—monochromaticity, intensity and collimation. We will now discuss some of the most popular applications.

17.2.4 Lasers—Facts

- Laser generation was invented by Charles Townes and Arthur Schawlow of Bell Laboratories (USA) in 1958.
- Semiconducting lasers are multilayer semiconductor devices that generate a coherent beam of monochromatic light by laser action.
- Stimulated emission: Incident photon + atom with excited electron → atom with unexcited electron + emitted photon + incident photon.
- Lasers have good coherence, that is, their wavelengths are in phase in space and also in time.

17.3 APPLICATIONS OF LASERS

17.3.1 Fluorescence Spectroscopy

In this technique (discussed in Chapter 10), the sample is excited by light and the emission from the sample is then recorded. The emission from the sample serves as a good fingerprint of the sample being studied, and intensity of the emission, is a measure of the concentration of the sample. In many fluorescence spectrometers, a Xe lamp with a monochromator provides the excitation wavelength—the use of lasers for excitation adds a new dimension to this technique. In fluorescence spectroscopy, the number of molecules excited by the incident radiation depends on the intensity of the incident radiation. Intense sources therefore result in a larger fluorescence emission, and therefore allow for smaller concentrations to be detected. The use of intense laser sources has therefore pushed the limits of detection in fluorescence spectroscopy to smaller values. For example, limits as low as ng/mL to pg/mL have been achieved through the use of lasers, in the estimation of uranium in aqueous solutions. The monochromaticity of lasers also allows the selective excitation of species in a mixture, by taking advantage of the difference in absorption wavelengths of different molecular species. Lasers of short pulses are also used for the determination of fluorescence lifetimes, as described in Chapter 10.

17.3.2 Multiphoton Process

The intensity of the lasers has also opened a completely new dimension in spectroscopy—multiphoton processes. Normally, an atom or molecule absorbs one photon and makes a transition from a state *i* to *j* where the energy of the photon equals the energy difference between the two states. However, under conditions where the light source is intense, it is possible for a molecule to absorb two photons simultaneously, and make a transition from a state *i* to *j* such that the sum of the energy of the two photons equals the energy difference between the two states in question. Such a process is called a multiphoton process and is possible only when the light source has a large photon flux. The technique of multiphoton processes has become a possibility only after the advent of lasers.

Multiphoton processes have a number of advantages over single photon process. First, since two photons are used to span the energy difference $i \leftrightarrow j$, each photon needs to have only half the energy of the energy difference between the two states. That is, if the energy difference between two states is 65,000 cm^{-1} (which translates to ~150 nm), two photons, each of 32,500 cm^{-1} (~300 nm) would be required to conduct a two-photon excitation from state *i* to *j*. While radiation of wavelength ~150 nm would be required to conduct a one-photon excitation, radiation of ~300 nm would be required for a two-photon process. Experimentally, this is an advantage, since 150 nm corresponds to the vacuum ultraviolet region, while 300 nm is not. The vacuum ultraviolet region, which constitutes the region below ~190 nm is not transmitted through air, as oxygen in the air strongly absorbs in this region of the electromagnetic radiation. Experiments in this region are therefore conducted with some difficulty, as the radiation must be passed through specially designed vacuum chambers. Experiments that use radiation longer than 190 nm are more easily handled. Hence, two-photon processes convert the experiments that fall in the vacuum ultraviolet region for a one-photon process, to the more easily handled near- and far-ultraviolet region.

Another important advantage of a two-photon process has to do with the modified selection rules compared to those of a one-photon process. For a molecule that has a centre of symmetry, such as benzene, parity considerations prohibit transitions from states of gerade symmetry (*g*) to other states of the same symmetry, that is, $g \leftrightarrow g$ and $u \leftrightarrow u$ transitions are prohibited and only $g \leftrightarrow u$ and $u \leftrightarrow g$ transitions are allowed for a dipole-allowed one-photon transition. This selection therefore prohibits observation of excited states that have the same symmetry as the ground state. For a two-photon process however, $g \leftrightarrow g$ and $u \leftrightarrow u$ transitions are allowed; such transitions provide for the observation of states, that was prohibited by a one-photon process. This feature makes it possible to observe states that were hitherto impossible to be observed by a conventional one-photon process.

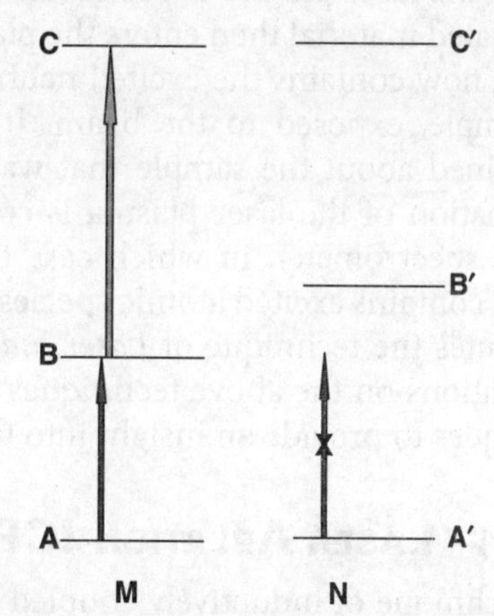

Fig. 17.3 Schematic showing a two-colour two-photon experiment, where one species M is selectively excited in the presence of another species N, which otherwise would have caused interference in a one-photon experiment

Multiphoton excitation can also be performed with photons of two different wavelengths. The first photon excites the atoms or molecules to an excited state, say B, while a second photon of a different wavelength, promotes this excited atom or molecule to a further excited state C, from where the molecule may relax emitting fluorescence (Fig. 17.3). In other words, fluorescence can be observed by exciting the atom or molecule to a predetermined excited state C, through an intermediate state B. One may of course argue that this process has no particular advantage than that conducted by directly exciting to the state C. The advantage becomes apparent in cases where two different species M and N (atoms or molecules), have excited states placed at nearly equal energies. Here, it can be seen that when one tries to excite species of interest M, the other species N may also be excited to the state C′, that lies at nearly the same energy as state C of M, causing interference in the observation of species M (Fig. 17.3). Such spectral interference is quite common in spectroscopic studies, as we have already seen in Chapter 9. Two-photon experiments can be used to advantage in such cases, which can be explained by referring to Fig. 17.3. While the final excited states C and C′, may be located at nearly equal energies for the two species, it is possible to select an intermediate state that does not have an interference. For example, as shown in Fig. 17.3, the intermediate state B of species M, has energy that is different from that of the intermediate state B′ of species N. Hence one can selectively reach state C of species M, by first exciting it to B. The photon that excites state B would not be resonant with state B′ of species N, and therefore causes no excitation of species N. Hence species M can be excited selectively, without the interference of the second species, in a two-photon process. The use of two different wavelengths in the excitation process provides this flexibility and consequent selectivity.

17.3.3 Laser Ablation Processes

The availability of high intensity lasers has opened up the area of laser ablation processes. In this technique, a high energy laser beam is focussed onto a sample surface. At the focal point, the power density of the laser beam may exceed many tens of megawatts/cm^2. For example, if a 10 ns Nd:YAG laser of pulse energy 10 mJ/pulse is focussed to a spot size of 50 μm, which is quite typical, the power density at the focal point would be ~50 GW/cm^2. At these power densities, a laser plasma is produced, which ablates the material exposed to the laser beam. The ablated material then enters the plasma where the atoms are excited and ionised. The laser plasma now contains the excited neutrals and ions characteristic of the material constituting the sample, exposed to the beam. If this plasma is now examined, valuable information is obtained about the sample that was ablated. This is the technique of laser ablation. The examination of the laser plasma is conducted by hyphenating the laser ablation process to a mass spectrometer, in which case the process is *laser ablation mass spectroscopy*. As the plasma contains excited atomic species, emission from the plasma can also be observed, which constitutes the technique of *Laser Induced Breakdown Spectroscopy* (LIBS). While a number of variations on the above techniques can be seen in the literature, we will discuss these two techniques to provide an insight into the basic working.

17.3.4 Laser Ablation ICP-MS

The technique of inductively coupled plasma spectroscopy has been discussed in Chapter 9. We will therefore discuss only the process of hyphenation between laser ablation and ICP-MS. The experimental set up is shown in Fig. 17.4. The sample is exposed to a focussed laser beam leading to the ablation of the sample. The ablated sample is flushed with Ar and then carried through a tubing into the ICP-MS. The typical tubing length is ~1 m. The material that enters the ICP, which is representative of the sample that was ablated, is then atomised and ionised, and detected by the mass spectrometer. An important experimental consideration in laser ablation ICP-MS is that sample must be rastored (vapourised) during the experiment. If the ablation is conducted at the same spot on the sample, the signal intensity decreases with time. The decrease is due to the formation of a crater, which causes the sample surface to recede, so that as the laser ablation process proceeds, the laser beam is no longer focussed on the surface. To alleviate this problem, the sample must be rastored using a X–Y translator so that a fresh sample surface is exposed for successive laser pulses.

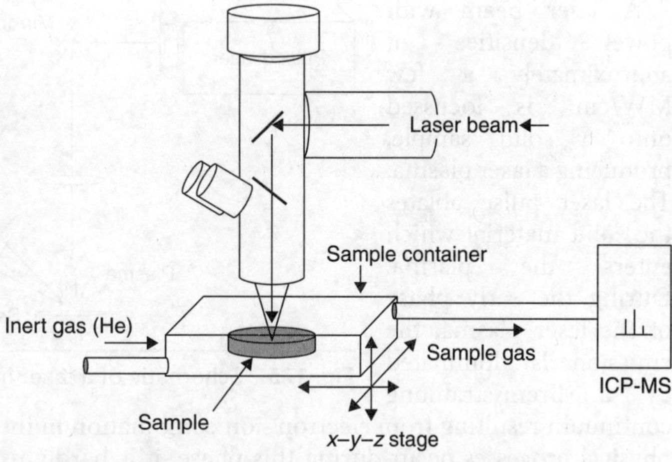

Fig. 17.4 Schematic diagram of laser ablation inductively coupled mass spectrometer

The advantage of the laser ablation process is that very little sample pre-treatment is necessary. Usually, the sample is introduced into the ICP as a solution that is sprayed into the plasma using a nebuliser. However, this sampling technique entails dissolution of the solid sample. The laser ablation process, on the other hand, does not need dissolution of the sample and is therefore convenient particularly when handling difficult-to-dissolve refractory materials. Furthermore, the laser ablation process uses very little of the sample and hardly leaves a discernible impression on the sample, so that the technique essentially turns out to be non-destructive. This is an extremely important advantage when dealing with precious samples.

Another important advantage of the laser ablation process is that it can be used for determining the concentration of analytes as a function of spatial coordinates, that is, spatial concentration profiling can be done using this technique. This is made possible as the laser beam is focussed to about 50 μm spot size, so that the concentration of the analytes can be determined for every ~75 to 100 μm aliquot of the sample. This is a unique feature of the technique as the solution sampling technique cannot retain the concentration profile during the dissolution process.

The detection limits for this technique is in the sub-ppm region, but more importantly this technique has a significantly larger dynamic range than the solution technique. The larger dynamic range is achieved by simply turning down the laser energy when estimating analytes that have a higher concentration and vice versa. This flexibility is not available with the solution sampling technique and the only way high concentration analytes can be estimated is by diluting the sample solution.

The technique has also been hyphenated with ICP emission spectroscopy, mainly to derive the advantage of direct solid sampling and spatial sample profiling.

17.3.5 Laser Induced Breakdown Spectroscopy (LIBS)

The technique of *laser induced breakdown spectroscopy* is somewhat of a recent introduction into the long list of laser techniques applied to analytical chemistry. This technique has the laser ablation process as the front end of the technique, while the detection process is different when compared to laser ablation ICP-MS.

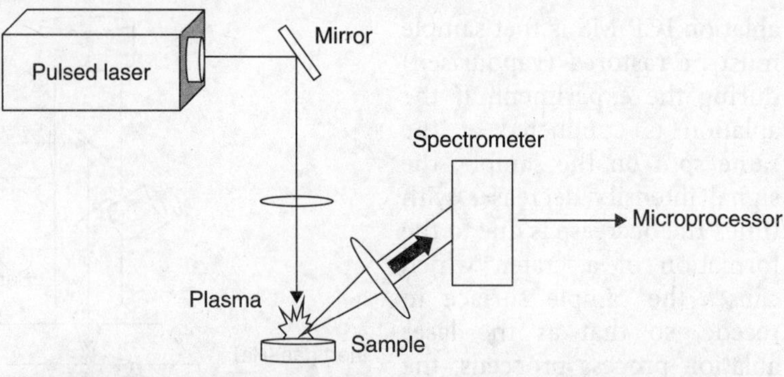

Fig. 17.5 Schematic of a laser induced breakdown spectrometer

A laser beam with power densities of approximately a few MW/cm^2 is focussed onto a solid sample, producing a laser plasma. The laser pulse ablates the solid material which enters the plasma. During the early phase of the laser plasma, the emission is dominated by a Bremsstrahlung continuum resulting from electron–ion combination in the plasma. While several interesting physical processes occur during this phase, it is hardly useful for the purposes of chemical analysis. The continuum emission is however short-lived and extends to just a few hundred nanoseconds after the laser pulse. At the end of this phase, when the plasma expands and cools, sharp emission lines from atoms and ions begin to appear. The emission observed from ions and atoms are characteristic of the sample which was ablated and hence the emission from the laser plasma provides an analytical tool for the characterisation of the solid. The emission from the laser plasma is monitored by focussing the emission onto a spectrometer, fitted with a detector that can be time gated. Figure 17.5 shows the schematic of the LIBS experimental set up. *Time gating* is a process where one records the emission from the laser plasma after a specific time delay following the laser pulse and the emission is recorded for a definite predetermined period called the *time window*. Delaying the observation of the emission from the laser plasma is essential, since the initial phase contains only the continuum emission, which, as mentioned earlier, is not of much use from a chemical analysis point of view. Delaying the observation till the continuum emission dies off ensures that one observes the characteristic emission lines of the ions and neutrals of the elements constituting the solid sample, lending analytical utility to this method. An appropriate choice of the delay and the gate window is necessary to optimise the emission intensity. The emission observed from the laser plasma at various delay times and the choice of the delay time are important aspects of this analytical technique. Figure 17.6 shows the atomic emission lines of metal M in a stainless steel sample. If appropriate standards are available, the technique can be used for quantification of these elements. Similar to laser ablation ICP-MS, for the LIBS signal to be steady, the sample must be rastored to expose a fresh surface for every laser pulse.

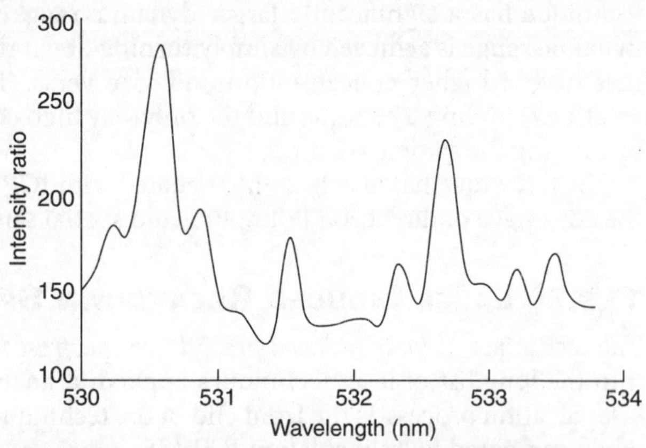

Fig. 17.6 A typical LIBS spectrum: metal M in an alloy

One of the major advantages of the LIBS technique is the simplicity of sample handling. While techniques such as solution-based ICP techniques involve sample dissolution, which at times can be difficult, the laser ablation technique is a direct solid handling method. Furthermore, since the excitation and detection processes are photon-based, it is amenable to fibre-optic adaptation. The laser beam can be made incident onto the sample using a fibre-optical cable, and the emission, likewise, can be collected and transmitted to a spectrometer using an optical fibre. This enables this technique to be used for remote analysis of hazardous materials.

While LIBS has been applied to the analysis of solids and gases, its application to the analysis of liquid samples requires imaginative sampling techniques. Focussing a laser pulse onto the surface of a liquid causes splashing and consequent fogging of the focussing lens or window. Hence a variety of ingenious methods for liquid sampling have been reported in the literature. One method is to spot the liquid sample onto an absorbent paper, dry the paper containing the solutions and laser ablate the solid film left on the paper. Wood has also been used to serve as a vehicle for the liquid sample. Another interesting method is to electrochemically deposit the elements in the aqueous solution onto an electrode; the electrode is then subjected to a LIBS analysis. The detection limits for the LIBS technique for the analysis of liquids is typically 1 μg/mL. Though this limit is inferior to that obtained in laser ablation ICP-MS, the ease of sampling and amenability for remote operation make this technique attractive.

While nanosecond laser pulses have been routinely used for LIBS experiments, more recently pico and femtosecond laser pulses have been shown to be useful in these experiments. Ultrashort pulses produce very little heating, and ablation occurs with very little matrix effects. The intensities of the emission lines therefore are reasonably independent of the matrix in which they occur. This is a considerable advantage as matrix matched standards are not necessary for the quantification of the elements.

17.3.6 Matrix-Assisted Laser Desorption and Ionisation (MALDI)

This technique has found extensive applications in the field of biosciences as well as chemical sciences. In these studies, it is important to determine the molecular weight and structure of large molecules, such as peptides, polymers and dendrimers (repetitively branched molecules). However, these molecules are non-volatile and introducing them into a mass spectrometer for molecular weight determination is a challenge. Heating the sample is not advisable as the molecules tend to decompose on heating. MALDI is a technique that serves to gently introduce these high molecular weight samples into the mass spectrometer. The utility and importance of this technique can be quickly gauged when one notes that the pioneers of this technique, John Fenn and Koichi Tanaka, received the Nobel Prize in 2002.

In this technique, the polymer to be studied is embedded in a matrix. The matrix is appropriately chosen to absorb the laser energy that is incident on it. The absorbed energy causes the matrix together with the sample embedded in it, to desorb, which results in the large molecular weight polymer to be brought into the gas phase. During the process of desorption, the polymer gets protonated to form species such as MH^+, which can be extracted into a mass spectrometer for mass analysis.

The choice of the matrix is important in this technique and the ones usually employed are nicotinic acid, sinapinic acid, glycerol and nitrobenzoic acid. A solution of the sample is mixed with a solution of the matrix in ratios where the matrix is in large excess, ranging from typically 100:1 to ~10,000:1. A small amount of this mixture, typically a few μL is placed on a metal disk and dried to remove the solvent. The sample disk is placed in the vacuum system of a mass spectrometer. A short pulse (~10 ns) UV laser, usually from a N_2 laser, is incident on the sample film. The sample disk is rotated to expose a fresh sample surface to every laser pulse, to obtain a steady signal intensity. The matrix absorbs the UV radiation

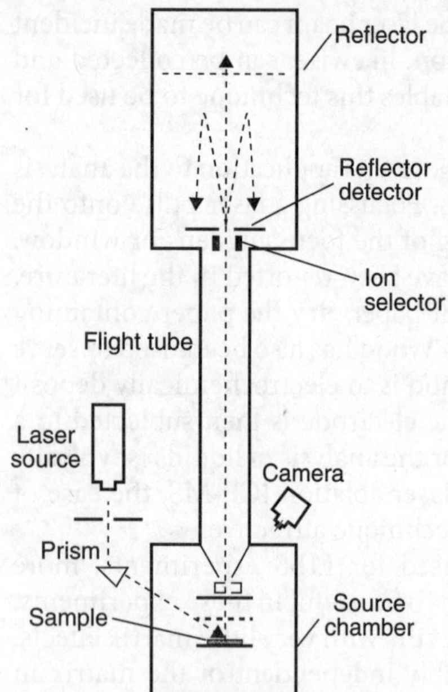

Fig. 17.7 Schematic of MALDI instrument

and desorbs, carrying with it the sample polymer into the gas phase. Concomitantly, the desorption process also produces the ions of the desorbed sample. In MALDI, sample ions are not produced by ionisation, as in e-impact ionisation mass spectrometry, but rather by proton attachment. The matrix provides a proton that attaches to the polymer molecules, to produce MH^+. This positive ion is then extracted into a mass spectrometer for a mass analysis, which is usually performed with a time-of-flight analyser. Since the process of ion production is due to a soft proton attachment process, a MALDI mass spectrum usually displays just a single peak at the mass corresponding to MH^+, with hardly any fragmentation. This feature is extremely useful when one needs to determine the molecular weight of the peptide, particularly when the sample contains a mixture of peptides. If fragmentation is required for the sake of structural inferences, one can always increase the laser pulse energy to cause fragmentation. Figure 17.7 shows the schematic of the MALDI experimental set up. A typical MALDI spectrum is shown in Fig. 17.8.

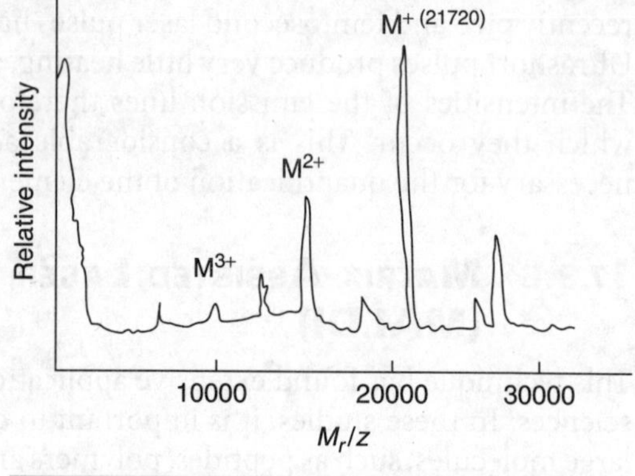

Fig. 17.8 A typical MALDI spectrum of a polypeptide.

17.3.7 Cavity Ring Down Spectrometry

Absorption spectroscopy is a popular tool for many analytical chemistry applications. However, this technique does not offer low detection limits. To overcome the problem of poor absorption or low concentration, *multipass cells* (Fig. 17.9) are used, where the light beam, instead of making just one pass through the absorption cell, is made to pass several times over (Fig. 17.9a), so that the effective pathlength is large. In a multipass cell, the light enters the cell at a small angle and is incident onto one of the mirrors (A). The light is then reflected to fall on mirror B and after several reflections exits the cell for detection. The increased pathlength enables the determination of low concentrations or molecules with small absorption coefficients.

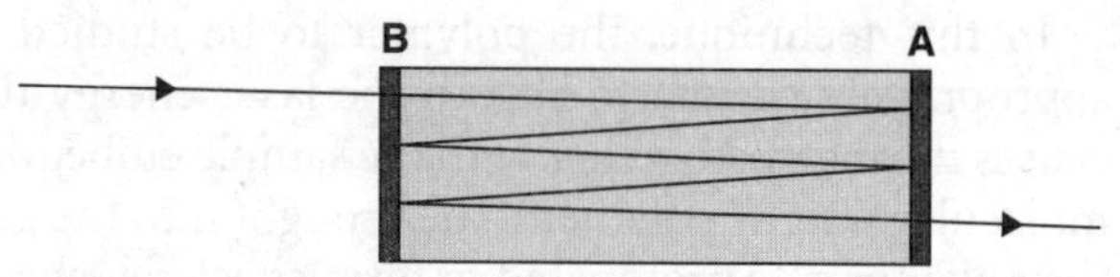

Fig. 17.9(a) Schematic of a multipass cell used in absorption spectroscopy

Figure 17.9a represents a conventional multiply cell. Figure 17.9b denotes a linear multipass cell invented by Herriott and Schulte in 1965 at Bell Laboratories (USA). It consists of two

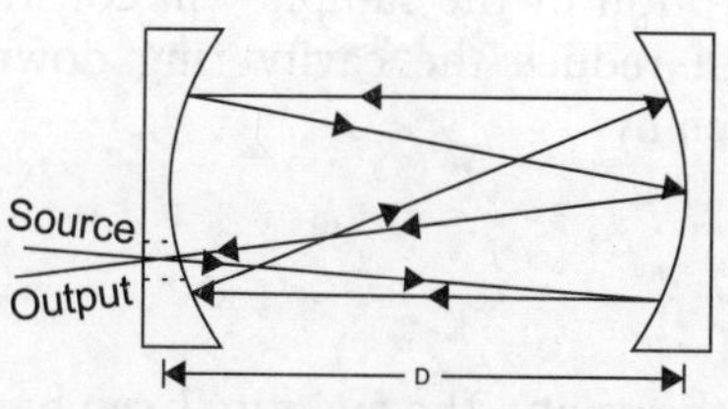

Fig. 17.9(b) Classical multipass absorption cells

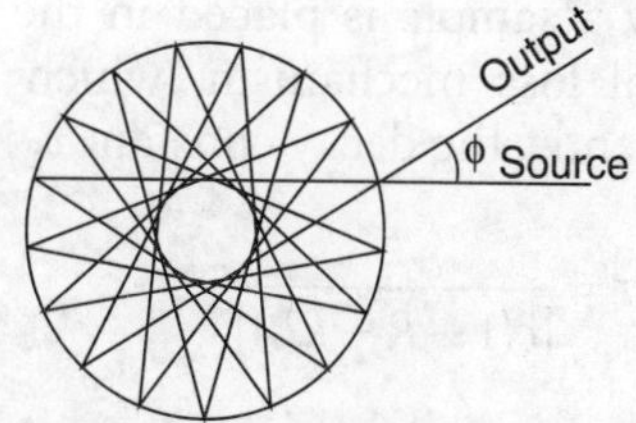

Fig. 17.9(c) Circular multipass absorption cells

opposing spherical mirrors. A hole in one of the mirrors enables the input and output beams to enter and also exit. Figure 17.9c denotes a circular multipass cell invented by Thoma and his coworkers in 1994. It consists of an arrangement of spherical mirrors in a concentric manner. The beam is made to enter this cell under an angle and propagate inside the cell on a star-shaped pattern. This cell helps in recording the spectra of extremely low volumes of analytes.

With the advent of lasers, the multipass method has led to the development of a new coencept—*cavity ring down spectroscopy*. In this technique, a laser pulse is injected into a cavity consisting of two plano-concave mirrors of very high reflectivities (R > 0.999) (Fig. 17.10). The spatial width of the laser pulse is shorter than the cavity round trip time. Each time the laser beam is incident on the mirror, a small amount of light leaks out of the cavity, while a major part of the beam is retained inside the cavity. If the intensity of the light injected into the cavity is I_o, then at the first bounce off mirror B, the light leaking out of the cavity would be $(1 - R)I_o$. The light that is reflected off mirror B back into the cavity will have an intensity I_oR. This pulse is reflected off mirror A and returns to mirror B with an intensity I_oR^2, where a fraction of this light leaks out. The intensity that leaks out during the second bounce of mirror B would be smaller than that at first. Likewise, every subsequent bounce of mirror B causes progressively smaller intensities of light to leak out. A detector positioned beyond mirror B would detect pulses of light with progressively smaller intensities, with the decay showing an exponential envelope of time constant τ_o (Eq. 17.7).

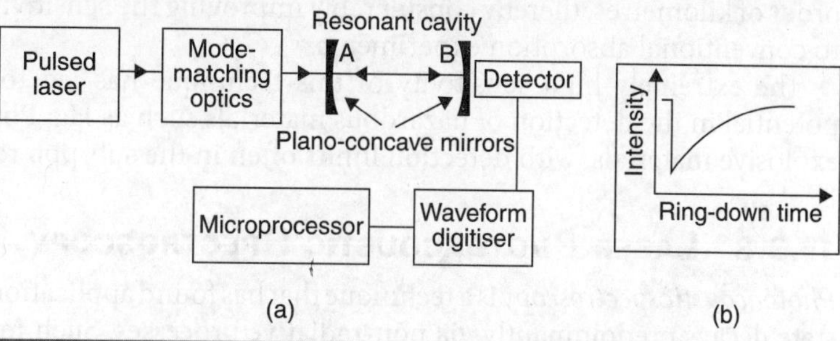

Fig. 17.10 (a) Schematic of cavity ring down spectrometer; (b) A typical spectrum

$$I = I \exp\left(\frac{-t}{\tau_o}\right) \tag{17.7}$$

The time constant of the decay process τ_o, is called the cavity ring down time, which for an empty cavity (with no sample) is determined mainly by mirror reflectivities (Eq. 17.8).

$$\tau_o = \frac{L}{[c(1-R)]} \tag{17.8}$$

where R is the mirror reflectivity, L is the cavity round trip length and c is the velocity of light.

If now a sample is placed in the cavity, the absorption of the sample will constitute an additional loss mechanism, which consequently will reduce the cavity ring down time. Consequently, the decay constant τ, in this case, is given by

$$\tau = \frac{L}{[c(1 - R + kL)]} \tag{17.9}$$

where k is the absorption coefficient of the sample, in the cavity. The quantity k can be written in terms of the decay constants τ_o and τ, as

$$k = c^{-1}(\tau^{-1} - \tau_o^{-1}) \tag{17.10}$$

The absorption of the sample is therefore measured in terms of a decrease in the cavity ring down *time*, and not by measuring the decrease in the intensity of light which is done in routine absorption experiments. Furthermore, the high reflectivities of the mirrors cause the light pulse to make innumerable transits within the cavity, so that the effective pathlength is of the order of kilometres, thereby considerably improving the sensitivity of the technique, compared to conventional absorption experiments.

The extremely high sensitivity of this technique has led to this technique having great potential in the detection of hazardous materials such as Hg, Pb, NO_x in ambient air, and also explosive materials, with detection limits often in the sub-ppb regime.

17.3.8 Laser Photoacoustic Spectroscopy

Photoacoustic spectroscopy is a technique that has found applications for molecules whose excited state decays predominantly via non-radiative processes. Such molecules are not amenable for observation using fluorescence methods and photoacoustic spectroscopy provides a strong alternative. In this method, a laser source is used to excite a sample. The molecules that are excited return to the ground state by colliding with the surrounding molecules, which causes the energy of the excited state to be lost through non-radiative processes. Consequently, the translation energy of the surrounding molecules increases, which results in an increase in its temperature. Larger the absorption by the sample, the larger will be the increase in the temperature rise; monitoring the temperature increase will therefore yield the absorption by the sample. If the incident light is pulsed at a certain frequency, the temperature rise of the sample will also pulse at the same frequency. In a closed cell, the temperature rise will manifest as a pressure pulse that oscillates at the same frequency as the frequency of the input radiation. If the frequency is in the audio regime, the pressure pulse can be picked up as an audio signal by using a microphone as the pressure transducer. A schematic view of the laser photoacoustic spectrometer is shown in Fig. 17.11.

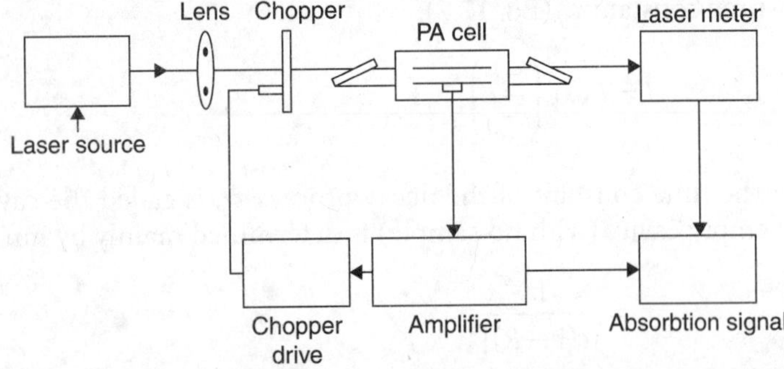

Fig. 17.11 Schematic of laser photoacoustic spectrometer

The linewidth of the laser used in these experiments must be small so that one can tune through individual absorption bands. It is possible to conduct photoacoustic experiments, by exciting ro-vibronic or electronic levels, by a suitable choice of laser wavelength. The strength of the photoacoustic signal is proportional to the intensity of the incident light and hence the laser intensity must be appropriately high to ensure small detection limits.

This technique is amenable for use with gas, liquid or solid samples. With gas or liquid samples, the pressure pulse produced in the sample can be easily monitored. When studying solid samples, a gas fills the cell in which the solid sample is taken. The heat evolved from the sample is transferred to the ambient gas, which serves to couple the temperature pulse produced in the sample, to the microphone.

The technique has found applications in the study of many trace components in the air such as, methane, oxides of nitrogen, carbon dioxide, hydrogen sulphide and ammonia. The detection limits are usually in the realm of a few ppb by volume. The technique has also found applications in the detection of actinides such as plutonium, which has strong non-radiative decay channels.

17.3.9 Thermal Lensing Spectroscopy

The technique of *thermal lensing* is closely related to photoaccoustic spectroscopy, in that this technique also monitors the heat deposited in the ambient through non-radiative decay processes. However, the method of monitoring the heat deposited is different. The heat deposited in the surrounding medium is monitored by changes in its refractive index.

The experimental set up for this technique is shown in Fig. 17.12. Two laser beams are used in this technique. The pump beam excites the sample to an excited state, from which the molecules eventually relax, depositing heat into the surrounding medium causing local heating. The local heating produces a spatially varying density, which causes a spatially varying refractive index. This in turn effectively has the effect of a lens—an effect that is referred to as a thermal lens. Since most liquids have a negative temperature coefficient of refractive index, the lens that is produced is equivalent to a concave lens. The ensuing concave lens is monitored by the second laser beam, called the probe beam. Usually, a He–Ne laser is used as the probe beam. The concave lens causes the probe beam to diverge, which is monitored by measuring the intensity of the probe beam through a pin-hole aperture. When the sample absorbs strongly and deposits heat into the medium, a larger local temperature rise in the medium is produced. The lens that is produced causes the probe beam to diverge, which reduces the intensity through the pin-hole. A strong absorption therefore results in a drop in the intensity of the probe medium, measured through the pin-hole aperture. In practice, the pump beam is either pulsed or chopped, so that a time-varying thermal lens is produced. The probe beam intensity is synchronously detected at the frequency of the pump beam by a lock-in amplifier.

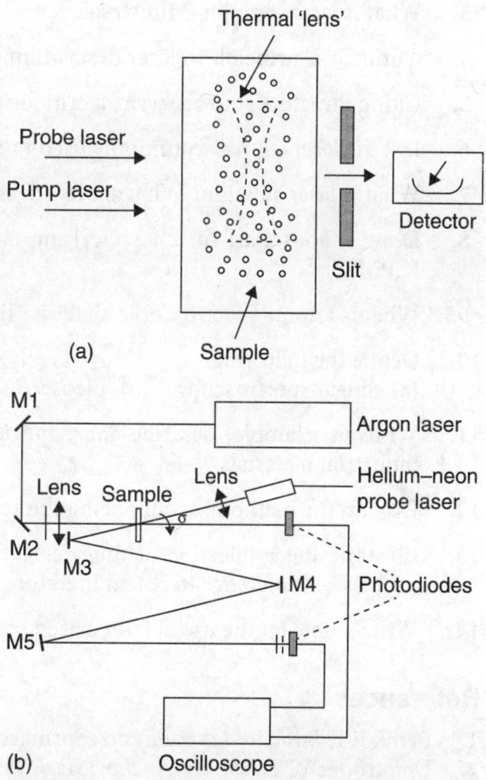

Fig. 17.12 **(a)** Thermal lens formation **(b)** Schematic of thermal lens spectrometer

There are two different configurations for the experimental set up. In the collinear configuration, the pump and the probe beam are aligned nearly parallel to the sample. In this arrangement, the two beams interact over a long path length, thereby yielding high detection sensitivity. In an alternative set up, the pump and the probe beam cross each other at right angles—this arrangement is referred to as the transverse configuration.

The technique has been applied particularly for the detection of systems that have poor fluorescence quantum yields with dominant non-radiative processes. In addition to applications in analytical chemistry, the thermal lens technique has been used in the field of biology, materials science and environment studies.

The advent of the laser has opened up many new analytical techniques, with superior detection limits and capable of handling a variety of samples. It is not unusual to find the practice of laser-based analytical techniques in most advanced analytical chemistry laboratories. Research in laser-based methods is actively pursued and the use of lasers in chemical analysis can only increase in future.

EXERCISES

1. The advent of lasers has vastly refined the classical spectral techniques: substantiate this with examples.
2. Write the principles of laser microprobe.
3. What is laser sampling? Illustrate.
4. Outline the principle of laser desorption source used in a mass spectrometer.
5. Citing literature sources, write a critique on laser-assisted photoluminescent spectroscopy.
6. List the laser sources commonly used in Raman spectroscopy and write on their relative utility.
7. What is laser ablation? What are its advantages in spectroscopy?
8. Draw a flow-chart for characterising experimentally a sample of monazite by laser ablation/ICPMS.
9. What is remote spectroscopic analysis? Illustrate.
10. Define the following:
    (a) linear spectroscopy (b) picosecond laser spectroscopy (c) time-resolved spectroscopy
11. With an example, describe the application of laser spectroscopy in the surface analysis of industrial materials.
12. Explain the methods of enhancing the sensitivity in laser spectroscopic methods.
13. Illustrate the application of time-resolved laser-assisted spectroscopy in the study of biological processes. (Reference to recent literature is required.)
14. Write a note on the use of laser-based spectroscopy in cancer diagnosis.

References

1. Renik R F, *Basics of Laser Physics*, Springer, 2012.
2. Demtröder W, *Laser spectroscopy: Basic Principles*, Springer, 2014.
3. Andrews D L and Demidov A A, *An Introduction to Laser Spectroscopy*, Springer, 2011.

18 Mössbauer Spectroscopy

18.1 INTRODUCTION

The nucleus of an atom has energy levels; it can exist in two or more energy levels at different moments. A nucleus in the ground state can acquire energy and go to an excited state. Mössbauer spectroscopy is the study of transitions of nuclei between energy levels, that is, *nuclear energy changes.* This effect is now called the *Mössbauer effect* or *nuclear gamma ray resonance.* That a nucleus can undergo energy changes was discovered by Rudolf L Mössbauer in 1958. He received a Nobel Prize in 1961 for this discovery.

Mössbauer

Source: http://nobelprize.org/nobel_prizes/physics/laureates/1961/mossbauer-bio.html, Public Domain, https://commons.wikimedia.org/w/index.php?curid=6148339

Rudolf Ludwig Mössbauer was born in Munich on 21 January 1929. While working for his doctoral degree at the Institute for Physics of the Max Planck Institute for Medical Research in Heidelberg, he observed the phenomenon of Recoilless Nuclear Resonance absorption in ^{191}Ir, now called the Mössbauer effect. He was appointed Professor of Physics at the California Institute of Technology in 1961. His work in the field of recoilless nuclear resonance absorption earned him the Nobel Prize in physics in 1961. He worked also in the 'neutrino puzzle'. He died on 14 september 2011. His work provided the impetus to hundreds of chemists and physicists to pursue research on Mössbauer spectroscopy. Now, the scientific literature is replete with thousands of articles on this subject.

Some elements, especially the heavier ones, are initially produced in an excited (high energy) nuclear state during nuclear reactions. After a short time – in microseconds – the excited nucleus reaches the ground state by emitting its excess energy; this emitted energy is in the γ-ray region of the electromagnetic spectrum. Thus, nuclear energy transitions involve γ-rays. Mössbauer spectroscopy is the study of this γ-ray emission and subsequent reabsorption.

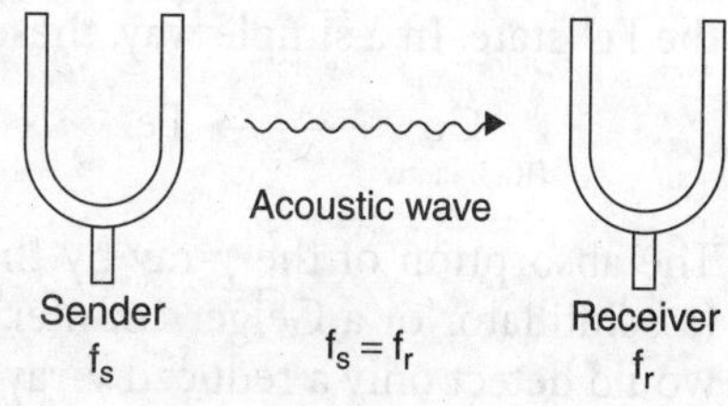

Mössbauer effect is recoilless nuclear resonance absorption of γ-rays. It is similar to acoustic resonance between two tuning forks with the same frequency (f).

18.2 PRINCIPLES OF MÖSSBAUER SPECTROSCOPY

The principles of Mössbauer spectroscopy are explained in this section using the example of the iron nucleus. The isotope ^{57}Fe is produced by the decay of radioactive ^{57}Co by electron capture. In electron capture, an atomic nucleus captures an orbital electron to form the nucleus of the element just prior to it in the periodic table:

$$^{57}_{27}Co \xrightarrow{\text{Electron capture}} {}^{57}_{26}Fe^*$$

The half-life of ^{57}Co is 270 days. In this decay, the ^{57}Fe is formed in an excited energy state; therefore, in the equation, it is denoted as Fe*. Then, Fe* rapidly (in 10^{-6} s) comes to the ground state emitting its excess energy.

$$Fe^* \rightsquigarrow Fe + \gamma\text{-ray}$$

This is called an *isomeric transition*, whereby the nucleus in an excited state emits a gamma ray and forms its ground state without any change in mass number or charge. Only the energy of the isotope changes.

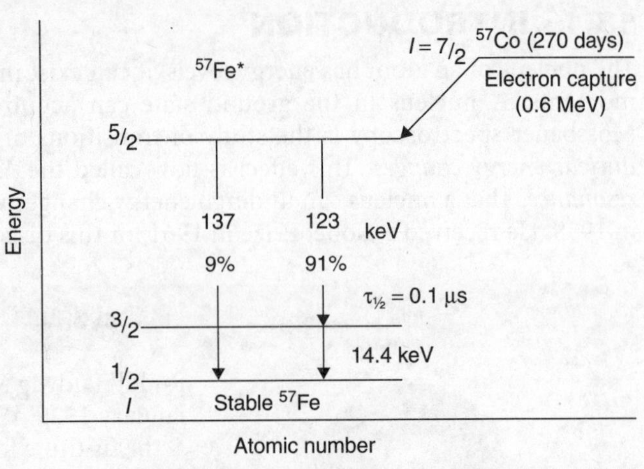

Fig. 18.1 Energy-level diagram for the decay of ^{57}Co to ^{57}Fe showing the isomeric transition to ^{57}Fe

A simplified energy level diagram for this process is shown in Fig. 18.1. The energy change associated with this process is

$$\Delta E = 2.30 \times 10^{-15} \text{ J per nucleus}$$

Therefore, the frequency of the emitted γ-ray

$$\nu = \frac{\Delta E}{h} = \frac{2.30 \times 10^{-15}\,\text{J}}{6.63 \times 10^{-34}\,\text{J.s}}$$

$$= 0.347 \times 10^{19}\ \text{s}^{-1} = 3.5 \times 10^{18}\ \text{Hz}$$

Let us place *another Fe nucleus* (absorber) in the beam of the emitted radiation. This nucleus, in its ground state, would be expected to absorb energy from the beam, get excited and go to the Fe* state. In a simple way, these processes can be written as

$$\underset{\text{(Radioactive)}}{Co} \longrightarrow Fe^* \rightsquigarrow Fe + \text{energy } (\gamma\text{-ray}) \xrightarrow{\text{Absorber Fe}} Fe^*$$

The absorption of the γ-ray by the absorber Fe nucleus can be detected by a γ-ray detector (a scintillator or a Geiger counter). The detector, placed in the beam behind the absorber Fe would detect only a reduced γ-ray count when there is absorption of energy by the second Fe nucleus.

The study of γ-ray emission from an excited nucleus and the subsequent absorption of this γ-ray by another nucleus is Mössbauer spectroscopy. It is called also *γ-ray spectroscopy.*

The nucleons (protons and neutrons) in the nucleus occupy quantised energy levels in the nucleus. Transitions among these energy levels are possible with absorption or emission of energy; thus, *resonant absorptions* can occur in the nucleus. Such absorptions are called the *Mössbauer effect.*

Resonance absorption can be observed only if the emission and absorption lines overlap sufficiently. When the lines are too narrow (Fig. 18.2a) or too broad (Fig. 18.2b); it cannot be observed.

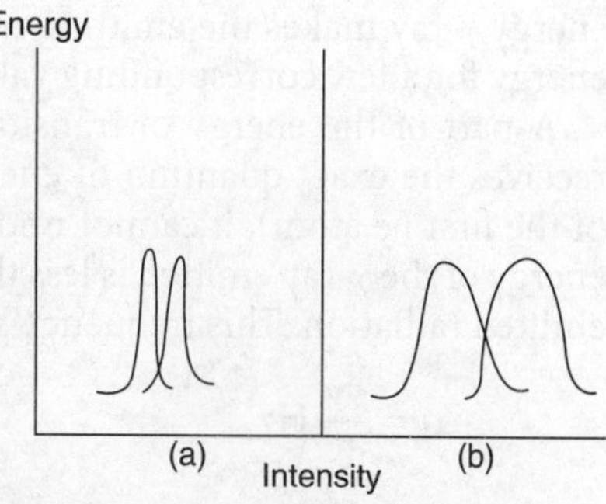

Fig. 18.2 Possibility of Mössbauer resonance absorption **(a)** Emission and absorbance lines are too narrow **(b)** Emission and absorbance lines are too broad

18.2.1 Doppler Shift

Let us consider a free nucleus of mass *M* which undergoes a transition from the excited state to the ground state by the emission of a γ-ray. Let the energy of the γ-ray be E_γ. Actually, the total energy of the nuclear transition is not emitted as a γ-ray; a part of it is used for recoil of the nucleus. As the nucleus emits photons in one direction, it recoils in the opposite direction. Thus, there is loss of a part of the transition energy.

The momentum of the γ-ray

$$P_\gamma = \frac{E_\gamma}{c} \tag{18.1}$$

where *c* is the velocity of light. To conserve momentum, the recoiling atom must have an identical momentum ($= P_\gamma$). By definition, the recoil energy of the nucleus

$$E_r = \frac{P_\gamma^2}{2M} \tag{18.2}$$

Substituting the value of p_γ from Eq. (18.1) in Eq. (18.2),

$$E_r = \frac{(E_\gamma / c^2)}{2M} \tag{18.3}$$

$$E_r = \frac{E_\gamma^2}{2Mc^2} \tag{18.4}$$

For *M* in atomic mass unit and the energies in millions of electron volts (MeV), Eq. (18.4) can be simplified as

$$E_r = \frac{E_\gamma^2}{1862M} \tag{18.5}$$

Thus, the recoil energy of an atom is directly proportional to the emitted gamma ray energy and inversely proportional to the nuclear mass. A high-

Table 18.1 Recoil energies in electron volts imparted to nuclei by emitted gamma rays

M	$E_\gamma =$ 2 MeV	4 MeV	6 MeV
		E_r	
20	107	430	967
50	43	172	387
100	21	86	193
150	14	57	129
200	11	43	97

energy γ-ray makes the emitting nucleus move in the opposite direction. The values of recoil energy for a few corresponding values of E_γ and M are given in Table 18.1.

A part of the energy of transition is lost as recoil energy. Unless the second atom of Fe receives the exact quantum of energy required for transition (equal to the transition energy of the first Fe atom), it cannot undergo a nuclear transition (resonance reabsorption). As the energy of the γ-ray emitted is less than the transition energy, there is a shift in the frequency of emitted radiation. This frequency shift Δν – called the *Doppler shift* – is given by

$$\Delta\nu = \frac{v\nu}{c}\ \text{Hz} \tag{18.6}$$

where ν and c are the frequency and velocity of the emitted radiation, respectively; v is the relative velocity of the source and observer.

When a moving body emits radiation (or sound), a stationary observer sees (or hears) a shifted frequency; this effect is called the *Doppler effect.*

- The Doppler effect is an increase or decrease in the apparent frequency of sound, light, or other waves as the source and the observer move toward (or away from) each other. This effect was discovered by the Austrian physicist Johann Christian Doppler.

The partial use of the emitted energy for recoil of the emitting nucleus precludes resonant absorption by the same type of nucleus.

18.2.2 Thermal Motion of Nuclei

At ordinary temperatures, the nuclei in the emitter and absorber are in thermal motion. Therefore, in addition to the recoil, dissipation of the γ-ray energy takes place. In his initial investigations, Mössbauer did not observe the expected resonant absorption. Realising that elimination of energy dissipation (wastage) through recoil and thermal vibrations of nuclei was necessary for observing resonant absorption, Mössbauer modified the experimental conditions:

- He used solid crystal lattices as emitters: the emitting nucleus is firmly fixed to surrounding nuclei in the crystal – locked in the lattice – and therefore, it has a very large apparent mass. This 'increase' in mass considerably reduced the recoil and hence reduced energy loss (larger the mass, lesser is the recoil; the kinetic energy is inversely proportional to mass). By going from individual nuclei to a small crystal lattice, the mass will be raised by a factor of about 10^{18}, and therefore the kinetic energy involved in the emission and absorption process will become negligible.
- He cooled both the source and the absorber to low temperatures so that thermal motions of the lattice atoms are reduced to a minimum.

These two experimental conditions led to *recoilless emission* by Fe* and resonant absorption by the second Fe.

A further requirement for resonance absorption is that the recoil energy not be sufficient to excite any optical modes of vibration in the crystalline lattice. Vibrational excitation would heat the lattice and modulate the energy of the emitted gamma ray; this would nullify the conditions for resonant absorption. Therefore, only gamma rays with an energy *less* than about 150 keV are usable for Mössbauer spectroscopy. This means that not all isomeric nuclear transitions are suitable for this study.

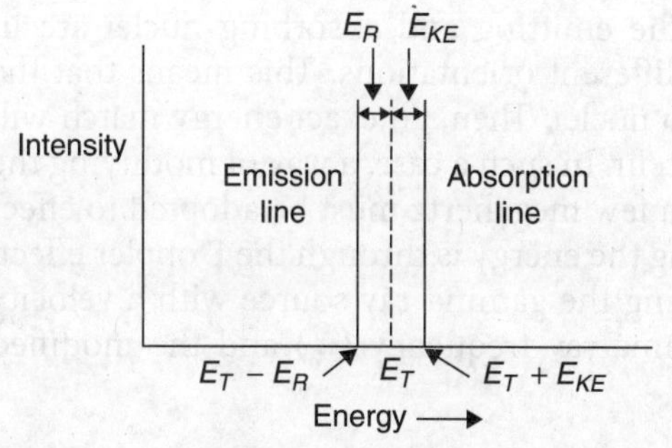

Fig. 18.3 Diagram showing the relationship among line width, transition energy and recoil energy

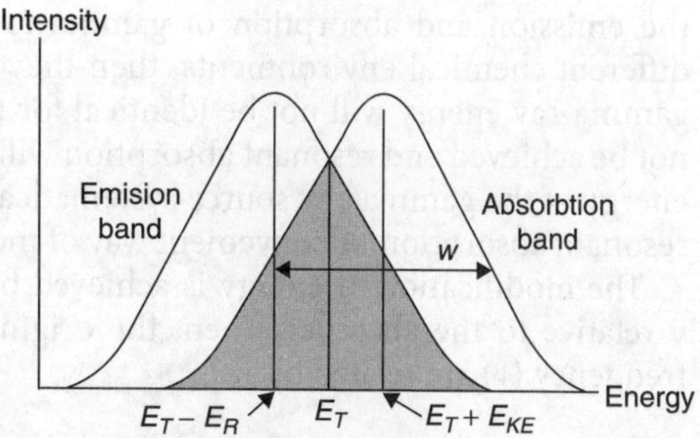

Fig. 18.4 Diagram showing emission and absorbtion line with finite width w

18.2.3 Width of Emission and Absorption Lines

Theoretically, the emission and absorption lines should not have any width, but should be infinitely thin; therefore in the spectrum, the transition should be recordable as a line. If the gamma-ray emission and absorption lines were infinitely thin, the Mössbauer effect would not be possible, since even the smallest loss of emission energy (as recoil energy) would make absorption impossible. The emission and absorption are energetically identical processes. These facts are shown in Fig. 18.3.

Here E_T is the actual energy level separation in the nucleus (= transition energy), $E_T - E_R$ is the energy of the emitted gamma ray, E_R is the recoil energy, $E_T + E_{KE}$ is the energy required for resonance absorption, E_{KE} is the kinetic energy requirement of the absorber. (The absorber also recoils on absorbing energy, and therefore, a little energy more than the resonance energy is required by the absorber nucleus.)

As the energy of the emitted gamma ray ($E_T - E_R$) and the energy required for resonant absorption ($E_T + E_{KE}$) are different and do not overlap or match, resonant absorption becomes impossible under such normal circumstance.

Actually, however, all absorption and emission lines have a finite width (Fig. 18.4). This width can be calculated from the lifetime of the nuclear excited state using the Heisenberg uncertainty principle. These line widths are thus calculated to be of the order of 10^{-7} eV (about 10 MHz) for most Mössbauer radioisotopes. Such line widths are extremely narrow. Assuming that a typical Mössbauer gamma ray has an energy of 100 keV, a line width of 10^{-7} eV is only 10^{-12} th of the energy of the gamma ray. This means that the energy of the gamma ray is defined to an accuracy of 1 part in 10^{12}; thus, the gamma ray is the most accurately defined electromagnetic radiation used for physical measurements.

The recoil energy E_R of a nucleus locked in a crystal lattice is very much smaller than the line width. Typically, the recoil energy for a crystal might be 10^{-19} eV, much smaller than w (the line width at half maximum peak height). Therefore, the emission band overlaps the absorption band (shaded area of Fig. 18.4). Actually, the two bands are almost superimposed, minimising the effect of the recoil energy on absorption.

18.2.4 Use of the Doppler Effect to Vary the Gamma Ray Energy

A nucleus may have different nuclear orientations; that is, its energy may vary. It can interact with its surrounding electrons and undergo changes in energy. These two factors influence the emission and absorption of gamma rays. If the emitting and absorbing nuclei are in different chemical environments, then they have different orientations. This means that the gamma-ray energy will not be identical for the two nuclei. Then, an exact energy match will not be achieved and resonant absorption will not occur. In such a case, a way of modifying the energy of the gamma-ray source systematically by a few megahertz must be adopted to effect resonant absorption. A convenient way of modifying the energy is through the Doppler effect.

The modification of energy is achieved by moving the gamma-ray source with a velocity v relative to the absorber. Then, the original gamma-ray frequency (ν_o) and the modified frequency (ν) are related by

$$\nu = \nu_o\left(1 + \frac{\mathrm{v}}{c}\cos\theta\right)$$

where θ is the angle between the axis of symmetry and the optical axis. As the frequency is modified, energy is changed ($E = h\nu$).

When an absorber and a gamma-ray source move directly toward each other with a velocity v, the *energy* will amount to $E_o\,(1 + \mathrm{v}/c)$, where E_o is the inherent energy of the emitted gamma ray and $\cos\theta = 1$. When the absorber and the gamma-ray source move directly away from each other ($\cos\theta = -1$), the energy will amount to $E_o\,(1 - \mathrm{v}/c)$. The magnitude of the Doppler shift $\Delta\nu$ is given by

$$\Delta\nu = \nu_o\frac{\mathrm{v}}{c}$$

For example, with ^{57}Fe emitting gamma rays of 14.4 keV, a velocity of 1 cm/s would give a frequency shift of 116 MHz. The line width of ^{57}Fe is only about 1.6 MHz, and therefore a frequency scan of 116 MHz is more than adequate to scan an entire Mössbauer spectrum.

In a Mössbauer instrument, the source is moved by mounting the source on a vibrating microphone coil. The Doppler velocity given to the source relative to the absorber is necessary because of the finite width of the resonance line and also because the nuclear energy level separation in the source may be different from that in the absorber with a different electronic environment. The energy shift ΔE is given by

$$\Delta E = \pm E\frac{\mathrm{v}}{c}$$

18.2.5 Lamb–Mössbauer Factor

This factor is based on Lamb's theory of γ-ray emission. According to this theory, recoilless emission and absorption of gamma rays occur when the nucleus concerned is embedded in solid lattices. Most of the gamma-ray energy is emitted without loss (loss as kinetic energy) in such an embedded system. The recoilless, emitted fraction of γ-rays from an embedded source is called the *Lamb–Mössbauer factor* (*f*); this factor is given by the expression,

$$f = \exp^{(-E_r/h\omega_E)}$$

where E_r is the recoil energy and ω_E is the angular frequency of the oscillator. A large *f* indicates least recoil of nuclei. Therefore, from the *f* values, the possibility of resonant transition can be predicted; higher *f* means greater transition probability.

18.3 MÖSSBAUER SPECTROMETER

The Mössbauer spectrometer records the counts of γ-ray photons per second against the velocity (mm s^{-1}) with which the source is moved. The block diagram of a typical Mössbauer spectrometer is given in Fig. 18.5.

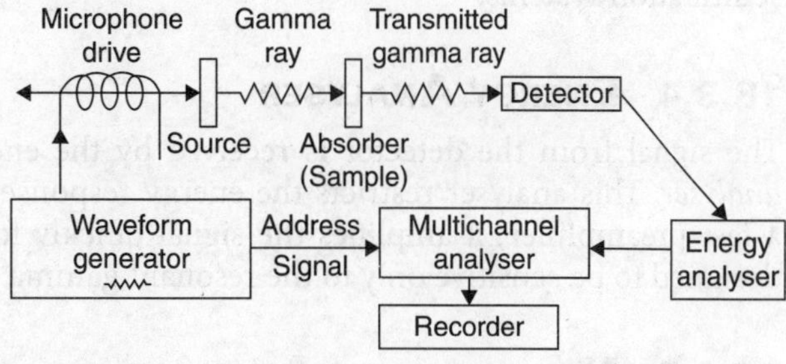

Fig. 18.5 Block diagram of Mössbauer spectrometer

18.3.1 Source

The radioactive source – which emits gamma rays – is made into a thin foil (0.1 mm thick). The source is incorporated in a crystal lattice; the material which constitutes the crystal traps the radioactive nuclei rigidly and minimises recoil of the source nuclei. For example, the radioactive ^{57}Co source may be incorporated in iron foil.

The source is attached to a moving microphone coil, whose motion is controlled by a *waveform generator.* Generally, a sawtooth variation of velocity with time is used; the entire velocity range is scanned several times a second. The Doppler effect is used to tune the energy of the source in and out of resonance with the absorber.

A gamma quantum of energy E_γ, which is emitted from a source moving at velocity v_o receives a Doppler energy E_d, such that

$$E_d = \frac{E_\gamma v_o}{c}$$

For a resonant transition, it is enough to shift the photon energy of the source by an amount equal to H, the gamma line width. Therefore, E_d should be equal to or greater than H. The Doppler velocities required to shift the gamma-ray energy for some Mössbauer nuclei are given in Table 18.2.

Table 18.2 Doppler velocities for some Mössbauer nuclei

Mössbauer nucleus	Doppler velocity (cm.s^{-1})
^{57}Fe	9.5×10^{-3}
^{119m}Sn	3.0×10^{-2}
^{67}Zn	1.5×10^{-5}
^{99}Ru	7.3×10^{-3}
^{129}I	3.0×10^{-2}
^{153}Eu	1

The mechanical device in the spectrometer provides a precisely controlled velocity to the source to impart appropriate energy modulation for resonance absorption.

18.3.2 Absorber

The absorber is the sample whose spectrum has to be recorded and whose nucleus can undergo resonant absorption with the γ-ray released by the source. It is also incorporated in a crystal lattice similar to the source. It is cooled by liquid He or N_2. The absorber as a foil is fixed so that it covers the window of the detector; in such an arrangement any unabsorbed gamma photons will directly enter the detector. The absorber, which must contain the same species as the gamma ray emitter (for example, ^{57}Fe), is stationary.

18.3.3 Detector

The γ-ray detector is a scintillator; generally, a NaI (thallium-activated) scintillation crystal is used in the detector. However, it is better to use a proportional counter (Geiger counter) for gamma energies below 20 keV. This is because at low energies, the background is high with scintillation systems.

18.3.4 Energy Analyser

The signal from the detector is received by the energy analyser, also called *single-channel analyser*. This analyser restricts the energy response by the single resonant gamma ray. It is a fast-preamplifier; it amplifies the signal quickly for clear recording of the spectrum. It is designed to be sensitive only to the resonant gamma ray.

18.3.5 Multichannel Analyser

It receives the amplified signal from the energy analyser. It is synchronised with a signal generator. This analyser assigns each channel to a specific narrow increment of velocity. A built-in oscilloscope displays the response as a function of source velocity. The counts at each source velocity are fed over equal time intervals, into separate channels of the multichannel analyser; then the channel for each velocity is determined by an address signal appropriately derived from the wave form generator. Each channel denotes one velocity on the abscissa (X-axis) of the spectrum. After a 2 to 4-hour counting period, each channel will have accumulated enough counts to allow an accurate readout of the γ-ray transmittance at that velocity.

Table 18.3 Some Mössbauer nuclei

Mössbauer nucleus	Gamma ray energy(keV)	Half-life of excited state (nanoseconds)
^{57}Fe	14.4	98
^{119}Sn	23.9	18
^{129}I	28	16
^{40}K	29.4	3.9
^{61}Ni	67.4	5.3
^{67}Zn	93	9400
^{73}Ge	67	1.6
^{83}Kr	9.3	147
^{107}Ag	93	44×10^9
^{121}Sb	37	3.5
^{125}Te	36	1.5
^{129}Xe	40	1.0
^{133}Cs	81	6.3
^{182}W	100	1.4
^{186}Os	137	0.8
^{191}Ir	129	0.1
^{195}Pt	99	0.2
^{197}Au	77	1.8

18.3.6 Typical Source–Absorber System

A typical source is ^{57}Co, a radioactive isotope, which decays to ^{57}Fe through $^{57}Fe^*$ by emitting low-energy (14.4 keV) gamma radiation. The iron nucleus which undergoes the Mössbauer effect is called the Mössbauer nucleus. Some Mössbauer nuclei are listed in Table 18.3. Each of these nuclei is formed in an excited state by an isomeric transition (like $^{57}Co \rightarrow {}^{57}Fe^*$).

The half-life values given in Table 18.3 refer to the Mössbauer nuclei in their excited states. The absorber in each case is the corresponding isotopic nucleus in its ground state. All the isotopes listed have gamma emissions with energies below the 150 keV limit. The half-life of each isotope determines the line width of the gamma emission. Thus, ^{107}Ag and ^{67}Zn, with the longest half-lives, have the narrowest line width.

18.4 CONDITIONS FOR MÖSSBAUER SPECTROSCOPY

A satisfactory Mössbauer spectrum can be obtained only if the following conditions are fulfilled.

- A suitable radioactive source decaying to the Mössbauer nucleus (excited state) should be available.
- The average lifetime of the excited source emitting γ-radiation should be in the range 10^{-10} to 10^{-4} s.
- The energy of the emitted γ-ray should be in the range 10– 200 keV.
- The half-life of the parent nuclide producing the γ-emitter nuclide should be large (about a year) so that it can be used for a number of experiments. For example the $t_{½}$ for ^{57}Co, the parent for $^{57}Fe^*$, is 270 days.
- The nucleus should not be too light as to recoil greatly and dissipate the γ-ray energy (elements lighter than K are not suitable for Mössbauer spectral studies).
- The γ-ray emitted should be of low energy, because high energies result in recoil, precluding resonant absorption.
- The sample which absorbs the γ-radiation should be present in high isotopic abundance.

The standard convention in presenting the abscissa (X-axis) is to represent the motion of the source toward the absorber by positive velocities and motion of the source away from the absorber by negative velocities.

18.5 MÖSSBAUER SPECTRUM

A Mössbauer spectrum is a plot of gamma-ray counts (per second) being transmitted through the absorber versus the velocity of the source (millimetre per second). A typical spectrum, that of $[Fe(CN)_6]^{4-}$, is shown in Fig. 18.6. The features are discussed below.

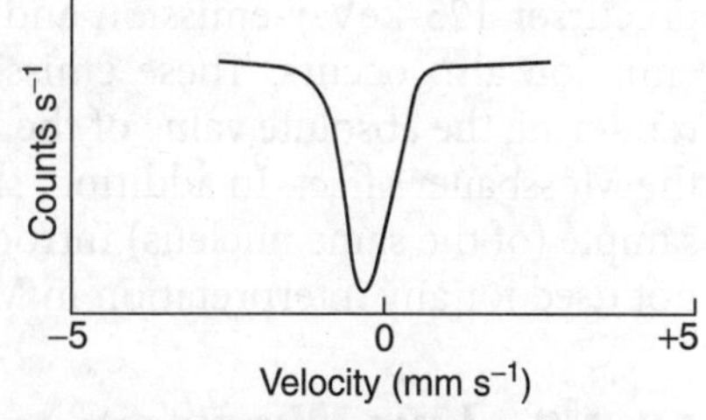

Fig. 18.6 The Mössbauer spectrum of $[Fe(CN)_6]^{4-}$

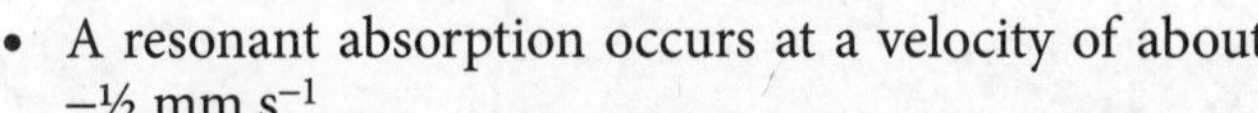

- A resonant absorption occurs at a velocity of about $-½$ mm s^{-1}.

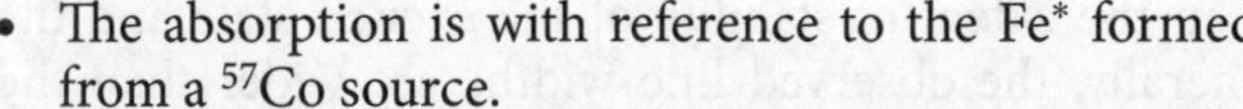

- The absorption is with reference to the Fe* formed from a ^{57}Co source.
- The source is Fe metal but the absorber is an iron compound; that is why, the absorption is shifted from the 0 mm.s^{-1} value on the x-axis. If the source and the absorber are chemically identical, then the absorption would occur at 0 mm.s^{-1}; this is so when both are Fe metal or the same iron compound.
- As resonant absorption occurs, the γ-photons are absorbed and hence the count drops; that is why the absorption curve is inverted. When there is no absorption, the counts are a constant per second (as shown by the straight line portions on the two upper sides of the curve).

Some instruments are designed to record the absorption as percentage; the maximum count rate is taken to be 100% transmittance (0% absorption), and a zero count rate (or background). Count rate is taken as 0% transmittance (100% absorption). Then the y-axis is calibrated from 0% to 100%. The x-axis is calibrated in mm/s.

18.5.1 STANDARD ABSORBER

A standard absorber (reference) for each type of nucleus is used. For example, for the Mössbauer spectra of iron compounds, sodium nitroprusside $[Na_2Fe(CN)_5NO.2H_2O]$ is used as the standard absorber. The isomer shift values for the various iron systems are then reported with reference to this absorber. Sometimes, the absorber is enriched to about 80% for ^{57}Fe content for greater sensitivity of absorption and clear recording of the spectrum. For the ^{119}Sn source, barium stannate ($BaSnO_3$) is used as the standard absorber.

18.6 PARAMETERS AND APPLICATIONS OF MÖSSBAUER SPECTROSCOPY

Five Mössbauer spectral parameters are useful for chemists in understanding molecular properties. These are:

(i) the size of the absorption peak ε,
(ii) the line width ω,
(iii) the isomer shift IS,
(iv) the quadrupole splitting QS, and
(v) the magnetic hyperfine structure MHFS.

18.6.1 Size of the Absorption Peak ε

Theoretically, the size of the absorption peak – the area inside the signal – is proportional to the number of absorbing nuclei in the path of the γ-ray. However, this factor is not used for quantitative interpretation because of a variety of interference effects and background scattering from the environment near the absorber. For example, with the ^{57}Fe absorber, the primary γ-ray emission pertaining to the Mössbauer effect is 14.4 keV; in addition, there is a precursor 123-keV γ-emission and also a 137 keV emission. In addition to these two, x-ray emission also occurs. These emissions also contribute to the measured counting rate thus rendering the absolute value of the Mössbauer peak height variable, and only partly related to the Mössbauer effect. In addition, slight variations in the isotope composition from sample to sample (of the same nucleus) introduce variation in peak heights. Therefore, peak heights are not used for any interpretation in Mössbauer spectroscopy.

18.6.2 Line Width ω

Theoretically, the line width depends on the extent of stability of the excited state and the Heisenberg uncertainty principle. Generally, the observed line widths are wider than the theoretical values because of experimental complications, erratic functioning of the velocity drive, crystal defects and impurities in the absorber crystal, thermal effects and the finite thickness of both the source and the absorber. The important use of the line width is a check on the quality of the absorber used; the purest absorber sample shows the least width. Thus, the width may not be a constant for a particular type of nucleus of different samples. In addition, it varies for different chemical types of the absorbing nucleus.

18.6.3 Isomer Shift IS

Isomer shift is called also *chemical shift* (cs) as it depends on the chemical state of the absorber. It is defined as the displacement of the resonance maximum from zero velocity (Fig. 18.7). Isomer shift arises when the source nucleus and the absorber nucleus are in different chemical oxidation states, for example $^{57}Fe^{0}$ and $^{57}Fe^{3+}$. The absorbing frequency of Fe^{3+} is not exactly equal to the frequency of the emission from the source Fe^{0}. Figure 18.7a denotes

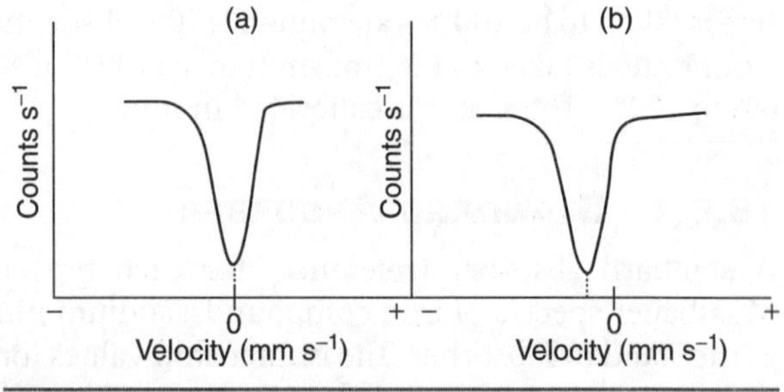

Fig. 18.7 Isomer shift **(a)** The Mössbauer spectrum of Fe^{0} with Fe^{0} source, **(b)** The Mossbauer spectrum of Fe^{3+} compound with Fe^{0} source

the Mössbauer spectrum of $^{57}Fe^0$ with $^{57}Fe^0$ as the source. Figure 18.7b denotes the spectrum of $^{57}Fe^{3+}$ with the same ($^{57}Fe^0$) source. The chemical shift is zero in the first spectrum as the source and the absorber are chemically identical, both in the Fe^0 state. In the second spectrum, a chemical shift occurs due to difference in the chemical nature between the source (Fe^0) and the absorber (Fe^{3+}). *As the chemical environment of a nucleus changes, changes in nuclear energy levels occur; this is the origin of the Mössbauer chemical shift.* The nucleus interacts with the extranuclear electrons leading to nuclear energy changes.

18.6.3.1 Chemical Shift and Electron Density

The electron density around the nucleus is the main factor which affects the magnitude of chemical shifts. The *p* and *d* orbitals, due to their shapes, have zero density at the nuclei and therefore do not significantly influence chemical shifts. On the other hand, the *s* orbitals being close to the nucleus influence IS. Therefore, the IS values are indicative of the *s* electron densities around the Mössbauer nuclei. The IS values give the measurement of relative *s* electron density and hence an estimate of the bond character of atoms or ions chemically linked to the Mössbauer nucleus. The valence state of an atom in a compound – which decides the chemical environment of the atom – can be guessed from the IS values (see Problem 18.1).

Another factor, the nuclear radius, also affects IS. A nucleus in its excited state has a radius different from the radius in its ground state; it can be smaller or larger. The relationship between IS and the nuclear radius is given by the equation.

$$\text{IS} = \text{Constant}(\rho_{ex}^2 - \rho_{gd}^2)\left(\frac{R_{ex} - R_{gd}}{R_{gd}}\right)$$

where, ρ^2 = *s* electron density at the excited (*ex*) and ground (*gd*) state nuclei and R = radius of each nucleus. The constant is a proportionality factor. For any particular nucleus, $(R_{ex} - R_{gd})/R_{gd}$ is constant and therefore, using this equation, the relative electron densities can be calculated.

IS can be positive or negative; it is positive when R_{ex} is larger than R_{gd} and negative when R_{ex} is smaller than R_{gd}. For example, with ^{57}Fe, the excited state is physically smaller than the ground state (a negative radius effect), and therefore an increase in electron density in the absorber will lead to a negative isomer shift. When the absorber is changed from Fe^{2+} to Fe^{3+}, the charge density at the nucleus increases and a considerable IS results. The *changes* in IS with changes in chemical environment – not the absolute values of isomer shifts – are important in the study of chemical environments. The magnitude of shifts depends on the bonded groups, whether the Mössbauer nucleus is bonded to say, a chloride, bromide, or some other ion.

The isomer shift for an absorber is modified by

- the mean radius dR/R, and
- the *s* electron density of the absorber.

If the mean radius is positive, the positive isomer shift corresponds to increased *s* electron density at the nucleus. If it is negative, a *positive* isomer shift corresponds to decreased *s* electron density at the nucleus. These relationships can be illustrated by $FeSO_4$ and $FeCl_3$. Fe in $FeSO_4$ is d^6, whereas Fe in $FeCl_3$ is d^5. The six *d* electrons in high-spin Fe^{2+} provide more screening of its *s* electrons than the five *d* electrons in high-spin Fe^{3+}. It implies that the *s* electron density in Fe^{2+} is effectively more than that in Fe^{3+}. Hence, the IS is more for Fe^{2+} compared to that for Fe^{3+}.

Generally, the IS decreases as the *s* electron density decreases in a set of related absorber nuclei. As the oxidation state of the metal M increases, the effective *s* electron density around the nucleus of M decreases and hence the IS. The IS values for some iron compounds are given in Table 18.4.

The Fe^{2+} species have larger IS values than the Fe^{3+} species. The value is the least for $FeCl_3$; the d^5 electron structure in $FeCl_3$ is less screening; in addition, the three electronegative chlorine atoms draw electrons away from the Fe nucleus. These factors decrease the *s* electron density and hence the IS is low.

Table 18.4 Isomer shifts for some iron compounds (source ^{57}Fe)

Absorber	IS (mm s^{-1})
FeF_2	1.55
$FeC_2O_4 \cdot 2H_2O$	1.52
$FeSO_4$	1.50
$FeCl_2$	1.40
$FePO_4 \cdot 4H_2O$	0.68
$FeCl_3$	0.66

18.6.3.2 Isomer Shift and Ionicity

A direct relationship between the isomer shifts and ionicity of a set of related compounds has been noted. The following data prove this.

Compound	:	AuI	AuBr	AuCl
IS (mm s^{-1})	:	0.125	0.143	0.161
% ionicity	:	< 2	25	60

(Source: ^{197}Au)

As the ionicity increases, IS also increases; the difference in the chemical nature between Au^0 (source) and Au^+ (absorber) increases as ionicity increases, and hence the IS increases.

18.6.4 Quadrupole Splitting QS

To understand what is QS, let us consider the Mössbauer spectra of $(C_6H_5)_4Sn$ and $(C_6H_5)_3SnCl$ (Fig. 18.8). The spectrum of $(C_6H_5)_4Sn$ has a single absorption, as the electron environment for the Mössbauer nucleus Sn is symmetrical. The four identical C_6H_5 groups in this compound provide such a symmetrical or spherical electron distribution (environment). The unsymmetrical electron environment around the Mössbauer nucleus is called *electric gradient*. The Sn nucleus in $(C_6H_5)_3SnCl$ does not have a symmetrical electron distribution; its electron environment is said to have an electric gradient. Such an electric gradient splits the absorption into two; this is called quadrupole splitting.

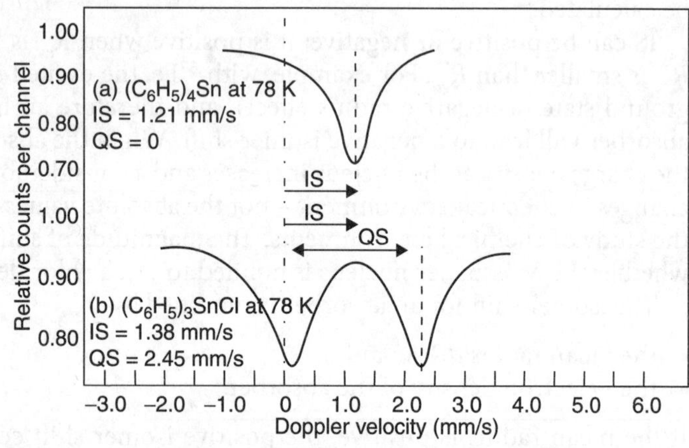

Fig. 18.8 Mössbauer spectrum of **(a)** $(C_6H_5)_4Sn$ and **(b)** $(C_6H_5)_3SnCl$

The nonsymmetrical electric field removes the degeneracy of the spin states in the excited nuclear state (Fig. 18.9). The energy levels for the free nucleus are shown in (a). Transitions between these states denote resonance at zero relative velocity. The displacements of energy levels due to isomer shift are shown in (b). The effect of an unsymmetrical electric field (electric field gradient) at the nucleus is shown in (c). The quadrupole coupling between the electric field and the spin of the nucleus causes a splitting of the upper spin state; one state is raised by an energy E_Q, and one is lowered by the same amount. As per the selection rules, transitions to the two new states are equally probable. Hence, the spectrum is split and has two lines of equal intensities. Such a splitting has already been shown for $(C_6H_5)_3SnCl$. A typical spectrum with QP is shown in Fig. 18.10.

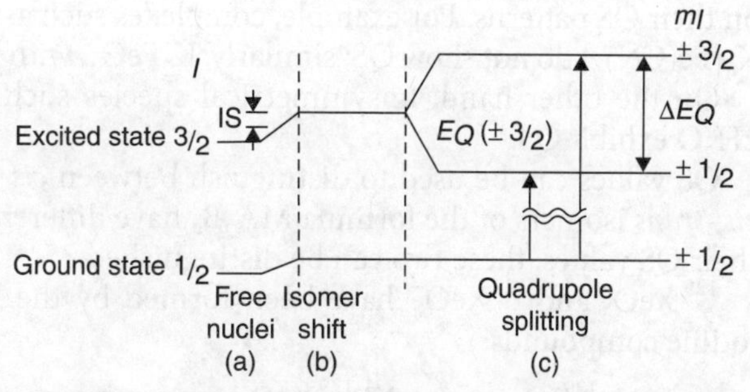

Fig. 18.9 The origin of quadrupole splitting interaction

18.6.4.1 Nuclear Spins and Quadrupole Effect

The majority of Mössbauer nuclei have a non-zero spin; most of them have half-integral values. The spin of the excited state is different from that in the ground state as per selection rules. Therefore, either or both of the nuclear states must involve a spin greater than ½, that is, one or both will have a quadrupole moment. Such spins lead to interaction of the nucleus with the electric field gradient in the vicinity.

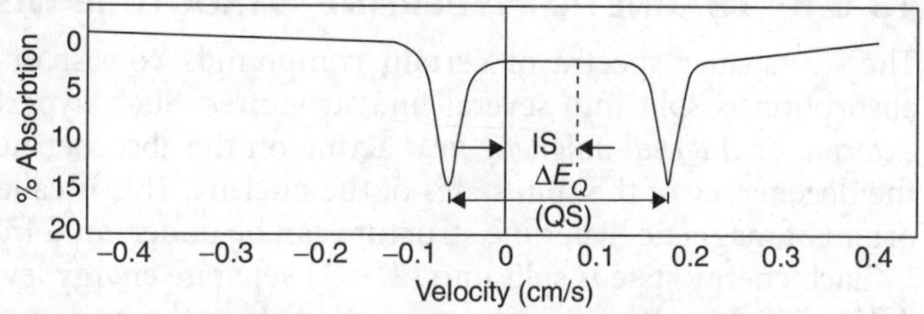

Fig. 18.10 A typical Mössbauer spectrum with quadrupole splitting.

For example, in each of ^{57}Fe, ^{119}Sn and ^{129}Xe, the excited state nucleus has $I = 3/2$ and therefore, these nuclei have quadrupole moment. In an electric field along the vertical z direction in such a case, four $(2I + 1)$ possible orientations of the excited nucleus will be possible. The nucleus is assumed to acquire a cigar-shape (not spherical) because it has a *positive* quadrupole moment. The angle which the nucleus makes with the field gradient is the same in the $I_z = +½$ and the $I_z = -½$ states, and hence these two states have the same energy in the field. Similarly, $I_z = \pm 3/2$ states have the same energy, though this energy will be different from that of the ±½ states. Therefore, the nuclear energy in the excited state splits into two levels due to an electric field gradient at the nucleus. When the quadrupole moment is positive, the ±3/2 states are raised in energy and the ±½ states are lowered. If the moment is negative (tangerine-shaped nucleus) the reverse occurs. In these cases, splitting of spectral absorption is due to the electric field inherent in the absorber; it is *not* dependent on the external, applied field.

QS is helpful in understanding the nature of electron distribution in the absorber species and the magnitudes of internal crystal fields. Spin-paired and spin-free complexes can be distinguished using the data on QS. For example, $[Fe(CN)_6]^{4-}$, a spin-paired complex, with a symmetrical field around Fe produces a single-line spectrum; $[Fe(CN)_5NO]^{2-}$ containing a spin-free electron – and hence an electric gradient – shows a doublet in its spectrum.

QS is a sensitive property used for knowing the symmetry of certain compounds. Several complexes of iron and also those of some other metals have been assigned symmetries based on their QS patterns. For example, complexes such as octahedral, symmetric $K_3[Fe(CN)_6]$ and $K_4[Fe(CN)_6]$ do not show QS; similarly, K_2FeO_4, with tetrahedral symmetry does not show QS.

On the other hand, unsymmetrical species such as $(C_6H_5)_3SnCl$ and $Na_2[Fe(CN)_5NO].2H_2O$ exhibit QS.

QS values can be used to distinguish between *cis–trans* isomers. For example, octahedral, *cis–trans* isomers of the formula MA_2B_4 have different electric field gradients; therefore, from their QS values, these two can be distinguished.

$^{129}XeO_3^-$ and $^{129}XeO_4^-$ have been formed by the radioactive decay of the corresponding iodine compounds:

$$Na^{129}IO_3 \xrightarrow{-\beta} Na^{129}XeO_3^-$$

$$Na^{129}IO_4 \xrightarrow{-\beta} Na^{129}XeO_4^-$$

The QS values have proved that XeO_3 has a pyramidal structure; the electron environment for Xe is asymmetric. But, the electron environment for Xe in XeO_4^- is symmetric; this ion, unlike XeO_3 produced only a single Mössbauer spectral line.

18.6.5 Magnetic Hyperfine Structure MHFS

The Mössbauer spectra of certain compounds consist of hyperfine structure, that is, an absorption is split into several fine structures. Such hyperfine structures are caused by an *external* or *internal magnetic field* acting on the absorber nucleus. A magnetic field removes the degeneracy of the spin states of the nucleus. This is called the *nuclear Zeeman effect.* The origin of magnetic hyperfine structure can be understood from Fig. 18.11.

Each energy state is split into $(2I + 1)$ separate energy levels. The spacing between them is $\Delta E = g\beta_N B_z/h$, where B_z is the magnetic field at the nucleus, g is the Lande splitting factor, β_N is the nuclear magneton and h is Planck's constant. Generally, the g values of the excited and ground states differ; therefore, the splitting in each state is different. In addition, the g values may have opposite signs (as in the case of Fe), with positive g in the ground state and negative g in the excited state.

In Fig. 18.11, the energy levels are shown in the absence of a magnetic field in (a); the magnetic field splits the ground state ($I = ½$, g positive) into two sub-levels and the excited state ($I = 3/2$, g negative) into four in (b). In the ground state, the $I_z = +½$ sublevel has lower energy than the $I_z = -½$ sublevel. The sublevel energies of the excited state increase in the order $I_z = -3/2, -½, +½, +3/2$. All transitions for which $\Delta I_z = 0$ or $+1$ are allowed. The relative transition probabilities differ according to the states involved. Each m_I (magnetic spin value) is split into $(2I + 1)$ values. Hence, for an absorber with an excited state spin of 3/2 and ground state spin of ½, six transitions are possible.

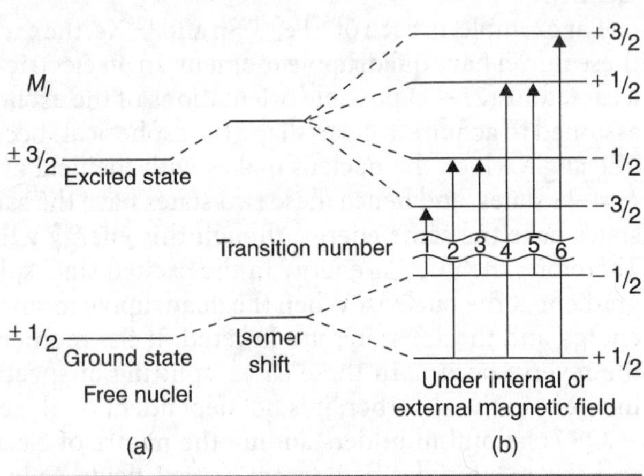

Fig. 18.11 The origin of magnetic hyperfine struture

Considering the six transitions in pairs, and starting with Fe*, there are three sets of transitions:

(i) 3/2 ↔ ½, −3/2 ↔ −½
(ii) ½ ↔ ½, −½ ↔ −½
(iii) −½ ↔ +½, +½ ↔ −½

The two members in each pair have the same probability. The relative probabilities of the three pairs (i), (ii), (iii) are 3:2:1. The observed spectrum for Fe is in accord with these facts.

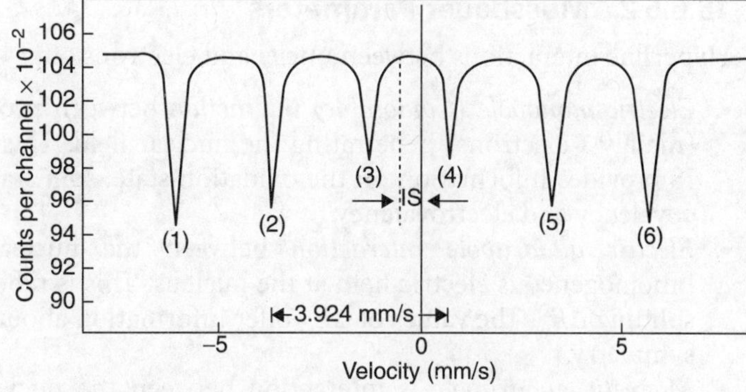

Fig. 18.12 Mössbauer spectrum of metallic iron at room temperature

The hyperfine magnetic field can arise in different ways:

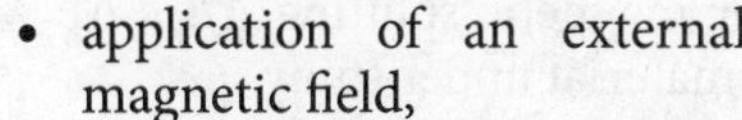

- application of an external magnetic field,
- antiferromagnetic exchange as in Fe_2O_3,
- ferromagnetic exchange interaction as in metallic iron, and
- paramagnetic species [due to the presence of spin-free electron(s)] with spin-lattice relaxation time longer than the lifetime of the Mössbauer excited state.

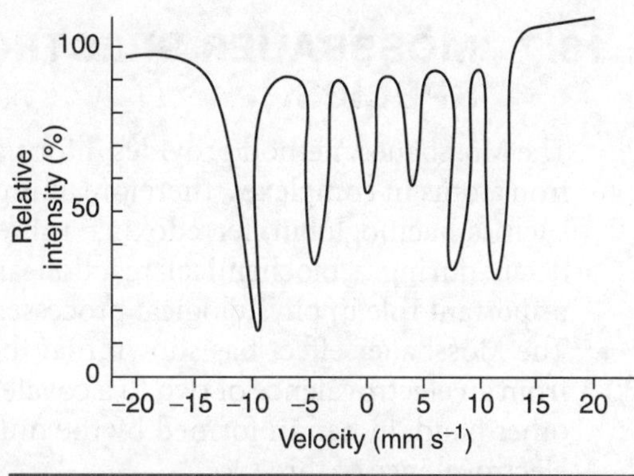

Fig. 18.13 Mössbauer spectrum of Fe_2O_3

The Mössbauer spectrum of ^{57}Fe at room temperature is shown in Fig. 18.12. The two resonance lines at either end are the −1/2 to −3/2 and 1/2 to 3/2 transitions respectively. The separation between these two can be directly related to the magnetic field. The separation between lines 2 and 4 (or between lines 3 and 5) is just the ground state splitting. This splitting is 3.924 mm/s in metallic iron at room temperature.

In some unsymmetrical iron compounds such as Fe_2O_3, simultaneous magnetic and electric quadrupole coupling may occur. The ferromagnetism in Fe_2O_3 leads to magnetic hyperfine splitting into six lines, but the electrical asymmetry of the compound can superimpose on an electric quadrupole coupling. When this happens, the lines are no longer equally spaced (Fig. 18.13).

18.6.5.1 Determination of Excited State Nuclear Spins

The energy difference between adjacent absorption maxima is called the *splitting energy.* This energy can be calculated from the source velocity differences; it is related to the product of the nuclear magnetic moment and the magnetic field strength. Therefore, the moment of the excited nuclear state can be evaluated from the field strength. Thus, the analysis of the Mössbauer absorption spectrum can furnish nuclear spin values in the excited state, if the spin in the ground state is known.

An application of the Mössbauer effect is the study of internal magnetic fields in metallic compounds and alloys which have magnetic properties. The magnetic moment of the nucleus in the excited state can be measured independently and then used to determine internal magnetic field strengths from the splitting energy calculated from the spectrum. These internal fields are determined by the arrangement of electrons in the atom.

18.6.5.2 Mössbauer Parameters

Hyperfine interactions between nuclei and electrons offer three kinds of parameters:

- *Electric monopole (Coulombic) interaction* between protons of the nucleus and electrons (mainly *s*-electrons) penetrating the nuclear field. This is observed as the isomer shift δ. IS provides information on the oxidation state, spin state and bonding properties such as covalency and electrovalency.
- *Electric quadrupole interaction* between the nuclear quadrupole moment and an inhomogeneous electric field at the nucleus. This is reflected in the parameter quadrupole splitting ΔE_Q. The values of ΔE_Q offer information about oxidation state, spin state and site symmetry.
- *Magnetic quadrupole* is interaction between the nuclear magnetic dipole moment and magnetic field at the nucleus. This provides the parameter magnetic splitting ΔE_M. ΔE_M provides information about the magnetic properties of the material under study.

18.7 MÖSSBAUER SPECTROSCOPY OF BIOLOGICAL SPECIES

- The Mössbauer method provides information on the chemical state and the environment of iron atoms in complexes, therefore, it is used to study iron-containing biological molecules such as haemoglobin, ferredoxins, rubredoxins, and so on. The electronic changes which occur during a biochemical reaction are centred around the iron atoms. Iron plays an important role in physiological processes.
- The Mössbauer effect has shown that the iron atom in the hemoglobin molecule changes from an electrovalence of two to a covalence of two upon combination with oxygen. On the other hand, in hemin formed by the mild decomposition of haemoglobin, the iron has an electrovalence of three.
- The Mössbauer spectroscopy of some biological molecules has established the nature of energy levels, wave function, electron environment, the type of ligand field and the extent of spin–orbit coupling. With rubredoxin, the relationship between the electron environment around the iron and its biological functions has been correlated based on the chemical shifts and magnetic hyperfine splitting. The CS values for some of the biological molecules in their reduced and oxidised states are given in Table 18.5.

Table 18.5 Chemical shift values for some biological molecules

Molecule	Chemical shift (mm s^{-1})	
	Fe (II)	Fe(III)
Rubredoxin	0.65	0.25
Ferredoxin	0.56	0.22
Andrenodoxin	–	0.26
Deoxyhaemoglobin	0.90	–
Methhaemoglobin	–	0.20

18.8 TEMPERATURE COEFFICIENTS OF MÖSSBAUER PARAMETERS

The Mössbauer parameters are dependent on temperature. Data on such parameters are obtained by changing the temperature for the sample or for both the source and sample; these two materials are kept in isothermal enclosures through which the γ-ray can pass. Temperature studies give information on the chemical state and the solid state properties of the host lattice. The fraction of recoil-free emissions depends on the state of excitation of the lattice vibrations.

Ferromagnetic and antiferromagnetic properties can also be understood from temperature effects. Temperature coefficients of Mössbauer data provide information about crystal-field effects and relaxation times.

Mössbauer Effect and Gravitational Shift of Spectral Lines

Einstein's theory of relativity predicts the gravitational shift of spectral lines. According to this theory (mass–energy equation $E = mc^2$), a photon of energy E should have an effective mass m equal to E/c^2. If this photon drops through a vertical distance d under the influence of gravity, its energy should increase by mgd.

$$mgd = \frac{Egd}{c^2}$$

where g is the acceleration due to the earth's gravity. For better understanding of the gravity effect on energy, fractional energy is quoted. It is the actual energy increase divided by the original energy E,

$$= \frac{Egd/c^2}{E} = \frac{gd}{c^2}$$

If a photon were to move a distance of d upward, away from the earth, its energy would decrease by some amount. For example, for a fall of 100 feet, the fractional energy increase for a photon is about 3×10^{-15}. The fraction is the same for a photon which moves upward by 100 feet. The shift in Mössbauer absorption can be used for calculating the fractional energy changes due to gravity change.

18.9 APPLICATIONS OF MÖSSBAUER SPECTROSCOPY IN THE STUDY OF METAL COMPLEXES

The Mössbauer spectral data are extensively used in the study of metal complexes. The following information about complexes can be obtained from the spectra.

- The nature of electron environment around the metal and its oxidation state.
- The chemical state of some species.

For example, Mössbauer spectroscopy has proved that Prussian blue and Turnbull's blue are identical compounds with the formula $\overset{\text{III}}{Fe_4}[\overset{\text{II}}{Fe}(CN)_6]_3$. The formula is constituted by high spin Fe(III) and low spin Fe(II).

- The geometry of the complex—symmetric or unsymmetric.
- The spin – high or low – of the complex, the magnetic nature.
- The extent of π-bonding and the relative π-bonding capacities of ligands.

π-Back donation in metal complexes influences the magnitude of δ values. The δ values for a set of $[Fe(CN)_5X^{n-}]^{(3-n)-}$ complexes are listed on the right:

Ligand (X)	δ (mm s^{-1})
NO^+	0
CO	+ 0.15
NO_2^-	+ 0.26
NH_3	+ 0.26
H_2O	+ 0.31

The δ values are given relative to that of pentacyanonitrosylferrate as zero. The variation in δ is due to varying effects of d_π–p_π backdonation for the different ligands X. The increasing δ values form NO^+ to H_2O ligand indicates increasing d-electron density around iron centre as

d_π–p_π backdonation decreases. Thus, there is strong shielding of *s*-electron density at the iron nucleus in the aqua complex compared to that in the nitrosyl complex. The nuclear factor $\Delta R/R$ is negative for ^{57}Fe and therefore the increasing positive δ values from the nitrosyl to the aqua complex.

Problem 18.1 Explain the following Mössbauer spectra.

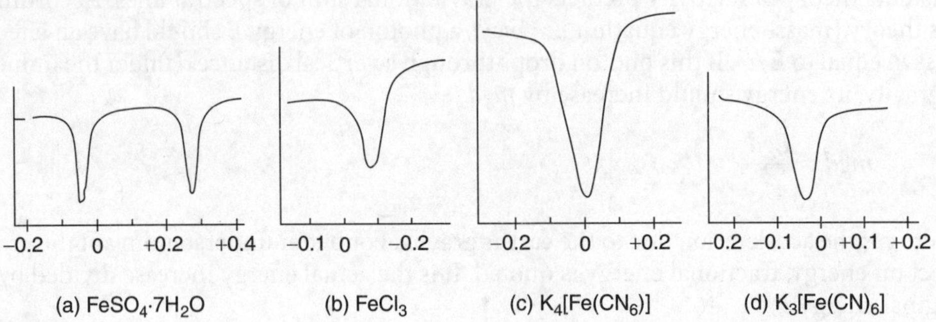

(a) $FeSO_4{\cdot}7H_2O$ (b) $FeCl_3$ (c) $K_4[Fe(CN_6)]$ (d) $K_3[Fe(CN)_6]$

Solution

(a) **$FeSO_4.7H_2O$:** In this salt, iron(II) has a spin free electron configuration (d^6). The electric field around the iron nucleus is not spherical; therefore, there is a field gradient at the nucleus. This field gradient produces quadrupole splitting and consequently the Mössbauer spectrum is split into two peaks.

(b) **$FeCl_3$:** The iron in $FeCl_3$ has a d^5 electron configuration; each of its five *d* orbitals has one electron. Such an arrangement provides the iron nucleus with a spherical electric field. In this system, there is no electric field gradient at the nucleus and therefore the spectrum is not split.

(c) **$K_4[Fe(CN)_6]$:** CN^- is a strong field ligand and therefore the electron configuration for Fe in this complex is $t_g^6\, e_g^o$; it is a spin paired complex. The electric field at the iron nucleus has spherical symmetry and consequently there is no quadrupole splitting. The Mössbauer spectrum of each of the strong field ligands (six equivalent ligands) of the iron(II) consists of a single sharp resonance line.

(d) **$K_3[Fe(CN)_6]$:** The electron arrangement in Fe in this complex is $t_{2g}^5\, e_g^o$ which produces an electric field gradient at the iron nucleus. Therefore, quadrupole splitting is possible.

The spectrum of each of the strong field ligands (6 equivalent ligands) of the iron(III) consists of a pair of peaks due to quadrupole splitting.

Problem 18.2 Explain the following Mössbauer data.

Absorber	FeF_2	$FeCl_2$	$FeBr_2$	FeI_2	FeS
δ/mm s^{-1} at 4.2K relative to iron metal	1.48	1.16	1.12	1.04	0.59

Solution

The δ value decreases with increasing covalent character.

The increase in covalent character decreases the effective 3*d* shielding because of the nephelauxetic effect of electron withdrawal towards the ligands. This results in a corresponding decrease in δ.

If the Fe^{2+} forms covalent bonds with the surrounding groups, the higher the covalency of the bonds, the lesser is the density of *d* electrons in the vicinity of the nucleus. Higher the covalency, the lesser is the quadrupole splitting and the greater is the *s* electron density at the nucleus, that is, the lower is the isomer shift.

Problem 18.3 The Mössbauer spectrum of $[Fe(CN)_6]^{4-}$ shows a single resonance absorption but that of $[Fe(CN)_5 NH_3]^{3-}$ shows a pair of resonances. Explain.

Solution

In $[Fe(CN)_6]^{4-}$, the six ligands are equivalent and therefore, there is no electric field gradient at the iron nucleus. However, in $[Fe(CN)_5NH_3]^{3-}$, the six ligands are not identical; this produces an electric field gradient at the nucleus and hence a quadrupole splitting of the spectrum.

Problem 18.4 Explain the following Mössbauer spectra.

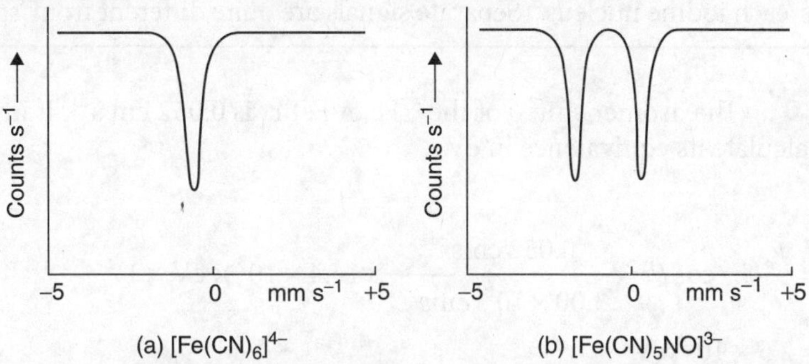

(a) $[Fe(CN)_6]^{4-}$ (b) $[Fe(CN)_5NO]^{3-}$

The ion $[Fe(CN)_6]^{4-}$ is symmetrical . The electric field around the Fe nucleus is symmetrical; therefore, there is no net field gradient at the iron nucleus. Thus its Mössbauer spectrum has a single absorption without any splitting.

When one of the CN^- ligands is replaced by the NO group, the symmetrical electric field is lost; the NO produces an internal field. (NO group is electronically different from the CN^- group). Then electric field splits the spectrum. In this example, the electric field gradient existing in the system itself, produces splitting of the spectrum.

Problem 18.5 Explain the following spectra.

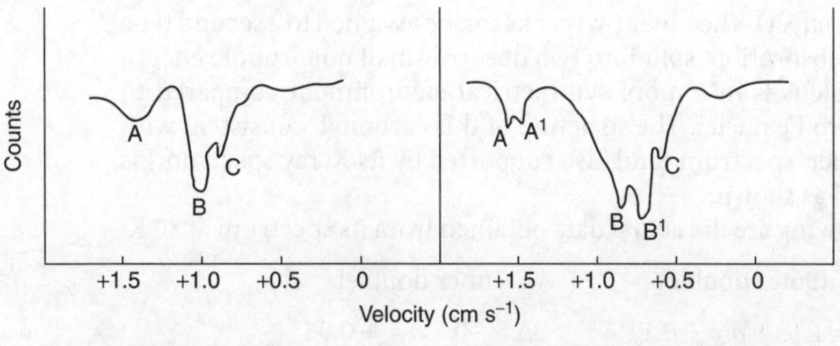

(a) Partial ^{129}I spectrum of I_2Cl_6 (b) Partial ^{129}I spectrum of $I_2Br_2Cl_4$

Solution

The spectrum of $I_2Br_2Cl_4$ on comparison with that of I_2Cl_6 indicates that the two iodine atoms in $I_2Br_2Cl_4$ are in different environments (unlike the iodine atoms in I_2Cl_6). The structure of I_2Cl_6 can be written as shown. In this structure, the two iodine nuclei have identical environments. Based on the bridged structure of I_2Cl_6, three possible structures for $I_2Br_2Cl_4$ may be considered:

Cl Cl Cl / I I / Cl Cl Cl

(i)	(ii)	(iii)
Cl, Cl – I – (Br, Br bridges) – I – Cl, Cl	Cl, Br – I – (Cl, Cl bridges) – I – Br, Cl	Cl, Cl – I – (Cl, Cl bridges) – I – Br, Br

Structures (i) and (ii) are symmetrical and the two iodines are in identical environments. Then, there can be no splitting of the absorption peaks. On the other hand, in structure (iii), the iodine atoms are structurally inequivalent and hence the spectrum as observed consists of two separate signals, one for each iodine nucleus. (Separate signals are quite different from 'split' signals.)

Problem 18.6 The isomer shift δ of the ^{57}Fe in $FeBr_3$ is 0.052 cm.s^{-1}. It involves 14.4 keV γ ray decay. Calculate its equivalence in eV.

Solution

$$\Delta E_s = \frac{v_o}{c} E_\gamma \cos\theta = \frac{0.052 \text{ cms}^{-1}}{3.00 \times 10^{10} \text{ cms}^{-1}} \times 14.4 \times 10^3 \times \text{eV} \times 1$$

$$= 2.5 \times 10^{-8} \text{ eV}$$

Problem 18.7 Interpret the Mössbauer spectrum obtained for $Fe_3(CO)_{12}$.

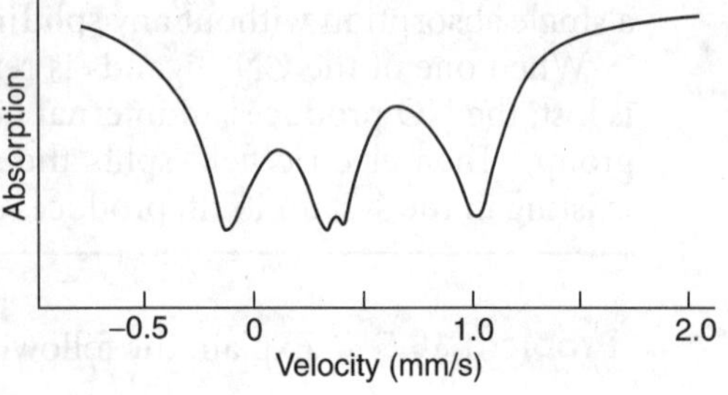

Solution

This spectrum indicates the presence of more than one type of iron in the structure of the carbonyl (the multiple asymmetric absorption peaks are not of the type expected only because of quadrupole splitting). The outer two peaks can be assigned to one type of iron (an absorption, split into two due to a large quadrupole effect). The inner two peaks can be assigned to a second type of iron (an absorption, split into two due to a small quadrupole effect). This Fe nucleus is in a more symmetrical environment compared to the other two Fe nuclei. The structure of this carbonyl, consistent with its Mössbauer spectrum (and also supported by its X-ray spectrum) is represented as shown.

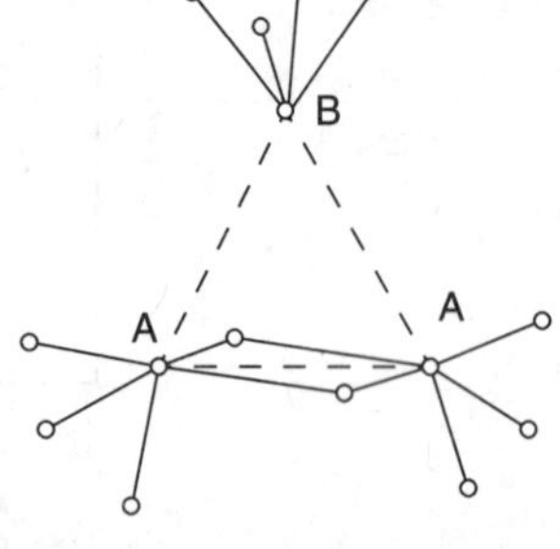

The following are the actual data obtained from its spectrum at 80 K:

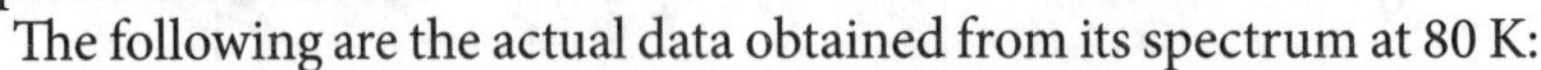

Outer doublet	Inner doublet
$\Delta = 1.13$ $\delta = +0.11$	$\Delta = \sim 0$ $\delta = +0.05$

Problem 18.8 Interpret the Mössbauer spectrum of $Fe(CO)_5$ shown.

Solution

This spectrum consists of a doublet; this indicates the existence of a field gradient at the nucleus. The excited state of Fe nucleus must obviously be split by the field gradient. This is expected of an asymmetric trigonal bipyramidal geometry, as in iron pentacarbonyl. The two expected transitions, denoted by arrows, are shown in the figure on the right.

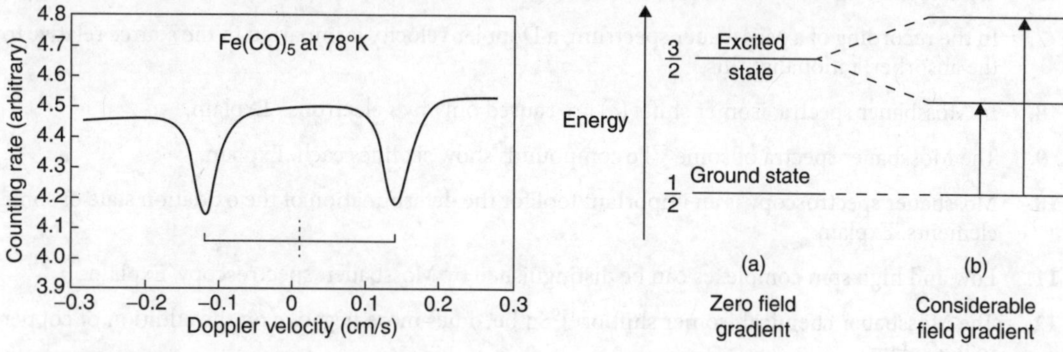

Problem 18.9 What structural features of $Fe_2(CO)_9$ may be predicted from the given spectrum?

[% transmission = (100 × number of counts in the absence of transition) / number of counts during transition]

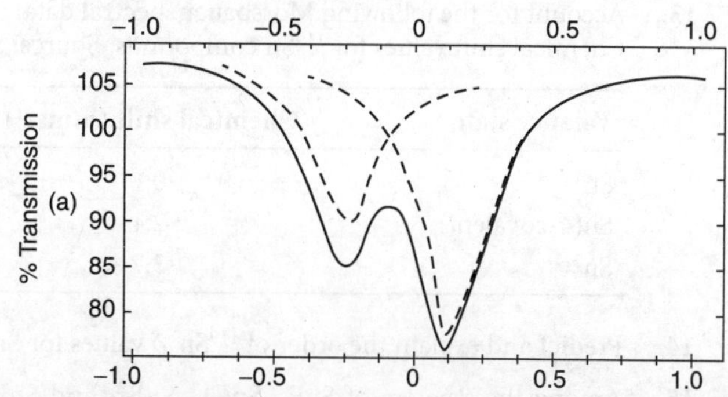

Solution

The spectrum has a pair of split peaks but not two independent peaks. This indicates that the two iron atoms are in an identical state of bonding. If the two iron atoms were bonded differently to CO groups, then two independent peaks would have occurred. The quadrupole splitting points to lack of total symmetry in the structure of the carbonyl. This asymmetry may arise from a slight distortion in the octahedral geometry of each Fe centre.

EXERCISES

1. Rationalise the following:
   (a) In Mössbauer spectra, only *s* electrons but not *p* and *d* electrons cause isomer shifts.
   (b) The isomer shifts are positive for some nuclei, but negative for others.
   (c) For a pair of *cis–trans* isomers, the δ values may be identical.
   (d) Covalency and δ values are correlative.
2. Predict and explain the ^{127}I Mössbauer spectrum of $CsIF_6$.

3. Explain how Mössbauer spectroscopy can be applied in the study of *cis–trans* isomerism in octahedral metal complexes.

4. Mössbauer spectroscopy can be applied only to the solid state. Explain.

5. In the Mössbauer method, there is only a slight probability that the gamma ray energy from the source nucleus will match that required for absorption by the sample nucleus, especially if the source and sample are in the liquid or gaseous state; rationalise.

6. What is the origin of the Doppler broadening in Mössbauer spectroscopy?

7. In the recording of a Mössbauer spectrum, a Doppler velocity is imparted to the source relative to the absorber; rationalise this.

8. In Mössbauer spectra, isomer shifts (δ) are caused only by *s* electrons. Explain.

9. The Mössbauer spectra of some ^{57}Fe compounds show six lines each. Explain.

10. Mössbauer spectroscopy is an important tool for the determination of the oxidation state of some elements. Explain.

11. Low and high spin complexes can be distinguished by Mössbauer spectroscopy. Explain.

12. The Mössbauer chemical isomer shift of ^{119}Sn becomes more negative on the addition of copper to it; explain.

13. Account for the following Mössbauer spectral data:
Chemical shift values for ^{119}Sn compounds. Source: Sn^{4+}

Valance state	Chemical shift (mms^{-1})
Sn^{4+}	0
Sn(4-covalent)	2.1
Sn^{2+}	3.7

14. Predict and explain the order of ^{119}Sn δ values for SnF_4 $SnCl_4$, $SnBr_4$ and SnI_4.

15. Among the spectra of SnF_4, $SnCl_4$, $SnBr_4$ and SnI_4, the spectrum of SnF_4 alone indicates the occurrence of quadrupole splitting. Explain.

16. The ^{127}I and ^{129}I spectra of $Na_3H_2IO_6$ are characterised with δ values of opposite signs. Explain.

17. The ^{119}Sn spectrum of SnO shows a quadrupole splitting of 1.45 mm s^{-1} whereas the spectrum of SnTe shows a sharp line with no quadrupole splitting. Rationalise this.

18. The ^{121}Sb spectrum of solid SbF_5 does not indicate any resolved quadrupole splitting. Explain.

19. The Mössbauer chemical shifts are positive for some nuclei, but negative for others. Justify.

20. The δ values for both the *cis* and *trans* isomers of $[Fe(EtCN)_4(CN)_2]$ are identical, namely +0.05 mm s^{-1}. Explain.

21. With Fe(II) complexes, the isomer shift and also the quadrupole splitting are strongly dependent on the nature of the donor atoms. Justify.

22. Which of the two, *cis*-$Fe(CO)_4Cl_2$ or *trans*-$Fe(CO)_4Cl_2$ would have the larger quadrupole splitting for iron?

23. Justify the following Mössbauer spectral data:

System	Quadupole spitting ΔE_Q/mm s^{-1}
a) $Na_3[Fe(CN)_5NH_3]$	0.60
b) $Na_2[Fe(CN)_5NO]$	1.76
c) $FeCl_2.4H_2O$	3.00

24. Explain the following isomer shift values (source is Au-197):

Compound	AuI	AuBr	AuCl
δ/mm s^{-1}	0.125	0.143	0.161

25. Justify the following Mössbauer data (source is ^{57}Co):

Complex	δ/mm s^{-1}	ΔE_Q/ mm s^{-1}
$K_3[Fe(CN)_6]$	−0.413	0.373
$Ag_3[Fe(CN)_6]$	−0.439	0.860
$Cu_3[Fe(CN)_6]$	−0.454	0.760

19 X-Ray Techniques

19.1 X-RAYS

X-rays were discovered by Roentgen in 1895. These rays are generated by electron bombardment of heavy metal targets. They are electromagnetic radiation like ordinary light, but of very much shorter wavelength. The wavelength range for visible light is of the order 10^{-4} cm, whereas the range for X-rays is about 10^{-8} cm or 1 Å.

- *The wavelength of X-rays is of the same order of magnitude as molecular diameters in gases and the interatomic distances in solids.* This property of X-rays renders these rays suitable for studying crystal structures.
- X-ray spectroscopy is based upon measurement of scattering emission, absorption and fluorescence of electromagnetic radiation. This spectroscopy is similar to optical spectroscopy and is used to obtain useful information about qualitative and structural aspects of materials.
- X-rays are produced when high-speed electrons collide with a solid target. These X-rays are called *primary X-rays*. The emission of X-ray spectral peaks produced are characteristic of elements present in the target. The wavelengths of the peaks can be related to the atomic numbers of the elements producing them; therefore, this method is used to identify elements. Under controlled conditions, the intensity of the peaks is used to determine the amounts of the elements.

Wilhelm Roentgen

Roentgen was a German physicist (1845–1923). He discovered X-rays when working with a Crookes tube. He received the first Nobel Prize in physics in 1901 for this discovery. In recognition of his achievement in physics, IUPAC named element 111 Roentgenium, after him. X-rays are called *Roentgen rays*. The first picture he took using X-rays was his wife's hand.

Today, Roentgen is considered the father of diagnostic radiology, the medical study which uses imaging to identify diseases. He died of carcinoma of the intestine, believed to have been caused by the ionising radiation with which he worked. He refused to apply for patents on his discoveries, not wanting to commercialise science. He donated his Nobel Prize money to the University of Munich where he worked as a professor.

Source: Public Domain, https://commons.wikimedia.org/w/index.php?curid=5985289

19.1.1 Production of X-rays

X-rays required for analytical studies are obtained by three methods:

(i) by bombardment of a metal target with a beam of high energy electrons,
(ii) by the exposure of certain substances to a primary beam of X-rays; then, secondary beam of fluorescent X-rays are generated, and
(iii) by using a radioactive source which decays producing X-rays.

Artificial radioactive isotopes provide a simple source of X-rays. For example, the artificial isotope $^{55}_{27}Fe$ undergoes K-capture producing X-rays.

$$^{55}_{26}\text{Fe} \longrightarrow \, ^{55}_{25}\text{Mn} + h\nu \text{ (X-rays)}$$

The resulting K_α line at 210 pm (2.1 Å) is used in X-ray methods. ^{57}Co, ^{60}Co and ^{241}Am, synthetic isotopes, can also serve as X-ray sources for analytical investigation of materials.

19.1.2 Monochromatic X-rays

Monochromatic X-rays have to be used in the application of X-ray methods. An X-ray beam of a selected narrow range of wavelength (limited bandwidth) is obtained by using filters (monochromators) which absorb most of the wavelengths, allowing only a narrow beam to pass through. The filtered X-ray is monochromatic. For example, the K_β line and most of the continuous radiation from the X-ray emitted by Mo is filtered by a zirconium filter (Fig. 19.1). The X-ray after filtration consists of a monochromatic beam of radiation of K_α line. The thickness of the filter in addition to its absorbing characteristics, is important in the production of monochromatic X-rays. Elements such as V, Mn, Fe, Co, Ni, Zr and Pd can act as filters. The thickness of the filters range from 15–40 μm, depending upon the constituent elements of the filters. For example, a thickness of 15 μm is effective for absorbing 99% of the Cr-K_β X-rays by a V filter but a thickness of 42 μm is required for absorbing the Ag-K_β X-ray by a Pd filter.

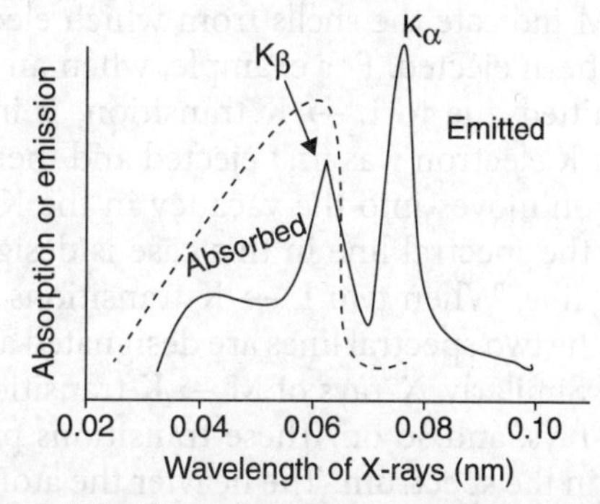

Fig. 19.1 Absorption of K_β X-ray by Zr filter, giving monochromatic K_α X-ray beam (source Mo)

19.2 MOSLEY'S LAW

When a beam of electrons impinges on a target material, the incident electrons are decelerated due to their interaction with the orbital electrons of the target atoms. When the energy of the incident electrons is low, a part of the energy lost by them on interaction with the target is converted into a continuum of X-radiation called *Bremsstrahlung* or breaking radiation. When the energy of the incident electrons is increased, sufficient energy will be transferred to the target atoms and the orbital electrons of the atoms will get ejected. Such ejection creates a vacancy in the electron level and consequently, an electron from a higher level falls into this vacancy. In such a transition, a photon of X-radiation is emitted from the atom concerned. The wavelength of the emitted X-radiation is dependent on the type of electronic transition and hence is characteristic of the element.

When high-energy incident electrons hit the atom, the electrons closest to the nucleus are the principal ones affected. When such electrons, say a K electron is ejected, a series of electronic transitions, such as L → K, M → L, N → M occurs. Each new vacancy is filled by an electron from a higher shell, until the excited atom returns to its ground state. These changes in the electronic levels release X-radiations characteristic of the target element.

The inner electrons are not involved with the state of atom, or the chemical combination of the atom (except for the lighter atoms) and therefore the nature (λ) of the X-rays emitted by the elements is independent of elements' chemical state.

The wavelengths of emitted X-rays are short and in the order 1–1000 pm; this range corresponds to high energies. Each electronic transition results in a characteristic X-ray spectral line. The energy $h\nu$ of such a spectral line is equal to the difference between the binding energies of two electronic levels. The spectral peaks are designated by symbols such as K_α, K_β, L_α, M_α, and so on. The prefixes K, L and M indicate the shells from which electrons have been ejected. For example, when an X-ray is emitted due to L → K transition, it implies that a K electron was first ejected and then an L electron moves into the vacancy in the K shell. Thus the spectral line in this case is designated as K_α line. When two L → K transitions occur then the two spectral lines are designated as $K_{\alpha 1}$ and $K_{\alpha 2}$ lines. Similarly, X-rays of M → K transitions are called K_β X-rays, and so on. These transitions produce sharp lines in the spectrum. The heavier the atom, the greater is the number of X-ray lines found in the spectrum due to higher number of electronic transitions. The origin of characteristic X-ray lines is shown in Fig. 19.2(a).

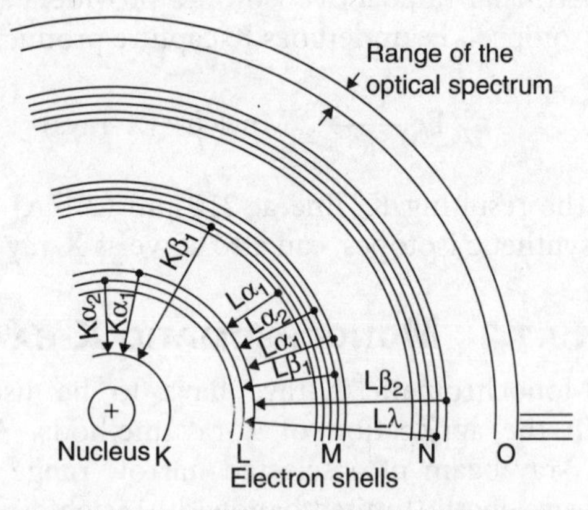

Fig. 19.2(a) Origin of characteristic X-ray

An X-ray spectrum of an element is a plot of relative intensity versus wavelength of the emitted X-rays. A typical X-ray emission spectrum of an element M is shown in Fig. 19.2(b). As there is only a limited number of possible inner shell transitions, the resulting X-ray spectrum is much simpler than the complex optical spectrum; optical spectra originate from valence (outer) electrons, giving rise to complex spectra.

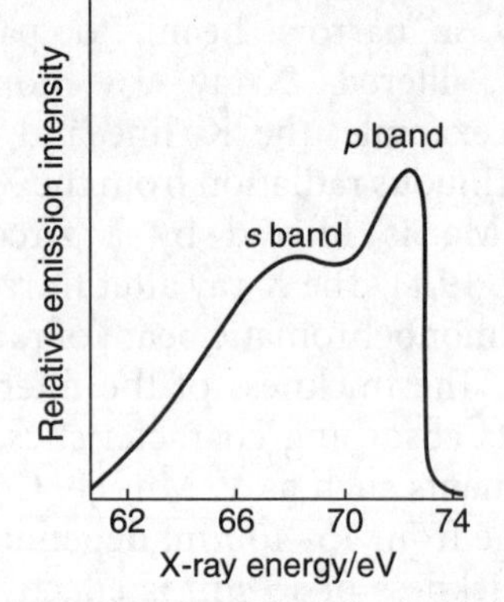

Fig. 19.2(b) A typical X-ray emission spectrum: aluminium

A linear relationship exists between the reciprocal values of wavelength of each X-ray transition series and square of the atomic number Z of the excited element. This is mathematically denoted as

$$\frac{1}{\lambda} = K\,(Z-1)^2 \tag{19.1}$$

This is *Mosley's law*. Mosley's law is the basis for X-ray spectral chemical analysis.

The elements in a sample can be identified by matching the measured wavelengths of emitted X-rays with those listed in literature; for easy comparison, the wavelengths are given in terms of 2θ values in accordance with the Bragg equation, $n\lambda = 2d\sin\theta$.

Analytical Applications of X-radiations

X-rays are used in several analytical investigations. These applications are of the following types:

- The formation of X-rays by bombarding a material with electrons and measuring the wavelengths of emitted X-rays can be used to identify the elements and determine their *Z* values.
- The diffraction of X-rays by crystalline materials is used for the determination of crystal structures.
- The absorption of X-rays by a material can be used to determine elements of high atomic numbers.
- The absorption of X-rays by a material and the consequent emission of electrons from it, X-ray photoelectron spectroscopy (XPS) can be used for chemical analysis. The XPS is an excellent method for surface analysis.
- In the electron microprobe method, the elements on the surface of a matrix can be identified and determined. This is an X-ray emission procedure known as Energy Dispersive X-ray Analysis (EDXA).
- In *X-ray fluorescence spectroscopy*, a material absorbs incident X-rays and emits X-rays of energy different from that of the incident X-rays. The emitted X-ray spectrum is used to identify the constituents of materials. This is an X-ray absorption–X-ray emission method.
- X-ray diffraction is the most widely used and least ambiguous method for determining the positions of atoms in a molecule.
- The X-ray diffraction method is more useful for structural determination of inorganic molecules than that of organic molecules. Spectroscopic data for inorganic molecules are not as unambiguous as for organic molecules. But, X-ray diffraction data are precisely applicable to diverse structures encountered among inorganic molecules.
- The bond angles and distances required for characterising the structures of inorganic molecules are accurately obtained from X-ray diffraction data.
- An indication that a solid is ionic is provided by X-ray diffraction for, the coordination number of ionic lattices is generally low.

19.3 STRUCTURE OF SOLIDS

Strong forces hold the atoms, ions or molecules together in solids. When the atoms in a solid are arranged in a definite pattern in space, the solid is said to be *crystalline*. When there is no such definite crystal form, the solid is called *amorphous.* For example, sodium chloride is crystalline and glass is amorphous. The crystalline forms have definite characteristics such as sharp melting point, shape and density. The internal structure of a crystal, called the *lattice structure*, is characteristic of a crystal. A knowledge of the types of crystal structures is required. This is understood in terms *of crystal systems and space lattices.*

19.3.1 Crystal Systems

Crystals form different geometric forms with different arrangements of the constituent atoms. On the basis of symmetry, there are six crystal systems (Table 19.1). This classification is based on crystallographic axes, the relative length of the various axes and the angles of inclination between axes. Crystallographic axes are straight lines passing through a common origin and inclined at definite angles (Fig. 19.3). Thus, crystals of a particular crystal system have the same *relative length* of axes and the same angles of inclination between axes.

Table 19.1 Crystal systems and their characteristics

System	Axes and angles	Essential symmetry	Examples
1. Cubic	$a=b=c$	Four three-fold axis	NaCl
	$\alpha=\beta=\gamma=90°$		Diamond
2. Tetragonal	$a=b\neq c$	One four-fold axis	Rutile
	$\alpha=\beta=\gamma=90°$		Zircon
3. Hexagonal	$a=b\neq c$	One six-fold axis	Mg
	$\alpha=\beta=90°, \gamma=120°$	or one three-fold axis	
Trigonal*	$a=b=c$		Calcite
	$\alpha=\beta=90°, \gamma=120°$		
4. Orthorhombic	$a\neq b\neq c$	Three mutually perpendicular two-fold axes, or two planes intersecting in a two-fold axis	Rhombic sulphur KNO_3
	$\alpha=\beta=\gamma=90°$		
5. Monoclinic	$a\neq b\neq c$	One two-fold axis, or one plane of symmetry	Monoclinic sulphur $Na_2SO_4.10H_2O$
	$\alpha=\gamma=90°, \beta\neq 90°$		
6. Triclinic	$a\neq b\neq c$	No planes, no axis-of symmetry	$CuSO_4.5H_2O$
	$\alpha\neq\beta\neq\gamma\neq 90°$		$K_2Cr_2O_7$

**The trigonal system is considered to be a sub-group of the hexagonal system*

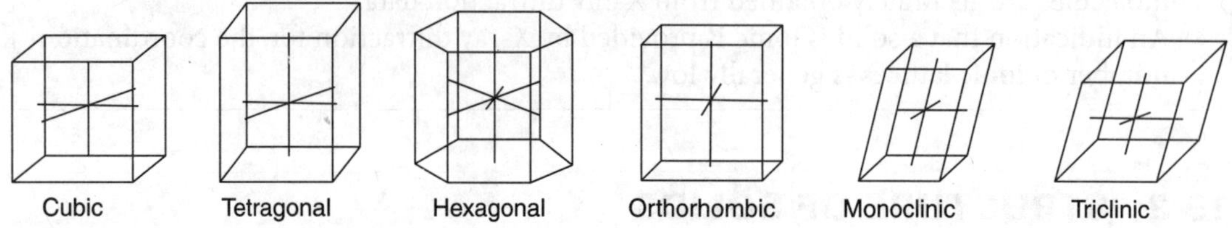

Fig. 19.3 The six crystal systems

19.3.2 Space Lattices (Bravais Lattices)

Unit crystal lattice (*space group*) is the fundamental structure of a crystal. Each unit lattice is constituted by atoms, molecules or ions arranged in a particular geometrical configuration. A crystal can be built up by repetition and extension in all directions of the unit crystal lattice. The geometric shape of the macroscopic crystal is the same as that of the unit cell. For example, the unit cell of NaCl is a cube and this salt is formed in tiny cubes.

The internal structures of crystals are of 14 basic arrangements. These 14 arrangements are called the *space lattices* or the *Bravais lattices* (Fig. 19.4). The black circles in each space lattice diagram represent atoms.

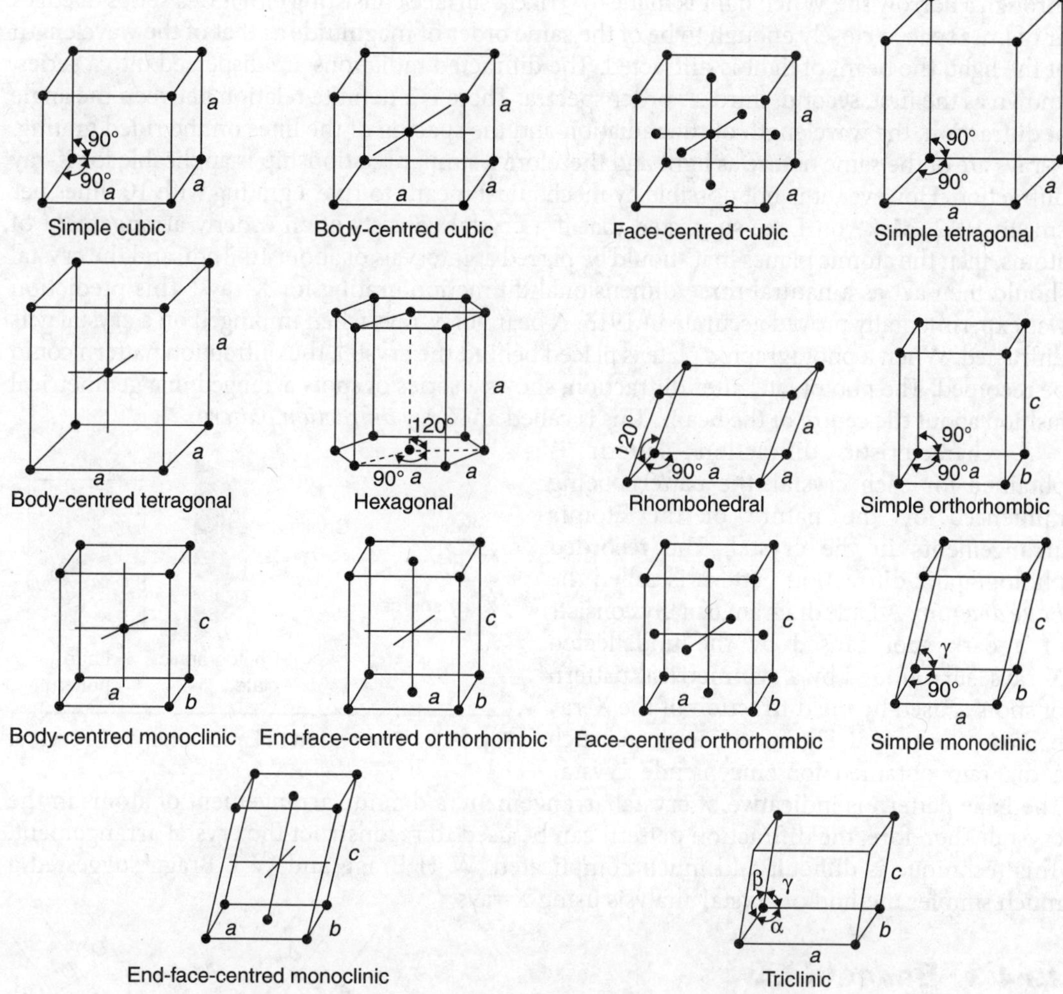

Fig. 19.4 The fourteen space (Bravais) lattices

19.4 DIFFRACTION METHODS

X-ray diffraction is the chief method of studying crystal structures. Let us see how X-rays are used in determining crystal structures,

19.4.1 MONOCHROMATIC X-RAYS

For X-ray diffraction, a monochromatic X-radiation such as the K_α radiation (1.54 Å) is used. This is obtained from an X-ray tube using copper as the target. The K_β radiation (1.39 Å) formed along with K_α radiation can be eliminated by using a nickel foil as filter. Nickel strongly absorbs K_β radiation but not K_α radiation.

19.4.2 PRINCIPLE OF X-RAY DIFFRACTION (XRD)

Diffraction is the *breaking up* of a ray into dark and bright bands caused by the interference of one part of the beam with another when the ray is deflected by an opaque object on passing through a narrow slit. When light is made to strike a surface consisting either of a series of edges or of lines spaced closely enough to be of the same order of magnitude as that of the wavelength of the light, the beam of light is diffracted. The diffracted radiations are dispersed into a series, known as the first, second, third ... order spectra. There is a definite relation between the angle of diffraction, the wavelength of the radiation and the spacing of the lines on the ruled grating. X-rays are of the same nature as light and therefore a similar relationship is applicable for X-ray diffraction. However, it is not possible by mechanical means to rule a grating with 10^8 lines per cm. In 1912, Max von Laue suggested that if a crystal consists of an orderly arrangement of atoms, then the atomic planes in it should be placed at intervals of about 10^{-8} cm, and the crystal should then act as a natural three dimensional diffraction grating for X-rays. This prediction was experimentally proved accurate in 1913. A beam of X-rays when impinged on a crystal gets diffracted. When a photographic plate is placed behind the crystal, the diffraction pattern could be recorded. The photoplate, after diffraction, shows a series of spots arranged in a geometrical fashion about the centre of the beam. This is called an *X-ray diffraction pattern.*

A characteristic diffraction pattern is obtained for each crystal, the pattern being influenced by the nature of the atomic arrangements in the crystal. The recorded photographic diffraction pattern is called the *Laue diagram.* A Laue diagram usually consists of a dark spot caused by the undeflected X-rays, surrounded by a symmetrical pattern of spots caused by the diffraction of the X-ray beam by the crystal. Figure 19.5 indicates such a diagram obtained for zinc blende crystal. The Laue pattern is indicative of crystal arrangement, a definite arrangement of atoms in the crystal. Therefore, the diffraction pattern can be used to reconstruct the crystal arrangement. This technique is difficult and much complicated. W H Bragg and W L Bragg suggested a much simpler method of crystal analysis using X-rays.

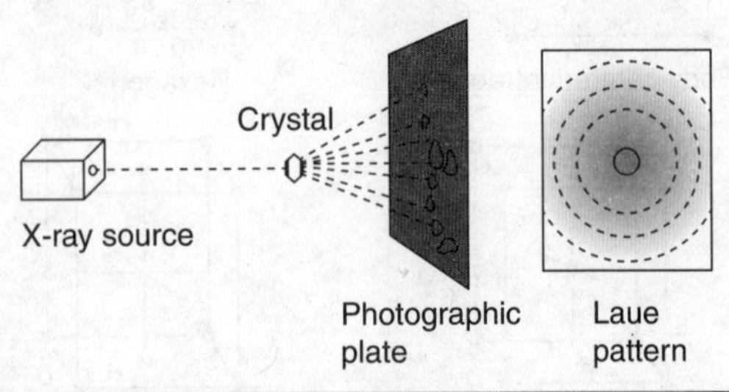

Fig. 19.5 Formation of Laue pattern of a crystal

19.4.3 Bragg's Law

When a beam of monochromatic X-rays impinges on a crystal at an angle θ, some of the rays will be diffracted by the layers (L, M, N) of atoms in the crystal (Fig. 19.6). The wave front F consists of a bundle of rays in phase. After diffraction, the wave front is at D, D′, D″. For the rays diffracted from the first layer the path length is FCD and the path length for the second layer is FC′D′. The path length FC′D′ is longer than FCD by AC′B. AC′B is equal to 2AC′.

Fig. 19.6 Diagram for proving that $n\lambda = 2d \sin\theta$

$$AC' = d \sin\theta$$

where d is the interplanar distance. The difference in path length is $2d \sin\theta$. The X-ray will be diffracted without destructive interference only if the difference in path length is an integral number n of the wave length λ. Therefore,

$$2d \sin \theta = n\lambda \qquad (19.2)$$

$$n = 1, 2, 3...$$

This is *Bragg's law*. Using this law, the spacing between layers (d) can be calculated if λ is known. Using the Bragg relationship, the wavelength of monochromatic X-rays can be determined with a crystal of known layer spacing. For X-rays of a definite wavelength a series of angles θ_1, θ_2, θ_3, ..., gives reflections corresponding to values of n equal to 1, 2, 3, ... which are called the first, second, third order reflections. Thus the total geometry of a crystal can be worked out by rotating a crystal through many values of θ and finding d for rows of particles viewed in various directions.

Bragg and Bragg

William Henry Bragg working at University College, London, discovered the relationship between the spacing of the planes of atoms inside the crystal and strong reflections of X-rays by the crystal. This is now called the Bragg law. He developed the X-ray spectrometer and improved the instrument to obtain reliable diffraction data.

His son William Lawrence Bragg also studied X-ray crystallography and together with his father established the structures of several crystals, such as rock salt, zinc blende, diamond and so on. Lawrence pursuing crystallography remarked that his discoveries were like looking for gold and finding nuggets lying around everywhere. In 1915, the Braggs jointly received the Nobel Prize in Physics. Lawrence was only twenty-five, the youngest Nobel laureate!

Source:

1. By Nobel foundation - http://www.archive.org/details/lesprixnobel1913nobe, Public Domain, https://commons.wikimedia.org/w/index.php?curid=33407292
2. By Nobel foundation - http://nobelprize.org/nobel_prizes/physics/laureates/1915/wl-bragg-bio.html, Public Domain, https://commons.wikimedia.org/w/index.php?curid=6201237

19.4.4 Miller Indices

The faces of a crystal and the internal layers of atoms are identified by a set of three numbers called *Miller indices*. In Fig. 19.7(a), the shaded centre face is parallel to the b and c axes, and it intersects the a axis at a distance which is one unit cell length. The intercepts on b and c axes are taken as infinite. The Miller indices are the reciprocals of the intercepts, 1/1, 1/∞, 1/∞ or (100). In the general case, the indices are represented as (hkl). The parallel face through the atoms in the centre of the cubes would cut the a-axis at 1/2 a, the

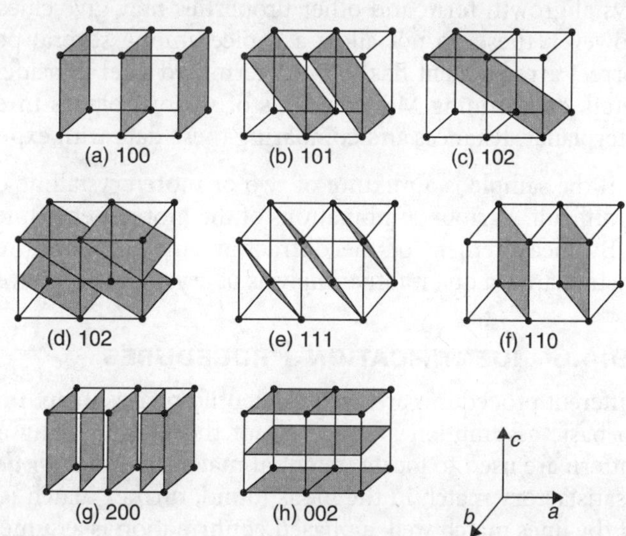

Fig. 19.7 Miller indices of planes in a body-centred cubic lattice

Miller indices being (200). The face in the plane of the paper is parallel to the *a* and *c* axes and cuts the *b*-axis at one unit cell length. The Miller indices are $1/\infty$, $1/1$, $1/\infty$ or (010). The shaded plane in Fig. 19.7(b) has the intercepts 1, ∞ and 1 and the indices (101). In Fig. 19.7(c), the plane shaded has the indices $1/2$, $1/\infty$, $1/1$ or multiplying by 2 to give whole numbers (102). In Fig. 19.7(d), the lower parallel shaded plane gives the indices (102) directly. Equivalent, parallel planes are identified by the same set of indices containing the smallest whole numbers. The Figs 19.7(e) to (h) indicate several other planes.

The reflections from a set of equivalent planes in a crystal are referred to by the Miller indices of the plane, that is, the (100) reflection, (111) reflection, and so on. Higher orders ($n > 1$) of the reflections from the same planes are equivalent to reflections from parallel planes which are more closely spaced. For example, the second order reflection ($n = 2$) from the (100) planes would occur at the same angle θ as a first order reflection from a (200) plane. This reflection is called the (200) reflection. The third order reflection from the (111) plane is called the (333) reflection.

19.4.5 Determination of Crystal Structure

Three steps are involved in the determination of a crystal structure:

- finding the crystal system to which the substance belongs,
- determining the spacings of the various planes in the crystal, and
- finding the shape of the *unit cell* and the exact atomic arrangement in it.

The analysis of a crystal structure involves determination of inter-planar spacings by the measurement of the angles at which X-rays are deflected from different crystal faces. The reflection of light is almost entirely from the surface of a crystal but the reflection of X-rays is only after considerable penetration through the layers of the crystal. X-rays are highly penetrating as shown by the formation of Laue's spots after passing through a whole crystal. Most of the reflection of X-rays occurs inside the crystal from planes of atoms within a millimetre from the crystal surface.

Visual observations may sometimes give an idea about the crystal system. In addition, crystal growth form and other properties may give clues to the nature of the crystal lattice. However, these do not allow a choice among several possible arrangements of atoms. The correct arrangement has to be determined after considering different possible structures in detail, determining Miller indices of various planes in each, calculating the corresponding interplanar distances and comparing these data with experimental results.

- If the sample is a mixture of two or more crystalline compounds, identification would be difficult. Various combinations of the more intense lines are used to find a match.
- By measurement of the diffraction line intensities and comparing them with those of standards, a quantitative analysis of crystalline mixtures can be made.

19.4.6 Identification Procedures

Different procedures are used to identify phases in an unknown mixture. In the first method, no basic assumption is made about the sample being analysed. The strongest lines in the pattern are used to locate potential matches in the *Powder Data File* (PDF) Index. Each time a satisfactory match in the file is found, further match is made with the complete pattern. If all the lines match well, a phased confirmation is assumed. In the second method, a series of guesses is made based on preconceived ideas of what phases might be present in the sample. In this search, the two basic parameters, *d* values and the relative intensities of the lines in the pattern are analysed to identify the phases in the sample. The d values are calculated from the measured 2θ values in the *diffractogram*. Normally, the d values thus obtained have accuracy of about 5%. However, the intensities are not that accurate.

19.4.7 Interpretation of Diffraction Patterns

- The position of the lines – in terms of θ and 2θ – and their relative intensities are the basis for the interpretation of diffraction patterns.
- The intensities of the lines depend upon the number and kind of atomic reflection centres in each set of planes.
- The diffraction angle 2θ is calculated by the spacing between a particular set of planes. This spacing d is calculated from the known wavelength of the incident X-ray and the measured angle.
- Computerised X-ray data are now available and therefore the recorded data can be compared with the literature data through computer search programs. For example, Swanson H E, Tagte E and Fuyat R K; *digital.library.unt.edu*. The data in computer files pertain to d spacings and relative line intensities, arranged in the order of decreasing line intensities for each material. Comparing the most intense experimental line with the file information may help identify the material being studied. The d spacings of the most intense line and also those of the second most intense line, the third most intense line, and so on, may also help confirm the identity of the material.

19.4.8 Phase Characterisation by XRD

XRD is used to obtain qualitative and quantitative information on the presence of phases of elements or compounds in an unknown mixture. A diffraction pattern recorded with a sample has three parameters:

(i) position of the diffraction maxima,
(ii) peak intensities, and
(iii) intensity distribution as a function of diffraction angle.

These parameters can be used to arrive at

- identification of the sample constituents,
- quantities of the constituents,
- crystalline size,
- distribution patterns of crystals in the sample matrix,
- degree of crystallinity, and
- stress and strain in the crystal.

Advantages of XRD are:

- it is applicable to both inorganic and organic crystals,
- the detection limit is much less compared to XRF (ppm level),
- a diffraction pattern is characteristic of the atomic arrangement within a given phase, and to this extent it acts as a fingerprint of that particular phase,
- X-ray methods cover many techniques based on the scatter, emission and absorption properties of X-radiation,
- X-ray fluorescence (XRF) spectrometry and X-ray powder diffratometry (XRD) are the most common X-ray methods,

- XRF is based on the diffraction power of a single crystal, or the proportional characteristics of photon detector, to separate the polychromatic beam of radiation from the sample into separate wavelengths; this enables qualitative and quantitative elemental analyses of materials, and
- the X-ray diffractometer and the X-ray spectrometer are commonly used to give complementary information on crystals.

Limitations of XRD are the following.

- The X-ray diffractometer is expensive.
- The chance of misinterpreting the XRD data during the course of a qualitative analysis procedure is not low. This problem arises from the fact that considerable similarity exists between diffraction patterns and can cause confusion. Out of about two million possible unique 'phases', only 120000 phases are listed in the literature!
- The XRD method has low sensitivity; its sensitivity is not comparable to the other X-ray based techniques. For example, XRF is sensitive to the extent of ppm level, whereas XRD is not sensitive below 1% of a matrix.

Fig. 19.8 100 and 110 planes in a cubic crystal

19.5 STRUCTURES OF SOME CUBIC CRYSTALS

By the X-ray diffraction method, the distance (d) between planes in a crystal can be determined. Then, the positions of different atoms relative to one another can be determined. Figure 19.8 represents a two-dimensional segment of a cubic crystal. The circles in the figure represent atoms in the crystals, spaced out and confined to a two dimensional representation for clarity. The layers of atoms joined by solid lines are separated by greater distances than those joined by dotted lines ($d = d'\sqrt{2}$).

Certain metals have simple cubic crystalline forms (Fig. 19.9a). The crystalline units are identical positive ions. Simple cubic (sc), body-centred cubic (bcc) and face-centred cubic (fcc) lattices are the most symmetric arrangements for crystals. These structures have

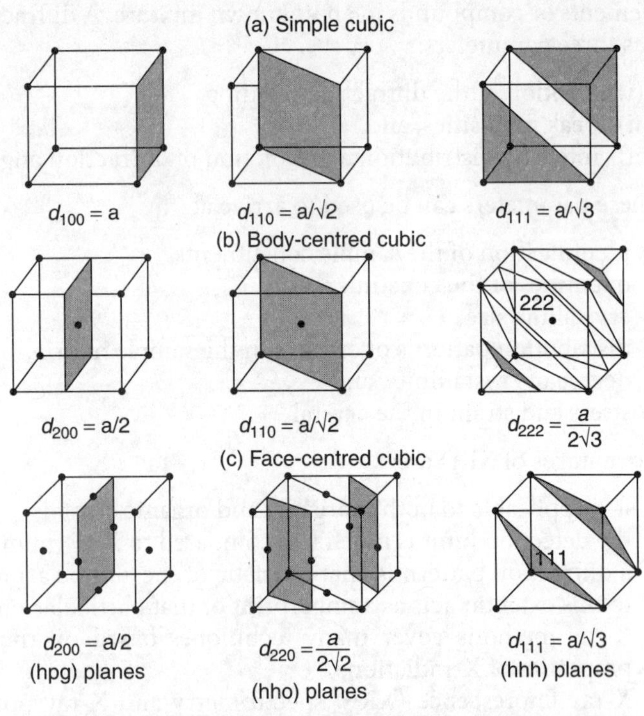

Fig. 19.9 Indexing of planes and their spacings in there cubic systems

identical external symmetry. However, they differ in the relative spacing of characteristic sets of planes. Figure 19.9 represents unit cubes of the three different types cut by the characteristic sets of planes.

The edge of the unit cube in each is designated as a. In the simple cube lattice, these characteristic planes are (100), (110) and (111). Their spacings are:

$$d_{100} = \frac{a}{\sqrt{1}} = a \qquad d_{hkl} = \frac{a \text{ (lattice constant)}}{\sqrt{(h^2 + k^2 + l^2)}}$$

$$d_{110} = \frac{a}{\sqrt{(1^2+1^2)}} = \frac{a}{\sqrt{2}} \qquad \text{(lattice spacing)} \quad \text{(Miller indices)}$$

$$d_{111} = \frac{a}{\sqrt{(1^2+1^2+1^2)}} = \frac{a}{\sqrt{3}}$$

The body-centred atom and face-centred atom in these two crystal lattices lie on the (110) and (111) planes respectively. But they do not fall on (100) planes but fall on (200) planes ($d_{200} = 1/2\ d_{100}$). Face-centred atoms introduce (220) planes and body-centred atoms introduce (222) planes. The relative spacings of the three simplest planes characteristic of the different cubic lattices are given in Table 19.2.

Table 19.2 Interplanar spacings in three cubic crystals relative to $d_{h00} = 1$ and to longest spacing = 1

Crystal lattice	$d_{h00} : d_{hh0} : d_{hhh}$	$d_{h00} : d_{hh0} : d_{hhh}$
Simple cubic	$1 : 1/\sqrt{2} : 1/\sqrt{3}$	$1 : 0.707 : 0.577$
Body-centred cubic	$1 : 2/\sqrt{2} : 1/\sqrt{3}$	$1 : 1.414 : 0.577$
Face-centred cubic	$1 : 1/\sqrt{2} : 2/\sqrt{3}$	$1 : 0.717 : 1.155$

The indexing of crystal planes and their spacings in the three cubic systems are depicted in Fig. 19.9.

19.5.1 Measurement of Scattering Angles

Several types of instrumental methods, all based upon the Bragg principle, are used to determine interplanar distances in crystals. Two of the commonly used methods are the *rotating crystal method* and the *powder method.*

19.5.1.1 Rotating Crystal Method: X-ray Spectrometer

This instrument allows the determination of spacings parallel to a selected plane and measures the intensity of reflection with an ionisation chamber or a Geiger–Muller counter. This unit is called ionisation spectrometer (Fig. 19.10). X-rays from tube T are collimated by lead slits S_1 and S_2 and fall on crystal C. The rays are diffracted from the face of the crystal through a third slit S_3 and pass into the ionisation chamber I, which measures their intensity. Careful adjustment of the crystal brings a prominent face perpendicular to the surface of the table. As the table is rotated through any angle θ, the ionisation chamber is moved through 2θ to receive diffracted

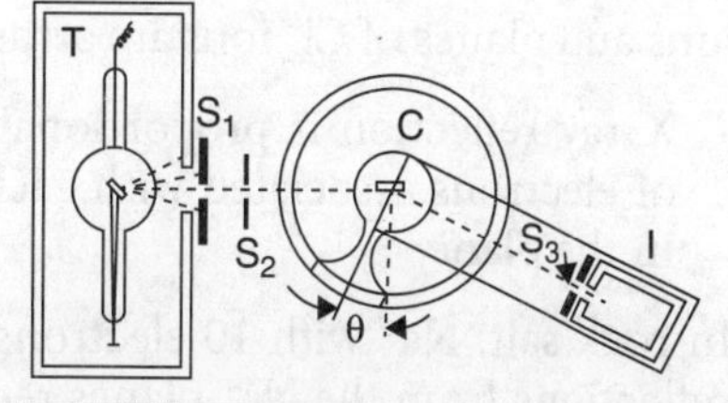

Fig. 19.10 Bragg X-ray spectrometer

X-rays. The intensity of this diffracted beam is measured by the current from the ionisation chamber. A plot of current against angle produces a series of peaks (Fig. 19.11).

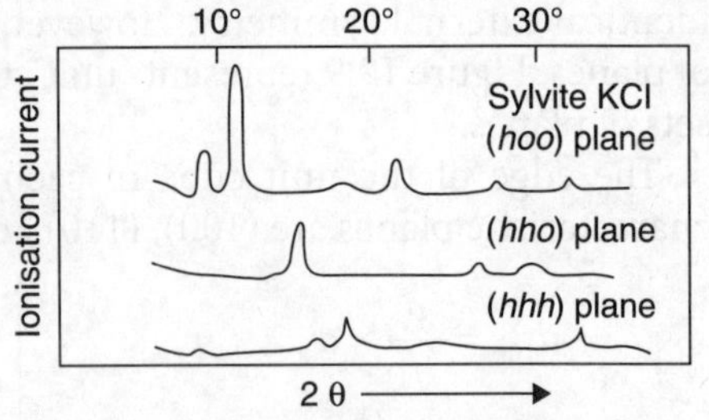

Fig. 19.11 X-ray spectra of KCl

After a plot has been obtained from one reflecting plane, the crystal is turned to reflect from other principal faces, until sufficient evidence is obtained for determining the crystal structure. With a cubic crystal three sets of planes are investigated, parallel to the (100), (110) and (111) planes and designated as *(h00), (hh0) and (hhh)* where *h* is any integer but zero.

The diffracted pattern obtained depends upon the geometry of the unit cell. The various portions of the diffracted pattern vary considerably in their relative intensities and these relative intensities are measured to provide the experimental data required for a structure determination. The intensities of the reflections are dependent upon the positions of the atoms within the unit cell. The X-ray spectrometer is an accurate method of crystal analysis, but requires a large single crystal than is ordinarily available.

Sylvite (KCl) structure KCl forms the fcc lattice. The top section in the X-ray spectrum of KCl shows the stronger lines in the doublets at $\theta = 5°23'$, $10°49'$ and $16°20'$ (Fig. 19.11). Therefore, sin 5°23′: sin 10°49′ : sin 16°20′ = 0.0938 : 0.1877: 0.2812 = 1 : 2 : 3.

These peaks represent the first, second and the third order reflections from the *(h00)* plane. Therefore, $\sin\theta$ *(h00)*: $\sin\theta$ *(hh0)* : $\sin\theta$ *(hhh)* = 0.0938:0.1325:0.1630 = 1:1.413: 1.738. Using the Bragg equation, $d_{h00} : d_{hh0} : d_{hhh} = 1 : 1/\sqrt{2} : 1/\sqrt{3}$.

This ratio agrees with that expected for a simple cubic crystal (Table 19.2). Therefore, KCl deceptively appears to have a simple cubic lattice.

The spectrum for rock salt is similar to that for KCl, except that in addition to the strong *(hhh)* reflection at 10°18′, there is a weak reflection at 5°6′. This could not come from a simple cubic structure. K^+ and Cl^-, each having 18 electrons, scatter equally. Therefore in KCl, the (222) planes lying halfway between the (111) planes cause reflections, equal in amplitude and exactly out of phase, which completely cancel the (111) reflections. In other words, KCl reflects X-rays like a simple cubic crystal with a unit cell edge half that of the rock salt structure, though it has fcc lattice.

Rock salt (NaCl) structure Bragg assumed that NaCl crystallised in a lattice consisting of alternate sodium and chloride ions. The unit cube of such a structure is shown in Fig. 19.12. In this rock salt structure, the (200) and (220) planes all contain identical arrangement of Na^+ and Cl^- ions. The (222) planes are different. In these, planes of Na^+ ions and planes of Cl^- ions are arranged alternately.

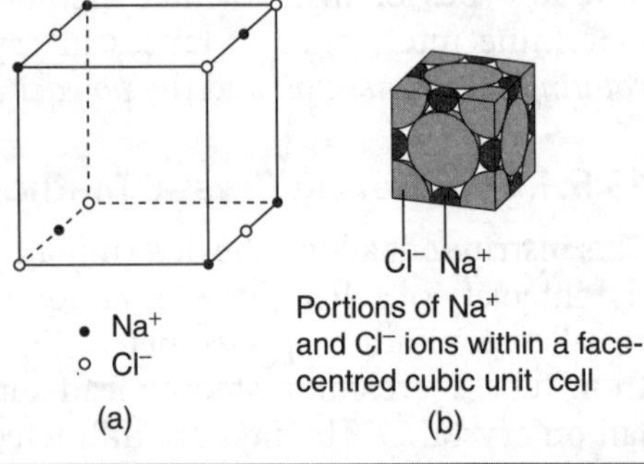

Fig. 19.12 Unit cube of rock salt crystal

- X-ray reflection is proportional to the number of electrons associated with each reflecting unit in the plane.

In rock salt, Na^+ with 10 electrons scatters much less than Cl^- with 18 electrons. Therefore, reflections from the Na^+ planes reduce but do not cancel completely the reflections from the intervening Cl^- planes. Hence, these reflections appear feebly, corresponding to reflections from the (111) planes. The plot of current versus angle for this crystal is shown in Fig. 19.13.

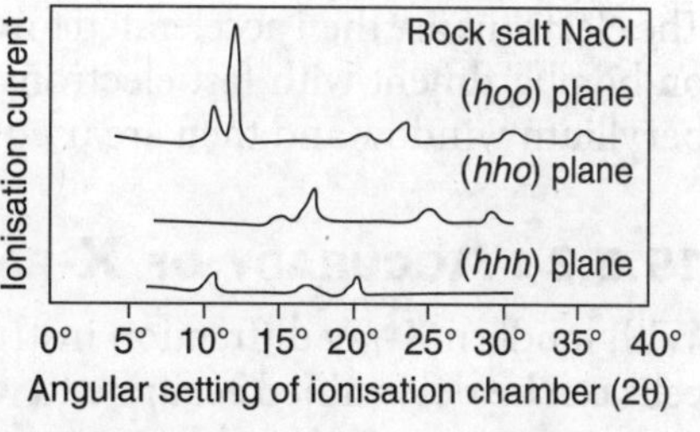

Fig. 19.13 X-ray spectra of NaCl

19.5.1.2 Powder Method

Peter Debye and Paul Scherrer devised in 1916 a method of analysing the structure of crystalline powders. Albert Hull independently developed the same method in 1917. In this technique, a beam of monochromatic X-rays, collimated by two pin holes in lead sheets S_1, and S_2 is made to fall on a crystalline powder *P* (Fig. 19.14a). The many small crystals arranged at random in the powder present all possible orientations of their faces to the X-ray beam. Those faces which lie at the correct angle to the beam will reflect it at an angle θ given by

$$\sin\theta = \frac{\lambda}{2d} \tag{19.3}$$

The rays reflected at the same angle to the incident beam fall on a cone having this beam as axis. Rays reflected at a greater angle fall along a broader cone. The reflected beams are recorded on a photographic film, *F*. After exposure, the film is developed. It shows lines corresponding to all planes in the crystal (Fig. 19.14b). From the relative spacings of these lines, the spacings of the planes and the crystal structure can be found out. This method is not applicable to very complicated crystal structures because with such structures many lines on the film are found, making the interpretation difficult. This method is especially useful in comparing similar crystalline compounds and, in determining relative spacing with greater accuracy. The film showing the powder pattern for NaCl is shown in (Fig. 19.14c).

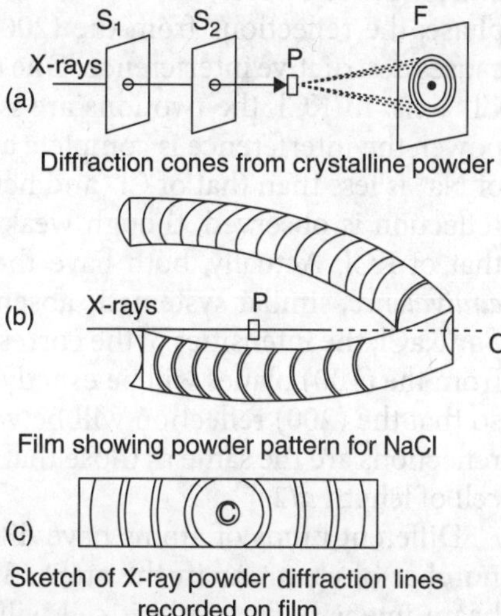

Fig. 19.14 The Debye–Scherrer–Hull powder method

- Crystalline materials diffract a beam of X-rays in a characteristic manner. Therefore, X-ray powder diffractometry is used to identify components of mixtures.
- The X-ray methods are non-destructive methods.

19.5.2 X-Ray Tube

An *X-ray tube*, called also a *Coolidge tube* (Fig. 19.15) is commonly used as the source of X-rays in X-ray methods. It consists of a tungsten filament cathode and an anode of the target metal which produces X-rays.

The target metal is plated on a bar of copper. The target metal may be one of the metals—Cu, Mo, Ag or Co. The tungsten cathode is electrically heated to produce electrons.

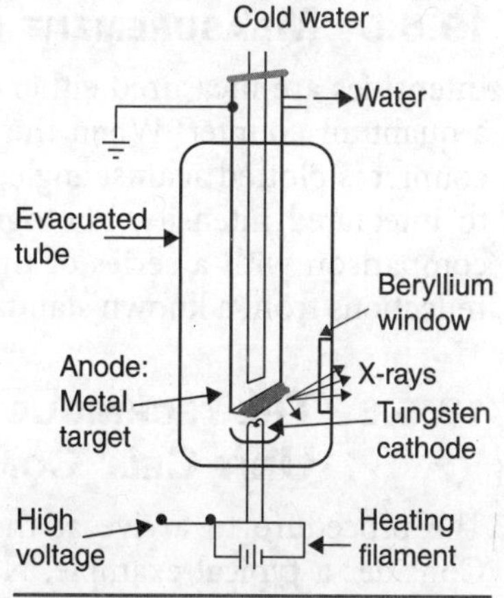

Fig. 19.15 Coolidge tube

The electrons are then accelerated toward the anode by an applied potential. The anode surface, on bombardment with fast electrons, produces X-rays. The X-rays formed escape through a beryllium window and then are used for the required X-ray method.

19.5.3 Accuracy of X-ray Diffraction Data

With modern X-ray diffraction instruments, coupled with computers, the dimensions of unit cells can be determined accurate to within ± 0.001 Å.

19.5.4 Intensities of Reflections

The intensities of reflections depend on the scattering power of the atoms within the planes and on the extent of destructive interference. For a simple cubic structure, reflections corresponding to all possible combinations are observed. However, the situation is different for a face-centred lattice (NaCl or KCl). In this case, when the X-rays scattered from the (100) planes are in phase, the reflections from the (200) planes are retarded by exactly half a wavelength. This causes destructive interference. One of these planes contains metal ions and the other contains Cl^- ions. In KCl, the two ions are isoelectronic and therefore they have the same scattering power, the interference is complete and reflection is missing. With NaCl, the scattering power of Na^+ is less than that of Cl^- and hence the interference is not complete. Therefore, the (100) reflection is observed, though weak. Therefore it appears to have a structure different from that of KCl. Actually, both have the same structure. Since K^+ and Cl^- ions have *scattering equivalence*, similar systematic absences are noted for all planes containing odd values of *hkl*. For NaCl, the intensities of the corresponding reflections are weak. The second order reflection from the (100) planes will be exactly in phase with first order reflection from the (200) planes so that the (200) reflection will be very strong for both NaCl and KCl. For KCl, the observed reflections are the same as those that would be expected of a simple cubic structure with a unit cell of length $a/2$.

Different kinds of atoms have different scattering powers for X-rays depending upon the number of electrons in the atom. This is expressed as *scattering power.* The total diffracted beam intensity from a unit cell will be the sum of contributions from different atoms, and addition or cancellation effects on the intensity will result from the particular geometrical arrangement of the atoms and the differences in their scattering factors.

19.5.5 Measurement of Intensities

Intensities are measured either by observation of photographic density on films or by using a quantum counter. When the photographic density or beam intensity as indicated by the counter is plotted against angle, a curve is obtained. The area under the curve is proportional to integrated intensity. Photographic intensities may be reduced to absolute intensities by comparison with a series of timed exposures of the incident beam or by comparison with reflections from a known standard structure, say, NaCl.

19.5.6 The Technique of Indexing and Determination of Unit Cell Constants

The procedure to arrive at the crystal structure from diffraction data is called *indexing.* Consider a typical example, NaCl. In Table 19.3 are given some values of angles at which maxima have been observed along with their sines when X-rays of $\lambda = 0.5869$ Å were used. Substituting these sines along with the value of λ in the equation,

$$\lambda = 2d_{hkl}\sin\theta \qquad (19.4)$$

the distances can be obtained (third column of the table). Since NaCl is cubic, these distances should also be given by the equation,

$$d_{hkl} = \frac{a}{\sqrt{h^2+k^2+l^2}}$$

or $$a = (h^2 + k^2 + l^2)^{1/2} \times d_{hkl} \qquad (19.5)$$

Table 19.3 X-ray diffraction data for NaCl obtained with X-rays of $\lambda = 0.5869$ Å

θ	$\sin\theta$	d_{hkl} observed (Å)	Miller indices (hkl)	d_{hkl} calculated (Å)
5.2	0.091	3.24	111	3.24
5.9	0.103	2.85	200	2.81
8.4	0.146	2.01	220	1.99
10.5	0.182	1.62	222	1.62
11.9	0.208	1.41	400	1.41
17.9	0.292	1.00	440	0.990
18.2	0.312	0.941	600	0.937

The length of the unit lattice a must be a constant. Therefore, the quantity on the right side in Eq. 19.5 must also be a constant. The question now arises, what values of h, k and l are to be given to the various planes such that these along with the observed d_{hkl} values will make a constant. The method used in the determination h, k, l for each observed value of d_{hkl} is called indexing.

From Eq. 19.5, it is clear that indexing cannot be done in a straightforward manner since the equation involves more than one unknown. This problem is solved by adopting a trial and error method. The values of h, k and l are integers and for large values of d these integers must have low values. In Table 19.4 are given values of $(h^2 + k^2 + l^2)$ and their square roots. These are given for low values of h, k and l. If one assumes that the highest observed value of d in Table 19.3 is due to reflection by (100) planes, then, using Eq. 19.5, $a = 3.24$ Å. With this value of a, the second reflection should give $d = 3.24/1.414 = 2.96$ Å. This is obviously incorrect. If it is assumed that the highest observed distance is due to (110) planes, $a = 4.59$ Å and $d = 2.67$ Å for the next reflection. This is also not correct. Let us assume that the first reflection is due to the (111) planes. Then, $a = 5.62$ Å and for the next reflection $d = 5.62/2 = 2.81$ Å. This value agrees with the observed value for the second reflection. Therefore, the first two maxima must correspond to indices of (111) and (200) respectively. Using similar methods, further indices and other distances can be obtained. There is good agreement between the calculated values of distances with those observed. This indexing procedure gives a value of 5.62 Å for a. This indicates that the length of the edge of the unit cube of NaCl is 5.62 Å.

Table 19.4 Values of $(h^2 + k^2 + l^2)$ and square root for various Miller indices

hkl	$(h^2+k^2+l^2)$	$(h^2+k^2+l^2)^{1/2}$	hkl	$(h^2+k^2+l^2)$	$(h^2+k^2+l^2)^{1/2}$
100	1	1.000	211	6	2.449
110	2	1.414	220	8	2.828
111	3	1.732	300, 221	9	3.000
200	4	2.000	310	10	3.162
210	5	2.236			

19.5.7 Number of Molecules in a Unit Lattice

The number of molecules present in the unit cell of a crystal can be determined from the dimensions of the unit cell, its volume and the molecular weight of the substance. The volume (v) per molecule of the substance,

$$v = \frac{M}{dN} \tag{19.6}$$

where M is the molecular weight, d the density and N the Avogadro number. If the volume of the unit cell is v_c, then the number of molecules present in it (n) is given as,

$$n = \frac{v_c}{v} = v_c \cdot \frac{Nd}{M} \tag{19.7}$$

Considering sodium chloride, $M = 58.443$, $d = 2.165$ g cc^{-1}

$$v_c = a^3 = (5.628 \times 10^{-8})^3 \text{ cc}$$

Substituting these values in Eq. 19.7,

$$n = \frac{(5.628)^3 \times 10^{-24} \times 2.165 \times 6.023 \times 10^{23}}{58.443}$$

$$n = 3.98 \approx 4$$

Therefore, the unit cell of NaCl lattice contains four molecules of NaCl.

19.5.8 Crystal Structure and the Avogadro Number

The Avogadro constant can be accurately evaluated from the structure and dimensions of unit cell of crystals with known density. The unit cell of each crystal has a definite number of ions. For example, the unit cell of the rock salt structure contains four cations and four anions. The volume of the unit cube is a^3, where a is the length of the unit cell. One molecular weight of the compound contains N ions of each element in the molar volume V.

$$\text{Volume of one molecule} = \frac{a^3}{4}$$

$$\text{Therefore,} \quad V = \left(\frac{a^3}{4}\right) \times N$$

$$\text{or} \qquad N = \frac{4V}{a^3}$$

The accurate spacings in various crystals can be determined from the wavelengths of various characteristic X-rays. For example, the a-value for the unit cube of NaCl is 5.628×10^{-8} cm. The density of the solid is 2.165 g cm^{-3} at 18°C. The molecular weight of the salt is 58.443. Therefore, the Avogadro constant is,

$$N = \frac{4 \times 58.443}{2.165 \times (5.628 \times 10^{-8})^3} = 6.057 \times 10^{23}$$

Similar studies on several salts and metals give an average value of 6.02252×10^{23} for the Avogadro constant.

Conversely, using the Avogadro number and density, the length of the unit cube of a crystal can be calculated.

19.5.9 Difficulty in the Detection of Hydrogen

The scattering of an X-ray beam by an atom is proportional to its atomic number. For example, a uranium atom scatters X-rays 92 times more strongly than does a hydrogen atom. Therefore, it is difficult to resolve the position of light atoms accurately in crystals since their reflections are swamped by those of heavier atoms. Thus hydrogen atoms are difficult to detect by X-rays even in organic molecules even though they contain no elements other than carbon and oxygen. In some cases, where the positions of all other atoms have been obtained accurately, the hydrogen atoms have been located from a *difference synthesis*. This technique amounts to using the calculated positions and observed intensities to obtain an electron density map. The contributions of the other atoms to the electron density are subtracted in the electron density map and thus the positions of the hydrogen atoms can be inferred.

19.6 SOME CRYSTAL STRUCTURES

Simple cubic lattice Several inorganic crystals are constituted by cubic crystal cells. In the cubic crystal system, three types of arrangements are found.

- Simple cubic (primitive cube)
- body-centred cubic, and
- face-centred cubic.

The simplest of these is the simple cubic cell structure (Fig. 19.16). This unit cell has a lot of empty space; it is not an efficient way of packing atoms. Only very few crystals are formed with the SCL. Alpha-polonium is an example. In a body centred cell, one atom is located in the middle of the cube apart from those at each corner.

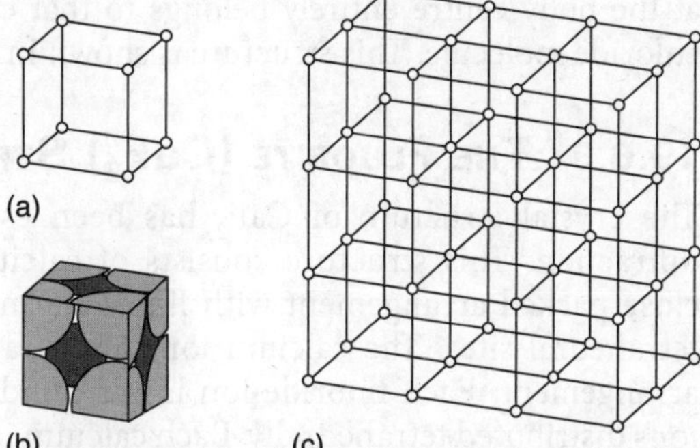

Fig. 19.16 **(a)** A simple cubic unit cell **(b)** a simple cubic unit cell with atoms having their nuclei at the corners **(c)** a part of a simple cubic lattice built by stacking simple cubic unit cells

In a face centred cell, one atom is located at each corner of the cube and one at the centre of each face. It has 14 identical lattice points. fcc structure is known also as cubic close-packed (ccp). Al, Cu, Ni, Au and Ag adopt fcc structures. There is more empty space in fcc than in bcc.

19.6.1 Sodium Chloride

The crystal structure of NaCl is shown in Fig. 19.17. In this structure, ions of sodium are located at the corners of the cube and in the centre of each of the six faces. A chloride ion is located half-way between every two sodium ions. The crystal has two interpenetrating face-centred cubic lattices, one composed entirely of sodium ions and the other of chloride ions. Each sodium ion at each corner of the cube is shared by eight cubes. Hence to each cube, this share is $8 \times 1/8 =$ 1 sodium ion. In addition, each sodium ion at each of the six faces is shared by another cube. Hence this share for the cube is $6 \times 1/2$ $= 3$ sodium ions. Thus the unit cube contains 4 sodium ions. Each of the 12 edges of the cube has a chloride ion shared by 4 cubes, or $1/4 \times 12 = 3$ chloride ions are part of the cube. Adding to these, the

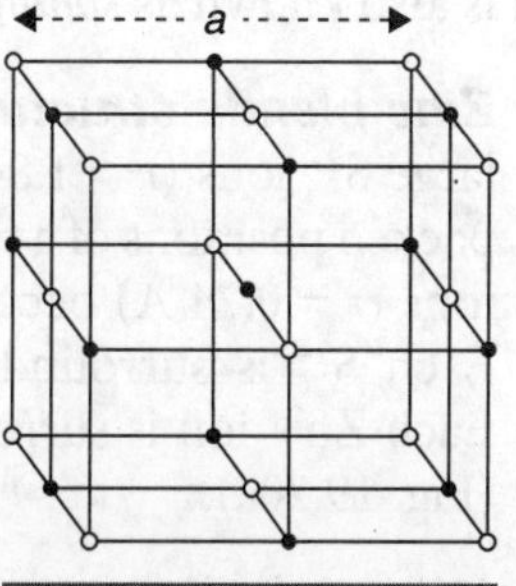

Fig. 19.17 The crystal structure of NaCl

one chloride ion at the centre of the cube, the total number of chloride ions in the unit cube becomes 4. Therefore, each unit lattice of sodium chloride contains 4 sodium and 4 chloride ions, that is, 4 NaCl molecules.

19.6.2 Cesium Chloride (bcc)

The structure of this crystal has been established clearly by the X-ray diffraction technique. It has a body-centred cubic lattice. Eight ions of one kind are at the corners of a cube and an ion of the other kind is at the body-centre of the cube. An ion at a corner is shared by 8 cubes so that effectively in each cube there is only $8 \times 1/8 = 1$ ion of that kind. The other ion at the body centre entirely belongs to that cube. Thus each unit cube contains one cesium chloride molecule. This structure is shown in Fig. 19.18.

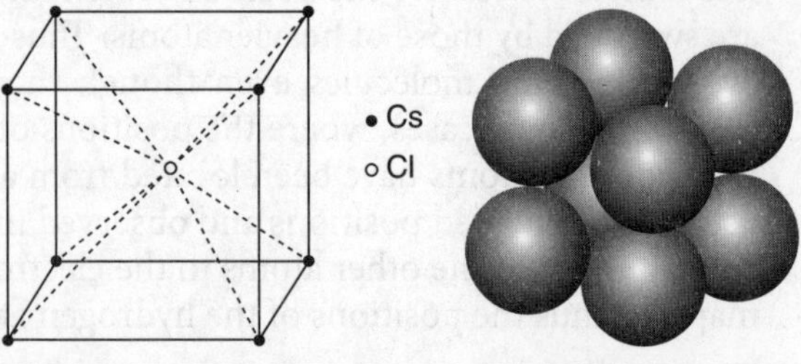

Fig. 19.18 Unit cube of cesium chloride

19.6.3 The Fluorite (CaF_2) Structure

The crystal structure of CaF_2 has been established by X-ray diffraction. This structure consists of calcium ions in a cubic close packed arrangement with fluoride ions occupying all the tetrahedral sites. The calcium ions are in a face-centred cubic arrangement. Each fluoride ion is surrounded by four calcium ions distributed tetrahedrally. Each calcium ion is surrounded by eight fluoride ions disposed towards the corners of a cube. This structure is an example of 8:4 coordination. The radius of the F^- ion is too great for it to be accommodated in the tetrahedral holes of a face-centred cubic lattice of Ca^{2+} ions. Therefore, a body-centred lattice is adopted. The Ca^{2+} ions occupy one half of the positions of the cube centres (Fig. 19.19).

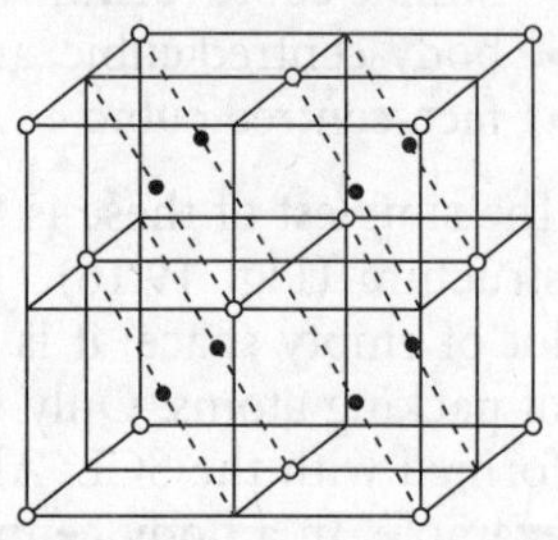

Fig. 19.19 Fluorite lattice structure

19.6.4 Structure of Zinc Sulphide

X-ray diffraction study on this salt indicates the following features. Zinc sulphide is *dimorphic*. One crystal form is known as *zinc blende* and the other as *wurtzite*. Zinc blende is also known as *sphalerite*.

Zinc blende structure This has 4 : 4 coordination. The large S^{2-} ions ($r = 1.84$ Å) of zinc blende occupy the close packed positions of a face-centred cubic lattice and the Zn^{2+} ions ($r = 0.74$ Å) occupy one half of the tetrahedral holes. Each S^{2-} is surrounded tetrahedrally by four Zn^{2+} ions. Each Zn^{2+} ion is surrounded tetrahedrally by four S^{2-} ions (Fig. 19.20a).

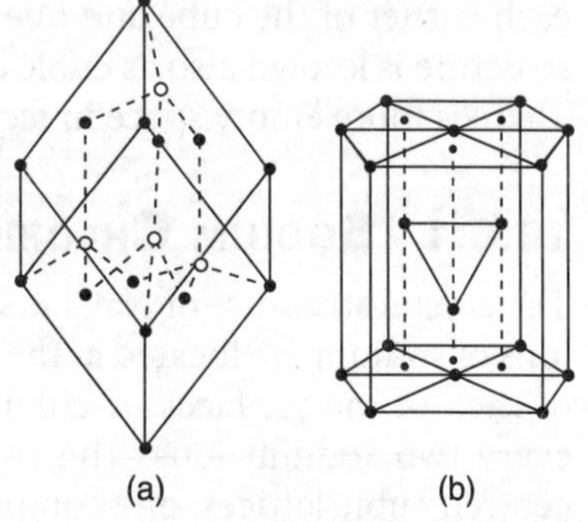

Fig. 19.20 Crystal structure of zinc sulphide: **(a)** zinc blende, **(b)** wurtzite

Wurtzite structure This also has 4 : 4 coordination. The sulphur atoms are in a hexagonal close packed arrangement. Zinc ions occupy half of the tetrahedral holes (Fig. 19.20b).

The names of some crystals and the characteristic crystal structures they adopt are given in Table 19.5.

Table 19.5 Some crystals and their structures

Crystal structure	Examples	
Rock salt	NaCl	LiCl, KBr, AgCl, CaO, TiO, UC
Cesium chloride	CsCl	CaS, CuZn
Fluorite	CaF_2	Na_2O, $BaCl_2$, UO_2, PbO_2
Rutile	TiO_2	MnO_2, SnO_2, WO_2, NiF_2
Zinc blende (sphalerite)	ZnS	CdS, HgS, GaP, InAs
Wurtzite	ZnS	ZnO, BeO, MnS, SiC
Antifluorite	K_2O	K_2S, Li_2O, Na_2S
Perovskite	$CaTiO_3$	$BaTiO_3$, $SrTiO_3$
Nickel arsenide	NiAs	NiS, FeS, CoS

Closest Packed Crystal Type

A simple cube, with 8 atoms at its 8 corners has only one atom *effectively* in its unit cell. A body-centred cube, with one whole atom in the centre and 8 at the corners, contributing one-eighth each has a total of two atoms in its unit cell. A face-centred cube with 8 atoms at the corners (1/8 each) and 6 at the six faces (contributing ½ atom each); has effectively 4 atoms in its unit cell. Therefore, the face-centred cube is the densest.

Au, Ag, Cu and Ni have fcc structures. A hexagonal close packed crystal also has 4 atoms in its crystal structure though it is different from a fcc crystal. Zn and Ti have hcp structure.

19.6.5 ORTEP Diagram

The structure of a molecule can be guessed based on X-ray diffraction data analysed by a computer program.

Figure 19.21 is a computer-generated drawing of $[Re(CN)_7]^{4-}$, based on X-ray diffraction intensities and positions of reflections. Such a drawing is called an *Oak Ridge Thermal Ellipsoid Plot diagram* (ORTEP diagram). Such a diagram denotes the bond distances and bond angles. In this diagram, the atoms are displayed as ellipsoids, taking into account their thermal motion. The stretching of bonds is restored more powerfully than the restoration of bond angle bending (both occur in a molecule at all temperatures above 0 K). Therefore, the ellipsoids are shown elongated in directions perpendicular to the bonds.

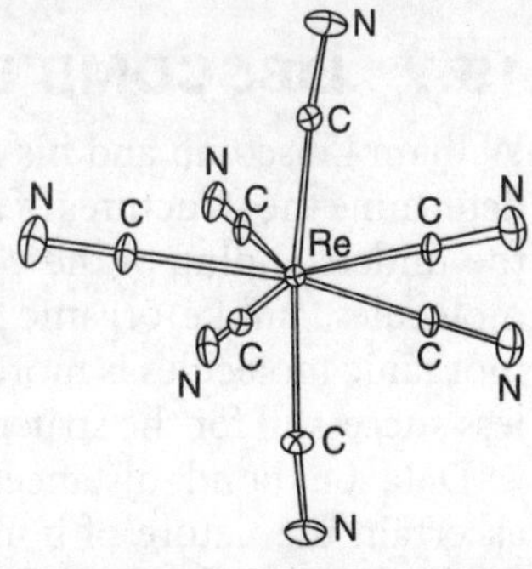

N C N C N C N C Re C N C N C N

Fig. 19.21 ORTEP diagram for $[Re(CN)_7]^{4-}$

19.6.6 XRD—A Probe for Polymorphism

When a substance crystallises in two or more distinct crystalline forms, the phenomenon is called *polymorphism*. For example, calcium carbonate is polymorphic; it is actually dimorphic and crystallises in two solid structures, calcite and aragonite. Polymorphic crystals can be studied by X-ray diffraction and their differences in crystalline states clearly understood. Titanium dioxide is trimorphic; its three forms as established by XRD, are brookite, anastase and rutile. Polymorphism of an element results in allotropy. Polymorphism among some crystals was discovered by Eilhard Mitscherlich in 1821. The word polymorphism means different shapes.

Under a given set of experimental conditions, only a single crystalline structure of a substance is the stable structure. However, if two forms exist that are nearly equal in stability, both the forms may exist simultaneously. Kinetic control can be adopted to form only one of the two crystalline forms, avoiding the simultaneous formation of the thermodynamically more stable second form. The formation of artificial diamond from graphite uses this principle of kinetic control of crystal formation.

19.6.7 Variants of XRD Techniques

Small-angle X-ray scattering (SAXS), *thin-film X-ray scattering* (TFXS) and *low-angle diffraction* are variants of XRD techniques. Low-angle XRD profiles of solids can provide detailed information about the multilayer periodicity and thickness of the individual layers that make up a multilayer in a crystal.

In SAXS experiment, a sample is illuminated by narrow beams of X-rays and the scattered radiation is detected and recorded. As the SAXS measurements are done very close to the primary beam, it is called 'small angles' scattering. Intense, narrow X-ray beams generated by particle accelerators (synchrotrons) are used in this method. This method is applied specially to study the crystallography of proteins. The scattering data are used to provide high resolution crystal models of individual domains of the solid and using this information the entire macromolecular complex protein crystallography can be inferred.

TFXS is used to characterise industrially important thin films, especially coating materials. Grain size, porosity, density, preferred orientation of polymer units in thin films are important parameters in using thin films in some industrial products. These are characterised precisely by TFXS. Polycrystalline thin films are studied both by low angle and high angle XRD.

19.7 LIBSCOMB'S STUDY ON BORON COMPOUNDS

William Libscomb and his research team in the USA used single-crystal X-ray diffraction to determine the structures of a large number of boranes and borohydrides. Their studies enabled the understanding of the concept of multicentre bonding in inorganic molecules. Inorganic molecules, unlike organic molecules are structurally diverse. In addition, the bonding in inorganic molecules is more varied than that in organic molecules. Therefore, spectroscopy is less successful for the structural determination of inorganic molecules.

Data on bond distances and bond angles are important to ascertain the nature of bonds in inorganic molecules. The X-ray method gives the positions of atoms in inorganic molecules and solids, and in turn provides insight into bond distances and bond angles. Libscomb's X-ray diffraction studies on diboron tetrachloride at low temperatures have shown that its structure is planar in the solid state with the molecular dimensions as shown:

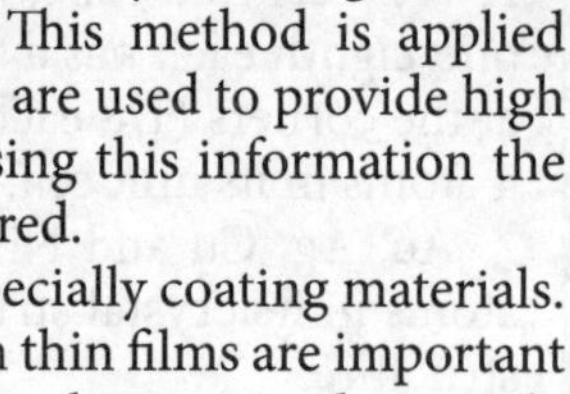

Cl Cl
1.75 Å
B—B 120.5°
1.73 Å
Cl Cl

Each molecule exists as a part of an orthorhombic unit cell containing four diboron molecules. The B-B bond is longer than those in other similar boron compounds.

An indication that a solid is ionic is provided by X-ray diffraction: the coordination number of an ionic solid is low; the X-ray diffraction method clearly indicates the coordination number and such a low number suggests ionic character.

William Nunn Libscomb, Jr. (1919–2011)

Libscomb, an American scientist, researched in nuclear magnetic resonance, theoretical chemistry, boron chemistry and biochemistry. He was one of the early chemists to use NMR to study chemical structures. His research on boron compounds earned a Nobel prize for him in 1976. Three of his students also received separate Nobel prizes in chemistry. He established the structure of proteins. His research group applied X-ray diffraction for ascertaining the three dimensional structure of proteins. This led to a better understanding of the biological action of enzymes. *Carboxypeptidase A* was the first protein structure established by Lipscomb's group.

Source: By Jslipscomb James S. Lipscomb - Own work [1], , https://commons.wikimedia.org/w/index.php?curid=10173896

19.8 X-RAY ABSORPTION METHODS

A material under investigation can be made to absorb X-rays and the absorption peaks recorded to identify the component of the material. A monochromatic X-radiation from a radioactive source may serve as the incident radiation in this method. Alternatively, the X-rays from an X-ray tube may be passed through a suitable monochromator and X-rays of suitable wavelength made to fall on the absorber.

The X-ray absorption method is similar to the optical absorption method in which the attenuation of a band or line of X-radiation serves as the analytical parameter. X-ray absorption measurements are relatively free of matrix effects. However, the absorption peaks are broad and therefore, this method is useful only when a single element with high atomic number has to be determined in a matrix consisting of only lighter elements.

19.8.1 X-Ray Photoelectron Spectroscopy

19.8.1.1 Principle

X-ray photoelectron spectroscopy (XPS) is called *electron spectroscopy*. The electrons are emitted by atoms on bombardment with incident X-ray. In this method, the kinetic energy of emitted electrons is recorded. The XPS spectrum is a plot of the number of emitted electrons as a function of the energy (expressed as ν or λ) of the emitted electrons.

What is the origin of the XP spectrum? Consider an atom *A* (in an elemental form or in a molecule) on which a beam of monochromatic X-rays is made to fall. Then, the changes in

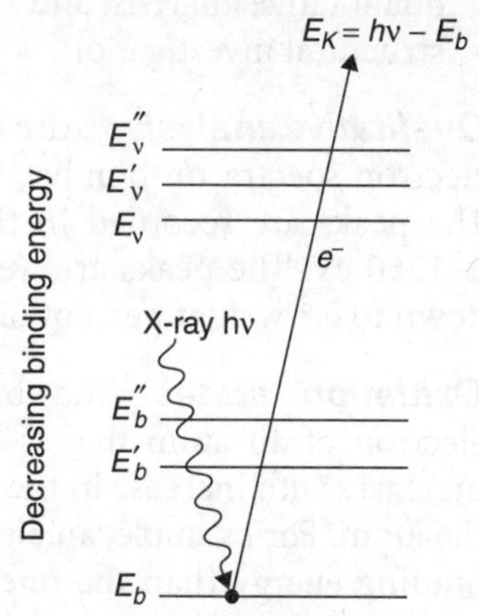

Fig. 19.22 Origin of X-ray photoelectron spectrum:

- the incident beam is monoenergic X-ray photons,
- the emitted beam is made up of electrons.

this atom may be denoted as in Fig. 19.22. The three lower lines denote the energy levels of the inner K and L shell electrons of atom A. Let their binding energies be BE_1, BE_2 and BE_3. The upper three lines denote the energy levels of some of the outer shell or valence electrons. When a photon of a monochromatic X-ray beam of known energy ($h\nu$) hits the atom, an electron from a K orbital is ejected.

$$A + h\nu \longrightarrow \underset{\text{excited state}}{A^{+*}} + e^-$$

A^{+*} is an electronically excited ion.

The emitted electron has a kinetic energy E_k. This energy is measured in an electron spectrometer. This kinetic energy is related to $h\nu$ of the incident X-ray photon and the binding energy of the electron. This relationship is given by the equation,

$$BE = h\nu - E_k - w$$

The term w is the work function; it is a correction factor to account for the electrostatic environment in which the electron is formed and whose energy is measured in the spectrometer.

The value of w can be experimentally determined using the various methods available. The binding energy of an electron is a fixed value that is characteristic of the atom and the orbital from which it was emitted.

- X-Ray absorption spectroscopy is applied in the structural analysis of several biologically important compounds. For example, the structure of nitrogenase consists of two distinct proteins; one is the 'Fe–Mo protein' or molybdoferredoxin and the other is 'Fe protein' or azoferredoxin. These structural aspects of nitrogenase have been established by X-ray absorption spectroscopy in conjunction with esr and Mössbauer spectroscopy.

19.8.1.2 Applications of XPS

XPS is useful in

- qualitative analysis,
- quantitative analysis, and
- structural investigation.

Qualitative analysis All elements except H and He emit electrons and produce characteristic electron spectra on bombardment with X-rays from magnesium or aluminium K_α source. The peaks are recorded in the 250–1500 eV range, corresponding to binding energies of 0–1250 eV. The peaks are well-resolved, offering easy identification of elements. Quantities down to 0.1 weight percent of an element in a solid can be identified with certainty.

Oxidation states The binding energy of an electron of an atom that is bonded in a molecule increases with increase in the positive (ionic) state of the atom. For example, an electron in Fe^{3+} has more binding energy than the one in Fe^{2+} or the one in Fe^0. Therefore, the position of the *peak maximum depends* – to a small extent – on the oxidation state. In other words, the peak position depends upon the chemical environment of the atom concerned. Consequently *chemical shifts* are observed in the electron spectrum; for example, the copper 1*s* electron.

Species	Cu^0	Cu^+	Cu^{2+}
Chemical shift (eV)	0	+0.7	+4.4

Arbitrarily, a value of 0 eV has been assigned to the binding energy of the 1*s* electron in Cu^0. For Cu^+, the peak is shifted from that of Cu^0 by +0.7 eV.

Chemical shift in XPS depends upon:

- the number of valence electrons,
- the type of bonds formed by the atom, and
- the atomic environment, that is, the other atoms to which the atom concerned is bonded.

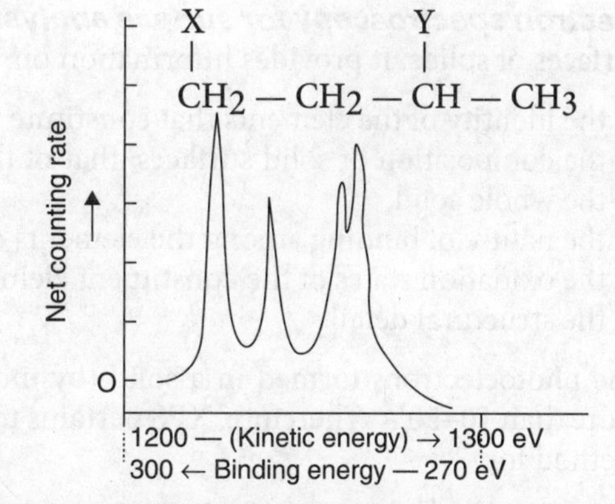

Fig. 19.23 The XP spectrum of $XCH_2CH_2CHYCH_3$

Chemical shifts and structure The positions of peaks of an element are influenced by the structure of the molecule in which the element is bonded. Figure 19.23 represents the XP spectrum of the molecule,

$$XCH_2-CH_2-CHY-CH_3$$

where X and Y are two different substituents. The spectrum consists of four peaks; each peak corresponds to the 1*s* electron of a carbon atom.

Four different peaks are obtained, though all of them denote the carbon 1*s* electrons—because of chemical shift. The four 1*s* electrons in the four carbon atoms are not in an identical structural environment and experience different effective nuclear charge. When a carbon atom is attached to an electron withdrawing group (such as fluorine or bromine), that carbon is more positive and consequently its 1*s* electron has more binding energy (as this electron is more tightly bound by the positive carbon nucleus).

The spectrum reveals that X is more electron withdrawing than Y. The carbon carrying X has a 1*s* electron with maximum binding energy.

In the XP spectra, the position of peaks for sulphur in its various oxidation states in compounds varies; this is due to isomer shifts.

Sulphur 2*s* electron binding energies:

Species	(2⁻) R–S–H	(0) S	(4⁺) SO_3^{2-}	(6⁺) SO_4^{2-}
Binding energy (eV)	161	162	166	167

The sulphur electron spectrum of thiosulphate, $S_2O_3^{2-}$ shows two peaks. This indicates that the two S atoms are in two different oxidation states.

XPS can provide information not only about the types of atoms present, but also about the relative number of each type. For example, in the nitrogen 1*s* spectrum of potassium azide ($K^+N_3^-$), two peaks with relative areas in the 2:1 ratio are recorded. This shows that the two N atoms are structurally identical and different from the third nitrogen. This observation is in accordance with the structure of the azide ion $[N{=}N{=}N]^-$.

Quantitative applications XPS is suited for determining quantitatively the elemental composition of both inorganic and organic substances. The peak area is proportional to the quantity of an element. The peak height is also a measure of elemental quantity. Before the analysis of the test material, a standard spectrum of a pure sample of the element is recorded to relate the peak area with quantity. An internal standard may also be used to calculate the quantity. However, the precision of quantitative analysis is not high.

- Liquids also can be analysed by XPS.

Electron spectroscopy for surface analysis XPS is a convenient method of analysing the surfaces of solids. It provides information on:

- the identity of the elements that constitute the solid surface,
- the composition of solid surfaces; that of the whole solid if the surface is representative of the whole solid,
- the nature of binding among the elements of the solid surface,
- the oxidation states of the constituent elements of the solid surface, and
- the structural detail.

The photoelectrons formed in a solid (by incident X-rays) cannot pass through the solid to more than 10–50 Å. Therefore, XPS pertains to the study of only surfaces of solids. It is a handy method for

- studying heterogeneous catalysis, especially identification of active sites of catalytic surfaces,
- identifying and determining impurities on the surfaces of semiconductors,
- the analysis of the composition of human skin, and
- the study of oxide films on corroded metal structures.

X-ray analysis of electron bands Evidence for the existence of electron bands and a map of their electron densities in metals can be obtained experimentally with X-ray emission spectroscopy. Using monochromatised Al K_α radiation and a single crystal specimen, incisive information on the valence band electron map of gold has been obtained. Such studies on metals and semi-conductors are helpful in understanding the conduction phenomena in them.

19.8.2 Electron Spectroscopy for Chemical Analysis

XPS provides information not only about the atomic composition of a material but also about the structure and the oxidation state of the element and as well as the type of species it is bonded to. Therefore, this technique is called *electron spectroscopy for chemical analysis* (ESCA).

The XPS of an organic compound whose molecule is constituted by C, H, O and S is shown in Fig. 19.24. The spectrum is a plot of electron counting rate versus energies of the emitted electrons.

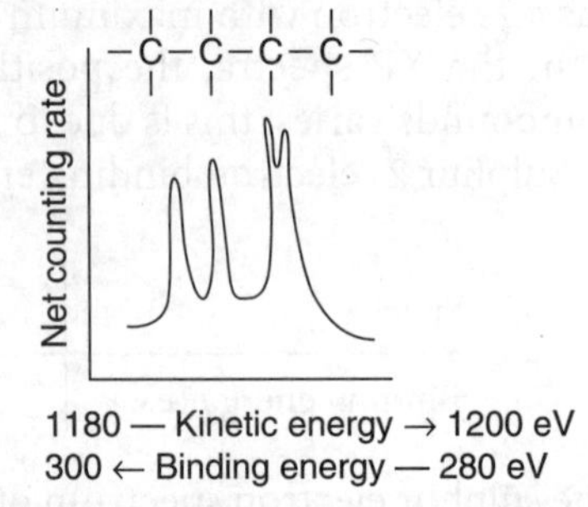

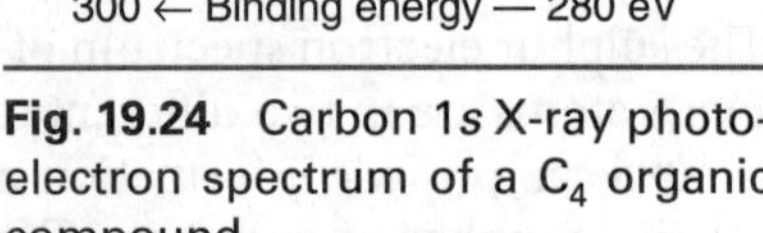

Fig. 19.24 Carbon 1*s* X-ray photoelectron spectrum of a C_4 organic compound

The following are the important features of this spectrum:

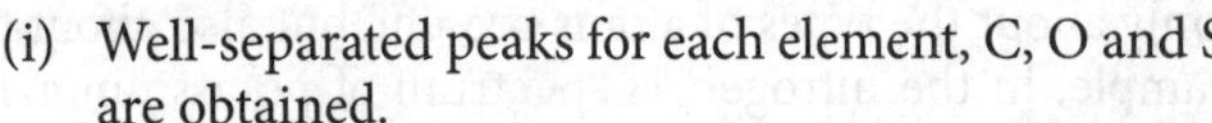

(i) Well-separated peaks for each element, C, O and S are obtained.

(ii) No peak has been recorded for H. ESCA is not suitable for the identification of light elements such as H and He.

- ESCA is an excellent method for all the elements in the periodic table except H and He.

(iii) According to the spectrum, the binding energies of the 1*s* electrons of the three elements are in the order C < O < S.

(iv) The increasing energies are in the order of atomic numbers, namely, increasing positive charges on the nuclei.

- More than one peak has been recorded for sulphur. These denote 2*s* and 2*p* electrons.

(v) XPS may have more than one peak for each element present in a compound. In a high-resolution spectrometer, the peaks corresponding to the 2*s* and 2*p* electrons, for example, can be resolved, though their energy separation is not high. This resolution may not occur in a low-resolution spectrometer.

(vi) The electron spectrum is characteristic of the element and therefore, it provides a means for identifying the element.

(vii) When a subshell has two electrons (for example, $2p^2$), only one peak will be obtained in the spectrum as both the electrons have the same energy.

- The spectrum shows a large background count. This originates from the formation of a tail with each peak. The tail arises from inelastic collisions of the ejected electrons within the solid sample. The ejected electrons lose a part of their energy. Such electrons have lower energies than those which have not undergone collision. Therefore, these electrons appear at lower kinetic energies or at upper binding energies, as indicated by the equation,

$$E_b = h\nu - E_k - w$$

19.8.2.1 ESCA Instrument

The block-diagram of an instrument used for ESCA is shown in Fig. 19.25.

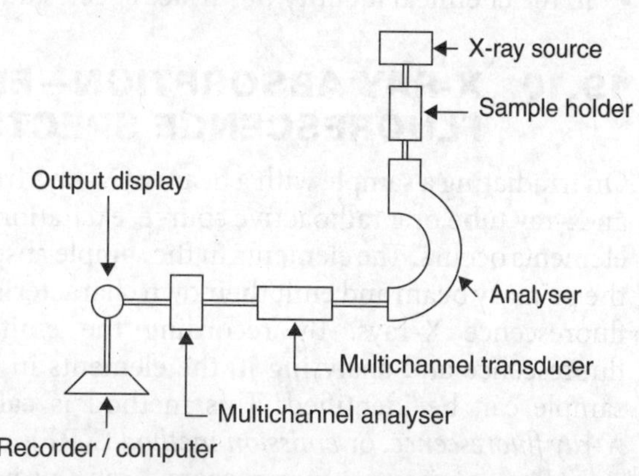

Fig. 19.25 Block diagram of an ESCA instrument

The *source* is an X-ray tube with an aluminium or magnesium target. On hitting the target element with an electron beam, X-rays are produced. Filters choose narrow X-ray bands (K_α). The X-rays falling on the test material should have narrow bandwidths for clear resolution of the peaks. A crystal monochromator gives an X-ray beam of narrow bandwidth. The beam is collimated on a small spot on the test material.

The *sample holder* is an evacuated (10^{-5}–10^{-10} torr) cell. It is located close to the source so that the radiation emerging from the slit falls effectively on the sample.

The *analyser* is a curved tube providing a hemispherical magnetic field. This field makes the electron describe a semicircular path. The radius of curvature of the path depends upon the kinetic energy of the electrons. Electrons of different kinetic energies describe paths of different radii and hence get separated. Separated electron beams then enter the detector.

The *detector* is a *transducer.* Its working is based upon solid-state, channel electron-multipliers—it consists of glass tubes, doped with lead. A potential of several kilovolts is applied across the tubes. For each incident electron, a pulse of 10^6–10^8 electrons is produced in this unit. The pulses produced are then counted electronically in the multichannel analyser. The data are displayed, recorded as a spectrum and can be stored in a computer.

19.9 X-RAY EMISSION METHOD: THE ELECTRON MICROPROBE

In the electron microprobe method, the elements on the surface of a material are bombarded with a beam of electrons. This produces X-rays characteristic of the surface elements. The

X-ray emission is stimulated by the incident narrowly focussed electron beam (diameter 0.1 to 1 μm). The fluorescent X-rays produced are collimated, dispersed by a single crystal and then detected by a gas-filled transducer. The X-rays produced are analysed with a wavelength spectrometer or an energy dispersive spectrometer.

- In *electron probe microanalysis*, a small target area of the sample is chosen for analysis. This X-ray method is applied in the study of geological samples, industrial metals and alloys, metallic elements in biological samples.

An optical microscope is used to select and locate the surface area to be bombarded.

Applications The electron microprobe is applied:

- to study the physical and chemical properties of surfaces,
- in understanding the nature of grain boundaries in alloys,
- in phase studies with ceramics,
- in the investigation of active sites in heterogeneous catalysis, and
- in the chemical identity of surface species during catalytic reactions.

19.10 X-RAY ABSORPTION—EMISSION METHOD: X-RAY FLUORESCENCE SPECTROSCOPY

On irradiating a sample with a beam of X-rays from an X-ray tube or a radioactive source, excitation of elements occurs. The elements in the sample absorb the primary beam and emit their own characteristic fluorescence X-rays. By recording the emitted fluorescence and analysing it, the elements in the sample can be identified. This method is called *X-ray fluorescence*, or *emission method* (XRF).

X-Ray emission spectroscopy can provide information on the existence of electron bands and a map of their densities of states. As a metal target is bombarded with an electron beam, electrons are ejected from the inner closed shells of the atoms. Then, X-rays are emitted as electrons from the valence bands fall into the vacancy created (Fig. 19.26). In this process, a range of X-ray frequencies is produced, corresponding to electrons originating from the occupied states of the valence bands. The intensity profile of the emitted X-rays depends on the densities of states in the band; therefore, electron densities in the bands can be deduced from the spectrum.

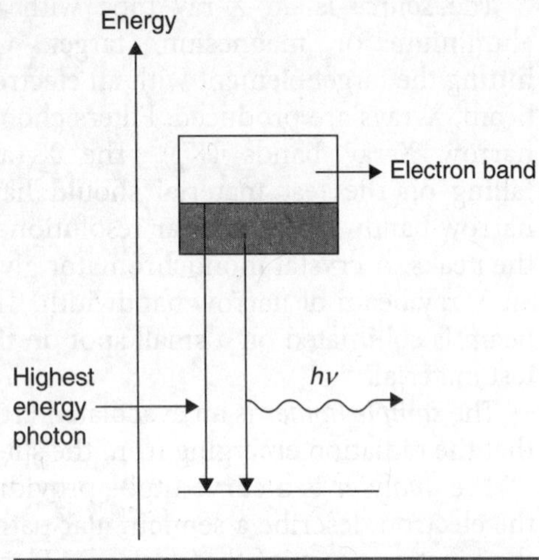

Fig. 19.26 Formation of X-ray emission spectral band

- When a beam of short-wavelength primary X-ray strikes a solid target, the target may emit X-rays at wavelengths characteristic of the atoms involved. Such an X-ray emission is called *secondary* or *fluorescence emission*. This emission also originates by a mechanism similar to the formation of primary X-rays. The peak height of fluorescence emission is proportional to the amount of an element; therefore, the composition of the sample can be determined by X-ray fluorescence analysis. This analysis is routinely used for studying the compositions of industrial materials such as ores, metals, alloys and cement samples.

Instrument X-rays originating from a radioactive source or an X-ray tube is made to fall on the sample (Fig. 19.27) The radioactive material (X-ray source) is kept in an annular ring. The sample, kept inside a sample holder is placed above this ring. X-rays impinge upon the sample. The X-ray fluorescence emitted passes through Si(Li) detector-cum-pre-amplifier. Then the rays reach the amplifier. The amplified energy is analysed in a multichannel pulse height analyser and recorded. The analyser measures all the emitted X-ray lines simultaneously.

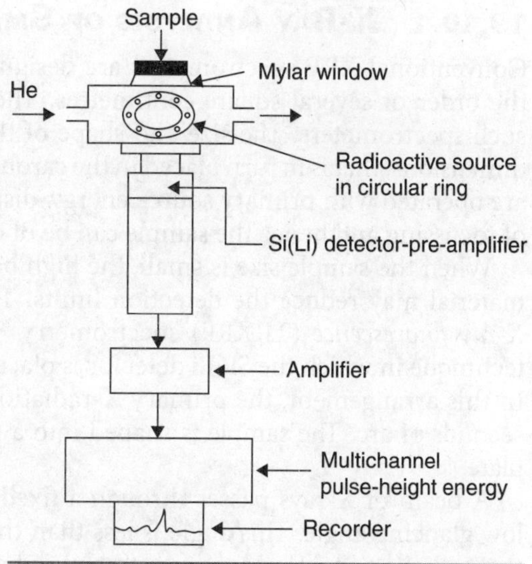

Fig. 19.27 Block-diagram of an X-ray fluorescence spectrometer

A typical X-ray fluorescence spectrum is shown in Fig. 19.28. It shows a plot of ion intensity versus 2θ. The 2θ values can be converted to wavelengths with knowledge of the crystal spacing of the monochromator (using the equation, $n\lambda = 2d \sin\theta$). The peaks can be identified by reference to tables of emission lines of the elements.

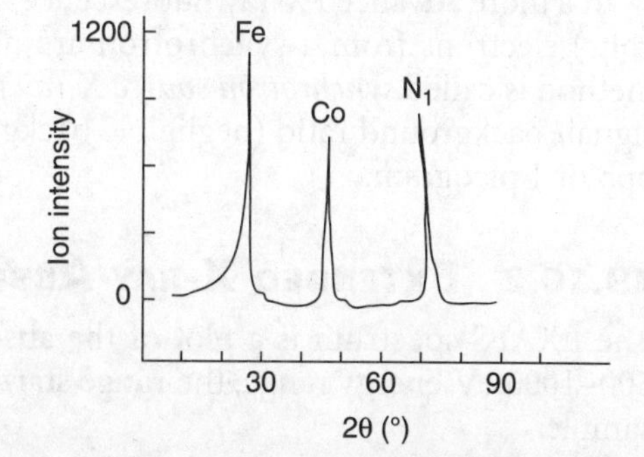

Fig. 19.28 The X-ray fluorescence spectrum of an alloy of Fe–Co–Ni

Quantitative analysis The estimation of an element in the sample may be done using the equation,

$$P_x = P_s W_x$$

where P_x is the relative line intensity measured in terms of the number of counts for a fixed period and W_x is the weight fraction of the element in the sample. The term P_s is the relative intensity of the line observable under identical counting conditions if W_x were unity. The P_s value is evaluated with a pure sample of the element.

- X-ray fluorescence spectroscopy is a simple method, with no spectral line interference.
- It is a non-destructive method. Therefore, it can be applied to studying valuable objects such as archaeological specimens, jewellery and paintings.
- It can be performed on samples ranging from microgram quantities to macro quantities.
- It is suitable for multi-element analysis in a mixture; it is a rapid method.
- It is applied in quality control in metal and alloy industries.
- The method has high precision and accuracy.

However, it has two disadvantages:

- It is not suitable for elements of low atomic numbers (< 23).
- The instrument required is expensive.

X-ray absorption methods are useful for determining lead in petrol and sulphur and halogens in hydrocarbons.

19.10.1 X-Ray Analysis of Small Specimens and Thin Films

Conventional XRF spectrometers are designed to use large specimens with surface areas of the order of several square centimetres. Therefore, small specimens cannot be analysed by such spectrometers. The size and shape of the sample should fit into a cup of fixed external dimensions, that is in turn placed in the carousel unit of the instrument. Modern spectrometers are operated with primary source energy-dispersive systems that do not require a high degree of focussing and hence the sample can be of any size or shape, including thin films.

When the sample size is small, the high background noise due to scatter from the support material may reduce the detection limits. This problem is reduced by using *total reflection X-ray fluorescence* (TRXRF) spectrometry. The TRXRF method involves energy-dispersive technique in which the Si–Li detector is placed close to (5 mm) and directly above the sample. In this arrangement, the primary X-radiation enters the sample at a glancing angle of a few seconds of arc. The sample is shaped into a thin film on the optically flat surface of a quartz plate.

A beam of X-rays passes through a fixed aperture and impinges on the sample at a very low glancing angle. This angle is less than the critical angle for total reflection, and therefore the radiation does not penetrate the substrate media appreciably. Consequently, scatter and fluorescence from the substrate become negligible. The low background permits the measurement of low amounts of constituents in the ppb range.

In a more advanced X-ray fluorescence method, very high energy (typically of giga electron volts) electrons from a synchrotron are used to generate X-rays required for analysis. This method is called *synchrotron source X-ray fluorescence* (SSXRF). This method offers very high signal/ background ratio (negligible background) which increases the detection limits to < 1 ppb or 1 picogram.

19.10.2 Extended X-ray Absorption Fine Structure (EXAFS)

The EXAFS spectrum is a plot of the absorption coefficient of a sample versus energy in a 500–1000 eV energy range, the range starting before an absorption edge of an element in the sample.

X-rays of narrow energy resolution are made to fall on the sample. The incident X-ray energy (I_o) is increased simultaneously recording the increasing intensity of the incident radiation. A part of this incident radiation is absorbed by the sample and the unabsorbed radiation (photon), I_t is transmitted through the sample. The relationship between I_o and I_t is given by the equation

$$I_t = I_o\, e^{-\mu x}$$

where μ is the absorption coefficient and x is the thickness of the sample.

The absorption coefficient is calculated from the ratio of the incident X-ray intensity to the transmitted X-ray intensity.

$$\mu = \frac{-\ln (I_t/I_0)}{x}$$

When the energy of the incident X-rays equals the binding energy of an electron of an atom in the sample, the number of X-ray photons absorbed increases dramatically; this causes a drop in the intensity of the transmitted radiation. This energy situation is called *absorption edge*. Below the absorption edge, the photons cannot excite the electrons of the relevant atomic level and therefore absorption is low. As a 'sweep' of photon energy over a range is required to effect absorption, the use of synchrotron radiation is a necessity in the EXAFS method.

- In X-ray absorption spectroscopy (XAS) the material under investigation is targetted with a monochromatic X-ray beam. Then, the rate of absorption is measured versus the X-ray photon energy.
- EXAFS study is useful to determine the atomic number, atomic distances and coordination number of the atoms in the element whose absorption edge is being examined.

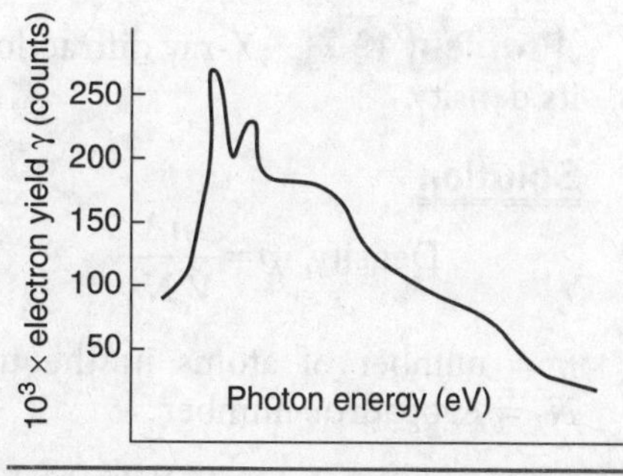

Fig. 19.29 EXAFS spectrum of Al with adhering Al_2O_3 film

EXAFS is useful for probing the local structure around almost any element in the periodic table (except the lightest elements). Even trace amounts (<1000 ppm) of species can be characterised by this spectroscopy.

An EXAFS spectrum is obtained by plotting the electron yield (counts) against photon energy (eV). Figure 19.29 depicts the spectrum of a sample of aluminium with a thin layer of aluminium oxide formed due to exposure to air. The energy sweep used is in 500–800 eV range. The spectrum shows a sharp increase in count rate of around 530 eV; this corresponds to the oxygen K edge. The absorption falls off rapidly above the edge (> 530 eV).

> XAS is a versatile technique for understanding the details of structures in
>
> - elements,
> - defect lattices,
> - alloys,
> - metal clusters,
> - industrial products, such as glass, ceramics, and so on,
> - ion-implanted semiconductors,
> - proteins, and
> - electrolyte solutions.

EXAFS is useful in

- determining the oxidation state of the element in a sample,
- determining the structures of biomolecules, such as nitrogenase and haemoglobin,
- understanding the coordination environment of the absorbing atom in a sample, and
- the identity of samples by matching the recorded spectra with those of standards.

The dependence of the scattering on the type of atomic species renders it possible to obtain information listed from EXAFS data.

Problem 19.1 For a crystal with bcc lattice, the first order X-ray ($\lambda = 0.162$ nm) reflection maximum for a set of (200) planes was recorded at 21°. What is the edge length (a) of its unit cell?

Solution

$$n\lambda = 2d\sin\theta; \qquad d = \frac{n\lambda}{2\sin\theta}$$

$$\therefore \qquad d_{200} = \frac{1\times 0.162}{2\sin 21^\circ} = \frac{0.162}{2\times 0.3584} = 0.226 \text{ nm} = 226 \text{ pm}$$

For a cubic lattice $d_{200} = \dfrac{a}{\sqrt{h^2+h^2+l^2}} = \dfrac{a}{\sqrt{2^2+0+0}} = 226$ pm

$$\therefore \qquad a = 226 \text{ pm} \times 2 = 452 \text{ pm}$$

Problem 19.2 X-ray diffraction data show that $a = 4.05$ Å for Al with fcc lattice. Calculate its density.

Solution

$$\text{Density, } \rho = \frac{nA}{V_c N_A}$$

n = number of atoms in the unit cell, A = atomic weight, V_c = volume of unit cell, N_A = Avogadro's number

$$\therefore \quad \rho = \frac{4 \times 26.98}{(4.05 \times 10^{-8})^3 \times 6.023 \times 10^{23}} = 2.697 \text{ g/cc}$$

Problem 19.3 In an X-ray emission, a metal M emits X-rays of $\lambda = 0.1402$ nm when an electron from its L-shell falls into a vacancy in its K-shell. What is the energy of the emitted X-ray?

Solution

The energy per proton $E = h\nu = \dfrac{hc}{\lambda}$

The energy of emitted X-ray in the transition $L \rightarrow K$

$$\Delta E = \frac{N_A hc}{\lambda} = \frac{6.022 \times 10^{23} \times 6.626 \times 10^{-34} \times 2.998 \times 10^{8}}{0.1402 \times 10^{-9}}$$

$$= \frac{119.623}{0.1402} \times 10^{6} = 8.53 \times 10^{8} \text{ J/mol}$$

Problem 19.4 Calculate the short-wavelength (λ_o) limit of the continuum generated by an X-ray tube having a metal target and operated at 100 kV.

Solution

The *Duane–Hunt law* is used for calculating the λ_o:

$$h\nu_o = \frac{hc}{\lambda_o} = Ve$$

Substituting the values for the constants h, c, the equation reduces to

$\lambda_o = 12\,398/\text{V}$ where λ_o is in angströms and V in volts.

Therefore, in this case

$$\lambda_o = \frac{12398}{100\,000} \text{ V} = 0.124 \text{ Å}$$

EXERCISES

1. Explain why elements of high atomic numbers are used as targets in Coolidge tubes.
2. Write a critical account of the quantitative analysis of elements by X-ray methods.
3. What are the limiting factors in the sensitivity of X-ray methods?
4. $K_{\alpha 1}$ radiation, the characteristic X-ray emitted from Fe when one of the electrons in its L-shell falls into a vacancy in its K-shell has a wavelength of 0.1936 nm. Calculate the energy difference pertaining to this transition.
5. Calculate the volume of empty space in the unit cell of a bcc structure with the lattice parameter *a*.
6. A crystal M^+X^- has a cubic structure as revealed by XRD study. M^+ occupies the centre position of a unit cell and the corners are occupied by X^- ions. The density of the sample is 3.97×10^6 g/m^3. The ionic radii values for M^+ and X^- are 0.169 and 0.181 nm respectively. Calculate the length (*a*) of the cube edge for the unit cell.
7. Explain the characteristics expected of X-ray sources used in XRD studies.
8. Prove that the packing efficiency of fcc is 74% and that of bcc is 68%.
9. fcc metals are ductile while bcc and hcp metals are not: explain.
10. The density of a metal M is 10.22 g/cc and its atomic weight is 95.94. Its atomic radius is 0.136 nm. Predict its lattice geometry, between bcc and fcc.
11. Suggest an X-ray spectral method for determining the thickness of an electroplated film of Cr on steel. Explain the experimental process.
12. Illustrate with diagrams (100), (110), (111) and (112) planes in a cubic lattice.
13. How are the volumes of voids calculated in crystal lattices?
14. CsCl has a bcc lattice. Its density is 3.97×10^6 g/m^3. The ionic radius for Cs^+ is 0.169 nm and for Cl^- 0.181 nm. Calculate its lattice parameters.
15. Citing literature, outline the *Hanawalt method* of identification of unknown samples by X-ray diffraction.

20 Isotopic Analytical Methods

20.1 INTRODUCTION

The discovery of radioactivity and production of isotopes have led to the use of these in several applications in basic research, industry, agriculture, diagnosis of diseases and therapy. The uses of isotopic methods have helped us understand clearly reaction mechanisms, devise better methods of making and using machines, in diagnosis and cure, to improve agricultural practices, finding routes of producing energy, and so on. The basis for all of these applications is the evolution of elegant and accurate analytical methods in which isotopes – both active and inactive – are used. Currently, about two hundred isotopes of various elements are being produced and used in radiochemical methods.

20.2 ISOTOPIC TRACER TECHNIQUE

Isotopic tracer technique uses an isotope to study a physical or chemical change. The change is monitored by following a characteristic property – mass or radioactivity – of the isotope used. To understand this technique, let us consider the reaction:

$$2\ \text{A–B}(s) \longrightarrow \text{A}_2(s) + \text{B}_2(g)$$

where A–B is a molecule giving a gaseous product B_2. To monitor this reaction, first the ordinary isotope of B in A–B is replaced by its radioactive isotope (denoted as B^*); then, this reaction is denoted as

$$2\ \text{A–B}^*(s) \longrightarrow \text{A}_2(s) + \text{B}_2^*(g)$$

As this reaction proceeds, the radioactivity of the reactant A–B^* would decrease due to loss of B^* as B_2^* (*g*). Therefore, the rate of this reaction can be calculated by measuring the decrease in radioactivity of the reactant with time. Such a technique is called *tracer technique*. B^* is called a *radioactive tracer* or *radioactive indicator.*

B is called the tracer element. It serves as the tag for identifying the change in the system. A–B^* is said to be *labelled* or *tagged*. As B^* is radioactive, giving off a characteristic radiation, its radiation is measured to monitor the reaction. Instead of a radioactive tag, a non-radioactive tag, an isotope of mass different from that of the ordinary isotope, can also be used in the tracer technique. In such a case, the mass of B^* is monitored; the *change in mass* is an indication of the course of the reaction. The course of this reaction may be followed by estimating the amount of B_2^* formed during the reaction.

Two molecules containing different isotopes of an element have different vibrational modes; these can be detected by infrared spectroscopy. Hence, IR spectroscopy may be used for estimating labelled species. Nuclear magnetic resonance can also be applied to find out the location of isotopes.

20.2.1 Conditions for Tracer Technique

- The tracer technique can be used only when a suitable isotope – radioactive or non-radioactive – is available as the tag.
- The half-life of the radioactive tag should be compatible with the duration of analysis of the reaction or system. For example, an isotope whose $t_{1/2}$ is less than the reaction time, is not suitable for the study.
- The radioactivity of the tag should not interfere with the nature or course of the system being studied. For example, the emission from the radioactive tag may induce reactions in the chemicals under investigation.

20.2.2 Basis for Tracer Technique

The tracer technique is based on the following factors.

- The chemical and physical properties of the radioactive isotopes are *similar* to the corresponding non-radioactive isotopes. However, this is not true when D is substituted for H, because in this case, the mass of the substituted atom is doubled.
- The radioactivity of the isotopes used enables the labelling of an element and determination of its position among a great excess of the non-radioactive species.
- By this method, very small quantities of a material can be detected, the quantities being many times smaller than those detected by any other known chemical or physical method.

20.2.3 Tracers

Radioactive isotopes are more useful than stable (non-radioactive) isotopes in tracer methods as the former are more easily detected and monitored through a sequence of physical or chemical changes. In addition, radioactive isotopes are more readily available for a large number of elements. Even low quantities of radioisotopes can be accurately determined.

20.2.4 Sources of Isotopes

Isotopes required for radiochemical methods can be sourced by three methods.

- *Accelerator products*: On bombarding appropriate target nuclides with accelerated projectiles, new isotopes are formed.
- *Fission products:* Fission of uranium in nuclear reactors produces numerous isotopes.
- *Naturally occurring isotopes:* These are isolated from minerals.

Practically, all artificial isotopes used in tracer methods are β-emitters. The continuous decay of these nuclides lowers the concentration of such tracers during investigations. Radioisotopes of very short lives or very long lives are not suitable for tracer methods. In tracer methods, an electroscope, an electrometer or a Geiger counter is used for measuring the quantities of active isotopes. A mass spectrometer is used when the tracer is a stable isotope. The commonly used isotopic tracers are listed in Table 20.1.

Table 20.1 Commonly used isotopic tracers

Element	Isotope	Detection of
Hydrogen	^{2}H	mass
	^{3}H	β particle
Oxygen	^{18}O	mass
Carbon	^{13}C	mass
	^{14}C	β particle
Nitrogen	^{15}N	mass
Fluorine	^{19}F	mass
Sodium	^{24}Na	β particle
Phosphorus	^{32}P	β particle
Sulphur	^{34}S	mass
Iodine	^{131}I	β particle

20.2.4.1 Production of Isotopes

The isotopes required to be used as tracers are produced by a variety of methods. Most of the stable isotopes are obtained by the electromagnetic separation method using a mass spectrometer. The production of some of the isotopes commonly used in the tracer method is summarised in Table 20.2.

Table 20.2 Production of common isotopic tracers

Isotope	Production method
H-2	from D_2O
H-3	(n, α) reaction on Li-6
C-13	chemical exchange
C-14	(n, p) reaction on N-14
N-15	fractional distillation
O-17	fractional distillation
O-18	fractional distillation
F-18	(t, n) reaction on O-16
Na-22	(d, ∞) reaction on Mg-24
Na-24	(n, γ) reaction on Na-23
P-32	(n, γ) reaction on P-31
S-34	chemical exchange
S-35	(n, p) reaction on Cl-35
Cl-37	(d, p) reaction on Cl-36
K-38	(α, n) reaction on Cl-35
K-40	by hot-atom reaction
Ca-45	(n, γ) reaction on Ca-44
Tc-99m	by decay of Mo-99
Cs-137	extraction from fission products
I-128	(n, γ) reaction on I-127
I-131	extraction from fission products
Fe-59	(n, γ) reaction on Fe-58
Co-60	(n, γ) reaction on Co-59
Zn-65	(n, γ) reaction on Zn-64

20.2.4.2 Synthesis of Radio-labelled Compounds

When an isotope is used as a tracer, it is necessary to introduce the tracer element into the compound to be studied. For example, to study the way in which phosphorus is taken up by a plant, a suitable phosphorus compound is labelled by introducing certain proportion of isotopic phosphorus into the compound. Sometimes, as in the investigations of kinetics, the tracer atom should be inserted at a definite site of the molecule being investigated. For example, in the study of the kinetics of ester hydrolysis, the tracer element should be either the alkyl carbon or the acyl carbon. Thus, the preparation of labelled compounds is important in tracer studies. Some methods of such preparations are illustrated in the following section (only schemes of reactions producing labelled compounds are given and not the experimental procedures). These syntheses involve the familiar and simple organic synthetic methods.

Labelled acids

(i) $\overset{*}{C}O_2 \rightarrow K\overset{*}{C}N \rightarrow CH_3\overset{*}{C}N \rightarrow CH_3\overset{*}{C}OOH$

(ii) $CH_3CN \xrightarrow{D_2O} CH_3COOD$

(iii) $Ba\overset{*}{C}O_3 \rightarrow \overset{*}{C}O_2 \rightarrow \overset{*}{C}H_3OH \rightarrow \overset{*}{C}H_3I$

$\rightarrow \overset{*}{C}H_3CN \rightarrow \overset{*}{C}H_3COOH$

Labelling at three sites of acetic acid molecule is illustrated by these equations.

Labelled hydrocarbons

(i) $CaC_2 \xrightarrow{D_2O} C_2D_2$

(ii) $CO + D_2 \xrightarrow[\text{reduction}]{\text{Catalytic}} CD_3OD \rightarrow CD_4$ (Tetradeuteromethane)

By exchange reaction H and D atoms have the tendency to undergo exchange, and this tendency is used for preparing labelled compounds; for example, by passing a mixture of ethylene (C_2H_4) and deuterium (D_2) over nickel catalyst at 120°C, C_2H_3D is obtained

$$C_2H_4(g) + D_2(g) \longrightarrow C_2H_3D(g) + HD(g)$$

Labelled alkyl halides

(i) $CCl_3COOD \xrightarrow{\text{heat}} CDCl_3$

(ii) $CH_2 = CH_2 \xrightarrow{\text{H}\overset{*}{\text{Br}}} CH_3 - CH_2\overset{*}{Br}$

A molecule labelled with a radioactive tag is called a *radio-labelled molecule;* for example, CH_3COOT, labelled with a radioactive tritium atom, is a radio-labelled molecule. Irradiating a target molecule by a projectile such as neutrons can produce a radio-labelled molecule.

$$C_2H_5I \xrightarrow{n} C_2H_5I^*$$

In such a process, an atom in the target molecule absorbs a neutron and gets changed to its radioactive atom. However, the breaking away of this atom from the product molecule is a possibility, which would reduce the yield of the labelled product.

20.2.5 Applications of Tracer Technique

The tracer technique can be applied to a variety of investigations:

- physical processes such as evaporation, condensation, solubility, mobility of gases and liquids and adsorption,
- chemical processes, especially kinetics and mechanisms of reactions,
- structural investigations,
- analytical estimations,
- radiobiology,
- nuclear medicine, and
- industrial applications.

These applications can now be illustrated.

(i) **Physical Processes**

Surface area of an adsorbent: A labelled material (adsorbate) can be equilibrated with an adsorbent, then the adsorbent–adsorbate system is isolated, and its surface analysed for radioactivity. This will give the quantity of adsorbate, and also the surface area of adsorption. Similarly, the traces of a substance adsorbed on a precipitate can be determined by labelling the substance.

Leak detection: The leakage of a fluid, gas or liquid flowing through an underground pipeline can be detected by the tracer method. A radioactive source, say, a γ-emitter is added to the fluid at its starting point. A detector is moved over the surface of the submerged fluid pipeline; it will register a count at the point of leakage. Then, only that portion of the pipeline can be dug out and replaced by a new one and the leakage stopped. Leaks in long, buried waterlines and crude oil lines are repaired by this method.

Solubility: The solubility of a sparingly soluble salt such as lead chromate or silver iodide can be measured by the tracer method. This procedure was adopted first in 1913 by A Hevesy and F A Paneth. It is based on the fact that a radioactive element, added to a sample of its non-radioactive counterpart, remains in the same ratio (amount of radioactive element /amount of non-radioactive element) irrespective of the state of the element (solid, liquid, gas, solution or precipitate). The experiment involves comparing the activity of an aliquot of a saturated solution of the labelled substance with that of a known amount of the labelled substance. This method can be illustrated with reference to AgI. A stock solution of potassium iodide, labelled with ^{131}I, is diluted such that it gives about 10,000 to 50,000 counts min^{-1} mL^{-1}. An excess of silver nitrate solution is added to it to precipitate silver iodide. AgI(*s*) is filtered off and washed twice with distilled water to remove all excess KI. The precipitate is then dried under an infrared lamp, and the specific activity of the Ag ^{131}I sample is determined (s_1 counts $min^{-1}mg^{-1}$).

Now, an accurately weighed amount of the precipitate is shaken in distilled water at about 50°C and then cooled to the temperature (say 25°C) at which the solubility has to be determined. When the system has attained a constant temperature, 0.1 mL of the clear saturated solution from the supernatant is drained into a cupped planchette and the contents are carefully dried under an infrared lamp. When dry, the planchette is covered with a film of collodion (to avoid loss of the minute amount of the precipitate) and the activity measured (s_2 counts min^{-1} mg^{-1}). Then the solubility (*s*) of AgI

$$s = \left(\frac{s_2}{s_1}\right) 10^4 \text{ mg L}^{-1}$$

(ii) **Chemical Processes**

Study of hydrogen exchange processes: The ability of a compound to undergo hydrogen exchange with water or some other compound can be qualitatively and also quantitatively studied by the tracer method.

For example, to check whether or not phenol takes part in hydrogen exchange with water, a sample of phenol is added to D_2O and then it is recovered in its pure form. The recovered sample on mass spectral analysis shows that the OH group in some of the phenol molecules has been converted to –OD, confirming that the molecule can undergo exchange, namely, replacement of its protium with deuterium. Exchange occurs only with the hydroxyl proton and not with the H atoms in the benzene ring.

$$C_6H_5\text{–}OH + D_2O \rightleftharpoons C_6H_5\text{–}OD + HOD$$

Electron transfer reactions: Isotopic tracers can be used to study simple electron transfer reactions such as the exchange reactions between different oxidation states of the same element. For example, the electron exchange between the Fe(II) and Fe(III) species can be studied by using radioactive iron. When Fe^{2+} is mixed with radioactive Fe^{3+} and then the reaction mixture analysed, radioactivity is found in both the ferrous and ferric species.

Exchange with unlabelled reactants: $Fe^{2+} + Fe^{3+} \rightleftharpoons Fe^{3+} + Fe^{2+}$

Exchange with labelled Fe^{3+}: $Fe^{2+} + \overset{*}{Fe}{}^{3+} \longrightarrow Fe^{2+} + \overset{*}{Fe}{}^{2+} + \overset{*}{Fe}{}^{3+} + \overset{*}{Fe}{}^{3+}$

Though with ordinary reactants, there is no apparent change in the overall concentrations of the Fe(II) and Fe(III) species, the rate can be measured by the rate at which the tracer becomes randomly mixed between the two oxidation states. During the reaction, one of the species, either the ferrous or the ferric species should be isolated and its radioactivity measured. This rate exchange, though normally fast, can be made measurable by reducing the concentrations of the reactants and maintaining a very low temperature, close to 0°C.

Study of reaction mechanisms: A carboxylic acid, RCOOH, can undergo decarboxylation either in its unionised form itself or through its carboxylate ion.

(i) $R{-}\underset{\underset{O}{\|}}{C}{-}O{-}H \xrightarrow{\text{Slow}} RH + CO_2\uparrow$

(ii) $R{-}COOH \longrightarrow R{-}COO^- + H^+$

$R{-}\underset{\underset{O}{\|}}{C}{-}O^- \xrightarrow{\text{Slow}} R^- + CO_2\uparrow$

To decide between these two mechanisms, the rate constants for the decarboxylation of RCOOH and RCOOD are determined. If these two rate constants are identical, then it should be concluded that the decarboxylation occurs by mechanism (ii) because here the –O–D (or –O–H) bond is not involved in the rate determining step. If the decarboxylation of the free RCOOH molecular occurs, then the replacement of H of COOH group by D will change the rate constant.

Study of equilibria: The occurrence and nature of certain equilibria can be established using isotopic tracers. For example, when an alcohol R–O–H is dissolved in D_2O and then the alcohol recovered, the hydroxyl proton is exchanged with D atoms in some of the R–OH molecules. This establishes the equilibrium

$$R{-}O{-}H + DOD \rightleftharpoons R{-}O{-}D + H{-}O{-}D$$

When labelled ammonium chloride $^{15}NH_4Cl$ is dissolved in liquid NH_3 and then recovered by evaporating the solvent, ^{15}N is equally distributed between ammonium chloride and NH_3 molecules. This is possible only if the liquid NH_3 ionises:

$$2NH_3 \rightleftharpoons NH_4^+ + NH_2^-$$

In a solution containing C-14 labelled CN^- and $Fe(CN)_6^{3-}$, no exchange occurs between the labelled and unlabelled CN^- groups. This proves that the six CN^- groups in the complex ion are not labile, that is, they do not ionise in solution.

Mechanism of electrodeposition: The mechanism of electrodeposition of metals is fascinating chemistry. It is influenced by the nature of the metal, electrolyte, temperature and so on. For example, in the electroplating of base metals with chromium, a solution of chromate, Cr(VI) is used as the electrolyte in the electrolytic bath. In this process, Cr(VI) is converted to Cr(0). This conversion may occur directly involving a six-electron transfer or in stages, say Cr(VI) to Cr(III) and then to Cr(0). Thus, the Cr(III) species could be formed as an intermediate in the electrolysis. The mechanism between these two routes was decided by the isotopic tracer method. The deposition was carried out using an electrolytic bath containing Cr(VI) and labelled Cr(III) species. The deposit was then checked, and it did not contain any tracer chromium. This proved that the mechanism did not involve the formation of a Cr(III) intermediate; presumably, six electrons were rapidly and directly transferred to Cr(VI) to form the Cr(0) deposit. When the deposition was carried out with labelled Cr(VI) species, the tracer was found in the deposit, further proving the direct reduction of this species.

(iii) **Structural Studies**

The tracer method can be applied to establish structures of both inorganic and organic molecules; some examples are considered.

The thiosulphate ion $S_2O_3^{2-}$ may be represented by either of the two structures:

(i) $(-O-S-O-S-O-)^{2-}$

(ii) $\left[-O-\overset{\overset{\displaystyle O}{\|}}{\underset{\underset{\displaystyle O}{\|}}{S}}-S- \right]^{2-}$

In structure (i), the two S atoms are bonded identically whereas in structure (ii) they are unequally bonded. The actual structure of this ion has been established by the tracer method.

The usual method of preparing $S_2O_3^{2-}$ involves boiling an aqueous sulphite with flowers of sulphur:

$$SO_3^{2-} + S \longrightarrow S_2O_3^{2-}$$

When the product thiosulphate is treated with a dilute mineral acid, the reverse reaction occurs, namely it is converted to SO_3^{2-} and S.

$$S_2O_3^{2-} \xrightarrow{H^+} SO_3^{2-} + S$$

To establish its structure, a sample of thiosulphate is made using radioactive S-35 isotope. Then the labelled thiosulphate is decomposed with an acid. The products are then checked for radioactivity. No activity (no presence of S-35) is noticed in the SO_3^{2-} product; all the S-35 activity is present in the elemental S product; therefore, it is obvious that the S atoms in $S_2O_3^{2-}$ are structurally non-equivalent as represented in (ii). The S atom which enters the SO_3^{2-} in the formation of $S_2O_3^{2-}$ is the one formed as elemental sulphur in the reverse reaction:

$$SO_3^{2-} + S^* \longrightarrow S^*SO_3^{2-}$$

$$S^*SO_3^{2-} \longrightarrow S^* + SO_3^{2-}$$

If the S atoms in $S_2O_3^{2-}$ were identical, then S^* is expected in both the products.

To understand the nature of the five chlorine atoms in PCl_5 – whether or not they are structurally similar – it is synthesised using PCl_3 and ^{36}Cl-labelled chlorine:

$$PCl_3 + \overset{*}{C}l_2 \longrightarrow P\overset{*}{C}l_5$$

The product is hydrolysed to the oxychloride and hydrogen chloride. All the $\overset{*}{C}l$ was present in HCl proving that the five Cl atoms in PCl_5 do not occupy structurally equivalent positions.

$$P\overset{*}{C}l_5 + H_2O \longrightarrow POCl_3 + 2H\overset{*}{C}l$$

The isotopic study reveals that two of the Cl atoms occupy positions different from those occupied by the other three chlorine atoms. This agrees with the trigonal bipyramidal structure assumed for PCl_5.

(iv) **Analytical Determinations**

Radiometric titration: Radiometric titration (RT) is an analytical technique that involves the use of a radioactive indicator to track the transfer of a material between two liquid phases in equilibrium. It is also a method of detecting the equivalence point in a titration by labelling one of the reactants. Let us study a couple of examples.

Titration of KCl(*aq*) with $AgNO_3$ (*aq*): The titrant, $AgNO_3$ is labelled with ^{110}Ag; then, $^{110}Ag^+(aq)$ is added to the analyte, KCl(*aq*). During the titration, the activity of the solution is monitored. As the titration proceeds, the added active silver is converted to $^{110}AgCl(s)$. No activity will be noticed in solution until the equivalence point. After the equivalence point, the excess active silver added will remain in solution. The initiation of activity in solution signals the equivalence point. In the reverse titration, that is, titration of active $AgNO_3$ with KCl, the cessation of activity in solution will signal the end point. RT is suitable for determining traces of a material when the conventional titration method does not work.

Titration of hexachloroplatinate(IV) ion with $Cs^+(aq)$: The analyte reacts with Cs^+ to form an insoluble product.

$$PtCl_6^{2-}\ (aq) + 2\ Cs^+\ (aq) \rightarrow Cs_2\ [PtCl_6]\ (s)$$

In a radiometric titration, this reaction is conducted using radioactive Cs-137 as the indicator cum titrant. The appearance of radioactivity due to excess of Cs^+-127 in the liquid phase of the reaction mixture immediately after the equivalence point signals the end point for the titration.

Radiogravimetry: Radiogravimetry is the gravimetric determination of an analyte using a radionuclide. The measurement of the activity of the precipitated analyte is the basis for calculating weights in this method. This method can be illustrated with the estimation of, say, Ag^+ ions present in traces in a material. As Ag^+ is present only in traces, the conventional methods such as volumetry and gravimetry are not suitable for this estimation. However, it can be accurately estimated by radiogravimetry. Assuming that there is no interference by other species in this estimation, Ag^+ ions are precipitated using aqueous radioactive I^- ions. The AgI^* formed is then quantitatively adsorbed on $Fe(OH)_3(s)$ and the activity of I^* measured. From this measured activity, the amount of Ag^+ can be calculated. This method is suitable even for very small amounts of Ag^+, so that as little as 10 ppm can be detected and determined.

The activity of a known weight of a pure sample of radioactive I^- is also measured for comparing it with the activity of the adsorbed AgI^* and calculating the amount of AgI^*. The isotope, I-131, a beta-emitter, with a half life of 8.06 days can be used as the tag in this determination. As even a few counts per second from a radioactive material can be measured accurately, this method gives accurate results even for traces of analytes.

(v) **Radiobiology**

Radiobiology deals with the effects of radioactive substances on living organisms and also the use of radioactive tracers to study metabolic processes. The study of photosynthesis by isotopic labelling – a radiobiology study – is an example of radiobiology. Isotopes are used in pest control, genetic engineering of crops, to study the mechanism of nutrient uptake by plants, and other radiobiology studies.

Tracer study on photosynthesis: Photosynthesis in plant cells can be represented as

$$6CO_2 + 6H_2O \xrightarrow[\text{Chlorophyll}]{\text{Energy}} C_6\,H_{12}O_6 + 6O_2$$

Does the oxygen liberated come from CO_2, H_2O or from both? This question was settled by Ruben using labels, in 1941 at the University of California, Berkeley. The synthesis was allowed to occur with labelled water, H_2O^*:

$$6CO_2 + 6H_2O^* \longrightarrow C_6H_{12}O_6 + 6O_2^*$$

The oxygen formed contained O*. When the synthesis was made with labelled carbon dioxide CO_2^*, no O* was detected in the product oxygen.

$$6CO_2^* + 6H_2O \longrightarrow C_6H_{12}O_6^* + 6O_2$$

These experiments proved that the oxygen formed in photosynthesis comes from water and not from carbon dioxide.

Pest control: Radioisotopes are used in understanding the migration of pests and also in their population control. Some insects are collected, dipped in a solution of Co-60 and then released. Their movements are monitored by tracking the gamma ray emission from the Co-60 in their bodies. After locating their preferential areas for breeding, they can be destroyed by spraying a pesticide. Another method using radiation for insect population control involves sterilising the male insects. These insects are collected, exposed to gamma radiation and then released. When they mate, no offspring are produced or only unhealthy offspring that die soon are produced. In some cases, the eggs of the insects do not hatch. These procedures reduce the insect populations.

Genetic engineering for crop improvement: Seeds on exposure to gamma radiation undergo mutation. Controlled mutations effected by gamma radiation can be used to grow plants for increasing yields, enhancing pest-resistance and shortening crop maturation time. Radiation can be used to select and combine different desirable characteristics in plant crops. Co-60 is used as the gamma-ray source for such genetic engineering. Radiation can alter genetic codes, as changes in the DNA molecules in chromosomes may result in biological mutations.

Nutrient uptake by plants: Calcium is an important nutrient required for the growth of plants. Studies with ^{45}Ca tracer (β-active, $t_{1/2}$ = 164 d) indicates that the uptake of Ca by plants is efficient and equal with CaO and $CaCO_3$; however, it is poor with $CaSO_4$. With ^{32}P, it has been established that the uptake of phosphorus is best when the phosphate fertiliser is added at the time of sowing seeds but poor when it is added during plant growth. Thus, the selection of fertilisers and also that of micronutrients for high plant produce can be done after the tracer method.

Radiolabels

A radiolabel (noun) is a radioactive atom in a molecule.

To radiolabel (verb) means to label something, say, a molecule with a radioactive atom.

- Radiolabels are used in several biological studies.
- H-3, a very low-energy emitter is used to label proteins, nucleic acids, drugs and toxins.
- C-14 is used as radiolabel in proteins and nucleic acids.
- S-35 is used to label proteins and nucleic acids.
- P-33 and P-32 are used to label nucleotides.
- I-125 is used for labelling tyroxine.

(vi) **Nuclear Medicine**

Nuclear medicine is a branch of medicine involving the use of radioactive isotopes in the diagnosis and treatment of diseases. For example, ^{131}I is a beta and gamma emitter with a half-life of 8.0197 days. It is used both diagnostically and therapeutically. It is used in radiation therapy—treatment of *thyrotoxicosis* and thyroid cancer. Diagnostic tests are based on its ability to get absorbed on the normal cells of the thyroid gland. It can be used to check how well the thyroid in a patient functions. ^{131}I is used also as a radioactive label for radiopharmaceuticals that in turn can be used for organ imaging and therapy. In therapy, the patient is made to drink a solution containing ^{131}I as iodide ions. The active iodide ions reach the thyroid, emit beta rays which preferentially destroy the cancerous cells; the radioactivity affects only a small proportion of healthy cells.

Bone imaging: Fracture and abnormal growth in bones can cause severe pain to the patient. Such cases can be diagnosed by bone imaging. The patient is given an injection containing ^{99m}Tc. This radioisotope is a gamma ray emitter with a half life of 6 hours. Several hours after taking the injection, the patient undergoes bone imaging. The area of the body that has unusually high bone growth or contains a fracture will show up as a different image compared to the normal image on the screen. Erosion of bones (osteoporosis) in arthritic patients can also be studied by bone imaging.

Radioimmunoassay: Radioimmunoassay (RIA) is a method of determination of hormones, drugs, vitamins and other compounds at nanogram and smaller concentrations. This method was invented by Berson and Yallow. For example, small quantities of insulin can be estimated by RIA. It involves mixing a known quantity of a radioactive antigen (labelled with a gamma-active isotope of iodine) with an antibody, then adding the unlabelled antigen and measuring the amount of antigen displaced. The procedure is denoted as

$$\begin{pmatrix} \text{(antibody)} \\ + \\ \text{radio-labelled antibody} \\ + \\ \text{antigen in sample} \\ \text{(or standard)} \end{pmatrix} \xrightarrow{\text{Cu}} \begin{pmatrix} \text{(antigen–antibody)} \\ + \\ \text{(radio-labelled antigen–antibody)} \\ + \\ \text{free antigen} \\ + \\ \text{free radio-labelled antigen} \end{pmatrix}$$

$$\xrightarrow{\text{Separation}} \text{radio-labelled products} \xrightarrow{\text{activity measurement}} \text{estimation of antigen}$$

From the measured radioactivities and using a calibration curve, the antigen in the sample (say blood) can be determined.

Study of blood circulation disorder: $^{24}_{11}Na$ is used to diagnose blood clots. Labelled NaCl solution containing ^{24}Na is injected into the veins of the patient, and the circulation of blood in the veins is monitored from outside by tracking the activity of ^{24}Na using a GM counter. The timings of distribution of the activity in the blood are observed and compared with standard data for a normal person. Any obstruction as a clot (thrombosis) in a body part

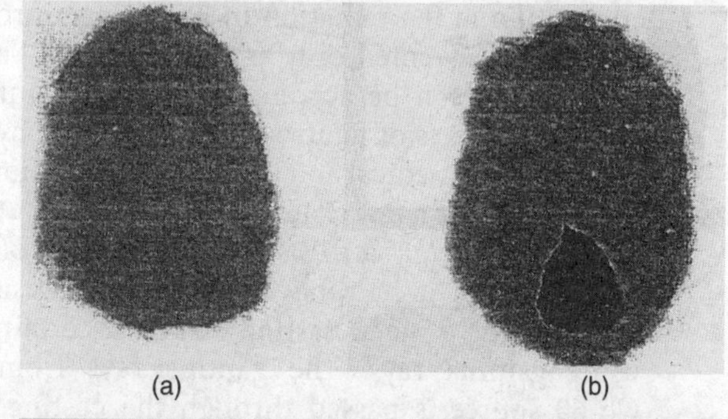

Fig. 20.1 Isotopic organ imaging; the dark area indicates tumour; **(a)** normal organ **(b)** organ with tumour

will be indicated by a slowing down of blood circulation over that part. The efficacy of a prescribed anti-hypertension drug is measurable by the improvement in blood circulation as revealed by the activity of Na-24.

Brain tumour location: Certain dyes such as fluorescein and Rose Bengal can preferentially be adsorbed by cancerous cells in the brain. One such dye is labelled with ^{131}I and administered to the patient; the labelled dye migrates to the brain and gets adsorbed on cells. Then, the brain is mapped (imaged on a photo-plate) using the activity of ^{131}I. The areas of the brain with the tumour will be revealed as darker spots in the photo and thus the exact location of the tumour can be ascertained (Fig. 20.1). This procedure is called *isotopic organ-imaging*.

Table 20.3 Isotopes used in nuclear medicine

Radioisotope	Use
F-18	Bone imaging
Na-24	Diagnosis of blood circulation disorder and other metabolic disorders
P-32	Treatment of blood cancer
K-42	Diagnosis of metabolic disorders
Fe-59	Diagnosis of anemia
Ga-67	Lung ventilation assessment
Co-60	Cancer therapy
Sr-90	Treatment of corneal cancer
Tc-99*m*	Imaging diseased organs (thyroid, brain, kidneys)
I-123	Diagnosis of thyroid tumour
I-131	Treatment of thyroid cancer
Au-198	Study of liver and spleen malfunction
Tl-201	Diagnosis of heart disorders
Pu-238	In heart pacemakers

Cancer cure: Radiothereapy is used for curing cancer; it involves exposing cancerous cells to gamma radiation. Normally, radiation damages rapidly-reproducing tissues such as the bone marrow, blood-forming tissues, lymph nodes and embryonic tissues. Ironically, this ability of radiation is applied in cancer cure; the fast-multiplying cancerous cells are more easily killed than are the slower growing, healthy cells surrounding the cancer. The isotopes used in nuclear medicine are listed in Table 20.3.

(vii) **Industrial Applications of Active Isotopes**

Applications of isotopes in industries are routine practices. A few such applications are considered here. Certain active nuclides are used to ascertain the location of a material with which the tracer gets itself associated. Gamma and beta sources are used in such applications.

Radiography: Radiography is the recording of shadow images of objects on photographic emulsion by the action of ionising radiation. The image is the result of the differential attenuation of the radiation in its passage through the object radiographed. When this method was invented, only X-rays were used—it is called *roentgenography*. However, now, radiography can be accomplished with gamma rays, proton rays or neutron rays. Radiography is used for both medical and industrial applications. Let us consider a few examples.

Testing of metal castings: The presence of a flaw, such as a hairline crack or an invisible cavity inside a metal casting can be ascertained using gamma rays. The gamma rays from a Co-60 source is passed through the casting. A photographic plate is kept on the other side of the casting. On developing the plate, the presence, location and profile of the flaw will be revealed

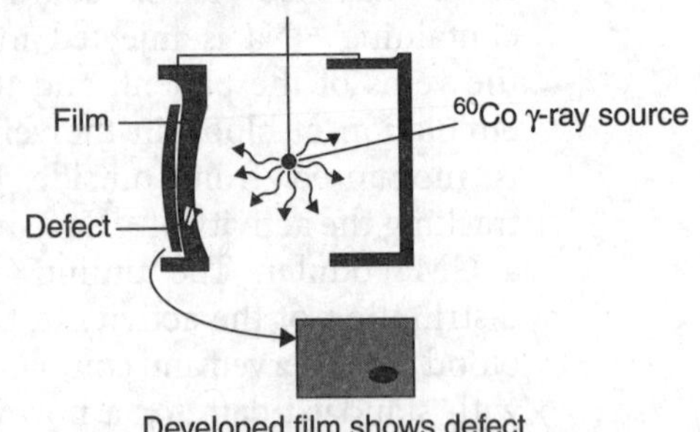

Fig. 20.2 Radiography

(Fig. 20.2). The components of expensive machines such as petroleum rigs and lathes are tested by radiography for proper quality. The presence of flaws in aircraft components, which may lead to accidents and endanger lives of passengers, is routinely checked by gamma-ray radiography.

Metal structures develop *fatigue*, namely, changes in their crystal aggregation, causing cracks. Constant friction and extreme weather patterns may cause such fatigue. This happens with an aircraft body; then, detection of such cracks by radiography and replacement of damaged parts save human lives and reduce cost of operation.

Measurement of film thickness: Certain industrial films made of polymers should have uniform thickness. The uniformity of the thickness of such films can be checked using a Sr-90 beta source; this source is kept below and a GM counter above the sheet. As the sheet is moved between these two, the γ counts are monitored; a uniform count indicates uniformity in thickness. The strength of the signal from the detector is an inverse measure of the thickness. This method, called *radionuclide-gauge* is used to measure the thickness of sheets of paper, cellophane, plastic, rubber and steel. When thick sheets such as steel sheets have to be gauged, more penetrating (high energy) gamma rays are used. When one metal is coated on another metal, the thickness of the coat can be measured by back-scattering of beta particles. The extent of back-scattering, as observed by a detector on the same side of the sheet as the source, is related to the thickness.

Leak detection: The detection of a leak of a fluid – liquid or gas – flowing through submerged (underground) pipes can be done by the tracer technique.

Smoke detector: Americium-241 is used in smoke detecting gadgets. ^{241}Am is an alpha particle emitter ($t_{½}$ = 432 y). The alpha particle emitted ionises O_2 and N_2 in the air. This causes a small constant current to flow through the circuit (Fig. 20.3). When smoke is formed due to fire, it enters the ionisation chamber and disrupts the current flow. The detector senses a decreased O_2 and N_2, and drop in current that sets the alarm on.

Table 20.4 Common gamma ray sources

Source	Half-life	Energy (MeV)
Fe-55	2.7 y	0.0059
Co-60	5.27 y	1.17, 1.33
Cs-137	30.17 y	0.662
Tm-176	128.60 d	0.084
Ir-192	74.2 d	0.2

The common gamma ray sources used in tracer methods are listed in Table 20.4.

20.3 ISOTOPIC DILUTION ANALYSIS

20.3.1 Principle

Isotopic dilution analysis is the estimation of a component of a mixture *without separating the component* from the mixture. For example, the amount of an amino acid in a mixture of amino acids can be estimated without isolating it by adopting the isotopic dilution analysis; for example, estimation of aureomycin in a fermented broth. This analysis involves the following steps.

Procedure	Example
(i) A pure radioactively labelled sample of the compound for which analysis has to be performed is obtained.	Radioactive aureomycin.

(*Continued*)

Continued

Procedure	Example
(ii) Its radioactivity is measured.	Let the activity of 1 mg of labelled aureomycin be s_i counts min^{-1} mg^{-1}.
(iii) To a definite amount of the mixture containing the compound to be estimated, a known weight of the same but radioactively labelled compound is added.	To one kg of the broth containing x mg (unknown) of aueromycin, one mg of the labelled aueromycin is added.
(iv) Now, the activity of the added compound is diluted by the non-radioactive compound in the mixture. The 'diluted' activity of the mixture is measured.	Let the diluted specific activity of the labelled compound be s_f counts min^{-1} mg^{-1}.
(v) The extent of dilution of the initial activity is proportional to the amount of the particular compound in the mixture. Therefore, the concentration of the compound can be calculated from the two measured activities.	Therefore, x, the quantity of aueromycin in the sample can be calculated using the formula, $(x + 1)\, s_f = s_i$.

20.3.2 Advantages

- Isotopic dilution analysis is useful for estimating a component in a complex mixture without isolating that constituent; sometimes, isolation may be impossible or laborious.
- It can be used for accurate estimation of the traces of a component in a mixture.

20.3.3 Applications of Dilution Analysis

20.3.3.1 Assessing the Volume of Blood in a Patient

Sometimes, it is necessary for a surgeon to know the volume of blood in a patient, say an anemia patient or one who has had a hemorrhage in an accident. The volume of blood in the body of the patient can be assessed by isotopic dilution analysis by the following procedure. One cm^3 of a healthy donor's blood is withdrawn and it is labelled with a solution of ^{24}Na (as NaCl). The initial specific activity of the labelled blood is measured in 0.1 cm^3. Let this be s_i min^{-1} cm^{-3}. The rest of the labelled blood sample (0.9 $cm^3 = y$) is injected intravenously into the patient. The labelled blood now gets mixed with the blood in the patient due to blood circulation. After about 15 minutes, when thorough homogenisation of blood has been established, 1 cm^3 of the mixed blood is withdrawn from the patient and its specific activity s_f measured. Then, the volume of blood (x) in the patient's body is calculated from the equation,

$$ys_i = (x + y)\, s_f$$

$$= xs_f \text{ (because } y << x)$$

$$x = \frac{ys_i}{s_f} \text{ cm}^3$$

A healthy adult human being should have 5–6 litres of blood.

20.3.3.2 Analysis of Proteins

Proteins on hydrolysis produce complex mixtures of amino acids. Analysing such mixtures quantitatively is an elaborate procedure. An amino acid in such a mixture can be estimated without isolating it by adopting the isotopic dilution technique. For example, to determine the amount of glycine in a mixture, a specimen of this amino acid is prepared in which some of the normal N-14 is replaced by N-15 (non-radioactive) to act as the tracer. The ratio of the two isotopes present is determined by a mass spectrometer. Then, a known quantity of this labelled acid is added to the mixture of amino acids. From the mixture, a specimen of glycine is extracted and subjected to mass spectral analysis. From the change in the ratio of N-15 to N-14, compared to their ratio in the added glycine, the extent of dilution can be calculated. This ratio is called the *dilution factor*. Multiplication of the amount of labelled glycine added by the dilution factor gives the total amount of glycine in the mixture.

20.4 RADIOCARBON DATING

Radiocarbon dating is a method of estimating the age of an antique (ancient material) by measuring the $^{14}_{6}C$ content of the antique and comparing this value with the present $^{14}_{6}C$ content in living matter.

Radiation from the stars, called cosmic rays, are constituted by high energy particles such as H^+ and He^{2+}. These particles reach the Earth's atmosphere and react with stable nuclei in the upper atmosphere. Neutrons are one of the products of such nuclear reactions. A neutron thus produced interacts with ^{14}N present in the atmosphere forming ^{14}C:

$$^{14}_{7}N + ^{1}_{0}n \longrightarrow ^{14}_{6}C + ^{1}_{1}H$$

$^{14}_{6}C$ is beta-active with a half life of 5730 years.

$$^{14}_{6}C \longrightarrow ^{14}_{7}N + ^{0}_{-1}\beta$$

The $^{14}_{6}C$ gradually gets oxidised to $^{14}CO_2$ in the atmosphere and then gets assimilated in plants through photosynthesis. It enters animals through the food chain. It is then returned to the atmosphere through respiration of animals.

This cycle involving ^{14}C has been occurring for thousands of years. It is believed that an equilibrium with respect to the concentration of ^{14}C was attained in nature several thousand years ago. This equilibrium implies a constant amount of ^{14}C per gram of carbon in a *living system*. This amount corresponds to 15.3 disintegrations per minute per gram of carbon. This value was arrived at after a careful estimation of ^{14}C in several living systems. When a plant dies, it is removed from the natural equilibrium; then the ^{14}C content in the dead matter would decrease with time due to its decay. This cannot be compensated as the dead matter is no more capable of photosynthesis. For example, a piece of wood dead 20,000 years ago would now contain less ^{14}C than a piece of wood dead 5000 years ago; the amount of active carbon in a dead matter is inversely proportional to its age. This fact is used for estimating the age of antiques.

The radioactive decay of ^{14}C follows the equation,

$$2.303 \log \frac{N_0}{N} = kt$$

$$\therefore \quad t = \frac{2.303}{k} \log \frac{N_0}{N_t}$$

where $N_0 = 15.3$ disintegrations per minute per gram of carbon, N_t = number of disintegrations per minute per gram of carbon in the dead matter at present.

$$k = \text{decay constant} = \frac{0.693}{t_{1/2}} = \frac{0.693}{5730}$$

where t = time (age of antique in years). Therefore, to determine the age of an antique, the C-14 content (N_t) at present has to be determined. Then its age t, can be calculated.

This technique is based on the presumed validity of the following assumptions;

- The flow of $^{14}_{6}C$ into the biosphere is constant over a time. The material under study when it was alive had the same activity as the 'living' carbon now.
- The decay of ^{14}C in the antique is independent of its present chemical environment.

20.4.1 Applications of Radiocarbon Dating

Radiocarbon dating has been adopted for determining the ages of archaeological and geological materials. Some of these interesting dating results are given in Table 20.5.

The ages reported in Table 20.5 may not be accurate. However, these values indicate the approximate century. The ages of antiques in the range 500–50,000 years can be determined satisfactorily by radiocarbon dating.

Table 20.5 Ages of antiques determined by radiocarbon dating

Material	Age (years)
Certain ocean bottom sediments	25,000
Skeleton from a grave in UP (India)	10,050
Charcoal from Maharashtra (India)	3,500
Charcoal from Egyptian tombs	2,800
Wood from a Roman ship	2,100
Dead Sea scroll	1,940
Shroud of Turin	600
Human bones from Incan temple	500

W F Libby

The radiocarbon dating method was suggested by Willard Frank Libby (1909–1980), an American chemist. His suggestion was later experimentally applied and ages of antiques were determined. Libby received the Nobel Prize in chemistry in 1960 for this suggestion. He invented the gaseous diffusion method of separating U-235. This method enabled the use of enriched U-235 in the atom bomb dropped over Hiroshima.

Problem 20.1 A sample of rock obtained from the moon is found to contain 18% K-40 and 82% Ar-40 by mass spectral analysis. Estimate the age of the rock. (The radioactive K-40 decays to Ar-40 with a $t_{1/2}$ of 1.2×10^9 years.)

Solution

The decay constant for the nuclear change,

$$k = \frac{0.693}{t_{1/2}} = \frac{0.693}{1.2 \times 10^9\ \text{y}} = 0.5775 \times 10^{-9}\ \text{y}^{-1}$$

$$k = \frac{2.303}{t} \log \frac{N_0}{N_t}$$

$$0.5775 \times 10^{-9} = \frac{2.303}{t_{1/2}} \log \frac{100}{82}$$

$$\therefore \quad t_{1/2} = \frac{2.303}{0.5775 \times 10^{-9}} \log \left(\frac{100}{82}\right) = 3.44 \times 10^9 \text{ years}$$

The age of the rock is 3.5×10^9 years.

20.5 ACTIVATION ANALYSIS

Activation analysis is a method of qualitative or quantitative analysis of a substance by artificially activating an element in the substance.

20.5.1 Principle

A stable isotope of an element is converted into a radioactive nucleus by bombarding it with projectile particles, say, neutrons. The active product is then identified by its characteristic decay mode and half-life. A known amount of the element being analysed is also bombarded with particles under identical experimental conditions; the decay of the standard is also measured. By comparing the decay of the test material with that of the standard, identification and estimation of the element can be effected. Though the test element can be activated by neutrons, protons or photons (X-ray), activation by neutrons is the commonest technique; this technique is called *neutron activation analysis* (NAA).

Invention of NAA

G Hevesy and H Levi (Denmark) first introduced NAA in 1936. They accidentally found that a sample containing rare earth elements became highly radioactive after exposing it to neutrons. They realised the potential of neutron activation followed by measurement of the induced radioactivity to facilitate both qualitative and quantitative analyses of elements. The basic requirements for carrying out an analysis of a sample by NAA are a source of neutrons, instrumentation suitable for detecting gamma rays and a detailed knowledge of the reactions that occur when neutrons interact with the target nuclei.

George Hevesy

George Karl von Hevesy (1885–1966) was born in Budapest, Hungary. He specialised in radiochemistry and received the Nobel Prize in chemistry (1943) for his research on chemical processes such as the metabolism of animals. In 1923, along with Dirk Coster, he discovered the element hafnium, validating the prediction of the existence of this element by Mendeleev in 1869.

During the Second World War, Hevesy worked at the Neils Bohr Institute, Germany. He dissolved the Noble Prizes of his colleagues, Max von Laue and James Frost into aqua regia and kept the solutions in the laboratory to avoid the Nazis stealing the gold. After the war, the dissolved gold was recovered and new prizes were awarded to Laue and Frost.

20.5.2 Prompt Versus Delayed NAA

NAA can be categorised according to whether gamma rays are measured during neutron irradiation [prompt gamma NAA (PGNAA)] or at some time after the end of irradiation [delayed gamma NAA (DGNAA)]. The DGNAA is performed by using a beam of neutrons obtained through a reactor beam port. Fluxes on samples irradiated in beams are of the order of one million times lower than on samples inside a reactor, but detectors can be placed very close to the sample compensating for much of the loss in sensitivity due to low flux. The PGNAA is applicable to elements with extremely high neutron capture cross-sections (such as B, Cd, Sm and Gd), elements which decay too rapidly to be measured by DGNAA and elements that produce only stable isotopes of elements with weak decay gamma-ray intensities. DGNAA (conventional NAA) is useful for the vast majority of elements that produce radioactive nuclides. The sequence of events involved NAA is shown in Fig. 20.3.

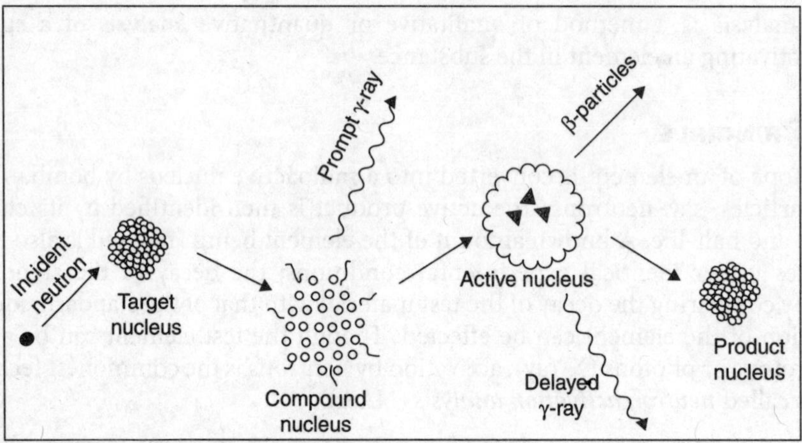

Fig. 20.3 Sequence of events in neutron activation analysis

20.5.3 Theory

If the atoms of a stable element are irradiated with neutrons, the most common resultant nuclear reaction is one whereby a certain proportion of the nuclei of the stable atom absorb neutrons to become heavier by one atomic mass unit. Since only γ-rays are emitted, there is no change in the atomic number, and the product species is an isotope A* of A. The rate of increase in A* is proportional to the number of atoms (A) of the stable element taken. Simultaneously, A* decays and its rate of decrease is proportional to the number of A* formed.

On exposure to a flux of neutrons, the rate of formation of radioactive nuclei from a single isotope is denoted by the equation,

$$\frac{dA}{dt} = A\phi\sigma$$

where dA / dt is the formation rate of active nuclei per second, A is the number of stable target nuclei. The radioactive nuclei formed, decay at a rate $- dA^* / dt$: it is given by

$$-\frac{dA^*}{dt} = \lambda A^*$$

Therefore, during radiation with a uniform flux of neutrons, the net rate of formation of active nuclei is

$$\frac{dA^*}{dt} = \phi\sigma A - \lambda A^* \tag{20.1}$$

The incident neutron flux ϕ is usually given in neutrons $cm^{-2}\ s^{-1}$, σ is the absorption cross-section of X (cm^2/target atom) (the effective area presented by one X-nucleus to the neutron stream), commonly measured in barns (1 barn = $1 \times 10^{-24}\ cm^2$), λ is the decay constant for A^* and A is the number of target nuclei available.

The number of target nuclei is given by

$$A = wN_A \frac{r}{M} \tag{20.2}$$

where w is the weight of the parent nuclide, N_A is the Avogadro number, M is the atomic number of the nuclide and r is the fractional abundance of the target nuclei. During irradiation, ϕ will be essentially constant as will be A, since only a tiny fraction of the nuclei is expected to absorb the incident neutron. Thus, Eq. (20.1) may be integrated for the initial condition $A^*(0) = 0$, to give

$$A^* = \frac{\phi\sigma A}{\lambda}(1 - e^{-\lambda t}) \tag{20.3}$$

A^* is proportional to the activity (the disinntegration rate) D_s, of the radioactive sample, which in turn is directly proportional to the observed counting rate, R_s.

$$D_s = -\frac{dA^*}{dt} = \lambda A^* \tag{20.4}$$

$$R_s = ED_s \text{ (for particles)}$$

$$R_s = F_\gamma ED_s \text{ (for } \gamma\text{-ray photons)}$$

The factor E measures the efficiency of the counting device being used; this factor has values $0 < E < 1$. F_γ is the fraction of the decays that may result in the particular photon that is being counted.

$$\therefore \quad R_s = EF_\gamma \phi\sigma A\,(1 - e^{-\lambda t}) \tag{20.5}$$

If D_o is the initial activity just at the termination of irradiation, then,

$$D_o = \lambda A^*$$

$$D_o = A\,\phi\sigma\,(1 - e^{-\lambda t})$$

But, $\lambda = \dfrac{0.693}{t_{1/2}}$

$$\therefore \quad D_o = \phi\sigma A\left(1 - e^{-0.693t/t_{1/2}}\right) \tag{20.6}$$

where t is the duration of irradiation. During the irradiation period, some radionuclides will decay. The term,

$$1 - e^{-0.639t/t_{1/2}}$$

gives the saturation factor S.

$$S = \frac{\text{Amount of activity produced during the irradiation period}}{\text{Amount of activity produced at infinite time}}$$

At $t/t_{1/2}$ value of		1	2	3	4	5	6	…	∞	
S	=	0.50	0.75	0.87	0.94	0.97	0.98	…	1	respectively

The induced activity will reach 98% of saturation value for an irradiation period equal to six half-lives.

The element under study may have several isotopes, but let us assume that only one of these with a relative abundance of r% is activated under the conditions chosen, or better, the radiation emitted by other isotopes or elements present can be eliminated by absorption. Then, it is easy to obtain the relation between the weight of the element w and the measured R_s:

$$w = \frac{R_s M\,100}{N_A \phi \sigma r\,(1 - e^{-\lambda t})}; \quad (R_s = ED_s)$$

For a given neutron flux and time of irradiation, the sensitivity of the method increases with capture cross section σ. The isotopic abundance r% decreases with increase in half life and increase in atomic weight.

20.5.4 Irradiation Time

Because of the rapid asymptotic approach of the saturation factor to unity, in practice, a sample is seldom irradiated for a period of time longer than a few half-lives of the induced activity of interest. Short-lived activities are enhanced by a shorter irradiation period, followed quickly by counting. Similarly, longer-lived activities are enhanced by longer irradiation periods.

20.5.5 Analytical Procedures: Comparative Method

In quantitative determinations, the comparative method is used. This involves only a simple calculation. The standard is weighed and packed in duplicate, together with the test sample of appropriate size, also in duplicate. Both the sets are irradiated in the same physical location and under the same flux conditions. Then the relative activities,

$$\frac{D_s \text{ sample}}{D_s \text{ standard}} = \frac{w \text{ sample}}{w \text{ standard}} \times \frac{(e^{-\lambda t_d}) \text{ sample}}{(e^{-\lambda t_d}) \text{ standard}}$$

where D_s = activity, w = weight of the element and t_d = decay time.

The above ratio simplifies as

$$C_{\text{sample}} = C_{\text{standard}} \times \frac{w' \text{ standard} \times D_s \text{ sample}}{w' \text{ sample} \times D_s \text{ standard}}$$

where C = concentration of the element and w' = weight.

In a typical NAA, the nuclides (A_z the target nuclide) in the sample are bombarded with a flux of (incident) neutrons. Each A_z absorbs a neutron to form an active compound nucleus $(A + 1)_z$. Then, the active nucleus decays through the emission of a beta particle and gamma ray with a characteristic half life. A high resolution gamma ray spectrometer is used to detect these delayed gamma rays from the artificially induced radioactivity in the sample for both qualitative and quantitative analyses.

Problem 20.2 The presence as well as the amount of arsenic in a material can be established by NAA. The natural ${}^{75}_{33}\text{As}$ nucleus in the material absorbs a neutron to form ${}^{76}_{33}\text{As}$, which is β-active:

$$ {}^{75}_{33}\text{As} + {}^{1}_{0}n \longrightarrow [{}^{76}_{33}\text{As}] \longrightarrow {}^{76}_{34}\text{Se} + {}^{0}_{-1}e \quad t_{1/2} = 26.5\text{ h} $$

The number of beta particles emitted per unit time from the activated material is measured from which the amount of As in the material can be calculated. A known weight of pure ${}^{75}_{33}\text{As}$ is also irradiated with neutrons simultaneously with the test sample under identical experimental conditions. The number of beta particles emitted per unit time from this standard sample is also measured. Then, comparison of the two radioactivities would give the amount of arsenic in the test material. The following relationship is used for this calculation:

$$ \frac{w}{w_0} = \frac{A_t}{A_0} $$

where, w = weight of arsenic in the test material, w_o = weight of arsenic taken as standard, A_t = activity of arsenic in test material and A_o = activity of arsenic in standard.

20.5.6 Decay Scheme

In NAA, the element in the test material is identified by fingerprinting the decay undergone by the activated material. Each type of active nucleus has a characteristic decay mode. The pictorial depiction of this decay mode is called the *decay scheme*. For example, the decay scheme for ${}^{24}_{11}\text{Na}$ is given in Fig. 20.4.

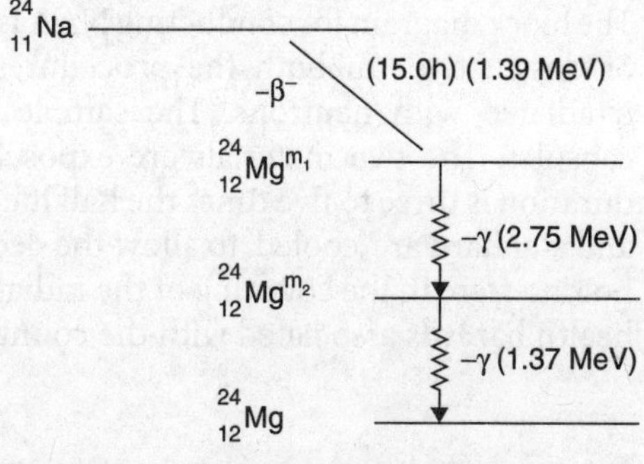

Fig. 20.4 Decay scheme for ${}^{24}_{11}\text{Na}$

Based on the decay scheme, the active element can be identified by its radiation, that is beta particles or gamma rays, and also by its half life. NAA can be carried out by counting the number of gamma rays of specific energy emitted by the active nuclides. For example, ${}^{109}\text{Ag}$ on NA, forms ${}^{110}\text{Ag}$ which decays to ${}^{110}\text{Cd}$ and γ ray:

$$ {}^{109}\text{Ag} + n \longrightarrow [{}^{110}\text{Ag}] \longrightarrow {}^{110}\text{Cd} + {}^{0}_{-1}e + \gamma(658)\text{ keV} $$

The amount of silver in the original sample can be determined by measuring the number of 658 keV gamma-rays emitted from the sample in a given time interval after the sample has been irradiated with a flux of neutrons.

The measured count rate R of the gamma rays from the decay of a specific isotope (${}^{110}\text{Ag}$) in the irradiated sample can be related to the amount (actually, the number of atoms of silver, n) in the original sample by the equation,

$$ R = \varepsilon \, \text{I}_\gamma A $$

$$ R = \varepsilon I_\gamma n \varphi \sigma (1 - e^{-\lambda} t_i) \, e^{-\lambda t_d} $$

where R = measured gamma ray counts per second, A = absolute activity of isotope ^{A+1}Z in the sample, ε = absolute detector efficiency, I_γ = absolute gamma ray abundance, n = number of atoms of isotope ^{A}Z in the sample, φ = neutron flux (neutrons.cm^{-2}.s^{-1}), σ = neutron cross section (cm^2 or barn, b = 10^{-8} m^2) for isotope ^{A}Z, λ = radioactive decay constant (s^{-1}) for isotope ^{A+1}Z, t_i = irradiation time (*s*) and t_d = decay time (*s*).

If the values of φ, σ, ε and I_γ are known, the number of atoms n of the isotope ^{A}Z can be calculated directly using this equation. However, the calculation can be simplified by irradiating a standard simultaneously with the test material.

Then, $$w_{\text{test}} = w_{\text{std}}\left(\frac{R_{\text{test}}}{R_{\text{std}}}\right)$$

where, w_{test} = mass of element (g) in test, w_{std} = mass of element (g) in standard, R_{test} = gamma ray count (c/s) from the test and R_{std} = gamma ray count (c/s) from the standard.

The limit of detection of a particular element will depend upon the measured count rate (R) of the gamma ray being monitored and the background upon which that gamma ray peak is situated. The measured count rate for a given isotope can be increased by

- increasing the detector efficiency (moving the sample closer to the detector), and
- increasing the irradiation time (t_i).

20.5.7 Instrument

The block diagram for conducting NAA is shown in Fig. 20.5. The analysis can be nondestructive or destructive. In both the procedures, the sample and the standard are simultaneously irradiated with neutrons. The sample and standard are contained in small polyethylene capsules. The two materials are exposed to the same neutron flux. Usually, the irradiation duration is three to five times the half life of the activated product. After irradiation, the sample and standard are 'cooled' to allow the decay of any short-lived nuclides formed so that they do not interfere in the counting of the radiation selected for analysis. In addition, cooling reduces health hazards associated with the counting material.

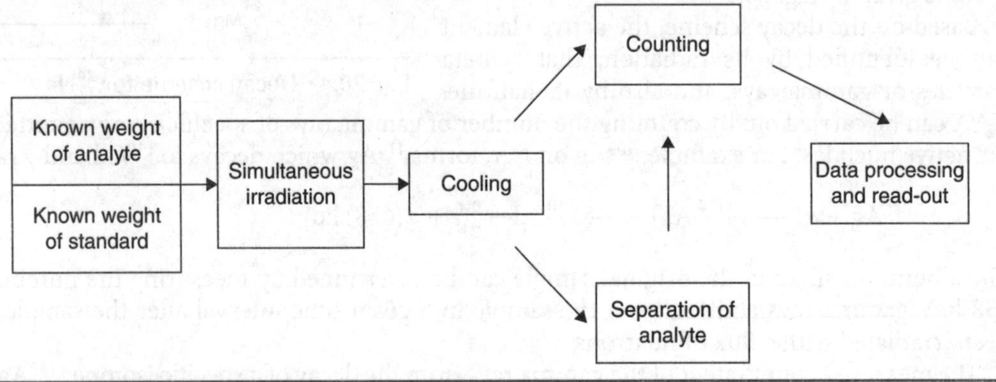

Fig. 20.5 Flow diagram for neutron activation analysis

20.5.7.1 Nondestructive Method

In this method, after cooling, counting is performed directly for both the sample and the standard. Though, some of the constituents other than the analyte in the mixture may get activated, the γ rays produced by these activated nuclides vary in energy; the spectrometer can differentiate energies and identify the gamma ray emitted by the analyte constituent. The amount of analyte in the mixture can be calculated from the weight of the standard taken and the two measured activities.

The gamma ray spectrometer can identify the particular gamma ray signal produced by the analyte from all the signals produced by the components of the mixture and count that signal alone. The nondestructive method is simple and requires less time than the destructive method. The flow diagram for the two routes of NAA is shown in Fig. 20.6.

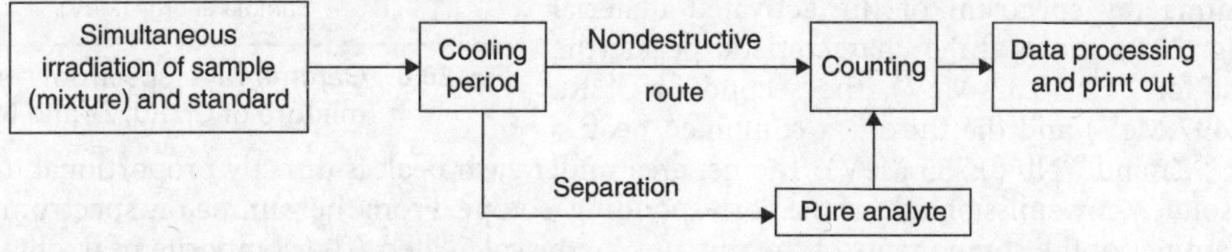

Fig. 20.6 Flow diagram for two types of NAA

20.5.7.2 Destructive Method

In the destructive method, the original material is lost as the analyte is separated from the other components of the mixture after irradiation. The irradiated components of the solution are separated by a suitable procedure (solvent extraction, chromatography or ion exchange). The isolated active analyte is then subjected to γ counting.

20.5.8 Neutron Sources

A common radioactive source of neutrons is a transuranium element that undergoes spontaneous nuclear reaction to give neutrons. Cf-238 is one such source ($t_{½}$ = 2.6 y). It gives 3.8 neutrons per decay. Neutrons can also be produced by intimately mixing an alpha emitter such as Pu with a light element such as Be.

$$^{9}_{4}\text{Be} + {}^{4}_{2}\text{He (from Pu)} \longrightarrow {}^{12}_{6}\text{C} + {}^{1}_{0}n + 5.7\text{ MeV}$$

20.5.9 Estimation of Mn in a Sample by NAA

When a sample containing ^{55}Mn has to be analysed, it is bombarded with a neutron flux. The following decay scheme denotes the changes:

$$^{55}_{25}\text{Mn} \xrightarrow{n} {}^{56}_{25}\text{Mn} \xrightarrow{-\beta^-} {}^{56}_{26}\text{Fe}^* \longrightarrow {}^{56}_{26}\text{Fe} + \gamma$$

The gamma ray spectrum of the activated nucleus (Fig. 20.7) shows a sharp symmetrical peak at 0.847 MeV, the result of total absorption of gamma ray energy by the detector. This peak is used for qualitative identification of the element. Normally, it is referred to as the *full-energy peak* or *photopeak*.

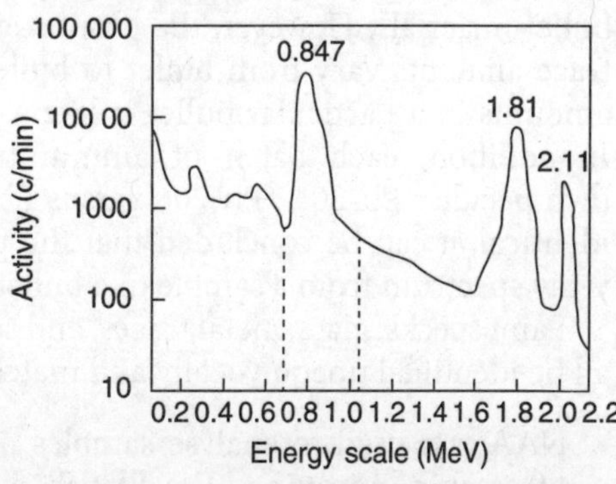

Fig. 20.7 Gamma ray spectrum of ^{56}Mn

20.5.10 NAA of Multi-component Material

More than one element in a material can also be identified and estimated by a single NAA. Consider, for example, a mixture (a mineral) containing ^{51}Cr, ^{103}Ru, ^{95}Zr and ^{95}Nb. On irradiation of this mixture with a neutron beam, all the four nuclides get activated by capturing a neutron each. The gamma ray spectrum of the activated material (Fig. 20.8) shows three characteristic peaks, the first for ^{51}Cr (0.32 MeV), the second for ^{103}Ru (0.497 MeV) and the third – a combined peak – for ^{95}Zr and ^{95}Nb (0.765 MeV). The net area under each peak is directly proportional to the absolute γ-ray emission rate of the corresponding isotope. From the gamma ray spectrum, the quantities of the components of the mixture can be calculated. The composite peak obtained for Zr and Nb can be enhanced by the addition of pure ^{95}Zr or ^{95}Nb, and then activating the mixture. Comparison of the two peaks obtained before and after the addition will give the concentrations of these two components.

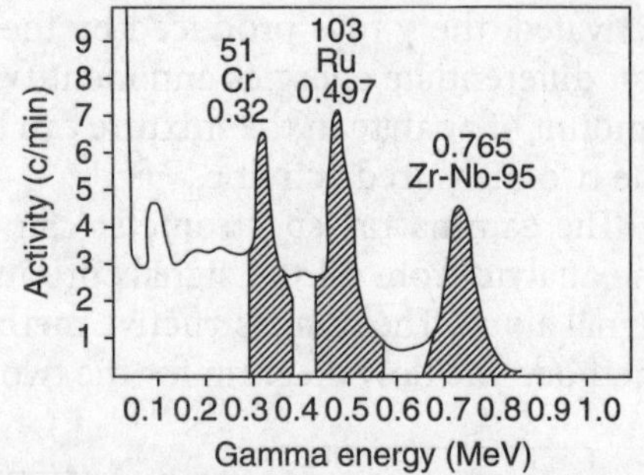

Fig. 20.8 Gamma-ray spectrum of a mixture of Cr, Ru, Zr and Nb

- NAA is a sensitive analytical technique useful for performing both qualitative and quantitative multi-element analysis of major, minor and trace elements in samples from almost every conceivable field of scientific and technical interest.

20.5.11 Applications of NAA

20.5.11.1 Forensic Science

Forensic chemical analysis generally involves trace quantities of materials. NAA is suitable for such analyses. For establishing that a bullet recovered from a crime scene had been fired from the pistol of the accused, the bullet material scraped from the pistol barrel and the actual bullet material obtained from the crime spot are activated by neutron flux and their gamma ray spectra recorded. Typically, traces of As and Sb, along with Pb are present in bullet materials. However, the proportions of these trace amounts vary from bullet to bullet and their amounts in a particular bullet is like a fingerprint. In addition, each batch of ammunition has its own peculiar Pb-204 : Pb-206 versus Pb-207 : Pb-208 ratio. Therefore, if the two spectra are identical, it can be concluded that the pistol under study must be the murder weapon. The γ-ray spectrum from a sample of a bullet material is shown in Fig. 20.9.

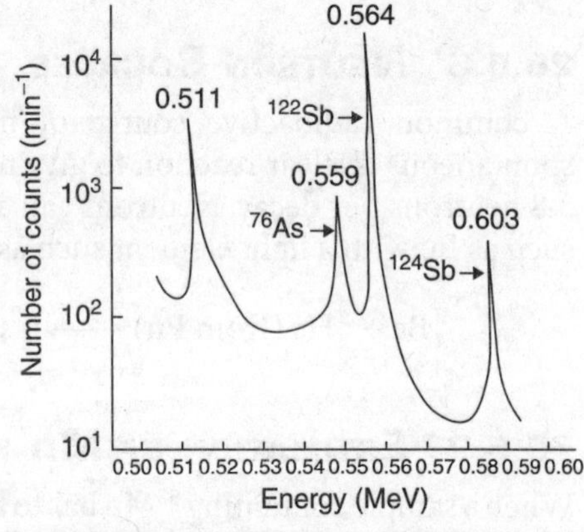

Fig. 20.9 Gamma-ray spectrum of a bullet material (traces of As and Sb)

Paint specks, glass, metal traces, and so on, gathered in a hit-and-run automobile crime, can all be identified unequivocally and matched in forensic investigations.

- NAA was used to analyse samples of the hair of Napoleon to investigate the possibility of arsenic poisoning. The British were accused of poisoning him to death during his incarceration in St Helena Island. His hair contained a higher quantity of arsenic than the normal quantity. Arsenic is one of the trace elements normally present in human hair.

- NAA was applied to fingerprint the trace elements in the bullet lead obtained from the body of the US President John F Kennedy after his assassination.

20.5.11.2 Isotope Geochemistry

Isotope geochemistry is a branch of geology based upon the study of the relative and absolute concentrations of the elements and their isotopes in the earth. This study can be illustrated with reference to the occurrence of lead in natural samples of materials. Lead has four stable isotopes, Pb-204, Pb-206, Pb-207 and Pb-208 and one radioactive isotope, Pb-202 ($t_{½} = 53{,}000$ years). Lead is formed in the earth via the decay of transuranic elements, primarily U and Th. By measuring the relative amounts (ratio) of the four lead isotopes in natural materials, such as igneous rocks or ice blocks in the Arctic Shelf, the age of the material can be calculated. The lead contents of ancient volcanic ashes can also be determined to understand the history of the volcano.

20.5.11.3 Prospecting of Natural Resources

The occurrence of natural resources such as water, coal, petroleum and minerals deep below the surface of the earth can be ascertained by neutron activation. A deep hole is drilled in the terrain to be assessed for resources and a neutron probe is inserted into it (Fig. 20.10). The neutron probe is a Po–Be source of flux 10^7 n/s. As the probe is lowered to different depths, the neutrons from the source activate the elements present at these depths; characteristic radiations are emitted from the activated nuclei. These radiations are collimated and the γ-ray made to fall on NaI(Tl) scintillation detector attached to the probe. The signals of the detector are amplified and recorded by a γ-ray spectrometer. From such spectra, the nature of resources and also their quantities can be known. On activation, H gives 2.2 MeV, O gives 22.7 MeV and C gives 4.94 MeV gamma rays respectively. Subsoil resources such as Mg, K, Cl, Ca, S, U, Th, diamond and beryl deposits can be identified by this method from their characteristic gamma emissions.

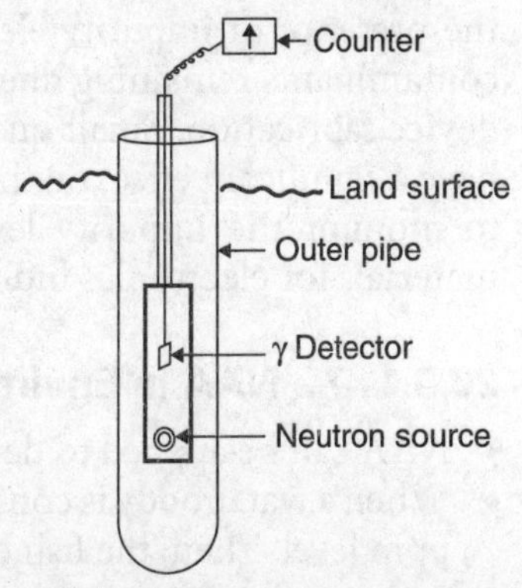

Fig. 20.10 Neutron probe for prospecting natural resources

20.5.11.4 Analysis of Minerals for Metallurgy

NAA is applied to assess the commercial viability of extracting rare metals from their minerals. The quantity of the rare metal present in a mineral should be sufficient for profitable metallurgical extraction of the metal. This can be ascertained by activating the mineral and evaluating the percentage of the rare metal in the mineral. For example, U and Th occur in some varieties of quartz. These metals, used in nuclear industries, can be isolated from such quartz minerals after checking the extent of their occurrence by NAA.

Neutron activation of sea water has indicated the presence of substantial quantities of ^{47}Ca, ^{59}Fe, ^{60}Co and ^{140}La in the sea water. In future, on depletion of mineral resources on land, sea water will have to be exploited for such minerals.

20.5.11.5 Assessment of Micronutrients

Certain micronutrients, such as Se and Mo are needed in extremely low quantity for the healthy function of living tissues. These nutrients help proper biological activity of enzymes, and their deficiency adversely affects the health of animals and human beings. Their concentrations are so low in tissues that they cannot be estimated by conventional analytical methods. NAA on the other hand, can be applied to estimate them precisely. For example, the adverse effects of selenium deficiency on the thyroid hormone were studied with NAA. Deiodination of thyroxin to form the active form of thyroid hormone (3,5,3[1]-triiodothyroxine) is important for the functioning of the thyroid. Type I deiodinase contains selenocysteine at its active site thus defining a dietary selenium requirement to growth and development through thyroid hormone function.

$$^{80}_{34}\text{Se} + n \longrightarrow {}^{81}_{34}\text{Se} \xrightarrow{t_{1/2}=19\text{ min}} {}^{81}_{35}\text{Br} + \beta^- + \gamma 1.38\text{ MeV}$$

The gamma sensitivity of the decay is 5 μg of Se. Therefore, Se up to as low as 5.0×10^{-6} g can be accurately estimated by the gamma ray spectrum of ^{81}Se.

20.5.11.6 Study of Semiconductor Materials

NAA is applied to measure trace and ultra-trace concentrations of impurities and/or dopants in semiconductors. The behaviour of semiconductor devices is strongly influenced by the presence of impurity elements either added intentionally (doping with B, P, As, Au) or contaminants remaining due to incomplete purification of the semiconductor material during device fabrication. Small quantities of impurities present at concentrations below 1 ppb can have a significant effect on the quality of semiconductor devices. NAA is a convenient method to monitor the impurity levels in semiconductor raw materials, and prepare appropriate materials for electronics industries.

20.5.11.7 NAA in Environmental Pollution Studies

- NAA can be applied to detect and determine environmental pollutants even in traces.
- When a water body is contaminated with mercury, the metal gets accumulated in fish at 1–2 ppm level. Then, the fish can be analysed by NAA and quantitative determination of ^{197}Hg activity effected.
- Metallic pollutants in air can be detected and estimated by NAA. The air quality in areas of metal mines and metallurgical factories can be monitored for metallic pollutants. Similarly, water and soil in such places can be analysed for pollutants on routine basis by NAA.
- The presence of hazardous elements in industrial chimney gases can be monitored by NAA, and remedial measures adopted when the levels of toxins increase.

Problem 20.3 A sample of ground water was analysed for its arsenic content by NAA. To 10.0 ml of this water, 1.0 ml of a standard solution containing 1.0 mg of As^{3+} was added and the mixture irradiated by a neutron flux. This gave a counting rate of 1280 cpm. To another 10.0 ml of the water sample, 1.0 ml of deionised water was added and the diluted solution after similar irradiation with the neutron flux, gave a counting rate of 840 cpm. Calculate the arsenic content in the 10 ml of the ground water.

Solution

$$R_s = Rw_s$$

$$R_x = Rw_x$$

$$840 = Rw_x\,;\; R = \frac{840}{w_x}$$

$$R_s + R_x = k\,(w_x + w_s) = k\,(w_x + 1.0)$$

(as $w_s = 1.0\ \mu g$)

$$R_s + R_x = 1280$$

$$\therefore \quad 1280 = \frac{840}{w_x}(w_x + 1) = 840 + \frac{840}{w_x}$$

$$\therefore \quad \frac{840}{w_x} = 1280 - 840 = 440$$

$$w_x = \frac{840}{440} = 1.91\ \mu g$$

10.0 ml of the ground water contains 1.91 μg of arsenic.

20.5.12 Sensitivities of Elements for NAA

The sensitivities (detection limits) of elements for NAA depends upon (i) the irradiation parameters—neutron flux, irradiation time and decay time, (ii) nuclear parameters of the elements being measured—isotope abundance, neutron cross section, half life and emitted gamma ray abundance. The accuracy of an individual NAA determination usually ranges between 1% and 10% of the reported value. The sensitivities for determination of most elements range from 10^{-16} to 10^{-11} g.

20.5.13 Advantages of NAA

- NAA is a non-destructive method.
- It is highly sensitive; an element present even at microgram level in a material can be accurately detected and estimated by NAA.
- The accuracy and precision of NAA are such that it is a reliable method used to certify concentrations of elements in Standard Reference Materials (SRMs, NIST, USA publication).
- The analyte can be in the solid, liquid, solution or gaseous state.
- It is nearly free of any matrix interferences as the majority of the constituents of the samples are completely transparent to both the probe (neutron) and the analytical signal (gamma ray).
- This method can be applied directly to the sample; there is no risk of contamination or loss of the analyte.
- It can be applied to a variety of samples such as minerals, clothes, forensic samples, archaeological specimens, and so on.

20.5.14 Drawbacks of NAA

- NAA is an expensive method.
- For measurement requiring a high degree of sensitivity, a large flux of the bombarding particles is required from a nuclear reactor or particle accelerator. Therefore, NAA cannot be carried out in ordinary laboratories; a radiochemical laboratory is required for this.
- With some samples, the activity generated by the irradiation of the bulk matrix is large, and hence it would mask the signal of interest. This happens when the element being determined is in a mixture and the other components of the mixture also get activated. In such a case,

one has to employ time delays or chemical separations to improve both selectivity and sensitivity of count measurement.

20.6 HOT-ATOM CHEMISTRY

Hot-atom chemistry is the chemistry of producing isotopes by artificial nuclear reactions. It includes the study of chemical reactions resulting from the transfer of energy produced in nuclear processes of various kinds to valence bonds of certain target molecules. For example, let us consider the following steps in a hot-atom process.

- Ethyl iodide (target) is irradiated with a beam of neutrons.
- The iodine nucleus ^{127}I in C_2H_5I captures a neutron and forms ^{128}I.
- ^{128}I in the molecule (C_2H_5–^{128}I) has now acquired energy from the projectile (*n*).
- ^{128}I is radioactive, and emits prompt gamma ray.
- This radioactive atom is called a hot-atom. This extra energy acquired by the molecule breaks the C–^{128}I bond in C_2H_5–^{128}I; a free ^{128}I atom is formed:

$$C_2H_5 - {}^{128}I \longrightarrow C_2H_5 + {}^{128}I$$

The ^{128}I atoms combine to form I_2 molecules which can be extracted with water; as the amount of $^{128}I_2$ formed is low, water itself can extract it, though the solubility is low. Alternatively, the active iodine formed can be reduced to I^- and precipitated as AgI.

The new isotope (^{128}I) is in a different chemical (bonded) form compared to the iodine in the target molecule. The energy acquired by ^{127}I is more than sufficient for the C–I bond breakage; therefore, the excess energy is emitted as gamma ray. Now, the whole process can be represented as

$$\underset{\text{Target molecule}}{C_2H_5 - {}^{127}I} \xrightarrow{n} C_2H_5 - {}^{128}I^*$$

$$C_2H_5 - {}^{128}I^* \longrightarrow C_2H_5 + \underset{\text{Hot atom}}{{}^{128}I^*}$$

$$2\,{}^{128}I^* \longrightarrow {}^{128}I - {}^{128}I + \gamma$$

$$2C_2H_5 \longrightarrow \text{various products: } C_4H_{10}, C_2H_4 \ldots$$

^{128}I with excess energy is called a hot atom and it is denoted as $^{128}I^*$; it decays to the ground state by emitting a gamma ray:

$$\underset{\text{hot atom}}{{}^{128}I^*} \rightarrow {}^{128}I + \gamma$$

This process of formation and isolation of isotopes, invented by Szilard and Chalmers is called the *Szilard–Chalmers process*. It is used for the preparation and separation of isotopes. In this example, an (*n*, *γ*) reaction has been performed. The Szilard–Chalmers process can be effected also by other types of nuclear reactions: (*γ*, *n*), (*n*, 2*n*) and (*d*, *p*). In each type, an isotope of an atom in the target molecule is formed. For example, ^{15}O can be prepared by a (*d*, *n*) reaction on ^{14}N, containing traces of oxygen.

$$^{14}N_2 + O_2 \xrightarrow{d} {}^{15}O{-}O$$

Unlike with (*n*, *γ*) processes, several products (isotopes) are formed with the other types of particle fluxes.

Leo Szilard (1898–1964)

Leo Szilard was born on 11 February 1898 in Budapest, Hungary. He studied physics under Max van Laue at the University of Berlin and earned his doctorate in 1922. He obtained several patents for his inventions, including the one on a new type of refrigerator. He migrated to England and worked with T A Chalmers. They developed the Szilard–Chalmers process. It was on a street corner in London in October 1933, that Szilard first conceived of the possibility of nuclear chain reaction. This theory was rejected by Lord Ernest Rutherford, a leading atomic physicist of that time. Szilard proved Rutherford wrong and his theory is now the basis for producing atomic energy. He moved to the US, and in 1942 demonstrated the first nuclear chain reaction; this was conducted at the University of Chicago campus.

After the bombing of Hiroshima and Nakasaki, Szilard became an active antagonist for the use of nuclear bombs. Szilard was a great thinker and his theories on physics were proved correct by experimentation later.

20.6.1 Conditions for the Szilard–Chalmers Process

Three conditions have to fulfilled to effect a Szilard–Chalmers isotope separation.

(i) The radioactive atom in the process of its formation must be broken loose from the target molecule; for example, $C_2H_5{-}I^* \rightarrow I^*$

(ii) The active atom must neither recombine with the molecular fragment from which it is separated nor rapidly interchange with inactive atoms in other target molecules.

$$C_2H_5 + I^* \rightarrow C_2H_5{-}I^* \quad \text{Unfavourable recombination}$$

$$C_2H_5{-}I + I^* \rightarrow C_2H_5{-}I^* + I \quad \text{Unfavourable exchange}$$

(iii) A chemical method for the separation of the target compound from the radioactive material in its new chemical form must be available.

Why does a hot atom break away? Most chemical bond energies are in the range of 1 to 5 eV (20000 to 100000 calories per mole). When an atom captures a thermal neutron, the incident neutron does not impart enough energy to the nucleus to cause any bond rupture. Then, how does bond rupture occur in the Szilard–Chalmers process?

The answer to this question can be derived if we consider the γ-ray emission by the nucleus after it has captured a thermal neutron. Neutron capture is always followed by γ-ray emission. When γ-ray is emitted, the emitting nucleus receives some energy (recoil energy).

Let the energy of the emitted γ-ray be E_γ. Its momentum P_γ is given as

$$P_\gamma = \frac{E_\gamma}{c} \tag{20.6}$$

where c is the velocity of light. In the emission process, the momentum should be conserved, and therefore the recoiling atom must have an identical momentum. The recoil energy E_r is given by the expression,

$$E_r = \frac{P_\gamma^2}{2M} \tag{20.7}$$

where M is the mass of the atom. It is difficult to measure the momentum, therefore, substituting Eq. 20.6 in Eq. 20.7,

$$E_r = \frac{(E_\gamma/c)^2}{2M} = \frac{E_\gamma^2}{2Mc^2} \tag{20.8}$$

For M in atomic mass units and energy in MeV, Eq. 20.8 becomes

$$E_r = \frac{1862\,E_\gamma^2}{M} \tag{20.9}$$

In this equataion, the recoil energy is in eV. Equation 20.9 indicates that the recoil energy is directly proportional to the square of the gamma ray energy and inversely proportional to the atomic mass. Using this equation, the recoil energies expected for various nuclei can be calculated for known gamma ray energies (Table 20.6).

The recoil energies are higher than the bond energies and therefore, the probability of bond breakage is high. Thus, in most (n, γ) processes, the probability of bond rupture is high.

A few other isotope separation effected by the Szilard–Chalmers process are denoted below.

$$CCl_4 \xrightarrow{(n,\gamma)} {}^{38}Cl$$

$$C_2H_4Cl_2 \xrightarrow{(n,\gamma)} {}^{38}Cl$$

$$C_2H_5Br \xrightarrow{(n,\gamma)} {}^{80}Br$$

$$CH_3I \xrightarrow{(n,\gamma)} {}^{128}I$$

$$C_2Br_6(s) \xrightarrow[-196°C]{(n,\gamma)} {}^{82}Br$$

Table 20.6 Recoil energies in electron volts for various nuclei emitting gamma rays

M	$E_\gamma = 2$ MeV	$E_\gamma = 4$ MeV	$E_\gamma = 6$ MeV
20	107	430	967
50	43	172	387
100	21	86	193
150	14	57	129
200	11	43	97

In each of these cases, the halogen isotope formed is reduced to X^- and then extracted with water.

In these processes, only those halogen atoms which have captured a neutron each get separated; the remaining ordinary halogen atoms remain attached in the target molecule itself. Therefore, the sample of separated isotope is *isotopically pure*.

The maximum energies of γ photons accompanying (n, γ) reactions with halogen atoms together with the resulting recoil energies and the carbon–halogen bond energies are given in Table 20.7.

Table 20.7 Szilard–Chalmers process data for halogens

Halogen atom	E_γ / MeV	E_r / eV	Carbon–halogen bond energy / eV
Cl	22.2	543	3.4
Br	5.1	174	2.2
I	4.8	96	2.3

The E_r values are much higher than the bond energies indicating that the C–X bond breaks can occur easily in the Szilard–Chalmers process.

- The active halogen atoms from the irradiated compounds can be separated by other methods also; adsorbing them on activated charcoal and collecting them on charged plates (electrodes) are two such methods. Active arsenic has been collected on charged metal plates from irradiated AsH_3.
- High yields of active halogens have been isolated by irradiating solid or aqueous chlorates, bromates, iodates, perchlorates and periodates. Halogen carriers can be used to form halides from the halogen isotopes formed.
- The difference in oxidation states before and after neutron capture can be used for the Szilard–Chalmers separation of isotopes. For example, ^{56}Mn formed on neutron irradiation of permanganate solution can be separated as $^{56}MnO_2$ after reduction of Mn (VII). Similarly, arsenic can be separated by the addition of an arsenite carrier to an irradiated arsenate solution and precipitating the product as As_2S_3.
- Metal complexes have been used for successful Szilard–Chalmers separation. For example, U-239 has been separated from irradiated unanyl benzolacetonate, $UO_2(C_6H_5COCHCOCH_3)_2$. U-238 in the complex becomes U-239 and gets separated as a free hot atom. The freed and hot uranium does not exchange with uranium in the target complex.
- Another example for using metal complex as target involves the copper complex: Bisacetylacetoneethylenediimino $^{64}Cu(II) \xrightarrow[n]{} {}^{65}Cu$. The recoiling ^{65}Cu can be isolated by extracting it with an aqueous inert electrolyte.
- Rare isotopes of some of the elements, that do not occur naturally and can be produced only with difficulty by other methods, have been successfully produced by the Szilard–Chalmers method. For example, ^{98}Tc, ^{239}U

20.6.2 Chemistry of Recoil Atoms

A recoil atom, having high energy is expected to undergo chemical reactions with species with which it is in contact. The following types of reactions are possible for a hot atom:

(i) The hot atom can recombine with the fragment of the target molecule.

$$C_2H_5I \xrightarrow{n} C_2H_5 + I^* \text{ Formation of hot atom}$$

$$I^* + C_2H_5 \longrightarrow C_2H_5I^* \text{ Recombination}$$

This recombination reaction is called *retention;* lesser the retention, higher is the yield of the isotope under preparation. Quantitatively, retention is the fraction of the active atoms not separable from the target compounds. The retention, in addition to other factors, depends upon the physical state of the target. The retention in a separation is of the order,

$$\text{gaseous phase} < \text{liquid phase} < \text{solid phase}$$

As the species are far apart from one another in the gaseous phase, the retention is the least. For example, the retention of bromine for $C_2H_5Br(g)$ target is 5% whereas that for $C_2H_5Br(l)$ target is 75%. Retention decreases with decreasing concentration; for example, in the separation of hot bromine from C_2H_5Br in an inert solvent, the retention is 42% with 0.05 M but only 7% with 0.002 M solution.

(ii) The hot-atom may replace its other isotope in the unaffected target molecule.

$$C_2H_5I + I^* \longrightarrow C_2H_5I^* + I$$

Such a replacement also increases retention and decreases the efficiency of the Szilard–Chalmers separation.

(iii) The hot atom, in addition to replacing its own isotope, may replace an atom of another element in the target.

$$C_2H_5\text{–}I + I^* \longrightarrow {}^*I\text{–}C_2H_4\text{–}I + H$$

Such a substitution has been shown to be independent of temperature; therefore, it is not a thermal reaction. However, this type of reaction can be used to prepare labelled molecules. This decreases the yield of free hot atom.

20.6.2.1 Enrichment Factor

The three processes discussed so far decrease the yield of free (separated) isotope. These effects together are represented by a factor called the *enrichment factor*. This factor is the ratio of the specific activity of the separated isotope to the specific activity of the irradiated target molecule. Some of the target molecules become and remain active after irradiation due to retention. Higher the enrichment factor, better is the separation of the isotope. Higher this factor, lesser is the retention.

The excited atom formed on irradiation can even substitute groups such as –OH, $-NH_2$, –COOH, and so on, giving labelled products. For example, aniline hydrobromide on irradiation with neutrons gives labelled C_6H_5Br.

$$C_6H_5NH_2 \cdot HBr \xrightarrow{n} C_6H_5Br^*$$

An atom of an element in a molecule may be converted to an atom of another element on irradiating the molecule. For example, by slow-neutron irradiation of a nitrogenous molecule, the N atom in it absorbs a neutron and becomes ^{14}C by (n, p) reaction. Acridine, for example, forms labelled anthracene. This type of reaction is unique in that a labelled molecule is elegantly formed without adopting any conventional chemical reaction route.

20.6.2.2 Hot-atom Reactions in Inorganic Systems

Several inorganic species in aqueous medium undergo hot-atom reactions on irradiation with neutrons. For example, on irradiating permanganate with a neutron flux, the following were observed.

(i) The retention is independent of the concentration of permanganate (an unusual behaviour).

(ii) The manganese in the primary recoil fragment is in its +7 state, but in various forms:

$$MnO_3^+, MnO_2^{3+}, MnO^{5+}, \ldots$$

(iii) These unstable manganese species formed undergo reactions with water:

$$MnO_3^+ + 2OH^- \longrightarrow MnO_4^- + H_2O$$

$$4MnO_3^+ + 2H_2O \longrightarrow 4MnO_2 + 3O_2 + 4H^+$$

(iv) The retention is pH-dependent; at pH >12, the retention is nearly 100%, due to predominant hydration. Below pH 12, the retention decreases and becomes a constant (7%) for pH values between 8 and 2. Below pH 2, the retention increases slightly. The reduction by water is faster than hydration in neutral and acidic solutions.

Thus, neutron irradiation is able to effect several reactions in inorganic target species; some of these reactions are unique because they do not occur in normal solution chemistry. The hot-atom chemistry of phosphates and arsenates has also been studied. With PO_4^{3-}, under all conditions, 50% retention occurs, the other 50% of the phosphate species undergoes hot-atom reactions. With AsO_4^{3-}, the retention is nearly 100% over a wide range of pH. Hydration occurs predominantly over oxidation with the arsenate. Bromates, chromates and iodates have also been studied similarly by neutron bombardment. However, the hot-atom reactions of these species in solution are complex.

20.6.2.3 Hot Atoms from Radioactive Decay

A hot atom may be formed from radioactive decay; for example,

$$TeO_3^{3-} \longrightarrow I^*O_3^- + \beta^-$$

Radioactive Te-127 (β-active) in TeO_3^{3-} decays to I-127 with a half-life of 9.3 hours; the hot iodine in $^*IO_3^-$ gives off γ-rays.

$$^*IO_3^- \longrightarrow IO_3^- + \gamma$$

Another process of this type is the decay of Mn in MnO_4^-. Radioactive Mn-52 in MnO_4^- decays to Cr-52 and a positron, and in this process, CrO_4^{2-} is the product.

$$^{52}MnO_4^- \longrightarrow {}^*CrO_4^{2-} + \beta^+$$

$$^*CrO_4^{2-} \longrightarrow CrO_4^{2-} + \gamma$$

The gamma ray decay *(isomeric transition)* may be followed by bond ruptures in the product chemical species in these reactions. Hot-atom chemistry has also been studied by other modes of reactions, such as (*n*, *d*), (*n*, *p*), and so on.

20.7 EFFECT OF RADIATION ON MATTER

All the three radioactive rays, α, β and γ, interact with matter. These rays remove electrons from atoms or molecules present in matter and produce ions. However, their ionising powers are different; the order of their ionising power is

$$\alpha > \beta > \gamma$$

When a radiation falls on matter, ion pairs, each consisting of an electron and a positive ion, are formed. The number of such ion pairs formed is a measure of the ionising power of the radiation. The electrons produced initially by interaction between the radiation and matter are called *primary electrons.* These electrons may interact with matter and lead to further ionisation; this gives rise to *secondary electrons.* Among the three types of radiation, the γ radiation produces the least number of primary electrons; however, as these electrons cause further ionisation, the total ionisation produced by this radiation is substantial.

The interaction of radiation with matter need not always cause ionisation. When the energy of the radiation is *insufficient* for ionisation, it may excite some of the electrons in matter to higher atomic or molecular energy levels. When these electrons return to their ground states, radiation is emitted from the matter. This radiation may occur in X-ray, ultraviolet or visible region.

20.7.1 Gamma Ray Induced Reactions

Gamma rays can induce chemical reactions in matter. The following are typical examples:

$3C_2H_2 \rightarrow C_6H_6$: polymerisation

$2NH_3 \rightarrow N_2 + 3H_2$: radiolysis

$H_2O \rightarrow H^{\bullet} + {}^{\bullet}OH$ + other products : radiolysis

Radiolysis is the decomposition of a molecule into small fragments induced by radiation. The radiolysis of water produces solvated electrons, $e^-(aq)$. This species has a very short life. Simple organic molecules readily get radiolysed on irradiation:

$$CH_4 \rightarrow {}^{\bullet}CH_3 + {}^{\bullet}H$$

$$R\text{–}COOH \rightarrow R^{\bullet} + CO_2 + {}^{\bullet}H$$

A polymer may be deploymerised on irradiation:

$$A_n \rightarrow n\,A$$

20.7.1.1 Radiolysis of Organic Compounds

Some organic compounds are radiolysed on irradiation with gamma rays. Such reactions are complicated, forming more than one product in each reaction. Most of these radiolysis reactions have been done in the aqueous medium. Oxidation and hydroxylation are predominant. In addition to simple oxidations, gamma rays can degrade the substrate molecules. Frequently, after initial radiolysis, secondary reactions – unaided by gamma rays – may also occur by interactions among the radiolytic products, especially among free radical species. Another important feature of radiolysis of aqueous organic compounds is the aftereffects, that is, reactions occurring after the cessation of irradiation. Such aftereffects may continue for several hours increasing the yields of products. The aftereffects are mainly due to the formation of peroxides in radiolysis.

A few examples for radiolysis of aqueous organic compounds are given.

(i) $H - OH \rightsquigarrow H^{\bullet} + OH^{\bullet}$

$${}^{\bullet}OH + HCOOH \longrightarrow {}^{\bullet}COOH + H_2O$$

$$2\,{}^{\bullet}COOH + O_2 \longrightarrow H_2O + 2CO_2 + H^{\bullet}$$

$$H^{\bullet} + O_2 \longrightarrow HO_2^{\bullet}$$

$$2HO_2^{\bullet} \longrightarrow H_2O_2 + O_2 \ldots$$

(ii) $H\text{–}OH \rightsquigarrow H^{\bullet} + {}^{\bullet}OH$

$$CHCl_3 + H^{\bullet} \longrightarrow {}^{\bullet}CHCl_2 + HCl$$

$${}^{\bullet}OH + CHCl_3 \longrightarrow {}^{\bullet}CCl_3 + H_2O$$

(iii) $H\text{–}OH \rightsquigarrow H^{\bullet} + {}^{\bullet}OH$

$$H^{\bullet} + RSH \longrightarrow RS^{\bullet} + H_2$$

$$2RS^{\bullet} \longrightarrow RS\text{–}SR \ldots$$

(iv) $C_6H_6 \xrightarrow{H_2O} H_2 + H_2O_2 + C_6H_5OH$

(v) $C_6H_5NO_2 \xrightarrow{H_2O}$ *o*, *m* and *p*-nitrophenols

A common feature of these radiolysis reactions is the initial radiolysis of H_2O, and then $H^\bullet$ and $^\bullet OH$ formed reacting with the organic molecules.

- Gamma ray induced organic reactions are complex, more complex than even photochemical reactions.
- Products which may not be formed in thermal reactions are formed in these reactions.
- The extent of reaction and nature of products depend upon the energy of the incident gamma ray as well as upon the duration of irradiation.

20.7.1.2 Irradiation of Polymers

The effect of gamma rays on polymers has been extensively researched. On irradiating a polymer with a flux of gamma rays, two types of chemical changes occur.

(i) *Cross linking of linear chains*: Gamma rays induce cross-linking in the linear polymer chains so that the relative molecular mass increases steadily with the dose. This process can be denoted as:

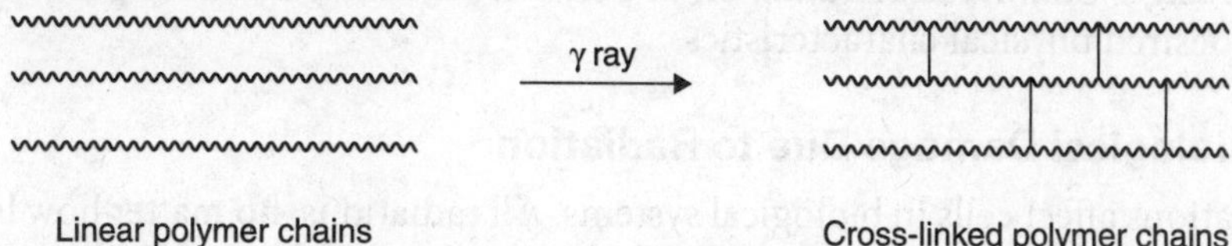

Cross-linking is initiated through the removal of a hydrogen atom from one of the chains by irradiation. This creates a radical site on the chain and the hydrogen atom produced will abstract another hydrogen atom from an adjacent chain. The two radical sites created on the chains can then be linked to form a cross-link. This can be illustrated with polythene:

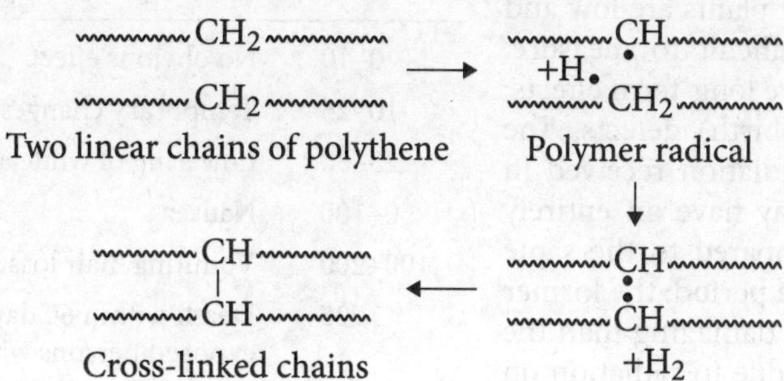

(ii) *Degradation of polymer chains*: Gamma rays can degrade a polymer by breaking several bonds:

γ ray → +

γ ray → + +

γ ray → +

Experiments have established that the polymers bearing the structures $[CH_2–CH_2]$ or $[CH_2–CHR]$ get cross-linked, while those bearing the structure $[CH_2–CR_1R_2]$ get degraded.

In both types of reactions, some gas is evolved. The gases may be of hydrogen and volatile monomers or small fragments of the polymer. In many polymers, the degree of unsaturation increases on irradiation; but in some rubbers which contain a large number of double bonds, the unsaturation decreases on irradiation. Irradiation of the polymer in the presence of oxygen enhances polymer degradation. The polymer chains break and react with O_2 forming carbonyl groups:

$$\sim\sim CH_2 \sim\sim \xrightarrow{O_2} \sim\sim CO \sim\sim$$

$$\sim\sim CH_2 \sim\sim CH_2 \sim\sim \xrightarrow{\gamma,\, O_2} \sim\sim CHO + OHC - CH_2 \sim\sim$$

In addition to these changes, peroxides and hydroperoxides can be formed.

Irradiation of a polymer may produce a variety of products depending on the nature of the polymer, energy of the gamma rays and the duration of irradiation. Irradiated polymers usually show physical changes—the mechanical properties, electrical conductivity, colour and so on, may change. Gamma ray irradiation of polymers is thus a means to produce industrial polymers of desired physical characteristics.

20.7.1.3 Biological Damage Due to Radiation

Nuclear radiations affect cells in biological systems. All radiations, no matter how low the dose is, are hazardous, even if the effect cannot be observed immediately in a healthy person. This is called the *linear hypothesis of radiation damage.* Another theory assumes that low-level doses of radiations, up to a certain limit, are not likely to be harmful to biological systems. This theory is called the *threshold hypothesis.*

The doses of radiation received for medical diagnosis, from television or from nuclear power plants are low and their effects are difficult to measure. Such doses may have long-term effects, including genetic (birth) defects. The same amount of radiation received in one single dose may have an entirely different effect compared to the same dose received over a period; the former is likely to be more damaging than the latter. The damage due to radiation on the human body depends on the dose received by the body (Table 20.8).

Table 20.8 Effect of radiation on the human body

Dose (rems)	Probable effect
0–10	No obvious effect
10–25	Temporary changes in blood
25–30	Lowering of white and red blood cells
50–100	Nausea
100–200	Vomiting, hair loss
225	Death within 60 days for 5% of the exposed persons without medical care
400	Death within 60 days for 50% of the exposed persons without medical care

The effects of radiation on the human body are of two types—*somatic effects* and *genetic effects.* The somatic effects are confined to the actual persons exposed to radiation (skin rash and cancer are examples of somatic effects). Genetic effects not only affect the person exposed to radiation but also his or her children and subsequent generations. The genetic effects of radiation result from damage to the cells of the testes (sperm) or ovary (egg cells) due to radiation. Radiation causes ionisation in the cell; this may break a DNA strand or alter its structure. The damaged DNA, on replication would give new messages to successive generations; this is called *mutation of cells.* Such mutations lead to birth disorders. The fast-dividing cells in the body are the ones most affected by radiation. The cells in bone marrow, blood, and gonads are some of the fast-dividing ones (Fig. 20.11). The neutrons cause the worst radiation problems for human beings. The human body contains a high percentage of H_2O which absorbs neutrons very efficiently.

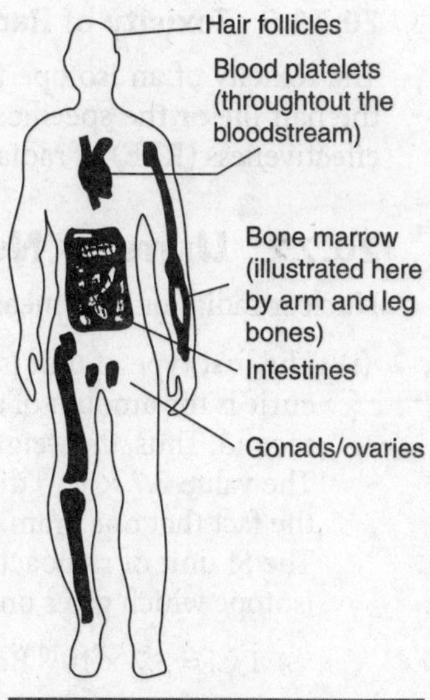

Fig. 20.11 Mutation of cells in human body

20.7.1.4 Biological Concentration of Radioisotopes

Certain radioisotopes tend to concentrate in certain human organs; for example, I-131. It is released to the atmosphere in nuclear explosion testing and from nuclear power plants. This isotope gets into the food chain: plant–animal–(cow's milk or meat)–human route is the most common route. It accumulates in the thyroid gland and creates health problems.

20.7.1.5 The Chemical Basis of Radiation Damage

Radiations – α, β and γ – can ionise molecules in matter. When any of these radiations fall on human tissue, the molecules in the tissue get ionised to form free radicals. The physiologically important organic molecules in the body get destroyed; then, they fail to function normally in the cells and therefore cause diseases. The interaction of water molecules in the cells with radiation produces the superoxide ion ($.O_2^-$) and other radicals. These species then attack cell membranes and several organic molecules in the cell, such as enzymes and DNA.

Radiation therapy for cancer also involves the destruction of cancerous cells. The radiation to which the patient is exposed must be sufficient to destroy the cancer cells without destroying the normal cells significantly. The radiation used should not induce another type of cancer in the patient. In radiation therapy, beams of gamma rays must be directed as closely as possible towards the cancerous tissue.

Problem 20.4 The energy required to split a water molecule into a hydrogen and a hydroxyl radical is 25 eV. A gamma ray of wavelength 5×10^{-13} m is absorbed by a tissue sample (which is mostly water). Calculate the number of OH radicals produced.

Solution

The total energy absorbed by the tissue,

$$E = h\nu = \frac{hc}{\lambda}$$

$$= \frac{(6.62606 \times 10^{-34}\,\text{Js})\,(3.0 \times 10^{8}\,\text{ms}^{-1})}{5 \times 10^{-13}\,\text{m}} = 3.978 \times 10^{-15}\,\text{J}$$

$$1\,\text{eV} = 1.602177 \times 10^{-19}\,\text{J}$$

$$\therefore \quad 3.976 \times 10^{-15}\,\text{J} = \frac{1\,\text{eV} \times 3.976 \times 10^{-15}}{1.602177 \times 10^{-19}\,\text{J}} = 2.482 \times 10^{4}\,\text{eV}$$

25 eV can split one H_2O molecule

$$\therefore \quad 2.482 \times 10^{4}\,\text{eV will split} = \frac{2.482 \times 10^{4}}{25} = 993\ H_2O\ \text{molecules}$$

Therefore, the number of OH radicals formed is 993.

20.7.1.6 Toxicity of Radioactive Isotopes

The toxicity of an isotope for human beings depends on the nature of the radioactivity and the half life or the specific activity of the isotope. Table 20.9 indicates the relative biological effectiveness (RBE) of radiations. The data in Table 20.10 illustrate the types of toxic isotopes.

20.7.2 Units of Nuclear Radiations

Nuclear radiations are measured in two kinds of unit.

(i) The first type of unit is *curie* (Ci), used to describe the intensity of radiation source. One curie is the amount of a radioactive substance that produces 3.7×10^{10} disintegrations per second. Thus, the weight of 1 curie of U-238 is different from the weight of 1 curie of K-40. The value 3.7×10^{10} disintegrations per second (dps) is chosen as the standard based on the fact that one gram of radium produces 3.7×10^{10} dps.
The SI unit of radioactivity is *becquerel* (Bq). It is defined as the amount of a radioactive isotope which gives one disintegration per second.

$$1 \text{ Ci} = 3.7 \times 10^{10} \text{ Bq}$$

$$1 \text{ Bq} = 27 \times 10^{-12} \text{ Ci}$$

(ii) The second type of unit describes the measure of absorption of radiation by tissues or air. Such a unit gives the dosage of radiation received. Three units of radiation dosage are used, *roentgen, rem* and *rad*.

Roentgen A roentgen is the amount of gamma or X-radiation required to produce ions carrying 1 electrostatic unit of charge in 1 cubic centimetre of dry air at standard temperature and pressure. This unit was named in honour of the German physicist Whilhelm Roentgen, the discoverer of X- rays.

Rad A rad is an absorption of 100 ergs of energy per gram of absorbing tissue.

Rem The rem unit is defined as the product of the absorbed dose in rads and the relative biological effectiveness (RBE) of the incoming radiation.

$$\text{rem} = \text{rads} \times \text{RBE}$$

The RBE denotes the relative ability of various kinds of radiation to carry out ionisation. An RBE value of 1 has been assigned to gamma rays (Table 20.9).

It is also 1 for X-rays. For α particles, it is 10. Therefore, a dose of 1 rad of gamma rays or 0.1 rad of alpha particles would each be equal to 1 rem and would have the same effect on the tissue. For neutrons, the RBE values range from 2.5 to 10.5 depending on their velocities and energies. A person's body receives about 50 millirems per year from terrestrial radiation (from the earth's crust) and about 50 millirems from cosmic rays. In a chest X-ray, the patient receives 100–200 millirems. When a person watches colour television for 2 hours per day, then in one year, he would receive about 4 millirems of radiation. A person living at the boundary of a nuclear power plant would receive at most

Table 20.9 Relative biological effectiveness of radiations

Radiation	RBE
γ rays, X-rays	1
β particles	1
Thermal neutrons	2.5
α particles, protons and fast neutrons	10
Heavy nuclei	20

5 millirems of radiation per year. This is much less than the background radiation exposure. The toxicity of radiations to human beings varies with nuclides (Table 20.10).

Table 20.10 Toxicity of isotopes

Toxicity	Example	Nature of possible health hazard
Very highly toxic	Sr-90	Long-lived bone-seeker
Highly toxic	Ca-45	Bone-seeker
Moderately toxic	Na-24	Not specific
Slightly toxic	C-14	Does not damage any critical organ

EXERCISES

1. A 1.0 ml solution containing 0.160 microcurie per millilitre of tritium was injected into the bloodstream of a guinea pig. After waiting for homogenisation, a 1.0 mL sample of the blood from the guinea pig was found to have a count rate of 60 counts per second. Calculate the blood volume of the animal. (Ans. 267 mL)
2. A small quantity of D_2O is added to aqueous hydrogen chloride. The mixture is evaporated and the vapour analysed by IR spectroscopy. Predict and explain the spectrum expected of this mixture.
3. Explain how the tracer technique can be used to prove that the equilibrium

   $PbCrO_4 \rightleftharpoons Pb^{2+} + CrO_4^{2-}$ lies far to the left.
4. The specific activity of carbon present in an antique wooden article is 2.70 dm^{-1} g^{-1}. Calculate its age. (Ans. 14344 y).
5. Predict and explain the nature and extent of isotopic exchange between

   (a) D_2O and H_2SO_4 (b) $H_2{}^{18}O$ and NaOH and (c) citric acid and T_2O.
6. The penicillin in 1000 g of a broth was estimated by the addition of 3.0 mg of the pure antibiotic labelled with ^{14}C. The specific activity of this mixture was 400 cpm /mg for a 30 minute count. 0.250 mg of pure penicillin was isolated from this mixture and it gave 902 counts in 60.0 minutes. Calculate the quantity of penicillin (in ppm) in the broth.

A1 List of Elements in the Increasing Atomic Numbers

No.	Atomic weight	Symbol	Name	Electronic configuration	No.	Atomic weight	Symbol	Name	Electronic configuration
1	1.008	H	Hydrogen	$1s^1$	27	58.933	Co	Cobalt	$[Ar]\ 3d^7\ 4s^2$
2	4.003	He	Helium	$1s^2$	28	58.693	Ni	Nickel	$[Ar]\ 3d^8\ 4s^2$
3	6.941	Li	Lithium	$[He]\ 2s^1$	29	63.546	Cu	Copper	$[Ar]\ 3d^{10}\ 4s^1$
4	9.012	Be	Beryllium	$[He]\ 2s^2$	30	65.390	Zn	Zinc	$[Ar]\ 3d^{10}\ 4s^2$
5	10.811	B	Boron	$[He]\ 2s^2\ 2p^1$	31	69.723	Ga	Gallium	$[Ar]\ 3d^{10}\ 4s^2\ 4p^1$
6	12.011	C	Carbon	$[He]\ 2s^2\ 2p^2$	32	72.640	Ge	Germanium	$[Ar]\ 3d^{10}\ 4s^2\ 4p^2$
7	14.007	N	Nitrogen	$[He]\ 2s^2\ 2p^3$	33	74.922	As	Arsenic	$[Ar]\ 3d^{10}\ 4s^2\ 4p^3$
8	15.999	O	Oxygen	$[He]\ 2s^2\ 2p^4$	34	78.960	Se	Selenium	$[Ar]\ 3d^{10}\ 4s^2\ 4p^4$
9	18.998	F	Fluorine	$[He]\ 2s^2\ 2p^5$	35	79.904	Br	Bromine	$[Ar]\ 3d^{10}\ 4s^2\ 4p^5$
10	20.180	Ne	Neon	$[He]\ 2s^2\ 2p^6$	36	83.800	Kr	Krypton	$[Ar]\ 3d^{10}\ 4s^2\ 4p^6$
11	22.990	Na	Sodium	$[Ne]\ 3s^1$	37	85.468	Rb	Rubidium	$[Kr]\ 5s^1$
12	24.305	Mg	Magnesium	$[Ne]\ 3s^2$	38	87.620	Sr	Strontium	$[Kr]\ 5s^2$
13	26.982	Al	Aluminium	$[Ne]\ 3s^2\ 3p^1$	39	88.906	Y	Yttrium	$[Kr]\ 4d^1\ 5s^2$
14	28.086	Si	Silicon	$[Ne]\ 3s^2\ 3p^2$	40	91.224	Zr	Zirconium	$[Kr]\ 4d^2\ 5s^2$
15	30.974	P	Phosphorus	$[Ne]\ 3s^2\ 3p^3$	41	92.906	Nb	Niobium	$[Kr]\ 4d^4\ 5s^1$
16	32.065	S	Sulphur	$[Ne]\ 3s^2\ 3p^4$	42	95.940	Mo	Molybdenum	$[Kr]\ 4d^5\ 5s^1$
17	35.453	Cl	Chlorine	$[Ne]\ 3s^2\ 3p^5$	43	98.000	Tc*	Technetium	$[Kr]\ 4d^5\ 5s^2$
18	39.948	Ar	Argon	$[Ne]\ 3s^2\ 3p^6$	44	101.070	Ru	Ruthenium	$[Kr]\ 4d^7\ 5s^1$
19	39.098	K	Potassium	$[Ar]\ 4s^1$	45	102.906	Rh	Rhodium	$[Kr]\ 4d^8\ 5s^1$
20	40.078	Ca	Calcium	$[Ar]\ 4s^2$	46	106.420	Pd	Palladium	$[Kr]\ 4d^{10}$
21	44.956	Sc	Scandium	$[Ar]\ 3d^1\ 4s^2$	47	107.868	Ag	Silver	$[Kr]\ 4d^{10}\ 5s^1$
22	47.867	Ti	Titanium	$[Ar]\ 3d^2\ 4s^2$	48	112.411	Cd	Cadmium	$[Kr]\ 4d^{10}\ 5s^2$
23	50.942	V	Vanadium	$[Ar]\ 3d^3\ 4s^2$	49	114.818	In	Indium	$[Kr]\ 4d^{10}\ 5s^2\ 5p^1$
24	51.996	Cr	Chromium	$[Ar]\ 3d^5\ 4s^1$	50	118.710	Sn	Tin	$[Kr]\ 4d^{10}\ 5s^2\ 5p^2$
25	54.938	Mn	Manganese	$[Ar]\ 3d^5\ 4s^2$	51	121.760	Sb	Antimony	$[Kr]\ 4d^{10}\ 5s^2\ 5p^3$
26	55.845	Fe	Iron	$[Ar]\ 3d^6\ 4s^2$	52	127.600	Te	Tellurium	$[Kr]\ 4d^{10}\ 5s^2\ 5p^4$

No.	Atomic weight	Symbol	Name	Electronic configuration
53	126.905	I	Iodine	[Kr] $4d^{10}\ 5s^2\ 5p^5$
54	131.293	Xe	Xenon	[Kr] $4d^{10}\ 5s^2\ 5p^6$
55	132.906	Cs	Cesium	[Xe] $6s^1$
56	137.327	Ba	Barium	[Xe] $6s^2$
57	138.906	La	Lanthanum	[Xe] $5d^1\ 6s^2$
58	140.116	Ce	Cerium	[Xe] $4f^1\ 5d^1\ 6s^2$
59	140.908	Pr	Praseodymium	[Xe] $4f^3\ 6s^2$
60	144.240	Nd	Neodymium	[Xe] $4f^4\ 6s^2$
61	145.000	Pm*	Promethium	[Xe] $4f^5\ 6s^2$
62	150.360	Sm	Samarium	[Xe] $4f^6\ 6s^2$
63	151.964	Eu	Europium	[Xe] $4f^7\ 6s^2$
64	157.250	Gd	Gadolinium	[Xe] $4f^7\ 5d^1\ 6s^2$
65	158.925	Tb	Terbium	[Xe] $4f^9\ 6s^2$
66	162.500	Dy	Dysprosium	[Xe] $4f^{10}\ 6s^2$
67	164.930	Ho	Holmium	[Xe] $4f^{11}\ 6s^2$
68	167.259	Er	Erbium	[Xe] $4f^{12}\ 6s^2$
69	168.934	Tm	Thulium	[Xe] $4f^{13}\ 6s^2$
70	173.040	Yb	Ytterbium	[Xe] $4f^{14}\ 6s^2$
71	174.967	Lu	Lutetium	[Xe] $4f^{14}\ 5d^1\ 6s^2$
72	178.490	Hf	Hafnium	[Xe] $4f^{14}\ 5d^2\ 6s^2$
73	180.948	Ta	Tantalum	[Xe] $4f^{14}\ 5d^3\ 6s^2$
74	183.840	W	Tungsten	[Xe] $4f^{14}\ 5d^4\ 6s^2$
75	186.207	Re	Rhenium	[Xe] $4f^{14}\ 5d^5\ 6s^2$
76	190.230	Os	Osmium	[Xe] $4f^{14}\ 5d^6\ 6s^2$
77	192.217	Ir	Iridium	[Xe] $4f^{14}\ 5d^7\ 6s^2$
78	195.078	Pt	Platinum	[Xe] $4f^{14}\ 5d^9\ 6s^1$
79	196.967	Au	Gold	[Xe] $4f^{14}\ 5d^{10}\ 6s^1$
80	200.590	Hg	Mercury	[Xe] $4f^{14}\ 5d^{10}\ 6s^2$
81	204.383	Tl	Thallium	[Xe] $4f^{14}\ 5d^{10}\ 6s^2\ 6p^1$
82	207.200	Pb	Lead	[Xe] $4f^{14}\ 5d^{10}\ 6s^2\ 6p^2$
83	208.980	Bi	Bismuth	[Xe] $4f^{14}\ 5d^{10}\ 6s^2\ 6p^3$
84	209.000	Po*	Polonium	[Xe] $4f^{14}\ 5d^{10}\ 6s^2\ 6p^4$
85	210.000	At*	Astatine	[Xe] $4f^{14}\ 5d^{10}\ 6s^2\ 6p^5$
86	222.000	Rn*	Radon	[Xe] $4f^{14}\ 5d^{10}\ 6s^2\ 6p^6$

No.	Atomic weight	Symbol	Name	Electronic configuration
87	223.000	Fr*	Francium	[Rn] $7s^1$
88	226.000	Ra*	Radium	[Rn] $7s^2$
89	227.000	Ac*	Actinium	[Rn] $6d^1\ 7s^2$
90	232.038	Th	Thorium	[Rn] $6d^2\ 7s^2$
91	231.036	Pa	Protactinium	[Rn] $5f^2\ 6d^1\ 7s^2$
92	238.029	U	Uranium	[Rn] $5f^3\ 6d^1\ 7s^2$
93	237.000	Np*	Neptunium	[Rn] $5f^4\ 6d^1\ 7s^2$
94	244.000	Pu*	Plutonium	[Rn] $5f^6\ 7s^2$
95	243.000	Am*	Americium	[Rn] $5f^7\ 7s^2$
96	247.000	Cm*	Curium	
97	247.000	Bk*	Berkelium	
98	251.000	Cf*	Californium	
99	252.000	Es*	Einsteinium	
100	257.000	Fm*	Fermium	
101	258.000	Md*	Mendelevium	
102	259.000	No*	Nobelium	
103	262.000	Lr*	Lawrencium	
104	261.000	Rf*	Rutherfordium	
105	262.000	Db*	Dubnium	
106	266.000	Sg*	Seaborgium	
107	264.000	Bh*	Bohrium	
108	277.000	Hs*	Hassium	
109	268.000	Mt*	Meitnerium	
110		Ds*	Darmstadium	
111		Rg*	Roentgenium	
112		Cn*	Copernicium	
113		Nh*	Nihonium	
114		Fl*	Flerovium	
115		Mc*	Moscovium	
116		Lv*	Livermorium	
117		Ts*	Tennessine	
118		Og*	Oganesson	

*Artificial elements

References

1. Mendham J, Denney R C, Barnes J D and Thomas M J K, *Vogel's Textbook of Quantitative Chemical Analysis*, Pearson Education Asia, New Delhi, 2000.
2. Skoog A D, Heller F J and Nieman T A, *Principles of Instrumental Analysis*, Thomson, Singapore, 2005.
3. Christian G D, *Analytical Chemistry*, John Wiley & Sons Pte. Ltd, Singapore, 2004.
4. Belcher R and Gordon L, Eds, *International Series of Monographs on Analytical Chemistry*, New York, Pergamon, Multivolume Series, Annual.
5. Kolthoff I M and Elving P J, Eds, *Treatise on Analytical Chemistry*, New York, Interscience, Multivolume Series, 1980.
6. Wilson C L and Wilson D W, *Comprehensive Analytical Chemistry*, Elsevier, Amsterdam, 1959.
7. Christian G D, *Analytical Chemistry*, 5th Ed., John Wiley, Chichester, 2004.
8. Crouch S, West, Donald, Heller, F and Skoog D A, *Fundamentals of Analytical Chemistry*, Cencage Learning Inc., U.S., 2013.
9. Tredwell F P, *Analytical Chemistry*, John Wiley & Sons, 1996.
10. Banwell C N and McCash E M, *Fundamentals of Spectroscopy*, McGraw Hill International UK Limited.
11. Williams D H and Fleming I, *Spectroscopic Methods in Organic Chemistry*, Tata McGraw-Hill Publishing Company Limited, New Delhi, 1987.

FURTHER READING

1. Long D A, *Raman Spectroscopy*, McGraw-Hill, Maidenhead, 1977.
2. Thomas M J K, *Ultraviolet and Visible Spectroscopy*, 2nd Ed., ACOL-Wiley, Chichester, 1996.
3. Skoog D A, *Principles of Instrumental Analysis*, 3rd Ed., CBS College Publishing, Philadelphia, PA, 1997.
4. Dean J R, *Atomic Absorption and Plasma Spectroscopy*, 2nd Ed., ACOL-Wiley Chichester, 1997.
5. Wendlandt W W, *Thermal Analysis*, 3rd Ed., John Wiley, Chichester.
6. Culity B D, *X-Ray Diffraction*, Wiley.
7. Glasstone S, *Source Book on Atomic Energy*, Van Nostrand, 1950.
8. Gibbs T C, *Principles of Mossbauer Spectroscopy*, Chapman and Hall, London, 1976.
9. *Sadtler Handbook of Proton NMR Spectra*, Heydon, London.
10. Naganishi K, *Infrared Absorption Spectroscopy Honden-Day*, San Franscisco, 1977.
11. Howe I, Williams D H and Bowen R D, *Mass Spectrometry—Principles and Applications*, McGraw-Hill, New York, 1981.
12. Workman J J, *The Concise Handbook of Analytical Spectroscopy*, World Scientific Publishing Co. Pvt Ltd, US, 2016.

Index

A

B

E

F

P

Q

R

S

T